The Czech and
Slovak Republics

written and researched by

Rob Humphreys

with additional contributions by

Susie Lunt and Tim Nollen

ROUGH
GUIDES

www.roughguides.com

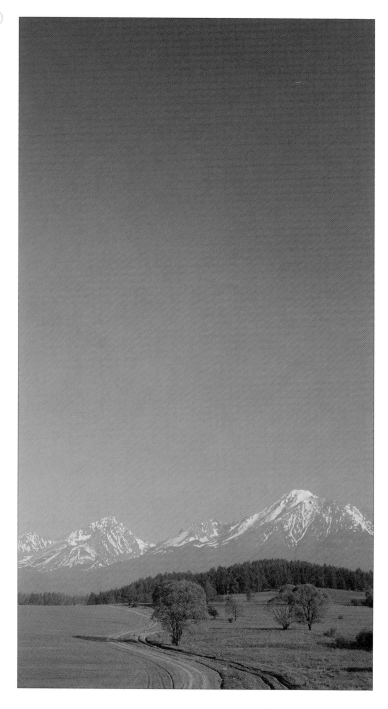

Introduction to

The Czech and Slovak Republics

**The only thing I know about Slovakia is what I learned
first-hand from your foreign minister, who came to Texas.**

George W. Bush replying to a Slovak journalist. Bush had, in fact, met the

leader of Slovenia.

The complexities of central European
politics can be baffling to outsiders. In
fact, even those who knew their Slovaks
from their Slovenes were surprised
when, on New Year's Day 1993, after
seventy years of (sometimes turbulent)
cohabitation, the Czechs and Slovaks
went their separate ways and
Czechoslovakia ceased to exist. To the outsider, at least, it had looked like a
match made in heaven. Yet just three years after the Velvet Revolution – when
true to their pacifist past, the Czechs and Slovaks shrugged off 41 years of
Communist rule without so much as a shot being fired – came the Velvet
Divorce.

In the ten years since then, the two republics have continued to change at an
unprecedented rate and are now more accessible today than at any time since
the 1930s. The major cities buzz with a cultural and commercial diversity, and
– apart from the obligatory high-rise suburbs – fail to conform to most people's
idea of former Eastern Europe. Luxury hotels have sprouted up all over Prague
and, while the remoter regions can sometimes seem more reminiscent of the
early twentieth century than the twenty-first, private shops and restaurants now

Fact file

● The Czech and Slovak Republics are landlocked countries in the geographical centre of Europe, roughly equidistant from the Baltic and Adriatic seas. The highest **mountains** are Sněžka (1602m) in the Czech Republic, and Gerlachovský štít (2655m) in Slovakia.

● The **population** of the Czech Republic is 10.23 million, of whom roughly 95% are Czech, with significant Romany, Slovak, Polish and German minorities. Slovakia's population is 5.38 million, including over half a million Hungarians and an estimated quarter of a million Romanies.

● 40% of the Czech Republic's **trade** is with Germany and 8% with Slovakia. 27% of Slovakia's trade is with Germany and 16% with the Czech Republic.

exist in even the most provincial of rural villages. Instead of posters exhorting the country's citizens to fulfil the next five-year plan, there are now billboards advertising mobile phones, investment portfolios and cars. Inevitably, the pace of change in both republics has been bewildering for those who lived through the Communist era, and along with the new-found freedom have come the usual suspects: multinationals, mafia and all the vices that plague the western world. Few Czechs or Slovaks would want to turn the clock right back, but when the Czech Communists receive eighteen percent of the vote, and the most popular Slovak politician is a nationalist who inveighs against the EU and NATO, it's clear that not everybody's happy with the changes.

Most Czechs and Slovaks, however, simply shrug their shoulders at the

> In contrast to the political upheavals that have plagued the region, the Czech and Slovak Republics have suffered very little physical damage over the last few centuries.

problems, since neither nation has ever felt in full control of its historical destiny. When **Czechoslovakia** was founded in 1918, it was always a marriage of convenience: the Czechs reasoned that the Slovaks would help dilute the number of ethnic Germans in the new country; the Slovaks needed to escape the unwanted attentions of the Hungarians, who were keen to reform Greater Hungary. The Nazis broke up the marriage in 1938 by forcing the Slovaks into a Faustian pact; ten years later, any thoughts of divorce were thrown out of the window as the country disappeared behind the Iron Curtain; and in 1968, Warsaw Pact tanks trampled on the country's dreams of "socialism with a human face". The 1989 **Velvet Revolution** only took place because the Soviet leader Gorbachev allowed it to. Even the break-up of the country was cooked up by the intransigent leaders of the two main political parties, and went ahead without a popular referendum.

In contrast to the political upheavals that have plagued the region, the Czech and Slovak Republics have suffered very little physical damage over the last few centuries. Gothic castles and Baroque chateaux have been preserved in abundance, town after town in

Wooden churches

The Czech and Slovak Republics boast an amazing number of **wooden churches**. While timber-framed houses have, on the whole, been superseded by bricks and mortar, wooden churches have survived in many villages. The densest cluster is to be found in the Rusyn villages in the far east of Slovakia, and most, though by no means all, are Greek-Catholic. Elsewhere in Slovakia, vast Lutheran churches survive from the days when Protestants were forbidden to build their churches in stone. One or two survive in Bohemia, but for Czech wooden churches, you need to head into Moravia, to the Wallachian region of the Beskydy hills, where there's a varied collection of Roman Catholic wooden churches.

Bohemia and Moravia has retained its old medieval quarter, and even the wooden architecture of Slovakia has survived beyond all expectations. Geographically speaking, the two republics are the most diverse of all the former Eastern Bloc states. Together they span the full range of central European cultures, from the old German towns of the west to the Hungarian and Rusyn villages in East Slovakia. In physical terms, too, there's enormous variety: Bohemia's rolling hills, lush and relentless, couldn't be more different from the flat Danube basin, or the granite alpine peaks of the High Tatras, the beech forests of the far east, or the coal basins of the Moravian north.

Where to go

Before the fall of Communism, a staggering ninety percent of foreign tourists visiting Czechoslovakia never strayed from the environs of the Czech capital, **Prague**. While that no longer holds true, Prague is still the main focus of most people's trips to the Czech Republic, certainly English-speaking tourists. Of course, much of the attention heaped on Prague is perfectly justified. It is one of the most remarkable cities in Europe,

> **Geographically speaking, the two republics are the most diverse of all the former Eastern Bloc states.**

having emerged virtually unscathed from two world wars. Baroque palaces and churches shout out from the cobbles, Gothic pinnacles spike the skyline, and Art Nouveau and functionalist edifices line the boulevards.

The rest of the Czech Republic divides neatly into two: Bohemia to the west and Moravia to the east. Prague is the perfect launching pad from which to explore the rolling hills and forests of Bohemia, at their most unspoilt in South Bohemia, whose capital is **České Budějovice**, a grid-plan medieval city and home to the original Budweiser beer. The real gem of the region is **Český Krumlov**, arguably the most stunning medieval town in the country, beautifully preserved in a narrow U-bend of the River Vltava. To the west, **Plzeň** produces the most famous of all Czech beers, Pilsener Urquell, the original golden nectar from which all other lagers derive. Meanwhile, along the German border, a triangle of relaxing **spa towns** – Karlovy Vary, Mariánské Lázně and Františkovy Lázně – retain an air of their halcyon days in the last years of the Habsburg Empire. Pine-covered mountains form Bohemia's natural borders, and the weird **sandstone "rock cities"** of the České Švýcarsko and Český raj and Krkonoše, in the north and east of the region, make for some of the most memorable landscapes.

Moravia, the eastern province of the Czech Republic, is every bit as beautiful as Bohemia, though the crowds here thin out significantly. The largest city, **Brno**, has its own peculiar pleasures – not least its interwar functionalist architecture – and gives access to the popular Moravian karst region, or **Moravský kras**, plus a host of other nearby castles and chateaux. The southern borders of Moravia comprise the country's main wine region, while in the uplands that

Walking and hiking

The Czechs and Slovaks are keen **walkers**, and both countries are crisscrossed with a dense, easily followed, 48,000-kilometre network of way-marked, colour-coded paths ranging from a gentle stroll to a serious hike, leaving no excuse not to get into the countryside and take some exercise. All 1:50,000 hiking maps show the trails and each path has regular signposts, with distances and approximate walking times. To make sure you don't lose your way there's even a colour-coded marker or *značka* every 100m or so, maintained annually by teams of local volunteers.

form the border with Bohemia are two of the most perfectly preserved medieval towns in the entire country, **Telč** and **Slavonice**. To the north, **Olomouc** is perhaps Moravia's most charming city, more immediately appealing than Brno, and just a short step away from the region's highest mountains, the **Jeseníky** in Moravian Silesia, and the **Beskydy**, renowned for their folk architecture.

Although the Slovak capital, **Bratislava**, can't compare with Prague, it does have its virtues, not least its compact old town and its position on one of Europe's great rivers, the Danube. The flat plain of the Danube basin is of little visual interest, but there are two historic towns that make worthwhile day-trips from the capital: **Trnava**, Slovakia's most important ecclesiastical town, and **Nitra**, the spiritual centre of Slovak Catholicism.

In the central mountain regions, well-preserved medieval mining towns like **Banská Štiavnica** and **Kremnica** still smack of their German origins. Other towns, like those in the Váh valley, are mainly of interest as bases for exploring the chief attractions of the region, the **mountains** of the Malá Fatra, Low Tatras, and – tallest and most spectacular of the lot – the **High Tatras**. These jagged granite peaks are Slovakia's most popular tourist destination, and justifiably so. Within easy reach, however, is the **Spiš region**, the country's architectural high point. The area is dotted with intriguing medieval towns, like **Levoča**, originally built by German settlers, now preserved almost untouched since the sixteenth century. And just a step away is the **Slovenský raj**, a thickly wooded region of verdant ravines and rocky outcrops.

Further east still is **Prešov** the cultural centre of the Rusyn minority who inhabit the villages to the north and east. Here, you'll find an extraordinary wealth of **wooden churches**. Finally, **Košice**, Slovakia's second largest city, boasts Europe's easternmost Gothic cathedral and has a strongly Hungarian ambience. It's also a good launch pad for exploring the Slovak karst region or **Slovenský kras**, and the beech forests of the Vihorlat region by the Ukrainian border.

When to go

I n general, the climate is continental, with short, fairly hot summers and chilly winters. **Spring** can be a good time to visit, as the days tend to warm quickly, with consistently pleasant, mild weather for most of May. This is also the

Trains

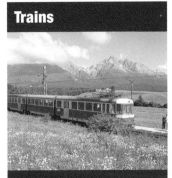

The most relaxing way to travel round the Czech and Slovak Republics is by train. The system, bequeathed by the Habsburgs in 1918, is one of the most dense in Europe, and has changed little since those days, with only five percent of lines allowing train speeds of over 120kph. In addition, many are wonderfully scenic, such as the single-track one that winds its way through the Šumava, or the Slovak line that follows the Hron valley and includes a 360-degree switchback. Heritage railways are beginning to emerge, too, with several old forest railways now running steam train excursions on summer weekends.

Average temperatures (°C)

	Jan	Feb	Mar	Apr	May	June	July	Aug	Sept	Oct	Nov	Dec
Prague												
Average temp (°C)	-1	0	4	9	14	17	19	18	14	9	4	0
Brno												
Average temp (°C)	-2	-1	3	8	13	16	18	17	14	8	3	-1
Bratislava												
Average temp (°C)	-1	0	5	10	15	18	20	19	16	10	4	0
Banká Štiavnica												
Average temp (°C)	-3	-2	2	7	12	15	18	17	13	8	2	-1
Košice												
Average temp (°C)	-3	-2	3	9	14	17	19	18	14	9	3	-1

Note that these are **average daily temperatures**. At midday in summer, Bratislava can be blisteringly hot. Equally, in most mountainous regions it can get extremely cold and wet at any time of the year.

blossom season, when the fruit trees that line so many Czech and Slovak roads are in full flower. **Autumn** is also recommended, with clear and settled weather often lasting for days on end in September and October. With both countries

heavily forested, this is also a great time to appreciate the changing colours of the foliage.

Winter can be a good time to come to Prague: the city looks beautiful under snow and there are fewer tourists to compete with. Other parts of the country have little to offer during winter (aside from skiing), and most sights stay firmly closed between November and March. **Summer** is, of course, still the season that sees the largest number of tourists descend on the two countries. Certainly, temperatures are at their highest, with the occasional heat wave pushing readings above 30°C. While that can be advantageous if you fancy swimming in a lake or river, it's not fun in Prague, which is at its most crowded in July and August.

29

things not to miss

It's not possible to see everything that the Czech and Slovak Republics have to offer in one trip – and we don't suggest you try. What follows is a selective and subjective taste of the two countries' highlights, from historical castles and striking Renaissance architecture to handsome mountain ranges. They're all arranged in five colour-coded categories to help you find the very best things to see, do and experience. All entries have a page reference to take you straight into the guide, where you can find out more.

01 **Budvar Beer** Page **190** • Taste the original Budweiser beer in the former medieval butchers' stalls of the Masné kramy in České Budějovice.

02 **Třeboňsko** Page **185** • South Bohemian flatlands with the pretty walled town of Třeboň at its heart, surrounded by medieval carp ponds.

03 **Český ráj** Page **285** • Natural playground within easy reach of Prague, with densely wooded hills, sandstone "rock cities" and a smattering of ruined castle.

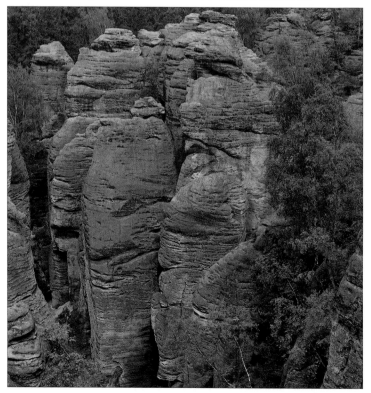

04 **České Švýcarsko (Bohemian Switzerland)** Page **266**
Switzerland it may not be, but this forested border region features outlandish sandstone outcrops and boat trips down the River Kamenice.

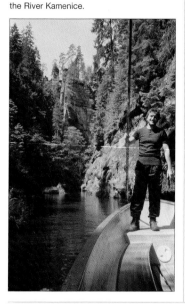

05 **Terezín** Page **258** • This Habsburg-era military fortress was transformed into a "model" Jewish ghetto by the Nazis, though in reality it was simply a transit camp en route to Auschwitz.

06 **Jindřichův Hradec, Zámek** Page **182** • This chateau's forbidding exterior gives no hint of the exuberant interior executed by Italian architects in the sixteenth century.

08 **Levoča** Page **532** • Attractive walled medieval town, originally settled by Saxons, whose church is packed full of the finest Gothic altarpieces in Slovakia.

07 **Raft trips in the Pieniny** Page **531** • Ride a log raft down the River Dunajec, which forms the border between Slovakia and Poland.

09 **Litomyšl** Page **319** • This pint-sized Bohemian town, which is the birthplace of Bedřich Smetana, is home to a very handsome Renaissance chateau and the weird and wonderful Portmoneum, designed by self-taught artist Josef Váchal.

10 **Rožnov pod Radhoštěm** Page **411** • Moravian town that's home to the largest and most impressive open-air folk museum in either republic.

11 **Plzeň Brewery** Page **217** • World-famous brewery, where, in 1842, the world's first lager, Pilsner Urquell, was produced.

12 **Žďár nad Sazavou, Zelena Hora** Page **368** • Star-shaped Gothic–Baroque pilgrimage church by Giovanni Santini, dedicated to the martyr Saint John of Nepomuk.

14 Banská Štiavnica Page **483**
Well-preserved former silver and
gold-mining town, settled by German miners
in medieval times, and beautifully situated
on terraced slopes.

13 **High Tatras** Page **512** • The jagged,
granite peaks of the High Tatras,
which rise up dramatically from the Poprad
plain, are the most spectacular mountains in
Slovakia.

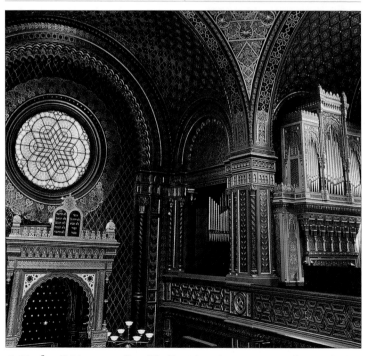

15 **Španělská synagoga** Page **102** • Prague's most ornate synagogue houses a fascinating exhibition on the fate of the city's Jewish population since 1848.

16 **Spišský hrad** Page **536** • This sprawling medieval castle is quite simply the most stunning hilltop ruin in Slovakia.

18 **Moravský kras** Page **345** • Moravia's karst region, just outside Brno, replete with cave systems featuring superb stalagtites and stalagmites and an underground river.

17 **Veletržni palác, Prague** Page **123** The finest modern art museum in the Czech Republic, and a functionalist masterpiece in its own right.

19 **Karlovy Vary** Page **237** • Grandiose late nineteenth-century spa town lying in a steep valley, and home to the Czech Republic's premier film festival.

20 **Mariánské Lazně** Page **225** • Elegant fin-de-siècle Bohemian spa town set in verdant wooded hills – and once a firm favourite with European royalty.

22 **Český Krumlov** Page **192** • Medieval town of steep cobbled streets, picturesquely situated in a tight U-bend of the River Vltava.

21 **Slovenský raj** Page **537** • Scramble up the ravines of the pine-forested Slovenský raj, with the aid of chains and ladders.

23 **Slavonice** Page **363** • Slavonice's tiny old town sports more pictorial sgraffito facades than any other town in either republic.

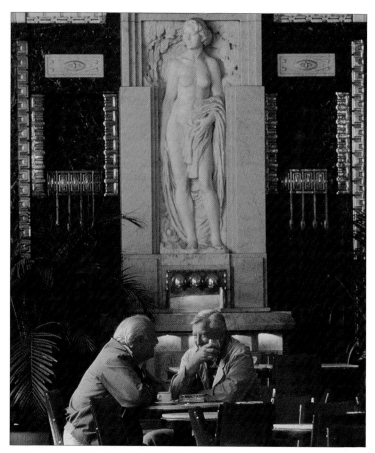

24 **Obecní dům** Page **112** • Prague's Art Nouveau jewel from 1911, housing a café, several restaurants, an exhibition space and a concert hall.

25 **Vlkolínec** Page **506** • UNESCO-listed, hillside Slovak village, lined with pristinely preserved timber-built cottages.

26 **Prague Castle** Page **68** • Landmark castle that's home to the cathedral, royal palace, several museums and galleries, and the president.

27 **Bardejov** Page **550** • Walled medieval town, originally built by Saxon colonists, now home to Slovakia's finest collection of icons.

28 **Pernštejn** Page **348** • Highly atmospheric hilltop Gothic castle with dizzying sheer walls and spectacular views across the wooded hills.

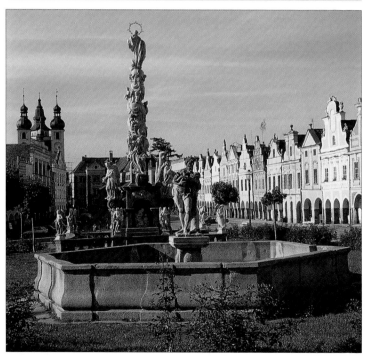

29 **Telč** Page **362** • Telč's vast, arcaded main square is one long parade of perfectly preserved sixteenth-century facades and gables, culminating in a handsome Renaissance chateau.

Contents

Using the Rough Guide

We've tried to make this Rough Guide a good read and easy to use. The book is divided into six main sections, and you should be able to find whatever you want in one of them.

Colour section

The front colour section offers a quick tour of the Czech and Slovak Republics. The **introduction** aims to give you a feel for the countries, with suggestions on where to go. We also tell you what the weather is like and include a basic country fact file. Next, our author rounds up his favourite aspects of the two countries in the **things not to miss** section – whether it's great scenery, amazing architecture or a special museum. Right after this comes a full **contents** list.

Basics

The Basics section covers all the **pre-departure** nitty-gritty to help you plan your trip. This is where to find out which airlines fly to your destination, what paperwork you'll need, what to do about money and insurance, about internet access, food, security, public transport, car rental – in fact just about every piece of **general practical information** you might need.

Guide

This is the heart of the Rough Guide, divided into user-friendly chapters, each of which covers a specific region. Every chapter starts with a list of **highlights** and an **introduction** that helps you to decide where to go, depending on your time and budget. Likewise, introductions to the various towns and smaller regions within each chapter should help you plan your

itinerary. We start most town accounts with information on arrival and accommodation, followed by a tour of the sights, and finally reviews of places to eat and drink, and details of nightlife. Longer accounts also have a directory of practical listings. Each chapter concludes with **public transport** details for that region.

Contexts

Read Contexts to get a deeper understanding of what makes the Czech and Slovak Republics tick. We include introductions to their histories, plus a further-reading section that reviews dozens of **books** relating to the country.

Language

The **Language** section gives useful guidance for speaking Czech and Slovak, and pulls together all the vocabulary you might need on your trip, including a comprehensive food glossary. Here you'll also find a glossary of words and terms peculiar to each country.

Index + small print

Apart from a **full index**, which includes maps as well as places, this section covers publishing information, credits and acknowledgements, and also has our contact details in case you want to send in updates and corrections to the book – or suggestions as to how we might improve it.

Chapter list and map

- Colour section
- Contents
- **B** Basics
- **1** Prague and around
- **2** South Bohemia
- **3** West Bohemia
- **4** North Bohemia
- **5** East Bohemia
- **6** South Moravia
- **7** North Moravia
- **8** Bratislava and west Slovakia
- **9** The mountain regions
- **10** East Slovakia
- **C** Contexts
- **L** Language
- **I** Index

Contents

Colour section   i–xxiv

Colour map of the Republics ....ii–iii
Where to go ix
When to go xii
Things not to miss xiv

Basics   9–28

Getting there 11
Red tape and visas 18
Insurance and health 19
Costs, money and banks 21
Information, websites and maps 22
Trouble and the police 25
Travellers with disabilities 26
Directory 27

Guide   29–564

The Czech Republic 30–414
Introduction 33
Getting around..............................33
Accommodation 37
Communications 39
Eating and drinking 41
Castles, churches and museums 45
Public holidays, festivals and
   entertainment 47

❶ **Prague and around** 51–165
Chapter highlights 52
Arrival and information..................56
City transport.................................58
Accommodation 62
Hradčany 67
Malá Strana 80
Staré Mesto 87
Josefov 98

Nové Mesto 104
Vyšehrad 117
The suburbs................................119
Eating and drinking 129
Entertainment 137
Listings 141
North along the Vltava 143
East of Prague 147
Kutná Hora and around 151
Průhonice and the Sázava
   Valley..155
Přuíbam 158
Along the Berounka river 160
Around Kladno............................163
Travel details 165

❷ **South Bohemia** 167–209
Chapter highlights 168
Up the Vltava 171

Tábor 174
West of Tábor 178
East of Tábor 179
Třeboňsko 182
České Budějovice and around 187
Český, Krumlov 192
The Šumava.........................197
Travel details 209

❸ **West Bohemia** 211–243
Chapter highlights 212
Plzeň 215
Klatovy and around 221
Domažlice 223
Mariánské Lázně 225
Cheb 231
Františkovy Lázně 234
Karlovy Vary...........................237
Travel details 243

❹ **North Bohemia** 245–281
Chapter highlights 246
Up the River Ohře 249
The North Bohemian brown
  coal basin 252
Teplice 255
Terezín 258
Litoměřice 261
Ústí nad Labem 264
České Svýcarsko.......................266
The Česká Lípa region..............272
Liberec and around 274
Travel details 281

❺ **East Bohemia** 283–323
Chapter highlights 284
Český ráj 285
The Krkonoše 293
East to Broumov 300
Náchod and around...................302
Hradec Králové 306
Around Hradec Králové 311
Pardubice 315
Litomyšl and around 319
Travel details 323

❻ **South Moravia** 325–381
Chapter highlights 326

Brno 329
Around Brno 345
Mikulov and around 351
Lednicko-Valtický aréal 353
Znojmo.................................355
Podyjí 358
Třebíc and around 359
Telč 362
Slavonice 363
Jihlava 364
Zďár nad Sázavou 368
The Slovácko region 369
Luhačovice 373
Zlín...................................374
Kroměříž and around 378
Travel details 381

❼ **North Moravia** 383–414
Chapter highlights 384
Olomouc 385
Around Olomouc 393
The Jeseníky 397
Ostrava 403
The Beskydy 406
Travel details 413

The Slovak Republic 415–564
Introduction 417
Getting around.........................417
Accommodation 420
Communications 421
Eating and drinking 423
Castles, churches and
  museums 424
Public holidays, festivals and
  entertainment..........................425

❽ **Bratislava and
West Slovakia** 427–471
Chapter highlights 428
Bratislava.............................429
Arrival................................431
Transport and information 431
Accommodation 434
The stare mesto........................435
From the Dóm to the Hrad.........440
Hviezdoslavono námestie and the
  waterfront 443

Námestie SNP and the suburbs 445
Eating..447
Entertainment and nightlife 448
Listings 449
Out from the city 450
The Small Carpathians 451
Trnava 454
Nitra 457
The Danube basin 460
Piešťany and the Váh valley........465
Trenčín and around 469
Travel details 471

❾ The mountain regions..473–521
Chapter highlights 474
Banksá Bystrica..........................475
South to Zvolen 480
Banská Štiavnica 483
Kremnica 485

The road to Lučenec 487
The Turiec valley 486
The Malá Fatra............................492
The Orava region 500
The Liptov region........................504
The Low Tatras (Nízke Tatry) 508
The High Tatras (Vysoké Tatry) ..512
Travel details 521

❿ East Slovakia................523–564
Chapter highlights 524
The Spiš region 526
The Slovenský, raj 537
The Slovenský kras 540
Carpatho-Ruthenia 545
Košice 556
East to Michalovce and
  the Vihorlat 562
Travel details 564

Contexts   481–601

The historical frmaework...................567   Books 593

Language   603–619

Pronunciation 605
A Czech/Slovak language guide........607
Czech food and drink glossary 610
Slovak food and drink glossary 612
An A–Z of Czech and Slovak
  street names 614

A glossary of Czech and Slovak words
  and terms.....................................614
An architectural glossary 618
Historical and political terms 618
Abbreviations 619

Index + small print   621–632

Full index...622
Rough Guide credits 630
Publishing information 630

Help us update 630
Acknowledgements 631
Photo credits.....................................632

Map symbols

maps are listed in the full index using coloured text

▬▪▬▪▬	International boundary		◓	Cave
▬ ▪ ▬ ▪ ▬	Regional boundary		⊙	Statue
▬ ▬ ▬ ▬	Chapter division boundary		ⵌ	Fountain
▬▬▬	Motorway		◔	Swimming pool
═══	Road		⚠	Campsite
┄┄┄	Pedestrianized street/alley		🅿	Parking
⊞⊞⊞⊞	Steps		Ⓜ	Metro station
┈┈┈	Footpath		✈	Airport
▬━▬	Railway		ⓘ	Information office
┅┅┅	Funicular		©	Telephone
─ ─	Ferry route		✉	Post office
═══	River		@	Internet access
⌣	Bridge		▬	Building
⬥	Point of interest		✚	Church
▲	Mountain peak		✡	Synagogue
⌐ⵗⵗⵗⵔ	Cliffs		▤	Park
♙	Castle		⁘	Forest
⚔	Battle site		✝	Cemetery
▬▪▪▬	Wall		⊡	Jewish cemetery
⊠ ⊠	Gate			

7

Basics

Basics

Getting there 11

Red tape and visas 18

Insurance and health 19

Costs, money and banks 21

Information, websites and maps 22

Trouble and the police 25

Travellers with disabilities 26

Directory..27

Getting there

BASICS | Getting there

Unless you're coming from a neighbouring European country, the quickest and easiest way to get to either the Czech or Slovak republic is by plane. There are direct flights from just about every European capital to Prague and Vienna, which is only a brief bus ride from the Slovak capital, Bratislava. If you're heading straight for eastern Slovakia, flying to Budapest is also an option worth considering. There are also one or two non-stop flights from North America to Prague or Vienna, though you'll get a much wider choice – and often lower fares – if you fly via London or another more popular European gateway.

Airfares depend primarily on availability, but they also vary with season, with the **highest fares** charged from Easter to October, and around Christmas and New Year. Fares will ordinarily be cheaper during the rest of the year, which is considered **low season**, though some airlines also have a **shoulder season** – typically April to mid-June and mid-September to October – and a correspondingly shorter high season. Note also that flying at weekends may add to the round-trip fare; price ranges quoted below assume midweek travel.

You can often cut costs by going through a **specialist flight agent** – either a consolidator, who buys up blocks of tickets from the airlines and sells them at a discount, or a **discount agent**, who in addition to dealing with discounted flights may also offer special student and youth fares and a range of other travel-related services such as travel insurance, rail passes, car rentals, tours and the like.

Another option if you're travelling from Britain or elsewhere in Europe, is to go by **train**, **bus or car**, though these usually take considerably longer than a plane and may not work out that much cheaper. For more details, see p.15

Booking flights online

Many airlines and discount travel **websites** offer you the opportunity to book your tickets online, cutting out the costs of agents and middlemen, and often giving you a discount at the same time. Good deals can often be found through discount or auction sites, as well as through the airlines' own websites.

Online booking agents and general travel sites

ⓦ **travel.yahoo.com** Incorporates a lot of Rough Guide material in its coverage of destination countries and cities across the world, with information about places to eat, sleep and other practicalities.

ⓦ **www.cheapflights.com** Bookings from the UK and Ireland only. Flight deals, travel agents, plus links to other travel sites.

ⓦ **www.cheaptickets.com** Discount flight specialists.

ⓦ **www.deckchair.com** Bob Geldof's online venture, drawing on a wide range of airlines.

ⓦ **www.etn.nl/discount.htm** A hub of consolidator and discount agent web links, maintained by the nonprofit European Travel Network.

ⓦ **www.expedia.com** Discount airfares, all-airline search engine and daily deals.

ⓦ **www.flyaow.com** Online air travel info and reservations site.

ⓦ **www.gaytravel.com** Gay online travel agent, concentrating mostly on accommodation.

ⓦ **goeasterneurope.about.com** US site with good links to discount airfares to, and accommodation in, Prague.

ⓦ **www.hotwire.com** Bookings from the US only. Last-minute savings of up to forty percent on regular published fares. Travellers must be at least 18 and there are no refunds, transfers or changes allowed. Log-in required.

ⓦ **www.lastminute.com** Offers good last-minute holiday package and flight-only deals.

ⓦ **www.orbitz.com** Discounted airline tickets from the US only.

ⓦ **www.priceline.com** Name-your-own-price website that has deals at around forty percent off standard fares. You cannot specify flight times (although you do specify dates) and the tickets are non-refundable, non-transferable and non-changeable.

ⓦ **www.skyauction.com** Bookings from the US only. Auctions tickets and travel packages using a "second bid" scheme. The best strategy is to bid the maximum you're willing to pay, since if you win you'll pay just enough to beat the runner-up regardless of your maximum bid.

ⓦ **www.smilinjack.com/airlines.htm** Lists an up-to-date compilation of airline website addresses.

ⓦ **www.travelocity.com** Destination guides, hot web fares and best deals for car hire, accommodation and lodging as well as fares. Provides access to the travel agent system SABRE, the most comprehensive central reservations system in the US.

ⓦ **www.travelshop.com.au** Australian website offering discounted flights, packages, insurance and online bookings.

Flights from Britain and Ireland

The most competitive airfares from Britain are with the no-frills budget airlines. At the time of going to press, Go were offering return fares from Stansted **to Prague** from around £100 upwards, with prices roughly the same from Bristol and East Midlands airports. British Midland's budget arm, bmibaby, were offering matching fares from East Midlands. Buzz, meanwhile, were offering similar fares from Stansted **to Vienna**. Note, however, that the cheaper tickets need to be booked well in advance, and often apply to specific (early or late) flights on specific days, and are either non-refundable or only partially refundable, and non-exchangeable.

British Airways (BA) and Czech Airlines (ČSA) both have a wider choice of flight times from London **to Prague**; BA only fly from Heathrow, while ČSA fly from Heathrow, Stansted, Birmingham and Manchester. Austrian Airlines, BA and Lauda Air all have a wide choice of flight times from London **to Vienna**; BA fly from Heathrow, Austrian Airlines fly from Heathrow and Manchester and Lauda fly from Gatwick. The national airlines are rarely the cheapest option, though their special offers can bring return fares down to as low as £120, though a fare between £150 and £200 is more common.

ČSA operates a regular non-stop service **from Dublin** to Prague, costing around €350 return, and Tyrolean and Austrian Airlines run a direct service from Dublin to Vienna, costing around €390 return. However, in both cases it may still be cheaper to fly via London.

Finding **the best deal** involves ringing round, or checking the websites of a few of the discount specialist agents (see below), and comparing prices, routes and timings. Students under 32 and those under 26 should enquire about discounts on scheduled flights, or contact the likes of STA Travel (see opposite). Note, however, that in peak season, discount flights are often booked up weeks in advance. If this is the case, it might be worth considering flying to a neighbouring European city like Berlin, Budapest, Leipzig or Munich.

Airlines

Austrian Airlines UK ☎0845/601 0948; Ireland ☎1-800/509142, ⓦwww.austrianairlines.co.uk.
British Airways UK ☎0845/773 3377; Ireland ☎1-800/626747, ⓦwww.britishairways.com.
bmibaby UK ☎0870/264 2229; Ireland ☎01/407 3036; ⓦwww.bmibaby.com.
Buzz UK ☎0870/240 7070, ⓦwww.buzzaway.com.
Czech Airlines (ČSA) London ☎020/7255 1898; Manchester ☎0161/489 0241; Ireland ☎01/814 4626, ⓦwww.csa.cz.
Go UK ☎0870/607 6543, ⓦwww.go-fly.com.
Lauda Air UK ☎0845/601 0948; Ireland ☎1-800/509142, ⓦwww.austrianairlines.co.uk.
Tyrolean Airlines UK ☎0845/601 0948; Ireland ☎1-800/509142, ⓦwww.austrianairlines.co.uk.

Specialist agents and operators in Britain

Bridgewater Travel ☎0161/703 3003, ⓦwww.bridgewater-travel.co.uk. Accommodation and package deals.
ČEDOK ☎020/7580 3778, ⓦwww.cedok.co.uk. Unreconstructed former state-owned tourist board offering flights, accommodation and package deals.
CIE Tours International Ireland ☎01/703 1888, ⓦwww.cietours.ie. General flight and tour agent.
Czech & Slovak Tourist Centre ☎020/7794 3263, ⓦwww.czech-slovak-tourist.co.uk. Accommodation, bus tickets, flights and tourist information.
Czech Birding ⓦwww.czechbirding.com. Regular bird-watching tours of the Czech Republic.

Czech Travel ☎01376/560592,
ⓦwww.czechtravel.freeuk.com. Rooms and flats for rent in Prague, plus flights.
Explore Worldwide ☎01252/760 000,
ⓦwww.exploreworldwide.com. Tailor-made trips to Prague and walking in the Tatras.
Hotel Connect ☎020/8731 7000,
ⓦwww.hotelconnect.co.uk. Accommodation in Prague.
Joe Walsh Tours Ireland ☎01/676 0991,
ⓦwww.joewalshtours.ie. General budget fares agent.
Martin Randall Travel UK ☎020/8742 3355,
ⓦwww.martinrandall.com. Small-group cultural tours led by experts on art, archeology and music.
McCarthy's Travel Ireland ☎021/427 0127,
ⓦwww.mccarthystravel.ie. General flight agent.
Neenan Travel Ireland ☎01/607 9900,
ⓦwww.neenantrav.ie. Specialists in European city breaks.
New Millennium ☎0870/240 3217,
ⓦwww.newmillennium-holidays.com. Cheap coach and hotel packages to the Czech Republic.
North South Travel UK ☎01245/608 291,
ⓦwww.northsouthtravel.co.uk. Friendly, competitive travel agency, offering discounted fares worldwide – profits are used to support projects in the developing world, especially the promotion of sustainable tourism.
Ramblers Holidays ☎01707/331133,
ⓦwww.ramblersholidays.co.uk. Trips to Prague and occasional walking holidays on offer.
Slovak Wildlife Society ☎020/8451 7555,
ⓦwww.slovakwildlife.org.uk. Holidays seeking out wolves, bears and eagles in Slovakia.
STA Travel UK ☎0870/1600 599,
ⓦwww.statravel.co.uk. Worldwide specialists in low-cost flights and tours for students and under-26s, though other customers welcome.
Student & Group Travel Ireland ☎01/677 7834. Student and group specialists to Europe.
Trailfinders UK ☎020/7628 7628; Ireland ☎01/677 7888; ⓦwww.trailfinders.com. One of the best-informed and most efficient agents for independent travellers.
Travelscene ☎0208/427 4445,
ⓦwww.travelscene.co.uk. Two-night breaks and upwards in Prague.

Flights from the USA and Canada

Czech Airlines (ČSA) are the only airline to offer non-stop flights from North America **to Prague**. Their most frequent service is from New York's JFK airport, with only a couple of flights a week departing from Toronto and Montréal. Flying time from New York to Prague is about eight and a half hours; Toronto to Prague is around ten hours. Austrian Airlines fly non-stop from New York and Washington DC **to Vienna**, the best gateway for Bratislava. A direct flight from the east coast to Vienna takes around nine hours.

Fares depend very much on the flexibility of the ticket and on availability. Tickets tend to be comparatively expensive if you buy directly from the national airlines, with an economy class New York–Prague or Vienna return costing between $800 and $1000, and a Toronto–Prague return rarely going below C$1200. By contrast, agents and consolidators regularly offer New York–Prague or Vienna return fares of between $600 and $800, and Toronto–Prague return fares of around C$1000. Note that the cheaper fares usually mean that the ticket is non-exchangeable and non-refundable.

You'll get a much wider choice of flights and ticket prices if you opt for the one- and two-stop flights offered by the major carriers (a selection of which are listed below), allowing you to depart from any number of North American gateways via one of the major European cities. Another option is to fly into Berlin, Leipzig or Munich. If the Czech and Slovak republics are part of a longer European trip, you'll also want to check out details of the Eurail pass (see p.16).

Airlines

Air Canada ☎1-888/247-2262,
ⓦwww.aircanada.ca.
Air France US ☎1-800/237-2747; Canada ☎1-800/667-2747; ⓦwww.airfrance.com.
American Airlines ☎1-800/433-7300,
ⓦwww.aa.com.
Austrian Airlines ☎1-800/843-0002,
ⓦwww.aua.com.
British Airways ☎1-800/247-9297,
ⓦwww.british-airways.com.
Czech Airlines (ČSA) US ☎1-877/359-6629 or 212/765-6022; Canada ☎416/363-3174;
ⓦwww.czechairlines.com.
Delta Air Lines ☎1-800/241-4141,
ⓦwww.delta.com.
Lufthansa US ☎1-800/645-3880; Canada ☎1-800/563-5954; ⓦwww.lufthansa-usa.com.
United Airlines ☎1-800/538-2929,
ⓦwww.ual.com.

Discount agents and tour operators

Airtech ☎1-877/247-8324 or 212/219-7000, ⓦwww.airtech.com. Standby seat broker; also deals in consolidator fares and courier flights.
Backroads ☎1-800/462-2848 or 510/527-1555, ⓦwww.backroads.com. Cycling in the Czech Republic.
BCT Scenic Walking ☎1-800/473-1210, ⓦwww.bctwalk.com. Hiking trips to the Czech Republic and to Prague.
Central Europe Holidays ☎1-800/800-8891, ⓦwww.tourdeal.com/ceheurope. Tour packages to Prague.
Council Travel ☎1-800/226-8624, ⓕ617/528-2091, ⓦwww.counciltravel.com. Nationwide organization that mostly, but by no means exclusively, specializes in student/budget travel.
Escapade Tours ☎1-800/356-2405, ⓦwww.isram.com. City breaks and multi-city Czech packages.
Europe Train Tours ☎1-800/551-2085, ⓦwww.ettours.com. Customized tours by rail, with special rates on Swiss and Finnair.
General Tours ☎1-800/221-2216, ⓦwww.generaltours.com. City breaks to Prague.
New Frontiers/Nouvelles Frontières ☎1-800/677-0720, ⓦwww.newfrontiers.com. French discount-travel firm based in New York City. Other branches in LA, San Francisco and Québec City.
REI Adventures ☎1-800/622-2236, ⓦwww.rei.com/travel. Cycling and hiking tours in the Czech Republic.
Romantic Czech Tours ☎206/522-4559, ⓦwww.romanticczechtours.com. Walking, biking, and customized tour operator specializing in Eastern Europe.
Skylink US ☎1-800/247-6659 or 212/573-8980; Canada ☎1-800/759-5465; ⓦwww.skylinkus.com. Consolidator.
Summit International Travel ☎1-800/527-8664, ⓦwww.summittours.com. Highly-regarded specialists in the area. Walking, bicycling and car packages plus customized tours.
STA Travel ☎1-800/777-0112 or 1-800/781-4040, ⓦwww.sta-travel.com. Worldwide specialists in independent travel; also student IDs, travel insurance, car rental, rail passes, etc.
TFI Tours International ☎1-800/745-8000 or 212/736-1140, ⓦwww.lowestairprice.com. Consolidator.
Travac ☎1-800/872-8800, ⓦwww.thetravelsite.com. Consolidator and charter broker with offices in New York City and Orlando.
Travel Avenue ☎1-800/333-3335, ⓦwww.travelavenue.com. Full-service travel agent that offers discounts in the form of rebates.
Travel Cuts Canada ☎1-800/667-2887; US ☎1-866/246-9762; ⓦwww.travelcuts.com. Canadian student-travel organization.

Flights from Australia and New Zealand

Flight time from Australia and New Zealand to Prague or Vienna is over twenty hours, and can be longer depending on routes, with those flights touching down in Southeast Asia the quickest and cheapest on average. To reach Prague, you'll have to change planes in one of the main European gateways; the same is true for Vienna, unless you fly with Lauda Air. Given the length of the journey involved, you might be better off including a night's stopover in your itinerary, and indeed some airlines include one in the price of the flight.

The cheapest direct scheduled flights to European gateways (including Vienna) are usually to be found on one of the Asian airlines. Average return fares (including taxes) from eastern gateways to London are A$1500–2000 in low season, A$2000–2500 in high season (fares from Perth or Darwin cost around A$200 less). You'll then need to add A$100–200 onto all these for the connecting flight on to Prague. Return fares from Auckland to London range between NZ$2000 and NZ$2500 depending on the season, route and carrier.

Airlines in Australia and New Zealand

Aeroflot Australia ☎02/9262 2233, ⓦwww.aeroflot.com.
Air New Zealand Australia ☎13 24 76; New Zealand ☎0800/737 000; ⓦwww.airnz.com.
Alitalia Australia ☎02/9262 3925, ⓦwww.alitalia.com.
American Airlines Australia ☎1300/650 747, ⓦwww.aa.com.
British Airways Australia ☎02/8904 8800; New Zealand ☎0800/274 847; ⓦwww.britishairways.com.
Czech Airlines (ČSA) Australia ☎02/9247 7706, ⓦwww.csa.cz/en.
Garuda Australia ☎02/9334 9970; New Zealand ☎09/366 1862; ⓦwww.garuda-indonesia.com.
KLM Australia ☎1300/303 747; New Zealand ☎09/309 1782; ⓦwww.klm.com.
Lauda Air Australia ☎02/9251 6155; New

Zealand ☎09/522 5948; ⓦwww.laudaair.com.
Lufthansa Australia ☎1300/655 727; New
Zealand ☎09/303 1529; ⓦwww.lufthansa.com.
Malaysia Airlines Australia ☎13 26 27; New
Zealand ☎09/373 2741; ⓦwww.mas.com.my.
Qantas Australia ☎13 13 13; New Zealand
☎09/661 901; ⓦwww.qantas.com.au.
Singapore Airlines Australia ☎13 10 11; New
Zealand ☎09/303 2129;
ⓦwww.singaporeair.com.
Sri Lankan Airlines Australia ☎02/9244 2234;
New Zealand ☎09/308 3353;
ⓦwww.airlanka.com.
Swiss Australia ☎1800/221 339,
ⓦwww.swiss.com.
Thai Airways Australia ☎1300/651 960; New
Zealand ☎09/377 3886; ⓦwww.thaiair.com.
Virgin Atlantic Airways Australia ☎02/9244
2747; New Zealand ☎09/308 3377;
ⓦwww.virgin-atlantic.com.

Travel agents and tour operators in Australia and New Zealand

Australians Studying Abroad ☎02/9509 1955,
ⓦwww.asatravinfo.com.au. Cultural, historical and
political package tours of Prague and Bohemia.
Budget Travel New Zealand ☎09/366 0061 or
0800/808 040, ⓦwww.budgettravel.co.nz. Long-
established agent with budget airfares and
accommodation packages.
Destinations Unlimited New Zealand ☎09/373
4033. Discount fares with a good selection of tours
and holiday packages.
Flight Centres Australia ☎13 31 33 or 02/9235
3522; New Zealand ☎09/358 4310;
ⓦwww.flightcentre.com.au. Concentrates on
discounted airfares.
Gateway Travel Australia ☎02/9745 3333,
ⓦwww.russian-gateway.com.au. Packages to the
Czech Republic.
Silke's Travel Australia ☎1800/807 860 or
02/8347 2000, ⓦwww.silkes.com.au. Gay and
lesbian specialist travel agent.
STA Travel Australia ☎1300/733 035,
ⓦwww.statravel.com.au; New Zealand
☎0508/782 872, ⓦwww.statravel.co.nz. Fare
discounts for students and under 25s as well as
student cards, rail passes and accommodation.
Student Uni Travel Australia ☎02/9232 8444,
ⓔaustralia@backpackers.net. Discounted airfares
and student/youth travel specialists.
Trailfinders Australia ☎02/9247 7666,
ⓦwww.trailfinders.com.au. Discounted flights, car
rental, tailor-made tours, rail passes and RTW tours.

By train

You can travel from London to Prague or
Bratislava (via Vienna) overnight in around
twenty hours by **train**. The fares, however,
only really compete with standard scheduled
airline tickets.

The routes

There are several possible routes from
London to Prague via **Eurostar**. The quickest option is to catch the train just after 2pm
from Waterloo, arriving in Brussels Midi an
hour before the departure of the
Brussels–Köln service. From **Köln**, there's an
overnight service to Prague, which gets into
the Czech capital just after 10am the following morning. If you set off a couple of hours
earlier from Waterloo, and change at
Brussels, Köln and **Frankfurt**, you can pick
up an earlier overnight service and arrive at
around 8am in Prague. If you're heading
straight for Bratislava, there's a direct
overnight service from **Brussels** to Vienna.
Arriving at Vienna's Westbahnhof, you must
make your way to the city's Südbahnhof and
catch a train to Bratislava.

Although you can simply crash out on the
seats on the overnight service from Köln to
Prague or from Brussels to Vienna, it makes
sense to book a **couchette** which costs
around £15 one-way in a six-berth compartment, rising to £20 in a four-berth compartment. Couchettes are mixed-sex and allow
little privacy; for a bit more comfort, you can
book a bed in a single-sex three-berth
sleeper for around £35 one-way, or £45 for
a two-berth compartment. You should be
able to book your couchette or sleeper when
you buy your ticket, but if you have any
problems, contact German Railways
(Deutsche Bahn) – see p.16. However you
decide to sleep, if you're heading for Prague,
you'll probably be woken up in the early
hours of the morning when the train crosses
the Czech border.

Tickets and passes

Fares for continental rail travel are much
more flexible than they used to be, so it's
worth shopping around for the best deal,
rather than taking the first offer you get. The
cheapest deals for a return ticket from
London–Prague or London–Vienna tend to

hover around £200; tickets are usually valid for two months and allow as many stopovers as you want on the specified route. To qualify for the most heavily discounted fares, however, there are usually various restrictions: you may have to stay over a Saturday night, and your Eurostar ticket may be non-exchangeable and non-refundable. If you're travelling with one or more companions, you may be eligible for a further discount.

Those **under 26** can purchase discounted tickets from one of the rail agents listed on below, thus saving up to 25 percent on the return fare. Travellers **over 60** can also get discounts of up to thirty percent between, but not within, European countries by purchasing a **Rail Plus** card at a cost of £12. However, before you can buy this card, you must already possess a British Senior Rail Card (£18); both are valid for a year.

Virtually the only way to buy an international train ticket at the moment is via a travel agent or over the phone with one of the rail agents listed on below. However, while Eurostar can book you as far as Paris or Brussels from any station in the UK, they can't book your onward travel; conversely, Rail Europe and the other national rail agents can only book your journey from London onwards – for travel within the UK, contact National Rail Enquiries (☎08457/484950). Both European Rail and Trainseurope can book you from anywhere in the UK to anywhere in Europe. The only British stations that can sell you an international train ticket over the counter (further than Paris or Brussels) are Euston and Charing Cross in London.

If you're planning to visit the Czech and Slovak republics as part of a more extensive trip around Europe, it may be worth purchasing an **InterRail pass**, which gives you unlimited rail travel within certain countries; you must, however, have been resident in Europe for at least six months. InterRail tickets are currently zonal: to travel to the Czech and Slovak republics and back, you'll need at least a three-zone pass, costing £209 for one month for those under 26, and £299 a month for those aged 26 and over. Passes are not valid in the UK, though you're entitled to discounts in Britain and on Eurostar and cross-Channel ferries. Either way, though, you're only really going to get your money back if you do a lot of travelling.

North Americans, Australians and New Zealanders who don't qualify for the InterRail pass can obtain a **Eurail pass**, which comes in various forms, and must be bought before leaving home. For more information, and to reserve tickets, contact: Rail Europe in North America (US ☎1-877/456-7245; Canada ☎1-800/361-7245; ⓦwww.raileurope.com); and CIT World Travel (☎02/9267 1255 or ☎03/9650 5510, ⓦwww.cittravel.com.au) or Rail Plus (☎1300/555 003 or ☎03/9642 8644, ⓔinfo@railplus.com.au) in Australia.

Rail contacts

Belgian Railways UK ☎020/7593 2332, ⓦwww.b-rail.be. Sells tickets from London across Europe, with discounts on journeys through Belgium.

European Rail ☎020/7387 0444, ⓦwww.europeanrail.com. Rail specialists that consistently offer competitive prices on international rail tickets from anywhere in the UK.

Eurostar ☎0870/160 6600, ⓦwww.eurostar.com. Latest fares and youth discounts (plus online booking) on the London–Paris and London–Brussels Eurostar service, and competitive add-on fares from the rest of the UK.

German Railways (Deutsche Bahn) UK ☎0870/243 5363, ⓦwww.bahn.de. Competitive discounted fares for any journey from London across Europe, with very reasonable prices for those journeys that pass through Germany.

Rail Europe UK ☎0870/584 8848, ⓦwww.raileurope.co.uk. SNCF-owned information and ticket agent for all European passes and journeys from London.

Trainseurope UK ☎020/8699 3654, ⓦwww.trainseurope.co.uk. Travel agent specializing in organizing discounted international rail travel.

By bus

One of the cheapest ways to get to Prague, Brno or Bratislava is by **bus**. There are direct services from London's Victoria Station more or less daily throughout the year. Some bus companies continue their journeys via Brno and Bratislava, though you may have to change in Prague. For Bratislava, it may be more convenient to go to Vienna, and change buses there. The journey is bearable (just about), but only really worth it if you absolutely can't find the extra cash for a budget flight. Prices between companies vary very slightly so it's worth ringing round to find the best deal; a return ticket can cost as little as £65. Addresses and telephone numbers for all current operators are given below.

Another option worth considering if you're heading for other parts of Europe as well as the Czech and Slovak republics is a **Eurolines Pass**. The pass, which covers all the major cities in Europe (including Prague and Vienna, but not Bratislava), is valid for fifteen days (£155/£130, over 26/under 26), thirty days (£229/£186) or sixty days (£267/£205). Prices outside the peak period (June to mid-Sept) are around thirty percent cheaper.

From mid-April to mid-October **Busabout** offers a hop-on, hop-off bus service, which calls at Prague, plus numerous other cities in western Europe including Vienna, but, again, not Bratislava. The **Consecutive Pass** allows unlimited travel from two weeks (£179/£159, over 26/under 26) to seven months (£699/£629); the **Flexible Pass** gives you anything from ten days' travel in two months (£169/£149) to 25 days in four months (£549/£449). There's a ten percent discount for those travelling before mid-May.

Bus contacts

Busabout ☎020/7950 1661, ⓦwww.busabout.com. European bus passes. The passes are available from STA Travel (see p.13) in the US.
Capital Express ☎020/7243 0488, ⓦwww.capitalexpressuk.com. Regular London to Prague services via Eurotunnel.
Eurolines UK ☎0870/514 3219; Republic of Ireland ☎01/836 6111; ⓦwww.eurolines.co.uk. Tickets can also be purchased from any National Express agent – ☎0870/580 8080, ⓦwww.gobycoach.com.
Kingscourt Express ☎0800/496 0001, ⓦwww.kce.cz. Czech-based bus company running regular services from London to Prague via the ferry.

By car

With two or more passengers, **driving** to the Czech and Slovak republics can work out relatively inexpensive. However, it is not the most relaxing option, unless you enjoy pounding along the motorway systems of Europe for the best part of a day and a night.

The **Eurotunnel** service through the Channel Tunnel doesn't significantly affect total travel times, though it does of course speed up the cross-Channel section of the journey. Eurotunnel operates a 24-hour service carrying cars, motorcycles, buses and their passengers to Calais. At peak times, services run every fifteen minutes, with the journey lasting 35 minutes. Off-peak fares start at around £300 return (passengers included) – no bargain, though special offers do appear from time to time.

The alternative cross-Channel options for most travellers are the conventional **ferry** links between Dover and Calais, Ostend or Zeebrugge. Fares vary enormously with the time of year, month and even day that you travel, and the size of your car. If you book in advance, the cheapest off-peak summer fare on the Dover–Calais run, for example, can be as little as £170 return per carload. Journey times are usually around ninety minutes.

Once you've made it onto the continent, you've got some **1000km of driving** ahead of you. Theoretically, you could make it in twelve hours solid, but realistically it will take you longer. The most direct route from Calais or Ostend is via Brussels, Liège (Luik), Cologne (Köln), Frankfurt, Würzburg and Nuremberg (Nürnberg), entering the country at the **Waidhaus–Rozvadov** border crossing. Another possibility is to head east from Cologne through Hessen via Erfurt and Chemnitz, and enter at the **Reitzenhain–Pohraniční** border crossing. If you're heading straight for Slovakia, continue along the autobahn from Nuremberg (Nürnberg) in a southeasterly direction via Regensburg, Passau, Linz and Vienna, entering Slovakia at the **Berg–Bratislava** border crossing. Motorways in Belgium and Germany are free, but to travel on any motorways within Austria, the Czech Republic or Slovakia, you'll need to buy the relevant **tax disc** in each of those countries, available from all border crossings and most post offices and petrol stations.

If you're travelling by car, you'll need proof of ownership, or a letter from the owner giving you permission to drive the car. A British or other EU driving licence is fine; all other drivers are advised to purchase an International Driving Licence. You also need a red warning triangle in case you break down, a first-aid kit (both these are compulsory in the Czech and Slovak republics), and a "Green Card" for third party insurance cover at the very least. An even better idea is to sign up with one of the national motoring organizations, who offer continental breakdown assistance and, in extreme circumstances, will get you and your vehicle brought back home if necessary.

Cross-channel contacts

Eurotunnel ☎0870/535 3535, ⓦwww.eurotunnel.com. Through the channel tunnel.
Hoverspeed ☎0870/240 8070, ⓦwww.hoverspeed.co.uk. Dover to Calais and Ostend.
Norfolk Line ☎0870/870 1020, ⓦwww.norfolkline.com. Dover to Dunkirk.
P&O Stena Line ☎0870/600 0600, ⓦwww.posl.com. Dover to Calais and Zeebrugge.
Sea France ☎0870/571 1711, ⓦwww.seafrance.com. Dover to Calais.

Red tape and visas

US, New Zealand and all EU nationals need only a full passport to enter either the Czech Republic or Slovakia, though the passport itself must be valid for at least six months beyond your return date. US citizens can stay for up to 30 days; UK citizens can stay up to 180 days; all other EU citizens and New Zealanders can stay up to 90 days. All visitors must register with the police within three days of arrival (if you're staying in a campsite, hostel, pension or hotel, this will be done for you). Entry requirements do change, so if in doubt, check with your nearest embassy or consulate before you leave, or look on the Czech and Slovak foreign ministry websites ⓦwww.czech.cz or ⓦwww.foreign.gov.sk.

At the time of writing Canadians and South Africans need a **visa** for the Czech Republic, but not for Slovakia, while Australians need a visa for both countries. Visas (valid for up to thirty days) must be bought beforehand from a Czech embassy or consulate; prices vary (around £25 is the norm), and can take ten to fifteen working days to obtain by post. Along with your application form you'll need a valid passport and two passport photographs (four for a multiple entry visa) and a SAE if applying by post.

If you wish to extend your visa or your stay, you need to go to the Foreigners' Police headquarters in Prague or Bratislava (addresses are given in the directories of those cities).

For an updated list of Czech and Slovak embassies and consulates abroad, go to ⓦwww.mfa.cz. Foreign embassies and consulates in Prague are listed on p.141; those in Bratislava are listed on p.449.

Czech embassies and consulates

Australia 169 Military Rd, Dover Heights, Sydney, NSW 2030 ☎02/9371 8887.
Austria Penzingerstrasse 11–13, 1140 Vienna ☎0222/894 2125.
Canada 541 Sussex Drive, Ottawa, Ontario K1N 6Z6 ☎613/562 3875.
Germany Wilhelmstrasse 44, 10117 Berlin ☎030/226380.
Ireland 57 Northumberland Rd, Ballsbridge, Dublin 4 ☎01/668 1135.
New Zealand 48 Hair St, Wainuiomata, Wellington ☎44/939 1610.
South Africa 2 Fleetwood Ave, Claremont 7700, Cape Town ☎021/7979 835.
UK 26 Kensington Palace Gdns, London W8 4QY ☎020/7243 1115.
USA 3900 Spring of Freedom St NW, Washington DC 20008 ☎202/274 9100.

Slovak embassies and consulates

Australia Level 42 Gateway, 1 MacQuarie Plata, NSW 2000, Sydney ☎06/290 1516.
Austria Armbrustergasse 24,1190 Vienna ☎0222/318 9055.
Canada 50 Rideau Terrace, Ottawa, Ontario K1M 2A1 ☎613/749 4442.
Germany Pariser Strasse 44, 10707 Berlin ☎030/88926.
Ireland 20 Clyde Rd, Ballsbridge, Dublin 4 ☎01/660 0012.
New Zealand Level 11, ASB Bank Centre, 135 Albert St, PO Box 7359, Auckland ☎09/366 5111.
South Africa 930 Arcadia St, Arcadia, Pretoria ☎012/342 2051
UK 25 Kensington Palace Gardens, London W8 4QY ☎020/7243 0803.
USA 3523 International Court NW, Washington DC 20008 ☎202/237 1054.

Customs allowances into the Czech and Slovak republics are 250 cigarettes or 50 cigars, one litre of spirits and two litres of wine. Allowances when taking goods from either republic into EU countries are the same. However, these allowances may change in the future, so if in doubt, check with customs before you leave.

Border police in both republics have the power to ask visitors to prove they have sufficient funds for their visit. It has to be said that these restrictions are primarily aimed at visitors from the east, but it's as well to be aware of this. The easiest way around the problem is to have at least £30/$50 a day in travellers' cheques, cash or in a bank statement; credit cards on their own will not be accepted as proof. In addition, Slovak border police also have the power to ask visitors to provide proof of a comprehensive medical insurance policy.

Insurance and health

Before setting out, you'd do well to take out an insurance policy to cover against theft, loss and illness or injury. Before paying for a new policy, however, it's worth checking whether you are already covered: some all-risks home insurance policies may cover your possessions when overseas, and many private medical schemes include cover when abroad. In Canada, provincial health plans usually provide partial cover for medical mishaps overseas, while holders of official student/teacher/youth cards in Canada and the US are entitled to meagre accident coverage and hospital in-patient benefits. Students will often find that their student health coverage extends during the vacations and for one term beyond the date of last enrolment.

After exhausting the possibilities above, you might want to contact a specialist travel insurance company, or consider the travel insurance deal we offer (see box p.20). A typical travel insurance policy usually provides cover for the loss of baggage, tickets and – up to a certain limit – cash or cheques, as well as cancellation or curtailment of your journey. Most of them exclude so-called dangerous sports unless an extra premium is paid. Many policies can be chopped and changed to exclude coverage you don't need – for example, sickness and accident benefits can often

be excluded or included at will. If you do take medical coverage, ascertain whether benefits will be paid as treatment proceeds or only after return home, and whether there is a 24-hour medical emergency number. When securing baggage cover, make sure that the per-article limit – typically under £500 – will cover your most valuable possession. If you need to make a claim, you should keep receipts for medicines and medical treatment, and in the event you have anything stolen, you must obtain an official statement from the police (see p.25).

Rough Guides travel insurance

Rough Guides offers its own travel insurance, customized for our readers by a leading UK broker and backed by a Lloyd's underwriter. It's available for anyone, of any nationality and any age, travelling anywhere in the world.

There are two main Rough Guide insurance plans: **Essential**, for basic, no-frills cover; and **Premier** – with more generous and extensive benefits. Alternatively, you can take out **annual multi-trip insurance**, which covers you for any number of trips throughout the year (with a maximum of 60 days for any one trip). Unlike many policies, the Rough Guides schemes are calculated by the day, so if you're travelling for 27 days rather than a month, that's all you pay for. If you intend to be away for the whole year, the Adventurer policy will cover you for 365 days. Each plan can be supplemented with a "Hazardous Activities Premium" if you plan to indulge in sports considered dangerous, such as skiing, scuba-diving or trekking.

For a policy quote, call the Rough Guide Insurance Line on UK freefone ⊕0800/015 0906, US toll-free ⊕1-866/220 5588 or, if you're calling from elsewhere ⊕+44 1243/621 046. Alternatively, get an online quote or buy online at ⊚www.roughguidesinsurance.com.

Health matters

No inoculations are required for the Czech and Slovak republics, and on a short visit you're unlikely to fall victim to anything worse than an upset stomach. However, with both countries blighted by decades of ecological abuse, there is well-founded concern about the quality of the water, milk, meat and vegetables.

Reciprocal arrangements between the Czech and Slovak republics and most EU countries (including Britain and Ireland) mean that you're entitled to free emergency medical care, with a charge only for imported drugs and certain specialized treatments. Citizens of other countries should have their own health insurance, and even EU residents would be well advised to take out their own health policy, as the reciprocal agreement only covers emergency treatment and not a visit to a doctor. Indeed, it is now compulsory to have full medical insurance in order to enter Slovakia.

If you should fall ill, it's easiest to go to a **pharmacy** (*lékárna* in Czech, *lekáreň* in Slovak). Pharmacists are willing to give advice (though language may be a problem) and able to dispense many drugs available only on prescription in other Western countries. They usually keep normal business hours, but at least one in each major town will be open 24 hours for minor problems. If it's an emergency, dial ⊕155 for an ambulance and you'll be taken to the nearest hospital.

Health websites

⊚**http://health.yahoo.com** Information on specific diseases and conditions, drugs and herbal remedies, as well as advice from health experts.
⊚**www.istm.org** The website of the International Society for Travel Medicine, with a full list of clinics specializing in international travel health.
⊚**www.tripprep.com** Travel Health Online provides an online-only comprehensive database of necessary vaccinations for most countries, as well as destination and medical service provider information.
⊚**www.fitfortravel.scot.nhs.uk** UK NHS website carrying information about travel-related diseases and how to avoid them.

Costs, money and banks

In general terms, the Czech and Slovak republics are incredibly cheap for Westerners, with the exception of accommodation, which is comparable with many EU countries. That said, price differentiation across the country is now quite marked: costs in the centre of Prague (and, to a lesser extent, Bratislava) creep ever upwards, while in some parts of the countryside, they remain much more static.

Most of your daily allowance will go on **accommodation**, with even the cheapest places charging around £10/$16 a night. All other basic costs, like food, drink and transport, remain very cheap indeed. To put things in perspective, however, it's worth bearing in mind that the average monthly salary for Czechs is around 15,000Kč (£300/$450), and less than that for Slovaks.

Currency

The Czech and Slovak republics use separate currencies, both known as the crown. The Czech crown is fully convertible, so it's possible to buy some currency and bring it with you; the Slovak crown is not fully convertible, which theoretically means you can't buy any currency until you arrive in the country. For the most up-to-date exchange rates, consult the useful currency converter websites ⓦwww.oanda.com or ⓦwww.xe.com/ucc.

The currency in the Czech Republic is the **Czech crown** or *koruna česká* (abbreviated to Kč or CZK), which is divided into one hundred relatively worthless hellers or *halíře* (abbreviated to h). At the time of going to press there were around 50Kč to the pound sterling, 30Kč to the Euro and around 35Kč to the US dollar. Notes come in 20Kč, 50Kč, 100Kč, 200Kč, 500Kč, 1000Kč and 2000Kč (less frequently 5000Kč) denominations; coins as 1Kč, 2Kč, 5Kč, 10Kč, 20Kč and 50Kč, plus 10h, 20h and 50h.

The currency in Slovakia is the **Slovak crown** or *Slovenská koruna* (abbreviated to Sk), which is divided into 100 heller or *halér* (abbreviated to h). At the time of going to press there were around 70Sk to the pound sterling, 45Sk to the Euro and around 50Sk to the US dollar.

Notes come in 20Sk, 50Sk, 100Sk, 200Sk, 500Sk and 1000Sk (less frequently 5000Sk) denominations; coins as 1Sk, 2Sk, 5Sk and 10Sk, plus 10h, 20h, 50h.

Travellers' cheques, credit and debit cards

Although they are the traditional way to carry funds, **travellers' cheques** are no longer the cheapest nor the most convenient option – debit cards are better (see below) – although they do offer safety against loss or theft. The usual fee for buying travellers' cheques is one or two percent, though this fee may be waived if you buy the cheques through a bank where you have an account. Be sure to keep the purchase agreement and a record of the cheques' serial numbers safe and separate from the cheques themselves. In the event that cheques are lost or stolen, the issuing company will expect you to report the loss forthwith to their nearest office; most companies claim to replace lost or stolen cheques within 24 hours.

Credit cards are a very convenient way of carrying your funds, and can be used either in ATMs or over the counter. Remember that all cash advances are treated as loans, with interest accruing daily from the date of withdrawal; there may be a transaction fee on top of this. However, you may be able to make withdrawals from ATMs in the Czech and Slovak republics using your **debit card**, which is not liable to interest payments, and the flat transaction fee is usually quite small – your bank will be able to advise on this. Make sure you have a personal identification number (PIN) that's designed to work overseas.

Changing money

Most Czech and Slovak banks will be prepared to change travellers' cheques and

21

give cash advances on credit cards – look for the window marked *směnárna/ zmenáreň*. Commissions at banks are fairly reasonable (generally under three percent), but the queues and the bureaucracy can mean a long wait. Quicker, but more of a rip-off in terms of either commission or exchange rate, are the exchange outlets which exist in the bigger towns and cities.

Banking hours are usually Monday to Friday 8am to 5pm, often with a break at lunchtime. Outside of these times, you may find the odd bank open, but otherwise you'll have to rely on exchange outlets and international hotels.

Wiring money

Having money wired from home using one of the companies listed below is never convenient or cheap, and should be considered a last resort. It's also possible to have money wired directly from a bank in your home country to a bank in the Czech Republic or Slovakia, although this is likely to take a couple of days and will cost around £25/$40 per transaction. If you can last out the week, then an international money order, exchangeable at any post office, is by far the cheapest way of sending money. If you're in really dire straits, get in touch with your consulate in Prague or Bratislava, who will usually let you make one phone call home free of charge, and will – in worst cases only – repatriate you, but will never, under any circumstances, lend you money.

Money-wiring companies

American Express Moneygram Australia ☎1800/230 100; New Zealand ☎09/379 8243 or 0800/262 263; UK and Republic of Ireland ☎0800/6663 9472; US and Canada ☎1-800/926-9400; ⊛www.moneygram.com.
Thomas Cook Britain ☎01733/318 922; Canada ☎1-888/823-4732; Northern Ireland ☎028/9055 0030; Republic of Ireland ☎01/677 1721; US ☎1-800/287-7362; ⊛www.us.thomascook.com.
Western Union Australia ☎1800/649 565; New Zealand ☎09/270 0050; Republic of Ireland ☎1800/395 395; UK ☎0800/833 833; US and Canada ☎1-800/325-6000; ⊛www.westernunion.com.

Business hours

Business hours in both republics are generally Monday to Friday 9am to 5pm, though most supermarkets and tourist shops work longer hours. Smaller shops usually close for lunch for an hour sometime between noon and 2pm. Those shops that open on Saturday are generally shut by noon or 1pm, and very few open on Sunday. The majority of pubs and restaurants outside the big cities tend to close between 10pm and 11pm, with food often unavailable after 9pm.

Information, websites and maps

While the Czechs have a network of tourist centres across the world, where you can pick up maps and brochures, the Slovaks have yet to establish a similar global presence. In most countries, the Slovak embassy or consulate will have to be your first port of call. However, with lots of Czech and Slovak websites now available online in English, it should be easy enough to glean some useful information about either republic before you set out.

Czech tourist offices

Once in the Czech Republic, you'll find most large towns and cities now have a **tourist** office, usually known as an *informační centrum*, specifically designed to assist visitors. Most will hand out (or sell for a small fee) basic maps and pamphlets on local sights.

They may also be able to assist with finding accommodation, but don't rely on this. Hours vary and are detailed in the text. In those places where there is no information centre, your best bet is probably to try the reception at the nearest large hotel. In Prague itself, simply go to one of the branches of the **PIS** (*Pražská informační služba*), whose staff can book accommodation and theatre and concert tickets, and answer most questions.

Czech centres abroad

Austria Herrengasse 17, 1010 Vienna
℡ 0222/535 2361.
Belgium Boulevard Leopold II Laan 262, 1080 Brussels ℡ 02/644 9527, @ www.czechcenter.be.
Germany Friedrichstrasse 206, 10969 Berlin
℡ 030/208 2592, @ www.czech-berlin.de.
Slovakia Hviezdoslavovo nám 8, 811 02 Bratislava ℡ 02/5920 3305, @ www.czc.sk.
UK 95 Great Portland St, London W1 5RA
℡ 020/7291 9920, @ www.czechcentre.org.uk.
USA 1109 Madison Ave, New York, NY 10028
℡ 212/288 0830, @ www.czechcenter.com.

Useful websites

Czech language @ www.bohemica.com. Czech language and culture – especially language. You can learn it online and there are lots of links to Czech sites.
Downtown/Do města @ www.downtown.cz. Prague's fortnightly listings leaflet online in English and Czech.
High Tatras @ www.tatry.sk. Excellent guide to the High Tatras, with plenty of info, travel and accommodation details, and particularly good for walkers, climbers and skiers.
Maps @ www.mapy.cz. This site will provide you with a thumbnail map to help you find any hotel, restaurant, pub, shop or street in the Czech Republic.
News @ www.ceskenoviny.cz/news and @ www.tasr.sk. Weekly news in English from the Czech News Agency (ČTK) and the Slovak News Agency (TASR).
Prague Post @ www.praguepost.cz. A very useful site, not just for getting the latest news, but also for finding out what's on in Prague over the coming week.
Radio Prague @ www.radio.cz/english. An informative site well worth visiting, with updated news and weather as audio or text.
Romanies @ www.romnews.com. Official website

of the Roma/gypsies. Loads of news about Romanies all over Europe.
Slovak Spectator @ www.slovakspectator.sk. Online version of the Bratislava-based English-language weekly, with news, sport, weather and listings.
Slovak Tourist Board @ www.sacr.sk. The official Slovak Tourist Board website with basic, but useful information on the country.
Welcome to the Czech Republic
@ www.czech.cz. Basic information on the country in English, and on the worldwide network of Czech Centres, run by the Czech Foreign Ministry.

Slovak tourist offices

The **BIS** (*Bratislavská informačná služba*) in Bratislava is a tourist office specifically set up to give information to foreign visitors, selling maps, booking accommodation and helping with general enquiries. Most large towns and cities in Slovakia have followed suit, and now have their own tourist office, or centre for *informácie*. In the High Tatras, for instance, the PIA (*Popradská informačná agentúra*) fulfils much the same role. Otherwise, your best bet for local information and help with accommodation is probably the reception of the nearest hotel.

Slovak tourist offices abroad

Czech & Slovak Tourist Centre
℡ 020/7794 3263, @ www.czech-slovak-tourist.co.uk. In Britain, the Slovak embassy points callers in the direction of this friendly North London travel agent.
Slovak Information Center 406 East 67th St, New York, NY 10021 ℡ 212-737 3971, @ www.inx.net/~matica. This New York centre is the nearest you'll get to a national tourist office in the US.

Maps

There are lots of good maps available now in the Czech and Slovak republics. Geodézie produce an excellent range of **road maps**, with the 1:200,000 version probably the best general touring atlas; in Slovakia VKÚ, the military mapmakers, produce an incredibly detailed 1:100,000 version.

Shocart, along with several other competitors, do a series of 1:50,000 **walking maps**, which cover the whole of the Czech

Addresses and town names

The street name is always written before the number in **addresses**. The word for street (*ulice/ulica*) is either abbreviated to *ul.* or simply missed out altogether – Celetná ulice, for instance, is commonly known as Celetná. Other terms often abbreviated are *náměstí/námestie* (square), *třída/trieda* (avenue), and *nábřeží/nábrežie* (embankment), which become *nám., tř./tr.* and *nábř./nábr.* respectively.

Bear in mind when using a Czech or Slovak **index** that "Ch" is considered a separate letter and comes after H in the alphabet. Similarly, "Č", "Ď", "Ĺ", "Ř", "Š" and "Ž" are all listed separately, immediately after their non-accented cousins.

Many towns and villages in the Czech and Slovak republics were once (or still are) inhabited by **German** (or **Hungarian**) minorities. In these places we have given the German (or Hungarian) name in brackets after the Czech or Slovak, for example Mariánské Lázně (Marienbad).

Republic, marking all the colour-coded paths which criss-cross the countryside. In Slovakia, the 1:50,000 series is produced by VKÚ; again, it covers the whole country, and in the more popular walking areas there's usually a 1:25,000 version. Local **town plans** (*plán města* or *mapa mesta*), showing bus, tram and trolleybus routes, should be available from most bookshops and some hotels.

Map outlets

UK and Ireland

Easons Bookshop 40 O'Connell St, Dublin 1 ☎01/873 3811, ⓦwww.eason.ie.
Stanfords 12–14 Long Acre, WC2E 9LP ☎020/7836 1321, ⓦwww.stanfords.co.uk, ⓔsales@stanfords.co.uk. Maps available by mail, phone order, or email. Other branches within

British Airways offices at 156 Regent St, London W1R 5TA ☎020/7434 4744, and 29 Corn St, Bristol BS1 1HT ☎0117/929 9966.

USA and Canada

Rand McNally ☎1-800/333-0136, ⓦwww.randmcnally.com. Around thirty stores across the USA; dial ext 2111 or check the website for the nearest location.
World of Maps 1235 Wellington St, Ottawa, Ontario K1Y 3A3 ☎1-800/214-8524, ⓦwww.worldofmaps.com.

Australia and New Zealand

Specialty Maps 46 Albert St, Auckland 1001 ☎09/307 2217, ⓦwww.ubdonline.co.nz/maps.
Mapland 372 Little Bourke St, Melbourne, Victoria 3000 ☎03/9670 4383, ⓦwww.mapland.com.au.

Trouble and the police

Despite their change of name to *Policie* (in Czech) and *Polícia* (in Slovak), the national police are still extremely unpopular. Both republics have experienced a dramatic rise in crime since 1989. However, you shouldn't be unduly paranoid: the crime rate is still very low compared with most European or North American cities.

The **national police**, who wear navy blue, grey and white in the Czech Republic, and khaki-green with red lapels in Slovakia, are under the control of their respective ministries of interior. However, if you do need the police – and above all if you're reporting a serious crime – you should always go to the **municipal police**, run by the local authorities and known as *Městská policie* (in Czech) and *Mestská polícia* (in Slovak); their uniforms differ from region to region, though black is a popular choice.

In addition, there are various **private police forces**, who also dress in black – hence their nickname *Černí šerifové* (Black Sheriffs) – employed mostly by hotels and banks. They are allowed to carry guns, but have no powers of arrest, and you are not legally obliged to show them your ID.

Avoiding trouble

Almost all the problems encountered by tourists in the Czech and Slovak republics are to do with **petty crime** rather than more serious physical confrontations. Theft from cars and hotel rooms is commonplace, but Prague is also currently one of the worst cities in Europe for **pickpockets**. Sensible precautions include making photocopies of your passport, leaving passport and tickets in the hotel safe and noting down travellers' cheque and credit card numbers. If you have a car, don't leave anything in view when you park it, and take the cassette/radio with you if you can. Vehicles are rarely stolen, but lug-gage and valuables left in cars do make a tempting target and rental cars are easy to spot.

In theory, you're supposed to carry some form of **identification** at all times, and the police can stop you in the street and demand it. In practice, they're rarely bothered if you're clearly a foreigner (unless you're driving). In any case, the police are now so deferential that they tend to confine themselves to socially acceptable activities like traffic control and harassing Romanies.

What to do if you're robbed

If you are unlucky enough to have something stolen, you will need to go to the police to report it, not least because your insurance company will require a police report. It's unlikely that there'll be anyone there who speaks English, and even less likely that your belongings will be retrieved but, at the very least, you should get a statement detailing what you've lost for your insurance claim. Try the phrase *byl jsem oloupen* (pronounced something like "bill sem ollow-pen") or (if you're a woman) *byla jsem oloupena* – "I have been robbed".

Emergencies	
Ambulance	☎ 155
Police	☎ 158
Fire	☎ 150

Travellers with disabilities

Under the Communists very little attention was paid to the needs of the disabled. Attitudes are slowly changing – all new buildings now have to provide disabled access – but there is still a long way to go, and chronic shortage of funds in both countries makes matters worse.

Transport is a major problem, since buses and all except the newest trams and trains are virtually impossible for wheelchairs, though some Prague metro and train stations now have facilities for the disabled. The prevalence of cobbles, and general lack of ramps, make life hard even on the streets.

At the time of writing, none of the car rental companies could offer vehicles with hand controls in either republic. For help and advice obtaining one in Prague, contact the local Association of Disabled People (*Sdružení zdravotné postižených*), Karlínské nám. 12 (☏224 816 997, extension 238). If you're driving to Prague, most cross-Channel ferries now have adequate facilities, as does British Airways for those who are flying.

For a list of wheelchair-friendly hotels, restaurants, metro stations and so forth, in Prague, order the guidebook *Accessible Prague/Přístupná Praha* from the Prague Wheelchair Association (*Pražská organizace vozíčkářů*), Benediktská 6, Staré Město (☏224 827 210, ⓦwww.pov.cz). The association can organize airport pick-up in Prague if you contact them well in advance, and can help with transporting wheelchairs.

Contacts for travellers with disabilities

UK and Ireland

Access Travel 6 The Hillock, Astley, Lancashire M29 7GW ☏01942/888 844, ⓦwww.access-travel.co.uk. Tour operator that can arrange flights, transfer and accommodation. This is a small business, personally checking out places before recommendation. ATOL bonded, established seven years.
Holiday Care 2nd floor, Imperial Building, Victoria Rd, Horley, Surrey RH6 7PZ ☏01293/774 535, Minicom ☏01293/776 943, ⓦwww.holidaycare.org.uk. Provides free lists of accessible accommodation abroad. Information on financial help for holidays available.
Irish Wheelchair Association Blackheath Drive, Clontarf, Dublin 3 ☏01/833 8241, ⓕ833 3873, ⓔiwa@iol.ie. Useful information provided about travelling abroad with a wheelchair.
Tripscope Alexandra House, Albany Rd, Brentford, Middlesex TW8 0NE ☏0845/7585 641, ⓔtripscope@cableinet.co.uk, ⓦwww.justmobility.co.uk/tripscope. This registered charity provides a national telephone information service offering free advice on UK and international transport for those with a mobility problem.

USA and Canada

Access-Able ⓦwww.access-able.com. Online resource for travellers with disabilities.
Directions Unlimited 123 Green Lane, Bedford Hills, NY 10507 ☏1-800/533-5343 or 914/241-1700. Tour operator specializing in custom tours for people with disabilities.
Mobility International USA 451 Broadway, Eugene, OR 97401, voice and TDD ☏541/343-1284, ⓦwww.miusa.org. Information and referral services, access guides, tours and exchange programmes. Annual membership $35 (includes quarterly newsletter).
Society for the Advancement of Travelers with Handicaps (SATH) 347 5th Ave, New York, NY 10016 ☏212/447-7284, ⓦwww.sath.org. Non-profit educational organization that has actively represented travellers with disabilities since 1976.
Travel Information Service ☏215/456-9600. Telephone-only information and referral service.
Twin Peaks Press Box 129, Vancouver, WA 98661 ☏360/694-2462 or 1-800/637-2256, ⓦwww.twinpeak.virtualave.net. Publisher of the *Directory of Travel Agencies for the Disabled* ($19.95), listing more than 370 agencies worldwide; *Travel for the Disabled* ($19.95); the *Directory of Accessible Van Rentals* ($12.95); and *Wheelchair Vagabond* ($19.95), loaded with personal tips.

Wheels Up! ☎1-888/389-4335, ⓦwww.wheelsup.com. Provides discounted airfare, tour and cruise prices for disabled travellers, also publishes a free monthly newsletter and has a comprehensive website.

Australia and New Zealand

ACROD (Australian Council for Rehabilitation of the Disabled) PO Box 60, Curtin ACT 2605 ☎02/6282 4333; Suite 103, 1st floor, 1–5 Commercial Rd, Kings Grove 2208 ☎02/9554 3666. Provides lists of travel agencies and tour operators for people with disabilities.

Disabled Persons Assembly 4/173–175 Victoria St, Wellington, New Zealand ☎04/801 9100. Resource centre with lists of travel agencies and tour operators for people with disabilities.

Directory

BOTTLES Neither republic is quite yet a fully paid-up member of the throwaway culture, and many drinks still come in bottles with a deposit that can be reclaimed at most supermarkets. Otherwise, there are now bottle banks scattered around most towns and cities.

CHILDREN The attitude to kids is generally very positive in both republics. That said, you'll see few babies out in the open, unless snuggled up in their prams, and almost no children in pubs, cafés or even most restaurants. Children are generally expected to be unreasonably well behaved and respectful to their elders, and many of the older generation may frown at over-boisterous behaviour. Kids under six go free on public transport; six- to fourteen-year-olds pay half-fare. Disposable nappies are becoming more widely available, but convenience food for babies is still fairly thin on the ground.

ELECTRICITY This is the standard continental 220 volts AC. Most European appliances should work as long as you have an adaptor for continental-style two-pin round plugs. North Americans will need this plus a transformer.

GAY MEN AND LESBIANS Homosexuality is legal in both republics, with the age of consent at fifteen (in the Czech Republic) and sixteen (in Slovakia), whatever your sexuality. That said, on the whole attitudes remain very conservative.

LAUNDRY Self-service laundries don't exist, except in Prague, though you can get clothes beautifully service-washed or dry-cleaned for a very reasonable price at a *čistírna* as long as you've got a few days to spare.

LEFT LUGGAGE Most bus and train stations have lockers and/or a 24-hour left-luggage office.

LOST PROPERTY Most train stations have lost property offices – look for the sign *ztráty a nálezy*. If you've lost your passport, then get in touch with your embassy (see p.18).

SMOKING Like most continental Europeans, the Czechs and Slovaks are keen smokers, and you'll find very few no-smoking areas in cafés, pubs or restaurants, though there is no smoking on the public transport system. If you're a smoker and need a light, say *máte oheň?* Matches are *zápalky*.

TAMPONS Tampons (*tampóny*) and sanitary towels (*dámské vložky*) are cheap and easy to get hold of in department stores and supermarkets.

TIME The Czech and Slovak republics are generally one hour ahead of Britain and six hours ahead of EST, with the clocks going forward in spring and back again some time

27

in autumn – the exact date changes from year to year. Generally speaking, Czechs and Slovaks use the 24-hour clock.

TIPPING is normal practice in cafés, bars, restaurants and taxis, though this is usually done by simply rounding up the total. For example, if the waiter tots up the bill and asks you for 74 crowns, you should hand him a 100-crown note and say "take 80 crowns".

TOILETS Apart from the automatic ones in the big cities, toilets (*záchody*, *toalety* or *WC*) are few and far between. In some, you still have to buy toilet paper (by the sheet) from the attendant, whom you will also have to pay as you enter. Standards of hygiene can be low. Gentlemen should head for *muži* or *páni*; ladies should head for *ženy* or *dámy*. In dire straits you should make use of conveniences in restaurants and pubs, as most Czechs and Slovaks do.

Guide

Guide

① Prague and around..51–166

② South Bohemia...167–210

③ West Bohemia 211–244

④ North Bohemia 245–282

⑤ East Bohemia 283–324

⑥ South Moravia 325–382

⑦ North Moravia..383–426

⑧ Bratislava and west Slovakia 427–472

⑨ The mountain regions..473–522

⑩ East Slovakia 523–564

The Czech Republic

Introduction

With the official break-up of Czechoslovakia on January 1, 1993, the Czech Republic became one of Europe's newest nations, with a population of just over ten million. Compared to their former Slovak compatriots, the Czechs had comparatively few problems in gaining recognition on the international stage, entering NATO and now stand on the brink of EU membership. In playwright Václav Havel, the Czechs have had a president many people have actually heard of; they have a capital city – Prague – that has been one of the most popular tourist destinations of the last decade; and they have had, for much of that time, a stable government widely praised at home and abroad for the speed and efficacy of its economic reforms.

Geographically, the Czech Republic lies at the very heart of central Europe and, despite more than forty years' isolation behind the Iron Curtain, its towns and villages still bear the stamp of numerous, much older cultural influences. The millions of Germans who lived here for centuries before their postwar expulsion have left perhaps the most obvious traces: their splendid burgher houses line countless town squares and their timber-framed farmhouses still dot the borderlands. The Habsburg dynasty, which ruled over the Czechs for nearly four hundred years, has left the landscape punctuated by the onion domes of the Counter-Reformation and castellated follies of the old aristocracy. And for much of the modern era, the Czechs themselves have been at the forefront of European culture. Before World War I, Prague boasted a Cubist movement second only to Paris, and, between the wars, a modernist architectural flowering to rival Bauhaus. Even today, its writers, artists and film directors continue to exert a profound influence on European culture, out of all proportion to their numbers.

Getting around

The most relaxing way of travelling around the Czech Republic is by train. The system, bequeathed by the Habsburgs in 1918, is one of the most dense in Europe, and has changed little since those days, with only a small percentage of the tracks allowing train speeds of over 120kph. Though often wonderfully scenic, it's also extremely slow, so if you're in a hurry, buses are nearly always

faster. Bus and train timetables can be found in the "Travel Details" section at the end of each chapter.

Trains

The country's state-run train system, Czech Railways, **České dráhy** or **ČD** (Ⓦwww .cdrail.cz), remains the country's largest employer, largely due to overemployment, and runs at a huge loss. The constant threats to close down up to a third of the railway system – which cast a shadow over much of the last decade – look more likely than ever to become a reality. In the meantime, enjoy the system while you can.

There are two main **types of train** (*vlak*): *rychlík* (R) or *spěšný* (Sp) trains are the faster ones which stop only at major towns, while *osobní* (or *zastavkový*) trains stop at just about every station, averaging as little as 30kph. Fast trains are further divided into SuperCity (SC), which are first class only, EuroCity (EC) or InterCity (IC), for which you need to pay a supplement, and Expres (Ex).

Tickets and fares

Once you've worked out when your train leaves (for which, see overleaf), the best thing to do when buying a **ticket** (*lístek*) is to write down all the relevant information (date/time/destination) on a piece of paper and hand it to the ticket clerk. This avoids any linguistic misunderstandings – rectifying any mistakes involves a lengthy bureaucratic process and costs you ten percent of the ticket price.

If you want a return ticket (*zpáteční*) or you're travelling on a *rychlík* train, you must say so, though the former is no cheaper than buying two singles. Overall, fares, which are calculated by the kilometre, remain remarkably low; a second-class single from Prague to Brno still only costs around £6/$8.50. First-class carriages (*první třída*) exist only on fast trains; tickets are fifty percent more expensive, but should guarantee you a seat on a busy train. There are half-price **discount fares** for children under 16, and you can take two children under 6 for free (providing they don't take up more than one seat). There are even some "crèche carriages" on the slower trains – marked with a "D" on the timetable – where those with children under 10 have priority over seats.

For all international services (and any other trains marked with an "R" on the timetable), you can buy a **seat reservation** (*místenka*). It's advisable to get one if you're travelling at the weekend on one of the main routes and want to be sure of a seat. The *místenka* costs very little, but you must get it at least an hour before your train leaves, and either after or at the same time as you purchase your ticket.

Information and timetables

With very few English-speakers employed on the railways, it can be difficult getting **train information**. The larger stations have a simple airport-style arrivals and departures board, which includes information on delays under the heading *zpoždění*. Many stations have poster-style displays of arrivals (*příjezd*) and departures (*odjezd*), the former on white paper, the latter on yellow, with fast trains printed in red.

All but the smallest stations also have a comprehensive display of **timings and route information** on rollers. These timetables may seem daunting at first, but with a little practice they should become decipherable. First find the route you need to take on the diagrammatic map and make a note of the number printed beside it; then follow the timetable rollers through until you come to the appropriate number. Some of the more common Czech notes at the side of the timetable are *jezdí jen v...* (only running on...), or *nejezdí v* or *nechodí v...* (not running on...),

followed by a date or a symbol: a cross or an "N" for a Sunday, a big "S" for a Saturday, two crossed hammers for a weekday, "A" for a Friday and so on. Small stations may simply have a board with a list of departures under the title *směr* (direction) followed by a town. A platform, or *nástupiště*, is usually divided into two *kolej* on either side.

Buses

Buses (*autobusy*) go almost everywhere, and from town to town they're often faster than the train. Bear in mind, though, timetables tend to be designed around the needs of commuters, and tend to fizzle out at the weekend. Most services are run by the state-owned ČSAD, though private companies compete on the more popular, long-distance routes.

In many towns and villages, the **bus station** (*autobusové nádraží*) is adjacent to the train station, though you may be able to pick up the bus from the centre of town. The bigger terminals, like Prague's Florenc, are run with train-like efficiency, with airport-style departure boards and numerous platforms. Often you can book your ticket in advance, and it's essential to do so if you're travelling at the weekend or early in the morning on one of the main routes. For most minor routes, simply buy your ticket from the driver. Large items of **luggage** (*zavazadlo*) go in the boot, and you'll have to pay the driver a few crowns for the privilege. Minor bus stops are marked with a rusty metal sign saying *zastávka*. If you want to get off, ask *já chci vystoupit?*; "the next stop" is *příští zastávka*.

Bus **timetables** (ⓦwww.vlak-bus.cz) are even more difficult to figure out than train ones, as there are no maps at any of the stations. In the detailed timetables, each service is listed separately, so you may have to scour several timetables before you discover when the next bus is. A better bet is to look at the departures and arrivals board. Make sure you check on which day the service runs, since many run only on Mondays, Fridays or at the weekend (see the section on trains for the key phrases).

The following is a brief rundown of the most common **timetable symbols**: crossed hammers or an "X" denotes a service run only on weekdays; Saturday-only services are marked with a capital "S"; Sunday-only services are marked with a capital "N"; a cross denotes a Sunday or holiday service; Monday to Saturday services are marked with a "b"; Saturday, Sunday and holiday services are marked with an "a"; Monday-only services are marked with a "P"; Friday-only services are marked with a capital "V"; schoolday-only services are marked with a "c"; services running daily except Saturday are marked with a "g"; Monday to Thursday services are marked with a "d"; and Tuesday to Friday services are marked with a "y".

City transport

City transport is generally excellent, with buses (*autobus*), trolleybuses (*trolejbus*) and sometimes also trams (*tramvaj*) running from dawn until around midnight in most major towns (and all night in Prague and Brno). Ticket prices vary from place to place (generally around 10Kč for an adult; reduced rates for those aged 6–14; under-6s travel free), but are universally cheap. In Prague and Brno, various **passes** are available (see the "Getting Around" sections of the relevant city accounts).

With a few exceptions, you must buy your **ticket** (*lístek* or *jízdenka*) before getting on board. Tickets, which are standard for all types of transport, are available from newsagents, tobacconists and the yellow machines at major stops, and are validated in the punching machines once you're on board. There are no conductors, only plain-clothes **inspectors** (*revizoři*), who make spot checks and will issue an on-the-spot fine of 400Kč.

Taxis

Taxis are cheap and plentiful. Beware, however, that tourists are seen as easy prey by some taxi drivers, especially in Prague. The best advice is to hail a cab or have your hotel or pension call you one, rather than pick one up at the taxi ranks.

Driving

Czech car ownership is on the rise, but traffic outside the big cities is still pretty light. Road conditions are generally not bad,

though there's only a very limited motorway system. The only place where you might encounter difficulties is in the bigger cities and towns, where the lane system is confusing, tramlines hazardous and parking a nightmare. You have to be 18 or over to drive in the Czech Republic, and if you want to travel on long-distance motorways within the Czech Republic, you'll need a **motorway tax disc** or *dálniční známka*, which currently costs around 100Kč for ten days, 200Kč for a month, and is available from all border crossings and most post offices and petrol stations.

If you're bringing your own car, you'll need proof of ownership, or a letter from the owner giving you permission to drive the car. A British or other EU driving licence is fine; all other drivers are advised to purchase an International Driving Licence. You also need a red warning triangle in case you break down, a national identification sticker and a first-aid kit (these are all compulsory in the Czech Republic), and a "Green Card" for third party insurance cover at the very least. An even better idea is to sign up with one of the national motoring organizations, who offer continental breakdown assistance and, in extreme circumstances, will get you and your vehicle brought back home if necessary.

Rules of the road

Rules and regulations on Czech roads are pretty stringent, with on-the-spot fines regularly handed out, up to a maximum of 500Kč. The basic rules are driving on the right (introduced by the Nazis in 1939); compulsory wearing of seatbelts; headlights on at all times (Nov–March); no under 12s in the front seat, and no alcohol at all in your blood when you're driving. Theoretically, Czechs are supposed to give way to pedestrians at zebra crossings, but few do. However, Czechs do give way to pedestrians crossing at traffic lights when turning right or left. You must also give way to trams, and, if there's no safety island at a tram stop, you must stop immediately and allow passengers to get on and off. As in other continental countries, a yellow diamond sign means you have right of way, a black line through it means you don't; it's important to clock this sign before you reach the junction since the road markings at junctions rarely make priorities very clear.

Vehicle crime is on the increase and Western cars are a favourite target – never leave anything visible or valuable in the car. Restrictions on **parking** are becoming more common in Czech towns, with pay-and-display meters the easiest system to decipher; more complicated are the voucher schemes, which require you to buy a voucher from a newsagent, tourist office or bookshop. Illegally parked cars will either be clamped or towed away – if this happens, phone ☎158 to find out the worst.

Speed limits are 130kph on motorways (and if you travel any faster you will be fined), 90kph on other roads and 50kph in all cities, towns and villages – you need to remember these, as there are few signs to remind you. In addition, there's a special speed limit of 30kph for **level crossings** (you'll soon realize why if you try ignoring it). Many level crossings have no barriers, simply a sign saying *pozor* and a series of lights: a single flashing light means that the line is live; two red flashing lights mean there's a train coming.

Fuel and car rental

Petrol (*benzín*) comes in three types: super (96 octane), special (90 octane) and **lead-free** petrol (*natural* or *bezolovnatý*); diesel (*nafta*) is also universally available. The price of petrol is cheaper than in much of Western Europe, currently costing around 25Kč a litre (£0.50/$0.80). If you have **car trouble**, dial ☎154 at the nearest phone and wait for assistance. For peace of mind it might be worth taking out an insurance policy which will pay for any on-the-spot repairs and, if necessary, ship you and your passengers home free of charge.

Car rental is easy to arrange, with all the major companies operating out of Prague airport, with offices downtown and some in Brno. If you book in advance with a multinational you're looking at a whopping £60/$84 per day for a small car, £200/$280 a week. You'll get a much cheaper deal, however, if you go for a Škoda and book

your car through a local agent once you've arrived in Prague; prices can be as low as £10/$14 a day, though language may be a problem. To rent a car in the Czech Republic, you need to be at least 21, have a clean licence, and have been driving for at least a year.

Rental agencies

Abroad
Alamo US ☎1-800/522-9696, 🖳www.alamo.com.
Auto Europe US ☎1-800/223-5555; Canada ☎1-888/223-5555; 🖳www.autoeurope.com.
Avis Australia ☎13 63 33; Canada ☎1-800/272-5871; Ireland ☎01/605 7500; New Zealand ☎0800 655 111 or 09/526 2847; UK ☎0870/606 0100; US ☎1-800/331-1084; 🖳www.avis.com.
Budget Australia ☎1300/362 848; Ireland ☎01/9032 7711; New Zealand ☎0800/652 227 or 09/976 2222; UK ☎0800/181 181; US ☎1-800/527-0700; 🖳www.budgetrentacar.com.
Hertz Australia ☎13 30 39; Canada ☎1-800/263-0600; Ireland ☎01/676 7476; New Zealand ☎0800/654 321; UK ☎0870/844 8844; US ☎1-800/654-3001; 🖳www.hertz.com.
Holiday Autos UK ☎0870/400 00 99; Ireland ☎01/872 9366; 🖳www.holidayautos.com.
National Australia ☎13 10 45; New Zealand ☎0800/800 115 or 03/366 5574; UK ☎0870/5365 365; US ☎1-800/227-7368; 🖳www.nationalcar.com.
Thrifty Australia ☎1300/367 227; New Zealand ☎09/309 0111; UK ☎01494/751 600; US ☎1-800/367-2277; 🖳www.thrifty.com.

In Prague
Alimex Na Petynce 22 ☎220 961 414, 🖳www.alimex-rent.cz.
Avis Klimentská 46, Nové Město ☎221 851 229, 🖳www.avis.cz.
Czechocar Kongresové centrum 5 května 65, Nusle ☎261 222 079, 🖳www.czechocar.cz.
Hertz Karlovo nám. 28, Nové Město ☎220 102 424, 🖳www.hertz.cz.

Useful hiking terms

cesta/stezka/pěšina	road/path/trail
bouda	mountain refuge
hranice	border
jeskyně	cave
lanovka/lánova draha	chairlift/cable car
les	wood
lyžařský vlek	ski lift
pramen	spring
rozhled/vyhlídka	viewpoint
skála	rock
údolí	valley
vodopad	waterfall

Cycling and hiking

Cycling is now pretty popular as a leisure activity in the Czech Republic, and the rolling countryside, though hard work on the legs, is rewarding. Facilities for **bike rental** are improving, and the increasing number of bike shops makes repairs possible and spare parts slightly easier to obtain. To take your bike (*kolo*) on the train, you must buy a separate ticket before taking it down to the freight section of the station, where, after filling in the mountains of paperwork, your bike should be smoothly sent on to its destination.

Hiking is a very popular pastime with young and old alike, the most enthusiastic indulging in an activity curiously known as going *na trampu*; dressing up in quasi-military gear, camping in the wilds, playing guitar and singing songs round the campfire. There is a dense network of paths that covers the whole countryside – sometimes reaching even within the city boundaries of Prague. All the trails are colour-coded with clear markers every 200m or so and signs indicating roughly how long it'll take you to reach your destination.

Many of the walks are fairly easy-going, but it can be wet and muddy underfoot even in summer, so sturdy boots are a good idea, particularly if you venture into the mountains proper. There are no hiking guides in English, but it's easy enough to get hold of 1:50,000 maps which cover the whole country and detail all the marked paths in the area (see p.23).

Planes and boats

Domestic flights, run by ČSA and a variety of other carriers, link Prague with Brno and Ostrava, and there are regular international flights to the Slovak cities of Bratislava, Poprad and Košice. Though not exactly cheap, particularly when compared with the train or bus, they can prove useful if time is short and you want to get to eastern Slovakia quickly, reducing the travel time from Prague to Košice to two hours from twelve, for example. If you do decide to fly, make sure you book well in advance as demand is high, and flights to places like Poprad in the High Tatras are booked solid in the high season. Further details can be obtained from ČSA offices or agents in most large towns.

The opportunity for travelling by **boat** (*lod*) is pretty limited in the Czech Republic, but there are a few services worth mentioning. From Prague, boats sail all the way down to Orlík, with a change of vessel at each of the dams on the way. There's also a summer service on Lake Lipno in South Bohemia, and down the River Labe (Elbe) between Děčín and Hřensko (see box on p.171 for more information on boat trips).

Accommodation

Accommodation is likely to be by far the largest chunk of your daily expenditure, unless you're camping. Overall, standards in pensions, hotels and hostels have improved enormously. Prices are pretty uniform across the country; only in Prague, and, to a lesser extent, in Brno, is it difficult to find resonably-priced accommodation. For a run down on the **price codes** used in this book, see the inside front cover.

If you're going to Prague from late spring to late summer or over the Christmas holidays, it's as well to arrange accommodation before you arrive. There are inexpensive accommodation specialists who can arrange this for you (see pp.12 and 14 for a list of current operators). Another alternative is to use the listings in the guide to ring or email a hotel and book yourself in.

Hotels, pensions and private rooms

On the whole, the country has come a long way from the bad old days when foreign visitors were shepherded into high-rise monstrosities and charged three times as much as locals for services that were uniformly bad. That said, one or two hotel dinosaurs live on, some places still charge more for the foreigners and "service with a snarl" is still occasionally encountered.

All hotels operate a star system, though it's self-regulatory and therefore none too reliable. Prices vary wildly and, unsurprisingly, tend to be much higher in those areas which receive the most tourists. The vast majority of rooms now have en-suite bathrooms and TVs, with continental breakfast either included in the price or offered as an optional extra, and you'll find a restaurant and/or bar in almost every hotel.

Most guest houses bill themselves as **pensions**. Again, prices and standards can vary widely, and a well-run pension can often be cheaper, friendlier and better equipped than many hotels. **Private rooms**, too, are a case of pot luck. You can be sure that they will be clean and tidy, but in what proximity you'll be to your hosts is difficult to predict. You might be sharing bathroom, cooking facilities, etc, with the family – Czech hospitality can be somewhat overwhelming, although meals other than breakfast are not generally included in the price. In some parts of the countryside you'll see plenty of signs saying either *ubytování* or *pokoje* ("accommodation" and "rooms" in Czech) or, more frequently, *Zimmer Frei* ("rooms available" in German). In some towns and cities, you may be able to book rooms through the local tourist office (details are listed throughout the *Guide*).

Hostels and student rooms

A smattering of **hostels** are now affiliated to Hostelling International (@www.iyhf.org), but these are few and far between, vary wildly in size and quality, and are often in obscure, out-of-the-way places. For more details, get hold of a copy of Hostelling International's hostel booklet, published annually. There are, of course, lots of other unofficial hostels – especially in Prague – where you can pay very little and usually get very little in return, beyond a place to lay your sleeping bag.

A more reliable alternative to hostels in the big university towns is **student accommodation** – known as *kolej* – which is let out cheap to travellers from June to August. Though heavily booked up in advance by groups, they'll try their best to squeeze you in. Curfews operate in some hostels and can be as early as 10 or 11pm, so check before you book in. Addresses can change from year to year, so to find out the most recent, go to the local tourist office or the student organization, CKM, which has offices in most major towns.

Other dormitories, which go by the catch-all term of *ubytovna*, can be anything from sports halls to dorms used to house immigrant workers or workers on vacation. They are uniformly cheap and basic with few facilities beyond a bunk bed, toilet and cold shower, though they may remain unconvinced that a foreign tourist should demean themselves by staying there.

Camping and other options

Campsites (*autokemping*) are plentiful all over the Czech Republic. Some are huge affairs, with shops, swimming pools, draught beer and so on; others, known often as *tábořiště*, are just a simple stretch of grass with ad hoc toilets and a little running water. In the majority of sites, facilities are just about adequate, but don't get your expectations up too high. Many sites feature **chalets** (*chaty* or *bungolovy*), which vary in size and facilities from rabbit hutches to mini villas; prices start at around £10/$14 for two people.

Very few campsites are open all year round, most opening in May and closing in September. Even though prices are inflated for foreigners, costs are still reasonable; two people plus car and tent weigh in at around £5/$7. Campfires, though officially banned, are tolerated at many campsites, and the guitar-playing barbecues go on until well into the night.

Mountain huts

In the mountains of the Krkonoše, there are a fair number of **mountain huts** (*bouda* or *chata*) scattered about the hillsides. Some are little less than hotels and charge similar prices, but the more isolated ones are simple wooden shelters costing around £6/$8 per person, with no self-catering, but with a rudimentary evening meal included in the price. A few are accessible by road, and most are only a few miles from civilization. Ideally, these should be booked in advance through the various accommodation agencies in the nearest settlements. The more isolated ones work on a first-come, first-served basis, but if you turn up before 6pm, you're unlikely to be turned away.

Communications

Czech telecommunications have come a long way in the last ten years. The phone system, in particular, has improved enormously and has recently undergone a radical overhaul, with all numbers within the country now made up of nine digits. Czechs are also keen web-users and access to the internet is possible in most towns and cities across the country.

Post

Most **post offices** (*pošta*) are open from 8am to 5pm Monday to Friday, and Saturdays until noon. They're pretty baffling institutions with separate windows for just about every service. Look out for the right sign to avoid queueing unnecessarily: *známky* (stamps), *dopisy* (letters) or *balky* (parcels).

Outbound mail is reasonably reliable, with letters or postcards taking around four to five working days to reach Britain, a week to reach North America. You can buy **stamps** from newsagents, tobacconists and some kiosks, as well as at the post offices. Postal charges at the time of going to print were 9Kč for postcards within Europe and 12Kč to North America. See p.609 for a list of countries in Czech.

Poste restante (pronounced as five syllables in Czech) services are available in major towns, but remember to write Pošta 1 (the main office), followed by the name of the town. Get the sender to write their name and address on the back so that mail can at least be returned if something goes wrong.

Phones

The majority of public phones in the Czech Republic take only **phone cards** (*telefonní karty*), currently available in 50, 100 and 150 units from post offices, tobacconists and some shops (prices vary). You can make international calls from all card phones, though be warned that rates are expensive. There are instructions in English, and if you press the appropriate button the language on the digital read-out will change to English. If you have any problems, ring ☏1181 to get through to international information.

In **coin-operated phones**, you need to insert a minimum of 3Kč to make a local call, 5Kč for long-distance – if you stock up with enough coins, it is perfectly possible to make an international phone call. The **dialling** tone is a short followed by a long pulse; the ringing tone is long and regular; engaged is short and rapid (not to be confused with the connecting tone which is very short and rapid). The standard Czech response is *prosím*; the word for "extension" is *linka*.

You can also make phone calls from the local **telephone exchanges** situated in Prague, Brno and a few other cities. Write down the town and number you want, leave a deposit of around 200Kč and wait for your name to be called out. Keep a close watch on the time unless you've unlimited funds. Calls from a telephone exchange cost slightly less, but avoid making any calls from hotels, where the surcharge is usually outrageous.

Email

One of the best ways to keep in touch while travelling is to sign up for a **free internet email address** that can be accessed from anywhere, for example YahooMail or Hotmail – accessible through ⓦwww.yahoo.com and ⓦwww.hotmail.com. Once you've set up an account, you can use these sites to pick up and send mail from any internet café, or hotel with internet access.

You can get online at various cafés and bars in large Czech cities, though there aren't that many specialist cybercafés. The easiest way to find out how to get online is to ask the local tourist office. For details of how to plug your laptop in when abroad, plus information on country codes around the world, and electrical systems in different countries, check out the useful website ⓦwww.kropla.com.

Media

In Prague and Brno, it's possible to get day-old copies of most of the broadsheet **British papers**, though one that you can buy on the day of issue is the European edition of *The Guardian*, printed in Frankfurt (it arrives on the streets of Prague and Brno around mid-morning). As far as **American newspapers** are concerned, there's just the reliable old

International Herald Tribune. In addition, there's the weekly English-language *Prague Post*, a broadsheet with strong business coverage and a useful pull-out listings section.

It's a sign of the times that the majority of **Czech newspapers** are German-owned. The only Czech-owned paper is the left-wing *Právo*, formerly the official mouthpiece of the Communist Party (when it was known as *Rudé právo* or "Red Justice"). Its chief competitor is *Mladá fronta dnes*, former mouthpiece of the Communist youth movement, now a very popular centre-right daily. *Lidové noviny* (the best-known *samizdat* or underground publication under the Communists and the equivalent of *The Times* under the First Republic) is now a much less respected right-wing daily, while the orange-coloured *Hospodárské noviny* is the Czech equivalent of the *Financial Times* or *Wall Street Journal*. The country's most popular tabloid is *Blesk*, a sensationalist tabloid with lurid colour pictures, naked women and reactionary politics. If all you want, however, is yesterday's (or, more often than not, the day before yesterday's) international sports results, pick up a copy of the daily *Sport*.

As for **television**, Česká televize's two state-owned channels, ČT1 and ČT2, have both been eclipsed as far as ratings go by the runaway success of the commercial channel, Nova. The latter features lots of American sitcoms dubbed into Czech, plenty of game shows, striptease weather forecasts and the most comprehensive coverage of Czech football. Prima, the other commercial channel, has yet to make any significant inroads into Nova's audience monopoly. ČT2 is your best bet for foreign films with subtitles; it also shows news in English from the BBC on Monday to Friday at 8am, and on Saturday and Sunday at 7am.

On the **radio**, the BBC World Service (ⓦwww.bbc.co.uk/worldservice) broadcasts loud and clear on various FM wavelengths from the major cities, mostly in English, with occasional bits of Czech programming; you can also get the regular all-English European version on shortwave. The state-run Český rozhlas has four stations: ČR1 Radiožurnál (94.6FM), which is mainly current affairs; ČR2 (91.3FM), which features more magazine-style programming; Regina (92.6FM), which features news and pop music; and ČR3 Vltava (105FM), which plays classical music. The president broadcasts his presidential Sunday evening chat on ČR1; an English-language news summary goes out Monday to Friday at 5.30pm. The three top commercial channels are Evropa 2 (88.2FM), Radio Bonton (99.7FM) and Radio Kiss 98 FM (98FM), which dish out bland Euro-pop. More interesting is Radio 1 (91.9FM), which plays a wide range of indie rock.

Eating and drinking

The good news is that you can eat and drink very cheaply in the Czech Republic: the food is filling and the beer is divine. The bad news is that the kindest thing you can say about Czech food is that it is hearty. Forty years of culinary isolation under the Communists introduced few innovations to Czech cuisine, with its predilection for pork, gravy, dumplings and pickled cabbage. Fresh vegetables (other than potatoes) remain a rare sight on traditional Czech menus, and salads are still waiting for their day.

That said, the choice of places where you can eat has improved enormously over the last decade. In Prague, at least, you could spend a whole week eating out and never go near a dumpling, should you so wish. Czechs themselves are very keen on pizzas, and there are now some very good pizzerias in the larger towns and cities – there are even some passably authentic ethnic restaurants ranging from Japanese and Lebanese to Balkan and French in Prague, and, to a lesser extent, Brno.

For a comprehensive glossary of Czech food and drink terms, see the language section on p.605.

Breakfast, snacks and bufets

Despite the fact that breakfast cereal consumption is on the rise in the Czech Republic, Czechs generally have little time for **breakfast** (snídaně) as such. Many get up so early in the morning (often around 5 or 6am) that they don't have time to start the day with anything more than a quick cup of coffee or tea. Most hotels will serve the "continental" basics of tea, coffee, rolls and cold cheese and meat. Bear in mind, though, that if you get up much past 10am, you'll have missed it and may as well join the country's working population for lunch.

Pastries (pečivo) are available from most bakeries (pekařství), but rarely in bars and cafés, so you'll probably have to eat them on the go. The traditional pastry (koláč) is more like sweet bread; dry and fairly dense with only a little flavouring in the form of hazelnuts (oříškový), poppy-seed jam (makový), prune jam (povidlový) or a kind of sour-sweet curd cheese (tvarohový).

With breakfast, Czechs tend to have white **rolls**, which come in two basic varieties: rohlík, a plain finger roll, and houska, a rougher, tastier round bun. Czech **bread** (chléb) is some of the tastiest around when fresh. The standard loaf is domací or šumava, a dense mixture of wheat and rye, which you can buy whole, in halves (půl) or quarters (čtvrtina). Česky chléb is a mixture of rye, wheat and whey, with distinctive slashes across the top; kmínový chléb is the same loaf packed full of caraway seeds. Moskva remains popular, despite the name – a moist, heavy, sourdough loaf that lasts for days. Fresh **milk** (mléko) is available in most supermarkets either plnotučné (full fat) or nízkotučné (semi-skimmed). Look out, too, for kefír, deliciously thick sourmilk, or acidofilní mléko, its slightly thinner counterpart.

The ubiquitous street **takeaway** is the hot dog or párek, a dubious-looking frankfurter (traditionally two – párek means a pair), dipped in mustard and served with a white roll (v rohlíku). A greasier option is bramborák, a thin potato pancake with little flecks of bacon or salami in it. In Prague, felafal or kebabs (known as gyros) form another popular takeaway choice, usually with pitta bread and salad.

Stand-up **bufets** often open from as early as 6am and offer everything from light snacks to full meals. A cross between a British greasy spoon and an American diner, they're usually self-service (samoobsluha) and non-smoking, and occasionally have rudimentary seats. The cheapest of the wide range of meat sausages on offer is sekaná, bits of old meat and bread squashed together to form a meat loaf – for connoisseurs only. *Guláš* (goulash) is popular, though it may bear little relation to the original of that name – usually *Szegedinský* (pork with sauerkraut) after the Hungarian town. Less substantial fare boils down to *chlebíčky* – artistically presented **open sandwiches** with differing combinations of gherkins, cheese, salami, ham and aspic – and mountains of mayonnaise-based **salad** (*salát*), bought by weight (200g is a medium-sized portion).

Like the Austrians who once ruled over them, the Czechs have a grotesquely sweet tooth, and the coffee-and-cake hit is part of the daily ritual. The **cukrárna** is the place to go for cake-eating. There are two main types of cake: *dort*, like the German *Tort*, consist of a series of custard cream, chocolate and sponge layers, while *řez* are lighter square cakes, usually containing a bit of fruit. A *věneček*, filled with "cream", is the nearest you'll get to an eclair; a *větrník* is simply a larger version with a bit of fresh cream added; and a *kobliha* is a doughnut. One speciality to look out for is a *rakvička*, which literally means "little coffin", an extended piece of sugar like a meringue, with cream, moulded vaguely into the shape of a coffin. Whatever the season, Czechs have to have their daily fix of **ice cream** (*zmrzlina*), available in soft form from machines or scooped, either dispensed from little window kiosks in the sides of buildings, or dished out from within a *cukrárna*.

As for **fast food**, pizza places abound, though they can vary from vague approximations to quality imitations. Other staple Czech fast-food snacks include *hranolky* (chips/French fries) or *krokety* (croquettes) served with tartare sauce (*tartarská omačka*). Czech crisps (*chips*) have struggled to compete with foreign imports, but a few new brands are holding their own. Finally, it should also be noted that *McDonald's* now has a prime slice of real estate in almost every major Czech city.

Eating out

The division between cafés, bars, pubs and restaurants is pretty blurred. **Restaurants** (*restaurace* in Czech) are primarily there to serve you food, but some will also have a

bar area where you can simply have a drink. Others style themselves as *vinárna* or **wine-bars**, though they, too, often serve food. Equally, while many **cafés** (*kavárna* in Czech) realize most of their customers only want a drink and maybe a slice of cake, many serve up cheap, hot snacks and even full meals. Czech **pubs** (*pivnice*, *hostinec* or *hospoda* in Czech) are on the whole the cheapest places to eat, and almost exclusively serve standard Czech food. Cheaper still is the local stand-up *bufet*, usually a **self-service** café serving basic, hot Czech meals.

Czech menus

Away from the big hotels, the **menu** (*jídelní lístek*), which should be displayed outside, is often in Czech only, and deciphering it without a grounding in the language can be quite a feat. Just bear in mind that the right-hand column lists the prices, while the far left column usually gives you the estimated weight of every dish in grams; if what you get weighs more or less, the price will alter accordingly (this applies in particular to fish).

Most menus start with the **soups** (*polévky*), one of the region's culinary strong points and mainly served at lunchtimes. Posher restaurants will have a serious selection of starters, such as *uzený jazyk* (smoked tongue), *tresčí játra* (cod's liver) or perhaps *kaviárové vejce* (a hard-boiled egg with caviar on top). *Šunková rolka* is another favourite, consisting of ham topped with whipped cream and horseradish. You're more likely, though, to find yourself skipping the starters, which are usually little more than a selection of cold meats.

Main courses tend to be divided into several separate sections. *Hotová jídla* (ready-made meals), which should arrive swiftly, and *jídla na objednávku* or *minutky* (meals made to order), for which you'll have to wait. In either case, dishes are overwhelmingly based on **meat** (*maso*), usually pork, sometimes beef. The Czechs are experts on these meats, and although the quality could often be better, the variety of sauces and preparative techniques is usually good. The difficulty lies in decoding names such as *klašterny tajemství* ("mystery of the monastery") or even a common dish like *Moravský vrabec* (literally "Moravian sparrow", but actually just roast pork).

Fish (*ryby*) is generally listed separately, or along with chicken (*drůbez*) and other fowl like duck (*kachna*). River trout (*pstruh*) and carp (*kapr*) – the traditional dish at Christmas – are the cheapest and most widely available fish, and, although their freshness may be questionable, they are usually served, grilled or roasted, in delicious buttery sauces or breadcrumbs.

Vegetarians

Czech meat consumption has dropped dramatically since 1989, but it still remains one of the highest in the world. It's hardly surprising then that **vegetarianism** is still a minority sport. Needless to say, you're better off in Prague than anywhere else in the country. For a start, places which cater mostly for expats usually have one or two veggie options, and there are plenty of pizzerias.

Even in traditional Czech places, most menus have a section called *bez-masa* (literally "without meat") – don't take this too literally, though, for it simply means the main ingredient is not dead animal; dishes like *omeleta se šunkou* (ham omelette) regularly appear under these headings, so always check first. The staple of Czech vegetarianism is *smažený sýr*, a slab of melted cheese, deep-fried in breadcrumbs and served with tartar sauce (*tartarská omačka*) – beware, though, as it's sometimes served *se šunkou* (with ham). Other types of cheese can also be melted and deep-fried, as can other vegetables such as *smažené žampiony* (mushrooms) and *smažený květák* (cauliflower). Emergency veggie standbys which most Czech pubs will knock up for you without too much fuss include *knedlíky s vejci* (dumplings and scrambled egg) or *omeleta s hráškem* (pea omelette).

Veggie phrases to remember are "*jsem vegeterián/vegeteriánka. Máte nejaké bezmasa?*" (I'm a vegetarian. Is there anything without meat?); for emphasis, you could add "*nejím maso nebo ryby*" (I don't eat meat or fish).

Side dishes (*přílohy*), most commonly served with fish and fowl, generally consist of potatoes (*brambory*), though with meat dishes you'll more often be served **dumplings** (*knedlíky*), one of the mainstays of Bohemian cooking. The term itself is misleading for English-speakers, since they resemble nothing like the English dumpling – more like a heavy white bread. *Houskové knedlíky* are made from flour and come in large slices (four or five to a dish), while *bramborové knedlíky* are smaller and made from potato and flour. Occasionally, you may be treated to *ovocné knedlíky* (fruit dumplings), the king of *knedlíky* and usually served with melted butter and soured cream as a sweet main course.

Fresh salads rarely rise above the ubiquitous *obloha*, usually a bit of tomato, cucumber and lettuce, or cabbage (*zeli*), often swimming in a slightly sweet, watery dressing. *Šopský* salads, made with a feta-like cheese, are a pale imitation of Greek salads (without olives), but are generally fresher and more substantial than most other salads on offer.

With the exception of *palačinky* (pancakes) filled with chocolate or fruit and cream, **desserts** (*moučníky*), where they exist at all, can be pretty unexciting.

Drinking

Traditional Czech **pubs** are smoky, male-dominated places, where 99 percent of the customers are drinking copious quantities of Czech beer by the half-litre. If you want a more mixed environment, you're better off heading for a wine cellar or café, where you'll get a better selection of wine and spirits, but probably only bottled beer.

Coffee and tea

Coffee (*káva*) is drunk black and is usually available in espresso (*presso*) form: small, black and strong, though by no means as diminutive as in Italy. Occasionally, you may still come across the original pre-1989 Czech coffee, called somewhat hopefully *turecká* (Turkish) – it's really just hot water poured over coffee grains. Downmarket *bufets* sell *ledová káva*, a weak, cold black coffee, while at the other end of the scale *Vídeňská káva* (Viennese coffee) is a favourite with the older generation, served with a dollop of whipped cream. Another rather rich option is a mix with advocaat, *Alžírská káva*.

Tea (*čaj*) is drunk weak and without milk, although you'll usually be given a glass of boiling water and a tea bag so you can do your own thing – for milk, say "*s mlékem*". If you want really good tea, you should look out for a *čajovna*, one of the country's growing number of tea-houses: calm, no-smoking cafés that take their tea drinking very seriously.

Beer

Alcohol consumption among Czechs has always been high, and in the decade following the events of 1968 it doubled, as a whole generation found solace in drinking, mostly **beer** (*pivo*). The Czechs have been top of the world league table of beer consumption for some time now, though it's a problem which seldom spills out onto the streets; violence in pubs is uncommon and you won't see that many drunks in public.

Czech beer ranks among the best in the world and the country remains the true home of most of the lager drunk around the world today. It was in the Bohemian city of Plzeň (Pilsen) that the first **bottom-fermented** beer was introduced in 1842, after complaints from the citizens about the quality of the top-fermented predecessor. The new brewing style quickly spread to Germany, and is now blamed for the bland rubbish served up in the English-speaking world as lager or Pils.

The distinctive flavour of Czech beer comes from the famous hand-picked Bohemian hops known as Žatec (Saaz) Red, the Moravian barley, and the soft local water; it should then be served with a high content of absorbed carbon dioxide – hence the thick, creamy head. Under the Communists, brewing methods in the Czech Republic remained stuck in the old ways, but the 1990s have seen many breweries opt for modernization: pasteurization, de-oxidization, rapid maturation and carbon dioxide injections – all of which mean less taste, more fizz. It's a development against which the Czech Beer Party and Britain's own Campaign for Real Ale (CAMRA) are fighting hard.

Czech etiquette

It's common practice to share a table with other eaters or drinkers; *je tu volno?* ("Is this seat free?") is the standard question. Waiter-service is the norm, even in pubs, so sit tight and a beer should come your way. You may have to ask to see the menu (*jídelní lístek*) in pubs and some cafés to indicate that you wish to eat. When food arrives for your neighbours, it's common courtesy to wish them bon appetit (*dobrou chuť*). When you want to leave, simply say *zaplatím, prosím* (literally "I'll pay, please"), and your tab will be totted up. A modest form of tipping exists in all establishments, generally done by rounding up the bill to the nearest few crowns, though beware that the waiters haven't already done this for you. On leaving, bid your neighbours farewell (*na shledanou*).

Beer (*pivo*) is served by the half-litre; if you want anything smaller, you must specifically ask for a *malé pivo* (0.3 litres). The average jar is medium strength, usually about 1050 specific gravity or 4.2 percent alcohol. Somewhat confusingly, the Czechs class their beers using the **Balling scale**, which measures the original gravity, calculated according to the amount of malt and dissolved sugar present before fermentation. The most common varieties are 10° (*desítka*), which is generally slightly weaker than 12° (*dvanáctka*). Light beer (*světlé*) is the norm, but many pubs also serve a slightly sweeter dark variety (*černé*) – or, if you prefer, you can have a mixture of the two (*řezané*).

Wine and spirits

Czech **wine** (*víno*) will never win over as many people as has Czech beer, but since the import of French and German vines in the fourteenth century, it has produced a modest selection of medium-quality wines. The main wine region is South Moravia, though a little is produced around the town of Mělník (see p.145). Suffice to say that most domestic wine is pretty drinkable –

Frankovka is a perfectly respectable, though slightly sweet, red; Veltlínské zelené a good, dry white – and rarely much more than £1/$1.40 a bottle in shops, while the best stuff can only be had from the private wine cellars (*sklepy*), hundreds of which still exist out in the regions. A Czech speciality to look out for is *burčák*, a very young, misty wine of varying (and often very strong) alcoholic content, which appears on the streets in the vine harvest season in September.

All the usual **spirits** are on sale and known by their generic names, with rum and vodka dominating the market. The home production of brandies is a national pastime, which results in some almost terminally strong liquors. The most renowned of the lot is *slivovice*, a plum brandy originally from the border hills between Moravia and Slovakia. You'll probably also come across *borovička*, a popular Slovak firewater, made from pine trees; *myslivec* is a rough brandy with a firm following. There's also a fair selection of intoxicating **herbal concoctions**: *fernet* is a dark-brown bitter drink, known as *bavorák* (Bavarian beer) when it's mixed with tonic, while *becherovka* is a supposedly healthy herbal spirit made to a secret recipe from the Bohemian spa town of Karlovy Vary, with a very unusual, almost medicinal taste; it can also be mixed with tonic, when it's known as *beton*.

The Czech Republic is one of the few countries in the world where **absinthe** is still legal. The preferred poison of Parisian painters and poets in the nineteenth century, absinthe is a nasty green spirit made from fermented wormwood – it even gets a biblical mention in Revelation: "and the name of the star is called Wormwood: and the third part of the waters became wormwood; and many men died of the waters, because they were made bitter". St John wasn't wrong: at 170 degrees proof, it's dangerous stuff and virtually undrinkable neat. To make it vaguely palatable, you need to set light to an absinthe-soaked spoonful of sugar, and then mix the caramelized mess with the absinthe.

There's not much to say about Czech **soft drinks**, with the exception of the high-energy drink Semtex, a can of which will amuse friends back home. Last of all, if you're looking for a decent **mineral water** (*minerální voda*), ask for the ubiquitous Mattoni, a mild and not too fizzy option.

Castles, churches and museums

The Czech Republic boasts well over a thousand castles, many of which have been converted for modern use, while others have been returned to their former owners. The country's churches and monasteries are similarly blighted by years of structural neglect and, more recently, by art thefts; most now lock their doors outside worshipping hours. Museums and galleries, by contrast, thrived under the Communists, filled to the gunwales with dull propaganda. Many have bitten the dust, others have changed out of all recognition, but most are now much more interesting to visit.

Castles and guided tours

Czech castles divide into two categories: a **hrad** is a defensive castle, usually medieval in origin and character, while a **zámek** is more of a chateau, built for comfort rather than for military purposes. The basic **opening hours** for both are the same: Tuesday to Sunday 8 or 9am to noon, then 1 to 4pm or later. From the end of October to the beginning of April, most castles are closed. In April and October, opening hours are often restricted to weekends and holidays only.

Whatever the time of year, if you want to see the interior of the building, nine times out of ten you'll be compelled to go on a **guided tour** (*průvodce*) that usually lasts for an hour. More and more places are now offering a choice of tours, of varying length, and some places insist on a minimum number of people before they begin a tour. Since most tours are in Czech (occasionally German) ask for an *anglický text*, an often unintentionally hilarious English resumé of the castle's history. You may also be asked to wear special furry overshoes (*papučky*), which protect and polish the floors at the same time. Tours almost invariably set off on the hour, and the last one leaves an hour before the lunchtime break (in other words, 11am) and an hour before the final closing time. **Entrance charges** are still comparatively low, rarely exceeding 100Kč – only the exceptions are quoted in the text – and students and children usually get in for half-price.

Churches, monasteries and synagogues

Getting into **churches** can present something of a problem. While the really important churches operate in much the same way as museums, occasionally charging an entry fee, particularly for their crypts or cloisters, the hundreds of more minor Baroque churches that litter the countryside – a legacy of the Counter-Reformation – are usually kept locked due to the enormous number of art thefts that have taken place. Usually, you can at least have a peek inside through the railings of the porch, but the only time you can guarantee the church is open is just before and after services in the early morning (around 7 or 8am) and/or evening (around 6 or 7pm); times are posted outside the main doors. Otherwise, it's worth asking around for the local *kněz* (priest) or *kaplan*, who's usually only too happy to oblige with the key (*klíč*).

In the Czech Lands, widespread agnosticism and the punitive policies of the last regime (self-confessed believers were not allowed to join the Party or take up teaching posts) have left many churches in a terrible state of disrepair. A similar fate has befallen the country's **monasteries** (*klášter*), many of which were closed down by the Emperor Joseph II in the late eighteenth century, while the remainder fell prey to the Communists. Nowadays, the buildings have become schools, factories and prisons, or been returned to their former orders, but a few remain as museums, which keep similar opening hours to the country's castles.

The country's once considerable Jewish population has been whittled down to an official figure of around 2000, over half of whom live in Prague, one of only a handful of places where regular worship still takes place. A few **synagogues** and graveyards have been saved from neglect, and some are well worth visiting, such as those in Plzeň, Děčín, Kolín, Mikulov and Třebíč.

Museums and galleries

Czech **museums** have tended to be stronger on quantity than quality, with exclusively Czech labelling designed to baffle any passing foreigner. This is changing slowly as tourism becomes more important, and many places do have at least an *anglický text* on offer. There are two main types of museum outside Prague: a **krajské**, **okresní** or **oblastní muzeum** or district museum traces the local history through arts, crafts and old photos, while a **mestské muzeum** or town museum is more provincial still, with stuffed animals and displays of mushrooms the only diversion. Occasionally you'll come across a real gem, but many of the local museums are far from riveting, and school groups are often the only visitors.

The big cities boast the best **art galleries** (*galerie umění*), though even the collections of Prague's Národní galerie (National Gallery) pale in comparison with those of most major Western European and North American cities. The impact of Socialist Realism was as heavy here as elsewhere in the Soviet empire, and the repercussions can still be seen in the country's provincial art galleries. In addition, many of the country's best artists – like Kupka and Mucha – worked abroad for much of their careers, and their works now grace the galleries of Paris and New York. However, previously unshown work from the 1950s and '60s has now found its way onto gallery walls, alongside exhibitions of up-and-coming contemporary artists.

Closed for technical reasons

A regular feature of the region is for museums, galleries and chateaux to be temporarily "closed for technical reasons", or, more permanently, "closed for reconstruction". Notices are rarely more specific than that, but the widespread shortage of staff and funds is often the reason. It's impossible to predict what will be closed when, but it's as well to make alternative plans when visiting galleries, museums and castles, just in case.

Opening hours for museums and galleries tend to be from 9 or 10am to 4pm or later, usually without a break at lunch. Most stay open all year round and some switch from a Tuesday–Sunday summer routine to Monday–Friday during the winter. Full opening hours are detailed in the guide. Ticket prices are still negligible outside Prague, and students usually go for half-price.

Public holidays, festivals and entertainment

There are remarkably few large-scale national festivals. Aside from the usual religious-oriented celebrations, most annual shindigs are arts-, music- and sports-based events, confined to a particular town or city. In addition, there are also folkloric events in the nether regions, the Strážnice folk festival in Moravia being by far the most famous.

Public holidays

National holidays were always a potential source of contention under the Communists, and they remain controversial even today. May Day, once a nationwide compulsory march under dull Commie slogans, remains a public holiday, though only the skinheads, anarchists and die-hard Stalinists take to the streets nowadays. Of the other *slavné májové dny* (Glorious May Days), as they used to be known, May 5, the beginning of

---

Public holidays

January 1 New Year's Day
March/April Easter Monday
May 1 May Day
May 8 VE Day
July 5 Introduction of Christianity
July 6 Death of Jan Hus
September 28 Czech State Day
October 28 Foundation of the Republic
November 17 Battle for Freedom and Democracy Day
December 24 Christmas Eve
December 25 Christmas Day
December 26 Saint Stephen's Day

---

the 1945 Prague Uprising, has been binned, and VE Day is now celebrated along with the Western Allies on May 8, and not on May 9, as it was under the Communists, and still is in Russia. September 28, the feast day of the country's patron saint, St Wenceslas, is now Czech State Day. Strangely, however, October 28, the day on which the First Republic was founded in 1918, is still celebrated, despite being a "Czechoslovak" holiday (and, for a while, Communist Nationalisation Day).

Festivals and annual events

At **Easter** (*Velikonoce*), the age-old sexist ritual persists of whipping girls' behinds and calves with braided birch twigs tied with ribbons (*pomlázky*) – objects you'll see being furiously bought and sold from markets in the run-up to Easter Sunday. To prevent such a fate, the girls are supposed to offer the boys a coloured Easter egg and pour a bucket of cold water over them. What may once have been an innocent bucolic spring frolic has now become another excuse for Czech men to harass any woman who dares to venture onto the street during this period.

Two ancient rituals which herald the end of winter continue in some parts of the country. The **"Slaughter of the Pig"**, known as *zabíjačka*, takes place in rural parts towards the end of January, traditionally a time when all other winter provisions are exhausted. Every single bit of the animal is prepared as food for the feast that accompanies the event. Halloween comes early to the Czech Republic on April 30, when the **"Burning of the Witches"** (*pálení čarodějnic*) takes place. It's an old pagan ritual, during which huge bonfires are lit across the country and old brooms are thrown out and burned to ward off evil spirits.

As in the rest of the Christian world, **Christmas** (*Vánoce*) is a time for over-consumption and family gatherings, and is therefore a fairly private occasion. On December 4, the feast day of **St Barbara**, cherry-tree branches are bought as decorations, the aim being to get them to blossom before Christmas. On the eve of **December 5**, numerous trios, dressed up as St Nicholas (*svatý Mikuláš*), an angel and

Festivals diary

April
Late April to early May Brno: International Trade Fair.
Late April to early May Šumperk: home-grown Jazz Festival.

May
Early May Prague: Czech-Moravian soccer cup final at the Strahov stadium.
May 12 to June 2 Prague Spring International Music Festival.
Mid-May Olomouc: Flower Festival.
Mid-May Zlín: International Children's Film Festival.
Late May Vlčnov: Folk Festival.
Late May Prague: Puppet Festival.
Late May to early June Ostrava: Janáček International Music Festival.

June
June Olomouc: Spring Music Festival.
Mid-June Český Krumlov: Five-Petalled Rose Festival.
Mid-June Litomyšl: National Opera Festival.
Mid-June Mariánské Lázně: International Festival of Mime.
Mid-June Pelhřimov: Festival of Records and Curious Performances.
Late June to early July Strážnice: International Folk Festival.

July
July Karlovy Vary: International Film Festival.
Early July Chrudim: Puppet Festival.
Late July Uherské Hradiště: Czech/Slovak Film Festival.
Late July/early Aug Telč: International Folk Festival.

August
Early Aug Valtice: Baroque Music Festival.
Mid-Aug Domažlice: Chodové Folk Festival.
Late Aug Brno: International Grand Prix motorcycling event.
Late Aug Strakonice: Biennial International Bagpipers' Festival.

September
Early Sept Kroměříž: Chamber Music Festival.
Early Sept Žatec: Hop (and beer) Festival.
Mid-Sept Tábor: Setkání Festival.
Late Sept to early Oct Brno: International Music Festival.
Late Sept to early Oct Teplice: Beethoven Music Festival.

October
Early Oct Pardubice: Velká Pardubická steeplechase.
Early Oct Plzeň: Beer Festival.

---

a devil, tour round the neighbourhoods, the angel handing out sweets and fruit to children who've been good, while the devil dishes out coal and potatoes to those who've been naughty. The Czech St Nicholas has white hair and a beard, and dresses not in red but in a white priest's outfit with a bishop's mitre.

With a week or so to go, large barrels are set up in the streets from which huge quantities of live *kapr* (carp), the traditional Christmas dish, are sold. **Christmas Eve** (*Štědrý večer*) is traditionally a day of fasting, broken only when the evening star appears, signalling the beginning of the Christmas feast of carp, potato salad, schnitzel and sweet breads. Only after the meal are the children allowed to open their presents, which miraculously appear beneath the tree thanks not to

Santa Claus but to *Ježíšek* (Baby Jesus).

Birthdays are much less important in the Czech Republic than in English-speaking countries. Even their Czech equivalent, saints' name days, which fall on the same day each year, are a fading tradition. Saints' days for popular names like Jan or Anna were once practically national celebrations since everyone was bound to know at least one person with those names.

The arts

Theatre (*divadlo*) has always had a special place in Czech culture, one which the events of 1989 only strengthened. Not only did the country end up with a playwright as president, but it was the capital's theatres that served as information centres during those first few crucial weeks.

In Prague, tourists are also a lucrative source of income and there are several English-language theatre companies now based there, but outside of Prague there's obviously precious little in English. Ticket prices are low, and the venue and the event itself are often interesting enough to sustain you – older-generation Czechs go as much for the interval promenade as for the show itself. There's less of a linguistic problem with **opera**, of course, and Janáček and Smetana's works in particular are regularly performed.

With numerous permanent puppet theatres across the country, Czech **puppetry** is still very popular. Sadly, few traditional marionette or puppet-only theatres survive; the rest have introduced live actors into their repertoire, making the shows less accessible if you don't speak the language. However, this trend has produced innovative and highly professional companies like Hradec Králové's Drak, which has toured extensively throughout Europe and now only occasionally uses puppets in its shows. If you want to see a performance, look out for the words *loutkové divadlo*.

The **cinema** (*kino*) remains a cheap and popular form of entertainment in the Czech Republic. Hollywood blockbusters form a large part of the weekly fare, but the Czech film industry has enjoyed something of a renaissance in the late 1990s, with Jan Svěrák collecting an Oscar in 1997 for his film *Kolja*. The majority of films are usually shown in their original language with subtitles (*titulky*) rather than dubbed (*dabing*). The month's film listings are usually fly-posted up around town or outside each cinema. Film titles are nearly always translated into Czech, so you'll need to have your wits about you to identify films such as *Prci, prci, prcičky 2* as *American Pie 2*.

Sport

For a small nation, the Czechs have a pretty good record when it comes to sporting triumphs: over the last two decades, they have consistently produced world-class tennis players, a strong national football team and several of the world's top ice hockey players. The two sports which pull in the biggest crowds, by far, are football and ice hockey. Getting tickets to watch a particular sport is easy (and cheap) enough on the day – only really big matches sell out. Participating in sports activities is also getting easier, though the Czechs are fairly lacklustre about the health kick.

Football

The Czech national football or soccer (*fotbal*) team have enjoyed mixed fortunes since splitting from the Slovaks in 1993. After losing the Euro '96 final in extra time, they failed to qualify for the 1998 and 2002 World Cups, and performed badly in Euro 2000, despite winning all ten of their qualifying matches. On the domestic front, however, things have been much worse. As with most former Eastern Bloc countries, the best home-grown players have, almost without exception, chosen to seek fame and fortune abroad. As a result, domestic teams usually struggle in European competitions, during which it's common to hear Czech fans racially abusing the opposing team's black players.

The most consistent team in the *Českomoravského liga* (Ⓦwww.fotbal.cz) is Sparta Praha, though 2002 saw Slovan Liberec emerge as the league champions for the first time ever. The season runs from August to late November and late February to late May, and matches are usually held on Saturdays. Tickets for domestic games are under 100Kč and four-figure crowds remain the norm. For the moment, however, the best thing about Czech football is that, somewhat unbelievably, you can still drink inexpensive and delicious beer on the terraces.

Ice hockey

Ice hockey (*lední hokej*) runs soccer a close second as the nation's most popular sport. It's not unusual to see kids playing their own form of the game in the street, rather than kicking a football around. As with soccer, the fall of Communism prompted an exodus by the country's best players who left to seek fame and fortune in North America's National Hockey League (NHL). In fact, Jaromír Jágr (Ⓦwww.jaromirjagr.cz), by far the most famous Czech player, remains one of the NHL's top scorers, and currently plays for the Washington Capitals. The Czech national team has been the team to beat in the last five years or so, winning the World Championships three years on the trot.

Unlike in soccer, there are several teams usually in close contention for the *Extraliga* title. Games are fast and physical, cold but compelling, and can take anything up to three hours. They are held in the local *zimní* *stadión* (winter stadium), usually on Saturday afternoons. The season starts at the end of September and culminates in the annual World Championships, when the fortunes of the national side are subject to close scrutiny, especially if pitched against the Slovaks or the Russians. A double victory against the latter in 1969 precipitated riots in towns across the country, culminating in the torching of the Aeroflot (Soviet airlines) offices in Prague.

Prague and around

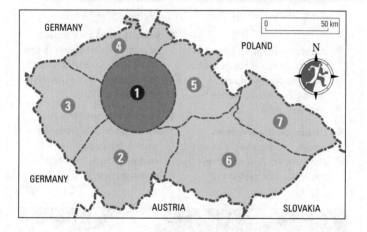

CHAPTER 1 # Highlights

✱ **Pražský hrad** – Perched high above the city, and the seat of power for over a millennium, Prague Castle is home to the cathedral, the royal palace, several museums and art galleries, and the president. **See p.68**

✱ **Malá Strana terraced gardens** – Ornamental Baroque gardens hidden away in the steep backstreets of Malá Strana. **See p.84**

✱ **Josefov** – Prague's former Jewish ghetto is still home to six synagogues and an atmospheric medieval cemetery. **See p.98**

✱ **Obecní dům** – The most ornate and accessible of all Prague's Art Nouveau masterpieces, completed in

1911, now houses cafés, restaurants, exhibition spaces and a concert hall. **See p.112**

✱ **Vyšehrad** – Habsburg fortress with zigzag walls, underground tunnels and the most prestigious cemetery in the city, resting place of Dvořak, Smetana and the artist Alfons Mucha, among others. **See p.118**

✱ **Veletržní palač** – Prague's vast modern art gallery is the finest in the country and an architectural sight in its own right. **See p.123**

✱ **Prague tea-houses** – A 1990s reaction against the smoky, boozy pub, tea-houses provide the perfect chill-out zone. **See p.133**

Prague and around

With some six hundred years of architecture virtually untouched by natural disaster or war, few other cities, anywhere in Europe, look as good as **Prague**. Straddling the winding River Vltava, with a steep wooded hill to one side, the city retains much of its medieval layout, the street facades remain smothered in a rich mantle of Baroque, and the historical core has successfully escaped the vanities and excesses of postwar redevelopment. During the postwar decades of Soviet-imposed isolation, very few westerners visited Prague. However, since the 1990s, all that has changed: the city is now one of the most popular city breaks in Europe, and the streets around the main sights are jam-packed with tourists for much of the year.

Prague is surprisingly compact, its city centre divided into two unequal halves by the **River Vltava**. The steeply inclined left bank is dominated by the castle district of **Hradčany**, which contains the most obvious sights – the castle or Hrad itself, the city's cathedral, and the old royal palace and gardens – as well as a host of museums and galleries. Squeezed between the castle hill and the river are the picturesque Baroque palaces and houses of the "Little Quarter" or **Malá Strana** – around 150 acres of twisting cobbled streets and secret walled gardens – home to the Czech parliament and most of the city's embassies, and dominated by the green dome and tower of the church of sv Mikuláš.

The city's twisting matrix of streets is at its most confusing in the original medieval hub of the city, **Staré Město** – literally, the "Old Town" – on the right bank of the Vltava. The Karlův most, or Charles Bridge, its main link with the opposite bank, is easily the city's most popular historical monument, and the best place from which to view Prague Castle. Staré Město's other great showpiece is its main square, Staroměstské náměstí, where you can view Prague's famous astronomical clock. Enclosed within the boundaries of Staré Město is the former Jewish quarter, or **Josefov**. The ghetto walls have long since gone and the whole area was remodelled at the end of the nineteenth century, but six synagogues, a medieval cemetery and a town hall survive as powerful reminders of a community that has existed here for over a millennium.

South and east of the old town is the large sprawling district of **Nové Město**, whose main arteries make up the city's commercial and business centre. The nexus of Nové Město is Wenceslas Square (Václavské náměstí), focus of the political upheavals of the modern-day republic. Further afield lie various **suburbs**, most of which were developed only in the last hundred years or so. The single exception is **Vyšehrad**, one of the original fortress settlements of the newly arrived Slavs in the last millennium, now the final resting place of leading Czech artists of the modern age, including the composers Smetana and Dvořák.

If Prague's city centre is a revelation, the city's outer suburbs, where most of the population live, are more typical of Eastern Europe: seemingly half-built, high-rise housing estates, known locally as *paneláky*, swimming in a sea of mud. However, once you're clear of the city limits, the traditional, provincial feel of **Bohemia** (Čechy) immediately makes itself felt. Many Praguers own a *chata*, or country cottage, somewhere in these rural backwaters, and every weekend the roads are jammed with weekenders. Few places are more than an hour from the centre by public transport, making an easy day-trip for visitors.

The most popular destinations for foreign day-trippers are the castles of **Karlštejn** and **Konopiště**, both of which suffer from a daily swarm of coach parties. You're better rewarded by heading north, away from the hills and the crowds, to the chateau of **Veltrusy** near Dvořák's birthplace of Nelahozeves, or to the wine town of **Mělník**. The wooded hills around **Křivoklát** in the northeast or **Kokořín** in the southwest, both around 40km from Prague, are also good places to lose the crowds. Even further afield is the undisputed gem of the region, the medieval silver-mining town of **Kutná Hora**, 60km east of Prague, with a glorious Gothic cathedral.

Prague (Praha)

The Czechs have a legend for every occasion, and the founding of **PRAGUE** is no exception. Sometime in the seventh or eighth century AD, the Czech prince Krok (aka Pace) moved his people south from the plains of the River Labe (Elbe) to the rocky knoll that is now Vyšehrad (literally "high castle"). His youngest daughter, **Libuše**, who was to become the country's first and last female leader, was endowed with the gift of prophecy. Falling into a trance one day, she pronounced that they should build a city "whose glory will touch the stars", at the point in the forest where they would find an old man constructing the threshold of his house. He was duly discovered on the Hradčany hill overlooking the Vltava, and the city was named **Praha**, meaning "threshold". Subsequently, Libuše was compelled to take a husband and again fell into a trance, this time pronouncing that they should follow her horse to a ploughman, whose descendants would rule over them. Sure enough, a man called **Přemysl** (meaning "ploughman") was discovered and became the mythical founder of the Přemyslid dynasty, which ruled Bohemia until the fourteenth century.

So much for the legend. **Historically**, Hradčany and not Vyšehrad appears to have been the site of the first Slav settlement. The Vltava was relatively shallow at this point, and it probably seemed a safer bet than the plains of the Labe. Under the Přemyslids the city prospered, benefiting from its position on the central European trade routes. Merchants from all over Europe came to settle here, and in 1234 the first of Prague's historic towns, the **Staré Město**, was founded to accommodate them. In 1257, King Otakar II founded the **Malá Strana** on the slopes of the castle as a separate quarter for Prague's German merchants. When the Přemyslid dynasty died out in 1306, the crown was handed over by the Czech nobles to the Luxembourgs, and it was under **Charles IV** (1346–78) that Prague enjoyed its **first golden age**. In just thirty years, Charles transformed Prague into one of the most important cities in fourteenth-century Europe, establishing institutions and buildings that survive today – the Charles University, St Vitus Cathedral, the Charles Bridge, a host of monasteries and churches – and founding an entire new town, **Nové Město**, to accommodate the influx of students and clergy.

Surprisingly enough, it was under a Habsburg, **Rudolf II** (1576–1612), that the city enjoyed its **second golden age**, inviting artists, scientists (and quacks) from all over Europe, and filling the castle galleries with the finest art. However, following the defeat of the Protestants at the 1620 **Battle of Bílá hora** (White Mountain) on the outskirts of the city, came the period the Czechs refer to as the **dark ages**, when the full force of the Counter-Reformation was brought to bear on the city's people. Paradoxically, though, the spurt of Baroque rebuilding during this period lent Prague its most striking architectural aspect, and the majority of the city's impressive palaces date from this period.

The next two centuries saw Prague's importance gradually whittled away within the Habsburg Empire. Two things dragged it out of the doldrums: the first was the **industrial revolution** of the mid-nineteenth century, which brought large numbers of Czechs in from the countryside to work in the factories; and the second was the contemporaneous **Czech national revival** or *národní obrození*, which gave Prague a number of symbolic monuments, such as its Národní divadlo (National Theatre), the Národní muzeum (National Museum), the Rudolfinum concert and exhibition hall and the Obecní dům (Municipal House). The national revival led eventually to the foundation of Czechoslovakia in 1918, which once again put Prague at the centre of the country's political events and marked the beginning of the city's third golden age, the **First Republic**. Architecturally, the first three decades of the twentieth century left Prague with a unique legacy of Art Nouveau, Cubist, Rondo-Cubist and Functionalist buildings.

The virtual annihilation of the city's Jews and the expulsion of the German-speaking community changed Prague forever, though the city itself survived World War II physically more or less unscathed and industrially intact, before disappearing completely behind the Iron Curtain. Internal centralization only increased the city's importance – it hosted the country's macabre show trials, and at one time boasted the largest statue of Stalin in the world. The city briefly re-emerged onto the world stage during the cultural blossoming of the **1968 Prague Spring**, but following the Soviet invasion in August of that year, Prague vanished from view once more. Just over twenty years later, the **1989 Velvet Revolution** finally toppled the Communist government without so much as a shot being fired. The exhilarating popular unity of that period is now history, but there is still a sense of new-found potential in the capital, which has been restored and transformed visually out of all recognition over the past ten years or so.

Arrival and information

Prague is one of Europe's smaller capital cities, with a population of one and a quarter million. The airport lies just over 10km northwest of the city centre, with only a bus link or taxi to get you into town. By contrast, both the **international train stations** and the main **bus terminal** are linked to the centre by the fast and efficient metro system.

By air

Prague's **Ruzyně** airport (☏220 111 111 ⊛www.csl.cz), 10km northwest of the city centre, is connected to the city by **local bus #119** (daily 5am to midnight; every 15–20min; journey time 20min), which stops frequently and ends its journey outside Dejvická metro station. You can buy your ticket from the public transport (DP) information desk in arrivals (daily 7am–10pm), or from the nearby machines or newsagents. If you arrive after midnight, you can catch a night bus #510 to Divoká Šárka, the terminus for night tram #51, which will take you to Národní in the centre of town. More convenient if you've a lot of luggage is to take the ČEDAZ **express minibus service** (daily 5.30am–9.30pm; every 30min), which stops first at Dejvická metro station, at the end of metro line A (journey time 20min) and ends up at náměstí Republiky (journey time 30min); the full journey currently costs 90Kč. Express minibuses will also take you straight to your hotel for around 360Kč per drop-off – a bargain if there's a few of you.

Of course, it's easy enough to take a **taxi** from the airport into the centre, though Prague taxi drivers have a reputation for overcharging. If you do end up taking a taxi, head for "Airport Cars", which offer a "fixed price" system depending on your destination; fares start at 260Kč to the northwest of the city, but will be more like 350Kč for somewhere in the centre.

By train and bus

International trains arrive either at the old Art Nouveau **Praha hlavní nádraží**, on the edge of Nové Město and Vinohrady, or at **Praha-Holešovice**, which lies in an industrial suburb north of the city centre. At both stations you'll find exchange outlets (there's even a branch of the PIS tourist office at Hlavní nádraží), as well as a 24-hour left-luggage office and accommodation agencies (see p.62). Both stations are on metro lines, and Hlavní nádraží is only a five-minute walk from Václavské náměstí (Wenceslas Square).

Domestic trains usually wind up at Hlavní nádraží or the central **Masarykovo nádraží** on Hybernská, a couple of blocks east of náměstí Republiky. Slower *osobní* trains and various provincial services arrive at a variety of obscure suburban stations: trains from the southwest pull into **Praha-Smíchov** (metro Smíchovské nádraží); trains from the east arrive at **Praha-Vysočany** (metro Českomoravská); trains from the west at **Praha-Dejvice** (metro Hradčanská); and trains from the south occasionally rumble into **Praha-Vršovice** (tram #24 to Václavské náměstí).

If you're catching a **train out of Prague**, don't leave buying your ticket until the last minute, as the queues can be long and slow. You can buy international train tickets (*mezinárodní jízdenky*) at either Praha hlavní nádraží or Praha-Holešovice, or at the main office of ČEDOK on Na příkopě, in the centre of town.

Prague's **main bus terminal** is **Praha-Florenc** (metro Florenc), on the eastern edge of Nové Město, where virtually all long-distance international and domestic services terminate. It's a confusing (and ugly) place to end up, but it has a left luggage office upstairs (daily 5am–11pm) and you can make a quick exit to the adjacent metro station. For destinations around Prague, you may need to head out to one of the more obscure bus terminals, all of which are easy enough to reach by metro. To find out which one you want, ask at any of the PIS offices in town or check the comprehensive (and extremely complicated) timetables at Praha-Florenc: *stání* is the bus stand; *odjezd* is the departure time.

Information

Once in Prague, the main tourist office is the **Prague Information Service** or **PIS** (Pražská informační služba), whose main branch is at Na příkopě 20, Nové Město (April–Oct Mon–Fri 9am–7pm, Sat & Sun 9am–5pm; Nov–March Mon–Fri 9am–6pm, Sat & Sun 9am–3pm; ⓦ www.pis.cz). The staff speak English, but their helpfulness varies enormously; they can usually answer most enquiries, and can organize accommodation, sell maps, guides and theatre tickets.

PIS also distributes and sells some useful **listings** publications, including *Culture in Prague/Česká kultura* (ⓦ www.ceskakultura.cz), a monthly English-language booklet listing the major events, concerts and exhibitions, and a free fortnightly leaflet, *Do města/Downtown* (ⓦ www.downtown.cz), which concentrates on cinema, art exhibitions and club listings. There are additional PIS offices in the main train station, Praha hlavní nádraží, within the Staroměstská radnice on Staroměstské náměstí, plus a summer-only office in the Malá Strana bridge tower on the Charles Bridge. Another good source of information is the weekly **English-language paper**, *Prague Post* (ⓦ www.praguepost.com), which carries selective listings on the latest exhibitions, shows, gigs and events around the capital.

The PIS should be able to furnish you with a quick free reference **map** of central Prague, but to locate a specific street, or find your way round the suburbs, you'll need a detailed city map (*plán města*). Kartografie Praha produces the cheapest and most comprehensive ones: the 1:20,000 map (available in both booklet and fold-out form), which covers the city centre as well as many of the suburbs, has a full street index and marks the metro, tram and bus routes. Maps are available from PIS offices, street kiosks, most bookshops (*knihkupectví*) and some hotels.

City transport

The centre of Prague, where most of the city's sights are concentrated, is reasonably small and best explored on foot. At some point, however, in order to cross the city quickly or reach some of the more widely dispersed attractions, you'll need to use the city's cheap and efficient public transport system, which comprises the metro and a network of trams and buses. To get a clearer picture, it's essential to invest in a **city map** (see p.57), which marks all the tram, bus and metro lines.

Tickets and passes

Prague's **public transport system** (*dopravní podnik* or DP; ⓦ www.dp-praha.cz) used to have a simple ticketing system – not any more. Most Praguers simply buy monthly passes, and to avoid having to understand the complexities of the single ticket system, you too are best off buying a travel pass (for more on which, see below).

Probably the single most daunting aspect of buying a ticket is the machines found inside all metro stations and at some bus and tram stops. The machines are covered in buttons, but only two are really relevant, since for a single **ticket** (*lístek* or *jízdenka*) in the two central zones (*2 pásma*), there are just two basic choices. The 8Kč version (*zlevněná*) allows you to travel for up to fifteen minutes on the trams or buses, or up to four stops on the metro (not including the one you start at); it's known as a *nepřestupní jízdenka*, or "no change ticket", although you can in fact change metro lines (but not buses or trams). The 12Kč version (*plnocenná*) is valid for one hour at peak times (an hour and a half off-peak), during which you may change trams, buses or metro lines as many times as you like, hence its name, *přestupní jízdenka*, or "changing ticket". Half-price tickets are available for those aged 6 to 15, bikes and other large objects, including suitcases; under-6s travel free.

If you're **buying a ticket** from one of the machines, you must press the appropriate fare button – press it once for one ticket, twice for two and so on – followed by the *výdej/enter* button, after which you put your money in. The machines do give change, but if you don't have enough coins, you may find the person on duty in the metro office by the barriers can give you change or sell you a ticket. Tickets can also be bought, en masse, and rather more easily, from a tobacconist (*tabák*), street kiosk, newsagent, PIS office or any place that displays the yellow DP sticker. When you enter the metro, or board a tram or bus, you must validate your ticket by placing it in one of the electronic machines to hand.

To save hassle, it's best to buy a **travel pass** (*časová jízdenka*). These are available for 24 hours (*na 24 hodin*; 100Kč), three days (*na 3 dny*; 200Kč), seven days (*na 7 dní*; 250Kč), fifteen days (*na 15 dní*; 280Kč), thirty days (*30 denní*; 560Kč), ninety days (*90 denní*; 1600Kč) or yearly (*roční*; 5900Kč); no photos or ID are needed, though you must write your name and date of birth on the reverse of the ticket, and punch it to validate when you first use it. All the passes are available from DP outlets, and the 24-hour pass is also available from ticket machines.

TRANSPORT SYSTEM

Legend:
- A line
- B line
- C line
- Tram route
- ⑦ Terminus

Prague addresses, house signs and numbers

In order to help locate **addresses** more easily, we have used the names of the city districts as they appear on street signs, for example Hradčany, Staré Město, etc. Prague's **postal districts**, which also appear on street signs, are too large to be of much help in orientation, since the city centre lies almost entirely within Prague 1.

In the older districts, many houses have retained their original medieval **house signs**, a system that is still used today, though predominantly by pubs, restaurants and wine bars, for example U zeleného hroznu (The Green Grape). In the 1770s, the Habsburgs, in their rationalizing fashion, introduced a numerical system, with each house in the city entered onto a register according to a strict chronology. Later, the conventional system of progressive **street numbering** was introduced; so don't be surprised if seventeenth-century pubs like U medvídků (The Little Bears) have, in addition to a house sign, two numbers, in this case 345 and 7; when written down the numbers are separated by a forward slash; on the building, the former Habsburg number appears on a red background, the latter modern number on blue.

Most Praguers buy a monthly (*měsíční*), quarterly (*čtvrtletní*) or yearly (*roční*) pass, with an ID photo attached, which is why you see so few of them punching tickets. Passes with ID photos are slightly cheaper: 420Kč for the monthly; 1150Kč for the quarterly; 3800Kč for the yearly. To obtain one, simply present your ID and a passport-sized photo to the windows marked DP at major metro stations. There's nothing to stop people from freeloading on the system, of course, since there are no barriers. However, plain-clothes **inspectors** (*revizoři*) make spot checks and will issue an on-the-spot fine of 400Kč to anyone caught without a valid ticket or pass; controllers should show you their ID (a small metal disc), and give you a receipt (*paragon*).

Metro

The futuristic Soviet-built **metro** is fast, smooth and ultra-clean, running daily from just before 5am to midnight, with trains every two minutes during peak hours, slowing down to every four to ten minutes by late in the evening. Its three lines (with a fourth planned) intersect at various points in the city centre, and the route maps are easy to follow. The stations are discreetly marked above ground with the logo shown on the map on p.59, in green (line A), yellow (line B) or red (line C). The constant bleeping at metro entrances is to enable blind people to locate the escalators. Once inside the metro, it's worth knowing that *výstup* means exit and *přestup* will lead you to one of the connecting lines at an interchange. The digital clock at the end of the platform tells you not only what time it is, but also how long it's been since the last train.

Trams and buses

The electric **tram** (*tramvaj*) system, in operation since 1891, negotiates Prague's hills and cobbles with remarkable dexterity. After the metro, trams are the fastest and most efficient way of getting around, running every five to eight minutes at peak times, and every five to fifteen minutes at other times – check the timetables posted at every stop (*zastávka*), which list the departure times from that specific stop.

Tram #22, which runs from Vinohrady to Hradčany via the centre of town and Malá Strana, is a good way to get to grips with the lie of the land, and a cheap method of sightseeing, though beware of pickpockets. From Easter to October, an interwar tram #91 runs from Výstaviště to náměstí Republiky via

Malá Strana (Sat & Sun hourly 1–7pm) and back again; the ride takes forty minutes and costs 15Kč. **Night trams** (*noční tramvaje*; #51–58) run roughly every thirty to forty minutes from around midnight to 5am, and all of them pass by Lazarská and Spálená in Nové Město.

Unless you're intent on staying in the more obscure suburbs, you'll rarely need to use Prague's **buses** (*autobusy*), which, for the most part, keep well out of the centre of town; they operate similar (though generally less frequent) hours to the trams, and route numbers are given in the text where appropriate. **Night buses** (*noční autobusy*) run just once an hour between midnight and 5am from náměstí Republiky.

Taxis, cars and bikes

Taxis come in all shapes and sizes, and, theoretically at least, are extremely cheap. However, Prague taxi drivers have a terrible reputation, and many will almost certainly attempt to rip you off if they think they can. Needless to say, the drivers with the worst reputations hang out at the ranks closest to the tourist sights. Officially, the initial fare on the meter should be 25Kč, plus 19Kč per kilometre within Prague. The best advice is to hail a cab or have your hotel or pension call you one, rather than pick one up at the mafia-controlled taxi ranks. The following cab companies have fairly good reputations: Profitaxi ☎261 314 151; and AAA ☎233 113 311.

You really don't need a **car** in Prague, since much of the city centre is pedestrianized and the public transport system is so cheap and efficient. The city authorities, quite rightly, make it very awkward for drivers to enter the city centre, and finding a parking space is also extremely difficult. Much of the centre is pay-and-display (Mon–Sat only); illegally parked cars will either be clamped or towed away – if this happens, phone ☎158 to find out the worst. A sensible option is to park near one of the metro stations out of the centre, several of which have park-and-ride schemes: try Hradčanská, Opatov or Skalka.

Cycling is seen as more of a leisure activity in the Czech Republic, rather than a means of transport. Prague has a handful of brave cycle couriers but the combination of cobbled streets, tram lines and sulphurous air is enough to put most people off. Facilities for **bike rental** are still not that widespread, but if you're determined to give cycling a go, head for City Bike, Králodvorská 5, Staré Město ☎776 180 284; they also organize group rides through Prague.

Boats on the Vltava

In the summer months there's a regular **boat** service on the River Vltava run by the PPS (Pražská paroplavební služba; ⊛ www.paroplavba.cz) from just south of Jiráskův most on Rašínovo nábřeží. From April to October there's three or four boats a day to Troja in the northern suburbs (April, Sept & Oct Sat & Sun; May–Aug daily). There are also much less frequent services north to Mělník (see p.145) and south to Slapy via Zbraslav.

In addition, the PPS also offers two-hour **boat trips** around Prague – and less frequently, to Slapy – on board a 1930s paddlesteamer. EVD (⊛www.evd.cz), who set off from Čechův most, near the *Hotel Intercontinental* at the far end of Pařížská, offer one-hour cruises or longer trips with food and drink thrown in. Another option is to hop aboard the much smaller boats run by Prague-Venice (⊛www.prague-venice.cz), which depart for half-hour meanders over to the Čertovka by Kampa Island. The boats depart from the north side of the Charles Bridge on the Staré Město bank.

Accommodation

Accommodation is twice as expensive in Prague as anywhere else in the country, and is still likely to be by far the largest chunk of your daily expenditure, with most half-decent hotels happily charging 5000Kč and upwards for a double room. The problem is that there's a chronic shortage of decent, inexpensive to middle-range places in Prague. At the bottom end of the scale, there are plenty of hostel beds, starting at a mere 200Kč per person, but the number of private rooms available has dwindled since the early 1990s.

Prague is pretty busy for much of the year, so if you're going to visit anytime from Easter to September, or over the Christmas and New Year period, it's almost essential to arrange accommodation before you arrive, either directly with the hotels or through one of the specialist agencies listed on pp.12, 14 & below. Prices are at their highest over the public holidays, but drop by as much as a third in the low season (Nov–March excluding New Year), and sometimes come down a bit in July and August when business custom is low.

If you arrive in Prague without having booked a room, there are several **accommodation agencies** you can turn to (see below), most of which will book you into either a hotel or pension, and some of which can also help you find a hostel bed or a private room in an apartment. Before agreeing to part with any money, be sure you know exactly where you're staying and check about transport to the centre – some places can be a long way out of town.

Accommodation agencies

AVE ☎257 555 176, 🌐www.avetravel.cz; hours vary but the airport desk is open daily 7am–10pm. AVE is the largest agency in Prague, with offices at the airport, both international train stations, and several points throughout the city, and is therefore an excellent last-minute fallback. They offer rooms in a selection of hotels, pensions and hostels, plus a few private rooms.

Mary's Travel Services Italská 31, Vinohrady ☎222 254 007, 🌐www.marys.cz; metro náměstí Míru; daily 9am–7pm. Good-value agency that will book hotels, pensions and private rooms in Prague, and a few other locations in the Czech Republic.

Pragotur Za Poříčskou bránou 7, Karlín ☎221 714 130, 🌐www.prague-info.cz. The main office is situated just across the road from Florenc bus station, but they also operate through the various PIS tourist offices (see p.57). They can book anything from hotels and hostels, but they specialize in private rooms.

Tom's Travel Ostrovní 7, Nové Město ☎224 990 991, 🌐www.travel.cz; metro Národní třída; daily: June–Aug 8am–10pm; Sept–May 8am–8pm. Well-established, upmarket travel agency that can book you into hotels, pensions and apartments in Prague, and help you with accommodation outside Prague, too.

Hotels and pensions

Prague now boasts a huge variety of **hotels** and **pensions**, from big multinational chain hotels to places with real character in the old town. The vast majority of rooms have en-suite bathrooms and TVs, with continental breakfast either included in the price or offered as an optional extra. There's no hard and fast rule as to what constitutes a hotel and what a pension – though if you come across a "residence", then there's likely to be some kind of self-catering facilities – and it's certainly not reflected in the price. Standards overall can still vary wildly, though "service with a snarl", once commonplace, is now only occasionally encountered.

With plenty of centrally located hotels, there's really no need to stay out in the suburbs unless you're on a very tight budget. The quietest central areas to stay in are on the left bank in Malá Strana, though there's more choice, more transport and more nightlife in Staré Město and Nové Město. Rather than trekking around any of the places listed below on the off chance that they will have vacancies, you're better off making a reservation by email or phone before you arrive in Prague, or using one of the agencies listed in the box on p.62.

Most of the places listed below are marked on the map on p.64.

Hradčany and Malá Strana

Dientzenhofer Nosticova 2 ☏257 316 830. Birthplace of its namesake, and a very popular pension due to the fact that it's one of the few reasonably priced places (anywhere in Prague) to have wheelchair access. Just seven rooms on offer. ❼

Dům U velké boty (The Big Shoe) Vlašská 30 ☏257 311 107, ✉rippl@mbox.vol.cz. The sheer anonymity of this pension, in a lovely old building in the quiet backstreets, is one of its main draws. Run by a very friendly couple, who speak good English, it has a series of characterful, tastefully modernized rooms, some with en-suite, some without. Breakfast is extra, but worth it. ❼

Na Kampě 15 Na Kampě 15 ☏257 531 432, ⓦwww.nakampe15.cz. Situated on a lovely tree-lined square, just off the Charles Bridge, the rooms in this former brewery have real character, despite the modern fittings. ❾

Nosticova Nosticova 1 ☏257 312 513, ⓦwww.nosticova.com. A Baroque house with ten beautifully restored apartments replete with antique furnishings, sumptuous bathrooms and small kitchens, on a peaceful square not far from the Charles Bridge. ❾

U kříže (The Cross) Újezd 20 ☏257 313 272. No airs and graces at this modernized hotel on a busy street in the south of Malá Strana; B&B prices reduced in July and August. ❻

U raka (The Crayfish) Černínská 10 ☏220 511 100, ⓦwww.romantikhotels.com; tram #22 from metro Malostranská to Pohořelec stop. The perfect hideaway, six double rooms in a little half-timbered eighteenth-century cottage in Nový Svět. No children under 12 or dogs, and advance reservation a must. ❾

Staré Město

Avalon-Tara Havelská 15 ☏224 228 083, ✉avalon-tara@volny.cz; metro Můstek. Perfect location right over the market on Havelská, with seven very small, plainly furnished but clean rooms, with or without en-suite facilities. ❹

Betlém Club Betlémské nám. 9 ☏222 221 574, ⓦwww.betlemclub.cz; metro Národní třída. Small rooms, but acceptable decor, plus a Gothic cellar for breakfast, and a perfect location on a quiet square at the heart of the old town – a rare bargain. ❺

Černá liška (The Black Fox) Mikulášská 2 ☏224 232 250, ✉cerna.liska@volny.cz; metro Staroměstská. Well-appointed rooms, all with lovely wooden floors, some with incredible views onto Old Town Square, quieter ones at the back. ❾

Černý slon (Black Elephant) Týnská 1 ☏222 321 521, ⓦwww.hotelcernyslon.cz; metro náměstí Republiky. Another ancient building tucked away off Old Town Square by the north portal of the Týn church, now tastefully converted into a very comfortable hotel. ❽

Cloister Inn Konviktská 14 ☏224 211 020, ⓦwww.cloister-inn.com; metro Národní třída. Pleasant, well-equipped hotel housed in a nunnery in one of the backstreets; the rooms are basic, but a bargain for the location. There are even cheaper rooms in the *Pension Unitas*, in the same building (see below). ❺

Expres Skořepka 5 ☏224 211 801, ⓦwww.hotel-expres.wz.cz; metro Národní třída. Friendly little hotel with few pretensions: cheap and cheerful fittings, low prices and an excellent location right in the thick of Staré Město. ❹

U krále Jiřího (The King George) Liliová 10 ☏224 248 797, ⓦwww.kinggeorge.cz; metro Staroměstská. Eight small, cosy en-suite rooms with repro furnishings above a set of bars, hidden in the network of lanes off Karlova. ❻

U medvídků (The Little Bears) Na Perštýně 7 ☏224 211 916, ⓦwww.umedvidku.cz; metro Národní třída. The rooms above this famous Prague pub are plainly furnished, quiet considering the locale, and therefore something of an Old Town bargain; booking ahead essential. ❻

Unitas Bartolomějská 9 ☏224 211 020, ⓦwww.unitas.cz; metro Národní třída. Run by the *Cloister Inn* (see above), with hostel rooms, plus bargain rooms in converted former secret police prison cells (Havel stayed in P6), now owned by Franciscan nuns. No smoking and no drinking, but unbelievably cheap. ❸

Nové Město

Alcron Šteřánská 40 ☏222 820 000, ⓦwww.radisson.com/praguecs; metro Muzeum/Můstek. Giant 1930s hotel, just off Wenceslas Square, that has been superbly restored to its former glory by the Radisson SAS chain. Double rooms, at around 10,000Kč, are without doubt the most luxurious and tasteful you'll find in Prague. ❾

ACCOMMODATION

Alcron	27	Dům U velké boty	10	Petr	29
Avalon-Tara	15	Expres	16	Salvator	5
Betlém Club	17	Grand Hotel Evropa	22	Travellers Hostel	2
Černá liška	8	Hostel Sokol	18	Triška	28
Černý slon	7	Hostel Týn	6	U krale Jiřího	14
City	30	Imperial	4	U kříže	24
Cloister Inn	19	Jerome House	26	U medvíků	21
Clown and Bard	9	Klub Habitat	25	U raka	3
Crowne Plaza	1	Na Kampě 15	11	Unitas	20
Dientzenhofer	13	Nosticova	12	Vesta	23

PRAGUE: ACCOMMODATION

Grand Hotel Evropa Václavské nám. 25 ☎224 228 117, ⓦwww.hotelsprague.org/evropa; metro Můstek/Muzeum. Without doubt, the most beautiful hotel in Prague, built in the 1900s and sumptuously decorated in Art Nouveau style; the rooms are furnished in repro Louis XIV, and there are some cheaper ones without en-suite facilities. Yet despite its prime location and its incredible decor, this place is run like an old Communist hotel – a blast from the past in every sense. ❽
Imperial Na poříčí 15 ☎222 316 012, ⓦwww.hotelimperial.cz; metro náměstí Republiky. The café on the ground floor is a 1914 period piece; the vast hotel above it is much more basic – clean, simply furnished doubles, triples and quads with shared facilities only. ❻
Jerome House V jirchářích 13 ☎224 911 011, ⓦwww.jerome.cz; metro Národní třída. Discreetly tucked away in a nice, quiet area just south of Národní, the Jerome offers plain, bright rooms with upbeat, modern design, plus the odd original feature. Very basic, clean rooms. ❽
Salvator Truhlářská 10 ☎222 312 234, ⓦwww.salvator.cz; metro náměstí Republiky. Very good location for the price, just a minute's walk from nám. Republiky, with small but clean rooms (the cheaper ones without en-suite facilities), and

a sports bar on the ground floor; advance booking advisable. ❹

Further afield

City Belgická 10, Vinohrady ☎222 521 606, ⓦwww.hotelcity.cz; metro náměstí Míru. Quiet locale, cheap, clean en-suite rooms with TVs and within walking distance of the top of Wenceslas Square. ❸
Crowne Plaza Koulova 15, Dejvice ☎224 393 111, ⓦwww.crowneplaza.cz; tram #20 or #25 from metro Dejvická to Podbaba terminus. Prague's classic 1950s Stalinist wedding-cake hotel, with its dour socialist realist friezes and large helpings of marble, is now run by the Austrians. ❻
Triška Vinohradská 105 ☎222 727 313, ⓦwww.hotel-triska.cz; metro Jiřího z Poděbrad. Large turn-of-the-twentieth-century hotel with comfortable rooms; they've made an effort with the interior decor, the service is good and it's close to the metro. ❸
Petr Drtinova 17, Smíchov ☎257 314 068, ⓦwww.hotelpetr.cz; tram #6, #9 or #12 from metro Anděl to Kinského zahrada stop. Situated on a leafy street at the foot of Petřín hill, close to Malá Strana; not that promising from the outside, but modern and pleasant inside. ❸

Hostels

There are a fair few **hostels** in Prague which cater for the large number of backpackers who hit the city all year round – and these are supplemented further by a whole host of more transient, high-season-only hostels. Prices in hostels range from 200Kč to 600Kč for a bed, usually in a dormitory. A few operate curfews – it's worth asking before you commit yourself – and, although many rent out blankets and sheets, it's as well to bring your own sleeping bag. Note that some of the accommodation agencies in Prague also deal with hostels; see p.62 for details.

Some Prague hostels give discounts to HI (Hostelling International; ⓦwww.iyhf.org), and a few can be booked via the HI's online booking service, but, for the most part, you're better off contacting a centrally located organization like the **Traveller's Hostels**, whose chain of hostels is very popular with US students. Their main booking office is at Dlouhá 33, Staré Město (☎224 826 662, ⓦwww.travellers.cz), where there is also a hostel (see p.67); dorm beds go for 350Kč and upwards per person.

Prague's university, the Karolinum, rents out over a thousand very basic **student rooms** from June to mid-September, starting at around 220Kč for a bed. Go to the central booking office at Voršilská 1, Nové Město (Mon–Fri only; ☎224 913 692; metro Národní třída).

Arena Hostel U Výstaviště 1, Holešovice ☎220 870 252, ⓦwww.arena.hostel.com; metro Holešovice, or tram #5 from Hlavní nádraží to stop Výstaviště. Newish, clean hostel with dorm beds from 290Kč and lively bar.
Clown and Bard Bořivojova 102, Žižkov ☎222

716 453, ⓦwww.clownandbard.com; tram #5, #9 or #26 from metro Hlavní nádraží to Husinecká stop. So laid-back it's horizontal, and not a place to go if you don't like hippies, but it's clean, undeniably cheap, stages events, has laundry facilities and rents out doubles (❶) as well as dorm beds

for 250Kč per person.
Hostel Sokol Újezd 40, Malá Strana ☏257 007
397; tram #12, #22 or #23 from metro
Malostranská to Hellichova stop. Shambolic student hostel with basic dorm beds for 300Kč, plus a
communal kitchen, in a great location in Malá
Strana; the entrance is on Všehrdova.
Hostel Týn Týnská 19, Staré Město ☏222 734
590, ⊛www.hostel.cz; metro náměstí Republiky.
The most centrally located hostel, just metres from
Old Town Square. Simple doubles (❸), and six-
bed dorms at 400Kč a bed.
Klub Habitat Na Zderaze 10, Nové Město ☏224
921 706, ⊜hostel@iol.cz; metro Karlovo náměstí.
The best of Prague's hostels, offering a discount to
HI members, located a short walk from Karlovo

nám. Dorm beds for 400Kč per person, with
breakfast. Book ahead.
Traveller's Hostel Dlouhá 33, Staré Město
☏224 826 662, ⊛www.travellers.cz; metro
Náměstí Republiky. Very centrally located hostel
and booking office above the *Roxy* nightclub – if
there's not enough room here, they'll find you a
bed somewhere for 350Kč per person and
upwards.
Vesta Wilsonova 8, Nové Město ☏224 617 118,
⊛www.vestack.cz; metro Hlavní nádraží. Vesta, an
accommodation agency with several offices in the
main train station (Praha hlavní nádraží), can book
you into various places including their very own
hostel in the station itself; beds cost 300Kč, and
you can ask for sole occupancy.

Campsites

Prague abounds in **campsites** – there's a whole rash of them in Troja (see
p.127) – and most are relatively easy to get to on public transport. Facilities, on
the whole, are rudimentary and poorly maintained, but the prices reflect this,
starting at around 300Kč for a tent and two people.

Džbán Nad lávkou 5, Vokovice ☏235 359 006;
tram #20 or #26 from metro Dejvická to Nad
Džbánem stop. Large field with tent pitches, bungalows and basic facilities, 4km west of the centre, near the Šárka valley. Open all year.
Kotva U ledáren 55, Braník ☏244 461 712. The
oldest, and nicest, site, with a riverside location
6km south of the city. Tram #3 or #16 from metro

Karlovo náměstí to Nádraží Braník stop. Open
April–Oct.
Trojská Trojská 375, Troja ☏283 850 487; bus
#112 from metro Nádraží Holešovice. Good loca-
tion, one of several along the road to Troja
chateau, situated in someone's large back garden,
3km north of the centre. Open all year.

Hradčany

HRADČANY is wholly dominated by the city's omnipresent landmark,
Prague Castle, or Pražský hrad, the vast hilltop complex that looks out over
the city centre from the west bank of the River Vltava. Site of a Slav settlement
in the seventh or eighth century AD, there's been a castle here since at least the
late ninth century, and since then whoever has had control of the Hrad has exer-
cized authority over the Czech Lands. It continues to serve as the seat of the
president, though the public are free to wander round from the early hours until
late at night, since the castle is also home to several museums and galleries.

The rest of the castle district, or Hradčany, has always been a mere appendage, its
inhabitants serving and working for their masters in the Hrad. Even now, despite
the odd restaurant or *pivnice* (pub) in amongst the palaces (and even in the Hrad
itself), there's very little real life here beyond the stream of tourists who trek
through the castle and the civil servants who work either for the president or the
government, whose departmental tentacles spread right across Hradčany and down
into neighbouring Malá Strana. All of which makes it a very peaceful and attractive area in which to take a stroll, and lose the crowds who crawl all over the Hrad.

Stretched out along a high spur above the River Vltava, Hradčany shows a suitable disdain for the public transport system. There's a choice of **approaches**
from Malá Strana, all of which involve at least some walking. From Malostranská

ACCOMMODATION
U raka **1**

▼ Petřín

metro station, most people take the steep short cut up the Staré zámecké schody, which brings you into the castle from its rear end. A better approach is up the stately Zámecké schody, where you can stop and admire the view, before entering the castle via the main gates. The alternative to all this climbing is to take tram #22 from Malostranská metro, which tackles the hairpin bends of Chotkova with ease, and deposits you either outside the Královská zahrada (Royal Gardens) to the north of the Hrad, or, if you prefer, outside the gates of the Strahovský klášter (monastery), at the far western edge of Hradčany.

Pražský hrad (Prague Castle)

Viewed from the Charles Bridge, **Pražský hrad** (known to the Czechs simply as the Hrad), stands aloof from the rest of the city, protected, not by bastions and castellated towers, but by a rather austere palatial facade – an "immense unbroken sheer blank wall", as Hilaire Belloc described it – above which rises the great Gothic mass of St Vitus Cathedral. It's the picture-postcard image of Prague, and is spectacularly lit-up at night, though for the Czechs the castle has been an object of disdain as much as admiration, its alternating fortunes mirroring the shifts in the nation's history. The golden age of Charles IV and Rudolf II and the dark ages of the later Habsburgs, interwar democracy and Stalinist terror – all have emanated from the Hrad. When the first posters appeared in December 1989 demanding "HAVEL NA HRAD" (Havel to the Castle), they weren't asking for his reincarceration. Havel's occupancy of the Hrad was the sign that the reins of government had finally been wrested from the Communist regime.

Visiting the Castle

Pražský hrad (Ⓦ www.hrad.cz) is open daily April–October 5am–midnight, November–March 6am–11pm; sights within the castle (unless otherwise stated) are open daily April–October 9am–5pm, November–March 9am–4pm.

You can wander freely through most of the streets, courtyards and gardens of the castle and watch the changing of the guard without a ticket. A single ticket, costing 220Kč, will give you entry to five sights within the castle: the choir, crypt and tower of the Cathedral; the Starý královský palác (Old Royal Palace); the Basilica of sv Jiří; the Zlatá ulička and the Mihulka or Prašná věž (Powder Tower). Tickets which cover all the above sights except the Basilica cost 180Kč and tickets for just the Zlatá ulička cost just 40Kč. Tickets are available from the main information centre in the third courtyard, opposite the cathedral, where you can also hire an audioguide (in English) for another 145Kč for two hours.

The art collections of the Jiřský klášter and the Obrazárna Pražského hradu, the toys at the Muzeum hraček, the museum in the Lobkovický palác, and the exhibitions held in Císařská konírna and Jízdárna, all have different opening hours and separate admission charges.

Within the castle precincts there are several cafés and restaurants, which are not quite as extortionate as you might expect from their location. If you simply want a quick cup of coffee and a place to write some postcards, head for the *Café Poet*, which has tables outside in the shade and is hidden away in the peaceful and little-visited Zahrada na baště.

The site has been successively built on since the Přemyslid princes erected the first castle here in the ninth century, but two **architects** in particular bear responsibility for the present outward appearance of the Hrad. The first is **Nicolo Pacassi**, court architect to Empress Maria Theresa, whose austere restorations went hand in hand with the deliberate run-down of the Hrad until it was little more than an administrative barracks. For the Czechs, his grey-green eighteenth-century cover-up, which hides a variety of much older buildings, is unforgivable. Less apparent, though no less controversial, is the hand of **Josip Plečnik**, the Slovene architect who was commissioned by T.G. Masaryk, president of the newly founded Czechoslovak Republic, to restore and modernize the castle in his highly distinctive style in the 1920s.

The first and second courtyards

The **first courtyard** (první nádvoří), which opens on to Hradčanské náměstí, is guarded by Ignaz Platzer's blood-curdling *Battling Titans* – two gargantuan figures, one on each of the gate piers, wielding club and dagger and about to inflict fatal blows on their respective victims. Below them stand a couple of impassive presidential sentries, sporting blue uniforms that deliberately recall those of the First Republic. The hourly **Changing of the Guard** is a fairly subdued affair, but every day at noon there's a much more elaborate parade, accompanied by a brass ensemble which appears at the first-floor windows to play a gentle, slightly comical, modern fanfare.

To reach the **second courtyard** (druhé nádvoří), you must pass through the early Baroque Matyášova brána (Matthias Gate), originally a freestanding triumphal arch in the middle of the long since defunct moat, now set into one of Pacassi's blank walls. Grand stairways on either side lead to the presidential apartments in the south wing, and to the **Španělský sál** (Spanish Hall) and the **Rudolfova galerie** (Rudolf Gallery) in the north wing – two of the most stunning rooms in the entire complex. Sadly, both are generally out of bounds, though concerts are occasionally held in the Španělský sál.

Surrounded by monotonous Pacassi plasterwork, the courtyard itself is really just a through-route to the cathedral. The most visible intrusion is Anselmo Lurago's **chapel of sv Kříž**, which cowers in one corner. Its richly painted interior, dating mostly from the mid-nineteenth century, used to house the cathedral treasury, a macabre selection of medieval reliquaries. In the north wing of the courtyard are the former **Císařská konírna** (Imperial Stables), which still boast their original, magnificent Renaissance vaulting dating from the reign of Rudolf II, and are now used to house temporary exhibitions (Tues–Sun 10am–6pm).

Obrazárna Pražského hradu (Prague Castle Picture Gallery)

The remnants of the imperial collection, begun by the Habsburg Emperor Rudolf II, are housed in the **Obrazárna Pražského hradu** (daily 10am–6pm), opposite the old imperial stables. The surviving collection is definitely patchy, but it does contain one or two masterpieces that are well worth seeing, and visiting the gallery is a great way to escape the castle crowds. One of the collection's finest paintings is **Rubens'** richly coloured *Assembly of the Gods at Olympus*, featuring a typically voluptuous Venus and a slightly fazed Jupiter. The illusionist triple portrait of Rudolf (when viewed from the left), and his Habsburg predecessors (when viewed from the right), by Paulus Roy, is typical of the sort of tricksy work that appealed to the emperor. Elsewhere, there's an early, very beautiful *Young Woman at her Toilet* by **Titian**, and a superbly observed *Portrait of a Musician* by one of his pupils, Bordone. **Veronese**'s best offering is his portrait of his friend Jakob König, a German art dealer in Venice, who worked for, among others, Rudolf II. Look out, too, for **Tintoretto**'s *Flagellation of Christ*, a late work in which the artist makes very effective and dramatic use of light.

St Vitus Cathedral

St Vitus Cathedral (chram sv Víta) is squeezed so tightly into the third courtyard that it's difficult to get an overall impression of this chaotic Gothic edifice. Its asymmetrical appearance is the product of a long and chequered history, for although the foundation stone was laid in 1344, the cathedral was not completed until 1929 – exactly 1000 years after the death of Bohemia's most famous patron saint, Wenceslas.

The inspiration for the medieval cathedral came from Emperor Charles IV, who, while still only heir to the throne, had not only wangled an independent archbishopric for Prague, but had also managed to gather together the relics of Saint Vitus. Inspired by the cathedral at Narbonne, Charles commissioned the Frenchman **Matthias of Arras** to start work on a similar structure. Matthias died eight years into the job in 1352, with the cathedral barely started, so Charles summoned **Peter Parler**, a precocious 23-year-old from a family of great German masons, to continue the work, but the cathedral got no further than the construction of the choir and the south transept before his death in 1399.

Little significant work was carried out during the next four centuries, and the half-built cathedral became a symbol of the Czechs' frustrated aspirations of nationhood. Not until the Czech national revival or *národní obrození* of the nineteenth century did building begin again in earnest, with the foundation, in 1859, of the **Union for the Completion of the Cathedral**. A succession of architects, including Josef Mocker and Kamil Hilbert, oversaw the completion of the entire west end, and with the help of countless other Czech artists and sculptors, the building was transformed into a treasure-house of Czech art. The cathedral was finally given an official opening ceremony in 1929, though in fact work continued right up to and beyond World War II.

The sooty Prague air has made it hard now to differentiate between the two building periods. Close inspection, however, reveals that the **western facade**, including the twin spires, sports the rigorous if unimaginative work of the neo-Gothic restorers (their besuited portraits can be found below the rose window), while the **eastern section** – best viewed from the Belvedér – shows the building's authentic Gothic roots. The south door (see Zlatá brána, p.73) is also pure Parler. Oddly then, it's above the south door that the cathedral's tallest steeple reveals the most conspicuous stylistic join: Pacassi's Baroque topping resting absurdly on a Renaissance parapet of light stone, which is itself glued onto the blackened body of the original Gothic tower.

The nave

The cathedral is the country's largest, and once inside, it's difficult not to be impressed by the sheer height of the **nave**. This is the newest part of the building, and, consequently, is decorated mostly with twentieth-century furnishings. The most arresting of these is the cathedral's modern **stained-glass** windows, which on sunny days send shafts of rainbow light into the nave. The effect is stunning, though entirely out of keeping with Parler's original concept, which was to have almost exclusively clear-glass windows. The most unusual windows are those by František Kysela, which look as though they have been shattered into hundreds of tiny pieces, a technique used to greatest effect in the rose window over the west door with its kaleidoscopic *Creation of the World* (1921). In keeping with its secular nature, two of the works from the time of the First Republic were paid for by financial institutions: the *Cyril and Methodius* window, in the third chapel in the north wall, was commissioned from Art Nouveau artist Alfons Mucha by the Banka Slavie; while on the opposite side of the nave, the window on the theme *Those Who Sow in Tears Shall Reap in Joy* was sponsored by a Prague insurance company.

Of the cathedral's 22 side chapels, the grand **Chapel of sv Václav**, by the south door, is easily the main attraction. Although officially dedicated to St Vitus, spiritually the cathedral belongs as much to the Přemyslid prince, Václav (Wenceslas, of "Good King" fame; see box below), the country's patron saint, who was killed by his pagan brother, Boleslav the Cruel. Ten years later, in 939, Boleslav repented, converted, and apparently transferred his brother's remains to this very spot. Charles, who was keen to promote the cult of Wenceslas in order to cement his own Luxembourgeois dynasty's rather tenuous claim to the Bohemian throne, had Peter Parler build the present chapel on top of the original grave; the lion's head **door-ring** set into the north door is said to be the one to which Václav clung before being killed. The chapel's rich, almost Byzantine decoration is like the inside of a jewel casket: the gilded walls are inlaid with semi-precious Bohemian stones, set around ethereal fourteenth-century frescoes of the Passion; meanwhile the tragedy of Wenceslas unfolds above the cornice in the later paintings of the Litoměřice school.

Though a dazzling testament to the golden age of Charles IV's reign, it's not just the chapel's artistic merit which draws visitors. A door in the south wall gives access to a staircase leading to the coronation chamber (closed to the public) which houses the **Bohemian crown jewels**, including the gold crown of Saint Wenceslas, studded with some of the largest sapphires in the world. Closed to the public since 1867, the door is secured by seven different locks, the keys kept by seven different people, starting with the president himself – like the seven seals of the holy scroll from Revelation. Replicas of the crown jewels can be seen in the Lobkovický palác (see p.76).

Good King Wenceslas

As it turns out, there's very little substance to the story related in the nineteenth-century Christmas carol, *Good King Wenceslas looked out*, by J.M. Neale, itself a reworking of the medieval carol *Tempus adest floridum*. For a start, **Václav** was only a duke and never a king (though he did become a saint); he wasn't even that "good", except in comparison with the rest of his family; the St Agnes fountain, by which "yonder peasant dwelt", wasn't built until the thirteenth century; and he was killed a full three months before the Feast of Stephen (Boxing Day) – the traditional day for giving to the poor, hence the narrative of the carol.

Born in 907, Václav inherited his title at the tender age of thirteen. His Christian grandmother, Ludmilla, was appointed regent in preference to Drahomíra, his pagan mother, who had Ludmilla murdered in a fit of jealousy the following year. On coming of age in 925, Václav became duke in his own right and took a vow of celibacy, intent on promoting Christianity throughout the dukedom. Even so, the local Christians didn't take to him, and when he began making conciliatory overtures to the neighbouring Germans, they persuaded his pagan younger brother, Boleslav the Cruel, to do away with him. On September 20, 929, Václav was stabbed to death by Boleslav at the entrance to a church just outside Prague.

The chancel and crypt

Having sated yourself on the Chapel of sv Václav, buy a ticket from the nearby box office and head off to the north choir aisle – the only place where you can currently enter the **chancel**. Slap bang in the middle of the ambulatory, close to the Saxon Chapel, is the perfect Baroque answer to the medieval Chapel of sv Václav, the **Tomb of St John of Nepomuk**, plonked here in 1736. It's a work of grotesque excess, designed by Johann Bernhard Fischer von Erlach's son, Johann Michael, and sculpted in solid silver with free-flying angels holding up the heavy drapery of the baldachin. Where Charles sought to promote Wenceslas as the nation's preferred saint, the Jesuits, with Habsburg backing, replaced him with another Czech martyr, John of Nepomuk (Jan Nepomucký), who had been arrested, tortured, and then thrown – bound and gagged – off the Charles Bridge in 1393 on the orders of Václav IV, allegedly for refusing to divulge the secrets of the queen's confession. A cluster of stars was said to have appeared over the spot where he drowned, hence the halo of stars on every subsequent portrayal of the saint.

The Jesuits, in their efforts to get him canonized, exhumed his corpse and produced what they claimed to be his tongue – alive and licking, so to speak (it was in fact his very dead brain). In 1729, he duly became a saint, and, on the lid of the tomb, back-to-back with the martyr himself, a cherub points to his severed tongue, sadly no longer the "real" thing. The more prosaic reason for John of Nepomuk's death was simply that he was caught up in a dispute between the archbishop and the king over the appointment of the abbot of Kladruby, and backed the wrong side. John was tortured on the rack along with two other priests, who were then made to sign a document denying that they had been maltreated; John, however, died before he could sign, and his dead body was secretly dumped in the river. The Vatican finally admitted this in 1961, some 232 years after his canonization.

Before you leave the chancel, check out the sixteenth-century marble **Imperial Mausoleum**, situated in the centre of the choir, and surrounded by a fine Renaissance grille, on which numerous cherubs are irreverently larking about. It was commissioned by Rudolf II and contains the remains of his grandfather Ferdinand I, his Polish grandmother Queen Anne, and his father Maximilian II, the first Habsburgs to wear the Bohemian crown. Rudolf himself rests beneath them, in one of the two pewter coffins in the somewhat cramped **Royal Crypt** (Královská hrobka). Rudolf's coffin (at the back, in the centre) features yet more cherubs, brandishing quills, while the one to the right contains the remains of Maria Amelia, daughter of the Empress Maria Theresa. A good number of other Czech kings and queens are buried here, too, reinterred last century in incongruously modern 1930s sarcophagi, among them the Hussite King George of Poděbrady, Charles IV and, sharing a single sarcophagus, all four of his wives. The exit from the crypt brings you out in the centre of the nave.

In the summer months (April–Oct daily 9am–4.15pm), you can get a great view over the castle and the city from the cathedral's **Hlavná věž** (Great Tower), the entrance to which is in the south aisle – be warned, there are around three hundred steps before you reach the top. Be sure, too, to check out Parler's **Zlatá brána** (Golden Gate), over the doorway to the south transept, which is decorated with a remarkable fourteenth-century mosaic of the *Last Judgement*, recently restored to something like its original, rich colouring.

Starý královský palác (Old Royal Palace)

Across the courtyard from the Zlatá brána, the **Starý královský palác** (Old Royal Palace) was home to the princes and kings of Bohemia from the eleventh to the sixteenth centuries. It's a sandwich of royal apartments, built one on top of the other by successive generations, but left largely unfurnished and unused for the last three hundred years. The original Romanesque palace of Soběslav I now forms the cellars of the present building, above which Charles IV built his own Gothic chambers; these days you enter at the third and top floor, built at the end of the fifteenth century.

Immediately past the antechamber is the bare expanse of the massive **Vladislavský sál** (Vladislav Hall), the work of Benedikt Ried, the German mason appointed by Vladislav Jagiello as his court architect. It displays some remarkable, sweeping rib-vaulting which forms floral patterns on the ceiling, the petals reaching almost to the floor. It was here that the early Bohemian kings were elected, and since 1918 every president from Masaryk to Havel has been sworn into office in the hall. In medieval times, the hall was also used for banquets and jousting tournaments, which explains the ramp-like **Riders' Staircase** in the north wing (now the exit). At the far end of the hall, to the right, there's an outdoor **viewing platform**, from which you can enjoy a magnificent view of Prague (at its best in the late afternoon).

From a staircase in the southwest corner of the hall, you can gain access to the Ludvík Wing. The rooms themselves are pretty uninspiring, but the furthest one, the **Bohemian Chancellery**, was the scene of Prague's **second defenestration** (see p.113 for details of the first). After almost two centuries of uneasy coexistence between Catholics and Protestants, matters came to a head over the succession to the throne of the Habsburg Archduke Ferdinand, a notoriously intolerant Catholic. On May 23, 1618, a posse of more than one hundred Protestant nobles, led by Count Thurn, marched to the chancellery for a showdown with Jaroslav Bořita z Martinic and Vilém Slavata, the two Catholic governors appointed by Ferdinand. After a "stormy discussion", the two councillors (and their personal secretary, Filip Fabricius) were thrown out of the window. As a contemporary historian recounted: "No mercy was granted them and they were both thrown dressed in their cloaks with their rapiers and decoration head-first out of the western window into a moat beneath the palace. They loudly screamed *ach, ach, oweh!* and attempted to hold on to the narrow window-ledge, but Thurn beat their knuckles with the hilt of his sword until they were both obliged to let go." There's some controversy about the exact window from which they were ejected, although it's generally agreed that they survived to tell the tale, landing in a medieval dungheap below, and – so the story goes – precipitating the Thirty Years' War.

Back down in the Vladislavský sál, there are more rooms to explore through the doorways on either side of the Riders' Staircase, but you're better off heading down the ramp to the **Gothic and Romanesque chambers** of the palace. Although equally bare, they contain a couple of interesting models showing the castle at various stages in its development, plus copies of the busts by Peter Parler's workshop, including the architect's remarkable self-portrait; the originals are hidden from view in the triforium of the cathedral.

The Basilica and Convent of sv Jiří

The only exit from the Old Royal Palace is via the Riders' Staircase, which deposits you in Jiřské náměstí. Don't be fooled by the russet red Baroque facade of the **Basilica of sv Jiří** (St George) which dominates the square; inside is Prague's most beautiful Romanesque building, meticulously scrubbed clean and restored to recreate something like the honey-coloured stone basilica that replaced the original tenth-century church in 1173. The double staircase to the chancel is a remarkably harmonious late-Baroque addition and now provides a perfect stage for chamber music concerts. The choir vault contains a rare early thirteenth-century painting of the New Jerusalem from Revelation – not to be confused with the very patchy sixteenth-century painting on the apse – while to the right of the chancel, only partially visible, are sixteenth-century frescoes of the **burial chapel of sv Ludmila**, grandmother of St Wenceslas, who was strangled by her own daughter-in-law in 921 (see box on p.72), thus becoming Bohemia's first Christian martyr and saint. There's a replica of the recumbent Ludmilla, which you can inspect at close quarters, in the south aisle.

Rudolfine and Baroque art collection

Next door is Bohemia's first monastery, the **Jiřský klášter** (St George's Convent) founded in 973 by Mlada, sister of the Přemyslid prince Boleslav the Pious, who became its first abbess. Closed down and turned into a barracks by Joseph II in 1782, it now houses the Národní galerie's **Rudolfine and Baroque art collection** (Rudolfinské a barokní umění). To be honest, this is a collection of only limited interest to the non-specialist. The art collection begins upstairs with a brief taste of the overtly sensual and erotic **Mannerist paintings** that prevailed during the reign of Rudolf II, including Bartolomeus Spranger's colourfully erotic works, Hans von Aachen's sexually charged *Suicide of Lucretia* and Josef Heintz's riotous orgy in his *Last Judgement*.

The rest of the gallery is given over to a vast collection of Czech **Baroque art**, as pursued by the likes of Bohemia's Karel Škréta and Petr Brandl, whose paintings and sculptures fill chapels and churches across the Czech Lands. Perhaps the most compelling reason to wade through the gallery is to admire the vigorous, gesticulating sculptures of Matthias Bernhard Braun, and, to a lesser extent, Ferdinand Maximilian Brokof.

Zlatá ulička and the castle towers

Around the corner from the convent is **Zlatá ulička** (Golden Lane), a seemingly blind alley of miniature sixteenth-century cottages in dolly-mixture colours, built for the 24 members of Rudolf II's castle guard. The lane takes its name from the goldsmiths who followed (and modified the buildings) a century later. By the nineteenth century, it had become a kind of palace slum, attracting artists and craftsmen, its two most famous inhabitants being Jaroslav Seifert, the Nobel prize-winning Czech poet, and Franz Kafka, who came here in the evenings in the winter of 1916 to write short stories. Finally, in 1951, the Communists kicked out the remaining residents and turned most of the houses into souvenir shops for tourists.

At no. 24, you can climb a flight of stairs to the **Obranná chodba** (defence corridor), which is lined with wooden shields, suits of armour and period costumes. The **Bílá věž** (White Tower), at the western end of the corridor, was the city's main prison from Rudolf's reign onwards. In the opposite direction, the corridor leads to **Daliborka**, the castle tower dedicated to its first prisoner, the young Czech noble Dalibor, accused of supporting a peasants' revolt at the beginning of the fifteenth century, who was finally executed in 1498. According to Prague legend, he learnt to play the violin while imprisoned here, and his playing could be heard all over the castle – a tale that provided material for Smetana's opera, *Dalibor*.

To get inside the castle's other tower, the **Prašná věž** (Powder Tower) or Mihulka, which once served as the workshop of gunsmith and bell-founder Tomáš Jaroš, you'll have to backtrack to Vikářská, the street which runs along the north side of the cathedral. The Powder Tower's name comes from the lamprey (*mihule*), an eel-like fish supposedly bred here for royal consumption, though it's actually more noteworthy as the place where Rudolf's team of alchemists was put to work trying to discover the philosopher's stone. Despite its colourful history, the exhibition currently on display within the tower is dull, with just a pair of furry slippers and hat belonging to Ferdinand I to get excited about.

Muzeum hraček (Toy Museum) and the Lobkovický palác

If you continue east down Jiřská, which runs parallel with Zlatá ulička, you'll come to the courtyard of the former Purkrabství (Burgrave's House) on the left, which hides a café, exhibition space and **Muzeum hraček** (daily 9.30am–5.30pm). With brief, Czech-only captions and unimaginative displays, this is a disappointing venture, which fails to live up to its potential. The succession of glass cabinets contains an impressive array of toy cars, robots and even Barbie dolls, but there are too few buttons for younger kids to press, and unless you're really lost for something to do, you could happily skip the whole enterprise.

The hotchpotch historical collection in the **Lobkovický palác** (Tues–Sun 9am–5pm; Ⓦwww.nm.cz), on the opposite side of Jiřská, is marginally more rewarding, despite the ropey English text provided. The exhibition actually begins on the top floor, but by no means all the objects on display deserve attention. The prize exhibits are replicas of the Bohemian crown jewels, an interesting sixteenth-century carving of *The Last Supper*, originally an altarpiece from the Bethlehem Chapel, and the sword (and invoice) of the famous Prague executioner Jan Mydlář, who could lop a man's head off with just one chop, as he demonstrated on 24 Protestant Czechs in 1621 (see p.92).

The Castle Gardens

For recuperation and a superlative view over the rest of Prague, head for the **Jižní zahrady** (South Gardens), accessible via Plečnik's copper-canopied Bull Staircase on the south side of the third courtyard. Alternatively, make a short detour beyond the castle walls from the second courtyard, by crossing the **Prašný most** (Powder Bridge), erected in the sixteenth century to connect the newly established royal gardens with the Hrad. Beyond the bridge, opposite Jean-Baptiste Mathey's plain French Baroque Jízdárna (Riding School), now an art gallery, is the entrance to the Royal Gardens or **Královská zahrada** (April–Oct daily 10am–6pm), founded by Emperor Ferdinand I on the site of a former vineyard. Today, this is one of the best-kept gardens in the capital, with fully functioning fountains and immaculately cropped lawns. Consequently, it's a very popular spot, though more a place for admiring the azaleas and almond trees than lounging around on the grass. It was here that tulips brought from Turkey were first acclimatized to Europe before being exported to the Netherlands, and every spring there's an impressive, disciplined crop.

Built into the gardens' south terrace is Rudolf's distinctive Renaissance ballgame court, known as the **Míčovna** (occasionally open to the public for concerts and exhibitions) and tattooed with sgraffito. At the far end of the gardens is Prague's most celebrated Renaissance legacy, the **Belvedér**, a delicately arcaded summerhouse topped by an inverted copper ship's hull, built by Ferdinand I for his wife, Anne. Unlike the gardens, the Belvedér is open most of the year and is now used for exhibitions of contemporary artists. At the centre of the palace's miniature formal garden is the **Zpívající fontána** (Singing Fountain), built shortly after the palace and so named from the musical sound of the drops of water falling in the metal bowls below. From the garden terrace you can enjoy an unrivalled view of the castle's finest treasure – the cathedral.

From Hradčanské náměstí to Strahovský klášter

The monumental scale and appearance of the rest of Hradčany, outside the castle, is a direct result of the **great fire of 1541**, which swept up from Malá Strana and wiped out most of the old dwelling places belonging to the serfs, tradesmen, clergy and masons who had settled here in the Middle Ages. With the Turks at the gates of Vienna, the Habsburg nobility were more inclined to pursue their major building projects in Prague instead, and, following the Battle of Bílá hora in 1620, the palaces of the exiled (or executed) Protestant nobility were up for grabs too. The newly ensconced Catholic aristocrats were keen to spend some of their expropriated wealth, and over the next two centuries they turned Hradčany into a grand architectural showpiece. As the Turkish threat subsided, the political focus of the empire gradually shifted back to Vienna and the building spree stopped. For the last two hundred years, Hradčany has been frozen in time, and, two world wars on, its buildings have survived better than those of any other central European capital.

Hradčanské náměstí

Hradčanské náměstí fans out from the castle gates, surrounded by the oversized palaces of the old Catholic nobility. For the most part, it's a tranquil space that's overlooked by the tour groups marching through, intent on the Hrad. The one spot everyone heads for is the ramparts in the southeastern corner, by the top of the Zámecké schody, which allow an unrivalled view over the red rooftops of Malá Strana, past the famous green dome and tower of the church of sv Mikuláš and beyond, to the spires of Staré Město.

Until the great fire of 1541, the square was the hub of Hradčany, lined with medieval shops and stalls but with no real market as such. After the fire, the developers moved in; the powerful Lobkowicz family replaced seven houses on the south side of the square with the over-the-top sgraffitoed pile at no. 2, now known as the **Schwarzenberský palác** after its last aristocratic owners (the present-day count, Karl, is one of the republic's leading capitalists). The palace now houses the **Vojenské historické muzeum** (Museum of Military History; May–Oct Tues–Sun 10am–5.30pm). Predictably enough, it was the Nazis who founded the museum, though the Czechs themselves have a long history of manufacturing top-class weaponry for world powers (Semtex is probably their best-known export), so it's no coincidence that one of the two Czech words to have made it into the English language is pistol (from *pišt'ale*, a Hussite weapon) – the other is *robot*, in case you're wondering. Among the endless Habsburg uniforms and instruments of death – all of which are pre-1914 – you'll find the first Colt 45 produced outside the USA, manufactured in 1849 for the Austrian Navy.

Šternberský palác - the Old European art collection

A passage down the side of the Arcibiskupský palác leads to the early eighteenth-century **Šternberský palác** (Tues–Sun 10am–6pm ⓦ www.ngprague.cz), which houses the Národní galerie's **old European art collection**, mostly ranging from the fourteenth to the eighteenth century, but excluding works by Czech artists of the period (you'll find them in the Jiřský klášter in the Hrad). It would be fair to say that the collection is relatively modest, in comparison with those of other major European capitals, though the handful of masterpieces makes a visit here worthwhile.

The **first floor** kicks off with Florentine religious art, most notably a series of exquisite miniature triptychs by Bernardo Daddi, plus several gilded polyptychs by the Venetian artist Antonio Vivarini. Moving swiftly into the gallery's large Flemish contingent, it's worth checking out Dieric Bouts' *Lamentation*, a complex composition crowded with figures in medieval garb, and the bizarre *Well of Life*, painted around 1500 by an unknown artist. The latter features a squatting Christ depicted as a Gothic fountain issuing forth blood which angels in turn serve in goblets to passing punters. One of the most eye-catching works is Jan Gossaert's *St Luke Drawing the Virgin*, an exercise in architectural geometry and perspective which used to hang in the cathedral. The section ends with a series of canvases by the least famous members of the Brueghel family; before you head upstairs, though, don't miss the side rooms containing Orthodox icons from Venice and the Balkans to Russia.

The **second floor** contains one of the most prized paintings in the whole collection, the *Feast of the Rosary* by Albrecht Dürer, depicting, among others, the Virgin Mary, the Pope, the Holy Roman Emperor, and even a self-portrait of Dürer himself (top right). This was one of Rudolf's most prized acquisitions (he was an avid Dürer fan), transported on foot across the Alps to Prague (he didn't trust wheeled transport with such a precious object). There are other outstanding works here, too: two richly coloured Bronzino portraits, a Rembrandt, a Canaletto of the Thames, a whole series by the Saxon master, Lucas Cranach, and a mesmerizing *Praying Christ* by El Greco. Rubens' colossal *Murder of St Thomas* is difficult to miss, with its pink-buttocked cherubs hovering over the bloody scene. Nearby, in the hugely expanded (and uneven) Dutch section, there's a wonderful portrait of an arrogant "young gun" named Jasper by Frans Hals. A few of the rooms in the gallery have preserved their original decor, the best of which is the Chinoiserie of the činský kabinet.

From Nový Svět to Loretánské náměstí

At the other end of Hradčanské náměstí, Kanovnická heads off towards the northwest corner of Hradčany. Nestling in this shallow dip, **Nový Svět** (meaning "New World", though not Dvořák's) provides a glimpse of life on a totally different scale from Hradčanské náměstí. Similar in many ways to the Zlatá ulička in the Hrad, this cluster of brightly coloured cottages, which curls around the corner into Černínská, is all that's left of Hradčany's medieval slums, painted up and sanitized in the eighteenth and nineteenth centuries. Despite having all the same ingredients for mass tourist appeal as Zlatá ulička, it remains remarkably undisturbed, save for a few swish wine bars, and Gambra, a surrealist art gallery at Černínská 5 (Wed–Sun noon–6pm), which sells works by, among others, the renowned Czech animator, Jan Švankmajer, and his wife Eva, who live nearby.

Up the hill from Nový Svět, Loretánské náměstí is dominated by the phenomenal 135-metre-long facade of the **Černínský palác** (Černín Palace), decorated with thirty Palladian half-pillars and supported by a swathe of diamond-pointed rustication. For all its grandeur, it's a miserable, brutal building, whose construction nearly bankrupted future generations of Černíns, who were forced to sell the palace in 1851 to the Austrian state. Since the First Republic, the palace has housed the Foreign Ministry, and during the war it housed the Nazi bureaucracy and the German State Minister for Bohemia and Moravia, Karl Hermann Frank. On March 10, 1948, it was the scene of Prague's third – and most widely mourned – defenestration. Only days after the Communist coup, **Jan Masaryk**, only son of the founder of Czechoslovakia and the last non-Communist in the cabinet, plunged 45 feet to his death from a top-floor bathroom window. Whether it was suicide (he had been suffering from bouts of depression, partly induced by the country's political path) or murder will probably never be satisfactorily resolved, but for most people Masaryk's death cast a dark shadow over the newly established regime.

The facade of the **Loreta** (Tues–Sun 9am–12.15pm & 1–4.30pm), immediately opposite the Černínský palác, was built by the Dientzenhofers, a Bavarian family of architects, in the early part of the eighteenth century, and is the perfect antidote to the Černíns' humourless monster. It's all hot flourishes and twirls, topped by a tower which lights up like a Chinese lantern at night, and by day clanks out the hymn *We Greet Thee a Thousand Times* on its 27 Dutch bells (it does special performances of other tunes from time to time, too).

The facade and the cloisters are, in fact, just the outer casing for the focus of the complex, the **Santa Casa**, founded in 1626 and smothered in a mantle of stucco depicting the building's miraculous transportation from the Holy Land. Legend has it that the Santa Casa (Mary's home in Nazareth), under threat from the heathen Turks, was transported by a host of angels to a small laurel grove (*lauretum* in Latin, hence Loreta) in northern Italy. News of the miracle spread across the Catholic lands, prompting a spate of copycat shrines. During the Counter-Reformation, the cult was actively encouraged in an attempt to broaden the popular appeal of Catholicism. The Prague Loreta is one of fifty to be built in the Czech Lands, each of the shrines following an identical design, with pride of place given to a limewood statue of the *Black Madonna and Child*, encased in silver.

Behind the Santa Casa, the Dientzenhofers built the much larger **Church of Narození Páně** (Church of the Nativity), which is like a mini-version of sv Mikuláš, down in Malá Strana. The Santa Casa's serious financial backing is evident in the **treasury** on the first floor of the west wing, much ransacked over the years but still stuffed full of gold. The light fittings are a Communist period piece, but most folk come here to gawp at the master exhibit, a tasteless Viennese silver monstrance designed by Fischer von Erlach in 1699, and studded with diamonds taken from the wedding dress of Countess Kolovrat, who had made the Loreta sole heir to her fortune.

Strahovský klášter

Continuing westwards from Loretánské náměstí, Pohořelec, an arcaded street-cum-square, leads to the chunky remnants of the zigzag eighteenth-century fortifications that mark the edge of the old city, as defined by Charles IV back in the fourteenth century. Close by, to the left, is the **Strahovský klášter** (Strahov Monastery; ⓦ www.strahovmonastery.cz), founded in 1140 by the Premonstratensian order. Having managed to evade Joseph II's 1783 dissolution of the monasteries, it continued to function until shortly after the Communists took power, when, along with all other religious establishments, it was closed down and most of its inmates thrown into prison; following the events of 1989, the monks have returned.

It's the monastery's two ornate **libraries** (daily 9am–noon & 1–5pm; 50Kč), though, that are the real reason for visiting Strahov; the entrance for both is to the right as you enter the outer courtyard. The first library you come to is the later and larger of the two, the **Filosofický sál** (Philosophical Hall), built in some haste in the 1780s in order to accommodate the books and bookcases from Louka, a Premonstratensian monastery in Moravia (see p.357) that failed to escape Joseph's decree. The walnut bookcases are so tall they touch the library's lofty ceiling, which is busily decorated with frescoes by the Viennese painter Franz Maulbertsch on the theme of the search for truth. Don't, whatever you do, miss the collection of curios exhibited in the glass cabinets outside the library, which features shells, turtles, crabs, lobsters, dried-up sea monsters, butterflies, beetles, plastic fruit and moths. There's even a pair of whales' penises set amidst a narwhal horn, several harpoons and a model ship. The other main room is the low-ceilinged **Teologický sál** (Theological Hall), studded with ancient globes, its wedding-cake stucco framing frescoes on a similar theme, executed by one of the monks seventy years earlier. Outside the hall the library's oldest book, the ninth-century gem-studded Strahov Gospel, is displayed – look out, too, for the cabinet of books documenting Czech trees, each of which has the bark of the tree on its spine.

If you leave the monastery through the narrow doorway in the eastern wall, you enter the gardens and orchards of the **Strahovská zahrada**, from where you can see the whole city in perspective. The gardens form part of a wooded hill known as Petřín, and the path to the right contours round to the Stations of the Cross that lead up to the miniature Eiffel Tower known as the Rozhledna (see p.87). Alternatively, you can catch tram #22 from outside Strahov's main entrance to Malostranská metro or the centre of town.

Malá Strana

Foolishly, many visitors never stray from the well-trodden route that links the Charles Bridge with the Castle, thus bypassing most of **MALÁ STRANA**, Prague's picturesque "Little Quarter" that sits below the Hrad. This is easy enough to do given that the whole town takes up a mere 600 square metres of

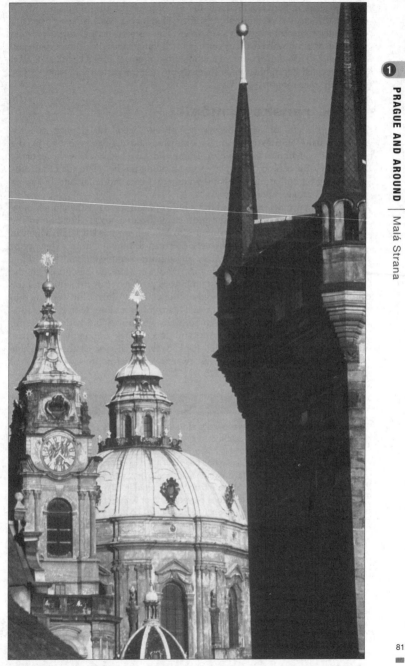

△ Rooftops, Prague

land squeezed in between the river and Hradčany, but it means missing out on one of the city's most enjoyable pastimes: exploring Malá Strana's peaceful, often hilly, eighteenth-century backstreets. These streets have changed very little since Mozart walked them during his frequent visits to Prague between 1787 and 1791, and they conceal a whole host of quiet terraced gardens, as well as the wooded Petřín hill, which together provide the perfect inner-city escape in the summer months.

Malostranské náměstí

The main focus of Malá Strana has always been the sloping, cobbled **Malostranské náměstí**, which is dominated and divided into two by the church of sv Mikuláš (see below). Trams and cars hurtle across it, regularly dodged by a procession of people – some heading up the hill to the Hrad, others pausing for coffee and cakes at the numerous bars and restaurants hidden in the square's arcades and Gothic vaults.

Towering above the square, and the whole of Malá Strana, is the church of **sv Mikuláš** (St Nicholas), easily the most magnificent Baroque building in the city, and one of the last great structures to be built on the left bank, begun in 1702. For Christoph Dientzenhofer, a German immigrant from a dynasty of Bavarian architects, this was his most prestigious commission and is, without doubt, his finest work. For the Jesuits, who were already ensconced in the adjoining college, it was their most ambitious project yet in Bohemia, and the ultimate symbol of their stranglehold on the country. When Christoph died in 1722, it was left to his son Kilian Ignaz Dientzenhofer, along with Kilian's son-in-law, Anselmo Lurago, to finish the project, which they did with a masterful flourish, adding the giant green dome and tower – now among the most characteristic landmarks on Prague's left bank. Sadly for the Jesuits, they were able to enjoy the finished product for just twenty years, before they were banished from the Habsburg Empire in 1773.

Mozart in Prague

Mozart made the first of several visits to Prague with his wife Constanze in 1787, staying with his friend and patron Count Thun in what is now the British Embassy (Thunovská 14). A year earlier, his opera *The Marriage of Figaro*, which had failed to please the opera snobs in Vienna, had been given a rapturous reception at Prague's Nostitz Theater (now the Stavovské divadlo; see p.96); and on his arrival in 1787, Mozart was already flavour of the month, as he wrote in his diary: "Here they talk about nothing but Figaro. Nothing is played, sung or whistled but Figaro. Nothing, nothing but Figaro. Certainly a great honour for me!" Encouraged by this, he chose to premiere his next opera, *Don Giovanni*, later that year, in Prague rather than Vienna. He arrived with an incomplete score in hand, and wrote the overture at the Dušeks' Bertramka villa in Smíchov (now the Mozart Museum; see p.129), dedicating it to the "good people of Prague". Apart from a brief sojourn whilst on a concert tour, Mozart's fourth and final visit to Prague took place in 1791, the year of his death. The climax of the stay was the premiere of Mozart's final opera, *La Clemenza di Tito*, commissioned for the coronation of Leopold II as King of Bohemia (and completed whilst on the coach from Vienna to Prague). The opera didn't go down quite as well as previous ones – the empress is alleged to have shouted "German hogwash" from her box. Nevertheless, four thousand people turned out for the funereal memorial service, held in Malá Strana's church of sv Mikuláš to the strains of his *Requiem Mass*.

Nothing about the relatively plain west facade prepares you for the overwhelming High Baroque **interior** (daily 9am–4pm). The vast fresco in the nave, by Johann Lukas Kracker, portrays some of the more fanciful miraculous feats of St Nicholas. Apart from his role as Santa Claus, he is depicted here rescuing sailors in distress, saving women from prostitution by throwing them bags of gold, and reprieving from death three unjustly condemned men. Even given the overwhelming proportions of the nave, the dome at the far end of the church, built by the younger Dientzenhofer, remains impressive, thanks, more than anything, to its sheer height. Leering over you as you gaze up at the dome are Ignaz Platzer's four terrifyingly oversized and stern Church Fathers, one of whom brandishes a gilded thunderbolt, leaving no doubt as to the gravity of the Jesuit message. Before you leave, check out the church's superb organ, its white case and gilded musical cherubs nicely offsetting the grey pipes.

Nerudova, Tržiště and Vlašská

The most important of the various streets leading up to the Hrad from Malostranské náměstí is **Nerudova**, named after the Czech journalist and writer Jan Neruda (1834–91), who was born at *U dvou slunců* (The Two Suns), at no. 47, an inn at the top of the street. His tales of Malá Strana immortalized bohemian life on Prague's left bank, though he's perhaps best known in the West via the Chilean Nobel prize-winner, Pablo Neruda, who took his penname from the lesser-known Czech. Historically, this was the city's main quarter for craftsmen, artisans and artists, though the shops and restaurants that line Nerudova now are mostly predictably and shamelessly touristy.

Architecturally, the Baroque houses that line the steep climb up to the Hrad are fairly restrained, many retaining their medieval barn doors, and most adorned with their own peculiar house signs (see p.60). Halfway up the hill, Nerudova halts at a crossroads where it meets the cobbled hairpin of Ke Hradu, which the royal coronation procession used to ascend; continuing west along **Úvoz** (The Cutting) takes you to the Strahovský klášter (see p.79). On the south side of Úvoz, the houses come to an end, and a view opens up over the picturesque jumble of Malá Strana's red-tiled roofs, while to the north, narrow stairways squeeze between the towering buildings of Hradčany, emerging on the path to the Loreta.

Running (very) roughly parallel to Nerudova – and linked to it by several side streets and steps – is **Tržiště**, which sets off from the south side of Malostranské náměstí. Halfway up on the left is the **Schönbornský palác**, now the US Embassy. The entrance, and the renowned gardens, are nowadays watched over by closed-circuit TV and twitchy Czech policemen – a far cry from the dilapidated palace in which Kafka rented an apartment in March 1917, and where he suffered his first bout of tuberculosis.

As Tržiště swings to the right, bear left up **Vlašská**, home to yet another **Lobkovický palác**, now the German Embassy. In the summer of 1989, several thousand East Germans climbed over the garden wall and entered the embassy compound to demand West German citizenship, which had been every German's right since partition. The neighbouring streets were soon jampacked with abandoned Trabants, as the beautiful palace gardens became a muddy home to the refugees. Finally, the Czechoslovak government gave in and organized special trains to take the East Germans over the federal border, cheered on their way by thousands of Praguers, and thus prompted the exodus that eventually brought the Berlin Wall down.

Valdštejnský palác and around

To the north of Malostranské náměstí, up Tomášská, lies the **Valdštejnský palác**, which takes up the whole of the eastern side of **Valdštejnské náměstí** and Valdštejnská. As early as 1621, Albrecht von Waldstein started to build a palace which would reflect his status as commander of the Imperial Catholic armies of the Thirty Years' War. By buying, confiscating, and then destroying 26 houses, three gardens and a brick factory, he succeeded in ripping apart a densely populated area of Malá Strana to make way for one of the first, largest and, quite frankly, most undistinguished Baroque palaces in the city – at least from the outside.

The Czech upper house, or **Senát**, is now housed in the palace, and can be visited on a guided tour at weekends (Sat & Sun 10am–4pm). The former stables are also accessible to the public, as they contain the **Pedagogické muzeum** (Museum of Education; Tues–Sat 10am–12.30pm & 1–4.30pm; Ⓦwww.pmjak.cz). This is a small and none too exciting exhibition on Czech education and, in particular, the influential teachings of Jan Amos Komenský (1592–1670) – often anglicized to John Comenius – who was forced to leave his homeland after the victory of Waldstein's Catholic armies, eventually settling in Protestant England. To get to the exhibition, go through the main gateway and continue straight across the first courtyard; the museum is on your right.

If you've no interest in pedagogical matters, the palace's formal gardens, the **Valdštejnská zahrada** (April–Oct daily 10am–6pm) – accessible only from a doorway in the palace walls along Letenská – are a good place to take a breather from the city streets. The focus of the gardens is the gigantic Italianate *sala terrena*, a monumental loggia decorated with frescoes of the Trojan Wars, which stands at the end of an avenue of sculptures by Adriaen de Vries. The originals, which were intended to form a fountain, were taken off as booty by the Swedes in 1648 and now adorn the royal gardens in Drottningholm. In addition, there's a number of peacocks, a pseudo grotto along the south wall, with quasi-stalactites, a door that once led to Waldstein's observatory, and a small aviary.

One of the chief joys of Malá Strana is its **terraced gardens**, hidden away behind the Baroque palaces on Valdštejnská, on the slopes below the castle, where the royal vineyards used to be, and commanding superb views over Prague. If you're approaching from below, you enter via the **Ledeburská zahrada** on Valdštejnská (April–Oct daily 10am–6pm), which connect higher up with the Jižní Zahrady (see p.76) beneath the Hrad itself. Another option is to seek out the **Vojanovy sady** (May–Sept daily 9am–7pm), securely concealed behind a ring of high walls off U lužického semináře. Originally a monastic garden belonging to the Carmelites, it's now an informal public park, with sleeping babies, weeping willows, and lots of grass on which to lounge about; outdoor art exhibitions and occasional concerts also take place here.

Southern Malá Strana

Karmelitská is the busy cobbled street that runs south from Malostranské náměstí along the base of Petřín towards the industrial suburb of Smíchov, becoming Újezd at roughly its halfway point. Between here and the River Vltava are some of Malá Strana's most picturesque and secluded streets. Although there are no major sights around here, the island of **Kampa**, in particular, makes up one of the most peaceful stretches of riverfront in Prague.

Before you set off to explore this part of town, however, you should pop through the doorway at no. 25, on the corner of Karmelitská and Tržiště, to see one of the most elusive of Malá Strana's many Baroque gardens, the **Vrtbovská zahrada** (April–Oct daily 10am–6pm), founded on the site of the former vineyards of the **Vrtbovský palác**. Laid out on Tuscan-style terraces, dotted with ornamental urns and statues of the gods by Matthias Bernhard Braun, the gardens twist their way up the lower slopes of Petřín Hill to an observation terrace, from where there's a spectacular rooftop perspective on the city.

Maltézské náměstí and around

From the trams and traffic fumes of Karmelitská, it's a relief to cut across to the calm restraint of **Maltézské náměstí**, one of a number of delightful little squares between here and the river. It takes its name from the Order of the Knights of St John of Jerusalem (better known by their later title, the Maltese Knights), who in 1160 founded the nearby church of **Panna Maria pod řetězem** (Saint Mary below-the-chain), so called because it was the knights' job to guard the Judith Bridge. The original Romanesque church was pulled down by the knights themselves in the fourteenth century, but only the chancel and towers were successfully rebuilt by the time of the Hussite Wars. The two bulky Gothic towers are still standing and the apse is now thoroughly Baroque, but the nave remains unfinished and open to the elements.

The Knights have now reclaimed (and restored) the church and the adjacent Grand Priory, which backs onto **Velkopřevorské náměstí**, another pretty little square to the south, which echoes to the sound of music from the nearby Prague conservatoire. Following the violent death of John Lennon in 1980, Prague's youth established an ad hoc shrine smothered in graffiti tributes to the ex-Beatle along the Grand Priory's garden wall. The running battle between police and graffiti artists continued well into the 1990s, with the Maltese Knights taking an equally dim view of the mural, but a compromise has now been reached and the wall's scribblings legalized. On the opposite side of the square from the priory, sitting pretty in pink behind a row of chestnut trees, is the Rococo **Buquoyský palác**, built for a French family and appropriately enough now the French Embassy.

Kampa

Heading for **Kampa**, the largest of the Vltava's islands, with its cafés, old mills and serene riverside park, is the perfect way to escape the crowds on the Charles Bridge, from which it can be accessed easily via a staircase. The island is separated from the left bank by Prague's "Little Venice", a thin strip of water called **Čertovka** (Devil's Stream), which used to power several mill-wheels until the last one ceased to function in 1936. In contrast to the rest of the left bank, the fire of 1541 had a positive effect on Kampa, since the flotsam from the blaze effectively stabilized the island's shifting shoreline. Nevertheless, Kampa was still subject to frequent flooding right up until the Vltava was dammed in the 1950s.

For much of its history, the island was the city's main wash house, and it wasn't until the sixteenth and seventeenth centuries that the Nostitz family, who owned Kampa, began to develop the northern half of the island; the southern half was left untouched and is today laid out as a public park, with riverside views across to Staré Město. To the north, the oval main square, **Na Kampě**, once a pottery market, is studded with slender acacia trees and cut through by the Charles Bridge, to which it is connected by a double flight of steps.

Definitely worth a visit if you're wandering around Kampa is the **Museum Kampa** (Tues–Sun 10am–5pm), a brand new art gallery housed in an old mill by the river in the park. Established in 2001, but only half-completed at the time of going to print, the museum is devoted to the private art collection of Jan and Meda Mládek. As well as short-term exhibitions, there's a permanent display of Czech art by the likes of František Kupka, the father of abstract art, the sculptor Otto Gutfreund and postwar surrealist Jiří Kolář.

Panna Maria Vítězná

Halfway down busy Karmelitská is the rather plain church of **Panna Maria Vítězná** (Mon–Sat 9.30am–5.30pm, Sun 1–5pm; Ⓦwww.pragjesu.com), which was begun in early Baroque style by German Lutherans in 1611, and later handed over to the Carmelites after the Battle of Bílá hora. The main reason for coming here is to see the **Pražské Jezulátko** or *Bambino di Praga*, a high-kitsch wax effigy of the infant Jesus as a precocious three-year-old, enthroned in a glass case illuminated with strip lights, donated by one of the Lobkowicz family's Spanish brides in 1628. Attributed with miraculous powers, the *pražské Jezulátko* became an object of international pilgrimage equal in stature to the Santa Casa in Loreta, similarly inspiring a whole series of replicas. It continues to attract visitors (as the multilingual prayer cards attest) and boasts a vast personal wardrobe of expensive swaddling clothes – approaching a hundred separate outfits at the last count – regularly changed by the Carmelite nuns. If you're keen to see some of the infant's outfits, there's a small museum, up the spiral staircase in the south aisle. Here, you get to see his lacy camisoles, as well as a selection of his velvet and satin overgarments sent from all over the world. There are also chalices, monstrances and a Rococo crown studded with diamonds and pearls to admire.

Petřín

The scaled-down version of the Eiffel Tower is the most obvious landmark on the wooded hill of **Petřín**, the largest green space in the city centre. The tower is just one of the exhibits built for the 1891 Prague Exhibition, whose modest legacy includes the **funicular railway** (*lanová dráha*; every 10–15min; daily 9.15am–8.45pm), which climbs up from a station just off Újezd. As the carriages pass each other at the halfway station of Nebozízek, you can get out and soak in the view from the restaurant of the same name. At the top of the hill, it's possible to trace the southernmost perimeter wall of the old city – popularly known as the **Hladová zed'** (Hunger Wall) – as it creeps eastwards back down to Újezd, and northwestwards to the Strahovský klášter. Instigated in the 1460s by Charles IV, it was much lauded at the time (and later by the Communists) as a great public work which provided employment for the burgeoning ranks of the city's destitute (hence its name); in fact, much of the wall's construction was paid for by the expropriation of Jewish property.

Follow the wall southeast and you come to the aromatic **Růžový sad** (Rose Garden), whose colour-coordinated rose beds are laid out in front of Petřín's observatory, the **Štefánikova hvězdárna** (March & Oct Tues–Sun noon–5pm & 7–9pm; April–Aug Tues–Fri 2–7pm & 9–11pm, Sat & Sun 10am–noon, 2–7pm & 9–11pm; Sept Tues–Sun 1–6pm & 8–10pm; Nov–Feb Tues–Fri 6–8pm, Sat & Sun 10am–noon & 2–8pm; Ⓦwww.observatory.cz), run by stargazing enthusiasts. The small astronomical exhibition inside is hardly worth bothering with, but if it's a clear night, a quick peek through the observatory's two powerful telescopes is a treat. Follow the wall northwest and you'll come to Palliardi's twin-towered church of **sv Vavřinec** (St Lawrence), from which derives the German name for Petřín – Laurenziberg.

Opposite the church is a series of buildings from the 1891 Exhibition, starting with the diminutive **Rozhledna** (April–Oct daily 10am–7pm; Nov–March Sat & Sun 10am–5pm), an octagonal interpretation – though a mere fifth of the size – of the Eiffel Tower which shocked Paris in 1889, and a tribute to the city's strong cultural and political links with Paris at the time; the view from the public gallery is terrific in fine weather. The next building along is the **Bludiště** (April–Oct daily 10am–7pm; Nov–March Sat & Sun 10am–5pm), a mini neo-Gothic castle complete with mock drawbridge. The first section of the interior features a **mirror maze**, followed by an action-packed, life-sized diorama of the Prague students' and Jews' victory over the Swedes on the Charles Bridge in 1648. The humour of the convex and concave mirrors that lie beyond the diorama is so simple, it has both adults and kids giggling away. From the tower and maze, the path with the Stations of the Cross will eventually lead you to the perimeter wall of the Strahovský klášter (see p.79), giving great views over Petřín's palatial orchards and the sea of red tiles below.

Staré Město

STARÉ MĚSTO, literally the "Old Town", is Prague's most central, vital ingredient. Most of the capital's busiest markets, shops, restaurants and pubs are in this area, and during the day a gaggle of shoppers and tourists fills its complex and utterly confusing web of narrow streets. The district is bounded on one side by the river, on the other by the arc of Národní, Na příkopě and Revoluční, and at its heart is **Staroměstské náměstí**, Prague's showpiece main square, easily the most magnificent in central Europe.

Merchants and craftsmen began settling in what is now Staré Město as early as the tenth century, and in the mid-thirteenth century it was granted town status, with jurisdiction over its own affairs. The fire of 1541, which ripped through the quarters on the other side of the river, never reached Staré Město, though the 1689 conflagration made up for it. Nevertheless, the victorious Catholic nobles built fewer large palaces here than on the left bank, leaving the medieval street plan intact with the exception of the Klementinum (the Jesuits' powerhouse) and the Jewish quarter, Josefov, which was largely reconstructed in the late nineteenth century (see p.98). Like so much of Prague, however, Staré Město is still, on the surface, overwhelmingly Baroque, built literally on top of its Gothic predecessor to guard against the floods which plagued the town.

In their explorations of Staré Město, most people unknowingly retrace the **králová cesta**, the traditional route of the coronation procession from the medieval gateway, the Prašná brána (see p.112), to the Hrad. Established by the Přemyslids, the route was followed, with a few minor variations, by every king until the Emperor Ferdinand IV in 1836, the last of the Habsburgs to bother having himself crowned in Prague. It's also the most direct route from the Charles Bridge to Prague's main square, Staroměstské náměstí, and therefore a natural choice. However, many of the real treasures of Staré Město lie away from the *králová cesta*, so if you want to escape the crowds, it's worth heading off into the quarter's silent, twisted matrix of streets, then simply following your nose – for details of specific sights to the south of Karlova, see p.95.

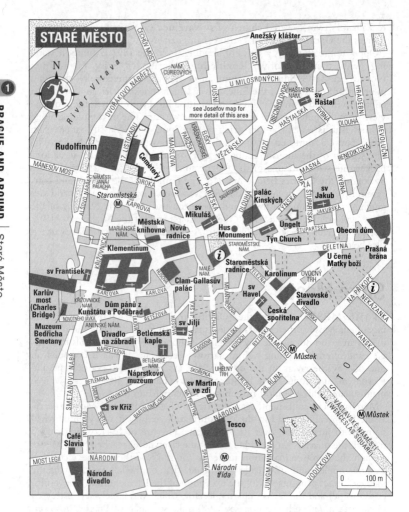

Karlův most (Charles Bridge)

The **Karlův most**, or Charles Bridge – which for over four hundred years was the only link between the two halves of Prague – is by far the city's most familiar monument. It's an impressive piece of medieval engineering, aligned slightly askew between two mighty Gothic gateways, but its fame is due almost entirely to the magnificent, mostly Baroque statues, additions to the original structure, that punctuate its length. Individually, only a few of the works are outstanding, but taken collectively, set against the backdrop of the Hrad, the effect is breathtaking.

The bridge was begun in 1357 to replace an earlier structure that was swept away in 1342 by one of the Vltava's frequent floods. Charles IV commissioned his young German court architect, Peter Parler, to carry out the work, which was finally completed in the early fifteenth century. For the first four hundred years it was known simply as the Prague or Stone Bridge – only in 1870 was it officially named after its patron. Since 1950, the bridge has been closed to vehicles, and is now one of the most popular places to hang out, day and night: the crush of sightseers never abates during the day, when the niches created by the bridge-piers are occupied by souvenir hawkers and buskers, but at night things calm down a bit, and the views are, if anything, even more spectacular.

A bronze **crucifix** has stood on the bridge since its construction, but its gold-leaf Hebrew inscription, "Holy, Holy, Holy Lord", from the Book of Isaiah, was added in 1696, paid for by a Prague Jew who was ordered to do so by the city court, having been found guilty of blasphemy before the cross. Somewhat incredibly, the local Jewish community recently succeeded in persuading the local council to erect a plaque below the statue, explaining that the charges were drummed up and the inscription designed to humiliate Prague's Jews. The first of the sculptures wasn't added until 1683, when a bronze statue of **St John of Nepomuk** appeared as part of the Jesuits' persistent campaign to have him canonized (see p.73); this later inspired hundreds of copies, which adorn bridges throughout central Europe. On the base, there's a bronze relief depicting his martyrdom, the figure of John now extremely worn through years of being touched for good luck. The statue was such a propaganda success with the Catholic Church authorities that another 21 were added between 1706 and 1714. These included works by Prague's leading Baroque sculptors, including Matthias Bernhard Braun and Ferdinand Maximilian Brokof; the remaining piers (and a few swept away in the 1890 flood) were filled in with unimaginative nineteenth-century sculptures. The originals, mostly crafted in sandstone, have weathered badly over the years and have now been replaced by copies and put into storage in the Lapidárium (see p.127).

The **bridge towers** (April–Oct daily 10am–6pm) at each end of the bridge, can be climbed for a bird's eye view of the masses pouring across. On the Malá Strana side, two unequal towers, connected by a castellated arch, form the entrance to the bridge. The smaller, stumpy tower was once part of the original Judith Bridge (named after the wife of Vladislav I, who built the twelfth-century original); the taller tower is crowned by one of the pinnacled wedge-spires more commonly associated with Prague's right bank. On the Staré Město side is arguably the finest bridge tower (daily: April–Oct 10am–7pm; Nov–March 10am–5pm) of the lot, its eastern facade still encrusted in Gothic cake-like decorations from Peter Parler's workshop. The severed heads of twelve of the Protestant leaders were displayed here for ten years, following their executions on Staroměstské náměstí in 1621 (see p.92). In 1648, it was the site of the last battle of the Thirty Years' War, fought between the besieging Swedes and an ad hoc army of Prague's students and Jews, which trashed the western facade of the bridge tower.

Křížovnické náměstí to Malé náměstí

Pass under the Staré Město bridge tower and you're in **Křížovnické náměstí**, an awkward space hemmed in by its constituent buildings and, with traffic hurtling across the square, a dangerous spot for unwary pedestrians.

The two churches facing onto the square are both quite striking and definitely worth exploring. The half-brick church of **sv František z Assisi** (St Francis of Assisi) was built in the 1680s to a design by Jean-Baptiste Mathey for the Czech Order of Knights of the Cross with a Red Star, the original gatekeepers of the old Judith Bridge. The design of the church's interior, dominated by its huge dome, decorated with a fresco of *The Last Judgement* by Václav Vavřinec Reiner, and rich marble furnishings, served as a blueprint for numerous subsequent Baroque churches in Prague. The **Galerie Křižovníků** (Tues–Sun 10am–1pm & 2–6pm), next door, houses a stunning collection of silver and gold chalices, monstrances and reliquaries. Don't miss the subterranean chapel on your way out, whose unusual stalactite decor was completed in 1683.

Over the road is the church of **sv Salvátor**, its facade prickling with saintly statues which are lit up enticingly at night. Founded in 1593, but not completed until 1714, sv Salvátor marks the beginning of the Jesuits' rise to power and, like many of their churches, its design copies that of the Gesù church in Rome. It's worth a quick look, if only for the frothy stucco plasterwork and delicate ironwork in its triple-naved interior.

Karlova and the Klementinum

Running from Křižovnické náměstí all the way to Malé náměstí is the narrow street of **Karlova**, packed with people wending their way towards Staroměstské náměstí, their attention divided between checking out the souvenir shops and not losing their way. With Europop blaring out from several shops, jesters' hats and puppets in overabundance and a strip club for good measure, the whole atmosphere can be oppressive in the height of summer, and is better savoured (if at all) at night. While much of what's on offer in Karlova is eminently missable, there is one sight worth seeking out, and that's the **Muzeum loutkářkých kultur** (Puppet Museum; daily 10am–8pm; Ⓦ www.puppetart.com), in the cool Gothic cellars of Karlova 12. Despite the appalling lack of information in either Czech or English, the museum boasts a highly impressive display of historic Czech puppets, both string and rod, mostly dating from the late nineteenth and the early twentieth centuries.

As they stroll down Karlova, few people notice the **Klementinum** (April–Oct Mon–Fri 2–8pm, Sat & Sun 10am–8pm; Nov–March Sat & Sun 10am–8pm), the former Jesuit College on the north side of the street, which covers an area second in size only to the Hrad. In 1556, Ferdinand I summoned the Jesuits to Prague to help bolster the Catholic cause in Bohemia, giving them the church of sv Kliment, which Dientzenhofer later rebuilt for them. Initially, the Jesuits proceeded with caution, but once the Counter-Reformation set in, they were put in control of the entire university and provincial education system. From their secure base at sv Kliment, they began to establish space for a great Catholic seat of learning in the city by buying up the surrounding land, demolishing more than thirty old town houses, and, over the next two hundred years, gradually building themselves a palatial headquarters. In 1773, soon after the Klementinum was completed, the Jesuits were turfed out of the country and the building handed over to the university authorities.

Nowadays, the Klementinum houses the National Library's collection of over five million volumes, but much of the original building has been left intact. The **entrance**, inconspicuously placed just past the church of sv Kliment, on Karlova, lets you into a series of rather plain courtyards. The entrance to the **Zrcadlová kaple** (Mirrored Chapel) is immediately to the left after passing through the archway on the far side of the first courtyard; its interior of fake marble, gilded stucco and mirror panels boasts fine acoustics but is only open for concerts. Nearby is the visitors' entrance, where thirty-minute guided tours (in English) set off for the Klementinum's two most easily accessible attractions. The most spectacular sight is the **Barokní sál** (Baroque Library), a long room lined with leather tomes, whose ceiling is decorated by one continuous illusionistic fresco praising secular wisdom, and whose wrought-iron gallery balustrade is held up by wooden barley-sugar columns. Upstairs, at roughly the centre of the

Klementinum complex, is the Jesuits' **Astronomická věž** (Astronomical Tower), from which you can enjoy a superb view over the centre of Prague.

Malé náměstí

After a couple more shops, boutiques, hole-in-the-wall bars and a final twist in Karlova, you emerge onto **Malé náměstí**, a square originally settled by French merchants in the twelfth century. The square was also home to the first apothecary in Prague, opened by a Florentine in 1353, and the tradition is continued today by the pharmacy **U zlaté koruny** (The Golden Crown) at no. 13, which boasts chandeliers and a restored Baroque interior. The square's best-known building, though, is the russet-red, neo-Renaissance **Rott Haus**, originally an ironmonger's shop founded by V.J. Rott in 1840, whose facade is smothered in agricultural scenes and motifs inspired by the Czech artist Mikuláš Aleš. At the centre of the square is a (non-functioning) fountain from 1560, which retains its beautiful, original wrought-iron canopy.

Staroměstské náměstí

East of Malé náměstí is **Staroměstské náměstí** (Old Town Square), easily the most spectacular square in Prague, and the traditional heart of the city. Most of the brightly coloured houses look solidly eighteenth-century, but their Baroque facades hide considerably older buildings. From the eleventh century onwards, this was the city's main marketplace, known simply as Velké náměstí (Great Square), to which all roads in Bohemia led, and where merchants from all over Europe gathered. When the five towns that made up Prague were united in 1784, it was the Old Town Square's town hall that was made the seat of the new city council, and for the next two hundred years the square was the scene of the country's most violent demonstrations and battles. In summer, cafés spread out their tables, in winter there's a Christmas market, and all year round tourists pour in to watch the town hall clock chime, to sit on the steps of the Hus Monument, and to drink in this historic showpiece.

The most recent arrival in the square is the colossal **Jan Hus Monument**, a turbulent sea of blackened bodies – the oppressed to the right, the defiant to the left – out of which rises the majestic moral authority of Hus himself (for more on whom, see p.204), gazing to the horizon. For the sculptor Ladislav Šaloun, a maverick who received no formal training, the monument was his life's work. Commissioned in 1900 when the Art Nouveau style Viennese Secession was at its peak, but strangely old-fashioned by the time it was completed in 1915, it would be difficult to claim that it blends in with its Baroque surroundings, yet this has never mattered to the Czechs, for whom its significance goes far beyond aesthetic merit. The Austrians refused to hold an official unveiling; in protest, on July 6, 1915, the 500th anniversary of the death of Hus, Praguers smothered the monument in flowers. Since then it has been a powerful symbol of Czech nationalism: in March 1939, it was draped in swastikas by the invading Nazis, and in August 1968, it was shrouded in funereal black by Praguers, protesting at the Soviet invasion. The inscription along the base is a quote from the will of Comenius, one of Hus's later followers, and includes Hus's most famous dictum, *Pravda vítězí* (Truth Prevails), which has been the motto of just about every Czech revolution since then.

Staroměstská radnice

It wasn't until the reign of King John of Luxembourg (1310–46) that Staré Město was allowed to build its own town hall, the **Staroměstská radnice**.

Short of funds, the citizens decided against an entirely new structure, buying a corner house on the square instead and simply adding an extra floor; later on, they added the east wing, with its graceful Gothic oriel and obligatory wedge-tower. Gradually, over the centuries, the neighbouring merchants' houses to the west were incorporated into the building, so that now it stretches all the way across to the richly sgraffitoed **Dům U minuty**, which juts out into the square.

On May 8, 1945, on the final day of the Prague Uprising, the Nazis still held on to Staroměstské náměstí, and in a last desperate act set fire to the town hall – one of the few buildings to be irrevocably damaged in the old town in World War II. The tower was rebuilt immediately, but only a crumbling fragment remains of the neo-Gothic **east wing**, which once stretched almost as far as the church of sv Mikuláš. Set into the paving nearby are 27 **white crosses** commemorating the Protestant leaders who were condemned to death on the orders of the emperor Ferdinand II, following the Battle of Bílá hora. They were publicly executed in the square on June 21, 1621: 24 enjoyed the nobleman's privilege and had their heads lopped off; the three remaining commoners were hung, drawn and quartered.

Today, the town hall's most popular feature is its *orloj* or **Astronomical Clock** – on the hour (daily 8am–8pm), a crowd of tourists gathers in front of the tower to watch a mechanical dumbshow by the clock's assorted figures. The Apostles shuffle past the top two windows, bowing to the audience, while perched on pinnacles below are the four threats to the city as perceived by the medieval mind: Death carrying his hourglass and tolling his bell, the Jew with his moneybags (since 1945 minus his stereotypical beard), Vanity admiring his reflection, and a turbaned Turk shaking his head. Beneath the moving figures, four characters representing Philosophy, Religion, Astronomy and History stand motionless throughout the performance. Finally, a cockerel pops out and flaps its wings to signal that the show's over; the clock then chimes the hour.

The powder-pink facade on the south side of the town hall now forms the **entrance** to the whole complex (Mon 11am–5pm, Tues–Sun 9am–6pm). A twenty-minute guided tour of the four rooms that survived World War II sets off every hour when the clock has finished striking (more frequently in summer). Despite being steeped in history, there's not much of interest here, apart from a few decorated ceilings with chunky beams and a couple of Renaissance portals. You'll probably get more enjoyment from climbing the tower for the panoramic sweep across Prague's spires. You can also visit the chapel, designed by Peter Parler, which has patches of medieval wall painting, and wonderful grimacing corbels at the foot of the ribbed vaulting. If you get there just before the clock strikes the hour, you can watch the apostles going out on their parade; the figures all had to be re-carved by a local puppeteer after the war.

The church of sv Mikuláš and palác Kinských

The destruction of the east wing of the town hall in 1945 rudely exposed Kilian Ignaz Dientzenhofer's church of **sv Mikuláš**, built in just three years between 1732 and 1735 for the Benedictines. Dientzenhofer's hand is obvious: the south front is decidedly luscious – painted creamy white, with Braun's blackened statuary popping up at every cornice – promising an interior to surpass even its sister church of sv Mikuláš in Malá Strana, which Dientzenhofer built with his father immediately afterwards (see p.82). Inside, however, it's a curious mixture. Although caked in the usual mixture of stucco and fresco and boasting an impressive dome, the church has been stripped over the years of much of its ornament and lacks the sumptuousness of its namesake on the left bank. This is partly due to the fact that Joseph II closed down the monastery and turned the church into a storehouse, and partly because it's now owned by the very "low", modern, Czech Hussite Church.

The largest secular building on the square is the Rococo **palác Kinských** (Tues–Sun 10am–6pm; ⓦwww.ngprague.cz), designed by Kilian Ignaz Dientzenhofer and built by his son-in-law Anselmo Lurago. In the nineteenth century it became a German *Gymnasium*, which was attended by, among others, Franz Kafka (whose father ran a haberdashery shop on the ground floor). The palace is perhaps most notorious, however, as the venue for the fateful speech by the Communist prime minister, Klement Gottwald, who walked out on to the grey stone balcony one snowy February morning in 1948, flanked by his Party henchmen, to address the thousands of enthusiastic supporters who packed the square below. It was the beginning of *Vitězná února* (Victorious February), the bloodless coup which brought the Communists to power and sealed the fate of the country for the next 41 years. The upper floor now hosts top-flight exhibitions of graphic art put on by the Národní galerie.

The Týn church and Ungelt

Staré Město's most impressive Gothic structure, the mighty **Týn church** (Matka boží před Týnem), whose two irregular towers, bristling with baubles, spires and pinnacles, rise like giant antennae above the arcaded houses which otherwise obscure its facade, is a far more imposing building than sv Mikuláš. Like the nearby Hus monument, the Týn church, begun in the fourteenth century, is a source of Czech national pride. In an act of defiance, George of Poděbrady, the last Czech and the only Hussite King of Bohemia, adorned the high stone gable with a statue of himself and a giant gilded *kalich* (chalice), the mascot of all Hussite sects. The church remained a hotbed of Hussitism until the Protestants' crushing defeat at the Battle of Bílá hora, after which the chalice was melted down to provide the newly ensconced statue of the Virgin Mary with a golden halo, sceptre and crown.

Despite being one of the main landmarks of Staré Město, it's well-nigh impossible to appreciate the church from anything but a considerable distance, since it's boxed in by the houses around it, some of which are actually built right against the walls. The church's **interior** has recently been restored and the rather appealing gloom of the place has been swept away. Instead, the lofty, narrow nave is now bright white, and punctuated at ground level by black and gold Baroque altarpieces. The pillar on the right of the chancel steps contains the red marble **tomb of Tycho Brahe**, the famous Danish astronomer, who arrived in Prague wearing a silver and gold false nose, having lost his own in a duel in Rostock. Court astronomer to Rudolf II for just two years, Brahe laid much of the groundwork for Johannes Kepler's later discoveries – Kepler getting his chance of employment when Brahe died of a burst bladder in 1601 after joining Petr Vok in one of his notorious binges.

Behind the Týn church lies the **Týn** courtyard, better known by its German name, **Ungelt** (meaning "No Money", a pseudonym used to deter marauding invaders), which, as the trading base of German merchants, was one of the first settlements on the Vltava. A hospice, church and hostel were built for the use of the merchants, and by the fourteenth century the area had become an extremely successful international marketplace; soon afterwards the traders moved up to the Hrad, and the court was transformed into a palace. The whole complex has now been restored, and the Dominicans have reclaimed one section, while the rest houses various shops, restaurants, and a luxury hotel.

Dům U zlatého prstenů

Back on Týnská, you'll come to the handsome Gothic townhouse of **Dům U zlatého prstenů** (House of the Golden Ring; Tues–Sun 10am–6pm; Ⓦ www.citygalleryprague.cz), now used by the City of Prague Gallery to show some of its twentieth-century Czech art. If you're not heading out to the modern art museum in the Veletržní palác (see p.123), then this is a good taster. The permanent collection is spread out over three floors, and arranged thematically rather than chronologically, while the cellar provides space for installations by up-and-coming contemporary artists; there's also a nice café across the courtyard.

On the first floor, symbolism looms large, with *Destitute Land*, Max Švabinský's none-too-subtle view of life under the Habsburg yoke, and a smattering of works by two of Bohemia's best-loved eccentrics, Josef Váchal and František Bílek. There's a decent selection of dour 1920s paintings, too, typified by *Slagheaps in the Evening II* by Jan Zrzavý, plus the usual Czech Surrealist suspects, Josef Šíma, Toyen and Jiří Štyrský. More refreshing is the sight of Eduard Stavinoha's cartoon-like *Striking Demonstrators 24.2.1948*, an ideological painting from 1948 that appears almost like Pop Art. Antonín Slavíček's easy-on-the-eye Impressionist views of Prague kick off proceedings on the second floor, along with works by Cubist Emil Filla, and abstract artist Mikuláš Medek. Also on this floor, there's the chance to see a lot of 1980s works that don't often see the light of day nowadays, such as Michael Rittstein's political allegory *Slumber beneath a Large Hand*. Highlights on the third floor include an excellent collection of mad collages by Jiří Kolář, abstract Vorticist works by Zdeněk Sýkora, and studies for kinetic-light sculptures by Zdeněk Pešánek.

From Celetná to Anežský klášter

Celetná, whose name comes from the bakers who used to bake a particular type of small loaf (*calty*) here in the Middle Ages, leads east from Staroměstské náměstí direct to the Prašná brána, one of the original gateways of the old town. It's one of the oldest streets in Prague, lying along the former trade route from the old town market square, as well as on the *králová cesta*. Its buildings were smartly refaced in the Baroque period, and their pastel shades are now crisply maintained. Most of Celetná's shops veer towards the chic end of the Czech market, making it a popular place for a bit of window-shopping. Dive down one of the covered passages to the left and into the backstreets, however, and you'll soon lose the crowds, and eventually end up at the atmospheric ruins of Anežský klášter, now home to the Národní galerie's Gothic Czech art collection.

Two-thirds of the way along Celetná, at the junction with Ovocný trh, is the **Dům U černé Matky boží** (House at the Black Madonna; Tues–Sun 10am–6pm; Ⓦ www.ecn.cz/cmvu), built as a department store in 1911–12 by Josef Gočár and one of the best examples of Czech Cubist architecture in Prague (see p.117 for more). Appropriately enough, the building now houses a small but excellent permanent exhibition of **Český kubismus** (Czech Cubism), on the top two floors. There's a little bit of everything, from sofas and sideboards by Gočár himself to paintings by Emil Filla and Josef Čapek, plus some wonderful sculptures by Otto Gutfreund. If the above has only whetted your appetite, there are more Czech Cubist exhibits in the Veletržní palác (see p.123), and more Cubist buildings in Vyšehrad (see p.117). The first, second and third floors are currently given over to temporary exhibitions of twentieth-century art.

Celetná ends at the fourteenth-century Prašná brána (see p.112), beyond which is náměstí Republiky, at which point, strictly speaking, you've left Staré Město behind. Back in the old town, head north from Celetná into the backstreets which conceal the Franciscan church of **sv Jakub** or St James (Mon–Sat 9am–12.30pm & 2.30–4pm, Sun 2–4pm), with its distinctive bubbling, stucco portal on Malá štupartská. The church's massive Gothic proportions – it has the longest nave in Prague after the cathedral – make it a favourite venue for organ recitals, Mozart masses and other concerts. After the great fire of 1689, Prague's Baroque artists remodelled the entire interior, adding huge pilasters, a series of colourful frescoes and over twenty side altars. The most famous of these is the tomb of the Count of Mitrovice, in the northern aisle, designed by Fischer von Erlach and Prague's own Maximilian Brokof.

Anežský klášter

Further north through the backstreets, the **Anežský klášter** (Convent of St Agnes), Prague's oldest surviving Gothic building, stands within a stone's throw of the river as it loops around to the east. It was founded in 1233 as a Franciscan convent for the Order of the Poor Clares, and takes its name from Agnes (Anežka), youngest daughter of Přemysl Otakar I, who left her life of regal privilege to become the convent's first abbess. Agnes herself was beatified in 1874 to try to combat the spread of Hussitism amongst the Czechs, and was officially canonized on November 12, 1989, just four days before the Velvet Revolution.

The convent itself was closed down in 1782 and fell into rack and ruin. It was squatted for most of the next century, and although saved from demolition by the Czech nationalist lobby, its restoration only took place in the 1980s. The convent now houses the Národní galerie's **medieval art collection** (Tues–Sun 10am–6pm; Ⓦwww.ngprague.cz), in particular the Gothic art, which first flourished here under the patronage of Charles IV.

The exhibition is arranged chronologically, starting with a remarkable silver-gilt casket from 1360 used to house the skull of St Ludmilla. The nine panels from the altarpiece of the Cistercian monastery at Vyšší Brod in South Bohemia, from around 1350, are among the finest in central Europe: the *Annunciation* panel is particularly rich iconographically. The real gems of the collection, however, are the six panels by **Master Theodoric**, who painted over one hundred such paintings for Charles IV's castle chapel at Karlštejn (see p.160). These larger-than-life half-length portraits of saints, church fathers and so on, are full of intense expression and rich colours, their depictions spilling onto the embossed frames.

The three late fourteenth-century panels by the **Master of Třeboň** show an even greater variety of balance and depth, and the increasing influence of Flemish paintings of the period. Since the quality of the works in the gallery's largest room is pretty uneven, it's worth moving fairly swiftly on to the smaller rooms beyond, where you'll find woodcuts by Cranach the Elder, Dürer and the lesser-known Hans Burgkmair – the seven-headed beast in Dürer's *Apocalypse* cycle is particularly Harry Potter. Finally, don't miss the superb sixteenth-century wood sculptures, including an incredibly detailed scene, *Christ the Saviour and the Last Judgement*, in which Death's entrails are in the process of being devoured by a frog.

Southern Staré Město

The southern half of Staré Město is bounded by the *králová cesta* (the coronation route) to the north, and the curve of Národní and Na příkopě, which follow the course of the old fortifications, to the south. There are no showpiece squares like Staroměstské náměstí here, but the complex web of narrow lanes and hidden passageways, many of which have changed little since medieval times, makes this an intriguing quarter to explore, and one where it's easy to lose the worst of the crowds (and yourself).

From Ovocný trh to Uhelný trh

Heading southwest from the Dům U černé Matky boží (see p.94), you enter **Ovocný trh**, site of the old fruit market, its cobbles fanning out towards the back of the lime-green and white **Stavovské divadlo** (Estates Theatre). Built in the early 1780s by Count Nostitz (after whom the theatre was originally named) for the entertainment of Prague's large and powerful German community, the theatre is one of the finest Neoclassical buildings in Prague, reflecting the enormous self-confidence of its patrons. The Stavovské divadlo has a place in Czech history too, for it was here that the Czech national anthem, *Kde domov můj* (Where is My Home), was first performed, as part of the comic opera *Fidlovačka*, by J.K. Tyl. It is also something of a mecca for Mozart fans, since it was here, rather than in the hostile climate of Vienna, that the composer chose to premiere both *Don Giovanni* and *La Clemenza di Tito*. This is, in fact, one of the few opera houses in Europe which remains intact from Mozart's time, though it underwent major refurbishment during the nineteenth century – it was here that Miloš Forman filmed the concert scenes for his Oscar-laden *Amadeus*.

On the north side of the Stavovské divadlo is the home base of the **Karolinum** or Charles University, named after its founder Charles IV, who established it in 1348 as the first university in this part of Europe. To begin with, the university had no fixed abode; it wasn't until 1383 that Václav IV bought the present site. All that's left of the original fourteenth-century building is the Gothic oriel window which emerges from the south wall; the rest was trashed by the Nazis in 1945. The new main entrance is a modern red-brick curtain wall building by Jaroslav Fragner, set back from the street and inscribed with the original Latin name *Universitas Karolina*. Only a couple of small departments and the chancellor's office and administration are now housed here, with the rest spread over the length and breadth of the city. The heavily restored Gothic vaults, on the ground floor of the south wing, are now used as a contemporary **art gallery**.

The junction of Melantrichova and Rytířská is always teeming with people pouring out of Staroměstské náměstí and heading for Wenceslas Square. Clearly visible from Melantrichova is Prague's last surviving **open-air market** – a poor relation of its Germanic predecessor, which stretched all the way from Ovocný trh to Uhelný trh. Traditionally a flower and vegetable market, it runs the full length of the arcaded Havelská, and sells everything from celery to CDs, with plenty of souvenirs and wooden toys in between. The market runs west into **Uhelný trh**, which gets its name from the *uhlí* (coal) that was sold here in medieval times. Nowadays, however, it's Prague's red-light district – particularly Perlová and Na Perštýně – and although you'll see little evidence during the day, it can get busy at night, as a result of which the local authorities are constantly trying to move the trade elsewhere.

Sv Martin ve zdi and Bartolomějská

South of Uhelný trh, down Martinská, the street miraculously opens out to make room for the twelfth-century church of **sv Martin ve zdi** (St Martin-in-the-Walls), originally built to serve the Czech community of the village of sv Martin, until it found itself the wrong side of the Gothic fortifications. It's still essentially a Romanesque structure, adapted to suit Gothic tastes a century later; it was, however, closed down in 1784 by Joseph II and turned into a warehouse, shops and flats. The city bought the church in 1904 and thoroughly restored it, adding the creamy neo-Renaissance tower, and eventually handing it over to the Czech Brethren. For them, it has a special significance as the place where communion "in both kinds" (ie bread and wine), one of the fundamental demands of the Hussites, was first administered to the whole congregation, in 1414. To be honest, there's very little to see inside, which is just as well as it's only open for concerts nowadays.

Around the corner from sv Martin ve zdi is the gloomy, lifeless street of **Bartolomějská**, dominated by a tall, grim-looking building on its south side, which served as the main interrogation centre of the universally detested Communist secret police, the *Statní bezpečnost*, or *StB*. The building is now back in the hands of the Franciscan nuns who occupied the place prior to 1948, and its former police cells now serve as rooms for a small *pension* – it's even possible to stay in Havel's old cell (see p.63).

Betlémské náměstí

After leaving the dark shadows of Bartolomějská, the brighter aspect of **Betlémské náměstí** comes as a welcome relief. The square is named after the **Betlémská kaple** (Bethlehem Chapel; daily: April–Oct 9am–6pm; Nov–March 9am–5.30pm), whose high wooden gables face on to the square. This was founded in 1391 by religious reformists, who, denied the right to build a church, proceeded instead to build the largest chapel in Bohemia, with a total capacity of three thousand. Sermons were delivered not in the customary Latin, but in the language of the masses – Czech. From 1402 to 1413, **Jan Hus** preached here (see box on p.204), regularly pulling in more than enough commoners to fill the chapel. Hus was eventually excommunicated for his outspokenness, found guilty of heresy and burnt at the stake at the Council of Constance in 1415.

The chapel continued to attract reformists from all over Europe for another two centuries until it was handed over to the Jesuits. The chapel was demolished following the expulsion of the Jesuits in 1773, and only three outer walls now remain from the medieval building, with patches of their original biblical decoration. The rest is a scrupulous reconstruction by Jaroslav Fragner, using the original plans and a fair amount of imaginative guesswork. The initial reconstruction work was carried out after the war by the Communists, who were keen to portray Hus as a Czech nationalist and social critic as much as a religious reformer.

At the western end of the square stands the **Náprstkovo muzeum** (Tues–Sun 9am–noon & 12.45–5.30pm; ⓦwww.aconet.cz/npm), whose founder, Czech nationalist Vojta Náprstek, was inspired by the great Victorian museums of London while in exile following the 1848 revolution. Despite the fact that the museum could clearly do with an injection of cash, it still manages to put on some excellent temporary ethnographic exhibitions on the ground floor, and does a useful job of promoting tolerance of different cultures. The permanent collection of Náprstek's American, Australasian and Oceanic collections occupies the top two floors. Náprstek's technological exhibits now form part of the collections of the Národné technické muzeum (see p.123), while his Asian and Oriental collections are housed in the chateau at Liběchov (see p.146).

Muzeum Bedřicha Smetany

A few blocks west, in a gaily decorated neo-Renaissance building on the riverfront, is the **Muzeum Bedřicha Smetany** (daily except Tues 10am–noon & 12.30–5pm). Bedřich Smetana (1824–84) was without doubt the most nationalistic of all the great Czech composers, taking an active part in the 1848 revolution and the later national revival movement. He enjoyed his greatest success as a composer with *The Bartered Bride*, which marked the birth of Czech opera. However, he was forced to give up conducting in 1874 with the onset of deafness, and eventually died of syphilis in a mental asylum. Sadly, the museum fails to capture much of the spirit of the man, though you get to see his spectacles, and the garnet jewellery of his first wife. Still, the views across to the castle are good, and you get to wave a laser baton around in order to listen to his music.

Josefov

It is crowded with horses; traversed by narrow streets not remarkable for cleanliness, and has altogether an uninviting aspect. Your sanitary reformer would here find a strong case of overcrowding.

Walter White, "A July Holiday in Saxony, Bohemia and Silesia" (1857)

Less than half a century after Walter White's comments, all that was left of the former ghetto of **JOSEFOV** were six synagogues, the town hall and the medieval cemetery. At the end of the nineteenth century, a period of great economic growth for the Habsburg Empire, it was decided that Prague should be turned into a beautiful bourgeois city, modelled on Paris. The key to this transformation was the "sanitization" of the ghetto, a process, begun in 1893, which reduced the notorious malodorous backstreets and alleyways of Josefov to rubble and replaced them with block after block of luxurious five-storey mansions. The Jews, the poor, the Gypsies and the prostitutes were cleared out so that the area could become a desirable residential quarter, rich in Art Nouveau buildings festooned with decorative murals, doorways and sculpturing. This building frenzy marked the beginning of the end for a community which had existed in Prague for almost a millennium.

In any other European city occupied by the Nazis in World War II, what little was left of the old ghetto would have been demolished. But although Prague's Jews were transported to the new ghetto in Terezín, by a grotesque twist of fate the ghetto itself was preserved by Hitler himself in order to provide a site for his planned "Exotic Museum of an Extinct Race". With this in mind, Jewish artefacts from all over central Europe were gathered here, and now make up one of the richest collections of Judaica in Europe, and one of the most fascinating sights in Prague.

The former ghetto

Geographically, Josefov lies to the northwest of Staroměstské náměstí, between the church of sv Mikuláš and the River Vltava. The warren-like street plan of Josefov disappeared during the sanitization, and through the heart of the old

Visiting Josefov

All the "sights" of Josefov (@www.jewishmuseum.cz), bar the Staronová synagoga, are covered by an all-in-one 280Kč ticket, available from the quarter's numerous ticket offices. Opening hours vary but are basically daily except Saturday April–October 9am–6pm, November–March 9am–4.30pm. In order to try and regulate the flow of visitors, at peak times a timed entry system comes into operation, giving you around twenty minutes at each sight, though don't worry too much if you don't adhere rigidly to your timetable.

Prague's Jews

Jews probably arrived in Prague as early as the tenth century and, initially at least, are thought to have settled on both sides of the river. In 1096, at the time of the first crusade, the earliest recorded **pogrom** took place, which may have hastened the formation of a much more closely-knit "Jewish town" within Staré Město during the twelfth century. However, it wasn't until much later that Jews were actually herded into a **walled ghetto** (and several centuries before the word "ghetto" was actually first coined in Venice), sealed off from the rest of the town and subject to a curfew. From the beginning, though, they were subject to laws restricting their choice of profession to usury and the rag trade; in addition, some form of visible identification, a cap or badge (notably the Star of David), remained a more or less constant feature of Jewish life until the Enlightenment.

During the **1389 pogrom**, 3000 Jews were massacred over Easter, some while sheltering in the Old-New Synagogue – an event commemorated every year thereafter on Yom Kippur. By contrast, the reign of Rudolf II (1576–1612) was a time of economic and cultural prosperity for the Prague Jewish community. The Jewish mayor, **Mordecai Maisel**, Rudolf's minister of finance, became one of the richest men in Bohemia and the success symbol of a generation. This was the "golden age" of the ghetto: the time of **Rabbi Löw**, the severe and conservative chief rabbi of Prague, who is now best known as the legendary creator of the Jewish "golem" (a precursor of Frankenstein's monster).

It was the enlightened **Emperor Joseph II** (1780–90) who did most to lift the restrictions on Jews. His 1781 Toleration Edict ended the dress codes, opened up education to all non-Catholics, and removed the gates from the ghetto. The community paid him homage in the following century by officially naming the ghetto Josefov, or Josefstadt. It was not until the **1848 revolution**, however, that Jews were granted equal status as citizens and permitted to settle outside the ghetto. Gradually, the more prosperous Jewish families began to move to other districts of Prague, leaving behind only the poorest Jews and strictly Orthodox families, who were rapidly joined by the underprivileged ranks of Prague society: Gypsies, beggars, prostitutes and alcoholics. By 1890, only twenty percent of Josefov's population was Jewish, yet it was still the most densely populated area in Prague.

After the **Nazi occupation** of Prague on March 15, 1939, the city's Jews were subject to an increasingly harsh set of regulations, which saw them again barred from most professions, placed under curfew, and compelled once more to wear the yellow Star of David. In November 1941, the first transport of Prague Jews set off for the new ghetto in Terezín, 60km northwest of Prague. Of the estimated 55,000 Jews in Prague at the time of the Nazi invasion, over 36,000 died in the camps. Many survivors emigrated to Israel and the USA. Of the 8000 who registered as Jewish in the Prague census of 1947, a significant number joined the Communist Party, only to find themselves victims of Stalinist anti-Semitic wrath during the 1950s.

It's difficult to calculate exactly how many Jews now live in Prague – around a thousand were officially registered as such prior to 1989 – though their numbers have undoubtedly been bolstered by a new generation of Czech Jews who have rediscovered their roots, and by the new influx of Jewish Americans and Israelis.

ghetto runs the ultimate bourgeois avenue, **Pařížská**, a riot of turn-of-the-twentieth-century sculpturing, spikes and turrets, home to swanky boutiques and cafés. If Josefov can still be said to have a main street, though, it is really the parallel street of **Maiselova**, named after the community's sixteenth-century leader. The sheer volume of tourists – over a million a year – that visit Josefov has brought with it the inevitable rash of souvenir stalls flogging dubious

"Jewish" souvenirs, and the whole area is now something of a tourist trap. Yet to skip this part of the old town is to miss out on an entire slice of the city's cultural history.

Staronová synagoga and Židovská radnice

Walking down Maiselova, it's impossible to miss the steep sawtooth brick gables of the **Staronová synagoga** or Altneuschul (Old-New Synagogue), so called because when it was built it was indeed very new, though as time went on, it became anything but. Begun in the second half of the thirteenth century, it is, in fact, the oldest functioning synagogue in Europe, one of the earliest Gothic buildings in Prague and still the religious centre for Prague's Orthodox Jews. Since Jews were prevented by law from becoming architects, the synagogue was probably constructed by the Franciscan builders working on the convent of sv Anežka. Its five-ribbed vaulting is unique in Bohemia; the extra, purely decorative rib was added to avoid any hint of a cross.

To enter the synagogue, you must buy a separate ticket (200Kč) from the ticket office opposite the synagogue's entrance on Červená (or from one of the other ticket offices in Josefov). Men are asked to cover their heads out of respect – paper *kippahs* are available at the ticket office, though a handkerchief will do. To get to the **main hall**, you must pass through one of the two low vestibules from which women are allowed to watch the proceedings. Above the entrance is an elaborate tympanum covered in the twisting branches of a vine tree, its twelve bunches of grapes representing the tribes of Israel. The low glow from the chandeliers is the only light in the hall, which is mostly taken up with the elaborate wrought-iron cage enclosing the *bimah* in the centre. In 1357, Charles IV allowed the Jews to fly their own municipal standard, a moth-eaten remnant of which is still on show. The other flag – a tattered red banner – was a gift to the community from Emperor Ferdinand III for helping fend off the Swedes in 1648. On the west wall is a glass cabinet, shaped like Moses' two tablets of stone and filled with tiny personalized light bulbs, which are paid for by grieving relatives or friends and light up on the anniversary of the person's death (there's even one for Kafka).

Just south of the synagogue is the **Židovská radnice** (Jewish Town Hall), one of the few such buildings to survive the Holocaust. Founded and funded by Maisel in the sixteenth century, it was later rebuilt as the creamy-pink Baroque house you see now, housing an overpriced kosher restaurant. The belfry, permission for which was granted by Ferdinand III, has a clock on each of its four sides, plus a Hebrew one stuck on the north gable which, like the Hebrew script, goes "backwards".

Pinkasova synagoga

Jutting out at an angle on the south side of the Old Jewish Cemetery (see below), with its entrance on Široká, the **Pinkasova synagoga** was built in the 1530s for the powerful Pinkas family, and has undergone countless restorations over the centuries. In 1958, the synagogue was transformed into a chilling memorial to the 77,297 Czech Jews killed during the Holocaust. Of all the sights of the Jewish quarter, the Holocaust memorial is perhaps the most moving, with every bit of wall space taken up with the carved stone list of victims, stating simply their names, dates of birth and dates of transportation to the camps. It is the longest epitaph in the world, yet it represents only the merest fraction of those who died in the Nazi ghettos and concentration camps. All that remains of the synagogue's original decor is the ornate *bimah* surrounded by a beautiful wrought-iron grille, supported by barley-sugar columns. Upstairs in a room beside the women's gallery, there's now a harrowing exhibition of naive drawings by children from the Jewish ghetto in Terezín (see p.258), most of whom later perished in the camps.

Starý židovský hřbitov (Old Jewish Cemetery)

At the heart of Josefov is the **Starý židovský hřbitov** (Old Jewish Cemetery), called *beit hayyim* in Hebrew, meaning "House of Life". Established in the fifteenth century, it was in use until 1787, by which time there were an estimated 100,000 buried here, one on top of the other, as many as twelve layers deep. The enormous number of visitors has meant that the graves themselves have been roped off to protect them, and a one-way system introduced: you enter from the Pinkasova synagoga, on Široká, and leave by the Klausová synagoga (see p.102). The oldest grave, dating from 1439, belongs to the poet Avigdor Karo, who lived to tell the tale of the 1389 pogrom. Get there before the crowds – a difficult task at most times of the year – and you'll find the cemetery a poignant reminder of the ghetto, its inhabitants subjected to inhuman overcrowding even in death. The rest of Prague recedes beyond the sombre lime trees and cramped perimeter walls, the haphazard headstones and Hebrew inscriptions casting a powerful spell.

Obřadní síň and the other synagogues

Immediately on your left as you leave the cemetery is the **Obřadní síň**, a lugubrious neo-Renaissance house built in 1906 as a ceremonial hall by the Jewish Burial Society. Appropriately enough, it's now devoted to an exhibition on Jewish traditions of burial and death, good to peruse before you head off into the cemetery.

On Kafka's trail

Franz Kafka was born on July 3, 1883, above the *Batalion* Schnapps bar on the corner of Maiselova and Kaprova (the original building has long since been torn down, but a gaunt-looking modern bust now commemorates the site). He spent most of his life in and around Josefov. His father was an upwardly mobile small businessman from a Czech-Jewish family of kosher butchers (Kafka himself was a vegetarian), his mother from a wealthy German-Jewish family of merchants. The family owned a haberdashery shop, located at various premises on or near Staroměstské náměstí. In 1889, they moved out of Josefov and lived for the next seven years in the beautiful Renaissance Dům U minuty, next door to the Staroměstská radnice, during which time Kafka attended the *Volksschule* on Masná (now a Czech primary school), followed by a spell at an exceptionally strict German *Gymnasium*, located on the third floor of the palác Kinských.

At eighteen, he began a law degree at the German half of the Karolinum, which was where he met his lifelong friend and posthumous biographer and editor, Max Brod. Kafka spent most of his working life as an accident insurance clerk, until he was forced to retire through ill health in 1922. Illness plagued him throughout his life and he spent many months as a patient at the innumerable spas in *Mitteleuropa*. He was engaged three times, twice to the same woman, but never married, finally leaving home at the age of 31 for bachelor digs on the corner of Dlouhá and Masná, where he wrote the bulk of his most famous work, *The Trial*. He died of tuberculosis at the age of 40 in a sanatorium just outside Vienna, on June 3, 1924, and is buried in the Nový židovský hřbitov in Žižkov (see p.120).

Nowadays, thanks to his popularity with Western tourists, Kafka has become an extremely marketable commodity, with his image plastered across T-shirts, mugs and postcards all over the city centre. The small **museum** (Tues–Sat 10am–6pm), on the site of Kafka's birthplace next door to the church of sv Mikuláš, retells Kafka's life simply but effectively with pictures and quotes (in Czech, German and English), and flogs souvenirs.

Close to the entrance to the cemetery is the **Klausová synagoga**, a late seventeenth-century building, founded in the 1690s by Mordecai Maisel on the site of several medieval prayer halls (*klausen*), in what was then a notorious red-light district of Josefov. The ornate Baroque interior contains a rich display of religious objects from embroidered *kippah* to *Kiddush* cups, and explains the very basics of Jewish religious practice.

Founded and paid for entirely by Mordecai Maisel, the neo-Gothic **Maiselova synagoga**, set back from the neighbouring houses on Maiselova, was, in its day, one of the most ornate synagogues in Josefov. Nowadays, its whitewashed interior is almost entirely bare apart from the rich offerings of its glass cabinets, which contain gold and silverwork, *hanukkah* candlesticks, *torah* scrolls and other religious artefacts.

East of Pařížská, up Široká, stands the **Španělská synagoga** (Spanish Synagogue), built in 1868. By far the most ornate synagogue in Josefov, every available surface of its stunning, gilded Moorish interior is smothered with a profusion of floral motifs and geometric patterns, in vibrant reds, greens and blues, which are repeated in the synagogue's huge stained-glass windows. The interior houses an interesting exhibition on the history of Prague's Jews, from the time of the 1848 emancipation. Lovely, slender, painted cast-iron columns hold up the women's gallery, where the displays include a fascinating set of photos depicting the old ghetto at the time of its demolition. There's a section on Prague's German-Jewish writers, including Kafka, and information on the planned Nazi museum and the Holocaust.

Around náměstí Jana Palacha

As Kaprova and Široká emerge from Josefov, they meet at **náměstí Jana Palacha**, previously called náměstí Krasnoarmejců (Red Army Square) and embellished with a flower bed in the shape of a red star, in memory of the Soviet dead who were temporarily buried here in May 1945. It was probably this, as much as the fact that the building on the east side of the square is the Faculty of Philosophy where Palach (see p.108) was a student, that prompted the authorities to make the first of the post-Communist street-name changes here in 1989 (there's a bust of Palach on the corner of the building). By a happy coincidence, the road which intersects the square from the north is called 17 listopadu (17 November), originally commemorating the day in 1939 when the Nazis closed down all Czech institutions of higher education, but now equally good for the 1989 march (see p.110).

The north side of the square is taken up by the **Rudolfinum** or Dům umělců (House of Artists), designed by Josef Zítek and Josef Schulz. One of the proud civic buildings of the nineteenth-century national revival, it was originally built to house an art gallery, museum and concert hall for the Czech-speaking community. In 1918, however, it became the seat of the new Czechoslovak parliament, only returning to its original artistic purpose in 1946. It's now one of the capital's main exhibition and concert venues (and home to the Czech Philharmonic), with a wonderfully grand café on the first floor (see p.133).

UPM – the Decorative Arts Museum

A short way down 17 listopadu from the square is the **UPM**, or Uměleckopřymyslové muzeum (Tues–Sun 10am–6pm), installed in another of Schulz's worthy nineteenth-century creations, richly decorated in mosaics, stained glass and sculptures. Literally translated, this is a "Museum of Decorative Arts", though the translation hardly does justice to what is one of the most fascinating museums in the capital. The museum's consistently excellent temporary exhibitions are staged on the ground floor, with the permanent collections on the floor above. Audioguides to the collections are available, at no extra cost, though they're by no means essential, as there's lots of information and labelling in English.

The displays start with the **Votivní sál** (Votive Hall), which is ornately decorated with trompe l'oeil wall hangings, lunette paintings and a bewhiskered bust of Emperor Franz-Josef I. Next door is the **Story of a Fibre**, which displays textile exhibits, ranging from a sixteenth-century Brussels tapestry of Samson bringing down the temple to some 1930s curtains by the Surrealist artist Toyen. The room is dominated by a double-decker costume display: above, there are richly embroidered religious vestments from the fifteenth to eighteenth centuries; below, fashionable attire from the eighteenth century to contemporary catwalk concoctions.

More rooms are planned to open on this side of the Votive Hall, but at the time of going to press, you have to backtrack to reach the **Arts of Fire**, home to the museum's impressive glass, ceramic and pottery displays, ranging from eighteenth-century Meissen figures to Art Nouveau vases by Bohemian glassmakers such as Lötz. To catch the best examples of Cubist works on display, head for the room's Gočár-designed Cubist bookcase, and look out, too, for Jan Zrzavy's three-piece glass mosaic from the 1930s.

The **print and images** room is devoted mainly to Czech photography, and includes numerous prints from the art form's interwar heyday, including several of František Drtikol's remarkable 1920s geometric nudes, Jaromír Funke's superb still-lifes and Josef Sudek's contemplative studio shots. Finally, in the **treasure**

hall, there's a kind of modern-day *Kunstkammer* or cabinet of curiosities: everything from ivory objets d'art and seventeenth-century Italian *pietro dure* or hardstone mosaics, to miniature silver furniture and a goblet made from rhino horn.

Nové Město

NOVÉ MĚSTO is the city's main commercial and business district, housing most of its big hotels, cinemas, nightclubs, fast-food outlets and department stores. Architecturally, it comes over as big, bourgeois and predominantly late nineteenth century, yet Nové Město was actually founded way back in 1348 by Emperor Charles IV as an entirely new town – three times as big as Staré Město – intended to link the southern fortress of Vyšehrad with Staré Město to the north. Large market squares, wide streets, and a level of town planning far ahead of its time were employed to transform Prague into the new capital city of the Holy Roman Empire. However, this quickly became the city's poorest quarter after Josefov, renowned as a hotbed of Hussitism and radicalism throughout the centuries. In the second half of the nineteenth century, the authorities set about a campaign of slum clearance similar to that inflicted on the Jewish quarter; only the churches and a few important historical buildings were left standing, though Charles' street layout survived pretty much intact. The leading architects of the day began to line the wide boulevards with ostentatious examples of their work, which were eagerly snapped up by the new class of status-conscious businessmen – a process that continued well into the last century, making Nové Město the most architecturally varied part of Prague.

The obvious starting point, and probably the only place in Prague most visitors can put a name to, is Wenceslas Square, known to the Czechs as **Václavské náměstí**, hub of the modern city and somewhere you'll find yourself passing through again and again. The two principal, partially pedestrianized, streets which lead off it are **Národní třída** and **Na příkopě**, which together form the *zlatý kříž* or "golden cross", Prague's commercial axis and for over a century the most expensive slice of real estate in the capital. The *zlatý kříž*, and the surrounding streets, also contain some of Prague's finest late-nineteenth-century, Art Nouveau and twentieth-century architecture. The rest of Nové Město, which spreads out northeast and southwest of the square, is much less explored and, for the most part, still heavily residential; unusually for Prague, using the tram and metro systems to get around here will save some unnecessary legwork.

Václavské náměstí (Wenceslas Square)

The natural pivot around which modern Prague revolves, and the focus of the events of November 1989, **Václavské náměstí** (Wenceslas Square) is more of a wide, gently sloping boulevard than a square as such. It's scarcely a conventional – or even convenient – space in which to hold mass demonstrations, yet the square's **history of protest** goes back to the 1848 revolution, whose violent denouement began here on June 12 with a peaceful open-air mass organized by Prague students. On the crest of the nationalist disturbances, the square – which had been known as Koňský trh (Horse Market) since medieval times – was given its present name. Naturally enough, it was one of the rallying points for the jubilant milling crowds on October 28, 1918, when Czechoslovakia's independence was declared. At the lowest point of the Nazi occupation, on July 3, 1942, some two weeks after the capture of Reinhard Heydrich's assassins (see p.114), over 200,000 Czechs gathered to swear allegiance to the Third Reich. Just six years later, in February 1948, a similar-sized crowd showed their support for the Communist coup. Then in August 1968, it was the scene of some of the most violent confrontations between the Soviet invaders and local Czechs. On January 16, 1969, at the top of the square, Jan Palach set fire to himself in protest at the continuing occupation of the country by Warsaw Pact troops. And, of course, it was here that night after night, in late November 1989, more than 250,000 people crammed into the square, until the Communist old guard finally threw in the towel.

Despite the square's medieval origins, its oldest building dates only from the eighteenth century, and the vast majority are much younger. As the city's money moved south of Staré Město during the industrial revolution, so the square became the architectural showpiece of the nation, and it is now lined with self-important six- or seven-storey buildings, representing every artistic trend of the last hundred years, from neo-Renaissance to Constructivist. In addition, the square has a very good selection of period-piece arcades or *pasáže*, preserved from the commercial boom of the First Republic.

Up the square

The busiest part of Wenceslas Square and a popular place to meet up before hitting town is around **Můstek**, the city's most central metro station, at the northern end of the square. The area is dominated by the **Palác Koruna**, a hulking wedge of sculptured concrete and gold, built for an insurance company in 1914 by Antonín Pfeiffer, one of Jan Kotěra's many pupils. The building is a rare mixture of heavy constructivism and gilded Secession-style ornamentation, but the *pièce de résistance* is the palace's bejewelled crown which lights up at night.

Opposite Palác Koruna, adjacent to one another, are two functionalist buildings designed by Ludvík Kysela in the late 1920s, billed at the time as the first glass curtain-wall buildings. Along with the former *Hotel Juliš* (see below), they represent the perfect expression of the optimistic mood of progress and modernism that permeated the interwar republic. The building on the right, as you face them, was erected by the chocolate firm Lindt; the **Baťa** store, on the left, followed a few years later. The latter was built for the Czech shoe magnate Tomáš Baťa, one of the greatest patrons of avant-garde Czech art, whose company's assets were nationalized by the Communists in 1948; the store was returned to the family, along with a number of their shoe factories, after 1989.

Twenty-five years earlier, Czech architecture was in the throes of its own version of Art Nouveau, one of whose earliest practitioners was Jan Kotěra. The **Peterkův dům**, a slender essay in the new style, was his first work, undertaken at the age of 28. Kotěra, a pupil of the great architect of the Viennese Secession, Otto Wagner, eventually moved on to a much more brutal constructivism. Another supreme example of Czech functionalism, a few doors further up at no. 22, is the former **Hotel Juliš**, designed by Pavel Janák, who had already made his name as one of the leading lights of the short-lived Czech Cubist (and later Rondo-Cubist) movement (see p.117).

Further up on the same side of the square is the **Melantrich** publishing house, whose first floor is occupied by the offices of the Socialist Party newspaper, *Svobodné slovo* (The Free Word). For forty years the Socialist Party was a loyal puppet of the Communist government, but on the second night of the demonstrations in November 1989, the newspaper handed over its well-placed balcony to the opposition speakers of the Občanské fórum (Civic Forum). Melantrich House faces two of the most famous and most ornate buildings on the entire square, the Art Nouveau **Grand Hotel Evropa** and its slim neighbour, the *Hotel Meran*, both built in 1903–5. They represent everything the Czech modern

NOVÉ MĚSTO

WILSONOVA

Muzeum Prahy Ⓜ

Florenc ▲❷

TĚŠNOV

KLIMENTSKÁ

SVOBODY

PETRSKÁ

Bílá labuť

sv Petr

Café Imperial

Banka legií

ZLATNICKÁ

NA PORÍČÍ

NA FLORENCI

Masarykovo nádraží

Praha hlavní nádraží

WILSONOVA

HAVLÍČKOVA

Ⓘ

WASHINGTONOVA

NÁBR. LUDVÍKA

KLIMENTSKÁ

SOUKENICKÁ

TRUHLÁŘSKÁ

NA POŘÍČÍ

Lidový dům

HYBERNSKÁ

SENOVÁŽNÉ NÁM.

❸ Jubilejní synagoga

Hlavní nádraží Ⓜ

JERUZALÉMSKÁ

Poštovní muzeum

sv Kliment

Náměstí Republiky Ⓜ

Ⓜ U hybernů

Prašná brána

SENOVÁŽNÁ

RŮŽOVA

JINDŘIŠSKÁ

POLITICKÝCH VĚZŇŮ

OPLETALOVA

REVOLUČNÍ

NÁMĚSTÍ REPUBLIKY

Ⓘ PIS

NEKÁZANKA

PANSKÁ

Kotva

DLOUHÁ

Obecní dům

CELETNÁ

Mucha Museum

NA PŘÍKOPĚ

Ⓜ Můstek

PANSKÁ

Ⓜ Můstek

VÁCLAVSKÉ NÁMĚSTÍ

Wax Museum Prague

JUNGMANNOVO NÁM.

Panna Maria Sněžná

Palác Adria

JUNGMANNOVA

NA FRANTIŠKU

PAŘÍŽSKÁ

KAPROVA

J O S E F O V

17 LISTOPADU

British Council

Tesco

Národní třída

Ⓜ Národní třída

MIKULA...

see Staré Město map for more detail of this area

MÁNESŮV MOST

KARLŮV MOST (CHARLES BRIDGE)

SMETANOVO NÁBŘ.

Café Slavia

sv Voršila

R i v e r   V l t a v a

Střelecký ostrov

MOST LEGIÍ

ACCOMMODATION

Club Habitat	4
Gay Penzion David	7
Hotel Balkán	8
Hotel Hlávkova kolej	5
Hotel Kafka	2
Hotel Legie	6
Libra	3
Hotel sv Salvator	1
Pension City	9

movement stood against, chiefly, ornament for ornament's sake, not that this has in any way dented their renown. The *Evropa*, in particular, has kept many of its sumptuous original fittings intact, though at the time of writing, the whole place was at a particularly low ebb in terms of service and popularity.

① The Wenceslas Monument and the Národní muzeum

A statue of St Wenceslas (sv Václav) has stood at the top of the square since 1680, but the present **Wenceslas Monument**, by the father of Czech sculpture, Josef Václav Myslbek, was only unveiled in 1912. It's worthy and heroic but pretty unexciting, with the Czech patron saint sitting resolutely astride his mighty steed, surrounded by smaller-scale representations of four other Bohemian saints – his grandmother Ludmilla, Procopius, Adalbert and Agnes – added in the 1920s. In 1918, 1948, 1968, and again in 1989, the monument was used as a national political noticeboard, festooned with posters, flags and slogans and, even now, it remains the city's favourite soapbox venue.

A few metres below the statue, on January 16, 1969, a 21-year-old student, **Jan Palach**, set himself alight in protest against the continuing occupation of his country by the Soviets. The spot is marked by a simple memorial to the *obětem komunismu* (the victims of Communism), adorned with flowers and photos of Palach and Jan Zajíc, another student who followed suit a month or so later.

Dominating the top, southern end of Wenceslas Square sits the broad, brooding hulk of the **Národní muzeum** (daily: May–Sept 10am–6pm; Oct–April 9am–5pm; ⓦwww.nm.cz), built by Josef Schulz and deliberately modelled on the great European museums of Paris and Vienna. Along with the Národní divadlo (see p.111), this is one of the great landmarks of the nineteenth-century Czech national revival, sporting a monumental gilt-framed glass cupola, worthy clumps of sculptural decoration and narrative frescoes from Czech history.

The museum is old-fashioned and underfunded, but it's worth taking at least a quick look at the ornate marble entrance hall and the splendid monumental staircase leading to the **Pantheon** of Czech notables at the top. Arranged under the glass-domed hall are 48 busts and statues of distinguished bewhiskered Czech men (plus a couple of token women and Czechophile Slovaks), including the universally adored T.G. Masaryk, the country's founding president, whose statue was removed by the Communists from every other public place. The rest of the museum is dowdy and badly labelled, though those with children might like to head upstairs for the fossils and stuffed animals. The museum's temporary exhibitions, displayed on the ground floor, can be very good indeed, so it's always worth checking to see what's on.

Wilsonova

At the southern end of Wenceslas Square is some of the worst blight that Communist planners inflicted on Prague – above all, the six-lane highway that now separates Nové Město from the residential suburb of Vinohrady to the east and south and effectively cuts off the National Museum from Wenceslas Square. Previously known as Vítězného února (Victorious February) after the Communist coup, the road was renamed **Wilsonova** in honour of US President Woodrow Wilson (a personal friend of the Masaryk family), who effectively gave the country its independence from Austria-Hungary in 1918 by backing the proposal for a separate Czechoslovak state.

The Prague stock exchange building alongside the National Museum, only completed in the 1930s but rendered entirely redundant by the 1948 coup, was another victim of postwar "reconstruction". The architect Karel Prager was given the task of designing a new "socialist" **Federal Assembly** building on the same site, without destroying the old bourse. He opted for a supremely unappealing, bronze-tinted, plate-glass structure, supported by concrete stilts and sitting uncomfortably on top of its diminutive predecessor. Since the break-up of the country, the building has lost its *raison d'être* once more, and now provides a home for, among other things, Radio Free Europe's headquarters.

Next to the old parliament building, the grandiose **Státní opera** (State Opera; ⓦ www.opera.cz), built by the Viennese duo Helmer and Fellner, looks stunted and deeply affronted by the traffic which now tears past its front entrance. It was opened in 1888 as the *Neues Deutsches Theater*, shortly after the Czechs had built their own National Theatre on the waterfront. Always second fiddle to the Stavovské divadlo, though equally ornate inside, it was one of the last great building projects of Prague's once all-powerful German minority. The velvet and gold interior is still as fresh as it was when the Bohemian-born composer Gustav Mahler brought the traffic to a standstill, conducting the premiere of his *Seventh Symphony*.

The last building on this deafening freeway is **Praha hlavní nádraží**, Prague's main railway station. One of the final glories of the dying empire, it was designed by Josef Fanta and officially opened in 1909 as the *Franz-Josefs Bahnhof*. Arriving in the subterranean modern section, it's easy to miss the station's surviving Art Nouveau parts. The original entrance on Wilsonova still exudes imperial confidence, with its wrought-iron canopy and naked figurines clinging to the sides of the towers. You can sit and admire the main foyer from the *Fantová kavárna* (daily 6am–11pm); it's also worth heading north from the foyer to take a peek at the ceramic pillars in the former station restaurant.

Národní and Na příkopě

Národní and **Na příkopě** trace the course of the old moat, which was finally filled in 1760. Their boomerang curve marks the border between Staré Město and Nové Město (strictly speaking, the dividing line runs down the middle of both the streets). Ranged around here is a variety of stylish edifices, including some of the city's most flamboyant Art Nouveau buildings.

Jungmannovo náměstí and around

Heading west from Můstek, before you hit Národní třída proper, you must pass through **Jungmannovo náměstí**, which takes its name from Josef Jungmann (1772–1847), a prolific writer, translator and leading light of the Czech national revival, whose pensive, seated statue was erected here in 1878. This small, ill-proportioned square boasts one of Prague's most endearing architectural curiosities, Emil Králíček and Matěj Blecha's unique **Cubist streetlamp** (and seat) from 1912, which is currently crumbling away beyond the Jungmann statue in the far eastern corner of the square.

On the south side stands the square's most imposing building, the chunky, vigorously sculptured **Palác Adria**. It was designed in the early 1920s by Pavel Janák and Josef Zasche, with sculptural extras by Otto Gutfreund and a central *Seafaring* group by Jan Štursa. Janák was a pioneering figure in the short-lived, prewar Czech Cubist movement; after the war, he and Josef Gočár attempted to create a national style of architecture appropriate for the newly founded republic. The style was dubbed "Rondo-Cubism" – semi-circular motifs are a recurrent theme – though the Palác Adria owes as much to the Italian Renaissance as it does to the new national style.

Originally constructed for the Italian insurance company *Reunione Adriatica di Sicurità* – hence its current name – the building's *pasáž* still retains its wonderful original portal featuring sculptures by Bohumil Kafka, depicting the twelve signs of the zodiac. The theatre in the basement of the building was once a studio for the multimedia **Laterna magika** (Magic Lantern) company. In 1989, it became the underground nerve centre of the Velvet Revolution, when Civic Forum found temporary shelter here shortly after their inaugural meeting on the Sunday following the November 17 demonstration. Against a stage backdrop for Dürenmatt's *Minotaurus*, the Forum thrashed out tactics in the dressing rooms and gave daily press conferences in the auditorium during the crucial fortnight before the Communists relinquished power.

Through the unpromising courtyard back near the Jungmann statue, you can gain access to the church of **Panna Maria Sněžná** (St Mary-of-the-Snows). Once one of the great landmarks of Wenceslas Square, towering over the backs of the old two-storey houses that lined the square, it's now barely visible from any of the surrounding streets. Charles IV, who founded the church, envisaged a vast coronation church on a scale comparable with St Vitus Cathedral, on which work had just begun. Unfortunately, the money ran out shortly after completion of the chancel; the result is curious – a church that is short in length, but equal to the cathedral in height. The hundred-foot-high vaulting – which collapsed on the Franciscans who inherited the half-completed building in the seventeenth century – is awesome, as is the gold and black Baroque altar which touches the ceiling. To get an idea of the intended scale of the finished structure, take a stroll through the **Františkánská zahrada**, to the south of the church, which links up with one of the arcades off Wenceslas Square.

Wax Museum Prague

A short walk down ulice 28 října, which connects Jungmannovo náměstí with Wenceslas Square, is one of Prague's new commercial museums, the **Wax Museum Prague** (Muzeum voskových figurín; daily 9am–8pm; 120Kč; Ⓦwww.waxmuseum.cz), laid out on the ground floor of the Art Nouveau palác Rapid at no. 13. The current entrance fee is steep for most Czechs, yet the museum is aimed primarily at a domestic audience. For anyone familiar with London's Madame Tussaud's, the formula is predictable enough, but unless your grasp of Czech history, past and present, is pretty good, many of the wax tableaux will remain slightly baffling. The most popular section with the locals is the podium of commie stooges ranging from Lenin to the Czechs' home-grown Stalinist, Klement Gottwald, followed by today's generation of Czech politicians dressed in bad suits, sat amidst naff office furniture.

The Masakr – November 1989

On the night of Friday, November 17, 1989, a 50,000-strong, officially sanctioned student demo, organized by the students' union, *SSM* (League of Young Socialists), worked its way down Národní with the intention of reaching Wenceslas Square. Halfway down the street they were confronted by the *bílé přilby* (white helmets) and *červené barety* (red berets) of the hated riot police. For what must have seemed like hours, there was a stalemate as the students sat down and refused to disperse, some of them handing out flowers to the police. Suddenly, without any warning, the police attacked, and what became known as the **masakr** (massacre) began. No one was actually killed, though it wasn't for want of trying by the police. Under the arches of Národní 16, there's a small symbolic bronze relief of eight hands reaching out for help, a permanent shrine in memory of the hundreds who were hospitalized in the violence.

Národní třída

The eastern end of **Národní** is taken up with shops, galleries and clubs, which begin to peter out as you near the river. Three-quarters of the way down on the north side is an eye-catching duo of Art Nouveau buildings designed by Osvald Polívka in 1907–8. The first, at no. 7, was built for the **pojišt'ovna Praha** (Prague Savings Bank), hence the beautiful mosaic lettering above the windows, advertising *život* (life insurance) and *kapital* (loans), as well as help with your *důchod* (pension) and *věno* (dowry). Next door, the slightly more ostentatious **Topičův dům**, built for a publishing house, provides the perfect accompaniment, with a similarly ornate wrought-iron and glass canopy.

At the western end of Národní, overlooking the Vltava, is the gold-crested **Národní divadlo** (National Theatre), proud symbol of the Czech nation. Refused money by the Habsburg state, Czechs of all classes dug deep into their pockets to raise funds for the venture themselves. The foundation stones were laid in 1868 and in June 1881, the theatre opened with a premiere of Smetana's opera *Libuše*. In August of the same year, fire ripped through the building, destroying everything except the outer walls. Within two years the whole thing was rebuilt – even the emperor contributed this time – opening once more to the strains of *Libuše*. The grand portal on the north side of the theatre is embellished with suitably triumphant allegorical figures, and inside, every square inch is taken up with paintings and sculptures by leading artists of the Czech national revival.

Standing behind and in dramatic contrast to the National Theatre is its state-of-the-art extension, the ultra-modern glass box of the **Nová scéna** (New Stage), designed by Karel Prager, the leading architect of the communist era, and completed in 1983. It's one of those buildings most Praguers love to hate – it has been memorably described as looking like "frozen piss" – though compared to much of Prague's communist-era architecture, it's not that bad.

The **Café Slavia**, opposite the theatre, has been a favourite haunt of the city's writers, dissidents and artists (and, inevitably, actors) since the days of the First Republic. The Czech avant-garde movement, *Devětsil*, led by Karel Teige, used to hold its meetings here in the 1920s; the meetings are recorded for posterity by another of its members, the Nobel prize-winner Jaroslav Seifert, in his *Slavia Poems*. The café has been carelessly modernized since those Arcadian days, but it still has a great riverside view and Manet's famous *Absinthe Drinker* canvas on the wall.

Na příkopě

Heading northeast from Můstek, at the bottom end of Wenceslas Square, you can join the crush of bodies ambling down **Na příkopě** (literally "on the moat"). The big multinational franchises have staked their claim on this stretch of Prague, with the **Pasáž Myslbek**, fronted by Marks & Spencer, one of the few contemporary works of architecture in central Prague. The street has, of course, been an architectural showcase for more than a century and was once lined on both sides with grandiose Habsburg-era buildings; the Art Nouveau **U Dörflerů**, at no. 7, is one of the few survivors along this stretch, its gilded floral curlicues gleaming in the midday sun.

There are another couple of interesting buildings at nos. 18 and 20, designed by Polívka over a twenty-year period for the **Zemská banka** and connected by a kind of Bridge of Sighs suspended over Nekázanka. The style veers between 1890s neo-Renaissance and later Art Nouveau elements, such as Jan Preisler's gilded mosaics and Ladislav Šaloun's attic sculptures. It's worth nipping upstairs to the main banking hall of what is now the **Živnostenka banka**, at no. 20, to appreciate the financial might of Czech capital in the last decades of the Austro-Hungarian Empire. Yet more financial institutions, this time from the dour 1930s, line the far end of Na příkopě, as it opens up into náměstí Republiky, including the palatial Národní banka (National Bank), which underwent a controversial and very expensive makeover in the 1990s.

Mucha Museum

Dedicated to **Alfons Mucha** (1860–1939), probably the most famous of all Czech artists in the West, the **Mucha Museum** (daily 10am–6pm; 120Kč; ⓦwww.mucha.cz), housed in the Kaunicky palác on Panská, southwest of Senovážné náměstí, has proved very popular indeed. Mucha made his name in fin-de-siècle Paris, where he shot to fame after designing the Art Nouveau poster *Gismonda* for the actress Sarah Bernhardt. "Le Style Mucha" became all the rage, but the artist himself came to despise this "commercial" period of his work, and in 1910, Mucha moved back to his homeland and threw himself into the national cause, designing patriotic stamps, banknotes and posters for the new republic.

The whole of Mucha's career is covered in the permanent exhibition, and there's a good selection of informal photos, taken by the artist himself, of his models, and Paul Gauguin (with whom he shared a studio) playing the harmonium with his trousers down. The only work not represented here is his massive *Slav Epic*, but the excellent video (in English) covers the decade of his life he devoted to this cycle of nationalist paintings. In the end, Mucha paid for his Czech nationalism with his life; dragged in for questioning by the Gestapo after the 1939 Nazi invasion, he died shortly after being released.

Náměstí Republiky

The oldest structure on **náměstí Republiky** is the **Prašná brána** (Powder Tower; April–Oct daily 10am–6pm), one of the eight medieval gate-towers that once guarded Staré Město. The present tower was begun by Vladislav Jagiello in 1475, shortly after he had moved into the royal court, which was situated next door at the time. A small historical exhibition inside traces the tower's architectural metamorphosis up to its present remodelling by the nineteenth-century restorer Josef Mocker. Most people, though, ignore the displays and climb straight up for the modest view from the top.

Attached to the tower, and built on the ruins of the old royal court, the **Obecní dům** (Municipal House) is by far the city's most exciting Art Nouveau building, one of the few places that still manages to conjure up the atmosphere of Prague's turn-of-the-twentieth-century café society. Conceived as a cultural centre for the Czech community, it's probably the finest architectural achievement of the Czech national revival. Designed by Osvald Polívka and Antonín Balšánek, it is extravagantly decorated inside and out with the help of almost every artist connected with the Czech Secession. From the lifts to the cloakrooms, just about all the furnishings remain as they were when the building was completed in 1911, and every square inch of the interior and exterior has recently been lovingly renovated.

The simplest way of soaking up the interior – peppered with mosaics and pendulous brass chandeliers – is to have a drink in the cavernous café, or a meal in the equally spacious *Francouská restaurace* or the *Plzeňská restaurace* in the basement. For a more detailed inspection of the building's spectacular interior (which includes paintings by Alfons Mucha, Jan Preisler and Max Švabinský, among others), you can sign up for a **guided tour** (150Kč); tickets are available from the new information and ticket centre (daily 10am–6pm; ⓦwww.obecni-dum.cz) on the ground floor, beyond the main foyer. Several rooms on the second floor are given over to temporary art exhibitions, while the building's **Smetanova síň**, Prague's largest concert hall, stages numerous concerts, including the opening salvo of the *Pražské jaro* (Prague Spring Festival) – traditionally a rendition of Smetana's *Má vlast* (My Country) – which takes place in the presence of the president.

Around Karlovo náměstí

The streets south of Národní and Wenceslas Square still run along the medieval lines of Charles IV's town plan, though they're now lined with grand nineteenth- and twentieth-century buildings. Of the many roads which head down towards Karlovo náměstí, **Vodičkova** is probably the most impressive, running southwest for half a kilometre from Wenceslas Square. You can catch several trams (#3, #14 or #24) along this route, though there is a handful of buildings worth checking out on the way. The first, **U Nováků**, is impossible to miss, thanks to Jan Preisler's mosaic of bucolic frolicking (its actual subject, *Trade and Industry*, is confined to the edges of the picture) and Polívka's curvilinear window frames and delicate, ivy-like ironwork – look out for the frog-prince holding up a window sill. Originally built for the Novák department store in the early 1900s, for the last sixty years it has been a cabaret hall, restaurant and café all rolled into one, and the original fittings have long since been destroyed.

Halfway down the street stands the imposing neo-Renaissance **Minerva** girls' school, covered in bright-red sgraffito. Founded in 1866, it was the first such institution in Prague and later became notorious for the antics of its pupils, the "Minervans" – most famously Milena Jesenská, the epistolary lover of Franz Kafka – who shocked bourgeois Czech society with their experimentations with fashion, drugs and sexual freedom.

Karlovo náměstí

Vodičkova eventually curves left into Prague's biggest square, **Karlovo náměstí**, created by Charles IV as Nové Město's cattle market (Dobytčí trh). Unfortunately, its once impressive proportions are no longer so easy to appreciate, obscured by a tree-planted public garden and cut in two by the busy thoroughfare of Ječná. The Gothic **Novoměstská radnice** (New Town Hall; April–Sept daily 10am–5.30pm), at the northern end of the square, sports three steep, triangular gables embellished with intricate blind tracery. It was built, like the one on Staroměstské náměstí, during the reign of King John of Luxembourg, though it has survived rather better, and is now one of the finest Gothic buildings in the city. It was here that Prague's **first defenestration** took place on July 30, 1419, when the radical Hussite preacher Jan Želivský and his penniless religious followers stormed the building, mobbed the councillors and burghers, and threw twelve or thirteen of them out of the town hall windows onto the pikes of the Hussite mob below. Václav IV, on hearing the news, suffered a stroke and died just two weeks later. So began the long and bloody Hussite Wars. Nowadays, you can visit the site of the defenestration, and climb to the top of the **tower** (added shortly afterwards) for a view over central Prague; the town hall also puts on temporary art exhibitions.

The crypt of sv Cyril and Metoděj

West off Karlovo náměstí, down Resslova, the noisy extension of Ječná, is the Orthodox cathedral of **sv Cyril and Metoděj** (Tues–Sun 10am–4pm), originally constructed for the Roman Catholics by Bayer and Dientzenhofer in the eighteenth century, but since the 1930s the main base of the Orthodox church

The assassination of Reinhard Heydrich

The assassination of Reinhard Heydrich in 1942 was the only attempt the Allies ever made on the life of a leading Nazi. It's an incident which the Allies have always billed as a great success in the otherwise rather dismal seven-year history of the Czech resistance. But, as with all acts of brave resistance during the war, there was a price to be paid. Given that the reprisals meted out on the Czech population were entirely predictable, it remains a controversial, if not suicidal, decision to have made.

The target, **Reinhard Tristan Eugen Heydrich**, was a talented and upwardly mobile anti-Semite (despite rumours that he was partly Jewish himself), a great organizer and a skilful concert violinist. He was a late recruit to the Nazi Party, signing up in 1931 after his dismissal from the German Navy for dishonourable conduct towards a woman. However, he swiftly rose through the ranks of the SS to become second in command to Himmler and, in the autumn of 1941, *Reichsprotektor* of the puppet state of *Böhmen und Mähren* – effectively, the most powerful man in the Czech Lands. Although his rule began with brutality, it soon settled into the tried-and-tested policy which Heydrich liked to call *Peitsche und Zucker* (literally, "whip and sugar").

On the morning of May 27, 1942, as Heydrich was being driven by his personal bodyguard, *Oberscharführer* Klein, in his open-top Mercedes from his house north of Prague to his office in Hradčany, three Czechoslovak agents (parachuted in from England) were taking up positions in the northern suburb of Libeň. The first agent, Valčík, gave the signal as the car pulled into Kirchmayer Boulevard (now V Holešovičkách). Another agent, a Slovak called Gabčík, pulled out a gun and tried to shoot. The gun jammed, at which Heydrich, rather than driving out of the situation, ordered Klein to stop the car and attempted to shoot back. At this point, the third agent, Kubiš, threw a bomb at the car. The blast injured Kubiš and Heydrich, who immediately leapt out and began firing at Kubiš. Kubiš, with blood pouring down his face, jumped on his bicycle and fled downhill. Gabčík meanwhile pulled out a second gun and exchanged shots with Heydrich, until the latter collapsed from his wounds. Gabčík fled into a butcher's, shot Klein – who was in hot pursuit – in the legs and escaped down the backstreets.

Meanwhile back at the Mercedes, a baker's van was flagged down by a passer-by, but the driver refused to get involved. Eventually, a small truck carrying floor polish was commandeered and Heydrich was taken to the Bulovka hospital. Heydrich died eight days later from the fragments of horsehair and wire from the car seat which had infected his spleen, and was given full Nazi honours at his Prague funeral; the cortège passed down Wenceslas Square, in front of a crowd of thousands. As the home resistance had forewarned, revenge was quick to follow. The day after Heydrich's funeral service in Berlin, the village of **Lidice** (see p.163) was burnt to the ground and its male inhabitants murdered; two weeks later, the men and women of the village of **Ležáky** (see p.319) suffered a similar fate.

The plan to assassinate Heydrich had been formulated in the early months of 1942 by the Czechoslovak government-in-exile in London, without consultation with the Czech Communist leadership in Moscow, and despite fierce opposition from the resistance within Czechoslovakia. Since it was clear that the reprisals would be horrific, the only logical explanation for the plan is that this was precisely the aim of the government-in-exile's operation – to forge a solid wedge of resentment between the Germans and Czechs. In this respect, if in no other, the operation was ultimately successful.

in the Czech Republic. Amid all the traffic, it's extremely difficult to imagine the scene here on June 18, 1942, when seven of the Czechoslovak secret agents involved in the most dramatic assassination of World War II (see box on p.114) were besieged in the church by over 700 members of the Waffen SS. Acting on a tip-off by one of the Czech resistance who turned himself in, the Nazis surrounded the building just after 4am and fought a pitched battle for over six hours, trying explosives, flooding and any other method they could think of to drive the men out of their stronghold in the crypt. Eventually, all seven agents committed suicide rather than give themselves up. There's a plaque at street level on the south wall commemorating those who died, and an exhibition on the whole affair in the crypt itself, which has been left pretty much as it was; the entrance is underneath the church steps on Na Zderaze.

The islands and the embankments

Magnificent turn-of-the-twentieth-century mansions line the Vltava's right bank, almost without interruption, for some two kilometres from the Charles Bridge south to the rocky outcrop of Vyšehrad. It's a long walk, even just along the length of **Masarykovo** and **Rašínovo nábřeží**, though there's no need to do the whole lot in one go; you can hop on a tram (#17 or #21) at various points, drop down from the embankments to the waterfront itself, or escape to one of the two islands connected to them, Střelecký ostrov and Slovanský ostrov, better known as Žofín.

The islands

Access to either of the two islands in the central section of the Vltava is from close to the Národní divadlo. The first, **Střelecký ostrov**, or Shooters' Island, is where the army held their shooting practice, on and off, from the fifteenth until the nineteenth century. Closer to the left bank and accessible via the most Legií (Legion's Bridge), it became a favourite spot for a Sunday promenade and is still popular, especially in summer (see p.135). The first *Sokol* sports festival took place here in 1882, while the first May Day demonstrations were held here in 1890.

The second island, **Slovanský ostrov**, more commonly known as **Žofín** (after the island's concert hall, itself named after Sophie, the mother of the Emperor Franz-Josef I), came about as a result of the natural silting of the river in the eighteenth century. By the late nineteenth century it had become one of the city's foremost pleasure gardens, where, as the composer Berlioz remarked, "bad musicians shamelessly make abominable music in the open air and immodest young males and females indulge in brazen dancing, while idlers and wasters . . . lounge about smoking foul tobacco and drinking beer." On a good day, things seem pretty much unchanged from those heady times; concerts, balls, and other social gatherings take place here, and there are rowing boats for hire from May to September.

Along the embankment

Most of the buildings along the waterfront are private apartments and therefore inaccessible. One exception to this, and architecturally atypical of this part of Prague, is the striking white functionalist mass of the **Mánes** art gallery (Tues–Sun 10am–6pm), halfway down Masarykovo nábřeží. Designed in open-plan style by Otakar Novotný in 1930, it spans the narrow channel between Slovanský ostrov and the waterfront, close to the onion-domed Šítek water-tower. The gallery is named after Josef Mánes, a traditional nineteenth-century landscape painter and Czech nationalist, and houses consistently interesting exhibitions, as well as two cafés and an upstairs restaurant suspended above the channel. Clearly visible from Mánes is the **Tančící dům** (Dancing House), also known as "Fred and Ginger" after the shape of the building's two towers, which look vaguely like a couple ballroom dancing. It was designed in the 1990s by the Canadian-born Frank O. Gehry and the Yugoslav-born Vlado Milunič, and stands next door to the block of flats where Havel lived before becoming president (when he wasn't in prison).

Further along the embankment, at **Palackého náměstí**, the buildings retreat for a moment to reveal an Art Nouveau sculpture to rival Šaloun's monument in Staroměstské náměstí (see p.92): the **Monument to František Palacký**, the great nineteenth-century Czech historian, politician and nationalist, by Stanislav Sucharda. Like the Hus Monument, which was unveiled three years later, this mammoth project – fifteen years in the making – had missed its moment by the time it was completed in 1912, and found universal disfavour. The critics have mellowed over the years, and nowadays it's appreciated for what it is – an energetic and inspirational piece of work. Ethereal bronze bodies, representing the world of the imagination, shoot out at all angles, contrasting sharply with the plain stone mass of the plinth and, below, the giant seated figure of Palacký himself, representing the real world.

Vyšehradská and Ke Karlovu

Behind Palackého náměstí, off **Vyšehradská**, the intertwined concrete spires of the **Emauzy** monastery are an unusual modern addition to the Prague skyline. The monastery was one of the few important historical buildings to be damaged in the last war, in this case by a stray Anglo-American bomb. The cloisters contain some extremely valuable Gothic frescoes, but since the return of the monks from their forty-year exile, access has become unpredictable.

Heading south from here, Vyšehradská descends to a junction, where you'll find the entrance to the university's **Botanická zahrada** (Botanic Gardens; daily 10am–5pm), laid out in 1897 on a series of terraces up the other side of the hill. Though far from spectacular, the garden is one of the few patches of green in this part of town, and the 1930s greenhouses (*skleníky*) have recently been restored to their former glory.

On the far side of the gardens, Apolinářská runs along the south wall and past a grimly Gothic red-brick maternity hospital with steep, stepped gables, before joining up with **Ke Karlovu**. Head north up here and the first street off to the right is Na bojišti, usually packed with tour coaches. The reason for this is **U kalicha** (ⓦwww.ukalicha.cz), on the right, the pub immortalized in the opening passages of the consistently popular comic novel *The Good Soldier Švejk*, by Jaroslav Hašek. In the story, on the eve of the Great War, Švejk (*Schweik* to the Germans) walks into *U kalicha*, where a plain-clothes officer of the Austrian constabulary is sitting drinking and, after a brief conversation, finds himself arrested in connection with the assassination of Archduke Ferdinand. Whatever the pub may have been like in Hašek's day (and even then, it wasn't his local), it's now unashamedly orientated towards reaping in the Euros, and about the only authentic thing you'll find inside – albeit at a price – is the beer.

Further north along Ke Karlovu, set back from the road behind wrought-iron gates, is a more rewarding place of pilgrimage, the russet-coloured **Vila Amerika** (Tues–Sun 10am–5pm), now a museum devoted to the Czech composer **Antonín Dvořák** (1841–1904), who lived for a time on nearby Žitná. Even if you've no interest in Dvořák, the house itself is a delight, built as a Baroque summer palace around 1720 and one of Kilian Ignaz Dientzenhofer's most successful secular works. Dvořák, easily the most famous of all Czech composers, for many years had to play second fiddle to Smetana in the orchestra at the Národní divadlo, where Smetana was the conductor. In his forties, Dvořák received an honorary degree from Cambridge before leaving for the "New World", and his gown is one of the very few items of memorabilia to have found its way into the museum's collection, along with the programme of a concert given at London's Guildhall in 1891. However, the tasteful period rooms echoing with the composer's music and the tiny garden dotted with Baroque sculptures compensate for what the display cabinets may lack.

Vyšehrad

At the southern tip of Nové Město, around 3km south of the city centre, the rocky red-brick fortress of **VYŠEHRAD** (Ⓦ www.praha-vysehrad.cz) – literally "High Castle" – has more myths attached to it per square inch than any other place in Bohemia. According to Czech legend, this is the place where the Slav tribes first settled in Prague, where the "wise and tireless chieftain" Krok built a castle, and whence his youngest daughter Libuše went on to found Praha itself (see p.55). Alas, the archeological evidence doesn't bear this claim out, but it's clear that Vratislav II (1061–92), the first Bohemian ruler to bear the title "king", built a royal palace here, to get away from his younger brother who was lording it in the Hrad. Within half a century the royals had moved back to Hradčany and into a new palace, and from then on Vyšehrad began to lose its political significance.

Czech Cubism in Vyšehrad

Even if you harbour only a passing interest in modern architecture, it's worth seeking out the cluster of **Cubist villas** below the fortress in Vyšehrad. Whereas Czech Art Nouveau was heavily influenced by the Viennese Secession, it was Paris rather than the imperial capital that provided the stimulus for the short-lived but extremely productive Czech Cubist movement. In 1911, the *Skupina výtvarných umělců* or *SVU* (Group of Fine Artists) was founded in Prague and quickly became the movement's organizing force. **Pavel Janák** was the *SVU*'s chief theorist, **Josef Gočár** its most illustrious exponent, but **Josef Chochol** was the most successful practitioner of the style in Prague.

Cubism is associated mostly with painting, and the unique contribution of its Czech offshoot was to apply the theory to furniture (some of which is now on permanent display at the Dům U černé Matky boží, see p.94) and **architecture**. In Vyšehrad alone, Chochol completed three buildings, close to one another below the fortress, using prismatic shapes and angular lines to produce the sharp geometric contrasts of light and dark shadows characteristic of Cubist painting.

The most impressive example of Czech Cubist architecture, brilliantly exploiting its angular location, is Chochol's apartment block **nájemný obytný dům** at Neklanova 30; begun in 1913 for František Hodek, and now housing a restaurant on the ground floor. Further along Neklanova, at no. 2, there's Antonín Belada's Cubist street facade, and around the corner is the largest project of the lot – Chochol's **Kovařovicova vila**, which backs onto Libušina. From the front, on Rašínovo nábřeží, it's possible to appreciate the clever, slightly askew layout of the garden, designed right down to its zigzag garden railings. Further along the embankment is Chochol's largest commission, the **rodinný trojdům**, a large building complex with a heavy mansard roof, a central "Baroque" gable with a pedimental frieze, and room enough for three families.

Keen to associate himself with the early Přemyslids, Emperor Charles IV had a system of walls built to link Vyšehrad to the newly founded Nové Město, and decreed that the *králová cesta* (coronation route) begin from here. These fortifications were destroyed by the Hussites in 1420, but over the next two hundred years the hill was settled again, until the Habsburgs turfed everyone out in the mid-seventeenth century and rebuilt the place as a fortified barracks, only to tear it down in 1866 to create a public park. By the time the Czech national revival movement became interested in Vyšehrad, only the red-brick fortifications were left as a reminder of its former strategic importance; they rediscovered its history and its legends, and gradually transformed it into a symbol of Czech nationhood. Today, Vyšehrad is a perfect place from which to escape the human congestion of the city and watch the evening sun set behind the Hrad.

The fortress

There are several **approaches to the fortress**: if you've come by tram #3, #7, #16, #17 or #21, which trundle along the waterfront to Výtoň stop, you can either wind your way up Vratislavova and enter through the Cihelná brána, or take the steep stairway from Rašínovo nábřeží that leads up through the trees to a small side entrance in the west wall. Alternatively, from Vyšehrad metro station, walk west past the ugly Kongresové centrum, and enter through the twin gateways, between which there's an **information centre** (daily: April–Oct 9.30am–6pm; Nov–March 9.30am–5pm).

However you come, head for the blackened sandstone church of **sv Petr and Pavel**, rebuilt in the 1880s by Josef Mocker in neo-Gothic style (with further, even more ruthless additions in the 1900s) on the site of an eleventh-century basilica. The twin open-work spires are now the fortress's most familiar landmark, and if luck is on your side, you should be able to view the church's polychrome interior, though opening times can be a bit erratic (March–Nov Tues–Fri 9am–noon & 1–5pm, Sat 9am–noon & Sun 11am–3pm; Dec–Feb Wed–Sun 11am–3pm).

Vyšehradský hřbitov (Vyšehrad Cemetery)

One of the first initiatives of the national revival movement was to establish the **Vyšehradský hřbitov** (daily: May–Sept 8am–7pm; March, April & Oct 8am–6pm; Nov–Feb 9am–4pm), which spreads out to the north and east of the church. It's a measure of the part that artists and intellectuals played in the foundation of the nation, and the regard in which they are still held, that the most prestigious graveyard in the city is given over to them: no soldiers, no politicians, not even the Communists managed to muscle their way in here (except on artistic merit).

To the uninitiated only a handful of figures are well-known, but for the Czechs the place is alive with great names (there is a useful plan of the most notable graves at the entrance nearest the church). Ladislav Šaloun's grave for **Dvořák**, situated under the arches, is one of the more showy ones, with a mosaic inscription, studded with gold stones, glistening behind wrought-iron railings. **Smetana**, who died twenty years earlier, is buried in comparatively modest surroundings near the Slavín monument. The Prague Spring Festival begins on the anniversary of his death (May 12) with a procession from his grave to the Obecní dům.

The grave of the Romantic poet **Karel Hynek Mácha** was the assembly point for the 50,000-strong demonstration on November 17, 1989, which triggered the Velvet Revolution. This was organized to commemorate the 50th anniversary of the Nazi closure of all Czech higher education institutions in 1939.

The focus of the cemetery, though, is the **Slavín monument**, a bulky stele, covered in commemorative plaques and topped by a sarcophagus and a statue representing Genius. It's the communal resting place of over fifty Czech artists, including the painter Alfons Mucha, the sculptors Josef Václav Myslbek and Ladislav Šaloun, the architect Josef Gočár and the opera singer Ema Destinová (see p.184).

The rest of the fortress

The next best thing to do after a stroll around the cemetery is to head off and explore the **Kasematy** or dungeons (daily: April–Oct 9.30am–6pm; Nov–March 9.30am–5pm), which you enter via the Cihelná brána. After a short guided tour of a section of the underground passageways underneath the ramparts, you enter a vast storage hall, which shelters several of the original statues from the Charles Bridge, and, when the lights are switched off, reveals a camera obscura image of a tree.

The rest of the deserted fortress makes for a pleasant afternoon stroll; you can walk almost the entire length of the ramparts, which give some superb views out across the city. The heavily restored **rotunda of sv Martin** – one of a number of Romanesque rotundas scattered across Prague – is the sole survivor of the medieval fortress, built by Vratislav II in the eleventh century; it's only open for services. Time is probably better spent lounging on the grass to the south of the church, where you'll come across the gargantuan legendary statues by Myslbek that used to grace the city's Palackého most.

The suburbs

By the end of his reign in 1378, Charles IV had laid out his city on such a grand scale that it wasn't until the industrial revolution hit Bohemia in the mid-nineteenth century that the first **suburbs** began to sprout up around its boundaries. A few were rigidly planned, with public parks and grid street plans; most grew with less grace, trailing their tenements across the hills and swallowing up existing villages on the way. The majority still retain a distinctive individual identity, and are free from the crowds in the centre, all of which makes them worth checking out on even a short visit to the city.

Vinohrady

Southeast of Nové Město is the predominantly late-nineteenth-century suburb of **VINOHRADY**, Prague's most resolutely bourgeois suburb up until World War II. In one of its two main squares, **náměstí Jiřího z Poděbrad** (metro Jiřího z Poděbrad), stands Prague's most celebrated modern church, **Nejsvětější Srdce Páně** (Most Sacred Heart of Our Lord), built in 1928 by Josip Plečník, the Slovene architect responsible for much of the remodelling of the Hrad. It's a marvellously eclectic and individualistic work, employing a sophisticated potpourri of architectural styles: a Neoclassical pediment and a great slab of a tower with a giant transparent face in imitation of a Gothic rose window. Plečník also had a sharp eye for detail; look out for the little gold crosses set into the brickwork both inside and out, and for the celestial orbs of light suspended above the heads of the congregation.

Žižkov

Though they share much the same architectural heritage, **ŽIŽKOV**, unlike Vinohrady, is a traditionally working-class area, and was a Communist Party stronghold even before the war, earning it the nickname "Red Žižkov". Its peeling turn-of-the-twentieth-century tenements are home to a large proportion of Prague's Romany community, and it boasts more pubs per head than any other district in Prague. The main reason for venturing into Žižkov is to visit the ancient landmark of Žižkov hill, the city's main Olšany cemeteries, at the eastern end of Vyšehradská, and the aforementioned pubs.

Žižkov TV tower

At over 100m in height, the **Žižkov TV tower** (Televizní vysílač; daily 10am–11pm; 120Kč; ⦾ www.tower.cz) is the tallest building in Prague – and the most unpopular. Close up, it's an intimidating futuristic piece of architecture, made all the more disturbing by the addition of several statues of giant babies crawling up the sides, courtesy of artist David Černý. Begun in the 1970s in a desperate bid to jam West German television transmission, the tower only become fully operational in the 1990s. In the course of its construction, however, the Communists saw fit to demolish part of a nearby Jewish cemetery, that had served the community between 1787 and 1891; a small section survives to the northwest of the tower. From the fifth-floor café or the viewing platform on the eighth floor, you can enjoy a spectacular view across Prague. To get to the tower, take the metro to Jiřího z Poděbrad and walk northeast a couple of blocks – it's difficult to miss.

The cemeteries

Approaching from the west, the first and the largest of the **Olšanské hřbitovy** (Olšany cemeteries; metro Flora) – each of which is bigger than the entire Jewish quarter – was originally created for the victims of the great plague epidemic of 1680. The perimeter walls are lined with glass cabinets, stacked like shoeboxes, containing funereal urns and mementoes, while the graves themselves are a mixed bag of artistic achievement, reflecting funereal fashions of the day as much as the character of the deceased. The cemetery's two most famous incumbents are an ill-fitting couple: Klement Gottwald, the country's first Communist president, whose ashes were removed from the mausoleum on Žižkov hill after 1989 and reinterred here; and the martyr Jan Palach, the philosophy student who set himself alight in protest at the continuing Soviet occupation in January 1969.

Immediately east of Olšany is the **Nový židovský hřbitov** (New Jewish Cemetery; daily except Sat: April–Aug 8am–5pm; Sept–March 8am–4pm), founded in the 1890s when the one by the Žižkov TV tower was full. It's a melancholy spot, particularly in the east of the cemetery, where large, empty allotments wait in vain to be filled by the generation who perished in the Holocaust. In fact, the community is now so small that it's unlikely the graveyard will ever be full. Most people come here to visit **Franz Kafka**'s grave, 400m east along the south wall and signposted from the entrance (for more on Kafka, see p.102). He is buried, along with his mother and father (both of whom outlived him), beneath a plain headstone; the plaque below commemorates his three sisters who died in the camps.

Žižkov hill

Žižkov hill (also known as Vítkov) is the thin green wedge of land that separates Žižkov from Karlín, a grid-plan industrial district to the north. From its westernmost point, which juts out almost to the edge of Nové Město, is probably the definitive panoramic view over the city centre. It was here, on July 14, 1420, that the Hussites enjoyed their first and finest victory at the **Battle of Vítkov**, under the inspired leadership of the one-eyed general, Jan Žižka (hence the name of the district). Ludicrously outnumbered by more than ten to one, Žižka and his fanatically motivated troops thoroughly trounced Emperor Sigismund and his papal forces.

Despite its overblown totalitarian aesthetics, the giant concrete **Žižkov monument** which graces the crest of the hill was actually built between the wars as a memorial to the Czechoslovak Legion who fought against the Habsburgs – the gargantuan equestrian statue of the mace-wielding Žižka, which fronts the monument, is reputedly the world's largest. The building was later used by the Nazis as an arsenal, and eventually became a Communist hacks' mausoleum. In 1990, however, the bodies were cremated and quietly reinterred in Olšany, and at present there's an ongoing legal battle over what should happen next with the monument.

To get to the monument, take the metro to Florenc, walk under the railway lines and then up the steep lane U památníku. On the right as you climb the hill is the **Armádní muzeum** (Army Museum; April–Oct Tues–Sun 10am–6pm; Nov–April Mon–Fri 8.30am–5pm; Ⓦ www.militarymuseum.cz), guarded by a handful of unmanned tanks, howitzers and armoured vehicles. Before 1989, this museum was a glorification of the Warsaw Pact, pure and simple; its recent overhaul has produced a much more evenly balanced account of both world wars, particularly in its treatment of the previously controversial subjects of the Czechoslovak Legion, the Heydrich assassination (see p.114) and the Prague Uprising.

Holešovice and Bubeneč

The late-nineteenth-century districts of **HOLEŠOVICE** and **BUBENEČ**, tucked into a huge U-bend in the Vltava, have little in the way of magnificent architecture, but they make up for it with two sizeable areas of green: to the south, **Letná**, where Prague's largest gatherings occur; and to the north, the **Stromovka park**, bordering the Výstaviště funfair and international trade fair grounds. In addition, Holešovice boasts a couple of excellent museums: the city's **Národní technické muzeum**, which shows off the Czechs' past scientific and industrial achievements, and the **Veletržní palác**, Prague's impressive modern art museum.

Chotkovy sady and the Bílkova vila

This first sight is, strictly speaking, a part of the Hradčany that lies to the northeast of the castle, but it makes a convenient starting point for this account. The easiest way to this part of town is to take tram #22 one stop from Malostranská metro to the Královský letohrádek stop, to the east of which lies the **Chotkovy sady**, Prague's first public park, founded in 1833. You can enjoy an unrivalled view of the bridges and islands of the Vltava from its south wall, or check out the elaborate, grotto-like memorial to the nineteenth-century Romantic poet Julius Zeyer, from whose blackened rocks emerge life-sized, marble characters from his works.

Across the road from the park and hidden behind its overgrown garden, the **Bílkova vila** (mid-May to mid-Oct Tues–Sun 10am–6pm; mid-Oct to mid-May Sat & Sun 10am–5pm), at Mieckiewiczova 1, honours one of the most unusual Czech sculptors, František Bílek (1872–1941). Born in Chýnov (see p.179), in a part of South Bohemia steeped in Hussite tradition, Bílek lived a monkish life, spending years in spiritual contemplation, reading the works of Hus and other Czech reformers. The villa was built in 1911 to Bílek's own design, intended as both a "cathedral of art" and the family home. At first sight, it appears a strangely mute red-brick building, out of keeping with the extravagant Symbolist style of Bílek's sculptures: from the outside, only the front porch, supported by giant sheaves of corn, and the sculptural group, the fleeing Comenius and his followers, in the garden, give a clue as to what lies within.

Inside, the brickwork gives way to bare stone walls lined with Bílek's religious sculptures, giving the impression that you've walked into a chapel rather than an artist's studio: "a workshop and temple", in Bílek's own words. In addition to his sculptural and relief work in wood and stone, often wildly expressive and anguished, there are also ceramics, graphics and a few mementoes of Bílek's life. His work is little known outside his native country, but his contemporary admirers included Franz Kafka, Julius Zeyer and Otakar Březina, whose poems and novels provided the inspiration for much of Bílek's art. Bílek's living quarters have also now been restored and opened to the public, with much of the original wooden furniture, designed and carved by Bílek himself, still in place: check out the dressing table for his wife, shaped like some giant church lectern, and the wardrobe decorated with a border of hearts, a penis, a nose, an ear and an eye, plus the sun, stars and moon.

Letná

Cross over the bridge at the eastern end of the Chotkovy sady and you'll find yourself on the flat green expanse of the **Letná plain**, traditional assembly point for invading and besieging armies. It was laid out as a public park in the mid-nineteenth century, but its main post-1948 function was as the site of the May Day parades. For these, thousands of citizens were dragooned into marching past the south side of the city's main football ground, the Sparta stadium, where the old Communist cronies would take the salute from a giant red podium. The post-Communist Party parades still take place here, but are a shadow of their former selves.

The Stalin monument

Letná's – indeed Prague's – most famous monument is one which no longer exists. The **Stalin monument**, the largest in the world, was once visible from almost every part of the city: a thirty-metre-high granite sculpture portraying a procession of people being led to communism by the Pied Piper figure of Stalin, popularly dubbed *tlačenice* (the crush) because of its resemblance to a communist-era bread queue. Designed by Jiří Štursa and Otakar Švec, it took 600 workers 500 days to erect the 14,200-ton monster. Švec, the sculptor, committed suicide shortly before it was unveiled, as his wife had done three years previously, leaving all his money to a school for blind children, since they at least would not have to see his creation. It was eventually revealed to the cheering masses on May 1, 1955 – the first and last popular celebration to take place at the monument. Within a year, Khrushchev had denounced his predecessor and, after pressure from Moscow, the monument was blown to smithereens by a series of explosions spread over a fortnight in 1962. All that remains above ground is the statue's vast concrete platform and steps, on the southern edge of the Letná plain, now graced with David Černý's symbolic giant red **metronome** (which is lit up at night); it's also a favourite spot for skateboarders and another good viewpoint.

Národní technické muzeum (National Technical Museum)

Despite its dull title, the **Národní technické muzeum** (Tues–Sun 9am–5pm; ⓦ www.ntm.cz) on Kostelní is a surprisingly interesting museum. Its showpiece hanger-like main hall contains an impressive gallery of motorbikes, Czech and foreign, and a wonderful collection of old planes, trains and automobiles, from Czechoslovakia's industrial heyday between the wars, when the country's Škoda cars and Tatra soft-top stretch limos were really something to brag about. The oldest car in the collection is Laurin & Klement's 1898 *Präsident*, more of a motorized carriage than a car; the museum also boasts the world's oldest Bugatti. Upstairs, there are interactive displays (a rarity in a Czech museum) tracing the development of early photography, and a collection of some of Kepler's and Tycho Brahe's astrological instruments. Below ground guided tours are offered of a mock-up of a coal mine (11am, 1pm & 3pm).

Veletržní palác

Situated at the corner of Dukelských hrdinů and Veletržní, some distance from the nearest metro station, the **Veletržní palác** (Tues–Sun 10am–6pm; 180Kč; ⓦ www.ngprague.cz), or Trade Fair Palace, gets nothing like the number of visitors it should. For not only does the building house the Národní galerie's excellent nineteenth- and twentieth-century Czech and international art collection, it is also an architectural sight in itself. A seven-storey building constructed in 1928 by Oldřich Tyl and Josef Fuchs, it is Prague's ultimate functionalist masterpiece, not so much from the outside, but inside, where its gleaming white vastness is suitably awesome.

The main exhibition hall is used for its original purpose, trade fairs, with the Národní galerie confined to the north wing. Nevertheless, the gallery is both big and bewildering, and virtually impossible to view in its entirety – you can even pay a reduced fee to visit just part of the collection: 130Kč for two floors or 80Kč for one floor. Special exhibitions occupy the ground, first and fifth floors, while the permanent collection occupies the second, third and fourth floors – the popular French art collection can be found on the third floor. The account below takes a chronological approach, beginning on the fourth floor, with nineteenth-century art.

To reach the Veletržní palác by public transport, catch tram #5 from náměstí Republiky, tram #12 from Malostranská metro, tram #17 from Staroměstská metro, or tram #5, #12 or #17 from Nádraží Holešovice to Veletržní stop. If you need a bite to eat, the pub, *U houbaře* (*The Mushroom*), opposite the museum at Dukelských hrdinů 30, is a good bet.

Nineteenth-century art

The **nineteenth-century art** collection kicks off with a series of bronze sculptures from the second half of the century by **Josef Václav Myslbek**, the father of Czech sculpture. The painting collection, however, begins earlier in the century with Antonín Machek's well-crafted portraits of the Czech bourgeoisie, and his 32 naive scenes depicting Bohemian rulers from Krok to Ferdinand IV. Close by are Ludvík Kohl's fantasy paintings: the one of Vienna's Stephansdom shows the cathedral with two complete towers (instead of one); his imaginary completion of Prague's St Vitus Cathedral was eventually fulfilled more or less to the letter by nineteenth-century architects.

In this exhaustive survey of Czech nineteenth-century painting, the influential **Mánes family** have several sections to themselves. Antonín Mánes succeeded in getting the Czech countryside to look like Italy, and thus gave birth to romantic Czech landscape painting. Three of his offspring took up the brush: Quido specialized in idealized peasant genre pictures; Amálie obeyed her father's wishes and restricted herself to a little gentle landscape painting; Josef was the most successful of the trio, much in demand as a portrait artist, and one of the leading exponents of patriotically uplifting depictions of national events (he himself took part in the 1848 disturbances in Prague).

The next few sections can be taken at a steady trot, though make sure you check out the eye-catching paintings of Yugoslavia by **Jaroslav Čermák**, a man who lived life to the full, was decorated for his bravery by the Montenegran prince Nicholas I, and died of a heart attack at the age of just 48. **Mikuláš Aleš**, whose designs can be seen in the sgraffito on many of the city's nineteenth-century buildings, is under-represented, though you can admire his wonderfully decorative depiction of the historical meeting between George of Poděbrady and Matthias Corvinus.

Prize for most striking portrait goes to Václav Brožík's *Lady with a Greyhound*, possibly a portrayal of his wife, the daughter of a wealthy Parisian art dealer. **Antonín Chittussi**'s Corot-esque landscapes proved very popular in the Parisian salons of the 1880s; beyond hang several misty, moody streetscapes by Jakub Schikaneder (one of whose ancestors was Mozart's librettist).

Several wood sculptures by **František Bílek** offer a taste of his anguished style, but for a more comprehensive insight into his art, you should visit the Bílkova vila (see p.121). **Jan Preisler**'s mosaics and murals, which can be found on Art Nouveau buildings all over Prague, tend to be ethereal and slightly detached, whereas his oil paintings, like the cycle of *Black Lake* paintings displayed here, are more typically melancholic, and reveal the influence of the Norwegian painter Edvard Munch (see below).

The most successful Czech exponent of moody post-Impressionism was **Antonín Slavíček**, whose depictions of Prague remain perennially popular. **Gustav Klimt**'s mischievous *Virgins*, a mass of naked bodies and tangled limbs painted over in psychedelic colours, hangs nearby; the gallery also owns one of the square landscapes he used to like painting during his summer holidays in the Salzkammergut.

Egon Schiele's Czech connection is that his mother came from Český Krumlov (see p.192), the subject of a tiny, gloomy, autumnal canvas, *Dead City*. The gallery also owns one of Schiele's most popular female portraits, wrongly entitled *The Artist's Wife*, an unusually graceful and gentle watercolour of a seated woman in green top and black leggings. In contrast, *Pregnant Woman and Death* is a morbidly bleak painting, in which Schiele depicts himself as both the monk of death and the life-giving mother. Perhaps the most influential non-Czech artist on show is **Edvard Munch**, whose two canvases hardly do justice to the considerable effect he had on a generation of Czech artists after his celebrated 1905 Prague exhibition.

The fourth floor collection ends in the foyer area, known rather wonderfully as the respirium, where sculptures by **Stanislav Sucharda** and **Jan Štursa**, two of the most important Czech Art Nouveau artists, predominate. On the balcony, there's a mixed bag of applied art from architectural drawings and models to lino patterning and wrought-ironwork. Architects whose work is featured include **Jan Kotěra**, Balšánek, Polívka and Oldřich, and there are several iridescent Lötz vases from Klášterský Mlýn to admire.

Art 1900–1930

On entering the **1900 to 1930 art** collection, on the third floor, visitors are confronted by **Otakar Švec**'s life-sized *Motorcyclist,* a great three-dimensional depiction of the optimistic speed of the modern age.

These are followed by a whole series of works by **František Kupka**, who was Czech by birth, but lived and worked in Paris from 1895. In international terms, Kupka is by far the most important Czech painter of the last century, having secured his place in the history of art by being (possibly) the first artist in the western world to exhibit abstract paintings. His seminal *Fugue in Two Colours (Amorpha)*, one of two abstract paintings Kupka exhibited at the Salon d'Automne in 1912, is displayed here, along with some earlier, pre-abstract paintings.

The aforementioned 1905 Edvard Munch retrospective prompted the formation in 1907 of the first Czech modern art movement, Osma (The Eight), one of whose leading members was **Emil Filla**, whose *Ace of Hearts* and *Reader of Dostoyevsky* – in which the subject appears to have fallen asleep, though, in fact, he's mind-blown – are both firmly within the Expressionist genre. However, it wasn't long before several of the Osma group were beginning to experiment with Cubism. Filla eventually adopted the style wholesale, helping found the Cubist SVU in 1911. **Bohumil Kubišta**, a member of Osma, refused to follow suit, instead pursuing his own unique blend of Cubo-Expressionism, typified by the wonderful self-portrait, *The Smoker*, and by the distinctly Fauvist *Players*.

To round out the Czech Cubist picture, there's furniture and ceramics (and even a Cubist chandelier) by Gočár, Janák and Chochol, as well as sculptures by **Otto Gutfreund**, a member of SVU, whose works range from the Cubo-Expressionist *Anxiety* (1911–12) to the more purely Cubist *Bust* (1913–14). After World War I, during which he joined the Foreign Legion but was interned for three years for insubordination, Gutfreund switched to depicting everyday folk in technicolour, in a style that prefigures Socialist Realism, examples of which can be seen a little further on in the gallery. His life was cut short in 1927, when he drowned while swimming in the Vltava.

Josef Čapek, brother of the playwright, Karel, is another Czech clearly influenced by Cubism, as seen in works such as *Accordion Player*, but like Kubišta, Čapek found Filla's doctrinaire approach difficult to take, and he left SVU in 1912. Another artist who stands apart from the crowd is **Jan Zrzavy**, who joined SVU, but during a long career pursued his own peculiarly individual style typified by paintings such as his 1909 self-portrait, in which he appears Chinese, and *Valley of Sorrow*, his own personal favourite, painted while still a student, and depicting a magical, imaginary and very stylized world.

At this point, signs begin to appear tempting you on to the ever popular **French art** collection, which features anyone of note who hovered around Paris in the fifty years from 1880 onwards. There are few masterpieces here, but it's all high-quality stuff, most of it either purchased for the gallery in 1923, or bequeathed by art dealer Vincenc Kramář in 1960.

The collection kicks off with several works by **Auguste Rodin**, particularly appropriate given the ecstatic reception that greeted the Prague exhibition of his work in 1902. Rodin's sculptures are surrounded by works from the advance guard of Impressionism: Courbet, Delacroix, Corot, Sisley and early Monet and Pissarro. Among the other works here, there's a characteristically sunny, Provençal *Green Wheat* by **Vincent van Gogh**, and *Moulin Rouge* by Toulouse-Lautrec, with Oscar Wilde looking on. Beyond, the loose brushwork, cool turquoise and emerald colours of **Auguste Renoir**'s *Lovers* are typical of the period of so-called High Impressionism. *Bonjour Monsieur Gauguin* is a tongue-in-cheek tribute to Courbet's painting of a similar name, with **Paul Gauguin** donning a suitably bohemian beret and overcoat. Also on display is the only known self-portrait by **Henri Rousseau**, at once both confident and comical, the artist depicting himself, palette in hand, against a boat decked with bunting and the recently erected Eiffel Tower.

There's also a surprisingly good collection of works by **Pablo Picasso**, including several paintings and sculptures from his transitional period (1907–08), and lots of examples from the heights of his Cubist period in the 1910s; his *Landscape with Bridge* from 1909 uses precisely the kind of prisms and geometric blocks of shading that influenced the Czech Cubist architects. In addition, there's a couple of late paintings by Paul Cézanne, a classic *pointilliste* canvas by Georges Seurat and Cubist works by Braque. *Joaquine* painted by **Henri Matisse** in 1910–11 is a first-rate portrait, in which both Fauvist and Oriental influences are evident. Look out too for Marc Chagall's *The Circus*, a typically mad work from 1927, and a rare painting by Le Corbusier himself, which clearly shows the influence of Fernand Léger, one of whose works hangs close by.

Art from 1930 to the present day

On the second floor, the section covering **art from 1930 to the present day** has been greatly expanded; it's mostly Czech in origin, and gives a pretty good introduction to the country's artistic peaks and troughs.

First off, there's a wild kinetic-light sculpture by **Zdeněk Pešánek**, a world pioneer in the use of neon in art, who created a stir at the 1937 Paris Expo with a neon fountain. Devětsil, founded back in 1920, was the driving force of the Czech avant-garde between the wars, and is represented here by the movement's two leading artists: **Toyen** (Marie Čermínová) and her lifelong companion **Jindřich Štyrský**, whose abstract works – they dubbed them "Artificialism" – reveal the couple's interest in the French Surrealists.

Avant-garde photography featured strongly in Devětsil's portfolio, and there are several fine abstract works on display. One Czech artist who enthusiastically embraced Surrealism was **Josef Šíma**, who settled permanently in Paris in the 1920s; several of his trademark floating torsoes and cosmic eggs can be seen here.

Fans of Communist kitsch should make their way to the excellent **Socialist Realism** section, heralded by Karel Pokorný's monumental *Fraternisation* sculpture, in which a Czechoslovak soldier is engaging in a "kiss of death" with a Soviet comrade. Among the paintings on display are works with wildly optimistic titles such as *We Produce More, We Live Better*, and Eduard Stavinoha's cartoon-like *Listening to the Speech of Klement Gottwald, Feb 21, 1948*. Note, too, the model of Otakar Švec's now demolished Stalin statue, which once dominated central Prague (see p.122).

In the 1960s, **performance art** (umění akce) was big in Czechoslovakia, and it, too, has its own section. Inevitably, it's difficult to recapture the original impact of some of the "happenings": the paltry "remnants of an installation" by Zdeněk Beran look a bit forlorn. Other photographs, such as those of Zorka Ságlová's *Laying out Nappies near Sudoměř*, give you a fair idea of what you missed. Eva Kmentová's *Footprints* betray their ephemeral intentions by being reproduced in a gallery: her plastercasts were originally exhibited for one day only in 1970 before being signed and given away.

The gallery owns several works by **Jiří Kolář** – pronounced "collage" – who, coincidentally, specializes in collages of random words and reproductions of other people's paintings. Close by hangs one of **Joan Miró**'s characteristically abstract Surrealist works called simply *Composition*, a couple of Henry Moore sculptures and a perforated Lucio Fontana canvas. The rest of the contemporary Czech art collection is interesting enough, if taken at a canter. Ivan Kafka's phallic *Potent Impotency* installation should raise a smile, and there's the occasional overtly political work such as *Great Dialogue* by Karel Nepraš, in which two red figures lambast each other at close quarters with loudspeakers.

Výstaviště and Stromovka

Five minutes' walk north up Dukelských hrdinů takes you right to the front gates of the **Výstaviště** (Tues–Fri 2–10pm, Sat & Sun 10am–10pm), a motley assortment of buildings, originally created for the 1891 Prague Exhibition, that have served as the city's main trade fair arena and funfair ever since. The Communist Party held its rubber-stamp congresses in the flamboyant stained-glass and wrought-iron **Průmyslový palác**, at the centre of the complex, from 1948 until the late 1970s, and more recently several brand new permanent structures were built for the 1991 Prague Exhibition, including a circular theatre, Divadlo Spirála, and Divadlo Globe, a reconstruction of Shakespeare's Globe Theatre in London, used for summer-only productions of the bard in English and Czech.

The grounds are at their busiest on summer weekends, when hordes of Prague families descend on the place to down hot dogs, drink beer and listen to traditional brass-band music. Apart from the annual fairs and lavish special exhibitions, there are a few permanent attractions, such as the city's **Planetárium** (Mon–Fri 8.30am–noon & 1–8pm, Sat & Sun 9.30am–noon & 1–8pm; ⓦwww.planetarium.cz), which has static displays and shows videos, but doesn't have telescopes (for which you need to go to the Štefánikova hvězdárna – see p.128); the **Maroldovo panorama** (Tues–Fri 2–5pm, Sat & Sun 11am–5pm), a giant diorama of the 1434 Battle of Lipany (see p.571); and the **Lunapark**, a run-down funfair and playground for kids. In the long summer evenings, there's also an open-air **cinema** (*letní kino*), and regular performances by the **Křižíkova fontána**, dancing fountains devised for the 1891 Exhibition by the Czech inventor František Křižík, which perform a music and light show to packed audiences; for the current schedule, ask at the tourist office, or check the listings magazines or the website ⓦwww.krizikova-fontana.cz. Lastly, to the right as you enter the fairgrounds, there's the much overlooked **Lapidarium** (Tues–Fri noon–6pm, Sat & Sun 10am–6pm; ⓦwww.nm.cz), official depository for the city's monumental sculptures that are under threat from demolition or the weather.

To the west is the *královská obora* or royal enclosure, more commonly known as **Stromovka**. Originally a game park for the noble occupants of the Hrad, it's now Prague's largest and leafiest public park. From here, you can wander northwards to Troja and the city's zoo (see p.128), following a path that leads under the railway, over the canal, and on to the Císařský ostrov (Emperor's Island) – and from there to the right bank of the Vltava. Bus #112, which runs hourly, will take you back to metro Nádraží Holešovice.

Troja

Though still well within the municipal boundaries, the suburb of **TROJA**, across the river to the north of Holešovice and Bubeneč, has a distinctly provincial air. Its most celebrated sight is Prague's only genuine chateau, the late-seventeenth-century **Trojský zámek** (April–Sept Tues–Sun 10am–6pm; Nov–March Sat & Sun 10am–5pm; 120Kč; bus #112 from metro Nádraží Holešovice), perfectly situated against a hilly backdrop of vines. Despite a recent renovation and rusty red repaint, its plain early Baroque facade is no match for the action-packed, blackened figures of giants and titans who battle it out on the chateau's monumental balustrades. To visit the **interior**, you'll have to join one of the guided tours. The star exhibits are the gushing frescoes depicting the victories of the Habsburg Emperor Leopold I (who reigned from 1657 to 1705) over the Turks, which cover every inch of the walls and ceilings of the grand hall; ask for the *anglický text* when you enter. You also get to wander through the chateau's pristine trend-setting French-style formal **gardens**, the first of their kind in Bohemia.

On the other side of U trojského zámku, which runs along the west wall of the chateau, is the city's capacious but underfunded **zoo** (zoologická zahrada; daily: April 9am–5pm; May 9am–6pm; June–Sept 9am–7pm; Oct–March 9am–4pm; Ⓦwww.zoopraha.cz), founded in 1931 on the site of one of Troja's numerous hillside vineyards. Despite its rather weary appearance, all the usual animals are on show here, and kids, at least, have few problems enjoying themselves. Thankfully, a programme of modernization is currently under way, though some cramped cages still remain. In the summer, you can take a "ski-lift" (*lanová dráha*) from the duck pond to the top of the hill, where the prize exhibits – a rare breed of miniature horse known as Przewalski – hang out.

Dejvice to Smíchov

Spread across the hills to the northwest of the city centre are the leafy garden suburbs of **Dejvice** and **Střešovice**, peppered with fashionable villas built between the wars for the upwardly mobile Prague bourgeoisie and commanding magnificent views across the north of the city.

Müllerova vila

The most famous of these villas, the **Müllerova vila** (Müller Haus; Tues, Thurs, Sat & Sun 10am, noon, 2pm & 4pm; 300Kč; 100Kč more for an English guide; ℡224 312 012, Ⓦwww.villamuller.cz) at Nad hradním vodojemem 14, has recently been restored and is now open to the public. Designed by the Brno-born architect, Adolf Loos – regarded by many as one of the founders of modern architecture – and completed in 1930, it's a typically uncompromising box, wiped smooth with concrete rendering. However, Loos' most famous architectural concept, the Raumplan, or open-plan design, is apparent in the living room, which is overlooked by the dining room on the mezzanine level, and, even higher up, by the boudoir, itself a Raumplan in miniature. The house is also decorated throughout in the rich materials and minimal furnishings that were Loos' hallmark: green and white Cipolino marble columns, with an inset aquarium in the living room and mahogany panelling for the dining room ceiling. To visit the house, you must phone in advance as each guided tour is limited to seven people; to reach the house, take tram #1 or #18 from metro Hradčanská, four stops to Ořechovka.

Hvězda

A couple of kilometres southwest of Dejvice, trams #1, #2 and #18 terminate close to the hunting park of **Hvězda** (May–Sept Tues–Sun 9am–5pm), one of Prague's most beautiful and peaceful parks. Wide, green avenues of trees radiate from a bizarre star-shaped building (*hvězda* means "star" in Czech) designed by the Archduke Ferdinand of Tyrol for his wife in 1555. It houses a worthy but dull museum devoted to the reactionary writer Alois Jirásek (1851–1930), who popularized old Czech legends during the national revival, and to the artist Mikuláš Aleš (1852–1913), whose drawings were likewise inspired by Czech history. On the top floor there's a small exhibition on the **Battle of**

Bílá hora (White Mountain), the first battle of the Thirty Years' War, which took place in 1620 a short distance southwest of Hvězda. However, it's the building itself – decorated with delicate stucco work and frescoes – that's the greatest attraction; it makes a perfect setting for the chamber music concerts occasionally staged here.

Bertramka (Mozart Museum)

In the hills above the late-nineteenth-century suburb of **Smíchov** is Prague's Mozart Museum, known as the **Bertramka** (daily: April–Oct 9.30am–6pm; Nov–April 9.30am–5pm; 50Kč; ⓦwww.bertramka.cz), where, so the story goes, the composer put the finishing touches to his *Don Giovanni* overture, the night before the premiere at the Stavovské divadlo (see p.96). As long ago as 1838, the villa was turned into a shrine to Mozart, though very little survives of the house he knew, thanks to a fire on New Year's Day 1871 – not that this has deterred generations of Mozart-lovers from flocking here. These days, what the museum lacks in memorabilia, it makes up for with its Rococo ambience, lovely garden and regular Mozart recitals. To get to Bertramka, take the metro to Anděl, walk a couple of blocks west or go one stop on a tram up Plzeňská, then turn left up Mozartova.

Zbraslav

One of Prague's more intriguing museums is situated in the little-visited village of **ZBRASLAV**, 10km south of the city centre, though within the municipal boundaries. Přemyslid King Otakar II built a hunting lodge here, which was later turned into a Cistercian monastery – more recently, the buildings used to house the National Gallery's modern Czech sculptures, a few of which still pepper the grounds. Now, however, **Zámek Zbraslav** (Tues–Sun 10am–6pm; ⓦwww.ngprague.cz) shelters the gallery's remarkably extensive Asian art collection.

The collection starts downstairs with Japanese art ranging from late-nineteenth-century lacquerwork lunchboxes and exquisite landscapes of birds and flowers on silk, to seventeenth-century travelling altarpieces and cracked glaze porcelain. Upstairs, there's a vast array of Chinese exhibits from Neolithic axes and ancient funerary art to Ming vases, dishes and even roof tiles. Highlights include an incredibly naturalistic eleventh-century wooden statue of one of the Buddha's aged disciples, a large standing gilded and lacquered Burmese Buddha, and an erotic Yab-Yum, a central icon of Tantric Buddhism.

Appropriately enough, the museum has a teahouse (*čajovna*) in the cloisters, and plenty of grass outside, on which to picnic. To reach the gallery, take bus #129, #241, #243, #255 or #360 from metro Smíchovské nádraží or the local train from Smíchovské nádraží to Praha-Zbraslav – there's even the occasional PPS boat (see p.61).

Eating and drinking

While traditional Czech food still predominates in the city's pubs, the choice of places where you can eat has improved enormously over the last decade. You can spend a whole week eating out and never go near a dumpling, should you so wish. Praguers themselves are very keen on pizzas, and there are now some very good pizzerias in the capital – there are even some passably authentic ethnic restaurants ranging from Japanese and Lebanese to Balkan and French.

RESTAURANTS

Angel	Y	Kampa Park	N	Radost FX Café	aa	
Bar Bar	U	Kogo	O&P	Rybářský klub	T	
Bellevue	Q	Maestro	G	Rybí trh	H	
Circle Line	M	Náprstek	R	Le Saint-Jacques	I	
Le Crêperie	A	Obecní dům	J	Sushi Bar	Z	
Faros	L	Pálffy palác	E	U patrona	K	
Góvinda	B	Petřínské terasy	S	U sádlů	C	
Jarmark	V	Pizzeria Kmotra	W	Zahrada v opeře	X	
Jerusalem	D	Pizzeria Rugantino	F			

PRAGUE: EATING & DRINKING

Snacks and fast food

Czechs are beginning to get into sandwiches, and the best city-wide chain is **Paneria** (ⓦwww.paneria.cz), which specializes in providing sandwiches, toasted panini and pastries for Prague's hungry office workers; there are branches at Kaprova 3 and Maiselova 4 (both metro Staroměstská) and elsewhere in the city. For more traditional Czech open sandwiches or *chlebíčky*, you need to go to **Na zlatém kříži**, Jungmannova 34 (closed Sun; metro Můstek). Expat favourites include the self-service breakfast, bagel and soup outfit, **Bohemia Bagel**, Újezd 16 (ⓦwww.bohemiabagel.cz; tram #6, #9, #12, #22 or #23, stop Újezd) and Masná 2 (metro Staroměstská), both of which have an internet café attached. More varied and upmarket sandwiches, wraps, bread and cakes can be had from **Bakeshop Praha**, V Kolkovně 2 (metro Náměstí Republiky), which has a few eat-in bar stools. Czech veggies head for the multinational health food café **Country Life**, Melantrichova 15 (metro Můstek) and Jungmannova 1.

Obviously the usual multinational burger chains have their outlets splattered all over Prague. For something more uniquely Czech, head for **Havelská Koruna**, Havelská 21 (metro Můstek), an authentic no-frills, self-service Czech *jídelna* serving Czech comfort food classics such as *sekaná*, goulash and *zelí*, all for under 50Kč (you pay at the exit). Other quick-bite options include the Middle Eastern kebab and falafel outlet, **Safir** at Havelská 12 (ⓦwww.safirgrill.czrb.cz; metro Můstek), or the similar **Anis-Adonis** at Jungmannova 21 (metro Národní třída).

In addition, there's also a whole range of new, slightly more expensive restaurants aimed at the palates (and wallets) of the passing tourist, the expat community, wealthy Czechs and the diplomatic crowd. So while it's fun to sample authentic Czech food, and experience Czech eating habits, many visitors are happy to pay a bit more for food that is tastier and more imaginative, albeit not always very Czech.

Not surprisingly, the places in the main tourist areas along Mostecká and Karlova, on either side of the Charles Bridge, and on Staroměstské náměstí and Wenceslas Square, tend to be overpriced, relying on their geographical position, rather than the quality of their food, to bring in custom. Venture instead into the backstreets, such as those north of Celetná, south of Karlova, or south of Národní, and you're more likely to find better service, better value and perhaps even better food.

Cafés

At the beginning of the twentieth century, Prague boasted a café society to rival that of Vienna or Paris. A handful of these classic Habsburg-era haunts have survived, or been resurrected, and should definitely be sampled. The cafés listed below are a mixed bunch. The majority serve just coffee and cakes, and more often than not, alcohol; others also serve up cheap and filling (though rarely gourmet) meals.

Malá Strana

U zavěšeného kafe Úvoz 6; tram #12 or #22 from metro Malostranská to Malostranské náměstí. A "hanging coffee" is one that has been paid for by the haves for the have-nots who drop in. That apart, this place is a pleasant smoky cross-over café/pub, serving cheap beer and traditional Czech food in a handy spot on the way up or down from the Hrad. Daily 11am–midnight.

Staré Město

Chez Marcel Hašt'alská 12 ⓦwww.chezmoi.cz; metro Náměstí Republiky. Effortlessly chic French café-bistro. A good place to grab a coffee or a *tarte tatin*, read a French mag or eat some moderately priced bistro-style food. Mon–Sat 8am–1am, Sun 9am–1am.

Érra Konviktská 11; metro Národní třída. Vaulted cellar café in the backstreets off Betlémské náměstí that's popular with a professional mixed straight/gay crowd. Tasty salads and snacks on offer too. Mon–Fri 10am–midnight, Sat & Sun 11am–midnight.

Montmartre Řetězová 7; metro Staroměstská. Surprisingly small, barrel-vaulted café that was once a famous First Republic dance and cabaret venue. Mon–Fri 9am–11pm, Sat & Sun noon–11pm.

Rudolfinum Alšovo nábřeží 12; metro Staroměstská. Gloriously grand nineteenth-century café on the first floor of the old parliament building (see p.103) – you don't have to go to the exhibition to go to the café. Tues–Sun 10am–6pm.

Nové Město

Arco Hybernská/Dlažděná; metro Náměstí Republiky. Once the haunt of a clique of Prague-German writers (including Kafka), now approximately reproduced, though a café is more than the sum of its fittings. Mon–Fri 3–9.30pm, Sat & Sun 10am–9.30pm.

Globe Pštrossova 6 ⓦwww.globebookstore.cz; metro Národní třída/Karlovo náměstí. Large, buzzing café, at the back of the English-language bookstore of the same name, that's a serious expat hang-out, but enjoyable nevertheless. Mon–Thurs & Sun 10am–midnight, Fri & Sat 10am–1am.

Imperial Na poříčí 15 ⓦwww.hotelimperial.cz; metro Náměstí Republiky. An endearingly shabby yet grand Habsburg-era *Kaffeehaus* which has retained its original, over-the-top ceramic tiled decor. The locals clearly approve of its unpretentious air, too, and the free doughnuts go down a treat. Mon–Thurs 9am–midnight, Fri & Sat 9am–1am, Sun 9am–11pm.

Louvre Národní 20 ⓦwww.kavarny.cz/louvre; metro Národní třída. Turn-of-the-twentieth-century café, closed down in 1948, but now back in business and a very popular refuelling spot for Prague's shoppers. Dodgy colour scheme, but high ceiling, mirrors, daily papers,

Prague's tea-houses

Prague's tea-houses are a post-Communist phenomenon, though they have their historical roots in the First Republic. Partly a reaction to the smoke-filled, alcohol-driven atmosphere of the ubiquitous Czech pub, and partly a reaction against the multinational, fast-food culture that has now arrived in Prague, tea-houses tend to be non-smoking, slightly hippified places to enjoy a quiet cuppa and chill out. The tea-drinking is taken very seriously and there's usually a staggering array of leaves on offer, some commanding pretty high prices.

Dahab Dlouhá 33, Staré Město ⓦwww.dahab.cz; metro Náměstí Republiky. The mother of all Prague tea-houses, a vast Bedouin tent of a place serving tasty Middle Eastern snacks, couscous and hookahs to a background of funky world music. Daily noon–midnight.

Dobrá cajovna Boršov 2, Staré Město ⓦwww.cajovna.com; metro Staroměstská. The original, slightly precious, mellow, rarefied tea-house, with an astonishing variety of teas (and a few Middle Eastern snacks) served by waiters who slip by silently in their sandals. This place is off Karoliny Světlé and you'll need to ring the bell. Small branch at Václavské náměstí 14, Nové Město; metro Můstek/Muzeum. Mon–Fri 10am–9.30pm, Sun 3–9.30pm.

Malà Buddha Úvoz 46, Malá Strana; tram #12, #22 or #23 from metro Malostranská to Malostranské náměstí. Typical Prague tea-house decor, with a Buddhist altar in one corner and vegetarian Vietnamese snacks on the menu. A very useful haven just down from the Hrad. Tues–Sun 1–10.30pm.

U zeleného čaje Nerudova 19, Malá Strana; tram #12, #22 or #23 from metro Malostranská to Malostranské náměstí. The "green tea" is a great little stop-off for a pot of tea or a veggie snack en route to or from the Hrad; the only problem is getting a place at one of the four tables. Daily 11am–9.30pm.

U zlatého kohouta Michalská 3, Staré Město; metro Můstek. Hidden away in a courtyard off Michalská, this is another secretive, relaxing *čajovna* worth knowing about, located in the heart of Staré Město. Mon–Fri 10am–9.30pm, Sat & Sun 2–9.30pm.

lots of cakes, a billiard hall and window seats overlooking Národní. Mon–Fri 8am–11.30pm, Sat & Sun 9am–11.30pm.

Obecní dům Nám. Republiky. The vast *kavárna*, with its famous fountain, is in the more restrained south hall of this huge Art Nouveau complex, and has recently been glitteringly restored – an absolute aesthetic treat. Daily 7.30am–11pm.

Slavia Národní 1; metro Národní třída. Famous Prague riverside café that has a special place in the city's cultural and political history (see p.111).

Despite losing much of its former character, it still pulls in a mixed crowd from shoppers and tourists to older folk and the pre- and post-theatre mob. Daily 9am–11pm.

Terminal Bar Soukenická 6 ⓦwww.terminal.cz; metro Náměstí Republiky. Definitely the number-one choice in terms of atmosphere when it comes to going online, this is a funky, loud bar, with a groovy chill-out basement littered with kitsch sofas and weird lighting. Daily 10am–2am.

Pubs and bars

In the last ten years the Prague **pub** scene has diversified enormously, with the establishment of expat American-style bars, "Irish" pubs and smarter, designer places that attract a more mixed crowd of young professionals. Nevertheless, there are still plenty of traditional Czech *pivnice*: smoky, male-dominated places, primarily designed for drinking copious quantities of Czech beer. Food, where served, is almost always of the traditional Czech variety – cheap and filling, but ultimately it could shorten your life by a couple of years.

Hradčany and Malá Strana

Jo's Bar Malostranské náměstí 7; metro Malostranská. A narrow bar in Malá Strana that is the original expat/backpacker hang-out. Tex-Mex food served all day, bottled beer only and a heaving crowd guaranteed most evenings. Downstairs is the nightclub *Jo's Garáž*. Daily 11am–4am.

Na Kampě Na Kampě 15; metro Malostranská. Round the corner from the formal restaurant of the same name is this friendly (and even child-friendly) *pivnice* offering tasty pub snacks; you can sit outside or wander down to the riverside with your *Pilsner Urquell*. Daily noon–midnight.

U černého vola (The Black Ox) Loretánské náměstí 1; tram #22 from metro Malostranská to Pohořelec stop. Great traditional Prague pub doing a brisk business providing the popular light beer *Velkopopovický kozel* in huge quantities to thirsty local workers, plus a few basic pub snacks. Daily 10am–10pm.

U hrocha (The Hippo) Thunovská 10; metro Malostranská. A genuine smoky, Czech local in the heart of Malá Strana – difficult to believe but true. Cheap grub and beer. Daily noon–11.30pm.

U malého Glena Karmelitská 23 ⓦwww.maly-glen.cz; metro Malostranská. Smart-looking pub/jazz bar that attracts a fair mixture of Czechs and expats thanks to its better-than-average food and live music in the basement. Daily 10am–2am.

U kocoura (The Cat) Nerudova 2. One of the few surviving pubs on Nerudova, owned by the Beer Party, but, for the most part, abandoned by its old clientele. Some of the best Budvar in town, plus

the obvious Czech stomach-fillers. Daily 11am–11pm.

Staré Město

Legends Týn (Ungelt) ⓦwww.legends.cz; metro náměstí Republiky. Heaving, loud, full-blown expat bar in the Týn courtyard, which shows the big TV sports events and has disco theme nights. Daily 11am–3am.

Marquis de Sade Templová 8; metro náměstí Republiky. Great space: huge high ceiling, big comfy sofas, and a mostly expat crowd. Crap beer and limited snacks, but a good place to start the evening (before the live band kicks in) or end it (after they've packed up). Daily noon–2am.

Molly Malone's U Obecního dvora 4 ⓦwww.mollymalones.cz; metro Staroměstská. Best of Prague's Irish pubs with real Irish staff (who speak very little Czech), an open fire, draught Kilkenny and Guinness (neither of them very cheap), and decent Irish-themed food. Daily 11am–2am.

Radegast Templová 2; metro náměstí Republiky. Typically smoky, boozy pub divided into booths, serving its namesake plus decent Czech food. Attracts Czechs and expats. Daily 11am–12.30pm.

U medvídků (The Little Bears) Na Perštýně 7; metro Národní třída. A Prague beerhall going back to the thirteenth century and still much as it ever was (make sure you turn right when you enter, and avoid the new bar to the left). The Budvar comes thick and fast, and the food is absolutely standard. Mon–Sat 11.30am–11pm, Sun 11.30am–10pm.

U mravence (The Ant) U radnice 20; metro Staroměstská. Incredibly, given the top tourist location, this is an all right Czech pub, serving typical Czech pub food at reasonable prices. Daily 11am–midnight.

Nové Město

Branický sklípek Vodičkova 26; metro Můstek. Convenient downtown pub decked out like a pine furniture showroom, serving typical Czech fare, and jugs of Prague's *Braník* beer. The rough and ready *Branická formanka* next door opens and closes earlier. Mon–Fri 9am–11pm, Sat & Sun 11am–11pm.

Ostroff Střelecký ostrov ⓦwww.ostroff.cz; metro Národní třída. Very popular sleek, long bar and summer terrace overlooking the National Theatre from the first island you come to on the most Legií. The terrace gets packed in summer, as does the Italian restaurant below. Terrace daily 2–11pm.

Pivovarský dům Corner of Lipová/Ječná; metro Karlovo náměstí. Busy micro-brewery dominated by its big shiny copper vats, serving light, mixed and dark unfiltered beer (plus banana, coffee and wheat varieties), and all the standard Czech pub dishes (including *pivný sýr*). Daily 11am–11.30pm.

U Potrefená husa (The Wounded Goose) Jiráskovo náměstí 1; metro Karlovo náměstí. Smart, convivial brick cellar pub that attracts a mix of young and middle-aged professionals; *Staropramen* and decent pub food on offer. Daily 11.30am–1am.

U Fleků Křemencova 11; metro Karlovo náměstí. Famous medieval *pivnice* where the unique dark 13° beer, *Flek*, has been exclusively brewed and consumed since 1499. Seats over 500 German tourists at a go, serves short measures (0.4l), slaps an extra charge on for the music and still you have to queue. This is a tourist trap and the only reason to visit is to sample the beer, which you're best off doing during the day. Daily 9am–11pm.

U kotvy (The Anchor) Spalená 11; metro Národní třída. All-night spot that's perfect for a last *Staropramen* before you attempt to work out how to catch a night tram home. Daily 24hr.

Further afield

Hospoda na verandách Nádražní 90, Smíchov; metro Anděl. The new official *Staropramen* brewery tap, and therefore the place to taste Prague's most popular beer. Daily 11am–11pm.

Letenský zámeček Letenské sady, Holešovice ⓦwww.letenskyzamecek.cz; tram #1 or #25 from metro Vltavská to Letenské náměstí. Convenient beer garden opposite the Národní technické muzeum serving *Velkopopovický kozel*, and slightly upgraded Czech pub food, including some veggie options, in the *Ullman* restaurant inside. Daily 11am–11.30pm.

U buldoka (The Bulldog) Preslova 1, Smíchov ⓦwww.ubuldoka.cz; metro Anděl. A half-decent Smíchov pub is hard to find, but this is one, serving *Gambrinus* and with occasional DJ nights. Mon–Fri 11am–midnight, Sat & Sun noon–midnight.

U Houdků Bořivojova 110, Žižkov; tram #5, #9 or #26 from metro Hlavní nádraží to Husinecká stop. Friendly pub in the heart of Žižkov with a beer garden, *Velkopopovický kozel* and cheap Czech food. Daily 10am–11pm.

U vystřelenýho oka (The Shot-Out Eye) U božích bojovníků 3, Žižkov; metro Florenc. Big, loud, smoky, heavy-drinking pub just south of Žižkov Hill, off Husitská, with (unusually) good music playing and lashings of *Měšťan* beer, plus absinthe chasers. Mon–Sat 3.30pm–1am.

Zvonařka (The Bell) Šafaříkova 1, Vinohrady ⓦwww.zvonarka.cz; tram #6 or #11 from metro I. P. Pavlova to Nuselské schody stop. The slick, futuristic interior hosts DJs at the weekend, while the terrace has great views over the Nuselské schody and Botič valley. Mon–Sat 11am–2am, Sun 11am–midnight.

Restaurants and wine bars

The influx of tourists has, of course, pushed the prices in some restaurants out of the reach of many Czechs, who tend more than ever to stick to pubs when eating out. However, even in the city's top restaurants, you can't guarantee faultless food and service, so keep an open mind. Service is gradually becoming more sophisticated, though surly staff are still no rarity, nor are unscrupulous waiters who exercise dubious arithmetics when totting up the bill. Beware of extras in the pricier restaurants, where you will be charged for everything you touch, including the almonds you thought were courtesy of the house.

The restaurant listings are divided into geographical areas that correspond to the chapters, and into price categories, too – inexpensive, moderate and expensive. You should be able to get a soup, a main course, a dessert, plus a couple of beers in the price bracket indicated: **Inexpensive** under 300Kč a head;

Moderate 300–600Kč a head; **Expensive** 600Kč and upwards. While 500Kč for a meal is hardly extravagant compared to meal prices in the EU or US, it's still pricey for most Czechs. At popular and/or upmarket restaurants, it's advisable to book a table beforehand either by calling in or by telephoning ahead.

Malá Strana

Bar Bar Všehrdova 17 ☎257 312 246. Arty crêperie with big cheap salads, savoury and sweet crêpes/*palačinky* on offer. Daily noon–11pm. Inexpensive.

Circle Line Malostranské náměstí 12 ☎257 530 023. The fresh seafood and sumptuous salads are the main draw at this luxurious restaurant, though the meat and veggie courses are equally good. Mon–Fri noon–11pm, Sat & Sun 11am–11pm. Expensive.

Faros Šporkova 5 ☎257 533 964, ✆www.faros.cz. Cosy little Greek restaurant in the backstreets of Malá Strana that makes a nice change from other Prague restaurants and is relatively veggie-friendly. Daily noon–11pm. Moderate.

Kampa Park Na Kampě 8b ☎257 532 685, ✆www.kampapark.com. Pink house exquisitely located right by the Vltava on Kampa Island with a superb fish and seafood menu, top-class service and tables outside in summer. Daily 11.30am–1am. Expensive.

Petřínské terasy Seminářská zahrada 13 ☎290 000 457. Gay-owned, but with mixed clientele, superb views over Prague, beer and barbecues – get off at the Nebozízek stop on the funicular up Petřín, but walk away from the restaurant of the same name. Daily 11am–10pm. Inexpensive.

Rybářský klub U sovových mlýnů 1 ☎257 534 200; tram #12, #22 or #23 from metro Malostranská to Hellichova stop. Fresh fish – carp, trout, pike and others – simply prepared at this unpretentious riverside restaurant, situated in the park on Kampa Island. Daily noon–11pm. Inexpensive.

Pálffý palác Valdštejnská 14 ☎257 530 522, ✆www.czechreality.cz/palffy. Grand candle-lit room on the first floor of the conservatoire, and a wonderful outdoor terrace from which you can survey the red rooftops of Malá Strana; the international menu doesn't always live up to the setting. Daily 11am–midnight. Moderate.

U patrona Dražického náměstí 4 ☎257 530 725. An excellent, intimate little restaurant very close to the Charles Bridge, offering beautifully prepared local dishes – in the same stable as *Circle Line* et al. Mon–Sat 6–11.30pm. Expensive.

Staré Město and Josefov

Bellevue Smetanovo nábřeží 18 ☎222 221 438, ✆www.praguefinedining.cz; metro Národní třída. The view of Charles Bridge and the Hrad is out-

standing and they serve imaginative Czech-centred cuisine – hardly surprising then that it's around 1000Kč a head and you need to book ahead to eat here. Mon–Sat noon–3pm & 5.30–11pm, Sun 11am–3pm & 7–11pm. Expensive.

Jerusalem Břehová 6; metro Staroměstská. One of a rash of kosher places on Břehová, on the edge of the old Jewish quarter; decor is very plain, service relaxed and the menu vast and tasty, ranging from breakfasts and savoury pancakes to full meals. Daily 8am–11pm. Inexpensive.

Kogo Havelská 27 ☎224 214 543, metro Můstek; and Na příkopě 22 ☎221 451 259, metro náměstí Republiky; ✆www.kogo-prague.cz. The Havelská site is divided into two intimate spaces by a passageway and has a small courtyard; the Na příkopě site is much larger and more showy, with a more spacious courtyard. Either way, you'll get decent pasta, pizza and salads served by courteous and efficient waiters. Daily 9am–midnight. Moderate.

Le Saint-Jacques Jakubská 4 ☎222 322 685, ✆www.saint-jacques.cz; metro Náměstí Republiky. Excellent French brasserie cuisine on offer here in the heart of the so-called "French quarter", with tasteful live music nightly. Mon–Fri noon–3pm & 6pm–midnight, Sat 6pm–midnight. Moderate.

Maestro Křižovnická 10; metro Staroměstská. Very good pizza place close to the metro (and to Charles Bridge); the chicken cacciatore is also worth sampling, as are the profiteroles. Mon–Fri 11am–11pm, Sat & Sun 1–11pm. Inexpensive.

Náprstek (Thimble) Náprstkova 8; metro Národní třída ☎222 221 019, ✆www.restaurant-naprstek.cz. Award-winning, elegant restaurant serving a mouth-watering international menu. Daily 11am–midnight. Expensive.

Pizzeria Rugantino Dušní 4 ☎222 318 172; metro Staroměstská. This pizzeria, just off Dlouhá, is the genuine article: an oak-fired oven, gargantuan thin bases, numerous toppings to choose from, and *Bernard* on tap. Mon–Sat 11am–11pm, Sun 5–11pm. Inexpensive.

Rybí trh Týn 5 ☎224 895 447, ✆www.flambee.cz; metro náměstí Republiky. Swish fish and seafood restaurant in the Týn (Ungelt) courtyard, where you pick your victim, and tell the chef how to cook it. Daily 11am–midnight. Expensive.

Nové Město

Angel Opatovická 3 ☎224 930 019, ✆www.the-cafe.cz; metro Národní třída. Sleek, light, minimalist decor and seriously delicious designer cooking available at this resolutely expat café-restaurant. Mon–Wed & Sun 11am–3pm, Thurs–Sat 11am–3pm & 7–10pm. Moderate.

Góvinda Soukenická 27; metro Náměstí Republiky. Hare Krishna (*Haré Kršna* in Czech) restaurant serving organic Indian veggie slop for knock-down prices. Mon–Sat 11am–5.30pm. Inexpensive.

Jarmark Vodičkova 30 ☎224 233 733, ⓦwww.jarmark.com; metro Můstek. Popular, inexpensive self-service steak and salad buffet in the Lucerna pasáž, where the chef prepares your food in front of you; a few veggie dishes on offer, too. Mon–Fri 8–10am & 11am–10pm, Sat & Sun 11am–10pm. Inexpensive.

Obecní dům Nám. Republiky 5 ☎222 002 770, ⓦwww.obecni-dum.cz; metro náměstí Republiky. The *Francouzská restaurace* has stunning Art Nouveau decor and the French-style food is very good and not really that expensive. Daily noon–4pm & 6–11pm. The *Plzeňská restaurace* in the cellar is a cheaper Czech-style pub-restaurant. Daily 11am–11pm. Moderate–expensive.

Pizzeria Kmotra (Godmother) V jirchářích 12 ☎224 915 809, ⓦwww.kmotra.cz; metro Národní třída. This sweaty basement pizza place is one of Prague's most popular, and justifiably so – if possible book a table in advance. Daily 11am–midnight. Inexpensive.

U sádlů (The Lard) Klimentská 2 ☎224 813 874, ⓦwww.usadlu.cz; metro náměstí Republiky.

Deliberately over-the-top themed medieval banqueting hall serving inexpensive hearty fare and lashings of frothing ale. Daily 11am–1am. Inexpensive.

Zahrada v opeře Legerova 75 ☎224 239 685, ⓦwww.zahradavopere.cz; metro Muzeum. Striking modern interior and beautifully presented food from around the world at democratic prices. The entrance is around the back of the Radio Free Europe building at the top of Wenceslas Square. Daily 11.30am–1am. Moderate.

Further afield

La Crêperie Janovského 4, Holešovice; tram #5, #12 or #17, stop Strossmayerovo náměstí. Stylish French-run crêperie serving sweet and savoury pancakes, French liqueurs and even the rare *Nová Paka* beer. Mon–Sat noon–11pm, Sun 11am–10pm. Inexpensive.

Sushi Bar Zborovská 49, Smíchov ☎290 001 517, ⓦwww.sushi.cz; tram #6, #9, #12, #22 or #23, stop Újezd. Minimalist sushi bar in the part of Smíchov just south of Malá Strana. The sushi and sashimi set dishes are delicious, but beware of mounting bills. Daily noon–10pm. Moderate.

Radost FX Café Bělehradská 120, Vinohrady; metro I. P. Pavlova. Without doubt the best choice of vegetarian dishes in town (okay, so there's not much competition), drawing in a large expat posse, particularly for the Sunday brunch. Daily 11.30am–4am. Moderate.

Entertainment

For many Praguers, **entertainment** is confined to an evening's drinking in one of the city's beer-swilling *pivnice*. But if you're looking for a bit more action, there's plenty to keep you from night-time frustration. To find out **what's on**, check the **listings** sections in *Prague Post* (ⓦwww.praguepost.com), the bilingual bi-weekly free listings handout *Do města/Downtown* (ⓦwww.downtown.cz), or the Czech listings monthly *Culture in Prague/Česká kultura* (ⓦwww.ceskakultura.cz), and keep your eyes peeled for flyers and posters.

Clubs and live venues

While most Praguers go to bed pretty early, a dedicated minority, including many of the city's expats and tourists, stay up until the wee small hours. To service this crowd, Prague has a good selection of late-night drinking holes (see p.134) and a handful of half-decent **clubs**. Local DJs, and the odd international one, perform at most of these, and there are a few good one-off raves throughout the year (a case of scouring the fly posters around), but many clubs double as **live music venues**. As well as indigenous live acts, spanning the entire range of musical tastes from Czech reggae to thrash, a surprising array of world music bands find their way to Prague, along with a few big names from the USA and UK.

Rock, pop and dance music

Major Western **bands** often include Prague in their European tours and, to be sure of a full house, many offer tickets at below their usual price in the West. There are gigs by Czech bands almost every night in the city's clubs and discos – a selection of the better venues is listed below, though you should always check in the local listings before setting out.

Futurum Zborovská 7, Smíchov ⓦwww.musicbar.cz; metro Anděl. Impressive, futuristic, high-tech club whose DJs take their house and techno seriously. Daily until 3am.

Karlovy lázně Novotného lavka 1, Staré Město ⓦwww.karlovylazne.cz; metro Staroměstská. Mega, high-tech club on four floors of an old bathhouse by the Charles Bridge; techno on the top floor, progressively more retro as you descend to the internet café on the ground floor. Daily until 5am.

Lucerna music bar Vodičkova 36, Nové Město, ⓦwww.musicbar.cz; metro Můstek. Without doubt the best gig venue in Prague, a gilded turn-of-the-twentieth-century hall with balcony, situated underneath the Lucerna pasáž. Doors open at 7pm.

Mecca U Průhonu 3, Holešovice, ⓦwww.mecca.cz; tram #12 or #14 from metro Nádraží Holešovice to U Průhonu stop. Despite being out in Prague 7, this converted factory is one of the best, and most popular, clubs in Prague.

Daily 7pm–2am.

Palác Akropolis Kubelíkova 27, Žižkov ⓦwww.palacakropolis.cz; tram #5, #9 or #26 to Lipanská stop. Two live venue spaces and a whole complex of bars in scruffy Žižkov, this place is the nerve centre of the city's alternative world music and puts on the most eclectic programme of gigs in Prague. Live venue doors open 7pm.

Radost FX Bělehradská 120, Vinohrady ⓦwww.radostfx.cz; metro I. P. Pavlova. Still the slickest (and longest-running) all-round dance club venue in Prague, attracting the usual mix of clubbers and despots; good veggie café upstairs. Daily until 5am.

Roxy Dlouhá 33, Staré Město ☎224 826 296, ⓦwww.roxy.cz; metro náměstí Republiky. The *Roxy* is a great little venue: a laid-back rambling old theatre with an interesting programme of events from arty films and exhibitions to live acts and DJ nights. Daily from 8pm–late.

Gay and lesbian nightlife

Prague Post does the occasional update on gay and lesbian nightlife; otherwise you'll need to get hold of the bi-monthly gay magazine *Amigo* (ⓦwww.amigo.cz), or the lesbian publications *Promluv* and *Alia*. You'll also find useful flyers at the places listed below.

"A" Klub Milíčova 32, Žižkov ☎222 781 623; tram #5, #9 or #26 to Lipanská stop. The city's premier lesbian bar with women-only Friday nights. It's small but stylish and definitely worth checking out. Daily 7pm–6am.

Arco Voroněžská 24, Vinohrady ☎271 742 908, ⓦwww.arco-guesthouse.cz; tram #4, #22 or #23 from metro Náměstí Míru to Krymská stop. Gay internet café and guesthouse. Mon–Fri 8am–1am, Sat & Sun 9am–1am.

Babylonia Martinská 6, Staré Město; metro Národní třída. Prague's most centrally located gay sauna, with steam baths, pools and massage on offer. Daily 2pm–3am.

Friends Náprstkova 1, Staré Město ☎221 635 408, ⓦwww.friends-prague.cz; metro Národní třída.

Friendly, laid-back mixed gay/lesbian cellar bar in the centre of the old town. Daily 4pm–3am.

Gejzee...r Vinohradská 40, Vinohrady ☎222 516 036, ⓦwww.gejzeer.cz; metro Náměstí Míru. Prague's largest and most popular gay club with dance floor, DJs and the inevitable darkroom. Tues–Thurs 6pm–4am, Fri & Sat 9pm–5am.

Pinocchio Seifertova 3, Žižkov ☎222 710 773, ⓦwww.pinocchio-club.cz; metro Hlavní nádraží. Bar, club, internet café and even hotel, all rolled into one, a short stroll into Žižkov.

Stella Lužická 10, Vinohrady ☎224 257 869; metro náměstí Míru. One of the most popular and relaxed mixed gay/lesbian hot spots in the capital – ring the bell to gain entry. Daily 8pm–5am.

Jazz

Prague has a surprisingly long indigenous jazz tradition, and is home to a handful of good jazz clubs. With little money to attract acts from abroad, the artists are almost exclusively Czech and tend to do virtually the entire round of venues each month. The one exception to all this is *AghaRTA*, which attracts a few big names each year. More often than not, it's a good idea to book a table at the jazz clubs listed below – this is particularly true of *AghaRTA* and *Reduta*.

AghaRTA Jazz Centrum Krakovská 5, Nové Město ☎222 211 275, ⊛www.agharta.cz; metro Muzeum. Probably the best jazz club in Prague, with a good mix of Czechs and foreigners and a consistently good programme of gigs; situated in a side street off the top end of Wenceslas Square. Mon–Fri 5pm–1am, Sat & Sun 7pm–1am.

Metropolitan Jazz Club Jungmannova 14, Nové Město ☎224 216 025; metro Můstek. Small jazz restaurant that tends to stick to a traditional menu on stage and in the kitchen. Daily until 1am; gigs start at 9pm.

Reduta Národní 20, Nové Město ☎224 912 246; metro Národní třída. Prague's best-known, but strangely unfashionable, jazz club – Bill Clinton played his sax here in front of Havel. Gigs daily from 9pm; box office open from 3pm.

U malého Glena Karmelitská 23, Malá Strana ☎257 531 717, ⊛www.malyglen.cz; tram #12, #22 or #23 one stop from metro Malostranská. Tiny downstairs stage worth checking out for its eclectic mix of Latin jazz, bebop and blues. Daily 7pm–2am.

U staré paní (The Old Woman) Michalská 9, Staré Město ☎224 228 090, ⊛www.ustarepani.cz; metro Můstek. Decent old town jazz restaurant that really gets going when the live contemporary jazz kicks in from 9pm onwards. Daily 7pm–1am.

The arts

Alongside the city's numerous cafés, pubs and clubs, there's a rich **cultural life** in Prague. Music is everywhere, especially in the summer, when the streets, churches, palaces, opera houses, concert halls and gardens are filled with the strains of classical music. True, there are too many Mozart concerts pandering to the tourist trade, but equally there are some very high-quality chamber concerts. Czech theatre and film both struggled to find their way in the 1990s, following the virtual ending of both subsidies and censorship. Even if you don't understand Czech, there are theatre performances worth catching – Prague has a strong tradition of mime, "black theatre" and puppetry, and many cinemas show films in their original language.

You can obtain **tickets** from the box office (*pokladna*) of the venue concerned, but you might find it easier to go to one of the city's numerous **ticket agencies** – it will cost you more, but might save you a lot of hassle. Ticketpro has branches all over the city, including at the Staroměstská radnice (Old Town Hall), Staroměstské náměstí, Staré Město (Mon–Fri 9am–7pm, Sat & Sun 9am–6pm; ☎224 816 020, ⊛www.ticketpro.cz), plus at Salvátorská 10, Staré Město and in the Lucerna pasáž, Štěpánská 61, Nové Město. Another option is Bohemia Ticket International (⊛www.ticketsbti.cz), which has offices at Malé náměstí 13 (Mon–Fri 9am–5pm, Sat 9am–2pm; ☎224 227 832) and Na příkopě 16, Nové Město (Mon–Fri 10am–7pm, Sat 10am–5pm, Sun 10am–3pm; ☎224 215 031). Ticket **prices**, with a few notable exceptions, are still good value, starting at just 250Kč. Lastly, don't despair if everything is officially sold out (*vyprodáno*), as standby tickets are often available at the venue's box office on the night, an hour before the start of the performance.

By far the biggest annual event is the *Pražské jaro* (Prague Spring), the country's most prestigious **international music festival**, which traditionally begins on May 12, the anniversary of Smetana's death. The main venues are listed on p.140, but keep an eye out for concerts in the city's churches and palaces, gardens and courtyards; note that evening performances tend to start fairly early, either at 5 or 7pm.

The main opera houses and concert halls

Národní divadlo (National Theatre) Národní 2, Nové Město ☎224 913 437, ✆www.narodni-divadlo.cz; metro Národní třída. Prague's grandest nineteenth-century theatre is the living embodiment of the Czech national revival movement, and continues to put on a wide variety of mostly, though by no means exclusively, Czech plays, plus the odd opera and ballet. Worth visiting for the decor alone. Box office Mon–Fri 10am–6pm, Sat & Sun 10am–12.30pm & 3–6.30pm. Closed July & Aug.

Obecní dům – Smetanova síň Nám. Republiky 5, Nové Město ☎222 002 105; metro náměstí Republiky. Fantastically ornate and recently renovated Art Nouveau concert hall which usually kicks off the Prague Spring festival, and is home to the excellent Prague Symphony Orchestra. Box office Mon–Fri 10am–12.30pm & 1.30–6pm.

Rudolfinum Alšovo nábřeží 12, Staré Město ☎224 893 352, ✆www.rudolfinum.cz; metro Staroměstská. A truly stunning Neo-Renaissance concert hall from the late nineteenth century, that's home base for the Czech Philharmonic (✆www.czechphilharmonie.cz). The Dvořákova síň

is the large hall; the Sukova síň is the chamber concert hall. Box office Mon–Fri 10am–6pm, plus 1hr before performance.

Státní opera Praha (Prague State Opera) Wilsonova 4, Nové Město ☎224 227 266, ✆www.opera.cz; metro Muzeum. A sumptuous nineteenth-century opera house, built by the city's German community, which once attracted star conductors such as Mahler and Zemlinsky. Now it's the number two venue for opera, with a repertoire that tends to focus on Italian pieces. Box office Mon–Fri 10am–5.30pm, Sat & Sun 10am–noon & 1–5.30pm, plus 1hr before performance. Closed mid-July to mid-Aug.

Stavovské divadlo (Estates Theatre) Ovocný trh 1, Staré Město ☎224 215 001, ✆www.narodni-divadlo.cz; metro Můstek. Prague's oldest opera house, which witnessed the premiere of Mozart's *Don Giovanni*, puts on a mixture of opera, ballet and straight theatre (with simultaneous headphone translation available). Box office Mon–Fri 10am–6pm, Sat & Sun 10am–12.30pm & 3–6pm, plus 30min before performance. Closed mid-July to mid-Aug.

Theatres

Divadlo Archa Na poříčí 26, Nové Město ☎221 716 333, ✆www.archatheatre.cz; metro Florenc. By far the most innovative venue in Prague, with two very versatile spaces, an art gallery and a café. The programming includes music, dance and theatre with an emphasis on the avant-garde. Box office Mon–Fri 10am–6pm, plus 2hr before performance.

Divadlo minor Vodičkova 6, Nové Město ☎222 232 530, ✆www.minor.cz; metro Karlovo náměstí. The former state puppet theatre puts on children's puppet shows most days, plus adult shows on occasional evenings – sometimes with English subtitles. Box office Mon–Fri 2–5pm, plus 1hr before performance.

Divadlo Spejbla a Hurvínka Dejvická 38, Dejvice ☎224 316 784, ✆www.spejbl-hurvinek.cz; metro Dejvická/Hradčanská. Features the indomitable puppet duo, Spejbl and Hurvínek, created by Josef Skupa in the twentieth century and still going strong at one of the few puppet-only theatres in the country. Box office Tues, Thurs & Fri 10am–2pm & 3–6pm, Wed 10am–2pm & 3–7pm, Sat & Sun 1–5pm.

Divadlo v Celetné Celetná 17, Nové Město, ☎224 809 168, ✆www.divadlovceletne.cz; metro náměstí

Republiky. Home of several fringe companies, and a student drama venue, which puts on tourist-friendly productions (occasionally puppetry and black theatre or *černé divadlo*). Box office in café Mon–Fri 9am–7.30pm, Sat & Sun noon–7.30pm.

Duncan Centre Branická 41, Braník ☎244 461 342, ✆www.osf.cz/dc; tram #3, #16, #17 or #21, stop Přístaviště. Interesting dance pieces by resident and visiting artists at this theatre based in a school for contemporary dance in the southern suburb of Braník.

Laterna magika (Magic Lantern) Nová scéna, Národní 4, Nové Město ☎224 914 129, ✆www.laterna.cz; metro Národní třída. The National Theatre's *Nová scéna*, one of Prague's most modern and versatile stages, is now the main base for Laterna magika, founders of multimedia theatre way back in 1958, now content just to pull in crowds of tourists. Box office Mon–Sat 10am–8pm.

Ta Fantastika Karlova 8, Staré Město ☎222 221 369; metro Staroměstská. Probably the best of the "black theatre" venues, albeit strategically located close to the Charles Bridge, offering dialogue-free shows specifically aimed at tourists. Box office daily 11am–9.30pm.

Cinemas

Aero Biskupcova 31, Žižkov ☎271 771 349, ✆www.kinoaero.cz; tram #1, #9, #16 or #19, stop

Biskupcova. Crumbling arthouse cinema that shows rolling mini-festivals, interspersed by more

popular movies.
Dlabačov Bělohorská 24, Břevnov ☎233 359 058; tram #8, #22 or #23, stop Malovanka. Excellent film club on the ground floor of the ugly *Hotel Pyramid*, showing a discerning selection of new releases and plenty of art-house classics.
Lucerna Vodičkova 36, Nové Město ☎224 216 972; metro Můstek. Without doubt the most ornate film theatre in Prague, decked out in Moorish style by Havel's grandfather, in the *pasáž* the family once owned.

MAT Studio Karlovo náměstí 19, Nové Město ☎224 915 765; metro Karlovo náměstí. Café and cinema popular with the film crowd, with an eclectic programme of shorts, documentaries and Czech films with English subtitles. Entrance is on Odborů.
Ponrepo – Bio Konvikt Bartolomějská 11, Staré Město ☎224 237 233; metro Národní třída. Really old classics from the black-and-white era, dug out from the National Film Archives. Membership cards (150Kč) can only be bought Mon–Fri 2–5pm, and you need to bring a photo.

Listings

Airlines Austrian Airlines, Revoluční 15, Nové Město ☎224 826 199, ☎www.awa.com; metro Staroměstská. British Airways, Ovocný trh 8, Staré Město ☎222 114 444, ☎www.britishairways.cz; metro Můstek. British Midland, Kozí 3, Staré Město ☎224 810 180, ☎www.britishmidland.cz; metro Staroměstská. Czech Airlines (ČSA), V celnici 5, Nové Město ☎220 104 310, ☎www.csa.cz; metro náměstí Republiky. Delta, Národní 32, Nové Město ☎224 946 733, ☎www.delta.com; metro Národní třída. KLM, Na příkopě 21, Nové Město ☎233 090 933, ☎www.klm.cz; metro Můstek.
American Express Amex, Václavské náměstí 56, Nové Město ☎222 800 111, ☎www.americanexpress.cz; metro Muzeum; daily 9am–7pm.
Books Anagram, Týn 4, Nové Město ☎www.anagram.cz; metro náměstí Republiky. Well-stocked, central English-language bookstore. Mon–Sat 10am–8pm, Sun 10am–6pm. The Globe, Pštrossova 6 ☎www.globebookstore.cz; metro Národní třída/Karlovo náměstí. *The* expat bookstore *par excellence*: both a social centre and superbly well-stocked ramshackle store, with an adjacent café and friendly staff. Mon–Thurs & Sun 10am–midnight, Fri & Sat 10am–1am.
Cultural centres American Center for Culture and Commerce, Hybernská 7A, Nové Město ☎224 231 085, ☎www.usis.cz; metro náměstí Republiky. Austrian Cultural Institute (Rakouský kulturní institut), Jungmannovo náměstí 18, Nové Město ☎224 234 875, ☎www.austria.cz/kultur; metro Můstek. British Council (Britská rada), Národní 10, Nové Město ☎221 991 111, ☎www.britishcouncil.org; metro Národní třída. Goethe Institut, Masarykovo nábřeží 32, Nové Město ☎221 962 111, ☎www.goethe.de; metro Národní třída. Hungarian Cultural Centre (Maďarské kulturní středisko), Rytířská 25–27, Staré Město ☎224 222 424; metro Můstek. Institut Français (Francouzský institut), Štěpánská 35, Nové Město ☎222 230 577,

☎www.ifp.cz; metro Muzeum. Instituta Italiana di Cultura (Italský kulturní institut), Šporkova 14, Malá Strana ☎257 533 600. Polish Institute (Polský institut), Václavské náměstí 51, Nové Město ☎224 214 708, ☎www.polskyinstitut.cz; metro Muzeum. Slovenský institut Purkyňova 4, Nové Město ☎224 948 137; metro Národní třída.
Dentist Václavské náměstí 33, Nové Město ☎224 228 984.
Department stores Bílá labuť, Na poříčí 23, Nové Město. Kotva, nám. Republiky 8, Nové Město. Tesco, Národní 26, Nové Město.
Embassies/consulates Australia, Klimentská 10 ☎251 018 350, ☎www.austrade.gov.au; metro náměstí Republiky. Austria, Viktora Huga 10, Smíchov ☎257 090 511, ☎wwwvol.cz/Austria/. Britain, Thunovská 14, Malá Strana ☎257 402 111, ☎www.britain.cz; metro Malostranská. Canada, Mickiewiczova 6, Hradčany ☎272 101 800, ☎www.dfait-maeci.gc.ca; metro Hradčanská. Germany, Vlašska 19, Malá Strana ☎257 113 111, ☎www.german-embassy.cz; metro Malostranská. Ireland, Tržiště 13, Malá Strana ☎257 530 061; metro Malostranská. New Zealand, Dykova 19, Vinohrady ☎222 514 672; metro Jiřího z Poděbrad. Poland, Valdštejnská 8, Malá Strana ☎257 530 388, ☎www.polamb.cz; metro Malostranská. Slovakia, Pod hradbami 1, Dejvice ☎233 321 442; metro Dejvická. Ukraine, Charles de Gaulle 20, Dejvice ☎224 226 157; metro Dejvická. USA, Tržiště 15, Malá Strana ☎257 530 663, ☎www.usembassy.cz; metro Malostranská.
Exchange offices 24hr service at 28 října 13, Nové Město; metro Můstek.
Football Prague's (and the Czech Republic's) most successful club is Sparta Praha (☎www.sparta.cz), who play at a stadium by the Letná plain (five minutes' walk from, or one tram stop east of, metro Hradčanská); Prague's second most successful team, Slavia Praha (☎www.slavia.cz), play at

Eden, on Vladivostocká in Vršovice, just off U Slavie (tram #22 or #23 from metro Náměstí Míru or tram #6, #19, stop Slavia); snapping at their heels are Viktoria Žižkov (❀www.fkviktoriazizkov.cz), whose stadium is on Seifertova in Žižkov (tram #5, #9 or #26 from metro Hlavní nádraží to Husinecká stop); Prague's least successful professional side, Bohemians (❀www.fc-bohemians.cz), play just south of Vršovické náměstí (tram #4, #22 or #23 from metro Náměstí Míru to Vršovické náměstí stop).

Hospitals For an English-speaking doctor, you should go to the private Nemocnice na Homolce, Roentgenova 2, Motol ☏257 271 111; bus #167 from metro Anděl. If it's an emergency, dial ☏155 for an ambulance and you'll be taken to the nearest hospital.

Ice Hockey Prague's top hockey team is Sparta Praha (❀www.hcsparta.cz), and their *zimní stadión* (winter stadium) is at Za elektrárnou, next door to the Výstaviště exhibition grounds in Holešovice (metro Nádraží Holešovice). Prague's only other first division team is Slavia Praha (❀www.hc-slavia.cz), who play at the *zimní stadión* near the Slavia football ground on Vladivostocká in Vršovice (tram #22 or #23 from metro Náměstí Míru or tram #6, #19, stop Kubánské náměstí).

Laundrettes Laundry Kings, Dejvická 16, Dejvice ☏233 343 743; metro Hradčanská; Mon–Fri 6am–10pm, Sat & Sun 8am–10pm. Laundryland, Na příkopě 12, Nové Město ☏221 014 632, ❀www.laundryland.cz; metro Můstek; Mon–Fri 9am–8pm, Sat 9am–7pm & Sun 11am–7pm.

Left luggage Prague's main bus and train stations have lockers which have instructions in English. The train stations also have 24hr left luggage offices.

Lost property The main train stations have lost property offices – look for the sign *ztráty a nálezy*

– and there's a central municipal one at Karoliny Světlé 5, Staré Město. If you've lost your passport, then get in touch with your embassy (see p.18).

Markets Havelská, Staré Město; metro Můstek. Food, flowers and wooden toys are sold in the only open-air fruit and veg market in central Prague. Mon–Fri 8am–6pm, Sat & Sun 9am–6pm.

Newspapers You can get most foreign dailies and magazines at the kiosks at the bottom of Wenceslas Square, outside metro Můstek.

Pharmacies 24hr chemists at Palackého 5, Nové Město (☏224 946 982).

Police If you wish to extend your visa or your stay, you need to go to the Cizinecká policie (Foreigners' Police), Olšanská 2, Žižkov. In an emergency dial ☏158.

Post office Main office/poste restante at Jindřišská 14, Nové Město; 24hr post office at Hybernská 15, Nové Město.

Records and music Bontonland, Palác Koruna, Václavské nám. 1 ❀www.bontonland.cz; metro Můstek. Prague's biggest record store in the *pasáž* at the bottom of Wenceslas Square, with rock, folk, jazz and classical, and headphones for previews to boot. Classical branch at Jungmannova 20, Nové Město. Mon–Sat 9am–8pm, Sun 10am–7pm.

Soccer See "Football".

Swimming Divoká Šárka, Vokovice; tram #20 or #26 from metro Dejvická to the Divoká Šárka terminus. Idyllically located in a craggy valley to the northwest of Prague, with two small outdoor pools filled with cold but fresh and clean water – great for a full, hot day out. Food and drink and plenty of shade available, too. May to mid-Sept daily 9am–7pm. YMCA, Na poříčí 12, Nové Město ☏224 875 811; metro náměstí Republiky. Has a new, clean, 25-metre indoor pool, the best in central Prague, though it often closes during the main part of the day for private classes. Mon–Fri 6.30–10pm, Sat & Sun 10am–9pm.

Central Bohemia

Few capital cities can boast such extensive unspoilt tracts of woodland so near at hand as Prague. Once you leave the half-built high-rise estates of the outer suburbs behind, the softly rolling hills and somnolent villages of central **Bohemia** (Čechy) take over.

To the north, several chateaux grace the banks of the Vltava, including that of the wine-producing town of **Mělník**, on the Labe (Elbe) plain. Beyond Mělník lie the wooded gorges of the **Kokořínsko** region, too far for a day-trip unless you've your own transport, but perfect for a weekend in the country. One of the most obvious day-trip destinations is to the east of Prague: **Kutná Hora**, a medieval silver-mining town with one of the most beautiful Gothic cathedrals in the country and a macabre gallery of bones in the suburb of **Sedlec**.

Further south, there are a couple of chateaux worth visiting along the **Sázava valley**; while nearby, two more, **Průhonice** and **Konopiště**, are set in exceptionally beautiful and expansive grounds – with a car, you could take in several in a day. Southwest of Prague, a similar mix of woods and rolling hills surrounds the popular castle of **Karlštejn**, a gem of Gothic architecture, dramatically situated above the River Berounka. There are numerous possibilities for walking in the region around Karštejn and, further upstream, in the forests of **Křivoklátsko**. West of Prague, near Kladno, there are two places of pilgrimage: **Lány** is the resting place of the founder of the modern Czechoslovak state and summer residence of the president; and **Lidice**, razed to the ground by the SS, recalls the horror of Nazi occupation.

Transport throughout Bohemia is fairly straightforward, thanks to a comprehensive network of railway lines and regional bus services, though connections can be less than smooth and journeys slow. However, if you're planning to see a few places outside Prague, or one of the destinations more difficult to reach, it might be worth hiring a car.

North along the Vltava

One of the quickest and most rewarding trips out of the capital is to follow the Vltava as it twists northwards across the plain towards the River Labe at Mělník. This is the beginning of the so-called **záhrada Čech** (Garden of Bohemia), a flat and fertile region whose cherry blossoms are always the first to herald the Bohemian spring and whose roads in summer are lined with stalls overflowing with fruit and vegetables. But the real reason to venture into this relatively flat landscape is to visit the **chateaux** that lie along the banks of the river, all easily reached by train from Prague's Masarykovo nádraží (with a possible change at Kralupy).

Beyond Kralupy

The Nobel prize-winning poet Jaroslav Seifert didn't beat around the bush when he wrote that **KRALUPY NAD VLTAVOU** "is not a beautiful town and never was". Seifert had happy childhood memories of the place, but it was heavily bombed in World War II, and postwar industrial development left it with "smokestacks . . . like phantom trees, without branches, without leaves, without blossoms, without bees". Now, Kralupy's oil refineries and chemical plants have spread across both sides of the river, but it's still worth making the thirty-minute train journey from Prague, as just a few kilometres to the north, on either side of the Vltava, are two fine chateaux: Nelahozeves on the left bank and Veltrusy on the right – again, both accessible by train.

Nelahozeves

Shortly after pulling out of Kralupy, the train passes through a short tunnel and comes to rest at Nelahozeves zastávka, the first of two stations in the village of **NELAHOZEVES** and the one to get off at. Above the railway sits the village's monumentally large **zámek** (Tues–Sun 9am–5pm), built in the 1550s by

Italian builders for one of the lackeys of the Habsburg Ferdinand I, and totally smothered in sgraffito. In the early 1990s, the chateau was returned to the Lobkowicz family, who bought the place way back in 1623, and it's now enjoying a wonderful renaissance as the family's museum showpiece.

The interior is well worth a visit, having been restored and replenished with paintings given back to the family after the end of Communism in 1989. There's a choice of tours, and often the possibility of paying extra for an English-speaking guide, but since the family's vast **art collection** is one of the highlights, there seems little point in opting for the half-hour tour (*trasa 2*), which skips the European masters, rather than the hour-long tour (*trasa 1*). Only the most exceptional works are on display, among them Pieter Breughel the Elder's sublime *Haymaking* from the artist's famous cycle of seasons, a view of St Paul's Cathedral across the Thames by Canaletto, and a portrait of the Infanta Margarita Teresa (possibly by Velázquez), who was betrothed to her uncle the emperor Leopold I from the age of three. The family also has a long history of musical patronage (most notably Beethoven) and the musical scores on show are pretty impressive, while the family library's prize possession is a Gutenberg Bible.

The other reason for stopping at Nelahozeves is that **Antonín Dvořák** (1841–1904) was born and bred under the shadow of the chateau, at the house (no. 12) next door to the post office. Dvořák was originally apprenticed to a butcher but, on the recommendation of his schoolmaster, was sent to the Prague Organ School instead. He went on to become director of the Prague conservatoire and by far the country's most famous composer. If there's someone around at the house (Tues–Thurs, Sat & Sun 9am–noon & 2–5pm, Fri 9am–noon), you can have a quick look at the great man's rocking chair and various other personal effects.

Veltrusy

The industrial suburbs of Kralupy stop just short of the gardens of the zámek of **Veltrusy** (May–Sept Tues–Sun 9am–noon & 1–5pm). The classic Baroque symmetry of the chateau is more hospitable than the one at Nelahozeves, its green shutters and four hennaed wings pivoting round a bulbous, green-domed building that recalls earlier country houses in France or Italy. It was built in the early eighteenth century as a plaything for the upwardly mobile Chotek family, its 290 acres of surrounding woodland perfect for a little light hunting. It was also the unlikely venue for the world's first trade fair, which took place in 1754 under the title "The Veltrusy Large Trade Fair of Products of the Czech Kingdom", and drew a distinguished audience including the empress Maria Theresa.

Once again, there are two **guided tours**, both lasting half an hour: *trasa 1* concentrates almost exclusively on the period furniture, while *trasa 2* intersperses period interiors with a lot of porcelain and a peek at the library. Don't, whatever you do, miss out on the **Zámecký park**, as the Choteks were keen gardeners, and the grounds are liberally dotted with fallow deer and follies. To get to the chateau from the train station at Nelahozeves (one stop on from Nelahozeves zastávka), it's a 1.5km walk across the busy road bridge, or the smaller bridge further south. There are also regular buses to Veltrusy from Prague's Florenc bus station.

Practicalities

If you fancy staying, there are several houses also offering inexpensive **private rooms** on the road to Veltrusy, and just outside its chateau grounds, there's a very good **campsite**, *ATC Obora* (Feb–Dec). It's a great spot for watching the barges on the Vltava, but, given the pollutants that seep into the river further upstream, no place for a dip. There are a couple of pubs in Nelahozeves, but the nicest place to **eat** is the *Zámecká restaurace* in the courtyard of Nelahozeves zámek, where you can quaff *Lobkowicz* wine or beer with your meal.

Říp

Czech legend holds that the founding father of the nation, called Praotec Čech ("Forefather Czech"), led a group of his Slavic followers to the top of **Říp** (461m), some 20km north of Kralupy, sometime around the sixth century AD, and proclaimed all the land around as Čechy. The name has certainly stuck – Čechy translates as "the Czech lands" or Bohemia – and the legend itself renders the hill a fairly important point of pilgrimage. Říp is an upside-down bowl of a hill that forms an intriguing lump in this otherwise monotonous landscape, and is quite a popular summertime hike. At its top, the twelfth-century Romanesque rotunda of sv Jiří a Vojtěch (usually closed) commemorates the legend. The walk up is not difficult, and judging from the splendid views of flat fields spreading for miles around, it's not hard to recognize the peaceful agrarian roots of the Czech nation. Getting to Říp is easiest via the red-marked path from Roudnice nad Labem, 5km to the north, which is on the secondary rail line between Prague and Děčín; if travelling by car, park in the village of Ctiněves just south of the hill.

Mělník

Occupying a spectacular, commanding site at the confluence of the Vltava and Labe rivers, **MĚLNÍK**, 33km north of Prague on route 9, lies at the heart of Bohemia's tiny wine-growing region. The town's history goes back to the ninth century, when it was handed over to the Přemyslids as part of Ludmilla's dowry on her marriage to Prince Bořivoj (see p.568). And it was here, too, that she introduced her heathen grandson, Václav (later to become St Wenceslas, aka "Good King"; see p.72), to the joys of Christianity. Viticulture became the town's economic mainstay only after Charles IV, aching for a little of the French wine of his youth, introduced grapes from Burgundy (over which he also ruled).

The old town

Mělník's greatest monument is its Renaissance **zámek** (daily March–Dec 10am–5.30pm; Ⓦwww.lobkowicz-melnik.cz), perched high above the flat plains and visible for miles around. The present building, its courtyard covered in familiar sgraffito patterns, is back in the hands of its last aristocratic owners, the Lobkowicz family, who have restored the chateau's magnificently proportioned rooms, which also provide great views out over the plain. Visits are by guided tour only, and you've a choice between a half-hour trawl (60Kč) round seven beautifully painted rooms of the castle interior, filled with artefacts and Old Masters returned to the family since 1989, or touring the wine museum in the cellars (25Kč), finishing up with samples of plonk; alternatively, you can do both tours. In addition, there's a museum of prams, pushchairs and baby carriages which forms part of the local museum (April–Oct Tues–Sun 9am–5pm) on the first floor of the chateau.

Below the chateau, vines cling to the south-facing terraces, as the land plunges into the river below. From beneath the great tower of Mělník's onion-domed church of **sv Petr and Pavel**, next door to the chateau, there's an even better view of the rivers' confluence and the subsidiary canal, once so congested with vessels that traffic lights had to be introduced. The church itself contains a compellingly macabre **ossuary** or *kostnice* (Tues–Sun 10am–12.30pm & 1.15–4pm), filled with over 10,000 bones of medieval plague victims, fashioned into weird and wonderful shapes by students around a hundred years ago.

The rest of the old town is pleasant enough for a casual stroll. One half of the main square, **náměstí Míru**, is lined with Baroque arcades typical of the region, and there's an old medieval gateway nearby, the **Pražská brána**, which has been converted into an art gallery. Finally, the other part of the city museum (Tues–Sun 9am–5pm) is in a burgher house at no. 54, and contains a moderately interesting model of medieval Mělník as well as displays on regional folk life.

Practicalities

The main line from Prague veers northwest beyond Nelahozeves, so it's easiest to take a fast **train** from Prague's Hlavní nádraží to Všetaty, and change, which gets you to Mělník in around an hour. There's a regular **bus** service from Prague, too, which takes around fifty minutes. To reach the older part of town from the **bus station**, simply head up Krombholcova in the direction of the big church tower. If your next destination is Liběchov or Litoměřice, you have the choice of either the bus or the train; the **train station** is further still from the old town, a couple of blocks northeast of the bus station, down Jiřího z Poděbrad.

The **tourist office** is on náměstí Míru, and can help with accommodation, if you're hoping to stay over. There are **private rooms** available on Legionářů, to the north of the old town, and on Palackého náměstí, off the main square. In the shadow of the chateau to the south you'll find the relatively plush *Hotel Jaro*, 17 listopadu 174 (☎315 626 852; ℉315 626 851; ❹), and diagonally opposite, the spotless *Penzion V podzámčí*, J. Seiferta 167 (☎ & ℉315 622 889, ✉hrzi@post.cz; ❸). The nearest **campsite** (closed Christmas & New Year) is around 750m north of the old town, on Klášterní (a continuation of Fügnerova).

As for **food and drink**, the *Zámecká restaurace* is as good (and cheap) a place as any to sample some of the local wine (and enjoy the view): the red Ludmila is the most famous of Mělník's wines, and there's even a rare Czech rosé produced by the castle vineyards, but if you prefer white, try a bottle of Tramín. Equally good views can be had from the *Stará škola* restaurant, behind the church; otherwise, you could try *Na hradbách*, on náměstí Míru, which serves up big portions of rabbit and game with local wines, plus Guinness and Kilkenny, in a cosy brick and wood-panelled interior.

Liběchov

Seven kilometres north and ten minutes by train from Mělník – just out of sight of the giant coal-fired power station that provides most of Prague's electricity – is the rhubarb-and-custard-coloured **zámek** (Tues–Sun 9am–5pm) at **LIBĚCHOV** (Liboch). Even without the sickly colour scheme, it's a bizarre place: formal and two-dimensional when viewed from the French gardens at the front, but bulging like an amphitheatre around the back by the entrance. Inside is another surprise, a **Museum of Asian and Oriental Cultures**, based around the collections of Czech explorer Vojta Náprstek and featuring endless Buddhas, Mongolian printing equipment, Balinese monster gear and Javanese puppets – all of which make for a fascinating half-hour tour. The main dining hall, now full of Asian musical instruments, is curious, too, smothered in its original barley-sugar decor with little sculpted jesters crouching mischievously in the corners of the ceiling.

For all the chateau's excesses, the **village** itself is little more than a *hostinec* (pub) and a bend in the road, but straggling up the valley are the remains of what was once an attractive spa resort for ailing Praguers. Many of the old *Gasthäuser* are still standing, including the *Pension Stüdl* where **Franz Kafka** spent the winter of 1918. It was here that he met and became engaged to Julie Wohryzek, daughter of a Jewish shoemaker from Prague – a match vigorously opposed by his father. Kafka was prompted to write his vitriolic *Letter to His Father*, which he passed on to his mother, who wisely made sure it never got any further. On the other side of the trickling River Liběchovka, there's a **campsite** (mid-May to mid-Sept), a possible starting point for hikes into the Kokořín region (see below).

Kokořínsko

Northeast of Mělník, you leave the low plains of the Labe for a plateau region known as **Kokořínsko**, a hidden pocket of wooded hills which takes its name from the Gothic castle rising through the treetops at its centre. The sandstone plateau has weathered over the millennia to form sunken valleys and bizarre rocky outcrops, providing great scope for some gentle hiking. With picturesque valleys, such as the Kokořínský důl, dotted with well-preserved, half-timbered villages and riddled with marked paths, it comes as a surprise that the whole area isn't buzzing all summer.

At the centre of the region is the village of **KOKOŘÍN**, whose dramatic setting and spectacular fourteenth-century **hrad** (April & Oct Sat & Sun 9am–4pm; May–Sept Tues–Sun 9am–5pm) greatly inspired the Czech nineteenth-century Romantics. The castle is a perfect hideaway, ideal for the robbers who used it as a base after it fell into disrepair in the sixteenth century. Not until the end of the nineteenth century did it get a new lease of life, from a jumped-up local landowner, Václav Špaček, who bought himself a title and refurbished the place as a family memorial. There's precious little inside and no incentive to endure the guided tour, as you can explore the ramparts and climb the tallest tower on your own.

If you've got your own transport, Kokořínsko makes a pleasant day-trip from Prague. For those using public transport, take a bus to Mělník and change there. Alternatively, you could catch the local train from Mělník to Mšeno, from where it's a three-kilometre walk west to Kokořín on the green-marked path. Finding **accommodation** shouldn't be too much of a problem, with plenty of private rooms available in Kokořín, and Kanina 2km further east, plus a decent pension, *Myslivna* (☎315 695 036; ❸), and a cluster of **campsites** (May–Oct) at Kokořínský důl, a couple of kilometres down the valley.

East of Prague

The scenery **east of Prague** is as flat as it is around Mělník, a rich blanket of fields spreading over the plain as far as the eye can see. Two places you might consider heading for are **Mladá Boleslav**, where Škoda cars are produced, and **Přerov nad Labem**, an open-air museum of the kind of folk architecture that was common in Bohemia less than a century ago. The towns of **Poděbrady** and **Kolín** are not likely to be high on most people's itineraries, but make convenient stop-off points when heading east.

Přerov nad Labem

The **open-air museum** or **skansen** (April–Oct Tues–Sun 9am–5pm) of folk architecture at the village of **PŘEROV NAD LABEM** was the first of its kind in central Europe when it was founded in 1895 (it is called a *skansen*, after the first such museum founded in a Stockholm suburb in 1891). Later, in the 1950s and 1960s, *skansens* became quite a fad, as collectivization and urbanization wiped out traditional rural communities, along with their distinctive folk culture and wooden architecture. During the summer, Přerov's *skansen* is busy with tour groups from Prague, wandering through the various half-timbered and stone buildings, some brought here plank by plank from nearby villages, some from Přerov itself. Particularly evocative is the reconstructed eighteenth-century village school, with a portrait of the Austrian emperor taking pride of place amid the Catholic icons, and a delicate paper theatre that was used in drama lessons.

To get to the village, take one of the three daily **buses** from Prague (Černý Most metro) to Poděbrady, which drop you off right in front of the *skansen*. If you're driving, the village is around 25km east of Prague (take exit 18 off the E67 at Bříství and follow the signs).

Mladá Boleslav

Fast trains from Praha hlavní nádraží take an hour to reach **MLADÁ BOLESLAV** (Jungblunzau), 30km or so northeast of Prague on the E65, where Václav Laurin and Václav Klement set up a bicycle factory in the mid-nineteenth century. They went on to produce the country's first car in 1905, and in the 1920s merged with the Škoda industrial empire. Škoda Auto, as the company is now known, is one of the largest employers in the republic, and is entirely separate from the heavy engineering arm of the Škoda empire, which is based in Plzeň (see p.215).

The main reason for coming here is to visit the **Škoda Museum** (daily 9am–5pm), which exhibits over 25 old Škodas and Laurin & Klements in its showroom. The exhibition starts off, as the factory itself did, with an L & K bicycle and a couple of motorbikes. There are also several vintage vehicles and a 1917 fire engine, but the vast majority of the cars date from the 1920s and 1930s – big, mostly black, gangster-style motors. You can even admire the new fleet of Škoda cars produced since the company was acquired by Volkswagen (see box) – Czechs are very proud of their new international-quality Octavias and Fabias. The museum is suitably situated on třída Václava Klementa, northeast of the town centre near the edge of the massive car plant, and badly signposted. Diagonally opposite the museum, and handy for orientation, is a park with a palatial neo-Baroque *Gymnasium* at the far end. Close by, there's a wonderfully provincial Art Nouveau theatre from 1912, brightly painted in white, gold and blue.

The **staré město** lies to the east of the River Jizera, in a tight bend of one of its tributaries, the Klenice. It has little going for it besides its pristinely painted Renaissance **radnice** and the Gothic **hrad** tucked into the southernmost part of town, used as a barracks by the Habsburgs and now home to the local museum (Tues–Sun 9am–noon & 1–5pm). However, if you're looking for somewhere to **eat**, the *Jihočeská hostinec*, beside the castle entrance, has a big fish restaurant adjacent to it, called the *Rybářská restaurace*, with an amazing menu

The story of Škoda

For Czechs, the **Škoda industrial empire** is a great Czech achievement and a source of national pride. It's therefore doubly ironic that the word *škoda* means "shame" or "pity" in Czech – a marketing own-goal were it not the name of the founding father of the Czech car industry, **Emil Škoda**. The last Škoda model produced under the Communists was very favourably received, even in the West (whence a large proportion of its components derived). In 1989, there was a three-year waiting list for the car, despite a retail price equivalent to over twice the average yearly salary. Then in 1991, in one of the many controversial deals in the country's privatization programme, the German company Volkswagen bought a majority stake in Škoda for a song. Volkswagen invested heavily in the company, and set its design teams aggressively to work, bringing forth new models such as the Felicia, Octavia and Fabia. VW ultimately acquired all the remaining shares of Škoda in 2000, so that the Czech "family silver" is now completely in the hands of a foreign entity, and while the Czechs may not feel quite the same way about the company, the new models brought out under VW guidance have vastly improved the international image of Škoda Auto. In addition, observers of the Czech economy may note that this VW-Škoda joint venture/privatization programme has turned out the best of all major Czech company privatization efforts.

that includes pike, eel and plaice. **Accommodation** in town is on the pricey side, no doubt as it caters to the occasional foreign executive visiting Škoda. *Hotel U hradu* (☎326 721 049, ℉326 721 039; ❹) by the zámek is the top pick, while the smaller pension *Zlatý kohout* (☎326 721 937; ❹) sits opposite the radnice. The nearest **campsite**, *Škoda* (May–Sept), is 2km north of town in the suburb of Kosmonosy.

Poděbrady

If spa towns evoke turn-of-the-twentieth-century hotels for you, then **PODĚBRADY** will come as something of a disappointment. The spa waters were actually only discovered this century, with the town's previous existence simply due to its strategic position on the east–west trade routes. However, the **spa** itself is pleasant enough, attracting thousands of patients every year, most of whom can be seen promenading through the town's park around teatime, admiring the fully functioning floral clock. For a glimpse of the town's halcyon days in the last years of the Empire, check out the local **Polabské muzeum** at Palackého 68 (Tues–Sun 9am–5pm).

Facing onto the main square, **Jiřího náměstí**, is the **zámek** (May–Oct Tues–Sun 9am–5pm), birthplace of the town's most famous son, **George of Poděbrady** (Jiří z Poděbrad to the Czechs), the only Hussite (and last Czech) king of Bohemia. The present structure was actually built a hundred years after his death and houses the minutest of historical exhibitions. The only other trace of George is the green copper equestrian statue in the main square.

Poděbrady does provide a convenient stop on the road heading east from Prague, and is less than an hour by train or bus from the capital. To get to the main square and castle from the train and bus stations, simply walk south through the park of náměstí T.G. Masaryka. Furthermore, Poděbrady has a wide choice of **hotels**. The *Bellevue-Tlapák* (☎325 616 483, ⓦwww.bellevue.cz; ❺), overlooking the park on náměstí T.G. Masaryka, is a fairly modern spa fixture with all manner of treatments available, from natural spring bathing pools to massage therapy. Cheaper alternatives include the nicely redone

Soudek at Palackého 174 (☎ & ℱ325 613 191; ❷); try to get a room in the back to avoid the noisy street below. You can even stay in the zámek itself (*Zámek Poděbrady;* ☎325 614 456, ℮zdenek.bouda@seznam.cz; ❷): a small section of the chateau has been converted by the youthful proprietors of the Klub Netopýr (see below) into rooms that are comfortable enough for the budget-minded. Alternatively, there's a **campsite**, *Golf* (April–Oct), a little further upstream from the castle.

With visitors of one kind or another all summer, there's a fair selection of films and classical concerts on offer, as well as some varied **eating** options: the *Klub Netopýr* in the castle courtyard is indeed clubby, and serves inexpensive Czech food, while *Bašta U krále Jiřího*, on the main square, is a step up the scale. For something different, try the Chinese food at the nearby *Savoy*, or a floating dinner aboard the *Král Jiří*, moored by the castle.

Kolín

In addition to its railway sidings and industrial plants, **KOLÍN** – 16km south of Poděbrady along the Labe – has actually managed to preserve its central medieval core. One of numerous towns in Bohemia founded by German colonists in the thirteenth century, its streets are laid out in chessboard fashion, so finding the cobbled main square, Karlovo náměstí, should present few problems. There's a wonderfully imposing Renaissance **radnice**, covered in sgraffito and decorated with four rose-coloured panels from the nineteenth century, and four unusual Baroque gables on the west side, but the rest of the square is unspectacular.

Kolín's most significant monument is actually tucked away in the southeast corner of the old town. On raised ground at the end of Karlova, on a rather cramped site, stands the Gothic church of **sv Bartoloměj** (St Bartholomew), begun in 1261. The church's fairly gloomy nave is suffused with an unusually intense blue light from the modern stained-glass windows, which disturbs the otherwise resolutely medieval ambience. But it's the choir, rebuilt and extended in the fourteenth century by Peter Parler, which provides the highlight, taking up almost half the church with its seven chapels, intricate tracery and spectacular ribbed vaulting.

Like many towns in Bohemia and Moravia, Kolín had a significant **Jewish community**, which was subsequently all but wiped out in the Holocaust. The ghetto was situated in the southwest corner of the old town, in what is now Na Hradbách and Karoliny Světlé, and after descending into dereliction over the past six decades, it is now largely cleaned up. There's a plaque commemorating the 2200 Jews deported during the Holocaust at Na Hradbách 157; inside is the **tourist office** (Mon–Fri 9am–5pm, Sat 10am–3pm; ☎321 712 021), which gives guided tours of the marvellously renovated seventeenth-century **synagogue**, hidden in the rear courtyard. Though much was damaged or has disappeared in the intervening years, the bright stuccoed interior still contains portions of Hebrew writings lovingly restored on the walls, amid flourishing floral designs. This mini-complex once contained a Jewish school and residence hall for the rabbis, though these have long since been turned into offices. The synagogue is no longer active, but because of the building's fine acoustics, concerts are held here on occasion; ask at the tourist office. A few streets away on Sluneční, outside the former city walls, is an overgrown Jewish cemetery – a faint image of the famous one in Prague.

Fans of the turn-of-the-twentieth-century sculpture of František Bílek should check out his **statue of Jan Hus**, which is hidden behind the Hussite church in the town park. Though slightly weathered, it's an impressive, and typically expressive, piece of work, rising a good three metres off the ground. To get there, head west down Kutnohorská, turn right into Smetanova, then right again for the park.

If you need **to stay overnight**, there's the *Hotel Theresia*, Na Petříně (☎321 711 117; ❹), on a busy road west of the old town, or two excellent pensions in the old town itself, both with equally commendable restaurants: *Pension pod věží*, Parléřova 40 (☎321 723 877; ❸), or *U rabína*, near the synagogue on Karoliny Světlé (☎ & ℱ321 724 463; ❸). Kolín also happens to be closely associated with **František Kmoch** (1848–1912), king of Bohemian oompah music, and every year, during the last weekend of June, a brass band festival is held in the town in his honour, featuring a wide range of music from Kmoch to Dvořák and a huge parade of bands from all over the country.

Kutná Hora and around

For 250 years or so, **KUTNÁ HORA** (Kuttenberg) was one of the most important towns in Bohemia, second only to Prague. At the end of the fourteenth century its population was equal to that of London, its shantytown suburbs straggled across what are now green fields, and its ambitious building projects set out to rival those of the capital itself. Today, Kutná Hora is a small provincial town with a population of just over 20,000, but the monuments dotted around it, the superb

Gothic cathedral, and the remarkable monastery and ossuary in the suburb of **Sedlec**, make it one of the most enjoyable of all possible day-trips from Prague. In addition to the new influx of tourists, Kutná Hora has also benefited from a large injection of cash from the American tobacco giants Phillip Morris, who now run the local tobacco factory as a joint venture.

A brief history

Kutná Hora's road to prosperity began in the late thirteenth century with the discovery of **silver deposits** in the surrounding area. German miners were invited to settle and work the seams, and around 1300 Václav II founded the royal mint here, importing Italian craftsmen to run it. Much of the town's wealth was used to fund the beautification of Prague, but it also allowed for the construction of one of the most magnificent churches in central Europe and a number of other prestigious Gothic monuments in Kutná Hora itself.

At the time of the Hussite Wars, the town was mostly German-speaking and staunchly Catholic; local miners used to throw captured Hussites into the deep mineshafts and leave them to die of starvation. Word got out, and the town was besieged and eventually taken by Žižka's fanatical Táborites in 1421, only to be recaptured by Emperor Sigismund and his papal forces shortly afterwards, and again by Žižka the following year.

While the silver stocks remained high, the town was able to recover some of its former prosperity, but cheap Spanish imports of silver from South America caused a collapse in the price of silver during the sixteenth century. By the end of the century the mines had dried up, and Kutná Hora's wealth and importance came to an abrupt end – when the Swedes marched on the town during the Thirty Years' War, they had to be bought off with beer rather than silver. The town never fully recovered, shrivelling to less than a third of its former size, its fate emphatically sealed by a devastating fire in 1770.

The Town

The small, unassuming houses that line the town's medieval lanes and main square, **Palackého náměstí**, give little idea of its former glories. A narrow alleyway on the south side of the square, however, leads to the leafy Havlíčkovo náměstí, on which lies the **Vlašský dvůr** (Italian Court), originally conceived as a palace by Václav II, and for three centuries the town's bottomless purse. It was here that Florentine minters produced the Prague Groschen (*pražské groše*), a silver coin widely used throughout central Europe until the nineteenth century. The building itself has been mucked about with over the years, most recently – and most brutally – by nineteenth-century restorers, who left only the chestnut trees, a fourteenth-century oriel window (capped by an unlikely looking wooden onion dome) and the miner's fountain unmolested. The original workshops of the minters have been bricked in, but the outlines of their little doors and windows are still visible in the courtyard. The short **guided tour** (daily: April & Oct 9am–5pm; May, June & Sept 9am–6pm; July & Aug 10am–6pm) of the old chapel, treasury and royal palace gives you a fair idea of the building's former importance.

Outside the court is a statue of the country's founder and first president, **T.G. Masaryk**; twice removed – once by the Nazis and once by the Communists – it has now been returned to its pride of place. Before you leave, take a quick look in the court gardens, which descend in steps to the Vrchlice Valley. This is undoubtedly Kutná Hora's best profile, with a splendid view over to the Cathedral of sv Barbora (see opposite).

Behind the Vlašský dvůr is **sv Jakub** (St James), the town's oldest church, begun a generation or so after the discovery of the silver deposits. Its grand scale is a clear indication of the town's quite considerable wealth by the time of the fourteenth century, though in terms of artistry it pales in comparison with Kutná Hora's other ecclesiastical buildings. The leaning tower is a reminder of the precarious position of the town, the church's foundations prone to subsidence from the disused mines below. If you want to see some of these, head for the **Hrádek**, an old fort which was used as a second mint and now serves as a **Mining Museum** (Muzeum a středověké důlní dílo; Tues–Sun: April & Oct 9am–5pm; May, June, Sept 9am–6pm; July & Aug 10am–6pm; 110Kč). Here you can pick up a white coat, miner's helmet and torch, and follow a guide through narrow sections of the medieval mines that were discovered beneath the fort in the 1960s – some of which tunnel over 100 metres below the surface. To do so, though, you have to endure a visit to the castle's collection of city artefacts; the whole package takes about ninety minutes.

The Cathedral of sv Barbora

Kutná Hora's **Cathedral of sv Barbora** (Tues–Sun: April & Oct 9–11.30am & 1–3.30pm; May–Sept 9am–5.30pm; Nov–March 9–11.30am & 2–3.30pm; 30Kč) is arguably the most spectacular and moving ecclesiastical building in central Europe. Not to be outdone by the great monastery at Sedlec (see p.154) or the St Vitus Cathedral in Prague, the miners of Kutná Hora began financing the construction of a great Gothic cathedral of their own, dedicated to St Barbara, the patron saint of miners and gunners. The foundations were probably laid by Parler in the 1380s, but work was interrupted by the Hussite wars, and the church remained unfinished until the late nineteenth century, despite being worked on in the intervening centuries by numerous architects, including Master Hanuš, Matouš Rejsek and Benedikt Ried.

The approach road to the cathedral, Barborská, is lined with a parade of gesticulating Baroque saints and cherubs that rival the sculptures on the Charles Bridge; and on the right-hand side is the palatial seventeenth-century former **Jesuit College**. The cathedral itself bristles with pinnacles, finials and flying buttresses which support its most striking feature, a roof of three tent-like towers added in the sixteenth century, culminating in unequal, needle-sharp spires. Inside, cold light streams through the plain glass windows, illuminating Ried's playful vaulted nave, whose ribs form branches and petals stamped with coats of arms belonging to Václav II and the local miners' guilds. The wide spread of the five-aisled nave is remarkably uncluttered: a Gothic pulpit – half-wood, half-stone – creeps tastefully up a central pillar, and black and gold Renaissance confessionals lie discreetly in the north aisle. On the south wall is the Minters' Chapel, its walls decorated with fifteenth-century frescoes showing the Florentines at work, while in the ambulatory chapels are some fascinating paintings – unique for their period – of local miners at work.

The rest of the town

There are a few minor sights worth seeking out in the rest of the town. On Rejskovo náměstí, the squat, polygonal **Kašna** (fountain), built by Rejsek in 1495, strikes a very odd pose – peppered with finials and replete with blind arcading, anything less like a fountain would be hard to imagine. At the bottom of the sloping Šultyskovo náměstí is a particularly fine **Morový sloup** (Plague Column), giving thanks for the end of the plague of 1713; while just around the corner from the top of the square is one of the few Gothic buildings to survive the 1770 fire, the **Kamenný dům**, built around 1480, with an oriel window and a steep gable, covered in an ornate sculptural icing. This now contains an unexceptional local museum (hours as at the Hrádek, see p.153). A couple of blocks down Poděbradova stands Kilian Ignaz Dientzenhofer's unfinished **Voršilský klášter** (Ursuline Convent; April & Oct Sat & Sun 9am–4pm; May–Sept Tues–Sun 9am–5.30pm). Only three sides of the convent's ambitious pentagonal plan were actually finished, its neo-Baroque church (now buried under scaffolding) being added in the late nineteenth century while sv Barbora was being restored.

Sedlec

Buses #1 and #4 run from the inner ringroad, 3km northeast to **SEDLEC**, once a separate village but now a suburb of Kutná Hora. Adjoining Sedlec's defunct eighteenth-century Cistercian monastery (now the largest tobacco factory in Europe, owned by Phillip Morris) is the fourteenth-century church of **Panna Maria** (Virgin Mary; Tues–Sat 9am–noon & 1–5pm) imaginatively redesigned in the eighteenth century by Giovanni Santini, who specialized in melding Gothic with Baroque. Here, given a plain French Gothic church gutted during the Hussite wars, Santini set to work on the vaulting, adding his characteristic sweeping stucco rib patterns, relieved only by the occasional Baroque splash of colour above the chancel steps.

Cross the main road, following the signs, and you'll come to the monks' graveyard, where an ancient Gothic chapel leans heavily over the entrance to the macabre subterranean **kostnice** or ossuary (daily: April–Sept 8am–6pm; Oct 9am–noon & 1–5pm; Nov–March 9am–noon & 1–4pm; 30Kč), full to overflowing with human bones. When holy earth from Golgotha was scattered over the graveyard in the twelfth century, all of Bohemia's nobility wanted to be buried here, and the bones mounted up until there were over 40,000 complete sets. In 1870, worried about the ever-growing piles, the authorities commissioned František Rint to do something creative with them. He rose to the challenge and moulded out of bones four giant bells, one in each corner of the crypt, designed wall-to-ceiling skeletal decorations, including the Schwarzenberg coat of arms, and, as the centrepiece, put together a chandelier made out of every bone in the human body. Rint's signature (in bones) is at the bottom of the steps.

Kačina and Žleby

Nothing quite so ghoulish confronts you at the early-nineteenth-century zámek of **Kačina**, 5km northeast of Kutná Hora hlavní nádraží along route 2 to Přelouč (or a much shorter walk if you catch one of the buses heading out to the satellite village of Nový Dvory). It's a colossal Neoclassical summer residence, the semicircular wings of the building stretching for over 200m across the lawn. For the owners, the up-and-coming Chotek family (who also owned Veltrusy), the chateau grounds came first, with planting begun a full fifteen years before a stone was laid. The Choteks forfeited their properties after collaborating with the Nazis, and the chateau now houses a **Zemědělské muzeum** (agriculture museum; April–Oct daily 8am–5pm). You can skip the museum entirely, but to view the chateau's surviving period interiors, you must sign up for an hour-long guided tour of the chateau; however, it's the wide informal expanse of the "English Park" that draws carloads of Czechs here throughout the summer.

For those who prefer more exotic castles, there's a flamboyant aristocratic haunt at **Žleby** (Schleb), 20km southeast of Kutná Hora, beyond Čáslav (where you must change trains; buses from Kutná Hora are direct but much less frequent). Here, in the mid-nineteenth century, Franz Schmoranz created a pseudo-Gothic extravaganza out of the original medieval **hrad** (April, Oct & Nov Sat & Sun 9am–noon & 1–4pm; May–Sept Tues–Sun 9am–noon & 1–5pm) for the Auersperg family. For once, the family failed to take the necessary precautions at the end of the war, and were forced to leave behind virtually all the castle's contents. The result is a full-blown neo-Gothic interior filled with lots of weaponry and heavy Baroque and quasi-medieval furnishings. There are two **guided tours** to choose from: *trasa 1* (1hr) includes pretty much everything except the Velká věž, the castle's lookout tower, which you only get to see on *trasa 2* (1hr 45min).

Practicalities

The simplest way to get to Kutná Hora is to take a **bus** from outside metro Želivského in Prague (1hr 15min). Fast **trains** from Prague's Masarykovo nádraží take around an hour (there's only one in the morning); slow ones take two hours; trains from Praha hlavní nádraží involve a change at Kolín. The main **train station** (Kutná Hora hlavní nádraží) is a long way out of town, near Sedlec; bus #1 or #4 will take you into town, or there's usually a shuttle train service ready to leave for Kutná Hora město train station, near the centre of town.

The town has a highly efficient system of orientation signs and, at almost every street corner, a pictorial list of the chief places of interest (beware, though, that the train station signposted is not the main one). The town's **tourist office** on Palackého náměstí (April–Oct Mon–Fri 9am–6.30pm, Sat & Sun 9am–5pm; Nov–March Mon–Fri 9am–5pm; ☎327 512 378, Ⓦwww.kutnahora.cz) can arrange reasonably priced private rooms or other **accommodation**. *U rytířů*, on Rejskovo náměstí (☎ & Ⓕ327 512 256; ❷) is a simple inexpensive pension, while *Hotel Anna*, Vladislavova (☎ & Ⓕ327 516 315; ❸) is a bit more upmarket. Continuing on up the price scale, *U vlašského dvora*, on Havlíčkovo náměstí (☎327 514 618, Ⓕ327 514 627; ❸), is quite comfortable and has a decent restaurant and a sauna, while *Zlatá stoupa*, on Tylova (☎327 511 540, Ⓕ327 513 808, Ⓔzlatastoupa@iol.cz; ❹), is the top of the ladder here, with mahogany furnishings and its own vinárna. The nearest **campsite** is the unlikely sounding *Santa Barbara*, northwest of the town centre on Česká (April–Oct).

On the **eating and drinking** front, you're spoilt for choice: *U bakaláře*, at the junction of Husova and Šultysova, is one of the better restaurants in town, with a reasonable choice for vegetarians; *Katakomby*, just up the street on Václavské náměstí, is a deep gothic cellar, with slightly upmarket Czech cuisine, while *Piazza Navona*, on Palackého náměstí, is an excellent pizzeria, run by an Italian. There are plenty of good pubs, too, where you can get more simple fare: try *U havíře* on Šultysova (closed Mon), which offers a variety of brews and has a quiet back patio.

Průhonice and the Sázava Valley

A short train ride **southeast** of Prague is enough to transport you from the urban sprawl of the capital into one of the prettiest regions of central Bohemia, starting with the park at **Průhonice**. Until the motorway to Brno and Bratislava ripped through the area in the 1970s, the roads and railways linking the three big cities followed the longer, flatter option, further north along the

Labe Valley. As a result, commerce and tourism passed the **Sázava Valley** by, and, with the notable exception of **Konopiště**, it remains relatively undeveloped, unspoilt and out of the way.

Průhonice

Barely outside Prague's city limits, and just off the country's chief motorway, **PRŮHONICE** is a popular weekend destination in the summer. A whole series of new buildings, including a large conference centre, have been erected over the last decade, and have somewhat spoilt the character of the original village – now stuffed with villas full of expatriates and well-to-do Czechs and known locally as "Beverly Hills". Nevertheless, it's still worth a visit, not for the newly restored neo-Renaissance **zámek**, which as a botanical and horticultural research centre is out of bounds, but for the 625-acre **park** (daily: April–Oct 7am–7pm; Nov–March 8am–dusk), founded by Count Emanuel Sylva Taroucca, which boasts an unusually fine array of flora and several picturesque lakes.

Another good reason for coming to Průhonice is to have a beer at the family-run *U Bezoušku* at Květnové náměstí 5, one of the republic's finest microbreweries, which serves up its very own *Bernard* brew and *Bizon amber* beer. Alternatively, tuck into a slap-up fish lunch in front of the fire or on the terrace of *Hliněná Bašta* at Újezdská 619, or wade through plates of pancakes just off the main square at *U slepíček*, Říčanská 89. You can also stay at the *Bezoušku* (℡267 750 551; ❷), and there are two well-equipped **campsites** a couple of kilometres west of the park: *Apple Garden* (April–Oct), to the north of Šeberov, and *Prager* (mid-May to Sept), to the south. To get to Průhonice, you can either catch the ČSAD **bus** service, which leaves three times an hour from metro Opatov, or else you can walk the 4km along the red-marked route, via the Hostivař lake (a good place for a dip in summer), starting from the penultimate tram stop on the #22 or #26 routes.

Sázava and Český Šternberk

Rising majestically above the slow-moving Sázava river, is the **Sázavský klášter** and **zámek** (daily: May–Aug 9am–6pm; Sept 9am–5pm; April & Oct 9am–noon & 1–5pm; last tour one hour before closing). The monastery was founded by the eleventh-century Prince Oldřich, on the instigation of a passing hermit called **Prokop** (St Procopius), whom he met by chance in the Sázava forest. Prokop became the first abbot of what was initially a Slavonic Basilian monastery, and, for a while, Sázava became an important centre for the dissemination of Slavonic texts. Later, a large Gothic church was planned, and this now bares its red sandstone nave to the world, incomplete but intact. The chancel was converted into a Baroque church, later bought by the Tiegel family, who started to build themselves a modest chateau. Of this architectural miscellany, only the surviving Gothic frescoes – in the popular "Beautiful Style", but of a sophistication unmatched in Bohemian art at the time – are truly memorable. The village itself thrived on the glass trade, and the rest of the monastery's hour-long guided tour concentrates on the local glassware.

Without your own transport, it'll take a good hour and a half by bus or train to cover the 55km from Prague to Sázava. Of the two, the **train** ride (change at Čerčany) is the more visually absorbing, at least by the time you join the branch line that meanders down the Sázava Valley; the train station is a fifteen-minute walk across the river from the monastery. Try the *Hostinec za vodou*, on your right as you walk from the monastery to the village, for huge portions and a summer terrace.

Český Šternberk

Several bends later in the Sázava river, the village of **ČESKÝ ŠTERNBERK** is overlooked by the great castellated mass of its **hrad** (April & Oct Sat & Sun 9am–4pm; May & Sept Tues–Sun 9am–5pm; June–Aug daily 9am–5pm; 75Kč for English tour; open year-round for groups of ten or more; last tour 45min before closing; ☏317 855 101, ✉hradcs@iol.cz), strung out along a knife's edge above the river. It's a breathtaking sight, rising out of thick woods, though not much remains of the original Gothic castle, headquarters of the powerful Šternberk family (who still own it now and have renovated it beautifully). The highlight of the 45-minute guided tour is the Italian stucco work that survives from the seventeenth century. If you have a car, however, it's worth driving past for the view – though there's an even better one from the lookout tower (*rozhledna*), a fifteen-minute walk through the woods behind the castle. If you're coming by train, you'll need to change trains at Čerčany and get out at Český Šternberk zastávka, one stop past Český Šternberk's main station. If you're coming by car, go 12km to Uhlířské Janovice, then turn right for Český Šternberk along twisting country roads via Mitrov. If you need to stay, ask for a room at the *Parkhotel* (☏317 855 168; ❸), with a view overlooking the castle and, if you're hungry, the fur-strewn castle restaurant provides cheap, hot Czech nosh.

Konopiště

The popularity of **Konopiště** (daily: April & Nov 9am–3pm; May, June & Oct 9am–4pm; July–Sept 9am–5pm; 130Kč for tours I and II, 260Kč for tour III; ☏317 721 366, ⊕www.zamek-konopiste.cz), with a quarter of a million visitors passing through its portcullis every year, is surpassed only by the likes of Karlštejn (see p.160). Of the two, Konopiště is the more interesting, though Karlštejn looks more dramatic from the outside. Coach parties from all over the world home in on this Gothic castle, which is stuffed with dead animals, weaponry and hunting trophies. Most interesting are its historical associations: King Václav IV was imprisoned for a while by his own nobles in the castle's distinctive round tower, and the Archduke Franz Ferdinand, heir to the Habsburg throne, lived here with his wife, Sophie Chotek, until their assassination in Sarajevo in 1914. In addition to remodelling the chateau into its current appearance, the archduke shared his generation's voracious appetite for hunting, eliminating all living creatures foolish enough to venture into the grounds. However, he surpassed all his contemporaries by recording, stuffing and displaying a significant number of the 171,537 birds and animals he shot between the years 1880 and 1906, the details of which are recorded in his *Schuss Liste* displayed inside.

There's a choice of **guided tours**. The *I okruh* explores several salons, which contain some splendid Renaissance cabinets and lots of Meissen porcelain, while the *II okruh* takes you through the chapel, past the stuffed bears and deer teeth, to the assorted lethal weapons of one of the finest armouries in Europe. Both the above tours take 45 minutes, and, you'll be relieved to know, include the hunting trophies. The *III okruh* takes an hour, is restricted to just eight people per tour, and concentrates on the personal apartments of the archduke and his wife. The couple hid themselves away in Konopiště, as they were shunned by the Habsburg court in Vienna, due to the fact that Sophie was a mere countess, and not an archduchess. Occasionally there are tours in English, French and German, too, so ask at the box office before you sign up, or give them a call and book one in advance.

Even if you don't fancy a guided tour, there are plenty of other things to do in Konopiště. In the main courtyard of the chateau, you can pop into the purpose-built **Střelnice** (Shooting Range; times as at the castle), where the archduke used to hone his skills as a marksman against moving mechanical targets, all of which have been lovingly restored. Tucked underneath the south terrace is the **Galerie sv Jiří** (Tues–Sun: April, May, Sept & Oct 9am–1pm & 2–3pm, June–Aug 9am–1pm & 2–5pm), which is stuffed to the gunwales with artefacts from Franz Ferdinand's collection – from paintings to statuettes and trinkets relating to St George, the fictional father of medieval chivalry, with whom the archduke was obsessed. Much the best reason to come to Konopiště, though, is to explore its 555-acre **park**, which boasts a marked red path around the largest lake, sundry statuary, an unrivalled rose garden (with café by the greenhouses) and a deer park. There are also regular one-hour displays of **falconry** in the chateau's grounds (April & Oct Sat & Sun 10am–noon & 2–4pm, May–Sept Tues–Sun same times) in English and Czech.

Practicalities

To get to Konopiště take a fast (50min) or slow (1hr 5min) **train** from Praha hlavní nádraží to **Benešov** u Prahy, 45km southeast of Prague, on the main line to České Budějovice; the castle is a pleasant two-kilometre walk west of the railway station along the red- or yellow-marked path (buses are relatively infrequent). Since train connections are good from Prague, you don't need to **stay** the night, but if you do, the *Nová Myslivna* (☎317 723 017; ❷) is a modern hotel right by the main car park (with cart rides offered up to the castle). If that's full, there's a **campsite** (May–Sept) a kilometre to the southeast of the castle, near the ugly *Motel Konopiště* (☎317 722 732; ❹), which has a good restaurant; or you might want to consider staying at the newly restored *Pecínov* (☎317 763 111, ✉pecinov@quick.cz; ❾), a luxurious, Victorian-style mansion with French restaurant, pool, riding school and wine cellar, a couple of kilometres southeast of Benešov. If the weather's fine, though, you might as well come equipped with a picnic; otherwise, there are numerous food stalls by the main car park, and decent Czech fare available in the nineteenth-century *Stará Myslivna*, on the path to the castle, and in the bistro in the main courtyard. Back in Benešov, it's perfectly possible to while away some time before your train departs at the *Galerijní čajovna* on Malé náměstí.

Příbram

PŘÍBRAM (Pibrans), like Kutná Hora (see p.151), was once a royal silver-mining town, though it contains nothing like the same treasures. Among older Czechs, however, the town is better known for its notorious uranium mines, where thousands of political prisoners worked and died in appalling conditions in the 1950s. Since 1989, all mining operations have ceased here, and there's now a museum to those terrible years called **Muzeum třetího odboje** (Museum of the Third Resistance; Tues–Sun 10am–4pm; 25Kč), housed in an unprepossessing block at Mariánská 260. Bus #15 from the train station passes close by every half-hour, or you can walk in ten minutes by crossing over the tracks, heading west up Anenská, and then first left down Aloise Jiráska to the crossroads with Mariánská.

In the southwestern suburb of Březové Hory, there's also an extensive and smartly laid-out **Hornické muzeum** (Mining Museum; hourly guided tours April–Oct Tues–Sun 9am–5pm; Nov–March Tues–Fri 9am–4pm; ⓦ www.pb.cz/muzeum.html), accessible via bus #1 or #14 from the train station. The museum is divided between five separate buildings, and you'll need to buzz the doorbell in building 1 for tickets. The most impressive of the endless number of sections is the splendidly ornate pithead of the UNESCO-protected Ševčínský důl (Ševčín Shaft), which was built in 1813. The other buildings, which include a traditional miner's cottage, contain displays on mineralogy, and numerous Bethlehem folk scenes filled with wooden figurines. If you fancy walking ten minutes back along the main road to the second section of the museum, you can also take a short train trip (25Kč) with a minimum of five people down one of the old mineshafts, the Prokop Adit, in the company of a retired miner, after which you're encouraged to pay a visit to the nearby miners' pub *Na vršíčku* (closed off season).

The real reason most people trek out to Příbram, however, is to see the beautiful Marian shrine of **Svatá hora** (Holy Mountain; daily 8.30am–5pm), whose pepperpot domes rise up above the town on a wooded hill to the east of the main square. According to legend, the first shrine was built here in the thirteenth century, but was transformed out of all recognition by the Jesuits, who in 1658 employed Carlo Lurago to produce the striking set-piece of Italianate Baroque you see now. The best way to reach the shrine is via the Svatohorské schody or covered stairway off Dlouhá, built by Kilian Ignaz Dientzenhofer in 1728. From the stairs, you enter the arcaded ambulatory which surrounds the main church, whose restored frescoes, dating from the late nineteenth century, recount the history of Svatá hora. Thick stucco work surrounds the hell, fire and damnation ceiling paintings, with cherubs fighting and hugging, skulls surrounded by swags made from bones, and egg timers on more skulls. At the centre of the complex is the pilgrim church or basilica, its balustrade dotted with saintly statuary; inside, pride of place goes to a kitsch Gothic statue of the Madonna and Child, whose clothes are regularly changed.

Since 1997, Příbram has also been the home town of the old army football team, **Dukla Praha** – immortalized in the pop song *All I Want for Christmas is a Dukla Prague Away-Kit* by British band Half Man Half Biscuit – after they were forced to leave the capital due to financial difficulties, and merge with the town's local team. Dukla have since bounced back into the first division, and now play rent-free in Příbram's Na Litavce stadium, which is situated a couple of kilometres south of the town centre.

Practicalities

Příbram itself is around 50km southwest of Prague along motorway route 4. The easiest way to get there on **public transport** is by bus from Prague's Na Knížecí bus station, next to metro Anděl; the train from Prague's Smíchovské nádraží takes longer and often involves a change at Zdice, on the main line to Plzeň. Příbram is not a great place to stay the night, though the *Modrý hrozen* (ⓣ318 628 007, ⓔhotel@modryhrozen.cz; ⑤), on the main square, is a pleasant and comfortable enough **hotel**, and boasts a restaurant with an original seventeenth-century ceiling. For cheaper food and drink, undoubtedly the best **pub** around is the *Březohorka*, on náměstí J.A. Alise 235, just above the main part of the mining museum; back in the town centre, there's *U havlínů*, on Václavské náměstí.

Along the Berounka river

The green belt area to the **west of Prague** is easily the most varied of the regions around the city, and consequently one of the most popular escapes for citizens of the Czech capital. The **River Berounka** carves itself an enticingly craggy valley up to Charles IV's magnificent country castle at **Karlštejn**, the busiest destination of all, and further upstream is the more isolated stronghold of **Křivoklát**.

Karlštejn and around

KARLŠTEJN (Karlstein) is a small ribbon of a village, strung out along one of the tributaries of the Berounka – no doubt once pretty, it boasts a pricey golf course and is now jam-packed with tacky souvenir stands and tourists visiting its **hrad** (Tues–Sun: Jan–March 9am–noon & 1–3pm; April & Oct 9am–noon & 1–4pm; May, June & Sept 9am–noon & 1–5pm; July–August 9am–noon & 1–6pm; video cameras and cameras forbidden inside the castle; ☏274 008 154, ⓦwww.hradkarlstejn.cz), which occupies a spectacular, defiantly unassailable position above the village. Designed in the fourteenth century by Matthias of Arras for Emperor Charles IV as a giant safe-box for the imperial crown jewels and his large personal collection of precious relics, it quickly became Charles' favourite retreat from the vast city he himself had masterminded. Women were strictly forbidden to enter the castle, and the story of his third wife Anna's successful break-in (in drag) became one of the most popular Czech comedies of the nineteenth century.

Ruthlessly returned to a replica of its original Gothic style in the late nineteenth century by Josef Mocker, the castle now looks much better from a distance, with its giant wedge towers rising above a series of castellated walls. Most of the rooms visited on the overpriced forty-minute guided route I (200Kč) contain only the barest of furnishings, the empty spaces taken up by uninspiring displays on the history of the castle. Theoretically, the top two chambers would make the whole trip worthwhile: unfortunately, on the basic guided tour you can only look into (but not enter) the emperor's residential **Mariánská věž**, where Charles shut himself off from the rest of the world, with any urgent business passed to him through a hole in the wall of the tiny ornate chapel of **sv Kateřina**.

As for the castle's finest treasure, the **Holy Rood Chapel** (Kaple svatého kříže), connected by a wooden bridge that leads onto the highest point of the castle, the **Velká věž**, this is only open to those who book Route II in advance (300Kč). Traditionally, only the emperor, the archbishop and the electoral princes could enter this gilded treasure-house, whose six-metre-thick walls contain 2200 semi-precious stones and 128 breathtakingly beautiful painted panels, the work of Master Theodoric, Bohemia's greatest fourteenth-century painter (a small selection of his panels is exhibited in Prague's Anežský klášter; see p.95). The imperial crown jewels, once secured here behind nineteen separate locks, were removed to Hungary after an abortive attack by the Hussites, while the Bohemian jewels are now stashed away in the cathedral in Prague.

Elsewhere in the village – transformed over the last decade, with every other house offering rooms to rent or selling souvenirs – most of what you see, including the decidedly iffy **Wax Museum** at no. 173 (daily 9am–6pm), is eminently missable, with the exception of the **Muzeum Betlémů** (Tues–Sun 9am–6pm), which occupies a fourteenth-century house towards the top of the village at no. 11. You can admire an impressive array of nativity scenes dating back to the early nineteenth century. They range in size from complex mechanical set-ups to miniature affairs that can fit into small sea shells – there are even some made out of gingerbread.

Practicalities

Trains for Karlštejn leave Prague's Smíchovské nádraží roughly every hour, and take about 35 minutes to cover the 28km. The village is ten minutes' walk across the river from the station, and it's a further fifteen- to twenty-minute climb up to the castle entrance. If you're looking for somewhere to grab a beer and a fairly bog-standard bite to **eat**, try hunting-lodge-style *U Janů*, which has an outdoor terrace, or the slightly posher *Koruna*, both on the main street. Alternatively, bring a picnic with you and eat by the banks of the river or, if you've got a car, nip down the road to *Pivovarský Berounský medvěd* at Tyršova 135, next to the railway station in Beroun, a three-tun, in-house brewery pub and restaurant, serving its own *Brown Bear* beer in a former sugar factory.

There are loads of **accommodation** options in Karlštejn, but since prices are something like fifty percent higher than most places in the country, only a masochist would choose to stay here. If you are stuck here for some reason, your best bet is the *Hotel Mlyn* (☎311 681 194; ❹), an unpretentious, but well-run converted fishing lodge, on the same side of the river as the train station, ten minutes' walk downstream. Karlštejn's **campsite** (open all year) is on the opposite bank, upstream from the village, and allows fires, but there's a nicer site at **Řevnice** (April–Sept), two stops on the train before Karlštejn (and, incidentally, the village in which Martina Navrátilová spent her tennis-playing childhood), with a small pool, restaurant, draught beer, and good train links with Prague.

Walks around Karlštejn and the Český kras

There are some great possibilities for **hiking** in the countryside around Karlštejn. Several marked paths cover the stiff climb through the forests of the Hřebeny ridge. If you're armed with a *Praha okolí* map, these are easy enough to follow; you can pick up a bus back to Prague from Mníšek on the other side of the hills.

If you're feeling energetic, you could go for a swim at the popular flooded quarry, **Malá Amerika**, 1km from the castle. Getting there is tricky and access is prohibited to motor vehicles: either take the red-marked path from near the castle at Karlštejn, and head off northwest through the woods at *Hajovna U dubu* (you may need to ask a local to point you in the right direction), or head west down the track, which comes off the road between Mořina and Bubovice.

From **SRBSKO** (one stop on from Karlštejn), a red-marked path winds its way through the woods to **sv Jan pod Skalou** (St John Under the Rock), a strikingly situated monastery, as the name suggests, underneath a steep bluff in a landscape full of dramatic craggy flourishes. Designed by Christoph Dientzenhofer, the monastery was used as a training camp for the Communist secret police, but is now an ecological research centre. This is also the place where the country's remaining aristocrats were imprisoned following the 1948 coup. Again, you can catch a bus back to Prague easily enough from Vráž, a kilometre or so to the north.

Another option from Srbsko is to take the yellow-marked path west into the **Český kras** (Bohemian Karst). The geology of this region has fascinated scientists since the early nineteenth century, but the one set of caves open to the public, the **Koněpruské jeskyně** (April–Oct daily 8am–4pm), 3km west of Srbsko, lay undiscovered until 1950. Nowadays it's not so easy to miss, thanks to the Hollywood-style giant white lettering on the hillside above. Much more fascinating than the dripstone decorations, however, was the simultaneous discovery of an illegal mint in the upper level of the caves. A full set of weights, miners' lamps and even the remains of food were found here, dating back to the second half of the fifteenth century. To reach the caves other than by foot, you'll need to catch one of the infrequent **buses** from the nearby soap-producing town of **Beroun** (50min by train from Praha hlavní nádraží). Finally, just for the record, Czech film buffs may like to know that the station at **Loděnice**, two stops up the line from Beroun, was used as the location for Jiří Menzel's classic, Oscar-winning, 1966 film, *Closely Observed Trains*, based on the novel by Bohumil Hrabal.

Křivoklátsko

Further up the Berounka is the beautiful, mixed woodland of a UNESCO nature reserve, **Křivoklátsko**. Just out of reach of day-trippers, it's an altogether sleepier place than the area around Karlštejn.

The agonized twists (*křivky*) of the Berounka river cast up the highest crags of the region, which cluster round the lofty castle of **Křivoklát** (Pürglitz), first mentioned in the twelfth century and heavily renovated by the Fürstenbergs at the end of the nineteenth century (March, Sept & Dec Sat, Sun & state holidays 9am–noon & 1–3pm; April & Oct Tues–Sun 9am–noon & 1–3pm; May & Sept Tues–Sun 9am–noon & 1–4pm; June Tues–Sun 9am–noon & 1–5pm; July & Aug daily 9am–noon & 1–5pm). With such a perfect location in the heart of the best hunting ground in Bohemia, and a refuge from the deprivations of the plague, Křivoklát naturally enjoyed the royal patronage of the Přemyslids, whose hunting parties were legendary. Charles IV also spent the early part of his childhood here before being sent off to Burgundy. From the outside, it's a scruffy but impressive stronghold, dominated by the round tower in which English alchemist Edward Kelley was incarcerated for two and a half years for failing to reveal the secret of the philosopher's stone to Rudolf II. Kelley was, by all accounts, a slippery character, a swindler and a seducer, with a hooked nose and no ears (they were cut off by the Lancastrians as a punishment for forgery). In an attempt to escape, he jumped out of the window, only to break his leg so badly it had to be amputated.

There are now two tours round this ancient castle to choose between, with the 70-minute guided tour (*trasa 1*) round the interior taking in most of the castle's good points, including the dungeon and pit, and the Royal Hall and the Chapel. The last two, dating back to the thirteenth century, have kept their original late-Gothic vaulting, studded with corbels carved with colourful figureheads, and retain an austere beauty quite at odds with the castle's reputation as a venue for bacchanalian goings-on. An appealing alternative for those with kids (or an aversion to guided tours) is the 40-minute scramble around the fortifications (*trasa 2*) and viewing of the hunting exhibition in the grand tower. During high season, you can watch traditional woodcarving demonstrations and visit the hunting exhibition in the castle's outbuildings, too. Look out for the summer festival in the first week of August, plus one-off concerts, theatrical performances and Easter and Advent fairs.

Practicalities

Virtually all journeys by **train** from Prague to Křivoklát require a change at Beroun. **Buses** from the Praha-Dejvice terminal run frequently only at weekends, less regularly during the week, and take around an hour and a half. Křivoklát is just one of several castles in the region, and you could happily spend days exploring the surrounding countryside on a network of well-marked footpaths. There's an **information centre** (June & Sept Sat & Sun 10am–6pm; July & Aug Tues–Sun 10am–6pm) right in the centre of the village, which can advise on walks, and also book private **accommodation**. If the office is closed, try the nearby *Sýkora* (☎313 558 114; ❸), which could do with a lick of paint on the outside but is fine inside, or one of the many **campsites** in the vicinity, such as *Višňová II* (June–Aug) by the river. Be warned that Křivoklát hosts an annual **film festival** at the end of August, during which it will be all but impossible to find anywhere to stay.

Around Kladno

No Czech would seriously suggest you should visit **KLADNO**, just under 30km west of Prague, but if you're heading for Lány by bus, you may need to change here. As you approach the town, nicknamed "Black Kladno", it's difficult to miss the low, blue barracks of the giant Poldi Kladno steelworks, insensitively built on a section of the old town in the heyday of central planning in 1975. Founded way back in 1855, the steelworks was one of the first foundries in the world to produce stainless steel in 1910. It was here, too, that the Czech Communist Party was founded in 1921, and Kladno's workers were rewarded with some of the best wages in the country after the 1948 coup.

Poldi's problems began in earnest in 1992 when the factory, which once employed a majority of the town's 70,000 inhabitants, was forced to shut down for eight months due to a lack of orders. Then, two years later, it was sold to the fiery entrepreneur Vladimír Stehlík, who was known to shoot his pistol in the air on the shop floor in order to gain the attention of his employees. During the 1996 elections, he gave his entire workforce the day off so that they could march in Prague against prime minister Václav Klaus's government. The following year, having failed to pay their workers for several months, Stehlík and his son Marko were behind bars, awaiting trial for defaulting on bank loans. They were released, after four months inside, only on condition that they sell the steelworks, which they duly did to a Liechtenstein-based company. However, the factory remains firmly shut, and the citizens of Kladno have now more or less got used to commuting to Prague for their work.

Lidice

The small mining village of **LIDICE**, 18km northwest of Prague, hit the world headlines on June 10, 1942, at the moment when it ceased to exist. On the flimsiest pretext, it was chosen as the scapegoat for the assassination of the Nazi leader Reinhard Heydrich (see p.114). All 173 men from the village were rounded up and shot by the SS, the 198 women were sent off to Ravensbrück concentration camp, and the 89 children either went to the camps or, if they were considered Aryan enough, were packed off to "good" German homes, while the village itself was burnt to the ground.

Knowing all this as you approach Lidice makes the modern village seem almost perversely unexceptional. At the end of the straight, tree-lined main street, 10 června 1942 (June 10, 1942), there's a dour concrete memorial with a small but horrific **museum** (daily: April–Oct 8am–5pm; Nov–March 8am–4pm) where you can watch a short film about Lidice, including footage shot by the SS themselves as the village was burning. The spot where the old village used to lie is just south of the memorial, now merely smooth green pasture punctuated with a few simple symbolic reminders and a new bronze memorial to the 82 local children who were gassed in the camps.

After the massacre, the "Lidice shall live" campaign was launched and villages all over the world began to change their name to Lidice. The first was Stern Park Gardens, Illinois, soon followed by villages in Mexico and other Latin American countries. From Coventry to Montevideo, towns twinned themselves with Lidice, so that rather than "wiping a Czech village off the face of the earth", as Hitler had hoped, the Nazis inadvertently created a symbol of anti-fascist resistance.

There's no place nor reason to stay, and most people come here as a day-trip from Prague on one of the regular buses from Praha Dejvická, getting off at the turn-off to the village on the main road.

Lány

On summer weekends, Škoda-loads of Czech families, pensioners and assorted pilgrims make their way to **LÁNY**, a plain, grey village on a hill by the edge of the Křivoklát forest, 12km beyond Kladno. They congregate in the town's pristine cemetery to pay their respects to one of the country's most important historical figures, Tomáš Garrigue Masaryk, the founding father and president of Czechoslovakia from 1918 to 1935.

The Masaryk plot is separated from the rest of the cemetery (*hřbitov*) by a little wooden fence and flanked by two bushy trees. Tomáš is buried alongside his American wife, Charlotte Garrigue Masaryková, who died some fifteen years earlier, and their son Jan, who became foreign minister in the post-1945 government, only to die in mysterious circumstances shortly after the Communist coup (see p.79). The Masaryks have since been joined by their daughter, Alice, who founded the Czechoslovak Red Cross and died in exile in 1966.

TGM

Tomáš Garrigue Masaryk – known affectionately as TGM – was born in 1850 in Hodonín, a town in a part of Moravia where Slovaks and Czechs lived harmoniously together. His father was an illiterate Slovak peasant who worked for the local bigwig, his mother a German. Tomáš himself trained as a blacksmith. From such humble beginnings, he rose to become professor of philosophy at the Charles University, a Social Democrat MP in the Viennese *Reichsrat*, and finally the country's first, and longest-serving, president. A liberal humanist through and through, Masaryk created what was, at the time, probably the most progressive democracy in central Europe, featuring universal suffrage, an enviable social security system and a strong social democratic thrust. The whole country went into mourning when he died in 1937, leaving Czechoslovakia one of the few remaining democracies in central Europe, "a lighthouse high on a cliff with the waves crashing on it on all sides", as Masaryk's less fortunate successor, Edvard Beneš, put it. A year later the Nazis marched into Sudetenland.

After the 1948 coup, the Communists began to dismantle the myth of Masaryk, whose name was synonymous with the "bourgeois" First Republic. All mention of him was removed from textbooks, street names were changed, and his statue was taken down from almost every town and village in the country. However, during liberalization in 1968, his bespectacled face and goatee beard popped up again in shop windows, and his image returned once more in 1989 to haunt the beleaguered Communists.

After laying their wreaths, the crowds generally wander over to the presidential summer **zámek**, with its blue-liveried guards, on the other side of the village. The chateau still serves as the president's out-of-town retreat, and its rooms are strictly out of bounds, but the large English gardens, orangerie and deer park, which were landscaped by Josip Plečnik, are open to the public (April–Oct Wed & Thurs 2–6pm, Sat & Sun 10am–6pm). To get to Lány, either change buses at Kladno, or take the slow train to Chomutov from Prague's Masarykovo nádraží, getting out at Stochov – the nearest station to Lány, 3km away to the southwest – which boasts a presidential waiting room.

Travel details

Trains

Beroun to: Křivoklát (11–12 daily; 40–50min); Prague (5–9 daily; 50min–1hr).
Čerčany to: Český Šternberk (7–8 daily; 1 hr); Sázava (7–8 daily; 30min).
Mělník to: Liběchov (7 daily; 8min); Litoměřice město (7–9 daily; 35min).
Prague Hlavní nádraží to: Benešov (hourly; 40min–1hr 5min); Čerčany (hourly; 55min); Kolín (1–2 hourly; 45min); Kutná Hora (4 daily; 55min–1hr); Mělník (2–3 daily; 1hr 30min); Mladá Boleslav (7–8 daily; 1hr 10min–1hr 50min); Poděbrady (hourly; 50min–1hr).
Prague Masarykovo nádraží to: Kladno (hourly; 40–55min); Kolín (hourly; 1hr 10min); Nelahozeves (3 daily; 30min–55min); Roudnice nad Labem (3 daily; 50min–1 hr 20min); Stochov (hourly; 1hr–1hr 15min).
Prague Holešovice to: Kolín (5 daily; 40min).

Prague Smíchov to: Beroun (5–9 daily; 50min–1hr); Karlštejn (1–2 hourly; 30min); Příbram (2–4 daily; 1hr 15min); Řevnice (1–2 hourly; 25min).

Buses

Prague (Černý Most) to: Přerov nad Labem and Poděbrady (up to 3 daily, 30min/50min).
Prague (Dejvická) to: Lidice (1–2 hourly; 25–35min); Kladno (1–2 hourly; 45–50min).
Prague (Florenc) to: Konopiště (up to every 45min; 1hr); Kutná Hora (Mon–Fri 1 daily; 1hr 15min); Mělník (up to 10 daily; 50min); Mladá Boleslav (frequently; 1hr 15min).
Prague (Na Knížecí) to: Příbram (10 daily; 1hr).
Prague (Opatov) to: Průhonice (every 30min–1hr; 15min).
Prague (Želivského) to: Kutná Hora (up to 5 daily; 1hr 15min); Sázava (5–12 daily; 1hr 10min).

South Bohemia

CHAPTER 2

Highlights

✳ **Zámek, Jindřichův Hradec**
– Despite its forbidding exterior, this chateau boasts one of the finest Italianate Renaissance interiors in the country. **See p.182**

✳ **Třeboň** – Perfectly preserved walled town and spa set amidst the medieval carp ponds of Třeboňsko. **See p.185**

✳ **Budvar at Masné Krámy, České Budějovice** – Down a glass of the original Budweiser in the atmospheric former butchers' stalls of the South Bohemian capital. **See p.190**

✳ **Český Krumlov** – South Bohemia's most picturesque medieval town is tucked into an S-bend of the River Vltava and overlooked by a Renaissance castle. **See p.192**

✳ **Hiking through the Šumava** – The most unspoilt mountain range in the Czech Republic is the perfect place to do some summer hiking. **See p.201**

✳ **Sgraffito in Prachatice** – This tiny walled town, on the edge of the Šumava mountains, boasts the finest sgraffito facades in Bohemia. **See p.202**

✳ **Kašperské Hory** – Pretty little town with a motorcycle museum and one of the most impressive glass museums in the Czech Republic. **See p.207**

South Bohemia

South Bohemia (Jižní Čechy), more than any other region, conforms to the popular myth of Bohemia as a bucolic backwater of rolling hills and endless forests. A century of conspicuous industrialization and destruction from two world wars have pretty much passed it by. The only city to speak of is the regional capital, **České Budějovice**, which makes up for its urban sprawl with a good-looking old town and a beer of no less standing. The rest of the countryside is dotted with a series of exceptionally beautiful medieval walled towns, known collectively as the **"Rose Towns"** after the emblems of the two most powerful families: the red rose of the Rožmberks and the black rose of the lords of Hradec. Both dynasties died out at the beginning of the seventeenth century, and their prize possessions have been in almost terminal decline ever since, despite the subsequent rise of the Bavarian-based Schwarzenbergs.

Český Krumlov is by far the most popular of the Rose Towns; others, like **Pelhřimov** and **Třeboň**, are equally well preserved, if not quite as picturesquely located. The latter lies in an uncharacteristically flat part of the country, known as **Třeboňsko**, a unique ecosystem of medieval fishponds that still supply much of the country's Christmas carp. Bohemia's chief river, the **Vltava**, runs through South Bohemia and provides the setting for the region's most popular **castles**, some, like **Zvíkov**, almost monastic in their simplicity, and others, such as **Orlík**, **Hluboká** and **Rožmberk**, marvels of aristocratic decadence.

To the south, the **Šumava**, which forms the natural border with Austria and Germany, is one of the most unspoiled mountain ranges in the country. The German-speaking foresters and traders who settled on the northern slopes have left their mark on the architecture of the Bohemian towns and villages in that area. Following the postwar expulsions, however, the local population is now greatly reduced, their number augmented only by a seasonal influx of walkers, fishermen, canoeists and inland beachniks, drawn by the natural beauty of the region, which is probably the least affected by acid rain in the Czech Republic.

Regional **transport** in South Bohemia isn't as bad as might be expected, given the overwhelmingly hilly, rural nature of the terrain. Travelling by train allows you to experience more of the countryside, and even parts of the Šumava are served by a scenic single-track railway that winds its way from České Budějovice to Český Krumlov, along the shores of Lake Lipno and then north to Prachatice. While they can be less frequent than trains, buses go virtually everywhere and are almost invariably faster.

Boats on the Vltava

There are **boat services** three times a day from Orlík to Zvíkov (June & early Sept Sat & Sun; July & Aug Tues–Sun; 45min), which also head north to the Orlík dam, via the Trhovky, Podskalá, Radava and Velký Vír campsites. Another less frequent service plies between Zvíkov and Podolsko (July & Aug Tues & Wed; 1hr 45min; 1 daily), to the south, which lies close to Červená nad Vltavou train station. In addition, there are round-trip boat excursions, both short and long, on offer from the pier below Orlík castle. For more information on the timetable, call ℡ 382 275 333.

Up the Vltava

South of Prague and the Slapy dam, the **River Vltava** has been transformed into a series of long, winding lakes, which remain a favourite destination for Czechs in the summer. The campsites, many of them fairly ad hoc affairs, are full to capacity, and campfires burn into the night every night. There are also two **castles** worth visiting: **Orlík** and **Zvíkov**, both of which overlook the Vltava and are difficult to reach without your own transport. A possible base from which to see them is the nearby town of **Písek**, which has recently been prettily spruced up, and is easily accessible by bus or train.

Orlík nad Vltavou

With its vanilla-coloured rendering and mock castellations, you're unlikely to be disappointed by your first impressions of **Orlík** (which means "eagle's nest"), a creamy nineteenth-century castle which juts out into this wide stretch of the Vltava. No doubt the view was a great deal more spectacular before the valley was dammed in the 1960s; nowadays the water laps rather tamely at the foot of the castle, and concrete has been injected into its foundations to prevent it from being swept away.

As some of the region's greatest self-propagandists, the Schwarzenbergs turned this old Gothic **hrad** (Tues–Sun: April, Sept & Oct 9am–4pm; May–Aug 9am–5pm) into a pseudo-Gothic money-waster in the second half

Romany memorial at Lety

It has taken fifty years, but there is now a memorial at **Lety**, 7km west of Orlík, to the Czech Romanies who died here during World War II. Between 1942 and 1943, some 1300 Romanies passed through the transit camp in Lety, amidst what is now a rather insensitively placed pig farm (which is still a source of great contention and unhappiness for Roma), en route to Auschwitz. Thousands more were imprisoned in Hodonín, Moravia. About a quarter of those interned at Lety died in the camp – in the end around ninety percent of the prewar Czech Romany population was killed. Touching the raw nerve of Czech-Gypsy relations, it is inevitable that the memorial has provoked controversy, not least because of the accusation that the camp was staffed not by Germans, nor even Sudeten Germans, but by Czechs. The small-scale memorial is made up of a series of slabs of rock, already overgrown, with an information panel in Czech, Roma and English. To get there, take the road from Lety to Kožlí u Orlíka, and follow the inconspicuous sign *památník* into the woods, a fifteen-minute walk.

of the nineteenth century. There's nothing among the faïence, weaponry and Schwarzenberg military memorabilia on the hour-long guided tour to hint at its seven-hundred-year history, and even the gardens were only laid out in the last century, but if you're interested in the Schwarzenbergs, this is one of the best places to find out about them.

For moderately priced **food**, head for the restaurant *U Toryka* (named after the current count's pet fox terrier); for cheaper fare, try the café in the orangery, or go off into the castle grounds for a picnic. In the high season, there are also falcons and other birds of prey on display in the grounds. Of the many **campsites** in the area, the nearest to the castle is 2km downriver at Velký Vír (June–Sept; ☎382 275 161). En route, there's a nice **pension**, *U Nováku* (☎602 467 886; ❷), with a friendly pub downstairs serving cheap food and *Gambrinus* and *Purkmistr* beers.

Zvíkov

Fourteen kilometres upstream, hidden amid the woods of an isolated rocky promontory at the confluence of the Vltava and the Otava, is the bare medieval husk of **Zvíkov** (April & Oct Sat & Sun 9.30am–noon & 1–4pm; May & Sept Tues–Sun 9.30am–noon & 1–4.30pm; June–Aug Tues–Sun 9am–5.30pm), its simplicity a welcome relief after the "romantic interiors" of Orlík. You can wander at will among the light honey-coloured stone buildings, left to rack and ruin by the Rožmberks as long ago as the 1500s, then further destroyed by imperial troops during the Thirty Years' War. A small dusty track passes under three gatehouses before leading to the central courtyard, which boasts a simple, early Gothic, two-storey arcade, reconstructed in the nineteenth century from the few bays that still stood. Even the meagre offerings in the museum are more than compensated for by the absence of tour groups, the cool stone floors and the wonderful views over the water. A further incentive to visit are the chapel's faded fifteenth-century frescoes, featuring a particularly memorable scene "where nimbed souls in underpants float uncomfortably through a forest", as one critic aptly described it.

Buses from Písek (weekdays only) generally only go as far as the village of **ZVÍKOVSKÉ PODHRADÍ**, 1km south of the castle, from where the castle is signposted. Here you'll find private **rooms**, as well as plusher accommodation at the *Hotel Zvíkov* (☎382 285 659; ❹).

Temelín

The cooling towers of **Temelín**, which rise up beside the main road from Písek to České Budějovice, are a chastening sight. Built to a Soviet design similar to the one used at Chernobyl, Temelín was designed to be the largest nuclear power station in the world – reason enough to give the place a wide berth. A long campaign of protest by local and international groups persuaded the first post-Communist government to postpone the opening of the power station, which is situated on a tectonic fault line. However, in 1992, the US energy giant Westinghouse was commissioned to complete at least two of the four reactor units. With so much of the countryside devastated by the effects of coal-produced energy, however, the majority of Czechs think the plant should be completed, while top politicians such as Zeman and Havel have taken vociferous stands, the former in favour and the latter against it; Austria, meanwhile, has said that it will block Czech entry into the EU if the government goes ahead with the reactor. Border demonstrations and slanging matches between Austria and the Czech Republic continue at the time of going to press, with completion not yet on the horizon. Once and if on-line, Temelín will provide twenty percent of the nation's electricity, as does the republic's only other (much older) nuclear reactor in the southern Moravian town of Dukovany.

Písek

Twenty kilometres south of Zvíkov is the pretty little town of **PÍSEK**, which gets its name from the gold-producing sand (*písek*) of the Otava. Gold fever has waxed and waned in the town over the centuries (an annual gold-panning championship is now held every August on the river around Slaník). At present, commercial exploration, mostly around the nearby village of Mokrsko, has been suspended, and the likelihood of any company getting the go-ahead to mine looks very slim indeed. The problem is that the gold is dispersed in microscopic particles, which means for every tonne of gold, the mining companies would have to shift half a million tonnes of rock, crush it into powder and then leach the gold out in pools of cyanide. Obviously, the environmental consequences would be disastrous, and so far the locals (and even the government) are against any mining.

The Town

Písek experienced its last gold rush in the thirteenth century, but its prosperity was later demolished by the Thirty Years' War. The chief reminder of those days is the town's wonderful **medieval stone bridge** (Kamenný most), which predates even the Charles Bridge in Prague and which likewise accrued a fine selection of beatific Baroque statuary during the Counter-Reformation. Located in the westernmost edge of the staré město, it is now closed to traffic, and has recently been restored.

From the bridge, it's a short hop to the main square, **Velké náměstí**, overlooked by the magnificent golden yellow Baroque **radnice**. Behind the town hall, at the far end of the courtyard, you'll find the entrance to the **Prácheňské muzeum** (Tues–Sun 9am–6pm), which occupies the only surviving wing of the medieval riverside castle, built by Přemysl King Otakar II in the thirteenth century and destroyed by fire in 1532. The highlight of this recently refurbished and vast museum is the Gothic Knights' Hall, which has retained its original black floor tiles, and contains a model of how the castle once looked. The rest of the museum is also worth a quick canter for its unusually frank account of the area's history, including a section on the Gypsy concentration camp of Lety (see p.171), and the more recent events of 1968 and 1989; and before you leave, don't miss the gold exhibits in the basement.

A few doors down the main square from the *radnice* is the pretty little former monastery church of **sv Kříž**, with its gabled sgraffitoed facade. If you can get inside (it's unlocked for services Mon–Wed & Fri 5pm, Thurs 5.30/6pm, Sun 7.30am), it has a superbly kitsch Baroque main altar, sporting a golden sunburst in the shape of a love heart and a backdrop of blue, ruched curtains dotted with gold stars. There are several other buildings around the town which boast more recent sgraffito decoration, mostly the work of the late-nineteenth-century artist (and local student) Mikuláš Aleš. A short walk up Fráni Šrámka brings you to the **Putimská brána**, the only remaining bastion, adjoined by a number of quiet backstreets heading east. These lead to a small market which takes place under the aegis of the 74-metre-high, onion-domed *hláska* (watchtower) of the Dominican church.

Finally, the technically turned-on might consider paying a visit to Písek's latest attraction, the **Městská elektrárna** (power station; Tues–Sun 9am–noon & 1–4pm), a short walk upstream from the Kamenný most. It became operational in 1887, thus making Písek the first Czech town to have electric lighting supplied by its very own power station.

Practicalities

Písek has a useful **information centre** (Mon–Fri 10am–5pm; July & Aug daily 9am–6pm, ☎382 213 592, ⓦwww.webhouse.cz/pisek) at Hejduková 97, just off the main square, which offers **internet** services, organizes accommodation and has a computerized information screen outside (in Czech, English and German) for when it's closed. For a fairly quaint Bohemian **meal**, book a table under the stone vaults at *U Přemysla Otakara II*, at Velké náměstí 114, in the courtyard of the museum, or try *Ostrov*, on a leafy island in the river just downstream of the bridge, complete with kids' playground and mini-golf. *U Zlatého Byka*, Kocínova 1, offers good steaks and a view of the city walls. The *City Hotel* (☎382 213 592, ⓦwww.cityhotel.cz; ❹) is a smart and pricey Gothic **hotel** with a vaulted restaurant, in the old town at Alšovo náměstí 35; a cheaper alternative is *U Kloudů* (☎382 215 018; ❷), a **pension** on Nerudova with a café-bar and bustling restaurant downstairs – follow Heyduková through Havlíčkovo náměstí. The two **campsites** nearest Písek are a long way out of town and a couple of kilometres from the nearest train stations: *Soutok* (May–Oct) is to the south, nearest Rutim station, while the *Vrcovice* site (open all year) is north of town, nearest Vrcovice station. In the novel by Jaroslav Hašek, the Good Soldier Švejk of the title makes his fictional appearance at Písek in a blizzard, handcuffed to a lance-corporal in the Austrian constabulary "for comfort", before moving on to Tábor on the next train. Should you wish to do the same, the main **bus** and **train stations** are both a kilometre or so south of town, at the end of Nádražní (bus #1).

Tábor

Founded in 1420 by religious exiles from Prague, 88km away to the north, **TÁBOR** – named after the mountain where the transfiguration of Christ took place – was the spiritual and strategic centre of the social and religious revolution which swept through Bohemia in the first half of the fifteenth century. It gave

▲ Prague & Autokemp Malý Jordán

its name to the radical wing of the reformist Hussite movement, the **Táborites**, whose philosophy – that all people should be equal on earth as in heaven – found few friends among the church hierarchy and feudal-minded nobility of the time, Hussite or Catholic. Under constant threat of physical attack, they developed into a formidable fighting force, declaring war on the established Church and remaining undefeated until 1452, when the town was taken by a force led by the moderate Hussite King Jiří of Poděbrady.

Anti-authoritarianism persists here, and despite the efforts of the Jesuits and others over the centuries, Tábor still boasts the smallest percentage of Catholics in the country. Considering its pugnacious history, though, and despite being a major bus and rail junction, Tábor is a relatively quiet little town nowadays, especially in the beautifully preserved old quarter, which is virtually devoid of traffic and has kept its labyrinthine street plan. In the staré město's back alleys, many houses have retained their rich sgraffito decoration and pretty Renaissance gables, while the main square boasts the country's premier museum devoted to the Hussite movement.

The Town

To reach the staré město from the new town or **nové město**, walk west from the train or bus station through the Husův park, making sure you take note of the unusual and passionate **statue of Jan Hus** by local turn-of-the-twentieth-century sculptor František Bílek (you can see more of his work at the nearby village of Chýnov; see p.179). Continue past the statue down třída 9 května until you reach the busy square, náměstí Fr. Křižíka, which straddles the ridge between the new and old towns, then head up Palackého into the old town.

The street plan of the **staré město**, with its vast maze of narrow medieval streets designed to confuse the enemy, has changed very little since its foundation back in the fifteenth century. No fewer than twelve streets lead onto the central square, **Žižkovo náměstí**, with its brightly coloured houses and stunning variety of gables and gargoyles, all of which had to be rebuilt after fires in the fifteenth and sixteenth centuries. The square is dominated by the **Děkanský kostel**, with its unusual triple gable; for a bird's-eye view of Tábor's weblike street layout, climb the 199 steps of the church's extremely tall **bell-tower** (May–Aug daily 10am–5pm), and try to time your climb between the hourly tolling, since you have to pass within inches of the bell to reach the top.

It was on Tábor's main square in 1420 that the Táborites threw theological caution to the wind and set up a religious commune under the principle of *není nic mé a nic tvé, než všecko v obec rovně mají* ("nothing is mine, nothing is yours, everything is common to all"). Large urns were set up in the square and any-one – male or female – wishing to live in the commune had first to place all their possessions in them, after which they were given work on a daily rota. Men and women were granted equal rights, there was a complete ban on alcohol, and from the stone table which still stands outside the stará radnice, communion was given to the people "in both kinds" – as opposed to the established practice of reserving the wine (the blood of Christ) for the priesthood. The Hussites had this last symbolic act emblazoned on their flag – a red chalice on a black back-ground – which, like the rousing religious war songs they sang before going into battle, struck fear into the crusaders from thirty nations who came against them.

Matching the church's triple gable on the west side of the square are the three steeply stepped neo-Gothic gables of the **stará radnice**, which now houses the **Husitské muzeum** (Hussite Museum; April–Oct daily 8.30am–5pm; rest of the year Tues–Fri only). Inside, in amongst the nasty-looking pikes, there's a model of medieval Tábor, and several versions of Myslbek's late-nineteenth-century statue of **Jan Žižka**, the Táborites' brilliant, blind military leader (tra-ditionally depicted with one eye still functioning), which stands on the square in front of the church. You also get the chance to peek inside the Gothic hall, with its diamond rib-vaulting and irreverent medieval corbels. The museum also runs hourly guided tours of a small section of the huge network of **under-ground passages** (*podzemí*); originally used to store beer barrels, they also served as a refuge from fire and siege, and as the town prison.

△ Tábor

As for the rest of the town, its hotchpotch of backstreets, enlivened by the occasional sgraffito flourish, are perfect for a spot of aimless wandering – there's a great view of the surrounding countryside from the town's southern walls along Na parkánech. To give direction to your strolling, head down Klokotská to the **Bechyňská brána**, the town's only remaining gateway; its adjoining tower, now housing the Muzeum života a práce středověké společnosti (Museum of Life and Work in Medieval Society; May–Oct daily 8.30am–5pm; Nov–April advance booking required on ☏381 254 286), has display cases full of farm tools and dioramas of house-building, and shows a video in English on life in Bohemia in medieval times.

Another place to aim for is the pilgrimage church and monastery of **Klokoty**, a kilometre west of the old town (turn right off Klokotská up Sady, telephone at least two days before, ☏381 232 584) and a steep down-and-up scramble. An ensemble of nine onion domes rises above the peeling walls, making this one of the most endearing and least pompous of Bohemia's Counter-Reformation monasteries. The domes form the corner towers of a set of cloisters with a lovely rose garden as its centrepiece. The church, surprisingly, has a flat and unadorned ceiling, but the putti-strewn pulpit and main altar don't disappoint.

Practicalities

Fast trains from Prague take under two hours to reach Tábor. If you wish to stay the night, you can arrange **private rooms** through the friendly and efficient **information centre** at Žižkovo náměstí 2 (May–Sept Mon–Fri 8.30am–7pm, Sat 9am–1pm, Sun 1–5pm; Oct–April Mon–Fri 9am–4pm; ☏381 486 230, ⓦwww.tabor.cz). Without doubt, the best **accommodation** option is the *Penzion Černy leknín*, a grandiose neo-Gothic villa on Příběnická (☏381 256 405; ❹), beyond the Bechyňská brána. Cheaper alternatives include the pensions *U Husicky Tábor*, Tržní 274 (☏381 256 419; ❸) in the historic centre, or *Dáša Tábor*, Bílková 736 (☏381 256 253, ⓦwww.travel-guide.cz/pensiondasa; ❷), off the Husův park close to the station, with a sauna attached. As for the big **hotels**, go for *Kapitál* (☏381 256 096, ⓕ381 252 411; ❸), on třída 9 května, which also has a decent restaurant. All the **campsites** are well out of the centre. The best of the bunch is *Autokemp Malý Jordán*, with basic chalets (mid-May to mid-Sept, ☏381 235 103; buses #20 and #21; ❶), situated north of the town in the woods between Lake Jordán – formed by the oldest dam in Europe (built in 1492) and once a favourite spot for baptizing children – and its smaller sister lake, after which it's a pleasant kilometre's walk along the lakeside.

If it's **food** you want, there's traditional Czech fare and *Budvar* and *Bernard* beers at *Beseda* (closed Sun eve), the popular, old-fashioned restaurant at no. 5 at the top of the main square in the old town, whose patio spills out onto the square itself. *U dvou koček*, Svatošova 310, to the west of the Děkanský kostel, is a bit of a tourist trap but offers dark *Purkmistr* beer and light *Pilsner* to go with good solid cooking, or there's the *Dobra čajovná* (tea house) at Tomkova 2. For your afternoon coffee break, there's a good *cukrárna* on the main square, or for pizza, try *Pizza Napoli* on Husovo náměstí near the stations. As for **nightlife**, Tábor has its very own theatre, Divadlo Oskara Nedbala, on Palackého, though the plays are all in Czech, and a rock club, *Orion*, on náměstí Fr. Křižíka, featuring the occasional live band. If you're in town around the middle of September, be prepared for a lot of medieval fooling around as part of Tábor's annual **festival**, *Setkání*.

West of Tábor

Tábor's old town will keep you occupied for the best part of a day. However, if you've an afternoon to spare, a couple of side-trips are possible west of Tábor, both of them just a short train journey from the town.

Milevsko

Halfway along the branch line from Tábor to Písek, **MILEVSKO** has a couple of interesting sights besides its impressive array of late-nineteenth-century buildings. The most unusual is the former **synagogue**, on Sokolovská, designed by Oldřich Tyl and completed in 1919, which has been used by the local Hussite congregation since 1965. Its Neoclassical facade is disrupted by a double staircase that leads to the women's gallery, and by the distinctive Cubist prisms in the tympanum. There's a memorial to the town's hundred-strong Jewish community, which was wiped out in the Holocaust. The town's sturdy, twelfth-century **Basilica of sv Jiljí**, just off the main Tábor–Plzeň road, used to attract a stream of royal and ecclesiastical admirers until the Hussites wrecked it; despite repairs and later additions, it's currently in a desperate state. The nearby Premonstratensian monastery houses the small **Milevské muzeum** (Tues–Fri 9am–5pm, Sat & Sun 9am–4pm) charting the history of the town, with details as fascinating as the price of a fifteenth-century chicken.

Bechyně

Every hour and a half, a dinky electric train covers the 24-kilometre journey from Tábor to the small soporific spa and pottery-producing town of **BECHYNĚ**. The line from Tábor to Bechyně was the empire's first electrified line when it was opened in 1903, and on Saturdays in July and August, you can travel there and back on the original train. As you enter the town, both rail and road cross a spectacular viaduct over the Lužnice gorge, known locally as the "Rainbow". The old town teeters on the edge of the gorge, ten minutes' walk southwest of the station down Libušina.

At the far side of the leafy main square, which has long since lost its function as a marketplace, is the **Alšova jihočeská galerie** (May–Oct Tues–Sun 9am–noon & 12.30–5pm), housed in the old town castle brewery, which has an impressive collection of locally produced ceramics and hosts regular international exhibitions. Opposite is the medieval **Zámecká sýpka** (Tues–Sun 11am–6pm), now home to local history and temporary art exhibitions. Just beyond lies the Rožmberks' Renaissance **zámek**, whose treasures, unfortunately, are off-limits to the public. The Franciscan **monastery** nearby is now a school, but the church is open on Sundays for mass, and the gardens host summer concerts and afford excellent views of the gorge. Also worth exploring before you leave town is the **Hasičské muzeum** (Firefighting Museum; May–Oct Tues–Sun 9am–1pm & 1–5pm) in Široká, to the north of the main square, interesting less for its old fire engines than for the fact that it occupies the town's former **synagogue**. There's also a well-kept **Jewish cemetery** just beyond the old town walls on Michalská; ask at the museum.

The last **train** back to Tábor leaves at around 7.45pm; the last **bus** much earlier. If you wish to **stay the night**, head for the *Pichlův dům* (☎381 811 075; ❹), a lovely little Baroque cottage on the main square, with a bar and ceramics shop downstairs; alternatively, there's the *Hotel Jupiter*, a newly renovated late-nineteenth-century villa on Libůšina (☎381 962 131; ❹), which has a good restaurant and also offers spa treatment. For **beer and food**, try the *Hospoda u města Bechyně*, a popular pub on the main square, or the *Hostinec pod skálou*, by the riverside at the bottom of the steps leading down from the corner of the square.

East of Tábor

East of Tábor, there are several more possible day-trips: to the village of **Chýnov**, where the turn-of-the-twentieth-century sculptor František Bílek built his own house, now a museum to his exceptional talents; and, for those with an interest in the country's motorcycling history, to **Kámen**. Even **Pelhřimov** is possible as a day-trip by train or bus, though you're more likely to pass through en route to Moravia. Only devotees of Jaroslav Hašek will journey even further east beyond Humpolec to the village of **Lipnice**, to pay their respects to the last resting place of the author of *The Good Soldier Švejk*. Likewise, admirers of Gustav Mahler might want to make the trip to **Kaliště**, northwest of Humpolec, to visit his birthplace, though unfortunately there's no dedicated museum there.

Chýnov

The little village of **CHÝNOV**, three stations east of Tábor, is the birthplace of the sculptor **František Bílek** (1872–1941), whose former home (though not his birthplace), the **Bílkův dům** at Údolní 133 (June–Sept Tues–Sun 10am–5pm), has recently been restored, and is an absolute must if you're in the area. Far from being a simple house-museum, this is a remarkable piece of architecture, designed by Bílek himself in 1897. Built in red bricks, with a large overhanging wooden roof and balcony, it stands out, above all, thanks to Bílek's biblical plaster relief on the south facade, and the miniature wooden chapel on the north side of the house. A large part of the interior is taken up with Bílek's studio, which is suffused with natural light and filled with studies for his large-scale works, but there is no attempt to re-create Bílek's home as it would have been in his day; instead, the building simply serves as a gallery for his works. Trained in Paris, Bílek was clearly influenced stylistically by Art Nouveau, though the tortured gestures and expressions of his subjects are derived more from the religious fervour that imbues all his work, which he himself described as "a sacrifice for the recovery of the brethren".

The Bílkův dům is situated on the south side of the river, across from the main part of town, signposted off the road to Tábor, and is a good 1.5km from Chýnov train station. While you're in the vicinity, you might consider paying a visit to the **Chýnovská jeskyně** (April–Oct Tues–Fri 10am–4pm, Sat & Sun 9am–4pm), a three-kilometre walk northeast across the fields from the train station on the blue-marked path. Amid gentle meadows and orchards, the entrance to the caves consists of a fifty-metre plunge down narrow, precipitous steps, to the sounds of Bach's *Toccata and Fugue in D minor*. What's fun about the thirty-minute guided tour is that it's a lot more like real potholing than the larger caves in Moravia or Slovakia, and there are even some stalactites and stalagmites to admire when you reach the bottom.

Kámen

There's a sporadic branch-line service between Tábor and Pelhřimov, but you'll have to take the bus along route 19 to reach the one-street village of **KÁMEN** (meaning "Rock"), whose castle was once a fortified staging post between these two strongly pro-Hussite walled towns. It's worth a detour, since in 1974, after centuries of neglect, the castle was reopened – somewhat incongruously – as a **Motorcycle Museum** (April & Oct Sat & Sun 9am–noon & 1–4pm; May–Sept Tues–Sun 9am–noon & 1–5pm). Some wonderful old Czech bikes are on display, from the very first Laurin & Klement Model TB from 1899 – not much more than a bicycle with a petrol tank tacked on – to stylish examples from the heyday of Czech biking between the wars. Other machines include ČZs and Jawas, which may have cut some ice back in the 1940s when they were designed, but now only exacerbate the country's environmental problems. To trace the sad demise of the Czech motorcycle industry, you have to join the short guided tour of the castle before reaching the machines.

Pelhřimov

If you're heading east into Moravia and need a place to stay, make for the tiny, sleepy medieval town of **PELHŘIMOV**, only 16km further east along route 19. Barely 200m across, the walled town still retains two sixteenth-century tower gates, on one of which, the **Rynárecká brána**, two rams tirelessly butt each other on the hour. In one corner of the extremely pretty, cobbled main square stands the beautiful Renaissance **Šrejnarovsky dům**, and the Venetian-red sixteenth-century **zámek Říčanskych**, with a splendid clocktower, both now part of the local **museum** (April–Oct, Tues–Fri 9–11am & 1–4pm, Sat & Sun 10am–noon; Nov–March Tues & Thurs 9–11am & 1–4pm). On the main square itself, just opposite the museum, it's surprisingly easy to miss a minor work of Cubist architecture by Pavel Janák, who in 1913 adapted the Baroque **Fárovy dům** at no. 13 into a slightly bizarre combination of pale pink Baroque and Cubism. You can get a good feel for the angled interior by stopping for a drink at the *Denní* bar upstairs. If you're on the Cubist trail, head through the chateau's archway and a short distance north up Strachovská to check out Janák's **Drechselův dům** at no. 331, right by the town brewery. The maroon and mustard colour scheme looks snazzy, especially on the stripey columns of the garden canopy, but it's not on the quietest of roads.

On one weekend in the middle of June the rather unlikely spectacle of Pelhřimov's **Festival of Records and Curious Performances** takes place, during which Czech eccentrics attempt to enter the *Guinness Book of World Records*, by whatever means necessary: recent new records include 157 people on one tractor, and a man with 82 socks on one foot, while "Železný Zekon" allowed seven cars to roll over him whilst lying on a bed of 970 nails. A museum cataloguing these great feats, the **Muzeum rekord a kuriozit** (nominally June–Aug Tues–Sat 9am–4.30pm, though hours are unpredictable), is open in the Dolní (Jihlavská) brána, to the east of the main square. Inside, you can see the world's longest paper chain, the largest picture made from pasta, a giant toothbrush and pyjamas, the smallest paper boat (2 x 5mm) and a bicycle made entirely of wood. There's also photographic evidence of one-off achievements, and various rather tedious displays of strength. All in all, it's a fun museum, which children will probably love.

The **train** station is, unfortunately, a good 2km south of the town centre; the **bus** station is about halfway along the road into town. Pelhřimov still brews its own **beer**, which you can sup to your heart's content at *U Vlasáků*, right next to the brewery, beyond the chateau; they also do passable Czech **food**, though the atmosphere is decidedly grungy. In addition to housing the best restaurant, cocktail bar and pizzeria in town, the Secessionist-era *Hotel Slavia* (☎565 321 540, ℗565 321 857; ❷), at no. 29 on the main square, is also by far the nicest place **to stay**. The other option is the unlovely Communist-era *Rekrea* (☎565

350 111; ❸), just outside the historical centre, though its rooms are fine, with en-suite facilities and TVs.

Kaliště

Devotees of composer Gustav Mahler might want to make a detour to his birthplace in **KALIŠTĚ**, a tiny village 24km northeast of Pelhřimov and 10km northwest of Humpolec. Several years of fundraising have finally resulted in the renovation of the building in which the great symphonist was born, in an apartment above the former town pub. The pub is now operating again (although the thoroughly modern decor lends little character), but the upstairs is, frustratingly, still used as an apartment and is firmly closed to the public. If you still want to make the trip, you can catch the rare bus from Humpolec, 16km northeast of Pelhřimov and linked by regular buses, and look for the white house opposite the church with "Mahler" painted across one side. While you're in **Humpolec**, you might want to visit the **Muzeum Dr Alše Hrdličký** (April–Oct Tues & Thurs–Sat 8–11am & 1–4pm, Wed 8–11am & 1–6pm, Sun 9–11am), which has a room full of photos and newspaper clippings of Mahler, with extensive captions in Czech only.

Lipnice nad Sázavou

Around 20km northeast of Pelhřimov, just beyond Humpolec and the Prague–Brno motorway, in the midst of some glorious Bohemian countryside, is the village of **LIPNICE NAD SÁZAVOU**. Here, Bohemia's ultimate bohemian, the writer **Jaroslav Hašek**, died on January 3, 1923, his most famous work still unfinished. The village has changed little over the intervening years; the pub he lived, drank and died in is still going strong, and the castle, ruined even in Hašek's day, is still mostly rubble. A flattering bust of the author has been erected on the way up to the castle, and his gravestone is a little less ignominious these days. Beside the castle, in the house where he died, the **Memorial to Jaroslav Hašek** (May–Sept Tues–Sun 9am–noon & 1–4pm) is respectfully vague about the many contradictions in Hašek's life, not least the alcoholism which eventually cost him his life. If you want to pay homage to Hašek at Lipnice, roughly five buses a day make the ten-kilometre trip from Humpolec.

Jaroslav Hašek

Stories about Hašek's life – many propagated by the author himself – have always been a mixture of fact and fiction, but at one time or another he was an anarchist, dog-breeder, lab assistant, bigamist, cabaret artist and people's commissar in the Red Army. He alternately shocked and delighted both close friends and the public at large with his drunken antics and occasional acts of political extremism. When, towards the end of his life, he made his home in the *Česká koruna* pub in Lipnice, he wrote happily, "Now I live bang in the middle of a *pivnice*. Nothing better could have happened to me." Few friends attended his funeral, and none of his family, with the exception of his eleven-year-old son, who had met his father only two or three times. In a final act of contempt, the local priest would only allow his body to be buried alongside the cemetery wall, among the unbaptized and suicide victims. Before long, however, the protagonist in Hašek's *The Good Soldier Švejk* had become the most famous (fictional) Czech of all time, culminating in Hašek's "canonization" by the Communist regime – his works even being published by the military publishing house.

Třeboňsko

The **Třeboňsko** region, with the picturesque town of **Třeboň** at its heart, is unlike the rest of South Bohemia – characterized not by rolling hills but by peat bogs, flatlands and fishponds. This monotonous marshland, broken only by the occasional Gothic fortress, was moulded into an intricate system of canal-linked **ponds** (totalling over 6000) as early as the fifteenth century, ushering in profitable times for the nobles who owned the land. The fish industry still dominates the region, and around September the ponds are drained to allow the fish to be "harvested". Larger ponds, like the Rožmberk, are drained only every other year, and for several days people from the surrounding district gather to feast, sing and participate in a great local event that's worth seeking out if you're in the vicinity. Wildlife also thrives on the soggy plains – as do mosquitoes in the summer – and in 1977 UNESCO declared a large area, from Soběslav south as far as the Austrian border, a **nature reserve**.

Jindřichův Hradec

JINDŘICHŮV HRADEC (Neuhaus) is the largest of the towns set amongst Třeboňsko's fish ponds. Hemmed in by walls and water, it's typical of the region – blessed with a glorious medieval past and, structurally at least, untouched by modern conflicts. Although the staré město was robbed of much of its rich medieval dressing by a fire in 1801, the main square, **náměstí Míru**, still displays an attractive array of wealthy merchants' houses, sporting brightly coloured early-nineteenth-century facades, and an exceptionally fine Baroque Trinity column. Only one house, the **Langrův dům** from 1579, hints at the Renaissance riches that were once the norm here. The diamond vaulting in the arcaded ground floor, and the sgraffito biblical scenes that cover the facade bear closer inspection, especially the depiction of Jonah being swallowed by what looks like a giant crocodile, on the side of the oriel window.

Rybniční leads down from the main square to a bridge that bisects the Vaygar fish pond, creating a small harbour. From here, the town's thirteenth-century **zámek** (Tues–Sun: April & Oct 10am–4pm; May & Sept 10am–5pm;

The White Lady

If you're in the castle in Jindřichův Hradec and you hear a clinking of keys or a door unexpectedly slamming, or notice a figure in white floating about in the evening, it could be the *Bílá paní* or **White Lady**, the most famous ghost in the Czech Republic, whose favourite haunt is the castle. According to legend, she is the spirit of Perchta Rožmberková, born in 1430, who fell in love with the young Count Šternberk but was married against her wishes to Count Liechtenstein of Styria. On her wedding night, she secretly met Šternberk to bid him farewell, but was caught *in flagrante* by her husband, who thenceforth mistreated his wife. Many years later, Perchta returned to Jindřichův Hradec as a widow and used to hand out porridge, warm beer and honey to the poor. Since her husband never pardoned her, she was condemned to roam the castle as a ghost, though a benevolent one, prophesying births and deaths in the Rožmberk family by wearing white gloves for the former and black for the latter, and pointing out hidden treasure in the various family properties through-out Bohemia. Evenings in August are her favourite spooking time, when she is reg-ularly spotted handing out porridge along the approach to the castle, outside the restaurant that bears her name.

June–Aug 9am–5pm; 140Kč for each tour; 400Kč for all three) – chief residence of the lords of Hradec, and later the Černíns – is picturesquely mirrored in the water, its forbidding exterior giving no hint of the exuberant interior renovations by Italian architects in the sixteenth century, which make a visit here an absolute must.

To get to the chateau's main entrance, head down Dobrovského. You currently have a choice of three different forty-five-minute **guided tours** (only occasionally in English), which set off from the second courtyard. *Trasa 1* (the *Adamovo stavení*) leads you through the Neoclassical and Baroque "Green Rooms", and past Petr Brandel's painting of St Joseph curing the lepers; *trasa 2* (May Sat & Sun 10am–4pm; June–Sept Tues–Sun 10am–5pm), the Gotický hrad, explores the Gothic interiors, and features the starkly beautiful thirteenth-century chapel, fourteenth-century frescoes and the black kitchen; *trasa 3* (July & Aug Tues–Sun 9.30am–4pm), the *Interiéry 18. a 19. století*, despite its title ("interiors of the eighteenth and nineteenth centuries"), takes you round the slender, triple-tiered, Renaissance loggia (which you can view without a guide) and the Černíns' bizarre collection of dog portraits, as well as gaining you entrance to the chateau's pride and joy, the striking bubble-gum pink garden rotunda, known as the "Rondel", with its incredible gilded stucco work. The Spanish Wing, which was designed as a Communist conference centre,

183

complete with lift and cinema, is under lengthy restoration. The chateau's Černá věž (Black Tower), accessible from the second courtyard, is open to the public without a guided tour (May Sat & Sun 10am–4pm; June–Sept Tues–Sun 10am–4pm), and you can peek through the windows into the Rondel anytime.

With most tour groups visiting only the chateau, there's hardly anyone exploring the cobbled alleyways northwest of the main square at the top of Komenského. You can climb the tall **tower** (daily 10am–noon & 1–4pm) of the Gothic church of Nanebevzetí Panny Marie, which doubled as the town's watchtower, and pay a visit to the former Jesuit seminary on Balbínovo náměstí, founded by Adam II of Hradec and Catherine de Montfort in 1604, and now home to the local **museum** (April–Dec Tues–Sun 8.30am–noon & 12.30–5pm; June–Sept daily). One room is devoted to Ferenc Rákóczi II, leading light of the Hungarian War of Independence (1703–11), who studied here, while another honours the composer Bedřich Smetana, who seems to have moved from one brewery to another; born in one in Litomyšl (see p.321), he lived in another here, below the castle, from 1831 to 1835. Still another room features folk costumes from the vicinity, plus the reconstructed parlour of opera singer Ema Destinnová, who lived nearby in Stráž nad Nežárkou (see box below). However, the museum's chief exhibit is its eighteenth-century 3-D Bethlehem Nativity scene, allegedly the largest in the world, with fully mechanized figures.

Practicalities

To get to the staré město from the **bus and train stations** to the north, it's a fifteen-minute walk along Nádražní, then left down Klášterská. This brings you to the edge of the old town, where the walls have long since been replaced by a park, the Husovy sady; the old town lies beyond. There's a **tourist office** on Panská (Mon–Fri 8am–5pm, Sat & Sun 8am–noon; ℡384 363 546,

Ema Destinnová

Halfway between Jindřichův Hradec and Třeboň lies the town of Stráž nad Nežárkou, whose chateau was once the estate of Czech diva **Ema Destinnová** (1878–1930) – her initials "ED" are emblazoned on the gates – one of the world's premier sopranos of the early twentieth century. Born Ema Kittlová, she took her stage name as a tribute to her first singing teacher. She won huge critical acclaim in Berlin at the age of just nineteen as Santuzza in *Cavalleria rusticana*. As Donna Anna in Mozart's *Don Giovanni* at Covent Garden, she sang so well that they had her back for every performance of it for the next ten years. She sang opposite Enrico Caruso in the London premiere of *Madame Butterfly*, was chosen by Richard Strauss for the Berlin premiere of *Salome*, and enjoyed eight seasons as the *prima donna* at New York's Metropolitan Opera. However, she also had strong ties to the Czech independence movement, and in 1916, during the height of World War I, she decided to return to Stráž for a visit, where she was arrested for smuggling revolutionary plans over the border. She was sentenced to confinement at her estate – though given that the penalty for espionage was, in fact, death without trial, Destinnová got off relatively lightly. When the war ended, Destinnová threw herself into promoting Czech opera and went on a European tour with an exclusively Czech repertoire. Her great days as a diva were over, however, and she spent her last twelve years writing plays, novels and poetry and living off the fish she caught from the Nežárka river. After her death from a stroke at the age of 52, Destinnová was given a lavish burial at Prague's Vyšehrad cemetery, and in 1996, the Czech treasury placed Ema Destinnová on its new 2000Kč note. Her chateau, however, is closed to the public, and up for sale or rent.

@www.jh.cz), just off the main square, who should be able to give information about the state-owned **narrow-gauge railway** (*úzkorozchodná železnice*) run by JHMD (@www.jhmd.cz), that winds its way north to Obrataň, and south to Nová Bystřice, with occasional steam trains on the latter branch line.

On the main square, the best of the **hotels** is the *Concertino* (☎384 362 320, @www.concertino.cz; ➍). Much better value, though, is the *Bílá paní* (☎384 363 329; ➌), in a lovely old house right by the chateau at Dobrovského 5, with a restaurant on the ground floor, and real character to the rooms. Another option is *U tkadlen* (☎384 321 348, @www.sthubert.cz; ➌), a geranium-bedecked, converted sixteenth-century tannery in a peaceful spot to the west of the castle walls at Pod hradem 7; the year-round pension and restaurant also serves as an **HI hostel** (July–Sept), with dorm bed-and-breakfast for 280Kč.

The **restaurants** in the *Bílá paní* and *U tkadlen* are both reasonable places to eat, but the locals seem to prefer *U Kateřiny* (closed Sun), opposite the tourist office on Panská. There's a pleasant café in the zámek courtyard, and an **internet** café, *Bistro pod hradem* (closed Sun) to the north of *U tkadlen* on Pod hradem.

Červená Lhota

In the middle of nowhere, off the main road between Jindřichův Hradec and Soběslav, the red sugar-lump castle of **Červená Lhota** (April & Oct Sat & Sun 9am–4pm; May, June & Sept Tues–Sun 9am–4pm; July & Aug 9.30am–4.30pm) is reflected perfectly in the still waters that surround it. This breathtaking sight – a Gothic waterfort converted into a Renaissance retreat for the rich in 1551 – appears on almost every regional tourist handout, but its isolated location makes it a nightmare to reach on public transport. Given this, and the unremarkable nature of the chateau's interior, it's really only for dedicated fans of Karl Ditters von Dittersdorf, Mozart's composing chum who died here in 1799. That said, the lakeside grounds around the chateau are perfect for a picnic, and in high season there are boats for hire, and a horse and carriage available in which to take a turn. You can also stay in the simple **rooms** at *U zámku Červená Lhota* (☎384 384 305; ➋) in some of the chateau's outbuildings.

Třeboň

Right in the midst of some of the region's largest fish ponds, the spa town of **TŘEBOŇ** (Wittingau) is as medieval and minute as they come. The houses lining the long, thin main square, Masarykovo náměstí, make an attractive parade, but the *Bílý koníček* (*White Horse*) – now a hotel – built in 1544, steals the show with a stepped gable of miniature turrets. The entire **staré město** is made up of just three more streets, a fourteenth-century monastery and a chateau. Three gateways (including the impressive double south gate, next to the local brewery) and the entire ring of walls have survived from the sixteenth century, though many houses suffered badly during the last great fire in 1781.

Out of all proportion to the rest of the town is the huge Renaissance **zámek** (April–Oct Tues–Sun 9am–noon & 1–4pm; June–Aug closes 5pm), built by Petr Vok, a colourful character, notoriously fond of sex, drugs and alchemy, friend of the mad Emperor Rudolf II, legendary thrower of parties, and the last heir of the Rožmberk family. The chateau, daubed in blinding white sgraffito and taking up almost a fifth of the town, is a pretty clumsy affair, but the interior is definitely worth visiting. There's a choice of two guided tours: *trasa 1* is the one to go for as it concentrates on Petr Vok and the chateau's Renaissance legacy; the Baroque and nineteenth-century period furniture imported by the later owners, the Schwarzenbergs, forms the bedrock of *trasa 2*. Adjacent to the chateau and equal in size to the old town is a very pleasant "English park", where the town's spa patients can take a stroll.

South of the town is the Svět pond, beside which stands the local **fishery** on Novohradská, which handles the region's huge fish harvest and, most importantly, its *kapr* (carp) culling. **Carp**, not turkey, is the centrepiece of the Christmas meal in the Czech Lands, traditionally sold live and wriggling from town squares across the country, then transferred to the family bathtub until the big day.

The Schwarzenberg mausoleum

Head south out of Třeboň in the direction of Borovany along the lake, and you'll pick up signs to the **Schwarzenberg mausoleum** (Schwarzenberská hrobka; April & Oct Sat & Sun 9am–4pm; May & Sept Tues–Sun 9am–4pm; June–Aug Tues–Sun 9am–5pm), twenty minutes' walk from the town centre. Hidden among the silver birch trees south of the Svět pond, it's a rather subdued, out-of-the-way site for a family so fond of ostentatious displays of wealth. The building itself is equally strange: a seemingly brand-new neo-Gothic building, with a bare chapel above and a dark crypt below (guided tours only). Třeboň was the first Bohemian town to be bought up by the Bavarian-based Schwarzenberg family in 1660 who, having sided with the Habsburgs in the Counter-Reformation, became the unofficial heirs of ousted or defunct Czech aristocrats like the Vítkovci and Rožmberks. By 1875, the family owned more estates in Bohemia than anyone else and decided to "honour" Třeboň by establishing the family mausoleum in the town. After 1945, the family's possessions were expropriated and, along with all their fellow German-speakers, they were thrown out of the country. Today, the most famous descendant is probably Count Karl von Schwarzenberg, a former emigré and one of the republic's leading businessmen.

Practicalities

The local **tourist office** (Mon–Fri 9am–5pm; ☎384 721 169, ⓦwww.trebon-mesto.cz), on the main square in the old town, can book **private rooms**. There are also two **hotels** on the main square: the aforementioned *Bílý koníček* (☎384 721 213; ❷) is, in fact, not as pretty inside, but offers cheap en-suite rooms; the *Zlatá hvězda* (☎384 757 111, ⓦwww.zhvezda.cz; ❹), opposite, has much more comfortable en-suite rooms with TV for roughly twice the price. Another option is *U míšků* (☎384 721 698, ⓦwww.misek.cz; ❹), a pension and café-gallery, with a tiny indoor pool, in a prettily gabled building just north of the main square at Husova 11. For **camping** (and swimming), head for the *Třeboňský ráj* campsite (May–Sept), south of the fish-pond, near the mausoleum.

For a taste of the local beer, there's no better place to go than the *Regent* brewery's own **pub**, to the south of the main square, a simple *pivnice* just on the right inside the brewery archway. The very popular local fish **restaurant** *Supina Supinka*, lies opposite; if it's full, the folky *Rožmberská bašta*, Rožmberská 59, between the main square and the brewery, offers lots of fish dishes. If you're camping and cooking your own food, buy fresh fish from the *rybárna* (fishmonger) right by the carp pools, to the south of town. For a game of pool with the locals, head for *U zámku*, en route to the brewery; for bowling, head for the back end of the *Zlatá Hvězda*; while the town's liveliest spot is *Torpedo*, in the passageway that leads from the main square, through the chateau to the park.

Třeboň **train station** is 2km north of the old town, off the road to Tábor; Třeboň lázně station is only ten minutes' walk east of the old town. A couple of express trains stop at the latter station en route to Vienna, via Gmünd. However, there are no direct trains to or from České Budějovice or Jindřichův Hradec; for them, you're best off heading for the **bus station**, a five-minute walk west of the old town.

České Budějovice and around

The flat, urban sprawl of **ČESKÉ BUDĚJOVICE** (Budweis) comes as something of a surprise after the small-town mentality of the rest of South Bohemia. But first impressions are deceptive, for at its heart it's a laid-back city, no more cosmopolitan than anywhere else in the region, with a perfectly preserved staré město that attracts a good number of Bavarian and Austrian tourists. Founded by King Otakar II in 1265 as a German merchants' colony, the town's wealth was based on medieval silver mines and its position on the old salt route from Linz to Prague. All this was wiped out in the seventeenth century by the twin ravages of war and fire. But, perhaps because it remained a loyal Catholic town in a hotbed of Hussitism, the Habsburgs lavishly reconstructed most of České Budějovice in the eighteenth century. Miraculously, in the face of two centuries of rapid industrial growth, the city's staré město has been carefully preserved. Besides, its renown nowadays is due to its local brew *Budvar*, better known abroad under its original German name, *Budweiser* (see box p.189).

▲ Budvar Brewery (1 km)

ČESKÉ BUDĚJOVICE

ACCOMMODATION
Grand Hotel Zvon	3
Hotel Bohemia	1
Hotel Malý pivovar	5
Penzion Klika	2
Hotel U solné brány	4

CAFES, RESTAURANTS & BARS
Dobrá čajovna	B
Masné krámy	C
Pizzeria Regina	A

187

Arrival, information and accommodation

Ten minutes' walk from the **train and bus stations** down Lannova třída will bring you to Na sadech, the busy ring road flanked by small parks that encloses the staré město in place of the greater part of the old town walls.

The **tourist office** at no. 2 on the main square (June–Sept Mon–Fri 8.30am–noon & 12.30–6pm, Sat 8.30am–noon & 12.30–5pm, Sun 10am–4pm; Oct–May Mon–Fri 9am–noon & 12.30–5pm, Sat 9am–3pm; ☎386 801 413, ⓦwww.c-budejovice.cz) can help with accommodation. České Budějovice's popularity with neighbouring Austrians and Germans means that **hotels and pensions** tend to charge over the odds. From July to September rooms are available in **student halls**, located west of the Vltava at Studentská 15 (☎387 774 201; ❶); take bus #1 or #3 from Na Sadech. Another guaranteed cheap sleep is to **camp** or rent a **bungalow** at the *Dlouhá louka* site (☎387 210 601; open all year), southwest of the centre on Litvínovská silnice; bus #16 from the station (which stops running around 7pm). The *Stromovka* site (April–Oct), a little further along the same road, is even cheaper and also has bungalows.

Hotels and pensions

Grand Hotel Zvon náměstí Přemysla Otakara II 28 ☎387 311 383, ⓦwww.hotel-zvon.cz. Luxurious hotel right on the spectacular main square, and the best place to head for if you're feeling flush or are on business expenses. ❽

Hotel Bohemia Hradební 20 ☎386 360 691, ⓦwww.hotel-bohemia-cb.cz. A comfortably modernized option on the northern edge of the old town, with its own little courtyard and vaulted cellar restaurant. ❹

Hotel Malý pivovar Karla IV 8–10 ☎386 360 471, ⓦwww.budvar.cz. Slick, Budvar-run hotel, just off the main square, with tasteful modern en-suite rooms. ❺

Penzion Klika Zátkovo nábřeží 17 ☎387 318 360, ⓦwww.klika-penzion.cz. Newly expanded pension-restaurant in a nice quiet position by an arm of the Malše, on the western edge of the old town. ❸

U solné brány Radniční 11 ☎386 354 121, ⓦwww.hotelusolnebrany.cz. Hotel, tucked into the old town walls, with pleasant, relaxed service and tasteful, plain rooms. ❹

The Town

České Budějovice's medieval grid plan leads inevitably to the town's showpiece, the magnificent **náměstí Přemysla Otakara II**, one of Europe's largest squares. The buildings are supremely elegant, testifying to the last three centuries of German burgher power (it wasn't until the 1890s that the first Czech was able to buy one of the houses here), but it's the square's arcades, its magnificent Baroque radnice, whose clock tinkles out tunes, and the octagonal **Samson's Fountain** – once the only tap in town – that make the greatest impression. It was German merchants, too, who paid in silver and salt for the 72-metre status symbol, the **Černá věž** (Black Tower), one of the few survivors of the 1641 fire, which leans gently to one side of the square; its roof gallery (April–June, Sept & Oct Tues–Sun 10am–6pm; July & Aug daily 10am–6pm) provides a superb view of the staré město. Next to the tower is the cathedral of **sv Mikuláš**, a church of Gothic proportions heavily overlaid with eighteenth-century plasterwork and furnishings, including a spectacular white marble pulpit with gold trimmings and cherubs.

The streets immediately off the square – Krajinská, Česká and Kněžská – are worth wandering down, and if the weather's fine, folk promenade by the banks of the Malše, where parts of the original town walls have survived along with some of České Budějovice's oldest buildings, like the fifteenth-century prison tower, named after its most infamous torture instrument, **Železná panna** (literally "Iron Maiden"). All that is left of the bishop's palace is his serene **garden**, occasionally accessible in summer through a small gateway in the walls a little further on. At the second bridge, a right turn down Hroznová will lead you round into Piaristické náměstí, where the rough-looking, thoroughly medieval **solnice** (salt store) stands, its stepped gables proof of its former importance; later it was used as the town's arsenal and the building now houses a **Motocyclové muzeum** (Motorcycle Museum; March–Oct Wed–Sun 9am–5pm). Incidentally, the nearby church is worth a peek as it retains some of its Gothic cloisters, and patches of medieval fresco, too.

Two further refuges in wet weather are the grandiose **Jihočeské muzeum** (Tues–Sun 9am–5.30pm), southeast of the old town on Dukelská, which contains all the usual thrills of a regional museum (stuffed birds, mushrooms, armoury, coins, etc), but occasionally puts on an interesting exhibition. Further south, at the bottom of F.A. Gerstnera, beyond the pencil factory, there's a meagre museum dedicated to the **Horse-Drawn Train Station** (Nádraží koněspřežská; May–Sept Tues–Sun 9am–noon & 12.30–5pm), which tells the history of continental Europe's first horse-drawn railway link, constructed between Linz and České Budějovice in 1827. With only a few photos and maps to accompany the video presentation, it's really only for aficionados. En route to the museum, you pass a vacant lot where the city's main **synagogue** stood until it was destroyed by the Nazis in July 1942, a few months after the city's 909 Jews had been deported to Terezín – thirty returned after the war.

The **Budvar brewery** is 2.5km up the road to Prague, on Karolíny Světlé, and has a modern *pivnice* (daily 10am–10pm) inside the nasty titanium-blue headquarters; despite appearances, the beer and food are both inexpensive.

Budvar v Budweiser

As far as taste goes, Czech *Budvar* bears little resemblance to the bland American *Budweiser* or *Bud* as it's universally known – it wins hands-down. However, the fact that two of the world's beers are sold under the same name has caused over a century of problems.

The story begins in 1857 when a German brewer named Adolphus Busch moved to the US. German beer names sold well in the States, so in 1876, Busch adopted the name *Budweiser*. At that time, the only beer brewed in what is now České Budějovice (but at the time was better known as Budweis) was *Samson* – another excellent brand which is still brewed today. It was only in 1882, that local Czech brewers registered the name *Budweiser* for one of their beers. As early as 1911, the Czechs and the American brewers, now known as Anheuser-Busch, came to an agreement, allowing the Czechs to call their beer *Original Budweiser*; in return, the Americans could market their *Budweiser* anywhere in the world, except Europe.

More negotiations followed over the course of the century, until the issue was forgotten behind the Iron Curtain. Then in the 1990s, the two breweries came together for talks once more, with the scales tipped heavily in Anheuser-Busch's favour. Not only were the American brewers now the largest brewing company in the world, the Czechs were desperate for cash to try and modernize their operation. A takeover seemed the most obvious solution. However, thanks to Britain's Campaign for Real Ale (CAMRA), worried that Czech *Budvar* would not be safe in Anheuser-Busch's hands, the issue became widely publicized. For the moment České Budějovice's *Budvar* brewery is safely protected, as it remains the only one in the country still to be state-owned, and as of 2000, the beer is now finally available in the US under the name *Czechvar*. However, further litigious skirmishes across the globe look likely.

Those who wish to make a pilgrimage should phone (☎387 705 341, ⓦwww.budweiser.cz) to find out if they can join up with one of the guided tours. To reach the brewery, take bus #2 or a slow-stopping train to Tábor one stop to České Budějovice severní zastávka.

Eating, drinking and entertainment

Drinking is obviously an important activity in České Budějovice, and without doubt the most atmospheric place to quaff *Budvar* is at the *Masné krámy*, on Krajinská, formerly a sixteenth-century covered meat market, which also serves typical Czech **food**. For slightly more sophisticated pub food, the *Malý pivovar* is recommended, as is the *Bohemia's* brick-vaulted restaurant. If you've had your fill of Czech pub food, head for the *Pizzeria Regina*, on Hradební. For chilling out, there's no better place than the *Dobrá čajovna*, on Hroznová right behind the Černá věž, a typically relaxing branch of the teashop chain. There's also an **internet café** called *Xfiles*, at Senovážné náměstí 6 (ⓦwww.xfiles.cz).

Those with kids might consider giving the local **puppet theatre**, Malé divadlo, Hradební 18, a go; it puts on shows every Saturday and daily in the school holidays. The city's largest **theatre**, the Jihočeské divadlo (ⓦwww.jiho-ceskedivadlo.cz), puts on theatre mostly, so for non-Czech speakers your best bet is to go and listen to the local **chamber orchestra** at the Koncertní síň Otakara Jeremiáše, next to the church of sv Anna on Kněžská. More raucous **nightlife** is still thin on the ground, though *Legend Pub*, at Radniční 9, is a Harley-Davidson-inspired bar that thumps away until late.

Across the Českobudějovická pánev

To the northwest of České Budějovice lies the flat basin of soggy land known as the **Českobudějovická pánev**. Most people head for **Hluboká**, whose chateau receives an incredible number of tourists each year. Its neo-Gothic pastiche is not to everyone's taste – in many ways you'd be better off seeking out the more elusive gems of Holašovice's folk-Baroque architecture or Kratochvíle's simple Renaissance beauty.

Hluboká nad Vltavou

HLUBOKÁ NAD VLTAVOU (Frauenberg), 8km northwest of České Budějovice, is a modest little village which sits below possibly the republic's most famous **zámek** (April, Sept & Oct Tues–Sun 9am–4.30pm; May–June Tues–Sun 9am–5pm; July & Aug daily 9am–5pm). Originally founded as a Přemyslid stronghold as early as the thirteenth century, the royal family sold the property to the Lords of Hradec in 1562, only to confiscate it in 1622 after the Hradec clan backed the Protestant side in the Thirty Years' War. Eventually, it was given to the arriviste Schwarzenberg family, who, during the course of the nineteenth century, made Hluboká their chief seat, and spent some of their considerable fortune turning it into its present crenellated, mock-Gothic incarnation. In 1945, when all the German estates were nationalized, the Schwarzenbergs decamped with most of the loot, but they've since returned and filled the interior with the odds and ends they left behind at their numerous other castles. The results are impressive, both inside and out, and pull in a quarter of a million visitors every year, with regular guided tours in English during high season.

If Hluboká's reproduction interiors fail to move you, it's possible to seek sanctuary in the former riding school (*Zámecká jízdárna*), which now houses the **Alšova jihočeské galerie** (daily: May–Sept 9am–6pm; Oct–April 9–11.30am & 12.30–4pm), a permanent collection of Gothic religious art, Dutch and

Flemish seventeenth-century masters and a large hall filled with a superb collection of twentieth-century Czech art, including Art Nouveau works by Bílek and Jan Preisler, a smattering of Cubist canvases by Čapek, Kubišta and Filla, a good selection of Surrealist paintings by the likes of Toyen and Štyrský, through to 1960s Pop Art. Alternatively, you can head off into the chateau's very beautiful English-style grounds, where South Bohemia's wild boars are reputed to roam; other distractions include occasional displays of falconry and hot-air balloon flights (ask at the tourist office for details).

There are plenty of places **to stay** in Hluboká, but prices are no cheaper than in České Budějovice; ask at the **tourist office** (Ⓦ www.hluboka.cz) in the village about private rooms. There's also the lakeside *Křivonoska* **campsite** (mid-May to Sept), 3km to the northwest up route 105. **Eating** options are good: *Na růžku*, on the corner of the main street, serves *Budvar* and reasonably priced food, and there's an excellent fish restaurant, *Ka.pr*, further down the road. Regular **buses** run from České Budějovice, dropping passengers off in the main square. If you're arriving by **train**, two out-of-the-way stations (nominally) serve the village: Hluboká nad Vltavou station, 3km to the southwest on the Plzeň line; and Hluboká nad Vltavou-Zámostí station, 2km to the east on the main line to Prague. There's also a **cycling path** from České Budějovice to Hluboká along the Vltava; ask the tourist office for a leaflet.

Holašovice

If you have the time (and preferably your own car or bike), it's worth making a quick detour to the village of **HOLAŠOVICE**, 15km west of České Budějovice off the road to Lhenice, where you can see some of the finest examples of **Baroque folk architecture** unique to this part of Bohemia. The stone farmhouses (including the one and only pub) date from the first six decades of the nineteenth century, and face onto the original green. Every house on the square follows the same basic design, though the decorative details on barn doors and gables are unique to each. There are other nearby villages displaying similar architectural treats – like Záboří, 2km north, and Dobčice, another 2km west – but none can compete with the consummate effect of Holašovice.

Kratochvíle

Further west along route 145, and 2km beyond Netolice, lies **Kratochvíle** (Kurzweil), without doubt the most charming Renaissance chateau in Bohemia. It stands unaltered since its rapid six-year construction by Italian architects between 1583 and 1589, commissioned by the last generation of Rožmberks to while away the time – the literal meaning of *kratochvíle*. The attention to detail is still clearly visible in the exquisite stucco work and painted vaults, but the rest of the place is now given over to the **Museum of Animated Film** (April & Oct Sat & Sun 9am–noon & 1–4pm; May & Sept Tues–Sun 9am–noon & 1–4.15pm; June–Aug Tues–Sun 9am–noon & 1–5.15pm), which is aimed primarily at a young, domestic audience, with original puppet "actors" and drawings from well-known Czech kids' cartoons like *Boris* and *Mach a Šebestová*. However, the thoughtfully laid out exhibition, demonstrating all the painstaking processes involved in animation, should interest anyone, particularly with Josef Lada's amusing drawings of the Good Soldier Švejk and two typically disturbing new sculptures by Jan Švankmajer: a weird bird skeleton with butterfly wings and crab claws, and a human face formed of seashells. Kratochvíle is served by several daily buses plying the České Budějovice–Prachatice route, though as usual service is cut short at weekends.

The foothills of the Šumava

An alternative to heading up the Českobudějovická pánev is to aim for the large bulge of forest, known as the **Blanský les**, to the southwest of České Budějovice. Its highest point is **Mount Kleť** (1083m), which stands slightly apart from the rest of the Šumava range and looks all the more impressive for it, towering above the Vltava basin to the north. From the summit on a clear day, you can see the undulating forested peaks of the Šumava laid out before you. As well as the obligatory TV tower, the hill boasts the astronomical **Observatoř Kleť** (Oct–June Sat & Sun 10.30am–3.30pm; July & Aug Tues–Sun 10.30am–3.30pm; closed Sept; ☏380 711 242, ⓦwww.klet.org). To reach the top, either hop into one of the single-seat chairlifts (Tues–Sun hourly) or opt for the stiff but enchanting four-kilometre hike through the woods. To reach Mount Kleť from České Budějovice or Český Krumlov, catch a train to the idyllic rural station at Holubov and walk the last 2km to Krasetín, where the chairlift starts.

There's little **accommodation** in this neck of the woods, aside from a few private rooms and a basic **campsite** (May–Sept) in **ZLATÁ KORUNA** (Goldenkron), a tiny village on the Vltava, 6km along the line from Holubov. Here you can visit the strongly fortified **Cistercian monastery** (Tues–Sun: April, May, Sept & Oct 9am–noon & 1–4pm; June–Aug 9am–noon & 1–5pm), founded in 1263 by Přemysl King Otakar II. As a wealthy bastion of Catholicism, it suffered badly at the hands of the Hussites, but parts of the original medieval structures survive. In one building there's a worthy museum on Czech literature, but the main focus of interest is the vaulted chapterhouse dating from 1280 and the Gothic church, built in part by Peter Parler's masons and one of the first to employ ribbed vaulting without any accompanying capitols.

Český Krumlov

Squeezed into a tight S-bend of the Vltava, in the foothills of the Šumava, **ČESKÝ KRUMLOV** (Krumau) is undoubtedly one of the most exquisite towns in the Czech Republic. Rose-brown houses tumble down steep slopes to the blue-green river below, creating a magical effect whose beauty has barely changed in the last three hundred years. Under the Communists, few foreign visitors made it here, but nowadays the huge rise in tourism has made this the one place outside Prague where the warren of narrow streets can get uncomfortably crowded with day-trippers, including a steady parade of young backpackers. The whole town is a UNESCO-designated site, but with rich pickings now on offer, many of its residents are renovating their properties, causing great concern among conservationists, who foresee overdevelopment and insensitive restoration – not to mention the loss of character that occurs when virtually every building is turned over to pensions and restaurants. For all that, it's a place that never fails to impress.

Arrival, information and accommodation

The old town is divided into two separate quarters by the twisting snake of the River Vltava: the circular staré město on the right bank and the Latrán quarter on the hillier left bank. The **train station** is twenty minutes' walk north of the old town up a precipitous set of steps, while the main **bus station** is closer to the heart of town, on the right bank – either way, the best method of exploring Český Krumlov is on foot. There are two main **tourist offices**, one on náměstí

ACCOMMODATION

Barbakán	8
Dvořák	2
Hotel Konvice	6
Na louži	4
Hotel Růže	7
Hostel Ryba	9
Travellers Hostel	3
Pension ve věži	1
Zlatý anděl	5

RESTAURANTS

Cikánská jizba	B
Krčma šatlava	F
Laibon	C
Maštal	D
Papa's Living	A
Rybářská bašta	E

ČESKÝ KRUMLOV

(map labels: Train Station (1 km), Budljovická brána, Jelení zahrada, Convent of Poor Clares, Zámecké divadlo, Krumlovský zámek, LATRÁN, Brewery, Former arsenal, Zámecká zahrada, STARÉ MĚSTO, Schiele Centrum, Radnice, River Vltava, Museum, Bus Station, NÁMĚSTÍ SVORNOSTI, Church of sv Vit, Městské sady, N)

Svornosti (daily 9am–5pm; ☎380 711 183, ⓦwww.ckrumlov.cz), and one oppo-site the police station within the castle (daily 10am–4pm). It's also worth know-ing about the town's useful laundrette, *Lobo*, Latrán 73, which is open daily.

Accommodation is not in short supply, but there's an awful lot of people in town in high season. As well as the places listed below, there are also numer-ous small pensions and **private rooms** in town: Parkán is literally heaving with them, as is Rooseveltova. There's a huge number of lively **hostels** cater-ing for the young travellers who pass through all year round: the HI *Travellers Hostel* at Soukenická 43 (☎380 711 345, ⓦwww.iyhf.cz) has bike rental, a bar-becue and other amenities, and is very popular; a better bet is *Hostel Ryba* (☎380 711 801), which has a nice river terrace and pub attached. There's also a primitive **campsite** (May–Sept; ⓦwww.pavelec.cz), 2km south on route 160 to Nové Spolí, primarily aimed at summer canoeists (rental available). More and better campsites lie several kilometres further south along the road to Rožmberk nad Vltavou.

Hotels and pensions

Barbakán Horní 26 ☎380 717 017. A wonderfully refurbished place with tastefully decorated rooms and terrace dining. ❸

Hotel Dvořák Radniční 101 ☎380 711 020, ⓦwww.hoteldvorak.cz. Smart, efficient hotel in an

uncharacteristically grand late nineteenth-century building right by the river, overlooking the castle. ❼

Hotel Růže Horní 154 ☎380 772 100, ⓦwww.hotelruze.cz. Originally built by the Rožmberks to house their guests, the Růže is right

193

in the heart of the staré město, and is the hotel of choice, with pool, sauna, casino and the odd original Renaissance feature. ❾
Na louži Kájovská 66 ☎ 380 711 280, ⓦ www.nalouzi.cz. An excellent pension, kitted out with antique furniture, and situated above a great pub near the Schiele Centrum. ❸
Konvice Hotel Horní 144 ☎ 380 711 611. None of the history of the *Růže*, opposite, but a good option

nevertheless and a lot cheaper. ❹
Pension ve věží Pivovarská 28 ☎ 380 711 742. Four bargain doubles hidden inside one of the town's medieval bastions, right by the Eggenberg brewery. ❸
Zlatý anděl Nám. Svornosti 10 ☎ 380 712 310, ⓦ www.zlatyandel.cz. Tall, thin hotel, with no lift, but pleasant modern decor – ask for a room overlooking the old town square. ❺

The Town

Český Krumlov's **history** is dominated by those great seigneurs of the region, the Rožmberks and the Schwarzenbergs. Thanks to special privileges won after the Battle of Leipzig in 1813, the Schwarzenbergs were permitted to keep a private army of twelve soldiers dressed in Napoleonic uniform (who also doubled as the castle's private orchestra), one of whom would sound the bugle at 9am every morning from the thirteenth-century round tower. In 1945, Krumau awoke abruptly from this semi-feudal coma when the Schwarzenbergs and the majority of the town's inhabitants, who were also German-speaking, were booted out; three years later, repopulated by Czech-speakers, the town went back into aspic as the Iron Curtain descended. Now the economy relies increasingly heavily on the ebb and flow of foreign tourists, a dependency which has thrown up the dubious delights of a waxworks and a torture museum, neither of which is worth visiting.

Krumlovský zámek

For centuries, the focal point of the town has been its chateau, **Krumlovský zámek** in the **Latrán quarter**, as good a place as any to begin. Once you've passed through the first gateway, you enter the sprawling first courtyard, which belongs to the older, lower castle; from here you can climb the beautifully restored castle tower, the **Zámecká věž** (daily: April & Oct 9.30am–5pm; May–Sept 9am–6pm), for a superb view over the town. Cross the medvědí příkop (bear moat), where the latest batch of unfortunate bears is incarcerated, and head for the ticket office, located between the two smaller prettily painted courtyards of the upper castle, added in the fifteenth century. There are currently two hour-long **guided tours** (Tues–Sun: April & Oct 9am–noon & 1–4pm; May & Sept 9am–noon & 1–5pm; June–Aug 9am–noon & 1–6pm) to choose between, each costing 140Kč, occasionally in English: *trasa 1* is the one to go for as it takes you through the surviving Renaissance rooms, the Rococo excesses of the blue and pink marble chapel, and the Maškarní sál, a ballroom exquisitely decorated with trompe l'oeil murals of *commedia dell'arte* scenes; *trasa 2* concentrates on portraits of the Schwarzenbergs and doles out rich helpings of nineteenth-century opulence.

The castle's unique gem, however, is its ornate eighteenth-century Rococo **Zámecké divadlo** (Tues–Sun: May–Sept 10am–4pm; Oct 10am–3pm; 170Kč), on the other side of the covered Plášťový most, a many-tiered viaduct with a superb view over the town. This is one of the few Rococo theatres in the world to retain so much of its original scenery and wardrobe. An ingenious system of flies and flats meant that a typical comic opera of the kind the theatre specialized in could have more than forty scene changes without interrupting the action. Visits to the theatre are by thirty-minute guided tour only.

Another covered walkway takes you high above the town into the unexpectedly expansive and formal terraced **Zámecká zahrada** (daily: April & Oct 8am–5pm; May–Sept 8am–7pm), whose tranquillity is disturbed only by the operas and ballets performed in the gardens' modern, revolving, **open-air theatre** (otáčivé hlediště) during July and August; details from the tourist office.

The staré město

Latrán, lined with shabby, overhanging houses, leads to a wooden, ramp-like bridge that connects with the **staré město**. There's a compelling beauty in the old town, whose precarious existence is best viewed from the circling River Vltava. Turning right down Dlouhá, where the houses glow red at dusk, will bring you to the site of the town's former arsenal. From here, if the river's not swollen, you can walk across the gangplanks of the footbridge to Rybářská, which then follows the left bank to the southernmost bridge, taking you back into the old town.

Heading straight up the soft incline of Radniční brings you to the main square, **náměstí Svornosti** – look back for a great view of the castle. Occupying one side of the cobbled square is the former **radnice**, which was created out of two and a half Gothic houses, and sports a strikingly long, white, Renaissance entablature of blind arcading. To the southeast, the high lancet windows of the church of **sv Vít** rise vertically above the ramshackle rooftops. Inside, the church retains its Gothic lierne vaulting, patches of medieval fresco and the remarkable tomb of Vilém of Rožmberk. One or two of the later furnishings are notable, too, particularly the Rococo organ case and the fabulously gilded pulpit.

If you continue east off the square, down Horní, you'll meet the beautiful sgraffitoed sixteenth-century Jesuit college, which now houses the *Hotel Růže*, among other things. Opposite the *Růže*, the local **museum** (Okresní vlastivědné muzeum; May–Sept daily 10am–12.30pm & 1–5pm; Oct–April Tues–Fri 9am–noon & 12.30–4pm, Sat & Sun 1–4pm; ⓦ www.muzeum.ckrumlov.cz) puts on small, temporary exhibitions relating to the history of the town. Also on display are models of the town and the 2000-seater theatre at nearby Hořice, where elaborate Passion Plays have been staged on and off since 1816.

Schiele in Krumau

In 1911, the Austrian painter **Egon Schiele** decided to leave Vienna and spend some time in Krumau, his mother's home town. During his brief sojourn here, Schiele painted a number of intense townscapes of Krumau, like *Houses and Roofs near Krumau* and *Dead City*, in which he managed to make even the buildings look sexually anguished. At the time, he was not making much money from his art, and was forced to shuffle from rooming house to rooming house with his 17-year-old lover, Wally Neuzil, a model handed down to him by Gustav Klimt. Finally he succeeded in buying a studio, a crumbling Baroque cottage by the river in Plešivec, south of the old town. Schiele and his bohemian companions, Erwin Osen and Moa Mandu, caused more than a little controversy in this resolutely petit-bourgeois town – hiring young local girls for nude modelling and painting Wally naked in the orchard were among his more famous *faux pas*. Forced to leave before the year was out, he vowed never to return.

Under the Communists, the town made no attempt to advertise Schiele's brief but productive stay; now, however, Schiele is for Krumlov what Kafka is for Prague. Fans of the artist should head for the **Schiele Centrum** (daily: April–Sept 10am–6pm; Oct–March 11am–5pm; ⓦ www.schieleartcentrum.org; 120Kč), a vast, rambling art complex housed in a fifteenth-century former brewery in Široká, where a smattering of the artist's lithographs, watercolours and pencil sketches – including one of Český Krumlov – are on permanent display. In addition, there's some furniture designed by the artist for his studio, a small exhibition on Schiele's life, and regular shows by contemporary artists.

Eating, drinking and entertainment

As far as **eating** goes, there's certainly plenty of choice – the same goes for pubs. If you need to check email, there's an **internet café** just inside the zámek gates; for **teas** from around the world, slip into the *Dobrá čajovna* on Latrán.

Restaurants

Cikánská jizba Dlouhá 31. Nifty, cheap little place with a country theme and lots of Czech and Slovak specialities including goulash and *halušky*. Closed Sun.

Krčma šatlava Šatlavská. Wonderfully intimate little restaurant with a medieval theme, just off the main square.

Laibon Parkán. Has a surprisingly long, all-vegetarian menu and great riverside seating.

Maštal Nám. Svornosti 2. A smoky Gothic cellar restaurant on the main square serving typical Czech pub food and local beers.

Papa's Living Restaurant Latrán 13. Despite the naff name, this cosy, vaulted restaurant offers funky Mexican, Italian and veggie dishes.

Rybářská bašta Na louži. Excellent, reasonably-priced fish restaurant in the Krčinův dům off Široká.

Nightlife and entertainment

Na louži, on Široká, is the town's most historic **pub**, with fine food to boot, or else there's the Eggenberg brewery tap, *Formanka*, which also puts on occasional live events and gigs (Ⓦ www.eggenberg.cz). If it's late-night action you're after, *U Hada*, across the river from the old town on Rybářská, rocks on into the wee hours. Theatre performances take place in the **open-air revolving theatre** (otáčivé hlediště), in the castle gardens (June–Aug; Ⓦ www.jihoceske-divadlo.cz), and there's an **open-air cinema** 500m or so west of the main road junction, off route 39 to Volary. In summer, you can also **rent canoes** from outfits at the ends of both Parkán and Kajovská and float downstream (with a shuttle minibus bringing you back).

Sensitive to the huge high season audience of tourists, there are now more and more cultural events throughout the summer. If you arrive in town at the weekend nearest the summer solstice, you'll witness the **Five-Petalled Rose Festival** (Slavnosti pětilisté růže), an excuse for the townsfolk to don medieval dress worn in the days of the Rožmberks, as well as let off fireworks, sing, dance and generally make merry. The town also hosts several **music festivals** (Ⓦ www.czechmusicfestival.com): a chamber music festival in early July, one dedicated to early music, held in mid-July, an international one which takes place over three weeks in August, plus a pop (*bigbít*) festival in mid-July and a jazz festival in late August (Ⓦ www.jazz-krumlov.cz).

The Šumava

The dense pine forests and peat bogs of the **Šumava** region (Ⓦ www.sumava -info.cz) stretch for miles along the Austrian and German borders southwest of Český Krumlov, part of the much larger Böhmerwald which spreads across into Bavaria forming one of the last wildernesses in central Europe. The original inhabitants of this sparsely populated region were German-speaking foresters, who scraped a living from its meagre soil – their Austrian lilt and agricultural poverty separating them from their "civilized" Sudetenland brothers in western and northern Bohemia. Up to the declaration of the First Republic in 1918, the economic armlock of the all-powerful Schwarzenberg and Buquoy dynasties kept the region in a permanent semi-feudal state. Even in the nineteenth century, peasants had to have permission from their landlords to marry, and their customary greeting to the local squire was *Brotvater* (literally "Breadfather").

Following the expulsion of the German-speakers in 1945, all links with the past were severed, and despite financial incentives for Czechs to move here the Šumava has remained underpopulated. Poor, provincial and out of the way compared to the rest of the former Sudetenland, it had the added misfortune of lying alongside one of the most sensitive stretches of the East–West border during the Cold War – in the 1970s, large areas of forest along the south shore of Lake Lipno were closed off by the military. Much of this land has now been relinquished, the border dismantled, and contact between the two areas re-established, all of which has revived the area considerably. Ironically, while the Iron Curtain was there, the area was safely protected from overdevelopment, and local campaigners are now fighting hard to try and keep it that way. As a consequence, most of the roads to the south of Lake Lipno are still closed to vehicles except bicycles.

Aside from the region's one truly medieval town, **Prachatice**, the majority of visitors come here for the scenery, which is among the most unspoilt in the country, thanks to the lack of heavy industry and minimal acid rain damage. Most tourists crowd round the northern shore of the artificial **Lake Lipno**, creating their own peculiar brand of beach culture, while others head for the hills, which rise up more gently than those on the Austrian and German side. The deepest part of the forest, hugging the German and Austrian borders between Lake Lipno and Železná Ruda, is preserved as the **Šumava National Park** (Národní park Šumava), where tiny villages blend into the silent hills, meadows and peat bogs. The most scenic way of **getting around**, apart from walking, is the single-track České Budějovice–Volary train line. Local buses are much more convenient, though at weekends services begin to peter out. Look out, too, for the special **summer bus** services, which run three to four times daily through the heart of the national park. Due to its gently hilly landscape, the park is also great **cycling** territory, and in summer, Czechs often float down the Vltava in **canoes**, which can be rented from towns along the river.

Rožmberk nad Vltavou

Buses from Český Krumlov follow the Vltava valley to the pretty village of **ROŽMBERK NAD VLTAVOU** (Rosenberg), which is tucked into a U-bend of the river, and overlooked by a spectacular, sgraffitoed **fortress** which teeters on a knife's edge high above it. As the name suggests, its *raison d'être* was as the headquarters of the powerful and single-minded Rožmberk family, regional supremos from the thirteenth century until their extinction in 1611. Only one round tower remains from the Rožmberk era, though the highlight of the guided tour, the castle's banquet hall with its sixteenth-century Italian frescoes, is also a Rožmberk legacy. The rest of the interior speaks little of that family, but volumes of its later French owners, the Buquoys, who stuffed the dull, mannerless rooms with heavy neo-Gothic furnishings and instruments of torture, the latter being displayed in the Katovna, separate from the tour. In summer, Czech tour groups fall over one another for a place on the 45-minute **guided tours** (April & Oct Sat & Sun 9am–4pm; May & Sept Tues–Sun 9am–4pm; June–Aug Tues–Sun 9am–5pm; Ⓦwww.pamatky-jc.cz): *trasa 1* is the main tour; *trasa 2* is specifically aimed at (Czech) kids.

Finding **accommodation** down in the village is relatively easy at any of the many private rooms on offer. Otherwise, the *Hotel Růže* (Ⓣ380 749 715, Ⓦwww.angelfire.com/va/hotelruze; ❸) has well-appointed rooms and a restaurant, while the *Hotel Studenec* (Ⓣ380 749 888, Ⓦwww.hotelstudenec.rozmberk.cz; ❸), up a hill north of the village, off route 160 to Český Krumlov, rents out canoes and bikes.

Vyšší Brod

Upriver from Rožmberk, just fifteen minutes south by bus, is **VYŠŠÍ BROD** (Hohenfurth), notable for its white Cistercian monastery on the western edge of town, founded in the thirteenth century in response to the Přemyslids' founding of nearby Zlatá Koruna (see p.192). Its proximity to the border and its extreme wealth gave rise to a set of immodest fortifications that withstood two sieges by the Hussites. Despite its pews, the essentially Gothic **klášterní kostel** (May–Sept daily 9am–5pm) was for the exclusive use of the monks, who sat in the fancy gilded stalls that take up almost half the church – only on religious holidays were the locals allowed in at the back. In the blue side chapel rests Petr Vok, the last of the Rožmberks, who died of drink and drugs but was nonetheless given pride of place as the monastery's rich patron. Suppressed during the Communist period, Vyšší Brod is once more inhabited by monks.

The only way to see the church's interior properly is by **guided tour** (at 9, 10 & 11am, 1, 3 & 4pm), which also takes you through the beautiful Gothic chapterhouse and ends with the star attraction, a be-frescoed Rococo library decorated with 24-carat gold, accessible only via a secret door in one of the bookcases. The monastery's outer buildings house a mildly diverting **Poštovní muzeum** (April–Oct Tues–Sun 9am–5pm), charting the history of the republic's postal system since the late medieval period, with displays of period uniforms, old phones and typewriters, new stamps and old stage and post coaches.

If you need a place **to stay**, there's the vile, bile green *Hotel Panský dům* (☎380 746 669; ❷), which has unfortunate decor throughout, but very cheap rooms with or without en-suite shower. There are also several private rooms and pensions, including *Pension Inge* (☎380 746 482, ✉inge@pavelec.cz; ❷), right by the monastery, which also rents out boats and canoes; you can even stay in the monastery itself (☎380 746 457; ❶). The *Pod hrází* **campsite** (June to mid-Sept) is a basic riverside site with cold showers only, a short walk along route 163 towards Lipno nad Vltavou.

There are **buses** from Rožmberk to Vyšší Brod, or else you can catch a **train** from Rybník, 10km east on the Prague–Linz main line (get out at Vyšší Brod klášter, not Vyšší Brod, for the monastery). Local buses and trains continue 10km to Lipno nad Vltavou, at the eastern edge of Lake Lipno, where a host of other facilities is available (see below). If you are walking from Vyšší Brod, be sure to take the red route to the viewpoint at **Čertova stěna** (Devil's Walls), a giant scree of granite slabs that tumble into the river below.

Lake Lipno

Upstream from the giant paper mill at Loučovice on the Vltava, a dam marks the southeastern end of **Lake Lipno**. The barrage turns the turbines of a huge underground hydroelectric power station, and on the face of it, there's not much to get excited about. The northern shore is punctuated by small beach resorts, which have developed rapidly over the last thirty years, originally to give workers some well-needed fresh air, now with more of an eye to attract euros from across the border. The area is popular with Czechs, Germans and Austrians, so the **hotels** are often full in July and August, but you're rarely far from **private rooms** – look for the *Unterkunft/ubytování* signs dotted about – or a **campsite**, often with cheap bungalows for rent. **Buses** link most places, supplemented by trains from Černá v Pošumaví westwards.

Lipno nad Vltavou and Frymburk

About the only reason to come to **LIPNO NAD VLTAVOU** is to take the one- or two-hour **cruise** on the lake. From May to October there are three boats leaving daily from the small pier in town. The town has a couple of run-down hotels, though you're almost certainly better off trying any of the

Border crossings

Before 1989, the main road from Horní Planá northwest to Volary was punctuated at regular intervals by little red signs warning about the impending Iron Curtain; all villages on the right bank of the Vltava were closed to road vehicles, with trains the only legal means of transport. The military have now given up their patch, and today there are numerous **border crossings** into Austria and Germany, with varying restrictions. The only 24-hour checkpoints open to all vehicles are Přední Výtoň/Guglwald and Strážný/Philippsreuth, 50km to the west. In between there are six more crossing points, open only to cyclists and/or pedestrians, all with more limited opening hours – check with the local tourist office for the current restrictions.

numerous pensions signposted off the road to Frymburk, or one of the campsites by the lake. Note that the train station at Lipno is situated below the dam, a couple of kilometres east of the town itself. Beyond Lipno, you can hardly miss the brand new **Lipno Marina** (Ⓦwww.landal.de), run by the Dutch leisure group, Landal Greenparks, and the largest single development on the lake. To stay there, you need to book in for at least three nights, or you can simply make use of the yacht rental and sailing school.

Some 9km along the shore from Lipno is **FRYMBURK** (Friedberg), probably the most attractive village on the lake, with its delicate white, octagonal spire and leafy, oval main square. **Accommodation** is plentiful, and first choice on the leafy main square is the family-run *Hotel Maxant* (Ⓣ380 735 229, Ⓦwww.lipnonet.cz/maxant; ❸), which has a sauna and pool, or else there's the *Hotel Vltava* (Ⓣ380 735 605, Ⓦwww.hotel-vltava.com; ❹), opposite, the newest and flashiest accommodation in the village. *Camping Frymburk* (May–Sept) is a well-run lakeside site, just 500m from the village back along route 163 to Lipno, with cycle and boat hire.

Černá v Pošumaví

There are plenty more accommodation options 10km down the road in **ČERNÁ V POŠUMAVÍ** (Schwarzbach), a village divided into two by the lake: on the eastern shore is the village proper and the road junction; on the western shore, across the road bridge, is the train station. In addition to the regular service between České Budějovice and Volary, a **historic steam train** plies the rails at weekends (July to mid-Sept) from here to Nové Údolí, right next to the German border to the west. There's a **windsurfing** school in Černá (Ⓦwww.lipno-windsurfing.cz), but if you're just looking for a dip, head off to nearby **DOLNÍ VLTAVICE**, 6km south on a secluded thumb of land, where a small crowd enjoys the grassy "beach" with a view over to (and a ferry link with) the opposite shore, which is hard against the Austrian border.

Horní Planá

HORNÍ PLANÁ (Oberplan), 7km west of Černá, is the lake's chief resort, and has a useful **tourist office** (Mon–Sat 9am–4pm; July–Aug daily 9am–6pm; Ⓦwww.hplana.ckrumlov.cz) in the Česká spořitelna building on the leafy main square, which can help you fix up some accommodation and also rents out **mountain bikes**. A little cultural distraction can be experienced at the birthplace (*rodný domek*) of the German-speaking writer and painter **Adalbert Stifter**, who cut short his life in 1868 by slashing his throat to escape cancer of the liver. The house (mid-Jan to March & Nov to mid-Dec Tues–Sat 9am–noon & 1–4pm; April–June & Sept Tues–Sun 10am–noon & 1–6pm; July

& Aug daily 10am–noon & 1–6pm), on the road into town from the east, is now a small memorial to his life and work; his statue stands behind the church, and there's another memorial to him overlooking the waters of the Plešné jezero, which sits below Plechý (Plockenstein) close to the meeting of the German, Austrian and Czech borders, the Trojmezí.

There's no shortage of **accommodation**, with the smart *Pension Šejko* (T380 738 330; ❸), a short way along the road to the lake shore, a good choice. A better place to camp (May–Oct) than the concrete-surfaced site by the car ferry slipway is **JENIŠOV**, beside the lake, a couple of kilometres south of Horní Planá. There's a sprinkling of hotels here, too, including the *Penzion na Ježere* (T380 738 338; ❸) and *Hotel sv Anežka* (❺), along with a bevy of newly-built villas (❺); closer to the shore is the much cheaper Communist-era *Hotel Jenišov* (T380 738 184, Wwww.hoteljenisov.cz; ❷).

Nová Pec to Volary

The first place of any size on the western shores, at the very northwestern tip of Lake Lipno, is **NOVÁ PEC**, little more than a couple of hotels, a train station and a crossroads. Still, it's a good base if you're up for a bit of hiking. Try *U jezera* (T0338 336051; ❷), a simple pension-restaurant, or if it's full, the pension across the road.

The railway divides at **ČERNÝ KŘÍŽ**: the main branch heads north to Volary (see p.202), while a short spur heads southwest to Nové Údolí station, just 300m from the German border (the historic steam trains run along this line as well). Another possible base for the area is **STOŽEC**, one station up the line from Černý Kříž to Nové Údolí, where there's a useful **tourist office** (daily: June–Oct 8am–4pm; Dec–May 9am–3pm). Up the road leading east up the hill and out of the village, is *U Mauritzů* (T388 335 166; ❷), a pleasant chalet-style pension with its own restaurant, and great views out across the forested hills. If it's full, try the well-appointed *Penzion Druid* (T388 335 134; ❸), back down near the centre of the village, which insists on half-board in the summer and winter high seasons.

Hiking in the Šumava

One of the most interesting Šumava hikes sets off from Ovesná station, the next one along from Nová Pec (and occasionally request only). Follow the yellow-marked route northwest through gigantic boulders and thick forest to Perník (1049m), before dropping down to Jelení, where the **Schwarzenberský kanál** emerges from a tunnel. Built at the turn of the eighteenth century to transport the Šumava's valuable timber straight to the Danube (less than 40km due south), the canal was abandoned as a waterway in 1962. A little further on you reach the **Medvědí kámen** (Bären Stein), marking the spot where the last bear in the Šumava was shot in 1856. The only threat now is the lynx, which was reintroduced hereabouts in 1985. Moving on, you should reach the village station at Černý Kříž in around six hours from Ovesná.

From Nové Údolí (only accessible by train, bike or foot), hard by the German border, you can take the red-marked trail south, 5km to the peak of **Třístoličník** or Dreisesselberg (1302m) right on the border. From here, it's another 5km to Trojmezí, the meeting-point of the German, Austrian and Czech borders, and 1km further to the summit of the Šumava's highest peak, **Plechý** or Plöckenstein (1378m), on the Austrian border. From Plechý you could make the steep descent to Plešné jezero, a glacial lake that sits in the shadow of the sheer northeast face of the mountain, from which it's another 8km via the green-marked path to Nová Pec train station.

Heading north by train from Černý Kříž brings you to **VOLARY** (Wallern), founded by colonists from the Tyrol and now a sizeable town for these parts, with an uneasy mixture of traditional wooden Šumava cottages, postwar *paneláky*, a handsome Baroque church and a fair amount of industry. You may have to change trains here for Vimperk or Prachatice. At the centre of Volary, you'll find the unreconstructed Communist-era *Hotel Bobík* (☎388 335 351; ❸), and a much more appealing pension, *Kukačka* (☎388 333 232; ❷). The nearest **campsite** is *Soumarský Most* (May–Sept), by the banks of the Vltava, 4km west along the road to Lenora or one stop on the line to Strakonice (request stop only).

Prachatice and around

The slopes of Libín (1096m) merge into the Otava and Vltava plain by the amiable little market town of **PRACHATICE** (Prachatitz), known as the "Gateway to the Šumava". Most people do come here en route to the Šumava, but it's a beautiful medieval town in its own right, as well as being a useful base for visiting **Husinec**, birthplace of Jan Hus (see p.203). Founded in 1325, Prachatice flourished in the following century, when it controlled the all-important salt trade route into Bohemia. A fire in 1507 is responsible for the uniformly sixteenth-century appearance of the town and its famous collection of sgraffito facades.

The Town

A short walk uphill from the bus and train stations brings you to Malé náměstí, the main square-cum-crossroads of the nondescript new part of town. Everything of interest is contained within the walls of the tiny circular **staré město**, reached through the bulky fifteenth-century **Písecká brána**, a gateway with a faded mural showing Vílem of Rožmberk on horseback and, above it, in among the battlements, the red rose symbol of his family, who acquired the town briefly in 1501.

The gate's double arches open out on the small Kostelní náměstí, where old women sell spices and vegetables in the shade of the trees. The Gothic church of **sv Jakub**, with its steeply pitched, rather peculiar red-ribbed roof, is the oldest building and most obvious landmark in town. Inside, the short, tall nave is decorated with delicate lierne vaulting; the Baroque main altar, meanwhile, is much more in-your-face, with four gilded barley-sugar columns wreathed in vines dividing gold and silver relief scenes of the Nativity. Prachatice is best known, however, for the exquisitely decorative **Heydlův dům** to the left, which sports bizarre depictions of men clubbing each other to death, unintentionally apposite given its present incumbents, a family butcher's. Next door is the Latin school or **Literátská škola**, also crowned with miniature Renaissance battlements, and which local heroes Hus and Žižka are said to have attended in their youth.

At this point the cobbles open out into the old town square, **Velké náměstí**, which has a thoroughly Germanic air. Its most striking aspect is the riot of **sgraffito** on the facades of many of the buildings; if you haven't already come across the style, Prachatice is as good a place as any to get to grips with it. The technique – extremely popular in the sixteenth century and revived in the nineteenth – involves scraping away painted plaster to form geometric, monochrome patterns or even whole pictorial friezes, producing a distinctive lace-work effect. The most lavish example of this style is the arcaded **Rumpálův dům**, at no. 41 on the east side of the square, which depicts a ferociously confused battle scene. At no. 45 is another arcaded building, the former **solnice** or salt house (also known as the Bozovského dům), through which the town accrued its enormous wealth in the Middle Ages and which features Vílem of Rožmberk once more on horseback.

On the west side of the square, the sixteenth-century **stará radnice** is decorated with copies of Hans Holbein's disturbing, apocalyptic parables, employing a much more sophisticated use of perspective; just a few doors down stands the **nová radnice**, whose sgraffito dates from the late nineteenth century. One of the fanciest houses on the square is the **Sittrův dům**, now the local museum (March–June & Sept–Dec Tues–Fri 9am–4pm, Sat & Sun 10am–4pm; July & Aug Tues–Sun 9am–5pm), on the north side of the square, distinguished not by its sgraffito, but by its colourful painted facade and ornate Renaissance gable. Four doors down at no. 9 is the **Knížecí dům**, which hides its sgraffito round the side, on which you'll find, among other things, a stag hunt, several devils and an elephant, a mermaid with two tails and Joseph being put into the pit by his brothers.

Practicalities

The **tourist office** (April–Oct Tues–Sun 9am–4pm; Nov–March Mon–Fri 8am–4.30pm; ⓦ www.prachatice.cz), in the Písecká brána, or the old town hall (Mon–Fri 7.30am–4pm), can help find private rooms in the old town. *Hotel Parkán* (☎ 388 311 868; ❹), on Věžní, is probably the nicest **place to stay**, with en-suite facilities and TVs in all its rooms, and a solid Czech restaurant; to get there head up Křišťanova by sv Jakub and take the first left. Alternatively, head for the friendly *Hotel Koruna* (☎ 388 310 177; ❸), tucked away just down an alleyway in the southwestern corner of the main square; the en-suite rooms are spartan, but the wood-beamed restaurant on the ground floor is cosy. Infrequent buses will drop you close to either the primitive **campsite**, 10km south by the lake at Křišťanovice (July & Aug only), or the riverside Blanický Mlýn site (open all year), 2km further on.

Prachatice's Indian **restaurant**, *Tandoor*, Horní 165 (closed Sun), in the backstreets, is a remarkable find; a real Indian chef cooks up tandoori dishes, masalas, kormas and thalis. For more traditional Czech food, head for the vaulted beer hall, *Královská restaurace* (closed Sun), opposite the Husův dům on Husova. To check your email, head for the **internet café** upstairs at Club 111 on Křišťanova. The town's big summer bash is the *Slavností solné Zlaté stezky*, a medieval knees-up held at a weekend towards the end of June.

Husinec

You may burn the goose [hus],
but one day there will come a swan,
and him you will not burn.

Martin Luther

Six kilometres north of Prachatice is the unassuming village of **HUSINEC**, birthplace of **Jan Hus** (see box p.204), the man whose death in 1415 triggered off the Hussite revolution. In the nineteenth century, when interest in Hus began to emerge after the dark years of the Counter-Reformation, the poet Jan Neruda visited Husinec and was horrified to find Hus' former home shabby and neglected. No expense has been spared since, with the family house at nos. 36 & 37 converted into a **museum** (Památník M.J. Husa; Tues–Sun 9am–noon & 1–4pm) and many of Hus' old haunts in the surrounding region turned into points of pilgrimage over the nineteenth century. That said, there are few visitors nowadays to the museum's small exhibition and only one original

Jan Hus

The legendary preacher – and Czech national hero – **Jan Hus** (often anglicized to John Huss) was born in the small village of Husinec around 1372. From a childhood of poverty, he enjoyed a steady rise through the Czech education system, taking his degree at Prague's Karolinum in the 1390s, and eventually being ordained as a deacon and priest around 1400. Although without doubt an admirer of the English religious reformer, John Wycliffe, Hus was by no means as radical as many of his colleagues who preached at the Betlémská kaple. Nor did he actually advocate many of the more famous tenets of the heretical religious movement that took his name: Hussitism. In particular, he never advocated giving communion "in both kinds" (bread and wine) to the general congregation.

In the end, it wasn't the disputes over Wycliffe, whose books were burned on the orders of the archbishop in 1414, that proved Hus' downfall, but an argument over the sale of indulgences to fund the papal wars that prompted his unofficial trial at the Council of Constance in 1415. Having been guaranteed safe conduct by Emperor Sigismund himself, Hus naively went to Constance to defend his views, and was burnt at the stake as a heretic. The Czechs were outraged, and Hus became a national hero overnight, inspiring thousands to rebel against the authorities of the day. In 1965, the Vatican finally overturned the sentence, and the anniversary of his death (July 6) is now a national holiday.

room, a tiny garret on the top floor. To give you an idea of Hus' place in the Czech nationalist canon, take a look at the stirring multicoloured sgraffito illustration on no. 42. Getting to Husinec is easiest on one of the regular **buses** from Prachatice; the train station is 3km east of the village.

Volary to Vimperk

The scenic train ride from Volary, 18km south of Prachatice, to Vimperk takes you deep into the Šumava forest, and it's worth breaking the journey at some point to delve further into the woods. At **LENORA**, there's a glass factory, several old, wooden, Šumava cottages and a picturesque covered wooden bridge over the river. There are some great walks possible from the next station along, Zátoň, 1.5km northeast of which is the primitive *Boubín* campsite (open all year) and *Penzión Ida* (☎388 436 214, ✉pensionida@iol.cz; ➋), a charming little country house by the railway, whose price includes dinner and breakfast – the park's summer bus service also pulls in here.

From Zátoň station, a green-marked path skirts the ancient **Boubínský prales** (Boubín Virgin Forest) that occupies the slopes of Boubín (1362m). It's forbidden to walk among the pines and firs of the forest, some of which are over 400 years old, but the green markers take you 4km around the perimeter past a small deer park and on to the summit; from here you can get back to the rail line without retracing your steps by following the blue-marked path 4km to the station at the ski resort of **KUBOVÁ HUŤ**, where there are several hotels and pensions to choose from, including the vast *Ingo Hotel Arnika* (☎338 436 326, ⊛www.hotel-arnika.cz; ➌), with sauna, pool and bike rental, and the modern mega ski-chalet, *Amber Hotel Kuba* (☎338 436 321, ⊛www.lconsulting.cz; ➍), which also does bike rental in the summer. Before reaching Kubová Huť, the train skirts the southwestern slopes of Boubín, stopping (on request) at Horní Vltavice station high above the village of the same name. The two-kilometre scramble down through the forest is worth it for the justly popular riverside *Vltava* **campsite** (May–Sept) and the *hostinec* below.

Vimperk

From Horní Vltavice, a few local buses cover the 13km to the 24-hour Strážný–Philippsreuth German border crossing; trains continue for 13km to **VIMPERK** (Winterberg), where the first printing press in Bohemia was established in 1484 – a few decades after Gutenberg's invention. The business of the day goes on in the lower part of town, leaving the steep narrow streets of the **staré město** virtually deserted. The leafy main square, náměstí Svobody, is overlooked by the town's **hrad**, originally built in the thirteenth century by Otakar II, and last owned by the Schwarzenbergs. The castle, a stiff fifteen-minute hike up from the square, has been knocked about a bit over the centuries, and now houses the local museum (May–Oct Tues–Sun 9am–noon & 1–4pm), with little of interest beyond a selective display of local glassware, though you're rewarded with great views over the old town.

Despite its relative lack of local attractions, Vimperk is another possible base for exploring this part of the Šumava. There are a couple of **hotels** by the train station, but that leaves you a good 1.5km from the town centre down Nádražní. A better idea is to head for the *Amber Hotel Anna* (℡ 388 412 050, ⓦ www.lcon-sulting.cz; ➍), a lovely old building, right in the centre, that's been rather brutally modernized, but a very comfortable place to stay all the same. The hotel also conveniently houses the **tourist office** (Mon–Fri 9.30am–12.30pm & 1–5pm), which can point you in the right direction if you want a private room. The nearest **campsite** is *Vodník* (May–Oct), at Hájná Hora, a kilometre or so up the hill to the west of town. For a cheap *Platán* **beer** and some traditional **food**, head for the *Hospoda na náměstí* on náměstí Svobody.

Strakonice

The remaining, mountainous part of the Šumava is only accessible from the east by an infrequent bus service. The railway meanwhile veers northwards 30km to **STRAKONICE** (Strakonitz), which qualifies as a large industrial town in these parts. It grew up as a textile town in the nineteenth century, and its factories now produce an unusual trio of products: Turkish fez hats, ČZ motorcycles, and *dudy*, the Bohemian equivalent of bagpipes.

There's a museum on these very subjects in the town's extremely large thirteenth-century **hrad** (Tues–Sun: May, Sept & Oct 8am–4pm; June–Aug 9am–5pm), at the confluence of the Volyňka and the Otava, on the south bank of the latter. It's a fun place to explore: there are plenty of old motorbikes to admire, an international selection of *dudy* in everything from velvet to sheepskin, and a fez-making machine. Ironically enough, the fez-making venture was established back in the nineteenth century by some enterprising local Jewish textile merchants. You also get to climb the castle watchtower, Rumpál. If you're really into *dudy*, there's an **International Bagpipe Festival** held in the castle courtyard every year in the middle of August, which attracts a regular contingent from Scotland and elsewhere.

The rest of the town, on the other side of the river, can't quite match the eclectic attractions of the castle, though **Velké náměstí** boasts two very attractive late-nineteenth-century buildings – one a savings bank, the other the old radnice – facing each other across the square. Both are designed in florid neo-Renaissance style, and decorated with pretty folk-inspired and floral murals and friezes. East along Lidická, on the south side of the street, there's also a former butchers' stalls worth inspecting, a lovely little Baroque building with a brightly-coloured naïve relief in the gable showing a butcher about to slaughter a bull.

From the **train** and **bus stations**, it's a five-minute walk to the castle – west down Alfonse Šťástného, then right down Bezděkovská. If you're **staying the night**, head for the excellent **information centre** (Mon–Fri 9am–noon & 1–5pm) in the mapové centrum, located in the main gateway of the castle, where you can book private rooms. Alternatively, try the *Fontána* (☎383 321 440; ❷), northeast of the main square on Lidická – it doesn't look much from the outside, but it's smart enough inside. Even less prepossessing on the outside is the Communist-era high-rise *Amber Hotel Bavor*, across from the castle (☎383 321 300, ⓦwww.lconsulting.cz; ❹), though, again, the interior has been thoroughly modernized. Strakonice's cheapie is the *Švanda dudák* (☎383 321 305; ❷), near the junction of Alfonse Šťástného and Bezděkovská, only one room of which is en suite, or else, you could aim for the HI-affiliated *Garnet*, in the northern suburbs on Dr Jiřího Fifky (☎383 321 984; ❶) – it's a good 2km from the station, so it might be worth hopping on bus #1 or #2, getting off on Zvolenská. There's a **campsite**, *Podskalí* (June to mid-Sept), by the banks of the Otava, fifteen minutes' walk west along Pod Hradem, which runs south of the castle. Strakonice brews its own **beer**, across the river from the castle, and you can sup the local *Nektar* (and *Dudák*) nearby at *U zborova*, a rough-and-ready pub at Bavorova 20, which heads off north from the western end of the main square; more civilized is the newly wood-panelled **restaurant** serving *Budvar* in the *Fontána*.

Rabí and Sušice

There are several ruined castles along the banks of the River Otava beyond Strakonice, but by far the most impressive – and the largest in Bohemia – are the vast and crumbling fortifications of **Rabí**, 25km away by train (change at Horažďovice). A key fortress in the Hussite Wars, and allegedly the place where the Hussite general Jan Žižka lost his second eye, it was deliberately allowed to fall into rack and ruin in the eighteenth century for fear of its strategic value should it fall into the wrong hands. The village sold the castle to the state for one crown in 1920, and recent renovation work, aimed at stabilizing some of the more dangerously disintegrating bits, has now allowed the public access to most of the site (April & Oct Sat & Sun 9am–noon & 1–3pm; May & Sept Tues–Sun 9am–noon & 1–4pm; June–Aug Tues–Sun 9am–noon & 1–5pm) – however, you must endure a 45min-long guided tour in English to explore it. The castle also hosts regular falconry displays in the high season (May–Sept Tues–Sun 11am, 2 & 4.30pm).

A few stops on from Rabí is **SUŠICE** (Schüttenhofen), which means just one thing to the Czechs – matches. The local SOLO match factory is one of the largest in Europe, and dominates the domestic market. Aside from that, there's little evidence of the town's wealthy medieval past, which, like Prachatice's, was based on the salt trade. The exception is the main square, náměstí Svobody, which boasts a handful of striking Renaissance houses; the most arresting are the **Rozacínovský dům** at no. 48, with a fantastic sgraffitoed gable sporting several tiers of mini-pilasters, and the **Voprchovský dům** at no. 40, featuring a similarly eye-catching gable with a triple tier of blind arcading. The latter now houses the **muzeum Šumavy** (May–Oct Tues–Sat 9am–noon & 12.45–5pm, Sun 9am–noon), established as far back as 1880, with exhibits ranging from local glassware to fifteenth-century woodcarvings and, of course, the match-making industry, though it's the carefully restored interior that makes it worth a visit.

Sušice's **train station** is a regrettable 2.5km northeast of the town centre, with only infrequent bus connections; if you arrive by bus, make sure to get off at the town centre and not at the train and bus station, if you have the option. Sušice has a couple of decent inexpensive **hotels**: the most central one is the smart *Gabreta*, just off the main square at Americké armády 73 (☎376 528 016; ❷), a bit of a bargain given that all its rooms have TVs and en-suite shower and toilet (and they offer bike rental); alternatively, there's the excellent *Sport Hotel Pekárna* (☎376 526 479, ⓦwww.sumava.net/sporthotel; ❷), painted up like a multi-flavoured ice-cream gateau and located at T. G. Masaryka 129, on the road in from the train station, with the added attraction of a bowling alley. In addition, there's a nice little upbeat pension, *Milli* (☎376 526 598, ⓔpension.mili@tiscali.cz; ❷), with its own restaurant, down Kostelní, by the side of the old *Hotel Fialka* (now just a pub). Cheapest of all are the rooms with shower only (❶) above the *Granát* pub on the main square. If you're looking to camp, you're best off heading up the Otava to one of the riverside **campsites** like *Annín* (May–Oct), 7.5km south of Sušice, and a favourite spot for canoeists.

Kašperské Hory and around

Twice daily from Vimperk, more frequently from Sušice, a local bus heads for **KAŠPERSKÉ HORY** (Bergreichenstein), an old German mining village on the River Otava, positioned below the ruined castle of Kašperk that was built by Charles IV to guard over the local gold mines. The town's smartest building is its pristine Renaissance **radnice** with its three perfect eighteenth-century gables, featuring – from left to right – a Czech lion, a clock and the town's mining emblem.

In addition, the town's **muzeum Šumavy** (Tues–Fri 9.30am–4pm; May–Oct also Sun 9.30am–noon), on the main square, displays some wonderful local glassware on its top floor, ranging from fourteenth-century to turn-of-the-twentieth-century gear, with pieces by local firms such as Lötz, Schmid and Kralik, from the neighbouring town of Klášterský Mlýn (Klöstermühle). In the late nineteenth century, Lötz in particular won many prizes in Brussels and Paris for its Tiffany-style iridescent glass vases and weird vegetal shapes, many of which inexplicably escaped the auctioneer's hammer and ended up here. There's yet more glassware on display in the next-door building, where the museum stages temporary exhibitions (Tues–Sun 9.30am–5pm).

Also on the main square is the **Moto muzeum** (May Sat & Sun 9am–noon & 12.30–5.30pm; June–Aug daily 9am–noon & 12.30–5.30pm), containing one of the finest collections of old motorbikes in the country, displayed rather surprisingly in the building's attic. More than forty bikes line the eaves, all in pristine condition, and ranging from interwar BMW boxers to domestic trials bikes; pride of place, though, goes to a beautiful red 1928 Indian. The exhibition of Czech toys (*České hračky*) in an adjacent attic, is more of a blatant moneymaker than a labour of love, and only really worth visiting if you want to buy something.

Top **accommodation** is available at the high-class *Park Hotel Tosch* (☎376 582 592, ⓦwww.tosch-parkhotel; ❺), converted from the town's brewery into a luxury hotel with German capital to cater for the German tourists who pass through, and also at a host of pensions and private rooms in the outskirts of the town. You can get a decent bite to eat and a *Gambrinus*, *Radegast* and *Velkopopovický kozel* beer at the nearby *Pod věží* restaurant (closed Sun), which also offers simple rooms (❷).

Srní and around

The most remote part of the Šumava National Park lies south and west of Kašperské Hory, and while there are few attractions in the way of museums or churches, it's the unblemished mountains that people come to see. The first stop of note south of Kašperské Hory is **ČEŇKOVA PILA**, a spot made up of little more than the *Hotel Bystřina* (☎376 599 221; ❷), and a bridge across the Vydra stream, where composer Bedřich Smetana is said to have been inspired to write the swirling flute introduction to his symphonic poem "Vltava" from *Má vlast*.

A few kilometres further on, the cute village of **SRNÍ** has a wooden-shingled church and a few hotels and pensions, such as *Hotel Srní* (☎376 599 212; ❹), with indoor pool, sauna, weight room and bowling; and *Penzión Liška* (☎376 599 386; ❷), a pretty little house with inexpensive rooms along the road to Modrava. A few kilometres deeper into the forest, **ANTÝGL** is nothing more than a few wooden houses that make up a picturesquely situated and very popular **campsite** (mid-May to mid-Oct) and basic lodging (☎376 599 331; ❶); right nearby is the *Hotel Antýgl* (☎376 599 444; ❶), a cheap but clean place with a very good, if smoky, restaurant. Srní and Antýgl both make fine bases for **hikes** in the area. One popular walk from Antýgl is to take the red-marked path 6km along the boulder-strewn Vydra stream (which was the setting for a scene from the film *Kolya*) back down to Čeňkova Pila, and you can make a longer day of it by returning via roundabout paths such as the blue-marked trail to Srní and eventually, via another red-marked path, to Modrava, or the yellow-marked trail that descends from Srní back down to the Vydra.

Pushing on, the quiet settlements of **MODRAVA**, 3km south of Antýgl, and **KVILDA**, another 4km further east, are both surrounded by peat bogs. These were restricted areas when the Iron Curtain was draped just a few kilometres beyond; because of this, the landscape is refreshingly underdeveloped, but there are just enough pensions and simple restaurants today to keep visitors happy. Buses from Sušice wind their way up here at fairly regular intervals.

Železná Ruda and Špičák

The northwestern tip of the Šumava centres on the town of **ŽELEZNÁ RUDA** (Eisenstein), 2km from the German border and best approached on the scenic railway line or bus from Klatovy (see p.221). In its triple role as a border town, ski resort and summer hiking base, the place has certainly lost much of its original charm. Souvenir shops, filled with "traditional" Czech art and garden gnomes, plus the odd strip club, attempt to coax every last euro out of the Germans who come here. In many ways, you're better off using quieter neighbouring resorts like Špičák as a base. Local sights are confined to the ludicrously oversized wooden onion dome over the nave of the village church, and the small **muzeum Šumavy** (Tues–Sat 9am–noon & 12.45–5pm, Sun 9am–noon), local repository for glassware and folk art.

Still, if you need to stock up on provisions or draw some cash, then Železná Ruda is a good place to come. The *Šumava* restaurant, opposite the Spar supermarket, is reasonably priced, and, as far as **accommodation** goes, you're spoilt for choice: try the *Bultas* (☎376 697 123; ❸), which has its own restaurant, or its cheaper cousin, *Richard* (☎376 697 458; ❷). An electronic board on the main road at the centre of town shows availability of many hotels and pensions, and provides a free phone from which you can call them; there's also a **tourist office** (daily 8am–6pm) further down the main road. Finally, the town's **campsite**, *U mlýna* (June–Sept), lies a kilometre or so out of town up route 27. The nearest **train station** to the town centre is Železná Ruda město, 500m north up the road to Špičák; meanwhile, the **rail link with Germany**, which was severed during the Cold War, has been re-established, with the two countries sharing the Železná Ruda/Bayerisch Eisenstein station on the border itself, 3km southwest of the town centre; hourly trains terminate 70km away at Plattling, with connections on to Regensburg.

From **ŠPIČÁK**, one stop back along the railway from Železná Ruda, a two-stage chairlift can take you to the top of **Pancíř** (1214m) all year round. The first stage takes you as far as Hofmanky, and the comfortable *Hotel Horizont* (☎376 397 219, ⓦwww.sumavanet.cz/horizont; ❸); more modest (and with just as good a view) is *Hotel Piák* (☎376 397 253; ❸), a few hundred metres back down the road. Towards the German border, there are two idyllically situated glacial lakes – Černé jezero and Čertovo jezero – surrounded by forests, which you can reach via the yellow-marked path from Špičák station.

Travel details

Trains

Prague to: České Budějovice (8–9 daily; 2hr 15min–3hr); Písek (1 daily, Fri 3 daily; 2hr 30min); Strakonice (1 daily; 2hr 40min); Sušice (1 daily; 3hr 45min); Tábor (every 1–2hr; 1hr 30min–2hr 20min).

České Budějovice to: Brno (4–5 daily; 4hr 20min); Černý Kříž (8 daily; 2hr 30min–2hr 45min); Český Krumlov (9 daily; 1hr); Horní Planá (8 daily; 1hr 45min–2hr 15min); Linz (2 daily; 3hr); Písek (6 daily; 50min–1hr 10min); Plzeň (10 daily; 1hr 45min–3hr); Strakonice (12 daily; 50min–1hr 20min); Tábor (13 daily; 1hr–2hr 15min); Volary (3 daily; 3hr).

Plzeň to: Špičák (4 daily; 2hr–2hr 35min); Železná Ruda (4 daily; 2hr 5min–2hr 40min).

Tábor to: Bechyně (9–10 daily; 50min); Brno (1 daily; 4hr); České Budějovice (12 daily; 1hr–1hr 40min); Jihlava (1 daily; 1hr 50min); Milevsko/Písek (9 daily; 40min/1hr 30min); Pelhřimov (8 daily; 55min–1hr 20min); Třeboň/Gmünd (2 daily; 1hr/1hr 30min).

Volary to: Prachatice (8 daily; 40min); Vimperk/Strakonice (6 daily; 1hr/2hr).

Buses

Prague to: České Budějovice (up to 6 daily; 2hr 25min–3hr); Český Krumlov (2 daily; 3hr 30min); Orlík/Písek (up to 6 daily; 1hr 30min/2hr 10min); Pelhřimov (up to 10 daily; 2hr 15min); Rabí/Sušice (2–3 daily; 2hr 30min/2hr 45min); Strakonice/Prachatice (up to 5 daily; 2hr/2hr 30min); Tábor (up to 8 daily; 2hr); Volary (up to 2 daily; 3hr 30min).

České Budějovice to: Český Krumlov (up to 15 daily; 45min–1hr); Hluboká nad Vltavou (hourly; 20min); Holašovice (2–5 daily; 40min); Jindřichův Hradec (9 daily; 1hr 10min); Prachatice (up to 14 daily; 1hr); Tábor (4–10 daily; 1hr 10min); Třeboň (hourly; 30min).

Český Krumlov to: Rožmberk/Vyšší Brod (3–9 daily; 45/50min); Lipno nad Vltavou (1–4 daily; 1hr 15min); Horní Planá (up to 7 daily; 45min–1hr); Zlatá Koruna (up to hourly; 15min).

Jindřichův Hradec to: České Budějovice (10–12 daily; 1hr 10min); Pelhřimov (3 daily; 45 min); Slavonice (up to 8 daily; 1hr 30min).

Pelhřimov to: Humpolec (up to 10 daily; 30min); Jihlava (up to 8 daily; 45min); Kámen (up to 7 daily; 30min).

Tábor to: Bechyně (up to 14 daily; 40min–1hr 15min); Kámen (up to 6 daily; 30min).

Sušice to: Srní/Modrava (1–2 daily; 45min/1hr).

West Bohemia

Highlights

* **Brewery at Plzeň** – Take a guided tour of the Pilsner Urquell brewery, home of the original lager. **See p.217**

* **Kladruby monastery** – A Baroque-Gothic master-piece by Czech-Italian architect Giovanni Santini. **See p.220**

* **Domážlice** – This Bohemian border region is renowned for its folk traditions and summer festival. **See p.222**

* **Mariánské Lázně** – Elegant fin-de-siècle spa, once the favourite watering hole of European royalty, set amidst gentle wooded hills. **See p.225**

* **Karlovy Vary** – Grandiose late nineteenth-century spa, stretched out along the steeply wooded Teplá valley, and venue for the country's most prestigious film festival. **See p.237**

* **Loket** – Miniature walled town, squeezed into a U-bend of a river, in this once German-speaking border region. **See p.242**

West Bohemia

For centuries, the rolling hills of **West Bohemia** (Západní Čechy) have been a buffer zone between the Slav world and the German-speaking lands. Encouraged by the Czech Přemyslid rulers, the border regions were heavily colonized by neighbouring Germans from the twelfth century onwards. The German settlers provided urgently needed skilled craftsmen and miners for the Bohemian economy, and for much of their history vast swathes of the region were almost exclusively German-speaking.

With the emergence of nationalism, and the subsequent rise of the pro-Nazi Sudeten German Party in the 1930s, the region became deeply divided along ethnic lines. The violent expulsions of the entire German-speaking population after World War II left vast areas of the countryside and several large towns virtually empty of people. Czechs and Slovaks were encouraged to resettle the area after the war; many Czechs used empty rural homes as country cottages, yet the countryside, particularly close to the border, remains eerily underpopulated even today.

The economic mainstay of the region for the last century has been the sprawling industrial city of **Plzeň**, home of the Škoda engineering works, centre of the country's beer industry, and capital of the region. It's by no means the most picturesque of cities, but it does have a certain nineteenth-century grandeur, and remains a magnet for anyone who admires Czech beer. Within easy reach of Plzeň are the monasteries of **Kladruby** and **Plasy**, monuments to the outstanding architectural genius of Giovanni Santini, the master of "Baroque-Gothic". Further south, the historic border town of **Domažlice** is one of the best-preserved towns in the region, and a jumping-off point to the neighbouring Šumava (see p.197).

West Bohemia's busiest tourist region, however, is the famous triangle of spas: **Mariánské Lázně**, **Františkovy Lázně** and **Karlovy Vary**. Conveniently scattered along the German border, these three Bohemian spa resorts were the Côte d'Azur of Habsburg Europe, attracting the European elite of the nineteenth century. Following the wholesale nationalization of the spa industry, under Communism every factory and trade union received an annual three weeks' holiday at a *lázně dům* (spa pension): a perk aimed at proving the success of socialism. Taking "the cure" remains very popular not only with Czechs, not so much as a holiday but as the serious treatment of a multitude of ills, but also with Russia's nouveaux riches, and, of course, with the neighbouring Germans. All three spa towns are very attractive visually, but they do tend to be full of the plethoric and elderly, so if you need a break from cure-seekers, head for **Cheb** or **Loket**, both beautifully preserved towns and largely crowd-free.

This being one of the most sparsely populated regions in the country, **public transport** is somewhat patchy. However, excellent rail and bus links exist between the major towns, so unless you're heading for the back of beyond, getting around should present few problems.

Plzeň

PLZEŇ (Pilsen) was built on beer and bombs. Founded in 1295 and now with a population of around 175,000, it's by far the largest city in Bohemia after Prague, but as recently as 1850 it was a small town of just 14,000, most of whom were German-speakers. Then in 1859, an ironworks was founded and quickly snapped up by the Czech capitalist **Emil Škoda**, under whose control it drew an ever-increasing number of Czechs from the countryside. Within thirty years, the overall population had trebled, while the number of Germans had decreased. Although initially simply an engineering plant, the Habsburgs transformed the place into a huge armaments factory (second only to Krupps in Germany), which, inevitably, was a key acquisition for the Germans when they annexed Czechoslovakia, soon attracting the attention of Allied bombers during World War II. Under the Communists, Plzeň diversified even further, producing trams, trains and buses, not to mention dodgy Soviet-designed nuclear reactors. Sadly, unlike Škoda's car-producing arm, based in Mladá Boleslav (see p.148), Škoda Plzeň is currently struggling economically, although Plzeň itself has attracted large-level foreign investment and is undergoing something of a minor renaissance. Despite the city's overwhelmingly industrial character, Plzeň has plenty of compensations: a large student population, eclectic late-nineteenth-century architecture, and an unending supply of (probably) the best **beer** in the world – all of which make Plzeň a justifiably popular stopoff on the main railway line between Prague and the West.

Arrival, orientation and accommodation

Fast trains from Prague take around one and a half hours to reach Plzeň, making it just about possible to visit on a day-trip from the capital. The town's **train stations** are works of art in themselves: there are numerous minor ones within the city boundaries, but your most likely point of arrival is Plzeň hlavní nádraží, the ornate main station east of the city centre. The irredeemably ugly **bus terminal**, for all national and international arrivals, is on the west side of town. From both the bus or main train station, the city centre is just a short walk away – or a few stops on tram #2 from the bus station, trams #1 and #2 from the train station.

Accommodation

Finding a vacancy in one of Plzeň's **hotels** presents few problems, though rooms don't come cheap. **Private rooms** can be arranged through the **tourist office** at no. 41 on the main square (Mon–Fri 10am–5pm, Sat–Sun 10am–3.30pm; ☏377 032 750, ⓦwww.plzen-city.cz). The city's university has cheap dorm accommodation available in the summer holidays at its **student hostels** (Bolevecká 30; take tram #4 north along Karlovarská; if in doubt ask at CKM on Dominikánská Mon–Fri 9am–5pm). There are two **campsites** – *Bílá hora* (April–Sept), on 28 října, and *Ostende* (May–Sept), to the west, on Malý Bolevec – both just under 5km north of the centre on the far side of the Velký ryb, where Plzeňites go to swim on summer days. To get to *Bílá hora*, take bus #20 from Šumavská, near the train station, or #39 from Sady Pětatřicátníků and get off at the last stop; for *Ostende*, you'll need to walk along the northern shore of the lake from *Bílá hora* or from the first stop on Plaská (tram #1). Alternatively, you could walk the last kilometre or two from Plzeň-Bílá Hora station – the slow trains from Plzeň to Žatec, which run roughly every two hours, stop here.

Pension Bárová Solní 8 ☏ 377 236 652. Best-value rooms in town are the three at this small pension, just off the main square. **②**
Pension City Sady 5 května 52 ☏ 377 326 069. Small, very central pension on the northeastern edge of the old town, with plainly furnished rooms with TV, and optional en-suite bathroom. **③**
Hotel Central Nám. Republiky 33 ☏ 377 226 757, ☏ 377 226 064, ⓦ web.telecom.cz/hotel-central. Communist-era eyesore, which enjoys the best possible position, with en-suite rooms looking out onto náměstí Republiky and a Seventies-style restaurant. **⑤**
Hotel Continental Zbrojnická 8 ☏ 377 235 292, ⓦ www.hotelcontinental.cz. Painstakingly restored to something like its former glory by its original

First Republic owners; the cheapest rooms here have en-suite shower, but no toilet. **③**
Hotel Rosso Pallova 12 ☏ 377 226 473. Large, new hotel on the edge of the old town, with comfortable, fully en-suite rooms. **④**
Hotel Roudná Na Roudné 13 ☏ 377 259 926, ⓦ www.tour-and-sports.cz. Small, fairly simple and only 300m from the centre; Gambrinus and Pilsner on tap plus guarded parking. **③**
Hotel Slovan Smetanovy sady 1 ☏ 377 227 256, ⓔ hotelslovan@iol.cz. Hotel in a peaceful park, once splendid, with a wonderfully ornate stairwell; partially reconstructed but otherwise communist-style. **②**
U Salzmannů Pražská 8 ☏ 377 235 855. Double rooms are available at Plzeň's renowned, seventeenth-century pub. **③**

The City

Stepping out of the main station onto Americká, you're confronted with a variety of bad-taste communist-era buildings. Close by, the river Radbuza – one of four rivers running through Plzeň – doesn't bear close inspection, but the historical core of the city beyond it certainly does.

Laid out in chessboard fashion by Václav II in 1295, the old town is still dominated by the exalted heights of the Gothic cathedral of **sv Bartoloměj**

ACCOMMODATION

Penzion Bárová	2	Hotel Continental	7	Hotel Slovan	8
Pension City	3	Hotel Rosso	6	U Salzmannů	5
Hotel Central	4	Hotel Roudná	1		

RESTAURANTS & PUBS

Archa	A	Na spilce	B
Barolo	D	Žumbera	E
Čajovna	C		

(St Bartholomew), stranded awkwardly in the middle of the main square. Inside, the late-Gothic vaulting of the Šternberská kaple, with its delicate pendant boss, is worth checking out, but the cathedral's prize possession is its thirteenth-century wooden statue of the Plzeň Madonna in the "Beautiful Style", on the high altar. The church used to boast two towers, but one was struck by lightning in 1525 and was never rebuilt. The cathedral's remaining bile-green **spire** reaches a height of more than a hundred metres, making it the tallest in the country; you can climb up to the viewing platform (*vyhlídková věž*; daily 10am–6pm) – which doubled as the town's lookout post – for a bird's-eye view of the local industrial complexes.

The rest of the main square, **náměstí Republiky**, presents a full range of architectural styles: some buildings, like the squat, grey *Hotel Central*, as recent as the 1960s; others, like the Italianate **stará radnice** (old town hall), smothered in sgraffito in the early twentieth century, but dating from the sixteenth century. Plzeň became an unlikely imperial capital in 1599, when the Emperor Rudolf II based himself next door at no. 41 for the best part of a year, in an effort to avoid the ravages of the Prague plague. The vast majority of Plzeň's buildings, however, hail from the city's heyday during the industrial expansion around the turn of the twentieth century. In the old town, this resulted in some wonderful variations on historical themes and Art Nouveau motifs, particularly to the north and west of the main square. West of Sady Pětatřicátníků, and south of Husova, there are still more blocks of late-nineteenth-century residential apartments, boasting vestiges of ornate mosaics and sculpturing, now barely visible beneath the black layer of pollution that's eating away at their fanciful facades.

On Sady Pětatřicátníků itself stands the flamboyant late-nineteenth-century **Divadlo J.K. Tyla** (Tyl Theatre), named after Josef Kajétan Tyl, composer of the Czech national anthem, who died in Plzeň in 1856. Diagonally opposite the theatre is the city's imposing red-brick **Velká synagóga** (Great Synagogue; daily except Sat 11am–5pm), reopened in 1998, and looking resplendent with its brightly coloured chevroned roof, and twin onion domes topped by gilded Stars of David. The largest surviving synagogue in the whole country, and claiming to be Europe's second-largest, it was built in 1888 and could just about have seated Plzeň's entire Jewish population of nearly 3500. The city's few remaining Jews use the winter synagogue at the back of the building, while the partially restored main hall now serves as a concert venue and exhibition space, although reconstruction work on paintings, furniture, the organ, upholstery and masonry is still continuing. The ornate interior, which boasts an organ at the east end, also contains a permanent exhibition on the history of the local Jewish community. The tourist office also has a free brochure detailing **Jewish sites** in the Plzeň region, listing cemeteries, homes, synagogues and the one remaining ghetto, plus four suggested routes by car.

Beer and the brewery

Whatever its other attractions, the real reason most people come to Plzeň is to sample its famous beer, the original *Plzeňský Prazdroj* or **Pilsner Urquell** (its more familiar Germanized export name). Beer has been brewed in the town since its foundation in 1295, but it wasn't until 1842 that the famous *Bürgerliches Brauhaus* was built by the German banker Bleichröder, after a near-riot by the townsfolk over the declining quality of their beer. The new brew was a bottom-fermented beer, which quickly became popular across central Europe, spawning thousands of paler imitations under the generic name of *Pilsner* – hence the brewers' addition of the suffix *Prazdroj* or *Urquell* (meaning "original"), to show just who thought of it first. The superiority of Plzeň's beer is allegedly due to a combination of the soft local water and world-renowned Žatec hops.

For a **guided tour** of the **brewery** (75Kč; ☎377 062 888, ⓦwww.pilsner -urquell.cz), you can either book in advance or simply show up and join one of the roughly hourly groups in English, Czech or German. Tours last about two hours, and include a brewery and bottling room visit, beer tasting and a brief and gloriously tacky video show, as well as a tour of the cellars. If the technological details of brewing don't appeal, you could just settle for the real thing at the vast *Na spílce* pub, the Czech Republic's largest (daily from 11am), beyond the brewery's triumphal arch. The arch itself, built in 1892 to commemorate the beer's fiftieth birthday, has been depicted on every authentic bottle of *Pilsner Urquell* ever since. Alternatively, you could try the historical angle at the Pivovarské muzeum (see p.219), or time your visit with Plzeň's annual **beer festival**, held early in October, as a preamble to the Munich Bierfest.

Plzeň's museums

Plzeň has a fair few museums, the biggest being the copper-topped **Západočeské muzeum** (West Bohemian Museum; Tues–Sun 10am–5pm), a neo-Baroque extravaganza, built in the nineteenth century to help educate the peasants who were flocking to the city. It's recently reopened, after more than a decade of restoration, and is worth a visit, if only for its ornate interior. The museum stages temporary exhibitions on the upper floor, and houses the impressive town armoury (*Plzeňská městská zbrojnice*) – established by Charles IV – on the ground floor.

More interesting than the city's big museum is the **Západočeské galerie** (Tues–Fri 10am–6pm, Sat 10am–1pm, Sun 9am–5pm), which puts on temporary exhibitions in a newly renovated Gothic building at Pražská 13, and is due to house its impressive permanent collection in the distinctive elongated vaults of the town's Gothic butchers' stalls or **Masné krámy** (times as above), which stand opposite the city's sixteenth-century water tower or *Černá věž* (now a commercial art gallery).

The American liberation of Plzeň

By May 6, 1945, General Patton's US Third Army had liberated much of West Bohemia, including Plzeň. Less than 100km of virtually open road lay between the Americans and Prague, by then into the second day of its costly uprising against the Nazis. However, the agreement between the big three Allies at Yalta was that Prague should be liberated by the Soviets, who at the time were still 200km from Prague, en route from Berlin. Patton offered to march on Prague, and in fact, on May 7, three US armoured cars reached the outskirts of the city, but the order was to stay put.

Following the 1948 coup, the Communists took down all the monuments and deleted all references in history books to the American liberation of Plzeň. They even went so far as to say that the Americans had deliberately hung back from Prague, allowing thousands to die in the uprising. However, in May 1990, the city was able once again to celebrate the liberation, and in the presence of large numbers of US army veterans, a new memorial was erected on Chodské náměstí, just off Klatovská třída. In 1995, the granite memorial planned after the war but never built was finally erected at the top of Americká, saying simply "Thank You America". Since the fall of communism, West Bohemia has held an annual celebration of Plzeň's liberation in early May, with parades of army vehicles both modern and veteran through the city.

At the end of Veleslavínova is the most popular of Plzeň's museums, the **Pivovarské muzeum** (Brewery Museum; daily 10am–6pm for booked groups; April–Dec 10am–6pm and Jan–March, tours at 10am, noon, 2pm & 4pm for individuals; 40Kč). Housed in what was originally a Gothic malthouse and later a pub, this is a more-than-sufficient consolation for those who fail to get into the brewery itself; ask the curator to get the old *Würlitzer* organ going while you check out the numerous exhibits on the long tradition of brewing in Plzeň, including the smallest beer barrel in the world (a mere one-centimetre cube) and case after case of kitsch Baroque beer mugs.

Also worth a quick once-over is the little-visited **Diecézní muzeum** (April, May, Oct & Nov Wed–Sun 9am–5pm; June–Sept Tues–Sun 9am–5pm), housed in the cloisters of the former Franciscan monastery on Františkánská. The highlight of the museum is the Gothic chapel of sv Barbora (Saint Barbara) in the presbytery, on whose walls beautiful rose-coloured frescoes survive from the 1460s. The frescoes depict Barbara's martyrdom, which was gruesome even by biblical standards. Condemned to death by her father for converting to Christianity, she was racked, birched, carded with a metal comb, forced to lie on a bed of shards, slashed with red-hot blades, paraded naked, dragged up a mountain and finally beheaded, upon which her father was struck down by lightning.

Of minor interest only are the **Plzeňské historické podzemí** or underground tunnels (April, May, Oct & Nov Wed–Sun 9am–5pm; June–Sept Tues–Sun 9am–5pm), accessible from Perlova 4, built as a defensive ploy in the fourteenth century, but also very useful for storing beer. The guided tours are in Czech only, but there's a fairly lucid English written commentary available on request.

Eating, drinking and entertainment

All the hotels in town have **restaurants** attached to them, but most Czechs prefer to head for the city's pubs or pizzerias. Apart from the aforementioned *Na spílce* **pub** (see p.218), you can get *Pilsner Urquell* (and cheap grub) at *U Salzmannů*, the town's famous wood-panelled pub at Pražská 8. *Gambrinus* and the dark *Purkmistr*, Plzeň's other beers, are best drunk at *Žumbera*, Bezručova 14. The city boasts several decent **Italian** joints: try the petite *Archa*, Veleslavínová 22, or *Barolo*, Prešovská 5, with a geranium-filled courtyard. Plzeň's very own *McDonald's* opened in 1994, a happy homecoming for the junk-food chain founder, Ray Krok, whose family originally hailed from the nearby village of Stupno. Those aiming for the healthy life should drop by the *čajovna* (tea house) at the tourist information centre on the main square, or that on Palackého.

Plzeň's wonderful Beaux-Arts Divadlo J.K. Tyla (Tyl Theatre) is the city's main venue for opera and ballet. Most other concerts and cultural events take place at the Dům kultury on Americká, though the **Festival of Folk Songs** (known as *Porta* and held over the first weekend in July) is held in the Vystaviště, on Radčická, off Palackého náměstí. Vystaviště is also home to the city's summer-only open-air **cinema** (*letní kino*), and there's an arthouse cinema complex called *Elektra*, at Americká 24, which also has a restaurant and occasional live music. The main **rock/DJ venue** is *C Music Club*, Americká 18, but check the flyposters for the latest.

Around Plzeň

Within easy reach of Plzeň are two monasteries that bear the hallmark of Giovanni Santini, arguably the most original Baroque architect to work in the

Czech Lands. Of the two, **Plasy** – 18km north of Plzeň – is the easiest to get to (by train or bus), though **Kladruby** – over 30km west – is without doubt a more rewarding day-trip.

Plasy

The **Cistercian monastery** at **PLASY** (Plass) is submerged in a green valley around 25km north of Plzeň. Originally founded in 1144 by Vladislav II, the present muddle of partially renovated Baroque outbuildings is the work of two of Prague's leading architects, Jean-Baptiste Mathey and Giovanni Santini (also known as Jan Blažej). Of the two, **Santini** (1667–1723), the Prague-born son of north Italian immigrants, is the more interesting: a popular architect, builder and stonemason whose personal, slightly ironic Baroque-Gothic style produced some of the most original works in the country. The brilliant white cloisters harbour palatial side chapels, while the rest of the monastery (April & Oct Sat & Sun 9am–3pm; May & Sept Tues–Sun 9am–4pm; June–Aug Tues–Sun 9am–5pm; regular concerts throughout July–Sept) is now an art gallery; the highlight of the 45-minute guided tour is a look at the tall side chapels off the cloisters, whose frescoes create an incredible splash of colour on the ceiling. The best time to visit the monastery is during the annual **Hermit Festival** of contemporary art and music in late June/early July, which draws avant-garde artists from all over Europe.

Shortly after its Baroque redevelopment, the monastery was dissolved and in 1826 fell into the hands of **Prince Clemenz von Metternich**, the arch-conservative Habsburg chancellor and political architect of the post-Napoleonic European order. Over the road, obscured by willow trees, the cemetery church was transformed by the prince into the family mausoleum. In tune with his politics, its oppressively Neoclassical forms dwarf the commoners' graveyard behind it.

Kladruby

If Plasy fails to move you, the **Benedictine monastery** (Tues–Sun: May & June 10am–3pm; July & Aug 9am–5pm; Sept 9am–4pm) at **KLADRUBY** (Kladrau), 35km west of Plzeň, should do the trick, particularly if you manage to catch a Christmas concert or join the August music festival. An altogether less gloomy affair, the monastery was founded by Vladislav I in 1114 (he's buried here, too) and was once the largest and richest monastery in Bohemia. Gutted by the Hussites and again during the Thirty Years' War, the whole place was transformed when the Counter-Reformation had set in – the monastery according to blueprints by Kilian Ignaz Dienzenhofer, and the monastery church under Santini's supervision. The huge monastery church, now restored, is the main attraction, where the original Romanesque and Gothic elements blend imperceptibly with Santini's idiosyncratic additions. The original lantern tower has been converted into an extravagant Baroque cupola, which filters a faded pink light into the transepts, themselves covered in stars and zigzags mirrored on the cold stone paving below. It's the perfect expression of Santini's style, and a work of consummate skill.

The easiest way to get from Plzeň to Kladruby on public transport is to go as far as **Stříbro** (Mies) by train, and then change onto one of the fairly frequent local buses that cover the last 6km to Kladruby. Dramatically poised over the Mže (Mies) river, Stříbro itself was previously the vague frontier post between the German- and Czech-speaking districts, its tidy square sporting arguably the most beautiful Renaissance **radnice** in Bohemia, paid for by the town's long-extinct silver mines (*stříbro* means silver).

Klatovy and around

Tightly walled in and nervously perched on high ground, **KLATOVY** (Klattau) warns of the approaching border with Germany. Founded by Přemyslid King Otakar II in 1260, the town's great prosperity in the middle ages is still visible in the main square, but it can't compete with the Rose Towns further east. Still, there's enough to keep you occupied for at least a couple of hours, and with Plzeň only an hour away by train it's another possible day-trip; or a potential base for exploring the northwest tip of the nearby Šumava region (see p.208).

The Town

Klatovy's best feature is undoubtedly the cluster of tall buildings jostling for position in the southwest corner of the cramped town square, **náměstí Míru**. The facade of the Renaissance radnice is decorated with 1920s sgraffito and features two liberation plaques: one to the Russians (who liberated the country), and one to the Americans (who liberated the town). Tucked in beside the town hall is the 76-metre, sixteenth-century **Černá věž** (April & Oct Sat & Sun 9am–noon & 1–4pm; May–Sept Tues–Sun 9am–noon & 1–5pm), the clearest evidence of the town's bygone prosperity. Its pinnacled parapet, once a look-out post to protect the town, offers views of the forests at the Bavarian border and, closer at hand, across the rooftops to the smaller and later **Bílá věž** (see below).

Next to the Černá věž, Dientzenhofer's white **Jezuitský kostel** exudes incense and cooled air from its curvaceous interior emblazoned with frescoes, including a spectacularly theatrical trompe l'oeil main altar and backdrop. More fascinating, though, are the church's musty **katakomby** (catacombs; May–Sept Tues–Sun 9am–noon & 1–5pm; Oct–April Tues–Fri 9am–noon & 1–4pm), where Jesuits and other wealthy locals are preserved in varying stages of decomposition underneath the radnice; the entrance is round the side of the church. Next door is **U bílého jednorožce** (The White Unicorn), a seventeenth-century Baroque *lékárna* or apothecary (April–Oct Tues–Sun 9am–noon & 1–5pm), which functioned until 1964 and has since become a UNESCO registered monument. The bottles and pots are all labelled in Latin, with swirling wooden pillars flanking the shelves, and a unicorn's horn (strictly speaking, it's a tusk from an arctic narwhal), the pharmacists' mascot, jutting out into the centre. The back room, where the drugs were mixed, comes complete with horror-movie flasks of dried goat's blood and pickled children's intestines. Adjacent to the pharmacy is the town's **art gallery**, Galerie U bílého jednorožce (daily 9am–noon & 1–5pm), a pristine vaulted white room used for temporary exhibitions.

Before you give up on sightseeing, it's worth strolling over to the **Bílá věž** (White Tower), built during the Renaissance period, but later Baroquified. Next door to the tower stands the Gothic church, **Arciděkanský chrám**, whose spires sport charming gilded crowns slipped on like rings on fingers. Inside, the church retains its medieval stellar vaulting, and features a fetching shell-shaped baldachin, held up by barley-sugar columns. Beyond the church and Bílá věž are the impressive remains of the town's medieval walls, which, if followed south, will bring you to the **local museum** (Okresní muzeum; Tues–Sun 9am–noon & 1–5pm), on Hostašova, more interesting for its salmon-pink Austro-Hungarian architecture than for its humdrum exhibits.

Practicalities

Klatovy's main **train and bus stations** are situated over a kilometre north-west of the old town (bus #1 or #2 to the main square); Klatovy-město station, just under a kilometre south of the old town, is only served by slow trains to and from Sušice. **Accommodation**, including private rooms, can be organized through the Pergolia **tourist office** by the Černá věž on the main square (Mon–Sat 9am–noon & 1–5pm, Sat 10am–noon; T376 313 515, Epergoliatour@worldonline.cz); they also offer bike rental.

There are a few decent pensions in the old town, such as *U Hejtmana* on ulice kpt. Jaroše (T376 317 918; ❷), just off the main square, plus the renovated Renaissance *Hotel Ennius*, Randova 111 (T376 320 564, F376 320 567; ❸), also in the old town, with a thriving restaurant, and owned by the same outfit who run the *Hotel Centrál*, at Masarykova 300 (T376 314 571, F376 314 745; ❸), which isn't really that central, but is at least conveniently situated between the old town and the train and bus stations. Another option is the *Klatovský dvůr* (T & F376 321 517; ❷), out on the road to Domažlice, or the *Rozvoj*, Procházkova 110/V (T376 311 609, Epkittlen@iol.cz; ❶–❹), an unusual circular building with three-bed rooms, apartments, a restaurant and disco. Alternatively, there's an excellent **campsite**, *Sluneční mlýn* (May–Sept) by an old water mill on the River Úhlava; it's signposted a couple of kilometres along the Domažlice, has a swimming pool, bungalows and tent space.

Back in Klatovy, you can admire the main square best from the tables outside the *Beseda* restaurant. The *Stará rychta*, on Denisova, west of the main square, is the town's liveliest **pub**, and serves Gambrinus, while the best **restaurant** is the *Zlatý drak*, Vídeňská 32, on the corner of Podbranská, which dishes up good Chinese-Czech food along with views of the town's towers.

Švihov

Ruined castles are ten-a-penny in these border regions; the virtue of the one at **ŠVIHOV**, 11km north of Klatovy, is that it still looks like a proper castle – and it's easy to reach by train, from either Plzeň or Klatovy. It was begun in 1480 by the Rožmberks as a vast concentric structure, with traditional double fortifications creating an inner and outer castle surrounded by a moat. Suspicious of such an unusually well-fortified stronghold, the Habsburgs ordered the owners to tear down the eastern section, and what remains today is a kind of cross-section of a castle, partially surrounded by its original moat. The highlights of the fifty-minute guided tour (April & Oct Sat & Sun 9–11am & 1–3pm; May & Sept Tues–Sun 9–11am & 1–4pm; June–Aug closes 5pm) are the late-Gothic chapel by Benedikt Ried, and a very fine Renaissance strapwork ceiling. It also frequently hosts concerts of classical music and theatrical performances.

Domažlice

Fifteen kilometres from the German border, **DOMAŽLICE** (Taus) is an attractive little town, situated in one of the few border areas that has always been predominantly Czech-speaking. For centuries the town was the local customs house, and the Chodové (see box opposite), as the folk round here are known, were given the task of guarding the border with Bavaria, but in 1707 the town lost much of its former importance when the border was fixed. The town's biggest bash is the annual Chod folk festival, **Chodské slavnosti**, held in the middle of August.

The Chodové

"The spearhead of the Slavic march into central Europe", as writer Josef Škvorecký described them, the **Chodové** are one of the few Czech peoples to have kept their identity. Very little is certain about their origin, but their name comes from *chodit* (to walk about), and undoubtedly refers to their traditional occupation as guardians of the frontier. Since the earliest times, their proud independence was exploited by a succession of Bohemian kings, who employed them as border guards in return for granting them freedom from serfdom, plus various other feudal privileges.

However, after the Battle of Bílá hora, the Habsburgs were keen to curb the power of the Chodové, and the whole region was handed over lock, stock and barrel to one of the victorious generals, Wilhelm Lamminger von Albenreuth (also known as Lomikar). At first the Chodové tried to reaffirm their ancient privileges by legal means, but when this proved fruitless, with the encouragement of one Jan Sladký – better known as Kozina – they simply refused to acknowledge their new despot. Seventy of the rebels were thrown into the prison in Prague, while Kozina was singled out to be publicly hanged in Plzeň on November 28, 1695, as an example to the rest of the Chodové. From the gallows, Kozina prophesied the death of Lomikar "within a year and a day" – the general died as Kozina foresaw, from a stroke following a banquet held to celebrate Kozina's demise.

Although the empire prevailed, the Chodové never allowed the loss of their freedom to quash their ebullience or their peculiar local dialect, which still survives in the villages. Stubbornly resistant to Germanization, they carried the banner of Czech national defiance through the Dark Ages. Even now, of all the regions of Bohemia, Chodsko is closest to its cultural roots, known above all for its local dialect and rich local costumes, still worn on Sundays and religious holidays, and for its *dudy* (bagpipes), now played only in folk ensembles and at festivals. If you're interested in seeing a "typical" Chod village, it's worth visiting Klenčí pod Čerchovem, close to Domažlice.

The Town

Like many small Bohemian towns, Domažlice starts and ends at its main square, **náměstí Míru**, a long, thin affair, positioned along a perfect east–west axis. Flanked by uninterrupted arcades under every possible style of colourful gable, the pretty, elongated cobbled square seems like a perfect setting for a Bohemian-Bavarian skirmish. Halfway down one side, the thirteenth-century **church tower** or *věž* (April–Sept daily 9am–noon & 1–5pm), now leaning to one side quite noticeably, used to double as a lookout post for the vulnerable town, and ascending its 196 steps provides a bird's-eye view of the whole area. The **Děkanský kostel** itself, whose entrance is round the corner in Kostelní, has a wonderful series of Baroque frescoes, colourful furnishings and a particularly fine trompe l'oeil scenic backdrop for the gilded main altar.

The town's other remaining thirteenth-century round tower lies to the southwest, down Chodská, and belongs to the **Chodský hrad**, seat of the Chodové self-government until it fell into the hands of Wilhelm Lamminger von Albreneuth. The castle has recently been renovated and now houses the **Muzeum Chodska** (Mon–Fri 10am–noon & 1–3pm), which worthily traces the town's colourful history.

More fascinating by half, though, is the **Muzeum Jindřicha Jindřicha**, east of the old town just beyond the medieval gateway (call ☏379 722 974 to arrange a visit), and founded by local composer Jindřich Jindřich. His extensive collection of Chod folk costumes, ceramics and other regional items, all displayed in a mock-up cottage interior, are ample compensation if you fail to catch the annual festival.

Practicalities

The town's **main train station**, called simply Domažlice, is 1km east of town; the Domažlice město station, five minutes' walk south of the old town down Jiráskova, is served only by slow trains to Bor and Tachov. The main **bus terminal** lies just north of the main square, on Poděbradova. The town's **tourist office** (Mon–Fri 7.30am–5pm, June–Aug also Sat 9am–noon) is situated in the nineteenth-century radnice on the main square; nearby there's a **cash machine**, useful if you've just crossed over from Germany.

As for **accommodation**, there are plenty of simple family-run pensions in the old town: try *Café-Pension Tiffany* (☎379 725 591; ❷), beside the church at Kostelní 102. Alternatively, check for vacancies at *Pension Viola* (☎379 722 435; ❷), an interwar villa north of the old town up Thomayerova (off the road to Luženice), with its own restaurant and garden, or *Hotel Koruna* (☎379 722 279; ❷), west of the main square at M.B. Staška 69, which has plain, cheap rooms. For those with a tent, there's a choice between the riverside *Babylon* **campsite** (mid-May to Oct), 6km south by bus or train, or the *Hájovna* site (May–Sept), a kilometre or so north of Kdyně (20min by train from Domažlice). As for **food**, the *Ural*, on the north side of the main square, is a regular Czech pub-restaurant serving the local, dark beer, *Purkmistr 11*; *Dalibor Kubů*, south off the main square on Branská, is slightly pricier and more used to tourists, or else there's *Chodská rychta*, a pleasant restaurant on M.B. Staška, opposite the town's art gallery. Domažlice has its own **brewery** by the bus station, though no brewery tap; instead, head for the *Štika*, a real drinkers' pub serving the local brew, on the road out to Plzeň.

If you're heading for Germany, there are now three trains a day from Domažlice to the Bavarian town of **Furth-im-Wald**, whose *Drachenstich* festival – during which the townsfolk fight a gory battle with a giant dragon – takes place shortly after the Chod Folk Festival on the second and third Sundays in August.

Horšovský Tyn

A lazy afternoon could happily be spent at **HORŠOVSKÝ TYN** (Bischofteinitz), just 10km north of Domažlice. Its main square, **náměstí Republiky**, is a picturesque grassy, sloping affair centred on the church of sv Petr and Pavel, and lined with Gothic houses sporting brightly coloured Baroque facades. At the top end, surrounded by a bear- and raccoon-inhabited moat, is the quadrilateral sgraffitoed **zámek** (April & Oct Sat & Sun 9am–noon & 1–3pm; May & Sept Tues–Sun 9am–noon & 1–4pm; June–Aug closes 5pm; ☎379 423 111), one of the most popular in West Bohemia and transformed by the Lobkowicz family into a rich Renaissance pile. There's a rather complicated choice of **guided tours**: the Hrad tour (*trasa 1*; 50min) takes you through the renovated Bishop's Palace, including the reconstructed interior of the Early Gothic bishop's chapel. The Zámek tour (*trasa 2*; 1hr) covers living quarters from the sixteenth to twentieth centuries, plus a gallery lined with portraits of Czech rulers; the Kuchyně tour (*trasa 3*; 45min) features a trawl round the kitchens, tacky china chandeliers equipped with their original Edison bulbs and other delights; and the Burgrave's Palace (*trasa 4*; 1 hour) leads visitors around the reconstructed Riding School. Behind the chateau, the vast **Zámecký park** stretches northwards, complete with hidden chapels, a large lake and hosts of peacocks. It's a ten-minute walk to the centre from the train station: head east up Nádražní to the main crossroads, then north over the river, and the main square will appear on your right. If you haven't brought your own picnic, the

Hotel Šumava restaurant, along from the chateau entrance (closed Mon), offers some fairly imaginative dishes.

Mariánské Lázně

At the end of the eighteenth century, what is now **MARIÁNSKÉ LÁZNĚ** (Marienbad) was unadulterated woodland. It was not until the 1790s that the local abbot, Karel Reitenberger, and a German doctor, Josef Nehr, took the initiative and established a spa here. Within a hundred years, Marienbad (as it was known in its heyday) had joined the clique of world-famous European spas, boasting a clientele that ranged from writers to royalty. The inveterate spa-man Goethe was among the earliest of the VIPs to popularize the place, and a few generations later it became the favourite holiday spot of King Edward VII (who visited it nine times), a passion he shared with his pal, the Emperor Franz-Josef I. During World War I, even the incorrigibly infirm Franz Kafka spent a brief, happy spell here with Felice Bauer, writing "things are different now and good, we are engaged to be married right after the war", though in fact they never were.

▲ *Lázně Kynžvart (7 km)*

MARIÁNSKÉ LÁZNĚ

Městské divadlo
Křížový pramen
Městské muzeum ②
Kolonáda
Zpívající fontána ●
Hotel Weimar
Nanebevzetí Panna Maria ✚
Spa Gardens
Karolinin pramen
dům Chopin ③
Anglikánský kostel
Ambrožův pramen
Casino
Nové lázně ⑥
Hotel Excelsior
Pravoslavný kostel
Kaiserturm

IBSENOVA
TŘEBÍZSKÉHO
MÍROVÉ NÁMĚSTÍ
NEHROVA
HLAVNÍ TŘÍDA
MASARYKOVA
ÚZKÁ
LESNÍ
GOETHOVO NÁMĚSTÍ
KARLOVARSKÁ
LÁZEŇSKÁ
RUSKÁ
REITENBERGEROVA
DUSÍKOVA
ANGLICKÁ
KLÍČOVA
POŠTOVNÍ

N

▶ & Chair Lift

RESTAURANTS, CAFÉS & BARS	
Classic	B
Helvetia	D
Irish Pub	E
Café Polonia	B
U zlaté koule	A
Villa Romana	C

ACCOMMODATION	
Hotel Bohemia	5
Hotel Esplanade	7
Hotel Helga	1
Hvězda	2
Hotel Kossuth/Suvurov	4
Nové Lázně	6
Hotel Polonia	3
Hotel Villa Butterfly	9
Zlatý zámek	8

0   100 m

Train & Bus Stations, ⑨ & ▼ ▼ Ⓓ   ▼ Ⓔ

Today, Mariánské Lázně is much less exclusive, though no less attractive – what was a fat-farm for the rich and famous only two generations ago is now eminently accessible to all and sundry. Over the last decade, the riotous, late-nineteenth-century architecture has been restored to its former flamboyance, and the whole place has been successfully brought back to life. Above all, though, it's the spa's beautiful setting, amidst thickly forested hills, that remains its most beguiling asset. The air around town is cool and refreshing and the centre of the spa is more or less free of cars, all of which comes as something of a relief after the usual traffic-choked streets.

The spa

Mariánské Lázně was the last of Bohemia's famous triangle of spas to be built, and as such is the most consistently flamboyant in its architecture. As far as the eye can see, sumptuously regal buildings rise up from the pine-clad surrounds, most dating from the second half of the nineteenth century. For all their sculptural theatricality and invention, there's an intriguing homogeneity in the fin-de-siècle opulence, with each building dressed up, almost without exception, in buttery *Kaisergelb* (imperial yellow) and white plaster-work.

The spa tradition

Following the Habsburg tradition, **spa treatments** remain extremely popular in the Czech and Slovak republics, which boast over a hundred spa resorts (*lázně* in Czech, *kúpele* in Slovak) between them. One of the chief perks of the Communist system, they were a form of healthcare open to all and usually paid for by one's employers (ie the state). Children, the elderly and the generally ill and infirm are still prescribed spa treatments by their doctors – it is often very difficult to book a cure, with huge waiting lists. Nowadays, the spas also attract an increasing number of Germans, Austrians and wealthy Russians, for whom stays are still relatively inexpensive compared to Western prices. At a few resorts, such as Mariánské Lázně, you can book in for half- or full-day "treatments", but most are intended for longer stays (three weeks is the norm for those sent by their doctors). If you're paying "foreign rates" for your visit, you don't actually have to be ill to be treated. Some people find spa resorts rather like open hospitals, but many are beautifully situated deep in the countryside, with fresh air and constitutionals very much part of the cure.

The basic treatment involves drinking the mineral waters from the spa's natural springs, for which many guests use their own ornate drinking vessels called *becher*. These curious miniature teapots each have a spout through which you sip the waters, thus preventing discolouration of the teeth. The waters come in an amazing variety: alkaline, chlorinated, carbogaseous and even radioactive, though they usually share one common characteristic: they are all pretty foul, or at least an acquired taste. In addition – and this is the more appealing bit – you can bathe in hot springs or sapropelic muds, breathe in pungent fumes or indulge in a new generation of complementary therapies, such as ultrasound and aerosol treatment, ultraviolet light baths, acupuncture and electrotherapy. Each spa resort tends to specialize in "curing" a particular ailment. For example, Františkovy Lázně is the best place for gynaecological problems; Luhačovice for respiratory diseases; Karlovy Vary for digestive complaints; and Trenčianske Teplice for motor problems. The most famous (and most oversubscribed) of the spa resorts are Karlovy Vary, Třeboň and Mariánské Lázně in Bohemia, Luhačovice in Moravia and Piešťany in Slovakia, but Ⓦwww.spas.cz, the official website, contains full information on all treatments going, and where they're on offer in the Czech Republic.

Hlavní třída

Hlavní třída, the spa's main thoroughfare, is several kilometres long, and forms an almost uninterrupted parade of luxury, four-storey mansions, most of which are hotels, glass shops or granny-filled cafés. The vast majority are thoroughly in keeping with the fin-de-siècle ambience of the place. There are, however, one or two hideous modern hotels built over the last decade, though even these have failed to impinge on the most impressive final section of the street, where layer upon layer of shapely balconies overlook the spa gardens. Several of the shops here sell tins of *oplatky*, the ubiquitous sugar- or chocolate-filled wafers which make the waters you are about to taste infinitely more palatable. At no. 47 is the *Bílá labut'* (The White Swan), a modest three-storey building where Frédéric Chopin stayed in 1836 on his way from Paris to Warsaw. Known as the **dům Chopin**, it serves as the spa's tourist office, and has a tiny museum to the composer on the first floor.

The spa's **synagogue**, which stood on Hlavní třída itself, was burnt down in 1938 on *Kristallnacht*, and no trace now remains. By contrast, the spa's small, red-brick **Anglikánský kostel** (Anglican church; Tues–Sun 9am–noon & 12.30–4pm) survives, hidden in the trees behind the *Hotel Bohemia*. Abandoned by its royal patrons and neglected under the Communists, the church has recently been restored, and is now used as an exhibition space. All that remains of the interior, however, is the pulpit, a rose window and a plaque to its most famous patron, King Edward VII. Better preserved is the nearby neo-Byzantine **Pravoslavský kostel** (Russian Orthodox church; May–Oct Mon–Fri 8.30am–noon & 1–4.30pm, Sat 8.30am–4.30pm; Nov–April daily 9.30–11.30am & 2–4pm) on Ruská, the road running parallel to Hlavní třída. Dating from 1902, the rather plain interior is made remarkable by the spectacular iconostasis that won the Grand Prix de France at the 1900 Paris World Exhibition. Designed in the shape of a miniature Orthodox church, and made from enamel and porcelain, it is coated in over nine kilograms of gold and cobalt, and is reputedly the largest piece of porcelain in the world. Mass is still held in the church every Sunday.

Around the Kolonáda

The focal point of the spa, overlooking the town, is the gently curving **Kolonáda**. Easily the most beautiful wrought-iron colonnade in Bohemia, it's rather like a whale-ribbed nineteenth-century railway station without the trains, and despite the lurid 1970s ceiling frescoes, the atmosphere is genteel and sober. In summer, there are daily concerts by Bohemian bands, occasional performances by the local symphony orchestra, and over-priced carriage rides around the spa (200Kč for ten minutes). Adjoining the northern tip of the colonnade is the spa's first and foremost spring, the **Křížový pramen**, housed in its very own Neoclassical colonnade and reputed to be good for one's kidneys. There are five further springs in the main Kolonáda with two more in Ušovice (see p.228). However, access to the life-giving faucets is restricted (daily 6am–noon & 4–6pm).

Beyond the southern end of the Kolonáda stands the **zpívající fontána**, a computer-controlled dancing fountain, no great beauty, which does its thing to a popular piece of classical music roughly every two hours until 10pm (the last two shows are accompanied by a light display – see the nearby poster for the latest programme). Beyond and, more importantly, out of earshot of the fountain, is the elegant Neoclassical colonnade of the **Karolinin pramen**, whose springs spurt forth water round the clock. The town is patrolled by special spa police, who impose strict fines on those discovered parking in the spa centre or committing crimes against health – it is still forbidden to smoke in this part of the spa.

Behind and above the colonnades lies **Goethovo náměstí**, which boasts a new aluminium, seated statue of Goethe; the original was carried off by the retreating Nazis, leaving just the granite plinth, to which the Czechs added a commemorative postwar plaque in Czech, Latin and French (but, significantly, not German). On his last visit in 1823, Goethe stayed at the house on the corner that now houses the **Městské muzeum** (Wed–Sun 9am–noon & 1–4pm). On the ground floor, the displays trace the history of the spa's development; upstairs, along with period furnishings from Goethe's time, there are new historical sections that are more frank about the spa's German roots (and about the American liberation), but still silent on the postwar expulsions that more or less cleared the spa of its remaining inhabitants.

The square is overlooked by yet more giant, ochre spa buildings, including the **Hotel Weimar**, at no. 9, in which King Edward VII preferred to stay (above the central portico there's a well-concealed German Gothic plaque commemorating his visit). Below, at the centre of the square, is the unusual octagonal church of **Nanebevzetí Panna Maria** (Assumption of the Virgin Mary), decorated inside in rich neo-Byzantine style. Still further down the hill are two buildings definitely worth checking out. The first is the old **Casino** building, now the spa's main social centre, with an old faded dance hall (discos on most nights) of fin-de-siècle marbled elegance; the other is the equally ornate **Nové lázně** (T & F354 644 111; Mon–Fri 9am–3pm, Sat 9am–noon; booking recommended at least two weeks in advance; ❽). Recently restored and over a century old, it accepts "outpatients" for nude wallows in the colonnaded Roman baths, massages, mud baths and peat packs (all heftily priced in euros); you can also stay here, although treatments are not available on Saturday afternoons and Sundays. Ask for a carbon dioxide bath in *kabina 1*, which was fitted out for Edward VII and large enough to encompass his considerable bulk.

Walks around the spa

Even if you're not booked in for treatment, you should participate in the other spa rituals – drinking the water, wolfing down the wafers and taking the obligatory constitutional. Mariánské Lázně's altitude lends an almost subalpine freshness to the air, even at the height of summer, and **walking** is as important to "the cure" as are the various specialized treatments. To this end, the expert nineteenth-century landscape gardener Václav Skalník was employed to transform the valley into an open park, providing an intricate network of paths leading to the many springs dotted around the surrounding countryside.

There are several maps posted up by the Kolonáda which show the various marked walks around the spa; armed with a *plán města* (available from most hotels, bookshops and newsagents), you can head off on your own. Goethe's favourite walk, up to the *Miramonte* for morning coffee, is retraced by most visitors, though the café has since been converted into a *lázně dům* (spa home) for kids; head north to the *Café Panoráma* for refreshment, instead. The energetic can continue to the lower town of **Úšovice** whence you can return to town via the Rudolfův and Ferdinandův springs, where, according to one tourist brochure, you can experience "hypotonic calcareous magnesium hydrogen carbonate ferrugineous acidulous waters".

There are several vantage points to head for in order to enjoy a **panoramic view** of the spa: Na Polomu (805m) or the Podhorn (847m), north along the strenuous red-marked paths; or, with considerably less exertion, the old **Kaiserturm** or *rozhledna* (723m), on the hillside southeast of the spa. Another option is to take the **chairlift** (*lánova draha*; daily: May–Sept 9.30am–5pm; Oct–April 9.30am–4.30pm) from the *Koliba* up Dusíkova, which will transport you to the *Hotel Krakanoš* (currently closed). Those with small kids might want to take a peek at the nearby **Miniaturpark**, a low-key, fairly risible stab at a miniature world.

Practicalities

Passengers arriving by train or bus are unloaded at a suitably discreet distance from the spa, some 3km south of the centre; trolleybus #5 covers the 3km up the former Kaiserstrasse, now Hlavní třída. The **tourist office** (daily 10am–noon & 12.30–6pm, ☎354 622 474, ⓦwww.marienbad.cz) is in the dům Chopin at Hlavní 47. Although none too friendly, it does have maps and basic information, should help with accommodation (see below) and features its own **internet** café (daily 9am–6pm), plus seven private rooms (❷) without bath or shower, which are the cheapest in town.

Accommodation

The tourist office can book **private rooms**, or, if you have your own transport, you can search for pensions and rooms for yourself in the suburbs of Úšovice and on Palackého street, where they predominate. There's also a vast choice of spa **hotels**, all run by Hungarian-owned Danubius Hotels (☎354 655 555, ⓦwww.marianbad.cz), based at Léčebné Lázně, Masaryková 22, which can be reserved one day in advance and are all fairly pricey (❹–❾). Be warned that, in high season, prices rise to a minimum of €100 for a double room in a central hotel, and those undergoing spa treatments will always get first refusal.

There are also two **campsites** to choose from: *Autokemping Luxor* (May–Sept), which is awkwardly located several kilometres to the west of the train station in Velká Hled'sebe, along the road to Cheb (bus #6 to Velká Hled'sebe, then walk 1km south down the Plzeň road; ☎354 623 504); and *Start*, on Plzeňská (open all year), a small campsite with motel and cheap bungalows (❷), walking distance from the train station, but a touch noisy.

Hotel Bohemia Hlavní třída 100 ☎354 623 251. Late-nineteenth-century hotel, somewhat brutally modernized, but still fairly classy and very comfortable: all rooms come with en-suite facilities and satellite TV. ❺

Hotel Esplanade Karlovarská 438 ☎224 193 876, ⓦwww.esplanade-marienbad.cz. Probably the snazziest of the bunch. ❽

Hotel Helga Třebízkého 10 ☎354 620 433. Friendly, fairly swish, family-run hotel with a decent restaurant, just beyond the top of Hlavní třída. ❹

Hvězda Goethovo nám. 7 ☎354 631 111, ⓔhvezda@marienbad.cz. Yet another comfortable, opulent pile in the centre of town, offering spa treatments and part of the spa hotel group. ❺

Hotel Kossuth/Suvurov Ruská 77 ☎354 622 861. Two cheap hotels, a few doors down from each other, that have joined forces. Quiet location, good views but absolutely no frills. ❸

Nové Lázně Reitenbergerova 53 ☎354 644 111 or 354 644 051, ⓔnovelazne@marienbad.cz. If you're staying for the cure, this is the place to stay, with its full-blown 1890s opulence. ❽

Hotel Polonia Hlavní třída 50 ☎354 622 451, ⓕ354 622 452. Simply modernized, but dripping with original fin-de-siècle features in the foyer and the café; ask for a room overlooking the spa gardens. ❺

Hotel Villa Butterfly Hlavní 131 ☎354 622 807, ⓔvillabutterfly@iol.cz. Luxurious and modern, with sauna, restaurant and *Café de Paris*. ❼

Zlatý zámek Klíčová 4 ☎ & ⓕ354 623 924. Clean to the point of sterility, but exceptional value for its central locale. ❶

Eating, drinking and entertainment

Café Polonia, at Hlavní třída 50, is probably Mariánské Lázně's most opulent surviving **café** offering stucco decoration as rich as its cakes. The choice of **restaurants** has improved over the last decade, with the moderately expensive *Villa Romana* on Anglická, a pretty stylish number, and romantic *U zlaté koule*, just east of Mírové náměstí at Nehrova 26, starring live violin and piano in the evenings. The *Classic* restaurant, just down from the *Excelsior* at Hlavní třída 50, has fewer pretensions, and is especially recommended for vegetarians. *Hotel Helvetia*'s basement features a typical Czech pub that's popular with the locals, but there's also a young, lively Irish pub at Poštovní 96.

There's usually a fair bit of highbrow **entertainment** on offer, including an international music festival in early summer, operetta three times a week in the theatre, once-weekly concerts by the Marienbad Symphony Orchestra, an annual week-long Chopin festival in mid-August, plus a Chopin music competition for young pianists every odd-numbered year in the first week in July. For **late-night spots**, you can try your hand in the splendid surroundings of the old casino. Mariánské Lázně also boasts the best **golf course** in the former Eastern bloc. Originally built for Edward VII, it was the first to hold a PGA Tour event in the 1990s; to get there, take one of the five daily buses (#12) to the *Hotel Golf* or simply walk for thirty-odd minutes from the town centre.

Lázně Kynžvart and Teplá

If you're looking for a longer excursion out of Mariánské Lázně, you could spend the afternoon walking over to **LÁZNĚ KYNŽVART** (Königswart), 10km northwest of town. Now an untypically designed, Swiss wooden chalet-style children's spa (W www.spas.cz/kynzvart), it was founded in the 1820s by the Metternich family as their own private spa, where they entertained Goethe, Beethoven and Dumas (among others) at their originally Baroque **zámek** (Tues–Sun 9am–12.30pm & 1–5pm; W www.top.cz/pamatky-plz/kynzvart), rebuilt as a Neoclassical, Empire-style mansion in the following decade by Pietro Nobile. Recently opened after more than a decade of renovation work, the chateau contains a valuable library stuffed with incunabula, rare prints and manuscripts and a museum full of lots of period furniture and Metternich mementoes; it's surrounded by a large English park. If your legs aren't up to the return journey, the nearest train station is 2km southeast of the chateau.

A longer day-trip is to the monastery at **TEPLÁ** (Tepl), 15km to the east off route 24, whose abbots used to own the springs at Mariánské Lázně. The **Klášter premonstrátů** (daily: May–Oct 9am–4.30pm; Feb–April, Nov & Dec 9am–3pm) – used as an army barracks until the 1960s, then renovated after 1989 – is 1km east of the village along the Toužim road. It's easy enough to spot, thanks to the plain stone towers of the original twelfth-century monastery church, though the rest of the monastery carries the universal stamp of the Baroque Counter-Reformation, courtesy of the Dientzenhofer duo. However, the real reason for coming here is to see the neo-Baroque library (*nová knihovna*); built in the 1900s, it boasts almost edible stucco decoration, triple-decker bookshelves and swirling black iron balconies framed by white pilasters. Many visitors choose to stay at the *Hospice Teplá monastery* (T 353 392 264; ❹), listen to the frequently-held summer organ concerts, or simply tuck into hearty meals at the excellent restaurant.

If your next stop is Karlovy Vary, be sure to take the train, which winds its way painstakingly slowly but picturesquely for 50km, via Teplá, through the **Slavkovský les**, the thick forest that lies between the two spas.

Cheb

CHEB (Eger), 10km from the German border, is a typical Czech frontier town, with prostitutes lining the main roads, and Vietnamese stallholders occupying the centre of town. For many Western visitors it's their first taste of the Czech Republic, and for most, it's a slightly bewildering introduction. Cheb is a beautiful historic town, but it is also primarily a German one, and postwar expulsion of the German-speaking population left it with less than a third of its prewar population, and an identity crisis of mammoth proportions (see box p.232). Money was poured into the town, but Czechs were reluctant to move here (not so Romanies, Hungarians and Slovaks who were financially encouraged here to work). The root of the malaise lay in the authorities' ambivalence to Cheb, simultaneously encouraging its future and denying its past. Nevertheless, the town's historic centre is worth an afternoon stopoff – even if it is overrun by German day-trippers for much of the summer.

ACCOMMODATION
Hostel 1
Hvězda 2

RESTAURANTS,
CAFÉS & PUBS
Café-Galerie U Kamene C
Radniční sklípek B
U koček A

CHEB

sv Bartoloměj

Chebský hrad

sv. Mikuláš

sv. Anna

Galerie G4

Chebské muzeum

Špaliček

Galerie výtvarného umění

District Library

Poor Clares Convent

Západočeské divadlo

0   100 m

Bus & Train Stations (500 m)

The Town

Cheb's showpiece main square, **náměstí krále Jiřího z Poděbrad**, is named after one of the few Czech leaders the *Egerländer* ever willingly supported. Established in the twelfth century, but today lined with handsome, mostly seventeenth-century houses, with steeply pitched red roofs, this was the old *Marktplatz*, the commercial and political heart of Egerland for eight centuries. After four decades of neglect, commercial life has returned once more, with numerous cafés and restaurants breathing life into the square. The batch of half-timbered buildings huddled together at the bottom of the square, known as **Špalíček** (*Stöckl* in German), forms a picturesque ensemble; originally medieval German-Jewish merchant houses, they now house a café and several shops.

In the backstreets to the west of the main square, the parade of seventeenth-century German merchants' houses continues unabated. Cheb's first medieval **Jewish ghetto** is recalled in the street name, Židovská (Jewish Street), though the community was wiped out in a bloody pogrom in 1350; Jews were later expelled on another two occasions, in 1430 and 1502. Nothing remains of the 500-strong Jewish community that came under sustained attack during the 1930s as the Sudeten German Party rose to prominence in the region. Fascist thugs butchered a pig in the local synagogue shortly before its official opening, and *Kristallnacht* demolished what was left.

Egerland

Most Germans still refer to Cheb as **Eger**, the name given to the town by the German colonists who settled here from the eleventh century onwards. The settlers were typically hard-working and proud of their folk traditions and peculiar dialect. Aided by its status as a Free Imperial City of the Holy Roman Empire, the town soon came to dominate trade between Bavaria and Bohemia. Shunted around between Babenbergs, Swabians and Přemyslids, Egerland finally accepted the suzerainty of King John of Luxembourg in 1322, in return for certain privileges, and in fact the *Egerländer* remained self-governing until well into the nineteenth century.

Hardly surprising, then, that the town was at the centre of the (anti-Semitic) **Pan-German Schönerer movement** of the late nineteenth century, which fought desperately against the advance of Czech nationalism, aided and abetted (as they saw it) by the weak and liberal Habsburg state. Here, too, was the most vociferous protest against the 1897 Badeni Decrees, which granted the Czech language equal status with German throughout the Czech Lands. The establishment of Czechoslovakia in 1918 was seen as a serious setback by most *Egerländer*, who made no bones about where their real sympathies lay; Eger remained the only town to successfully rebuff all attempts at putting up street names in Czech as well as German.

Thus, in the 1930s, the pro-Nazi **Sudeten German Party** (SdP) found Egerland receptive to its anti-Semitism as much as to its irredentism. Although it's estimated that a quarter of the German-speaking voters stubbornly refused to vote for the SdP, the majority of *Egerländer* welcomed their incorporation into the Third Reich, completed in 1938. At the end of World War II, only those Germans who could prove themselves to have been actively anti-fascist (Czechs were luckily exempted from this acid test) were permitted to remain on Czechoslovak soil; the others were bodily kicked out, reducing the population of Cheb to twenty-seven percent of its pre-war level. The mass expulsions were accompanied by numerous acts of vengeance, and the issue remains a delicate one. Havel's suggestion in his first presidential address that an apology to the Germans was in order remains one of the most unpopular statements of his entire presidency.

△ Cheb

Chebské muzeum and art gallery

Behind Špalíček lurks the **Chebské muzeum**, which first opened to the public
in 1874 on náměstí Krále Jiřího z Poděbrad 3 (March–Dec Tues–Sun
9am–12.30pm & 1–5pm; 50Kč, 100Kč to take photographs), in the former
Stadthaus where **Albrecht von Waldstein** (better known as Wallenstein from the
trilogy by Schiller, written during the author's stay here in 1791), generalissimo of
the Thirty Years' War, was murdered in 1634 following a decree by Emperor
Ferdinand II. The museum pays great attention to this event, and the heavy Gothic
woodwork of his reconstructed bedroom provides an evocative setting for
Waldstein's murder, graphically illustrated on the walls; however, Cheb's more
recent history is studiously avoided. (For more on Waldstein, see p.291).

The **Galerie výtvarného umění** (Gallery of Fine Arts; daily 9am–5pm), in
the Baroque nová radnice at no. 16 on the square, seems strangely out of context in a town with such rich traditions of its own, focusing as it does on Czech
modern art. Few of the town's predominantly German tourists pay a visit to the
temporary exhibitions, the superb collection of fourteenth- and fifteenth-century Bohemian sculpture, or to the wide-ranging permanent collection of modern Czech art. Kicking off with the 1890 generation, led by Jan Preisler and
Antonín Procházka, there are several memorable paintings depicting Prague
cityscapes, including the Belvedere, St Vitus Cathedral, and a red-and-cream city
tram. More surprising is the large contingent of Cubist and Fauvist canvases,
including a vivid blue *River Otava* by Václav Špála. In place of the usual Socialist
Realism, a thought-provoking postwar collection rounds off the gallery.

Another private gallery worth visiting is **Galerie G4** (Tues–Fri 10am–6pm,
Sat 10am–5pm), at Kamenná 2, which regularly puts on excellent temporary
photographic exhibitions.

Beyond the main square

Cheb's two largest buildings, dating from the town's early history, are out of
keeping with the red-roofed uniformity of the seventeenth-century *Altstadt*.
The church of **sv Mikuláš** has a bizarre multifaceted roof, like the scales of a
dinosaur, though since the renowned local-born architect Balthasar Neumann
restored the interior in the eighteenth century, only the bulky towers remain

from the original thirteenth-century building, conceived as a monumental Romanesque basilica. Very few of the original furnishings survive, and most of what you see is neo-Gothic infill, but there are two very fine Renaissance tombs worth inspecting inside the porch of the south door.

In the northwestern corner of the town walls, by the River Ohře (Eger), is the **Chebský hrad** (June–Aug Tues–Sun 9am–noon & 1–6pm; March & Oct 9am–noon & 1–4pm; May & Sept 9am–noon & 1–5pm; tours bookable on ☎354 422 942), or Kaiserburg as it used to be known; the sprawl of ruins built on and with volcanic rock is all that remains of the twelfth-century castle bequeathed by that obsessive crusader, the Holy Roman emperor Frederick Barbarossa, in 1179 on the foundations of a Slavic hill fort. In among the Baroque fortifications, the Gothic Černá věž (Black Tower) presents an impressive front and offers peeks at Cheb's chimneys and roof-tiles through its tiny windows. In the northeastern corner, the lower storey of the ruined chapel with its beautifully carved Romanesque capitals will give you an idea of the castle of Barbarossa's time. You may also want to catch some of the summer plays put on in the castle, if your Czech or German is up to it.

Practicalities

Had you arrived at Cheb's **train station** before 1945, you'd have had the impression of never having left Germany: by a quirk of railway history, the Deutsche Bundesbahn built and ran all the lines heading west out of Eger. It's a none too pleasant ten-minute walk from the ugly postwar station, north along **Svobody**, to the old town.

The **tourist office** is at no. 33 on the main square (Mon–Fri 9am–5pm, Sat 10am–2pm, also open on Sun May–Sept 10am–1.30pm; ☎354 422 705, ⓦ www.mestocheb.cz), has information about the annual festivals, such as the autumn Jazz Jamm and the summer organ concerts, and can sell you a Chebcard, giving discounted entry into the town's three main sights. They can also help with **accommodation**, though the choice is fairly limited, and, in many ways, you'd be better off staying the night in nearby Františkovy Lázně (see below). There's basically one half-decent **hotel** in Cheb, the *Hvězda*, on the main square (☎354 422 549; ❸), plus a number of small pensions, and a **hostel** at Židovská 7 (☎354 423 401). Otherwise, there's a **campsite**, *Camp Karel* (Jesenická přehrada, ☎354 430 033, mid-May to mid-Sept), 5km away at Dřenice by the artificial lake, Jesenickýpřehrada (plus the *Amerika* site in Františkovy Lázně) where windsurfing is all the rage.

There are several **places to eat** on the main square, which basically cater for German tourists – they're not bad for a drink and to soak in the surroundings, but for something more traditional try *U koček* for old Bohemian cuisine, at Kamenná 1, or *Radniční sklípek*, a cosy wine cellar on the main square. *Café-Galerie U Kamene* is a friendly source of coffee on the main square, and you can download your **emails** at the district library, Obrněné brigády 1, *Net Café* in the Economics Faculty building on Hradební 22, or *Arachna Web* at Hradební 17. *Rock Café Elektra*, opposite the train station on Žižkova, is the town's alternative nightspot, with regular gigs; *Kino Art*, Kamenná 5, puts on some interesting art-house films.

Františkovy Lázně

"The present Františkovy Lázně has nothing of historic interest", wrote Nagel's Guide in the 1960s, casually dismissing a town hailed by Goethe as "paradise

FRANTIŠKOVY LÁZNĚ

ACCOMMODATION
Květen	2
Melodie	1
Tři lilie	3

RESTAURANTS & CAFÉS
Café Milano	C
Sadová kavarna	A
Toša	B

Train Station (250m)

Campsite (1.5km)

Campsite (1.5km)

on earth".Yet while **FRANTIŠKOVY LÁZNĚ** (Franzensbad), 5km north of Cheb and linked by regular trains, may not boast any individual architectural gems, it is, in many ways, *the* archetypal spa town. Originally known as Egerbrunnen, the spa was founded in 1793 and named Franzensbad after the then Habsburg emperor Franz I. Laid out in the early nineteenth century, the Neoclassical architecture of the period finds its way into every building – even the cinema has Doric pillars – and virtually every conceivable building has been daubed in the soft ochre colour of *Kaisergelb*.The centre of the spa is barely five streets across, and surrounded on all sides by a backdrop of luscious greenery.The virtual absence of vehicles and rowdy nightlife makes it the most peaceful of the spas, though as patients stagger about and people in white coats run between buildings, it can resemble a large, open-plan hospital.

The Town

From the ochre-coloured train station, the road opens out onto the former *Kurpark* or **Městské sady**, whose principal path leads diagonally to a white, wooden bandstand at the head of pedestrianized **Národní**, the spa's modestly elegant main boulevard, lined with potted palms and diminutive lime trees. Beethoven stayed at no. 7 in 1812, as the German plaque by the entrance recalls; while *U tří lilie*, the eponymous garden café further down, features in a poem by the Czech surrealist Vítězslav Nezval.You can sit outside and take in the scene from *Café Corso* or one of the street's other cafés with al fresco tables.

At the bottom of Národní, a plain Neoclassical rotunda shelters the **Františkův pramen** (Franzensquelle; daily 8–11.30am & 12.30–4.30pm). While the faithful queue to have their receptacles filled from the dazzling brass pipes, the real spa snobs retire to drink from their beakers by the fruit-encrusted sphinxes or under the nearby modern colonnade. Don't worry if you've come unprepared, as you can buy a plastic cupful, though, like most spa water,

235

it's pretty unpalatable, on this occasion due to its high sulphur content. You've an even greater choice of tipple at the **Glauberovy pramen** (daily 7–11.30am & 1–5pm), to the south: more or less salty, and hot or cold. A different kind of faith drives women to touch the feet (and particularly another more specific part which is in danger of getting rubbed off) of a repulsive bronze cherub who sits holding a phallic fish, not far from the spring: in addition to treating diseases of the motor system and heart, Františkovy Lázně specializes in the treatment of gynecological problems, and popular myth has it that doing so will ensure fertility.

The Neoclassical church of **sv Kříž**, dating from 1820, strikes an appropriately imperial pose at one end of Jiráskova, another riot of princely mansions with wrought-iron balconies. A more intriguing church is that of **sv Olga**, a richly decorated Russian Orthodox church on Kollárova. Set apart from the other spa buildings, and a favourite with visiting Germans, is Františkovy Lázně's finest spa villa, the **Imperial**, its corner balconies held up by caryatids. In the **Městské muzeum**, dr. Pohoreckého 8 (Tues–Fri 10am–noon & 1–5pm, Sat & Sun 10am–4pm), you can see previous generations of Teutonic guests being subjected to gruesome nineteenth-century cures; don't miss the man with a leech on each buttock, held in place by two jam jars.

Walks and excursions

As with all the Bohemian spas, the formal parks quickly give way to untamed woodland, the difference being that in Františkovy Lázně the landscape is almost entirely flat, which is easier on the legs but shorter on views. A two-kilometre **walk** through the silver birches will take you to Lake Amerika (in dry weather a **mini-train**, or *mikrovláček*, runs every 30min), though swimming is not advisable. On the other side of town, a path marked by red hearts leads to the popular *Zámeček Café*, hidden away amidst the acacia.

A **longer walk** will take you to Cheb itself, just over 5km south; follow the red markers down Klostermannova. Alternatively, it's 7km northeast to **Soos**, a small area of peatland pockmarked with **hot gaseous springs**. As you approach the place in summer, the smell of salt emanating from the mini-geysers wafts across from the marsh. A nature trail raised above the bogland allows closer inspection of the springs that gurgle and bubble just above the surface, staining the land with a brown-yellow crust. A unique phenomenon in mainland Europe, the area attracts rare species of flora and fauna – not to mention insects, which make it no place to linger in the height of summer. Soos is also accessible by train from Cheb: three stops to Nový Drahov on the Luby u Chebu line.

Practicalities

Františkovy Lázně may not be the busiest spot in Bohemia, but with large numbers of Czech patients plus some tourists vying for **beds**, it can sometimes be difficult to find a place. It's occasionally possible to stay in spa hotels for one night, but spa guests always have priority and you'll have to pay in euros if you're not a Czech resident. Probably the nicest place to stay is the *Tři lilie*, Národní třída 3 (T & F354 208 900; ❺), which has been sensitively modernized and also houses the local **spa and tourist information office** (T & F354 542 430, Mon–Fri 8am–5pm, Sat 9am–1pm). Additional information offices exist at Četur, Anglická 5 (T354 542 210, spa info only) and FL-Tour, Americká 2 (T354 543 162, town info only). Cheaper options include the *Květen* (T354 542 025; ❸), the spa hotel opposite, and the private *Melodie* on Francouská (T354 543 577; ❸), whose green shutters overlook the Městské sady. The *Amerika* **campsite** (U Jezera, April–Oct, ☎354 542 518) with wooden **bungalows** is 1.5km southwest of the town by the lake; you can get there on the mini-train, and can hire boats once you're there. All the above-mentioned hotels have reasonable **restaurants**, with the *Tři lilie* far and away the best (and most expensive), with a pleasant café, and the *Goethe*, on Národní, locally renowned for its French restaurant. The *Café Milano*, next to the departure point of the *mikrovláček* on Máchova, is a popular outdoor place. *Toša* on Jirasková ulice serves decent coffee and cakes, and the *Sadová kavarna* and the *Lázeňský dům café* at the north entrance of the colonnade offers good set menus.

Karlovy Vary

KARLOVY VARY (Karlsbad) is the undisputed king of the famous triangle of Bohemian spas, with by far the most illustrious guest list of European notables. What makes it so special is its wonderful hilly setting – *Belle époque* mansions pile on top of one another along the steeply wooded banks of the endlessly twisting River Teplá. It is best known throughout the world by its German name, **Karlsbad** (Carlsbad in its anglicized form), and it was German-speakers who made up the vast majority of the town's population until their forced expulsion in 1945. Despite this violent uprooting, the spa has survived and continues to attract an international clientele – largely Russians – which annually doubles the local population, further supplemented in the summer by thousands of able-bodied day visitors, the greatest number of whom are, naturally, German.

Tradition credits the Emperor Charles IV (or rather one of his hunting dogs) with discovery of the springs (hence Karlsbad); in actual fact, the village of Vary (which means "boiling" in Czech) had existed for centuries before Charles' trip, though he did found a German town here in around 1350 and set a precedent for subsequent Bohemian rulers by granting Karlsbad various privileges. By the nineteenth century its position at the meeting point of two great German-speaking empires, and the much heralded efficacy of its waters, ensured the most impressive visitors' book in Europe. In addition, a lot of money has been spent over the last decade to ensure that Karlovy Vary returns to something like its former glory.

Arrival, information and accommodation

The main train station or **horní nádraží** is to the north of the River Ohře, while the **dolní nádraží** (where trains from Mariánské Lázně arrive), off Západní, and the **bus station**, on Varšavská, are next to each other, south of the river. Don't leave hopping off the Prague bus to the bus station; along with everyone else, get off at Tržnice, one stop before, which is rather more central. Wherever you arrive, you're basically in the unattractive, northern part of town, where the otherwise invisible local residents live and shop. The spa proper stretches south along the winding Teplá Valley and, in fact, the best way to approach Karlovy Vary is from the south. However, to do that you need your own transport, in which case you'll have the devil of a job finding somewhere safe to park it, as parking and traffic in the centre of the spa are strictly controlled.

For general **information** (and help with accommodation), there's a small kiosk called *City-Info*, opposite the post office on T.G. Masaryka (Mon–Fri 9am–5pm, Sat 8am–5pm, Sun 10am–4pm). For information, both general and specifically on **spa treatment**, go to the *Kur-Info* office in the Vřídelní kolonáda (Mon–Fri 7am–5pm, Sat 9am–4pm; ☏353 224 097, Ⓦwww.karlovyvary.cz).

Accommodation

Karlovy Vary can get pretty busy in the summer, especially in July during the film festival (see p.242), so it's best to start looking for **accommodation** early in the day. W Privat, an office on náměstí Republiky (Mon–Fri 8.30am–5pm, Sat & Sun 9am–1pm), can organize **private rooms**. If you're **camping**, head for the site with bungalows (❷) near the *Motel Gejzír* (April–Oct) on Slovenská, south and upstream from the *Grand Hotel Pupp*; take bus #7 from the local bus station.

Astoria Vřídelní 23 ☎353 228 224, ℻353 235 259. Central, quiet spa hotel, bang opposite the Kolonáda. ➍
Clara Na kopečku 23 ☎353 449 983. Very comfortable pension out of town beyond the railway station, at rock-bottom prices for this spa. ➋–➌
Grand Hotel Pupp Mírové náměstí 2 ☎353 109 111, ⓦwww.pupp.cz. They don't come better (nor more expensive) than this outside Prague – 6000Kč a double and upwards – and though the decor is pretty stunning, the service is not as good as it should be for the price. ➒
Heluan Tržiště 41 ☎353 225 756, ⒺHeluan@plz.pvtnet.cz. Peaceful hotel, with spacious, tastefully uncluttered en-suite rooms. ➍
Kavalerie T.G. Masaryka 43 ☎353 229 613, ℻353 266 171. Relatively cheap, but at the wrong end of town, near the bus station and not in the spa proper. ➌

Kolonáda I.P. Pavlova 8 ☎353 131 111, Ⓔreservation@kolonadahotel.cz. Very plush and efficient place; rooms have all mod cons, and there's even a sauna, and an acceptable cellar restaurant. ➍
Puškin Tržiště 37 ☎353 222 646, ⒺPuskin@volny.cz. Decent doubles with breakfast, in the central section of the spa. ➎
U tří mouřenínů Stará louka 2 ☎353 235 053, Ⓔpenkucera@plz.pvtnet.cz. Pension occupying two adjacent buildings; clean and reasonably priced for its prime central location. ➌
Vila Basileia Mariánskolázeňská 2 ☎353 224 132, ℻353 227 804. Secluded late-nineteenth-century villa at the quiet, southern end of the spa, close to the *Pupp*, with just six large en-suite rooms on offer. ➌

The spa

Unfortunately, many visitors' first impressions of Karlovy Vary are marred by the unavoidable sight of the **Thermal** sanatorium, an inexcusable concrete scab built in the 1970s, for whose sake a large slice of the old town bit the dust. It serves as home base for the annual film festival, and there's a certain perverse appeal to the faded 1970s kitsch interior decor, but the most useful aspect of the *Thermal* is its open-air *bazén*, a spring-water **swimming pool** set high up above the river (daily during daylight hours). The poolside view over the town is wonderful, but don't be taken in by the clouds of steam – the water is only tepid.

On the other side of the River Teplá from the *Thermal*, the late-nineteenth-century grandeur of Karlovy Vary begins to unfold along the river banks. The first of a series of colonnades designed by the Viennese duo Helmer and Fellner is the **Sadová kolonáda**, a delicate white-and-grey colonnade made of wrought iron. As the valley narrows, the river disappears under a wide terrace in front of Josef Zítek's graceful **Mlýnská kolonáda** (Mühlbrunnen Colonnade), whose forest of columns shelters four separate springs, each one more scalding than the last. At the next bend in the river stands the **Tržní kolonáda**, designed by Helmer and Fellner as a temporary structure, but one whose intricate whitewashed woodwork has lasted for over a century. Directly opposite is the **dům Zawojski** (now the Živnostenska banka), one of the best Art Nouveau houses in the spa, with its green wrought-iron and gilded detailing. Rising above the colonnade is the **Zámecká věž** (Schlossberg), the only link with the spa's founder, Charles IV, built on the site of his original hunting lodge.

Most powerful of the twelve springs is the **Vřídlo** or Sprudel, which belches out over 2500 gallons of water every hour. The old wrought-iron **Vřídelní kolonáda** (daily 6am–6.30pm) was melted down for armaments by the Nazis, and only finally replaced in the 1970s by a rather uninspiring modern building, which the Communists liked to call the Yuri Gagarin Colonnade (his statue once stood outside, but now resides at the local airport). The smooth marble floor allows patients to shuffle up and down contentedly, while inside the glass rotunda the geyser pops and splutters, shooting hot water forty feet upwards. Ensuing clouds of steam obscure what would otherwise be a perfect view of Kilian Ignaz Dientzenhofer's Baroque masterpiece, the church of **sv Maria Magdaléna**, pitched nearby on a precipitous site. The light, pink interior, full of playful oval shapes, is a striking contrast with the relentlessly nineteenth-century air of the rest of the town.

If you've forgotten your cure cup, you can buy the faintly ridiculous *becher* vessels from one of the many souvenir shops. The purpose behind these is to avoid colouring your teeth with the water, though plenty of people cut costs and buy a plastic cup. Popular wisdom has it that "when the disorder becomes a disease, doctors prescribe the hot waters of Carlsbad" – in other words, it's strong stuff. In the eighteenth century, the poor were advised to drink up to five hundred cups of the salty waters to cure the disease of poverty. The German playwright Schiller (who came here on his honeymoon in 1791) drank eighteen cups and lived to tell the tale, but generally no more than five to seven cups a day are recommended.

Stará and Nová louka

South of the Sprudel is Karlovy Vary's most famous shopping street, the **Stará louka** (Alte Wiese), described rather mystifyingly by Le Corbusier as "a set of *Torten* (cakes) all the same style and the same elegance". Its shops, which once rivalled Vienna's Kärntnerstrasse, are beginning once more to exude the snobbery of former days – there's even a branch of Versace at the far end of the street. Don't miss the Moser shop (everyone who's anyone, from Stalin to the Shah, has had a Moser glass made for them), where you can buy some of the local glassware, made in the factory in the suburb of Dvory, just off the Cheb road.

At the end of Stará louka is the **Grand Hotel Pupp**, named after its founder, the eighteenth-century confectioner Johann Georg Pupp. Rebuilt in the late-nineteenth-century by the ubiquitous Helmer and Fellner, *Pupp's* was *the* place to be seen, a meeting place for Europe's elite. Despite the odd spot of careless modernization and rather snotty service, it boasts an interior that can't fail to impress, and the cakes are allegedly still made to Mr Pupp's own recipe. On the opposite bank, the former Kaiserbad – now known rather more prosaically as Lázně I – is another sumptuous edifice, designed like a theatre by Helmer and Fellner, with a luscious velvet and marble interior.

Back round the corner in Nová louka, the spa's richly decorated, creamy white **Městské divadlo** is another Helmer and Fellner construction, where Dvořák gave the premiere of his *New World Symphony* in 1893. What makes this place special, though, is that the frescoes and main curtain were executed by a group of painters that included a young **Gustav Klimt**, later to become one of the most famous figures in the Viennese Secession. If you ask at the box office, you should be able to get a glimpse of the auditorium, though the curtain – by far the most interesting work – is rarely fully exposed to the audience. Nevertheless, you can spot Klimt's self-portrait in the bottom right-hand corner, playing the flute and looking at the audience.

A short distance beyond the casino is the spa's main **Galerie umění** (Tues–Sun 10am–noon & 1–6pm), on Goethova stezka, which contains a small but interesting cross-section of twentieth-century Czech canvases, and a disappointingly limited selection of glassware. Neither of Karlovy Vary's two museums are really worth bothering with: the **Karlovarské muzeum** (Wed–Sun 9am–noon & 1–5pm), on Nová louka, plods through the spa's history, glossing over the controversial (and interesting) bits, while the **Muzeum zlatý klíč**, Lázeňská 3 (same times), contains a fairly mediocre series of soft-focus oil paintings of the spa at its pre-World War I zenith, by Wilhelm Gause.

Walking in the hills

Of all the spas, Karlovy Vary's constitutional **walks** are the most physically taxing and visually rewarding. You can let the **funicular** (*lanová draha*) take the strain by hopping aboard one of the trains (9am–7pm; every 15min) from

Marx in Karlsbad

A certain Mr Charles Marx from London (as he signed himself in the visitors' book) visited the spa several times towards the end of his life, staying at the former *Hotel Germania*, at Zámecký vrch 41, above the Mühlbrunnen Colonnade. He was under police surveillance each time, but neither his daughter Eleanor's letters (she was with him on both trips) nor the police reports have much to say about the old revolutionary, except that he took the waters at 6am (as was the custom) and went on long walks. The Communists couldn't resist the excuse to set up a Karl Marx Museum, just down from the Mühlbrunnen Colonnade, at the house where Marx used to visit his doctor. Somewhat unbelievably, it was the only one of its kind in the entire communist world, Lenin being the orthodox choice. Needless to say, it has long since been dismantled, and is now the even duller Muzeum zlatý klíč (see p.240).

behind the *Grand Hotel Pupp* up to a café and viewpoint. Alternatively, you can climb up through the beech and oak trees to the wooden crucifix above Stará louka, and then on to the spectacular panorama where the **Peter the Great Memorial** commemorates the visiting Russian tsar and his dozen or so royal hangers-on. In season you can enjoy the (not so perfect) view northwards from the **Jelení skok** restaurant (Tues–Sun 10am–6pm).

The road below *Jelení skok* slopes down to **Zámecký vrch**, where Turgenev stayed at no. 22 in 1874–75 and which the English aristocracy used to ascend in order to absolve their sins at the red-brick Anglican church of **sv Lukáš** (Evangelical and Methodist services are still held here, although not in English). Clearly visible from here, high on the opposite bank, is the *Imperial* sanatorium, a huge fortress hotel built in 1912 to rival *Pupp*'s and flying in the face of the popular Art Nouveau architecture of the spa; it was converted into a hospital during World War II, handed over to the Soviets during the communist period, and has only recently been turned back into a hotel (it even has its own funicular to transport guests to and from the spa below).

An alternative route back down to the Sadová kolonáda is the street of **Sadová** itself, which is lined with some of the most gloriously flamboyant mansions in the whole spa. Topping the lot, though, is the fabulous white Russian Orthodox church of **sv Petr and Pavel** (daily 10am–5pm), built to serve the visiting Russian aristocracy and now equally popular with the spa's current crop of Russian visitors. It's the church's stunning exterior, crowned by a series of gilded onion domes, that steals the show, so don't worry if the janitor is out to lunch, thus preventing you from visiting the icon-filled interior.

Eating, drinking and entertainment

What I indulged in, what I enjoyed
What I conceived there
What joy, what knowledge
But it would be too long a confession
I hope all will enjoy it that way
Those with experience and the uninitiated.

Needless to say, Goethe had a good time here. His coy innuendoes are a reference to the enduring reputation of spas like Karlovy Vary for providing extra-marital romance. Dancing, after all, was encouraged by the spa doctors as a means of losing weight. These days, it's all a bit less racy. Nevertheless, if you're looking for a spot of opulence, you might as well head for the *Grand Hotel*

Pupp, whose bar and restaurant boast unrivalled Neoclassical decor. Otherwise, there's the *Zámecký vrch*, a more intimate restaurant up at no. 14 on the street of the same name; the Moravian wine cellar at *Promenáda*, Tržíště 31; or *Embassy*, Nová louka 21, one of the oldest Baroque houses in the spa, with superlative cuisine.

Karlovy Vary is, of course, the home of one of the country's most peculiar and popular drinks, **becherovka**, a liqueur made from a secret recipe of nineteen different herbs, which really does ease digestion and is fondly referred to as Karlovy Vary's "thirteenth spring". It was actually invented by the unlikely sounding Scot, Dr Frobig, in 1805, but only launched commercially two years later by the enterprising Dr Jan Becher. It's available in bars and restaurants all over town (and just about anywhere else in the country), though the company's factory shop is on T. G. Masaryka, near náměstí Republiky. Be warned: it's an acquired taste – a little like cough mixture – and perhaps best drunk with tonic, ice and a slice (ask for a *beton*). Not so good for you, but all part of the spa ritual, are coffee and cakes: the *Elefant café* on Stará louka is the nearest Karlovy Vary comes to an elegant Habsburg-style café, and as a result is very popular. You can also enjoy a marginally healthier cup of tea at *Dobrá čajovna*, by the market at Varšavská 13, and *Tusculum*, Sadová 31.

Karlovy Vary's **cultural life** is pretty varied, from classical concerts at the former *Kurhaus* (Lázně III) and occasionally at *Pupp*'s, to the rock club *Propaganda*, Jaltská 7. The town also plays host to an **International Film Festival** in July, which attracts at least a handful of big names. All showings are open to the public. For details on these and the town's other events, ask at City-Info or Kur-Info (see p.237).

Loket

The tiny hill-top town of **LOKET** (Elbogen) is an exquisite, virtually undiscovered, miniature gem, just 12km west of the crowds of Karlovy Vary. It takes its name from the sharp bend in the River Ohře – *loket* means elbow – that provides the town with its dramatic setting. The fourteenth-century **hrad** (Tues–Sun: April–Oct 9am–6pm; Nov–March 10am–4pm), which slots into the precipitous fortifications, displays porcelain manufactured in the town over the last couple of centuries; you can also explore the castle's former prison, climb the lookout tower, explore the ruined Romanesque rotunda, and enjoy the pretty tacky permanent exhibition on ghosts, plus the occasional concert, medieval market, and fencing match. Loket's beautifully picturesque streets form a garland around the base of the castle, sheltering half-timbered houses and secluded courtyards like Sklenařská, where the redundant German sign *Glaser Gasse* remains unmolested since the forced expulsions of 1945 stripped the town of its German-speaking inhabitants.

Accommodation is available at various pensions, including the friendly *Goethe* (☎352 684 184; ❸) or the *Actus* (☎352 684 103, @actus@mbox.cz; ❸), both on the main square and both with restaurants, or you can try the Info Centrum at Kostelní 4 (☎352 684 123, ⓦwww.loket.cz) for private rooms and pensions. It was at *Zum weissen Ross* – now the vanilla and pistachio coloured, neo-Gothic *Bílý kůň* – on the main square, that Goethe met his last love, Ulrike von Lewetzow, he in his seventies, she a mere seventeen. Hardly surprisingly, she refused his marriage proposal – his *Marienbader Elegie* describes the event – though she remained unmarried throughout her long life.

Loket is easily accessible by bus from Karlovy Vary, but by far the most inspiring way of getting there is to take the beautiful, blue-marked track from

Karlovy Vary, which crosses over to the left bank of the River Ohře at the halfway point and passes the giant pillar-like rocks of the **Svatošské skály** (Hans Heiling Felsen), which have inspired writers from Goethe to the Brothers Grimm.

Jáchymov

JÁCHYMOV (Joachimsthal), 20km northeast of Karlovy Vary and only 5km from the German border, is haunted by its past. In the early 1950s, literally thousands of citizens (many of them former Communist Party members) were rounded up during the country's Stalinist terror and sentenced to hard labour in the **uranium mines** to the north of the town. Underfed and subject to harsh treatment by their jailers, untold numbers died of exhaustion, starvation and leukemia.

Joachimsthal was founded in the sixteenth century when silver deposits were discovered. The royal mint established here struck the famous *Joachimsthaler* (eventually giving rise to the dollar, a corrupt form of the abbreviation *Thaler*). In 1896 the Frenchman Henri Bequerel discovered uranium, and it was from Joachimsthal uranium that Marie and Pierre Curie discovered radium in the early twentieth century. The experiment proved as fatal to them as it did to the generations of German miners who worked the pits: even under the First Republic their average life expectancy was 42 years. Although the mine was closed down in 1964, some three hundred houses are now thought to be so contaminated by radon that they represent a serious health risk to the occupants. Despite this, the citizens of Jáchymov continue to work in the local tobacco factory, and the *Radiumpalác* and *Curie* spa facilities still draw in thousands of patients annually, to be "cured" by treatment involving the town's radioactive springs.

Travel details

Trains

Connections with Prague: Domažlice (2 daily; 2hr 40min); **Františkovy Lázně** (3 daily; 3hr 45min); **Karlovy Vary** (3 daily; 3hr 20min–4hr); **Mariánské Lázně/Cheb** (every 2hr; 2hr/3hr 30min); **Plzeň** (hourly; 1hr 40min–2hr 15min).
Cheb to: Františkovy Lázně (10–14 daily; 10min); Karlovy Vary (15 daily; 50min–1hr 10min); Mariánské Lázně (11–13 daily; 30min); Nürnberg (5–6 daily; 2hr); Plzeň (10–12 daily; 1hr 35min–2hr 15min).
Domažlice to: Klatovy (5–6 daily; 1hr).
Karlovy Vary to: Kadaň (8–9 daily; 50min–1hr 15min); Leipzig (1 daily; 4hr 30min); Teplice (5 daily; 2hr).
Klatovy to: Železná Ruda (6–8 daily; 1hr 10min).
Mariánské Lázně to: Teplá (6–7 daily; 30min);

Karlovy Vary (6–7 daily; 1hr 40min).
Plzeň to: Domažlice (10–12 daily; 50min–1hr 25min); Furth-im-Wald (2 daily; 1hr 20min); Klatovy (8–12 daily; 45min–1hr); Munich (3 daily; 4hr 20min–7hr); Plasy (8–12 daily; 30–45min); Stříbro (12–14 daily; 25–45min); Železná Ruda (4 daily; 2hr 10min–2hr 40min).

Buses

Connections with Prague: Jáchymov (2 daily; 3hr); **Karlovy Vary** (hourly; 2hr 30min); **Plzeň** (hourly; 1hr 30min).
Karlovy Vary to: Františkovy Lázně (5 daily; 30min); Jáchymov (up to 18 daily; 50min); Loket (5–7 daily; 25min).
Plzeň to: Horšovský Týn (7 daily; 1hr); Karlovy Vary (7 daily; 1hr 30min).

North Bohemia

CHAPTER 4

Highlights

✷ **Terezín** – Habsburg-era fortress, used as a transit camp and "model ghetto" by the Nazis, which now stands as a chilling memorial to the Holocaust. See p.258

✷ **Litoměřice** – Ecclesiastical town with a remarkable collection of Baroque churches designed by the Broggio family. See p.261

✷ **České Švýcarsko** – Hilly, wooded border region with bizarre sandstone rock formations and boat trips along the Kamenice River. See p.266

4

North Bohemia

orth Bohemia (Severní Čechy) became a byword for the ecological disaster facing the country in the communist era. Its forests all
but disappeared, weakened by acid rain and finished off by parasites,
its villages were bulldozed to make way for opencast mines, and its
citizens literally choked to death – all due to the brown-coal-burning power
stations that have provided the region with employment for the last hundred
years. As in other parts of the country though, laborious environmental
clean-up efforts have finally turned the tide as green landscapes again pre-
vail in summertime, and the air, even in winter, is remarkably cleaner than
a decade ago. Parts of North Bohemia are popular with Czech and German
tourists, in particular the eastern half of the region, where the industrial
landscape gives way to areas of outstanding natural beauty like **České
Švýcarsko** and the **České středohoří**, and towns of architectural finesse,
like **Litoměřice**.

Geographically, the region is divided by the River Labe (Elbe) into two
roughly equal halves. To the east, where the frontier mountains are slightly
less pronounced, two rich German-speaking cities developed: **Liberec**
(Reichenberg), built on the cloth industry, and **Jablonec** (Gablonz), famed
for its jewellery. In addition, much of Bohemia's world-famous crystal and
glass is still based in the smaller settlements located in the very north of the
region. To the west of the Labe lie the **Krušné hory** (Erzegebirge or Ore
Mountains), which, as their name suggests, were once a valuable source of
iron ore and other minerals. Nowadays, however, the mountains are better
known for their depleted forests (albeit slowly coming back to life), and for
their brown coal deposits which have permanently altered landscapes and
cityscapes alike.

Historically, the region has been part of Bohemia since the first Přemyslid
princes, but from very early on, large numbers of Germans from neighbouring
Saxony drifted over the ill-defined border, some taking up their traditional
wood-based crafts, others working in the mines that sprang up along the base
of the mountains. By the end of the nineteenth century, **factories** and **mines**
had become as much a part of the landscape of North Bohemia as mountains
and chateaux. Then, with the collapse of the empire, the new-born
Czechoslovak state inherited three-quarters of the Habsburg Empire's industry, and at a stroke became the world's tenth most industrialized country.

German and Czech miners remained loyal to the Left until the disastrous
slump of the 1930s, when the majority of North Bohemia's German-speakers put their trust in the Sudeten German Party or SdP (see p.277), with disastrous consequences for the country – and for Europe. Allied bombings took

their toll during the war, and with the backing of the Big Three (Churchill, Roosevelt and Stalin) at Potsdam, the German-speaking population was forcibly (and bloodily) expelled in 1945. Economic necessity ensured that North Bohemia was quickly rebuilt and resettled, but its land and lives were irrevocably marred by forty years of unbridled industrialization under the communists.

While the rest of Europe was belatedly tempering sulphur emissions and increasing fuel efficiency, the Czechs were steadily sinking to fortieth place in the world league of industrial powers and rising to first place for male mortality rates, cancer and stillbirths. It's easy to blame all these calamities on the factory fetishism of the communists, but damage to the forests of the Krušné hory was noted well before 1948, and smog levels irritated the citizens of North Bohemia for the best part of the twentieth century. Yet the brown-coal industry that caused much of the havoc is gradually being wound down, as power generation is shifting to the newly completed nuclear plant at Temelín (see p.172), and the presence of filters on the remaining smokestacks has brought forth dramatic improvements. The downside is that these measures are likely to leave the region with one of the highest unemployment rates in the Czech Republic, something that can only exacerbate the smouldering tensions between the Czechs and Romanies who have shared this polluted home since 1945.

▼ Prague

Up the River Ohře

There are five historic towns along the **River Ohře** (Eger), overlooked by most travellers eager to reach Karlovy Vary and the spas of West Bohemia. With your own car, they can all be easily covered in a day; by public transport (preferably bus), it's best to concentrate on just one or two. If you are driving, be sure to take in one of the best **views** in the entire region, from the ridge shortly after Panenský Týnec on route 7: in the foreground, bizarre hillocks rise up like giant molehills, while behind, the entire range of the Krušné hory is stretched out in all its distant glory (close up it's not so pretty).

Libochovice

The first place of interest along the Ohře is **LIBOCHOVICE** (Libokowitz), a sleepy village nestling in the shadow of the Rožmberks' mighty ruined fortress of Hazmburk, whose Dracula-like profile is a prominent landmark. Libochovice has a **zámek** (April & Oct Sat & Sun 9am–noon & 1–4pm; May–June & Sept Tues–Sun 9am–noon & 1–5pm; July–Aug Tues–Sun 9am–noon & 1–6pm) of its own, given a Baroque cladding by the Lobkowicz family when they took it over in the seventeenth century, but with many of its original Gothic features intact. The entrance is presided over by a brooding bust of one of the heroes of the Czech national revival movement, Jan Evangelista Purkyně, father of Czech medicine, who was born in the chateau in 1787. Two lasting Lobkowicz additions provide the highlight of the chateau tour: the rather splendid *sala terrena* featuring trompe l'oeil frescoes by Italian artists, and the grandiose Saturn Hall. You could picnic with the noisy peacocks that stalk the carefully manicured French gardens, have a snack at the café in the courtyard of the chateau, or enjoy good Czech food at the *Zámecký šenk* next door.

Louny

LOUNY (Laun) is the first of the medieval fortified towns on route 7 (the road from Prague to Chomutov), its perfect Gothic appearance all but entirely destroyed by fire in 1517 – all, that is, except the strikingly beautiful church of **sv Mikuláš** (Tues–Sun 10am–5pm), whose spiky, tent-like triple roof, the town's most famous landmark, is thought to have been rebuilt by the German mason Benedikt Ried (he used a similar design to great effect on the cathedral in Kutná Hora; see p.151), who died here in 1534. Even if the church is closed, you can peek in at his skilful ribbed vaulting through the glass in the entrance lobby. If you do get inside, be sure to check out the intricately carved limewood altars, barleysugar pillars and remarkable knobbly filigree work; when the church is open you can also climb the tower.

A couple of other isolated buildings in Louny are worth inspecting: round the back of the church in Pivovarská, the local museum occupies the **Dům rytířů sokolů z Mor** (Tues–Fri 10am–5pm, Sat & Sun 1–5pm), with its distinctive Gothic stone oriel window and wedge-shaped roof, while the town's nineteenth-century **synagogue**, on Hilbertova, has now been restored and houses the district archives. The **Žatecká brána**, Louny's only remaining medieval gateway, is extremely impressive and marks the beginning of a pleasant walk along the town's surviving ramparts by the river on the northern edge of the old town.

Louny is less than an hour's drive from Prague airport. There are a few direct **trains** from Prague's Masarykovo nádraží, but for most you have to change at Kralupy nad Vltavou; the main train station is a kilometre or so east of the old town, while Louny předměstí, a short walk south of the old town, is only good for trains to Rakovník, and the once daily České Budějovice–Most express. If you need a place **to stay**, by far the best deal is the *Hotel Union* (☎415 653 330; ❷), literally in the shadow of sv Mikuláš on Beneše z Loun, with its own half-decent restaurant serving the local **beer**. There are good pizzas and grilled meats (and great views over the ramparts) to be had at the outdoor terrace at *Vivaldi*, or the usual Czech staples (plus the odd surprise, like eel in mustard sauce) at *U Daliborky*, both east of the main square on Hilbertova.

Žatec

ŽATEC (Saaz), 24km up the Ohře from Louny, is the centre of the hop-growing region that supports the famous Czech beer industry. In summer, from here as far south as Rakovník (Rakonitz), the roads are hemmed in by endless tall, green groves of hop vines. No one quite knows why Czech hops are the best in the world for brewing beer, but everyone accepts the fact, and even Belgian beer giants like Stella Artois import them in preference to their own. Since as long ago as the twelfth century, Bohemia's *Red Saaz* hops have been sent down the Elbe to the Hamburg hop market, and Žatec's biggest annual binge is still the September hop festival held in the town square.

The **old town** itself, on the hilltop opposite the train station, is a substantial, though scruffy, medieval affair, with two of its fifteenth-century western gates still intact. In those days the town was predominantly Czech, but during the next three centuries, wave upon wave of German immigrants gradually reversed the balance. These days, the central area contains a large Romany population. The central square, headed by the plain, grey Renaissance **radnice**, is pleasant enough, with arcades down one side and a very busy plague column in the middle. To the right of the radnice there's a small garden of hops – the perfect advertisement for the town's wares – beyond which lies the town's ruined synagogue. Behind the radnice, the town's Jesuitized church is guarded by a wonderful gallery of beatific sculptures, while the town **brewery** (no admission) occupies pride of place in the thirteenth-century castle.

The main square and the backstreets around are rather lonely and unpleasant places to hang around, though you can sit outside and have a coffee beside the Baroque statuary, or browse among the market stalls that have begun to appear in between the arcades. **Hotels** are inexplicably overpriced, and you'd probably be more comfortable spending the night in either Louny (see opposite) or Kadaň (see below). The *Motes* (☎415 711 169, ✉ikadnar@iol.cz; ❸), on Chelčického náměstí, is hidden in the grubby backstreets east of the main square, though it does offer good views. The more upscale *U hada* on the main square (☎415 711 000, ⓦhoteluhada.mujweb.cz; ❸) is a much better bet, and has its own decent **restaurant** and *vinárna*. Beyond this, there aren't too many other eateries you'd want to try, though *Na baště*, near the theatre on Dvořákova, has a reasonable offering of Czech dishes.

Kadaň

Very much in the same mould as Louny and Žatec, **KADAŇ** (Kaaden), 22km west, is an altogether more picturesque halt on the Ohře. From the train station, you enter the old town through the round, whitewashed barbican of the **Žatecká brána**. The town suffered badly during the Thirty Years' War, the population was driven out in 1945, and the whole place lived under a dusty air of neglect for the following fifty years. Now the town's handsome eighteenth-century buildings have all been more or less restored to their former glory, and the place has really come alive once more. The most striking sights on the partially arcaded town square are the prickly white conical octagonal spire of the **radnice** and the twin red onion domes of the imposing **Děkanský kostel**, which contains some good Baroque furnishings. Directly opposite the radnice, you'll find **Katová ulička** ("Hangman's Lane"), Bohemia's narrowest street, which is barely more than a passage, the light straining to make its way past the maze of buttresses. The hangman himself used to live in the small white house below the gate at the end of the lane, which has since been converted into a cute little tea and spice shop. From the end of Katová ulička, you can gain access to the best-preserved part of the town walls or **hradby**, which lead round to the southern tip of town, where Kadaň's partially renovated **hrad**, a modest provincial seat, sits overlooking the Ohře; it's currently undergoing restoration and looks set to remain closed for some time to come.

Accommodation shouldn't be a problem, with the lovely pension *Horoskop* (☎474 342 684, ✉horoskop@pension-kadan.cz; ❸), across from the hrad, easily the best of several good central places to stay. There are several **campsites** in the vicinity as well, with the *Hradec* site (mid-April to Sept) 3km southeast of the town, enjoying the nicest position on the banks of the Ohře, not far from Hradec train station. A good place to grab a bite **to eat** in Kadaň is the excellent *Slunce* restaurant on the main square, next door to the radnice; for serious drinking, you can quaff beer from Úštěk at the pub on Tyršova.

Klášterec nad Ohří

Also worth a visit is **KLÁŠTEREC NAD OHŘÍ** (Klösterle-an-der-Eger), 5km west of Kadaň, the pretty quadrilateral seat of one of the many branches of the Thun family. Although, as the name suggests, the town was originally centred on a Benedictine monastery, it was the Thuns who really determined its present appearance, commissioning the two colourful Baroque churches and establishing the porcelain factory and spa facilities that made the town wealthy in the previous two centuries.

The Thuns' **zámek**, built up the hill from the village in 1646, today houses a **Muzeum porcelánu** (April–Oct Tues–Sun 10am–noon & 1–5pm), containing over 6000 pieces of local and imported china from the vast collection belonging to Prague's UPM (Decorative Arts Museum); visits are by guided tour only and leave on the hour; replicas can be purchased in the museum shop. More accessible are the wonderful **gardens** (*zámecká zahrada*) sloping down to the river, filled with 46 varieties of rare trees – there's a map to show where each one stands – dotted with Baroque sculptures by Brokoff and boasting a *sala terrena*, whose gaudy red and cream colour scheme matches the church across the road. To get inside the family vault or **Thunská hrobka**, you need to ask at the museum, though it offers little of interest besides the odd quadruple-barrelled name – viz. Josef Oswald II Thun-Hohenstein-Salm-Reifferscheid, who has barely enough room on his coffin to fit his aristocratic credentials. The guide disappointedly concedes that all that remains of the first Thun of Klášterec is "a skull and a few bones" – rather impressive, considering that he died some 300 years ago and when all that's left of another, eighteenth-century, Thun is a shoe.

The chateau is a 1.5km trek from the main bus or train station. There are a few places to stay in Klášterec, though you're better off with the amenities in Kadaň.

The North Bohemian brown-coal basin

The **North Bohemian brown-coal basin** contrives to be even less enticing than it sounds. Stretching the sixty kilometres from Kadaň to Ústí nad Labem, it comprises an almost continuous rash of opencast mines, factories and prefabricated towns, earning it the nickname *Černý trojhelník* or "black triangle". The majority of the country's brown coal (lignite) is mined here, most of it from just ten metres below the surface. As a result, huge tracts of land at the foot of the **Krušné hory** have been transformed by giant diggers that crawl across fields of brown sludge like the last surviving cockroaches in a post-nuclear desert. Around one hundred villages have been bulldozed, rail and road links shifted, and the entire town of Most flattened to make way for the ever-expanding mines.

Not only is the stuff extracted here, but much of it is burnt locally, and brown coal is by far the filthiest and most harmful of all fossil fuels. To the credit of the Czech government (and not a little pushing from the EU), filters have been installed in the two main power stations at Tušimice and Prunéřov, situated less than 5km to the north and east of Kadaň, and the smoky yellow clouds that used to billow through the valley are now much less lethal. On certain winter days, when the nearby mountains cause thermal inversions, the smog can still be intense and authorities resort to distributing filter masks to local schoolchildren; but in the summer the pollution levels drop dramatically, and you'll hardly notice the effect. Nonetheless, the character of the region has been forever altered, and aside from a few engaging stops – or indeed to view the spectacle itself – there is little reason to visit.

Chomutov

CHOMUTOV (Komotau), a major road and rail junction that's difficult to avoid if you're passing through the area, has a history more notable for its repeated destruction than for anything else. Three devastating fires, sackings by the Hussites and Swedes, outbreaks of the plague, World War II bombs, the violent postwar expulsion of most of the German-speaking townsfolk, and finally the legacy of the communist period – an ironworks, a meat-processing factory and vast swathes of high-rise *paneláky* – have all taken a heavy toll on the town. For all this, the central square area is actually quite pretty, and if, by some unfortunate set of circumstances, you should find yourself here, you can survey the entire scene best from the top of the Renaissance **tower** (May–Oct Tues–Sun 9am–5pm), which dominates the main square; the landings on the way up trace the town's history. You can fritter still more time away at the local **museum** in the town's radnice/zámek (Tues–Fri 10am–5pm, Sat 9am–2pm, Sun 2–5pm), opposite, or the renovated Baroque church of sv Ignác, designed by the Italian Carlo Lurago. If by some unfortunate set of circumstances you should end up here, make tracks to *Hotel Český dům* on Lipska (☎474 624 287, Ⓦ www.ceskydum.cz; ❸), a pleasant small **hotel** 2km northwest of centre (follow the main road from the bus station), with its own restaurant and wine bar. For somewhere more central to eat, there's a passable pizzeria and a pub on the main square.

Prostitution

All Czech towns close to the German and Austrian borders suffer from a high level of **prostitution**, but the 17km along route 7 between Chomutov and the German border is one of the worst-affected areas. Sparsely populated since the expulsion of the German-speaking inhabitants in 1945, many of the derelict buildings have been turned into brothels, with women sitting bored in the doorways, or dancing half-heartedly in the windows; many ply their trade at the side of the road, wearing skimpy clothes, sometimes in temperatures way below freezing. There have been several highly publicized police raids in the area, highlighting the fact that many of the women are brought here against their will from other former Eastern bloc countries, but the authorities seem uncertain as to how to proceed: whether to legitimize the industry, which would be unpopular with the locals but safer for the women, or crack down on it. There have also been reports of overcrowding in the region's orphanages as many women have fallen pregnant, accidentally and even on purpose, since it is claimed that pregnant women are more highly prized by some punters who pay higher sums more for the privilege of their company. The whole scene is made all the more surreal by the fact that the brothels share roadside space with countless Vietnamese traders, whose stalls are lined with technicolour **garden gnomes** (a particular favourite of the neighbouring Germans).

Most, Litvínov and Libkovice

MOST (Brüx) is like a sort of architectural paean to the *panelák*, the prefabricated high-rise blocks that are perhaps the communists' most obvious visual legacy. The only historic building to survive the town's demolition in the 1960s was the late-Gothic church of **Nanebevzetí Panna Maria** (Tues–Sun: May–Sept 9am–6pm; Oct–April 9am–4pm), which was transported in one piece on a specially built railway to the edge of the mine, 841 metres away (the move took 28 days). Designed by Jakob Heilmann of Schweinfurt, a pupil of Benedikt Ried, in the early sixteenth century, it's now something of a lonesome sight, stranded between a motorway and the edge of the mining area, a short walk upriver from the train station. The original altar and numerous statues were preserved and reinstalled after the move, lending an odd juxtaposition to the otherwise clean, modern setup of the interior. Ask to see the video in the crypt which lauds the state's wonderful achievement in shifting the church – a hollow feat given that they relocated it above a polluted underground lake, whose sulphurous liquid has to be drained off to prevent the site from flooding. If your morbid fascination is captured, head for the vast **local museum** (Tues–Fri 9am–5pm, Sat & Sun 1–5pm), visible to the west beneath the hilltop castle of Hněvín; outside the museum is a new memorial to František Niedermertl, who was shot in 1952 for insubordination in one of the local forced labour camps.

Trams connect Most with **LITVÍNOV** (Leutensdorf), 6km north. En route, they pass a huge Chemopetrol plant just south of the town, which, coupled with the constant sulphur emissions from a neighbouring power station, creates a bank of cloud that in winter often blots out the sun and reduces all light to a grey haze. At the side of the road, special red lights illuminate the simple command (in Czech) "STOP! DON'T SMOKE! SWITCH OFF YOUR ENGINE!" when the authorities deem the chemical levels to be too dangerous. Amazingly, Litvínov still has the leftovers of its nineteenth-century *Ringstrasse*, now boarded up and long since overtaken by the town's new constructions.

The last settlement in the "black triangle" to be bulldozed to make way for opencast mining was the village of **LIBKOVICE**, 5km southeast of Litvínov (current maps mark the location *bývalé* Libkovice, "former Libkovice"). In 1994, on the eve of the village's demise, Czech environmentalists managed to pressurize the local mining company into sparing the village's Baroque church as a kind of monument to the postwar destruction that has marred the region. It remains to be seen whether the public will be granted access to the building in the future, or whether, as some fear, the whole structure will simply sink into the ground; for now, it sags in forlorn neglect off the side of an access road.

Duchcov

At first, **DUCHCOV** (Dux), 8km east of Litvínov, appears no different, encircled as it is by coal mines. But in this unlikely town there's a grandly conceived Baroque **zámek** (April & Oct Wed–Sun 9am–4pm; May–Sept Tues–Sun 9am–6pm), designed by Jean-Baptiste Mathey, which once hosted emperors and kings, as well as artistic luminaries such as Schiller, Goethe and Beethoven. The chateau's former librarian was none other than **Giacomo Casanova** (1725–98), who took refuge here at the invitation of Count Waldstein. Broke, almost impotent and painfully aware of his age, Casanova whiled away his final, fairly miserable thirteen years writing his steamy memoirs, the twelve-volume *Histoire de ma vie*. He took a vow of celibacy on entering Duchcov, though rumours continued to link him with various women, including the leading lady at the premiere of Mozart's *Don Giovanni* in Prague. The Venetians would like Casanova's remains, but no one is sure where they lie now, and the likelihood is that they have disappeared under the opencast mines.

The tour guides are well aware that today's trickle of visitors is more concerned with Casanova than with the chateau's period furniture, and so save the exhibition dedicated to the world's most famous bounder till last. Duchcov also boasts a vast collection of Czech Baroque art, including sculptures by Brokoff and Braun, and a series of obsequious portraits of the Waldstein family, mostly by Václav Vavřinec Reiner, who is also responsible for the fresco in the Great Hall. Much of the chateau park, along with the Baroque hospital designed by Octavio Broggio, was bulldozed in the 1950s by the Communists, who (wrongly) suspected that large coal deposits lay beneath the gardens. The priceless frescoes were shifted to a purpose-built concrete pavilion, where – forlorn, badly lit and brutally restored – they remain today; to see the frescoes, you must endure a thirty-minute guided tour.

If you need a bite **to eat**, the *Zámecká bašta* on Masarykova, just by the chateau, serves up the usual with dumplings.

Osek

Another monument worth visiting, just out of earshot of the region's mines, is **OSEK** (Ossegg), 7km northeast of Litvínov, whose twelfth-century **Cistercian abbey** (April, May, Sept & Oct Tues–Sat 10am–noon & 1–4pm, Sun 1–4pm; June–Aug closes 5pm) is a reminder of the wealth of the area before the dawn of industrialization. After the destruction of the Thirty Years' War, some of the country's leading Baroque artists – painter Václav Vavřinec Reiner, architects Broggio and Santini, and the sculptor Corbellini, whose vigorous stucco drapery upstages the lot – set to work restoring the place. The abbey's real artistic treasure, however, is the thirteenth-century chapel off the cloisters, where light filters through to illuminate a central altar and an elegant stone pulpit with a rotating lectern. Under the communists, the abbey was used as an internment camp for monks and nuns who refused to abandon their religious calling; now, happily, the Cistercians are back, putting the place to use as a refuge for the homeless and a religious education centre for a new generation of Czech monks. There's a **campsite** (May–Sept) and an inexpensive pension just west of the monastery, by the lake.

Teplice

In the midst of this polluted region lies the traumatized town of **TEPLICE-ŠANOV** (Teplitz-Schönau), the forgotten fourth spa of the once celebrated quartet of Bohemian resorts that included Mariánské Lázně, Františkovy Lázně and Karlovy Vary (see Chapter 3). In the early nineteenth century it became "the drawing room of Europe", prompting the likes of Beethoven, Liszt and Wagner to appear on its *Kurliste*. By the 1880s, however, the adjacent mining industry had already inflicted its first blow on Teplice's idyllic way of life: the nearby Döllinger mine breached an underwater lake, flooding the natural springs, which subsequently had to be artificially pumped to the surface. The lingering smell of lignite was a characteristic of the town even then, and is now complemented by several additional chemical vapours.

The accumulative cost of this assault on the environment is extremely serious, but it has been compounded by the fact that, following the expulsion of the spa's German-speaking inhabitants, the communists proceeded to wreck the place aesthetically too, dismembering much of the old town and erecting tasteless edifices. In addition, Teplice now has more than its fair share of social problems: there's a large and vocal skinhead movement here, which has come to blows with the town's Vietnamese and Romany communities on several occasions over the last decade; meanwhile, as at Chomutov, prostitution is endemic along route 8 to Dresden. All this doesn't make for a great introduction to the town, but elements of the old spa have survived, and if you're in the area, Teplice merits at least an afternoon's halt.

The Town

Arriving at the main train station, **Teplice v Čechách**, with its rich neo-Renaissance frescoes adorning the vaulted ceiling, injects a sense of hope in innocent minds, though this is soon dispelled by block after block of silent and peeling late-nineteenth-century houses as you head for the centre via 28 října or the main street, Masarykova třída, one block south.

At the end of Masarykova, behind the rather brutal Krušnohorské divadlo (an uncharacteristic, late work by Helmer and Fellner), the spa proper begins. Even the old *Kur Garten* – now the **Lázeňský sad** – has a somewhat diseased air about it, despite the lively sounds of birdlife. Nowadays, the communist-era white concrete **Dům kultury** is the dominant feature of the park, fronted by the **Nová kolonáda**, a glorified greenhouse made from some of Bohemia's great glass surplus.

Only when you cross the valley to the brightly coloured Neoclassical houses on **Lázeňská** is it possible to make the imaginative leap into Teplice's arcadian past. Beethoven once stayed in a house on Lázeňská, and it was in Teplice that he wrote his famous love letter to a woman he called his "Immortal

Beloved", but whose identity still remains a mystery. Beyond Lázeňská lies the town's monumental **zámek**, seat of the Clary-Aldringen family until 1945, when they and most other *Teplitzer* took flight from the approaching Red Army. It was here, in 1813, that Tsar Alexander I, the Emperor Franz I and Kaiser Friedrich Wilhelm of Prussia concluded the "Holy Alliance" against Napoleon. The countless rooms of the chateau are now part of the local museum (Tues–Sun 10am–noon & 1–5pm), with memorials to Beethoven, Pushkin, and (of course) Goethe, wall-to-wall Biedermeyer, displays of historical clocks, ceramics and spa porcelain, and much else besides.

Outside the main gates of the chateau is the cobbled expanse of **Zámecké náměstí** centred on Matthias Bernhard Braun's flamboyant charcoaled plague column. To the east, there are two churches: the first is the **Pravoslavný chrám**, a neo-Gothic Orthodox church; the second is the more handsome Baroque church of **sv Jan Křtitel**, whose richly painted interior is worth a quick peek. Hot water dribbles through a sculpted boar's mouth into the occasional tourist's palms from the original spring, known as the **Pravřídlo** (Urquelle), which is set into the wall opposite the southeast corner of the church on Lázeňská. Further east still, a splendid staircase, the Ptačí schody (Birds' Staircase), takes you past the twin turrets of the *U Petra* restaurant to the blissful **zámecká zahrada**, which spreads itself around two lakes still "enlivened with swans", just as Baedeker noted approvingly back in 1905.

Šanov

The rest of the spa lies in the eastern part of town, once the separate village of **Šanov** (Schönau) linked to Teplice by Lipová (Lindenstrasse), which clings to its lime trees. Like the bark on the trees, the paint is slowly dropping off many of the grandiose private villas and spa pensions that characterize this part of the spa, though at least some effort has been made to restore images of their former glory. Lipová culminates in the sady Československé armády, overlooked by a large, run-down, red-brick Protestant church and peppered with yellowing Neoclassical spa buildings. Unfortunately, the sky-blue Art Nouveau Termalní lázně, just off Lipová on Hálkova, once the city's public spa house, is completely broken down and disappearing behind exuberant arboreal growth. However, you could improve your health by climbing the 230 steps to the summit of Letná (accessible from Laubeho náměstí, at the eastern corner of the Lázeňský sad) for a great **view** over the spa.

Practicalities

By far Teplice's nicest (and most expensive) place to **stay** is the *Hotel Prince de Ligne* (☎417 537 733; ❺), a pristinely renovated late-nineteenth-century hotel overlooking Zámecké náměstí. Cheaper alternatives include the *Hotel de Saxe*, closed at the time of going to press, and visitors are being referred to the *Hotel Thermal* on U kamenných lázní (☎417 533 700, ⓦ www.abaka.com/czech/thermal; ❸), on the corner of Masarykova and Husitská, near the main train station, or the rooms above the *Pinocchio* ice cream parlour on U kamenných lázní (❸). One of the best restaurants in town is *U Petra*, on the zámecká zahrada staircase, which serves up Chateaubriand for 200Kč. Try also the *Beethoven*, a nearby daytime-only eatery, or the *U cedra*, round the corner on Lázeňská, which does Middle Eastern dishes as well as Czech ones (you can also buy warm *oplatky* in the same building). There's a pleasant café on the first floor of the smart nineteenth-century Císařské lázně; the *U palmy* pub in a converted eighteenth-century villa on the opposite side of Laubeho náměstí is also recommended for good beer and cheap food.

Moving on from Teplice, the main **bus terminal** and **train station** (Teplice v Čechách) are next to one another just off Masarykova; Teplice zámecká zahrada train station, to the west of the chateau garden, is served only by slow trains to Lovosice. Slow, scenic trains to Děčín leave from Teplice lesní brána, 1km northwest of the centre – a fifteen-minute walk down Dubská from the town hall and across the motorway, or bus #20 from the main train station, or buses #16 and #23 from Benešovo náměstí.

Terezín

The old road from Prague to Berlin passes through the fortress town of **TEREZÍN** (Theresienstadt), just over 60km northwest of the capital. Purpose-built in the 1780s by the Habsburgs to defend the northern border against Prussia, it was capable of accommodating 14,500 soldiers and hundreds of prisoners. In 1941 the population was ejected and the whole town turned into a **Jewish ghetto**, and used as a transit camp for Jews whose final destination was Auschwitz.

Hlavná pevnost (Main Fortress)

Although the **Hlavná pevnost** (Main Fortress) has never been put to the test in battle, Terezín remains intact as a garrison town. Today, it's an eerie, soulless place, built to a dour eighteenth-century grid plan, its bare streets empty apart from the residual civilian population and visitors making their way between the various museums and memorials. As you enter, the red-brick zigzag fortifications are still an awesome sight, though the huge moat has been put to good use by local gardening enthusiasts.

The first place to head for is the **Muzeum Ghetta** (Ghetto Museum; daily: April–Sept 9am–6pm; Oct–March 9am–5.30pm; 130Kč, or 150Kč for com-

Bohušovice & Jewish Cemetery

bined ticket with Malá pevnost), which was finally opened in 1991, on the fiftieth anniversary of the arrival of the first transports to Terezín. After the war, the communists had followed the consistent Soviet line by deliberately underplaying the Jewish perspective on Terezín. Instead, the emphasis was on the Malá pevnost (see p.260), where the majority of victims were not Jewish, and on the war as an anti-fascist struggle, in which good (communism and the Soviet Union) had triumphed over evil (fascism and Nazi Germany). It wasn't

A brief history of the ghetto

In October 1941 Reinhard Heydrich and the Nazi high command decided to turn the whole of Terezín into a Jewish ghetto. It was an obvious choice: fully fortified, close to the main Prague–Dresden railway line, and with an SS prison already established in the **Malá pevnost** (Small Fortress) nearby. The original inhabitants of the town – less than 3500 people – were moved out, and transports began arriving at Terezín from many parts of central Europe. Within a year, nearly 60,000 Jews were interned here in appallingly overcrowded conditions; the monthly death rate rose to 4000. In October 1942, the first transport left for Auschwitz. By the end of the war, 140,000 Jews had passed through Terezín; fewer than 17,500 remained when the ghetto was finally liberated on May 8, 1945. Most of those in the camp when the Red Army arrived had been brought to Terezín on forced marches from other concentration camps. Even after liberation, typhus killed many who had survived this far.

One of the perverse ironies of Terezín is that it was used by the Nazis as a cover for the real purpose of the *Endlösung* or "Final Solution", formalized at the Wannsee conference in January 1942 (at which Heydrich was present). The ghetto was made to appear self-governing, with its own council or *Judenrat*, its own bank printing (worthless) ghetto money, its own shops selling goods confiscated from the internees on arrival, and even a café on the main square. For a while, a special "Terezín family camp" was even set up in Auschwitz, to continue the deception. The deportees were kept in mixed barracks, allowed to wear civilian clothes and – the main purpose of the whole thing – send letters back to their loved ones in Terezín telling them they were OK. After six months' "quarantine", they were sent to the gas chambers.

Despite the fact that Terezín was being used by the Nazis as cynical propaganda, the ghetto population turned their unprecedented freedom to their own advantage. Since almost the entire Jewish population of the Protectorate (and Jews from many other parts of Europe) passed through Terezín, the ghetto had an enormous number of outstanding Jewish artists, musicians, scholars and writers (most of whom subsequently perished in the camps). Thus, in addition to the officially sponsored activities, countless clandestine cultural events were organized in the cellars and attics of the barracks: teachers gave lessons to children, puppet-theatre productions were held, and literary evenings were put on.

Towards the end of 1943, the so-called *Verschönerung* or "beautification" of the ghetto was implemented, in preparation for the arrival of the International Red Cross inspectors. Streets were given names instead of numbers, and the whole place was decked out as if it were a spa town. When the International Red Cross asked to inspect one of the Nazi camps, they were brought here and treated to a week of Jewish cultural events. A circus tent was set up in the main square; a children's pavilion erected in the park; numerous performances of Hans Krása's children's opera, *Brundibár* (Bumble Bee), staged; and a jazz band, called the Ghetto Swingers, performed in the bandstand on the main square. The Red Cross visited Terezín twice, once in June 1944, and again in April 1945; both times the delegates filed positive reports.

until the Prague Spring of 1968 that the idea of a museum dedicated specifically to the history of the Jewish ghetto first emerged. In the 1970s, however, the intended building was turned into a Museum of the Ministry of the Interior instead. Now that it's finally open, this extremely informative and well-laid-out exhibition at last attempts to do some justice to the extraordinary and tragic events which took place here between 1941 and 1945, including background displays on the measures which led inexorably to the *Endlösung* (Final Solution). There's also a fascinating video (with English subtitles) showing clips of the Nazi propaganda film shot in Terezín – *Hitler Gives the Jews a Town* – intercut with harrowing interviews with survivors.

The **Magdeburská kasárna** (Magdeburg Barracks), former seat of the *Freizeitgestaltung* – part of the *Judenrat*, the Jewish self-governing council – in the south of the ghetto, has recently been turned into a fascinating museum concentrating on the remarkable artistic life of Terezín. First off, however, there's a reconstructed women's dormitory, with three-tier bunks and all the luggage and belongings in place to give some kind of idea as to the cramped living conditions endured by the ghetto inhabitants. The first exhibition room has displays on the various Jewish musicians who passed through Terezín, including Pavel Haas, a pupil of Janáček, Hans Krása, a pupil of Zemlinsky, who wrote the score for *Brundibár*, and Karel Ančerl, who survived the Holocaust to become conductor of the Czech Philharmonic. The final exhibition room concentrates on the writers who contributed to the ghetto's underground magazines, but the greatest space is given over to the work of Terezín's numerous artists. Many were put to work by the SS, who set up a graphics department headed by cartoonist Bedřich Fritta, producing visual propaganda, showing how smoothly the ghetto ran. In addition, there are many clandestine works, ranging from portraits of inmates, to harrowing depictions of the cramped dormitories, the effects of starvation, and the transports. These provide some of the most vivid and deeply affecting insights into the reality of ghetto life in the whole of Terezín, and it was for this "propaganda of horror" that several artists, including Fritta, were eventually deported to Auschwitz.

Malá pevnost (Small Fortress)

On the other side of the River Ohře, east down Pražská, lies the **Malá pevnost** (Small Fortress; daily: April–Sept 8am–6pm; Oct–March 8am–4.30pm; 130Kč, or 150Kč combined ticket with the Muzeum Ghetta), built as a military prison in the 1780s, at the same time as the main fortress. The prison's most famous inmate was the young Bosnian Serb, Gavrilo Princip, who succeeded in assassinating Archduke Ferdinand in Sarajevo in 1914, and was interned and died here during World War I. In 1940 it was turned into an SS prison by Heydrich, and after the war it became the official memorial and museum of Terezín. The majority of the 32,000 inmates who passed through the prison were active in the resistance (and, more often than not, communists). Some 2500 inmates perished in the prison, while another 8000 subsequently died in the concentration camps. The vast cemetery laid out by the entrance contains the graves of over 2300 individuals, plus numerous other corpses, and is perhaps rather insensitively dominated by a large Christian cross, plus a smaller Star of David.

There are guides available (occasionally survivors of Terezín), or else you can simply use the brief guide to the prison in English, and walk around yourself. The infamous Nazi refrain *Arbeit Macht Frei* (Work Brings Freedom) is daubed across the entrance on the left, which leads to the exemplary washrooms, still as they were when built for the Red Cross tour of inspection. The rest of the camp has been left empty but intact, and graphically evokes the cramped conditions under which the prisoners were kept half-starved and badly clothed, subject to indiscriminate cruelty and execution. The prison's main **exhibition** is housed in the SS barracks opposite the luxurious home of the camp Kommandant and his family. A short documentary, intelligible in any language, is regularly shown in the cinema that was set up in 1942 to entertain the SS guards.

Practicalities

Terezín is about an hour's **bus** ride from Prague's Florenc bus terminal, or a short hop from Litoměřice, just 3km to the north; the bus drops you off in front of the tourist office around the corner from the museum. The nearest **train station** to Terezín (from which the transports used to leave) is at Bohušovice nad Ohří, on the main Prague–Děčín line; occasional buses run to and from Terezín, or else it's a two-kilometre walk southwest of the main fortress. The only acceptable **restaurant** in town is *U hojtašů*, on Komenského, just north of the museum. It's difficult to imagine a less appealing place **to stay**, but stay you may, at the badly run-down *Parkhotel*, on Máchova (☎416 782 260; ❷), or at the **campsite** *Kréta* (April–Sept) just west of town. Alternatively, the **tourist office** (Tues–Fri 9am–4pm) on the main square can advise you on the many accommodation possibilities in Litoměřice (see below).

Litoměřice

If the idea of lingering in Terezín is unappealing, you can walk or catch the bus 3km north to **LITOMĚŘICE** (Leitmeritz), at the confluence of the Ohře and the Labe rivers. The town has been an ecclesiastical centre since the Přemyslid Spytihněv II founded a collegiate chapter here in 1057. From the eleventh century onwards, German craftsmen flooded into Litoměřice, thanks to its strategic trading position on the Labe, and it soon became the third or fourth city of

Bohemia. Having survived the Hussite Wars by the skin of its teeth, it was devastated in the Thirty Years' War, but its most recent upheaval came in 1945, when virtually the entire population (which was predominantly German-speaking) was forcibly expelled. Since 1989 the town has begun to pick up the pieces after forty years of neglect. Restoration work is continuing apace, and the re-establishment here of a Catholic seminary has brought some pride back to the town.

The main reason people come here now is to pay their respects at Terezín, just south of the town (see p.258); however, Litoměřice is of more than passing interest, since the entire town is a virtual museum to **Octavio Broggio**. Broggio was born here in 1668 and, along with his father Giulio, redesigned the town's many churches following the arrival of the Jesuits and the establishment of a Catholic bishopric here in the mid-seventeenth century. The reason for this zealous re-Catholicization was Litoměřice's rather too eager conversion to the heretical beliefs of the Hussites and its disastrous allegiance to the Protestants in the Thirty Years' War.

The Town

Stepping out of the train station, you're greeted by the last remaining bastion of the old town walls across the road; behind it lies the historical quarter, entered via the wide boulevard of Dlouhá. The first church you come to is the hybrid church of **Kostel všech svatých** (All Saints) at the top of the street, which started life as a Romanesque church, and now boasts the only Gothic spires left on the skyline, a beautiful wedge-shaped affair reminiscent of Prague's right bank, plus three smaller spikier ones behind. Its present Baroque facade was designed by Broggio, but the oppressively low ceiling and dusty furnishings are disappointing, with the notable exception of the fifteenth-century panel painting by the Master of Litoměřice. More impressive is the light-infused interior of the nearby **Jezuitský kostel** (Jesuit Church), another work by Broggio, whose ceiling is adorned with colourful frescoes. While you're in the vicinity, check out the bizarre modern driftwood installation occupying the nearby flight of steps.

The town's vast cobbled marketplace, **Mírové náměstí**, once one of the most important in Bohemia, now boasts only a couple of buildings from before the Thirty Years' War. The best known is the **Mrázovský dům**, at no. 15 on the south side of the square, whose owner at the time, a devout Hussite, had a huge wooden *kalich* (chalice) – the symbol of all Hussites – plonked on the roof in 1537. The other building that stands out is the arcaded fourteenth-century **radnice**, at the eastern end of the square, topped by a shapely Renaissance gable. It now serves as the town museum (Tues–Sun 10am–5pm), worth a quick spin round, if only for the coffered sixteenth-century ceiling of the council hall; however, there's still precious little mention in the exhibition of the 1945 expulsions.

The town's art galleries

In the western corner of the square is the town's excellent **Diecézní muzeum** (Tues–Sun: April–Sept 9am–noon & 1–6pm; Oct–March 9am–noon & 1–5pm). As befits a rich ecclesiastical region, there are a lot of very fine religious paintings here beginning with the serene *Madonna with Child in an Enclosed Garden*, an early oil painting from 1494. In the gruesome *Donor, Christ and Death*, Christ's flesh appears almost translucent, while Death appears as a skeleton tightly wrapped in skin. Among the museum's most valuable paintings is Lucas Cranach the Elder's *St Anthony the Hermit*, which depicts the saint being tempted heavenwards by a grisly collection of devilish animals.

The most remarkable and unusual section of the gallery, however, is the timber-built building at the back of the museum, which contains a vast collection of "naive art": works from the last century by local amateur artists on a variety of themes from the religious to the political, from landscapes to portraits.

A few doors up nearby Michalská, the town's **Galerie výtvarného umění** (Gallery of Fine Art; Tues–Sun: April–Sept 9am–noon & 1–6pm; Oct–March closes 5pm) occupies a wonderfully rambling sixteenth-century building, whose inner courtyard is draped in ivy and echoes to the trickle of a modern fountain. Exhibitions doing the Bohemian circuit stop off here, supplementing the small permanent collection of late-nineteenth- and early-twentieth-century Czech canvases, including Impressionist work by Jan Preisler, Antonín Hudeček and Antonín Slavíček, plus a few pieces of Baroque art, and a bizarre Gothic statue of Mary Magdalene, depicted with her hair covering her entire body, except her knees. There's more Gothic art on the ground floor, in particular the surviving panels of the early-sixteenth-century winged altar by the Master of Litoměřice, whose paintings are peopled by folk with expressive, almost grotesque faces, whose poses and gestures are remarkably sophisticated for the period. Baroque dwarfs and other more modern sculptures pepper the gallery's terrace overlooking the ramparts.

Around sv Štěpán

On a promontory 500m southwest of the town centre, the **Dómský pahorek** (Cathedral Hill), where the bishop and his entourage once held residence, was originally entirely separate from the town, with its own fortifications. The small Orthodox chapel of **sv Václav** (St Wenceslas) on the northern slope is perhaps the younger Broggio's finest work, grand despite its cramped proportions and location, though suffering a little from a rather gaudy salmon-pink and silver-grey facelift. But the real reason to come out here is to wonder at the former cathedral of **sv Štěpán** (St Stephen), which looks out onto the quiet, grassy enclosure of Dómské náměstí. Redesigned by Giulio Broggio (among others) in the seventeenth century, sv Štěpán marked the start of the extensive rebuilding of Litoměřice. The cathedral's ceiling is disappointing, but the dark wood and the gloomy altar paintings from the school of Cranach the Elder add a bit of atmosphere. Outside, the freestanding Italianate campanile, designed by the Viennese architect Heinrich Ferstel in the 1880s, adds a peculiarly Tuscan touch.

A path along the north side of sv Štěpán leads down the cobbled lane of Máchova, where the Czech poet **Karel Hynek Mácha** died in 1836; there's a commemoration plaque at no. 3. In true Romantic style, Mácha died of consumption at the age of 26. His most famous poem, *Máj* (May), was hijacked by the communists as their May Day anthem, but remains a popular love poem. He used to be buried in the local cemetery, but when the Nazis drew up the Sudetenland borders, Litoměřice lay inside the Greater German Reich, so the Czechs dug up the poet and reinterred him in the Vyšehrad cemetery in Prague (see p.118). Once you've reached the bottom of the cathedral hill, the stairway of the Máchovy schody will take you back up into town.

Practicalities

All **buses** terminate at the Litoměřice město **train station**, at the southeast corner of the old town, terminus for trains to Mělník and Ústí nad Labem; trains to Lovosice, Úštěk and Česká Lípa depart from Litoměřice horní nádraží, to the north of the old town. The town's **tourist office** (May–Sept Mon–Sat 8am–6pm, Sun 9.30am–4pm; Oct–April Mon–Fri 8am–4pm, Sat 8–11am;

☎416 732 440, Ⓦwww.litomerice.cz) is in the Mrázovský dům on Mírové náměstí, and can arrange **private rooms** or point you to the **internet café** in the regional library opposite. If you want to treat yourself, stay at the friendly *Hotel Salva Guarda* (☎416 732 506, Ⓦwww.salva-guarda.cz; ❸), located in a lovely sgraffitoed building on Mírové náměstí and named after the house's sixteenth-century owner, who was an imperial bodyguard. Otherwise, the *Roosevelt*, on Rooseveltova (☎416 733 595, Ⓔreserve.hotel.roosevelt@email.cz; ❷) is perfectly comfortable. In a pinch, you could try the rooms above the pub *U pavouka*, Pekářská 7 (☎416 734 409; ❷). There's also the *Slavoj* **campsite** (May–Sept) with bungalows, near the open-air cinema (*letní kino*) on Střelecký ostrov, the woody island on the river. The **restaurant** in the *Salva Guarda* is the best choice in town; in warm weather, the locals congregate at the *Zahradní restaurace* on Zítkova, though don't be fooled by the name, as in fact there's no food on offer.

Ploskovice and Úštěk

An easy day-trip from Litoměřice, the village of **PLOSKOVICE**, 6km to the northeast, off route 15, hides one of Octavio Broggio's few secular works, a crisp, light summer **zámek** (April & Oct Sat & Sun 9am–4pm; May, June & Sept Tues–Sun 9am–5pm; July & Aug 9am–6pm). After his abdication in 1848, this became a favourite summer watering hole for the Habsburg emperor Ferdinand I, who commissioned the exuberant Rococo plasterwork – sometimes frivolous, sometimes tasteless, always fun. The whole place has recently undergone a lengthy restoration: the beautiful walled grounds (daily dawn–dusk) are beginning to flourish and the fountains are issuing forth once more. To reach the chateau from the train station, follow the little stream north for 1km.

Bypassed by the main road – and, it seems, by the entire last three centuries – **ÚŠTĚK** (Auscha) originally grew up around a now-ruined medieval fortress. On one side of the main square there's a line of fourteenth-century burgher houses, which, unusually for Bohemia, still retain their original triangular gables of wood or slate. The **Jezuitský kostel**, built after the devastating fire of 1765, occupies centre stage in the square, and features a trompe l'oeil main altar, a Karel Škréta altarpiece and several fine wooden sculptures. Down by the waters of the Úštěcký potok to the southwest of the town, in among the geese and hens, there are some fascinating wooden shacks known as **ptačí domky** (birds' houses). Perched on top of each other on the highest ledge of the steeply terraced banks, they provided ad hoc accommodation for Jewish families who were forced to live in ghettos until at least 1848, and for the Italian workers who built the town's railway link in the late nineteenth century.

It's fifty minutes by train from Litoměřice and about another half a kilometre's walk from the train station east to the old town. If you're **camping**, there's a site (mid-June–mid-Sept) by the pleasant sandy shores of Chmelař lake (boat rental available in season), behind the train station. You'll find alternative accommodation in the form of several modest pensions, and there are a couple of good restaurants: *Restaurace na růžku*, in a pink building off the square, and *Restaurace pod loubím*, behind the church on the main square.

Ústí nad Labem

Twenty kilometres north, on the other side of the beautiful České středohoří (Central Bohemian Hills), which part only to allow the River Labe to slither through, lies the vast metropolis of **ÚSTÍ NAD LABEM** (Aussig). From a small town, Aussig grew very rapidly into the second largest port on the Labe (Elbe) after Hamburg, and the busiest in the Habsburg Empire. Solidly German-speaking and heavily industrialized, Aussig suffered terrible bomb damage during World War II. Worse was to follow. On July 30, 1945, a devastating terrorist attack took place when Ústí's sugar refinery, being used to store ammunition confiscated from the Germans, was blown up, killing fourteen Czechs and triggering a riot. The attack was blamed on die-hard Nazis, and enraged Czechs stormed through the town, dragging off any German they could find, and lynching hundreds before throwing them into the Labe. The incident is thought to have been instrumental in persuading President Beneš to declare the three million ethnic Germans living in Czechoslovakia enemies of the state and call for their forceful expulsion from the country.

Ústí was resettled after the war, its industries further expanded, and it now has a population of 110,000, making it the third largest city in Bohemia. However, the city has lost almost all of its charm – even the tram system (once second only to Prague's) was wound up in 1970. More recently, it has hit the headlines across the world as the place where the local council tried to build a wall to divide some of the city's Romany residents from their white Czech neighbours (see box on below). Given the city's aesthetic limitations, and its almost unbearable historical baggage, most people give the place a wide berth. If, however, for whatever reason, you find yourself here, there are a couple of sights of minor interest, where you can while away an hour or so.

The Town

Trains usually stop at Ústí for only four or five minutes, which is long enough for most people – one whiff of the air and a glance at the discoloured river, tells you that this is yet another chemical town. For those venturing into town, it's just a couple of blocks west from the main train station to Ústí's chief sights, the Dominican church of **sv Vojtěch**, given a Baroque facelift by Octavio Broggio in the 1730s, and the fourteenth-century cathedral of **Nanebevzetí Panny Maria**. Destroyed by the Hussites during their bloody occupation of

The wall in Ústí

Ústí nad Labem leapt into the media spotlight in 1998 when the municipal authorities decided to erect a 2.65m-high "sound barrier" in Matiční, a street in the city's industrial eastern suburb of Krásné Březno. White Czech residents on one side of the street had complained about "antisocial and unhygienic behaviour" by the Romanies who lived in the housing block across the street. Ultimately, however, the plan was to subject the Romanies to a 10pm curfew, by locking them inside the compound. The decision was criticized by the EU, and by the Czech parliament, though few people actually believed the city council in Ústí – where fifteen percent of the population are Romany – would go ahead with the project. Then early one morning in October 1999, the council suddenly began construction. Human rights groups protested, the Romanies attempted to tear the wall down, and the Czech parliament declared the wall illegal. After several weeks of bad international publicity, and stalemate between the central government and the municipal authorities, the council was finally forced to back down. However, the gesture was not one of peace and reconciliation. The state has offered to buy up the houses of the non-Romany residents and pay for them to be rehoused. As one Czech government minister put it, "there are many streets like Matiční in our country" – in other words, this is not an issue that's going to go away overnight.

the town in 1426, the cathedral was rebuilt in late-Gothic style, and has recently been nicely restored. The building's outrageously leaning steeple is the result of bomb damage in World War II. From behind the churches you can view the 1930s road bridge over the Labe, opened in 1936 by President Beneš and somewhat optimistically named the "Bridge of Brotherhood" (between the Czech- and German-speakers).

The main square, **Mírové náměstí**, has had its entire northern side ripped out, and is now only really remarkable for the surviving Socialist Realist mosaic, depicting the inevitable road from the workers' revolution to world peace, which adorns the headquarters of the local council. One final building worthy of mention is the town's theatre or **Městské divadlo**, built in 1909 in the style of the Viennese Secession, and situated to the west of the main square, overlooking the concrete paving stones of Lidické náměstí.

On the opposite side of the Labe from the city centre is the suburb of **Střekov** (Schreckenstein), dominated by its ruined **hrad** (Tues–Sun: April & Sept–Dec 9am–4pm; May–Aug 9am–5pm), a dramatic nightmare fairy-tale pile built into a bleak, black rocky outcrop high above the river. Like the Lorelei on the Rhine, it was much loved by the nineteenth-century Romantics, and provided inspiration for one of Wagner's operas (in this case, *Tannhäuser*). Set amid the tantalizing hills of the České středohoří, it's easy to see why – and to forget for a moment that this lovely landscape has been pockmarked with industrial zones. Now back in the hands of the Lobkowicz family, you're free to explore the ruins, and revel in the utterly incredible views up the hilly Labe valley and over to Ústí's grim smokestacks and awesome *paneláky*. The castle kitchen is now the *Wágnerka* café and restaurant, with a shady terrace from which you can watch the barges negotiating the lock below.

Practicalities

Ústí's **bus station** is just south of Lidické náměstí, a couple of blocks west of the main square. Travelling by fast train from Prague, Dresden or Berlin, you're most likely to arrive at Ústí's main **train station**, hlavní nádraží, at the southeast corner of the old town by the river; trains from Most, Litoměřice and Mělník pass through Střekov station, on the other side of the river, and terminate at Ústí nad Labem západ, which is another couple of blocks west of the bus station, down Revoluční.

The **tourist office** (Mon–Fri 8am–5pm, Sat 8am–3pm; Ⓔinfo.ul@mbox. vol.cz) is on Hrnčířská 1, at the eastern edge of the main square, and can hand out a basic town map. If you do need to **stay the night** in Ústí, you might as well enjoy the communist-era luxury of the *Hotel Bohemia*, the high-rise monstrosity on the main square, Mírové náměstí (Ⓣ475 220 843, Ⓔbohemia@unl. pvnet.cz; ❹).

České Švýcarsko

The area of sandstone rocks around Děčín is popularly known as **České Švýcarsko** (Bohemian Switzerland), a nickname coined by artists of the Romantic movement, though the landscape is in fact far from alpine. The River Labe drives a deep wedge into the geographical defences of Bohemia, forging a grand valley through the dense forests, interrupted by outcrops of sandstone rock welded into truly fantastic shapes. While it has always been a popular spot for weekend recreation, it was only in January 2000 that a portion of České Švýcarsko was officially designated a national park, the **Národní Park České Švýcarsko**, and while the park certainly contains some of the most precious natural treasures of the region, the entire area surrounding Děčín is greatly appealing.

Like the other *skalní města*, or "rock-cities", in the Český ráj (see p.285) and the Broumov region (see p.301), the whole area was formed when volcanic rock thrust its way to the surface, causing fissures and cracks that later widened. The result is probably the most impressive geological amusement park in the country, a dense network of mini-canyons and bluffs all covered in a blanket of woodland – spectacular stuff, and a favourite with rock climbers, but also fairly easy **hiking** country.

Transport throughout the region is not great – just infrequent rural bus services to most places – though the distances are small enough to make hiking an attractive proposition. In season, there's plenty of inexpensive **private accommodation** throughout the region, making it possible for non-campers to spend more than just a day in the countryside.

Děčín

Despite being German-speaking for most of the last thousand years, **DĚČÍN** has long been the geographical gateway to Bohemia, its castle rising up to the east as you enter the country from Dresden. Modern Děčín is really two towns – **Děčín** (Tetschen) itself and **Podmokly** (Bodenbach) – amalgamated in 1942 but still divided by the River Labe, which has always been the driving force behind the town's economy. As a busy industrial port, its attractions are limited, but its position on the river is quite dramatic, and, lying at the heart of České Švýcarsko, it serves as a convenient base for exploring the region.

Podmokly

The main point of **arrival** is Děčín's grubby hlavní nádraží in **Podmokly**, which looks out onto a mass of grey concrete and an unsightly supermarket. It's not a great start, but then Podmokly was a late developer, only coming into existence in 1850 through the amalgamation of three villages on the left bank. Sixty years of furious building followed, funded by the town's flourishing shipping industry, the results of which are still visible in the four or five blocks west of the station, where the locals go shopping and wolf down ice cream.

With time to kill and an interest in stuffed birds, medieval Madonnas or seamanship and navigation, you can spend a happy hour in the **Okresní muzeum** (Tues–Sun 9am–noon & 1–5pm), situated in a former hunting lodge on Zbrojnická. There's even a hands-on knots section, and a bit of the chain from the 720m-long cable that was cooked up in the nineteenth century to help ships get upstream. A more miraculous sight is the Moorish Art Nouveau **synagogue**, round the corner on Žižkova, dating from 1907, which was saved from being torched on *Kristallnacht* by a local German, and is one of the few to survive in what was Sudetenland. Recently given a slightly injudicious lick of garish yellow and blue paint, it is now back in use by the local Jewish community for exhibitions (and services).

Afterwards, head for the meringue-coloured mansion (with ultraviolet lighting at night) atop the precipitous **Pastýřská stěna** (Hirtenfelswände or Shepherd's Wall); follow signs for the zoo up the hill past the synagogue. At the top there's a small **café** with an incredible view over Děčín, and, a little further back from the cliff, a small **zoo** (daily: April–Sept 8am–6pm; Oct–March 8am–4pm).

Děčín

To cross the river to **Děčín** from Podmokly, follow the crowds onto the buses from outside the station (buy your 10Kč ticket from a newsagent), or continue downstream from the above-mentioned Okresní muzeum until you reach the Tyršův most. Děčín itself is much older than Podmokly, as witnessed by the austerely impressive **Děčínský zámek** (Schloss Tetschen-Bodenbach) at its centre, elevated above the town and river on an isolated lump of rock. The chateau's current mostly Baroque appearance dates from the time of the Thun-Hohensteins, but it has been much abused since the family sold it to the state in the 1930s. Used as a barracks by the Germans, Czechs and lastly Russians, there's not much left of the original interior, though the exterior is finally getting a thorough make-over. Part of the newly restored interior has now been given over to a **Muzeum loutek** (Puppet Museum; Wed–Sun 10am–noon & 1–4pm), based on the private collection of Milan Knížák.

The chief attraction of the chateau, however, is the **Růžová zahrada** (May–Oct Tues–Sun 10am–5pm), a truly wonderful Baroque rose garden, laid out on a terrace cut into the north face of the rock high above the town. At one end is a befrescoed *sala terrena*, while at the far end is an ornate Baroque belvedere peppered with statuary. To gain access to the garden (and the chateau), you must walk up the sloping **Dlouhá jízda**, a gloomy 300-metre-long drive cut into the rock. Directly below the garden are the distinctive black dome and twin tower lanterns of the salmon-pink Baroque church of **sv Kříž**, which has a richly painted and furnished interior. Two other sights worth noting are the striking 1906 Art Nouveau **fountain** on Děčín's main square,

Masarykovo náměstí, and to the south of the castle, the slowly disintegrating stone bridge or **Kamenný most**, over the River Ploučnice, punctuated by Brokoff's Baroque statuary.

Practicalities

Most **trains** end up at Děčín hlavní nádraží in Podmokly; the town's **tourist office** (Mon–Fri 9am–5pm, Sat 9am–noon; ☎412 531 333, ⓔdezka@space.cz) is opposite on ulice Pokopa Holého. Děčín is the border town and all international trains to and from Germany stop here. The **bus** station is a few blocks south of the train station. A much more fun way to travel is on the **boat** to Hřensko, which sets off from the dock under Tyršův most (May–Oct Wed & Fri–Sun 8am & 1.45pm).

For **accommodation**, walk over or catch any bus to Děčín proper, where your best bets are probably the comfortable *Česká koruna* (☎412 516 104, ⓕ412 519 086; ❷), on Masarykovo náměstí, or the renovated *Hotel Faust*, on U plovárny (☎412 518 859, ⓔp.vitak@telecom.cz; ❷), just south of the zámek. With your own transport, you might also consider the pleasant *Pension Jana* (☎412 544 571, ⓕ412 527 030; ❷), a couple of kilometres out of town on route 13 to Teplice. There's also a small **campsite** (April–Oct) on the south side of the zámek, with an open-air swimming pool nearby, and some equally well-equipped sites in the České Švýcarsko itself (see below). The restaurant at the *Česká koruna* features fish from Třeboň, while the nearby *Pošta* is good for a beer. With a sense of adventure though, head for *Viadukt*, a few blocks west of Masarykovo náměstí on the corner of Anenská and Kamenická; it has a great selection of food and *Krušovice* beer on tap.

Exploring České Švýcarsko

Loosely defined, České Švýcarsko splits neatly in half, with Děčín as the meeting point. The small **České Švýcarsko National Park** occupies a stretch of land along the German border east of Hřensko. Whichever part you're heading for, it's a good idea to get hold of a proper walking **map**, which marks all campsites and footpaths in the area, including those on the German side. The popular **Jetřichovické stěny**, mostly within national park boundaries to the northeast of Děčín, is topographically more interesting and covers a much greater area than its western counterpart. At its base runs the Kamenice river, accessible in parts only by boat (for boat trips, see p.271). The smaller range to the west, the **Děčínské stěny**, is less spectacular but doesn't suffer the same human congestion and can easily be reached on a day's hike from Děčín itself.

Děčínské stěny

If your sole aim is to see the rocks, it's simplest to catch one of the few buses a day from Děčín to Tisá, or to take the train to Libouchec station and walk the 2.5km north to Tisá. If, however, you're intent on a day's walking, follow the red-marked path from the Tyršův most in Děčín for 10km to **Děčínský Sněžník** (723m), a giant table mountain thrust up above the decaying tree line, on top of which stands a handsome sandstone look-out tower (*rozhledna*), erected in 1864 by Count Thun-Hohenstein. The red-marked path eschews the direct route to Tisá and instead heads north to Ostrov, the last village before the border, where there's a simple **campsite** (April to mid-Nov) by a pretty lake, overlooked by the cliffs of the Ostrovské skály. (The nearest border crossing is the 24-hour one at Petrovice, northwest of Tisá.)

From the village of **TISÁ** itself, the **Tiské stěny** are hidden from view, but climb the hill and the whole "sandstone city" opens up before you. Sandy trails crisscross this secret gully, and it's fairly simple to get to the top of one or two of the gigantic boulders without any specialist equipment. You could spend hours here, exploring, picnicking and taking in the panoramic views. Via **Děčínský Sněžník**, it's a full day's walk from Děčín, but it's easy enough to hole up for the night, as there's plenty of private accommodation in the village, as well as a **campsite** (mid-April–mid-Oct).

Hřensko

Despite its dramatic mountainous setting, **HŘENSKO** (Herrnskretchen), at 116m above sea level, is in fact the lowest point in Bohemia. It was once a pretty village on the right bank of the Labe, dotted with half-timbered houses and redolent of Saxony on the opposite bank. However, Hřensko currently makes its living out of the German day-trippers flocking to the nearby rocks, and with their former East German neighbours now flush with euros, business is booming. Prostitutes line the road coming into Hřensko, and the village itself is barely visible under the sheer number of shops and garden-gnome stalls, the majority run by the republic's Vietnamese minority. It's unlikely you'll want to stay here, though there are several hotels to choose from; try the rather splendid *Hotel Labe* (☎412 554 088, ℱ412 555 268; ❷), right by the river front. With your own set of wheels, you'd be better off heading south to the tiny village of Labská Stráň (via Janov), set high above the deep Labe gorge, where the *Hotel Belveder* (☎ & ℱ412 553 121; ❷) has plain rooms but awe-inspiring views, plus a recommendable restaurant.

Jetřichovické stěny

The only way to get to the **Jetřichovické stěny** and the Kamenice gorge is by **bus**, with three or four a day making the roundabout journey to Jetřichovice, via Hřensko, Tří prameny, Mezní Louka and Mezná; car drivers should note that there is no parking between Hřensko and Mezní Louka, but there are additional daily buses between the two.

By far the most popular destination is the **Pravčická brána**, at 30m long and 21m high the largest natural stone bridge in Europe. It's a truly breathtaking sight, though not one you're likely to enjoy alone unless you get there very early or out of season. It's a two-kilometre hike up from Tři prameny, a clearing (and bus stop) 3km up the road from Hřensko, and you'll have to pay an admission fee to get up close. The German border is less than 1km away, but the red-marked path that appears to head towards it actually rejoins the road 4.5km further east at **MEZNÍ LOUKA**, where you can take your pick from the smelly **hotel** (☎412 554 084; ❷) of the same name, or the **campsite** (May–Sept) opposite with bungalows for rent (☎412 554 084; ❶).

From Mezní Louka, the red-marked path continues another 14km to Jetřichovice, meandering through the southern part of the complex of mini-canyons, taking in the **Malá Pravčická brána**, a smaller version of the bridge, and a couple of very ruined border castles. **JETŘICHOVICE** itself is a lovely old Saxon hamlet made up of huge wooden farmsteads typical of the region. Several serve as pensions, of which *Dřevák* (☎412 555 015, ☏412 555 222; ❸), an idyllic woodframe home with an impeccable restaurant in the centre of the village, stands out as one of the best places to stay in the entire region. There is also a **campsite**, *U Ferdinanda*, 1.5km to the south, across a ford, with its own swimming pool (April–Oct).

The Kamenice gorge

Another option from Mezní Louka is to walk the 2km southwest to **MEZNÁ**, an unassuming little village that basks in a sunny meadow above the River Kamenice. Several basic pensions offer affordable rooms: *Pension Na vyhlídce* (☎412 554 065, ⊛www.profidesign.cz/navyhlidce; ❷) has its own restaurant, while *Pension Taušner* (☎412 554 167; ❷) is a pretty house with a few simple rooms.

From the village green, a green-marked path plunges a hundred feet into the cool, dank shade of the river, traversed by the wooden bridge Mezní můstek. Here you have a choice of heading up or down the **Kamenice gorge** to landing stages, where boatmen punt you along a short but dramatic boat trip down (or up) the river. The trips (April, Sept & Oct Sat & Sun 9am–5pm; May–Aug daily 9am–5pm) are justifiably popular, but boats run every ten to twenty minutes, so you shouldn't have to wait long. The downstream trip, along the **Tichá soutěska** ("quiet gorge"), drops you at the edge of Hřensko (see p.270) – you can alternatively pick it up via the yellow-marked path in Hřensko; this is perhaps the more dramatic of the two, and certainly the longer. The upstream one unloads its passengers just 500m further up the **Divoká soutěska** ("wild gorge"). With the latter trip, you can either return to Mezní Louka via the blue-marked path, or continue along first the blue- then the yellow-marked path up a shallower gorge to Jetřichovice, about 5km east.

Česká Kamenice and Benešov nad Ploučnicí

With your own transport, **ČESKÁ KAMENICE** (Böhmisch Kamnitz), 18km east of Děčín on route 13 (or forty minutes by train), makes a great alternative base for exploring České Švýcarsko. For a start, it's a lot more pleasant to rest up in than Děčín, with its interesting blend of nineteenth-century Habsburg edifices, the odd wooden folk building and a splendid Baroque pilgrimage chapel. **Accommodation** is rather limited until the hotel on the main square reopens; meanwhile *Pension Kamenice* (☎412 584 290, ⊜jveidenthaler@seznam.cz; ❷), on náměstí 28 řijna east of centre, is your best bet. The **tourist**

office (Mon–Fri 9–11.30am & noon–5pm; ☎412 582 600, ✉ickam@dc. xion.cz) is on the main square, and you'll also find plenty of **restaurants** and pubs around here.

Five kilometres east of Česká Kamenice, on the other side of Kamenický Šenov, is another, much rarer geological phenomenon: the **Panská skála** (Herrnhausfelsen), a series of polygonal basalt columns like a miniature Giant's Causeway minus the sea. These are the result of a massive subterranean explosion millions of years ago, during which molten basalt was spewed out onto the surface and cooled into what are, essentially, crystals. They make a strange, supernatural sight in this unassuming rolling countryside, but are too small to be really awe-inspiring. Unlike Northern Ireland's major tourist attraction, the Panská skála are easily missed, even though they're only 500m south of route 13; look for the village of Prachen and ask the bus driver to tell you when to get out.

Halfway between Děčín and Česká Kamenice, and easily reached from either by train, is **BENEŠOV NAD PLOUČNICÍ**, a pretty little town characterized by its two connected **zámky** (April & Oct Wed–Sun 9am–4pm; May–Sept Tues–Sun 9am–6pm). The lower one is a neo-Gothic hunting lodge with meticulously restored interiors (restored after a fire in 1968); the upper one boasts Renaissance ceilings and an offbeat collection of Japanese and Chinese art. There is ample **accommodation**, though scout around before resorting to the rather dour *Jelen* (☎412 586 223; ❶), on the attractive main square; a safer bet, particularly for a longer stay, is one of the two basic self-service apartments at no. 6 on the square (☎412 586 262; ❷) – look for the "Apartma" sign.

The Česká Lípa region

The eastern border of České Švýcarsko marks the beginning of Bohemia's vast glass-making industry, stretching far into the east of the region. Bohemian glass and crystal has always been considered among the world's finest, though the industry suffered badly as a consequence of the postwar expulsions of the majority German-speaking population. If you're heading east towards Liberec (see p.274) or the Krkonoše (see p.293), there are several sights worth checking out for those interested in Bohemian glass, as well as a handful of chateaux en route.

Česká Lípa and Nový Bor

ČESKÁ LÍPA (Böhmisch Leipa) gets its name from the Czech national tree, the linden (*lípa*). The town itself has precious few trees now, thanks to the uranium boom of the 1970s that trebled the town's population, most of whom now live in endless high-rise estates around the town. There are, however, a few minor distractions: the prettified main square, a small sgraffitoed Renaissance hunting lodge, known as the Červený dům, an extraordinary tent-roofed chapel of sv Kříž and a former Augustinian monastery. However, the town's main virtue is its location at the meeting point of five railway lines, making it a good base for exploring the area; the main **train station** is around 2km south of the old town. For central **accommodation**, try *Penzión Monika*, on Jiráskova (❶); or the more upmarket *Hotel Olympia*, located in a building on Hrnčířská 854, which has a fine restaurant and bar (☎487 823 782, ✆487 823 800; ❸). There's also the lakeside *Neptun* **campsite** (June–Sept), 3km south-west of the station beyond Dubice.

NOVÝ BOR (Haida) is 8km north of Česká Lípa, on route 9, and best approached by train. Its **Sklářské muzeum** (Glass Museum; Tues–Sun 9am–noon & 1–4pm) was founded over one hundred years ago and boasts a particularly rich collection of glassware, including a functionalist tea set by Adolf Loos and a great Art Deco *vitraille*. The museum is on the main square, itself a typical mixture of folk cottages and late nineteenth-century industrial wealth. Nearby stands the *Parkhotel* (☎487 723 157; ✉agdpark@clnet.cz; ❸), a newly converted, very comfortable place to stay.

Máchovo jezero and Bezděz

Trains from Česká Lípa take less than half an hour to reach **DOKSY** on the southernmost sandy shores of the **Máchovo jezero**, 15km southeast on route 9. The lake, created in medieval times, has been a popular recreational spot since nineteenth-century Romantics like Karel Hynek Mácha (after whom the lake is named) used to trek out here. Nowadays it's surrounded by hotels, bungalows and campsites: the lakeside *Klůček* **campsite** (May–Sept) is the nearest to Doksy train station. There's a mercifully small museum dedicated to Mácha in Doksy itself, though you're infinitely better off going on the poet's favourite walk: the eight-kilometre hike southeast along the red-marked Máchova cesta up to the ruined hilltop castle of **Bezděz** (Bösig; April & Oct Sat & Sun 9am–4pm; May–Sept Tues–Sun 9am–5pm), clearly visible for miles around. It was one of the most important castles in Bohemia until its destruction in the Thirty Years' War, but there's not much to see now aside from a Gothic chapel and, of course, the unbeatable view from the top of the hill (604m) – still, at least you get to explore it without taking a guided tour. You can take the train another two stops to Bezděz to cut the walking distance down to just 2km.

East of Česká Lípa

Fifteen minutes by train east of Česká Lípa is the village of **ZÁKUPY** (Reichstadt), which boasts a rather fancy radnice and two prickly church towers – signs of the wealth that arrived when the Habsburg Emperor Ferdinand I chose it as one of his retirement homes after his abdication in 1848. The local **zámek** (April & Oct Sat & Sun 9am–4pm; May–Sept Tues–Sun 9am–5pm) was also lavishly renovated for him in neo-Renaissance style and adorned with a giant snooker table and Rococo paintings by, among others, Josef Navrátil. Outside in the moat, the brown bears pace up and down, but there's little life in the crumbling aviary or the formal terraced gardens with their mermaid fountains.

To the southeast of Zákupy is the strangely uninhabited tract of land known as **Ralsko**, after its highest peak. When the region's German-speaking population was expelled after the war, the Soviets took the opportunity to create a vast army base for their war games. When the troops finally withdrew in 1990, they left an estimated 3000 tonnes of pollutants, antitank mines and countless unexploded bombs. A ten-year clean-up operation is under way, as planners argue whether to build a giant international cargo airport here or turn the place into a safari park for the white rhino, which has been successfully bred at Dvůr Králové zoo (see p.313) for a number of years.

Fourteen kilometres northeast of Zákupy, the village of **JABLONNÉ V PODJEŠTĚDÍ** (Gabel) is dwarfed by the huge dome of the local Dominican church, an early work by the great Austrian Baroque architect Johann Lukas von Hildebrandt, dating from 1699. The inspiration for the church was the thirteenth-century wonder-worker Zdislava, wife of the lord of Lemberk (see p.274), who was beatified in 1907 and canonized in 1995, and whose remains (along with several mummified cadavers) lie in the crypt. Just over two kilometres northeast of the village is the military stronghold of **Lemberk** (April & Oct Sat & Sun 9am–4pm; May–Sept Tues–Sun 9am–5pm), a thirteenth-century zámek which owes its Baroque outer coating to one of Waldstein's Dutch generals, who held on to the place after Waldstein's murder (see box on p.233). The overlong guided tour (*trasa 1*) is probably worth skipping in favour of a stroll round the castle's displays about Zdislava and temporary exhibitions of local and international glassware (*trasa 2*).

Liberec and around

Lying comfortably in the broad east–west sweep of the Nisa Valley, framed by the Jizera Mountains to the north and the isolated peak of Ještěd to the south, **LIBEREC** (Reichenberg) couldn't hope for a grander location. The city itself, made prosperous and enormous by its famous textile industry, can't quite live up to its setting, but it's lively and bustling, with a smattering of interesting buildings and a couple of fairly good museums, all of which could keep you happily amused for the best part of a day. For further entertainment, you can while away a few hours in the glass and jewellery museum in the neighbouring town of Jablonec nad Nisou.

Arrival, information and accommodation

From the main **train and bus station** in Liberec, simply walk or jump on one of the trams heading down 1 máje to Soukenné náměstí, which is overlooked on one side by the city's eyesore Tesco superstore, and on the other by one of the functionalist Baťa shops designed by Vladimír Karfík in the 1930s. From here, it's a short steep walk up Pražská to the main square, náměstí Dr E. Beneše, where you'll find the **tourist office** (Mon–Fri 9am–5pm, Sat 9am–noon; ☏485 101 709, ⓦwww.infolbc.cz), which can arrange very reasonable private accommodation. If you're scouting about yourself, you'll find that Liberec's hotels tend to be rather pricey, relying as they do on German tourists and business travellers. The nearest **campsite** is at the well-equipped site with a swimming pool at the *Stadión Pavlovice*, Letná (May–mid-Oct), in the midst of a housing estate (bus #13, #24 or #26 to Letná stop).

Accommodation

Grandhotel Zlatý lev Gutenbergova 3 ☏485 104 093, ⓦwwwzlatylev.cz. Vast, turn-of-the-twentieth-century hotel, conveniently located behind the chateau. ❺

Ještěd Horní Hanychov ☏485 104 291, ⓕ485 104 295. Unbeatable location, view and kitsch 1960s decor in the TV tower on top of the mountain of the same name. ❸

Hotel Imperial 1. máje 29 ☏482 710 742, ⓕ482 710 063. Giant communist-era hotel on the way into town from the stations that undercuts the city's other big hotels. ❷

Hotel Orion Jizerská 250 ☏482 751 070, ⓔinfo@orion.lbc.cz. Modernized monster mountain chalet situated in the northeastern suburb of Starý Harcov, close to the woods (bus #19). ❸

Hotel Praha Železná 2 ☏485 102 655, ⓕ485 113 138. Very comfortable new hotel on the edge of the main square, which has preserved its original Art Nouveau entrance foyer, and a few other period fittings. ❹

Hotel Radnice Moskevská 11 ☏485 100 562, ⓔhotelradnicelb@mbox.vol.cz. Luxurious four-star hotel, on the edge of the main square, that's good value by international standards. ❺

Pension U muzea Vítězná 24 ☏ & ⓕ485 102 693. Large nineteenth-century villa located in the leafy district near the Severočeské muzeum. ❷

Unihotel Voroněžská 13 ☏485 352 211, ⓕ485 352 462. A real cheapie, just north of the main square, in a high-rise university complex. ❷

The City

Totally dominating the attractive main square of **Benešovo náměstí**, Liberec's magnificent, cathedral-like **radnice** is probably the most telling monument the chauvinistic *Reichenberger* could have bestowed on the city. Purposely designed to recall Vienna's own Rathaus, its lofty trio of neo-Renaissance copper cupolas completes the effect with an impressive Flemish flourish. Several cafés now spread their tables out onto the square, from which you can contemplate this great Germanic edifice. Liberec has the distinction of being one of the few places outside Prague where there was any real fighting following the Warsaw Pact invasion of 1968; a small memorial to the right of the town hall steps commemorates those who died.

Behind the radnice is the city's theatre, **Divadlo F.X. Šaldy**, a typically solid, showy affair designed by the Viennese architects Helmer and Fellner in the 1880s. While you're admiring the theatre, you can also check the

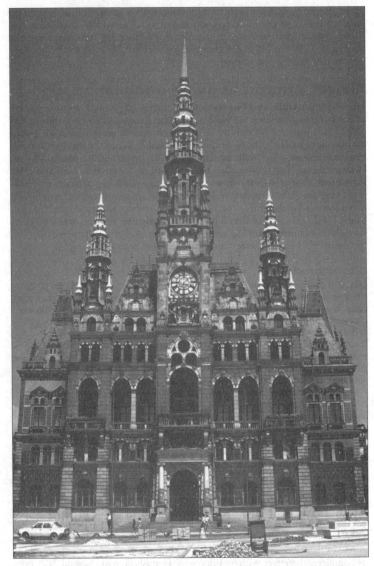

△ Liberec Town Hall

atmospheric pressure on the nineteenth-century weather machine opposite the main facade. At the beginning of Rumjancevova, behind the theatre, a brand new **Státní vědecká knihovna** (State Research Library) has been built on the site of the city's main synagogue, which was burnt down on *Kristallnacht* in 1938. As a gesture of reconciliation, the new building also houses a new synagogue, and the library's huge collection of German documents is now open to the public. The building itself is thoroughly contemporary, with a large open entrance hall and plenty of glass throughout to let in the light; the exposed steel infrastructure design is similar to that employed at the Myslbek centre in Prague. This is also a good place to get online, with several computers linked to the **internet** and an adjoining café providing the needed booster shots.

A couple of blocks west of the main square, on the far side of Sokolovské náměstí, the narrow side street of Větrná hides the town's most unusual treasure, the **Valdštejnské domky**, a terrace of four crisscross timber-framed houses dating from the early seventeenth century. To the east of the main square is the town's rouge-and-cream sixteenth-century **zámek**, previously owned by the Clam-Gallas family. It has recently been converted into a vast exhibition centre for the local glass giants Glassexport, and has been remarketed as the Skleněný zámeček. There's another, more historical, exhibition of glassmaking at the Severočeské muzeum (see p.278).

Oblastní galerie

Across the newly replanted formal gardens from the chateau is the **Oblastní galerie** (Tues–Sun 10am–6pm), a white nineteenth-century building off 8. března that has been an art gallery since 1873. Its unusually large collection includes a series of nineteenth-century French landscapes and some much earlier Dutch and Flemish masters, all of which were bequeathed to the gallery by the local German textile king, Johann Liebig.

Konrad Henlein in Reichenberg

Sited just the wrong side of the historical borders of Germany, the Reichenberger made up for this geographical oversight with their ardent pan-Germanism. Appropriately enough, it was the home town of Konrad Henlein, born in the nearby village of Reichenau (Rychnov) in 1898 and destined to become the leader of the Sudeten German Party (SdP). Henlein played an unheroic role in World War I, and after a spell as a bank clerk in Reichenau he became a gym teacher in the German-speaking town of Asch (Aš) in West Bohemia. The combined effects of the slump and the events in neighbouring Nazi Germany and fascist Austria, excited the Sudeten Germans, who proclaimed Henlein their Führer at a huge rally outside Saaz (Žatec) in 1933. Under Henlein, the SdP began to demand autonomy and self-determination for the German-speaking border districts of Bohemia and Moravia, and in the 1935 elections they won roughly two-thirds of the Sudeten German vote (thus becoming the largest single party in the country).

Yet despite his nationalist credentials, and the fact that the Nazis subsidized the SdP, Henlein was disliked in Nazi circles, due to his links with the Kamaradschaftbund, a secretive organisation inspired by Austrian clerical fascism rather than German National Socialism. The Nazis preferred the leader of the SdP's radical wing, Karl Hermann Frank, a one-eyed bookseller from Karlsbad, who wanted Sudetenland to be ceded to Germany. During the course of 1938, impressed by the Nazi takeover in Austria, Henlein foolishly agreed to push for the secession of Sudetenland. When the Nazis took over Sudetenland later that year, Henlein's closest associates, particularly those in the Kamaradschaftbund, were arrested and sent off to the camps. Henlein himself was too prominent a public figure to be interned; instead, he was appointed Gauleiter of Sudetenland, a position of little power, while Frank was eventually elevated to State Secretary, the second most powerful man in the Nazi Protectorate. In 1945 Henlein committed suicide after being captured by the Americans, while Frank was tried and hanged for war crimes in Prague in 1946.

The excellent collection of modern Czech paintings and sculptures includes two striking female portraits by the Impressionists Jiránek and Hudeček, a characteristic canvas by super-weird Symbolist Josef Váchal, and a lovely swaggering sculpture of a woman by Šaloun. The room of Cubist and Fauvist canvases includes Josef Čapek's much reproduced *Woman Over the City*, Kubišta's grim *Kiss of Death*, and one of the few extant sculptures by Otakar Švec, the man who gave Prague the Stalin Monument. In the new postwar section there's a bevy of Surrealist paintings, Abstract Expressionist works by the likes of Mikuláš Medek, and even a smattering of pieces from the 1980s.

Severočeské muzeum and beyond

Liberec's grandest museum is without doubt the **Severočeské muzeum** (Tues–Sun 9am–5pm), a wonderful period piece from the 1890s built in a theatrical neo-Renaissance style. The museum is a couple of tram stops up 5. května, which turns into Masarykova, a long, leafy avenue flanked by decadent turn-of-the-twentieth-century mansions, once the property of a wealthy *Reichenberger*, now converted into pensions, flats, clinics and the like. Inside the museum, the old communist-era displays on local and natural history are eminently skippable, but the glassware, jewellery and bronzework upstairs make a visit worthwhile. In addition to the locally produced stuff, there's an Art Nouveau lamp and vase by Lötz and another by Gallé, plus a Cubist tea set by Janák, some Wiener Werkstätte silverwork and some wacky shaggy tapestries from the 1970s.

At the top of the road is the city's chief park, and the popular **Botanical Gardens** (Botanická zahrada; daily: April–Sept 8am–6pm; Oct–March until 4pm), famous for their orchids. Here, too, you'll find the oldest **Zoo** (zoologická zahrada; same hours as above) in Bohemia, which boasts seven giraffes, two white tigers and a free-roaming peacock.

Ještěd

Liberec's top hotel – in every sense – sits on the summit of **Ještěd** (1012m) or Jeschken, from which you can look over into Poland and Germany on a clear day. Even if you don't stay the night, be sure to check out the bar-cum-diner and the restaurant with its crazy mirrors, either of which wouldn't look out of place in an episode of a 1960s sci-fi series. To get there from the centre of town, take tram #2 to the end of the line (Kubelíkova), then bus #3 to the **cable car** (*lanovka dráha*), which runs to the summit and hotel hourly 8am to 7pm all year (Mon from 2pm only).

Eating, drinking and entertainment

As for **restaurants**, the *Radniční sklipek* occupies the impressive vaults underneath the radnice and serves up typical Czech meals and *Krušovice* beer. For something a bit more special, head for the restaurant at the *Hotel Radnice*, whose food is a cut above the average (as are the prices). Whatever you do, you must check out the *Pošta* **café**, across the road from the theatre, on the corner of Mariánská. Decorated inside in white and gold Neoclassical style, with dazzling chandeliers, it conjures up late-nineteenth-century Reichenberg beautifully. *U salamandra*, the big modern **pub** halfway down Pražská, doles out heaps of Czech food and mugs of Gambrinus; *Balada* on the parallel street of Moskevská is a cosy place with good pasta and *Svijany* beer. Late-night drinking can be happily continued until the early hours at the *Rockový club* (aka *Golet*), at Tržní náměstí 11, which has live bands most nights. Alternatively, you can combine drinking with playing pool at *Edward's Billiards* on Sokolovské náměstí.

Followers of Czech football might be interested in watching the local team, Slovan Liberec, who surprised the entire country by winning the league in 2002 for the first time ever; Slovan's stadium is south of the centre – take tram #2 to three stops beyond the railway station.

Jablonec nad Nisou

JABLONEC NAD NISOU (Gablonz) starts where the southwestern suburbs of Liberec end. It began life as a small Czech village, but was cut short in its prime by the Hussite Wars, when the whole area was laid waste by the neighbouring Catholic Lusatians. Apocryphally, the only survivor was the large apple tree (*jabloň*) that stood on the village green and gave the subsequent town its name. From the sixteenth century onwards, it was better known as Gablonz, the name used by the Saxon glassmakers who began to settle in the area, but it wasn't until the late nineteenth century that the town's **jewellery trade** really took off.

By the turn of the twentieth century Gablonz was exporting its produce to all corners of the globe, and its burghers grew very rich indeed, erecting private mansions fit for millionaires and lavish public buildings. Everything changed in 1945, when almost the entire German-speaking population of 100,000 was expelled, throwing the local glass industry into crisis (the communists solved the problem by using forced labour in the factories). Meanwhile, uniquely for German refugees from eastern Europe, nearly a fifth of the exiled townsfolk stayed together and resettled in a suburb of Kaufbeuren, in Bavarian Swabia, which they named Neugablonz after their Bohemian home town.

The Town

The main reason for venturing into Jablonec is to visit the engaging **Muzeum skla a bižuterie** (Glass and Jewellery Museum; June–Sept Tues–Sun 9am–5pm; Oct–May Tues–Sun 9am–4pm), downhill from the town hall, in the palatial Zimmer & Schmidt building on U muzea, east off Dolní náměstí. The museum suffers from a lack of labelling but makes up for it with a 3m tower of bangles set against a backdrop of hundreds of earrings, and – on the stairs – the longest necklace in the world, 220m long and made in just four hours by local art students (it shows). Among the best items are the Lötz and Moser glass, the works by Adolf Loos, the Secession and Art Deco hatpins and the incredible collection of early twentieth-century jet jewellery.

The rest of the town centre boasts a number of dour, though impressive, 1930s structures, most notably the **Nová radnice**, whose slimline clock tower dominates the skyline. Up the hill from the town hall, the gargantuan brick-built church, **Nejsvětější Srdce Páně** (Most Sacred Heart of Our Lord), towers over Horní náměstí; local boy Josef Zasche was the architect responsible. The former wealth of the town is obvious from the leafy suburbs, though many of the buildings have not been well looked after. One that has recently been beautifully restored is the town theatre or **Městské divadlo**, designed by the ubiquitous Helmer and Fellner in 1907 and located west down Protofašistických bojovníků. Another that is finally receiving long overdue attention is the graceful **Starokatolický kostel** (open for services only), an earlier minimalist Art Nouveau church designed by Josef Zasche in 1900, situated 500m or so east of the centre, just off route 4 to Tanvald.

Practicalities

You can reach Jablonec on **tram** #11 from Liberec, which winds its way scenically and slowly up the Nisa Valley and deposits you close to the main **train station** to the southwest of the town centre. The choice of accommodation in Jablonec is more limited, though the town's **tourist office** (Mon–Fri 8am–5pm, Sat 8am–noon; Ⓦwww.jablonec.cz), on the main square, should be able to help. The best **hotel** is the fairly brutally modernized late-nineteenth-century *Rehavital* on Jugoslavská (Ⓣ483 317 591, Ⓔrehavital@iol.cz; ❹), which boasts a pool, sauna, gym and excellent restaurant; alternatively, there's the bland *Hotel na baště* opposite Zasche's church on Horní náměstí (Ⓣ483 711 640, Ⓕ483 320 914; ❷). For decent pizzas, head for *Pizzeria Franco*, just down from the radnice at Lidická 15; close by at no. 1 is *Balada*, a funky new place (with a twin in Liberec) that has a stab at some unusual dishes. On warm summer days, locals head out to the nearby **Mšeno lake**, north of the town centre, for a spot of sunbathing and swimming; to join them, take bus #1 or #10 from the centre.

Jizerské hory

Northeast of Liberec, the **Jizerské hory** (Isergebirge) form the western edge of the Krkonoše mountain range, which, in turn, makes up the northern border of Bohemia. Like their eastern neighbours, they have been very badly affected by acid rain, though extensive replanting has softened the impact visually. In fact, on first sight the mountains are undeniably dramatic, rising suddenly from Liberec's northern suburbs to heights over 1000m. Large numbers of Czech and German tourists flock here in summer and winter – and you can follow suit by taking tram #3 from Liberec, or bus #1 from Jablonec to Janov or Bedřichov.

Frýdlant

It was neither an old stronghold nor a new mansion, but a rambling pile consisting of innumerable small buildings closely packed together and of one or two storeys; if K had not known that it was a castle he might have taken it for a little town.

Franz Kafka, *The Castle*

No one is quite sure which castle Kafka had in mind when he wrote his novel, but a strong candidate is surely the hybrid sprawling castle at **FRÝDLANT** (Friedland), a town on the north side of the frontier mountains, forty minutes by train from Liberec. Like his fictional character K, Kafka himself came here on business, though not as a land surveyor but as an accident insurance clerk, a job he did for most of his brief life. In Kafka's time the **hrad** and **zámek** (Tues–Sun: April & Oct 9am–3.30pm; May, June & Sept 9am–4pm; July & Aug 9am–4.30pm) were still owned by the Clam-Gallas clan, but its most famous proprietor was Albrecht von Waldstein, Duke of Friedland, whose statue stands within the castle precincts. Such was the fame of Waldstein that the Clam-Gallas family opened the castle to the public as early as 1801. The guided tour (1hr 40min) might be a bit too much for some people, but the interior is, for once, richly furnished and in good condition, having been a museum now for two hundred years. The castle is ensconced on a rock over the river, a short walk southeast of the train station and town centre along a pretty, tree-lined avenue.

If you want to stay in the area, try the large, friendly *Frýdlant* **campsite** (May –mid-Sept) by a bend in the river beyond the castle, or the campsite (May–Sept) in **HEJNICE**, 10km southeast (30min by train; change at

Raspenava), a village dominated by its towering pilgrimage church, with an attractive frescoed interior. Hejnice also has a good choice of **hotels** and pensions; try the *Hotel Garni Lázně Libverda* (☏482 368 111, ✆www.lazne-libverda.cz; ❸) part of a small spa complex that offers various treatments. You can cross the border into Poland just 13km north of Frýdlant at Habartice-Zawidów, on the road to Zgorzelec/Görlitz.

Travel details

Trains

Prague Masarykovo nádraží to: Bohušovice (5–7 daily; 1hr); Chomutov (2–3 daily; 2hr 30min); Kadaň (2 daily; 2hr 50min); Louny (2–3 daily; 1hr 50min); Most (2 daily; 2hr 30min); Žatec (2 daily; 2hr).

Prague Hlavní nádraží to: Chomutov (3 daily; 2hr 30min); Kadaň (2 daily; 2hr 50min); Liberec (1 daily; 2hr 45min); Most (2 daily; 2hr 30min); Žatec (1 daily; 2hr).

Prague Holešovice to: Děčín (every 2hrs; 1hr 50min); Teplice (2 daily; 2hr); Ústí nad Labem (12–16 daily; 1hr 30min).

Česká Lípa to: Benešov nad Ploučnicí (8–10 daily; 20–30min); Děčín (7–8 daily; 35–50min); Liberec (11–12 daily; 1hr 5min–1hr 30min); Litoměřice (every 2–3hr; 1hr 10min); Jablonné v Podještědí (11–12 daily; 35–50min); Mimoň (11–12 daily; 20–30min); Zákupy (8–9 daily; 12min).

Chomutov to: Karlovy Vary (13–14 daily; 1hr–1hr 15min); Kadaň (hourly; 10–15min); Klašterec nad Ohří (15–17 daily; 20min); Most (16–18 daily; 25–30min); Plzeň (4 daily; 2hr 30min); Ústí nad Labem (hourly; 1hr 15min); Žatec (11–13 daily; 20–30min).

Děčín to: Benešov nad Ploučnicí (every 1–2hr; 15–20min); Česká Kamenice (10–12 daily; 35–40min); Liberec (5–6 daily; 2hr–2hr 30min);

Teplice lesní brána (7 daily; 1hr 30min); Ústí nad Labem (every 1–2hr; 20–30min).

Liberec to: Frýdlant (7–11 daily; 35min); Jablonec nad Nisou (every 1–2hr; 30min); Turnov (16 daily; 50min).

Litoměřice to: Mělník (10 daily; 30–45min); Ploskovice (every 2–3hr; 12min); Úštěk (every 2–3hr; 35min); Ústí nad Labem (7–10 daily; 25min).

Louny to: Libochovice (6–8 daily; 45min); Most (13–15 daily; 30–45min); Žatec (5 daily; 35min).

Most to: Děčín (4 daily; 1hr 15min–1hr 40min); Duchcov (every 1–2hr; 15–25min); Teplice (every 1–2hr; 30–40min); Ústí nad Labem (every 1–2hr; 45min–1hr).

Teplice to: Litvínov (4–6 daily; 35min); Osek (7–10 daily; 20min).

Buses

Prague to: Chomutov (up to 7 daily; 2hr 30min); Liberec (hourly; 1hr 40min); Litoměřice (9 daily; 1hr 15min); Terezín (9 daily; 1hr 10min).

Česká Kamenice to: Jetřichovice (Mon–Fri 4 daily; 25min).

Děčín to: Hřensko (8 daily; 20min); Mezná (up to 4 daily; 35min).

Jablonec to: Harrachov (6 or more daily; 1hr 15min).

East Bohemia

CHAPTER 5

Highlights

* **Český ráj** – Great rambling countryside, dotted with ruined castles, sandstone protrusions, chateaux and folk architecture. **See p.285**

* **Adršpach rocks** – A "rock city" that rises out of the woods to the east of the Krknoše mountains. **See p.300**

* **Nové Město nad Metují** – Picture-postcard square and a chateau whose interior includes work by early twentieth-century architects. **See p.304**

* **Hradec Králové** – A picturesque old town standing opposite an innovative new town, built between the wars by Rondo-Cubist architects. **See p.306**

* **Kuks** – Long defunct spa with the finest array of Baroque statues outside of Prague. **See p.312**

* **Pardubice** – As well as its old town and chateau, Pardubice boasts a Rondo-Cubist crematorium and the world's most challenging steeplechase course. **See p.315**

* **Litomyšl** – Attractive town with Renaissance chateau and the extraordinarily weird Portmonbeum, designed by Josef Váchal in the early twentieth century. **See p.319**

5

East Bohemia

ast Bohemia (Východní Čechy) is probably the most difficult Czech region to categorize. It has none of the polluting industry of its immediate neighbours, though it has suffered indirectly from their excesses; it contains some of the flattest landscape in Bohemia, but also its highest peaks; historically it has been predominantly Czech, though pockets of German settlement have left their mark in the culture and architecture. Lastly, the region has never really enjoyed fixed boundaries, a confusion compounded by the administrative borders currently in operation, which have arbitrarily added on parts of Moravia.

For variety of scenery, however, East Bohemia is hard to beat. Along the northern border with Poland, the peaks of the **Krkonoše** and the Orlické hory form an almost continuous mountain range, with excellent opportunities for hiking and skiing. The lower-lying **Český ráj**, to the south, and the area around **Broumov** to the east are wonderfully pastoral, and typically Bohemian, landscapes of rocky sandstone covered in thick forest. Further south still, the terrain on either side of the River Labe – the *Polabí*, as it is known – is flat, fertile and, for the most part, fairly dull. But the towns of the river basin do much to make up for it – **Hradec Králové**, the regional capital, and its historic rival, **Pardubice**, both boast handsomely preserved historic centres.

Český ráj

Less than 100km from Prague, the sandstone rocks and densely wooded hills of the **Český ráj** (Bohemian Paradise) have been a popular spot for weekending Praguers for over a century. Although the Český ráj is officially limited to a small nature reserve southeast of Turnov, the term is loosely applied to the entire swathe of hills from Mnichovo Hradiště to Jičín. **Turnov** is the most convenient base for exploring the region, though **Jičín** is infinitely more appealing, with its seventeenth-century old town preserved intact. But more interesting than either of the towns is the surrounding **countryside**: ruined fortresses, bizarre rock formations and traditional folk architecture, all smothered in a blanket of pine forests.

From Turnov, local **trains** run roughly every two hours to Jičín, and local **buses** from both towns infrequently wind their way through the otherwise inaccessible villages nearby. Generally, though, the distances are so small – Turnov to Jičín, for example, is just 24km – that you'd be better off buying a map and **walking** along the network of marked footpaths.

Turnov and around

TURNOV (Turnau), as the name suggests, can be less than stimulating, though its main square has recently been perked up, and the town has done a good job promoting itself as the logistical and accommodation centre for the region. Its chief attraction is the **Český ráj museum**, on Skálova (May–Sept Tues–Sun 9am–5pm; Oct–April Tues–Sun 9am–4pm), containing an interminable collection of semiprecious stones dug out of a nearby hillside, and temporary exhibitions of nature photography and the like. None of this matters, of course, if you're spending your days walking. The best **hotels** in town are the late-nineteenth-century *Korunní Princ* on the main square (☎481 313 520, ⓕ481 313 522; ❷), which also boasts the best restaurant in town, and the similarly remodelled *Cleopatra* (☎481 322 417, ⓔh.cleopatra@worldonline.cz; ❸), just up from the main square on 5 května. Hostel beds (160 Kč) and cheap rooms can be had at the clean and simple *Karel IV* at Žižkova 501 (☎481 323 855, ⓕ481 321 708; ❷); to get there, head left up Husova from 5 května, which then becomes Žižkova. In addition to the **restaurants** at the *Korunní Princ* and *Cleopatra* hotels, the smoky red *Pizzeria K* on the square does mini-pizzas from 35Kč. The town's **tourist office** (July–Aug Mon–Fri 8am–6pm, Sat 9am–4pm, Sun 9am–2pm; Sept–June Mon–Fri 8am–5pm, Sat 9am–noon; ☎481 366 255, ⓦwww.turnov.cz or www.ceskyraj.cz), also on the main square, can book all kinds of accommodation, including private rooms, as can Čechotour, located on Nádražní near the train station, a ten-minute walk away west of the old town on the other side of the river.

One place worth visiting, on the outskirts of Turnov, is the chateau of **Hrubý Rohozec** (April & Oct Sat & Sun 9am–3pm; May, June & Sept Tues–Sun 9am–4pm; July–Aug Tues–Sun 9am–5pm), high up on the left bank of the Jizera river, on the side of route 10 to Železný Brod. A Gothic castle redesigned in the Renaissance, it's a welcome contrast to the rest of the town, and its hour-long guided tour gives you access to some great views and a series of handsome Renaissance chambers.

Valdštejn and Hruboskalské skalní

A beautiful two-kilometre walk through the woods along either the red- or green-marked path from the Turnov-město train station (one stop down the Jičín line) brings you to the former Gothic stronghold of **Valdštejn** (April & Oct Sat & Sun 9am–4pm; May–Sept daily 9am–4.30pm), ancestral seat of the Waldsteins for many years. Already in ruins by the late sixteenth century, it was occupied by vagrants, and later attempts to restore it never came to fruition, though its position remains impressive – as does the eighteenth-century stone bridge, flanked by Baroque statues.

Another 2km southeast, the first (and arguably the best) of Český ráj's skalné města or "sandstone cities", **Hruboskalské skalní**, unfolds amidst the trees. It's easy to spend hours clambering up and down the bluffs and dodging the crevices, whose names – Myší díra (Mouse Hole), Dračí věž (Dragon's Tower) and Sahara – give some idea of the variety of rock formations. Various viewpoints, like Zamecká vyhlídka or Mariánská vyhlídka, range high above the tree line, with the protruding stone slabs emerging from the pine trees like ossified giants.

The nearby castle of **Hrubá skála** is a colossal nineteenth-century reconstruction of the original Gothic castle. It's very popular with Czech film crews, and is now a wonderful and very reasonably priced hotel, *Zámek Hrubá Skála* (☎481 389 681, ⓔhrskala@iol.cz; ❸), with a baronial restaurant open to non-residents. From here, a green-marked path descends through the Myší díra and the Dračí skály, zigzagging down to the large lakeside **campsite**, *Sedmihorky* (April–Oct), near the Karlovice-Sedmihorky station on the Turnov–Jičín line. Also down here is a well-sited, if faded, spa hotel, *Lázně Sedmihorky* (☎481 389 170, ⓔlsedmihor@iol.cz; ❷).

Trosky

The spectacular ruined castle of **Trosky** (April & Oct Sat & Sun 8.30am–4pm; May–Sept Tues–Sun 8.30am–6pm), which means literally "rubble", 5km southeast of Hrubá skála, is the Český ráj's number-one landmark. Its twin Gothic towers, Bába (Grandmother) and Panna (Virgin), were built on volcanic basalt rocks which burst through the sandstone strata millions of years ago. You can climb the ridge between Bába and Panna (the higher of the two) for a far-reaching view of the Jizera basin. The flash new **hotel** and restaurant complex, *Trosky* (☎ & ⓕ481 382 290; ❷), by the castle car park, offers cheap doubles, and there are two very basic **campsites**, the *Svitacka* site (May–Sept), a short

ČESKÝ RÁJ

distance to the south, and the *Vidlák* site (June–Aug), 2km northwest along the red-marked path, by the lake of the same name, with a cheap but decent *hospoda* across the road. Three or four **buses** a day run to Trosky from Turnov; trains are slower but more frequent and deliver you at Ktová station on the Jičín line, from where it's a two-kilometre walk uphill.

Sobotka and around

Compared to Turnov or Jičín, **SOBOTKA** is off the beaten track: 13km from either place, with limited accommodation, and only accessible by train from Jičín (50min; change at Libuň). Unless you're camping (and hiking) or staying in one of the handful of pensions, it's no good as a base for exploring the region, though it does harbour some good examples of the local brightly painted half-timbered architecture and – just northwest of the town, on a strange conical hill – the striking seventeenth-century **Humprecht** hunting lodge (April & Oct Sat & Sun 9am–noon & 1–4pm; May–Aug Tues–Sun 8am–noon & 1–5pm; Sept 9am–noon & 1–5pm), named after its eccentric aristocratic instigator, Jan Humprecht Černín. It's a bizarre building, worth a peek inside if only for the central trompe l'oeil dining room, a windowless sixteen-metre-high oval cylinder with the acoustics of a cathedral. On the other side of the hill from Sobotka is a rudimentary **campsite** (mid-June to Sept) and a swimming pool. The best **pension** in the immediate vicinity is the *Ort* (☎ & ℱ 493 571 137; ❷), 4km to the northeast in Mladějov.

Podkost

One bus daily (at around 1pm) covers the 3km northwest from Sobotka to **PODKOST**, a small settlement by a pond at the edge of the Žehrov forest. The village is dominated in every way by **Kost** castle (April & Oct Sat & Sun 9am–noon & 1–4pm; May–Aug Tues–Sun 8am–noon & 1–5pm; Sept Tues–Sun 9am–noon & 1–5pm), which sits on top of a gigantic sandstone pedestal and sports a characteristic rectangular keep. Thanks to a fire in 1635, after which it was used as a granary, Kost was spared the attentions of later architectural trends and retains the full flavour of its fourteenth-century origins, making it the best-preserved castle in the Český ráj. The late-Gothic art exhibition is well worth seeing, too, though it's only open to tours, which can be very popular at the height of summer. Down in the village, there's one cheap **hotel**, the *Helikar* (☎ 493 571 127; ❷), good for a bed or a beer.

Around Mužský

You're more likely to find suitable accommodation at **NOVÁ VES**, another 4km northwest along the scenic red-marked path through the woods of the Žehrovský les. This tiny village by the **Komárovský lake** has three campsites and plenty of pensions along its shore. North of the lake lies a matrix of paths that crisscross the complex rock systems within the forest, emerging 3km later at the hotel *Pod Kaštany* (☎ 326 789 737; ❷) and a **campsite** (May–Sept) in **Příhrazy**. Paths spread out west from here and back into the woods until they reach **Mužský** (463m), from where it's another 2km uphill to the prehistoric burial ground of Hrada and the rocky viewpoint at Drábské světničky. The truly amazing sight of **Valečov**, a ruined fort cut into the rock, lies another 2km to the south at the southwestern edge of the woodland. On a day's hike, you could easily do a round trip from Nová Ves or Příhrazy by heading east from Valečov, or else continuing another 3km west on the red-marked path to the station at Mnichovo Hradiště (see p.290), on the main railway line to Prague.

Mnichovo Hradiště

If you're thinking of exploring the area around Mužský, you could use the small industrial town of **MNICHOVO HRADIŠTĚ** (Münchengrätz), at the southwest corner of the Český ráj, as a base. The main square has a very handsome neo-Renaissance radnice smothered in sgraffito, as well as one of the region's better **hotels**, *U hroznu* (T 326 771 617, F 326 771 246; ❸), with its own *vinárna*. If you arrive by bus, you'll be deposited right on the main square; the **train station** is about five blocks to the southeast.

The town itself has an attractive Renaissance **zámek** (April & Oct Sat & Sun 9am–noon & 1–3pm; May–Sept Tues–Sun 9am–noon & 1–4pm), 1km north of the main square, that was owned by the Waldstein family right up to 1945. Interesting enough in itself, with lots of period furniture, a fine library, Chinese porcelain and attractive English-style grounds, the chateau is also the final resting place of **Albrecht von Waldstein**, who was murdered in Cheb (Eger) in 1634 (see opposite). Initially buried in Valdice, outside Jičín, the general's body wasn't brought to Mnichovo Hradiště until the eighteenth century, by which time the family couldn't afford the lavish mausoleum Albrecht himself had hoped for – instead, all you see is a modest plaque, which wasn't erected until 1934. Despite this, the Baroque chapel of **sv Anna**, in which Waldstein is buried, still merits a visit if only for its impressive stucco ceilings and lapidarium; the chapel is northeast of the chateau, accessible from the road to Podolí.

Jičín and around

At the southeastern tip of the Český ráj, where the fertile plain of the River Labe touches the foothills of the Krkonoše, **JIČÍN** (Gitschin), an hour by train from Turnov, is easily the most rewarding stop in the region. Its location, close to some of the Český ráj's most dramatic scenery, makes it a convenient base for some easy hiking, while its Renaissance zámek and arcaded main square make it by far the most attractive town in which to stay. Jičín is also easy to reach, with comprehensive bus connections throughout the region.

The Town

The town is closely associated with the infamous **Albrecht von Waldstein**, who, during his brief and meteoric rise to eminence (see opposite), owned almost every chateau in the region. Waldstein confiscated Jičín early on in the Thirty Years' War, and chose this rather unlikely town as the capital of his new personal empire, the Duchy of Friedland. He established a hospital to ensure his workers were not incapacitated for long, insisted everyone attend the Jesuit college he founded, and established a mint here; but for his murder, he would no doubt have fulfilled his plans for a bishopric and a university.

In the 1620s he rebuilt the main square – now named **Valdštejnovo náměstí** after him – in stone, in a late-Renaissance style, full of light touches. Waldstein even lent the local burghers money to adapt their houses to suit his plans for the square. One side is still dominated by Waldstein's **zámek** (Tues–Sun 9am–5pm), which now contains a dull local museum and, in the converted riding school, an art gallery, as well as the great conference hall in which the leaders of the three great European powers, Russia, Austria and Prussia, formed the Holy Alliance against Napoleon in 1813. A covered passage connects the chateau's eastern wing with the **Jesuit church** next door, allowing the nobility to avoid their unsavoury subjects while en route to mass. But this steeple-less Baroque church is eclipsed by the mighty sixteenth-century **Valdická brána** (April, May & Sept Tues–Fri 2–5pm, Sat & Sun 9am–5pm; June–Aug daily 9am–5pm) close by, whose newly restored tower gallery offers a panorama over the town.

Albrecht von Waldstein (known to the Czechs as Albrecht z Valdštejna, and to the English as Wallenstein – the name given to him by the German playwright Schiller in his tragic trilogy) was the most notorious warlord of the Thirty Years' War. If the imperial astrologer Johannes Kepler is to be believed, this is all because he was born at four in the afternoon on September 14, 1583. According to Kepler's horoscope, Waldstein was destined to be greedy, deceitful, unloved and unloving. Sure enough, at an early age he tried to kill a servant, for which he was expelled from his Lutheran school. Recuperating in Italy, he converted to Catholicism (an astute career move) and married a wealthy widow who conveniently died shortly after the marriage. Waldstein used his new fortune to cultivate a friendship with Prince Ferdinand, heir to the Habsburg Empire, who in turn thought that a tame Bohemian noble could come in handy.

Within five years of the Battle of Bílá hora in 1620, Waldstein owned a quarter of Bohemia, either by compulsory purchase or in return for money or troops loaned to Ferdinand. It was a good time to go into property: Ferdinand's imperial armies, who were busy restoring Catholicism throughout Europe, provided a ready-made market for agricultural produce. And as a rising general, Waldstein could get away with a certain amount of insider trading, marching armies with as many as 125,000 men over enemy territory or land owned by rivals, laying waste to fields and then selling his troops supplies from his own pristine Bohemian estates.

As Waldstein ranged further afield in Germany, conquering Jutland, Pomerania, Alsace and most of Brandenburg on Ferdinand's behalf, his demands for reward grew ever more outrageous. Already duke of Friedland and governor of Prague, Waldstein was appointed duke of Mecklenburg in 1628. This upset not only the existing duke, who had backed Ferdinand's opponents, but even the emperor's loyalist supporters. If Ferdinand thought fit to hand one of the greatest German titles to this Czech upstart, was any family's inheritance secure? By 1630 Waldstein had earned himself the right to keep his hat on in the imperial presence, as well as the dubious honour of handing the emperor a napkin after he had used his fingerbowl. However, at this point Waldstein's services became too expensive for Ferdinand, so the duke was relieved of his command.

The following year the Saxons occupied Prague, and the emperor was forced to reinstate Waldstein. Ferdinand couldn't afford to do without the supplies from Waldstein's estates, but knew he was mortgaging large chunks of the empire to pay for his services. More alarmingly, there were persistent rumours that Waldstein was about to declare himself king of Bohemia and defect to the French enemy. In 1634 Waldstein openly rebelled against Ferdinand, who immediately hatched a plot to murder Waldstein, sending a motley posse including English, Irish and Scottish mercenaries to the border town of Cheb, where they cut the general down in his nightshirt as he tried to rise from his sickbed. Some see Waldstein as the first man to unify Germany since Charlemagne, others see him as a wily Czech hero. In reality, he was probably just an ambitious, violent man, as his stars had predicted.

One of Waldstein's more endearing additions to the town is the **lipová alej** (now known as Revoluční), an avenue of 1200 lime trees, planted simultaneously in two dead straight lines, 2km long, by Waldstein's soldiers. At the far end is the once princely garden of **Libosad**, now an overgrown spinney but still worth a wander. The melancholy of its Renaissance loggia, last repaired at the end of the First Republic, is matched by the nearby Jewish cemetery, which boasts some finely carved tombstones and is overshadowed by the horror of one of the country's most brutal Communist prisons in nearby **VALDICE**. Originally a seventeenth-century Carthusian monastery, it was converted into a prison by the Habsburgs, and used after 1948 to keep the regime's political prisoners in a suitably medieval state of deprivation. It still functions as a prison today, housing some of the country's most hardened criminals.

Practicalities

The **tourist office** (Mon–Fri 9am–6pm; Sat 9am–2pm; Sun 9am–noon; ☎493 534 390), in the zámek, is very helpful with finding **accommodation**, including private rooms in and around town. Two central pensions provide simple rooms: *U České koruny* (☎493 531 241; ❷), on the main square, and *Na rynečku* (☎493 534 857; ❷) just off the square behind the run-down church of sv Ignác down Chelčického. There is also the friendly pension *Albrecht* (☎493 532 544; ❷), with just a pair of rooms in a family home 1km down the lime-tree avenue that leads to Valdice at Revoluční 712. Despite its prominent position just outside the Valdická brana on Žižkovo náměstí, *Hotel Paříž* (☎ & ℱ493 534 510; ❷) is poorly kept and is better avoided. Two kilometres down route 16 to Mladá Boleslav the *Rumcajs* **campsite** (May–Sept) is set behind a motel (☎493 531 078; ❶) which also has wooden chalets.

While accommodation is fairly run-of-the-mill, there are plenty of unusual **restaurants** to choose from in the old town: *U piráta*, outside the Valdická brana at Husova 127, comes as an unexpected new addition, with trout, tuna and even shark in addition to standard Czech main dishes, to back up its off-beat buccaneer theme. *U Matěje*, on Nerudova just off the northwest corner of the main square, offers everything from goulash to venison to Chinese dishes. Highly imaginative and filling pizzas, as well as what the menu describes as "food for those who say meat is meat", can be had in the pleasing little patio at *Pizzerie U Henryho*, just behind U České koruny on the main square.

Prachovské skály

Despite the very real attractions of the town, the reason most people come to Jičín is to see the **Prachovské skály**, a series of sandstone and basalt rocks hidden in woods 8km to the northwest. To get there, it's a gentle walk along the yellow-marked path, via the Rumcajs campsite, though there are local buses too. The rocks lack the subtlety of the Hruboskalské skalní, but make up for it in sheer size and area; their name derives from the dust (*prach*) that covers the forest floor, forming a carpet of sand. In high season, swarms of climbers cling to the silent, grey rocks like a plague of locusts, but out of season it's possible to find a tranquil spot; try the green-marked path. There are dorm beds available in the *ubytovna* right by the rocks, but these are usually booked solid in summer; try instead a private room, or the *Parkhotel Skalní město* (☎493 525 011, ⓦwww.skalnimesto.cz; ❸), a fine place back down the road to Jičín.

Železný Brod, Malá Skála and Sychrov

Heading northeast from Turnov, the railway follows the course of the Jizera river to **ŽELEZNÝ BROD** (Eisenbrod), one of the many centres of Bohemia's world-famous glass-making industry. It's a town of contradictions, its factories and high-rises spread along the banks of the river, while half-timbered cottages in the traditional Český ráj colours cover the hillside. The tiny main square is a typical mix of styles: one side is taken up by two wholly uninspiring 1950s buildings – the glass and crystal factory and the now-abandoned *Hotel Cristal* – while the other side shelters the nineteenth-century town hall and the timber-framed **museum** (May–Sept Tues–Sun 8.30am–noon & 1–4pm; Oct–April Sat & Sun only) of local arts and crafts. Up the hillside by the town church, which sports a nifty little wooden belfry, are some outstanding examples of **folk architecture**, usually confined to more inaccessible villages.

Železný Brod is really not an appealing town in which to stay, so you're much better off heading to the wonderful little village of **MALÁ SKÁLA**, 5km back down the valley towards Turnov (and also accessible by train and bus). Nothing much ever really happens here, but it's a supremely pretty place to be based for hikes into the surrounding hills. A steep red-marked path leads from behind the train station to the **Suché skály** (Dry Rocks) and a number of rock caves, used during the Counter-Reformation as safe houses for persecuted Protestants. A green-marked path then leads to the hamlet of Prosička, after which the blue-marked path heads back to Malá Skála; the whole route can easily be covered in a half day. Another red-marked path from Malá Skála follows a ridge on the other side of the river, from where the view across the valley to the ruined castle of **Frýdštejn** is the reward for your pains. You could extend the day by dropping into the castle, then continuing on up the blue-marked path to the viewpoint atop Kopanina, and returning to Malá Skála via the green-marked path. As for accommodation, there's a **campsite** on the right bank of the river, and a delightful little pension with a very good restaurant, *Teta Marta* (☎483 392 140, Ⓔtetamarta@hotmail.com; ❷), 1km up the road to Frýdštejn. Right near the train station is the larger, wooden *Hotel Skála* (☎483 342 299, Ⓦwww.cz-guide.cz/klient/hotelskala.html; ❷), a reasonable enough place that also serves up steaks and chops from its outdoor grill.

Six kilometres northwest of Turnov, off route 35, **Sychrov** (Tues–Sun: April, Sept & Oct 9am–noon & 1–3.30pm; May 9am–noon & 1–4.30pm; June–Aug 8am–noon & 1–4.30pm) is a relatively recent aristocratic pile, romantically remodelled in neo-Gothic style by the Rohans, who bought the estate in 1820 having been forced into exile by the French Revolution. Apart from the pseudo-medieval craftsmanship of its interior, the castle is famed for its long-standing connections with Dvořák, who enjoyed the family's patronage and visited often. This partly explains the excellent season of concerts that take place here each year. The castle is only about ten minutes by train from Turnov on the railway line to Liberec.

The Krkonoše

The **Krkonoše** (Giant Mountains) are the highest mountains in Bohemia and formed part of the historical northeastern border of its ancient kingdom. They were uninhabited until the sixteenth and seventeenth centuries, when glass-making and ore-mining brought the first German and Italian settlers to the Riesengebirge, as they were then known. The mountains' undoubted beauty ensured an early tourist following, and, for resorts like Špindlerův Mlýn and Pec pod Sněžkou, it's now the sole industry. Despite being one of the few protected national parks in the country, the Krkonoše suffered considerably from acid rain in the decades up to the 1990s – much of which was caused by heavy industries over the border in Poland. Once the trees were badly affected, insects did the rest, transforming them into grey husks, devoid of foliage. Extensive felling took place, aimed at stopping the spread of the destructive insects, but it was a bit like a smoker removing their lungs to prevent cancer. For many, the fate of Bohemia's ancient forests was the most damning indictment of the Communists' forty years of mismanagement, and as if to rub it in, the focus during the 1980s was on new hotels and chairlifts rather than environmental measures.

Since 1989, however, the condition of the mountains has improved remarkably, with plenty of new tree planting and rebirth on the heels of much stricter emissions controls in both Poland and the Czech Republic. Czechs will reassure you that things here were never as bad as in the Krušné hory (see p.252) anyway, and it's true: if you stay in the largely unspoiled valley, or come here in winter when the snow obscures much of the damage, it's possible to remain oblivious. In summer, though, when walking is the main pastime, you can still see the relics of barren hillsides and ashen tree trunks amid the general greenness.

Practicalities

The Krkonoše has long been the country's top outdoor resort area, which means **accommodation** should be booked in advance at the height of the winter ski season, and in July and August. That said, the entire mountain range is teeming with cheap **private rooms**, which can be booked through the numerous accommodation agencies in the resorts. Špindlerův Mlýn and Jánské Lázně are undoubtedly the prettiest towns in which to stay; theoretically, you can also sleep at one of the **bouda** (chalets) dotted across the mountains, originally hideouts for the fleeing Protestants in the seventeenth century, but even these often require advance planning. **Camping** is one way of ensuring a place for the night, although facilities are somewhat restricted. Within the strict boundaries of the national park are just two sites, though plenty more lie along the fringes.

As for transport, **buses** are the best way to get around, with plenty of fast connections to Prague and throughout east Bohemia. **Trains** can get you as far as Harrachov, Vrchlabí and Trutnov, though these connections can be awkward. There are also numerous **chairlifts** that operate even in summer. However, **hiking** is undoubtedly the best way of getting around, since each valley is basically a long, winding dead end for motor vehicles, with pretty hefty car-parking fees (and sometimes queues) aimed at dissuading drivers from bringing their vehicles into the park. There are now three 24-hour **border crossings into Poland**: Harrachov–Jakuszyce, Královec–Lubawka and Pomezní Boudy–Przelecz Okraj.

For those intent on serious hiking, a detailed **map** of the mountains, showing the network of colour-coded marked paths, is essential. **Warm clothing** is also important, no matter what the season – the summits are battered by wind almost every day, and have an average annual temperature of around freezing. Persistent mist – around for about 300 days in the year – makes sticking to the marked paths a must. In winter, most of the high-level paths are closed, and recently, even in summer, several have been closed to give the mountains a rest. To find out the latest details, head for the tourist information offices in any of the resorts. Keep in mind, too, that you will hardly be alone on the trails, as the mountains are immensely popular among Czechs, Poles and Germans.

The Krkonoše is also the most popular region in the Czech Republic for **skiing**, since it receives by far the longest and most reliable snowfall in the country. Pec pod Sněžkou is the largest resort, followed by Špindlerův Mlýn and Harrachov. Queues for lifts everywhere can be long and slow, but are more than compensated for by the cheapness of the ski passes and accommodation – although these have risen to levels formidable to the average Czech. Lift tickets cost upwards of 400Kč per day, and ski rental is easily had for around 250Kč per day. In summer, numerous outlets in each resort offer mountain bike rental, though this is not terribly recommended due to the dearth of roads and steepness of the hills.

Vrchlabí

VRCHLABÍ (Hohenelbe) is the hub of the Krkonoše for transport and supplies, and not as well situated for skiing or hiking as the other main towns. Reservations are recommended for the direct **buses** from Prague, some of which continue on to Špindlerův Mlýn (see below); if you're travelling by **train**, you'll need to change at Kunčice nad Labem, 4km south. Hotel **accommodation** boils down to the good-quality *Labut'* (☎499 421 964, ⓦwww.krkonose.cz/hotellabut; ❸) on the main street, Krkonošská. There are also many small, centrally-located pensions to choose from, such as the self-service apartments above the *Klasika* pizzeria and steakhouse just beyond (☎ & Ⓕ499 421 260, ⓦwww.klasika.com; ❷). Of the three local **campsites**, the *Výsplachy* (June to mid-Sept), just south of route 14, has the best locale, alongside a lake. For **food**, the aforementioned *Klasika* has become a local favourite for pizzas and steaks, or you can stretch out in the outdoor grill of the *Krušovická Restaurace* on the main square. This place also has an **internet café** upstairs.

Vrchlabí's official **tourist office** (Mon–Fri 9am–12.30pm & 1.30–5pm; ☎499 451 111) is in the sgraffitoed radnice on the main square, náměstí T.G. Masaryka. For comprehensive room booking and tour services right across the Krkonoše, check out the ING Tours travel agency (Mon–Fri 8am–6pm, Sat 9am–noon; ☎499 453 623, ⓦwww.ingtours.cz) in the IT Centrum near the square. This complex also contains the best **supermarket** in town.

Vrchlabí's long main street stretches for 3km along the banks of the Labe, taking you past the pleasing gardens and zoo of the sixteenth-century chateau and a number of traditional wooden arcaded folk buildings around the centre. A trio of folk houses at the far end of the street – one in stone flanked by two timber-framed neighbours – have been converted into the small **Krkonošské muzeum** (Tues–Sun 9am–noon & 1–4pm), containing folk art, sundry stones and displays on regional life through the ages. These houses also contain an office of the Krkonošský národní park (KRNAP) (Mon–Sat 9am–noon & 1–4pm), good for maps and information on weather conditions.

Špindlerův Mlýn and around

No doubt **ŠPINDLERŮV MLÝN** (Spindlermühle), 15km north up the Labe Valley, was once an idyllic, isolated mountain hamlet. Successive generations, however, have found it difficult to resist exploiting a town where seven valleys meet, and countless private pensions and hotels lie scattered across the hillsides. Still, the place retains a cosy feel, and makes a fine base for a few days of outdoor activity. The river Labe, here still a stream, flows through its tiny centre, which is just a convergence of a few roads.

It's important to book **accommodation** in advance during summer and winter high seasons, and the booking office of the Tourist Shop Pavilon (☎499 523 364, ⓦwww.spindleruvmlyninfo.cz), right in the centre, can help, as well as provide ski rental. This is a private agency with ties to particular local hotels; if you prefer impartial advice, make for the official **tourist office** (daily 9–11.30am & 12.30–5pm), hidden beyond the post office on the other side of the stream, which posts a complete list of accommodation possibilities in the vicinity. Recommendable hotels include the lovely wood-panelled mountain lodge *Start Hotel* (☎499 433 305, ⓦwww.hotelstart.cz; ❹), which stands on a slope just west of the central area. Equally well-appointed is the new *Hotel Praha* (☎499 523 516, Ⓔhotel.praha@spindleruvmlyninfo.cz; ❹), to the north of centre, with a slight Art Nouveau theme, and a nice restaurant with a terrace overlooking the town. Lower-end rooms can be found in the rustic *Pension Jaro* (T499 523 433; ❸), and the very pretty *Pension U Čeňků* (T499 523 700, Wwww.nahory.com; ❸), across the road from each other near the tourist office. Up the hill to the east in Svatý Petr is the modernized chalet *Pension Stráž* (T & F499 523 350; ❸). Another interesting option is to head for one of the **boudy** (chalets) up in the hills: armed with a map, you could aim for *Josefova bouda* (T & F499 523 422; ❷), near the end of the bus line at Špindlerova bouda, or *Bradlerovy boudy* (T499 422 056; ❷), along the green-marked trail east of the source of the Labe (*pramen Labe;* see below). There are two fairly pricey **campsites** a couple of kilometres north of the central area, both open all year.

A good place to grab a bite **to eat** is the terrace pizzeria in the Pavilon, by the edge of the stream. The aforementioned hotels both have good restaurants, and the *Pension U Čeňků* has a cute patio from which to sip a beer or have a meal. Finally, the *Špindlerovská hospoda* right bang in town is a decent pub with good food. If you're driving, keep in mind that **parking** is severely restricted in town, and unless your hotel has reserved space you'll have to leave your vehicle at the car park just to the south, and pay an exorbitant fee for the privilege.

Other than hanging around alongside the pretty riverbanks or poking into shops, there's little else to do in town other than ride the year-round Medvědín **chairlift** (*lánová dráha*) up the mountain of the same name (1235m), to the north of the central area (follow the signs from the left bank of the river; chair-lift runs every half-hour), or try out the new year-round **bobsleigh track** (*bobová dráha*) nearby. The **River Labe**, which flows into the North Sea (as the Elbe) near Hamburg, has its source in the Krkonoše. It takes about three hours to reach the source (*pramen Labe*): a long, boulder-strewn walk along the valley, followed by a short, sharp climb out of the forest. Characteristically for the Krkonoše, the summit is disappointingly flat and boggy, and the source itself (500m from the Polish border) no great sight. If you're carrying your pack with you, continue for three hours along the blue-marked track to Harrachov (see below). Otherwise, it's around two hours back to Špindlerův Mlýn, via Horní Mísečky and Medvědín. For a **glimpse of Poland**, you should catch a bus from Špindlerův Mlýn to Špindlerova bouda, where dead trees, Polish border guards and the odd grazing sheep provide the entertainment.

Harrachov

Five buses and three trains a day (change at nearby Tanvald) make the journey from Prague to the westernmost resort in the Krkonoše, **HARRACHOV** (Harrachsdorf), whose cottages are scattered about the Mumlava Valley. A glassworks was established here in 1712, and the **Muzeum skla** (Glass Museum; Mon–Fri 9am–5pm, Sat 9am–1pm) has a small sample of glassware throughout the ages, as well as a shop. There's also a new **Lyžařské muzeum** (Ski Museum; daily 9am–3pm), further up the road, which traces the history of skiing, and celebrates Harrachov's occasional hosting of a round of the world ski-jump championships (most recently in March 2002). Otherwise, you could aim for the rather pretty waterfall known as Mumlov, up a trail north of the bus station. Harrachov is basically a ski resort though, so unless you're aiming for the slopes, your time is best spent hiking the surrounding mountains. The official national park tourist office, KRNAP (daily 8am–noon & 1–4.30pm) is close to the bus station, and can help with maps and walking suggestions.

Accommodation in Harrachov can be significantly cheaper than in the neighbouring resorts, but it can still take some effort to secure a room in high season. The official **tourist office**, MIC (March–Oct Mon–Fri 9–11.30am &

noon–5pm, Sat 9am–noon; Nov–Feb daily 8am–8pm; ⓣ481 529 600), can book hotels, pensions and private rooms in the area; there's even a free phone outside the office so you can ring round yourself after hours. The office is on the main road at the western edge of town. There are dozens of pensions all over the valley, and in Harrachov itself these include the pleasing little *Pension Jitka* (ⓣ & ⓕ481 528 188; ❷), off the main road near the KRNAP office, and the equally appealing *Pension Ploc* (ⓣ & ⓕ481 528 194, 481 528 195 or 481 528 196; ❷), owned by a former Czech ski-jumping champion, located near the MIC office. Also near the MIC office is the basic dorm-style *Chata Kamenice* (ⓣ & ⓕ481 529 287, ⓦwww.vitrcomp.cz/kamenice; ❷). You could otherwise seek the modern comforts of the *Hotel Svornost* (ⓣ488 528 152, ⓕ481 528 144, ⓦwww.svornost@hr.bon.cz; at peak season book through ING Tours in Vrchlabí, ⓣ499 453 623, ⓦwww.ingtours.cz; ❹), a big, modern place just north of the centre, complete with indoor swimming pool, weight room, sauna and tennis courts. Alternatively, there's a **campsite** up the road towards the Polish border. The hotels generally have good **restaurants**, while the dining room in the *Pension Ploc* is also particularly atmospheric, and offers up sturdy Czech soups and main dishes. Those seeking a view with their meal would do well at the *Myslivna*, halfway up the **chairlift** to Čertova hora. For cheap thrills, continue on up above the dry tobogganing course to the top of the mountain, which at 1022m is high enough to view the barren hilltops around.

Pec pod Sněžkou and Janské Lázně

The sole attribute of **PEC POD SNĚŽKOU** (Petzer) is its proximity to the mountains. In winter this becomes the Czech Republic's chief ski centre, strung along an endless winding road. In summer it is the main hiking base for climbing **Sněžka** (Schneekoppe or Snow Peak), at 1602m the highest mountain in Bohemia and the most impressive in the entire range. Its bleak, grey summit rises above the tree line, relieving walkers of the painful sight of gently expiring pines, and making for a fine panorama – which you'll likely share with literally hundreds of others. If you don't fancy the six-kilometre ascent, take the **chairlift** from the village, which will take you in two stages right to the top (departing on the hour). The border, signified by discreet white-and-red stone markers, divides the rounded summit; there's an unappealing restaurant and a couple of snack stands on top. Border guards patrol with Kalashnikovs swinging nonchalantly at their sides, though they're unlikely to use them unless Czech–Polish relations take a dramatic turn for the worse.

Many Czechs use the chairlift as a launching pad for further **hiking**. To the east of the summit, a path follows the narrow mountain ridge (which also marks the border) for 2.5km to another peak, Svorová hora (Czarna Kopa to the Poles). To the west, there's a steep drop, again along the ridge, to *Slezská bouda*, a decent restaurant on the Polish side. To reach Špindlerův Mlýn from here (3hr 30min), follow the blue markers (via *Luční bouda*) forking off to the left, and not the red and blue ones that veer into Polish territory. Anyone wishing to cross the border should carry their passport, just in case the border guards want something to do.

There are regular **buses from Prague** to Pec pod Sněžkou, plus the occasional one to Janské Lázně (see opposite) and many to Trutnov. The Krkonoše National Park **information centre** (daily 9am–noon & 1–4.30pm), on the main road up from the bus station, has good maps and can provide hiking and skiing information. There is a second national park visitors' centre (same hours) with mundane exhibits on local flora and fauna, 2km up Obří důl, a valley to the north of town that provides an alternate hiking route to Sněžka. Ski rental is available from dozens of shops around town. As for **accommodation**, Pec has no campsite and its hotels are generally overpriced and booked-up, though the concentration of private rooms strewn across the hills is even denser here than in other Krkonoše resorts. The Turista information and travel agency (daily in winter 9am–7pm, shorter hours out of ski season; ☎499 736 280, ⓌＷwww.turistapec.cz) in the centre of town handles the whole range of accommodation, including cheap rooms and chalets (*boudy*) that can make a nice escape from the crowds. There is also an information stand down the road from the bus station with an electronic board posting hotel and pension vacancies, and you can call from the free telephone provided. One well-priced option is the *Penzion Veronika* (☎499 736 135, Ⓦwww.veronika-pec.cz; ❸), a comfortable, newly built place with its own restaurant a short drive or steep ten-minute walk uphill to the west of the centre, beyond the *Hotel Horizont*. A bit up the price scale is the *Pension Nikola* (☎499 736 151, Ⓕ499 731 251; ❸), near the park information centre. If you're travelling on a business-level budget, you'll find the plush and very central *Hotel Hořec* (☎499 736 422, Ⓕ499 796 424; ❹) to be a good deal; it also has self-contained apartments available (❺–❻). It's hard not to notice the eyesore (and expensive) *Hotel Horizont* (☎499 861 111, Ⓦwww.hotelhorizont.cz; ❺), Pec's most complete hotel with all conceivable amenities, though the rooms themselves are undistinguished. Many hotels and pensions have their own **restaurants**, and the *Hospoda na Peci* across from the Turista office provides a smoky mountain-lodge atmosphere to go with your cheap beer and goulash. Up the road toward the Pension Nikola, *Enzian Gril* is a tasty little pub and grill with outside tables round the back.

Janské Lázně

JANSKÉ LÁZNĚ (Johannisbad), hidden away in a sheltered, fertile valley on the southern edge of the national park, has a different atmosphere from the other resorts, and as such is probably the nicest and cheapest place to base yourself in the entire Krkonoše. Visitors tend to come here to take the cure rather than climb the surrounding peaks (although even the lazy can reach the top of Černá hora by the hourly cable car). On a hot summer's day all the classic images of spa life converge on the central stretch of lawn: a brass band plays oompah tunes in slightly lackadaisical fashion, while the elderly and disabled spill from the tearoom on to the benches outside. The best place to stay is the friendly, cosy *Villa Ludmila* (☎ & Ⓕ499 875 260, Ⓦwww.volweb.cz/villa.ludmila; ❷), followed by the more rustic *Lesní dům* (☎499 875 385, Ⓔlesni.dum@worldonline.cz; ❷), which has a sauna and hot tub and its own country-themed **restaurant**.

Trutnov

The modern factories and housing complexes that ring Bohemia's easternmost textile town, **TRUTNOV** (Trautenau), signal the end of the national park, though the town is easily within striking distance of the Krkonoše and an equally good base for exploring the Adršpach and Teplice rocks (see p. 000).

The busy arcaded main square, **Krakonošovo náměstí**, downstream and uphill from the railway station, has been beautifully restored. Alongside its plague column stands a fountain depicting Krakonoš (*Rübezahl* to the Germans), the sylvan spirit who guards the Giant Mountains and gave them their Czech name, both best appreciated from one of the cafés under the arcades of the main square. If you have time to kill, there's the odd exhibition at the **museum** (Tues–Sun 9am–5pm) in the former *stará škola*, just off the old town square. Trutnov's most recent claim to fame is that in the early 1970s, **Václav Havel** used to work in the local brewery, which produces a very good beer called, predictably enough, *Krakonoš*. His experiences later provided material for *Audience*, one of three plays centred around the character Vaněk (a lightly disguised version of himself).

The **tourist office** (Mon–Fri 8–11.45am & 12.30–5.30pm, Sat 8am–12.30pm; ☎499 803 111) in the radnice can point you towards some **private rooms**, or else you could try one of Trutnov's **hotels**: the *Grand* (☎ & Ⓕ499 811 901 or 499 811 099; ❸) on the main square, the *Bohemia* (☎499 811 951, Ⓕ499 811 953; ❸), just off the square on Palackého, or the four-star *Adam* (☎499 811 955, Ⓕ499 811 957; ❹), also near the square on Havlíčkova. Each of these hotels has its own **restaurant**, while the *No. 1*, on Horská between the bus station and the square, is recommended for good, cheap pub grub. The *Dolce Vita* **campsite** (open all year) is by a small lake, 4km southwest of Trutnov – take the blue-marked path from the centre of town. The town's annual August rock festival is the largest in the country, featuring mostly Czech bands, plus the odd headline Western band.

East to Broumov

Between Trutnov and Broumov, some 30km east, lie two seemingly innocuous hilly strips smothered in trees, which only on much closer inspection reveal themselves to be riddled with sandstone protrusions and weird rock formations on the same lines as those in the Český ráj (see p.285). Distances here are small and the gradients gentle, making it ideal for a bit of none-too-strenuous – but no less spectacular – **hiking**. If you're thinking of exploring the rocks, get hold of the extremely detailed *Teplicko-Adršpašské skály/Broumovské stěny* map before you get there, which shows all the colour-coded footpaths and the campsites. The local **buses** do serve the more out-of-the-way places like Broumov, but it's worth taking advantage of the slow but scenic **train** service from Trutnov to Teplice nad Metují, via Adršpach.

The Adršpach and Teplice rocks

The **Adršpach and Teplice rocks** (Teplicko-Adršpašské skály), 15km east of Trutnov, rise up out of the pine forest like petrified phalluses. Some even take trees with them as they launch themselves hundreds of feet into the air. German tourists have flocked here since the nineteenth century, though nowadays they are outnumbered by Czech rock climbers and ramblers. The rocks are concentrated in two separate *skalní města*, or "rock cities": the Adršpach rocks, just south of the village of the same name, and the Teplice rocks, 2km south through the woods. The latter can also be approached from the villages of Janovice or Teplice.

Adršpach

ADRŠPACH (Adersbach) train station (one stop on from Horní Adršpach) lies at the northern extremity of the rock system, though you can't really miss it, since some of the rocks have crept right up to the station itself. In high season, there's a small entrance fee to enter the **Adršpašské skalní město** (your ticket includes a boat ride, see p.301). Once through the perimeter fence, the outside world recedes and you're surrounded by new sensations – sand underfoot, the scent of pine, boulders and shady trees. Most of the sandstone rocks are dangerous to climb without the correct equipment and experience, so you'll probably have to content yourself with strolling and gawping at the formations best described by their nicknames: Babiččina lenoška (Grandmother's Armchair), Španělská stěna (Spanish Wall) and the ironic Trpaslík (Dwarf).

The green-marked path winds its way along and over a stream, through narrow clefts between the rocks, eventually bringing you to a couple of waterfalls (*vodopády*). From here, steps hewn out of the rock lead up to the Adršpašské jezírko, a lake trapped above ground level between the rocks, where jovial boatmen pole you along in rafts a short distance to the other side. From here, the yellow-marked path continues through the woods for 2km to the entrance to the Teplice rocks (see opposite). If you fancy a swim or a spot of nude bathing, head for the Pískovna lake to the east of the Adršpach entrance, with its dramatic backdrop of craggy rocks and pine trees. The *Lesní zátiší* (☎491 586 018; ❸), right by the entrance to the rocks, offers simple **rooms** and **food**.

Teplice nad Metují

The easiest approach for the **Teplické skalní město** is from Teplice nad Metují-skály station, just across the river from the entrance to the rocks. A blue-marked path heads west for 1km, after which you need to switch to the green-marked path, which threads its way through the Anenské údolí, the main valley of the *skalní město* – another theatrical burst of geological abnormalities that form a narrow valley of rocks. Right by the woods' edge you can also explore the rock fortress of **Střmen**, which once served as a Hussite hide-out. The *Hotel Orlík* (☎491 581 025; ❷) is situated right by the entrance to the rocks.

Alternatively, **TEPLICE NAD METUJÍ** (Wekelsdorf) itself, 2km east, is a functional base, with a supermarket, a cinema, several pensions and a couple of hotels. There's also the *Bučnice* **campsite** (May–Sept), 1km up the road from Teplice nad Metují-skály station. If you're a keen rock-climber, then the annual **festival of mountaineering films**, held here in late August/early September, may be of interest. It's basically an excuse for a lot of boozing and boasting, though it attracts people from all over Europe, who come to share their experiences, many demonstrating their skills on the local formations.

The Broumov walls

The **Broumov walls** (Broumovské stěny) make up a thin sandstone ridge that almost cuts Broumov off from the rest of the country. From the west, there's no indication of the approaching precipice, from which a wonderful vista sweeps out over to Broumov and beyond into Poland, but from the east, the ridge is clearly spread out before you. The best place to appreciate the view is from Dientzenhofer's chapel of **Panna Maria Sněžná**, situated in among the boulders at the edge of the big drop. The best rock formations are 9km south of here, close by the highest point of the wall, **Božanovský Špičák** (733m), only a few hundred metres from the Polish border. You can approach the Dientzenhofer chapel from either Police nad Metují, 5km to the southwest, or Broumov (see below), 6km to the east. To get to the rocks around Božanovský Špičák, take the bus from Police to Machov, and walk the final 3.5km; alternatively, there's the train from Broumov to Božanov, followed by a walk of 3.5km.

Broumov

BROUMOV (Braunau), a predominantly German-speaking town before the war, 30km due east of Trutnov, is probably the best place to base yourself if you're thinking of exploring the Broumov walls. The town is particularly impressive from a distance, with its colossal Baroque **Benediktinský klášter**, perched on a sandstone pedestal above the River Stěnava. The monastery was used by the Communists to incarcerate much of the country's Benedictine priesthood after 1948, most of whom were old and passed their remaining days here. During the 1960s numerous nuns were also imprisoned here – up to 300 at one point – and forced to labour in local factories and fields, until they too eventually died. This sad recent past seems to echo throughout the monastery, which, apart from the nicely repainted entrance gates, stands mostly decrepit, unused and lonely. Guided tours (April–Oct Tues–Sun 9–11am & 1–5pm on the hour) lead through the stunning Baroque chapel, designed by Dientzenhofer, who lived here from 1727 to 1738, and featuring paintings by his contemporary Vratislav Vavřinec Reiner. Upstairs, the musty library contains what is said to be the only copy of the Shroud of Turin in central Europe. Aside from the monastery tour, the complex also houses the town museum (May–Sept Tues–Sun 8am–noon & 1–5pm). The rest of Broumov's compact old town is mildly interesting, with a handsome cobbled main square, Mírové náměstí, lined with lime trees and pastel-coloured houses, and centred on a fine barleysugar Marian column.

As for **accommodation**, the *Hotel Veba* (☎ & ℱ 491 523 633; ❸) is the town's finest, set in its own grounds and with an excellent restaurant, to the southwest of the centre off Šalounova. Other options in the old town include the newly refurbished *Winterswijk* (☎491 523 908, ℱ491 523 707; ❸), tucked in beside the town brewery on Pivovarská, and the Communist-era *Hotel Praha* (☎491 523 786; ❸) on the main square. Try to sample the local beer, *Opat*, if the restaurants at these places still offer it – the larger national brands are doing a good job of taking over pub menus. The **train** and **bus stations** are both close to one another, five to ten minutes' walk southeast of the old town.

One attraction you shouldn't overlook is the unusual Silesian **wooden church** on the Křivinice road out of town. With a car and a passion for Baroque churches, you could also happily spend a morning exploring the local Stěnava valley. In the eighteenth century, Kilian Ignaz Dientzenhofer, Bohemia's foremost ecclesiastical architect, was chosen by the local abbot to redesign the Broumov monastery. He was also commissioned to build numerous **Baroque churches** in the area (and in the Klodzko region, over the border in Poland), in an attempt to Catholicize the staunchly Protestant Silesian Germans who used to live here. For each church, he experimented with a different design – a simple oval plan at Verneřovice (Wernersdorf), an elongated octagon at Ruprechtice (Rupperdorf), and a crushed oval at Vižňov (Wiesen). Most are now down to their bricks and mortar and firmly closed, but the key is usually traceable, and the effort well rewarded.

Náchod and around

Cowering at the base of its large, lordly seat, built to guard the gateway to Bohemia from Silesia, **NÁCHOD** is one of the few Czech border towns that has been predominantly Czech for most of its life. Even the Nazis stopped short of annexing it when they marched into the Sudetenland in 1938, since at the time there were only four German-speaking families in the whole town.

Nowadays, most people just stop off in order to break the journey and spend their last remaining crowns en route to Poland. Although the Polish border is a couple of kilometres east of the town centre, Náchod actually makes a useful base for exploring the surrounding area, including the two exceptional **chateaux** at Nové Město nad Metují and Opočno.

The Town

Náchod is a lot better looking than your average border town: the main square, **náměstí T.G. Masaryka**, in particular, has had a new lease of life following its recent restoration. Its two most winsome buildings are the fourteenth-century church of **sv Vavřinec** (St Lawrence) at the centre of the square, its entrance flanked by two fat square towers sporting comically large wooden onion domes, and the Art Nouveau *Hotel U beránka*, with sinewy lines and marvellously detailed mosaic lettering and interior light fittings. At one corner of the square is the town **museum** (Tues–Sun 9am–noon & 1–5pm), with a quite good display on local history that includes folk dress and dioramas describing the 1866 Austro-Prussian wars waged in the area.

Peeking out of the foliage, high above the town, and a very stiff climb from the main square, is Náchod's sprawling, unassailable, sgraffitoed **zámek** (April & Oct Sat & Sun 9am–noon & 1–4pm; May–Sept Tues–Sun 9am–noon & 1–5pm). The original Gothic structure survives only in the pretty little round tower in the centre of the complex; everything else is the result of successive building projects spanning the Renaissance and Baroque periods. There's a choice of two tours: the *malý okruh* (short tour), which allows access to the tower, the dungeons and the viewing terrace, and the *velký okruh* (long tour), which guides you through the interior. Inside, you get to see the castle art collection courtesy of the exiled Duke of Kurland, and an interesting hotchpotch of furnishings and exhibits accrued over the centuries by descendants of the Italian Ottavio Piccolomini-Pieri, Waldstein's bodyguard, who was given the castle by Ferdinand II after informing the emperor of Waldstein's secret plans (see p.291). If you've children in tow, you might also like to peruse the phantasmagoric figures in **Strašidla** (May–Sept Tues–Sun 9am–5pm), in the bastions of the castle's fourth courtyard. The dimly lit tableaux of mythological creatures from Czech legends are guaranteed to keep the kids amused and the adults bemused.

The Cowards in Náchod

The exiled writer **Josef Škvorecký** was born and bred in Náchod – a "narrow cleavage between the mountains", as he characteristically dubbed it. During his wartime adolescence he was joined by film-director-to-be Miloš Forman, then only a young boy, who came to stay with his uncle when his parents were sent to a concentration camp from which they never returned. Later, in the cultural thaw of the 1960s, before they were both forced to emigrate, the two men planned (unsuccessfully) to make a film based on *The Cowards*, Škvorecký's most famous novel. Set in "a small Bohemian town" (ie Náchod) in the last few days of the war, the book caused a sensation when it was published (briefly) in 1958 because of its bawdy treatment of Czech resistance to the Nazis. Škvorecký also set the action of a later novel, *The Miracle Game*, in the nearby village of Hronov. In both novels, and in *The Engineer of Human Souls*, the name of the main character is Danny Smiřický, after Náchod's local aristo family.

The former riding school, or **jízdárna** (Tues–Sun 9am–noon & 1–5pm), situated beyond the bear-inhabited moat by the car park, houses a surprisingly healthy permanent collection of **Russian paintings**. The highlights include two finely studied female portraits by Ilya Repin, the most famous of the "Wanderers" who broke away from the official Russian academy of art, better known for his epic works filled with fiery bearded figures like the *Trial of Christ*. The leader of the Wanderers, Ivan Kramskoy, is responsible for the superbly aloof portrait of an aristocratic lady in a carriage, with a St Petersburg palace as a backdrop. Also on display are works by Serov and Makovsky, but best of all by far are the wildly colourful depictions of peasant women by turn-of-the-twentieth-century artist Filip Malyavin, who was a lay brother on Mount Athos in Greece before he took up painting full-time.

Practicalities

The town's **train** and **bus stations** are both five minutes' walk east of the centre, at the end of Kamenice. The **tourist office** (Mon–Fri 8.30am–5pm, Sat 8.30–11.30am; ☎491 420 420), in a travel agency near the square at Kamenice 144, should be able to help with **accommodation**. The aforementioned *U beránka* (☎491 433 118, ℱ491 433 119; ❸) is a comfortable option and probably the town's greatest institution: a hotel, café, theatre and restaurant (serving the local *Primátor* beer as well as traditional Czech food) in one. Up behind the zámek, the *Zámecký Hotel* (☎491 426 503, ℱ491 427 882; ❷), with its own good **restaurant**, is pleasingly refurbished. Broumov's pretty riverside **campsite** (mid-May to mid-Sept) is by the woods 1.5km east of the centre, signposted down Běloveská.

Nové Město nad Metují

NOVÉ MĚSTO NAD METUJÍ, 9km south of Náchod, boasts a stunningly beautiful old town square, with one of the country's most interesting chateaux crouched in one corner. While the town's modern quarter sprawls unattractively over the lower ground, the staré město sits quietly (and extremely prettily) on a high spur hemmed in by the River Metuje, a tributary of the River Labe. Restored sixteenth-century houses line each side of the rectangular arcaded main square, **Husovo náměstí**, though the most photographed set of gables are the identical cream-coloured ones that parade along the north side.

What makes Nové Město's old town extra special is its remarkable seventeenth-century **zámek** (May, June & Sept Tues–Sun 9am–4pm; July & Aug daily 9am–5pm), which looks out across the Labe basin (known as the *Polabí*) from the northeast corner of the square. After piecemeal alterations, it fell into disrepair in the nineteenth century, until the industrialist Josef Bartoň bought the place in 1908 and commissioned the quirky Slovak architect **Dušan Jurkovič** to entirely redesign it – which he did, most notably with the timber-framed structures, redolent of his native land, in the terraced gardens, and the bizarre wall-to-wall leather vaulting of the Žebrový sál (Ribbed Hall). The other rooms are lavishly furnished in every period from the original Renaissance to Cubism, including highly unusual works by Czech Cubists like **Pavel Janák**. Bartoň eventually died here in 1951, at the ripe old age of 98. In an uncharacteristically magnanimous gesture, the Communists had allowed him and his wife (and their cook) to live out their last days in three rooms at the top of the chateau. The place is now back in the hands of the Bartoň family, who actually live here and run it with great efficiency. Before you buy your ticket, be sure to check out the set of dwarves by the Baroque sculptor Braun, which stand along the terrace and bridge across the moat.

An extra treat is on hand in the outlying village of **Slavoňov** in the form of a precious little wooden church dating from 1533. The wood-panelled interior is exquisite, virtually all surfaces being painted in simple, yet rich designs. The flat ceiling panels are each distinct, while the almost cartoon-like paintings on the choir depict local scenes and nobility. Be sure to ask the tourist office in Nové Město to call ahead to the friar's office next door, so that someone will be on hand to let you in. To get to Slavoňov, follow the yellow-marked path 4km through the woods from Nové Město's main square, or catch the occasional bus which leaves from there too.

Nové Město nad Metují itself is a beautiful eight-kilometre **walk** from Náchod down the winding River Metuje (yellow-marked path, followed by red). If you arrive here by **train**, you'll end up 2km northwest of the chateau, in Nové Město's new town; infrequent local buses link the old town square with the station or you can follow the blue markers. If you arrive by **bus** from Náchod or Hradec Králové, you can get off at Husovo náměstí itself. If you want to **stay the night**, the *Hotel U Broučka*, on Husovo náměstí (T491 472 571; ❷), offers simple rooms with en-suite facilities. The **tourist office** (May–Sept Mon–Fri 8am–noon & 1–5pm; Oct–April Mon–Fri 9am–noon & 1–4pm) just off the main square can set you up in a private room or nearby pension. One good **restaurant** on the square is, surprisingly, the rather grubby *Restaurace U Pad'ourů*, where the standard Czech fare is cheap and tasty. Better yet, the chateau has its very own *Pivní sklep*, a nice cellar pub with an outside terrace, serving pub snacks and Náchod's excellent *Primátor* beer.

Opočno

Ten kilometres south of Nové Město nad Metují is the town of **OPOČNO**, whose **zámek** (April & Oct Sat & Sun 9–11.30am & 12.30–4pm; May–June & Sept Tues–Sun 9–11.30am & 12.30–5pm; July–Aug closes 6pm) is spectacularly poised on a knife's edge above the Polabí plain. The main attraction here is the triple-decker loggia, built in the sixteenth-century by Italian architects around the chateau's three-sided courtyard. Clinging to the chateau's foundations are the lovely wooded grounds (daily: April–Sept 7am–8pm; Oct–March 8am–3pm) with a summer palace or *letohrádek*, now used for temporary exhibitions. All these treats, and the view, can be appreciated without having to sign up for either of the two guided tours, though these are something of a must if you've made it here. You may as well go for the full load as well, as this includes the armoury for which Opočno is famous: a priceless collection of rifles, swords, a Roman helmet, and even a well-worn chastity belt. The rest of the chateau consists of beautifully-restored rooms in which are contained sundry possessions of the Colloredo family, who owned the place until 1945; the last remaining family member is in the process of reacquiring it. Highlights include hunting trophies, ivory-inlaid furniture, thirteenth-century crystal and numerous portraits, many of which hang underneath extravagant stucco ceilings that practically sag with the extra weight.

Buses are the most direct means of getting to Opočno; several connect with Hradec Králové daily. The train station (Opočno pod Orlicki horami) is a good 2km below the town to the west. You can eat or shoot pool in the very 1960s (but good) *Zámecká restaurace* next to the castle gates on Trčkovo náměstí.

The Babiččino údolí

Ten kilometres west of Náchod by train, the town of **ČESKÁ SKALICE** marks the beginning of the Úpa Valley, better known as the **Babiččino údolí** after the novel that has made it famous, *Babička* (Grandmother) by **Božena Němcová** (1820–62). A very precise and realistic portrait of Czech peasant life in the mid-nineteenth century, dominated by the kindly wisdom of the story's grandmother figure, the tale is still required reading for Czechs of all ages. Němcová's tragic life is almost as well known as the tale itself: forced to marry at seventeen to a man more than twice her age, Němcová wrote, "The years of my childhood were the most beautiful of my life. When I married I wept over my lost liberty, over the dreams and ideals forever ruined." Moving in Czech republican and literary circles in the 1840s, she caused considerable outrage with her numerous passionate and very public affairs. Her independent spirit, her championing of women's education, and her involvement in the 1848 revolution have endeared her to many Czech women. Nowadays, she is still very much a household name, and one of the few Czech women to have entered the country's literary canon; Němcová is featured on the 500Kč note.

There are now several **museums** dedicated to Němcová in the area, two in Česká Skalice itself. The first is in her old schoolhouse, the timber-framed Baruncina škola (Tues–Sun: May–Aug 8am–noon & 1–5pm; Sept 9am–noon & 1–4pm), northwest off the main square up B Němcové; the second is in the former pub, *U bílého českého lva*, in which she got married, now part of the town's Textilní muzeum (Textile Museum; Tues–Sun: April, Sept & Oct 9am–4pm; May–Aug 8am–5pm), further up B Němcové and across the river. Her birthplace in Červený Kostelec, 8km north of Česká Skalice, is also now a museum (times as for the škola). Perhaps the most rewarding of the lot, though, for the non-Czech-speaker is **Ratibořice**, 2.5km north of Česká Skalice, (April, Sept & Oct Sat & Sun 10am–3pm; May Tues–Sun 9am–3pm; June–Aug Tues–Sun 9am–5pm), the pretty little pink chateau with green shutters where Němcová's father was equerry, and her mother laundress.

An alternative to visiting one of the above is to explore the gentle valley, which was her childhood haunt and the main inspiration for the book – a very beautiful place in its own right. Be sure not to miss the modern statue group by Otto Gutfreund, north of the chateau; walk through the chateau's lovely English gardens (daily: May–Sept 8am–8pm; Oct–April 9am–5pm) and upstream through the fields.

Hradec Králové

Capital of East Bohemia and the largest city on the fertile plain known as the Polabí, **HRADEC KRÁLOVÉ** (Königgrätz) has a typically handsome historical quarter, paid for by the rich trade that used to pass through en route to Silesia. But there's another side to the town, too. To the west of the medieval centre is one of the great urban projects of the interwar Republic, built by the leading modern Czech architects of the day. The two towns don't really blend in with one another – in fact, they barely communicate – and these days the staré město is more like a museum piece. Even if you don't particularly take to the new town, it's a fascinating testimony to the early optimism of the First Republic, and gives the whole of Hradec Králové a unique, expansive and prosperous atmosphere.

▲ Campsite

Šimkovy sady

Former Synagogue

STARÉ MĚSTO

ŠIMKOVA

ČESKOSLOVENSKÉ ARMÁDY

DLOUHÁ

MALÉ NAMĚSTÍ

❷ ❸

Galerie
moderního umění

UZKA

❹

KLÍCPEROVA

TOMKOVA

Nanebevzetí
Panny Marie

KOMENSKÉHO

VELKÉ NAMĚSTÍ

SPITÁLSKÁ

DLOUHÁ

B

Swimming
Baths

Krajské
muzeum

V KOPEČKU

A

Bílá věž

❺

U Špuláků

sv Duch

Stadión

❻

DIVIŠOVA

PALACKÉHO

Hotel
Bystrica

ČESKOSLOVENSKÉ ARMÁDY

River Orlice

HERMANNA

JANA KOŽÍ

IHRADKA

SMETANOVO NÁBŘEŽÍ

PRAŽSKÝ
MOST

River Labe

NÁM.
SVOBODY

TŘÍDA NÁBŘEŽÍ

Jiráskovy
sady

Wooden Church

KRUPKOVA

PRŮMYSLOVÁ

SÁDOVSKÁ

RESSLOVA

MASARYKOVO
NAMĚSTÍ

GOČAROVA

JIŘÍHO-HO
NÁM.

MANESOVA

Gymnázium

V LIPKÁCH

TŘÍDA KARLA IV

MONKOVA

STREJCKA

DUKELSKÁ

NOVÉ MĚSTO

STREJCKA

NERUDOVA

Ambrožův
sbor

V LIPKÁCH

N

KARLA ČAPKA

HOŘIČKÁ

BLAŽÍČKOVO
NAMĚSTÍ

NAMĚSTÍ
28 ŘÍJNA

GOČAROVA

HOROVÁ

NERUDOVA

BAAROVA

V LIPKÁCH

Aquarium

Train Station

Bus
Station

ⓘ

HRADEC KRÁLOVÉ

0   100 m

ACCOMMODATION
Penzión Amálka   3
Amber Černigov   1
Penzión pod věží   5
Stadión   6
U královny Elišky   2
U svatého Lukáše   4
**RESTAURANTS, CAFÉS
& BARS**
Buvol   A
Na hradě   B
Sluneční čajovna   C
U knihomola   D

Hradec Králové spreads itself out on both banks of the Labe: on the left bank, the **staré město** (old town) sits on an oval rock between the Labe and the Orlice rivers; the **nové město** (new town) begins as soon as you leave the old town, straddling the river and then composing itself in fairly logical fashion between the river and the station to the west.

The staré město

In the eighteenth century, the **staré město** was entirely surrounded by zigzag red-brick fortifications (those at nearby Josefov can still be seen), though they've now been replaced by a modern ring road that keeps most of the traffic out of the old quarter. With nearly all daily business conducted over in the new town, a few shops and restaurants are all that remain to disturb Hradec Králové's two adjoining medieval squares, **Velké náměstí** and the much smaller **Malé náměstí**. At the western end of Velké náměstí, the skyline is punctuated by five towers. Two of them belong to the church of **sv Duch** (Holy Ghost), one of Bohemia's few great brick-built churches, a style more commonly associated with neighbouring Silesia. Jan Žižka, the blind Hussite warrior, died of the plague here in 1424, and was for a while buried in this church. Given its grand Gothic scale, though, the whitewashed interior, filled for the most part with neo-Gothic furnishings, is a letdown, despite Petr Brandl's *St Anthony* in the north aisle, and a superb stone tabernacle dating from 1497.

The church's twin towers are outreached by the once-white **Bílá věž** (White Tower; April–Oct Tues–Sun 9am–noon & 1–5pm), built in the sixteenth century from the profits of Bohemian–Silesian trade, and *the* place to get a bird's-eye view of the town. Also in this corner of the square is the town **brewery**, invisible but for the terrace of Baroque former canons' houses that leads to its gate. To the east, where the two sides of the square begin to converge, the older Renaissance houses on the north side have kept their arcades. Opposite stands the distinctive pink **Dům U Špuláků**, with its projecting oriel and copper dome, and, close by, the Jesuits' Baroque "barracks" and church of **Nanebevzetí Panny Marie**, the latter beautifully maintained, its trompe l'oeil altarpiece providing a suitable repository for Brandl's work.

The Galerie moderního umění

Hradec Králové's **Galerie moderního umění** (Tues–Sun 9am–noon & 1–6pm), opposite the Jesuit church, houses one of the country's finest permanent collections of twentieth-century Czech art. The building itself – designed by Osvald Polívka in 1910–12, the genius behind much of Prague's finest Art Nouveau structures – is also a treat: five storeys high, with a large, oval glass-roofed atrium at the centre that sheds light onto the corridors and ground-level foyer.

The ground floor is given over to temporary exhibitions, while on the first floor, the collection of works by fin-de-siècle artists is entirely in keeping with its surroundings. Among the highlights are a couple of lesser-known **Mucha** drawings, an early **Kupka**, and a whole series by **Jan Preisler**, including a study for the mural which now adorns the *Hotel Bystrica* (see opposite). The unexpected pleasure is **Josef Váchal**'s work, in particular the mysterious *Satanic Invocation* (*Vzývaci d'abla*), which spills over onto its carved wooden frame. Several wood sculptures by **Bílek** and three bronze reliefs by **Sucharda** make for a fairly comprehensive overview of Czech Secessionist art. The floor ends with the beginnings of the Czech obsession with Cubism, most famously **Emil Filla**'s own version of *Les Demoiselles d'Avignon* and *Salome's Dance*.

The second floor is almost wholly devoted to Czech Cubist and Fauvist painters, interspersed with a few from the Realist and Surrealist schools, prominent in the 1920s. **Josef Šíma**'s semi-surreal work is probably the most original (he was a member of the avant-garde group *Devětsil*), though only two canvases and a pen-and-ink sketch are displayed here. Postwar art up to 1968 is the subject of the third floor, interesting if only for the fact that many of the artists, like **Mikuláš Medek**, have only recently been exhibited in public galleries. The views from the top floor should be sufficient incentive to get you up there, and again there's plenty of previously censored post-1968 material to feast your eyes on, like the psychedelic *Přátelé*, though patently political works like *Red Wall* (*Červená zeď*) are the exception. Surrealism was always frowned upon, hence artists like **Jiří Kolář**, two of whose classic collages are shown here, are much better known in the West.

The nové město

Most of what you now see outside the old town is the result of an architectural master plan outlined between 1909 and 1911, though much of the work wasn't carried out until the 1920s. Building began on a grand scale with the **Muzeum východních Čech** (April–Oct Tues–Sun 9am–noon & 1-5pm; Nov–March by appointment; ☎495 512 462, ⓦwww.muzeumhk.cz) on the leafy waterfront, designed by the father of the Czech modern movement, **Jan Kotěra**. With the rest of central Europe still under the hold of the Viennese Secession, Kotěra's museum, crowned with one of his characteristic domes, represents a shot across the bows of contemporary taste, finished in what was at the time an unconventional mixture of red brick and concrete rendering. The entrance is guarded by two colossal sphinx-like janitors, but otherwise the ornamentation is low-key – as is the exhibition inside, a straightforward though attractive display of nineteenth- and twentieth-century arts and crafts, books and posters, plus a model of the town from 1865, showing the fortifications intact.

Further down the Labe embankment is the Hradec Králové Filharmonie building, a stern structure that nonetheless hosts a good year-round orchestral concert series. Just beyond is an excellent **swimming pool** open to the public, designed in the 1920s equipped with an artificial wave machine, a sauna, massage parlour, and, of course, a pub.

Close by, on the inner ring road, is another work by Kotěra, the *Hotel Bystrica* (originally called, simply, the *Grand Hotel*), built immediately after the museum. It's currently in such a desperate state it's difficult to see beyond the pollutant-caked rendering to appreciate the subtleties of the facade. If and when it is ever renovated, head for the Art Nouveau restaurant – the fruit of an earlier work by Kotěra – adorned with murals by Jan Preisler and František Kysela's graceful stained-glass cranes. Kotěra is also responsible for the distinctive **Pražský most** (Prague Bridge), with its squat kiosks at either end and wrought-iron arch decorated with fairy lights.

Before crossing the river into Gočár's new town, there are a couple of minor attractions around the inner ring road. To the northeast is the town's **former synagogue** (now a library), a very handsome Art Nouveau edifice with an oddly oriental flavour to the lantern above the dome and the adjacent pagoda-style tower. To the southwest, the **Jiráskovy sady** occupy the slip of land at the confluence of the rivers Labe and Orlice and boast a colourful rose garden and a sixteenth-century **wooden Greek-Catholic church** (invariably closed) in the Lemk style, transported here from Sub-Carpathian Ruthenia in 1935.

Gočár's new town

Kotěra died shortly after World War I, and it was left to one of his pupils, **Josef Gočár**, to complete the construction of the new town. Gočár had been among the foremost exponents of Czech Cubist architecture before the war, but, along with Pavel Janák, he changed tack in the 1920s and attempted to establish a specifically Czechoslovak style of architecture, which incorporated prewar Cubism. It was dubbed "Rondo-Cubism" because of its recurrent semicircular motifs, and though few projects got off the ground, elements of the style are reflected in the appealing homogeneity of the new town. On a sunny day, the light pastel shades of the buildings provide a cool and refreshing backdrop; bad weather brings out the brutalism that underlies much of Gočár's work.

This brutalism is most evident in his largest commission, the **Státní gymnázium** on the right bank, a sprawling series of buildings with an L-shaped, four-storey, red-brick structure, fronted by an atypically slender bronze nude by Jan Štursa. Up the side of the school, on V lipkách, is a later, still more uncompromising work, the Protestant **Ambrožův sbor**, built in functionalist style on a striking angular site. But by far Gočár's most successful set-piece is **Masarykovo náměstí**, which basks in the sun at the heart of the new town, shaped like a big slice of lemon sponge, with a pivotal statue of Masaryk back in its rightful place after a forty-year absence. Lastly, if you're travelling by train, be sure to admire the **train station**'s splendidly modernist design, again by Gočár, in particular the wonderfully slimline 1930s clocktower.

Hradec Králové's newest attraction is its mini **aquarium** (*Obří akvárium*; Tues–Sun 9am–6pm) at Baarova 10, a ten-minute walk south of the new town in an otherwise faceless neighbourhood. Though it's hardly "giant" as it claims to be, its centrepiece is a glass tunnel large enough to walk through and view Amazonian fish, while a small construction of a rainforest helps you forget briefly that you're still in central Europe.

Practicalities

By **train** or **bus**, you arrive in the nové město; to reach the staré město, either take bus #5, #6, #11, #15 or #17, all of which plough down Gočárova, or take trolleybus #2, #3 or #7 and get off by the Krajské muzeum. Hradec Králové's useful **tourist office** (June–Aug Mon–Fri 8am–6pm & Sat 9am–3pm; Sept–May weekdays only; ☎495 534 485, ⓦwww.ic-hk.cz) is located near the stations at Gočarova 1225.

Accommodation should not be a problem, as several hotels and pensions have opened up in recent years – happily driving prices down with them. On Velké náměstí, *Penzión pod věží* (☎495 514 932, ⓔpenzion-pod-vezi@iol.cz; ❸) is right under the tower as its name states, and offers comfortable, airy rooms overlooking the square. *U svatého Lukáše*, just off the main square on Úzká (☎495 518 616; ❹), is another nice place, but pricier, with rooms situated around a quiet courtyard. The brand new *Hotel U královny Elišky* (☎495 518 052, ⓦwww.hfc-hk.cz; ❸) is an excellent choice and better value, a tasteful, small four-star hotel on Malé náměstí. You can save your crowns at the more basic *Penzión Amátka* (☎495 515 543; ❷), also on Malé náměstí, or at the *Hotel Stadión* (☎495 514 664; ❷), just outside the staré město by the ice hockey stadium on Komenského. The latter is better than it looks from the outside. Otherwise, you can plump for the *Amber Hotel Černigov* (☎495 814 111, ⓦwww.cernigov.cz; ❹), opposite the train station, a perfectly comfortable communist-era high-rise hotel. The *Stříbrný rybník* **campsite** (mid-June to

Sept) is very popular in the height of summer, due to its cabins and adjacent lake; you can even rent **bicycles**. To get there, take bus #17.

A good number of **restaurants** in town dish up the usual plain but filling fare. Apart from those in the above pensions, of which *U svatého Lukáše* is the best, there are plenty of additional cafés on Velké náměstí with outdoor seating. *Kavárna U knihomola* is an appropriate complement to the modern art gallery opposite, a soothingly hip spot for coffee or a light lunch, while *Sluneční čajovna* is a neat little tea-room under the arcades of the town hall, by the Bílá věž. The *vinárna* at the *Hotel Černigov* (accessed down the broad steps along the side of the hotel) does surprising twists on the old theme – like curried chicken – and is equally surprisingly good value. For a mid-morning sausage or a late-night beer, head to *Na hradě* on Špitálská – it's open from 10am. **Nightlife** is rather slow in Hradec Králové, but the *Buvol* on V Kopečku is a lively Czech-Irish pub, sitting above the *Teen's Club*, open until 2am.

Around Hradec Králové

The flat expanse around Hradec Králové, known as the **Polabí**, is a fertile region whose hedgeless cornfields stretch for miles on end. It's pretty dreary to look at, baking hot in summer and covered in a misty drizzle most of the winter, but there are several places worth a day-trip or overnight stop within easy reach of Hradec Králové by bus or train.

Třebechovice, Častolovice and Doudleby

TŘEBECHOVICE POD OREBEM, 11km east of Hradec Králové along route 11, is a nondescript town, famous only for its wood-carved Nativity scene or *Betlém*, housed in a purpose-built **museum** (Tues–Sun: May–Sept 9am–noon & 1–5pm; Oct–April closes 4pm). It all began in 1871, when local joiner Josef Probošt and his wood-carving friend, Josef Kapucián, set out to create the largest Nativity scene in the world. Only the death of Kapucián forty years later brought the project to an end, by which time the two men had carved 400 moving figures, many of them modelled on their friends and neighbours. And if you think that's kitsch, take a look at the museum's other room, which displays *Betlém* scenes in glass, pottery and paper.

Eighteen kilometres on is the Renaissance chateau or **Častolovice** (April & Oct Sat & Sun 9am–5pm; May–Sept Tues–Sun 9am–5pm), recently returned to the Šternberk family, who acquired it back in 1694. It's a pretty hybrid pile, right by route 11, with a huge English-style park stretching away to the north. The inner courtyard is particularly beautiful, and the tour takes you through the glorious Rytířský sál (Knights' Hall), with a Renaissance painted panel ceiling and portraits of various regional noblemen. If you're heading in this direction, you could continue another 6km to **Doudleby** (April & Oct Sat & Sun 9am–5pm; May–Sept Tues–Sun 8am–5pm), a lovely little chateau, again right by route 11, but this time covered in intricate swirling sgraffito, not unlike the locally made lace displayed inside. Tours lead through predictably elaborate Baroque rooms, many with frescoes and paintings, including a satirical *Devil's Wedding*.

Jaroměř and Josefov

JAROMĚŘ, 36km northeast of Hradec Králové and accessible by train, is a pleasant enough town with a curving cobbled square, arcaded on one side and with one of its medieval gateways intact. The main attraction, though, is one of Gočár's early works, the **Wenke department store**, situated on route 33, the busy main road from Hradec Králové to the Polish border. In this exceedingly unpromising street (now called Husova), Gočár undertook one of the first self-conscious experiments in Cubist architecture in 1911. It's an imaginative, eclectic work, quite unlike the much plainer Cubism of Prague's Vyšehrad villas or the nearby spa of Bohdaneč, the plate-glass facade topped by a Neoclassical upper floor and the monochrome, geometric interior still intact. Instead of selling goods, it now serves as the **Městské muzeum a galerie** (Mon–Fri 9am–4pm, Sat & Sun 9am–noon), its tiny art gallery upstairs displaying works by all three of Jaroměř's home-grown artists: the sculptors Otakar Španiel and Josef Wagner, and the *Devětsil* painter Josef Šíma, whose wilfully optimistic painting of Jaroměř is just one of a number of his works on show.

One kilometre south of Jaroměř, where the Labe and the Metuje rivers converge, is the fortress town of **JOSEFOV** (Josefstadt). In the 1780s the Habsburgs created three fortified towns along the northern border with their new enemy, Prussia: Hradec Králové (which has since lost its walls), Terezín and Josefov – the last two purpose-built from scratch and preserved as they were. Terezín was put to terrible use by the Nazis during World War II (see p.258), but Josefov remains the great white elephant of the empire, never having witnessed a single battle. Their mutual designs are unerringly similar: two fortresses (one large, one small), identikit eighteenth-century streets, and a grid plan whose monotony is broken only by the imposing **Empire Church** on the main square. Again like Terezín, Josefov is still a garrison town, though there aren't many soldiers left; the empty buildings have mostly been taken over by Romany families. Though not a great day out, it's worth taking a stroll along the thick zigzag trail of red-brick fortifications, now topped by beautiful tree-lined paths, with views across the wheat fields of the Polabí. If you're really keen, you can even visit the town's **underground tunnel system**, where costumed soldiers lead you through claustrophobic candle-lit passageways; follow the signs to the Podzemí (April & Oct Sat & Sun 9am–noon & 1–4pm; May–Sept Tues–Sun 9am–noon & 1–5pm).

Kuks and around

Magnificently poised above a rustic village of timber-framed cottages, the great complex of Baroque spa buildings at **KUKS**, just 5km north of Jaroměř, on the banks of the Labe, was the creation of the enlightened Bohemian dilettante Count Franz Anton Graf von Sporck (Špork in Czech). Work began, largely according to Sporck's own designs, in the 1690s, after the discovery of a nearby mineral spring with healing properties – by 1730 he had created his own private **spa resort**, with a garden maze, a hospital, a concert hall (complete with its own orchestra) and a racecourse (surrounded by statues of dwarves). For a while, Kuks' social life was on a par with the likes of Karlsbad; then, in 1738, the impresario died, and two years later, on December 22, 1740, disaster struck when the river broke its banks, destroying all the buildings on the left bank and, worse still, the springs themselves.

All that remains of the original spa is an overgrown monumental stairway leading nowhere, and, on the right bank, the hospital building fronted by **Matthias Bernhard Braun**'s famous terrace, now the chief reason for visiting Kuks. Sporck became the Tyrolean sculptor's chief patron in Bohemia, commissioning from him a series of **allegorical statues** intended to elevate the minds of his spa guests: to the west, the twelve *Vices* culminate in the grim

Angel of Grievous Death; to the east, the twelve *Virtues* end with the *Angel of Blessed Death*. Over the years the elements have not been too kind to Braun's work, whose originals, including a few surviving dwarves, have retreated inside the hospital building and now provide the highlight of the 45-minute guided tour (April & Oct Sat & Sun 9am–noon & 1–4pm; May–Aug Tues–Sun until 6pm; Sept Tues–Sun until 5pm). Also in the tour is the beautifully restored eighteenth-century pharmacy and Baroque chapel, though Sporck's subterranean mausoleum is no longer on show.

There's a good **restaurant** next to the zámek, ladling out big portions of meat and gravy. Buses will either drop you at the main road, a short walk north of the village, or in the village itself; the **train station** lies to the south, behind the hospital building and formal gardens (follow the blue-marked path).

Betlém

One stop along the tracks, or a steep 5km walk along the blue-marked path, upriver from Kuks, is **Betlém** (Bethlehem), Braun's outdoor Nativity sculpture park, again sponsored by Sporck. It's an unlikely, ingenious location, deep in the midst of a silver birch wood, and used to include several working springs, including one that shot water high up into the foliage. However, centuries of neglect, pilfering and weathering have taken their toll (many of the sculptures have been covered with cheap wooden roof shelters in a much-belated attempt to prevent any further damage) and what you see now are the few survivors of what would once have been a remarkable open-air *atelier* – exclusively the ones that Braun hacked out of various boulders he found strewn about the wood. In contrast to Kuks, the theme here is more explicitly religious, with the best-preserved sculptural groups depicting *The Journey of the Magi* and the *Nativity*. The dishevelled man crawling out of his cave, and looking very much like a 3-D representation of William Blake's *Fall of Man*, is in fact an obscure Egyptian hermit called Garinus.

Dvůr Králové nad Labem

DVŮR KRÁLOVÉ NAD LABEM, 8km northwest of Kuks, is familiar to postwar generations of Czech kids as the site of the country's largest **zoo** (daily 9am–6pm or dusk). As underfunded eastern European zoos go, Dvůr Králové has tried harder than most to make the animals' lives bearable, but a "safari park" it is not. The section of the zoo nearest the entrance is full of caged animals like any other zoo; all the usual beasts are here – lions, elephants, monkeys and so on. In addition, the zoo specializes in breeding African hoofed animals, including the rare white rhino. There's a *dětský koutek* (kids' corner), where children can stroke the more domesticated animals. The "safari" bit consists of a free bus ride through a series of open enclosures, where there's a serious surfeit of antelopes. The safari bus sets off from the far side of the zoo – a long way to walk for smaller kids, so it's best to take the horse and cart or mini-train there.

Dvůr Králové **bus station** is on 17 listopadu; to get to the main square, walk north two blocks, then left down Švehlova. The **train station** is 2km southwest of the centre; a bus meets all trains and drops passengers in the centre, or you can walk down 5 května, which becomes 28 října before crossing the river, after which it's due north up Riegrova and Revoluční to the main square. The zoo is 1km west of the town, on Štefánikova, and is well signposted. The town itself has an arcaded main square, with a good **restaurant** called, appropriately, *Country Saloon* – the name gives you an idea of the decor and occasional live music within.

Hořice

Just about every Czech sculptor over the last hundred years was trained at the School of Masonry and Sculpture founded in 1884 at **HOŘICE V PODKRKONOŠÍ**, 23km northwest of Hradec Králové. As a result, the town now boasts one of the country's richest collections of sculpture and plays host to an annual **international symposium of contemporary sculpture** in July and August.

There are sculptures all over town and exhibitions of contemporary works in the town museum (Tues–Sun 9am–noon & 1–5pm) on the main square, but the largest collection is in the **Galerie plastik** (Tues–Sun 9am–noon & 1–4pm), halfway up the sv Gothard hill to the east of town (five minutes' walk down Janderova). Half the gallery is given over to temporary exhibitions, but the permanent collection is still impressive. All the leading lights of Czech sculpture are represented here, even Šaloun, famous for his Jan Hus Monument in Prague, and Bílek, neither of whom actually studied here, as well as one of the few extant works by Otakar Švec, the man responsible for Prague's since-dynamited Stalin Monument. In the meadows and orchards to the north of the gallery is the **symposium area**, with previous years' exhibits out on show. To the east is the local **cemetery** (*hřbitov*), which has a wonderful triumphal arch over the entrance and a scattering of well-sculpted headstones. To the west, the **Smetanovy sady** are dotted with mostly nineteenth-century sculptures of leading figures of the Czech national revival.

Despite the town's enormous artistic treasures, it sees very few visitors. Decent **accommodation** is available at the *Hotel Královský Dvůr* (℡ 493 624 124; ❷), on the main square. There are also no fewer than three **campsites** in the area – the nearest being the *U věže* site (mid-May to mid-Sept), 1km north of town on the road to Dvůr Králové. The **train station** (Hořice v Podkrkonoší) is 1km south of town down Husova (there's an occasional connecting bus).

Chlum

A short 9km northwest of Hradec Králové, the flat fields around **CHLUM** make an ideal **battleground**. And in 1866, the forces of the Prussian and Austro-Hungarian armies clashed here as part of a long-running disagreement over how to divide central Europe. Following the 1848 revolts against the Habsburgs, the Austro-Hungarian Empire found itself in a precarious position, with the Prussians gaining increasing power over German matters. Both sides flexed their muscles in the spring and summer of 1866, with several skirmishes taking place across what is now eastern Bohemia. By late June, the Austrians had established a tenuous position around the tiny village of Chlum, but early in the morning of July 3, the Prussians attacked on the northern and western flanks, and by early afternoon had clearly gained the upper hand. At day's end, over 5500 Austrian soldiers and some 2100 Prussians lay dead, and what remained of the Habsburg army had begun its retreat. This marked a decisive defeat for Austria, as it lost yet more control over its German-speaking constituency. Its weakened status had no benefits for the Czechs either, as they remained second-class citizens to the Germans in an increasingly unstable Habsburg Empire.

Despite its rather important role in the downfall of the Habsburgs, Chlum is really only appealing for war buffs. The site of the battle is marked with a monument, a mass grave, a viewing tower over the fields and a small **museum** (April–Oct Tues–Sun 9am–noon & 1–5pm), which displays uniforms worn by some of the fallen as well as a thorough description, with dioramas, of the battle – but only in Czech and German. Two or three mid-day buses run to Chlum from Hradec Králové (the stop is marked Všestary, Chlum), but service is curtailed at weekends.

Chlumec nad Cidlinou

CHLUMEC NAD CIDLINOU, 29km west of Hradec Králové, in the middle of the featureless, dusty Polabí, was the scene of one of the largest peasant uprisings in the country in 1775, after which 3000 of those who had taken part were burned to death in a nearby farm. Just over fifty years before that bloody incident, Count Kinský built himself one of Bohemia's most exquisite provincial chateaux, **Karlova Koruna** (April & Oct Sat & Sun 9am–noon & 1–4pm; May–Aug Tues–Sun 8am–noon & 1–5pm; Sept Tues–Sun 9am–noon & 1–5pm). Begun in 1721 by Giovanni Santini, it stands on a rare patch of raised ground to the northwest of the town, south of the train station. Santini's ground plan is a simple but intriguing triple-winged affair, dominated by a central circular hall, with a two-storey pink-and-grey marble dome and a grand staircase leading to the upper balcony. The building's exterior and grounds are both in need of some tidying up, however. In the grounds, the modest Baroque pleasure house displays copies of Braun's statuary.

Pardubice

There's always been a certain amount of rivalry between the two big cities of the Polabí, Hradec Králové and **PARDUBICE**, just under 20km to the south. On balance, Pardubice's historical core is probably more immediately appealing than Hradec Králové's, and it has a lovely newly-renovated chateau, but its new town lacks the logic and cohesion of its neighbour, which makes the whole place feel a lot smaller. Throughout the horse-racing world, Pardubice is best known for its **steeplechase course** (second only to Liverpool's Aintree course for difficulty), where the *Velká Pardubická* (first run in 1874) takes place in early October, usually accompanied by protests by Czech animal rights activists.

The Town

The **train** and **bus stations** lie at the end of Palackého in the new town, a busy thoroughfare and the beginning of Pardubice's long parade of shops. It's a good ten-minute walk from here (or a short ride on trolley bus #2) northeast to the old town, much of it along **Míru**, a busy commercial street that contains an arresting threesome of late Secession buildings on the left-hand side, with *U lva* at the centre, distinguished by the two tiny lion heads on its gable.

Míru comes to an end at **náměstí Republiky**, which marks the transition from the new town to the old. At one end, the seriously striking Art Nouveau **Městské divadlo** (Town theatre) is a deliberately Czech structure, designed by Antonín Balšánek (who collaborated with Polívka on Prague's Obecní dům), its magnificent facade flanked by multicoloured mosaics: Libuše founding Prague on one side and a blind Žižka leading the Hussites into battle on the other. The other truly arresting building on the square is the church of **sv Bartoloměj**, originally Gothic but more memorable for the Renaissance additions to its exterior – courtesy of local bigwigs, the Pernštejns – which makes up for its lack of a tower with a syringe-like central spike. Josef Gočár worked in Pardubice, as well as in Hradec Králové: the squat, grey Komerční banka, and the recently restored *Hotel Grand* opposite, are both his.

The soaring Gothic gateway, **Zelená brána** (May–Sept Tues–Sun 9am–noon & 1–5pm), with its twisted uppermost tower and wonderful baubled spikes, makes for a memorable entrance to the old town, and a good place from which to survey it. The main square, **Pernštýnovo náměstí**, is an intimate affair, an effect made all the more pronounced by the tall three-storey buildings on each side, handsome gabled sixteenth- and eighteenth-century houses for the most part, with the exception of the flamboyant neo-Renaissance **radnice**. The sculptural decoration throughout the old town is remarkable and at its most striking on **U Jonáše**, whose plasterwork includes an exuberant depiction of Jonah at the moment of digestion by the whale. A handful of picturesque backstreets spread north from here, with the buttressed beauty of Bartolomějská or the crumbling facades of Pernštýnská, both leading eventually to the romantic embankment, Wernerovo nábřeží, whose drooping willow trees provide a perfect spot of shade in summer.

At this point, you should head up Zámecká, and cross the vast dry moat to the newly restored **zámek** (Tues–Sun 10am–6pm), which is protected by an impressive series of walls, gates and barbicans, and occupies more space than the entire staré město. The chateau's sgraffitoed appearance, and its beautiful loggia in the main courtyard, amongst which a happy congregation of peacocks and turkeys

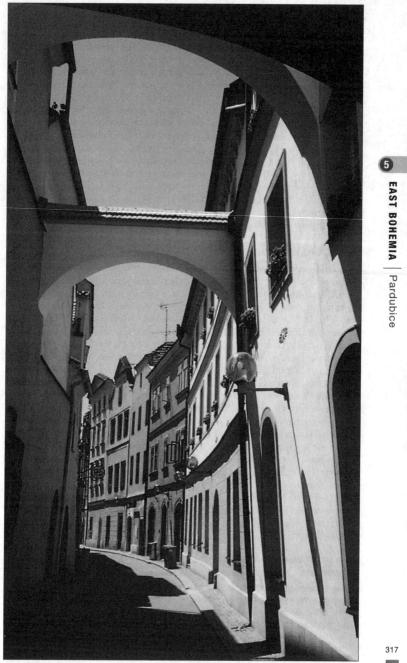

△ Pardubice

struts its stuff, date from the sixteenth century when it became the chief seat of the powerful Pernštejn family. The latter were also responsible for the chateau's precious Renaissance wall paintings, which have been partially preserved in the **Rytířské sály** on the first floor. There are trompe l'oeil doorframes and decorative motifs, plus two very large pictures: the first is of Moses being given the ten commandments, while the second (and best preserved) one features Delilah cutting the hair of the sleeping Samson, while a phalanx of Philistines arrives hotfoot. You can see the frescoes – and the tiny arms collection and the local museum, which are also housed in the chateau – without a guided tour; just make sure you buy the useful English information leaflets when you purchase your ticket.

On the other side of the outer courtyard is the **Východočeské galerie** (Tues–Sun 10am–5pm), which puts on temporary exhibitions on the ground floor, and contains a small collection of modern Czech art on the first floor. The gallery owns works by all the major Czech artists of the last century, from Čapek to Medek, but only a few pieces stick out: in particular Kamil Lhoták's realist canvases from the 1940s and 1950s, the giant (cracked) *Human Egg* by Eva Kmentová, and a great little pair of papier-maché wellingtons called *Homage to Jules Verne* by Jiří Kolář.

Practicalities

You could easily come to Pardubice on a day-trip from Hradec Králové (it's only 30min away by train); though there are at least a few reasonable **hotels** in the old town. *Bistro 100* (T466 511 179; ③) has a fine location and clean rooms on Kostelní, matched in appearance and price by *Penzión 102* right next door (T & F466 511 153; ③). *Hotel U Anděla* (T466 514 028, F466 516 575; ③), down the street on Zámecká, is a tad larger and dearer, but similarly well-kept. These are all recommended over the Communist-era *Labe* (T466 535 359; ③), by the Tesco department store in the new town. At the other end, both geographically and aesthetically, the *Sirius* (T466 511 548; ②) rises above the train station and is only recommended if you're pinching pennies. Otherwise, the town's *Cihelna* **campsite** (June to mid-Oct) is just north of the river up K cihelně.

There's a very pleasant chilled-out *čajovna* on Wernerovo nábřeží, and a great little *vinárna* named *Bazalka* across the way, which serves good salads at its wicker tables and chairs. You'll also find several **restaurants** on the old town square, most of which also have outdoor seating: *U černého orla* is a typical Czech goulash-and-dumplings kind of place, while *Pizzeria Galera* (whose entrance is actually on Bartolomějská) serves up decent fish and Italian entrées.

Note that accommodation is impossible to find over the weekend of the *Velká Pardubická* in early October. Less prestigious **horse races** take place every other weekend at Pardubice's **steeplechase course** (*závodiště*), which is 2km out of town; take bus #4 or #14. Pardubice's **tourist office** (daily 7am–7pm) is located at Míru 60.

Janák's crematorium and Gočár's spa

Pardubice boasts two fine buildings from a unique period in Czech architectural history. The first is the town's crematorium on Pod břízkami (trolley bus #1 from náměstí Republiky), designed by **Pavel Janák** in the 1920s, and, with its feast of semicircular motifs and garish colours, one of the finest extant Rondo-Cubist buildings in the country. The other architectural gem is **Josef Gočár**'s sanatorium at the nearby spa of Bohdaneč, accessible on trolley bus #3 (via Semtín). Built in 1909, it was, in all probability, the first Cubist structure ever built.

Chrudim and Ležáky

Twelve kilometres south of Pardubice, the pretty little town of **CHRUDIM** springs into life in early July for its annual **Puppet Festival**. At other times of the year, it's still worth the short train ride to visit the marvellous **Puppet Museum** (Muzeum loutkářských kultur; April–Sept daily 9–11am & 1–5pm; Oct–March Tues–Fri 9am–noon & 1–5pm, Sat & Sun 1–5pm), housed in the splendid sixteenth-century Mydlářovský dům on Břetislavova, just off the main square. The Czech Lands have a long tradition of puppetry, going back to the country's peasant roots, and the museum acts as a repository for marionettes and puppets donated from all over the world.

Southeast of Chrudim off route 37, in a quiet, shady glen, is a memorial to the village of **LEŽÁKY**, which suffered an even worse fate than Lidice (see p.163). On June 24, 1942, the SS rounded up the village's entire adult population and shot all 56 of them; two children were deemed fit for Germanization and the rest were sent off to the camps. The motive for Ležáky's destruction was the same as for Lidice's: Hitler wanted revenge for the assassination of Reinhard Heydrich, Reichsprotektor of Bohemia and Moravia. Exactly two weeks after Lidice was wiped out, Ležáky suffered the same fate for concealing a resistance transmitter. Today the foundation stones of the houses, which were all burned down, are all that remain of the village, and these have been carefully rearranged and topped with memorial stones. The main difference between Ležáky and Lidice, though, is that no new town was built here: the road simply passes through, with signs to mark the boundaries. A **museum** (May–Sept Tues–Sun 9am–5pm) displays photographs of the town after the destruction, as well as of each of the victims. There are no buses to Ležáky, only a few daily ones from Chrudim to Miřetice, 2km to the west.

Litomyšl and around

For a small town in the northern reaches of the Bohemian-Moravian Uplands, **LITOMYŠL** (Leitomischl) has big ideas. In 1992 a School for Restoration and Conservation was founded here and immediately set to work restoring the Portmoneum, a house decorated with fantastical murals and furniture by Josef Váchal, which opened the following year. Soon after the town pulled off an even more amazing coup by getting seven presidents of central Europe – including Václav Havel, Lech Walesa and Richard von Weizsäcker – to meet here for a summit. The prime mover behind these dramatic developments is the town's mayor, Miroslav Brýdl, who, along with his brothers, Jiří (mayor of neighbouring Svitavy) and Tomáš (who runs a local advertising agency), is determined to put Litomyšl on the map.

The Town

The town's picturesque main square, **Smetanovo náměstí**, is strung out like a juicy fat Czech sausage and lined with almost uninterrupted arcades, a pastel parade of Baroque and Neoclassical facades, all pristinely repainted in preparation for the presidents' visit. The sixteenth-century **U rytířů**, at no. 110 (Tues–Sun 10am–noon & 1–5pm), is the finest of the lot, decorated with medieval knights and merchants holding bags of money, clinging mischievously to their carved columns; the building now hosts art exhibitions, worth checking out if only to admire the coffered Renaissance ceiling inside. The

Train Station

Zámek ❶

Smetana's Birthplace

TOULCOVO NÁMĚSTÍ

Urytířů ❷

ŠANTOVO NÁMĚSTÍ

Portmoneum

LIDICKÁ

River Loučná

ROPKOVA

ⓘ

BRAUNEROVO NÁMĚSTÍ ❸

ACCOMMODATION & RESTAURANTS

Petra	2
Zámecká restaurace	1
Zlatá hvězda	3

N

0   100 m

Bus Station

Primátor Campsite ►

Svitavy ▼

town's most famous son is the composer **Bedřich Smetana**, who was born here in 1824, hence Jan Štursa's effete statue of the composer at the northwest corner of the main square. Every year in his honour, the town puts on a ten-day **international opera festival**, *Smetanova Litomyšl*, towards the end of June. Smetana was not the only Czech aesthete to stroll the streets of Litomyšl, though; Nationalist writers Božena Němcová and Alois Jirásek also lived here for short times, as plaques on their homes on the square recall.

To the northeast of the main square, a knot of ramshackle backstreets, punctuated by churches, leads up to the town's most celebrated monument, the Pernštejns' **zámek** (April & Oct Sat & Sun 9am–noon & 1–4pm; May–Aug Tues–Sun 9am–noon & 1–5pm; Sept Tues–Sun 9am–noon & 1–4pm), a smart, sgraffitoed affair that bursts into frivolous gables and finials on its roof and which boasts one of Bohemia's finest triple-decker loggia inside. You'll have to join a guided tour to view the interior, and you have a choice. *Trasa 1* leads you through state and banquet rooms richly decorated in porcelain and period furniture. The highlight, though, is the remarkable late eighteenth-century theatre where the young Smetana made his debut as a pianist, accompanied by much of the original scenery painted by Josef Platzer. *Trasa 2* extends the trip through a rather unanticipated collection of torture instruments, as well as a small gallery featuring local artists. If you don't fancy either tour, head instead for the former riding school, which now houses the **Muzeum antického sochařství a architecktury** (May–Oct Tues–Sun 9am–noon & 1–5pm), a bizarre collection of plaster and bronze casts of Greek and Roman classical statues from museums around the world.

Smetana himself was born in the adjacent former town brewery, one of eighteen children to an upwardly mobile beer maker. The building now houses the **Rodný byt Smetany** (April & Oct Sat & Sun 9am–noon & 1–5pm; May–Sept Tues–Sun 9am–noon & 1–5pm), a modest memorial museum to the composer. Smetana was a veritable *Wunderkind*, playing in a string quartet at the age of five and composing his first symphony at eight, but a year before that, the family moved to Jindřichův Hradec. Catalyzed by the events of 1848, Smetana became a leading figure in the Czech national revival (despite German being his mother tongue), helping to found Prague's Národní divadlo. In 1874 he had to resign as the theatre's chief conductor after becoming deaf through a syphilitic infection. He went on to promote the nationalist cause through works like *Má vlast* ("My Country"), a symphonic poem inspired by Czech legends, but sadly ended his days in a mental asylum.

A short walk southeast of the chateau, at Terézy Novákové 75, is without doubt Litomyšl's most extraordinary and unique artistic treasure, the **Portmoneum** (May–Sept Tues–Sun 9am–noon & 1–5pm), painstakingly restored and opened in 1993. From the outside, it looks like any other provincial town house, but inside, the walls, ceilings and furniture of two rooms are decorated with the strange and wonderful work of the self-taught artist **Josef Váchal** (1884–1969), from the early 1920s. Váchal's ghoulish art is difficult to categorize (though "weird" would be the simplest shorthand): the ceiling in one room is a whirlwind of devils, spirits and sinful creatures; elsewhere there are cherubs, Kupkaesque celestial orbs of light, quotations from Hindu religious poems and a Crucifixion, while Váchal himself appears at one point as a rat-catcher. The man who wanted his house decorated with such disturbing murals was **Josef Portman** (after whom the house is named), a civil servant, amateur printer and lifelong collector of Váchal's art, who died here in 1968.

Practicalities

Buses are probably the easiest way to get to Litomyšl, since the town lies on a little-used branch line from Choceň. The **bus station** is on Mařákova, five minutes' walk southeast of the centre, a pleasant stroll along (and across) the River Loučná; the **train station** is five minutes' walk west of the old town, again along (and across) the river. As befits a town with ambition, there's an efficient **tourist office** (Mon–Fri 9am–7pm, Sat 9am–4pm, Sun 10am–3pm; ☏461 612 161, ⓦwww.litomysl.cz) on the west side of the main square at no. 72, which can help with **accommodation**. The upmarket *Zlatá hvězda* on the main square (☏461 615 338, ⓦwww.hotel.cz/zl-hvezda; ❸), where Havel stayed, is the town's finest hotel, or there's the clean, modern pension *Petra* on B. Němcové (☏ & ⒻI461 613 061; ❷). The *Primátor* **campsite** (May–Sept) is 2km southeast of the town centre, off route 35/E442 to Moravská Třebová. If it's **food** you want, the *Hotel Zlatá hvězda* has an excellent restaurant and surprisingly good prices, or you can lunch at the fine *Zámecká restaurace*, in the chateau grounds.

Schindler's Svitavy

When Spielberg's Holocaust film, *Schindler's List*, reached the Czech Republic in 1994, it was premiered in **Svitavy** (Zwittau), a small Moravian town (currently in East Bohemia) 20km southeast of Litomyšl. The simple reason for this was that the "hero" of the film, Nazi industrialist **Oskar Schindler**, was born here in 1908, son of an insurance salesman, at Iglauerstrasse (now Poličská) 24. In Svitavy, he was known as a hard-drinking womanizer who was expelled from school for falsifying his school report and some years later arrested in the *Hotel Ungar*, on the town's main square, for supplying the German *Abwehr* with information.

Schindler became a member of the Nazi Party early on and, during the war, he used his Party contacts to establish a kitchenware factory in Kraków, using Jewish slave labour. It was here that Schindler began to shelter Jews, hiring them even though they were too sick or weak to work, in order to save them from certain death in the nearby camps. In 1943 he took 900 Jewish workers with him and set up an armaments factory in Brněnec, a town 15km south of Svitavy. In fact, Schindler made sure that not a single weapon was actually produced at the factory and by the end of the war he had saved 1200 Jews from deportation. He died in 1974 in Hildesheim in Germany, though his remains were transferred to Israel as a mark of gratitude.

The majority of Svitavy's population (most of whom were German-speaking) were expelled after the war, and only a few of the older inhabitants can remember Schindler from his Svitavy days. The film therefore came as something of a revelation to many of Svitavy's residents, who had previously been told only the Communists' postwar version of events: that Schindler was simply the Nazi chief of the local concentration camp. Despite the release of the film, the town council still had to overcome fierce local opposition in order to erect a memorial plaque – in Czech and German – in the park opposite Schindler's birthplace. The plaque was eventually unveiled by the republic's Chief Rabbi shortly after the film's premiere.

Polička

The Bohemian-Moravian Uplands are clearly a musically fertile region: Mahler spent his childhood in Jihlava (see p.364), while the town of **POLIČKA**, 18km south of Litomyšl, produced **Bohuslav Martinů**, who was born in 1890 at the top of the 75-metre tall fairy-tale neo-Gothic tower of the church of **sv Jakub**, just west of the main square. The composer's father – a cobbler by trade – was also the local watchman, and the single room in which the family of five lived until 1902, has to be one of the most memorable memorials to any composer. To climb the tower, you must first buy a ticket from the local **museum** (Tues–Sun 9am–5pm), on Tylova, north off the main square, where you can see an exhibition and watch a video on Martinů's life. Despite spending much of his life in exile, Martinů always carried a postcard of the view from the tower, and twenty years after his death in a Swiss hospital in 1959, he was finally buried in the town cemetery, within sight of the tower.

Apart from the composer, there's little other reason for coming to Polička, which had its aesthetic charms altered in a devastating fire in 1845. The main square was nicely rebuilt, however, and the town's beautifully preserved fortifications are pretty impressive (and clearly visible from the tower). The **train station** is north of the town, off route 359 to Litomyšl, but only connects with Svitavy and Česká Třebová, not Litomyšl. The best place to stay in town is the pretty blue *Penzion U purkmistra* (☎461 722 310; ❷), on Riegrova near the church of sv Jakub; alternatively there's a **campsite** (May–Sept), 1.5km south of the town off route 360 to Nové Město na Moravě.

Svojanov

In addition to being one of the prettiest castles in the charming Bohemian-Moravian Uplands, **Svojanov** (April & Oct Sat & Sun 9am–noon & 1–4pm; May–Sept Tues–Sun 9am–5pm), 15km southeast of Polička, commands admiration for its impressive stance atop a granite protuberance. It's a small place, and each stage of its many constructions ia clearly visible, from a thirteenth-century guard tower through to the Empire-style ornamentation of the interior halls. The guided tour takes you through the usual collection of paintings and glassware, along with an exceptional array of old clocks. If you're here in mid-July, you can also go to the annual **puppet festival**, where some of the country's leading artisans put on displays and shows of the craft particular to this region. You can **sleep** at the base of the rock in the very basic *Penzión Pála* (☎461 744 127; ❶), which also has a decent **restaurant**. Svojanov is served by fairly regular buses from Polička on weekdays, though at the weekend there's only one a day, which continues on to Brno.

Travel details

Trains

Prague: Hradec Králové (5–7 daily; 1hr 25 min–1hr 45 min); Jičín (2 daily; 1hr 50min); Pardubice (1–2 hourly; 1hr 10min–2hr 20min); Trutnov (1 daily; 4hr); Turnov (11 daily; 2hr–2hr 40min).
Hradec Králové to: Častolovice/Doudleby nad Orlicí (5–6 daily; 50min/1hr 10min); Chlumec nad Cidlinou (every 1–2 hours; 20–40min); Dvůr Králové (8 daily; 40min–1hr); Hořice (10 daily; 30–50min); Jaroměř (hourly; 20–30min); Jičín (8 daily; 1hr 15min); Kuks (6 daily; 40min); Pardubice (1–2 hourly; 30min); Třebechovice pod Orebem (10–15 daily; 15min).
Náchod to: Nové Město nad Metují/Opočno (10–14 daily; 15min/20–30min); Teplice nad Metují (9–12 daily; 40min).
Pardubice to: Chrudím (hourly; 20min); Liberec (2 daily; 3hr).
Trutnov to: Adršpach/Teplice nad Metují (6–8 daily; 1hr/1hr 15min); Česká Skalice/Jaroměř (10–12 daily; 1hr/1hr 15min); Kunčice nad Labem (10–12 daily; 30min); Chlumec nad Cidlinou (6–8 daily; 1hr–2hr 40min).
Turnov to: Hradec Králové (12 daily; 1hr 50min–3hr); Jičín (10 daily; 50min–1hr 10min); Železný Brod (8 daily; 20min).

Buses

Connections with Prague: Harrachov (up to 5 daily; 3hr); Hradec Králové (hourly; 1hr 30min–2hr); Jičín (up to 12 daily; 2hr); Litomyšl (up to 6 daily; 3hr 30min); Náchod (up to 8 daily; 3hr); Pec pod Sněžkou (up to 9 daily; 3hr); Špindlerův Mlýn (up to 6 daily; 2hr 40min); Trutnov (up to 15 daily; 2hr 45min); Vrchlabí (up to 11 daily; 2hr 30min–3hr).
Hradec Králové to: Jaroměř (hourly; 25min); Kuks (up to 10 daily; 30–40min); Litomyšl (hourly; 1hr 10min); Náchod (up to 12 daily; 1hr); Nové Město nad Metují (up to 6 daily; 1hr 20min); Pec pod Sněžkou (1 daily; 2hr); Trutnov (up to 10 daily; 1hr 10min); Vrchlabí (up to 8 daily; 1hr 30min).
Jičín to: Turnov (8 daily; 30min).
Náchod to: Broumov (up to 12 daily; 45min–1hr); Nové Město nad Metují (1–2 per hour; 30min).
Trutnov to: Jánské Lázně (hourly; 30min); Pec pod Sněžkou (hourly; 50min); Vrchlabí (12 daily; 30–40min).
Vrchlabí to: Špindlerův Mlýn (hourly; 20min).

South Moravia

CHAPTER 6 # Highlights

* **Moravský Kras** – Limestone karst region of caves, underground rivers and gorges within easy reach of the Moravian capital, Brno. See p.345

* **Pernštejn** – Classic hilltop medieval castle with dizzyingly high walls and equally awesome views. See p.348

* **Mikulov** – Quiet border town with a well-preserved synagogue and Jewish cemetery set amidst the vineyards of South Moravia. See p.351

* **Podyjí** – Former estate of the Liechtenstein family that boasts two fine chateaux, numerous follies, and abundant wildlife. See p.358

* **Telč** – Moravian Renaissance gem with the best-preserved sixteenth-century square in the country, and a chateau to match it. See p.362

* **Slavonice** – Border town with two remarkably well-preserved squares featuring Apocalyptic sgraffito facades. See p.363

* **Zelená Hora, Žďár nad Sázavou** – Star-shaped pilgrimage church on a hill beside a Cistercian monastery built by the Baroque-Gothic architect Giovanni Santini. See p.368

* **Kroměříž** – Set on the River Morava, this picturesque town is dominated by the chateau, art gallery, wine cellars and gardens of the former archbishops of Olomouc. See p.378

South Moravia

A t first sight, the landscape of **South Moravia** (Jižní Morava) appears little different from that of much of Bohemia, with rolling hills, dense forests and cultivation. Only as you move south towards Vienna does the land become noticeably more plump and fertile, with the orchards and vineyards continuing into Austria itself. **Brno** is the most obvious starting point: an engaging city, whose attractions are often underrated due to its heavy industrial base and conspicuous peripheral housing estates. Brno is also within easy reaching distance of a host of sights, most notably Moravia's karst region, the Moravský kras, which boasts the country's most spectacular **limestone caves**, and the atmospheric medieval castle of **Pernštejn**.

South of Brno a whole string of pretty villages, towns and chateaux punctuate the River Dyje (Thaya) as it meanders along the Austrian border. Historically, the land on either side of the Dyje was for centuries German-speaking, its buildings designed by Austrian architects and its sights set firmly on Vienna, just 60km to the south. However, as in the rest of the country, the ethnic German population was forcibly removed from South Moravia after 1945. The region's viticulture kept going on private plots even after nationalization in 1948, but in every other way the last half century has driven a great wedge between two previously identical regions on either side of the river. **Mikulov**, on the main road from Vienna, is a great introduction to the country; close by, at the chateaux of **Lednice** and **Valtice**, the Liechtensteins had their base for many centuries. Further west, another border town, **Znojmo**, harbours the country's most precious medieval frescoes, and is a great jumping-off point for the **Podyjí** national park, formed by the damming of the Dyje and dotted with castles and chateaux. Nevertheless, there are one or two real high spots that make this a region worth exploring.

Further west still, on the Bohemian border, **Telč** and **Slavonice** are two of the most beautiful Renaissance towns anywhere in Europe. Yet while Telč is a popular stopoff on whirlwind tours of the country, Slavonice – every bit as perfect – sees far fewer visitors. Telč and Slavonice sit at the southern end of the **Bohemian-Moravian Uplands** or Vysočina, a poor and sparsely populated area which separates Bohemia and Moravia, and which is viewed by most travellers only from the window of their bus, train or car en route to Brno. **Jihlava** is the area's most convenient starting point, but it won't hold you long. More compelling is the pilgrimage church at **Žďár nad Sázavou**, another of Santini's Baroque-Gothic confections.

To the east of Brno, the landscape around the River Morava is visually pretty uninspiring, but the wine and rich folk heritage are good reasons for stopping here. To the south, the area known as **Slovácko** hosts the country's two largest **folk**

festivals, in Vlčnov and Strážnice. Further north, the provincial treasure house and graceful gardens of **Kroměříž** provide a fascinating contrast with the modernist aesthetics of **Zlín**, where the multinational Baťa shoe empire has its roots.

Transport is fairly good throughout Moravia, though the train system is not quite as comprehensive as that of Bohemia, petering out in the Vysočina and degenerating into a series of overcomplex branch lines along the more industrialized River Morava. In such instances, buses are invariably quicker and more direct.

Brno

BRNO (Brünn) "welcomes the visitor with new constructions", as one communist-era tourist brochure euphemistically put it. In fact, the high-rise *paneláky* that surround the Moravian capital play a major part in discouraging travellers from stopping here. But as the second-largest city in the Czech Republic, with a population of over 400,000, a couple of really good museums and art galleries, a handful of other sights and a fair bit of nightlife, it's worth a day or two of anyone's time. For the most part, though, the city receives few foreign visitors outside the annual trade fairs, though of course this has its advantages too: tourists are welcomed here with genuine interest, and the pace of life is endearingly (some might say infuriatingly) provincial, compared to that of Prague.

Brno was a late developer, being no bigger than Olomouc until the late eighteenth century. The town's first cloth factory was founded in 1766, and within fifteen years was followed by another twenty, earning Brno the nickname of *rakouský Manchestr* (Austrian Manchester). With the building of an engineering plant early in the next century, the city began to attract Czech workers, along with Austrian, German, English and, in particular, Jewish entrepreneurs, making it easily the second largest city in the Czech Lands by the end of the nineteenth century. Between the wars, Brno enjoyed a cultural boom, heralded by the 1928 Exhibition of Contemporary Culture, which provided an impetus for much of the city's pioneering **functionalist architecture**.

Of the city's 10,000-strong prewar Jewish community, only around 670 survived, and immediately after the war, the city's German-speakers (some 25 percent of the population) were rounded up and ordered to leave, on foot, for Vienna (see p.350). Following the 1948 Communist coup and the subsequent centralization (and later federalization), state funds were diverted to Prague and Bratislava, pushing Brno firmly into third place. Since 1989, Brno has continued to play second fiddle to Prague, with reconstruction and restoration work progressing much more slowly here than in the capital. To add insult to injury, Brno was effectively demoted during the latest administrative reorganization, when the number of districts or *kraje* was increased from seven to fourteen, putting the likes of Jihlava and Ostrava on the same administrative footing as Brno.

Arrival, orientation and information

The fin-de-siècle splendour of the city's main **train station**, Brno hlavní nádraží, is a great introduction to the city; not so the main **bus station**, five minutes' walk south along the overhead walkway, though some buses arrive at the old bus station opposite the *Grand Hotel*. The main **tourist office** is in the stará radnice (Old Town Hall), on Radnická 8 (Mon–Fri 8am–6pm, Sat & Sun 9am–5pm; ☏542 320 758, ⓦwww.brno.cz); the staff are friendly enough, though the office is not as comprehensive as those in Prague or Bratislava.

Most of Brno's sights are within easy walking distance of the train station, although **trams** (ⓦwww.dpmb.cz) will take you almost anywhere in the city within minutes. Brno has, unfortunately, adopted Prague's complex system of ticketing: you need to buy either a 7Kč ticket for two zones (2 *pásma*), which will last you ten minutes without changing trams or buses, or a 12Kč ticket, again for two zones (2 *pásma*), which is valid for forty minutes and allows changes between trams or buses. Tickets must be bought beforehand from news kiosks or yellow ticket machines and validated in the electronic devices on board; if you're going to be whizzing about on the trams all day, you might want to buy a 24-hour *celodenní jízdenka*, currently 48Kč. A couple of trams run all night, but many have been replaced by night buses which run along the old tram routes – all gather together in front of the station on the hour, every hour. The same tickets are valid for the city's **buses** and **trolleybuses**, which congregate at Moravské náměstí and Mendlovo náměstí, though you're unlikely to need to use them unless you're staying right out in suburbia.

Accommodation

Finding **accommodation** in Brno is relatively easy, though prices are fairly high, thanks to the expense-account business people who come here for the various trade fairs (when prices can double). Taxatour Brno, the 24-hour agency in the train station, can arrange cheap **private rooms**, as can the tourist office in Radnická (see p.330); the latter also books hotels, though many of the ones on their books are out of the centre. **Hostels** do exist in Brno, but none of them are even remotely near the centre: the HI-affiliated *Student Pension Palacký* (☎541 641 111; open all year), for example, is a high-rise block on the far northern edge of the city at the end of Kolejní; take tram #12 or #13 to their terminus and then trolleybus #53 to the end of the line. The tourist office can also point you in the right direction for **student rooms** in July and August.

There are several **campsites** along the shores of the Brněnská přehrada (Brno Dam), 10km northwest of the city centre; the nearest one is *Radka* (June–Aug), on the east bank beyond the HI-affiliated hostel, *Hotel Přehrada* (☎546 210 167) and the Sokolské swimming pool; to reach the dam, take tram #1, #3 or #11. Less appealing, but easier to locate, is the *Bobrava* site, by the motorway 10km south of Brno at Modřice (open all year), a one-kilometre walk from Popovice train station under the motorway.

Hotels and pensions

Amphone Třída kpt. Jaroše 29 ☎545 211 783, ⓔamphone@brn.czn.cz. A really good choice: clean, plain and positioned on a lovely tree-lined boulevard, just ten minutes' walk from the city centre. ❸

Avion Česká 20 ☎542 214 055, ⓦwww.iqnet.cz/avion. Bohuslav Fuchs' slimline functionalist hotel has definitely seen better days; price and location are all right, but service and facilities could definitely be better. ❸

Grand Hotel Benešova 18–20 ☎542 518 111, ⓦwww.austria-hotels.co.at/grandhotel-brno. The Art Nouveau mural on the facade is sadly no indication of the interior, which retains no original features whatsoever. Still, it's Austrian-run and efficient enough, if somewhat overpriced. ❾

Pegas Jakubská 4 ☎542 210 104. Small, basic rooms located right in the old town above the micro-brewery/pub of the same name (although this doesn't make it especially noisy). ❹

Pyramida Zahradnická 19 ☎543 427 310. Perfectly comfortable and pleasant, communist-era high-rise hotel a couple of tram stops southwest of the old town, near Výstaviště. ❹

Royal Ricc Starobrněnská 10 ☎542 219 262, ⓦwww.romanctichotels.cz. Lovely position in the backstreets of the old town, and the odd original Renaissance feature and tasteful furnishings make this Brno's luxury hotel of choice. ❼

Slavia Solniční 15–17 ☎542 321 249, ⓦwww.slavia.hotel.cz. Communist-era hotel that's actually pretty comfortable, very central and competitively priced. ❺

Slovan Lidická 23 ☎541 321 207, ⓦwww.hotel-slovan.cz. Another comfortable and unpretentious communist-era hotel, just a step away from the Janáčkovo divadlo. ❹

U královny Elišky Mendlovo nám. 1a ☎543 216 898. Small, vaulted rooms in a cosy pension tucked behind the church in the grounds of the Augustinian monastery, slightly out of the centre. ❸

The City

One of the nicest things about Brno is that its historical centre is compact and almost entirely traffic-free. The city's main action goes on within the small, egg-shaped old town, pedestrianized for the most part and encircled by a swathe of parks and the inner ring road. Around **Zelný trh** and **náměstí Svobody** you'll find most of the city's shops and markets. In the southwestern corner raised above the old town are the quieter streets around **Petrov**, the lesser of Brno's two hills, topped by the cathedral. Further west, the squat fortress of **Špilberk** looks down on the old town to the east and Staré Brno to the south, site of the original early medieval settlement. Worth a visit, but still further from the centre, are Brno's

BRNO

Památník Leoše Janáčka (200 m) ▲

KOUNICOVA

VEVEŘÍ

GORKÉHO

JASELSKÁ

ÚVOZ

ÚDOLNÍ

Bílý dům

Červený kostel

ÚDOLNÍ

Masaryk University

TVRDÉHO

KOMENSKÉHO NÁM

ÚVOZ

Masaryk University

Špilberk

PELLICHOVA

PIVOVARSKÁ

8

Augustinian Monastery

ÚVOZ

PEKAŘSKÁ

ANENSKÁ

LEITNEROVA

Mendelianum

Brewery

MENDLOVO NÁMĚSTÍ

Výstaviště (300 m) ▲

HYBEŠOVA

HYBEŠOVA

RESTAURANTS

Aura	**B**
Haribol	**A**
Spolek	**E**
Schwarzův dům & Saurus	**D**
Taj	**C**
U císaře Leopolda	**F**

▼ 10

▲ **❶, Ⓐ & Ⓑ**   *Vila Tugendhat (750 m) &* **❷** ▲

ACCOMMODATION
Amphone	2
Astoria	6
Avion	3
Grand Hotel	7
Pegas	5
Pyramida	10
Royal Rice	9
Slavia	4
Slovan	1
U královny Elišky	8

0 ————— 100 m

MILADY HORÁKOVÉ

MORAVSKÉ NÁMĚSTÍ

Soviet War Memorial

KOLIŠTĚ

ŽEROTÍNOVO NÁMĚSTÍ

ČESKÁ

BRANOLOVA

Místodržitelský palác

BRATISLAVSKÁ

sv Tomáš

Janáčkovo divadlo

JOŠTOVA

Zemanova kavárna

JAMU

SOLNIČNÍ

Hotel Avion

JAKUBSKÉ NÁM.

sv Jakub

JEZUITSKÁ

BEETHOVENOVA

MOZARTOVA

ROOSEVELTOVA

Dům umění

KOLIŠTĚ

ČESKÁ

JAKUBSKÁ

RAŠÍNOVA

Ⓒ

BEHOUNSKÁ

KOZÍ

Besední dům

SKRYTA

DVOŘÁKOVA

SUKOVA

Divadlo 7a půl

Etnografické muzeum

Kabinet Múz

Mahenovo divadlo

KOBLIŽNÁ

Pražákův palác

NÁMĚSTÍ SVOBODY

Centrum Ⓖ

JÁNSKÁ

DIVADELNÍ

UPM

HUSOVA

ZÁMEČNICKÁ

Ⓓ

Minoritský kostel & Loretánská kaple

Měnínská brána

Nová radnice

sv Michal

PANSKÁ

MEČOVÁ

MINORITSKÁ

ORLÍ

Ⓔ

NOVOBRANSKÁ

DOMINIKÁNSKÁ

MASARYKOVA

Ⓕ

ORLÍ

ⓘ

Stará radnice

❼

❾

STAROBRNĚNSKÁ

ZELNÝ TRH

BENEŠOVA

BISKUPSKÁ

Kapucínská hrobka

JOSEFSKÁ

KOLIŠTĚ

PETROV

Moravské zemské muzeum

Brno train station

NÁDRAŽNÍ

HUSOVA

Cathedral of sv Petr & Pavel

Denisovy sady

NÁDRAŽNÍ

ⓘ

DORNYCH

Tesco

N

Prague ▼   *Bus Station (200 m)* ▼

333

modernist architectural sights: the exhibition grounds of **Výstaviště** and – on the opposite side of town – Mies van der Rohe's **Vila Tugendhat**.

Masarykova and Zelný trh

Most of Brno's trams pass in front of the station at some point, and there's an infectious buzz about the place in the afternoon, after work. A steady stream of people ploughs up and down **Masarykova**, with its cobbles, steaming manholes and defunct tram lines, which leads to náměstí Svobody (see p.336). Don't let that stop you from looking up at the five-storey mansions, laden with a fantastic mantle of decorations, and slowly being restored.

Immediately to the left as you head up Masarykova is Kapucínské náměstí, where you'll find the macabre **Kapucínská hrobka** (Tues–Sat 9am–noon & 2–4.30pm, Sun 11–11.45am & 2–4.30pm), a gruesome collection of dead monks and top nobs, mummified by chance in the crypt of the Capuchin church. Until the eighteenth century, Brno's moneyed classes forked out large sums to be buried here in the monks' simple common grave, in the hope of finding a short cut to heaven – righteousness by association, perhaps. The bodies lie fully clothed, some with the hollow expressions of skeletons, others still frozen in the last painful grimace of death. Just to drive the point home, signs in Czech chime in with "What we are, they once were; what they are, we will be." Not an experience for the faint-hearted.

To the west of the crypt steps lead up to the Biskupský dvůr, which, along with the neighbouring Dietrichsteinský palác, is home to the **Moravské zemské muzeum** (Tues–Sat 9am–5pm; Ⓦwww.mzm.cz). Brno is at the centre of quite an extensive area of early human settlement, and the museum contains an impressive collection of prehistoric finds from the surrounding region (there are more in the Anthropos annexe, see p.342), including the famous *Venus of Věstonice*, plus a large section on the Great Moravian Empire. Opening out to the north of Kapucínské náměstí is **Zelný trh** (literally "cabbage market"), the chaotic vegetable market on a sloping cobbled square, somewhat ill-served by the mishmash of buildings which line its edges. At its centre is the petrified diarrhoea of the huge *Parnassus* fountain by Fischer von Erlach, featuring mythological beasts and Hercules himself; now, as in the good old days, it's working properly, and live carp are sold from its waters at Christmas.

The stará and nová radnice

Tucked down a side street, but clearly visible from Zelný trh, is the **stará radnice**, whose best feature is Anton Pilgram's Gothic doorway on Radnická. The tallest of the five thistly pinnacles above the statue of Blind Justice is deliberately twisted as if it's about to fall on your head – Pilgram's testament to the corrupt town aldermen who shortchanged him for his work (he went on to help furnish Vienna's Stephansdom). Inside, the town hall's courtyards and passageways are home to the Brněnský drak (Brno dragon), the Brněnské kolo (Brno wheel) – for more on which see the box on p.335 – the town's main tourist office, an exhibition space, a café and an **observation tower** (*vyhlídková věž*; April–Sept daily 9am–5pm), worth a climb for the panorama across the city's red-tiled rooftops. Next door to the town hall at no. 6 is a small **akvárium** (Tues–Fri 9.30am–5.30pm, Sat & Sun 9.30am–4pm). At no. 5, **U zlaté koruny** (Mon–Fri 8.30am–6pm, Sat 8am–noon) is a well-preserved Baroque pharmacy, while no. 10 currently provides a temporary home for the **Panorama** (April–Oct daily 9am–5pm; Nov–March Mon–Fri 9am–5pm), a large wooden stereoscope built in 1890 and designed to allow several viewers to see its three-dimensional slides simultaneously (the slides are changed every fortnight or so).

The Brno mascots

Countless local legends surround the **Brněnský drak** (Brno dragon, though in fact it's a stuffed alligator), which hangs from the ceiling of the town hall entrance. The standard version is that the marauding beast was tricked into eating a carcass stuffed full of lime, upon which it rushed down to the River Svratka and drank so much it burst. The most likely origin of the creature is that it was a gift from the Turkish sultan to Archduke Matthias, who in turn bequeathed it to Brno in an attempt to ingratiate himself with the local aristocrats.

The other town mascot displayed here is the **Brněnské kolo** (Brno wheel), made in 1636 by a cartwright from Lednice, who bet a friend that he could fell a tree, make a wheel and roll it to Brno (some 50km away), all before sunset. He won the bet and the wheel has been given pride of place in the stará radnice ever since, though the story goes that following his great feat people began to suspect that the cartwright was in league with the devil: his business fell off and he died in poverty.

Round the back of the stará radnice, to the north, the cobbled square below the Dominican church of **sv Michal** serves as a car park for the functionaries of the present city council who hold office at the adjacent **nová radnice**, founded in 1935 in the former Dominican monastery. It's a passable effort by Mořic Grimm, the city's chief Baroque architect, "a provincial talent but a sound craftsman", as one critic described him. There are a couple of pretty sundials in the echoing first courtyard, and a modern fountain from the 1928 Exhibition in the second courtyard, but otherwise nothing much to get too excited about unless someone's getting married. The handful of cobbled streets that lead south from here to Petrov hill are the nearest Brno gets to a secluded, intimate spot: walk up Dominikanská from the cobbled square, and take a quick look inside the **Dům pánů z Kunštátu**, one of Brno's few Renaissance buildings.

Petrov

Continue up Biskupská to **Petrov**, the smaller of the city's two central hills and one of the best places in which to make a quick escape from the choked streets below. At the top of the hill stands the **Cathedral of sv Petr and Pavel**, whose needle-sharp Gothic spires dominate the skyline for miles around. Close up, the crude nineteenth-century rebuilding has made it a lukewarm affair, but it holds a special place in Brno's history for having been instrumental in saving the town from the Swedes during the Thirty Years' War. After months besieging the town during the course of 1645, the Swedish general Tortennson decided to make one last attempt at taking the place, declaring he would give up at midday if the town hadn't surrendered. In a fit of inspiration, the bell-ringer, seeing that the town was on the brink of defeat, decided to ring the midday bells an hour early. The Swedes gave up their attack, the city was saved, and as a reward the Habsburg emperor switched the Moravian capital from Olomouc to Brno (well, so the story goes). The clock strikes twelve at 11am to this day. Inside the lofty nave, there's a valuable fourteenth-century *Madonna and Child*, but the most intriguing art treasures are the aluminium *Stations of the Cross*, by Jiří Marek. Constructed in the early 1960s, these get progressively more outrageous and abstract as the story unfolds, until the final relief is no more than flailing limbs and anguished metal.

The cathedral is not the only reason to climb Petrov: from the nearby **Denisovy sady**, tucked into the city ramparts, there's a far-reaching view over the great plain south to Vienna, and an interesting angle on the cathedral itself.

In among the trees and courting couples, a slender obelisk, resting on several squashed lions, commemorates the end of the Napoleonic Wars (the Battle of Austerlitz took place just outside Brno – see p.349), lining up perfectly with the avenue of Husova which leads to the red-brick Protestant church, known as the **Červený kostel** (Red Church), and, beyond it, the bright white former Party headquarters, known affectionately as the **Bílý dům** (White House). When this was at the planning stages in the 1950s, the more committed cadres wanted to remove the offending Protestant church, which blocked the view up Husova. Fortunately, aestheticism triumphed over atheism and the plan was somehow foiled.

Náměstí Svobody

Back down on Masarykova, follow the flow north and you'll end up at **náměstí Svobody**, the city's main square and focus of the 1989 demonstrations for Brno's citizens. Compared with other squares across the country, Brno's is a second-division affair; nonetheless, it's the place where most of Brno comes to meet up, chat and shop. In summer, you can sit and drink coffee in the shadow of the square's gilded plague column (see box below) and admire the square's finer buildings, which together span almost four centuries. The earliest is the **Schwarzův palác** (aka Dům z panů Lipé), with an ornate Renaissance facade decorated with sgraffito, added as late as 1938. The building has recently been restored and its arcaded courtyard rather brutally converted into a "muzak"-filled shopping mall. However, it's worth venturing inside and taking the lift to the fifth floor, from which there's access to a rooftop **viewing platform** (*vyhlídková terasa*), which gives out great views over the old town, the cathedral and Špilberk. A few doors along, at no. 15, the **Kleinův palác** was designed around 1848 in neo-Renaissance style by Theophil Hansen, the Danish architect responsible for some of the finest buildings on Vienna's Ringstrasse; the Klein family owned a nearby ironworks, hence the elegant wrought-iron oriel windows held up with miniature Atlantes. Opposite, and totally lacking in such subtlety, is **Dům u čtyř mamlasů**, belonging to another of Brno's richest nineteenth-century Jewish industrialists, whose four muscle-bound employees (nicknamed the "four stupid boys") struggle to hold up both his building and their loincloths. And in the northwest corner of the square, Bohuslav Fuchs' functionalist **Moravská banka** (now simply the Komerční banka) has turned a rather nasty green since its inception in the 1930s.

Plague columns

The **plague column** (*morový sloup*) is a frequent feature of Catholic towns and cities across Central Europe. When the plague struck a city, as it did frequently right up until the eighteenth century, the locals would gather at the column and pray for deliverance. The plague columns you see today date from the Baroque period, when they took on an extra religious and political significance, as the image of the Virgin Mary praying for the sins of the world, surrounded by twelve stars, became a popular and distinctively Catholic image. Many columns, like the one in Brno, were in fact erected in 1648, in thanks for the town's liberation from the Protestant "plague", in this case the unsuccessful Swedish (Protestant) siege of the city. In the Czech Lands, the columns came to be regarded by Czech nationalists as symbols of the Austro-Hungarian hegemony, and a number were torn down during the celebrations following the foundation of Czechoslovakia in 1918, including the one which used to grace Prague's Old Town Square.

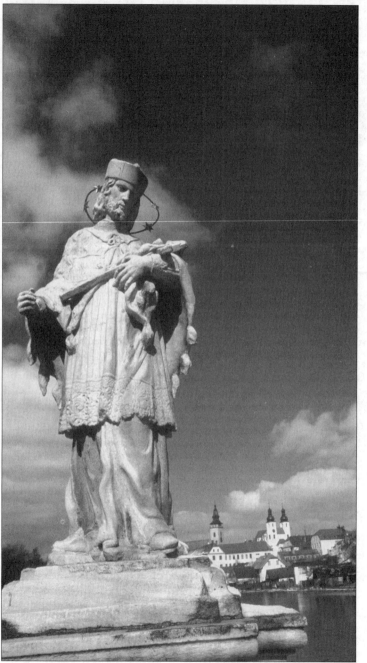

△ St John Nepomuk statue, Telč

Heading north from náměstí Svobody, a steady stream of people flows past the concentration of book and record shops, pubs and cafés on **Česká**, wolfing down takeaways and *zmrzlina* on the way and, at the top, waiting for the trams and buses that congregate on Joštova, which marks the end of the old town. On the northeast corner of the square is the wonderfully named, tonsil-twisting Palác Šlechtičen, which houses the **Etnografické muzeum** (Tues–Sat 9am–5pm). Under well-needed reconstruction at the time of going to print, this museum has a large permanent collection of Moravian folk costumes, ceramics, painted Easter eggs and old photos, as well as occasionally hosting exhibitions on ethnographic themes from other countries.

East of náměstí Svobody

The finest architectural work in Brno by the Grimm brothers (there really were two of them) is the **Minoritský kostel** on the corner of Minoritská and Jánská, whose vivacious frontage makes the most of its cramped site. The right-hand portal leads to the main gilded nave, whose interior represents much the best slice of Baroque in town, high to the point of giddiness, an effect that's intensified by the illusionistic frescoes. Linked to the church next door by double doors in the north aisle is an equally stunning chapel, with a steep altar staircase that must be ascended on bended knee, and full-size colour terracotta statues of Jesus and the two robbers looking down from the gallery above. The greater part of the church is taken up with a **Loretánská kaple** (Loreto Chapel), its outer walls smothered in grisaille depictions of the miracle; the atmospheric red-brick interior holds the standard *Black Madonna and Child* set against a rich marble backdrop.

At the bottom of Jánská, the department store **Centrum**, built in 1928 by the shoe magnate Tomáš Baťa, still cuts a bold figure. It was originally intended to be 28 storeys high (rather than its current seven), which would have made it the tallest building in Europe at the time, but not surprisingly the local council

---

Janáček in Brno

Although he was born in Hukvaldy (see p.410), in northern Moravia, **Leoš Janáček** (1854–1928) moved to Brno at the age of eleven and spent most of his life here, first as a chorister and then teacher and choirmaster at the local Augustinian monastery. Battling against the prejudices of the German-speaking town administration, he managed to drag Czech music out of the pub and into the concert hall, eventually founding the Brno Conservatoire and Organ School in 1882. All but one of his operas were premiered in Brno, and as a composer he remained virtually unknown outside Moravia until well into his sixties, when he began the last and most prolific creative period of his life. For much of the twentieth century, Janáček was overshadowed by his compatriots, Smetana (whom the Communists were particularly keen on) and Dvořák (whom the West has always revered), but in the last couple of decades his music has become increasingly popular, with works such as *The Cunning Little Vixen* enjoying international acclaim.

Across the park from the opera house named after him, at the junction of Kounicova and Smetanova, there's the fairly dull **Památník Leoše Janáčka** (Mon–Fri 8am–noon & 1–4pm) in the cottage where he lived at the back of the Organ School. Unlike his predecessors, Smetana and Dvořák, Janáček chose not to be buried in Prague's illustrious Vyšehrad cemetery, opting instead for Brno's municipal one. If you're on the Janáček trail, bus #62 from outside Tesco, behind the train station, terminates at the main entrance off Jihlavská; or else tram #2, #5, #6 or #8 will take you to within walking distance – the cemetery is easy enough to spot, thanks to the bright white pinnacles of Arnošt Wiesner's strikingly modern crematorium, designed in 1930.

refused planning permission. Beyond lies one of Brno's finest late-nineteenth-century buildings, the **Mahenovo divadlo**, a forthright structure designed by Helmer and Fellner, exuding the municipal confidence of its original German patrons with its Corinthian columns and pediment. Its insides are smothered in gold sculpturing and glittering chandeliers, and it had the distinction of being the first theatre in the Austro-Hungarian Empire to be fitted with electric light bulbs. In total contrast to the flamboyant Mahenovo is Bohuslav Fuchs' squat functionalist **Dům umění** (Tues–Sun 10am–6pm; Ⓦwww.dumb.cz), which puts on some of the city's most innovative art exhibitions, theatre performances, and even the occasional gig. A little further up Rooseveltova from the Mahenovo is the grey and fairly unappealing **Janáčkovo divadlo**, built in the 1960s as the city's – indeed the country's – largest opera house.

Moravská galerie: UPM, Pražákův palác and Místodržitelský palác

Brno's **Moravská galerie** (Wed–Sun 10am–6pm, Thurs until 7pm; Ⓦwww.moravska-galerie.cz) has one of the best art collections in the country, spread out over three premises. Probably the most universally appealing is the applied art collection in the recently renovated Uměleckoprůmyslové muzeum or **UPM**, on Husova, which forms the western limit of the old town. The building itself is a neo-Renaissance pile built as a museum in the 1880s by one of Brno's many wealthy Jewish industrialists. The richly decorated ground floor plays host to wacky installations and temporary exhibitions of anything from avant-garde photomontages to the work of the local art school. The gallery's permanent applied arts collection starts on the first floor, and continues on the top floor. Work was still ongoing at the time of going to press, but the first rooms completed are imaginatively designed, with captions in Czech and English throughout.

The museum begins with a room devoted to medieval craftsmanship, the centrepiece of which is a wonderful silver-gilt crozier from the 1330s belonging to the abbots of Rajhrad. The highlight of the Renaissance room is an incredible seventeenth-century Swiss ceramic stove with matching seta, all smothered in pictorial depictions of the months of the year. After a room of Baroque and Rococo glassware, snuff boxes, fans and pocket watches, and the simple, almost modernist lines of the Biedermeier or Empire period, you reach a whole selection of Thonet furniture. Thonet, whose factories were mostly located in Moravia, fitted out the fin-de-siècle cafés of the Habsburg Empire with their bentwood chairs and tables. The Art Nouveau or Secession section is particularly rewarding, with a vast, curvaceous Gaillard sideboard, some beautiful iridescent Lötz glassware from Klašterský Mlýn and a Klimt clay *jardinière*, which was bought in 1987 from an antique shop in Brno by a canny local collector.

Further up Husova is the Moravská galerie's **Pražákův palác**, another sturdy nineteenth-century edifice, designed by Theophil Hansen and now housing an excellent permanent collection of twentieth-century Czech art on its first and second floors. The pictures are re-hung every year or so, but you're bound to get to see at least some of the gallery's best works, which include sculptures by Bílek, Štursa and Gutfreund; some early Cubist works by Kubišta and Procházka, plus later pieces by Josef Čapek and Šíma; black-and-white photographs by Sudek and others; political works by Nepraš; and abstracts by Mikuláš Medek.

The third building belonging to the Moravská galerie is the **Místodržitelský palác**, the former residence of the governor of Moravia, originally built as an Augustinian monastery at the eastern end of Joštova. Under the Communists it served as a museum of the working class, but it now hosts temporary exhibitions put on by the Moravská galerie, plus a small permanent collection that includes a smattering of Gothic works, a few minor Baroque works by fresco specialists Kremser Schmidt, Maultbertsch and Daniel Gran, and some sentimental Biedermeier paintings. The final room contains the palace's only truly memorable work: a portrait of a woman by Hans Makart, painted with his characteristically dark, chocolate-brown palette, and Max Švabinský's striking *Red Sunshade*.

Špilberk

Skulking on a thickly wooded hill to the west of Husova and barely visible through the trees, the ugly, squat fortress of **Špilberk** (ⓦwww.spilberk.cz) acquired a reputation as one of the most god-awful prisons in the Habsburg Empire. As you walk up through the castle grounds, a monument featuring a wolf suckling Romulus and Remus commemorates the many Italians who died here, having been incarcerated fighting for their country's freedom in the northern regions – then under Austrian rule – of what is now Italy. The testimony of one Italian inmate, the poet Count Silvio Pellico, so shocked the empire's middle classes that the prison was closed down in 1855. In 1880 it was opened up to the public as a tourist attraction by the local military commander, Costa-Rosetti, who installed a model torture chamber and wrote the guide himself, recounting and embellishing myths and legends associated with the place. Sixty years later, it was put back into use by the Nazis who confined, tortured and killed countless prisoners here during the war.

There are now two entrances to the fortress, the first of which, on the east side, leads to the atmospheric **kasematy** (dungeons; Tues–Sun: May–Sept 9am–6pm; Oct–April 9am–5pm). The most chilling section is the reconstruction of the so-called "dark cells" in the north wing, installed by the great reforming Emperor Josef II, who first turned the barracks into a prison. In these, prisoners were chained by the neck and hands in complete darkness and given only bread and water – a practice eventually stopped by Josef II's successor, Leopold II. Silvio Pellico and his contemporaries were actually incarcerated in the upper storey of the fortress, in – as it were – the best cells. Before you set off round the dungeons, make sure you pick up a leaflet with a plan, since the place is a veritable labyrinth.

The entrance on the far, west side of the fortress leads to the exhibition rooms of the **Muzeum města Brna** (Museum of the City of Brno; April & Oct Tues–Sun 9am–5pm; May–Sept Tues–Sun 9am–6pm; Nov–March Wed–Sun 10am–5pm), which is best taken at a canter. Temporary exhibitions take place on the ground floor, along with a permanent display on the history of the prison (plus a few torture instruments and diagrams for good luck), and an *anglický text* in each room to help you decipher the exhibits. On the second floor, Baroque statues and sixteenth-century votive paintings from the church of sv Jakub, paid for by rich local burghers and painted by Dutch masters, hang alongside a decent collection of eighteenth- and nineteenth-century portraits of rich local townsfolk. There's also a modest selection of works from the first half of the last century, including a good spread by Antonín Procházka, from his Cubist *Girl with Garland* to the loose brushwork of *Bathing Horses* from the 1940s. Also worthy of note are Jaroslav Král's Cubist paintings, such as his portrait of Cubist architect Emil Králík; František Foltýn's pastel-shaded abstract works; and the minimalist egg cups and glasses designed by Bohuslav Fuchs.

But by far the most interesting part of the museum is the section on Brno's **interwar architecture**, a long overdue tribute to the city's modern golden age. The work of Bohuslav Fuchs occupies centre stage, and rightly so, as he was without doubt the most successful of the city's functionalist architects (see p.341).

There's a good section on the Nový dům colony (see p.342) and the original plans for the (unrealized) Centrum skyscraper. For the most part, it's an exhibition of photos and architectural drawings, but there are a couple of pieces of original furniture by the likes of Adolf Loos, Alvar Aalto and Mies van der Rohe.

Mendlovo náměstí and Výstaviště

The area south of the Špilberk hill, where the first settlements sprang up in the early Middle Ages, is known as Staré Brno. Few traces of these survive and nowadays there's nothing particularly old or interesting about this part of town, with the exception of the fourteenth-century **Augustinian monastery** on **Mendlovo náměstí**. Despite its unpromising locale – the square is little more than a glorified bus terminal – the monastery church is one of Brno's finest Gothic buildings, its pillars and walls smothered in delicate geometric patterning; sadly, though, it's only usually open for services. If you do get inside, be sure to take a look at the church's *Black Madonna* icon at the high altar, which dates from the thirteenth century and which, it was believed, protected the city from foreign troops.

The monastery is best known for one of its monks, **Gregor Mendel** (1822–84), whose experiments in the abbey gardens with peas and bees eventually led to the discovery of the principles of heredity and, subsequently, genetics. Despite the publication of several seminal papers outlining his discoveries, his work was ignored by the scientific establishment of the day, and in 1868 he gave up his research to become the monastery's abbot. Only after his death was he acknowledged as one of the greats of modern biology, and now several rooms in the western wing of the monastery have been given over to the **Mendelianum** (Mon–Fri 8am–5pm; July & Aug daily 8am–5pm). The garden Mendel used for his experiments was just to the left of the museum entrance; a multilingual memorial commemorates this fact, while nearby is a ridiculously heroic statue of Mendel, who was, in fact, a rotund and rather shy monk.

To the southwest of the city centre, where the River Svratka opens up to the plain (tram #1 from the station), is the **Výstaviště** (ⓦ www.bvv.cz) or exhibition grounds. The main buildings were laid out in 1928 for the city's Exhibition of Contemporary Culture, and most of the leading Czech architects of the day were involved in the scheme, which prompted a flurry of functionalist building projects across the city's burgeoning suburbs. The most arresting

Fuchs and Functionalism

Although Brno produced two great modern architects in Adolf Loos and Jan Kotěra, they spent most of their time in Vienna and Prague respectively, and it was left to another Moravian, **Bohuslav Fuchs**, who began working here in 1923, to shape the face of modern Brno. Fuchs and his functionalist cohorts turned their hand to everything from the town's crematorium to the Protestant church on Botanická, its interior decoration as "low-church" and prosaic as you can get. Fuchs' own hand is everywhere in the city, in the low-slung post office extension to the main train station, in the *pasáž* off Jánská, in the slimline *Hotel Avion*, and in Výstaviště itself. His most famous works are the open-plan boarding school and Vesna girls' school (on Lipová, just north of Výstaviště), two simple four-storey functionalist buildings, way ahead of their time, but already gone to seed in the intervening years. Perhaps the best way to appreciate Fuchs' work is to head out to the outdoor swimming pool he built in the city's eastern suburbs, just off Zábrdovická (tram #2, #3 or #7), where you can laze by the pool and take in the culture at the same time.

(and largest) building on the site, the circular crystal-and-concrete **Z pavilion**, is actually one of the postwar additions, but one which kept to the spirit of the original concept. The only building which predates the complex is the **Zámeček**, which features an interior by Brno-born arch-minimalist Adolf Loos. Even if you've no interest in modern architecture, the various fairs and exhibitions staged here between March and November are the largest in the country, and often interesting in their own right. Once the showpieces of socialism, they're now more an opportunity for foreign companies to tout their wares.

The part of the 1928 exhibition that really caused a sensation was the **Nový dům** settlement, worth a look if you're keen on Bauhaus-style architecture. Inspired by the Weissenhofsiedlung built a year earlier in Stuttgart, Bohuslav Fuchs and various others designed a series of boxy, white, concrete villas by the woods of the Wilsonův les, north of Výstaviště, up Žabovřeská (tram #1 from Výstaviště), in the streets of Drnovická and Petřvaldská. The brief for each architect was to create modest two-storey houses for middle-income families, using standard fittings and ordinary materials to keep the unit cost down. They are now grey, peeling and overrun by vegetation, and it takes a leap of imagination to appreciate the shock of the new that these buildings must have aroused at the time.

There are two other sights worth visiting, close, but entirely unrelated, to Výstaviště. The first, visible from the main trade-ground entrance, is a Louis XIV summer palace, **Letohrádek Mitrovských**, an unusual sight in this part of the world. Napoleon stayed here the night before the Battle of Austerlitz (see p.349), while his opposite number, the Russian general Kutuzov, stayed in the Dietrichsteinský palác on Zelný trh. On the opposite side of Výstaviště, over the River Svitava, is **Anthropos** (April–Nov Tues–Sun 8.30am–5pm), an annexe of the Moravian Museum, which concentrates on Ice Age geology and fauna, including remains of mammoths, Neanderthals and early *Homo sapiens*. As well as fossil bones and replicas of prehistoric cave paintings, the museum contains numerous paintings by Zdeněk Burian, a Czech painter who specializes in scientifically authentic illustrations of Stone Age life.

Vila Tugendhat

On the opposite side of town, in the northeastern suburb of Černá Pole, modernist guru Mies van der Rohe built the **Vila Tugendhat** (Wed–Sun 10am–6pm; ⓦwww.tugendhat-villa.cz) in the same functionalist style as the above-mentioned Nový dům settlement, but to a very different brief: the Tugendhats, an exceptionally rich Jewish family who ran a number of the city's textile factories, wanted a state-of-the-art house kitted out in the most expensive gear money could buy. It was completed in 1930, but the family had barely eight years to enjoy the luxury of the place before fleeing to South America (with most of the period furniture) in the wake of the Nazi invasion. For the next fifty years it was put to many uses – both the Nazis and Communists were particularly partial to it for exclusive social functions. Public access is a little unpredictable, so it's worth checking at the tourist office in the stará radnice before setting out. You enter through the top floor, but the main living space is actually downstairs, open-plan for the most part and originally decked out in minimalist monochrome furnishings offset by colourful Persian carpets. The Communists' "modernization" after the war was depressingly thorough, and the huge unbroken front window, which looked out over the garden and the whole cityscape beyond it, has been replaced by a series of much smaller panes, being all the Communists' glassworks could muster. The house is at Černopolní 45, off Merhautova, itself a continuation of M. Horákové; take tram #3, #5 or #11 three stops east from Joštova, and then walk north three blocks up Černopolní.

Eating, drinking and entertainment

There's no shortage of good **places to eat and drink** in Brno, but equally, there's nothing like the choice of cuisines available now in Prague. Brno also has nowhere near the same volume of expats, so prices are uniformly low, and the clientele predominantly Czech. As for **nightlife**, lovers of classical music and opera are well catered for, with two big opera houses/theatres, a philharmonic orchestra, and numerous smaller venues. With a large contingent of students, the city usually has something a bit less formal going on, particularly during term time. One word of warning, however: Brno (including most of its shops, and even some of its pubs and restaurants) tends to close down for the weekend at around noon Saturday, so if you want to experience city life to the full, come on a weekday.

Eating and drinking

For **Vietnamese fast food** head for one of the branches of the *Asijské bistro*, such as the one on Zelný trh, whose **vegetable market** is also worth a visit if you need provisions. Pameria, Česká 32, north of Joštova, is a great **bakery** offering a wide range of sandwiches and pastries. For tasty fresh take-away Bosnian **burek**, head for the outlet on Josefská. Also worth knowing about is the useful 24-hour bakery/**deli** called Jasa, upstairs at the bottom of Masarykova, opposite the train station.

For simple, traditional **Czech food**, the pubs listed overleaf are likely to be the cheapest; the restaurants, while offering much the same food, are likely to be a bit pricier and a lot more formal.

Restaurants

Aura Kabátníkova 2 ⓦ www.aura.cz. Clean, bright and pleasant veggie restaurant up Lidická just beyond Lužánky, that serves some very unusual and interesting dishes (take a dictionary). Daily 11am–11pm.

Hotel Slavia Solniční 15–17. Experience Czech cuisine as it was at its best under the Communists in the excellent hotel restaurant. Daily noon–11pm.

Haribol Lužánecká 4. Self-service Hare Krishna restaurant, off Lidická, with a cheap fixed menu of veggie slop. Mon–Fri 10.30am–5pm.

Saurus Nám. Svobody 17. Small, "healthy" veggie café in the basement of the Schwarzův dům, offering baguettes and one daily main course. Mon–Sat 9am–9pm, Sun 9am–6pm.

Spolek Orlí 22. Very pleasant bookshop café with an imaginative veggie-friendly menu featuring soups, risotto, pasta and *palačinky* dishes. Mon–Sat 10am–10pm, Sun 1–10pm.

Taj Běhounská 12/14. Large, first-floor Indian restaurant with a vast menu that includes lots of veggie dishes – if you want spice, go for the hottest dishes. Daily 11.30am–11pm.

U císaře Leopolda Orlí 3. Brno's best, most central pizzeria, with an al-fresco terrace. Mon–Thurs 11am–11pm, Fri & Sat 11am–midnight, Sun 2–10pm.

U královny Elišky Mendlovo náměstí 1a. A good

cellar *vinárna* tucked into the hillside behind the Augustinian monastery, offering the whole Moravian caboodle, including live folk music. Tues–Sat 7pm–3am.

Cafés

Brno is better for pubs than **cafés**, though of course you can get a coffee in either. During the summer, outdoor tables abound at the various cafés around náměstí Svobody and Zelný trh.

Adria Josefská. A wood-panelled, high-ceilinged café with coffee, cakes and pizzas, run by Yugoslavs but very much in the Viennese tradition. Daily 7am–midnight.

Blau Jakubské nám. Designer café, decked out in (you guessed it) blue, and something of a media hang-out, due to it being located in the same building as Czech TV's Brno studios. Mon–Fri 8am–10pm, Sat 11am–10pm, Sun 2–10pm.

Fischer Masarykova. Continuing the city's tradition for minimalism, this is a stylish designer café in a prime location. Mon–Fri 8am–10pm, Sat 9am–10pm, Sun 10am–10pm.

Pánů z Lípé Nám. Svobody 17. Congenial little café with old-fashioned furnishings, overlooking the main square from the second floor of the Schwarzův dům. Daily 8am–10pm.

Rendezvous Moravské nám. Small café next to the Scala cinema, opposite the Místodržitelský palác, serving sweet and savoury *palačinky*. Mon–Sat 8am–10pm, Sun 10am–10pm.

Zemanova kavárna off Jezuitská ⓦ www.zeman-ka.cz. Brno's newest café is an exact replica of Fuchs's functionalist café of 1923, which was torn down by the Communists in order to build the Janáčkovo divadlo; it stands in the park to the southeast of the theatre. Mon–Fri 10am–10pm, Sat & Sun 11am–10pm.

Pubs and bars

Starobrno is the local brew, though according to many the best pubs are those that don't serve it. Brno has its fair share of traditional old boozers, now joined by numerous trendy pubs for the city's young urban professionals.

Charlie's Hat Kobližná 12. Unpretentious pub down a passageway off Kobližná, with a nice shady courtyard and a louder cellar bar with occasional DJs. Mon–Thurs 11am–4am, Fri 11am–5am, Sat noon–5am, Sun 3pm–4am.

Elektra Běhounská ⓦ www.elektra.cz. Cellar pub with modernist decor, serving decent pub grub and *Starobrno* to a youngish, unpretentious crowd. Mon–Fri 11am–2am, Sat & Sun 5pm–late.

Mescalito Starobrněnská 3 ⓦ www.volny.cz/mescalito. Grotto-like basement bar that packs in a posey crowd, who like to shout over the loud house/dance or live music.

Mon–Thurs noon–3am, Fri & Sat until 4am.

Pegas Jakubská 4. If there are any foreigners in town, it's guaranteed they'll be drinking here – and fair enough, for this is a large and very pleasant pub that brews its own light and dark beers on the premises. Daily 9am–midnight.

Pivovarská pivnice Mendlovo nám. The true *Starobrno* experience: a rough-and-ready drinkers' pub right by the brewery itself, serving *Starobrno's* standard 12-degree and its rarer 14-degree *Baron Trenck* brews. Daily 10am–11pm.

Potrefená husa Joštova 2. Upwardly mobile drinkers head for this modern, designer pub, which shows sports on TV screens and serves the popular *Staropramen's* ale and stout, *Velvet* and *Kelt*. Daily 11am–1am.

Skleněná louka Kounicova 23 ⓦ www.sklene-nalouka.cz. Great barrel-vaulted cellar bar by Brno's *Moulin Rouge*, that has occasional live music, and, above it, the city's best internet café and *čajovna*. Mon–Fri 11am–1am, Sat & Sun 4pm–1am.

Špalíček Zelný trh 12. A pub overlooking the vegetable market, with tables outside in summer and lashings of *Starobrno*. Daily 11am–11pm.

Traubova Traubova. Dark, Gothic den, off M. Horákové, thick with smoke and filled to the cobwebs with the free-thinking youth of Brno.

U dvou kozlů Joštova 1. Old-style big, smoky, beery pub in the pea-green building opposite the church of sv Tomáš, with a youngish crowd supping *Velkopopovický kozel*. Mon–Thurs 9am–1am, Fri 9am–3am, Sat 9am–2am, Sun 10am–midnight.

Entertainment and nightlife

To find out what's on, get hold of the monthly **listings** pamphlet *Kam v Brně*, or the much flimsier fortnightly handout *Do města/Downtown* (ⓦ www.down-town.cz). **Tickets** for most shows can be bought in advance from the box office at Dvořákova 11 (Mon–Fri 9am–5.30pm, Sat 9am–noon; ⓦ www.brno-konz-ert.cz), or from the venue itself, half an hour before the performance starts.

The Mahenovo divadlo, which boasts the most ornate interior, puts on plays mostly in Czech; the Janáčkovo divadlo stages **opera and ballet**, while the Besední dům, home to the Státní filharmonie Brno orchestra (ⓦ www.filhar-moniebrno.cz), hosts regular **classical concerts**. For chamber music, check out the concert hall of the local music academy, JAMU, on Komenského náměstí. There's a lively **fringe theatre** scene, but unless you understand Czech or chance upon a particularly physical, visual show, the language is going to be an insurmountable barrier. Two places that are worth checking out are Kabinet múz, Sukova 4–6, home base for the fringe company HaDivadlo, and Divadlo 7 a půl, Koliště 51 (ⓦ www.7apul.cz), diagonally opposite Dům umění, both of which put on a variety of events and gigs, and are cool places to hang out in themselves.

The same few DJs tend do the rounds of Brno's **clubs**: *Remix*, Brandlova 4, *Základna*, Hybešova 21 and *Embargo*, Beethovenova 7. More varied fare from techno to live jazz goes down at *Edison Garden*, the music venue that forms part of the aforementioned Divadlo 7 a půl. One of the best places to catch jazz is at the Jazzová Kavárna Podobrazy in the Místodržitelský palác; more traditional jazz enthusiasts flock to Šelepova 1 to the club of the same name (tram #12 or #13 from Joštova, Klusáčkova stop; ⓦ www.selepova.cz). The local **folk music** club meets at the *Klub Leitnerova*, Leitnerova 2 (Tues & Thurs; tram #1 or #2 two stops west from the train station; ⓦ www.volny.cz/leitnerka).

There's an excellent **art-house cinema**, Kino Art, at Cihlářská 19, a short distance up Lidická from Moravské náměstí. The city hosts its own small-scale European film festival in April; a festival of spiritual music at Petrov around Easter; a summer music festival in the Špilberk courtyard; while in late September/early October, there's a three-week-long **international classical music festival**, known as Moravský podzim (Moravian Autumn).

Listings

Books Barvič & Novotný, Česká 13. Brno's best-stocked bookshop, with lots of maps, guides, CDs and posters. Daily until 7pm.
Currency exchange Komerční banka, nám. Svobody 21. 24hr exchange at the main train station.
Hospital Bratislavská 2; emergency medical attention ☎155.
Internet Skleněná louka, Kounicova 23 ⓦ www.sklenenalouka.cz; Čítárna, the municipal reading room on the corner of Kobližná and Poštovská; closed Sun.
Laundrette Self-service laundrette, Údolní 37 (tram #4); Mon–Wed noon–8pm, Thurs & Fri phone ☎604 347 537 to book an appointment.
Left luggage The main train station has 24hr left luggage and lockers.

Motorcycle Grand Prix Brno hosts a world championship motorcycle grand prix at the end of August at the Masarykův okruh (ⓦ www.brnograndprix.com). Special buses are laid on during the competition; otherwise take bus #52 or #54 and walk westwards for five minutes.
Newspapers The kiosk opposite the main train station has the best selection of foreign newspapers.
Pharmacy All-night service at Kobližna 7 ☎542 210 222.
Police The main police station is at Kounicova 46.
Post office The most convenient post office is next door to the train station. It runs a 24hr telephone exchange.
Taxis The main taxi ranks are outside the station and on Solniční, or dial ☎542 321 321 for City Taxi.

Around Brno

Brno has plenty to keep you occupied, but if you're staying any amount of time, follow the advice of the health authorities (and the example of most of its citizens) and get out of the city at the weekend. One of the few good things about living in Brno's drab concrete suburbs is that you can walk straight out into the woods and bump into a deer or chamois. If that doesn't take your fancy, the most popular day-trip is to the limestone caves of the **Moravský kras**, closely followed by the castle of **Pernštejn** and the battlefield at **Slavkov** (Austerlitz). Potentially more interesting than any of those, however, is the Renaissance chateau at **Moravský Krumlov**, which houses a museum dedicated to the work of the Art Nouveau painter Alfons Mucha.

Moravský kras

Well worth a visit is Moravia's number-one tourist attraction: the limestone **karst region** of the **Moravský kras** (ⓦ www.smk.cz), just over 25km northeast of Brno. There is a whole series of caves to visit, the most popular (and rewarding) being the Punkevní jeskyně, which is the most extensive cave system, and includes an underground river, a giant chasm and the possibility of a

Named after the Karst, the barren limestone plateau around Trieste, **karst** landscapes are formed by the action of rainwater on limestone. Rain picks up small amounts of carbon dioxide from the atmosphere, which, when it falls on limestone rock, slowly dissolves it. Gradually, over millions of years, the action of rain attacking the rock causes hairline cracks in the limestone, which are steadily enlarged by running water. In its early stages, karst scenery is characterized by narrow ridges and fissures; as these grow and deepen, the dry limestone is raked into wild, sharp-edged fragments – practically bare of vegetation since any topsoil is blown away – and bleached bright white, like shards of bone. Karst scenery is found throughout the Czech and Slovak republics, particularly in southern **Moravia** and central and eastern **Slovakia**.

Rivers do odd things in karst landscapes: they disappear down holes where the limestone is weakest, and flow for miles underground, suddenly bursting from rocks when the geology changes. When an underground river widens and forms a cavern, the drips of rainwater percolating through the soil deposit minuscule amounts of the calcium bicarbonate that it has dissolved from the limestone above. Over millions of years these deposits form stalactites hanging from the roof of the cavern; the drips on the floor form columns called stalagmites. Traces of other minerals such as iron and copper colour the stalactites and stalagmites, and the whole process forms cave systems like the **Punkevní jeskyně**.

cable-car ride. The other caves also feature spectacular stalactites and stalagmites and suffer much less from overcrowding. Quite apart from the caves, the whole karst region boasts some dramatic and varied scenery, all smothered in a thick coating of coniferous forest and riddled with marked paths, providing great **walking** country. If you're not in a hurry, the three churches in Křtiny, Jedovnice and Senetářov deserve a visit, providing a more relaxed alternative to the crush of tourists along the Punkva river.

The caves

The most popular tour target is the **Punkevní jeskyně**, at the deepest part of the gorge – get there early, or get the tourist office to book in advance for you, as tickets can sell out for the whole day in high season. In the summer, tours run every fifteen minutes (daily: Jan–March & Oct 8.20am–2pm; April–Oct 8.20am–3.50pm; Oct–April 8.20am–2pm; Nov & Dec 9am–2pm) and take around fifty minutes. The fantastic array of stalactites and stalagmites justifies the hassle of getting here. After a series of five chambers, you come to the bottom of the **Propast Macocha** (Macocha Abyss), a gigantic 138-metre mossy chasm created when the roof of one of the caves collapsed. The first man to descend into the abyss and return alive was Father "Lazarus" Erker in 1728, almost two hundred years before the caves themselves were properly explored. From the abyss, you're punted 500m along the slimy underground Punkva river, which gives the cave its name. Just beyond the entrance to the caves, there's a very steep **cable car** (*lanová dráha*), which can whisk you swiftly to the top of the abyss, so you can look down on where you've just been. If you're going to take the Eko-Train and the cable car, be sure to buy a *Kombi-Karte* when you first set out.

The two other caves open to the public are only slightly less spectacular, with the added advantage that the queues are correspondingly smaller. The **Kateřinská jeskyně** (30min tour; Feb & March 10am, noon & 2pm; April–Sept 8.20am–4pm; Oct 8.20am–2pm), 1.5km before the Punkevní jeskyně at the point where the Punkva river re-emerges, is the largest single cave in the karst region, one huge "cathedral" of rock formations, 100m long and 20m high. The smallest of the lot is the **Balcarka jeskyně** (50min tour; Feb & March 10am, noon & 1pm; April–Sept Mon–Fri 7.30am–3.30pm, Sat & Sun 8.30am–3.15pm; Oct Mon–Fri 7.30am–1.15pm, Sat & Sun 8.30am–2.30pm), which lies 2km east of the Propast Macocha. A fourth cave system called Sloupsko-Šošůvské jeskyně sits on the southern edge of the village of Sloup, but is really only worth visiting for the occasional concerts that take place there.

Křtiny, Jedovnice and Senetářov

Although buses run to Křtiny, the most rewarding way to reach the village is to take the train from Brno to Adamov zastávka (not Adamov itself) and walk east up the **Josefovské údolí** (the blue-marked path follows the road), a steep, craggy valley with remnants of the original primeval forest cover and open-air stalagmites. After 3km, at the top of the valley, there's a special nature trail round a mini-karst region of around five caves, none of which is actually accessible. Another 3km further east along the blue path, and out of the woods, leaps the enormous dome and tower of the pilgrimage church of **KŘTINY**, designed by the Baroque genius Giovanni Santini. One door is usually open to let you inside, where the nave has been handed over to a series of interlinking frescoed domes that fuse into one, giving the church a Byzantine feel. The interior decor is gaudy High Baroque, especially the main altar, sheltering under its marble baldachin, with technicolour cherubs and saints strewn about the place, but the overall effect is satisfyingly impressive and unified. Only one set of curvaceous cloisters was completed, now filled with the gifts of paintings from previous pilgrims.

Taking the yellow-marked path, skirt the edge of the woods to the northeast, which rise gently past the understated peak of Proklest (574m). Six kilometres on from Křtiny, you emerge from the trees at the small lake by the village of **JEDOVNICE**, no beauty itself, thanks to a fire in 1822, which also torched the late-eighteenth-century village church. From the outside the latter looks hurriedly restored; the interior, however, redesigned in the 1960s, contains symbolic art, stained glass and, as the centrepiece, a striking **altar** painting by Mikuláš Medek, *persona non grata* in Czechoslovakia in the 1950s for his penchant for abstract art, surrealism and social comment. His choice of colours is didactic: a blue cross for hope, and red for the chaos of the world. Unless it's a Sunday, you'll have to get the key from the *kaplan* who lives opposite the church and who can also furnish you with an *anglický text*.

There's no escaping the modernity of Ludvík Kolek's concrete church at **SENETÁŘOV**, completed in 1971, 4km down the road to Výskov; it's built in the shape of a ship, its "mast" visible as you approach from the plateau – though as a concept, its symbolism is reminiscent of the work of Santini. It's an uncompromising building, with huge plate-glass panels at the west end, through which you can clearly see the main altarpiece, an abstract version of the *Last Supper* against a vivid blue background. But it's Medek's *Stations of the Cross*, on the north wall and difficult to see without getting inside, that are the church's masterpiece. Starting with a deep red crown of thorns, the pictures progress in bold, simple colours and symbols, fusing into one long fourteen-piece canvas and signalling an original working of an otherwise hackneyed theme.

On a completely different note, there's a minute folk museum, the **Expozice tradičního bydlení a perlěvářství** (April–Oct Sat & Sun 8am–6pm) in a thatched house opposite the church, with displays on the region's mother-of-pearl button cottage industry, introduced in the 1880s, that flourished until World War I. It was all over by the 1930s, though there is a still a button-making factory in the area; ask for an *anglický text* to find out more.

Practicalities

Reaching the caves without your own transport is quite tricky – to find out the latest options, ask at the tourist office in Brno (see p.330). If getting there under your own steam, the best thing to do is to catch an early morning **train** from Brno out to Blansko station (not Blansko město), and walk 200m southwards to the bus station. From here, **buses** depart for **Skalní Mlýn**, location of the main ticket office and information centre for the **Punkevní jeskyně** caves. All visitors to the caves must either walk the 1.5km from Skalní Mlýn or catch the regular **Eko-Train** service; there are also bikes for hire. Alternatively, it's a very nice five-kilometre walk through the woods all the way from Blansko along the green-marked path. Make sure you take some warm clothing, as the temperature in the caves is always low.

Buses from Brno and Blansko run more regularly to Jedovnice, passing through Křtiny and occasionally continuing to Senetářov. Křtiny makes for a good base, with several new pensions such as the *Santini* (☎516 439 432; ❷). The *Hotel Skalní Mlýn* (☎516 418 113; ❸), in Skalní Mlýn itself, is busy with tourists, but the perfect place to stay if you're keen to visit several of the caves. The nicest **campsite** in the region is *Relaxa* (May–Sept; ☎516 435 237) in Sloup, to the north of the caves, though you'll have to walk or cycle the 5km to the caves, if you've no transport of your own.

Pernštejn

The Gothic stronghold of **Pernštejn** is many people's idea of what a medieval castle should look like, and is consequently one of the most popular targets around Brno. The nearest station to Pernštejn is at the village of **NEDVĚDICE** – from the platform, the castle is immediately visible to the west; to get there follow the yellow-marked track. After a series of outer defences, the **hrad** (April & Oct Sat & Sun 9am–noon & 1–4pm; May, June & Sept Tues–Sun 9am–noon & 1–5pm; July & Aug Tues–Sun closes 6pm) proper is a truly dramatic sight, with kestrels circling the dizzying sheer walls. It was originally built in the thirteenth century, and various reconstructions have left it a jumble of unpredictable angles and extras, including a death-defying covered wooden bridge that spans the castle's main keeps. The hour-long guided tour is highly atmospheric, giving out spectacular views across the mixed woodland of the nearby hills.

The picturesque **train** journey up the Svratka Valley to Nedvědice takes just over an hour from Brno, making this one of the easiest and most rewarding day-trips. If you have to change at **TIŠNOV**, be sure to check out the former Cistercian nunnery, **Porta Coeli** (Tues–Sun 8–11am & 1–3pm), named after the church's remarkable Romanesque portal; to get there, take the blue-marked path from the train station for 2km to the neighbouring settlement of Předklášteří.

Moravský Krumlov

Squeezed into a tight bend of the Rokytná river, southwest of Brno, is **MORAVSKÝ KRUMLOV**, whose **zámek**, to the west of town, boasts a delicate arcaded loggia from 1557, and an **art gallery** (Tues–Sun: April–June, Sept & Oct 9am–noon & 1–4pm; July & Aug closes 5pm), housed in one of the outbuildings, containing paintings and drawings by one of the better-known Czech artists, **Alfons Mucha** (1860–1939). Mucha was actually born in the mining town of Ivančice, a few kilometres to the north, an odd starting point for an artist who is best known for his graceful Art Nouveau posters. In the West he is known solely for the work he did while in Paris – particularly his Sarah Bernhardt posters – where he shared a studio with Gauguin (there's a photo of the latter playing the piano with his trousers down just to prove it). In fact, Mucha came to despise this "commercial" period of his work, and when the First Republic was declared in 1918, he threw himself into the national cause, designing its stamps, banknotes and numerous posters.

However, it was left to an American millionaire to commission him to do what he saw as his life's work: a cycle of twenty monumental canvases called the *Slovanská epopej* (Slav Epic), which constitute the bulk of the work on display here. In Czech terms they're well-worn themes – Komenský fleeing the "fatherland", the Battle of Vítkov and so on – but they were obviously heartfelt for Mucha. In the end he paid for his nationalism with his life: dragged in for questioning by the Gestapo after the 1939 Nazi invasion, he died shortly after being released. In this slightly forlorn chateau, Mucha's gloomy, melodramatic paintings take on a fascination all of their own.

Trains from Brno are fairly frequent and direct (those from Znojmo or Mikulov require you to change at Hrušovany nad Jevišovkou), but the station is a good 2km east of the town; **buses** from Brno and Znojmo will drop you in the centre, but timings are only really any good from Znojmo.

Slavkov and the Battle of Austerlitz

Twenty kilometres by train across the flat plain east of Brno, **SLAVKOV** (Austerlitz) would be just another humble ribbon village were it not for the great mass of Martinelli's late Baroque **zámek** (Tues–Sun: April, Oct & Nov 9am–noon & 1–4pm; May & Sept closes 5pm; June–Aug closes 6pm; Ⓦ www.slavov-austerlitz.cz). Like so many chateaux close to the Austrian border, its contents were quickly and judiciously removed by their owners before the arrival of the Red Army in 1945; in their place are changing exhibitions, usually on a military theme. The highlight of the 45-minute guided tour is the central concave hall, **Sál předků**, which has the most incredible acoustics. Every whisper of sound in the giant dome echoes for a full ten seconds, while outside not one word can be heard. Martinelli also designed the village's imposing Neoclassical church, with its massive Corinthian portico; inside there are some great high-relief sculptures along the walls and above the high altar.

On December 2, 1805, in the fields between Slavkov and Brno, the Austrians and Russians received a decisive drubbing at the hands of the numerically inferior Napoleonic troops in the **Battle of Austerlitz** (also known as the "Battle of the Three Emperors"). The Austrians and Russians committed themselves early, charging into the morning fog to attack the French on both flanks. From his vantage point on the Žuráň hill to the north, Napoleon, confident of victory, held back until the enemy had established its position, and then attacked at their weakest point, the central commanding heights of the Pratzen hill (Pracký kopec), splitting their forces and throwing them into disarray. It was all over by lunchtime, with over 24,000 troops dead. After the battle, all three emperors signed a peace treaty, marking an end to Napoleon's eastern campaign until the fateful march on Moscow in 1812. There's a graphic description of the battle in Tolstoy's epic novel *War and Peace*.

Just over one hundred years later, on the strategic Pratzen hill, 8km southwest of Slavkov, the **Mohyla míru** (Monument of Peace) was erected on the instigation of a local pacifist priest, and paid for by the governments of France, Austria and Russia, who within three years of pledging the money were once again at war with one another. There's a superb view of the surrounding killing fields, now just a series of ploughed fields peppered with crosses and dotted with the odd little Calvary. The tent-like stone monument, designed by the Art Nouveau architect Josef Fanta, contains a small chapel, and nearby there's a **museum** (April–Sept daily 8am–noon & 1–5pm; Oct–March Tues–Sun 9am–12.30pm & 1–3.30pm), including the obligatory toy soldier mock-up of the battle. Military enthusiasts without their own transport have a choice of uphill walks: 2km to the southeast from Ponětovice train station, 3km to the northeast from Sokolnice train station, or 1km to the south from the bus stop in Prace. If you happen to be here on the anniversary of the battle, the Friends of the French Revolution treat onlookers to a chilly re-enactment.

There's a **tourist office** next door to the zámek (April, May & Sept–Nov Tues–Sun 9am–4pm; June–Aug Mon–Sat 9am–noon & 12.30–5pm, Sun 11am–5pm; Dec–March Mon–Fri 9am–4pm). For **food**, head for the *Hotel Sokolský dům* (☎544 221 103; ❷), which also offers **rooms** for the night. Another good option is the *Stará pošta* (☎507 375 985, ⓦwww.austerlitz1805.cz; ❸), 4km northwest of Slavkov, on the north side of the motorway, where Napoleon stayed before the battle; it serves decent food, has very nicely furnished rooms, has a small museum of militaria and offers horse-drawn tours of the battlefield in the summer.

Bučovice

Ten kilometres further east, and accessible by train from Brno, the **zámek** (April & Oct Sat & Sun 9am–noon & 1–4pm; May–Aug Tues–Sun 9am–noon & 1–4.30pm; Sept Tues–Sun 9am–noon & 1–4pm) at **BUČOVICE**, circled by kestrels, gets a fraction of the visitors of Slavkov, partly perhaps because of its unpromising exterior: a dull grey fortress with four ugly squat towers. None of it prepares you for the subtle, slender Italianate arcading of the courtyard's three-sided loggia, with each set of supporting columns topped by a different carved motif. At the centre of the courtyard a stone fountain was added a few generations later – "a little too robust", as the guide puts it, and out of keeping with the rest of the masonry. The towers, the gardens and countless rooms once matched the charm and elegance of the courtyard, but the Liechtensteins, who obtained the chateau through marriage in 1597, soon turned it into little more than a storage house for the family records, scattering its original furnishings among their many other Moravian residences.

The Brno Death March

On May 30, 1945 an estimated 23,000 German-speaking Czechs from Brno and its environs were rounded up and forced to walk the 60km from Brno into Austria. Deportees were allowed to take only what they could carry (and no money or jewels). The following night, the refugees reached the village of **Pohořelice**, just over halfway from Brno to the border. Those who were too weak or ill with dysentery to continue were housed in a local brick factory. The Czechs maintain that their doctors treated the sick and that all those who died were victims of dysentery. Sudeten Germans argue that acts of brutality and mass murder were committed, while others died of starvation. No one knows quite how many Germans were buried in Pohořelice, but after years of official silence on the matter during the Communist period, a memorial to 890 known victims was finally erected in 1992 by the farm field in which the victims were buried, on route 52, just south of Pohořelice.

The only things they couldn't remove were the original sixteenth-century **ceiling decorations**, a fantastical mantle of sculpture and paint, coating just five or so rooms, none more than twenty feet across. The first few are just a warm-up for the thick stucco of the **císařský sál**, with the bejewelled relief figures of Mars, Diana, a half-naked Europa and, most magnificent of all, the emperor Charles V trampling a turbaned Turk into the paintwork. But the decoration of the **zaječí sál** (The Hall of Hares) is the real star turn, an anthropomorphic work reckoned to be one of the few of that period still in existence. It's a comical scene, with the hares exacting their revenge on the world of man and his closest ally, the dog. The aftermath of the hares' revolution sees them sitting in judgement (wigs and all) over their defeated enemies, as well as indulging in more highbrow activities – hare as Rembrandt, hare as scholar and so on.

Mikulov and around

Clinging on to the southern tip of the **Pavlovské vrchy**, the last hills before the Austrian plain, **MIKULOV** (Nikolsburg) is one of South Moravia's minor gems. Slap bang in the middle of the wine-producing region, it's been a border post for centuries – hence the narrow streets and siege mentality of much of the architecture. The town still functions as a busy crossing point between the two countries; if you're driving from Vienna, it's a great introduction to the country and, given its strategic locale, surprisingly tourist-free except after the **grape harvest** in late September, when the first bouquet of the year is being tried and tested in vast quantities at the local *sklepy* (wine caves) on the edge of town.

Raised above the jumble of red rooftops is the **zámek** (April & Oct Sat & Sun 9am–4pm; May–Sept Tues–Sun 8am–5pm), an imposing complex built right into the rocky hill on the west side of town. Close up, it's a plain, rather characterless building; used by the Gestapo to hoard confiscated art objects, it was then blown to smithereens by them in the last days of the war in a final nihilistic gesture. It was rebuilt in the 1950s to house a museum, which covers the town's history (minus the controversial episodes) and viticulture and dishes out amazing views over into Austria.

In 1575 castle and town fell into the hands of the fervently Catholic Dietrichsteins, who established various religious edifices and institutions here. They're also responsible for the hint of Renaissance in the town – the occasional arcade or pictorial sgraffito – and the main square itself, which is called simply **Náměstí**, appealingly misshapen and huddled below the castle. Later, behind the oversized plague column, they built the church of **sv Anna**, with a Loreto chapel within – this popular pilgrimage church burned down in the town fire of 1784. The imposing Neoclassical facade that you now see, with its stumpy square towers, dates from the mid-nineteenth century, when the Dietrichsteins decided to turn the church into the family mausoleum or **Dietrichsteinská hrobka** (April–Oct Tues–Sun 9am–5pm). The whole place has recently been thoroughly restored, though the main reason to have a wander inside is for the view from amidst the angels on the church's roof. The family was also responsible for the series of chapels visible to the east of the town on the bleak, exposed limestone hill of **Svatý kopeček**, well worth the climb for the view across the vineyards towards Vienna.

Mikulov boasted a thriving **Jewish community** until the advent of the Nazis: in the mid-nineteenth century it was the second largest in the Czech Lands and was the seat of the chief rabbi (Landesrabbiner) of Moravia from the sixteenth century until 1851. The old **Jewish ghetto** lies to the west of the castle, where the town's seventeenth-century **synagogue** (May–Sept Tues–Sun 1–5pm), on Husova, has recently been renovated and should theoretically be open at the times advertised. Uniquely for a Czech synagogue, the interior is in the Lvov style, with four central columns supporting the dome and bimah, and now houses an exhibition on the Jewish history of the town. Round the corner in Brněnská, a rugged path leads to the overgrown medieval **Jewish cemetery** (Židovský hřbitov), with finely carved marble tombstones dating back to 1618; to get into it, you'll need to pick up the key from Brněnská 28, though it's closed on Saturdays.

The town is rarely busy, except during the September wine festival, the majority of visitors pausing for a couple of hours at the most before moving on. The town centre is ten minutes' walk northeast of the **train station**, and there's a **tourist office** on the main square (daily: May–Sept 8am–6pm; Oct–April 8.30am–noon & 1–5pm; ⓦwww.rmm.cz), which can help with **accommodation** and any other queries. The best of the hotels is the *Rohatý krokodýl*, in the former Jewish quarter at Husova 8 (☎519 510 692, ⓦwww.rohatykrokodyl.cz; ❸), with the *Pension Moravia* (☎519 511 644; ❷), at Poštovní 1, off Česká, a useful fall-back. Alternatively, you can enquire about a cheap hostel bed at the *Národní dům* on the main square.

Apart from the *Rohatý krokodýl*'s **restaurant**, and the *Alfa* restaurant on the main square, both of which serve the usual Czech pub fare, there's *U nás doma*, at the far end of 1 května, ten minutes' walk northeast of the town centre, which is better than either.

Pálava

Mikulov is the starting point for hiking and exploring the **Pavlovské vrchy**, a big, bulging ridge of rugged and treeless limestone hills, and the surrounding region, known as the **Pálava**. Since the damming of the Dyje and the creation of the artificial Nový mlýn lake, the rare plant life on the Pavlovské vrchy has suffered badly. On the plus side, the lake has attracted much greater numbers

The Liechtensteins

The **Liechtensteins** (of Grand Duchy fame) were for many centuries one of the most powerful families in the Czech Lands, particularly in Moravia. At their peak in the seventeenth century they owned no fewer than 99 estates – one more and they would have had to maintain a standing army in the service of the emperor. The one who made the most of all this wealth was Prince-Bishop Karl Eusebius von Liechtenstein-Kastelcorn, who came into the family fortune in 1627, and whose motto – "Money exists only that one may leave beautiful monuments to eternal and undying remembrance" – can be seen in practice all over Moravia.

Like nearly all the ethnic Germans who lived in Czechoslovakia, the Liechtensteins were forced to leave in 1945 and retreat to their minuscule alpine country. For the next 45 years it looked like the long history of the Liechtensteins in the Czech Lands had come to an end. Then, in 1990, the new government passed a law of restituce (restitution), which meant that all property confiscated by the Communists from 1948 onwards was to be handed back to its original owners. Despite having had their property taken from them in the earlier appropriations of 1918 and 1945, the Liechtensteins continue to request compensation from the Czech government for the seizure of their former residences, which comprise something like 1600 square kilometres of land – ten times the area of present-day Liechtenstein.

of waterfowl, as well as eagles, falcons and black and red kites, and the whole area is now a protected region. It's also good, gentle **hiking country**, with wide-angle views on both sides and a couple of picturesque ruined castles along the ten-kilometre red-marked path to Dolní Věstonice.

Archeological research has been going on here since 1924, when an early Stone Age settlement was discovered. Brno's Moravské zemské muzeum (see p.334) displays the best findings, which include wolves' teeth jewellery and clay figurines such as the voluptuous *Venus of Věstonice*, a tiny female fertility figure with swollen belly and breasts. However, there is a small **Archaeologická expozice** (Tues–Sun 8am–noon & 1–5pm) in Dolní Věstonice, which, despite the lack of information in English, exhibits some interesting finds: skulls, a woolly mammoth's tooth, several animal and fertility statues, including, inevitably, a copy of the aforementioned Venus. From Dolní Věstonice you can either walk another 4km to the station at Popice or catch one of the hourly buses back to Mikulov.

Lednicko-Valtický areál

To the southeast of Mikulov, nose to nose with the Austrian border, is the UNESCO-protected **Lednicko-Valtický areál**, a landscape dominated by the twin residences of the Liechtensteins, one of the most powerful landowning families in the country until 1945 (see box on p.352). The chateaux lie 7km apart at either end of a dead-straight lime-tree avenue, in a vast, magnificent stately park, dotted with follies, including a sixty-metre minaret, and fish ponds and surrounded by acres of woodland – in many ways, it's this delightful setting that is the best feature of the whole area. However, being in a low-lying area prone to flooding, mosquitoes can be something of a problem in summer – worth bearing in mind if you're camping.

Lednice

The most popular of the two chateaux is undoubtedly the family's summer residence at **LEDNICE** (Eisgrub). Part of the Liechtenstein estate since 1243, the **zámek** (April & Oct Sat & Sun 9am–noon & 1–4pm; May–Aug Tues–Sun 9am–noon & 1–6pm; Sept closes 5pm; Ⓦwww.lednice.cz) was subjected to a lavish rebuild job in the 1840s, which turned it into a neo-Gothic extravaganza. Part of the chateau is occupied by an exhibition devoted to agriculture, but there's plenty to look at on the main guided tour, with vivid, over-the-top Romantic interiors crowding each of its wood-panelled rooms. If fake medievalism doesn't turn you on, however, head instead for the chateau's vast wrought-iron and glass palm house or **skleník** (April & Oct Sat & Sun 9am–4pm; May–Aug daily 9am–5pm; Sept closes 4pm). Those with kids in tow might want to seek out the new **Akvárium Malawi** (April–Oct daily 9am–5pm; Nov–March Sat & Sun 9am–4pm), in a wing of the old stables. It's something of an ad-hoc installation, and there's very little information on offer, but you're guaranteed to see piranhas, alligators, terrapins and countless colourful tropical fish.

Zámecký park

Best of all in Lednice is the expansive, watery **Zámecký park**, home to numerous herons, grebes and storks, as well as regular falconry displays in summer. You can either explore the park on foot, or catch one of the **boats**

(ⓦwww.lplavebni.cz) that head off for the minaret and the Janův hrad (also accessible by horse and cart). Piqued by local objections to their plan for a colossal church, the Liechtensteins decided in 1797 to further alienate the village by building the largest **minaret** (April & Oct Sat & Sun 10am–4pm; May–Aug Tues–Sun 10am–6pm; Sept Tues–Sun 10am–5pm) outside the Islamic world, which dominates the view of the park from the chateau; it's equally impressive close to, smothered in Arabic script, golden baubles and crescent moons, and you can climb to the top (60m) for a great view over the park. Further east is the **Janův hrad** (April & Oct Sat & Sun 9am–5pm; May–Sept Tues–Sun 9am–5pm), a ruined "Gothick" castle, round which there are guided tours every 45 minutes.

Valtice

VALTICE (Feldsberg), 7km southwest of Lednice, was ceded to the Czechs by the Austrians during a minor border adjustment dictated by the 1920 Treaty of St Germain, and from the end of the English-style gardens of the town's enormous Baroque **zámek** (Tues–Sun: April, Sept & Oct 9am–noon & 1–4pm; May–Aug 8am–noon & 1–5pm; ⓦwww.valtice.cz) you used to be able to see the watchtowers of the Iron Curtain in amongst the chateau's vineyards (which incidentally produce a good Moravian red). Once the family's foremost residence – over and above Liechtenstein itself – Valtice looks great from the outside, but was cleaned out just before the end of World War II, leaving its beautifully restored interior relentlessly bare. However, the east wing has been converted into a budget hotel and restaurant which does a brisk trade with holidaying Austrians.

The follies

Apart from the minaret and the ruined Janův hrad in Lednice's chateau grounds, numerous other **follies** were erected on a grand scale for the Liechtensteins in the early nineteenth century by Josef Kornhäusel and Josef Hardtmuth amidst the woods of the **Boří les** and the ponds that lie between Lednice and Valtice. The easiest to reach from Valtice, however, is the **Kolonáda na Rajstně**, a vast Neoclassical colonnade about 1km southwest of the town along the red-marked path or just off the road to Schrattenberg in Austria. To reach the Boří les, take the scenic red-marked path from Valtice train station, 2km through the woods, part of the way along a tree-lined avenue, to the triumphal arch called **Rendezvous**, which contains a concert hall and ballroom on the top floor. Another 1.5km deeper into the woods brings you to the Neo-Gothic chapel of **sv Hubert**, a popular picnic spot, and then for a similar distance north to the **Chrám Tří Grácií**, a curving colonnade sheltering a copy of the *Three Graces*; on the opposite bank of the nearby pond stands another Kornhäusel folly, the **Rybniční zámeček**.

A short distance east of the Tří Grácií stands the **Nový dvůr**, an ornate structure with a central rotunda-cum-cowshed, which featured glass partitions, built by the Liechtensteins for rearing sheep, rare-breed cattle and more latterly horses. Beyond, on the other side of the railway, is the **Apollonův chrám**, a Neoclassical pavilion overlooking one of the two fifteenth-century fish ponds, now a popular summer swimming spot. A couple of kilometres west of the Tří Grácií, on the other side of the village of **HLOHOVEC** (Bischofswarth), is the **Hraniční zámeček**, which used to stand on the historic border between Austria and Moravia (hence its name – *hranice* meaning "border"), and now houses a hotel and restaurant (see opposite).

Practicalities

Valtice is just twenty minutes by **train** from Mikulov and twenty-five from Břeclav, while Lednice is served only by a little-used branch line from Břeclav (April–Sept generally Sat & Sun); between Valtice and Lednice, however, there are just a couple of buses a day. The most convenient place to stay if you're travelling by train might well be the rather drab town of Břeclav (Lundenberg), 8km east of the two chateaux, on the main line from Prague to Bratislava, but you'll have a much better time in either Lednice or Valtice.

The best **accommodation in Lednice** is the large *Days Hotel* (☏519 340 130, ⓦwww.dayshotellednice.cz; ❹), up the road to Podivín, with good disabled access; alternatively, there's the by no means small *Pension Jordán* (☏519 340 285; ❷), further up the road to Podivín, which has clean, brightly painted en-suite rooms. The *U radnice*, just outside the chateau gates in Lednice, will furnish you with inexpensive Czech **food** and beer.

Accommodation in Valtice tends to be better value, particularly the plain rooms of the *Hubertus* (☏519 352 537; ❸) in the chateau itself, and the *Apollon* (☏519 352 625; ❷), set in its own gardens up the *lipovej alej* at P. Bezruče 720. The best place to **eat and drink** the local wine in Valtice is the *Vinářský dům*, opposite the church. An even better restaurant, with views across one of the lakes, can be found in the *Hraniční zámeček* (☏519 354 353, ⓦwww.hranicnizamecek.cz; ❸), in Hlohovec, which also offers excellent rooms, some with facilities for the disabled. Note, however, that all accommodation in the area tends to be fully booked in the middle of August when there's a Baroque Music Festival in Valtice.

Znojmo

Like Mikulov, 45km to the east, **ZNOJMO** (Znaim) enjoys a spectacular hilltop location, this time high above the Dyje, along with an old town blessed with an unrivalled set of Romanesque frescoes. What puts many first-time visitors off is that, unlike Mikulov, Znojmo's industry and suburbs have spread out in unsightly fashion to the north and east over the last hundred years. It's also something of a classic Czech border town, long blighted by the Iron Curtain, and now plagued by brothels and other institutions making a quick euro or two out of day-tripping Austrians.

The Town

Znojmo's main square, **Masarykovo náměstí**, was badly damaged in World War II, and the former Capuchin monastery at the bottom of the square is as uninspiring as the concrete supermarket that squats at the opposite end. The central Marian column survives, however, with its striking pink sandstone plinth and four accompanying saints. A couple of attractive surviving buildings on the east side of the square also deserve attention: the **Měšťanský dům**, which has a very fine sixteenth-century stone portal and matching pilasters, and the **Dům umění** (Tues–Sat 10am–6pm), a beautiful Renaissance building, two doors down. The latter has an arcaded courtyard out back, and diamond vaulting on the first floor, where temporary exhibitions are held. On the second floor there's a room devoted to local artist, Jan Tomáš Fisher, a pupil of Otakar Španiel, who, like his master, specialized in designing reliefs on medals. There's also a small collection of Gothic and Baroque art, particularly strong on sculpture, and a genial English-speaking curator to show you round.

Hope rears up at the top of the square, in the shape of the late-Gothic pin-nacled and baubled **radniční věž** (April & Oct Mon–Sat 9am–4pm; May–Sept daily 9am–5pm; Nov–March Mon–Fri 9am–4pm), all that's left of the old town hall, burnt down by the Nazis in the closing stages of the war. From this soaring romantic affair, its uppermost gallery twisting at an angle to the main body, the view through its wooden hatches is little short of spectac-ular – a good way to get your bearings and a feel for the old town. One block east on Slepičí trh (Chicken Market) is the entrance to the town's underground tunnels or **podzemí** (April & Oct Sat 10am–4pm; May–Sept daily 9am–4pm) that run for miles under the old town; originally built for defensive purposes, they were later used for storing wine.

At this point you can head off in a number of directions, but the most inter-esting is the narrow lane of Velká Mikulášská, which leads to the oldest part of Znojmo – a tight web of alleyways woven round the cathedral of **sv Mikuláš**, a plain Gothic hall church sporting an unusual gable embellished with blind arcading. Inside, it has retained its elegant Gothic net vaulting and slender round pillars, but the most amazing thing about the church is its Baroque pul-pit: a giant globe, with its top sliced off, crowned by a sounding board of free-flying clouds, sunbursts, cherubs and saints. Also worth inspecting is the glass coffin underneath the organ loft, containing the macabre clothed skeleton of a Christian martyr.

Set at a right angle to the cathedral is the much smaller **chapel of sv Václav**, tucked into the town walls, from which you get a commanding view up and down the Dyje valley as it blends into the Austrian plain. The chapel itself is a curious building, built literally on top of its Gothic predecessor in the sixteenth century, when the town's fortifications against the Turks were erected (and smothered the old building). The church now belongs to the local Orthodox community, and the priest will happily show you round the chapel and the bare Gothic original.

"Better a living brewery than a dead castle", goes one of the more obscure Czech proverbs, and as far as **Znojemský hrad** (May Sat & Sun 10am–6pm; June–Sept Tues–Sun 10am–6pm; ⓦ www.znojmuz.cz) goes it's hard to disagree. The parts that didn't become a brewery have since been turned into a deceptively large local **museum** distinguished, for the most part, by its trompe l'oeil Baroque fresco in the oval entrance hall, glorifying the Deblín family, who rebuilt the chateau in 1720 only to run out of male heirs in 1784. To reach the museum, take the special path (daily: May–Sept 9am–10pm; Oct–April 9am–8pm) that runs along the perimeter of the brewery. The castle's most precious relic is the **Rotunda** (times as above), home to the best-preserved twelfth-century frescoes in the country, including contemporary portraits of the Přemyslid princes. Note that access is sometimes restricted in bad weather in order to protect the paintings.

In fine weather the local museum in the former **Minoritský klášter**, opposite the brewery, is worth skipping in favour of a scramble in the thickly wooded deep gorge of the Podyjí national park, that begins as soon as you leave the town walls at the end of Přemyslovců. It's a gentle wander round the foot of the castle to the chapel of sv Václav, but for a longer **walk** and an unbeatable vista of Znojmo and the Dyje, take the blue-marked path down to the stream and then the green-marked path past the Stations of the Cross, up to the village and nunnery of Hradiště; bus #1 will run you back into town.

Architecture buffs may want to take a look at the huge yellow colossus of the Premonstratensian **convent** at **Louka** (Klosterbruck), now a suburb of Znojmo (10min walk or bus #4 down Vídeňská třída). It was begun but never finished by, among others, the Baroque architect Johann Lukas von Hildebrandt, and soon afterwards was turned into a barracks, its precious library carried off to Prague's Strahov monastery. From a distance it still manages to make an impression, and the main basilica has recently been restored, but the ongoing renovation work will take some years to bring the rest of the complex up to scratch.

Practicalities

Trains run fairly frequently from Mikulov to Znojmo, taking around an hour; trains from Brno take around two hours, often with a change (but no wait) at Hrušovany nad Jevišovkou. The old town is a stiff hike from the station: up 17 listopadu to Marianské náměstí, then west along Pontassievská and Zámečnická. If you're heading into Austria, there's a 24-hour **border crossing** at Hatě, 12km southeast on route 38 (the occasional bus goes there), and a railway border crossing at nearby Šatov; note, however, that the Hnanice-Mitterretzbach border crossing to the west is for Austrian and Czech passport holders only.

The **tourist office** (April–Sept Mon–Sat 8am–6pm: Oct–March Mon–Fri 8am–6pm, Sat 8am–12.30pm; ⓦ www.znojmocity.cz), at Obroková 12, can help with **accommodation**. Your best bet is to try one of the town's small pensions, such as the excellent *Havelka* (☎515 220 138; ❸), right by the church of sv Mikuláš, or the *Austis*, Václavské náměstí 5 (☎515 241 949; ❸). Another good choice is the *Cyklo Penzion*, Mikulášské náměstí 8 (☎603 836 693; ❷), a Dutch pub run by a couple of sculptor brothers keen on cycling. There are two good **campsites** to the north of Znojmo: the family-run *Country* **campsite** (May–Oct; ⓦ www.camping-country.com), in Hluboké Mašůvky, 7km up route 361, and the lakeside *Výr* site near Výrovice, 10km away off route 399 to Plaveč.

There are plenty of **restaurants** to choose from, but *Na Večnosti*, Velká Mikulášská 11 (Ⓦ www.navecnosti.cz), is a real find: a pleasant, mostly veggie restaurant-gallery, which offers *bryndzové halušky*, a whole range of *smažený sýr*, pasta and even fish dishes; they have internet access and even put on the occasional bit of live music. Another interesting option is *Bljus*, Dolní Česká 21 (closed Sat eve & Sun), which serves Russian staples like borscht and dumplings washed down with the local Hostan beer. Znojmo stages its own **wine festival**, *Znojemské vinobraní*, in the middle of September. Aside from booze, **pickled gherkins** (*kyselá okurka*) flavoured with paprika are another Znojmo speciality to look out for.

Podyjí

The meandering River Dyje and the artificial Vranov lake to the west of Znojmo are now part of the heavily forested and very pretty **Podyjí** national park, which provides a summer playground for large numbers of holidaying Czechs. There are plenty of opportunities for swimming and lazing around, plus a couple of interesting chateaux and lots of hiking possibilities. Without your own transport, getting about can be time-consuming, so you might want to plan to spend at least two or three days in the area.

Vranov

The village of **VRANOV NAD DYJÍ** (Frain), 20km west of Znojmo, is a scruffy place, but it sits below an incredible cliff-top **zámek** (April & Oct Sat & Sun 9am–noon & 1–4pm; May, June & Sept Tues–Sun 9am–noon & 1–5pm; July & Aug 9am–noon & 1–6pm; Ⓦ www.pamatky-jm.cz), magnificently poised on a knife's edge above the Dyje. Originally a medieval stronghold, it was converted into a beautiful Baroque chateau by the Viennese genius Johann Bernhard Fischer von Erlach after a fire in 1665. Nothing else on the guided tour of the sprawling complex (not even the medieval sauna) can quite compare to Fischer's trump card at the far end – the cavernous dome of the **Sál předků** (Ancestors' Hall), whose truly awesome overall effect is as much due to Rottmayr's wild frescoes as to Fischer's great oval skylights: its frenzied, over-the-top paintings depict the (fictitious) achievements of the Althan family who commissioned the work. One other piece of Fischer von Erlach genius worth inspecting is the palace's tiny **chapel** (June Sat & Sun 9am–5pm; July & Aug Tues–Sun 9am–6pm), a visit to which is not included in the chateau tour. Again, it's the frescoes, executed by a pupil of Rottmayr, that make the place so special: the main fresco features the Archangel Michael smiting Satan's followers who tumble over the cornice itself, while in the side chapels skeletons frolic and angels pray.

One of the most interesting **walks** in the area is to take the red-marked path from Vranov village along the Dyje, then up into the woods and hills until you reach the road from Čížov to the Austrian border (6km). From here, it's just 2km by either the blue-marked path by the road, or the green-marked path through the woods via the Hardeggská vyhlídka, a lookout post from which you can view the picturesque Austrian border village of Hardegg, accessible via a small footbridge. The round trip is about 16km and will take all day, so carry a picnic, or some euros, in order to grab a bite to eat in Hardegg (and, of course, your passport).

Practicalities

At the weekend **buses** run regularly from Znojmo to Vranov, less often during the week. Alternatively, you could take the more frequent **train** to Sumná station and walk the 4km along the green-marked path to Vranov. In the centre of Vranov, you can **stay** above the friendly, family-run *Country Saloon* courtyard pub (☎603 549 369, ⓦwww.country.saloon.web.wo.cz; ❷) or in the newly refurbished en-suite rooms of the grandiose *Zámecký hotel* (☎515 296 101, ⓦwww.zameckyhotel.cz; ❸), some of which have views of the chateau. From the village, it's a fifteen-minute walk to the dam (*přehrada*) and the sandy **beach** known as Vranovská pláž, accessible via the new footbridge across the lake. From May to September there's a fair bit of life here: a couple of **campsites** (May–Sept), chalets, boat rental, a couple of shops and an occasional **boat service** up the lake to Bítov and beyond. The sun-worshippers are shoulder to shoulder on the beach in the high season, but it's easy to lose the crowd by picking a rocky spot further upstream.

Bítov

The village of **BÍTOV**, 8km west up the lake, and high above the shore, is nowhere near as dramatically situated as Vranov. It does, however, have at least one decent **place to stay**: the popular café/pension *U Tesařů* on the main square (☎&ⓕ515 294 616; ❷), which offers modern comforts and decent Czech food. The nearby *Bítov-Horka* **campsite** (May–Sept) is ideally situated down by the lakeside. The only way to get from Vranov to Bítov – apart from hitching or walking – is to take the boat. There are just one or two buses from Znojmo to Bítov; connections with Jihlava (see p.364) are much the same.

The ruined castle that can be seen from the lake is a fourteenth-century defence fort of Cornštejn, and is unsafe to explore. Bítov's own **hrad** (April & Oct Sat & Sun 9am–noon & 1–4pm; May, June–Sept Tues–Sun 9am–noon & 1–5pm, July & Aug closes 6pm) has weathered slightly better and is located 2.5km to the west of the village, along the red-marked path. Like Vranov, it boasts a classic defensive location on a spit of grey rock high above the river, which the flooding of the valley has diminished only slightly, and for this reason alone it's worth clambering up to enjoy the view. In the castle's courtyard there's a lovely, cool thirteenth-century **wine cellar** where you can taste and purchase the local wine, and an *občerstvení* where you can get a snack and a glass of beer, but inside, lacking Fischer's ingenious touch, the castle's not a patch on Vranov. The hour-long **guided tour** (*1 trasa*) through the contrived neo-Gothic decor and soulless, unlived-in rooms is enlivened only by a pack of stuffed dogs. A better bet is take the short, unguided tour (*2 trasa*) of the castle's pink and white **chapel** in the main courtyard.

Třebíč and around

TŘEBÍČ, 70km due west of Brno, is best known for its Romanesque basilica and its newly restored Jewish ghetto. In most other respects, it's a fairly nondescript town, though it does serve as a useful jumping-off point for the tongue-twisting Baroque chateaux of Jaroměřice nad Rokytnou and Náměšť nad Oslavou.

The Town

Apart from a couple of sgraffito facades, the main square, **Karlovo náměstí**, is pretty undistinguished, though its grandiose scale gives some hint of the town's medieval importance. Třebíč's former glory is almost entirely down to the Benedictine monastery, which was founded in 1101 on a hill on the north bank of the River Jihlava, to the west of the town centre. The monastery was closed down as early as the fifteenth century, and transformed into a chateau, which now houses the local **museum** (Tues–Sun 8am–noon & 1–4pm; ⓦ www.zmm.cz), whose displays include an unusually large selection of nativity scenes. However, it's the former monastery church, the big grey **Basilica of sv Prokop** (May–Oct Tues & Wed 8–11.30am & 1–5pm, Thurs 9–11.30am & 1–5pm, Fri 8–11.30am & 1–4pm, Sat & Sun 1–5pm), that's the real draw here. Heavily restored in the Baroque period, and again between the wars, the church nevertheless retains much of its original mid-thirteenth-century architecture, a transitional style between Romanesque and Gothic, particularly in the vast north portal, the chancel, the galleried apse and the crypt.

Back down in the town, squeezed up against a hill, the northern bank of the river was for centuries the town's **Jewish ghetto** known as Zámostí. Třebíč's Jewish population peaked at the end of the eighteenth century, at over 1700 (nearly 60 percent of the total population of the town), but by the 1930s had dwindled to just 300, most of whom subsequently perished in the Holocaust. The ghetto was already a shadow of its former self by the outbreak of the war, but it's ironic that only now, with virtually no Jews left in Třebíč, is the Jewish quarter finally being restored. Architecturally, the ghetto remains remarkably intact – it's currently home to many of the town's local Romanies, though with renovation (and gentrification) continuing apace, probably not for long.

Now linked by a new pedestrian bridge to a passageway on the north side of the main square, the ghetto originally had to be approached from what is now Žerotinovo náměstí, by the road bridge to the west of the main square. Here, the narrow ghetto entrance by no. 114 was sealed off by a chain on the Sabbath, beyond which the quarter's two main cobbled streets run parallel with each other. At the western end of the ghetto, on Tiché náměstí, is the former **Přední synagoga** (Front Synagogue), which had to be reduced in height in the Baroque period after complaints by the Countess of Valdštejn; it was handed over to the Czechoslovak Hussite Church in the 1950s. At the eastern end of the two streets you can visit the **Žádní synagoga** (Rear Synagogue; daily 10am–noon & 1–5pm), whose walls are painted in Hebrew script and decorated with vegetal and floral motives. In the women's gallery there's an exhibition on the Jewish life of Třebíč, and, in the main body of the synagogue, a memorial to the 290 Jews who died in the Holocaust. To reach the **Jewish cemetery** (Židovský hřbitov; closed Sat), which contains some 3000 graves dating from the seventeenth century to the 1930s, follow the signs up the hill and down Hrádek.

You can gain a good overview of the town from the **Městská věž** (May–Sept daily 10am–5pm), which belongs to the church of sv Martin, to the south of the main square.

Practicalities

Třebíč is on the main line from Brno to Jihlava, and the **train station** is just five minutes' walk south of the main square; the **bus station** is a block or so west of the main square on Komenského náměstí, while the **tourist office** (Mon–Fri 8am–6pm, Sat 8am–1pm; ⓦ www.trebic-city.cz) is in the town hall, at the western end of the main square. **Accommodation** is thin on the ground, with the *Hotel Slavia*, Karlovo náměstí 5 (☎568 848 560; ❸), leading the charge; it's supremely ugly on the outside but inside is not so bad. A better bet is the *Penzion U synagogy* (☎723 082 131; ❷), next door to the Žádní synagoga. For **food** and **beer**, try the smart, new *V černem domě*, with outdoor seating, in the sgraffito house at no. 16, on the north side of the main square.

Jaroměřice nad Rokytnou

The small town of **JAROMĚŘICE NAD ROKYTNOU**, 14km south of Třebíč, is completely overwhelmed by its gargantuan russet-and-cream Baroque **zámek** (April & Oct Sat & Sun 9am–noon & 1–4pm; May, June–Sept Tues–Sun 9am–noon & 1–5pm, July & Aug closes 6pm), built over the course of 37 years by the wealthy and extravagant Johann Adam von Questenberg. For the most part it's the work of Dominico d'Angeli, but the two Austrian architects Jakob Prandtauer and Johann Lukas von Hildebrandt also appear to have been involved at various stages. The highlights of the chateau are the elegant Rococo halls, the Hlavní sál and the Táneční sál, where Questenberg used to put on lavish classical concerts. To see these you must join the fifty-minute *1. trasa*; the thirty-minute *2. trasa* only takes you round the later interiors and the porcelain collection. Alternatively, you could skip both tours and spend the morning exploring the great domed and frescoed chapel (now the local parish church) or pottering around the formal gardens. Even better, come during July and August, when the chateau stages a festival of classical music. Jaroměřice is on the train line from Znojmo to Jihlava, but from Třebíč you have to change trains, which means you'd be better off travelling by bus. Note that the train station is 2km west of the town in the village of Popovice. If you're stuck in town, you'll have the chance to check out the kitsch decor in the Communist-era *Hotel Opera* (☎568 440 232, ⓦwww.185.cz/hoopera.htm; ❷).

Náměšť nad Oslavou

Tucked into one of the many twists and turns of the River Oslava, the town of **NÁMĚŠŤ NAD OSLAVOU**, 18km east of Třebíč, sits below its big white Renaissance **zámek** (April & Oct Sat & Sun 9am–4pm; May, June & Sept Tues–Sun 9am–5pm; July & Aug closes 6pm), built by the Žerotín family in the sixteenth century. The grandiose double staircase leading to the main entrance, and the arcaded inner courtyard, give some indication of the chateau's former glories but belie the rather dull interior. What makes the chateau worth visiting are the large collection of remarkably well-preserved sixteenth- to eighteenth-century French tapestries and the Baroque library, whose barrel-vaulted ceiling is decorated with colourful frescoes. The gardens give out the most wonderful views, and are perfect for a picnic, but it's worth venturing down into the town to admire the **medieval bridge**, the country's third oldest, after Písek and Prague's Charles Bridge, and, like those two, lined with Baroque statues of saints and guarded by angels.

   Buses drop you on the main square, Masarykovo náměstí, where there's a **tourist office** (9am–noon & 1–5pm: Sept–June Mon–Fri; July & Aug daily) in the stará radnice; the **train station** is 1km or so to the west of the town centre. You can enjoy **food** and **drink** in the chateau's courtyard at the *Zámecký restaurace*, and you can even **stay** in the *Zámecký penzion* (☎568 620 319; ❷). There are several lovely **walks** to be had in the woods to the south of Náměšť, along the meandering Oslava: follow the red-marked path down to the river as far as the neo-Gothic hunting lodge of **Lovecký zámeček**, 5km to the south, and return via the green-marked path.

Telč

It's hardly an exaggeration to say that the last momentous event in **TELČ** (Teltsch) was the great fire of 1530, which wiped out all the town's wooden Gothic houses and forced it to start afresh. It is this fortuitous disaster that has made Telč what it is: a perfect museum-piece sixteenth-century provincial town. Squeezed between two fish ponds, the Štěpnický to the east and the Ulický to the west, the **staré město** is little more than two medieval gate towers, one huge wedge-shaped square and a chateau. Renaissance arcades extend the length of the main square, **náměstí Zachariáše z Hradce**, lined with pastel-coloured houses (including the town's fire station) that display a breathtaking variety of gables and pediments, none less than two hundred and fifty years old. At the eastern end of the square, you can climb the **věž sv Ducha** (June–Sept daily noon–5pm) for an overview of the ensemble.

At the narrow western end of the square, the **zámek** (Tues–Sun: April & Oct 9am–noon & 1–4pm; May–Sept until 5pm; Ⓦwww.zamek-telc.cz) in no way disturbs the sixteenth-century atmosphere of the town; it too was badly damaged in the fire and had to be rebuilt in similar fashion. Like the chateau at the nearby Bohemian town of Jindřichův Hradec (see p.000), it was the inspiration of Zachariáš of Hradec, whose passion for all things Italian is again strongly in evidence. Of the two guided tours on offer, the hour-long *trasa A* is the one to go for, as it concentrates on the Renaissance-era rooms, which boast a truly exceptional array of period ceilings. The shorter *trasa B* features living spaces from later periods, but even this can be fun as the whole place is refreshingly intimate and low-key after the intimidating pomposity of the Baroque chateaux of the region.

Even if you don't fancy going on a guided tour, you should take a look inside the chateau's exquisite All Saints' **chapel**, opposite the ticket office. The chapel was built in 1580 as the last resting place of Zachariáš of Hradec and his wife Kateřina of Valdštejn, who lie, arms outstretched in prayer, surrounded by a beautiful, multi-coloured wrought-iron grille. For a funereal chapel, the decor is surprisingly bright and upbeat, and the stuccowork is absolutely outstanding, with gilded trumpets erupting from a farrago of figs, olives, pomegranates and other fruit. In the central relief on the ceiling of the nave, a whole host of skeletons is being restored to life on the Day of Judgement, as prophesized by Ezekiel: "there was a noise, and behold a shaking, and the bones came together, bone to his bone".

You can also stroll through the cloistered formal garden at leisure, and pay a visit to the **Galerie Jana Zrzavého** (April–Oct Tues–Sun 9am–5pm; Nov–March Tues–Fri & Sun 9am–4pm, Sat 9am–1pm) in the east wing, dedicated to the Surrealist painter Jan Zrzavý (1890–1977), whose career spanned the first three quarters of the twentieth century. Born in nearby Havlíčkův Brod, Zrzavý's early works were Post-Impressionist, but he quickly adopted his own peculiar dreamlike, slightly surreal style. His paintings are definitely an acquired taste, though they are by no means monotonous; particularly striking are his pallid, grey, virtually uninhabited Breton landscapes painted between the wars.

The local branch of the **muzeum Vysočiny** (times as for the zámek) is housed in the chateau, too, with a model of the town, a miniature Bethlehem scene and displays on local history. More intriguing, though, is the exquisite ceramic World War I memorial, at the end of the covered passageway that leads to the town's church. Although the adjacent World War II memorial doesn't explicitly say so, it's clear that the majority of the town's victims in the last war were from the local Jewish community.

Practicalities

The **train station** is a ten-minute walk east of the old town along Masarykova, but with direct trains only connecting with Jihlava, you're more likely to find yourself arriving at the nearby **bus station**. The **tourist office** (Mon–Fri 8am–5pm, Sat & Sun 10am–5pm; winter Mon–Fri only; ⓦwww.telc.cz), at no. 10 on the main square, is very helpful and friendly and can book **private rooms**. Most tour groups come here only for a couple of hours, so **accommodation** shouldn't be too much of a problem and there's plenty of choice.

The *Hotel Celerin* (☎567 243 477, ⓦwww.czn.cz/celerin; ❹) enjoys a great location, at no. 43, at the wide end of the main square, as does the *Černý orel* (☎567 243 220, ⓦwww.cernyorel.cz; ❸), at no. 7, though neither has much character inside. The *Na hrázi* (☎567 213 150; ❷) is a pleasant new pub-hotel overlooking the fish ponds to the south of the old town on Na hrázi, and there are numerous other smaller pensions to choose from in the old town. The nearest **campsite** is the *Velkopařezitý* lakeside site (open all year), 7km north-west of Telč.

Bike rental is available from an outlet next door to *Celerin,* and there's an **ATM** at the wide end of the square. Nearby, *U Zachariáše* is a very popular **pub**, as is *Na kopečku,* a short walk north of the old town up Jihlavská. Another good choice is *U Marušky,* by the tower, at the opposite end of the square from the chateau, and the *Šenk pod věží* restaurant, next door. Telč can get busy in the summer, but it gets even busier for two weeks at the turn of July and August when the town hosts a non-traditional folk music **festival**.

Slavonice

SLAVONICE (Zlabings), 25km south of Telč and a stone's throw from the Austrian border, is in many ways even more remarkable. It's a monument to a prosperity that lasted for just one hundred years, shattered by the Thirty Years' War, which halved the population, then dealt its deathblow in the 1730s when the post road from Prague to Vienna was rerouted via Jihlava. In 1945 the forced removal of the local German-speaking inhabitants emptied Slavonice, and matters deteriorated even further when the Iron Curtain wrapped itself around the village, severing road and rail links with the West.

Even now, the **staré město** – not much larger than the one at Telč – still has a strange and haunting beauty. The impression is further enhanced by the bizarre biblical and apocalyptic sixteenth-century "strip cartoons" played out on the houses in monochrome sgraffito. The best way to start a tour of the town is to pick up an ice cream at the local *cukrárna,* on **náměstí Míru**, the larger of the town's two squares, if only for a closer look at the stunning diamond vaulting in the building's entrance hall. Next, you should pay a visit to the former **Lutheran prayer room** (*Protestantská modlitebna*; daily 9am–7pm or dusk; ☎384 493 048) at house no. 517 on Horní náměstí, known locally as *U itala,* as the very friendly owner's Italian. Here, on the first floor, they will show you the exceptional wall paintings of the Apocalypse, which miraculously survived the Counter-Reformation: look out, in particular, for the mischievous depiction of the Devil as a crocodile wearing the papal crown, not to mention the horse-riding Whore of Babylon. Last of all, you can now climb the **Městská věž** (8am–noon & 1–5pm: April, May & Sept Sat & Sun; June–Aug daily), which is attached to the town's central church.

Practicalities

Trains from Telč take fifty minutes, but from Jihlava they take an incredible two hours (with a change at Kostelec u Jihlavy); the train station is five minutes' walk south of the town centre, and a short walk from the **Austrian border** (daily 6am–10pm) and town of Fratres. Slavonice is also connected by the occasional **bus** to Jindřichův Hradec and points to the west. Most people come to Slavonice on a day-trip, but the **tourist office** on náměstí Míru (daily: June–Sept 9am–noon & 1–6pm; Oct–May Mon–Fri 10am–noon & 1–4pm; ⓦwww .slavonice-mesto.cz) provides information if you wish to **stay the night**. You can stay on náměstí Míru, at the *Hotel Alfa* (☎384 493 261; ❶), which is basically a pub with simple rooms upstairs, or at the more comfortable *U růže* (☎384 493 004, ⓦwww.dumuruze.cz; March–Nov; ❷). On Horní náměstí, there are rooms above the *Dům Besídka* bar and gallery (☎384 493 293, ⓦwww.mariz.cz; ❶), which runs arty workshops over the summer, or above the Lutheran prayer room at no. 517 (☎384 493 159; ❷). For **food**, you can also try *Appetito*, on the main square, with its own courtyard out back, which serves traditional Czech fare.

Jihlava

When silver deposits were discovered in the nearby hills in the 1240s, **JIHLA-VA** (Iglau) was transformed overnight from a tiny Moravian village into one of the biggest mining towns in central Europe. Scores of German miners came and settled here, and by the end of the century Jihlava could boast two hospitals, two monasteries and, most importantly, the royal mint. The veins of silver ran out in the fourteenth century, but the town continued to flourish thanks to the cloth trade, reaching its zenith around the latter half of the sixteenth century when over 700 master spinners worked in the town.

Jihlava retains a surprisingly attractive staré město, which has been painstakingly renovated over the last decade. That the town isn't quite as lovely as it should be is partly down to a fire in 1523 and the ravages of the Thirty Years' War, which drastically reduced Jihlava's population. Most of all, however, it was the expulsion of ethnic Germans from this *Sprachinsel* or "language-island" after 1945 that changed the face of the town for ever, or, as the Communist guidebooks euphemistically put it, "marked the beginning of a new stage in the development of Jihlava". In reality, the town immediately went into decline, plagued by an ignorant Communist council which, in its comparatively brief forty-year rule, left the most indelible mark on the town: the mud-brown, multistorey car park/supermarket complex plonked in the middle of Jihlava's huge main square in place of a block of medieval houses.

The Town

If you can look beyond Jihlava's most glaring addition, the cobbled main square, **Masarykovo náměstí**, is actually a wonderfully expansive space. Sloping steeply to the south and lined with restrained Baroque and Rococo houses, it sports two fountains, and a Marian column, beside which is a plaque to Evžen Plocek, the 41-year-old who set himself alight on April 4, 1969, in protest against the Soviet invasion. At the top of the square, in no. 58, is the **muzeum Vysočiny** (Tues–Sun 9am–noon & 12.30–5pm; ⓦmuzeum.ji.cz), worth a visit for the interior alone, being one of the few Renaissance houses to survive the 1523 fire. Its covered inner courtyard, with an arcaded gallery, patchy murals and diamond vaulting, is perfectly preserved. The museum's collections of stuffed animals and mushrooms are less remarkable, though there is a well-preserved eighteenth-century pharmacy from nearby Polná.

You can see different kinds of interior design in the **oblastní galerie Vysočiny** (Tues–Fri 9am–noon & 12.30–5pm, Sat & Sun 1–5pm), round the corner at Komenského 10, north off the main square, which houses a small but excellent permanent collection of nineteenth- and twentieth-century Czech art. You can also take a trip down into the town's extensive catacombs, known as **katakomby** (daily: April & Oct–Dec 10am–noon & 2–4pm; May, June & Sept 10am–noon & 2–4pm; July & Aug 9am–noon & 2–5pm) or *historické podzemí*. The entrance to the tunnels is beside the imposing early Baroque facade of the Jesuit church of **sv Ignác**, built at the top of the square in the 1680s. Unfortunately, the church is usually closed, so to see the ceiling fresco and the stupendous *trompe l'oeil* main altar, you'll need to get there before or after one of the services.

Apart from the Jesuit church, all the town's other churches comply with medieval requirements and are set back from the square. The most obvious of

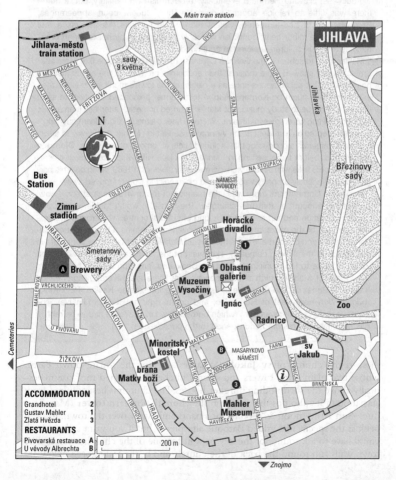

"I am thrice homeless, as a native of Bohemia in Austria, as an Austrian among Germans and as a Jew throughout the world. Everywhere an intruder, never welcomed." **Gustav Mahler's** predicament was typical of the Jews of Mitteleuropa, and it only exacerbated his already highly strung personality. Prone to Wagnerian excesses and bouts of extreme pessimism, he would frequently work himself into a state of nervous collapse when composing or conducting. It was this Teutonic temperament as much as his German-speaking background that separated him from his more laid-back Czech musical contemporaries.

Mahler was born in 1860 in the nearby village of **Kalištĕ** (Kalischt) on the Bohemian side of the border, the second son of Bernhard Mahler, an ambitious Jewish businessman. The very same year, the Mahlers, who were the only non-Czechs in the entire village, moved to **Iglau** (Jihlava), where there had been a strong Jewish community since the mid-fourteenth century. The family moved to **Wienerstrasse** (now Znojemská) 4, where there is now a plaque recording this fact. Mahler's father opened a pub here, a drunken dive by all accounts, and it proved a big success, allowing Bernhard eventually to open his own distillery, but at home there was little to rejoice about. Judging by his frequent court appearances, Bernhard was a bad-tempered, violent man, while his wife, Marie, was a frail woman, whose minor heart condition was only exacerbated by her fourteen pregnancies (only six children survived to adulthood).

Mahler went to school at the German Gymnasium on Hluboká (some fifty years after Smetana), but showed more musical, than academic, promise. At the age of just ten, he made his first public appearance as a pianist at the town's municipal theatre, then in a converted church on **Komenského**. A local farmer persuaded Bernhard to send his boy to **Prague** to study music, but Mahler returned homesick after less than a year. After completing his studies in **Jihlava**, where he later claimed "I didn't learn anything", he was accepted as a student at the **Vienna** conservatoire. Mahler then enjoyed a fairly stormy career as a conductor that included stints at, among other places, **Olomouc** and Prague, before finally settling in Vienna, the place with which he is most closely associated. His links with Jihlava were permanently severed in 1889, when both his parents died, the family property was sold, and his remaining siblings moved away.

Under the Communists there was little mention of the town's greatest son – now, predictably enough, all that has changed. The house in which Mahler grew up is under restoration and set to become a kind of cultural centre, while round the corner a branch of the muzeum Vysočiny (see overleaf) contains a permanent exhibition on him – and of course, there's the *Gustav Mahler* hotel. Mahler's parents' grave still stands in the Jewish cemetery, 1km west of the town centre on U cvičištĕ, off Žižkova, close to the municipal cemetery. Dedicated fans who wish to track down the village of Mahler's birth should beware that there are several villages called Kalištĕ in Bohemia: the right one is listed in map indexes as Kalištĕ (Pelhřimov), roughly 7km northwest of Humpolec, and confusingly not Kalištĕ (Jihlava). The house in which Mahler was born (which burned down in 1937 and had to be rebuilt) has recently been restored and opened to the public (see p.181).

these is the church of **sv Jakub** (St James), east of the square down Farní, whose two plain stone towers and steeply pitched, chevroned roof rise majestically above the surrounding burgher houses. The church is best admired from afar, though it's also possible to climb the church's northern **tower** (May–Sept Tues–Sun 10am–noon & 2–6pm) for a panoramic view over the town. You can peek at the spectacular gilded Baroque altarpieces, but if you want a closer look you'll have to ask round for the key or wait for one of the church services. The town walls run round the back of the church, and in the leafy gorge below are the woods of the Březinovy sady and the town's **zoo** (daily: April & Oct 9am–5pm; May–Sept 8am–6pm; Nov–March 9am–4pm), where tigers, zebras, kangaroos, monkeys, hippos and snakes share cramped quarters.

For a town originally built on silver, Jihlava lacks the vestiges of prosperity that grace, for example, Kutná Hora. A few finely carved portals and the remnants of fifteenth-century frescoes survive here and there, but just one gateway, **brána Matky boží** (May–Sept Tues–Sun 9am–noon & 12.30–5pm), guarding the road from the west, is all that's left of the town's five gates. Next door to the gateway is the beautifully restored **Minoritský kostel**, a remarkable little church that dates back to around 1250. The building's antiquity – it's the oldest stone building in the town – is evident in the thick Romanesque pillars and fragments of medieval frescoes in the nave. However, the Baroque fittings are no less interesting, particularly the technicolour Crucifixion scene opposite the pulpit, which is played out in front of a ruched silver drape. Make sure you venture into the choir to admire the mural depicting the medieval town, located above the sedilia, which harbours three finely sculpted female saints.

There is, however, just one more sight worth mentioning, the branch of the **muzeum Vysočiny** (mid-April to Sept Tues–Fri 9am–noon & 1–5pm, Sat & Sun 1–5pm; Oct to mid-April by appointment only; ☎567 309 728), at Kosmákova 9, off the southwest corner of the square, which houses a permanent exhibition on **Gustav Mahler**'s childhood in Jihlava (*expozice mladý Gustav Mahler a Jihlava*); for more on Mahler's time here, see the box on p.366. The captions for the black-and-white photos are in Czech and German only, so you'll need to buy the English catalogue to get anything out of the museum. That said, there's not a lot to get excited about: no original artefacts and little imagination to the displays.

Practicalities

The **main train station** – simply called Jihlava – is a good 2km northeast of the town centre, so hop on trolleybus #A or #B; slow trains to or from Tábor, Jindřichův Hradec or České Budějovice also stop at **Jihlava-město**, 1km north of the old town – there are no trolleybuses, but it's an easy walk to the staré město along třída Legionářů. From the **bus station**, northwest of the old town, it's a five-minute walk to the main square or a short hop on trolleybus #C. Jihlava's **tourist office** (Mon–Fri 9am–5pm, Sat 9am–noon) is at no. 18 on the main square and can organize **private rooms**.

Jihlava sees relatively few tourists, other than passing business folk, Austrians and homesick Sudeten Germans, so **accommodation** is limited to a few medium-priced choices. Perhaps the most reliable place to stay is the *Hotel Gustav Mahler*, Křížová 4 (☎567 320 501, ⓦwww.hotelgmahler.cz; ❹), which has taken over the former Dominican monastery north of the main square; the hotel is wonderfully spacious, though there's little original decor left – ask for a room with shared facilities if you want to save money. The sgraffitoed *Hotel Zlatá Hvězda* (☎567 320 782, ⓦwww.zlatahvezda.cz; ❹) is slightly cheaper and enjoys a good position on the main square, though it has a seedy non-stop bar in the basement. Other fallbacks include the Art Nouveau *Grand Hotel* (☎567 303 541; ❹), which has a few cheap rooms with shared facilities, and is at the junction of Komenského and Husova. If you're camping, take a local bus to the lakeside *Pávov* **campsite** (open all year) situated 4km north of Jihlava, not far from the motorway.

All the above accommodation choices will happily serve you food and drink, but Jihlava's most aesthetically pleasing **restaurant** is *U vévody Albrechta*, which occupies a banquet room decorated with Renaissance frescoes, on the first floor at no. 41 on the west side of the main square. If you want to sample Jihlava's local *Ježek* (hedgehog or *Iglau* in German) **beer**, head for the brewery's own cavernous *Pivovarská restaurace* on Vrchlického, which offers the entire range of *Ježek* beers including the 18-degree *Grand*, and the usual pub grub. A more mellow place to spend the evening is *Café Etage*, a trendy hangout on the first floor of no. 39 on the main square, or the *čajovna*, at the back of the bookshop on Brněnská (closed Sun eve). As for high culture, Jihlava's *Horácké divadlo* (Ⓦ www.webhouse.cz/hdj) boasts a brand new **theatre** building, and though it usually puts on plays, it does stage the occasional classical or jazz **concert**.

Žďár nad Sázavou

The highest point in the Bohemian-Moravian Uplands, or Vysočina, is around 40km northeast of Jihlava, though the whole range is actually more like a high rolling plateau. This has always been a poor region, but one really good reason for venturing into the hinterland is to visit **ŽĎÁR NAD SÁZAVOU** (Ⓦ www.zdarns.cz), established in the thirteenth century as a small settlement pitched near its Cistercian monastery. Since World War II the population has increased tenfold, making it one of the largest towns in the region, producing, among other things, ice skates. The only thing worth seeing, however, is the **monastery** complex, a three-kilometre walk (or short bus ride) north through the grey new town of Žďár – instructive if nothing else. As you approach the woods and fish ponds, there's a small bridge decorated with the familiar figures of eighteenth-century saints, on the other side of which is the monastery now back in the hands of the Kinský family.

The whole complex is the work of **Giovanni Santini** (who also had a hand in the monasteries of Plasy and Kladruby, near Plzeň), perhaps the most gifted architect of the Czech Counter-Reformation. His two great talents were marrying Gothic and Baroque forms in a new and creative way, and producing buildings with a humour and irony often lacking in eighteenth-century architecture. The monastery church isn't a particularly good example, but keys from the monastic office (daily: April–June, Sept & Oct 8am–4pm; July & Aug 9am–5pm), to the right of it, will allow you access to one that is: the UNESCO-protected **Zelená hora** (Green Hill) pilgrimage church, up through the wooded hill to the south of the monastery. It's a unique and intriguing structure, with zigzag cemetery walls forming a decagon of cloisters around the central star-shaped church, a giant mushroom sprouting a half-formed, almost Byzantine dome, dedicated to sv Jan Nepomucký (St John of Nepomuk). The interior is filled with details of his martyrdom, along with symbolic and numerical references to the saint and the Cistercians. On the pulpit, a gilded relief depicts his being thrown off the Charles Bridge in Prague by the king's men, while everywhere in macabre repetition are the saint's severed tongue and the stars that appeared above his head: above the pulpit, on the ceiling, in the shapes of the windows, and in the five side chapels.

Back in the main part of the monastery there's a **Muzeum knihy** (Book Museum), and a small exhibition dedicated to Santini (April & Oct Sat & Sun 8am–4pm; May, June & Sept Tues–Sun 8am–4pm; July & Aug Tues–Sun 9am–5pm), housed in the stables he himself designed, with swirling zigzag patterning on the ceiling. Packed with plans and photos of his other works in the Czech Lands, the exhibition traces Santini's influences and places him in the wider context of European architecture of the time. For more on Santini's work in the Žďár area, see the box opposite.

Santini in the Žďár region

A number of Santini's lighthearted minor buildings are dotted about the Žďár region. The first, a couple of hundred yards further north of the Cistercian monastery in Žďár, is the eerie **dolní hřbitov** (lower cemetery), whose three simple chapels symbolize the Trinity. Built to accommodate plague victims who never materialized, the grave-less space is empty but for a lonesome angel calling the tune for Judgement Day, and is enclosed by the gentle ripples of the cemetery walls.

Down the road at **Ostrov nad Oslavou** (7min by train), using a similar design to the one he employed in the chateau at Chlumec nad Cidlinou, Santini built a *hostinec* in the shape of a "W" in memory of his local patron, the Abbot of Žďár, Václav Vejmluva (the initials W.W. in German). It has seen a lot of use and abuse over the years, but is still the local boozer: buy a pint and appreciate the architecture at leisure.

Just 2km northeast of Ostrov and within easy walking distance, the local church at **Obyčtov** is another Santini design, built in the shape of a turtle, one of the Virgin Mary's more obscure symbols. Four chapels mark each leg, a presbytery the neck, and the west onion-domed tower the distorted head. Ask around for the key to the whitewashed interior, which features more turtle symbolism.

Practicalities

Žďár is only an hour's fast train ride from Brno; the town centre is 1km north of the train station, and it's another 2km to the monastery. It's easy to get a room in the town, whose **hotels** include the characterful *U labutě* (☎566 622 949, ⓦ www.oxygen.cz/u-labute; ❷), on the main square, and the less prepossessing high-rise *Hotelový dům Morava* (☎566 630 277; ❷), just below the square. There's a decent *hostinec* called *Teferna*, serving *Starobrno*, by the monastery, and, a little further up the road, the *Pilská nádrž* lakeside **campsite** (May–Sept).

The Slovácko region

What the Labe basin is to the Bohemians, the **Slovácko region**, around the plains of the River Morava 50km east of Brno, is to the Moravians. They settled in this fertile land around the late eighth century, taking their name from the river and eventually lending it to the short-lived Great Moravian Empire, the first coherent political unit in the region to be ruled by Slavs and the subject of intense archeological research (and controversy) over the last forty years. Geographically, the River Morava (along with the River Odra further north) forms a natural corridor between east and west, difficult to defend against intruders and consequently trashed by numerous armies marching their way across Europe, from the Turks to the Tatars. Nowadays, at various different points, the Morava forms the border between Slovakia and Austria, then, moving north, Moravia and Slovakia.

Ethnically, it's a grey area where Moravians and Slovaks happily coexist – the local dialect and customs virtually indistinguishable from West Slovakia – despite the new cross-border restrictions now in place. Tomáš Garrigue Masaryk, the country's founder and first president, hailed from here, and his mixed parentage – his mother was German-speaking, his father a Slovak peasant – was typical of the region in the nineteenth century. For the visitor, though, it's a dour, mostly undistinguished landscape – flat, low farming country, with just the occasional factory or ribbon village to break the monotony – and most people pass through en route to more established sights. In summer this can be a great mistake, for almost every village in the area has its own folk festival, and in early autumn the local wine caves are bursting with life and ready to demonstrate the region's legendary and lavish hospitality.

Uherské Hradiště and around

The industrial town of **UHERSKÉ HRADIŠTĚ** (Ungarisch-Hradisch), like many towns on the Morava, has made a remarkable recovery after the devastating floods of 1997. The town sees few visitors at the best of times, and the only reason travellers stray into its shapeless centre is in their search for the **Památník Velké Moravy** (April–Oct Tues–Fri 8.30am–4.30pm, Sat & Sun 8.30am–noon & 1–5pm), suspected site of the capital of the Great Moravian Empire, which is actually north of the centre, across the Morava, on Jezuitská in a part of town known confusingly as Staré Město (10min by foot, or bus #4 to the second stop after the bridge). The archeological remains, housed in what looks like a concrete bunker from the last war, include the foundations of a ninth-century church, discovered in 1949, and a lot of bones and broken crockery – a specialist's paradise, but less gripping for the rest of us.

A more accessible load of old rocks, along with a good selection of folk costumes and suchlike, is on display at the **Slovácké muzeum** (daily 9am–noon & 12.30–5pm) in the Smetanovy sady, to the east of town. The obligatory Jesuit church aside, the town's only other sight as such is the late Baroque **apothecary U zlaté koruny** on the main square; it's still functioning as a *lékárna* (pharmacy), and you can peep through into the frescoed back room.

Arriving at Uherské Hradiště by **bus**, simply walk west along Velehradská třída to the centre; arriving by train is more complicated – **trains** travelling north or south tend to arrive at Staré Město u Uherského Hradiště on the north bank of the river (bus #4 into town), while trains from the east or west arrive in the southern suburb of Kunovice (bus #2 into town). The more central Uherské Hradiště station, southwest of the main square, is only served by the occasional shuttle service between the two (or bus #1). When choosing a **hotel**, you might as well stay at the *Grand* (☎572 551 511, ℮hotel@grand.uh.cz; ❷) on Palackého náměstí, the best the town has to offer; the same management team runs the plainer *Morava* on Šafaříkova (☎572 551 508, ℱ572 552 975; ❷). Uherské Hradiště's **cinema**, Kino Hvězda, on náměstí

The apostles of the Slavs

The significance of saints **Cyril** (827–69) and **Methodius** (815–85) goes far beyond their mere canonization. Brothers from a wealthy family in Constantinople, they were sent as missionaries to the Great Moravian Empire in 863 at the invitation of its ruler, Rastislav, less for reasons of piety than to assert his independence from his German neighbours. Thrust headlong into a political minefield, they were given a hard time by the local German clergy, and had to retreat to Rome, where Cyril became a monk and died. Methodius, meanwhile, insisted on returning to Moravia, only to be imprisoned for two years at the instigation of the German bishops. The pope eventually got him released, but dragged him back to Rome to answer charges of heterodoxy. He was cleared of all charges, consecrated bishop of Pannonia and Moravia, and continued to teach in the vernacular until his death in 885.

More important than their achievements in converting the local populace was the fact that they preached in the tongue of the common people. Cyril in particular is regarded as the founder of Slavonic literature, having been accredited with single-handedly inventing the Glagolitic script, still used in the Eastern Church and the basis of the modern Cyrillic alphabet that takes his name, while Methodius is venerated by both Western and Eastern Christians as a pioneer of the vernacular liturgy and a man dedicated to ecumenism. After Methodius' death, his followers were duly chased out and forced to take refuge in Bulgaria. The Czech Lands and most of Slovakia came under Rome's sway once and for all, and had to wait until the end of the fourteenth century before they once more heard their own language used to preach the gospel.

Míru, puts on a good range of mainstream and art-house movies, stages exhibitions, and puts on a low-key film festival in April. It's also worth checking out what's on at *Klub Mír*, on náměstí Míru, which organizes a surprisingly good mix of **gigs**.

Velehrad

The **Cistercian monastery** at **VELEHRAD**, just 9km across the fields from Uherské Hradiště, is one of the most important pilgrimage sites in the Czech Republic. It's an impressive sight, too, with the twin ochre towers of its **church** (daily 9am–5pm) set against the backdrop of the Chřiby hills, a low beech-covered ridge that separates Brno from the Morava basin.

The monastery's importance as an object of pilgrimage derives from the belief (now proved to be false) that it was the seat of St Methodius' archbishopric, the first in the Slav Lands, and the place where he died on July 5, 885 (see box above). The 1100th anniversary of this last fact attracted over 150,000 pilgrims from across Czechoslovakia in 1985, the largest single, unofficial gathering in the country since the first anniversary of the Soviet invasion in August 1969 (July 5 is now a national holiday). Five years later, Velehrad entertained Pope John Paul II, and half a million people turned up.

There's certainly something about the place that sets it apart, whether it's the historical associations, the sheer magnificence of its High Baroque, or its strange limitless emptiness outside of the annual pilgrimage. The church owes its gigantic scale to the foundations of the original Romanesque church on which it's built. This burned down in 1681 after being sacked several times by marauding Protestants, but you can visit its remains in the crypt's **lapidárium** (9am–noon & 1–4pm: April–Sept daily; Oct & Nov Tues–Sun). Inside the church itself, the finer points of the artistry may be lacking in finesse, but the faded glory of the frescoed nave, suffused with a pink-grey light and empty but for the bent old women who come here for their daily prayers, is bewilderingly powerful.

There's a new **hotel**, *Hotel Mlýn Velehrad* (☎572 571 460, ⓔhotel-mlyn@hitech.cz; ❹), and a **campsite** (April–Oct) 1.5km up the road to Šalas, and the village is served by regular buses from Uherské Hradiště.

Buchlovice and Buchlov

Four kilometres west of Velehrad, still just out of reach of the Chřiby hills, is the village of **BUCHLOVICE** (Buchlowitz), easily accessible by bus from Uherské Hradiště. The reason for coming here is to see the Berchtolds' pretty little eighteenth-century **zámek** (April & Oct Tues–Sun 9am–noon & 1–4pm; May, June & Sept Tues–Sun 9am–noon & 1–5pm; July & Aug daily 9am–noon & 1–6pm), a warm and hospitable country house with a lovely arboretum bursting with rhododendrons, fuschias and peacocks. The house, composed of two symmetrically opposed semicircles around a central octagon, has been recently renovated, and the smallish suite of rooms still contains most of its original Rococo furniture, left behind by the family when they fled to Austria in 1945. Another prize exhibit abandoned in haste was a leaf from the tree beneath which Mary Queen of Scots was executed.

A stiff three-and-a-half-kilometre climb up into the forest of the Chřiby hills will take you to the Gothic hrad of **Buchlov** (May & June Tues–Sun 8am–5pm; July & Aug daily 9am–6pm; Sept Tues–Sun 9am–4pm), which couldn't be more dissimilar. In bad weather, as the mist whips round the bastions, it's hard to imagine a more forbidding place, but in summer the view over the treetops is terrific and the whole place has a cool, breezy feel to it. Founded as a royal seat by the Přemyslids in the thirteenth century, it has suffered none of the painful neo-Gothicizing of other medieval castles – in fact the Berchtolds had turned it into a museum as early as the late nineteenth century. Heavy, rusty keys open up a series of sparsely furnished rooms lit only by thin slit windows, and dungeons in which the Habsburgs used to confine the odd rebellious Hungarian. If you're on for a bit of hiking, the stillness and extraordinary beauty of the surrounding beech forests are difficult to match, but make sure you stock up with provisions as there are few shops in the area. There's a restaurant in the castle, and the *Smraďavka* **campsite** (April–Oct) is 2km southeast of Buchlovice.

Strážnice and around

For most of the year **STRÁŽNICE** (Strassnitz), 20km or so southwest of Uherské Hradiště, sees perhaps a handful of visitors, but on the last weekend of June thousands converge on this unexceptional town for the annual **International Folk Festival** – the largest in the country – held in three purpose-built stadiums in the grounds of the local chateau. During the festival, hotels are booked solid for miles around, and the only thing to do is to bring your own tent and try to squeeze onto the castle campsite (April–Oct) or just crash out somewhere in your sleeping bag.

If you're here at any other time of the year, there's only enough to keep you occupied for an hour or two. Though no work of art itself, the **zámek**, ten minutes' walk north of the centre, off the road to Bzeneč, contains an exceptionally good **folk museum** (May–Oct Tues–Sun 8am–5pm), part of the Institute of Folk Art. En route to the chateau, you'll pass the town's excellent **skanzen** (times as above), called variously Muzeum v přírodě or Muzeum vesnice jihovýchodní Moravy, with numerous restored thatched, timber-built cottages and peasant gear from the outlying villages.

The **train station** is five minutes' walk south of the town centre. Outside of the festival, it should be easy enough **to stay** at the *Strážnice Flag Hotel* (☎518 332 059, ℗518 332 098; ❷), which has comfortable en-suite rooms. The best place for a **meal** and to sample local wines is *Zámecká vinárna* in the chateau, with live music at weekends; the *Na rynku*, on the main square, is a decent pub serving *Starobrno* beer.

Wine caves and festivals around Strážnice

Strážnice makes a good base for visiting the private *sklepy* or **wine caves** that provide the focus of village life in the summer months before and after the grape harvest. Perhaps the easiest *sklepy* to visit for those without their own transport are the Plže caves at **PETROV**, a thin settlement strung out along the main road from Hodonín, one stop down the railway line from Strážnice. Hidden from sight, on the other side of the railway track, are around twenty whitewashed stone caves over two hundred years old, some beautifully decorated with intricate floral designs, others with just a simple deep-blue stripe. Around late September there are usually one or two locals overseeing their new harvest who'll be happy to show you around and no doubt invite you to sample (and of course buy) some of their wine. During the rest of the summer, merrymaking goes on in the evenings at weekends. Those with their own transport and a taste for the stuff could check out Polesovice, 12km north, or Mutěnice, 15km west, or better still the thatched *sklepy* at Prušánky.

There are countless other festivals in the area, such as the Dolmácké festival, held every four years in Hluk (next one is in 2005), and pilgrimages to places like Blatnice, held in September. The most famous festival of the lot after Strážnice is the annual *Jízda králů* or "Ride of the Kings" held over the weekend of Whitsuntide (the last Sunday in May) in **VLČNOV**, which lies south of route 50 between Uherské Hradiště and the pistol-producing town of Uherský Brod. Young villagers in traditional folk costumes ride through the town on horseback, and folk concerts and dances are staged all weekend.

Luhačovice

Twenty-seven kilometres east of Uherské Hradiště is the genteel spa town of **LUHAČOVICE**, decidedly lush after the rather demure Morava valley but without the pomp and majesty of the west Bohemian spas. Although its springs are mentioned as far back as the twelfth century, nothing much was done about developing the place until it was bought up in 1902 and building began on the first of Slovak Dušan Jurkovič's quirky, folksy, half-timbered villas, which have become the spa's hallmark.

The largest of these buildings, the **Dům Dušana Jurkoviče**, dominates the central spa gardens spreading northeast from the train station. The beams are purely decorative, occasionally breaking out into a swirling flourish, and the roof is a playful pagoda-type affair, creating a uniquely Slovak folk version of Art Nouveau. The blot on Luhačovice's copybook is the new **Kolonáda**, a graceless curving concrete colonnade that's nevertheless a good place to sit and watch the patients pass by as they sip the waters from their grotesquely decorated mugs. The rest of the spa forms a snake-like promenade boxed in by shrubs and trees, with folksy bridges spanning the gently trickling river. Soon enough you hit another cluster of Jurkovič buildings, one of which is the open-air natural spring **swimming pool**, good for a cheap, unchlorinated dip. The villas continue into the leafy suburbs, but unless you fancy a hike into the surrounding woods or are staying at the lakeside **campsite** 1km up the main road (mid-April to Sept), there's no reason to continue walking. If you're interested in finding out more about the folk traditions of the area, and the history of the spa, hop across to the west bank of the stream to the museum in the **Vila Lipová** (April–Oct Tues–Sun 9am–noon & 1–5pm, Nov & March Thurs only 9am–noon & 1–4pm).

To get to Luhačovice by train from Uherské Hradiště, you need to change at Uherský Brod; buses run direct, but less frequently. The **bus** and **train stations** are at the southwestern end of the spa. Reasonable **accommodation** can be found all over the spa, but call ahead as Luhačovice is a popular regional getaway. The pension-style *Hotel Lužná* (T & F 577 131 112; ❸) is very central, just south of the spa proper on Solné. *Dům Bedřicha Smetany* (T 577 682 111, W www.LazneLuhacovice.cz; ❸) is a more traditional spa hotel, in a pleasing manor house set in its own grounds. Although buses from all over the country run regular services to Luhačovice, it's still a bit out on a limb, stuck halfway up the Šťávnice Valley. If you're planning to continue into Slovakia, however, the scenic train journey from Uherský Brod through the White Carpathians to Trenčianska Teplá is as good a way as any to get there.

Zlín

Hidden in a gentle green valley east of the Morava, **ZLÍN** is one of the most fascinating Moravian towns. Despite appearances, it's not just another factory town, it is *the* factory town – a museum of functionalist architecture and the inspiration of one man, **Tomáš Baťa** (pronounced "Batya"). When Baťa founded his company in 1894 with his brother and sister, Zlín's population was less than 3000. Now, with suburbs trailing for miles along the River Dřevnice, it's approaching 90,000. The town's heyday was during the First Republic, when Baťa planned and started to build the ultimate production-line city, a place where workers would be provided with good housing, schooling, leisure facilities and a fair wage. "Work collectively, live individually" was one of Baťa's favourite aphorisms, and all along the approach roads to the town centre you can see the red-brick shoe-box houses that Baťa constructed for his workers as "temporary accommodation" – houses which have lasted better than anything built after 1948. The combined effects of Allied bombing, nationalization and economic stagnation have left only a hint of the model garden city Baťa had in mind. Zlín can't hope to appeal to everyone's aesthetic tastes, but it does present an entirely different side of the country from the usual provincial medieval staré město.

Some history

Son of a local cobbler, Tomáš Baťa worked his way up from nothing to become the First Republic's most famous millionaire. He grew rich supplying the Austro-Hungarian army with its boots during World War I, and between the wars quickly became the largest manufacturer of shoes in the world, producing over 50 million pairs annually. Baťa became the town's mayor in 1923, but died in a plane crash in 1932 at the peak of his power, and although his work was continued by his son (also called Tomáš), the firm and most of the family were forced to leave the country in 1938. Tomáš junior elected to go to

Map labels:
N
K PASEKÁM
SMETANOVA
TYRSOVO NÁBR.
Baťa's villa
River Dřevnice
BENEŠOVO NÁBR.
VODNÍ
ZÁRÁMÍ
Zlín-Dlouhá train station
DLOUHÁ
KVÍTKOVÁ
Zlín-střed train station
NÁMĚSTÍ MÍRU
GAHUROVÁ
Zámek
B i
Bus Station
C D
Městské divadlo
OSVOBODITELŮ
ŠTEFÁNIKOVA
Shoe Factory
TŘÍDA TOMÁŠE BATI
ŠTEFÁNIKOVA
Obuvnické muzeum
TŘÍDA TOMÁŠE BATI
HRADSKÁ
Obchodní dům
1
NÁMĚSTÍ PRÁCE
Velké kino
2
MOSTNÍ
NÁMĚSTÍ T. G. MASARYKA
HRADSKÁ
KOTĚROVA
BŘEZNICKÁ
Otrokovice
Slušovice
Dům umění
0   100 m

ACCOMMODATION
Garní 1
Moskva 2
RESTAURANTS & CAFÉS
Café Corso D
Kafírna Archa B
Pizzeria U čapa A
Valtická hospůdka C

6

Canada, taking his own management team (100 families) and shoemaking machinery with him. There, he quickly set about building another model factory town, known as Bataville, just outside Ottawa, and the company continued to expand into the vast multinational it is today; much of its production now takes place in low-cost Asia.

Nationalization in 1945 robbed Baťa of the company's spiritual home, and in 1949 zealous Party hacks added insult to injury by renaming the town Gottwaldov after the country's notorious first Communist president, Klement Gottwald, also known as the "Stalinist butcher". It was no doubt seen as a just revenge on Baťa, who rid his shop floor of Communists by decree in the 1920s. When the Communists fell from power in November 1989, Tomáš junior paid his first visit to Zlín for over forty years, and the whole town turned out to greet him, draping banners out of their windows proclaiming "ať žije Zlín" ("Long live Zlín"). In 1990 the town once more became officially known as Zlín, but due to alleged Nazi collaboration by members of his family, Baťa was unable to reclaim the factory through restitution. Nevertheless, Baťa now has a significant stake in the shoe market, with numerous outlets across the country, including the flagship modernist store on Wenceslas Square in Prague.

The Town

Baťa was a longstanding patron of modern art that he felt would reflect the thrust and modernity of his own business. In 1911 he had his own **villa** built on the north side of the river by the leading Czech architect of the time, Jan Kotěra; it's a very understated affair, virtually devoid of ornamentation, and now institutionalized. In the late 1920s Le Corbusier was called in to design the town, but after an abortive sketch of the place, this chance of a lifetime fell to local-born architect **František Gahura**, who had studied under Kotěra.

Unlike any other town in the country, Zlín does not revolve around the local chateau or marketplace but around the **shoe factory** itself, its sixteen-storey administrative offices designed by one of Gahura's assistants, the Slovene Vladimír Karfík. The style – concrete frame, red-brick infill and plate-glass windows – was intended to be "the leitmotif of Zlín's architecture", as Gahura put it, and is indeed typical of all the town's original 1930s buildings, later copied and barbarized by undistinguished postwar architects. Baťa's own office was a huge, air-conditioned, glass-encased lift, capable of visiting every floor. Nowadays, as well as serving as the corporation's administration office, it houses Zlín's main "sight", the Shoe Museum or **Obuvnické muzeum** (April–Oct Tues–Sun 10am–noon & 1–5pm, Nov–March Tues–Fri only). Even if you're not a foot fetishist, it's a wonderful 1930s-style museum, with shoes from all over the world from medieval *boty* to the sad attempts of the Communist Svit factory in Zlín, plus a "revised" final section on Baťa himself, and, tucked away in one corner, the old man's fantastic lift/office. It's also worth asking if you can see the museum's video on the architectural development of the town.

From out of the factory grounds rises the obligatory red-and-white-striped chimney, industriously spewing black smoke over the town – in its own way a reassuring guarantee of further employment (half the local workforce is employed by the company). When the siren goes at 2pm for the end of the day shift, workers pour out of the factory gates and onto the trolleybuses, as if part of some strange Orwellian dumb show. Directly opposite the main entrance, across třída Tomáše Bati, is Karfík's plate-glass department store, **Obchodní dům**, which naturally includes a shoe shop (the country still led the world in one respect in 1989 – in shoe consumption, which stood at an annual rate of 4.2 pairs per capita). Beyond here, on náměstí Práce (literally "Work Square"), lies Gahura's 1931 **Velké kino**, which holds 2000 movie-goers – now unfortunately redone with new white vinyl siding, it's undistinguished – and the eleven-storey Společenský dům, built by Karfík and Lorenz in 1932–33 and now occupied by the **Hotel Moskva**.

Gahura's master plan was never fully realized, and much of the town is accidental and ill-conceived. Only the sloping green of **náměstí T.G. Masaryka**, flanked by more boxy buildings, gives some idea of the trajectory of Gahura's ideas. The first block on the left is Gahura's Masarykovy školy, where Baťa pursued his revolutionary teaching methods still admired today. At the top of this leafy space is the **Dům umění** (Tues–Sun 9am–5pm), designed by Gahura in 1932 as a memorial to Baťa, where his (recently re-erected) statue, some memorabilia, and the wreckage of the biplane in which he crashed, used to stand. It now serves as the concert hall for the town's orchestra and for exhibitions of contemporary art – appropriate enough, given Baťa's tireless patronage of the **avant-garde**, which he not only utilized in his photographic advertising but also produced in the film studios that were built here between the wars, where many of the country's renowned animation films are still made.

The only other place of interest is the modest country **zámek** (Tues–Sun 9am–noon & 1–5pm) in the park opposite the factory, which houses the town's **Muzeum jihovýchodní Moravy** (South Moravian Museum) boasting a small, but excellent collection of **twentieth-century Czech art**, ranging from the Cubists Kubišta, Filla, Čapek and Procházka, to wacky Pop Art sculptures from the 1960s and more contemporary works.

Lastly, Zlín is the birthplace of two unlikely bedfellows: the not so avant-garde playwright **Tom Stoppard** and New York magnate, Donald Trump's ex-wife, Ivana. Stoppard's father was a Czech doctor by the name of Eugene Straussler, who fled with his wife and two-year-old son to Singapore to escape the Nazis. After his father's death, Tom's mother married a major in the British army (named Stoppard) and settled in England. These two snippets explain two otherwise puzzling points: why Stoppard has a slight foreign accent and why the Tom Stoppard Prize is given to Czech or Slovak authors in translation. **Ivana Trump** (Trumpová to the Czechs) was born here as Ivana Zelníčková, and rose to fame in her home country in the 1972 Olympic ski team. Her shocking blonde hair and formidable physique allowed her to pursue a modelling career in Canada before making the headlines as wife (and now ex-wife) of New York tycoon Donald Trump.

Practicalities

Arriving at Zlín's **train station** (Zlín-střed) or **bus terminal**, you're just a few minutes' walk from the centre and everything there is to see. The **tourist office** (Mon–Fri 8am–5pm, Sat 8am–noon; ☎577 214 138), in the radnice on náměstí Míru, should be able to help with any enquiries. **Accommodation** is uniformly overpriced, catering mostly for business clientele. At one time, *the* hotel to stay at was Gahura's high-rise *Hotel Moskva* (☎577 561 111, ✉3moskva_zlin@motylek.com; ❸), on náměstí Práce, though it's become something of an all-purpose building with offices, pseudo-glitzy shops and the centre of the town's fairly dubious nightlife. Next door, you can enjoy the gleaming white decor – and less fuss – of the *Hotel Garní* (☎577 211 941; ❸) for the same price.

Zlín does have a decent selection of **restaurants** and cafés. *Valtická hospůdka*, by náměstí Míru on třída Tomáše Bati, is a pleasant place for steak and potatoes, beer and Moravian wine. *Café Corso* (closed Sun), down the street and above the Česká spořitelna, has a good vegetarian selection and the usual Czech staples. Right by the tourist office, *Kafírna Archa* is a cool little coffee spot with computers linked to the **internet**. There's also a good pizzeria, *U čápa*, by the river on Benešovo nábřeží, east of Dlouhá. Avoiding the casino and disco in the *Moskva*, and the tacky *Flip* disco in the Dům kultury, your choices for **nightlife** boil down to watching a film in the cavernous Velké kino, listening to the local philharmonic orchestra in the Dům uměni, and catching a band or playing ten-pin bowling at the *Golem* on náměstí Práce.

Otrokovice

An alternative Baťa experience can be had in neighbouring **OTROKOVICE**, 11km west of Zlín, by the River Morava. As is evident from the architecture, this is another Baťa town, built as an extension of Zlín in the 1930s – in fact the town was originally named Baťov, and was only renamed Otrokovice (after *otrok*, meaning "slave") by the Communists. Despite the overwhelming presence of the local factory (in this case Barum), Otrokovice works better than Zlín as a planned "garden city". At its centre is the Constructivist *Společenský dům*, Karfík's three-winged radial building in reinforced concrete, shaped rather like the sails of a windmill.

The nearest **campsite** to Zlín is the *Pahrbek* site (open all year), 7km south of (and one stop down the line from) Otrokovice in **NAPAJEDLA**, on the River Morava.

Kroměříž and around

KROMĚŘÍŽ (Kremsier), 30km or so up the Morava from Uherské Hradiště and seat of the bishops of Olomouc from the Middle Ages to the nineteenth century, is one of Moravia's most graceful towns. Its once-powerful German-speaking population has long since gone, and nowadays the town feels pleasantly provincial, famous only for its Moravian male-voice choir and folk music tradition. Though quiet, Kroměříž is definitely worth a day-trip, if only for the chateau's rich collections and the town's very beautiful and extensive gardens.

Savagely set upon by the Swedish army in the Thirty Years' War, Kroměříž was rebuilt by order of **Prince-Bishop Karl Eusebius von Liechtenstein-Kastelcorn**, a pathological builder (see p.352) and a member of the richest dynasty in Moravia at the time. Vast sums of money were spent not only on hiring Italian architects, but also on enriching the chateau's art collection and establishing a musical life to rival Vienna. Liechtenstein founded a college for choristers, maintained a thirty-piece court orchestra and employed a series of prestigious *Kapellmeister*, though nowadays, aside from the chateau's extensive archives, there's little evidence of the courtly life.

The old town

Set back from the banks of the River Morava, the centre of the staré město is the former marketplace of **Velké náměstí**. A broad, gracious square, its sea of cobblestones is interrupted only by the lime trees that surround a gilded plague column and fountain (there's an even better column and fountain ensemble on

Riegrovo náměstí). Arcades have survived here and there round the square, the radnice has a fine white Renaissance tower, and the houses themselves, though they have suffered over the years, are now prettily painted up. Jánská, just off the square, hides the town's finest ensemble: a flourish of terraced canons' houses with bright Empire frontages in primary colours.

Arcibiskupský zámek

The houses at the northern corner of Velké náměstí part to reveal the **Arcibiskupský zámek** (Archbishop's Palace; April & Oct Sat & Sun 9am–5pm; May–Sept Tues–Sun 9am–5pm, July & Aug until 6pm; ⓦ www.azz.cz), a vast Baroque fortress whose severity is relieved only by the fifteenth-century lanterned tower, sole survivor of the Swedes' rampage in the Thirty Years' War. Inside, the chateau is a more gentle Rococo than its uncompromising exterior might suggest. The dark wood and marble decor of the small **Manský sál**, where the bishops held court, is overwhelmed by Maulbertsch's celebratory frescoes, which bear down on guests from the unusually low ceiling. The archbishop's bedroom rather alarmingly contains a double bed – the official story being that it was for his parents when they came to visit.

The showpiece of the palace is the fiddly white-and-gold excess of the **Sněmovní sál**, as high and mighty as anything in Prague, and featured in Miloš Forman's film *Amadeus*. In the first three months of 1849, Reichstag delegates from all parts of the Habsburg Empire met to thrash out a new liberal constitution in the face of the revolutionary events of the previous year. In the end, though, the "Kremsier Constitution" that came out of these brainstorming sessions and acknowledged "equality of national rights", was unceremoniously ditched by the new imperial government, who drew up their own version. Police were sent to Kremsier to close down the Reichstag, with orders to arrest the most radical delegates. The Habsburgs' final bout of absolutism had begun.

After – or instead of – the main guided tour (*trasa 1 – historické sály*) you can visit the **Zámecká obrazárna** (Chateau Gallery), which contains what's left of the Liechtensteins' vast art collection, still the best selection of sixteenth- and seventeenth-century European paintings in Moravia. There's plenty of bucolic frolicking supplied by the Flemish masters, including an earthy Breughel, a *trompe l'oeil* Hoogstraten, and a more sober portrait of Charles I of England and his wife Henrietta by Van Dyck. Others worth noting are Veronese's awestruck bearded *Apostles*, Cranach's richly coloured and exquisitely executed, but gruesome, *Beheading of St John the Baptist* (with a cute dog lapping up the spillage), and the gallery's prize possession, *Apollo Punishing Marsyas*, a late Titian, with characteristically loose brushwork, and yet another dog slurping up the remains.

Another minor episcopal sight is the **Biskupská mincovna** (times as above), round the back of the chateau, now a well laid-out museum, though really only of specialist interest. At the height of their powers in the seventeenth century, the Bishops of Olomouc minted their own coins, and commemorative coins are still struck to this day.

The rest of the old town

Like Olomouc (see p.385), Kroměříž is a place as rich in gardens as in buildings. The watery **Podzámecká zahrada** (daily dawn–dusk), established by one of the green-fingered Chotek family who held the archbishopric in the 1830s, stretches right down to the Morava, covering an area twice the size of the old town. Having long since lost its formality, it's now a pleasantly unruly park, reeking of wild garlic in spring and hiding an aviary and menagerie, harbouring raccoons, baboons and parrots, plus a deer park and a few stalking peacocks.

Ten minutes' walk west of the chateau is the early Baroque **Květná zahrada** (Mon–Fri 7.30am–6.30pm, Sat & Sun 9am–noon & 1–5pm), more formal but also more beautiful and generally in a better state of repair. The garden was laid out by the Liechtensteins in the 1670s, "ten years and no expense spared" as the Latin inscription reminds you. Its finest vista is the Neoclassical colonnade along the garden's north side, with each of the 46 columns topped by a Roman bust. There are chestnut and lime hedges and tall avenues of trees, plus two waist-high mazes and a wonderful greenhouse filled with orchids, palm and cacti. At the centre stands a huge domed **rotunda**, thickly stuccoed and gaudily frescoed by Italian artists, and featuring mini-grottoes stuffed with satyrs and strange wild creatures. Equally remarkable is the **Foucault pendulum**, suspended from the ceiling, which, as the guide proudly tells you, is one of only four in the world.

The **Muzeum Kroměřížska** (Tues–Sun 9am–noon & 1–5pm), on the main square, puts on temporary art exhibitions, and contains a large collection of work by Max Švabinský, a late-nineteenth-century artist and graphicist who was born at Panská 11 in 1872. There's no denying his skill nor his prolific output, but he's a mite too gushy and Romantic for some people's tastes, and the drawings of nudes and tigers, not to mention his collection of exotic butterflies and stuffed birds, displayed here are unlikely to make many new converts. Of the town's churches, the Gothic sv Mořic is the oldest, but its innards were ripped out by fire in 1836 and rebuilt without much feeling. A better bet is the Baroque church of **sv Jan Křtitel** at the top of Jánská, whose sensuous lines and frescoed oval dome combine to form one of the showpieces of Moravian Baroque.

Lastly, it's worth wandering round to Moravcova in the easternmost corner of the old town, which was formerly the Jewish ghetto. Jewish communities in places like Kroměříž, Uherské Hradiště and Prostějov were among the largest in the Czech Lands before World War II, and since they provided many essential services the local bigwigs left them alone. The **Židovská radnice** (Jewish Town Hall) in Moravcova – one of the few outside Prague – is remarkable not for its architectural beauty but for its mere existence, the result of a magnanimous gesture by the prince-bishop for services rendered in the Thirty Years' War; today it serves as a local cultural centre and gives little hint of its previous life.

Practicalities

The **train station** is on the opposite bank of the River Morava from the chateau gardens; head down Vejvanovského to reach the old town. The local **tourist office** (Mon–Fri 8am–6pm, Sat 9am–1pm, Sun 9am–noon; Ⓦwww.kromeriz.cz) is at Kovářská 1 and can arrange private rooms. The **accommodation** scene in Kroměříž is pretty limited, with a choice between the *Hotel Bouček* (Ⓣ573 342 777; ❹), on the main square, and the *Pension na jízdárně*, on Štěchovice (Ⓣ573 342 175; ❷), which has basic rooms above a pizzeria near the Květná zahrada. A good place to eat is the *Radniční sklípek*, Kovářská 20 (closed Sun), a wine **restaurant** in the cellars of the town hall, serving delicious food and a good range of wines from Valtice. The *Central* on the main square is back in business with a very pleasant restaurant on the ground floor and weekend dances in the café upstairs, and there's also a decent pizzeria beside the *Bouček*. To pick up and send emails, head for the **internet café** *U m@xe*, near the museum. You can buy the local **wine** and have a tour of the cellars at the *Arcibiskupské vinné sklepy*, behind the archway beside the chateau.

Holešov

HOLEŠOV (Holleschau), 15km northeast on route 432 (and just 15min by train), makes an interesting day-trip from Kroměříž. The town had one of the largest Jewish communities in Moravia, peaking at around 1700 in the mid-nineteenth century. It also has the dubious distinction of being a victim of the last Jewish pogrom on Czech soil in December 1918, during which two Jews were killed. The old ghetto lies to the northwest of the town square, náměstí dr. E. Beneše, centred on the bulky **Šachova synagoga** (Tues–Sun 9am–noon & 1–5pm), on Příční. Built in 1560, the synagogue retains its remarkably ornate eighteenth-century interior, with scallop shells and floral stucco on the ceiling, and ornate wrought-iron filigree work around the bimah. On the second floor there's an exhibition on, and a few relics from, the town's Jewish history, a model of the old ghetto gateway which was demolished in 1906, and of the new synagogue which was burned down in World War II by Czech collaborators. Further north, in a kink of the River Rusava, lies the **Jewish cemetery** (Židovský hřbitov), with graves dating back to 1647, including – enclosed within a protective glass case – the tomb of Rabbi Shabtai ben Meir Kohen, known as Shakh (after whom the synagogue is named). The town's seventeenth-century, dry-moated **zámek**, off the main square, is closed to the public, but its neglected formal French gardens are accessbile (daily 8am–5.30pm).

Travel details

Trains	Buses
Connections with Prague: Brno (hourly; 2hr 50min–3hr 30min); Žďár nad Sázavou (7 daily; 2hr 20min–3hr).	**Connections with Prague:** Brno (hourly; 2hr); Znojmo (up to 2 daily; 3hr).
Brno to: Blansko (hourly; 20–30min); Bratislava (8 daily; 2hr); Bučovice (every 2hr; 40min); České Budějovice (3 daily; 4hr 30min); Jihlava (hourly; 2hr–2hr 40min); Kroměříž (4 daily; 1hr 20min); Liberec (1 daily; 6hr); Moravský Krumlov (every 2hr; 45min–1hr); Náměšť nad Oslavou (hourly; 50min–1hr 20min); Olomouc (up to 6 daily; 1hr 40min); Pardubice (every 2hr; 1hr 40min); Slavkov (every 2hr; 25min); Třebíč (hourly; 1hr 15min–1hr 45min); Vienna (4 daily; 1hr 45min); Žďár nad Sázavou (every 1–2hr; 1hr–1hr 40min); Znojmo (up to 8 daily; 1hr 50min).	**Brno to:** Buchlovice (up to 10 daily; 1hr 10min); Jaroměřice nad Rokytnou (up to 6 daily; 1hr 30min); Jedovnice (up to 10 daily; 1hr); Kroměříž (up to 18 daily; 1hr 30min); Křtiny (up to 10 daily; 45min); Luhačovice (up to 4 daily; 2hr 10min); Mikulov (up to 10 daily; 1hr 20min); Zlín (up to 10 daily; 2hr–2hr 40min); Moravský Krumlov (3–5 daily; 1hr 15min); Telč (up to 5 daily; 2hr); Uherské Hradiště (up to 10 daily; 1hr 20min); Znojmo (up to 8 daily; 1hr 10min).
Znojmo to: Jaroměřice nad Rokytnou (up to every 2hr; 50min–1hr 10min); Jihlava (up to 8 daily; 1hr 45min); Mikulov (8–9 daily; 50min–1hr 5min); Šatov (5 daily; 12min); Retz (3–5 daily; 25min); Valtice (7–8 daily; 1hr–1hr 20min).	**Uherské Hradiště to:** Buchlovice (up to 10 daily; 20min); Kroměříž (up to 4 daily; 1hr); Luhačovice (up to 5 daily; 40min); Strážnice (up to 4 daily; 45min/1hr); Trenčín (up to 6 daily; 1hr 15min); Velehrad (up to 8 daily; 25min); Zlín (up to 10 daily; 40min–1hr).

North Moravia

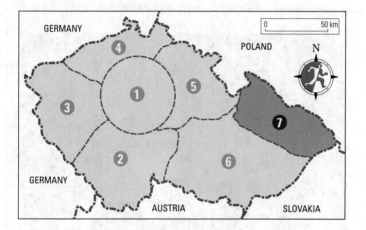

CHAPTER 7

Highlights

* **Olomouc** – Moravia's most handsome city is replete with cobbled squares, fountains and Baroque churches, and worth a day of anyone's time. See p.385

* **Wooden churches in the Beskydy** – The densely wooded countryside of the Beskydy boasts the largest concentration of wooden

churches in the Czech Republic. See p.407

* **Štramberk** – Hilly Beskydy village with a remarkable array of wooden architecture in situ. See p.407

* **Rožnov pod Radhoštěm** – The country's largest and most impressive open-air museum or skansen. See p.411

7

North Moravia

North Moravia (Severní Morava) is not the never-ending conglomeration of factories that its critics would have you believe, though it certainly has more than its fair share of ecological disaster zones, in particular the industrial belt in the Odra (Oder) basin, now in the grip of an economic depression. At the same time, the north also boasts some of Moravia's wildest and most varied countryside, including the **Jeseníky**, the region's highest peaks, which form part of what is still – nominally at least – known as Czech Silesia. As with the Sudetenland regions of Bohemia, Silesia's long-standing German community was forcibly expelled after World War II, leaving many villages and towns visibly underpopulated even today.

To the east, near the border with Slovakia, the traditional communities in the nether reaches of the **Beskydy** hills have fared much better. Wooden houses and churches are dotted along the valley, and a whole range of folk buildings has been gathered together and restored in the republic's largest open-air museum in **Rožnov pod Radhoštěm**. In addition to its folk culture and hiking potential, the Beskydy is endowed with some intriguing museums: a large car collection at the technical museum in **Kopřivnice**, a hat museum in **Nový Jičín**, and two memorials to famous local boys – Sigmund Freud, who was born in **Příbor**, and Leoš Janáček, who lived and composed in **Hukvaldy**.

The region's two largest cities typify North Moravia's contradictions: **Ostrava**, the country's largest mining and steel town, is a place no Moravian would ever recommend you visit (with some justification); **Olomouc**, on the other hand, the old medieval capital on the banks of the River Morava, is arguably Moravia's most attractive and vibrant city along with Brno, and a must on anyone's itinerary.

Olomouc

OLOMOUC (pronounced "Olla-moats" and known to the city's sizeable prewar German-speaking community as Olmütz) is easily the most immediately satisfying of Moravia's three big cities, thanks to its well-preserved staré město, sloping cobbled squares, Baroque fountains, and healthy quota of university students. Occupying the crucial Morava crossing point on the road to Kraków, Olomouc was actually the capital of Moravia from 1187 to 1641 and the seat of a bishopric (later archbishopric) for even longer. All this attracted the destructive attention of Swedish troops in the Thirty Years' War, and their occupation in the 1640s left the town for dead. During this period, Brno took over

as capital, in reward for its heroic stand against the Swedes; only the wealth of the church and its strategic trading position kept Olomouc alive. Meanwhile, the military threat from Prussia confined the town to within its eighteenth-century red-brick fortifications, and only after these were finally torn down in 1888 did the city begin to evolve into the industrial centre it is today.

Arrival, information and accommodation

The **train station** is 1.5km east of the old town, and the **bus terminal** is a good half-kilometre beyond this. On arrival, walk or take any **tram** from the train station heading west up Masarykova and get off after three or four stops; from the bus station take tram #4, which then proceeds down Masarykova, or tram #5, which runs along třída Svobody south of the old town. The city is divided into two zones: to go to the centre of town you need only an inner zone ticket (*vnitřní jizdenka*). Tickets should be bought beforehand from machines or news kiosks, and there is also a one-day ticket (*jednodenní lístek*), available from the main bus station. The **tourist office** in the arcades on the north side of the radnice (daily: 9am–7pm; ☎585 513 385, ⓦwww.olomoucko.cz) provides information as well as booking private rooms. **Internet cafés** seem to come and go rapidly in Olomouc, but at the time of writing you can get your fix at the simply named *Internet Café* at Denisova 35.

Accommodation

Hotel **accommodation** is uniformly pricey as the city receives mostly tour groups and flush business folk. For real budget accommodation head down Ztracená to the student travel agency CKM (Mon–Fri 9am–5pm) at Denisova 4; if you want to **camp**, ask at CKM, or head to the site in Šternberk (see p.396). A word of warning: rooms can be hard to come by in May when the Spring Music Festival (Olomoucké hudební jaro) follows the Flower Festival (Flora Olomouc).

Arigone Univerzitní 20 ☎585 232 351, Ⓕ585 232 350, ⓦhttp://arigone.web.worldonline.cz. Wonderful new hotel, with original wood ceilings and parquet floors. Small, so book early. ❹

Gemo Pavelčákova 22 ☎585 222 115, Ⓕ585 231 730, Ⓔgemo@hotel-gemo.cz. Something of a modern eyesore from the outside, but an efficiently run, centrally located place nevertheless, with all mod cons. ❼

Lafayette Alšova 8 ☎585 436 600, Ⓕ585 436 407, Ⓔhotel@lafayette.cz. Late-nineteenth-century hotel that's been fairly tastefully renovated, but is a good ten minutes' walk from the old town. ❹

Na hradbách Hrnčířská 14 ☎585 233 243, Ⓔaquaveri@iol.cz. Small, inexpensive, four-bed pension hidden away in one of the city's prettiest, quietest backstreets. ❷

Národní dům 8 května 21 ☎585 224 806, Ⓕ585

223 284. No doubt this late-nineteenth-century hotel was once a glorious place to stay, but, despite vestiges of its original decor, it's fallen well below standard. ❷

Palác 1 máje 27 ☎585 224 096. A communist-era hotel that needs a thorough going over, and is overpriced for what you get. ❸

Sigma Jeremenkova 36 ☎585 232 076. Cheapest hotel in town, and it looks it, located directly opposite the train station. ❷

U anděla Hrnčířská 10 ☎585 228 755, ⓦwww.uandela.cz. Just down from *Pension Na hradbách* and equally quaint, this little place sits above a soothing café. ❷

U dómu Dómská 4 ☎585 220 502, Ⓕ585 220 501, ⓦwww.mcs.cz/udomu. Small, centrally located pension near the cathedral, with six plain en-suite doubles. ❸

The city

Despite being a quarter the size of Brno, Olomouc has the same exciting buzz, with its main arteries clogged with shoppers in the afternoon rush. The **staré město** is a strange contorted shape, squeezed in the middle by an arm of the Morava.

Bus Station (1.5km) ▲ Train Station (1 km) & ⑤

OLOMOUC

N

0   100 m

ACCOMMODATION
Arigone	4
Gemo	6
Lafayette	9
Na hradbách	7
Národní dům	3
Palác	2
Sigma	5
U anděla	8
U dómu	1

RESTAURANTS
CAFÉS & BARS
Caesar	F
Café Mahler	D
Captain Morgan's	E
Kamenný šenk	C
Maruška	K
Moravská restaurace	G
U anděla	H
U bakaláře	B
U bílého slona	J
U červeného volka	A
U Huberta	L
U kapucínů	I

Přemyslovský hrad
Dóm
Arcibiskupský palác
Palacký University
Vlastivědné muzeum
Muzeum umění
Panna Maria Sněžná
Vila Primavesi
CKM
Sarkandrová kaple
sv Michal
Kapucínský kostel
Bezručovy sady
Botanická zahrada
sv Mořic
Radnice
Haunschildův palác
Holy Trinity Column
Moravské divadlo
Puppet Theatre
Zimní stadión

VÁCLAVSKÉ NÁMĚSTÍ
DOMSKÁ
KOMENSKÉHO
BISKUPSKÉ NÁMĚSTÍ
WURMOVA
MARIÁNSKÁ
1. MÁJE
KŘÍŽKOVSKÉHO
NÁM. REPUBLIKY
DENISOVA
KOŽELUŽSKÁ
DOBROVSKÉHO
SOKOLSKÁ
ZÁMEČNICKÁ
STUDENTSKÁ
8. KVĚTNA
SOKOLSKÁ
UNIVERZITNÍ
LIBRARIANSKÁ
ZBROJNICKÁ
MICHALSKÁ
UHELNÁ
OSTRUŽNICKÁ
OPLETALOVA
HORNÍ NÁMĚSTÍ
28. ŘÍJNA
RIEGROVA
ŠKOLNÍ
HRNČÍŘSKÁ
PANSKÁ
ŽEROTÍNOVO NÁM.
MALÉ NÁMĚSTÍ
KATEŘINSKÁ
DOLNÍ NÁMĚSTÍ
JAVORÍČKA
LAFAYETTOVA
DENISOVA
PAVELČÁKOVA
TŘÍDA SVOBODY
SLOVENSKÁ
VANČUROVA
KOLLÁROVO NÁM.
SPOJENCŮ
TYLOVA
ALBERTA
PALACHOVO NÁMĚSTÍ
VÍDEŇSKÁ
JAVORICKÁ
HAVLÍČKOVA
RAAPKOVA
ČECHOVY SADY
Čechovy sady
LEGIONÁŘSKÁ
PALACKÉHO

Football Stadium (150 m)
Flora Exhibition Grounds (300 m)

Horní and Dolní náměstí

In the western half of the staré město, all roads lead to the city's two central cobbled main squares, which are hinged to one another at right angles. The lower of the two, Dolní náměstí, is more or less triangular, but the upper one, **Horní náměstí**, is thoroughly irregular. At its centre is the **radnice**, a cream-coloured amalgamation of buildings and styles with the occasional late-Gothic or Renaissance gesture – a freestanding flight of steps, the handsome lanterned tower soaring up to its conclusion of baubles and pinnacles, and, tucked round the back, a lonely oriel window above a self-portrait of the mason holding out his hand for more money from the miserly town council. But it's the north side that draws the crowds, with its crude arcade of shops and **astronomical clock**, which was originally built by Master Hanuš, like its more famous successor in Prague, but destroyed in World War II. The rather soulless workerist remake chimes all right, but the hourly mechanical show of proletarians is disappointing.

Far more action-packed is the monumental, polygonal **Holy Trinity Column** (Sousoší nejvĕtší Trojice), erected in the first half of the eighteenth century to the west of the radnice, its ornamental urns sprouting dramatic gilded flames. It's big enough to be a chapel and is easily the largest plague column in either republic. It's also a favourite place for meeting up, eating your lunch, or just sitting and soaking it all in. Set into the west facade of the square is the **Moravské divadlo**, a Neoclassical theatre designed by Josef Kornhäusel in 1830, and previously known as the *Olmützer Stadttheater*, where the young Gustav Mahler arrived as the newly appointed *Kapellmeister* in 1883. The local press took an instant dislike to him: according to his own words, "from the moment I crossed the threshold . . . I felt like a man who is awaiting the judgement of God". No doubt there was a strong element of kneejerk anti-Semitism in his hostile reception, but this was not helped by Mahler's autocratic style, which caused a number of the local prima donnas to live up to their name. He lasted just three months.

Olomouc makes a big fuss of its sculpture, like that adorning the Edelmannův palác, at no. 28, and even more of its **fountains**, which grace each one of Olomouc's six ancient market squares. Horní náměstí boasts two of them: Hercules, looking unusually athletic for his years, and, to the east of the radnice, a vigorous depiction of Julius Caesar – the fabled founder of the city – bucking on a steed which coughs up water from its mouth. Jupiter and Neptune can be found in **Dolní náměstí**, which has a dustier feel to it, sloping down to the characteristically low-key Capuchin church. Of all the square's subdued Baroque facades, it's the **Haunschildův palác**, on the corner with Lafayettova, which stands out, its single Renaissance oriel decorated with scenes from Ovid.

The central side streets

From the bile-green late-Secession bank (now the main post office) on Horní náměstí, it's worth taking a quick turn northwest up **Riegrova** to see a cluster of fine Art Nouveau buildings: the first, at no. 10, has a ceramic facade and a delicate wrought-iron canopy, while the second, at no. 18, is decorated with low-relief figures, and the third, at no. 24, sports sapphire ovals. North of Horní náměstí, off Opletalova, is the church of **sv Mořic**, an oddly mutant building from the west at least, and defensive like a Norman fort, but inside overcome by a thick coat of pink paint that makes the original Gothic interior difficult to stomach. It does, however, boast the Engler organ, the largest in either republic; an ugly, dark, wooden affair with over 10,000 dirty grey pipes and a fair few cherubs, it sounds better than it looks (there's an organ festival held here in early September). You can also climb the church **tower** (May–Sept Mon–Fri 9–11.30am & 1–5pm, Sat 9–11.30am, Sun 2–5pm) for an overview of the staré město. Opposite its west door is a typical 1970s supermarket building, which muscled its way into the historic part of town with the connivance of the philistine Communist council.

Two of the city's best-looking backstreets, Školní and Michalská, lead southeast from Horní náměstí up to the long slope of Žerotínovo náměstí, which features an appealing ensemble of lime trees, streetlamps and Baroque statuary at its upper end. Overlooking them all is the Italianate church of **sv Michal**, whose rather plain facade hides a cool, spacious interior clad in the masterly excess of High Baroque. Three octagonal saucer domes rise up in Byzantine fashion atop Roman pilasters with gilded Corinthian capitals so large their acanthus leaves bear fruit. There's a very high cherub count on the side altars and a wonderful silver relief of sheep on the gilded pulpit; before you leave, look up at the equally exuberant late-nineteenth-century organ loft. Close to sv Michal, on the corner of Univerzitní, the late-nineteenth-century **vila Primavesi** is well hidden behind dense foliage and a coat of blackened pebbledash. It's currently in a parlous state, though you can still make out a blaze of gold-and-blue mosaic on the entrance steps. Fortunately, there are plans to restore the place, which was designed by, among others, the local sculptor Anton Hanak and the Viennese architect Josef Hofmann for the Primavesi family who went on to finance the Wiener Werkstätte in the 1920s.

More accessible is the mini-dome of the neo-Baroque **Sarkandrova kaple**, which replaced the old prison on Mahlerova at the beginning of the twentieth century. It's hardly big enough to kneel in, though this is perhaps its main charm. The chapel takes its name from a Catholic priest of Silesian origin, **Jan Sarkander** (1576–1620), who was incarcerated in the aforementioned prison and died after being tortured by local Protestants. In 1995 Pope John Paul II visited Olomouc and officially canonized Sarkander, whose relics now rest in the gilded casket opposite the pulpit in the local cathedral (see p.391). His canonization angered the local non-Catholic community, who charged that Sarkander was extremely anti-evangelical and a willing instrument of the Counter-Reformation, taking over the parish of Holešov after the local Protestants had been kicked out by the Jesuits, and that he was implicated in a very unsaintly treason plot involving Polish Cossacks.

Muzeum umění to the Dóm

Firmly wedged between the two sections of the staré město is the obligatory Jesuit church of **Panna Maria Sněžná**, deemed to be particularly necessary in a city where Protestantism spread like wildfire among the German community during the sixteenth century. Jutting out into the road, the church marks the former gateway from the old town to the archbishop's territory to the east, where the great mass of the former Jesuit College, now the **Palacký University**, dominates the neighbouring square, náměstí Republiky.

Above the Divadlo hudby, on the opposite side of the square, is the **Muzeum umění** (Tues–Sun 10am–6pm), which has a nice café (open until 10pm) and a permanent collection of fourteenth- to eighteenth-century Italian paintings, including one or two excellent sixteenth-century Venetian works. Best of all, though, is the **twentieth-century gallery** in the attic, which features a model of the town from 1895 with the zigzag fortifications still intact, 1930s photos of the city by, among others, the outstanding Otakar Lenhart (from a local-born family of fine artists), plus models of the city's modernist Konstandt Haus by Adolf Loos and Paul Engelmann and the Vila Primavesi. From the latter have been salvaged an Art Nouveau stained-glass window, table and chair by Anton Hanak, and a model of his strange *Child over an Ordinary Day* (a cherub standing over a four-headed plinth around which four snakes have wrapped themselves), originally positioned under the pergola in the villa's garden. There are lots of other great exhibits here, not least a model of the famous statue of Stalin and Lenin that once graced the city (see p.392), and you can gain access to the gallery's *vyhlídka věž* for a rooftop view over Olomouc. Next door is the town's **Vlastivědné muzeum** (May–Sept Tues–Sun 10am–6pm; Oct–April Wed–Sun 10am–4pm), housed in the former Poor Clares' convent and cloisters, with a pretty dull permanent display on the region's natural history.

The trams and cars hurtling across the cobbles make this one of Olomouc's least accommodating squares, so, after admiring the Bernini-esque Triton fountain, you'd be as well to slip down Mariánská to leafy **Biskupské náměstí**, one of the most peaceful spots in town. Among its fine Baroque buildings, erected after the destructive occupation of the Swedes, is the **Arcibiskupský palác** (Archbishop's Palace), financed by the multimillionaire Bishop Liechtenstein in the 1660s; it was here, at a safe distance from Vienna, that the eighteen-year-old Franz Josef I was proclaimed emperor in 1848. On the south side of the square is the former armoury, placed there by Maria Theresa after a disagreement with the archbishop. A popular spot nearby is the **student centre** (and British Council reading room) in the main university building, up Wurmova, which has a sunny terrace café.

On the other side of the tramlines, the Cathedral of sv Václav, or **Dóm**, started life as a twelfth-century Romanesque basilica, but, as with Brno and Prague, the current structure is mostly the result of nineteenth-century neo-Gothic restoration, which included the addition of the 100-metre-high eastern spire. However, the nave is bright and airy, its walls and pillars prettily painted in imitation of the great Romanesque churches of the West; the modern, high-relief Stations of the Cross are quite striking, and the **krypta** (Mon–Wed & Fri–Sat 9am–5pm, Thurs 9am–4pm & Sun 11am–5pm) has a wonderful display of gory reliquaries and priestly sartorial wealth. The exterior of the Dóm is currently undergoing repair and cleaning, as are other buildings around the secluded Václavské náměstí (Wenceslas Square) – a much calmer place than its counterpart in Prague.

Next door in the chapterhouse, you can view the fascinating remains of the original twelfth-century Románský biskupský palác or **Přemyslovský palác** (Tues–Sun 10am–6pm), now believed to have been built as a bishop's (and not a royal) palace. The common name refers to the Olomouc princes of the Přemysl dynasty, Czech rulers from the 9th century to the early 14th century, though recent archeological and historical research suggests it is more likely that the royal family lived in a part of the Přemyslid castle that used to stand at what is now the deanery, across the square. The bishop's palace was built in the early 12th century in the Romanesque style, but it was revised through several subsequent architectural styles over the centuries. A late Gothic cloister lies between the palace and the Dóm, while Renaissance frescoed corridors lead down to the restored chapel of sv Jan Křtitel (St John the Baptist), in which are exhibited fine statuary and fragments of the original palace. Upstairs the palace's origins are much more clearly on display, and you can peer down into what is now believed to be the bishop's living quarters from at least the year 1141, lined with Romanesque columns unrivalled in the Czech lands. Right by the entrance is the Baroque chapel of sv Anna (open for morning and evening services only) and, set back from it, the university deanery where the teenage King Václav III, the last of the Přemyslids, was murdered in mysterious circumstances in 1306, throwing the country into a blood-letting war of succession.

Beyond the staré město

The Habsburg defences to the west of the staré město were completely torn down in the late nineteenth century to make way for what is now a long, busy thoroughfare known as **třída Svobody**. Starting in the north with the former Edison cinema, a late-Secession building from 1913 decorated with caryatids worshipping light bulbs, it continues with the familiar trail of Habsburg bureaucratic architecture. Halfway down on the right, a leftover water tower is the only survivor on a square that contained a synagogue until the Nazis burnt it down in 1939, and where a double statue of Stalin and Lenin subsequently stood. The former (and only the former) was defaced badly towards the end of the 1980s, apparently by an outraged Gorby-supporting Soviet soldier; neither survived the iconoclasm of November 1989, and the square is now named after the 1969 martyr Jan Palach (see p.108).

If you're tired of Olomouc's uneven cobbles, the best places to head for are the **parks**, which practically encircle the town. A couple of blocks of *fin-de-siècle* houses stand between Svobody and the long, well-maintained patchwork strip of crisscross paths, flowerbeds and manicured lawns. It's just a small sample of what goes on show at the annual **Flower Festival** (Flora Olomouc), a minor international gathering of florists, held at the end of April or beginning of May in the Flora Výstaviště or exhibition grounds. The grounds also contain the city's **botanical gardens** (botanická zahrada; April–Sept Tues–Sun 10am–5pm), which are worth visiting at any time of the year. Another pleasant walk is out of the southern end of Dolní náměstí and left into the tiny Malé náměstí, which has a flight of steps leading down to the Bezručovy sady, once the city moat, where the local youth likes to hang out.

Eating, drinking and nightlife

For a big city, most of Olomouc goes to bed pretty early. As far as **nightlife** goes, there's always a good turnout at the Moravské divadlo, on Horní náměstí, which puts on a good selection of opera as well as regular concerts by the city's philharmonic orchestra. In late May, Olomouc has its own Spring Music Festival (Olomoucké hudební jaro), when concerts are spread evenly around the city's churches, monasteries and other venues. The Divadlo hudby, below the Muzeum umění at Denisova 47, puts on a more adventurous programme of **gigs**, films and videos. Olomouc has its own jazz club, the *Jazz Tibet Club*, Sokolská 48, which mostly features trad and swing bands, with the music kicking off at 8pm. It's also worth checking out what's on at the student clubs: *S-Klub*, třída 17. listopadu 43, is just outside the old town, while the *U-Klub* hosts gigs east of the city centre at the student union, Šmeralova 12. Art-house **films** can be seen on Tuesdays at the Metropol, Sokolská 25, but for a full rundown of the month's events, buy the listings magazine *Kdy, Kde Co v Olomouci* at the tourist office or newsagents around town. And before you leave town be sure to try out the city's famously pungent local cheese, *Olomoucký sýr*.

Caesar Horní nám. An excellent, popular pizzeria in the cobbled vaults of the radnice, from which the smell of garlic wafts enticingly across the main square. Mon–Sat 9am–1am, Sun 9am–midnight.

Café Mahler Horní nám. 11. Popular place to go for coffee and cake, with tables outside looking over to the radnice. Mon–Sat 8am–9pm, Sun 10am–9pm.

Captain Morgan's Mlynská. Hip dark café/bar/pizzeria situated in the old fortifications, with an outside patio and beer from nearby Litovel. Mon–Thurs 10am–1am, Fri & Sat 10am–3am, Sun 11am–midnight.

Kamenný šenk Žerotínovo nám. 13. Lively nighttime student cellar bar on the corner of Michalská. Mon–Sat 3pm–midnight.

Maruška 28 října 2. More functional than the *Mahler*, but a decent coffee-and-cake dispenser, with seating upstairs. Mon–Sat 8am–10pm, Sun 10am–10pm.

Moravská restaurace Horní nám. 23. Slap bang next to the main theatre on the main square, with traditional Moravian ambience; a good place for pre- or post-theatre food and drink. Daily 11.30am–11pm.

U anděla Hrnčířská 10. Popular little café/restaurant (topped by a pension) serving traditional Czech fare in the backstreets behind Dolní náměstí. Daily 11am–11pm.

U bakaláře Žerotínovo náměstí 3. Nice modern take on the traditional pub, with wooden benches and tables. Mon–Thurs 10am–10pm, Fri–Sat 10am–11pm, Sun 11am–9pm.

U bílého slona Univerzitní 10. The city's very own *čajovna* or teahouse/art gallery is housed in a lovely seventeenth-century building. Mon–Fri 11am–11pm, Sat 10am–11pm.

U červeného volka Dolní nám. 39. Wide choice of pasta and veggie dishes as well as the usual Czech pub-restaurant food. Daily 10am–11pm.

U Huberta 1 máje 3. A real drinkers' pub, which serves the local beer unfiltered and unpasteurized. Mon–Sat 10am–10pm.

U kapucínů Kapucínská. Odd combination of gothic and modern styles that works; a different menu from most, that includes pastas and fish. Mon–Fri 10am–10pm, Fri–Sat 10am–11pm, Sun 11am–8pm.

Around Olomouc

Olomouc sits happily in the wide plain of the **Haná region**, famous for its multifarious folk costumes and for its songs reflecting the fertility of the land. Naturally enough in a strongly agricultural area, the harvest festivals (*Hanácké dožínky* or *dožínkový slavnost*) are the highlight of the year, advertised on posters everywhere in the second half of September. All the places covered below are situated in the Morava plain, and easily reached by bus or train on day-trips from Olomouc, with the exception of Helfštýn and the area round Bouzov, which are really only accessible to those who have their own transport.

Přerov and around

Twenty-three kilometres southeast of Olomouc, and twenty minutes by train, **PŘEROV** (Prerau) is an important rail junction and ungainly town dedicated to the chemical and engineering industries. Apart from a brief jazz festival in late September, its chief redeeming feature is the endearing old town square, **Horní náměstí**, a tight semicircle of colourful houses elevated above the rest of the town. At its centre is a typically anguished statue by František Bílek, depicting the sixteenth-century religious reformer Jan Blahoslav brandishing his Czech translation of the New Testament. The straight side of the square is taken up by the sixteenth-century chateau, whose **Muzeum Komenského** (March & Nov Wed, Sat & Sun 9am–noon & 1–5pm; April–Oct Tues–Sun 9am–noon & 1–5pm) commemorates Blahoslav's more famous successor in the Protestant Unity of Brethren, Jan Ámos Komenský (aka Comenius; see box on p.394). The **bus** and **train stations** are about 1km southwest of the town centre.

If you're heading east into the Beskydy by rail or road, it's difficult to miss the spectacular ruined castle of **Helfštýn** (March & Nov Sat & Sun 9am–4pm; April, Sept & Oct Tues–Sun 9am–5pm; May–Aug closes 6pm), which looks down from the wooded hills to the south of River Bečva, 15km east of Přerov. Founded sometime in the fourteenth century, it's one of the largest medieval castles in the Czech Republic, and was used by the Hussites as a base from which to attack Olomouc, before being deliberately laid to waste by the

Comenius

Jan Ámos Komenský (John Amos Comenius) was born in 1592 in a village close to Uherský Brod, but his Latin schooling took place at the Unity of Brethren's school in Přerov. He served as a Protestant minister in Fulnek from 1616 to 1621, before being forced to flee the Czech Lands after the victory of the papal forces at the Battle of Bílá hora. Komenský and the Brethren set up an academy in the Polish city of Leszno, until forced to move on once more by the Swedish Wars of the 1650s. Of his many writings, Komenský's graded and pictorial Latin textbooks (the first of their kind) have proved more influential than his religious treatises, and he was called to put his educational theories into practice in Sweden, Hungary, Holland and England. He even received invitations from the Protestant-loathing Cardinal Richelieu in France, and from Harvard University, which wanted him as its president. He is buried in Naarden, Holland. Throughout the eastern part of Moravia, the Brethren rode out the Counter-Reformation to emerge in significant numbers once Austrian liberalism began to take effect in the late eighteenth century. They were later transformed into the Moravian Church, a body which continues to have an influence out of all proportion to its size, particularly in the Czech Lands and the USA.

Habsburgs following the Thirty Years' War. Sections of the complex have since been restored, but the place is still, for the most part, a ruin and you can wander at will. Concerts, mock battles and various other attractions are staged here over the summer, and there's a permanent display of modern **blacksmith** artistry in one of the castle wings (expozice kovářství; May–Sept Tues–Sun 9am–5pm), plus an annual blacksmiths' convention in late August. To get to the castle, you can either walk the 5km along the red-marked path from the train station at Lipník nad Bečvou, or catch one of the infrequent buses to Týn nad Bečvou, 1.5km below the castle.

Prostějov and around

Twenty kilometres and half an hour by train from Olomouc, the big textile town of **PROSTĚJOV** (Prossnitz) has a more grand and spacious old centre based around a large, well-laid-out main square, Masarykovo náměstí. Dominating this is the **nová radnice**, with its ludicrously large landmark tower built just before World War I and an asymmetrical appearance caused by the council's failure to purchase one of the neighbouring houses. The Renaissance **stará radnice**, in the opposite corner of the square, now houses the local **museum** (Tues–Sun 9am–noon & 1–5pm), with folk artefacts from the Haná region, including old clocks and watches, but very little on the town's brightest star, **Edmund Husserl** (1859–1938), the founder of phenomenology. A better bet is to pop into the nearby **church**, which has some terrific Baroque furnishings, a technicolour pulpit covered with carved figures and an extravagant crown-shaped baldachin, as well as a set of Stations of the Cross carved by František Bílek.

Just off the main square is the town's prettily sgraffitoed Renaissance **zámek** (times as at museum), which puts on art exhibitions and contains a permanent collection of graphics by Jan Köhler. The town's real architectural highlight, however, is Jan Kotěra's 1908 **Národní dům**, northeast of the main square near the last remaining bastion of the old town walls and now housing a theatre and restaurant. As in his museum at Hradec Králové (see p.309), Kotěra was moving rapidly away from the "swirl and blob" of the Secession, but here and there the old elements persist in the sweep of the brass door handles and the pattern on the poster frames. Apart from its furniture, the restaurant has been left unmolested, and the bold Klimt-like ceramic relief of the *Three Graces* above the mantelpiece is still as striking as ever.

To reach the old town from the main **bus** and **train stations**, head west down Svatoplukova. Prostějov doesn't get too many visitors, but there are a couple of **places to stay**, ranging from the expensive *Hotel Grand* (☎582 332 311, ⓕ582 332 323, ⓦwww.grandhotel.cz; ❺), on Palackého, a couple of blocks south of the main square, to the old stalwart *Hotel Avion* (☎582 330 514, ⓔhotel_avion@iol.cz; ❷), east of the main square on náměstí sv Čecha. Five kilometres west of Prostějov are two good **campsites**, *Přehrada* and *Žralok* (both May–Sept), whose lakeside locations provide plenty of opportunities for swimming. The latter sits below a high mound above the westernmost reservoir, on top of which stands the imposing slab of the chateau at **PLUMLOV** (Plumenau), another of the Liechtensteins' fancies. Designed by Prince-Bishop Karl Eusebius von Liechtenstein-Kastelcorn himself, only one wing of the four planned got off the drawing board. Reconstruction work continues slowly, but in high season you can now wander round the courtyards, and visit a small exhibition on the **zámek** (July & Aug Tues–Sun 10am–4pm), which makes a scenic backdrop if you're swimming.

Bouzov and around

The northernmost tip of the Drahanská vrchovina around **BOUZOV** (Busau) – an extension of the hills of the Moravský kras – has enough to keep you occupied on a lazy weekend. The village itself is nothing but its **hrad** (April & Oct Tues–Sun 9am–noon & 1–4pm; May–Sept Tues–Sun 9am–noon & 1–5pm; Nov–March Sat & Sun 10am–noon & 1–3pm), a Romantic neo-Gothic fortress right on the high point of the vrchovina, and perfectly suited as a base for its former proprietors, the Teutonic Knights. Predictably enough, it also took the fancy of the Nazi SS, who used it as a base during World War II. The pompous pseudo-medievalism of the interior decor is not to everyone's taste, and the place is absolutely huge, so there's a choice of guided tours: *trasa 1* (klasická) is the regular one that gives you an hour-long whirl around the place; *trasa 2* (velká) lasts an extra forty minutes and is for real enthusiasts; *trasa 3* takes you up the tower (věž) only. Tours are in Czech only, but ask for an English text (*anglicky text*).

Four kilometres south at **JAVOŘÍČKO**, the local SS burnt the village to the ground and shot 38 of the inhabitants in the last days of the war. This futile and tragic act aside, the reason for coming here is to visit the **Javoříčské jeskyně** (Tues–Sun: April & Oct 9am–3pm; May–Sept 9am–4pm), limestone karst caves on a par with those near Brno but without the crowds. Five kilometres east of Bouzov, **BÍLÁ LHOTA** has an eighteenth-century chateau worth visiting for its beautiful **arboretum** (April & Oct Sat & Sun 8am–5pm; May–Sept Tues–Sun 8am–6pm). The **Mladečské jeskyně**, a more extensive and popular limestone cave system another couple of kilometres on, is just off the main Olomouc–Prague road, at the end of the most twig-like of branch lines from Litovel.

Svatý Kopeček and Šternberk

If you're heading north from Olomouc on route 46, you can't fail to spot the twin clock towers of the gleaming yellow-and-white Baroque pilgrimage church on the nearby hill of **Svatý Kopeček** (Heiligberg), just 8km northeast of the city. Perched 200m above the plain and flanked by its vast convent

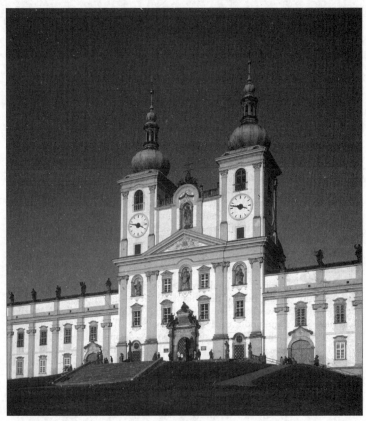

△ Olomouc

wings, the site and scale are truly spectacular. Close up, though, it doesn't live up to expectations, and is really only worth visiting for its adjoining **zoo** (daily 8am–7pm or dusk); bus #11 from Olomouc train station will take you there.

Further north on route 46, you hit the ridge of the Jeseníky foothills at **ŠTERNBERK** (Sternberg), where the annual *Ecce Homo* motor race is held in mid-September over the lethal switchbacks on the road to Opava. The town itself, a long two-kilometre haul north of the train and bus stations, is dominated by its giant Baroque church and **hrad** (April & Oct Sat & Sun 9am–4pm; May–Sept Tues–Sun 8am–5pm), the latter rebuilt in Romantic style in the late nineteenth century and worth a visit for its **Muzeum hodin** (Clock Museum), which houses a fabulous collection of timepieces and watches, from ancient Chinese alarm clocks through to the wild excesses of the Baroque era and examples of the substandard work churned out by the old state watch manufacturers, Prim, who are based in the town.

Šternberk has a **tourist office** (Mon–Thurs 9am–5pm, Fri 9am–4pm; ☏585 012 320, ⓦwww.sternberk.cz), at Horní náměstí 16, that can help with **accommodation**, though the *Šternberský dvůr* (☏585 012 990, Ⓕ585 015 042, Ⓔster.dvur@idop.cz; ➌) is a good place to start. Šternberk's two

campsites (both mid-May to mid-Sept) are the nearest you'll get to Olomouc: the *Šternberk* site is slightly closer to the town than *U zlatého muflona*, in Dolní Žleb, 3km north of Šternberk.

The Jeseníky

Extending east from the Bohemian Krkonoše are the **Jeseníky** (Altvatergebirge), the highest peaks in what is now Moravia. Sparsely populated since the postwar expulsion of its German-speakers, the region is worlds apart from the dense network of industrial centres in the north and east of the province, or even the vine-clad hills of the south. The highest reaches, to the northwest between Šumperk and Jeseník, have been damaged by acid rain, but the mountains as a whole are peaceful and green. One of the nicest areas to head for is the foothills on either side of the big peaks, which harbour some low-key spa resorts like Lázně Jeseník, Karlova Studánka, and the historical remains of Czech Silesia in Krnov and Opava.

Šumperk

ŠUMPERK (Schönberg) is the gateway to the upper Jeseníky, and has the feel of a mountain town, despite the fact that the shift from plain to hills is much less dramatic here than at Šternberk. For the last two centuries it was a thriving German-speaking textile town, at the vanguard of the language frontier, and though the town's original inhabitants may have been expelled, it still relies on its cloth-making tradition.

Unusually for a provincial town, there's no obvious centre to Šumperk. The main drag is **Hlavní třída**, beyond the park to the north of the train station, and, at the far western end of Hlavní, the tiny old town is easy to miss, its neo-Renaissance radnice standing on the pretty little square of **náměstí Míru**. Unreconstructed street names were a feature of most towns under the Communist regime, but Šumperk topped the lot with a Stalin Square, a Stalingrad Street and a statue of the man himself in a car park by the old town walls – all intact right up to November 1989.

Nowadays, there's not much to see here, but if you end up staying, details of current entertainments – such as at the beautifully-restored theatre – are available from the **tourist office** in the local museum by the park (Mon 8am–noon & 12.30–5pm, Tues–Fri 8am–5pm, Sat 8am–noon; ☎583 214 000, ✉icsumperk@seznam.cz). **Rooms** are available at the utterly basic *Grand* (☎583 212 141; ❶), by the park, or the more comfortable *Pension U Jiráska* (☎ & ⓕ583 213 849, ⓦwww.jirasek.cz; ❹), on the road heading northeast to the suburb of Vikýřovice.

Velké Losiny

One good reason for staying in Šumperk is to visit the tiny Moravian spa of **VELKÉ LOSINY** (Gross-Ullersdorf), 9km northeast of Šumperk and one of the last oases of civilization before you hit the deserted heights of the Jeseníky. The town's Renaissance **zámek** (April & Oct Sat & Sun 9am–noon & 1–4pm; May–Aug Tues–Sun 8am–noon & 1–5pm; Sept Tues–Sun 9am–noon & 1–4pm) is set in particularly lush grounds beside a tributary of the River Desná. It's a three-winged, triple-decker structure, part Renaissance and part Baroque, opening out into a beautifully restored sixteenth-century arcaded loggia, and for once the guided tour is really worthwhile. The chateau was the northernmost property of the extremely wealthy Žerotín family, but was inhabited for less than a hundred years; its grandest chamber is the Knights' Hall, which has retained its original parquet floor and leather wall hangings. Strong supporters of the Unity of Brethren, the Žerotíns were stripped of their wealth after the Battle of Bílá hora and the chateau was left empty – except as a venue for the region's notorious witch trials during the Counter-Reformation.

Velké Losiny is also home to the country's one remaining **paper mill** or *papírna* (Oct–April Mon–Fri 9am–noon & 1–3pm; May–Sept Tues–Sun 9am–noon & 1–5pm), which still produces handmade paper. Built in the 1590s by the Žerotín family, and still bearing the family's coat of arms on its water-mark, the mill is situated between the chateau and the spa and houses a small museum on the history of paper. The **train** and **bus stations** are in the spa itself, from which the chateau is a pleasant one-kilometre walk south through the verdant garden buildings.

Hrubý Jeseník

The River Desná peters out before the real climb into the central mountain range of **Hrubý Jeseník**. A bus from Šumperk runs roughly every two hours via the last train station, Kouty nad Desnou, to the saddle of Červenohorské sedlo (1013m) and beyond. The ascent by route 44 from Kouty is a dramatic series of hairpin bends, but the top of the pass is a disappointment. The tourist board may talk of "mountain meadows and pastures", but the reality is low-lying scrub and moorland: any spruce or pine trees that dare to rise above this are new growth, only recently conquering the effects of acid rain. There's a restaurant by the roadside for beer and food, and an impromptu and very basic **campsite**, 500m away to the northwest, along with plenty of private rooms. For a better view, it's a 45-minute walk northwest to **Červená hora** (1333m) and another hour and a half to **Šerák** (1351m), which looks down onto the Ramzovské sedlo, the much lower pass to the west that the railway from Šumperk to Jeseník wisely opts for. A chairlift here will take you down to the campsite and train station at Ramzová, or you could walk two hours in the opposite direction to **Praděd** (Altvater), at 1491m the highest and most barren peak in the range.

Below and to the east of Praděd is the picturesque Silesian spa resort of **KARLOVA STUDÁNKA**, strung out along the valley of the bubbling River Bílá Opava. The spa has a useful **information centre** (daily 9am–5pm), and is dotted with cold fizzy springs (with an extraordinarily high iron content) and attractive dark-brown weatherboarded spa buildings, many with cream shutters and balconies for enjoying the fresh mountain air. Most of the **accommodation** in the spa is for patients, but you could try the *Hotel Džbán* (☎554 772 014, ℻554 772 013; ❷), in the centre of town. There's also the *Dolina* **campsite** (mid-May to Sept), 7km northeast of the spa near Vrbno pod Pradědem (Würbenthal).

Another option is to stay in **MALÁ MORÁVKA**, 8km to the south down route 445, which has the advantage of being at the end of an idyllic little branch line from Bruntál (trains don't always run daily on this line so check it's running). M Service acts as a sort of **tourist office** (daily 8am–6pm; ⓦwww.malamoravka.cz) and can help with accommodation in the area; you can hire bikes and skis there, too. There are numerous inexpensive pensions and rooms along the valley between here and Karlova Studánka, so **accommodation** shouldn't be a problem.

BRUNTÁL (Freudenthal) is 14km east of Malá Morávka on the scenic railway line between Olomouc and Krnov, and has the dubious distinction of having one of the highest rates of unemployment in the country. It's worth a mention, though, for its Baroque **zámek** (Tues–Sun: April, Sept & Oct 9am–noon & 1–5pm; May–Aug 9am–noon & 1–6pm), another hangout of the Teutonic Knights. After the chateau's solid Baroque exterior, the beautiful sixteenth-century arcaded courtyard with loggia comes as something of a surprise; inside, amidst the lush furnishings, is a series of vast Baroque landscape frescoes.

Jeseník and around

On the other side of the pass, the road plunges down with equal ferocity to **JESENÍK** (Freiwaldau), a fairly nondescript town busy in summer with Polish day-trippers. Over the stream, north of the main square in the Smetanovy sady, there's a wonderful Art Nouveau monument to local farmer Vincent Priessnitz, founder of the nearby spa (see below), presiding godlike over the skinny and ill on his right and the "cured" (or at least plump) on his left. Otherwise, Jeseník is mainly useful as a base for exploring the surrounding area; there are several reasonably priced hotels and pensions, and a **campsite** (open all year) with a swimming pool less than 2km west along the valley en route to another spa resort, Lipová Lázně.

Two kilometres above the town, with fantastic views south to the Jeseníky and north into Poland, is **LÁZNĚ JESENÍK** (Gräfenberg). Here Priessnitz established one of the most famous Silesian spas in the nineteenth century, where the likes of Russian writer Gogol and King Carol I of Romania took the cure. Nowadays, the only grandish spa building is the grey rendered Priessnitz Sanatorium, built in 1910. Scattered about the surrounding countryside, and interspersed with numerous monuments erected by grateful patients, are the natural springs, which provide hot and sulphuric refreshment on the obligatory constitutionals (you can buy a map from the Priessnitz Sanatorium). If you'd prefer to get clean away from people, and particularly sickly spa patients, make your way to the viewpoint from the summit of Zlatý chlum, 2km east of Jeseník.

From Lipová Lázně, a tiny, picturesque branch line heads northeast, eventually terminating at Javorník (see below), in the northernmost Silesian salient. The first stop, though, is Lipová Lázně jeskyně, just over the ridge from the entrance to the **Jeskyně na pomezí** (April–Oct Tues–Sun 9am–4pm), a mini-karst cave system with colourful stalactites and stalagmites in the shape of fruit, vegetables and fungi. Another two stops along the line is **ŽULOVÁ**, whose local fortress, precipitously situated on a moated island of rock, was converted into a church in the nineteenth century, its Gothic round tower now the steeple of an otherwise Baroque building. You only have to look at the names on the World War I memorial in the porch to see that the village was once entirely German-speaking – the old German graves have since been stuck to the church wall to make way for postwar Czech ones.

Beyond Žulová, the countryside flattens out as it slips into Poland, and the train continues to **JAVORNÍK** (Jauernig), where the local chateau, **Janský vrch** (April & Oct Sat & Sun 9am–noon & 1–4pm; May–Aug Tues–Sun 8am–noon & 1–5pm; Sept 9am–noon & 1–4pm), perches high above the village. There's a choice of guided tours: the 45-minute tour (*trasa 1*) takes you round the period interior which features a collection of historical pipes and ornate smoking devices, as well as a small theatre, where the composer **Karl Ditters von Dittersdorf** used to stage operas (when he wasn't being the local forest warden); the half-hour tour (*trasa 2*) whisks you round the servants' quarters, the chapel and the lookout tower. If you need a place to stay, head for the *Hotel pod zámkem* (☎584 956 236; ❷), down in the village.

Krnov

As if to underline the arbitrary nature of the region's current borders, the railway line from Jeseník passes in and out of Polish territory en route to **KRNOV** (Jägerndorf), famous for its Rieger-Kloss organ factory – the largest in Europe – established here in 1873. The town was flattened in World War II, and lost most of its primarily German-speaking population in the postwar expulsions – the current population of 26,000 is only two-thirds of the town's prewar level – but it's still worth a brief stopover if you're heading for Opava or into Poland just 3km away.

From the town's otherwise nondescript main square, **Hlavní náměstí**, two buildings stand out: the salmon-pink-and-white **radnice** from 1902, topped by an excitable clock tower, modelled on the one in the Viennese suburb of Währing and decorated with patterned tiling; and the late-nineteenth-century **spořitelna**, a savings bank, in two shades of green. Beyond the Atlantes who guard the entrance to the latter, you can see the beautifully restored foyer and staircase, its stained glass, ironwork and plastering smothered in Art Nouveau floral motifs. On the ground floor is the *Městská kavárna*, restored and slightly modernized, but with enough of its original fittings – brass chandeliers, wooden panelling and so forth – to give some idea of its glory days. To the west on Zámecké náměstí, one side of the street features an unusual arcade held up by round, squat pillars, while beyond, to the north, lies the so-called **Švedská zed'** (Swedish Wall), a short, surviving stretch of the town's fortifications with decorative Renaissance battlements, later used in the unsuccessful defence of the town against the Swedes during the Thirty Years' War.

Krnov's main **train station** is 1km west of the centre along Mikulášská, though most trains heading to or from Opava and Ostrava also stop at Krnov-Cvilín, about half the distance northeast of the centre down Hlubčická. The **tourist office**, a few steps off the main square at Štursova 3 (Mon–Fri 8am–6pm, Sat 8am–noon), can help with private accommodation. **Accommodation** is in rather short supply, with the only two real options being the overpriced *Hotel Pepa* (☎554 611 005, ℻554 610 716, Ⓔpepa@krnov.cesnet.cz; ❹), on Zámecké náměstí, or the kitsch but cheap Communist-era *Hotel Praha* (☎554 610 741, ℻554 610 740; ❷), west of the historical core at Revoluční 10.

Opava and around

Right by the Polish border, 24km southeast of Krnov, **OPAVA** (Troppau) is one of the oldest towns in the country, an important trading centre on the Amber Road from the Adriatic to the Baltic Sea, but perhaps better known as **Troppau**, capital of Austrian (and later Czech) Silesia (see box opposite). Badly damaged in the last few weeks of World War II, then depopulated by the expulsion of the town's majority of Germans, it nevertheless retains enough grandiose nineteenth-century buildings to give some idea of how it looked in its heyday. Much has been rebuilt since 1945, and while Opava may not merit a detour, it's a good place to break a journey or do a bit of chateau-seeing.

From 1335 onwards, **Silesia** (*Slezsko* in Czech) was an integral part of the Historic Lands of the Bohemian Crown. In the 1740s the majority of it was carelessly lost to the Prussians by the young Habsburg Empress Maria Theresa. The three remaining Duchies – Troppau (Opava), Jägerndorf (Krnov) and Teschen (Těšín) – became known as Austrian Silesia, with Troppau as their capital, separated from each other by the Moravian salient around Ostrava. The population, though predominantly German, contained large numbers of Czechs and Poles – a mishmash typical of the region and one which caused often violent clashes and interminable territorial disputes. In 1920, after a few bloody skirmishes, the new state of Czechoslovakia lost part of Těšín to Poland and gained part of Hlučín from Germany, and in 1928 Czech Silesia was amalgamated with Moravia. This last act, in particular, annoyed the violently irredentist prewar German population. However, like the majority of the country's German-speaking minority, they were expelled in 1945, making the whole issue of a separate Silesia fairly redundant. Nevertheless, in the early 1990s, the newly formed Moravian nationalists teamed up with their Silesian counterparts (HSD-SMS) and scored some surprise election victories that briefly put the whole issue back on the agenda.

The most spectacular reminder of the town's former days, the huge church of **Nanebevzetí Panny Marie**, lies in the west of the old town, built in Silesian Gothic style in the late fourteenth century, and sheltering a lovely crown-shaped high altar. East of this giant red-brick church is the town's main square, **Horní náměstí**, above which rises the tall tower of the old *Schmetterhaus*, or **Hláska**, symbol of the town's forgotten prosperity, where foreign merchants were permitted to sell their wares. Opposite this stands another object of civic pride, the neo-Baroque **Slezské divadlo**. Opava's best-looking street is Masarykova třída, lined with noble Baroque palaces that once belonged to the likes of General Blücher and one of Beethoven's chief patrons, Count Razumovský. The **Silesian Diet** used to meet in the Jesuit college at the northern end of the street, while the Minorite monastery, further south, was the venue for the 1820 Troppau Conference, when the "Holy Alliance" of Austria, Russia and Prussia met to thrash out a common policy towards the revolutionary stirrings of post-Napoleonic Europe.

Set in the town's pretty semicircle of parks to the east is the grandiose **Slezské zemské muzeum** (Tues–Sat 9am–noon & 1–4pm, Sun 9am–noon & 2–4pm), built in neo-Renaissance style in 1893. It has been painstakingly restored since the war and houses a large but uninspiring exhibition that manages to avoid all the most controversial aspects of Silesian history. Opava does have one superb piece of twentieth-century architecture worth seeking out, the **church of sv Hedvik**, about 500m up Krnovská, one block to the south. The western facade is truly striking, made from big slabs of rusticated stone with concrete infill, plastered with giant Latin lettering and rising vertically in steps to form a strictly geometric tower. Begun in 1933 by local architect Leopold Bauer, it was used as a storehouse by the Nazis and Communists, and was only finished and opened for religious services in 1992.

Opava has two **train stations**; the main one – and the most central – is Opava východ, at the southeastern corner of the old town. Opava suffers from a dearth of accommodation, which makes the regional **tourist office** (Mon–Fri 8am–6pm, Sat 8–11am; ☎553 621 140, ⓔinfocentrum.opava

@coms.cz), on the main square behind the radnice, especially useful. There's just one central **hotel** to speak of at present, the none-too-cheap, dark-red, modern monstrosity known as the *Koruna*, náměstí Republiky 17 (☎553 621 132, ⓕ553 621 900; ❺), plus a few pensions in the suburbs. You may be better off heading to Hradec nad Moravicí (see below), or staying in Krnov or Ostrava. As for **food**, *U bílého koníčka*, on Dolní náměstí, is a vaulted beer hall, serving mugs of *Gambrinus* and all the usual Czech dishes, or else there's *Pizzeria Uno*, at the corner of Olbrichova and Otická. It only remains to say that lion-lovers all over the world might be interested to know that **Joy Adamson** (of *Born Free* fame) was born Friderika Viktoria Gessner at Na rybníčku 48 in 1910 – and there's a plaque on the house to prove it.

Hradec nad Moravicí

The castle high above the town of **HRADEC NAD MORAVICÍ**, 8km south on route 57, is a Hammer-horror neo-Gothic castle – or so it appears at first sight. In fact, the red-brick castle's magnificent gateway opens up to reveal another, earlier, Neoclassical zámek covered in smooth white plaster. The **Červený zámek**, or *Rotes Schloss* as the red-brick castle was known, is now home to the local museum, while the **Bílý zámek** or *Weisses Schloss* (April, Oct & Nov Sat & Sun 9am–noon & 1–4pm; May–Sept Tues–Sun 9am–noon & 1–5pm) contains a rather more interesting collection of porcelain and paintings. The latter used to belong to the Lichnovský family, who invited performances from the likes of Beethoven, Liszt and Paganini – in early June there's a Beethoven music festival, *Beethovenův Hradec*, held here. On a clear day it's well worth exploring the lovely grounds that stretch out along the ridge beyond the white castle.

Lying at the end of its very own branch line, and offering a wide range of **accommodation**, Hradec is a suitable base for visiting Opava and even Ostrava. First choice for a bed has to be the *Zámecký hotel* (☎553 783 021 or 553 786 775; ❷), in the neo-Gothic red-brick castle, which also has a restaurant open to non-guests, though there are other options. There's also the *Hradec* **campsite** (May–Sept) a short distance to the south of the town and castles, along route 57.

Hrabyně

No one driving between Ostrava and Opava on route 11 can fail to notice the ugly great slab of concrete which crowns the strategic heights around the village of **Hrabyně**. In the final few weeks of World War II, the Red Army was forced to engage in a costly pitched battle for the area. As recently as the 1980s, the sycophantic Communist regime decided to erect this bombastic tribute to the fallen, at a cost of millions' of crowns, thereby proving the indissoluble friendship between Czechoslovakia and the Soviet Union – "Together with the Soviet Union for ever and ever and never any other way", as the slogans used to say. The army vehicles that used to be scattered across the hilltop have been removed, but the monument still gives out superb views north into Poland. Inside, there's a typically lavish but dull permanent display on the military operation, and rather more enlightening temporary exhibitions upstairs (Tues–Sun 9am–3.30pm).

Ostrava

If you told a Czech you were going to **OSTRAVA** (Ostrau), they'd probably think you were mad. Although the situation has improved in recent years, the city used to be regularly shrouded in a pall of pungent sulphurous smog. Ostrava's coalmines were closed down in 1994 and since then huge efforts have been made to clean up the centre; however, it's hard to hide the fact that it's coal and steel that made the town, and pollution from nearby mining towns can still have an unfortunate effect on the city's air quality. From a village of less than 2000 inhabitants at the beginning of the nineteenth century, Ostrava has grown into the Czech Republic's third largest city with a population of 330,000, a significant number of whom are Polish due to its position as the main gateway into Poland. Ostrava does, however, have plenty of high culture and a packed sporting calendar, so if you should end up having to stay in the North Moravian coal basin, this is as good a place as any.

Mining Museum (3 km) ▲   ▲ Polish Consulate (100 m)

CENTRAL OSTRAVA

ACCOMMODATION	
Dom Polski	4
Imperial	5
Jindřich	1
Maria	3
Palace	6
Savoy	2
RESTAURANTS & BARS	
Astoria	C
España	B
Pivnice Radegast	D
Radniční restaurace	A
Staročeská pivnice	E

Nová radnice

Evangelický kostel

Husův sad

Dům umění

ČSA

Investiční banka

Bazilika

Puppet Theatre

sv Václav

Ostravské muzeum

Divadlo Antonína Dvořáka

Park kultury

River Ostravice

Main Train Station (1.5 km)

Hrad (750 m)

Hrad (400 m)

Ostrava střed & Bus Station

0   100 m

Arrival, information and accommodation

Ostrava's main **train station**, Ostrava hlavní nádraží, is 2km north of the city centre (tram #1, #2, #8 or #12). Trains from Krnov and Opava terminate at Ostrava-Svinov (most fast trains also call here), 5km west of the centre (tram #3, #4, #8, #9, or #10). One or two trains an hour from the main train station (including trains to and from Frýdek-Místek and Kroměříž) will take you to the most central of the city terminals, Ostrava střed, next door to the main **bus station** and just ten minutes' walk west of the centre (tram #2, #6, #12 or #13). The **tourist office** (Mon–Fri 7.30am–8.30pm, Sat 7.30am–3pm, Sun 1–8.30pm; ☎596 123 913, ⓦwww.ostravainfo.cz), on Nádražní, is helpful. Anyone needing a Polish visa can get one quickly and easily at the **Polish consulate** (Mon–Fri 8.30am–noon), at Blahoslavova 4, just north of the Nová radnice.

Accommodation

Despite the lack of tourists, Ostrava's **hotels** can get booked up by a combination of people on business and Polish migrant workers, so it's worth ringing in advance or starting your search early in the day.

Dom Polski Poděbradova 53 ☎596 122 001, Ⓔpolskydum@volny.cz. A striking Art Nouveau villa dating from 1899, that has been modernized inside, but is probably the place with most character in Ostrava. ❸

Imperial Tyršova 6 ☎596 116 621, ⓦwww.imperial.cz. A luxury, four-star hotel that has all the mod cons, but is expensive at nearly 4000Kč a double. ❼

Jindřich Nádražní 66 ☎596 112 979, ⒻW596 112 776. Smart, modern, red-brick hotel with a sauna, situated right by the disused nineteenth-century pithead of the same name. ❷

Maria Přívozská 23 ☎596 110 676, Ⓕ596 110 678, Ⓔobjednavky@hotel-maria.cz. A decent, medium-range hotel, a short walk from the city centre. ISIC and ITIC card holders receive a 10 percent discount. ❷

Palace 28 října 59 ☎596 158 111, Ⓔpalace@applet.cz. An old communist-era luxury hotel that can't quite pass muster in that category any more, hence the bargain prices. ❸

Savoy Macharova 16 ☎596 134 090, Ⓔreception@hotelsavoy.cz. Inexpensive, but comfortable, modernized hotel situated within walking distance of the main train station. ❸

The city

Ostrava divides into three distinct districts: **Slezská Ostrava**, on the east bank of the River Ostravice, where the first black-coal deposits were discovered back in the 1760s, **Vítkovice**, south of the centre on the opposite side of the river, where the first foundry was set up in 1828, and **Moravská Ostrava**, the largely pedestrianized downtown district.

It's in Moravská Ostrava that you'll find most of the town's shops and department stores, bunched up around the old marketplace and main square, **Masarykovo náměstí**. Under the Communists the square was known as náměstí Lidových milicí (People's Militia Square) – a once-proud reference to the city's strong working-class traditions and staunch postwar support for the Party (the Communists still capture a high percentage of the vote here). This largely unspoken alliance ensured high wages and well-stocked shops, and for the two decades after 1968, the commercial district was always crowded with Poles and Soviet soldiers gaping in awe at what to them was an unbelievably wide range of products. Hard times have now hit the local heavy industries, with steel production at less than half its 1989 level and thousands of workers being laid off. Similarly, the coal industry has drastically cut its workforce and closed down mines, owing to the decrease in demand for Czech coal stemming from greater environmental awareness, competition from other Eastern and

Western European countries, and since the Temelín nuclear plant began fuctioning (see p.172).

Though hardly an architectural masterpiece, the square still vaunts a handful of swanky late-nineteenth-century facades erected by the rich German and Austrian capitalists who owned the mines here until nationalization in 1945. The sixteenth-century **stará radnice**, in the southeastern corner of the square, is one of the oldest buildings in the city and now houses the less than thrilling **Ostravské muzeum** (Mon–Fri 9am–5pm, Sat & Sun 9am–1pm). Ostrava's most lavish museum, at Nádražní 10, was the one dedicated to the working-class movement, though it has now reverted to its original function as the **Investiční banka**, the muscular proletarians above the portico now simply employees. The city's purpose-built **Dům umění** (Tues–Sat 10am–noon & 12.30–6pm), a redbrick Functionalist building from the 1920s, on Jurečkova, one block west of Nádražní, displays an unexceptional collection of nineteenth-century Czech art on the ground floor, with temporary exhibitions upstairs.

With so much money sloshing around in the late nineteenth and early twentieth centuries, it comes as no surprise that Ostrava boasts one or two grandiose reminders of those golden years. The gargantuan salmon-pink-and-cream-coloured **Bazilika**, northwest of the main square, built in a heavy neo-Renaissance style in the 1880s, is the second largest church in Moravia, capable of seating a congregation of four thousand. One of the finest Art Nouveau buildings in the city stands to the north at the top of Milíčova, its facade decorated with delicate floral stuccowork – just don't look at the modern extension round the back. Directly opposite is Ostrava's imposing brick-built **Evangelický kostel** (Protestant Church), designed in Dutch Renaissance style in 1907. However, by far the most awesome monument to Ostrava's former municipal pride is the **nová radnice**, at the end of 30 dubna. Erected in the 1920s, it is the largest town hall in the country, and its slender, 72-metre-high, copper-clad clocktower has a viewing platform open to the public from May to October.

When the coal industry took off in the nineteenth century, the city just grew up around the pit heads – a convenient, but ecologically disastrous, piece of town planning. The **Karolina coking plant**, right in the city centre and pulled down only in the 1980s, spewed out lethal carcinogenic filth over the city's main shopping district for over a century, and you can still see the redbrick **Jindřich pithead** (těžní věž), just past 30 dubna on Nádražní. Elsewhere, antiquated derricks, silver snaking pipes and red-and-white-striped chimneys are very much a part of the cityscape: an awesome sight, lit up at night like proverbial satanic mills. Those with a passionate interest in the local mining industry should hop on bus #34, #52 or #56 at the top of Sokolská třída, east of the main train station, which provide a regular service north across the River Odra to the suburb of Petřkovice (get off at the U Jana stop). Here, at the now defunct Anselm mine (once owned by the Rothschilds), there's a **Hornický skanzen** or open-air mining museum (Tues–Sun guided tours at 9am, 11am, 1pm & 3pm), where you can descend into the pit, inspect the seams and take a look at the exhibition in the manager's villa.

The city continues to pay a high price for the mining exploitation of the last two centuries, especially when it comes to subsidence. The local **hrad**, originally built in the thirteenth century to guard the border between Moravia and Silesia, has already sunk fourteen metres and, according to city officials, is now beyond redemption. You can still visit it at any time by crossing one of the bridges over the Ostravice and negotiating the motorway (alternatively, take tram #9, #10, #13 or #18 and get off at the first stop across the river). If you're walking, as you cross the bridge, Sýkorův most, you'll pass by one of the few surviving monuments celebrating the city's liberation by the Soviets, which features a tank on a plinth.

Eating, drinking and nightlife

For a large city Ostrava is rather lacking in variety and quality of **dining** establishments. Options include thin-base pizzas from the popular *Astoria* pizzeria and steak restaurant, on the east side of the main square – one of the few places open on Sunday. The *Staročeská pivnice* on the ground floor of the *Hotel Palace* is a standard Czech pub where you can eat and drink cheaply, while the *Radniční restaurace*, through the arch to the right of the Nová radnice, allows you a glimpse of this magnificent interwar edifice from the inside; it also serves the local *Radegast* beer and even has disabled access. You can also sample the local pride in the *Pivnice Radegast*, a nice place in the Hotel Imperial. For something completely different, head for the new Spanish-themed restaurant, *España*, at Tyršova 31, decked like a Spanish galleon. The *Kavárna Elektra*, near the tourist office on Nádražní, was long the best café in town, a smart and spacious Viennese-style place, but is currently closed pending ownership changes.

Ostrava boasts a good **philharmonic orchestra**, once backed by big state funds, which plays in various venues across the city, while the Divadlo Antonína Dvořáka puts on a range of opera, ballet and theatre. Predictably enough, Janáček, who died in Ostrava, is the subject of the city's May music festival, **Janáčkův máj**. A more eclectic range of **jazz, rock and folk music** is staged upstairs at *Klub Parník*, the city's best alternative venue, housed in a striking late-nineteenth-century villa at the corner of Sokolská and Matiční; the pub downstairs (closed Sat & Sun lunch) is also a popular hangout. The city that produced Ivan Lendl is home to one of the republic's most important sports centres. Predictably enough, as a working-class city *par excellence*, Ostrava's strongest tradition is in **football**, and the city boasts two top-flight teams, Baník Ostrava and Vítkovice. A large number of the country's big sporting events are held here, so ask at the tourist office for the latest fixtures.

The Beskydy

Despite their proximity, the hilly **Beskydy** region and the Ostrava coal basin are poles apart. In the foothills there's a whole cluster of interesting sights not far from (and including) **Nový Jičín**. Further south and east, into hiking country proper, the old Wallachian traditions have been preserved both *in situ*, in the more inaccessible villages, and at the open-air folk museum or *skansen* at **Rožnov pod Radhoštěm**.

Nový Jičín

NOVÝ JIČÍN (Neu-Titschein) is a typical one-square town on the main road from Olomouc to Ostrava. That said, Masarykovo náměstí is a particularly fine square, with wide, whitewashed arcades tunnelling their way under a host of restrained, late-Baroque facades in pastel colours. The **radnice** is an unusual white, boxy affair rebuilt in the 1930s, its wonderfully jagged gable a reminder of its seventeenth-century origins. However, the one building that stands out (literally) from the rest is the **stará pošta**, where Tsar Alexander I and General Suvurov have both stayed the night; its pretty two-storey loggia dates from the town's boom time in the sixteenth century when it bought its independence from the Žerotín family.

Wooden churches in the Beskydy

If you can't make it out to the Greek-Catholic churches of East Slovakia (see p.554), the next best place for visiting **wooden churches** is the Beskydy region. Although numerous timber-framed houses were torn down during the course of the nineteenth century, churches appear to have fared a little better. Below is a selection of the region's best examples.

Bystřice nad Olší 12km southeast of Český Těšín. Polish/Czech town in the Olše valley, with a wooden neo-Gothic Catholic church, built in 1896 to replace the sixteenth-century stone one.

Guty 11km south of Český Těšín. Probably the most striking of all the Beskydy's wooden churches, with its bulky Lemk-style western tower erected in 1781 above the narthex or entrance porch.

Hodslavice 8km south of Nový Jičín. Birthplace of Czech nationalist and historian František Palacký, one of the chief political figures of the nineteenth-century Czech national revival. Hodslavice also boasts the sixteenth-century wooden church of sv Ondřej.

Kunčice pod Ondřejníkem 4km east of Frenštát pod Radhoštěm. This mountain village was a favourite summer resort of the wealthy steel and coal magnates of Ostrava, one of whom, in 1931, brought an entire Greek-Catholic church over from what is now the Ukraine for his wedding.

Radhošť 6km south of Frenštát pod Radhoštěm. You have to climb a mountain to see the wooden chapel of sv Cyril & Metoděj, built in neo-Byzantine style in 1905, from which there's an unbeatable view across the Beskydy.

Rybí 4km northwest of Štramberk. Fifteenth-century Gothic church with shingled roof, tower and onion dome steeple, plus a dinky little sundial in its main gable.

Nowadays, the town's chief attraction is its **Kloboučnické muzeum** or Hat Museum (Tues–Fri 8am–noon & 1–4pm, Sat & Sun 9am–3pm), laid out in the Žerotíns' old chateau, accessed through the covered passageway of Lidická underneath the radnice. Thankfully, the present exploits of the old state hat enterprise, Tonak (based in the town), are only lightly touched on, leaving most of the museum to a wonderful variety of hats produced in Nový Jičín since 1799 by the original firms of Hückel, Peschel and Böhm. The bit that gets the Czechs going is the array of hats worn by famous national personages – a bit esoteric for non-Czechs, though some might be stirred by the sight of Masaryk's topper.

Nový Jičín has two **train stations**, both located at the end of obscure and inconvenient branch lines, making the **bus** by far the easiest way to come and go. The **tourist office** (Mon–Fri 9am–noon & 1–4pm, Sat & Sun 9am–noon; ☎556 711 888), in the chateau, can book **private rooms** or find a pension in the area. This may be a good idea, as the local hotels are not up to snuff. If you're brave, the gaudy *Hotel Praha* (☎556 701 229, ℱ556 709 381; ❷), at Lidická 6, is a late-nineteenth-century building opposite the chateau that looks better outside than in.

Štramberk

Eight kilometres east of Nový Jičín, accessible by the occasional bus or an easy two-hour walk, the smokestack settlement of **ŠTRAMBERK** (Strallenburg) is one of the best places to take your first dip into Wallachian culture. Clumped under the conic Bílá hora (not to be confused with *the* Bílá hora in Prague) like an ancient funeral pyre, Štramberk feels very old indeed, yet many of its

As far as anybody can make out, the **Wallachs** or **Vlachs** were semi-nomadic sheep and goat farmers who settled the mountainous areas of eastern Moravia and western Slovakia in the fifteenth century. Although their name clearly derives from the Romanian Vlachs, it is believed that they arrived from eastern Poland and the Ukraine, and the name Vlach is simply a generic term for sheep farmer. Whatever their true origins, they were certainly considered a race apart by the surrounding Slav peasants. Successive Habsburg military campaigns against the Vlachs in the seventeenth century destroyed their separate identity, and nowadays Wallachian culture lives on only in the folk customs and distinctive wooden architecture of the region.

wooden cottages were built as recently as the first half of the nineteenth century. Its virtue is in displaying Wallachian architecture *in situ*, the cottages simply constructed out of whole tree trunks, unpainted and free of tourists rather than cooped and mummified in a sanitized *skansen*.

Despite being no more than a hillside village, Štramberk does have a nominal main square. At one end are several stone buildings in "folk Baroque", behind which rises up the galleried wooden *klopačka* (belfry) of the original church. At the other end is an old Jesuit church painted in sherbet orange, next door to a small **Muzeum Štramberk** (April–Oct Tues–Sun 9am–noon & 1–5pm) displaying archeological finds from the nearby Šipka cave (see below). The castle, laid waste by the Tatars and never rebuilt, has just one remaining round tower, **Trúba** (April–Oct daily 9am–5pm), which translates as "The Tube" and is now a lookout post, with a restaurant nearby.

Just below the main square is the newly established **Zdeněk Burian Museum** (May–Sept Tues–Sun 9am–noon & 1–5pm, Oct–April until 4pm), dedicated to the work of this prolific painter, who was born in nearby Kopřivnice and spent his childhood in Štramberk. Burian (1905–81) was a book illustrator and paleontologist, but is perhaps best known (to Czechs, at any rate) for his painstaking representations of the world of prehistoric humans. His inspiration came from the nearby **Šipka cave**, beneath the limestone hill of Kotouč (532m), where remains of Neanderthal man were discovered in the late nineteenth century. The caves are a short walk through the woods of the Národní sad, signposted off the road to Kopřivnice.

Štramberk is a fine place to spend a night, and *Hotel Šipka* (☎556 852 181, Ⓕ556 852 184, Ⓔhsipka@volny.cz; ❶), on the main square, lets out cheap, simple **rooms** and serves good Czech food and beer. A more comfortable option is the tastefully timber-clad *Hotel Roubenka* (☎ & Ⓕ556 852 566, Ⓔpavel.bajer@mailbox.cz; ❸), which enjoys great views up to the Trúba; to get there follow the signs off the road from Nový Jičín, or head down Dolní from the post office. Another, more expensive option is *Hotel Gong* (☎556 721 036, Ⓕ556 852 330, Ⓔgong.stramberk@applet.cz; ❹), a slightly unsightly modern edifice next door to the post office. At the bakery on the corner of the main square, you can sample the local speciality, *Štramberské uši* (Štramberk Ears), honeyed gingerbread (often filled with cream), which commemorates a particularly gruesome legend: during the Tatar invasion, the local people were saved by a judiciously timed flood which kept the marauders at bay – when the waters subsided, so the story goes, sacks full of the ears of Tatar victims were found.

Kopřivnice

On the other side of Bílá hora from Štramberk (and an easy half-hour walk), **KOPŘIVNICE** (Nesselsdorf) is an ugly, sprawling factory town, but nevertheless worth a quick visit for its **Technické Muzeum** (May–Sept Tues–Sun 9am–5pm; Oct–April until 4pm), in a new blue-and-white pavilion in the centre of town. The main draw here is the collection of Tatra cars, and even if spark plugs don't usually fire your imagination, there are some wonderful old cars here. Unlike the popular and ubiquitous Škoda, Tatra cars have always aimed to be exclusive: the first model, which came out in 1897, was called the "President", and from 1948 onwards that's exactly who rode in them. The silent and powerful black Tatra, looking like something out of a gangster B-movie, became the ultimate symbol of Party privilege. Ordinary mortals could buy any colour they liked except black – the colour reserved for Party functionaries. When you've seen the Tatra 87 and the 603, it's a slightly hysterical and somewhat frightening thought to imagine the country's top Stalinists cruising around in these cars, which were succeeded in the 1970s by the Tatra 613. The post-Communist leadership has decided to do away with the stigma of the Tatra, and with the Party no longer in a position to pay for its usual bulk order, the firm has had a hard time trying to modernize its Tonka-tough trucks and continue production of its super-luxury cars.

Příbor

Five kilometres and one train station north of Kopřivnice, **PŘÍBOR** (Freiberg) appears at first to be a rerun of Nový Jičín, with a similarly pleasant, arcaded main square. However, as the birthplace of **Sigmund Freud**, Příbor has a much greater claim to fame. Although the family's financial problems forced them to leave for Vienna when Sigmund was only four, it's difficult to resist the chance to visit the place where Freud went through his oral and anal phases: the ten-metre-square room at Freudova 117 (then belonging to Zajík the blacksmith; now, appropriately enough, a therapy centre offering reflexology and herbal remedies), which is now marked by a plaque. The local **Muzeum v Příboře** (Tues & Thurs 8am–noon & 1–4pm, Sun 9am–noon), situated in the former monastery on Lidická, has devoted only one of its four rooms to the man, and sadly there are no pictures of baby Sigi, only dull official photos of learned and bearded men (including Jung) at conferences on psychoanalysis. In the rest of the town, few associations present themselves, apart from Freud's bust, which stands just outside the pretty main square, náměstí S. Freuda.

> ### Freud in Freiburg
>
> Born in 1856 to a hard-up Jewish wool merchant and his third wife, Freud had no hesitation in ascribing significance to events that took place during the family's brief sojourn here. "Of one thing I am certain," Freud wrote later, "deep within me, although overlaid, there continues to live the happy child from Freiberg [Příbor], the first-born child of a young mother who received from this air, from this soil, the first indelible impressions." Things were not always so idyllic, and Freud later used a number of events from his early childhood to prove psychoanalytical theories. The family maidservant, "my instructress in sexual matters" in Freud's own words, was a local Czech woman who used to drag him off to the nearby Catholic church and in Freud's eyes was responsible for his "Rome neurosis." She was eventually sacked for alleged theft (and for encouraging baby Sigmund to thieve, too) and sent to prison. Things weren't too bad on the Oedipal front either, Freud suspecting his half-brother of being the father of his younger sister, Anna.

Hukvaldy

Moravians hold Janáček much dearer to their hearts than Freud, and the village of **HUKVALDY**, 6km east of Příbor, has become a modest shrine to the composer. Born just two years before Freud, **Leoš Janáček** was the fifth of nine children, too many for his impecunious father who taught at the local school. Thus, at the age of eleven, Janáček was sent to Brno to be a chorister, and from then on he made his home in the city, battling against the prejudices of the powerful German elite who ruled over the Moravian classical music scene. When at last he achieved recognition outside Moravia, through the success of the opera *Jenůfa*, he was already in his sixties. Having bought a cottage in Hukvaldy, he spent his last, most fruitful years based here and in Brno, composing such works as *The Glagolitic Mass*, *The Cunning Little Vixen* and *From the House of the Dead*. The music of this period was fired by his obsessive love for a woman called Kamila Strösslová, wife of a Jewish antique dealer in Písek, who had sent him food parcels throughout World War I. Although he never left his wife, Janáček wrote over 700 letters to Kamila, the most passionate ones written almost daily in the last sixteen months of his life. In August 1928 he caught a chill searching for her son in the nearby woods, and died in a hospital in Ostrava.

Even if you've no interest whatsoever in Janáček, Hukvaldy is a homely little village nestling into a wooded hill on top of which sits a ruined **hrad** (April & Oct Sat & Sun 9am–4pm; May–Sept Tues–Sun 9am–6pm), complete with deer park – there's a statue of the Cunning Little Vixen in the woods. The composer's **museum**, housed in his sandy yellow cottage, is pleasantly low-key (April & Oct Sat & Sun 10am–noon & 1–4.30pm; May & Sept Tues–Sun 10am–noon & 1–5pm; June–Aug Tues–Sun 10am–noon & 1–6pm), containing just a little modest furniture and his lectern (he always composed standing up). However, it's the gentle pastoral setting, an element underlying all Janáček's music, that provides the most instructive impression of the place. Should you wish to stay, there's a **tourist office** (Mon & Wed 7–11am & noon–5pm, Tues 7–11am & noon–3pm, Fri 7–11am; ☎ & ⨎558 699 221) in the village that can help with **accommodation**, if there's no room at the friendly *Hukvaldský dvůr* (☎558 699 241; ❷), opposite. Eight buses a day link Hukvaldy with Ostrava, and a few more run irregularly to Kopřivnice and Příbor.

Into the hills of the Beskydy

Between the sparsely wooded pastureland around Nový Jičín and the Rožnovská Bečva valley to the south are the **hills of the Beskydy**. Starting off in North Moravia and entering Poland, they actually extend right over into the Ukraine, shadowing the much higher Carpathian range to the south. Spruce has gradually given way to pine, which, though damaged by acid rain, is not too badly affected by pollutants, and in the westernmost reaches patches of beech forest still exist.

Around Radhošt'

During the Cold War, **FRENŠTÁT POD RADHOŠTĚM** (Frankstadt) was dominated by its Red Army barracks, but over the last decade the town has been spruced up, and the main square, which is peppered with Baroque statuary, is now looking very pretty indeed. Though not exactly in the thick of the Beskydy, it's easily the chief starting point for people heading off into the hills. There's a **tourist office** (Mon–Fri 9am–5pm, Sat 8.30–11.30am; ☎556 836

916, ⓦwww.frenstatpr.cz) in the town hall, and a couple of decent **hotels** in town. The *Přerov* (☏556 835 991, Ⓕ556 835 937; ❷), on the main square, is cheap, friendly and has a restaurant on the ground floor, and a cellar **pub** a few doors down, named after Oliver Hardy. A touch nicer is the *Radhošť'* (☏ & Ⓕ556 831 340; ❸), also on the square. Alternatively, there's the *Vlčina* (☏556 835 351, Ⓔvlcina@applet.cz; ❸), a communist-era mountain lodge complex southwest of the town with outstanding views over the valley – to get there either take the ski-lift (*lánova draha*) or walk 1.5km up the hill from town on the green-marked path. There's also the *Radhošť'* **campsite** (May to mid-Oct), on the north bank of the river, 1km northwest of the town centre.

Radhošť' (1129m), which Rožnov (see below) and Frenštát both dub themselves under (*pod*), is the most famous peak – thanks to its legends – though not the tallest. The view from the summit is still pretty good, and there's a fanciful wooden chapel, done out in neo-Byzantine style. Two kilometres east, there's a statue of Radegast, the mountain's legendary pagan god (who lends his name to the famous local beer). Another kilometre east, there's a series of late-nineteenth-century timber-slat buildings designed by Dušan Jurkovič, including the fantastical hotel, the *Tanečnica* (☏0656/83 53 41; ❸), named after the nearby mountain, as well as a nifty, carefully balanced *zvonička* (belfry). With the help of a chairlift (*lanovka*), the less athletic can reach the *Tanečnica*; the yellow- and/or green-marked path will take you down to the *Kněhyně* **campsite** (open all year) in Prostřední Bečva.

Rožnov pod Radhoštěm

Halfway up the Rožnovská Bečva valley, on the south side of Radhošť', lies the former spa town of **ROŽNOV POD RADHOŠTĚM**, now home of the biggest and most popular **skansen** of folk architecture in the Czech Republic, the main entrance to which lies on the other side of the river from the train station. The open-air museum – officially entitled **Valašské muzeum v přírodě** (admission to each of the three is 50 Kč; combined admission to all three is 120 Kč and a family pass is also available for 240 Kč) – is divided into three parts, each with a different opening time; guided tours (in Czech) are compulsory only in the Mlýnská dolina, so ask for the *anglický text*.

The moving force behind the first part, the Wooden Town or **Městečko dřeven** (Jan–March & Oct Tues–Sun 9am–4pm; April to mid-May & Sept daily 9am–5pm; mid-May to Aug daily 8am–6pm; Christmas season daily 9am–4pm), was local artist Bohumír Jaromek, who was inspired by the outdoor folk museum in Stockholm (from which the word *skansen* derives). In 1925 Rožnov's eighteenth-century wooden radnice was moved from the main square to its present site, followed by a number of other superb timber buildings from the town and neighbouring villages like Větřkovice u Příbora, which supplied the beautiful seventeenth-century wooden church (where services are still held). There are Wallachian beehives decorated with grimacing faces, a smithy and even a couple of *hospoda* selling food and warm *slivovice*.

The second part of the museum, the Wallachian Village or **Valašská dědina** (daily: late April to mid May & Sept 9am–5pm; mid-May to Aug 9am–5.30pm) was built in the 1970s on a hillside across the road from the Městečko dřevené. It takes a more erudite approach, attempting to recreate a typical highland sheep-farming settlement – the traditional Wallachian community – complete with a variety of farm animals and organic crops, plus a schoolhouse, dairy and blacksmith. Enthusiastic guides take you round the third and newest section, **Mlýnská dolina** (Mill Valley; times as at Valašská dědina), which is centred around an old flour mill and includes a water-powered blacksmith's and sawmill, peopled by period-dressed artisans.

Rožnov attracts a lot of coach parties who tend to book out the cheaper hotels, and oddly enough, there's no tourist office, so you may have to scout around for private **accommodation**. The best hotel in town is currently the flashy *Eroplán* (☎571 648 014, ☏571 648 222, ✉hotel-eroplan@iol.cz; ❹), with sauna, weight room and its own restaurant, and situated, like the nearby *Hotel Energetik* (☎571 654 045, ☏571 654 044; ❷), up the hill across from the *skansen*. The real bargain option in town is the high-rise *Pension Bečva* (☎ & ☏571 654 458, ✉majerz@quick.cz; ❷) – really a dorm-style hotel – opposite the *Billa* supermarket on the road to Valašské Meziříčí. Rožnov in general is not a great place to be laid up for the night; you may be more comfortable in Frenštát pod Radhoštěm, an easy bus ride 10km north, or in the pastoral mountain village of **Valašské Bystřica**, an equally simple bus ride 6km south of Rožnov. Here you'll find the snug *Penzion Horalka* (☎ & ☏571 646 428, ✉horalka@cm-group.cz; ❷) 1.5km west of the village centre in a fine setting, with a jacuzzi, sauna and restaurant on site. **Campsites** are thick on the ground to the east of the open-air museum in Rožnov, with one on either side of the road to Prostřední Bečva – the *Rožnov* (open all year) and the *Sport* (mid-June to mid-Sept) – and a third, *Pod lipami* (July & Aug), 3km up the road in Dolní Bečva. There's a nice **restaurant** in the Společenský dům, in the Městský sad, which also houses its own micro-brewery.

Frýdek-Místek

Lying halfway between the Beskydy and Ostrava, and accessible by train from either, **FRÝDEK-MÍSTEK** (Friedeck-Friedburg) is a rather rude re-entry into the Ostrava coal basin. Its charms are few – the tourist authorities call it "a city of possibilities" – and its soulless industrial quarter has assumed a much greater importance than its twin old towns straddling the River Ostravice: **Místek**, on the flat left bank, where the business of the town now goes on, and **Frýdek**, the prettiest and quietest part of town on the hill opposite. Frýdek's

---

Óndra L'ysohorsky

The ninth child of a Frýdek miner, the poet **Óndra Łysohorsky** (whose real name was Erwin Goy) took his pen name from the local Robin Hood rebel, Ondráš, who was imprisoned in, and escaped from, Frýdek castle back in the seventeenth century, when it was owned by the wicked Duke Pragma. His surname comes from the highest peak in the Beskydy, Lysa hora (Bare Mountain). Łysohorsky was brought up speaking German and the local Slav dialect, but, after writing his first verses in German, decided to change to Lachian, a written form of the local dialect which he himself invented, but which never really caught on. The dialect (or language, depending on your point of view), somewhere between Czech and Polish, survives in the towns and villages along the Polish border and was spoken by around a million people (mostly miners) at its peak between the two world wars. Łysohorsky's obstinacy on this linguistic point eventually brought him into conflict with the postwar Communist authorities, who accused him of supporting the region's Polish irredentists. Apart from a brief reprise in 1958, his verse remained unpublished in Czechoslovakia, despite his being one of the country's better-known poets abroad. Łysohorsky died shortly after the upheavals of 1989 in Bratislava, and the poet's vast archives are now safely deposited in Frýdek castle.

main square has now been beautifully restored, with a statue of St Florian, patron saint of firefighters, superintending the central fountain, and the town's landmark **zámek** (Tues, Wed & Fri 8am–noon & 12.30–4pm, Thurs closes 5pm, Sat & Sun 1–5pm) in one corner. Once the property of the lords of Těšín, it now contains an art gallery, and a small museum with tributes to Janáček, Óndra Łysohorsky (see box opposite) and the Silesian poet Petr Bezruč, who stayed in Místek for a while, championing the grievances of the poverty-stricken local miners; unfortunately, you have to go round the castle and the museum with a guide.

Český Těšín

If you fancy a quick jaunt into **Poland**, the easiest place is probably **ČESKÝ TĚŠÍN** (Cieszyn), 20km east of Frýdek-Místek, which found itself arbitrarily divided when the borders were drawn up following the collapse of the Habsburg Empire after World War I. The town was claimed by both Poland and Czechoslovakia, and it was finally decided in 1920 to use the fairly insignificant River Olše (Olza) as the frontier. In this instance, the Poles got the best deal, ending up with most of the town, including the staré město and the castle on the right bank. The Czech part is made up of grim, grey housing blocks built between the wars, and the only reason for coming here is to cross over to see the more interesting sights of the Polish side (see *The Rough Guide to Poland* for details).

When **crossing the border** into Poland, you have to use the Střelniční most (most Wolnolci), 400m due east of the train station; when returning to the Czech side, use Hlavní most (most Przyjazni), 700m downstream, at the end of Hlavní třída; both bridges are for pedestrians and cyclists only. Visa regulations and price disparities between the two countries have fluctuated over the years. At the height of Solidarity, during the 1980s, it was almost as difficult for Czechs to get into Poland as to travel to the West. Then the tables were turned and, with the Polish economy in free fall, the Czechs clamped down on Poles entering the country. Nowadays, people on either side of the border can cross using just their ID cards.

Travel details

Trains

Connections with Prague: Olomouc (every 1–2hr; 3hr–3hr 30min); Ostrava (every 2–3hr; 3hr 40min–5hr).
Jeseník to: Javorník (3 daily; 1hr 10min); Žulová (8 daily; 35min).
Lipová Lázně to: Javorník (6 or more daily; 50min); Žulová (8 or more daily; 20min).
Olomouc to: Bruntál (10 daily; 1hr 15min–1hr 45min); Jeseník (3 daily; 2hr 15min); Krnov (10 daily; 1hr 45min–2hr 30min); Lipová Lázně (3 daily; 2hr); Opava (4 daily; 2hr 20min–3hr); Ostrava (1–2 hourly; 1hr 30min–2hr 30min); Přerov (1–2 hourly; 20min); Prostějov (every 1–2hr; 15–25min); Šumperk (10 daily; 1hr

5min–1hr 25min).
Opava to: Hradec nad Moravicí (10 or more daily; 15min); Jeseník (4 daily; 2hr 10min); Krnov (every 1–2hr; 30–40min); Ostrava (hourly; 25–40min).
Ostrava to: Český Těšín (1–2 hourly; 50min); Frýdek-Místek (1–2 hourly; 40min/1hr).
Šumperk to: Jeseník (6 daily; 1hr 45min–2hr); Lipová Lázně (6 daily; 1hr 40min).

Buses

Connections with Prague: Nový Jičín (2 daily; 5hr); Olomouc (2 daily; 4hr); Ostrava (2 daily; 6hr).
Olomouc to: Nový Jičín (up to 6 daily; 1hr 15min); Opava (2–4 daily; 2hr); Ostrava (up to 6 daily; 2hr); Příbor (3–10 daily; 1hr 30min); Rožnov pod

Radhoštěm (2 daily; 1hr 15min).
Nový Jičín to: Frenštát pod Radhoštěm (hourly; 40min); Frýdek-Místek (up to 8 daily; 45min); Kopřivnice (hourly; 35min); Příbor (hourly; 25min);

Štramberk (1–2 hourly; 15–30 min).
Rožnov pod Radhoštěm to: Frenštát pod Radhoštěm (1–2 hourly; 15min); Valašské Bystřica (1–2 hourly; 10min).

The Slovak Republic

Introduction

After centuries of cultural repression by the Hungarians, followed by 75 years of playing second fiddle to the Czechs within Czechoslovakia, the **Slovaks** finally gained their independence on January 1, 1993. Since those heady celebratory days, however, life has been much harder for the Slovaks than for the Czechs. With no internationally popular figurehead to act as a public relations officer, the new Slovakia has found it difficult jockeying for a position in the new Europe. Political instability, corruption and slow-moving reforms initially deterred overseas investors and drew criticism from abroad, though more recently the country has rejoined the queue for membership to both NATO and the EU.

For the first-time visitor, however, perhaps the most striking difference between the Czechs and the Slovaks is their attitude to religion. **Catholicism** is much stronger in Slovakia and the country's churches are visibly fuller on a Sunday; indeed, it is not uncommon to see people crowded outside the entrance of an overflowing church with a service in progress. The republic also has a much more diverse population, with over half a million **Hungarian**-speakers in the area bordering Hungary, one of the largest **Romany** minorities in Europe and thousands of **Rusyns** in the east of the country bordering Ukraine. Geographically, Slovakia lies between two extremes: the flat, parched plains of the Danube basin in the west, and the limestone and granite peaks of the central mountains – including some of Europe's highest mountains outside the Alps – to the east. These have long formed barriers to industrialization and modernization, preserving and strengthening regional differences in the face of centralization from Vienna, Budapest, Prague and now Bratislava.

Getting around

Geographical considerations mean that Slovakia has nothing like the same density of **railways** as the Czech Republic. Some of the lines, however, are breathtakingly beautiful and serve most places along the chief valleys – after that you'll have to rely on the patchy **bus** network and, in some places (particularly in the far east of the country), you really need your own transport. Bus and train frequencies can be found in the "Travel Details" section at the end of each chapter.

Trains

With two-thirds of the Slovak train network made up of single-track lines, services are predictably slow. However, some **scenic journeys** are worth making for the views alone: try the Banská Bystrica–Diviaky line, the Brezno–Margecany trip in the Low Tatras, or any of the electric trains in the High Tatras. Ticket prices are still remarkably low at around 2Sk per kilometre.

The state railways, **Železnice Slovenskej Republiky** or **ŽSR** (ⓦwww.zsr.sk/english), run two main types of service: *rýchlik* trains are the faster, stopping only at major towns; the *osobný vlak*, or local train, stops everywhere and averages about 30km an hour. Fast trains are further divided into Euro-city (EC), Inter-city (IC), *expresný* (Ex) and *zrýchlený* (Zr). For EC trains, and occasionally for IC and Ex trains, you need to pay a supplement which you should purchase before boarding the train (it costs more otherwise).

Tickets and fares

Once you've worked out when your train leaves (for which, see p.418), the best thing to do when buying a ticket (*lístok*) is to write down all the relevant information (date/time/destination) on a piece of paper and hand it to the ticket clerk. This avoids any linguistic misunderstandings – rectifying any mistakes involves a lengthy bureaucratic process and costs you ten percent of the ticket price.

Fares are cheap, with a second-class single from Bratislava to Košice currently costing around £9/$13. First-class carriages (*prvá*

417

trieda) exist on all fast trains, and though tickets are fifty percent more expensive, they should guarantee you a seat on a busy train. There are half-price discounts (*zľavy*) for children (*deti*) aged 6 to 15, and you can take two under-6s for free. ŽSR also run reasonably priced night trains with sleepers (*lôžkový vozeň*) or couchettes (*ležadlový vozeň*), which should be booked as far in advance as possible and certainly no later than six hours before departure.

For all international services (and any other trains marked with an "R" on the timetable), you can buy a **seat reservation** (*miestenka*). It's advisable to get one if you're travelling at the weekend on one of the main routes and want to be sure of a seat. The *miestenka* costs very little, but you must get it at least an hour before your train leaves, and either after or at the same time as you purchase your ticket.

Information and timetables

As in the Czech Republic, obtaining train information can be problematic unless you have some knowledge of the language.

Reading Slovak train timetables

Select your route on the diagrammatic map and make a note of the number printed beside it, then find the appropriate number on the timetable rollers. Crucial notes and explanations are in Slovak: arrivals are often abbreviated to *pr.* or *prích.* and departures to *od.* or *odch.*; a platform or *nástupište* is usually divided into two *koľaj* on either side. At the side of the timetable you'll often find the notes *chodí v* (running on), or *nechodí v* (not running on), followed by a date or a number/symbol: 1–6 for Monday–Saturday, two hammers for a weekday and a cross for a Sunday. The main station in larger towns is known as *hlavná stanica*, while minor stations often have the suffix *mesto* or *zástavka* after the name. If you're planning on using the trains a lot, you could invest in a ŽSR timetable (*cestovný poriadok*), which comes out every May and is available from most bookshops and tobacconists.

Most stations have poster-style displays of arrivals (*príchod*) and departures (*odchod*), the former on white paper, the latter on yellow, with fast trains printed in red; timetables in the smaller stations are displayed on simple boards (*smer*). Rollers are an alternative source of information available in most stations. See the box below for advice on how to read them.

Buses

Trains will take you most places, but if you have to change a lot, it might be easier to take one of the regional **buses** (*autobus*), run by either the state bus company, Slovenská autobusová doprava (or SAD; Ⓦ www.sad.sk), or one of numerous private operations. Bus **stations** (*autobusová stanica*) are usually next to the train station, and where there's no office (or it's closed) you'll have to buy your ticket from the driver. It's a good idea to book your ticket in advance if you're travelling at the weekend or early in the morning on one of the main routes.

Tickets can be bought at the station before or on the day of departure; for more minor routes, tickets are on sale from the driver. Large items of luggage (*batožina*) have to go in the boot, for which the driver will charge you an extra 10–15Sk. Minor bus stops are signposted *zastávka*. To get off, say *ja chcem vystúpiť*; "the next stop" is *ďalšia zastávka*. For help with the symbols commonly used on bus timetables, see the Czech section on p.34.

City transport

Buses (*autobus*) and **trolleybuses** (*trolejbus*) – plus **trams** (*električka*) in Košice and Bratislava – combine to provide a generally excellent urban public transport system that operates from dawn until around 11pm in most major towns (and all night in Bratislava). **Ticket** prices are currently 12Sk in Bratislava for an adult (less elsewhere); with reduced rates for those aged 6–15; while under-6s travel free. Though costs can vary, they are universally cheap.

In most cases, you have to buy your ticket before travelling; these are available from newsagents, tobacconists and the yellow machines at major stops, and must be validated in the punching machine on board;

plain-clothes **inspectors** will impose an on-the-spot fine of 500Sk or more on anyone caught without a ticket.

Driving

Driving under your own steam is a viable alternative to public transport in Slovakia. Traffic is light and road conditions usually good. Only in Bratislava might you encounter difficulties, due to the confusing lane system, tramlines and lack of parking facilities. Although there are only a few short stretches of motorway to speak of, to use them, you'll need a **motorway sticker** (*úhrada* in Slovak) currently costing 60Sk for fifteen days and available from border crossings, post offices and some petrol stations. Note that many **border crossings** have special restrictions attached to them, with some operating only during hours of daylight, and others for use only by the nationals of the two countries who share the border.

Most foreign driving licences are valid – including all EU, US and Canadian ones – but getting an **International Driver's Licence** can set your mind at rest. If you're driving your own car, you are legally required to carry its registration document; if it's not in your name, you must have a letter of permission signed by the owner and authorized by an official motoring organization (not applicable to a rented car). Other legally required items are a red warning triangle, a first-aid kit, a set of replacement bulbs, and a national identification sticker. Your insurance company at home will advise you as to whether you need a green card; without one you may only be able to get third-party insurance.

Rules of the road

The strict **rules and regulations**, a legacy of the old police state, are less strictly adhered to nowadays, though on-the-spot fines are common and range from a paltry 50Sk to 500Sk or more. Basic rules are: drive on the right, always wear your seatbelt, never take the wheel with any alcohol in your bloodstream, and give way to pedestrians on zebra crossings, and those crossing the road at traffic lights if you're turning right or left. Road markings at junctions are sparse, so look out for the yellow diamond sign,

which means you have right of way; a black line through it means you haven't.

Speed limits are 130kph on motorways and 90kph on other roads, except in cities, towns and villages where the maximum is 50kph. There's a special speed limit of 30kph at **level crossings**, where instead of a barrier you'll often find simply the sign *pozor* and a series of lights: a single flashing light means the line is live; two red flashing lights mean a train is approaching. *Odchadzka* is a diversion; *prújezd zákazany* or *zákaz vjazdu* means no entry.

Fuel and car rental

Petrol (*benzín*) comes in super (95 octane) and *special* (91 octane); diesel (*nafta* or *TT diesel*) is also available. You can fill up with **lead-free** petrol (*natural*) at virtually all petrol stations from green-marked pumps. Bear in mind that petrol stations are few and far between in the more remote areas and that some close at lunchtimes and after 6pm (though the number of 24-hour ones is increasing steadily). The price of petrol is cheaper than in much of the EU, currently costing around 30Sk a litre (£0.50/$0.80). If you have **car trouble**, dial ☎154 and wait for assistance. You might consider an insurance policy that covers on-the-spot repairs, car rental and travel home for you and your passengers in case of an emergency.

Car rental is easy to arrange. To rent a car, you have to be at least 21 years of age (sometimes 25) and have a clean licence. Booking from abroad will cost you an incredible £280/$420 a week for a small car. Some of the multinationals have offices in Bratislava, but local agents offer far better deals. Car rental is cheaper from Vienna airport, and most companies allow customers to take their cars over the border into Slovakia, but do check before you book and inform them of your intention; you will incur an extra daily insurance charge. For details of international car rental agencies, see p.36.

Cycling and hiking

Cycling is now fairly popular as a leisure pursuit in Slovakia – less so as a means of getting to work – and in the more touristy areas

Useful hiking terms

cesta	path
chata	mountain refuge
dolina	valley
hranica	border
jaskyňa	cave
lanovka	chairlift/cable car
les	forest
lyžiarsky vlek	ski lift
prameň	spring
rozhladňa/prehliadka	viewpoint
skala	rock
vodopád	waterfall

such as the High Tatras, you'll find plenty of **bike rental** outlets. **Spare parts** are more difficult to obtain, so bring as many with you as you can. On the faster trains you can take your bike (*bicykel*) for a small supplement, and it's easy enough to persuade the guard on the slower trains to let you on, for a small fee. Special cyclists' **maps** (*cykloturistická mapa*), produced by both VNÚ and Freytag & Berndt, are also now available in the shops.

Walking is a popular pastime, with a dense network of trails covering the entire countryside; each path is colour-coded with clear markers every 100m or so and signs indicate how long it'll take you to reach your destination. The walks are usually fairly easy-going, but if you venture into the mountains proper, you'll need some sturdy boots. In the High Tatras, you must stick to the paths indicated and should really have some serious walking experience before attempting any ascent; this mountain range is one of the few areas on which **hiking guides** have been published in English, so you might consider investing in one before you leave home. Wherever you're going, it's a good idea to get hold of a 1:50,000 (or even better 1:25,000) *turistická* **map**, which details all the marked paths in the area (see p.23).

Accommodation

On the whole, **accommodation** in Slovakia is still relatively inexpensive. However, improvement in hotel standards is slow, and, in terms of quality of service, you'll often be better off staying in the privately owned pen-

sions, or private rooms in general, than in the old Communist-era hotels – even those that have been nominally "modernized". The further east you go, the more difficult it becomes to find accommodation, and service can be quite poor. For a run down on the **price codes** used in this book, see the inside front cover.

Hotels, pensions and private rooms

The modernization of Slovakia's **hotels** is proving a lengthy process, resulting in the temporary closure of large numbers while looking for new investors. In some areas, though, you'll still come across the old state-owned behemoths, whose standards are stuck in the Communist era. Prices vary enormously – they're at their highest in Bratislava and the High Tatras – but are generally lower than in the Czech Republic, even though many places still charge visitors from abroad roughly twice as much as Slovaks. Most hotels now operate some kind of star system, though it gives only a very vague indication of what to expect.

In many areas, the gap in the market has been filled by newly established **pensions** (often written as *penzión*), which are often excellent value, though not necessarily any less expensive than hotels. **Private rooms** are also available along many of the main roads and in the more tourist-frequented regions. You can be sure that these will be pristine, though how much privacy you'll have and to what extent you'll have to share facilities with the family will vary. Outside the bigger cities and more popular mountain areas, accommodation can be hard to come by and standards low, particularly in the eastern part of the country, so flexibility is a valuable asset.

Hostels and campsites

There is no real network of **hostels** in Slovakia, though a few are affiliated to Hostelling International and others come under the umbrella of CKM, the **student travel agency** (⦿www.ckm.sk). Other hostels do exist, ranging from places run much like hotels to dormitories primarily used by domestic tour groups or local workers but which may have a spare bed if you're lucky.

More useful are the **mountain huts** (*chaty*) on the hillsides of the High Tatras; though few are accessible by road, most are just a few kilometres' walk from civilization. Some cost as much as £10/$15 per person, while the more isolated and basic ones can cost as little as £6/$9 per person. These can really only be booked through local agencies or tourist offices within the republic, though you're unlikely to be turned away if you turn up before 6pm at the more isolated ones.

There are a large number of **campsites** (usually known as *autokemping*) scattered throughout Slovakia, varying enormously in standards and facilities. Many have **bungalows** (*chaty*), which are very cheap to rent but are often block-booked by groups. Most sites are open from April or May until September or October, with a handful open all year round. The more basic campsites (*táborisko*) are marked on hiking maps; open only in the height of summer, they provide just ad hoc toilets and a little running water. Prices are inflated for foreigners, but are still reasonable; two people plus car and tent weigh in at around £5/$8.

Communications

Like the Czechs, the Slovaks are currently in the middle of radically overhauling their telecommunications network. The **phone** system, in particular is being dragged kicking and screaming into the twenty-first century, with the result that a lot of the country's phone numbers and codes have been (and are still) changing. The Slovaks are nowhere near as wired up to the **internet** as the Czechs, though access is possible in most towns and cities across the country.

Post

Post offices (*pošta*) are usually open between 8am and 5pm Monday to Friday. Letters or postcards take around five working days to reach the UK, and a week to ten days to North America. **Stamps** (*známky*) are available from newsagents and kiosks as well as post offices, though often only for domestic mail. See p.609 for a list of countries in Slovak.

Poste restante (pronounced as five syllables in Slovak) is available in major towns. The sender should write Pošta 1 (the main office), followed by the name of the town, and their name and address on the back. It might be safer to have mail sent to your embassy in Bratislava, though you should inform them of this beforehand.

Phones

Slovak public **phones** (*telefón*) are pretty reliable, with instructions in English – despite the graphic description you may still encounter problems. Theoretically, you simply pick up the receiver, drop in the minimum fee demanded, then dial the number. When you run out of money, you'll hear a recorded message urging you in Slovak to insert more. Fortunately, most coin-operated phones are being replaced by more reliable **card phones**, which makes international calls much easier. Phone cards (*telefonní karty*), currently available in 75 and 150 units (prices vary), can be bought at post offices and most tobacconists and kiosks. Insert the card into the telephone, and the number of units remaining on the card appears on the phone's display.

The **dialling tone** is a short pulse followed by a long one; the **ringing tone** is long and regular; **engaged** is short and rapid, but shouldn't be confused with the very rapid tone which indicates the line is being connected; the standard Slovak response is *prosím*; and the word for extension is *linka*. If you have any problems, dial ☎149 and ask for an English-speaking operator.

You may still find it simpler to make international calls from one of the telephone exchanges found in the major towns. Write down the town and telephone number, leave a deposit of around 200Sk, then wait for your name to be called out; bear in mind that international calls are extremely expensive at any time. Calls can be made from most hotels, but the surcharge is usually quite heavy. An easier option is a **collect call**, which will cost the recipient less than it would cost you. Dial ☎0131 and ask for an English speaker. Calling cards issued by your home long-distance carrier often have the best rates, but be sure you know the direct number to call in order to place the call from Slovakia.

Ⓑ

Useful telephone numbers

Some Slovak regional prefixes have recently been changed, and others may follow in the future. In addition, the whole system is gradually being digitalized, which means all numbers are slowly getting longer or changing completely.

Phoning Slovakia from abroad

From Britain & Ireland ℡ 00 + 421 (Slovakia) + area code minus first 0 + number

From USA and Canada ℡ 011 + 421 (Slovakia) + area code minus first 0 + number

From Australia and New Zealand ℡ 0011 + 421 (Slovakia) + area code minus first 0 + number

Phoning abroad from Slovakia

To the UK: ℡ 0044 + area code minus 0 + number.

To the Republic of Ireland: ℡ 00353 + area code minus 0 + number.

To the USA & Canada: ℡ 001 + area code + number.

To Australia: ℡ 0061 + area code minus 0 + number.

To New Zealand: ℡ 0064 + area code minus 0 + number.

Email

One of the best ways to keep in touch while travelling is to sign up for a free **internet email address** that can be accessed from anywhere, for example YahooMail or Hotmail – accessible through ⓦ www.yahoo.com and ⓦ www.hotmail.com. Once you've set up an account, you can use these sites to pick up and send mail from any internet café, or hotel with internet access

You can usually get online somewhere in most Slovak towns and cities, though there aren't many specialist cybercafés. The easiest way to find out how to get online is to ask the local tourist office. For details of how to plug your laptop in when abroad, and electrical systems in different countries, check out the useful website ⓦ www.kropla.com.

Media

Besides the European edition of *The Guardian*, most of the broadsheet **British papers** on sale

in Bratislava are a day old. **American newspapers** are pretty much restricted to *USA Today* and the *International Herald Tribune*. In addition, there's the weekly *Slovak Spectator* (ⓦ www.slovakspectator.sk), a thin, broadsheet newspaper that concentrates on current affairs and finance, but carries a useful listings section on Bratislava. Unfortunately, it is hard to find anywhere but in Bratislava. Outside the capital, English-language newspapers are rare; your best bet is the more expensive hotels. If all you want are the soccer results, including Premiership ones, then the Slovak sports daily *šport* will do the job.

The **Slovak press** were under constant pressure when Mečiar and his allies were in power. Shortly after independence in 1993, Mečiar sacked the editor of the government-backed daily, *Smena*, for publishing critical articles. Eighty percent of the staff then left in protest and formed *Sme*, a paper whose readership quickly overtook that of *Smena*. As a further humiliation, *Sme* later took over *Smena* – it has a one-page English-language section covering the main news on Tuesdays and Thursdays.

The only good thing to be said about Czechoslovak state **television** under the Communists was that after federalization in 1969 it consistently broadcast in Czech and Slovak. This commitment to bilingual broadcasting was strictly adhered to, so that in the course of an ice hockey match, the first half would be commentated on in Czech and the second in Slovak. For twenty years, this helped nurture a generation for whom the differences between the two nations, at least linguistically, were irrelevant. Now the Slovaks and Czechs have gone their different ways, and both have their own commercial channels. The main Slovak commercial station, Markíza, now attracts by far the largest slice of the country's audience, pushing the more interesting state-run channels, STV1 and STV2, into second place.

As far as **radio** goes, most cafés and bars tune in to one of the new FM pop/muzak stations. You can pick up the **BBC World Service** (ⓦ www.bbc.co.uk/worldservice) fairly easily now from the two big cities, around the 100MHz mark, and on shortwave; most FM stations give out pretty weak signals, so don't expect much once you leave the suburbs.

Eating and drinking

Seventy-five years of close contact with the Czechs and forty years of Communist rule have left **Slovak cuisine** with many of the same predilections as the Czechs. The secret ingredient, however, is the Hungarian influence, which left a legacy of marginally spicier cooking.

For further **food and drink terms**, see p.605.

Food

The similarities between Slovak and Czech cuisine mean that much of the information contained in the section on Czech food starting on p.41 is relevant here. The few differences are outlined below.

There are several types of **eating establishments**: the *reštaurácia* is the most common and varies in formality; a *vináreň* (wine cellar), which often stays open later, will also guarantee a full meal; a *pivnica* or *piváreň* (pub) is based on the Czech version but less commonplace, usually serving filling food at a good price; and, at the budget end of the scale, you can stoke up with the local workers at very cheap self-service *bufet*.

Vegetarians

Though the Slovaks are a nation of carnivores, the outlook is not all bleak for **vegetarians**. Many menus have a section called *bezmäsité jedlá*; beware, however, that although this translates literally as "without meat", this can simply mean that meat is included to a lesser degree than usual. The most popular non-meat dish is *vyprážený syr*, a slab of melted cheese fried in breadcrumbs served with potatoes and a large dose of tartare sauce, though watch out – if it's *plnený* or *se šunkou*, then it will certainly include ham. The phrases to remember are *som vegetarián/vegeteriánka*, and for emphasis add *nejem ani mäso ani rybu* (I don't eat meat or fish), at which point your server may shake his or her head in disbelief.

Slovak cuisine

The usual mid-morning Slovak snack at the *bufet* (stand-up canteen) is *párek*, perhaps the most ubiquitous **takeaway food** in Central Europe: a hot frankfurter, dipped in mustard or horseradish and served inside a white roll. *Langoše* – deep-fried dough smothered in a variety of toppings, most commonly garlic butter – are very popular, too.

Most Slovak menus start with **soup** (*polievky*), followed by a main course of **meat** (*mäso*) – usually pork or beef – with potatoes, pickled cabbage and/or **dumplings** (*knedle*). Goulash (*guláš*) is popular, often *Szegedinský* (pork with sauerkraut) though it's usually more of a stew than a spicy soup. The Slovak national dish, *bryndzové halušky*, is potato gnocchi with a heavy sheep's cheese sauce, usually topped with specks of fried pork fat or bacon (veggies beware).

Main courses are overwhelmingly based on pork or beef, but trout and carp are usually featured somewhere on the menu and you may find catfish or pike-perch if you're lucky, and occasionally lamb. Most main courses are served with delicious potatoes (*zemiaky*) – but fresh salads or green vegetables are still a rarity in local restaurants. In addition to *palačinky* (pancakes) filled with chocolate, fruit and cream, Slovak **desserts** invariably feature apple or cottage-cheese strudel and ice cream.

For a fuller list of Slovak **food and drink terms**, see the "Language" section in Contexts, p.605.

Drinking

The Slovaks make some medium-quality **white wine**, though exports are low compared to neighbouring Hungary. The two main wine regions are along the hot southern edge of the republic; the vineyards of the Small Carpathians stretch right down to the suburbs of Bratislava, while those of the Slovak Tokaj, bordering onto the main Hungarian wine-producing region of the same name, produce a good dry white known as Furmint.

The most famous of the **spirits** available in Slovakia is the plum brandy *slivovice*, which originated in the western border hills but is now available just about everywhere. You'll probably come across *borovička* at some point, a popular firewater from the Slovak Spiš region, made from juniper berries; *myslivec* is another rough brandy with an ardent following.

Unlike the Czechs, the Slovaks have no great tradition of **beer** drinking, but union with the Czech Lands in 1918 gradually changed things, and since 1945, their beer consumption has increased tenfold. The Slovaks do, of course, brew their own. One of the most famous is the excellent *Zlatý bažant* (Golden Pheasant) from Hurbanovo, in the Danube basin. The central Slovak town of Martin also produces a distinctive porter, a dark, heady brew which is notoriously difficult to get hold of – try looking out for *Cassovar* instead. Other good Slovak beers include *Šariš* and *Smädný Mních*. Czech beers are also widely available, with the Bohemian *Pilsner Urquell*, *Gambrinus* and *Budvar* leading the field.

Castles, churches and museums

The Slovak countryside is dotted with **chateaux** (*zámok*) and **castles** (*hrad*), many of them reduced to rubble, others converted for modern use, into old people's homes, trade-union holiday retreats and even training centres for the secret police. Some have been returned to their former owners, and plenty more have been restored and opened to the public. The country's **churches** (*kostol*) and monasteries (*kláštor*) have generally been better looked after than those in the Czech Republic, though many lock their doors outside worshipping hours. **Museums** (*múzeum*) and **galleries** (*galéria*) thrived under the Communists, and those that have survived the subsequent ideological purging have little money to bring themselves up to date.

Castles and guided tours

Basic **opening hours** for castles and other historical buildings are usually May to September Tuesday to Sunday 9am to noon, then 1pm to 5pm; in April and October, opening times are usually restricted to weekends and holidays; the rest of the year the buildings are often closed. Access to the interior is usually only possible with a **guided tour** (*sprievodza*), which usually sets off on the hour, the last one leaving an hour before closing time. Tours are usually conducted in Slovak, occasionally in German or Hungarian, rarely in English, but it's always worth asking for a written English resumé (*anglický text*). Entrance tickets cost very little – rarely more than 50–100Sk – hence no prices are quoted in the text.

Churches, monasteries and synagogues

A few of the most popular **churches** operate in much the same way as museums, occasionally even charging an entrance fee. Other churches are usually closed except for services, for which times are often posted outside the main doors, but it is worth asking around for the local *kňaz* (priest) or *kaplan* (caretaker), who will usually be only too happy to oblige with the key (*kľúč*).

In the north and east of the country, there are a small number of **Orthodox** (*Pravoslavný*) believers and a much larger contingent who belong to the **Greek-Catholic Church** (*Grécko-katolícky*), an obscure branch of Roman Catholicism whose small wooden churches, packed with icons and Byzantine paraphernalia, appear just like Orthodox churches to the uninitiated. You'll find a much more thorough account of the Greek-Catholics and their churches in the section on Carpatho-Ruthenia in Chapter Ten. Suffice to say that the buildings are fascinating, especially their dark and poky interiors, but they are kept firmly locked with little indication of what time the next service will be held.

Slovakia once boasted a considerable **Jewish** population, but most fell victim to the Nazi Holocaust, helped on their way by certain members of the Slovak wartime government. Today, an estimated 2000 still live in the republic, but Bratislava is one of the few places where regular worship still takes place. Most of the country's **synagogues** still stand, but many need considerable repairs – notable exceptions are those at Trenčín, Liptovský Mikuláš and Prešov.

Museums and galleries

Outside of Bratislava, Slovak **museums** have changed little since the days of Communism, mostly, it has to be said, due to lack of funding. Nevertheless, you do still come across the odd gem, and most local museums boast decent collections of folk art. It's worth asking for an English commentary or *anglický text*, or else you'll normally have to make do with Slovak-only labelling. The **art galleries** of Bratislava and Košice will disappoint those hoping to find masterpieces by either Slovak or non-Slovak painters. In fact, some of the country's best indigenous art – Rusyn icons and the work of Pavol of Levoča – can only be found in the small-town galleries and churches of East Slovakia.

Opening hours for museums and galleries tend to be from 9am to 4pm or 5pm, usually without a break at lunch. Many stay open all year round or switch from a Tuesday–Sunday summer routine to a Monday–Friday one during the winter. Full opening hours are detailed in the guide, but ticket prices are not, since they are rarely more than 50–100Sk.

Public holidays, festivals and entertainment

Aside from **religious celebrations** and **pilgrimages**, the cultural calendar is dominated by **arts**- and **music-based festivals** unique to individual towns. In addition, summer is the season for village folkloric events, of which the most famous is the Východná folk festival, which takes place near Poprad. As for the arts and sport, both have had a bumpy ride whilst learning to live without massive state subsidies.

Festivals and other annual events

Slovakia may not have a bevy of international composers to its name, but it boasts an even stronger folk tradition than the Czech Republic. The Východná Folk Festival, in late June/early July, is the biggest and most prestigious of the many annual **folk festivals**, with groups from all over Europe performing. Others worth looking out for are the one in Detva in early July, a Rusyn-based one in Svidník in mid- to late-June, and a festival with a Hungarian flavour in Gombasek every August.

Public holidays

January 1 (Independence Day)
January 6 (Epiphany)
Good Friday
Easter Monday
May 1
May 8 (VE Day)
July 5 (Introduction of Christianity by ss Cyril and Methodius)
August 29 (Slovak National Uprising 1944)
September 1 (Constitution Day)
September 15 (Day of the Virgin Mary)
November 1 (All Saints' Day)
December 24
December 25
December 26

The 1980s witnessed a revival of **pilgrimages** (*púť*), usually centred around the cult of the Virgin Mary. The biggest gathering is on the first weekend in July at Levoča in the Spiš region of East Slovakia, when up to 250,000 people descend on the small pilgrimage church above the town. Lesser celebrations go on in the region for the following two months.

For the Orthodox rites churches, which predominate in the east of the country, **Easter** (*Veľká noc*) is much more important than Christmas (*Vánoce*), and the often elaborate and lengthy processions and services can be well worth catching.

The arts

As in the Czech Republic, the **theatre** (*divadlo*) industry in Slovakia played an important part in the events of 1989, leading the way in the strikes that eventually toppled the Communist regime. In 1997, the country's theatre community found itself once more thrown into the political arena, staging what was ultimately an unsuccessful strike against the government, after they replaced several key figures in the industry with people who supported the governing HZDS party. The problem is that theatres throughout the country are still heavily subsidized by the authorities, and this allows a certain amount of political leverage over appointments.

For those with no knowledge of Slovak, it's best to stick to productions with less of a linguistic problem, such as opera or ballet. That said, ticket **prices** are cheap, and the venue and the event itself are often interesting enough to sustain you. The other genre for which language is not always a barrier is **puppetry** or *bábkové divadlo* as it's known in Slovak. Unfortunately, few traditional marionette shows are put on nowadays, with live actors taking centre stage in more and more productions, making the shows less accessible if you don't speak the language.

The **cinema** (*kino*) is cheap and generally rudimentary in Slovakia. Most foreign films tend to be shown with Slovak subtitles (*titulky*), with only the big Hollywood blockbusters getting dubbed. Beware, however, that film titles are usually translated into Slovak, so you'll need a dictionary to identify films like *Pekelná Hora* as *Dante's Peak*.

Sport

If there's one thing that makes Slovak sports fans really angry, it's the way that everyone assumes all the best players in the old Czechoslovak teams were Czech. In fact, many of Czechoslovakia's finest sporting moments were Slovak-inspired, most notably the European Championship-winning soccer team of 1976. Even today, the Swiss tennis star Martina Hingis is frequently referred to in the Western press as Czech, when in fact her roots are Slovak. As a result, nothing makes Slovak sports fans happier than when they beat their former compatriots, as they have done since the split, in the country's two top sports, soccer and ice hockey. Getting tickets to watch either sport is easy (and cheap) enough on the day as matches rarely sell out. Taking part is much more difficult as there are still

relatively few facilities for the general public – your best bet is likely to be to go to the plusher hotels, whose sports facilities are often open to non-guests.

The 1998 World Cup **football** qualifiers pitched the Slovaks against the Czechs, and, contrary to everyone's expectations, the latter came off worse. Still, the national team are clearly a long way off qualifying for either of the two major international soccer finals. Slovak club football also looks a long way off repeating Slovan Bratislava's famous victory over Barcelona in 1969 to lift the European Cup Winners' Cup (the only European title won by either a Czech or Slovak club). Slovan remain one of the country's leading clubs, having won the first three Slovak league titles on the trot. Recently, however, they have lost ground to the likes of FC Košice and Spartak Trnava. The season runs from August to late November and from March to late June, with most matches held on Saturday afternoons.

As with football, so with **ice hockey**, the country's second most popular sport – the assumption has always been that it was Czech players who led the old Czechoslovak team to glory. However, that theory can now be safely set aside, as the Slovaks surprised everyone by winning the 2002 World Championships for the first time ever, beating the Russians in the final. Domestic games, which can take anything up to three hours, are held in the local *zimný štadión* (winter stadium) on Sunday afternoons. The season starts at the end of September and culminates in the annual World Championships, when the fortunes of the national side are subject to close scrutiny, especially if pitched against the Czechs.

Bratislava and west Slovakia

CHAPTER 8

Highlights

* **Bratislava** – The much maligned Slovak capital has a small but beautifully restored old town, its Baroque palaces interspersed with leafy squares. **See p.429**

* **Trnava** – Slovak ecclesiastical capital boasting a whole host of ornate churches, and a virtually complete circuit of town walls. **See p.454**

* **Čachtice** – Hilltop ruined castle with chilling associations with the "Blood Countess". **See p.467**

* **Trenčín** – Attractive town on the Váh river, overlooked by an impressive ruined castle. **See p.469**

* **Trenčianske Teplice** – Relaxing spa town with a functionalist thermal swimming pool. **See p.469**

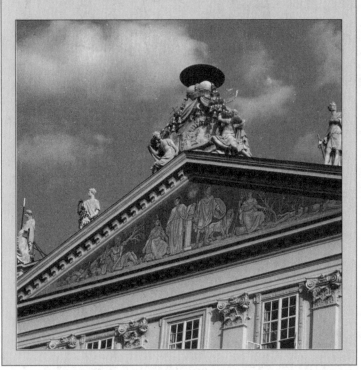

8

Bratislava and west Slovakia

I n many ways, the western third of Slovakia is the least typically Slovak part of the country. For a start, it's flat, fertile and fairly treeless, its only mountain range, the Small Carpathians, tame in comparison with the central mountains further east. Even the Slovak capital **Bratislava** was for centuries an Austro-Hungarian city in which the Slovaks, like the Romanies and Jews, were a distinct minority, and far removed from the true heart of the country in the central mountain regions. The great flat plain of the **Danube**, to the east of Bratislava, is inhabited largely by ethnic Hungarians, well over half a million at the last count. The two major cities on the plain – **Trnava** and **Nitra** – although now mostly Slovak, contain some of the most important religious institutions of the old Hungarian Kingdom; and in the Váh Valley, the spa town of **Piešťany** was, in its heyday, one of the favourite watering holes of the Hungarian nobility. Further up the Váh, however, begins the Slovak mountain region and the real heartland of Slovakia, heralded by the stronghold of **Trenčín**.

Bratislava

Caught between the westernmost tip of the Carpathians and the flat plain of the Danube, with both Austria and Hungary tantalizingly close, **BRATISLAVA** has two distinct sides to it. On the one hand, there's the old town or staré mesto, a manageable, attractive, mostly pedestrianized quarter lined with renovated baroque palaces; on the other hand, there's the rest of the city or nové mesto, a mixture of interwar tenements and postwar high–rises typical of the former Eastern bloc. More buildings have been destroyed here since the war than were bombed out during it, not least the Jewish quarter, bulldozed to make way for the colossal new suspension bridge, most SNP, symbol of the city's upwardly mobile thrust under Communism.

For centuries, Bratislava was known as *Pressburg* to the German-speaking world, which supplied around half its inhabitants until the 1945 expulsions, and as *Pozsony* to the Hungarians, who were forced to use it as their capital for several centuries during the Turkish occupation of much of Hungary, crowning their kings and queens in the cathedral and holding their Diet here until the Turks were finally beaten back from the Hungarian plain. At the turn of the twentieth century, the city had barely 60,000 inhabitants, most of whom were German, Hungarian and/or Jewish, with a smattering of Romanies and Slovaks. The balance shifted with the establishment of Czechoslovakia in 1918, which gave a leg-up to the Slovaks, who took over the cultural and political institutions and renamed the place Bratislava after Bratislav, the last Slav leader of the Great Moravian Empire.

Over the last eighty years, the population has increased more than sevenfold to 450,000, making it by far the country's largest city, occupied by roughly eight percent of the Slovak population. However, the historical centre is surprisingly small, with most of the population living in the city's mushrooming high-rise estates. Whatever Bratislava's previous identity, it's now Slovak through and through, its youthful centre packed out with students and the new Westernized generation of Slovakia's burgeoning population. The multicultural atmosphere of the prewar days is only vaguely echoed in the city's smattering of Magyars, Romanies and day-tripping Austrians, but there's still a ring of truth to Metternich's much-quoted aphorism, "East of Vienna, the Orient begins".

You'll need a couple of days at least to soak the city in; and with none of the sightseeing crowds of Prague, the relaxed feel of the old town, and some of the best weather in the country, you may want to stay longer.

Arrival

The geography of Bratislava is easy to get to grips with: the **staré mesto** – where you'll spend most of your time – lies on the north side of the Danube; on the rocky hill to the west is the city's most enduring landmark, the castle or **Hrad**. Equally difficult to miss is the spectacular suspension bridge over the Danube, **most SNP** (also called Nový most), leading to the vast **Petržalka** housing development that continues as far as the eye can see on the south bank. Northeast of the staré mesto are the late-nineteenth-century and early-twentieth-century residential blocks of **nové mesto**, which gradually give way to the postwar housing of the city's sprawling suburbs.

Points of arrival are less straightforward. A kilometre or so north of the staré mesto is the city's scruffy **main train station**, Bratislava-hlavná stanica, where most international and long-distance trains pull in. The station tourist information office is open Mon–Fri, 9am–2pm and 3–6pm, which arranges accommodation and provides maps and city guides (℡02/5443 3775). To get into town, go down to the tram terminus below the station and – having bought your ticket from one of the machines on the platform (see below) or from one of the many kiosks – hop on tram #1, which will deposit you on Obchodná, behind the *Hotel Fórum*. Buses and trolleybuses leave from directly outside the station steps.

For trains to and from destinations within West Slovakia, you're most likely to use **Bratislava-Nové Mesto** train station, situated on Bajkalská, 4km northeast of the centre; tram #6 will take you into town. The **main bus station**, Bratislava autobusová stanica (often written as Bratislava, AS on timetables) is a twenty-minute walk east of the centre on Mlynské nivy; trolleybus #208 will take you across town to the main train station, while #217 will drop you on Hodžovo námestie near the *Hotel Fórum*. The regional bus station is next door to the Bratislava-Nové Mesto train station (directions as above).

Most people flying into Bratislava simply use Vienna's **Schwechat Airport**, 45km away to the west, linked by a bus service running every two hours to the main bus station in Bratislava (payment only in euros) – be sure to book your seat for the return journey, as places sell out fast for some buses. Bratislava does have its own **airport**, the M.R. Štefánik (℡02/4857 3353), some 14km northeast of the city centre; bus #61 goes to the main train station, or else you could catch the ČSA bus, which runs a shuttle service to and from the ČSA office on Štúrova 13, timed to coincide with the flight schedule. Another possible arrival point from Vienna or Budapest is the **hydrofoil terminal** on Fajnorovo nábrežie, opposite the Slovenské národné múzeum, a very brief walk from the old town.

Transport and information

The best way to see Bratislava is to walk – in fact it's the only way to see the mostly pedestrianized staré mesto and the Hrad where the city's sights are concentrated. However, if you're staying outside the city centre or visiting the suburbs, you'll need to use the city's cheap and comprehensive **transport system** of buses, trolleybuses and trams (*električky* in Slovak). It's worth double-checking bus routes as these are constantly being changed. Tickets (12Sk for a one-way ticket at the time of going to press) are standard for all types of transport:

BRATISLAVA AND WEST SLOVAKIA

8

See 'Central Bratislava' map for more detail

River Danube

RESTAURANTS						CAFÉS			
Arkádia	dd	Modrá hviezda	cc	Rybársky cech	ii	Bystrica	ll	Impetus	K
Chez David	J	Passage	W	Slovenská pivnica	L	Café Français	Q	Kaffé Mayer	N
Corleone	Y	Rybárska brána		Umag	A	Galéria	G	Korzo – kaviareň	bb
Mária Terézia	I	Prašná bašta	H	Vegetarian	U	Gremium	V	Krym	hh
Mekong	ff								

432

▲ A

STEFANOVIČOVA UL.
TAZULOVA UL.
ŠKOLSKÁ UL.
RADLINSKÉHO UL.
BLUMENTÁLSKA UL.
KRÍŽNA UL.
ZÁHRADNÍCKA UL.

JUSTIČNÁ UL.

B

STAROHORSKÁ UL.

MÝTNA UL.

Americké nám

⑦

C

CHORVÁTSKA UL.

MOSKOVSKÁ UL.

Hospital

RADLINSKÉHO UL.

Technical University

JÁNSKA UL.

MICKIEWICZOVA UL.

UL. 29 AUGUSTA

Medická záhrada

SASINKOVA UL.

SOFIJSKÁ UL.

D

ODBOJÁROV...

MARIÁNSKA UL.

POČNÁ UL.

KARADŽIČOVA UL.

Ondrejský cintorín

REVOLUČNÁ UL.

HVIEZDOSLAVOVA...

Charlie Centrum

LAZARETSKÁ UL.

CINTORÍNSKA UL.

UL. 29 AUGUSTA

E

F

GORKÉHO UL.

ŠPITÁLSKA UL.

RAJSKÁ UL.

KOLÁRSKA UL.

Canadian Consulate

⑪

Tesco

DUNAJSKÁ UL.

UL. MLYNSKÉ NIVY ▶

Main Bus Station (100 m) & ⑭ ▶

N

KAMENNÉ NÁMESTIE

L

Štátne bábkové divadlo

GRÖSSLINGOVA UL.

LAZARETSKÁ UL.

M

ca, Vinohradicke Múzeum histórie mesta

⑮

GORKÉHO UL.

ŠTÚROVA UL.

Modrý kostolík

GAJOVA UL.

KLEMENSOVA UL.

BERNOLÁKOVA UL.

UL. TOVÁRENSKÁ

Slovenské národné divadlo

ff

MEDENÁ UL.

PARÍKOVÁ UL.

KÚPEĽNÁ UL.

DOBROVIČOVA UL.

⑨⑨

TOBRUCKÁ UL.

hh

ŠAFÁRIKOVO NÁM.

DOSTOJEVSKÉHO RAD

PRIBINOVA UL.

Komenský University

VAJANSKÉHO NÁBR.

kk

Prírodné múzeum

FAJNOROVO NÁBR.

Hydrofoil Terminal

STARÝ MOST

0   250 m

▼ Petržalka

ACCOMMODATION	
Arcus	7
Astra	14
Baronka	9
Bernolák	2
Botel Grácia	20
Chez David	13
Clubhotel	3
Danube	18
Devín	19
Fórum	8
Gremium	15
Hotel no. 16	10
Junior	5
Kyjev	11
Nešporák	12
Nivy	6
Perugia	16
Rybársky cech	17
Spirit	1
Turist	4

						BARS & CLUBS			
Kút	H	Olympia	D	Radnička	S	Charlie Centrum	E	Montana's Grizzly Bar	P
London Café	aa	Omama	C	Roland	O	Dubliner	R	Smirnoff Klub	gg
Maximilián	X	Piano Bar	T	U anjelov	M	Duna	B	Stará sladovňa	F
Múzeum	kk					Hradná Vináreň	Z	U-Club	jj
						Kelt	ee		

buy your ticket beforehand (from newsagents, kiosks or ticket machines), validate it as soon as you get on, and use a fresh ticket each time you change. If you're going to be using the system a lot, it might be worth buying a 70Sk one-day (*24 hodinový lístok*) or 130Sk two-day ticket (*48 hodinový lístok*), available from the main train station, and from some street-side yellow ticket machines. Trams and buses stop between 11pm and midnight (some even earlier, especially at the weekend), and **night buses** take over, congregating every quarter to the hour at námestie SNP.

The main branch of the city **tourist office**, Bratislavská informačná služba or BIS for short, is at Klobučnická 2 (June–Aug Mon–Fri 8am–7pm, Sat & Sun 8am–1pm; Sept–May Mon–Fri 8am–4.30pm, Sat 8am–1pm; ☎02/5443 3715 or 5443 161 86, ⓦwww.bratislava.sk/bis), good for general queries (English is spoken there) and getting hold of the monthly listings magazine, *Kam v Bratislave* (in Slovak but easily decipherable; ⓦmedia.gratex.sk/kam) and local English-language tourist brochures and freebies. They can also help with accommodation (see below) and sell you a detailed *orientačná mapa*; after working hours there is a touch-screen computer outside that can provide much of the same information. A smaller branch for information only is located in the main train station. One other excellent source of printed information is the *Slovak Spectator* travel guide, published by the English-language weekly newspaper (ⓦwww.slovakspectator.sk) and available from newsstands in the city centre and some tourist offices around the country. Although the coverage of the country focuses primarily on the main spots, the listings and off-beat advice are useful.

Accommodation

Bratislava has none of the logistical problems that plague Prague, but its status as capital, its proximity to Vienna, and the fact that it receives only a trickle of individual tourists, mean that **accommodation** is more expensive here than anywhere else in the country – inexpensive, or even medium-range hotels and pensions are few and far between, and for an old-town location, more often than not you'll pay through the nose. The cheaper hotels tend to lurk to the east and northeast of the centre, in amongst the high-rise *panelák* apartment blocks. While these are not the most appealing neighbourhoods, they are within easy striking distance of the centre by bus or tram. In all cases, try to reserve at least a day in advance to be sure of a room. There are relatively few accommodation agencies, but SATUR, Jesenského 3 (Mon–Fri 9am–6pm, Sat 9am–noon), and BIS, on Klobučnícká (see above), can book centrally located **private rooms** for around 300Sk and upwards per person (for a small fee), and the latter should have information on hostels too; at present all the city's hostels are open July and August only.

Hotels and pensions

Arcus Moskovská 5 ☎ & ℻02/55 57 25 22. Small pension within walking distance of the old town, just east of Americké nám., and a rarity in Bratislava: clean, quiet, comfortable and relatively affordable. Take any tram heading up Špitálska from Kamenné námestie. ❺

Astra Prievozská 14a ☎02/53 41 58 16. Just over 2km east of the centre, with pleasantly refurbished rooms; take trolleybus #218 from the main train station or walk from the main bus station. ❺

Baronka Murdorchova 2 ☎02/44 88 20 89, ⓦwww.baronka.sk. Comfortable, refurbished hotel with swimming pool, fitness centre and restaurant, outside the city centre on tram #3, with parking. ❸

Botel Grácia Rázusovo nábrežie ☎02/54 43 21 32, ⓦwww.botel-gracia.sk. Floating hotel moored on the main embankment. Overpriced and not everyone's cup of tea, especially in summer when the mosquitoes arrive. ❺

Carlton Hviezdoslavovo nám 3 ☎02/5939 0000, ⓦwww.radison.com/bratislavsl. Vast, imposing 1920s hotel, recently refurbished by the Radisson chain, with every conceivable creature comfort and a great position on one of Bratislava's finest squares. ❾

Chez David Zámocká 13 ☎02/54 41 38 24, ⓦwww.chezdavid.sk. Plush kosher pension with excellent kosher restaurant attached, superbly located in the old Jewish quarter behind the castle. Less expensive and better value than many other places in this price range. ❼

Clubhotel Odbojárov 3 ☎02/44 25 63 69. Drab but clean and with a decent restaurant, this is one of the city's few really inexpensive hotels. Located 3km northeast of the centre, but easily reached by tram #2 from the main train station and #4 or #6 from Kamenné nám. ❷

Danube Rybné námestie 1 ☎02/59 34 0 00, ⓦwww.hoteldanube.sk. This deluxe Austrian-run hotel, built in blue and grey titanium, has views of the castle, most SNP and the river, and charges for the privilege. ❾

Devín Riečna 4 ☎02/54 43 36 40, ⓦwww.hoteldevin.sk. On the riverfront, not quite as flash as the *Fórum* (see below) but pricey nevertheless. ❾

Fórum Hodžovo námestie 2 ☎02/59 34 81 11, ⓦwww.forumba.sk. The businessperson's hotel, on the northern edge of the staré mesto, with splendid suites, and beyond the means of most solo travellers. ❾

Gremium Gorkého 11 ☎02/54 13 10 25, Ⓕ054 43 06 53. This is really the only halfway decent, relatively inexpensive option in the whole of the old town. Centrally located, clean with extremely basic en-suite bathrooms, plus a great café on the ground floor. ❸–❹

Hotel no. 16 Partizánska 16a ☎02/54 41 16 72, ⓦwww.internet.sk/hotelno16. Opulent, wood-panelled villa, ten minutes' walk from the staré mesto. It's not cheap, but it's better value and more charming than the big hotels. ❼

Junior Drieňová 14 ☎02/43 33 74 49, Ⓕ43 33 80 65. Renovated 1970s-style hotel on the edge of a small lake 3km northeast of the city centre, with a disco, "funky bar" and erotic massage available, and a slightly dodgy clientele. Take bus #74 from the main train station or #54 from Hodžovo námestie. ❹

Kyjev Rajská 2 ☎02/5964 1111, ⓦkyjev-hotel.sk. Sky-rise communist-style 1960s hotel near Kamenné nám., with great views from the top floor. ❸–❻

Nivy Líščie Nivy 3 ☎02/55 41 03 89. A splash of blue amid the grey nové mesto high-rises, this new hotel is good value and has a swimming pool and weight room; take tram #8 from the main train station, #9 from Obchodná or #12 from Kamenné nám. ❹–❺

Perugia Zelená 5 ☎02/54 43 18 18, ⓦwww.perugia.sk. Probably the best of the old town's plush and pricey hotels, located right in the centre of the old town in a former palace. ❾

Rybársky cech Žižkova 1a ☎02/54 41 83 32/4, Ⓕ5441 8333. Pleasant rooms in an old fisherman's lodge by the busy road just below the Hrad, and, given its proximity to the old town, a bargain, although noisy thanks to passing trams. ❸

Turist Ondavská 5 ☎02/55 57 27 89, ⓦwww.turist.sk. Bargain communist-era high-rise hotel verging on the grotty; it's located 2.5km northeast of the centre, off Trnavská cesta, bus #22, #34, #106 or #110 from the main train station. ❷

Hostels and camping

Bernolák Bernolákova ☎02/52 49 77 24. The liveliest hostel in the city, only a short tram ride northeast of the centre; tram #7 or #11 from Kamenné námestie. Breakfast is included, and there's a bar and regular discos and gigs. Open July & Aug. ❷

Nešporák Svoradova 13 ☎02/54 41 53 86. Another bustling, youthful hostel, centrally located just two blocks north of the castle. Open July & Aug. ❷

Spirit Vančurova 1 ☎02/5477 7817,

ⓦunivers.host.sk. Welcoming yet bizarre hostel-cum-hotel round the back of the railway station that also houses a school for psychics. ❷

Zlaté Piesky Intercamp Zlaté Piesky ☎&Ⓕ02/44 25 73 73, ⓦwww.intercamp.sk. Two fairly grim campsites, 8km northeast of the city centre, near the swimming lake of the same name; tram #2 from the main train station or #4 from town. Bungalows (❶–❷) on offer all year round; tent camping May–Sept only.

The staré mesto

Bratislava's mostly pedestrianized **staré mesto** is, without a doubt, the nicest part of the city to explore. It's been massively overhauled over the last decade, and now looks really quite stunning. The best way to approach the old town is

CENTRAL BRATISLAVA

N

0   200 m

Archealogické múzeum

Národná rada

Hrad

Múzeum umeleckých remesiel

Múzeum židovskej kultúry

Múzeum mimoeuroúpskych kultúr

Kostol Trinitárov

Michalská veža

Mirbachov palác

Mozartov dom

sv Klára

Academia Istropolitana

Dom sv Martina

Dom na Beblavého 1

Múzeum hodín

STAROMESTSKÁ UL.

Kostol Františkánov

Jezuitský kostol

Stará radnica

Primaciálny palác

British Embassy

Pálffyho palác

Ganymedova fontána

US Embassy

Slovenské národné divadlo

Soviet War Memorial

Reduta

Hotel Carlton

Slovenská národná galéria

Hotel Devín

Hotel Danube

Hotel Kyjev

Tesco

Kamenné Námestie

NÁMESTIE SNP

Komensky University

Prírodovedné múzeum

Hydrofoil Terminal

River Danube

Petržalka

Židovská

MOST SNP

NÁBR. ARM. GEN. LUDVÍKA SVOBODU

from Obchodná – literally Shop Street – where trams #1, #5, #6, #7 and #9 all off-load their passengers to walk down to Hurbanovo námestie, a busy whizzing junction on the northernmost edge of the staré mesto.

Hurbanovo námestie and Michalská veža

On **Hurbanovo námestie** you'll find the city's biggest (albeit now rather dismal) shoe store **Dom obuvi** and, unmoved by the vulgar clamour of it all, the hefty mass of Galli da Bibiena's **kostel Trinitárov**. Inside, the single-domed nave is filled with red and grey stuccoed marble, lending the place a faded musty ambience, while the exuberant trompe l'oeil frescoes create a magnificent false cupola on the ceiling, typical of the Bibiena family who excelled in theatrical design.

Across the road and past the functionalist shoe shop, originally built for Baťa by the architect Vladimír Krafík and known locally as Veľký Baťa, a footbridge passes under the first tower of the city's last remaining double gateway. Below, in what used to be the city moat, is a tiny garden which serves as an open-air reading area in the summer. It belongs to the **Baroque apothecary** or Lekáreň U Červeného raka (At the Red Lobster), immediately on your left between the towers, which now houses a **Farmaceutická expozícia** (Pharmaceutical Museum; Tues–Fri 10am–5pm, Sat & Sun 11am–6pm), displaying everything from seventeenth-century drug grinders to Slovak herbal tea bags, with a series of reconstructed period interiors upstairs.

The second and taller of the two gateways is the **Michalská veža** (daily 10am–5pm), an evocative and impressive entrance to the staré mesto whose outer limits are elsewhere hard to distinguish. Climb the tower for a great rooftop view of the old town, pausing en route for a glance round to the vertical **expozícia zbraní a mestského opevnenia** (exhibition of weaponry and town fortifications).

Michalská and Ventúrska

Pedestrianized **Michalská** and **Ventúrska**, which run into each other, have both been beautifully restored and are lined with some of Bratislava's finest Baroque palaces. There are usually plenty of students milling about amongst the shoppers, as the main university library is on the right, in the building that once held the Palace of the Royal Hungarian Court Chamber, later the seat of the **Hungarian Parliament**. From here a passageway leads west to the **convent of sv Klara**, whose chapel spire is one of the city's most beautiful pieces of Gothic architecture. Sadly, the convent now houses another university library and, except for the occasional concert, the chapel can only be admired from its southern wall. The backstreets around sv Klara are among the most deserted (and evocative) in the staré mesto, and, at the time of writing, were still awaiting the forces of restoration. Back on Venturská 10, a few doors down on the corner of Zelená street, is the **Mozartov dom** (legend has it that Mozart once performed here at the age of six in December 1762), one of three Baroque palaces owned by the Pálffy family and rebuilt by Marshal Leopold Pálffy in 1747. Here, *Verejnost' proti násiliu* (People Against Violence), the Slovak sister of the Czech Civic Forum, seconded what was then the Institute for Political Education into their headquarters during the student strike of 1989 (it's now the Austrian embassy with its own internet café). Opposite the Mozartov dom is the **Academia Istropolitana**, the first Hungarian (or, if you prefer, Slovak) humanist university. Founded in 1465 as the Universita Istropolitana by King Matthew Corvinus, it continually lost out to the more established nearby universities of Vienna, Prague and

Kraków, and was eventually forced to close down in 1490. The buildings and inner courtyard were modernized in the 1960s for the faculty of performing arts, who put on some interesting shows and exhibitions in the chapel and crypt.

Pálffyho palác

The palaces of the Austro-Hungarian aristocracy continue right round into Panská, starting with the **Pálffyho palác**, which now serves as part of the Galéria mesta Bratislavy (Tues–Sun: June–Aug 10am–6pm; Sept–May 10am–5pm). Temporary exhibitions are held on the ground floor, basement and third floor, and occasionally on the first floor, too; the gallery's permanent collection seems to get shifted round a bit, but usually occupies the middle two floors. As well as a smattering of Gothic paintings and sculptures, there's a selection of pretty dreadful early-nineteenth-century landscapes and portraits, plus a few languid late-nineteenth-century works by Hungarian and Slovak artists.

The most interesting works, though, are by the founding generation of **twentieth-century Slovak artists**, such as Gustáv Mally and Martin Benka, whose depictions of Slovak peasantry from the 1930s gently portray a way of life that forms the backbone of Slovak national identity, but has now more or less disappeared. Peasant life is also the subject of Ľudovít Fulla's paintings which deliberately recall folk tapestries. Other eye-catching canvases include Janko Alexy's wonderfully exaggerated rendering of Košice's hoary Gothic cathedral, and Miloš Bazovský's *Devil Reading a Book*.

Hlavné námestie and Františkánske námestie

Slightly further east are the tranquil twin main squares of the staré mesto: the shady **Františkánske námestie** and **Hlavné námestie**, a delightful patch of cobbled granite focused on a Roland column, with a few acacia trees and a fountain sporting the usual cherubs seemingly peeing out of fishes' mouths; the dramatically renovated surrounding buildings indicate this was once the city's main marketplace. In summer craft stalls aimed at the tourist trade line the periphery, while in December the square heaves with locals enjoying roast sausages, pork and trout, mulled wine and hot meat at the traditional Christmas market.

On the east side of the square is the **stará radnica**, or Old Town Hall, a two-storey building in a lively hotchpotch of styles with a splash of beautifully patterned roof tiles. With a Gothic core, Renaissance innards and nineteenth-century detailing, it surpasses itself in the fanciful Baroque tower and serene half-moon crenellations and fragile arcading of the inner courtyard. The building itself, with its fine Gothic vaulting and superb Baroque ceilings, is the star of any visit, but the town hall also holds several collections: the **Vinohradícke múzeum** (Tues–Sun 9.30am–4.30pm; entrance at Radničná 1) is a scholarly tribute to Bratislava's position at the centre of the country's wine industry, and the **Múzeum histórie mesta** (Tues–Sun 10am–5pm), a less-than-fascinating collection of historical odds and sods, saved by some winsome Art Nouveau metalwork and a torture chamber (part of the feudal justice exhibition) in the basement. Sports fans will be thrilled to see the silver sequinned suit which belonged to 1970s Slovak ice-skating champion Ondrej Nepela, and, of course, pictures from Slovan Bratislava's famous victory over Barcelona in the 1969 Cup Winners' Cup.

The Counter-Reformation, which gripped the parts of Hungary not under Turkish occupation, exudes from the **Jezuitský kostol**, at Kostolná 1 just off the main square. This was nicked from the local German Protestant community – hence its lack of tower and its relatively plain facade (the gilded relief and the ornate main doors were added by the Jesuits during the Counter-Reformation). Inside, the nave seems to stop rather short, its best feature undoubtedly the richly decorated black and gold pulpit which is dripping with gilded tassles. Nearby, opposite the gaudy yellow Františkánov kostol, is the **Mirbachov palác** (Tues–Sun 10am–5pm), arguably the finest of Bratislava's Rococo buildings, still sporting much of its original stucco decor. The Galéria mesta Bratislavy puts on some interesting temporary exhibitions here, but the permanent collection of Rococo and Baroque art and sculpture isn't up to much, save for the room of wall-to-wall miniatures set into the wood panelling and busts by František Xaver Messerschmidt and canvases by František Xaver Palko. The recent addition of a few paintings by early-twentieth-century Slovak artists such as Miloš Bazovský and Mikuláš Galanda adds spice to the proceedings.

Primaciálny palác and around

Round the back of the old town hall, with the stillness of a provincial Italian piazza during siesta, is **Primaciálne námestie**, dominated by the pastel-pink Neoclassical **Primaciálny palác** (Tues–Sun 10am–5pm), built in 1778–81 for Cardinal Jozef Batthyány, head of the Hungarian Church. The palace's uninspiring pediment frieze, which dates from the 1950s, is topped by a 300-pound cast-iron archbishop's hat, for it was originally designed as the winter residence of the Archbishop of Esztergom. The palace's main claim to fame, however, is as the place where Napoleon and the Holy Roman emperor Francis I signed the Treaty of Pressburg in 1805, following the Battle of Austerlitz (see p.349). Fully renovated, it now houses yet more of the city's art collection, primarily portraits of the Habsburgs, but also minor works by seventeenth-century Dutch and Italian masters.

What also makes the palace worth visiting, though, is the dramatic **Zrkadlová sieň** (Mirror Hall), actually several interconnecting rooms, each lined with different-coloured damask, and, of course, with mirrors. The other highlight is the set of excellently preserved **seventeenth-century Bratislava tapestries**, discovered by chance during the building's restoration in 1903. Woven in Mortlake, London, how they ended up in Bratislava remains a mystery. The tapestries depict the tragedy of Hero, a priestess of Venus, and Leander, the lover who swam across the Bosphorus to be with her, until one night he drowned in a storm. The gallery terminates at a small balcony from which you can view the late-Baroque chapel of sv Ladislav, completed in less than a year in 1781, and sporting a lovely oval ceiling fresco by Maulpertsch or one of his followers.

All over the staré mesto, commemorative plaques make much of Bratislava's musical connections. But, apart from the reflected glory of its proximity to Vienna and Budapest – not to mention the prewar presence of a large German-speaking population who ensured a regular supply of Europe's best artistes – the city only produced a handful of composers, including **Johann Nepomuk Hummel** (1778–1837). Hummel's birthplace, **Rodny dom J.N. Hummela** (Tues–Sun 1–5pm), an apricot-coloured cottage swamped by its neighbours and hidden behind a row of fashionable shops at Klobučnícka 2 (Hat Street), is now a museum documenting his life and work and the musical history of Bratislava. Like Mozart, who was sufficiently impressed to give him free lessons and even put him up for a while in Vienna, Hummel was a *Wunderkind*, who began performing at the tender age of ten and was touted round Europe by his ambitious father. As a pianist in the 1820s, Hummel was one of the most celebrated performers in Europe, yet although he wrote many fine classical works, his music has been largely ignored since his death.

From the Dóm to the Hrad

On the side of the staré mesto nearest the castle, the most insensitive of Bratislava's postwar developments took place. As if the Nazis' annihilation of the city's large and visible Jewish population wasn't enough, the Communist authorities tore down virtually the whole of the **Jewish quarter** in order to build the brutal showpiece bridge, most SNP, in 1972 (see p.443). At the same time they sliced Rybné námestie in two, leaving its central plague column looking forlorn right by the motorway bridge. And finally, the best-preserved section of the old town walls now serves simply as a kind of sound barrier, protecting the rest of the staré mesto from the noise of the traffic. At least a memorial to Bratislava's Jews has finally been set up near the underpass to most SNP, a dense iron concoction of handprints and barbed wire, with a sign commanding "Zachor!" (Remember!).

Dóm sv Martina

Quite apart from the devastation of the ghetto, the traffic that tears along the busy thoroughfare of Staromestská has seriously undermined the foundations of the Gothic **Dóm sv Martina** (Rudnayovo námesti; Mon–Fri 10–11.45am & 2–4.45pm, Sat 10am–noon & 2–4.45pm, Sun 2–4.45pm), coronation church of the kings and queens of Hungary for over 250 years, whose ill-proportioned steeple is topped by a tiny gilded Hungarian crown. The new road misses the west facade by a matter of metres, engulfing the exterior in noise and fumes. The interior is disappointing, decorated mostly with neo-Gothic furnishings, the best of which are the carved animals and figures on the pews in the choir, but there are one or two outstanding Baroque features which survived the re-Gothicization. Perhaps the most striking piece is the dramatic **equestrian statue of St Martin**, executed in lead by the Baroque sculptor Georg Raphael Donner, which formed the centrepiece of the overblown main altar, erected in 1735 but removed in the nineteenth century. Far from being about to run the naked beggar through with his sword, St Martin, dressed in fashionable aristocratic garb and modelled on the donor, Count Esterházy, is depicted cutting his coat in two to share it with the supplicant. The only other slice of Baroque to have survived is the spectacular side chapel of **sv Ján Almužník** in the north aisle, once again the work of Donner, its red marble portal draped with stucco curtains and cherubs; unfortunately, you can only peer through the wrought-iron gates at the sarcophagus, baldachin and frescoed cupola within.

The Jewish quarter

Passing under the approach road for the new bridge, an old, thin yellow Rococo fancy called U dobrého pastiera (The Good Shepherd) houses the **Múzeum hodín** (Clock Museum; Židovská 1; Mon, Wed–Sun, 9.30am–6pm) with a display of – depending on your tastes – nauseatingly vulgar or brilliantly kitsch Baroque and Empire clocks.

Further north along Židovská, the former heart of the city's **Jewish quarter**, there's a **Múzeum židovskej kultúry** (no. 17; daily except Sat 11am–5pm), located in the Zsigrayova Kúria and tracing the history of the Jewish community in Bratislava and Slovakia and the basic religious practices of Judaism. There's also a memorial to the rabbis who perished in the camps and to the Slovaks who helped save Jews from deportation.

However, it's the **Múzeum mimoeurópskych kultúr** (Museum of Non European Cultures; Tues–Sun 9am–5pm), opposite at no. 18, that is particularly remarkable. Of all the unlikely places to find one of the most impressive collections of African sculpture outside of that continent, this has got to be one of

Jews probably settled in **Bratislava** during the thirteenth century, after which they were forced to move around the city, and expelled several times, before finally finding refuge in Podhradie (literally "under the castle"), just outside the city walls, in the sixteenth century. Before World War II, Jews made up ten percent of the city's population (the vast majority Orthodox), maintaining no fewer than nineteen synagogues and prayer rooms. Bratislava was also a significant centre of Jewish **education**; the *yeshivah* was founded here, in 1806, which became one of the most famous Orthodox institutions in Europe, a tradition carried on today by the Pressburger Yeshivah in Jerusalem. Its founder, Rabbi Hatam Sofer, died here in 1839, and his grave continues to attract Orthodox pilgrims from all over the world; it is situated in a grim mausoleum by the western exit of the tram tunnel under the castle, built by the Nazis over the original cemetery. Today, Bratislava's Jewish community is very small, with only one working synagogue escaping the attentions of both communism and fascism, at Heydukova 11–13, and a large cemetery, west of the city centre on Žižkova.

Of **Slovakia**'s considerable prewar Jewish population of 95,000, only an estimated 3000 remain. Slovak Jews were deported to Auschwitz from where two, Rudolf Vrba and Alfred Wetzler, were practically the only people to successfully escape. Their aim was to warn the last remaining Jewish community in occupied Europe – that of Hungary – about its forthcoming fate, and to get the Allies to bomb Auschwitz or the rail links leading to it. Their reports were dismissed as untenable and impractical. The fate of Slovak Jewry under the wartime **Tiso** regime is still a potent political issue – the suggestion made by the Czech ambassador to the USA that anti-Semitism was, and still is, "endemic" in Slovakia caused anger among many Slovaks, who argue that several leading members of Tiso's government did their best to prevent the Jews from being deported. Yet since 1989, there have been several disturbing developments: a plaque commemorating Tiso has been unveiled and several Jewish cemeteries have been vandalized across the country. These incidents do not necessarily confirm the widely held Czech view of Slovakia as a hotbed of anti-Semitism, but it is particularly distasteful that anti-Semitism should continue to be a useful political tool in a place where so few Jews remain.

them. Yet the range of work displayed here is staggering, from traditional masks and fetishes from the Congo to modern Zimbabwean stone carvings. Among the most remarkable works are the "Jamaa" family tree sculptures from Tanzania, featuring miniature figures piled on top of one another, carved from a single piece of wood. Equally compelling is the final room of huge Zimbabwean ironwood busts, carved from tree trunks, sections of which are left rough to create a contrast with the polished features of the wizened chiefs. What's more, labelling is in English and Slovak, African music plays in the background, and the differentiation between the various African cultures is sensitively addressed.

Meanwhile, the **Dom na Beblavého 1** (Museum of Folk Art; Mon, Wed–Sun 9.30am–4.30pm), which contains a few period dining rooms and a smallish collection of national folk art objects, lurks just a few steps around the corner at the bottom end of **Beblavého**, at no. 1.

From the folk, Jewish and clock museums, Beblavého begins the steep climb up to the castle. For many years this was one of the city's more infamous red-light districts, serving both town and barracks from its strategic point between the two, and described evocatively by **Patrick Leigh Fermor**, who passed through Bratislava en route to Constantinople in 1934:

During the day, except for the polyglot murmur of invitation, it was a rather silent place. But it grew noisier after dark when shadows brought confidence and the plum brandy began to bite home. It was only lit by cigarette ends and by an indoor glow that silhouetted the girls on their thresholds. Pink lights revealed the detail of each small interior: a hastily tidied bed, a tin basin and a jug, some lustral gear and a shelf displaying a bottle of solution, pox-foiling and gentian-hued; a couple of dresses hung on a nail.

Like the Jewish cafés Leigh Fermor also hung out in (along with, though not necessarily at the same table as, the young Orthodox Jew Ludvík Hoch – better known as Robert Maxwell), all this has long since gone, but there's only a vague hint of the bohemian about the ramshackle houses now slowly being turned into swish galleries, chic bars and restaurants.

Bratislavský hrad

Bratislava Castle itself (grounds open daily: 9am–8pm), frequently referred to as the "inverted bedstead", is an unwelcoming giant box, built in the fifteenth century by the emperor Sigismund in expectation of a Hussite attack, a one-time seat of the Habsburg empire, burned down by its own drunken Austrian soldiers in 1811, and restored under the Communists. Your first port of call should be the **Klenoty davnej minulosti Slovenska** (Tues–Sun 10am–noon & 1.30–4pm), a dimly lit treasury on the left as you enter the main gate, whose most precious exhibit is in the ticket office: the *Venus of Moravany*, a tiny fertility figure said to be made from a mammoth's tusk around 22,800 BC.

The rest of the castle, housing around half of the vast collections of the **Slovenské historické múzeum** (Tues–Sun 9am–5pm), is made up of two main parts. The second floor includes a long-winded exhibition of farm implements and wood- and metalworking tools; pass on through and up to the third floor until you get to the period furniture section, which ranges from heavy Renaissance wardrobes to Biedermayer dining-room sets to twentieth-century gear. The most interesting section, by far, begins with iridescent Art Nouveau glassware and bronze chandeliers, and features a whole set of bedroom furniture decorated with a peacock feather motif by Dušan Jurkovič, finishing up with a wild, Oriental-style Art Deco bed in golden-yellow. The castle's small collection of old clocks is also worth viewing, just in case you missed the museum on Židovská, and you also get the chance to climb to the top of the Korunná veža, one of the castle's four corner towers.

Even if you don't make it up the Korunná veža, you can get a pretty good view south across the Danube plain from outside the castle gates. From either vantage point, the panorama is nothing short of mind-blowing. Although you can gaze out over the meeting point of three countries, most of the immediate foreground is taken up with the infamous **Petržalka** estate, symbol of the new Slovak nation, dragged forcibly into the twentieth century at great social cost. A third of the city's population – an incredible 150,000 people – live in Petržalka, whose estates retain cruelly ironic names like Háje (Woods) and Lúky (Meadows), though barely a tree remains amid this expanse of mud and high-rises; until 1989 it had the added bonus of being surrounded by the barbed wire and watchtowers of the Iron Curtain. In many respects, most notably crime and drugs, it can't compete with the worst housing estates in the West, but with the highest suicide rate in the country and a dearth of amenities, it's not a place anyone would choose to live.

Around the castle

Before heading back down the hill, you might want to skip over to the north wall of the Hrad, which houses the **Hudobné múzeum** – **hrad** (Castle music museum; Tues–Sun 9am–5pm), including some unusual and colourful wooden horns, scores, recordings and Slovak folk instruments. From here, it's possible to take an alternative route back down to the staré mesto by following the path that winds down the hillside from west of the Leopoldova brána. This will bring you to a neglected couple of streets – the old fishing quarter, squeezed between the waterfront motorway and the castle hill, which harbours two little-visited minor branches of the Slovenské národné múzeum. The first is the **Archeologické múzeum** (Žižkova 12; Tues–Sun 9am–5pm), whose few notable Roman exhibits include a winsome stone lion, a sleeping marble cherub, a votive relief and a stone altar to Jupiter. The second, the **Museum of the Carpathian Germans** (Tues–Sun 10am–4pm) at Žižkova 14, examines the history of Germans living in the territory of current Slovakia.

Hviezdoslavovo námestie and the waterfront

Between the staré mesto and the waterfront lies the graceful, tree-lined boulevard of **Hviezdoslavovo námestie**, with restaurants and cafés along one side and, on the other, the mammoth *Hotel Carlton*, an amalgamation of three hotels originally built in the 1920s and recently restored to its former glory by the Radisson chain. Pride of place in the square, and a prime spot for casual loitering, is the larger-than-life statue of Pavol Orságh Hviezdoslav, "father of Slovak poetry", a minor government official in the Orava region whose poetry is still a source of great national pride.

At the square's eastern end are two magnificent late-nineteenth-century edifices: the first, fronted by the elaborate bronze **Ganymedova fontána** depicting the Trojan youth being kidnapped by Zeus disguised as an eagle, and featuring some wonderful frogs, tortoises, pike and crayfish, is now the **Slovenské národné divadlo** (Slovak National Theatre), built as a top-quality German-speaking opera house; the second, diagonally opposite, is the later, more Secessionist **Reduta**, a casino and restaurant as well as home to the Slovenská filharmónia (Slovak Philharmonic) and the site of the Bratislava Music Festival every autumn.

In between the two is a surprisingly playful **Soviet war memorial**, a complete contrast to the Slavín (see p.446), depicting a woman doing gymnastics with a laurel leaf. At the end of Mostova, which runs south along the side of Reduta, is **Štúrovo námestie**, its modern statue of **L'udovít Štúr** (see p.452) and his followers – appearing to levitate – a replacement for the grandiose statue of Maria Theresa blown up by Slovak nationalists in 1919 and erected in 1972.

The Danube and the Nový most (most SNP)

Beyond Štúrovo námestie and the fast dual carriageway of Rázusovo nábrežie, you can stroll along the banks of the (far from blue) **River Danube** – Dunaj in Slovak. At this point the Danube is terrifyingly fast – witness the speed to which the massive double-barges are reduced when going against the current and, by contrast, the velocity of those hurtling downstream. There's a regular (and hazardous) summer-only ferry service across the river, an alternative to crossing by either of the two bridges. The larger of these is the infamous **Nový most or most SNP** (Bridge of the Slovak National Uprising), for which the old Jewish Quarter was ripped up. However destructive its construction, it's difficult not to be impressed by the sheer size and audacity of this single open suspension bridge. Its one support column leans at an alarming angle, topped by a saucer-like penthouse café reminiscent of the *Starship Enterprise*. The view from the café is superlative (except after dark due to the reflection of the interior lights on the windows), but the cost of the lift and a drink puts many locals off: there's a cheaper and equally good view from the toilet. The best place from which to view the bridge is the rather forlorn funfair in the **Sad Janka Kráľa** on the opposite bank – all that's left of what Baedeker described in 1904 as "a favourite evening-promenade . . . with café and pleasant grounds" – its statue of the nineteenth-century poet Sándor Petöfi a reminder of the city's Hungarian heritage.

The Slovenská národná galéria

When the Slovaks took control of Bratislava in 1918, a town in which they had previously made little impression, they set about establishing their own cultural monuments to rival those of their predecessors, the Austrians and Hungarians. Three such buildings were put up in the waterfront district, of which the most rewarding is the **Slovenská národná galéria** (entrance on Rázusovo nábrežie 2; Tues–Sun 10am–6pm), housed in a converted naval barracks (*vodné kasárne*) and in the neighbouring Esterházyho palác (nám. Ľ. Štúra 4, same hours as above).

The latter now contains a collection of **thirteenth- to eighteenth-century European art** on its first and second floors, which repays merely selective viewing. Only the bizarre seventeenth-century Dutch painting of *A Frog Trial*, and two very fine portraits by the Scottish artists Henry Raeburn and David Wilkie really stand out. On the third floor, however, is a superb gallery concentrating on **twentieth-century Slovak design and architecture**, ranging from black-and-white photographs by the great Karol Plicka to zany contemporary jewellery. In between, there are some very dodgy modern ceramics and some equally dubious shaggy 1970s tapestries, but also a wonderful array of posters, from Mucha, Benka and Fulla in the 1920s to the present day, and models of the country's modern architectural masterpieces.

To reach the gallery's main building, known as the *vodné kasárne*, you must return to the second floor, where the two buildings are joined together, so to speak. Here, you'll usually find a couple of temporary exhibitions, as well as the gallery's collection of **Gothic art**, much of it from the German-speaking Spiš region in eastern Slovakia. The most compelling works in the **Baroque art** section are the hyperrealist "character heads", carved by the eccentric sculptor Franz Xaver Messerschmidt, each depicting a different grimace, and the icons, particularly the seventeenth-century *Last Judgement*, in which the sinful tumble into the mouth of a fish-devil. The nineteenth-century works, on the floor below, are less than inspiring, with the exception of the dark, expressionist works by Ladislav Medňanský (aka Mednyánszky) from the 1890s. For an overview of Slovak artists of the twentieth century, you need to go to the section of the Bratislava gallery based in Pállfyho palác at Panská 19 (see p.438).

The Slovenské národní múzeum and the Modrý kostolík

Further along the quayside, past the hydrofoil terminal, is the **Prírodovedné múzeum** (Tues–Sun 9am–5pm), the unremarkable natural history section of the Slovenské národní múzeum, housed in a dark and dingy 1930s building, and only really worth visiting for its excellent temporary exhibitions and its café round the back of the building. Further east along Vajanského nábrežie stands the equally dour **Komenský University**, founded along with the Republic in 1918, whose students spill out into the nearby bars and cafés and mingle with the crowds awaiting buses in Šafárikovo námestie.

The only specific sight around here is Ödön Lechner's sky-blue Art Nouveau **Modrý kostolík** (Little Blue Church) of St Alžbeta on Bezručova – a delicious, almost edible, concrete monument by one of Hungary's leading early twentieth-century architects. Decorated, inside and out, with the richness of a central European cream cake, it's dedicated to St Elizabeth, the city's one and only famous saint, who was born in Bratislava in 1207. Lechner quite clearly also designed the Gymnasium, one block north of the church, which shares the same shabby blue paint.

Námestie SNP and the suburbs

At the northern end of Štúrova, under the shadow of the high-rise *Hotel Kyjev* and the city's gargantuan Tesco department store, is **Kamenné námestie**. It's not exactly picturesque, but this is where the whole city seems to wind up after work, to shop, grab a beer or takeaway from one of the many stand-up stalls, gossip away the early evening and, above all, catch the bus or tram home.

To the northwest, Kamenné námestie melds imperceptibly into the slightly more accommodating **námestie SNP**, with a few trees and a host of sit-down cafés with outdoor terraces. In 1989 the Slovaks gathered here in their thousands for their part in the Velvet Revolution; nowadays it's a favourite spot for political activists. At its centre is the Monument to the Slovak National Uprising, the unsuccessful antifascist coup against the Nazis in the summer of 1944 which cost the country so dear. A macho bronze partisan guards the eternal flame, while two Slovak women (heads suitably covered) maintain a respectful distance. The one building worth noting on the square is the main **post office**, on the west side, whose Art Deco atrium of coloured glass has been lovingly restored.

Hodžovo námestie and beyond

Behind námestie SNP is the brown marble and onyx abomination of the *Hotel Forum*, which looks out onto **Hodžovo námestie**, nowadays one of the city's busiest intersections, though no doubt once a princely foil for the **Grassalkovičov palác** cowering in the top corner. Seat of the president under the clerico-fascist Jozef Tiso during World War II, and later home to the Communist youth organization, the palace is now once more the official residence of the Slovak president, though its gardens, which excel in ugly modern fountains, are open to the public in daylight hours. One block north of the park up Banskobystrická there's another grandiose Baroque palace, once the former summer residence of the archbishop of Esztergom and, until recently, home to the Slovak Parliament, which now occupies the ugly bunker to the west of the castle.

Devotees of totalitarian architecture might also visit **Námestie slobody**, a grandiose space designed by the local Party as a monumental setting for a giant statue of Klement Gottwald, the first Communist president. Gottwald has gone, thankfully, leaving only the wickedly unappealing Fountain of Friendship and the severe concrete mass of the General Post Office building, which takes up the entire length of the east side of the square and claims to be the largest in the world – although only a minute hall is actually open to the public. A more successful modern addition to the city is the striking inverted pyramid of the Slovak radio building, up Mýtna, northeast of the square. If you're on for a wander, head southeast two blocks or so to the **Medická záhrada** (summer 8am–9.30pm; winter 8am–6pm), a dog-free, peaceful garden marred only by the dodgy 1970s park benches and lights. Further southeast still, on the other side of Poľná, lies the city's oldest cemetery, the **Ondrejský cintorín** (daily 7am–dusk), established in 1784. More park than graveyard now, the predominantly Hungarian and German graves are rarely tended these days.

To the west of Hodžovo námestie, block after block of late-nineteenth-century buildings in faded colours squat under Slavín hill. The only sight as such is the pale-blue and exceedingly plain **Protestant Lycée** on Konventná (closed to the public), outside which a tall granite column commemorates the many leading Slovak men of letters who were educated here in the nineteenth century. Surprisingly for a fervently Catholic peasant country, the Protestants produced Slovak leaders far in excess of their numerical strength, including the entire 1848 triumvirate of Štúr, Hodža and Hurban. The city's Lenin Museum used to reside in a nineteenth-century neo-Baroque palace three-quarters of the way up Štefánikova at no. 25; to make up for this irrevocable loss, there's a **Múzeum polície SR** (Tues–Sat 10am–5pm) on the corner of Gunduličova itself, at no. 2, with a rather comical exhibition on the heroics of the Slovak police. It features a mock-up murder scene, detailed displays of feats such as nabbing bank robbers and drug smugglers, and a machine that recognizes counterfeit notes. The highlight is a model of the communist-era border crossing at Petržalka, with a double row of electrified razor-wire fences and lookout towers for the armed guards. The old Lenin Museum is now the Dom zahranizanych Slovákov (House of Slovaks Abroad) with a little-visited **Krajanské múzeum** (Compatriot's Museum; Tues–Sun 10am–6pm), at Štefánikova 25, run by the *Matica slovenská* (see p.489) and focusing on Slovaks who have made it big abroad and temporary exhibitions.

The Slavín Monument

Slavín hill, to the northwest of Hodžovo námestie, is crowned by the gargantuan **Slavín Monument** to the 7000 Soviet soldiers who lost their lives in the battle for Bratislava. Ceremoniously completed in 1960 to mark the fifteenth anniversary of the city's liberation, this is now one of the largest Soviet monuments still standing in the entire country, and visible from virtually every street corner in Bratislava. It's predictably militaristic, not to say phallic, a giant ribbed obelisk thrusting into the sky, topped by an anguished Soviet soldier holding the victory banner outstretched.

The villa quarter just below the monument has always been a well-to-do suburb, settled by the German middle class in the interwar period, later the exclusive territory of Party apparatchiks, and now something of an embassy enclave. The mild-mannered **Alexander Dubček** used to live at Mišikova 46 (Mouse Street). In 1968 he became probably the only Slovak ever to achieve world fame, a feat he accomplished by becoming the somewhat unlikely leader of a deeply divided Communist Party as it attempted to bring about *perestroika* twenty years ahead of its time. Crushed by the Soviet invasion, he spent his twenty years of internal exile here, under constant surveillance, working for the Slovak equivalent of the local forestry commission. He lived long enough to witness the happy events of 1989, appearing alongside Václav Havel to cheering crowds on Wenceslas Square and later becoming the parliamentary speaker. The circumstances of his death, in a car crash in 1992, are shrouded in controversy; his demise was a tragedy for Slovakia, which sorely lacks a politician of his international standing.

Eating

The choice of places **to eat** in Bratislava has improved enormously over the last few years, as have standards, though you're still unlikely to have the meal of a lifetime here. The most memorable aspect of the whole experience is often the ambience, and exploring the atmospheric streets of the old town by night is all part of the fun. In addition, you can also be fairly sure that, away from the places catering for those on expenses, prices remain uniformly low. Phone numbers are provided where reservations are advised.

Arkádia Zámocké schody ☎02/54 43 00 32. Great Slovak cuisine and a fantastic view over the Danube at this converted house halfway up the steps to the castle. Daily noon–11pm.

Chez David Zamocká 13 ☎02/54 41 38 24. Strictly kosher restaurant serving fresh, beautifully prepared Jewish cuisine, but pricey for Bratislava. Mon–Thurs & Sun 11.30am–10pm, Fri 11.30am–3pm.

Corleone Hviezdoslavovo námestie 21. The best pizza joint in the city, with a good range of moderately priced, thin-base pizzas. Daily 10am–11pm.

Mária Terézia Sedlárska 6 ☎02/52 92 55 90. Expensive but vastly popular with the expatriate population, offering snazzy international cooking and immaculate service. Mon–Fri noon–3pm & 6–11pm, Sat & Sun noon–11pm.

Mekong Palackého 18. Slap-up Thai food with all the classic dishes. Mon–Fri 11am–11.30pm, Sun 11am–10pm.

Modrá hviezda Beblavého 14. Restaurant en route to the castle serving decent Slovak and Hungarian specialities. Mon–Sat 10am–11pm.

Passage Rybárska brána Gorkého 1. Small complex of inexpensive restaurants, including *Spaghetti & Co*, a Balkan grill, a Chinese takeaway and a pseudo-English pub.

Prašná bašta Zámočnická 11. Soothing interior and a lovely courtyard, perfect for the tasteful cross-cultural cuisines on offer, with Mediterranean-influenced salads and creative main dishes. Live music. Daily 11am–11pm.

Ristorante Alvarez Bajkalská 24 ☎02/54 31 12 49. Good Italian nosh in a traditional Slovak pub with good grilled meats, veggie dishes and gnocchi. Reservations essential. Mon–Sat 11.30am–11.30pm.

Rybársky cech Žižkova 1 ☎02/54 41 30 49. Popular, reliably good but pricey fish restaurant on the ground floor of a former fisherman's house down by the waterfront below the castle (there's a posher, more expensive version upstairs). Reservations recommended. Daily 11am–midnight.

Slovenská pivnica Dunajská 18. A traditional Slovak beer hall in an unlikely setting just off noisy Kamenné nám., but its prices are low and the atmosphere is good. Mon–Sat 11.20am–11pm, Sun 11.30am–4pm.

Umag Žilinská 2. Small Croat-run pizzeria on the corner of Štefanovičova near the train station, with excellent thin-base pizzas. Daily 11am–10.30pm.

Vegetarian Laurinská 8. Plain and simple vegetarian lunch spot, with a short list of salads and soya-based main dishes. Mon–Fri 11am–3pm.

Cafés

For a relatively small city, Bratislava has an incredible number of **cafés**, ranging from coffee-and-cake pit stops for the older generation to smoky student dives. Many have tables outside in the summer, and warm snugs to sink into in the winter.

Bystrica most SNP. Sky-high café (prices as well as location) at the top of the city's main suspension bridge. Daily 10am–10pm.

Café Français Sedlárska 7. Decent croissants and other French snacks in the Institut Français. Mon–Fri 9am–9pm.

Galéria Panská 12. Nice café in the old town that's a favourite coffee and cigarette pit stop for students and arty types. Mon–Fri 9am–midnight, Sat & Sun 9am–midnight.

Gremium Gorkého 11. Wonderful, smoky café/gallery in the centre, with a high ceiling and a nice balcony where you can play pool. Daily 8.30am–midnight.

Impetus Michalská 2. Central internet café offering copy services, 1Sk/min for internet. Daily 8am–11pm.

Kaffé Mayer Hlavné nám. 4. A resurrected late-nineteenth-century café that tries very hard to emulate its Viennese-style ancestor – very popular with the city's older coffee-and-cake fans. Daily 10am–1am.

Korzo – kaviareň Hviezdoslavovo nám. 11. Passable shot at a Viennese-style café and a possible breakfast halt, with tables outside overlooking Rybné nám. and most SNP. Daily 9am–11pm.

Krym Šafaríkovo nám. Cheap, colourful pub/café with a short menu, that's also open for breakfast. Mon–Thurs 7am–10pm, Fri 1–11pm, Sat 9.30am–11pm, Sun 9.30am–10pm.

Kút Zámočnická 11. Light Mediterranean salads served in this café with burgundy walls, attached to the *Prašná bašta* restaurant. Mon–Fri 8am–11pm, Sat & Sun 4–11pm.

London Café Panská 17. Tiny British Council tearoom that's famous for its quiche and salad, popular with expats and a good place to catch up on the English press. Mon–Fri 9am–9pm.

Maximilián Hlavné nám. 5. Pleasant wood pannelled café on the main square in the staré mesto, with tables spilling onto the square in the warm months. Daily 8am–10pm.

Múzeum Vajanského nábr. 2. Appealingly gloomy mustard-yellow faux-marble foyer café round the back of the Prírodné múzeum, with an internet offshoot, *Klub Internet*, in the same building. Daily 9am–9pm.

Olympia Kollárovo nám. 20. Wonderfully tacky communist-era decor in this café above the Nová scéna theatre. Daily 11am–midnight.

Omama Sasinkovo 19. Fun, off-beat café decorated with classic old advertisements from the interwar period. Decent menu selection too. Mon–Fri 8am–10pm.

Piano Bar Laurinská 11. Popular little bar run by one of the stars of Slovak commercial TV, who occasionally treats his guests to an impromptu jam session. Mon–Sat 11am–midnight, Sun noon–midnight.

Radnička Hlavné nám. 1. Cosy café tucked into the Old Town Hall. Mon–Thurs 10am–7pm, Fri 10am–8pm, Sat & Sun 2–8pm.

Roland Hlavné nám. Pricey but splendid fin-de-siècle café overlooking the main square and spilling outdoors in summer. Open daily 8.30am–midnight.

U anjelov Laurinská 19. Cosy café/bar that attracts a discerning, black-clad crowd. Mon–Sat 9am–midnight, Sun 5pm–midnight.

Entertainment and nightlife

Bratislava's nightlife is still heavily biased towards high culture, with few out-and-out dance music venues or **nightclubs** to choose from. On the other hand, there are a number of bars and pubs that play loud music and stay open late, where dancing has been known to break out. For more mainstream fare, and cinema listings, pick up the monthly Slovak-language magazine, *Kam v Bratislave* (Ⓦ www.gratex.sk) from BIS or check the listings in the weekly English-language *Slovak Spectator*. In season, there are **opera and ballet** performances at the Slovenské národné divadlo (Ⓦ www.snd.sk) and **classical concerts** at Reduta, both on Hviedoslavovo námestie, as well as a more varied programme at the modern Istropolis complex on Trnavské mýto (tram #2 from the station; tram #4 or #6 from the centre).

Bratislava hosts a couple of annual large-scale **festivals**, the most prestigious being the classical music festival in October – without the big names of Prague's, but a lot easier to get tickets for. There's also a biennial international festival of children's illustrations held in September and October in odd-numbered years, as much of interest to adults as to kids. While on the subject, if you've **kids** in tow, it's worth finding out what's on at the Bibiana children's cultural centre on Panská, which stages events, shows and exhibitions aimed at kids.

Pubs, clubs and bars

Charlie Centrum Špitálska 4 Ⓦ www.charlies-pub.sk. Arts cinema complex that has a café upstairs and a spacious, loud, reasonably priced nightclub/pub downstairs. Situated behind the *Hotel Kyjev*, with its entrance on Rajská. Daily until 4am.

Dubliner Sedlárska 6. Very popular over-the-top Irish-themed pub, complete with mock cobbled

street. Daily noon–midnight.

Duna Radlinského 11 Ⓦ www.duna.sk. Probably the most reliable bet for a drink and a dance after *Charlie's*, this is a predominantly student hang-out in the basement of the Technical University. Mon–Thurs & Sun 5pm–1am, Fri & Sat 5pm–4am.

Hradná Vináreň Mudroňov 1. Stunning wine bar with separate restaurant, serving excellent wine and Slovak specialities with breathtaking views. Daily 11am–10pm.

Hystéria Odbojárov 9 ⊛www.hysteria-pub.sk. Worth the trek out to the Zimný štadión (tram #4 or #6 from Kamenné námestie) for this lively Tex-Mex pub, with regular pool and live music. Mon–Thurs & Sun 11am–2am, Fri & Sat 11am–5am.

Kelt Hviezdoslavovo nám. Young, lively bar decorated with questionable modern art with outdoor seating in good weather. Open daily 11am–1am.

Konik Mlynské nivy 8. Lively pub near the main bus station, which attracts a young crowd. Mon–Thurs & Sat 10am–1am, Fri until 2am, Sun until midnight.

Montana's Grizzly Bar Michalská 19 17. Music nights, a summer garden and US-style burgers,

steaks and cheesecakes. Mon–Thurs 11am–1am, Fri–Sat 11am–2am, Sun 11am–midnight.

Smirnoff Klub Štúrova (at the Šafárikovo nám. end). Lots of neon lights, bad DJs and dubious punters, but it can be fun if you're out late and still steaming. Daily 6pm–late.

Stará sladovňa Cintorínska 32. The city's malt-house until 1976, *Mamut*, as it's known, is Bratislava's most famous (and largest) pub. Czech Budvar on tap, big band and country & western music Thurs–Sat, and a bingo hall and casino on site as well. Daily 11am–11pm.

U-Club nábrežie arm. gen. L. Svobodu. Cheap, loud and slightly weird club located in an old nuclear bunker underneath the Hrad. Mon–Thurs until 2am, Fri & Sat until 4am.

Listings

Airlines Aeroflot, Laurinská 13 (☎02/54 43 51 92); Air France, Vazovova 1a (☎02/52 49 27 61, ⊛www.airfrance.com); Air Slovakia, Pestovateľská 2 (☎02/43 42 27 44); Austrian Airlines, Rybné nám. 1 (☎02/54 41 16 10, ⊛www.aua.com); British Airways, Štefánikova 22 (☎02/52 45 00 00, ⊛www.british-airways.com); ČSA, Štúrova 13 (☎02/52 96 10 42, ⊛www.czechairlines.com); Delta, Hotel Kyjev, Rajská 2 (☎02/52 92 09 40, ⊛www.delta-air.com); KLM, Dunajská 4 (☎02/52 92 11 11, ⊛www.klm.com); Lauda Air, Štúrova 4 (☎02/52 96 78 15, ⊛www.lauda-air.com); LOT, Špitálská 51 (☎02/5296 4007, ⊛www.lot.sk); Lufthansa, Štúrova 4 (☎02/52 96 78 15, ⊛www.lufthansa.com); Slov Air, Bratislava airport (☎02/43 29 14 09).

Boats Slovenská plavba dunajská (Slovak shipping) runs hydrofoil services from the terminal on Fajnorovo nábr. (☎02/54 41 03 36 or 5293 22 26, ⊛www.spap.sk) to various places along the Danube, including Budapest and Vienna (see box p.450 for details).

Car rental Two good local firms are Recar, Svätoplukova 1 (☎02/55 57 64 36), and Adecar, Hybešova 36 (☎ & ☞02/44 88 15 72).

Cultural centres Austrian Cultural Centre, Zelená 7; British Council, Panská 17; Canadian Bilingual Institute, Obchodná 43–49; České centrum, námestie SNP 12; European Information Centre, Panská 5; Goethe Institute, Konventná 1; Institut Français, Sedlárska 7; Kultúrny inštitút Maďarskej republiky (Hungarian Cultural Institute), Palisády 54; Pro Helvetia, Panská 15; Poľský inštitút, nám. SNP 27; United States Information Service, Hviezdoslavovo nám. 4.

Embassies and consulates Austria, Ventúrska

10 (☎02/54 43 29 85); Britain, Panská 16 (☎02/54 41 96 32); Canada, Mišíkova 28D (☎02/52 41 21 75); Czech Republic, Hviezdoslavovo nám. 8 (☎02/59 20 33 03); Hungary, Sedlárska 3 (☎02/54 43 05 41-4); Poland, Hummelova 4 (☎02/54 41 31 96); Russia, Godrova 4 (☎02/54 41 34 68); South Africa, Jančová 8 (☎02/531 15 82); Ukraine, Radvanská 35 (☎02/54 43 16 72); USA, Hviezdoslavovo nám. 4 (☎02/54 43 33 38).

Football Bratislava's premier team is Slovan Bratislava, the only Slovak club to have won a European competition. Slovan's ground is the Tehelné Pole stadium, built during World War II and also used for international games. For details of how to get there, see "Sports facilities" p.450.

Internet Internet cafés should cost between 1–2Sk per minute. Central cafés include: *Klub Internet*, in the *Múzeum* café at Vajanského nábr. 2 (Mon–Fri 9am–9pm, Sat & Sun noon–9pm); at *Internet Centrum Nextra* at Michalská 2 (open Mon–Sat 9am–midnight, Sun noon–midnight); or at *Heura*, Laurinská 14, a bookstore/gallery with a couple of computers (Mon–Fri 8am–9pm, Sat & Sun 8am–1pm).

Left luggage Lockers at both train and bus stations.

Libraries British Council Teaching Resource Centre, Panská 17 (Tues 1–5pm, Wed 1–6.30pm, Thurs 9.30am–noon & 1–5pm, Fri 1–5pm, Sat 9.30am–noon); French Institute library (Mon–Fri 2–6pm).

Markets The best fruit-and-vegetable market in town takes place Mon–Sat in the Tržnica covered market hall on Trnavské mýto (tram #4 or #6 from Kamenné námestie). Early Saturday morning is the busiest and best time to go. The stará tržnica, at nám. SNP 25, is a more Western-style shopping mall with an internet café (*Internet Te@*, nám. SNP 25, Mon–Fri 8am–10pm, Sat 10am–10pm), news kiosks and gifts.

Medical emergency Go to Mýtná 5 or Mickiewiczova 13.

Newspapers Interpress Slovakia, Sedlárska 2 (daily 7am–10pm) or one of the many kiosks dotted all over town.

Post office Main post office (Hlavná pošta), nám. SNP 35 (Mon–Fri 7am–8pm, Sat 7am–6pm, Sun 9am–2pm).

Sports facilities There are two main sports complexes, Tehelné pole and Pasienky, next to one another in the nové mesto (tram #2 from the station; tram #4 or #6 from the centre); facilities include an outdoor pool, ice-hockey stadium, cycle track and the big Slovan football stadium.

Taxis Not as bad a reputation as in Prague; try Yellow Expres (☎02/44 44 11 11) or Fun Taxi (☎02/167 77).

Telephones International calls are best made at the 24-hour exchange at Kolárska 12.

Out from the city

Most people find enough in the city centre to occupy them for the average two- or three-day stay, but if you're staying around for longer, or would prefer to be among the vine-clad hills which encroach on the city's northern suburbs, there are several places where you could happily spend a lazy afternoon, all within easy reach of the city centre.

Zlaté Piesky

Out on the motorway to Piešťany, just past the city's huge chemical works, **Zlaté Piesky** (the last stop on tram #2 from the train station and tram #4 from town) is a popular destination for weekending Bratislavans. Despite its name, meaning "Golden Sands", it's a far cry from the Côte d'Azur, though on a baking hot day in August not even the stench from the nearby chemical factory can deter large numbers of sweltering Slovaks from stripping off and throwing themselves into the lake's lukewarm waters.

Kamzík

North of the main train station the city immediately gives way to the vineyards and beechwood slopes of the suburb of Vinohrady (a world apart from its almost vine-less namesake in Prague), perfect for a quick escape from the city. From the station you can walk for 2.5km along a yellow-marked path through the woods to the summit of **Kamzík** (439m), topped by a 200m TV tower with a revolving restaurant from where you can see the Austrian alps if the weather's on your side. If you don't fancy the walk, take bus #33 to the chairlift on the north side of the hill, or simply trolleybus #213 from Mierové námestie or námestie Slobody to the last stop and walk along the red-marked path for 1km.

Devín

Bus #29 from beneath most SNP will get you to the village of **DEVÍN** (Theben), 9km northwest of Bratislava, whose ruined **hrad** (May–Oct

Tues–Sun 10am–5pm, July & Aug until 6pm), first established in the fifth century BC, perches impressively on a rocky promontory at the confluence of the Morava and the Danube. With the West just a stone's throw away across the river, border precautions used to be particularly excessive on the road to Devín – a continuous twenty-foot barbed-wire fence, punctuated at regular intervals by fifty-foot watchtowers and hidden cameras that monitored all passing vehicles. Today, though, such Cold War images seem as far removed from reality as the traditional Slovak legends that surround Devín.

In 864 and again in 871, the Slavs of the Great Moravian Empire gave the Germans two serious drubbings at Devín, the last of which is said to have left the Germans with so few prisoners with which to barter that they could only succeed in retrieving one half-dead hero named Ratbod. In the nineteenth century, Ľudovít Štúr and his fellow Slovak nationalists made Devín a potent symbol of their lost nationhood, organizing a series of publicity stunts in and around the castle in the run-up to 1848. Because of its importance in the national lore, Devín remains a symbol of Slovak strength and independence for its people, and its defining architectural feature, a lonesome round tower perched atop a spindle of rock, appears in many advertisements and political placards.

There's a good view over into Austria from the craggy ruins, as well as an **archeological museum** with objects from as far back as 1800 BC (Tues–Fri 10am–5pm, Sat–Sun 10am–6pm). A favourite place for weekend picnics, the castle also hosts nationalist events in July and sometimes performances in the open-air amphitheatre amongst its ruins; for details ask at BIS. If you fancy a walk, follow the red markers from just above the last stop on tram #4 or #9 for a pleasant two-hour trail through the woods to Devín. At the castle itself you can also pick up the *naučný chodník*, a twelve-kilometre-long educational walking trail along the Morava river floodplain to Vysoká pri Morave.

Rusovce

In 1945, to shore up its exposed western flank, Czechoslovakia was handed a small stretch of forested marshland on the previously Hungarian right bank of the Danube. Much of this land is now taken up with the unavoidable Petržalka housing estate (see p.442), but there are at least a couple more villages along the road to Györ, shortly before the Hungarian border; one of these is **RUSOVCE**, 17km southeast of Bratislava, a possible half-day trip by bus #116 which runs regularly from most SNP. Originally the Roman camp of Gerulata, it now harbours a small **Múzeum antická Gerulata** (May–Oct Tues–Sun 9am–5pm), signposted off the main road to the north, containing the results of extensive archeological excavations that have uncovered two large Roman burial sites. Nearby, a neo-Gothic **zámok**, or manor house, houses the SĽUK Folk Ensemble, although the English-style park is open at all times for picnicking under the oaks and plane trees and there's a series of reservoirs popular with naturists.

The Small Carpathians

From the Bratislavan suburbs to the gateway into the Váh valley, the **Small Carpathians** (Malé karpaty) form a thin, abrasive strip of limestone hills altogether different from the soft, pine-clad hills of the Czech Lands. These are the modest beginnings of the great Carpathian range that sweeps round through the back door into Romania. Throughout much of the year, a thoroughly Balkan heat bounces off the sun-stroked plains of the Danube and permeates even these first foothills, whose south-facing slopes are excellent for vine-growing. There's also a smattering of castles and a whole host of hiking opportunities, all making for a welcome release from the Bratislavan smog. Keen walkers might consider getting hold of the Turistická mapa Malé Karpaty – Bratislava (1:50,000) hiking map, published by VKÚ.

The Small Carpathians force their way right into the city boundaries, making Bratislava a good starting point for **hiking** in the hills. Kamzík (440m) is the first peak (see p.450), and on a clear day the view from its television tower is difficult to beat, but if you want to do some serious trekking in unmolested countryside, continue along the red-marked path (previously known as the cesta Hrdinov SNP) that wiggles its way along the ridge of the hills all the way to Brezová, 75km away at the end of the range. There are campsites and hotels peppered along the route, and it's easy enough to drop down off the hills and grab a bed for the night. Unfortunately, **biking** is still not brilliant as biking lanes are yet to be introduced in and around the capital; however, if you're interested, it may be worth investing in the Slovak-language *Okolo Bratislavy* (Pedál Publishing, 1998) for details of more than 700km of suggested tours around the region.

Modra and around

If you're going in search of víno, **MODRA** (Modern; Ⓦwww.tik.sk or www.modra.sk), just under 30km from Bratislava and entirely surrounded by the stuff, is the most convenient place to head for, particularly in September when fresh fermented grape juice known as *burčiak* is glugged at Vinobranie festivals. Modra is a typical ribbon-village with one long street lined with barn-door cottages growing fancier the nearer you get to the centre. There's an excellent little wine shop at no. 92, or you can imbibe the **local wines** at the co-op headquarters further down on the other side of the street or tuck in at the *Vinohradický dvor Modra* further along. Gracing the square at its widest point is a light stone statue of Slovak nationalist **Ľudovít Štúr**, who is buried in the local cemetery (see box below). The nearby **Štúr Museum** (Tues–Sat 9am–4pm), in the Renaissance former town hall, is predictable enough and makes a classic Slovak school trip, though kids are generally more interested in the ice cream outlet judiciously placed next door.

The *Modra*, at no. 111 on the main street (☎033/47 22 65; ❷), is the village's chief **hotel**, though the *Pension Club MKM* (☎033/647 5596; ❹) at Štúrova 25 is much better and has a decent restaurant and swimming pool. Alternatively, head 1km north to the Harmónia suburb, where you've a choice of pensions such as *Zita* (☎033/647 36 64; ❷), just along the road to Trnava; the nearest **campsite** (May–Sept) is 6km north at Piesok, in the hills above Modra. The tourist office (TIC Modra, Štúrova 84, ☎033/647 43 02, ⓦwww.tik.sk) can also help book accommodation. A good base for exploring the surrounding area, Piesok is just a five-kilometre walk from **Vysoká** (754m), quite the most rewarding peak in terms of views. For a more gentle stroll, you could head 5km east to the hulking chateau of **Červený Kameň** (April–Oct Mon–Fri 9am–3pm). Designed to put fear into enemies approaching from the plain, its defensive position and big fat bastions were created by the painter Albrecht Dürer for the unlikely sounding Fugger family. However, it was the powerful Pálffy dynasty who later transformed it into a more luxurious family residence, adding formal gardens and various other creature comforts. The castle now houses an impressive collection of period furniture, a medieval torture chamber and a seventeenth-century apothecary.

Brezová pod Bradlom and Košariská

Tucked away into a peaceful swathe of the northern Small Carpathians, the region around **BREZOVÁ POD BRADLOM** is the home of Slovak national hero Milan Rastislav Štefánik (see box below). Štefánik was born in the village of **KOŠARISKÁ**, 3km east of Brezová, in 1880, and his birthplace is now an engaging **museum** (April–Oct Tues–Sun 9am–5pm; Nov–March Mon–Fri 8am–4pm) tracing his adventurous life and untimely death. If you've any interest in Štefánik, you'll get a kick out of his personal photos, boyhood folk outfit, pipes, flying uniforms and personal letters from T.G. Masaryk. Much is made of his travels and diplomatic exploits, and the model and photos of the plane in which he was killed really bring to light how important his role was to the Slovak national cause.

Even more acclaim is bestowed upon Štefánik at his colossal **mausoleum** atop nearby Bradlo (543m), a short drive or steep one-hour hike up the red-marked path from Brezová. The imposing white stone really is overdone, as if you're standing at a temple, but at least the views from the hilltop are splendid. Košariská is connected by a few daily buses to Piešťany, though there are more connections in Brezová to Bratislava and Trnava. If you wish to **spend the night**, the *Penzión U Juhása* (☎033/624 2807; ❷) in Košariská has good rooms and a fine restaurant.

Trnava

Forty-five kilometres northeast of Bratislava, and just 35 minutes by fast train, **TRNAVA** (Nagyszombat) is one of the few towns on the plain to have survived with its walled-in medieval character intact. The town's rich ecclesiastical history took off in 1543, when the archbishop of Esztergom and primate of Hungary moved his seat here, and reached its zenith during the Counter-Reformation, with the founding of a Jesuit university in 1635. When the Turkish threat receded, these institutions moved out, and, despite the re-establishment of Trnava's archbishopric in 1990, and the frequent references in tourist literature of the town as a "Slovak Rome", its golden days are clearly over. Nowadays, it's a sleepy place, with a pleasant old town, a couple of very fine churches and a fairly good museum – enough for an afternoon or so, but by no means an essential overnight stop.

The staré mesto

From the bus and railway **stations**, cross the new footbridge over the main ring road, Hospodárska, and head north along the leafy banks of the River Trnavka. Parallel to this runs the most impressive section of the old **town walls**, reinforced in the sixteenth century (and up to six metres thick in places) in anticipation of the marauding Turks; the only surviving gateway is the red-brick Bernolákova brána, popularly known as the Franciscan gate after the nearby church of **sv Jakub**.

Soon after the church, you come to **Trojičné námestie**, the spacious main square centred on a lively plague column, pristinely restored and dramatically lit at night. Here, Trnava's institutions old and new congregate: the **mestská veža**, dating from the beginning of the town's golden age in the sixteenth century; the Neoclassical **radnica**; the salmon-pink, Empire-style **Trnavské divadlo**, the oldest theatre building in Slovakia, dating from 1831; and last, but in no way least, the **Dom kultúry**, just one of a number of modern eyesores in Trnava that have risen up from the rubble in the old quarter.

A short walk up Štefánikova from the square is the surprisingly interesting **Jesuitský kostol**. The typically High Baroque nave is suffused with a pink light emanating from the marble pilasters; more startling though is the deliciously decorative north chapel, with bounteous vegetative motifs and floral stucco. On the east side of the chapel is a bizarre watery grotto, with a statue of Mary lit only by a dramatic shaft of light, the grotto's grille entirely surrounded by plaques and graffiti in Hungarian, Slovak and even Latin, thanking the Virgin for her various intercessions in answer to prayers.

The modern-day focus of Trnava is the paved main boulevard, **Hlavná ulica**, which leads south from Trojičné námestie: a pleasant window-shopping stroll. Its southern end is marked by the church of **sv Helena**, the town's oldest and most beguiling church, whose bare and miniature Gothic style is untouched by the suffocating hand of the Counter-Reformation. Next door is the town's former hospital, a Neoclassical building in an inappropriately sickly version of imperial yellow. South of sv Helena, a swathe of parkland has replaced the old fortifications, and boasts a working fountain and a relatively new statue of Štefánik (see p.453).

The Dóm and Katedrálny chrám

East off Trojičné námestie, the **Dóm of sv Mikuláš** beckons with two rather clumsy but eye-catching Baroque steeples. Its Gothic origins are most obvious in the chancel, which boasts slender stained-glass windows and a fine set of

Piešťany

TRNAVA

N

RYBNÍKOVÁ
HORNÉ BAŠTY
HORNÉ BAŠTY
HLBOKÁ

Univerzitný kostol

INVALIDSKÁ

ŠTEFÁNIKOVA
PEKÁRSKA
HORNOPOTOČNÁ
HOLLÉHO

Book Museum
Dóm sv Mikuláš

Schneider-Trnavský muzeum

Arcibiskupský palác
KAPITULSKÁ

Jezuitský kostol
Mestská veža

HVIEZDOSLAVOVA
HAVLÍKA

sv Jakub
TROJIČNÉ NÁMESTIE
Dom kultúry

HALENÁRSKA

DIVADELNÁ
Trnavské divadlo

Západoslovenské múzeum

ZÁHRADNÍCKA
TRHOVÁ
PAULÍNSKA
DROTÁRSKA

River Trnávka
VAJANSKÉHO
HLAVNÁ ULICA

sv Helena

DOLNÉ BAŠTY
HALENÁRSKA

STRELECKÁ

HOSPODÁRSKA

0   100 m

ZÁRNOVA
KOLLÁROVA

KOLLÁROVA

KOLLÁROVA
STANIČNÁ

Train Station

Bus Station

ACCOMMODATION
Apollo	2
Barbakan	3
Koliba	1
Tulipán	4

RESTAURANTS & PUBS
Bašta	A
Billiard café	C
Pivnice nad baštem	F
Pizza Corleone	D
Prachareň	B
U Jozefa	E

choir stalls. It was promoted from a mere parish church following the Battle of Mohács in 1526, which caused the Hungarians to retreat behind the Danube; the royalty moved to Bratislava and the archbishop transferred his see to Trnava, setting up next door to sv Mikuláš. A century later, Trnava's position as a haven for Magyar cultural institutions seeking refuge from the Turks was further bolstered by the establishment of a university. In common with all Habsburg institutions of the time, it was under the iron grip of the Jesuits, and Trnava soon became the bastion of the Counter-Reformation east of Vienna.

The importance of religious over purely scholarly matters is most clearly illustrated by the sheer size of the **Univerzitný kostol**, down Hollého, one of the largest and most beautiful in Slovakia. The decor is mostly Italianate Rococo, with the apricot and peach pastels of the nave offset by darker stucco vegetation. The oval frescoes appear like giant lacquered miniatures, but the whole lot is upstaged by the vast wooden altarpiece, decked out in black and gold, peppered with saints, and looking more like an Orthodox iconostasis than a Catholic altar. These glory days were shortlived: with the expulsion of the Jesuit order from the Habsburg Empire and the defeat of the Turks, Trnava lost its university to Budapest, its archbishop's see to Esztergom, and consequently both its political and religious influence.

Trnava's museums

Kapitulská, the broad, leafy street that sets off south from the archbishop's palace, is probably the prettiest street in town, with a cathedral-close feel about it. At its end, the plain cream mass of the seventeenth-century convent of sv Klara, now the **Západoslovenské múzeum** (Tues–Sun: June–Sept 10am–6pm; Oct–May 11am–4pm), offers a variety of exhibitions including eight rooms of folk ceramics by local potter Štefan Cyril Parrák; best of all, though, is the glimpse of the convent's former chapel, and the bits and bobs salvaged from the town's now-defunct **Jewish community**.

Trnava's Jews were actually expelled from the city in the sixteenth century, when, on the usual trumped-up charge of ritual murder, the emperor Ferdinand sent them packing through the Sered' gate, walling it up with ripped-up Jewish gravestones to bar their return. For three hundred years, Trnava was *Judenfrei*, then in 1862 the gate was removed, and the Jews began to filter back to the unofficial ghetto, located about where the main supermarket car park lies today. The disused and weed-ridden orthodox **synagogue** on Havlíka is on the brink of collapse, but the more prominent Moorish onion-domed **synagogue** (Tues–Fri & Sun 9am–noon & 1–5pm) on the other side of the street has been at least structurally restored and is used as temporary exhibition space. The reason to visit, though, is to wander about the gloomy interior, damaged by fire in the 1980s, but still retaining fragments of gorgeous frescoes and stonework. Out front there's a large, black, tomb-like memorial to more than 2000 local Jews who were victims of the Holocaust.

The **Schneider-Trnavský museum** (June–Aug Tues–Sun 9am–5pm; Oct–May Mon–Fri 8am–4.30pm), at no. 5 ulica M. Schneidra-Trnavského, is devoted to the Slovak composer who was choirmaster at sv Mikuláš from 1909 until his death in 1958, and who clearly had very good taste in 1920s furniture. The little-visited **Book Museum** (Múzeum knižnej kultury; Mon–Fri 8am–4pm), further up the street opposite sv Mikuláš, was closed indefinitely at the time of writing, but if and when it reopens, it will focus on the many printing presses set up in Trnava by the Hungarians in the seventeenth century, and on the Slovak intellectual society here in the mid-nineteenth century.

△ Trnava, University Church, facade detail

Practicalities

The local **tourist office**, TINS (Oct–April Mon–Fri 9am–7pm; May–Sept Mon–Sat 8am–6pm; ☎033/55 11 022, ⓦ www.tranava.sk), is located in the mestská veža at Trojičné námestie 1, and can help with **accommodation**. There should, in any case, be few problems finding a room at the swankiest option in town, the *Apollo*, Štefánikova 21 (☎033/551 19 39, ⓕ 551 19 38; ❹); other central options include the comfortable *Barbakan* on Štefánikova 11 (☎033/551 40 22, ⓦ www.hotel-barbakan.sk; ❸) which features its own in-house brewery, and, cheapest of the lot, the pension *Tulipán*, Odbojárska 27 (☎033/551 19 03; ❷). Alternatively, you could try the quiet *Koliba* (☎033/533 44 59, ⓦ www.hotelkoliba.sk; ❷), 3km west on T. Vansovej (bus #1 or #2) in the Kammený mlýn recreation area, which also has a decent restaurant. For **eating**, *Prachareň* opposite the tourist office has a few vegetarian dishes on the menu, and the *Pizza Corleone*, Paulínska, does big pizzas (both closed Sun). In the northern part of the old town is the little restaurant *Bašta*, with good, standard Slovak fare; for beer pop into the *Pivnice nad baštem* on Hlavná ulica, while for wine, head for *U Jozefa*, an atmospheric *vináreň* on the same road. The billiard café on the corner of Trojičné námestie continues to be the only vaguely happening late-night place.

Nitra

While Trnava is stuck in the past, **NITRA** (Nyitra), 40km further east across the plain, has effectively shed its old skin and rushed headlong into the modern world. The result is a clearly divided town: on the one hand, the peaceful old quarter wrapped around the foot of the castle rock; on the other, the ungainly sprawl of modern Nitra, third largest city in the country with a population of 90,000, agricultural capital of the nation and a bustling market town with that symbol of development, a Tesco hypermarket. Sadly, to get to the former you must pass through the latter, since the sights are all situated in the old town, which has a certain national kudos attached to it as a centre of Slovak Catholicism, ancient and modern.

The City

The central axis of the nové mesto is the busy crossroads by the city's main **market** (*tržnica*) where the region's rich produce is sold daily. The staré mesto and the main sights are all north of here, except for the **Kalvária**, a kitsch mock-up of the Crucifixion, which crowns the summit of a small limestone hill southeast of the train station. The brutality of Nitra's modern development serves as the apocalyptic backdrop for three ugly concrete crosses, the two robbers grey and unpainted on either side of a technicolour Jesus.

Visible to the east of the market as you cross over Štúrova is the country's main **College of Agriculture**, a flying-saucer-shaped building, whose research department famously invented a strain of tree that could withstand acid rain – progress indeed. Beyond the college lies the Agrokomplex exhibition grounds, which also contain the marvellous **Slovenské poľnohospodárske múzeum** (Slovak Agricultural Museum or *skansen*; Tues–Sun 9am–5pm). Though you

ACCOMMODATION
Penzión Atrium 2
Olympia 3
Zlatý kľúčik 1

RESTAURANTS, BARS & CAFÉS
Boccaccio C
Café Piano F
Furmanská vináreň E
Izba starej matere B
Kaviareň Muzeum A
Thurzo D

NITRA

Swimming Pool

Cathedral

Nitriansky hrad

Ponitrianska galéria

ŽUPNE NÁMESTIE

PRIBINOVO NÁMESTIE

PODZÁMSKA

Puppet Theatre

MOSTNÁ

Divadlo A Bagara

Nitrianske múzeum

SVÄTOPLUKOVO NÁMESTIE

sv Michal

Former Synagogue

Piaristický kostol

Market

College of Agriculture

VIKÁRSKA
JESENSKÉHO
ĎURKOVÁ
SCHURMANNOVA
ČERVENEJ
FARSKÁ
KUPECKÁ
RADLINSKÉHO
ŠTEFÁNIKOVA TRIEDA
FARSKÁ
PÁROVSKÁ
PALÁNOK
PARISTICKÁ
JAŠÍKOVA
PALÁRIKOVA
WILSONOVO NÁBREŽIE
SLÁDKOVIČOVA
SLANČÍKOVEJ
TRIEDA ANDREJA HLINKU

ŠTÚROVA

ŠTÚROVA

River Nitra

MOSTNÁ

◀ Trnava & Bratislava

▲ Agricultural skanzen

0   100 m

▼ Bus & Train Stations (300 m)

wouldn't know it from the name or the setting – it's located at the rear of the Agrokomplex behind banks of ugly apartment blocks – this is a real gem, one of the very best museums of its kind in central Europe. In one large, barrack-like building there's a display on the history of farming and commerce in Slovakia up to the Middle Ages, with an impressive array of artefacts such as 3000-year-old wheat kernels and relics from the medieval amber trade route, which passed from the Baltic Sea to Italy through Slovakia. Another concrete structure holds a fun collection of interwar tractors, including a massive red Russian combine and a wooden thresher, claimed to be the only one of its kind in the world. In the vicinity are several smaller houses with a variety of folk displays inside; an early-twentieth-century bakery, a distillery, a mill, a honeycomb pressing shop and a one-room schoolhouse with original furnishings all vie for attention. In August, at the time of the National Agrocomplex Exhibition, the whole complex comes alive as costumed guides demonstrate how the old shops work (many are still operational), and an 1885 narrow-gauge railway toots around the grounds, much to the delight of visiting children. To get to the museum, you'll need to take bus #8, #12, #15, #19 or #31 to the last stop at the end of Dlhá.

North of Štúrova, the main street of Štefánikova trieda has been pedestrianized and leads north past the giant neo-Renaissance **Nitrianské múzeum** (Tues–Fri 8–11.30am & noon–5pm, Sat & Sun 10am–5pm), which puts on riveting exhibitions such as "Stones today and yesterday", to the town's octagonal, Communist-designed theatre, **Divadlo A. Bagara**, on the dusty expanse of Svätoplukovo námestie. On ulica pri synagóge, west off Štefánikova, the sheer size of Nitra's Moorish **synagogue** is an indication of the strength of the town's prewar Jewish community and is now restored. Currently used as an exhibition and concert hall, it is due to become a Holocaust museum at some point in the future. Farská, which leads you away from the chaos of the new town to the sights around the castle, is one of the most pleasant streets in the nové mesto, dotted with churches, grocery stores and snack bars.

The staré mesto

Nitra's **staré mesto** is actually very small, consisting of just a handful of streets huddled under the castle. The entrance is formed by the former Župny dom on Župné námestie, a handsome Art Nouveau building, now the **Ponitrianska galéria** (Tues–Sun 9am–4pm), which displays information about the Nitra region. The right-hand arch of the building leads to the steeply sloping old town square, **Pribinovo námestie**, a very modest affair but quite pretty and totally peaceful after the frenetic activity of the lower town. At its centre stands a recent (and fairly ugly) statue of **Prince Pribina**, the ninth-century ruler of Nitra, who erected the first church in what is now Slovakia here in 828. Though no great believer himself, he shrewdly realized such a gesture would keep him on good terms with his German neighbours. There's also a fair amount of evidence to suggest that St Methodius, the first bishop of (Great) Moravia, was stationed at Nitra and not at Velehrad in the Morava Valley, as was once claimed by the Czechs.

Nitriansky hrad is a scruffy little hybrid, saved only by its lofty position above the river, which allows a great view north over to Mount Zobor (588m), the southwesternmost tip of the Tribeč mountain range. A fortress since the time of the Great Moravian Empire (of which it may have been the capital), it provided refuge for various Hungarian kings over the centuries until its destruction by the

Turks in the seventeenth century. Crusty saints, a very fine plague column and two massive gateways mark the route to the remains, most of which have been turned over to the Archeological Institute and are closed to the public.

The one sight left in the complex is the **Hradná katedrála** (Mon–Fri 9am–1.30pm), an old structure which adjoins the bishop of Nitra's cosy Baroque residence. Confusingly, you enter the south door and pass through two antechambers – the first, the Pribinova kaplnka, is a Romanesque rotunda, the second is late-Gothic – before going up some more steps to the compact main church, its Baroquized marble interior in muted greys and reds. Frescoes adorn every possible space, and the modern blue stained glass in the chancel lends the whole place a magical quality. The cathedral is associated with two tenth-century Slovak saints, **Ondrej Svorad** and **Benedikt Junior**, both religious hermits who lived in the hills near Trenčín and spent most of their lives tending their gardens and vineyards. The locals, who had little time for able-bodied young men devoting their lives to spiritual contemplation, gave both of them a hard time; Ondrej Svorad escaped their wrath by diplomatically giving away a portion of his harvest, but Benedikt Junior failed to appease his enemies, who threw him off a nearby cliff and then drowned him in the River Váh.

Practicalities

If you're coming to Nitra from Bratislava, you're best off coming by **bus**, as there are no direct trains. Staff at Nitra's **tourist office**, NISYS, at Štefánikova 1 (Mon–Fri 8am–6pm, Sat 8am–1pm, July & Aug also Sat 9am–7pm, Sun 2–7pm; ☎037/161 86 or 741 09 07, ⊛www.nitra.sk), can help out with **accommodation**, though choice is limited to several (mostly ugly) large hotels and pensions outside the city centre. Nitra's finest hotel is the excellent *Zlatý kľúčik* (☎037/55 02 89; ❺), with great views from its position on the slopes of Zobor to the northeast of the centre (Svätourbánksa 27, take bus #10 or a taxi). Otherwise, you should try the *Penzión Atrium* (☎037/65 23 79 0; ❸), on Štefánikova 8, or the dormitory-style *Olympia* (☎037/65 36 72 7–9, ⓔolympia@hotelolympia.sk; ❷), fifteen minutes' walk east of the centre on trieda Andreja Hlinku – take bus #12, #13 or #23. The only time you may have problems finding a room is during the agricultural fair and the music festival, which take place in August and September respectively. The nearest **campsite with bungalows**, *chatová osada Jelenec* (May–Sept, ☎037/63 13 34 1; ❶), is a recreational centre 16km northeast of Nitra in the foothills of the Tribeč, near Jelenec.

Nitra has a fair range of **eating** establishments, including an Irish pub at Kupecká 12 and the boisterous, beery *Thurzo*, at Pri synagóge 3 by the synagogue; opposite is the semi-rustic *Furmanská vináreň* at no. 6, specializing in live music and fresh fish. Another good eatery is the *reštaurácia Izba starej matere*, at Radlinského 8, which has a nice garden and offers Slovak specialities plus *Nitria*, the local sweet white wine. *Boccaccio*, Farská 36, is a comfortable Italian-Slovak restaurant-pizzeria with a pleasant summer courtyard, and *Café Piano* at Farská 46 and *Kaviareň Muzeum* on Štefánikova 1 are both laid-back cafés.

The Danube basin

To the east of Bratislava lies the rich agricultural region of the **Danube basin** (*Podunajsko* to the Slovaks; *Felvidék* to the Hungarians), a flat, fertile expanse of land that benefits from some of the warmest temperatures in the country and is riddled with meandering rivers, ponds and steaming thermal springs. One of the few places in Slovakia where you can go for miles without spotting a hill, its chocolatey soil sprouts vast melons, plus apricots, grapes and peppers, all of which are sold road-side throughout the summer. Although originally Hungarian for about a millennium, and once an outpost of the Roman Empire with the remains of military camps by the Danube, the region has formed the border between Slovakia and Hungary since being handed over from Hungary to Czechoslovakia in 1918. However, it remains the traditional haunt of most of Slovakia's ethnic Hungarian minority. Sadly, this was one of the regions that suffered badly during World War II, and the subsequent rebuilding has made one place very much like another. The chief exception is **Komárno**, which, while not worth a detour in itself, has enough to make you pause en route to Hungary.

Senec

The towns of the Danube basin are probably the nearest either republic comes to seaside resorts, and in the summer the "beaches" are packed with wind-surfers, canoeists and sun-seekers slobbing out along reservoirs, lakes, swimming pools and any stretch of water they can find. If you're staying in Bratislava, **SENEC** (Szenc), 26km east and just over thirty minutes by train, is the warmest part of the country, the easiest place to get to and fairly indicative of the region. The Turks left one of their few monuments here, the creamy, crenellated **Turecký dom** (built in 1556 and now the town's poshest restaurant), which, along with the large, crumbling synagogue topped by a rusting Star of David, relieves the town's otherwise unprepossessing main street.

The Gabčíkovo-Nagymaros dam

The **Gabčíkovo-Nagymaros Hydroelectric Barrage** project was a megalomaniac idea dreamed up in 1977 by the Communist old guard of Hungary and Czechoslovakia, with the cynical collusion and capital of the Austrians, who were on the lookout for cheap electricity at someone else's environmental expense. However, following intense protest by the green lobby, the Hungarians unilaterally withdrew from the project in 1989 and called for an international enquiry into the environmental effects of the dam. The Czechoslovak government, however, having invested huge sums of money and desperate for an alternative source of energy to brown coal – the pollution from which continues to kill off the country's forests – pressed on and completed a scaled-down version of the scheme, diverting part of the Danube in 1993.

In 1997, after several years of verbal and legal sparring, the International Court in the Hague finally made a decision over the whole unhappy mess. It declared that Hungary had violated international law by reneging on the 1977 agreement. Most Slovaks rejoiced that, for once, their country had been found in the right, and that Hungarian propaganda had finally been unmasked. Unfortunately, however, the dispute is far from over. While deciding overall in Slovakia's favour, the court also ruled that the Slovaks had been wrong in diverting the Danube, which means that both sides can legitimately claim damages. Somewhat hopefully, the court ordered the two sides to come up with a joint proposal for the project (and for the damages), but this too has been stalled and generally the issue has slipped out of the limelight over the past five years. Sadly, in environmental terms, the damage has already been done, according to the WWF and ecologists on both sides of the border. You can visit the Danube barrage for yourself by boat (see p.450) or, better still, cycle along the new channel from Bratislava.

The real crowd puller is the **Slnečné jazerá** (Sunny Lakes), a couple of reasonably warm former gravel pits southeast of town, within sight of the train station, which simply heave with visitors during the hot months, especially August. By the larger lake you'll find water sports equipment for hire, two campsites (mid-June to mid-Sept), bungalows and rudimentary hotels, such as the *Amúr* (☎02/92 40 81; ❶), with bungalows and campsite. Alternatively, you can stay at the rather snazzy new *Penzión Labut'* on the banks of the northern lake (☎02/4592 3015, ✉office@baronka.sk; ❷). The tourist office at Mierové nám 19 (☎ & ✆02/4592 8224, ⓦwww.senec.sk) can also book accommodation. One place that doesn't draw the crowds (but should) is the extraordinary open-air **Museum of Bee-keeping** (Včelárska paseka; June–Sept Mon–Fri 9am–5pm, Sat & Sun 9am–1pm), signposted off route 62, close to the hamlet of Lučny dvor, and representative of a thriving local cottage industry. There's honey for sale and hives of all shapes and sizes spread out in a shady glade by the bee-keeping school.

Komárno

Situated right on the confluence of the Váh and the Danube, **KOMÁRNO** (Komárom) is a Hungarian town through and through, albeit divided by the Danube, which forms the Slovak-Hungarian border. Bilingual street and shop signs abound, and in shops you'll be greeted with *tessék* ("what would you like?") rather than the usual *prosím*. Ethnic niceties aside, however, Komárno is not going to win over many people's hearts; this Danube port town is only worth a stopoff if you're passing through on the way to Budapest.

The Town

When the Czechoslovak border was dreamed up in 1919, the Hungarians of Komárom found their town split in two, with by far the most significant part – and what few sights there are – on the Slovak side. Both sides now annually reunite in late April/early May for a week of joint cultural events, known as the *Komárňanské dni/Komáromi napok* or Komárno Days, which include sports events, markets and open days in the fortress.

To get to the town centre from the **train** and **bus stations** to the northwest, take Petőfiho and you'll hit the main street, Záhradníčka, which heads south to the bridge over the river and into Hungary. The pedestrianized section of town, and the cobbled main square, **námestie gen. Klapku**, lies to the east. The latter is named after the general who fought against the Austrians in the Hungarian uprising of 1848, and whose statue is overlooked by several solid late-nineteenth-century buildings.

The **Podunajské múzeum**, with two subsidiary branches, one at Palatínova 26 (Tues–Sun May–Oct 10am–noon & 2–4pm), west of Záhradníčka, and the other just down the street east of Záhradníčka at Palatínova 13 (Tues–Sun: May–Oct 10am–5pm; Nov–April 9am–4pm), pays tribute to the town's two most illustrious and somewhat controversial sons. The first is the composer **Franz Lehár**, whose father was military bandmaster with the local garrison. Lehár enjoyed the dubious privilege of having written one of Hitler's favourite works, the operetta *Die lustige Witwe* (*The Merry Widow*), and despite the fact that his native tongue was Hungarian and his own wife Jewish, he found himself much in demand during the Third Reich. The nineteenth-century Hungarian writer **Mór Jókai**, on the other hand, was an extremely patriotic Hungarian, who wrote a glowing account of the Hungarian aristocracy and would have had nothing good to say about Komárno's modern-day split nationality. The Palatínova 13 branch expands into greater detail about the two men's lives, while the Palatínova 26 branch is simply two small rooms containing photographs and furniture, but you won't get much from either exhibition unless you know Slovak or Hungarian.

More fascinating than either of the above is the disorientating sight of a small **Orthodox church** (Pravoslávny kostol) in the grounds of the museum at Palatínova 26, testifying to the Serbian colonists who settled around Komárno in the early eighteenth century in a desperate attempt to escape the vengeful Turks. Small pockets of Orthodox believers still exist in the region, and the seventeenth- and eighteenth-century Greek and Serbian icons on display here constitute one of the best collections outside Serbia. Opposite the museum at Palatínova 13 stands the stunning twin-spired Baroque **church of sv Ondreje**, which has a cool, peach-coloured interior.

The Hungarians of Slovakia

The creation of separate Czech and Slovak republics has brought into much sharper relief the rather more volatile relationship between the Slovaks and the 600,000 Hungarians who live along the southern border regions of Slovakia, and make up eleven percent of the country's total population. Like so many ethnic disputes in central Europe, it's an age-old conflict, one that remained fairly dormant during the communist period, but which has now returned with a vengeance.

For almost a millennium, Slovakia – known as the Upper Lands – was an integral part of Hungary where Slovaks were very much the peasants, and Germans and Hungarians the merchants and ruling classes. Both Slovak language and culture were severely suppressed right up until the foundation of the First Republic in 1918, when 750,000 Hungarians were left on the Slovak side of the Danube after the borders for the new republic were drawn up. Like the Germans who lived in the border regions of the Czech Lands for several centuries, Slovakia's Hungarians were not assimilated in the interwar period and were only too happy to unite with the fascist Magyar state during World War II, when Hungary was handed most of the Hungarian-speaking regions of Slovakia and Slovakia itself became an independent, albeit fascist, state for the duration (for the first time in its history). Unlike their Germanic counterparts, the attempt by Beneš to expel the Hungarians in 1945 was successfully blocked by the government in Budapest, although Slovakization of ethnic Hungarians was nonetheless enforced fairly brutally and many were forcibly moved to other regions of Czechoslovakia such as North Bohemia.

In 1989 the enforced fraternal friendship of the communist period finally came to an abrupt end with the dispute over the Gabčíkovo-Nagymaros dam (see p.461). The rise of Slovak nationalism that took place after the Velvet Revolution understandably worried the Hungarian community, which itself was wooed by increasingly chauvinistic politicians, keen to score cheap political points at home. On the Slovak side, former premier Vladimír Mečiar did little to calm the fears of the Hungarian community, rejecting an EU-backed ethnic-minority law, forbidding the public use of foreign languages and even suggesting the community should be expelled. Fortunately, the June 1999 election of Rudolf Schuster – a Hungarian-speaker from Košice and an advocate of governing "for all citizens" – to the presidency, combined with Prime Minister Dzurinda's EU-friendly multi-party government, paved the way to more productive dialogue and a considerable relaxing of tension. However, at the time of writing, the September 2002 elections could well see the return of Mečiar to power, much to the consternation of the international as well as Hungarian community and with the potential to cause serious damage to NATO- or EU-entry negotiations.

The town is also notable for its vast zigzag **fortifications** that seem much too big for the town, and its **fortress**, east of the town centre at the confluence of the Váh and the Danube, which has served as a strategic base for everyone from the Romans to the Russians, and is still in the hands of the military today. One of the town's bastions, **Bašta VI** (Tues–Sun 10am–5pm), on Okružná cesta, to the northwest of the town centre, beyond the railway lines, has been turned into a small museum (follow the signs to the *Fortezza* restaurant, see below). Summer visitors should also give the local thermal pools a whirl, such as the Komárno thermal swimming pool (☎035/771 30 14) on the main Bratislava–Komárno road.

Practicalities

The town **tourist office** (Mon–Fri 7am–3.30pm; ☎035/773 00 63, ⓦwww.komarno.sk) is at Župná 5, though **accommodation** should be no problem as the town has a smattering of hotels and pensions. The *Európa*, on the main street (☎035/773 13 49; ❷), looks unprepossessing on the outside, but the rooms have been splendidly modernized and feature ensuite facilities and TVs, something that cannot be said for the equally central, but run-down *Danubius* on Dunajské nábrežie (☎035/73 10 91; ❶). *Hotel Panoráma*, on Športova ulica (☎035/771 31 51–2; ❷) is a Socialist-style eggbox where you can also camp and park your caravan year-round (☎035/771 31 56; ❶), while the *Ring Bar Penzión*, just off the main square at Letná 4 (☎035/771 31 58; ❸), has fairly cosy rooms above a bar. Student hostels include the *Stredná priemyselna škola Komárno* on ul. Gazdovská (school holidays only; ☎035/773 14 18; ❶). You can **camp** at the local zimný stadión (July to mid-Sept), but the riverside sites 6km west (and just 8min by train) in Nová Stráž (mid-May to mid-Sept) and 16km east in Patince (☎035/778 77 33; mid-May to mid-Sept) are preferable. The Vel'ký Meder site with bungalows (❶) and campsite (☎031/555 21 04) also boasts a thermal swimming pool.

Basic **food** can be had at the *Litovel*, a nice pub on Dunajské nábrežie, or at the *Platán* on Alžbetin island. There are two popular Italian joints to try out: the trendy pizza parlour *Flinstonov cov*, on the main drag, and the Italian-Hungarian *Fortezza* restaurant in Bašta VI of the fortifications system to the north of the train station. The *Café Lehár*, a big fin-de-siècle building on Tržničné námestie, has potential, but the *Café Blik* on námestie gen. Klapku and the *Café Zichy-Europália* in the Europa Palace on Nádvorie Európy are both better bets. For those who know the language, there's a Hungarian theatre, Jókaiho divadlo, halfway down Petöfiho. **Trains for Budapest** leave more frequently from the station on the Hungarian side; simply cross the bridge and the border, and turn right.

Štúrovo

"The Danube threads towns together like a string of pearls", wrote Claudio Magris, but it's doubtful he had **ŠTÚROVO** (Párkány) in mind at the time. Its major saving grace is the unbeatable view of the great domed basilica of Esztergom (*Ostrihom* to the Slovaks), on the Hungarian side of the river, to which it's been linked by a ferry service ever since the bridge was blown up by the retreating German army in 1944. The new (partly EU-funded) bridge, symbolically linking the two, was finally opened in autumn 2001; a hugely positive step in Hungarian–Slovak relations. However, the town's name remains a bone of contention, with the current Slovak government insisting on keeping Štúrovo, the name given to the town by the Communists in 1948 after the Slovak nationalist (and virulent anti-Magyar) Ľudovít Štúr (see p.452), despite a local referendum which voted in favour of reverting to Párkány.

As the last town on the Slovak Danube, it's not a bad place to break your journey. Ferries over to Esztergom are frequent and you can take your car across, or you can hop on one of the international express trains that pause here en route to Budapest. The **train** and **bus stations** are actually an inconvenient 2.5km west of the town, though several local buses cover the distance. In the summer the focus of life is the town's outdoor swimming pool, fed by thermal springs, Termálne kúpalisko Vadaš, by the local **campsite** (☎036/751 14 10, with chalets and a mind-boggling range of water sports; mid-May to mid-Sept; ❶), just north of the town.

Brhlovce

The tiny village of **BRHLOVCE** nestles into the hills some 60km northeast of Štúrovo. Many of its 400-odd residents live in caves dug into the hills' soft rock faces, an oddity dating back to the sixteenth century when fears of Turkish attacks drove their ancestors into hiding. Simple holes in the short cliffs were expanded into habitable homes, and this inexpensive form of housing soon caught on. More cave homes were built in the late nineteenth and early twentieth centuries, and the troglodytes even made money by selling the rock they had hewn to local quarries. Once the living space was dug out, the walls were matted with straw and painted, and windows were carved out; in more recent years modern comforts, such as electricity and running water, have also been introduced. Although most of the cave homes are private residences, a pair of adjoining caves have been turned into a **museum** (Skalné obydlia; no regular hours but generally Mon–Fri 9am–4pm), where you can wander through the few tiny rooms. To get to Brhlovce, you'll have to rely on the infrequent **buses** from Levice, 10km west of Brhlovce, a fairly major bus and train stop in the region.

Piešťany and the Váh valley

Finding its source in the Tatras and carving a southwesterly course right the way to the Danube at Komárno, the **Váh** is one of the great rivers of Slovakia. Tourist office circles like to talk of the "Slovak Rhine", but despite the appearance of ruined cliff-top castles at every turn of the river, it lacks the magic of the Rhine valley. Heading north up the Váh from Piešťany to Trenčín, the mountains on either side keep their distance and the whole area still has the feel of the Danube basin. Beyond Trenčín, the industry, river dams and lorry-congested highway all dampen the effect of brigand hide-outs such as Vrsatec and Považský hrad. The best way to weigh up the relative merits of the region is on one of the fast and frequent **trains** from Bratislava that twist their way up the Váh valley en route to the Tatras.

Piešťany

The most convincing claim the local tourist board makes about **PIEŠŤANY**, just over an hour by train from Bratislava, is that it's the largest spa town in Slovakia. But, although the place is overrun with the unhealthily rich from different parts of the German- and Russian-speaking world, the town itself is slowly catching up with the rather grander late-nineteenth-century West

Bohunice and Mochovce

As you approach Piešťany from Bratislava, the cooling towers of the country's first nuclear power station at **Bohunice** are clearly visible on the western horizon. Built in the 1960s, but temporarily closed down in 1979 after two hushed-up accidents and only seven years of operation, Bohunice's A-1 reactor is currently being cleaned up at considerable cost to the Slovak taxpayer. The other four Soviet-designed reactors continue to function, despite being among the most dangerous in Europe, according to the US Department of Energy. The Slovaks, meanwhile, are trying to finish the second of two equally controversial Soviet-designed nuclear reactors at **Mochovce**, some 50km further east. Recent negotiations have resulted in an agreement to phase out Bohunice by 2007, as one of the two at Mochovce is now up and running, though of course protestors would rather both were shut down.

Bohemian spas. Millions of crowns have been injected into the spa facilities, which include freshly-painted Art Nouveau spa accommodation on the spa island, well-planted green spaces, clean swimming pools, and a host of other resources to which the public has access, making it a pleasant alternative to most of the "beachy" resorts further south.

The town divides conveniently into two parts: the spa island cut off from the mainland by a thin arm of the River Váh, and the rest of the town on the right bank between the main arm of the river and the **bus** and **train stations** to the west. It's a fifteen-minute walk into town down A. Hlinku and Štúrova (bus #3, #9 or #12) to **Winterova**, the main drag through the centre of town, a patchwork of muted fin-de-siècle and Secession buildings decorated with balconies and lined with cafés and trinkety shops. The main spa building at no. 29 is a typical example of Piešťany's understated architecture. Behind the bandstand in the Mestský park, there's a **Balneologické múzeum** (Spa Museum; Tues–Sun: April–Sept 9am–noon & 1–5pm; Oct–March closes 4pm) devoted to the local spa industry, but also displaying everything from a woolly mammoth's tusk to a mock-up of a Slovak folk cottage. The rest of the spa is on the opposite bank, a short stroll past **Barlolama**, the town's famous optimistic statue of a man breaking his crutches in two, and connected by the partially covered **Kolonádový most**, a graceful 1930s modernist structure, rebuilt under the Communists "for the benefit of the working class", in the words of the 1950s commemorative plaque.

One place that definitely wasn't built with the latter in mind is the vaguely Art Nouveau *Thermia Palace* hotel, which has regained its bygone opulence and – if the flash cars parked outside are anything to go by – now serves the new European aristocracy. The woods and park on the **Kúpeľný ostrov** (spa island) are decidedly verdant, with sculptures peeping out of every conceivable shrub and bush – part of the spa's annual international open-air sculpture symposium. The nearby low-lying annexes are still used for "mud wrapping and electro-treatment" to cure rheumatic illnesses (spa patients only). If you fancy a dip, the old-fashioned Eva swimming pool, 200m further north, is open to the public. From here, the sleek, ultramodern Balnea sanatorium spreads its luxurious wings the full length of the island.

Practicalities

Even if you haven't come here for treatment, you should have few problems finding **accommodation** on the left bank. *Pension Astra*, Pod Párovcami 21

(☎033/772 76 71; ❷), is a cheerful guesthouse just a few minutes' walk north of Winterova. Other options include splashing out at the opulent spa hotel *Thermia Palace* on the spa island (☎033/775 61 11, ✉reservations.thr @healthspa.sk; ❽), or playing it safe at the boxy but comfortable *Magnolia* with pool and spa facilities at Nálepkova 1 (☎033/762 62 51; ❸), and the *Eden*, Winterova 60 (☎033/762 47 09; ❷), which has a few cheap rooms in addition to more expensive ones with en-suite bath and satellite TV. Opposite is the pleasant, comfortable *City Hotel* (☎033/772 54 54; ❸), with a good restaurant. If these don't suffice, the staff at the efficient IVCO **tourist office** (Nalepkova 2; Mon–Fri 9am–5.30pm, Sat 8am–noon; ☎033/774 33 55, ✉incoming@ivco.sk, ⓦwww.ivco.sk) are only too pleased to help arrange accommodation. **Camping** is possible (June–Sept) on either side of the mouth of the action-packed Slňava lake (bus #12 or walk 1km to either the Piešťany or Banka sites, ☎033/762 6073), south of town; simple bungalows are also available (❶) and Sl'ňava boasts a thermal pool and water skiing. **Restaurant** prices are a little inflated, but you can get fairly cheap pizzas at *Pizzeria Orchidea*, overlooking the spa park at the end of Park pasáž, a side street off Winterova. *Čajovna Mystik* (A. Dubčeka 27) serves up a range of teas, while *Koliba* on Červená Veža will give you hearty Slovak grub. The obligatory bandstand and gleaming **Dom umenia** (which puts on plenty of free concerts of Bach, Mozart and oompah for the foreign guests in high season) are laid out in the nearby Sad Andreja Kmeťa.

Čachtice and Beckov

Halfway between Piešťany and Trenčín to the north is the industrial town of Nové Mesto nad Váhom, not a place to hang about in if you can help it, but a necessary halt if you're changing trains or buses to get to the ruined castles of Čachtice and Beckov (see below).

Of the two lofty piles of rubble perched on opposing sides of the Váh, the one at **ČACHTICE**, 8km southwest of Nové Mesto, has the edge on atmosphere, for it was here that the "Blood Countess" **Elizabeth Báthory** was walled in for almost four years before her death in 1612 to pay for her crimes (see p.468). Thirteenth-century **Čachticky hrad** was her favourite castle; "she loved it for its wildness", wrote one of her posthumous biographers, "for the thick walls which muffled every sound, for its low halls, and for the fact of its gloomy aspect on the bare hillside". The prize exhibit of the village **museum** (May–Oct Tues–Sun 9.30am–4.30pm), an impassive portrait of Elizabeth herself, was stolen in 1990 and has yet to be recovered. The quickest way up to the castle is actually the stiff climb from Višňové train station (15min from Nové Mesto), rather than the two-kilometre haul from Čachtice village itself.

There's substantially more of a **hrad** (May–Sept Tues–Sun 9am–1pm & 2–6pm) above the village of **BECKOV**, 5km northeast of Nové Mesto and accessible only by bus. Erected in the mid-twelfth century, this was another of Báthory's torture chambers, ruined by a fire that ripped through its apartments in 1729. The ruins are fun to explore and there's a Jewish cemetery at the base of the castle. If you're in need of refreshment, there's a *reštaurácia* just under the rock, where you can relax and watch the rock-climbers risk life and limb on the 245m cliff below the castle, not to mention a small **folk museum** (Tues–Sun 9am–5pm).

Born in 1560, **Countess Elizabeth Báthory** was the offspring of two branches of the Hungarian noble Báthory family, whose constant intermarriage may have accounted for her periodic fainting spells and fits of uncontrollable rage: other Báthorys, such as Prince "Crazy" Gábor, were similarly afflicted. As a child she was intelligent and well educated, being fluent in Latin, Hungarian and German at a time when many nobles, including the ruling prince of Transylvania, were barely literate. Brought up in the family castle at Nagyecsed, a humble town near what is now the Hungarian-Romanian border, she absorbed from her relatives the notion that peasants were little more than cattle – to be harshly punished for any act of insubordination.

As was customary in the sixteenth century, her marriage was arranged for dynastic reasons, and an illegitimate pregnancy hushed up. Betrothed in 1571 – the same year that her cousin István became Prince of Transylvania – she was married at 15 to 21-year-old Ferenc Nádasdy. Over the next decade Ferenc was usually away fighting Turks, earning his reputation as the "Black Knight", and Elizabeth grew bored at their home in Sárvár Castle. There she began to torture serving women, an "entertainment" that gradually became an obsession. With the assistance of her maids Dorothea Szentes and Anna Darvulia (who was also her lover), Elizabeth cudgelled and stuck pins into servants to "discipline" them; even worse, she forced them to lie naked in the snowy courtyard and then doused them with cold water until they froze to death. On his return, Ferenc baulked at this (although he too enjoyed brutalizing servants), and it wasn't until after his demise in 1604 that Elizabeth started torturing and murdering without restraint. Her victims were invariably women or girls, and – most importantly – always peasants, as killing peasants could be done with impunity. Poor women could always be enticed into service at Beckov and Čachtice – Elizabeth's residences after she quit Sárvár, both then located within the borders of Transylvania – and, should word of their deaths leak out, the authorities could hardly believe the accusations of the victims' parents against the Countess Báthory. With the assistance of Szentes, Darvulia, her son's former wet-nurse Helena Jo, and one man, the diminutive Fizcko, Elizabeth allowed her sadistic fantasies full rein. On occasion she bit chunks of flesh from servants' breasts and necks – probably the origin of the legend that she bathed in the blood of virgins to keep her own skin white and translucent.

In this fashion Elizabeth murdered over six hundred women and would probably have continued undetected had Darvulia not died. Grief-stricken, the countess formed an attachment to a local widow, Erzsi Majorová, who encouraged her to seek aristocratic girls for her victims. Enquiries by *their* parents could not be so easily ignored by the authorities, who in any case by now had their own motives for investigating *Die Blutgräfin*. Ferenc Nádasdy had loaned the Habsburg crown 17,000 gulden, which Elizabeth had persistently – and vainly – demanded back. Should she be found guilty of serious crimes this debt would be forfeited. Among Elizabeth's other adversaries were her son Paul, who had grown up apart from her at Sárvár, and one Count Thurzo, both of whom were anxious to prevent the confiscation of the Báthory estates and gathered evidence against her throughout 1610.

On December 29, Thurzo's men raided Čachtice castle, and on entry almost tripped over the corpse of a servant whom Elizabeth had just bludgeoned for stealing a pear. Thurzo secretly imprisoned the "damned woman" in her own castle immediately, so that (in his words) "the families which have won such high honours on the battlefield shall not be disgraced . . . by the murky shadow of this bestial female". Due to his cover-up the scandal was mainly confined to court circles, although when Elizabeth died in 1612 the locals protested at her burial in Čachtice cemetery. She was later reburied at Nagyecsed in the precincts of the family vault. Due to her sex (then considered incapable of such deeds) and rank, records of her trial were hidden and mention of her name subsequently prohibited by royal command.

Trenčín and around

Despite the usual high-rise accompaniments, **TRENČÍN**, 42km north of Piešt'any, is the most naturally appealing of the towns on the Váh. Its central historical core sits below by far the most impressive castle in the valley, best known as the centre of **Matúš Čák**'s (aka Csák Máté in Hungarian) short-lived independent kingdom, which even had its own currency. Čák was little more than a rebellious feudal despot who set up a mock royal court, crowning himself "King of the Váh and the Tatras". He supported the young Přemyslid Václav III in his unsuccessful quest for the Hungarian crown, and had John of Luxembourg and the Hungarian King Charles Robert on the run for a number of years. Defeated only once, near Košice, he remained in control of his fief until his death in 1321, and is now happily lauded as one of the first great Slovak heroes.

The Town

Trenčiansky hrad (daily April–Sept 9am–5pm; Oct–March 9am–4pm) itself – part ruins, part reconstruction – is a fiercely defensive sprawl of vaguely connected walls and ramparts on a steeply pitched and craggy site, spectacularly lit at night and hosting music, fencing, and folk displays in the summer months. Even in its present state, it's a great place to explore, though to visit the recently restored fifteenth-century palace complex, which contains a fairly dull gallery of rather dodgy oil paintings of nobility from the region, seals and coats-of-arms, you must sign up for a 45-minute guided tour in Slovak. Slovakia's one and only **Roman inscription** of any worth was carved into the rock face below the castle (you can see it from the back of the *Hotel Tatra*), commemorating Marcus Aurelius' victory over the German hordes in 179 AD, when the Romans had a fortified winter camp here known as Laugaritio.

Back down the cobbled lane which leads to the castle, in the elbow of the first sharp bend, is a radiant white-and-yellow **Farský kostol** (parish church) on its own paved plateau – packed on Sundays, closed the rest of the week. A covered walkway leads down Hradná to the main square, **Mierové námestie**, whose young plane trees give it a Mediterranean feel. Straight ahead is the **Piaristicky kostol**, ablaze with the fury of the Counter-Reformation and definitely worth checking out if it's open. Next door in the old monastery is the **Galéria M.A. Bazovského** (Tues–Sun 9am–5pm), named after the Slovak sculptor and painter who died here in 1968 and whose statues stand in the courtyard. Temporary exhibitions are held here beneath the building's surviving stucco ceilings, and on the top floor there's a permanent display of works by local artists, dominated by Bazovský's beguilingly simple depictions of peasant life from the 1930s.

One side of the square is closed by Trenčín's only remaining gateway, the **Dolná brána** – talk while you're walking beneath it and you'll never get married, according to locals. Once through it, take a sharp right and you'll discover the former **synagogue**, a grey hulk of a building – Moorism meets Modernism – completely ransacked during the war, but one of the few in Slovakia to have been fully restored. Now used as an exhibition hall, only the arcaded women's gallery and the vivid-blue painted dome give any hint of its former role.

Practicalities

The **bus** and **train stations** are located next to each other five minutes' walk east of the old town, which can be reached by crossing the park adjacent to the stations. The **tourist office** (mid-April to mid-Oct Mon–Fri 8am–6pm, Sat 8am–1pm; mid-Oct to mid-April Mon–Fri 8am–5pm; ☎032/16186,

@www.trencin.sk), at Štúrovo námestie 10, can fix balloon rides above the town, night-time guided tours of the castle and boat trips on the river, and generally helps with most problems, including with **accommodation**, which is rather limited. Trenčín's finest **hotel** is the grandiose late-nineteenth-century *Tatra* (☎032/650 61 11, @www.hotel-tatra.sk; ❺), a pricey and plush Canadian-Slovak joint venture, built into the crat at the very northeastern tip of the main square at ulica Gen. M.R. Štefánika 2, and which is also the home of an inscription carved into the rock by the second Roman legion in 179 AD (see p.469). Otherwise, try the moderate *Brezina*, Lesopark Brezina (☎032/652 81 71, ℱ652 81 73; ❸) or the central *Penzion Scarlet*, Mierové námestie 27 (☎032/743 04 16, ℯck-scarlet@post.sk; ❷). The *Autokemping na ostrove* **campsite** (June to mid-Sept; ☎032/743 40 13) includes tents, caravans and bungalows (❷); pass under the railway lines and look for signposts pointing off to the right. The *Tatra* has undoubtedly the best **restaurant** in town, or else you could eat at either of the two pretty basic pubs: the *Larnius*, Mierové námestie 20, and the *Plzenská pivnica*, in the Zlatá Fatima shopping arcade off the main square. Passable Chinese dishes can be had at *Zlatý lotos*, Hašická 5, and Slovak grub at *Koliba* on Mladežnická, while the relaxed *Čajovna pod hradom* on Mierové námestie 6 serves a range of good teas.

Trenčianske Teplice

While Trenčín bakes down in the valley, **TRENČIANSKE TEPLICE**, 12km northeast, marinates in the green glades of the Teplička valley. The nicest way to get there is on the narrow-gauge train-cum-tram that trundles up the valley from Trenčianska Teplá, less than ten minutes by train from Trenčín. Alternatively, you could follow the red-marked path 9km across the hills from Trenčín and end your walk with a dip in Bohuslav Fuchs' pool (see below).

The spa itself is little more than a collection of sanatoria, ranging from the typical nineteenth-century ochre mansion of the *Sina* to the concrete *Krym*. The town's most unusual building is the stripey *Hammam* bathhouse, whose Moorish interior is officially open only to male spa guests, though the attendants sometimes let visitors peek into this delightful Turkish bath; enter from the adjoining building around the side to the left. Architecture buffs should check out the *Mahnáč* sanatorium, a top-notch Bauhaus-style building by Jaromír Krejcar. From the same period, Brno-born Bohuslav Fuchs' swimming pool complex, **Zelená Žaba** (Green Frog; Mon, Wed & Fri 11.30am–6pm, Tues, Thurs, Sat & Sun 9am–6pm), has a much wider appeal; concealed in some woods to the north of the town and cut into the curve of the hillside, it looks as good as new seventy years on, and swimming in its spring water gives the weird sensation of bathing in warm lemonade. Like all spas, the strenuous stroll is an all-important part of the cure here; so continue up the valley from the Zelená Žaba, then, at the *Baračka* restaurant head up to **Heinrich's spring**, and thence on to Krájovec (557m) for the definitive view over the Teplička valley. The whole trip should take around two hours.

To complement its resort function, Trenčianske Teplice hosts two significant cultural **events** every summer. Art Film is a small international film festival held in mid-June, which nevertheless draws the occasional big-name star; in addition, *Hudobne léto* (Musical summer), spanning mid-June to mid-August, is a series of solo and chamber music performances. The tourist office at Dom služieb (M.R. Štefánika 2, ☎032/655 22 08, @www.sknet.sk/transbus) is happy to help and can also organize spa visits and accommodation.

Travel details

Trains

Bratislava hlavná stanica to: Brno (8 daily; 2hr); Budapest (8 daily; 3hr); Piešťany/Trenčín (1–2 hourly; 1hr–1hr 30min); Prague (8 daily; 5hr); Štúrovo (9 daily; 1hr 20min–2hr 20min); Trnava (14 daily; 35min); Vienna Südbahnhof (3 daily; 1hr 10min).

Bratislava-Nové Mesto to: Trnava (up to 15 daily; 35–50min); Komárno (6 daily; 2hr–2hr 30min).

Buses

Bratislava to: Brezová pod Bradlom (up to 8 daily; 1hr 30min–2hr 10min); Modra (every 30min–1hr; 35min–1hr); Komárno (up to 8 daily; 1hr 30min); Nitra (every 30–45min; 1hr 30min); Piešťany (hourly; 1hr); Senec (every 30min; 30min); Trnava (every 40min; 1hr); Vienna Schwechat Airport/city centre (7 daily; 1hr 10min/1hr 30min).

Trnava to: Nitra (hourly; 1hr–1hr 30min).

The mountain regions

Highlights

✳ **Banská Štiavnica** – Former mining town filled with interesting monuments to a bygone era and situated on a splendid sloping site. See p.483

✳ **Vratná dolina, Malá Fatra** – The finest hiking outside of the High Tatras. See p.495

✳ **Čičmany** – This village preserves a remarkable collection of uniquely and ornately decorated folk architecture. See p.498

✳ **Vlkolínec** – Hillside village of timber folk cottages set in blissful isolation near Ružomberok. See p.506

✳ **Demänovská dolina** – The chief northerly approach to the Low Tatras is also home to several underground caves. See p.509

✳ **Hron valley railway** – Spectacular scenic train ride that includes a 360-degree switchback. See p.510

✳ **High Tatras** – Jagged granite peaks of alpine proportions that offer the best hiking in either republic. See p.512

The mountain regions

The great virtue of Slovakia is its mountains, particularly the High Tatras, which, in their short span, reach alpine heights and have a bleak, stunning beauty. By far the republic's most popular destination, they are, in fact, the least typical of Slovakia's mountains, which tend on the whole to be densely forested and round-topped limestone ranges. The Low Tatras and Malá Fatra, for example, are less monumental but also much less crowded and developed and much more typical of the country.

Geographically speaking, the region splits into two huge corridors, with the Váh valley to the north and the Hron valley to the south. **Banská Bystrica**, in the Hron valley, is one of the many towns in the region originally settled by German miners, and its old quarter is still redolent of those times. Two other medieval mining towns worth visiting are **Banská Štiavnica**, best known for its silver, and **Kremnica**, a gold-mining town set in the nearby hills. For the Slovaks, by far the most important towns historically and culturally are **Martin** and **Liptovský Mikuláš**, both situated in and around the Váh valley, centres of the nineteenth-century Slovak national revival and bastions of Slovak nationalism to this day.

In general, though, the towns in the valley have been fairly solidly industrialized and are often best used as bases for exploring the surrounding **countryside**, most easily done by a combination of hiking, cycling and taking the bus. That said, **railways**, where they do exist, make for some of the most scenic train journeys in the country. As for the region's innumerable **villages**, from which many urbanized Slovaks are but one or two generations removed, they're mostly one-street affairs seemingly unchanged since the last century.

Banská Bystrica

Lying at the very heart of Slovakia's mountain ranges, **BANSKÁ BYSTRICA** (Neusohl) is a useful introduction to the area. Connected to the outlying districts by some of the country's most precipitous railways, it's a handsome historic town in its own right, once you've made it through the tangled suburbs of the burgeoning cement and logging industry. A prosperous royal free town in the Middle Ages, Banská Bystrica was the capital of seven Hungarian mining towns colonized by German miners who, in this case, extracted copper from the nearby hills until the seams ran dry in the eighteenth century. Since then, the town has shaken off its Teutonic past, and is perhaps best remembered today as the centre of the 1944 Slovak National Uprising, whose history, lavishly embellished and glorified by the Communists, is now undergoing a more critical reassessment.

The Town

On arrival, you'll find yourself in the monumental part of town, built up after the war and planned as a showpiece of Communist architecture. It's a thoroughly alienating space with few redeeming features, designed to culminate in a statue of Lenin (now removed), and, behind where he once stood, the high-rise cornflake-packet *Hotel Lux* (symbol of the town's inexorable progress and sophistication).

Beyond is the **Múzeum SNP** (May–Oct Tues–Sun 8am–6pm, Sept–April Tues–Sun 9am–4pm) at Kapitulská 23, resembling a giant mushroom chopped in half. Originally dedicated to a lavish though insubstantial display on the triumphant march of Communism from the Slovak National Uprising (Slovenské národné povstanie, or SNP, for more on which see box on pp.480–481) to the present day, nowadays the museum also deals with aspects of World War II, such as the deportation and extermination of Slovak Jews, through special exhibitions on the ground floor. The main collection of militaria on the top floor remains relatively unchanged, but the two multiprojector film and slide shows (also in English) have been remade. The current stance is anti-Tiso, with the Communists' huge contribution to the wartime resistance currently entirely ignored (though this may change). Whatever the outcome, the impressive facilities create a very powerful exhibition. Outside, between the town's last two surviving medieval bastions, there's a collection of hefty tanks and guns from the uprising.

From the giddy monumental heights of the Múzeum SNP, it's just a short step up Kapitulská to the town's restored centrepiece, **námestie SNP**, the old medieval marketplace and still the hub of life in Banská Bystrica. There are lots of cafés in which to soak up the local scene and admire the brutal fountain, the Marian column and the charcoal-black obelisk of the Soviet war memorial (although there is still talk of replacing this with the square's plague column that was moved in 1964 in preparation for a visit by Khrushchev). A plaque at the corner of the square and Lazovná commemorates the citizens of Banská Bystrica who were imprisoned under the Communists for their active religious beliefs. One or two of the Renaissance burgher houses bear closer inspection, particularly the so-called **Benického dom** (Venetian House), at no. 16, with a slender first-floor arcaded loggia. The sgraffitoed building opposite is now an art gallery, a few doors down from which is the most imposing building on the square, no. 4, the honey-coloured Thurzo Palace, decorated like a piece of embroidery and sporting cute oval portholes on the top floor. This now houses the **Central Slovak Museum** (Mon–Fri 9am–noon & 1–5pm, Sun 9am–4pm), which contains a fair selection of folk and "high" art.

At the top end of the square, beyond the leaning Baroquified clock tower, on námestie Š. Moyzesa, is all that's left of the old castle. The first building in this interesting ensemble is the last remaining **barbakan**, curving snugly round a Baroque tower. Next door, the boxy Renaissance **radnica** (Tues–Fri 9am–5pm, Sat & Sun 10am–4pm) is now the town's main art gallery, which puts on temporary exhibitions from its extensive catalogue of twentieth-century Slovak art, including works by the Slovak Jewish artist Dominik Skutecky, who spent much of his life in Banská Bystrica.

Behind the *radnica* is the most important building of the lot, the rouge-red church of **Panna Mária**, which dates back to the thirteenth century and contains the town's greatest art treasure, a carved late-Gothic **altarpiece** by Master Pavol of Levoča, in the north side chapel. At its centre stands the figure of St Barbara, the patron saint of miners, though more interesting are the side-panel reliefs, including one of St Ursula and her posse of shipwrecked virgins. Unfortunately, the church is only open for services, but if you get inside be prepared also for Schmidt and Kracker's fiery German frescoes, the result of heavy Baroquification in the eighteenth century. To the left of the main door, on the exterior of the church, is another Baroque addition, a wonderful 3D tableau of the Mount of Olives, surrounded by snakes and creepy crawlies, with a premonition of Judas's betrayal in relief above the main scene.

Practicalities

Banská Bystrica's main **bus** and **train stations** are in the modern part of town, ten minutes' walk east of the centre; if you're on a slow train, you can alight at Banská Bystrica mesto train station, just five minutes' walk south of the main square. There's a **tourist office** inside the barbakan (Mon–Fri 8am–7pm, Sat 8am–3pm; ☎048/16186 or 415 50 85, ⓦwww.isternet/sk/pkobb) which can help you arrange accommodation. The finest of the **hotels** is the luxurious *Arcadia* (☎048/430 21 11, ⓔarcade@mail.viapvt.sk; ➎–➏), a converted Renaissance building hidden away down a passageway beside the town's museum. The fourteen-storey Communist-era *Lux*, on Námestie slobody (☎048/414 41 41, ⓔhotellux@pcb.sk; ➎), enjoys great views over the town, but is overpriced; the other central option is the late-nineteenth-century *Národný dom* (☎048/412 37 37 or 412 50 14; ➋), at Národná 11, which has a wonderful café,

BANSKÁ BYSTRICA

Puppet Theatre A

NÁMESTIE SLOBODY B
C

Dom kultúry

Bus Station

Main Train Station

Brezno ▶

9

ACCOMMODATION
Arcadia	2
Lux	1
Národný dom	4
Privát Hodžová	3
Penzión U hlisko	5

RESTAURANTS, CAFÉS & BARS
Alfredo	E
Art Club	A
Copaline Baguette	D
Lotos	C
Reštaurácia U Tigra	G
Staročeska reštaurácia	B
Zlatý bažant	F

THE MOUNTAIN REGIONS | Banská Bystrica

casino and restaurant but is a little dated in decor and facilities. Two other cheap options are the *Penzión Uhlisko* (☎048/414 56 12, ☎411 55 05; ❷), at Lesná 3, across the river from the stations, and the private rooms offered at *Privát Hodžová*, M. Hodžu 5 (☎048/415 31 19; booking essential; ❶), east of the old town – walk to the end of Dolná, cross the bridge and turn right onto J. Kráľa, then left onto M. Hurbana. There's also a **campsite** (open all year), on Tajovského 180 (☎048/419 73 20), 1km west of the main square, just by the turn-off to Tajov.

Eating options in Banská Bystrica have improved greatly over the last decade. You can grab a freshly baked baguette sandwich at the self-service *Copaline Baguette*, námestie SNP 12, or drop into any of the cafés on the main square, such as *Alfredo* at no. 5. *EVIJO*, at no. 8 on the main square, dishes out huge pizzas made before your very eyes, or for hearty Bohemian fare, head for the *Staročeská reštaurácia* on námestie Slobody 9. Try *Lotos* for vaguely Asian delights at no. 3 or enjoy wonderful pub grub at *Reštaurácia U Tigra* at Dolná 36.

Surprisingly for provincial Slovakia, the **nightlife** scene here is fairly active. Most of the cafés on the main square stay open until midnight or beyond, and

479

The **Slovak National Uprising** was probably the most costly (and ultimately unsuccessful) operation undertaken by the resistance during World War II. Like the Prague Uprising of May 1945, it was portrayed in unambiguous terms by the last regime as yet another glorious (Communist-inspired) episode in the struggle to defeat fasasm. But no event in the minefield of central European history has ever been clear-cut, and the SNP is as controversial in its own way as the tragedy of the Warsaw Uprising.

As Hitler set about dismantling the western half of Czechoslovakia in 1938–39, the Slovaks under Jozef Tiso's Catholic People's Party established the first ever independent Slovak state. While for many this represented the fulfilment of a long-held aspiration, Slovakia under Tiso and his militia, the protofascist Hlinka Guards, was little more than a Nazi puppet state. With this realization, and the fact that, whatever the merits of independence, the country was clearly going to go down with the Nazis, Slovaks began to desert the army and join the partisans in the mountains. In December 1943, the Slovak National Council (SNR) was formed by the Communist and non-Communist opposition. The London-based Czechoslovak government-in-exile refused to acknowledge the council as a national organ, maintaining that it was only a regional body, such as the 1920 constitution permitted. These arguments continued to rage within the SNR itself, and between the SNR and London- and Moscow-based exiles throughout the preparations for a **national coup**, which Moscow hoped to co-ordinate with the arrival of Soviet troops.

By the summer of 1944, the Soviet army was massed on the Polish-Ukrainian side of the Carpathians, busy parachuting in Soviet partisans and seemingly poised to liberate Slovakia. **Lieutenant-Colonel Ján Golián**, meanwhile, established a secret military centre at Banská Bystrica and began forming partisan units from escaped prisoners and army deserters. But while the mountains were perfect for concealing their activities, they were not so good for communication. In the end, the uprising stumbled into action prematurely, set off by default rather than according to any plan. On the night of August 27, 1944, the German military attaché for Bucharest, General Otto, along with his personal entourage, was captured by Slovak partisans in Martin and shot. It was the most daring and provocative strike yet, immediately

the *Zlatý bažant*, at no. 11, is a popular watering hole with, no surprise, good *Zlatý bažant* beer on tap. There's also a collection of beer gardens through the passage at Dolná 36. For all-night dancing, try the passable *Disco Arcade* (open till 5am). Look out, too, on fly-posters for any gigs and events at the *Art Klub* on Rudlovská, northeast of the town centre just before the railway bridge. The **Štátna opera** is the town's bastion of high culture, while the local **puppet theatre** or Bábkové divadlo, on Jána Kollára, has regular shows for adults and kids and occasional performances by foreign touring companies.

South to Zvolen

The wide valley that stretches between Zvolen and Banská Bystrica provides a perfect site for the largest air-force base in the country, used by the Soviets until recently. Zvolen itself is worth visiting for its chateau, which contains one of the finest collections of European Masters in Slovakia. If you're travelling there by train, you could also take in Hronsek and Sliač en route, and given that Banská Bystrica's attractions are fairly limited, all three destinations make for pleasant day-trips.

prompting Hitler to demand that Tiso invite the German army into the country, and on August 29, five SS and two Wehrmacht divisions plus sundry other troops entered Slovakia. Events could not be delayed any longer, and the uprising was officially declared by partisan radio from Banská Bystrica.

In the eyes of the Czechs at home and abroad, the Slovaks, by starting the uprising, were at last making amends for their treacherous declaration of independence in 1939, which had helped Hitler to annex the Czech Lands. Yet the majority of Slovaks who took part in the uprising (there were fewer than 500 Czechs involved) were not fighting to restore Czechoslovakia, but to help liberate Slovakia from Tiso and the Nazis. For them the SNR was the new postwar Slovak government in waiting, and when the London-based Czechoslovak government sent a delegate, the Slovaks would only recognize him as a liaison officer, and not as a superior government official. The SNR were fighting to have an equal say in negotiations after the war was over, with a view to perhaps gaining a much greater degree of autonomy, if not independence, in the new postwar arrangement with the Czechs.

Ultimately, however, the uprising failed. The Soviets flew in 2500 paratroopers, along with hundreds of tonnes of weaponry and supplies, Russian advisers, and even a dozen American OSS and British officers. Yet it was not enough, and many blamed the Soviets for not launching a full-scale offensive to relieve the uprising. To be fair, though, their supply lines were already stretched, and breaching the Carpathians was no easy task. In the end, it took the 4th Ukrainian Army over two months and some 80,000 lives to capture the Dukla Pass and reach Svidník, the first major town to be liberated. More disheartening was the Soviet refusal to allow the Allies to use Soviet air bases to drop essential equipment into Slovakia. The Slovaks kept going for almost two months before the Nazis succeeded in entering Banská Bystrica on October 28, but apart from tying down a number of German divisions, it was a costly sacrifice to make. The reprisals went on for months: whole villages were given the "Lidice treatment" (see p.000), and women and children were no longer considered sacrosanct. All in all, well over 30,000 Slovaks lost their lives as a result of the uprising, even though by the end of the uprising, the Soviets had already begun to liberate the country.

Hronsek

Two stops further up the track towards Banská Bystrica is the small village of **HRONSEK**, by the banks of the River Hron. Here, on Hronsecká cesta, west off the road to Sliač, is one of Slovakia's more unusual wooden churches, erected in 1726 on what was originally an island in the river (the two giant lime trees were planted at the same time). With the Counter-Reformation still in full swing, as a Protestant church, it had to be built within a year according to strict guidelines: wood was the only material allowed, which is why there are no metal nails or plaster in the Scandinavian-style timber frame, and the belfry had to be separate. The interior, capable of squeezing in over 1000 worshippers, features seating rather like a theatre in the round. The church is normally kept locked; to get hold of the key, ask around for the local priest. If you'd rather stay out in the countryside, the local hunting lodge 2km north of Hronsek, *Kaštiel' Bocian* (☎045/418 83 92; ❸), has been nicely converted into a hotel.

Sliač

The nearby airstrip has made little impression on the sleepy hillside spa of **SLIAČ-KÚPELE**, 5km north of Zvolen by train. The springs were initially discovered back in the thirteenth century but were for years considered harmful rather than healing, since locals frequently came across the carcasses of birds and animals near the mouth of the source. Only in the eighteenth century was it discovered that fumes from carbonated waters, although therapeutic for humans, could, in sufficient concentration, asphyxiate small animals. A shot of the waters aside, there's nothing to do or see here as such, beyond a pleasant park, various mapped-out promenades and some far-reaching views across the valley basin. The **train station** lies between the village of Sliač and the spa, to the east, up the hill by the edge of the woods.

Zvolen

Once the effective capital of a Hungarian *župa* or regional district stretching as far as the Orava and Liptov regions, **ZVOLEN** (Altsohl), 20km and a forty-minute train ride south of Banská Bystrica, has come a long way since those halcyon days. Today, Zvolen lives off its logging industry and its key position in the country's road and rail system, and, thanks to the new bypass, its wide main thoroughfare, námestie SNP, is now a much more pleasant place to stroll. Although small, the **Vlastivedné múzeum** (Tues–Fri & Sun 9am–5pm), on the west side of the square at no. 43, is actually better than the one at Banská Bystrica, with a good selection of folk art that includes decorated crosses from nearby Detva.

The main reason for coming here, however, is to see the town's four-cornered **zámok** (Tues–Sun 10am–5pm), which squats on a big mound of earth at the southern end of the square, with a makeshift armoured train, built in Zvolen's railway workshops to protect the Slovak National Uprising, situated beneath it. Built in the fourteenth century, the chateau fell to the exiled Czech Hussite leader, Jiskra of Brandys, who for nearly twenty years ruled over much of what is now Slovakia. Later, it became the property of the powerful Hungarian Esterházy family, and, as the Turks got too close for comfort, it was transformed into the stern fighting fortress it now resembles. Nowadays, few rooms contain any of their original decor beyond some fine Renaissance portals, though one room boasts a splendid wooden ceiling decorated with no fewer than 78 portraits of successive Holy Roman and Habsburg emperors. The rest of the apartments have been turned into an **art gallery** displaying a decent range of mostly sixteenth- to nineteenth-century European masters belonging to the Slovenská národná galéria, including works by Hogarth, Brueghel, Caravaggio and Veronese, plus an exhibition by the Slovak National Gallery on forestry and the wood industry. Yet another section concentrates on Master Pavol of Levoča, easily the most original sculptor of the fifteenth century – a good opportunity to catch his work if you're going no further east – while the top floor hosts temporary exhibitions of Slovak art.

Practicalities

Zvolen is an easy day-trip from Banská Bystrica, but there are several places to stay, should you wish to, and a **tourist office** (Mon–Fri 8.30–4pm; ℡045/16186, ✆icko@zv.psg.sk) to help you, east off the main square at Trhová 4. Zvolen boasts several reasonable new **hotels** worth trying, including the very nice *Penzión Quatro* (℡045/532 32 56; ❸) on the main square at no. 32, and the almost as good *Mestsky hotel* (℡045/532 51 80; ❸) on the second floor of the building next door to the tourist office at Trhová 4. A short distance along route 66 to Krupina there's the *Neresnica* **campsite** (open all year, ℡045/533 26 51) at Neresnica cesta 19. For **food**, there's a branch of the ever-popular *Copaline Baguette*, on the east side of the main square, with a pizzeria out the back; the nearby *Jadran* is good for coffee, cakes and ice cream, while the *Victoria*, north of the main square by the main crossroads, is a good place for *Zubr* beer and pub food.

Banská Štiavnica

High above the Štiavnica river, on the terraced slopes of the Štiavnické vrchy, **BANSKÁ ŠTIAVNICA** (Schemitz), 25km southwest of Zvolen, couldn't wish for a more picturesque setting. An old German-speaking silver- (and gold-) mining town, its historic core has suffered from centuries of sheer neglect. The development of a modern lower town has saved the place in terms of its architecture, but turned the old town into little more than an ancient monument, as lifeless and isolated as it is beautiful. In 1993, however, the town gained UNESCO-protected status, and a concerted restoration effort is slowly taking effect.

The staré mesto

Banská Štiavnica earned its medieval wealth from the silver deposits discovered here in the thirteenth century. As at Banská Bystrica, skilled German miners were brought in to work the seams, the town was granted special privileges by the Hungarian crown, and the good times rolled – as testified by the handsome burgher houses and the wonderful red marble Trinity column erected on the main square, **Námestie sv Trojice**. Recently restored to their former glory, their names recall their German heritage: Baumgartner, Rubigall and Hellenbach. The last, the Kammerhof, served as the mining court from the fifteenth century, and now contains the geological section of the town's **Banské múzeum** (Mining Museum; May–Sept daily 8am–4pm; Oct–April Mon–Fri 7am–3pm, Sat & Sun 8am–3pm; ⓦwww.muzeumbs.sk). Of more universal interest, further up the square in a beautiful sgraffitoed building, is the **Galéria Jozefa Kollára** (May–Sept daily 8am–4pm; Oct–April Mon–Fri 7am–3pm), which puts on interesting temporary exhibitions as well as permanent exhibitions of paintings and sculpture from the thirteenth to twentieth centuries.

It's worth asking around for the key to the Gothic church of **sv Katerína**, at the bottom of the square alongside the old **radnica**; the hands of its Baroque clock are set back-to-front. Lutheranism caught on fast in Slovakia during the Reformation, especially among the German communities, and opposite the radnica is one of the most impressive Lutheran churches in the country, the black-roofed bulk of the **Protestant Church**, gilded urns atop its tympanum, built shortly after the 1781 Edict of Tolerance. Up the steps from the radnica is the thirteenth-to-eighteenth century walled **starý zámok** (old castle; May–Sept daily 8am–4pm; Oct–April Mon–Fri 7am–3pm; ⓦwww.hrady.sk/stary_zamok/english.html), once the town's most important building. It was built on the same lines as Kremnica's castle (see p.486), as the town's strongbox as well as a fortified residence for the local bigwigs, and the central church-turned-fortress testifies to the panic that beset the Hungarian Kingdom during the peak of Ottoman expansion in the sixteenth century. Currently undergoing slow but extensive restoration, it houses an exhibit of Baroque sculptures, Štiavnica tobacco pipes, religious art and medieval blacksmiths' works.

Below the castle, Sládkovičova leads past the **Belházyho dom**, a beautifully restored white Renaissance chateau, now a hospital, with an attractive arcaded loggia in the courtyard. Further up Sládkoviča is the seventeenth-century **klopačka** (May–Sept daily 8am–4pm; Oct–April Mon–Fri 7am–3pm), whose

BANSKÁ ŠTIAVNICA

0   100 m

Zvolen

Botanical
Gardens

Starý zámok

Galéria Jozefa Kollára

Banské múzeum

Academy of
Mining & Forestry

VODÁRENSKÁ

HORNÁ RUŽOVÁ

NÁM.
SV. TROJIČE

A

SV Katerína

B

i

Radničné
námestie

DOLNÁ RUŽOVÁ

ANTONA PECHA

Belházyho
dom

D

Protestant
Church

Former
synagogue

2

STRIEBORNÁ

A. KMETA

Klopačka

C

AKADEMICKÁ

J. PALÁRIKA

E **3** **F**

J. PALÁRIKA

KAMMERHOFSKÁ

4

Kammerhof

ANDREJA SLADKOVIČA

NOVOZÁMOCKÁ

KATOVA

N

Kaľvária (1 km)

Bus & Train Stations (1 km)

RESTAURANTS & CAFÉS

Banský dom	**D**
Červeny kohút	**A**
Etnočajovňa Klopačka	**G**
Jazz Café	**E**
Matej	**F**
Pizzeria Soragna	**C**
Spark IT	**B**

ACCOMMODATION

Bristol-Garni	**2**
Grand-Matej	**3**
Salamander	**4**
Tomino	**1**

Piargska
brána

Frauenberg
Church

Nový
zámok   Jewish
Cemetery

▼ *Open-air Mining Museum (1 km)*

wooden "clapper" used to raise the miners from their beds at 5am (nowadays
it "claps" at 10am and 2pm during the tourist season only). Inside, it's a low-
ceilinged building full of character – one of its functions in the past was as city
prison – and packed with displays of miners' lamps and tools. From here the
road continues uphill to the red-brick **Frauenberg Church** and the portly
Baroque **Piargska brána**, one of the town's former gateways that's now
stranded out on the road to Levice, giving an indication of Banská Štiavnica's
original size when it was the third largest town in the Hungarian Kingdom.

As further proof of this, there are no fewer than twelve cemeteries in this part
of town. On a nearby hillock, the white **nový zámok** (May–Sept daily
8am–4pm; Oct–April Mon–Fri 7am–3pm) – a turreted cross between a sugar
lump and a lookout tower – was yet another attempt by the town to guard
against a Turkish attack. The Turkish weaponry on display is far from gripping,
but there is a map showing the proximity of the Turks at the height of their
power, and a viewing gallery with a fantastic panorama of the town.

By far the most interesting section of the town's mining museum is the
open-air mining museum (Banské múzeum v prírode; J.K. Hella 12,
May–Sept daily 8am–4pm; Oct–April Mon–Fri 7am–3pm), set in some disused medieval mines, another kilometre beyond the nový zámok, along the
road to Levice. Above ground, a cluster of technical exhibits charts the technological innovations of the local mining school (information in German and
Slovak only), but the highlight of the museum is the trip down the Bartolomej
mine shaft in hard hat and overcoat. The tour of the narrow labyrinthine tunnel network gives a good impression of the appalling conditions medieval miners must have endured, and is not recommended for claustrophobes.

For the best view of Banská Štiavnica, though, head northeast, past the imposing nineteenth-century building of the **Academy of Mining and Forestry**, whose botanical gardens (daily dawn–dusk) boast one of the finest arboretums in Slovakia, replete with Californian redwoods, woodpeckers and tree creepers, to the copper-coloured hilltop church of **Štiavnica kalvária**. The green-marked path zigzags past a succession of Baroque chapels up the hill to the lower church, then on to the summit where the climactic uppermost chapel contains a gruesome, fantastical tableau of the Crucifixion.

Practicalities

Bus connections to and from Zvolen and Banská Bystrica are fairly good, but the scenic **railway**, built by "voluntary brigades" of Communist youth workers back in the 1950s, is easily the most rewarding way of getting to Banská Štiavnica (6–7 trains daily; 1hr from Zvolen – change at Hronská Dúbrava). The station is south of the new town, with the old town a long, steep hike away, but buses do a pretty good job of linking the two. Car drivers must buy a *celodenná karta* from one of the shops, restaurants or hotels in order to park (5Sk per hour). Any queries should be taken to the **tourist office** (Radničné nám. 1; Oct–April Mon–Fri 8am–4pm, Sat 8am–2pm; May–Sept daily 8am–6pm; ☎045/161 86 or 692 13 60, ⓦwww.banskastiavnica.sk), round the back of the radnica, which also offers guided tours in a multitude of languages.

Banská Štiavnica is justifiably popular with German and Austrian tourists, but there should be little problem getting a **room** for the night at either of the town's two best hotels, the excellent *Salamander*, J. Palárika 1 (☎045/691 39 92, ⓦwww.hotelsalamander.sk; ❸), and the equally good *Grand-Matej* at Kammerhofská 5 (☎045/691 37 82, ⓔgrand@spark.sk; ❸). The *Bristol Garni*, A Kmeťa 11 (☎045/691 13 87; ❷), is fine for a night, but lacks atmosphere, while *Penzión Tomino*, at Akademická 9 (☎045/692 13 07; ❶), has shared facilities, but is perfectly clean and a bargain for budget travellers. There are numerous other pensions and private rooms further out and in neighbouring villages. Campers can choose between **campsites** southwest of the town, in amongst the many artificial lakes; originally built in the eighteenth century as part of the town's ambitious water-pumping project, they're now popular summer bathing spots. The *Autocamp* at the Pučůvadlo lake (☎045/699 41 12; July & Aug) is recommended for both camping and basic bungalows.

For **food**, you can't beat the fine soups and great Slovak specialities prepared by the *Matej*, Akademická 4. The *Hubert* contains a splendid hunting restaurant and the *Banský dom* is a stylish café, opposite the tourist office, complete with chandeliers. Other recommendations include the *Jazz Café* on Kammerhofská 12, the *Etnočajovňa Klopačka* tea house on Sládkoviča, and the Asian restaurant within the *Tomino's* courtyard. For late-night boozing, the *Červeny Kohút* on Trojičné námestie has local flavour and a disco-bar, while *Pizzeria Soragna* on Akademická 9 offers the usual range of pizzas and pastas. Those who want to access their e-mails should drop by *Spark IT – Computer Club* on Námestie Sv. Trojice 3.

Kremnica

KREMNICA (Kremnitz) isn't really what you'd expect from a wealthy gold-mining town. Perched on a semi-plateau midway up the Rudnica Valley, it's a surprisingly modest place, little more than its duo of castle and square, and certainly no match for the wealth and beauty of Banská Štiavnica, though it attracts a few more visitors thanks to its gold mint. Accommodation can be something of a problem, particularly during the Festival of Satire and Humour in early September, so it's worth considering coming on a day-trip.

Founded by the Hungarian King Charles Robert in 1320, Kremnica's gold seams were once the richest in medieval Europe, keeping the Hungarian economy buoyant and booming throughout the Middle Ages. The thick walls and bastions that still surround the town and castle were built to protect what was effectively the Bank of Hungary – the royal mint. Yet **Štefánikovo námestie**, the steeply pitched main square on which the mint stands, is now little more than a provincial village green, dotted with pollarded ornamental trees, park benches and a particularly ornate **plague column** which, topped with a flash of gold, is the only obvious reference to the town's wealth. The heavily fortified **Mestský hrad** (May–Sept Tues–Sun 9am–noon & 1–5pm) sits amid fruit orchards above the square, and has been restored to sparkling cleanliness. To see it, though, you're supposed to join the two-hour tour – more than enough time to view every room, painting, and statue in the small lower living quarters, plus the richly decorated church of sv Katerína, which takes up most of the upper courtyard. The atypical Gothic nave is broader than it is long, and holds five altars, all bathed in local gold, plus a stupendous 3500-pipe organ. To cap off the tour, you can climb the adjoining tower for superlative views of the grassy square below and lolling hills around. If you don't want to go on the tour, you might be able to coax the ticket-sellers into letting you wander through the grounds on your own, or you can come and hear the organ in action during Sunday Mass (9.15am).

Back on Štefánikovo námestie, there's a **Museum of Coins and Medals** (Múzeum mincí a medailí; May–Sept Tues–Sat 8.30am–5pm, Sun 9am–4pm; Oct–April Tues–Sat 8am–1pm & 1.45–4.30pm) that's been attracting visitors from all around the world since 1890. From Stalin to Churchill, they've all had anniversary Kremnitzerducats minted for them in their time. As well as some exceptionally beautiful Renaissance coins, there's a whole room of paper money, which, during the First Republic, became an art in itself, with designs by top Czech artists like Alfons Mucha and Max Švabinský. The mines still produce a small amount of gold, and the odd commemorative coin is sporadically struck at the **Štátna mincovňa** (State Mint; no admission) on the northwest corner of the square. As an unlikely accompaniment to the coin museum, the **Ski Museum** (Lyžiarske múzeum; May–Sept Tues–Sat 9am–5pm; Oct–April Mon–Fri 8am–1pm), on the west side of the square, has a collection of antique skis, tins of dubbin and a whole range of ski memorabilia.

From Banská Štiavnica, it's simplest to catch a **bus** to Kremnica, but from Zvolen you also have the choice of the **train** with its wonderful views as the track switches back and forth through the hills, climbing over 460m in just 14km before depositing you above Kremnica itself, about a kilometre southeast of the centre. If you do need to stay the night, ask at the **tourist office** (TIC Kremnica, Námestie gen. M.R. Štefánika 35; Mon–Fri 8am–5pm; Sat 9am–2pm; ☎045/161 86 or 674 28 56, ⓦwww.kremnica.sk), in between the double gateway on the south side of the main square. The best hotel in town is the well-renovated *Centrál* at Dolná 40/3, just outside the double gateway (☎045/ 674 42 10; ❷), with a sauna and a bright restaurant. If this is full, try the *Veterník* (☎045/674 27 09; ❷), a few hundred metres south of the centre on Veternická 19 with a popular restaurant, or the pleasant pension *Stefanov Dvor* at Stefanshof, J. Horvatha 52 (☎045/674 40 97, Ⓔstefanshof@hotmail.com; ❷). The *Vofri* Gothic wine bar on Štefáníkovo námestie 34 and the *Rybárska reštaurácia Zlaty Sivon* on Langsfeldova 3 offer good Slovak and Hungarian grub and wine.

The road to Lučenec

Heading south or east from Zvolen by train takes you through the wilds of southern Slovakia to the Hungarian border. The southbound route 66 to Šahy is the more direct if you're heading for Budapest, but the eastbound route 50 via Lučenec is more interesting. For a start, it takes you past the imposing ruined castle of **Vígľašský zámok**, 15km east of Zvolen, just beyond Zvolenská Slatina. Originally a Gothic castle, later an anti-Turk fortress, and finally an aristocratic manor house, the whole place burnt down during fighting in World War II. The ruins are a stiff but straightforward climb up from the train station. Another 8km down the tracks is the village of **DETVA**, only really worth visiting in early July when the **folk festival** is on, reputedly one of the best in Slovakia. The traditional skills of the community lie in woodcarving, particularly the *fujara*, a cross between a flute and a bassoon, and an instrument commonly used in folk music right across central Europe. You can stay at the *Hotel Detva* (Záhradná 22, ℡045/545 5414; ❸) or contact the **tourist office** located in the same building (℡045/545 52 17, ⓦwww.alter.sk/hoteld) which can arrange accommodation.

Lučenec

Some 60km southeast of Zvolen, **LUČENEC** (Losonc) is, for the most part, a scruffy, ramshackle place typical of the border regions, with a population of Slovaks, Magyars and Romanies in roughly equal proportions. It gets few visitors, but if you're passing through it's worth checking out the two churches on the old town square, **Kubínyiho námestie**. Also worth a quick look is the **Novohradské múzeum** (Tues–Fri 9am–5pm, Sat & Sun 1–4pm), on the east side of the square, which puts on interesting temporary exhibitions. You might also take a closer look at the enormous disused Art Nouveau **synagogue**, a few blocks south of the square beyond the also disused *Hotel Pelikán*, one of the three that used to serve the town's large prewar Jewish population, and in line for reconstruction.

It's a good fifteen-minute walk south along Železnicná from the **bus** and **train stations** to the town centre, but once you've hit T.G. Masaryka, the main drag through town, there are a few places to break your journey. For **food** and **drink**, try the *Restaurácia Hviezda* at Zvolenská cesta 2 for standard Slovak nosh, or the *T&T* restaurant, T.G. Masaryka 2, which does some interesting Hungarian dishes. Due to its location right near the border, Lučenec has its fair share of **accommodation**, starting with the *Reduta* (℡047/433 12 37, 🖷047/433 12 40; ❸), a Best Western chain hotel dating back to 1810, just round the back of the wonderful neo-Gothic shopping precinct on the south side of Kubínyiho námestie at Vajanského 2. If you're minding your pennies, there's also the *Novohrad*, Novohradská 27 (℡047/433 12 11; ❷), or the even cheaper *P-7*, north of the main square at Kármána 22/A (℡047/ 432 12 55; ❷), which is new, kitschy but acceptable. For local and regional information, head for the **tourist office** (Mon, Tues, Thurs & Fri 8am–noon & 12.30–5pm, Wed 10am–7pm, Sat 8am–noon; ℡047/433 15 13) at T.G. Masaryka 14.

Fiľakovo and beyond

FIĽAKOVO (Fülek), a small Hungarian-speaking town just 13km southeast of Lučenec, is worth a brief stopoff, if only for the extremely photogenic ruins of **Fiľakovsky hrad** (daily 9am–6pm), perched on a craggy hilltop in the

Romany part of town and destroyed during the Turkish invasion in 1554, or the museum below (open Tues–Sun 10am–noon & 1–6pm), stuffed with local memorabilia. If you're heading south for Salgótarján in Hungary, you could also happily spend an afternoon exploring the Dolina Bukovinkého potoka, a gently wooded valley that starts 1km from the Hungarian border. Some 3km along the valley, you come to **Šomošský hrad**, another picturesque Gothic castle in ruins, right on the border, squatting upon vast blocks of eroded volcanic stone. Founded during the fifteenth century, its five towers survey impressive basalt formations, resembling giant organ pipes, some of which form part of a waterfall known as the *kammené vodopad*. Below the castle lies the Hungarian village of Somoskö, to which there is no access.

The Turiec valley

From Kremnica, the railway climbs another 18km or so before hitting the mill-pond flatness of the **Turiec valley**. Having climbed this far up a valley which gets progressively narrower and more dramatic, it comes as something of a surprise to find yourself in such a wide plateau: but for the cool mountain air and the Veľká and Malá Fatra in the distance, you could be back down in the Danube basin.

Turčianske Teplice

TURČIANSKE TEPLICE is the first stop on the railway as it romps across the valley floor to Martin (see p.489). A modern spa town (for the treatment of facial diseases and urinary tract problems), despite its fourteenth-century origins, it boasts very hot natural springs and a striking Bedouin-blue domed nineteenth-century **bathhouse**, the Modrý kúpeľ (call ☎043/491 33 89 to reserve spa treatments if you are not staying as a spa guest), with an ornate Moorish treatment. You can wander through the peaceful wooded spa park towards the **Dom Mikuláša Galanda** (Tues–Sun 10am–1pm & 2–5pm), southwest of the centre at Kollárova 74, where the influential Slovak painter Mikuláš Galanda was born in 1895. The home has been converted into a museum, with photos and personal effects of the artist to complement a small but vibrant collection of his works. Galanda studied in Budapest, where his early pen-and-ink sketches included cartoons published in the Hungarian magazine *Hárman* between the wars. In the 1920s and 1930s, he fell under the spell of Picasso, adopting the Spanish painter's styles in most of his subsequent works. Particularly striking among these are the gloomy Cubist *Pijani* (*Drinkers*), and the touching *Mother with Child and Poppy Flower*. Galanda won a silver medal at the Paris Exhibition in 1937, a year before he died prematurely, in Bratislava, of a stomach ailment.

The town also makes a good base for exploring the Veľká Fatra (the yellow-marked path from the station heads off into the hills), though, unfortunately, most of the town's hotels are filled with guests here for the spa (contact Slovenské liečebné kúpele Turčianske Teplice for further **information** about spa accommodation and treatments, ☎043/491 31 11, ✉turcslk@isternet.sk). You could, however, try *Penzión Milka* (☎043/492 26 31; ❷), a bright pink house on Partizánska, tucked behind the radnica just off the spa's pedestrianized main street, which offers comfortable **rooms**, plus a sauna and **restaurant** serving Slovak fare. The nearest **campsite** (mid-June to mid-Sept) is a two-

Hiking in the Veľká Fatra

To the east of the Turiec valley lie the **Veľká Fatra**, a line of craggy mountain tops surrounded by a sea of uninhabited, undulating forest. The ridge of brittle limestone peaks from Krížná (1574m) to Ploská (1532m), via the highest of the lot, Ostredok (1592m), is the most obvious area to aim for, but the thin craggy valleys leading up to the mountains are actually much more enthralling to walk along: the two most accessible and geologically exciting are the **Gaderská dolina** and the **Blatnická dolina**. The return trip along either, including ascending at least one of the big peaks, is a full day's hike (6–7hr); it's a good idea to get hold of a *Veľká Fatra* hiking map. Both valleys begin at **BLATNICA**, one of the most idyllic villages in the Turiec valley, with half-timbered cottages spread along both banks of the village stream. The local manor house, which features a lovely circular Neoclassical portico, is now a **museum** (Tues–Sun 9am–4pm) dedicated to the great grandfather of Slovak photography, **Karol Plicka**, whose images of the Slovak countryside are reproduced in countless coffee-table books. There are several pensions at the northern edge of the village, a *chata* colony at the entrance to the Gadierská dolina, and a **campsite** (open all year round) 1km south of Blatnica, which can be packed out in the summer season.

kilometre train journey north at Diviaky, across the river and the highway from the white seventeenth-century country house (closed to the public), but if you've got your own wheels, you'll find more appealing opportunities further north up the valley.

Martin

A town of considerable historic importance for the Slovaks, **MARTIN** and its industrial baggage occupy the last seven kilometres of the banks of the River Turiec before it joins forces with the mighty Váh. Perhaps unfairly, it's best known nowadays for its ZTS engineering works, but while this once had a monopoly on Warsaw Pact tank production, it's struggling to cope in the post-Cold War era and has had to halve its 16,000 workforce. Yet there's more to Martin than a five-minute drive through the town's confusing one-way system might suggest: for example, the country's most encyclopedic folk museum, a better-than-average Slovak art gallery and an open-air folk museum on the outskirts of the town. There's also the possibility of a day's hiking in the less visited southern range of the Malá Fatra, the Lúčanská Fatra (see box p.492).

Some history

Established back in the fourteenth century, Martin remained the extremely unexceptional town of Turčiansky Svätý Martin until well into the nineteenth century. Then, in 1861, a group of Slovak intellectuals and clergy gathered under the linden tree in front of the Protestant Church and proclaimed the **Martin Memorandum**, which declared boldly that the Slovaks "were as much a nation as the Magyars" and asked the Viennese Parliament to establish a North Hungarian Slovak District (which would remain an integral part of Hungary) with Slovak as the official language.

Their demands caused outrage among the Magyars and were studiously ignored by the Austrians. Nevertheless, a number of important Slovak institutions were founded in the town, of which by far the most important was the **Matica slovenská**, set up to promote the embryonic national culture through education, literature and the arts. It was short-lived. The infamous Ausgleich of 1867, which effectively gave the Hungarians a free hand in their half of the empire, ensured that all Slovak institutions of higher education were closed by the mid-1870s.

During the next forty years of heavy-handed Magyarization, Martin remained the spiritual centre of the Slovak nation, and on May 24, 1918, Slovak nationalists of all hues gathered for the last time at Martin to sign the **Martin Declaration**, throwing in their lot with the Czechs and scuppering the Hungarians' various proposals for a "Greater Hungary". At this point Martin was still seriously under consideration as the potential Slovak capital: it was centrally located, less exposed to attack and infinitely more Slav than the Austro-Hungarian town of Pressburg (Bratislava), the other main contender, to which it eventually lost out. Since 1989, however, the Matica slovenská has re-established itself in the town and is earning Martin a reputation as a hotbed of Slovak nationalism, not to say chauvinism.

The Town

There's not much to choose aesthetically between what might nominally be called the old town in the south and the industrial estates to the north, but the sights are all located in the south. From the train station, Martin's modern chessboard street-plan becomes quickly apparent as you hit the first major cross-roads, on which stand the **post office** and the adequate *Hotel Slovan*, along with the **Turčianské múzeum** (April–Oct Tues–Sun 9am–5pm; Nov–March Mon–Fri 9am–5pm), named after Andrej Kmeť – paradise for your average botanist, geologist or zoologist, but of limited appeal to anyone else. Of more general interest is the **Turčianská galéria** (Tues–Fri & Sun 10am–5pm, Sat 10am–noon), one block south on Daxnerova, which houses a good range of Slovak artists in its permanent collection on the first floor. Works by Miloš Alexander Bazovský, Ľudovít Fulla and Mikuláš Galanda are all featured, while the seminal Martin Benko, who lived and worked in Martin, has a whole room devoted to him – his simple form of Expressionism became a hallmark of much of Slovak art between the world wars. The plain interwar house at Kuzmanyho 34, where Benko lived from 1958 until his death in 1971, is now the **Múzeum Martina Benka** (Tues–Fri 9am–4pm, Sat & Sun 9am–5pm), containing his archive, much of the original furniture and plenty more of his paintings.

Straight ahead, two or three blocks up tree-lined Andreja Kmeťa (which then becomes Muzeálna), is the barracks-like mass of the **Slovenské národné múzeum** (Slovak National Museum; Tues–Sun 9am–5.30pm), which commands a great view of the Malá Fatra from its steps. The museum houses the country's Institute of Ethnography and one of the best and most extensive and exhaustive folk collections in the country. Richly decorated costumes and folk artefacts from every region of Slovakia are on display, with Slovak and English captions explaining the exhibits.

On the other side of the open-air amphitheatre, to the south, is the **Národný cintorín**, which, like the Slavín cemetery in Prague, contains the graves of most of the leading Slovaks of the národné obrodenie. It's nothing like as impressive as the Slavín, not least because of the subdued artistry of the head-stones, as demanded by Lutheranism, the religion of many of those buried here. Using the master plan near the entrance, you can find the graves of Andrej Kmeť, Janko Kráľ, Janko Jesenský, Martin Benko, Andrej Švehla, Karol Kuzmány and Svet Hurban-Vajanovský, all leading figures in the Slovak society of the nineteenth century.

Neither the old nor the new buildings of the **Matica slovenská**, founded in 1863, are anything to get excited about. The older of the two, on Osloboditeľov, has been nicely restored, and now serves as the **Slovenské národné literárne múzeum** (Slovak National Literary Museum; Tues–Fri 9am–5pm, Sat & Sun 10am–4pm). The Matica's current home, which looks rather like a giant domestic radiator, is easily spotted to the north of the Slovak National Museum.

Perhaps the most rewarding place to visit, though, is the **folk skanzen** (Múzeum slovenskej dediny; May–Oct Tues–Sun 9am–6pm, Nov–April until 5pm), 2km south of town near the Jahodnícky háj (bus #11 or #41, then follow the signs through the apartment blocks and into the woods), which gives some idea of what Martin was like during the nineteenth century. It's also one of the biggest open-air museums in the country and contains buildings from all over Slovakia, even retaining a feeling of some authenticity with a section of shops and homes laid along a road, rather than randomly strewn about.

Practicalities

Only one or two daily trains from Bratislava pass through Martin's small station; most use the train station at **Vrútky**, in a working-class suburb 7km north

Walking in the Lúčanská Fatra

The southern ridge of the Malá Fatra (see below), the **Lúčanská Fatra**, rises swiftly and dramatically from Martin's westernmost suburbs, making the town a suitable base for ascending the five big, bare peaks of the southern Malá Fatra. If you're staying in town, you can take a chairlift (*lanovka*) from Podstráne, 3km west of town (bus #41), which deposits you just over 1km below the highest peak, **Velká lúka** (1476m); on foot, it'll take nearly four hours. Ten kilometres north along the ridge are the ruins at Strečno (see p.497), about a two-hour walk. If you're camping at Vrútky, Martin's northern-most suburb, the nearest peak is the northernmost summit of **Minčol** (1364m).

(numerous buses go from here to the centre of Martin), while local trains to Žilina and Zvolen use both stations. **Accommodation** is not a problem, with at least a couple of cheaper options to challenge the comfortable *Turiec* (T & F 043/422 05 18; ❸), near the town's Catholic church at A. Sokolíka 2, and the pyramidical *Grandis* (T 043/422 00 15–6 W www.grandis.sk; ❹), which boasts a wealth of mod cons. Accommodation can also be arranged by the local **tourist office**, Stahl Reisen s.r.o. on ulica 29. Augusta 9 (Mon–Fri 9am–noon & 1–5pm; T 043/422 18 55 or 161 86, W www.stahl.sk). The *Penzión Čierná pani*, Kúzmanyho 24 (T 043/413 15 23, F 043/422 315; ❷), has modestly priced rooms and a popular restaurant, while *Hotel SI* (T 043/413 46 59, F 413 59 90; ❷), at Prieložtek 1, just off Jesenského, less than 1km south of the centre, is surprisingly nice inside despite its drab surroundings; hotel beds are cheap, and you can save even more by staying in dorm rooms for 200Sk per person.

Food options have improved over the last ten years as well: all the above hotels have good restaurants, and you can get Slovak pizzas at the simply-named *Pizza* restaurant on 29 augusta. This street forms part of Martin's small but nicely restored main square, and is also home to the *Rybarská Reštauracia*, with tables on the square and a menu that goes beyond the usual to include catfish and eel. The nearest **campsite** (mid-May to mid-Sept) is in the woods west of Vrútky; if you have a car, there is a better campsite south of Martin at Autocamping Blatnica (T 043/903 548 387 or 494 42 07), at Pod Záhorím, Blatnica.

The Malá Fatra

The **Malá Fatra** (W www.malafatra.sk) are the first real mountains on the road from Bratislava and are one of the most popular and accessible of the Slovak ranges. They are split in two by the sweeping meanderings of the Váh; the northern ridge is by far the more popular, boasting the highest peaks and the most spectacular valley, Vrátna dolina. The southern ridge, including the Lúčanská Fatra, is less geographically pronounced and drifts more gently south-westwards, but contains a couple of non-hiking attractions. Most people use **Žilina** as a base simply because it's on the main line from Bratislava, though in fact it's too far from the mountains to be really convenient. Accommodation in the area is now much easier to come by, but if you're serious about hiking, you'll solve a lot of problems by bringing your own tent.

Žilina and around

Throughout the summer season **ŽILINA** (Sillein/Zsolna) is awash with coach parties, school kids and backpackers, all heading for the mountains of the nearby Malá Fatra. Few bother to venture far from the bus and train stations, though the town itself has a pleasant, compact old quarter, originating from the fourteenth century when the town was colonized by German settlers. The whole place suffered badly during the Thirty Years' War and only really began to recover with the industrial development of this century. In October 1938, following the Munich Agreement ceding the Sudetenland to Hitler, the first Slovak government was formed in what became known as the Žilina Accord. It remains a bastion of Slovak nationalism, with the chief of the Slovak National Party, Ján Slota, as its mayor and with the nation's highest percentage of votes for local-boy Vladimír Mečiar's HZDS party.

The Town

Between the stations and the old town to the west is the pedestrianized street of **Národná**, the town's main shopping drag, which ends at the amorphous expanse of **námestie Andreja Hlinku**, featuring a larger-than-life statue of the cleric, known affectionately as *otec národa* (father of the nation). Statues of saints Cyril and Methodius look down from the Farské schody, the steps that lead up to the back end of the **Farský kostol** (parish church), with its freestanding belfry. Beside the Farské schody, and contemporary with them, is the **Mestské divadlo**, with its unusually tall Moorish arches, built during World War II.

A couple of minor sights lie just off the square to the southeast. First off, on Štefánikova, there's the main branch of the **Považská galéria umenia** (Tues–Fri 9am–5pm, Sat & Sun 10am–5pm), which puts on temporary art

▲ *Budatínsky Zámok*

ŽILINA

UL. FRAŇA · SASINKOVA UL · UHOĽNÁ UL.
HOLLÉHO UL. · UL. P.O. HVIEZDOSLAVA
RADLINSKÉHO UL · UL. ANDREJA KMEŤA

ACCOMMODATION

Astoria	1
GMK Centrum	4
Grand Hotel	3
Penzión Majovej	2

Train Station

HURBANOVA UL.
FRANTIŠKÁNSKE NÁM.
Tesco
NÁM. A. HLINKU
HURBANOVA UL.
NÁRODNÁ UL.
UL. JÁNA TVRDÉHO
MILCA

Bus Station

Former Synagogue
Farský Kostol
Považská galéria umenia
Mestské divadlo
Market
sv Pavel
MARIÁNSKE NÁM.
Múzeum židovskej kultúry

UL. J. KALINČIAKA · KUŽMÁNYHO UL · UL. DOLNÝ VAL · MÝDLARSKA UL · FARSKÁ UL · UL. DOLNÝ UL. ŠTÓLŇA · BURIANOVA MEDZIERKA · RADNIČNÁ UL · UL. HORNÝ VAL · PIVOVARSKÁ UL · STEFÁNIKOVA UL · KUKUČÍNOVA UL · UL. DANIELA DLABAČA · MOYZESOVA UL

VUROMA · MAKOVICKÉHO UL.
UL. NA PRÍKOPE · UL. HORNÝ VAL · UL. STUDNIČKY · UL. REKA · UL. REPUBLIKY · UL. 1. MÁJA
UL. ROMUALDA ZAYMUSA · UL. STUDNIČKY

N

HÁLKOVA UL · VEĽKÁ OKRUŽNÁ UL · KOMENSKÉHO UL · ŠTÚROVO NÁM. · UL. VOJTECHA SPANYOLA · PREDMESTSKÁ UL
UL. JÁNA KRÁĽOVA · KOLLÁROVA UL · VEĽKÁ OKRUŽNÁ UL · HRDZA UL

0   100m

RESTAURANTS

C-Klub	B
Radničná vináreň	C
Turecká reštaurácia	A

exhibitions; in addition, there's a small exhibition on Žilina's Jewish community in the **Múzeum židovskej kultúry** (daily except Sat 11am–5pm) on ulica Daniela Dlabača. Žilina had a large Jewish community of around 3500 before the war – as attested by the imposing 1930s functionalist synagogue (now a cinema) at the far end of Sladkovičova – though of the 700 who survived the Holocaust only a handful remain.

Beyond the Farský kostol is the staré mesto (old town), centred on **Mariánske námestie**, a very pleasant, partly arcaded square overlooked by the big ochre frontage of the Jesuit church of sv Pavel. There are several good cafés from which to admire the square's very Germanic, neat proportions and its fountain fringed by lofty lime trees. The backstreets are also great to wander round, but the staré mesto won't detain you long.

Žilina's most impressive sight, the attractive **Budatínsky zámok** (Tues–Sun 8am–4pm), is actually 2km north of the town centre, in the suburbs on the right bank of the Váh (bus #22 or #24). A characteristically hybrid Slovak affair, whitewashed over in the 1960s and now crumbling around the edges, the zámok now houses several exhibitions – a faintly hysterical Communist-era English commentary will guide you around the display of carved wooden furniture, and you can also climb the original thirteenth-century tower, but the most interesting section is the exhibition of *Slovenské drotárstvo* (wire sculptures and utensils) once sold by the region's tinkers (who made up an estimated two-thirds of the local population at the beginning of the nineteenth century).

Practicalities

Few people come to Žilina to sightsee in town, but a lot of people end up using it as an initial base – so many in fact that it may not be easy to get a bed in high season. The local **tourist office** (Mon–Fri 8.30am–4.30pm; ☎041/542 92 68), hidden off Mariánske námestie at Burianova medzierka 4, can organize private **accommodation** in town or in the mountains themselves.

The nicest **place to stay** is the plush *Astoria* (☎041/562 31 73; ❺), at the top of Národná by námestie Andreja Hlinku, followed by the *Grand Hotel*, (☎041/564 32 65, ⓦwww.grandhotel.sk; ❸), just off Mariánske námestie at Sladkovičova 1, which has pleasant modern rooms, some with views of the square (if you crane your neck). The best budget option is *GMK Centrum* (☎041/562 21 36; ❷), an office/restaurant/pension through a passage at Mariánske námestie 3; it's worth booking ahead as there are only three rooms. Otherwise, try the *Penzión Majovej*, Jána Mlca 3 (☎041/562 41 52; ❷), which is decent value, with en-suite showers and a location between the bus station and námestie Andreja Hlinku.

For **eating out**, there are a handful of outdoor cafés and cellar wine bars on Mariánske námestie, of which the *Radničná vinareň*, a designer wine cellar on the south side is probably the most likeable. The best restaurant in town is that at the *Astoria* hotel, with high ceilings, big windows overlooking the square, and a solid selection of Slovak dishes. Other, cheaper options include the *C-Klub* (closed Sun), a *palačinkáreň* by the Farský kostol, serving sweet and savoury pancakes, and the *Turecká reštaurácia*, at Andreja Kmeťa 11, off Kálov (closed Sun), a Slovak-style Turkish restaurant. For budget fare, pick up a tasty sandwich from the *Bagetéria* on the opposite side of námestie Andreja Hlinku from Tesco, or head for the self-service *Gastro*, on the corner of Hlavná and ulica J. Milca.

If you're here for the **nightlife** and want to drink with the locals, cut a path to the cheap *Kolečko*, ulica Jozefa Vuruma 13, play billiards at the *Zabavné centrum* on Sladkovičova, or head for the *Royal Pub*, by the Jesuit church, which throbs until late. There's a chilled-out *čajovna* called *Starinkova včeláreň* on the first floor of Štúrova 1, and you can get online at the basement **internet café** on Kálov, just off námestie Andreja Hlinku, behind Tesco.

Terchová and the Vrátna dolina

Twenty-five kilometres east of Žilina, at the mouth of the Vrátna dolina, **TERCHOVÁ** is a vast, straggling village, famous for being the birthplace of the Slovak folk hero **Juraj Jánošík** (see p.496). A small **museum** (Tues–Sun 8am–4pm) draws links between Jánošík and the partisans who took part in the 1944 Slovak National Uprising, and though all the texts are in Slovak, there's enough local folk art to keep you going, not to mention Jánošík's celebrated brass-studded belt (thought to bring good luck) and jaunty hat. On the low hill overlooking the town stands a giant futuristic aluminium statue of the man himself, one of the many mass-produced in the region. Late July and early August are good times to visit the village, during the international

Juraj Jánošík

Juraj Jánošík (1688–1713) is the most famous of the many Robin Hood figures who form an integral part of the songs and folklore of the Slovak mountain regions. Most originate from the turn of the seventeenth century when the central authority of the Habsburgs was at a weak point, worn down by the threat of Turkish invasion. Like many of the rural youth of his generation, Jánošík joined up with the anti-Habsburg army of the Hungarian rebel Ferenc Rákóczi II in 1703. When they were finally defeated by the imperial forces at Trenčín in 1711, large numbers fled into the hills to continue the fight from there. Jánošík, however, opted for the priesthood and left for Kežmarok to complete his religious training. While he was away, his mother fell ill and died, and his father – who had absconded from work in order to build a coffin for her burial – was given a hundred lashes, which proved fatal for the old man. With both parents dead, Jánošík finally took to the hills and gathered round him the obligatory band of merry men, indulging in the usual deeds of wealth redistribution.

Sadly – though this, too, is typical of Slovak folklore – the crucial difference between Robin Hood and characters like Jánošík is that the latter nearly always come to a sticky end. In March 1713 Jánošík was captured after the landlord of the pub he was drinking in betrayed him, and an old woman threw peas under his feet to make him fall over. The lords of Liptov cruelly tortured Jánošík in an attempt to extract a confession, and sentenced him to death in the central square of Liptovský Svätý Mikuláš, where he was hung by the ribcage. It's impossible to overestimate the importance of Jánošík to both the oral and written Slovak literary tradition, and more poems, novels and plays have been inspired by his exploits than by any other episode in Slovak history – except perhaps the Slovak National Uprising (see p.480).

folk festival of music and dance – the valley is said to produce a higher than normal concentration of musicians. There are several **hotels** and pensions, including the central *Penzión Covera* (☏041/569 52 63; ❷) above a bar, the newish *Hotel Terchová* (☏041/599 31 09; ❸), which sits overlooking the Jánošík statue, a short distance up the Vratna dolina road, and *Hotel Diery* (☏041/569 33 22; ❷), an old Communist-era hulk. There's also a good small, riverside **campsite** (May to mid-Oct), just 3km west of the village in Nižné Kamence. For **food**, try the *Pizzeria U Adama*, just west of the centre of Terchová, a typical Slovak cottage with a wood-burning oven.

The Vrátna dolina itself actually owes its winsome reputation to the gritty cliffs of **Tiesňavy**, the sharp-edged defile that acts as the gateway to the valley. A fair few buses go this way from Terchová, as well as several daily from Žilina, or it's a gentle twenty-minute walk. After such a dramatic overture, the valley itself is surprisingly sheltered and calm. The road continues a short way south through Lúky, a fairly major ski resort in winter, set against a scenic backdrop of thickly forested hilltops, and on to a smaller resort at Vratná. You can rent skis and bikes at a rental office along this road, some 2km short of Vratná. There's a wide choice of **accommodation** throughout the valley, cheapest of which is the hostel-style *Chata Vrátna* (☏&℻041/569 57 39; ❶) by the chairlift in Vratná, but you may do better in Štefanová, a small village at the end of a spur road heading east just before Lúky. Two good-value pensions here are the *Starek* (☏041/569 53 59; ❷) and the *Penzión pod Skalným mestom* (☏041/569 53 63; ❷), both clean and cosy, and both with **restaurants**.

Most people head for the **chairlift** at Vrátna, which takes you to Snilovské sedlo, a high saddle between **Veľký Kriváň** (1709m), the highest peak, and **Chleb** (1647m). The views are fantastic from either of the summits, but head away from the chairlift to lose the overwhelming coachloads of day-trippers; you can walk in either direction along the ridge and then head back down to Vrátna. If you're out for the whole day from Žilina, you could descend Chleb's southern face, tracking the blue-marked path that runs via the Šútovský vodopád (waterfall) to Šútovo, fifty minutes by train from Žilina. Otherwise it's over six hours across the peaks to Strečno (see below).

A pleasant alternative to the above is to turn left at the Vrátna dolina fork for Štefanová (2km), in the shadow of **Veľký Rozsutec** (1610m), whose sharply pointed rocky summit is arguably the most satisfying to climb. Follow the yellow-marked path to Podžiar, where you should change to the blue path up **Horné Diery**, an idyllic wet ravine that has to be traversed using ladders and steps. The ravine ends at sedlo Medzirozsutec, the saddle between Malý and Veľký Rozsutec. The ascent takes around four hours, and the descent via sedlo Medziholie about half that.

Strečno and Starý hrad

Impressive in scale and setting, the fourteenth-century ruins of **Hrad Strečno** (Tues–Sun: May, Sept & Oct 9am–5pm; June–Aug 9am–6pm) crown the summit of a 200-foot cliff 11km east of Žilina, commanding the entrance to the Váh valley as it squeezes through the Malá Fatra to Martin. You can climb up to the castle from the nearby train station, but the 45-minute guided tour round the cleaned-up insides and dull exhibition is worth skipping. More interesting is the nearby monument to the **French partisans**, escaped POWs from a camp in Hungary, who took part in the 1944 Slovak National Uprising.

There's a fairly basic **campsite** (May to mid-Oct), with its own swimming pool, in Varín, on the other side of the river, near the road to Terchová: if you don't have your own transport, it's actually a more convenient base for ascending the northern peaks of the Malá Fatra than Vrátna dolina. Alternatively, you could try the *Chata pod Suchým* hostel (☎041/569 73 94; ❶), a two-kilometre walk from Strečno along the red-marked path via the Váh gorge's other ruined castle, **Starý hrad** – it's over 1000m above sea level, so expect a chilly night.

The Kysuce region

Thirty kilometres north of Terchová, the little-known and little-visited **Kysuce region**, rubbing up against the Polish border and wedged in between the Malá Fatra and Orava regions to its south and east, respectively, is a tranquil area of rolling hills and small farming and logging towns. To maintain its withering folk traditions, the local authorities have established the open-air **Múzeum kysuckej dediny** (Kysuce folk museum; May–Oct Tues–Fri 9am–5pm, Sat & Sun 9am–6pm) in the hamlet of Vychylovka, near Nová Bystrica, which is well worth a visit if you're in the area. Timbered homes, barns, a functioning mill and a whitewashed church, most dating from the nineteenth and early twentieth centuries, were all rescued from imminent submergence when the nearby dam was built, and have been carefully relocated in a shady green glen. A **narrow-gauge forest railway**, originally built in the early twentieth century to carry logs out of the hills, now runs through the *skanzen* and a few kilometres into the hills around. Trains run about every hour from 9am to 3pm – try to visit at the weekend when the original steam engine pulls the single open carriage.

Transport to the region is very difficult – only the occasional bus makes it here from Čadca, 25km northwest (alight at Vychylovka-Riečky) – and there is no accommodation anywhere in the vicinity. You can, however, get simple *bryndzové halušky* and cabbage soup at the *Krčma z Korne*, one of the folk structures. If you're driving, you can continue on to the Orava region by taking the tiny, unsealed mountain road behind the *skanzen*, skirting within 1km of Poland, before linking up with route 520 at Oravská Lesná. Route 520 is permanently closed between Nová Bystrica and Oravská Lesná, even though maps show it goes through.

South of Žilina

Just south of Žilina, along route 64 or the railway, the cement works of Lietavská Lúčka coat the valley with a grey-white dust, before a bend in the River Rajčanka brings you into the verdant wooded spa town of **RAJECKÉ TEPLICE** (Ⓦ www.spa.sk). The town centre revolves around a small artificial lake, where you can hire boats, or tuck into some fish dishes at the *Rybárska bašta*, and the monstrous *Veľká Fatra* hotel (Ⓣ 041/549 37 27; ❸) on Osloboditeľov, which has a multi-coloured overhead walkway connecting it to the thermal swimming pools across the main road. For **accommodation**, however, you should plump for the *Hotel Talisman* (Ⓣ 041/549 32 94, Ⓦ www.talisman.miesto.sk; ❷), a chalet-style wine bar, restaurant and pension in a quieter part of the spa on ulica R. Suľovského; there's a nice pub called *Elán* nearby, too. The nearest **campsite** is the primitive but beautifully situated *Slnečné skály* campsite (May–Sept), 3km back down the valley (alight at Poluvsie station).

Rajecké Teplice is a convenient base for a series of day **hikes** in the surrounding hills. The most obvious is across the valley via **Zámok Kunerad**, an early twentieth-century chateau, where you can stay the night (Ⓣ 0907/360 000; ❷), and up Veľká lúka (1476m), which overlooks Martin and the Turiec valley. The blue-marked path is an alternative route back to the spa, and the whole trip is a full day's walk. A more leisurely afternoon's hike north along the green-marked path from the station takes you to the ruined castle of **Lietava**, a shade less spectacular than Strečno but still an impressive pile, some 100m above the village of the same name. The most popular destination, though, is across the hills to the **Súľovské skály** (3hr on the yellow-marked path via Zbyňov), a "rock city" made up of contorted slabs of limestone, with the ruined castle of Súľov at its centre. For a wet weather destination, pay a visit to the **Slovenský betlehem** (daily 10am–5pm), a vast nativity scene carved out of wood and dotted with automated figures, housed in a purpose-built building next door to the church in the village of Rajecká Lesná, 10km or so south of Rajecké Teplice.

Čičmany

ČIČMANY is probably one of the most hyped villages in the whole of Slovakia, and with good reason. Lying in a wide, gently undulating valley, it's a Slovak village *par excellence*: a cluster of typical wooden cottages-cum-farms haphazardly strewn about the banks of the River Rajčanka, which at this point is little more than a mountain stream. What makes Čičmany special, though, is the unique local tradition of **house-painting**, based on the patterns of the locally produced lacework. Each cottage is smothered in a simple, largely abstract, decorative mantle of white snowflakes, flowers and crisscrosses, and the only signs of modernity are electricity, telephone cables and the odd tractor. Only occasional tour groups break the spell, but even they don't stay longer

△ Čičmany

than it takes to visit the small branch of the **Považské múzeum** (Tues–Sun 8am–4pm), at no. 42. The disadvantage of Čičmany's isolated position is its inaccessibility; only infrequent **buses** cover the 38km from Žilina, and though you could try hitching, the traffic is light, especially on the last 7km from route 64. Somewhat remarkably, should you make it out here, there are a few **places to stay** – try the shady, arcaded *Kaštieľ* (☏041/549 21 19; ❷), with its own simple restaurant, or the *Penzion Katka* (☏041/549 21 32; ❷) in one of the painted houses to the north of the museum.

Prievidza and Bojnice

Continuing south for another 30km along route 64 will eventually bring you to **PRIEVIDZA**, an unlovely town after the joys of Čičmany, but an essential stop for those travelling by public transport. The only reason to pause at all in the town itself is to visit the eighteenth-century Piarist church situated between the bus and train stations and the town centre, which contains a spectacular array of trompe l'oeil Baroque ceiling paintings.

Most people, though, are simply passing through en route to the very photogenic **Bojnický zámok** (Tues–Sun: May–Sept 9am–5pm; Oct–April 10am–3pm), which stands on the slopes of a woody hill to the west of Prievidza, in neighbouring **BOJNICE**. From afar, it is indeed an arresting sight, a slice of French pastiche straight out of the Loire Valley, with its conical Gothic turrets and crenellations. In actual fact, what you see now is the result of Romantic reconstructions wrought by the last aristocratic owner, Count Ján Pálffy, who inherited the family pile in 1852. Such pseudo-Gothic splendour may not be everyone's cup of tea, but it sure pulls in the crowds; with some 350,000 visitors a year, this is by far the most popular castle in Slovakia. Ghost sightings are frequent, according to the chateau's efficient PR department, but not half as exciting as the unidentified goo that's been oozing out of Count Pálffy's neo-Romanesque sarcophagus in the castle chapel's crypt over the last few years.

To get to the chateau from Prievidza bus and train stations, take bus #3 or walk the 2.5km. Since Bojnice is not really a viable day-trip from Žilina, you may find yourself spending the night here. If so, your best bet is to head for the **tourist office** (Mon–Fri 8am–6pm, Sat 8am–1pm), námestie slobody 4, the main square in Prievidza – if you're given a choice, stay in Bojnice rather than Prievidza; *Hotel Lipa* (☎046/543 23 19; ❷), close to the castle, is a good bet, and it comes with a restaurant. There's also a **campsite** (mid-May to Sept), with nearby swimming pool, in the woods behind the chateau; take the road to Nitrianske Rudno. Those with children may be relieved to know that Slovakia's largest and oldest **zoo** (daily: March & April 7am–5pm; May 7am–6pm; June–Aug 7am–7pm; Sept & Oct 7am–4.30pm; Nov–Feb 7am–3.30pm) is situated beside the chateau.

The Orava region

Despite its wonderful mountainous backdrop and winding river valley, the **Orava region** (Ⓦ www.orava.sk), northeast of the Malá Fatra and flush with the Polish border, is generally fairly bleak. For centuries it remained an impoverished rural backwater on the main road to Poland, so poor that when the Lithuanian army marched through in 1683 en route to Vienna, they burned most of the villages to the ground (including the former capital of Veličná) in disgust at the lack of provisions. Emigration to America was widespread during the late nineteenth and early twentieth centuries, and after World War II, industry was hastily foisted onto the region in an attempt to save it from extinction. As a consequence, the towns are short on excitement and long on eyesores, but the artificial **lake** to the north is recommended for relatively clean swimming, and the **Western Tatras** provide a uniquely unspoilt alpine experience.

Accommodation can be a problem, so it's worth booking ahead from Dolný Kubín, the largest town in the region. **Transport** relies heavily on the branch line that stretches the length of the Orava valley from Kraľovany on the Váh to Trstená by the Polish border; elsewhere you're dependent on local buses or hitching.

Dolný Kubín and around

The Orava's administrative capital, **DOLNÝ KUBÍN**, is typical of the region, its faultlessly pretty, hilly locale lending a kind of surreal beauty to the gleaming white high-rise *paneláky* that house most of the town's residents. Despite its unattractive suburbs, the town makes for a convenient base and stopover, and its main square, **Hviezdoslavovo námestie**, is moderately pretty. Here, behind a statue of the square's eponymous poet, you'll find the town's **Oravské múzeum** (April–Sept Tues–Sun 8am–4pm; Oct–March Mon–Fri 8am–4pm), dedicated to the mild-mannered "father of Slovak poetry", Pavol Országh Hviezdoslav (1849–1921), who was born in neighbouring Vyšný Kubín. Next door to the museum is the town's blue-and-white Art Deco former **synagogue**, converted to the Choč cinema during the 1970s, with a plaque dedicated to the town's Holocaust victims.

A few doors down, the **Oravská galéria** (Tues–Sun 10am–5pm) is a surprisingly large gallery of art from the Orava region, located in a spiffed-up Baroque palace and well worth a visit. Chronologically, the gallery starts on the second floor, with several rooms of medieval icons, statuary and some very basic portraits of local noblemen. The focus then leaps to the twentieth century, with mostly local scenes of farmers, shepherds and the Orava hills painted by, among others, Miloš Alexander Bazovský and Mikuláš Galanda. The back rooms of the gallery contain some cutting-edge sculpture – look for Jozef Jankovič's gruesome *Red Wedge* – while the avant-garde theme continues upstairs, with 1980s and 1990s Slovak Pop Art predominating. Back down on the ground floor are some more gentle landscape paintings by Maria Medvecká, who hailed from nearby Tvrdošín (see p.503) and had a hand in the establishment of this gallery in 1965. Also down here are some beautiful examples of painted glass and Romantic-era folk sculpture.

Dolný Kubín is probably the best place to stay in the region, though you can book **accommodation** for here or for further up the valley, through the local **tourist office** (Mon–Fri 8am–noon & 12.30–6pm, Sat & Sun 8am–4pm; ☎0845/16186), just off the southwest corner of Hviezdoslavovo námestie. The *Marína* (☎043/586 43 51, ⓦwww.marina.sk; ❸), a fine little pension across from the Oravská galéria, is without doubt the best option. If this is full, you've a choice between the Communist-era *Severan* (☎043/586 46 67; ❷), just off the main square, or the nearby *Hotel Park* (☎043/586 41 10, ⓦwww.hotel-park.sk; ❹), a reliably comfortable option, with satellite TV and indoor swimming. There's also a **campsite**, the *Geceľ* (May to mid-Sept), with bungalows, 1km or so west beside the Orava river. For food, the excellent **restaurant** underneath the *Marína* is highly recommended and is open until midnight.

Istebné and Leštiny

The giant alloy plant and its attendant quarry at **ISTEBNÉ**, 6km west of Dolný Kubín, appear to offer little respite from the valley's depressing industry. Until a few years ago, the level of dust in the atmosphere was intolerable, regularly blackening the skies over the valley at midday. Only in the mid-1980s, when the local population threatened to move out en masse, were dust separators finally fitted onto the factory chimneys.

Miraculously, the pre-industrial settlement still exists, tucked into the hills to the north, fifteen minutes' walk from the bus and train stations. Among its few remaining wooden buildings, it boasts one of the country's four surviving **wooden Lutheran churches**, built in 1686 on slightly raised ground above the village, with the support of the Swedish king; a separate belfry was added in 1731. Inside, it's richly and prettily decorated with folk painting, especially around the pulpit and on the gallery parapet, which features naive eighteenth-century paintings of the apostles.

In the other direction in **LEŠTINY**, some 8km southeast of Dolný Kubín, there's another wooden Lutheran church, dating back to the late seventeenth century. It's a simple, barn-like structure from the outside, but the interior walls and ceiling are covered in eighteenth-century folk paintings. Once again, the gallery, and even the staircase leading to the pulpit, feature naive religious paintings from the period.

Oravský hrad

Eleven kilometres upstream from Dolný Kubín and accessible by train, **Oravský hrad** (Tues–Sun: May, Sept & Oct 8.30am–4pm; June–Aug 8.30am–5pm) is one of Slovakia's truly spectacular clifftop sights. Perched like an eyrie more than 100m above the village of Oravský Podzámok (literally "Below Orava Castle"), it's an impressive testament to the region's feudal past. Whoever occupied Orava Castle held sway over the entire region and made a fortune taxing the peasants and milking the trade into Poland. You may want to ask about the availability of English-speaking guides before signing up for a tour, as this takes over an hour. Inside, you'll be treated to hearty dollops of folk art, natural history, instruments of feudal justice and Romantic wood-panelled interiors courtesy of the last owners, the ubiquitous Pálffy family. Otherwise you can content yourself with the **mini-museum** of local artefacts in the village before heading on up the valley.

Podbiel and Zuberec

PODBIEL, thirty minutes by train up the valley from Oravský Podzámok, marks the entrance to the Studená dolina, the valley leading eastwards into the Western Tatras impressively arrayed on the horizon. Many of the village's collection of traditional wooden cottages have been converted into tourist accommodation. Ask at no. 71, on the road to Zuberec, during office hours on the off chance, but it's better to try and book in advance through the tourist office in Dolný Kubín or Zuberec; another alternative is the *Tatria penzion* (℡043/538 16 36; ❷), which also rents out *chaty*. In any case, the only reason to stop at Podbiel is to hitch, walk or catch one of the very few local buses going east up Studená dolina.

Fifteen kilometres east up the Studená dolina, **ZUBEREC** is only worth pausing in if you want to book accommodation through its Aices **tourist office** (Mon–Fri 8am–6pm, Sat 9am–6pm, Sun 10am–5pm; ℡043/539 51 97, ⓦwww.zuberec.sk). Three kilometres or so beyond lies the **Múzeum oravskej dediny** (May–June, Sept & Oct Tues–Sun 8am–4pm; July & Aug daily 8am–5pm; Nov–April Mon–Fri 8am–4pm), a *skanzen* of about twenty traditional wooden buildings from the surrounding area, including a fifteenth-century **wooden Catholic church** from Zábrež, one of the few to escape the pillaging of the local Protestants. Originally built in the fifteenth century, its simple exterior gives no indication of the intricate seventeenth-century folk panel paintings inside, at their best around the main altar. There's an English-language commentary if you want to go round on your own, but you'll get to see more of the interior with a guide.

The Western Tatras (Západné Tatry)

With the High Tatras reaching saturation point during most of the climbing season, the **Western Tatras** (Západné Tatry) are a refreshingly undeveloped alternative. They boast the same dog-tooth peaks and hand-mirror lakes, but with half the number of visitors. The best base is 3km beyond the folk *skanzen*, where you'll find the *Primula* **hotel** (℡043/539 51 79; ❷) and the *Zverovka*

From **Oravice**, two main trails head south 6km to the Polish border, of which the blue-marked one is the gentler. Once you reach the border, at the Bobrovecké sedlo, the blue-marked path will take you onto the ridge between the two countries and up to **Volovec** (2063m) and **Ostrý Roháč** (2084m), 1km from the border. It could easily take four hours to reach the more spectacular scenery around Volovec, making a return trip a full day's hike. If you're carrying a pack, it's possible to drop down onto the blue-marked path to the twin lakes of the Jamnicke plesá and then continue for 8km to the beautifully peaceful Račková dolina **campsite** (May–Oct) or a little further to the *Esperanto* **hotel** in Pribylina (☎044/529 32 31; **❸**); this is probably the quickest way to approach the High Tatras from the Orava region. If you do make it to Pribylina, take a turn around the *skanzen* behind the hotel (daily: mid-May to June 9am–4pm; July to mid-Sept 9am–6.30pm; mid-Sept to Oct 9am–4pm; Nov to mid-May 9am–3.30pm).

From the **Roháčska dolina**, everything happens much more quickly. As you head down the valley the brooding grey peaks begin to gather round and by the end of the road (8km from the *skanzen*; 3km from the final car park) it's only a steep 1.5-kilometre walk on the green path to the still, glacial waters of the **Roháčske plesá**, hemmed in by the Tatras' steep, scree-ridden slopes. A punishing 2.5km (reckon on about 2hr) along the blue path leads to the Smutne sedlo ("Sad saddle"– sad because it's the mountain's cold north face), which lies on the main Roháč ridge. Ostrý Roháč is less than an hour to the east and **Baníkov** (2178m) the same distance west, but the king of the lot is **Baranec** (2184m), a good two hours' ridge walk to the south.

9

and *Osobitá chaty*. Unless you've pre-booked from Dolný Kubín, however, you may have problems finding a room, though there is some private accommodation and plenty of discreet spots in which to pitch your tent. Alternatively, you could make your base further north, at Oravice, the only official **campsite** (April–Oct; Ⓦ www.oravice.sk) on this side of the mountains, with an adjacent swimming pool. The main problem is getting to Oravice, which either means catching one of the few buses from Trstená (the last station on the Orava rail line) or walking 7km from the Orava folk *skanzen*. Whatever you do, don't let the logistics get you down – you'll encounter similar problems in the other parts of the Tatras. More importantly, get hold of a decent *VNÚ* or *freytag & berndt* hiking map, plus the requisite camping gear, and you'll have a smooth trip. Don't, however, undertake any mountain hiking if you've no experience, and always get a weather check before you start on a long walk that goes above 1500m. For more **information** on hiking and climbing, and important **safety tips**, see p.516.

Around Lake Orava

Back at Podbiel, the rail line continues to the village of **TVRDOŠÍN**, which boasts a wooden church containing some fantastic primitive altar paintings, all dating from the fifteenth century. The last stop on the line is **TRSTENÁ**, 6km from the Polish border, which has several **accommodation** options: the *Skalka* (☎043/39 28 86; **❷**) is on the main square, while the ungainly *Košariská* (☎043/92 12 79; **❶**) is 2km north, overlooking the lake. If you're moving on to Poland, there's enough traffic to make hitching feasible.

What was once the Orava plain became **Lake Orava** in 1954 when five villages were submerged by the damming of the river. The wooded western shore has a fair smattering of *chata* settlements and two **campsites** (mid-June to mid-Sept). One of the lost villages, **SLANICA**, was the birthplace of an early pioneer of the Slovak language, the Catholic priest Anton Bernolák (1762–1813). Hidden in the trees, on Slanícky ostrov, is the village's only surviving building, a twin-domed **church of sv Kríž** (June–Sept 9am–5pm) with an attractive Neoclassical loggia set into its facade, now a museum of folk art and ceramics as well as a memorial to Bernolák. To reach the island, take the hourly boat from the pier next to the Slanická osada campsite, or from **NÁMESTOVO**, the big new town to the far west of the lake (and thankfully out of sight from the main recreational area). Standard Slovak food can be had at the *Šalaš*, a typical **pub** right near the Slanická osada campsite.

The Liptov region

The **Liptov region** (Ⓦ www.liptov.sk), to the south of the Orava region and the Western Tatras, offers a similar cocktail of traditional Slovak villages and depressed industrial towns against a backdrop of spectacular mountains. **Ružomberok**, the first town you come to, at another T-junction on the River Váh, has very little to offer except easy access to the surrounding peaks. East of Ružomberok, the Váh valley widens into a vast, partially flooded plain, whose main town, **Liptovský Mikuláš**, is similarly uninspiring, but the best placed for exploring the Low Tatras.

As in the Orava, the traditional way of life in these parts has disappeared over the last two generations. But while few mourn the demise of subsistence farming, more lament the fact that it was destroyed by forced collectivization and industrialization. Some things survive – the patchwork fields and terraces and the long timbered cottages – but give it a few more decades and the songs, dances and costumes will be of historical and folkloristic interest only.

Ružomberok and around

RUŽOMBEROK (Rosenberg), like so many big towns on the Váh, has more than its fair share of industrial suburbs and ungainly high-rise estates, not to mention a persistent smell of synthetic fabrics that's enough to put most people off. The place to head for is the church of **sv Ondrej**, pleasantly aloof from the rest of town up the graffiti-filled covered stairway, the Tmavé schody (Dark steps). Before the war, the local priest was **Andrej Hlinka** (see p.505), spiritual leader of Slovak separatism, *persona non grata* under the Communists but now fully rehabilitated. The church, on raised ground in the centre of town, stands on a square now named after him and sporting a statue of the cleric; on the south side of the church is his mausoleum. On one corner of the square is another curiosity – a monument in honour of the "Scotus Viator", Scottish academic R. W. Seton-Watson (1879–1951), "for defending the Slovak nation", erected in 1937 and miraculously still standing.

To the west of the church, the square stretches along a lovely avenue of lime trees, to the north of which lies námestie Š. N. Hýroša, home to the **Liptovské múzeum** (Mon–Fri 8am–4pm, Sat & Sun 9am–1pm; July & Aug Mon–Fri 8am–5pm, Sat & Sun 9am–4pm). It's a substantial museum, with Jánošík's jaunty hat hidden amidst the usual stuffed animals on the first floor, and a whole section on Hlinka on the top floor, which is at pains to refute the charges of anti-semitism regularly made against him. Behind the museum, you'll also find

Andrej Hlinka

Born in the neighbouring village of Černová in 1864, **Andrej Hlinka** served most of his life as a Catholic pastor of Ružomberok. He became a national martyr in 1906 when he was arrested by the Hungarian authorities and sentenced to two years' imprisonment for "incitement against the Magyar nationality", topped up by another eighteen months for "further incitement" in his inflammatory farewell address to the local parishioners.

Although at the time still in prison, he was also viewed by the authorities as the prime mover behind the demonstration of October 27, 1907, popularly known as the **Černová Massacre**, the Bloody Sunday of Hungarian rule in Slovakia. When the local Slovaks protested against the consecration of their church by a strongly pro-Magyar priest, the Hungarian police opened fire on the crowd, killing fifteen people and wounding countless others.

Although Hlinka was among those Slovaks who approved of the establishment of Czechoslovakia, it wasn't long before Hlinka began campaigning for Slovak autonomy, and travelled to Paris on a false Polish passport to press the point at the Versailles Peace Conference. This earned him a spell in a Czechoslovak prison, from which he was only released (without charge) after being elected leader of the newly founded **Ľudová strana** (People's Party, or HSĽS), strongly Catholic, vehemently nationalistic and the largest single party in Slovakia between the wars. From 1925 to 1928, the HSĽS's electoral clout ensured it a place in the Czechoslovak coalition government. However, the party's nationalist policies were constantly at odds with its collaboration in the Prague-based government, and eventually, in 1928, when the editor of the HSĽS newspaper was convicted of treason for publishing a seditious article, Hlinka withdrew from the coalition, never to return.

Hlinka's death in August 1938 was the only thing that saved him from suffering the fate of his successor in the People's Party, Jozef Tiso, who went on to become the Slovak Quisling, as leader of the Nazi puppet government, and was eventually executed as a war criminal in 1947. Nevertheless, his name lived on posthumously in the regime's elite **Hlinka Guards**, the wartime Slovak equivalent of the SS. Under the Communists, Hlinka was deemed a clerico-fascist pure and simple, but since 1989, Slovak nationalists have conducted a concerted campaign to rehabilitate Hlinka, Tiso and company. Most Slovaks are very much in sympathy with such moves, and town councils across the republic have successfully renamed streets and squares after Hlinka, although when a plaque in honour of Tiso was unveiled in his home town of Bánovce nad Bebravou, above the Catholic teacher-training college he founded, it provoked outrage in many quarters and was eventually removed. Undeterred, the Slovak government went ahead and chose Hlinka as one of the national figures to grace the country's new currency.

the **Galéria Ľudovíta Fullu** (Tues–Sun 10am–5pm), devoted to Ružomberok's talented painter of the same name,

The **train station** is northwest of the town centre, on the other side of the River Váh (bus #1 or #8). The **tourist office** (April–Sept Mon–Fri 8am–5pm, Sat & Sun 9am–noon; Oct–March Mon–Fri 8am–5pm; ℡044/432 10 96), at Madačova 3, can assist with finding **accommodation**, most of which is way out of the centre (no bad thing). The most central place is the good-value *Šport Penzión Blesk* (℡044/432 17 50, Ⓦwww.liptov.sk/penzion-blesk; ❸), fifteen minutes' walk west of the centre at Vajanského 9, which has a pleasant restaurant. Another option is *Hotel Hrabovo* (℡044/432 87 45, Ⓦwww.skipark.sk; ❷), which has a grassy banked lake in which you can swim, but is only accessible via the infrequent bus #3 or by taxi. Behind it, a four-seater cable car will take you, on the hour, to the renovated *Hotel Malina* (☎044/432 50 70; ❷). For **food**, the best bet in the centre is probably the *Koruna*, Mostová 13, which has a courtyard and cellar dining. You can also pick up fresh *bryndza* (sheep cheese) from a stand underneath the highway, near the end of Mostová.

Vlkolínec and Liptovská Štiavnica

One of the few redeeming features of Ružomberok is its proximity to the surrounding hills and villages. It's only a three-kilometre walk to the conic peak of **Sidorovo** (1099m) or 5km to **Malinné Brdo** (1209m), both of which are accessible via the cable car behind *Hotel Hrabovo* and guarantee extensive panoramas over the Váh and Revúca valleys.

Dropping down off the fell on the south side, head for the ribbon village of **VLKOLÍNEC**, on a windy hillside to the south (and thankfully out of view) of Ružomberok. The village is accessible by bus #2 or #7 from Ružomberok to Biely Potok, but the final two-kilometre walk from the bus stop is hard work and you might be better off approaching from Sidorovo or Malinné. This is one of the best environments in which to see Liptov wooden folk architecture, though as ever there's a note of melancholy about the place. It was badly damaged by the Nazis in September 1944 in the reprisals that followed the Slovak National Uprising, but those cottages that remain now form a protected natural *skanzen* of timber structures. One house, the Roľnícky dom, at no. 17, serves as a **museum** (July–Sept Tues–Fri 10am–4pm, Sat & Sun 9am–7pm), while another, by the car park, provides **information** (summer 9am–5pm; winter 10am–3pm) and offers guided **tours**.

With your own transport you could also explore nearby **LIPTOVSKÁ ŠTI-AVNICA**, east of Ružomberok, whose whitewashed manor house or *kaštieľ* was converted into the local church in 1973 and is worth a look for its shingled onion dome and conical turrets. Before you leave, be sure to appreciate the rare surviving socialist mural entitled *The Battle for Love and Truth*.

Liptovský Mikuláš and around

As in Orava, the broad sweep of the main Liptov plain east of Ružomberok has been turned, for the most part, into a vast lake, whose beautiful sandy shoreline is set against the distant backdrop of the Western Tatras. Quite why it deserves the title Liptovská Mara (Liptov Sea) while the one in Orava is simply a lake remains a linguistic mystery, but a similar number of villages bit the dust in the name of "progress". On its easternmost edge sits **LIPTOVSKÝ MIKULÁŠ**, which, like Martin and Ružomberok, played a major part in the Slovak national revival or *národné obrozenie*. Nowadays, it's really only worth coming here if you're intending to explore the Low Tatras.

The Town

You can get a taste of the literary milieu of nineteenth-century Mikuláš from the **Múzeum Janka Kráľa** (July & Aug daily 10am–5pm; Sept–June Tues–Fri 9am–4pm, Sun 10am–5pm), housed in a striking peach-coloured Baroque building on the town's large, pedestrianized main square, **Námestie oslobod-iteľov**. Local boy Kráľ was the foremost Slovak poet of the Romantic movement, "a lawyer who preferred the company of shepherds", or the Slovak Lord Byron as some would have it. Needless to say, he was a fervent nationalist, and only just escaped being executed for his beliefs in 1848. The museum also contains information on Jánošík, whose trial is thought to have taken place here, and who was sentenced to death in 1713 on the square outside, which currently sports a statue of the local artist Gašpar Belopotocký.

The first rumblings of the Slovak national revival in Liptovský Mikuláš occurred in the late 1820s when a Slovak reading room was founded, followed much later by the Tatrín literary society established by the Lutheran pastor Michael Miloslav Hodza, one of the leading lights of 1848. Hodža's house, by the Lutheran church east of the square, off ul. l. mája, at Tranovského 8, is now a rather uninspiring **Múzeum jaskyniarstva** (Tues–Fri 8am–2pm), which also touches on the events of May 10, 1848, when some of Mikuláš's leading Slovaks published the "Demands of the Slovak Nation" in response to the Hungarian uprising against the Habsburgs, then quickly fled the country to avoid arrest.

Opposite the museum, in a drab grey concrete building, is the much more palatable **Galéria P.M. Bohúňa** (Tues–Fri 9am–5pm, Sat & Sun noon–5pm), whose spacious interior houses an impressive array of Slovak art. Baroque, Gothic and pre-nineteenth-century works fill the ground floor, but it's the nineteenth- and twentieth-century collection on the top floor that justifies a visit here. In addition to depictions of peasant life by the likes of Martin Benka and Gustáv Mallý, there's a whole room devoted to Bohuň's own portrait of wealthy local burghers. Bazovský and Janko Alexy weigh in with a couple of mystical, almost ghostly canvases, and there are even works by contemporary artists like Rudolf Fila.

Like many Slovak towns, Liptovský Mikuláš had a large Jewish community before World War II, established back in the early eighteenth century when Jews moved here from Holešov in Moravia. The vast majority of the 885 Jews who were transported to the camps never returned, and there is now a plaque – a hand scraping its nails down a Jewish gravestone – outside the town's huge Neoclassical **synagogue** (mid-June to Sept Tues–Sun 10am–5pm), which has been restored and stands south of the main square on Hollého. When there's no exhibition on, you'll need to get hold of the key from the Múzeum Janka Kráľa to inspect the starkly beautiful, empty interior.

In the suburb of **Palúdza**, a kilometre west of Mikuláš town centre (bus #2 or #7 from Štúrova), is the *kaštieľ*, in whose dungeon Jánošík was tortured before his public execution on Mikuláš's main square. The largest **wooden Protestant church** in Slovakia (daily: June–Sept 9am–5pm; Oct–March; 9am–3pm; ☎044/559 26 22) used to stand opposite, but was transferred in the 1970s to the edge of **LAZISKO**, 5km to the southwest, beyond the village of Svätý Kríž. Built in 1774 for the local Lutheran community without a single nail being used, it's a remarkable building, with a vaguely cruciform ground-plan and a weatherboarded exterior. Inside, it seats over two thousand and looks almost new, with decoration only around the pulpit, gallery and organ gallery. There are one or two buses a day from Mikuláš to Lazisko.

Practicalities

The **bus** and **train stations** are next door to each other, a ten-minute walk north of the town centre. The efficient **tourist office** (mid-June to mid-Sept & mid-Dec to March Mon–Fri 8am–7pm, Sat 8am–2pm, Sun noon–6pm; April to mid-June & mid-Sept to mid-Dec Mon–Fri 9am–6pm, Sat 8am–noon; ☎044/552 24 18, ⒲www.lmikulas.sk), on Námestie mieru, can help with information and accommodation in the Low Tatras.

For a **place to stay**, the plain, newly furnished rooms at the *Kriváň*, Štúrova 5 (☎044/552 24 14; ❶), opposite the tourist office, are the cheapest in town, while the swankiest of the central hotels is the *Elan*, ulica 1 mája 35 (☎044/551 44 14;

❺), located east off Námestie osloboditeľov. In between, you have the *Janošík* (**☎**&**🖷**044/852 27 26; **❷**), a Communist-era high-rise at the busy road junction of Janošíkovo nábrežie and Jilemnického. If you've got your own transport or don't mind the long walk west of centre, the *Bocian* (**☎**044/554 12 76, **🖮**liptov.sk/hotelbocian; **❸**), near the *kaštieľ* in Palúdza, is a good choice.

The nearest **campsite** (May–Oct) is by the lake at Liptovský Trnovec (20min by bus) on the northern shores of the Liptovská Mara, with another, smaller, more secluded lakeside site, another 5km further on by *Villa Betula* (**🖮**www.villabetula.sk) in Liptovská Sielnica. If you're aiming to hike in the Low Tatras, you'd be better off at the *Borová Sihoť* site (June to mid-Sept) just 1km west of Liptovský Hrádok train station, 8km east (10min by train), or the *Bystrina* site (open all year) up the Demänovská dolina (see below). If you're staying in the area, it's worth knowing about the very popular and very hot outdoor **thermal swimming pool** complex (summer daily 10am–9pm; winter Thurs–Sun 1–9pm) in Bešeňová; the nearest train station is 1.5km west of the pool in Liptovská Teplá.

There's a very good **restaurant**, *Liptovská izba*, on Námestie osloboditeľov, serving *guláš* and Slovak specialities, along with an equally good pizzeria, the *Taverna*, upstairs. To send or receive **email**, head for *Z@vináč*.

Východná and Važec

The annual **Slovak folk festival** held around late June to early July in **VÝCHODNÁ**, 15km east of Liptovský Mikuláš and thirty minutes by train, is in every way equal to Strážnice's international affair (see p.372), attracting groups from every region of Slovakia. There's no accommodation in the village (a pleasant 2km hike north from the station), but during the festival there's a makeshift campsite, with many more people crashing out in the haylofts and barns of the local farmers (ask first). At any other time of the year, Východná is a modest little village, whose nondescript facades hide an array of interesting wooden buildings.

VAŽEC, one stop further on, was renowned for being one of the most beautiful villages in Slovakia and built almost entirely from wood, until it was destroyed by a catastrophic fire in 1931. However, its former reputation as a photographer's dream means that it is immortalized in many prints on display in the village **folk museum**. The purpose of most visits, though, is the **Važecká jaskyňa** (Tues–Sun: Feb to mid-May & mid-Sept to Nov tours at 10 & 11am, 12.30 & 2pm; mid-May to mid-Sept hourly tours 9am–4pm), a limestone cave system discovered back in the 1920s but only recently opened to the public. To get there from the train station, walk to the other side of the village.

The Low Tatras (Nízke Tatry)

The rounded peaks of the **Low Tatras** (Nízke Tatry) may have less of an immediate impact than the sharp craggy outline of the High Tatras on the northern horizon, but they do constitute a more extensive range, in parts much wilder and less explored, still home to the odd lynx and bear. The crudest development is on either side of the two tallest central mountains, **Chopok** and **Ďumbier**, but particularly to the east, the crowds are thin and, with the aid of a hiking map, the countryside is yours for the taking. If you're not planning anything as strenuous as hiking, you could happily spend a day or two visiting some of the **caves** in Demänovská dolina, swimming at the foot of the

Hiking around Chopok

Most people start walking from **Chopok** (2024m), the second highest peak in the range, reached by two consecutive (and extremely popular) chairlifts from Jasná (closed Oct & Nov). It's about two hours across the bare fell to the top of **Ďumbier** (2043m), king of the Low Tatras and the easternmost limit of this central ridge. From Ďumbier, it's six or more hours for each of the following routes: via Krupova hoľa, back down the yellow-marked path to the campsite at the bottom of Demänovská dolina; down Jánska dolina on the blue-marked path to the campsite in Podtureň, or further east to the campsite at Malužiná (turn right either at sedlo Javorie or Pred Bystrou). Westwards, it's about five hours along the ridge to the isolated hamlet of Magurka, which has a *chata* but no official campsite; otherwise it's a good ten hours' walk to the campsite and hotel at Donovaly, at the top of the pass from Banská Bystrica over to Ružomberok.

mountains at Tále or simply riding the chairlift to the top of Chopok and effortlessly soaking up the view.

On the practical front, **accommodation** is now no longer a problem, with plenty of private rooms available and several campsites, though still very few hotels outside the main resorts. **Transport** is also fairly good, with two rail lines serving the Váh and Hron valleys and buses taking you the rest of the way into the mountains: of course, to get the most out of the region, you'll need to walk – preferably armed with the map mentioned above and a stout pair of walking boots. **Ski rental** is possible both in Demänovská dolina and in Jasná.

Demänovská dolina and the caves

Extremely overloaded buses wend their way hourly up **Demänovská dolina**, by far the most popular valley on the north side of the mountains. As soon as you enter the narrow, forested part of the valley, signs point off to the left to the **Demänovská ľadová jaskyňa** (Tues–Sun: mid-May & Sept tours at 9 & 11am, 12.30 & 2pm; June–Aug hourly tours 9am–4pm), one of Slovakia's two "ice caves". After a sweaty fifteen-minute walk up through the woods to the entrance, there's a chilly forty-minute guided tour through the cave, starting in a vast hall-like chamber of mini-stalactites and stalagmites, its walls covered in eighteenth-century graffiti testifying to the early discovery of the caves. For the final section you descend into the claustrophobic **ice chamber**, where the temperature even in summer is well below zero. The best time to visit, though, is in the spring, when the ice formations are at their best, creating huge stalactites of frozen water that drip down onto a massive frozen lake. Two kilometres further on, signs indicate the **Demänovská jaskyňa slobody** (Tues–Sun: mid-Dec to May & mid-Sept to mid-Nov tours at 9 & 11am, 12.30 & 2pm; mid-May to mid-Sept hourly tours 9am–4pm), used for storage by frostbitten partisans during World War II – hence its name, "Cave of Freedom". It's an iceless cave (though no less freezing), with a much larger and more impressive variety of rock formations than Demänovská ľadová jaskyňa.

A little further on, the road swings violently to the right and begins to climb steeply for about 1.5km until it reaches **JASNÁ** (ⓦwww.chopok-jasna.sk), a major ski resort for this part of the world, with sundry chair and ski lifts, as well as a smattering of **hotels** wedged into the hillsides. The nicest of the bunch is the brand-new *Grand* (☎044/559 14 41; ➎), complete with indoor pool, weight-training room and billiards. The *Liptov* (☎044/559 15 06; ➍) and *Junior*

(☎044/559 15 71; ❹), both conveniently situated near the chair lifts, are cheaper Communist-era resort hotels offering many of the same features, while the smaller and nicely renovated *Mikulášská chata* (☎044/559 16 72; ❸) by the lakeside is another good option. It's worth enquiring about vacancies for all the above places beforehand at the tourist office in Liptovský Mikuláš; note, too, that prices vary wildly depending on the season, with the winter season being by far the most expensive.

If you're trying to save money, it's reassuring to know that there are plenty of **pensions** and private **rooms** back down in the bit of Demänovská dolina, just before the caves, such as the good-value *Kamenná chata* (☎044/554 81 69; ❷), which offers clean doubles as well as more basic, even cheaper dorm accommodation. In fact, Demänovská dolina is generally a more congenial place to be, and the hourly bus up to Jasná makes getting to the slopes a cinch.

As for **food**, practically all the hotels in Jasná have restaurants, and the one at *Mikulášská chata* stands out. In Demänovská dolina, the *Koliba* is a typically rustic Slovak pub with a fireplace in front of which to enjoy your mulled wine or a full meal.

Approaching from the Hron valley

If you're coming from Banská Bystrica and the Hron valley, you'll approach the Low Tatras from the south. The Hron valley as far as **BREZNO** has been marred by industry, and the latter only has one cheap hotel to recommend it, the *Ďumbier* (☎048/611 26 61; ❷), on námestie gen. M.R. Štefánika 31, the leafy main square. There's also a useful **tourist office** (mid-June to mid-Sept Mon–Fri 9am–5pm, Sat & Sun 10am–2pm; mid-Sept to mid-June Mon–Fri 8am–5pm; ☎ & ℱ048/6114 221, ⓦwww.brezno.sk – in Slovak only) in the central museum building at námestie gen. M. R. Štefánika 55, which can fix private and pension **accommodation** in and around the area.

The main approach to Chopok from this side is via **Bystrá dolina**, the flip-side valley of Demänovská dolina. At its southern base is **BYSTRÁ** (bus from Podbrezová station or 5km walk over the hills along the green-marked path from Brezno), a neat village riddled with private accommodation, and with a helpful **tourist office** (daily 10am–6pm). Close by is the **Bystrianska jaskyňa** (Tues–Sun: Jan to mid-May & mid-Sept to Oct tours at 9.30 & 11am, 12.30 & 2pm; mid-May to mid-Sept hourly tours 9am–4pm), the only underground cave system on offer on this side.

If you haven't booked **accommodation** in advance, scour the private rooms and pensions in Bystrá, or head 2.5km up the road to the fully equipped campsite (June to mid-Sept), in the clutter of hotels known as **TÁLE**. A little,

---

Railways around Brezno

The Brezno area pulls in a fair few railway enthusiasts, not least because the line from **Brezno to Margecany** is one of the country's most scenic, including a 360-degree switchback around Telgárt. In addition, though, the line to Tisovec, to the southeast, includes what is probably the only state-owned **rack-and-pinion** railway in the world, originally built to help trains, heavily laden with iron ore, make the ascent from Pohronská Polhora to Zbojská. Last, but by no means least, there's the Čiernohronská Železnica **forest railway**, built in 1896 between Hronec, 8km west of Brezno, to Čierny Balog. This last 17km-long narrow-gauge railway runs only in summer (May to mid-Sept), occasionally pulled by steam locomotives; for details enquire at the Brezno tourist office.

further on signs point to the ageing *Hotel Partizán* (☎048/617 00 31, ℮parti-zan@isternet.sk; ❹) which nonetheless enjoys every facility under the sun. However the nearby *Stupka* (☎048/617 00 24; ❹) is slightly better value, with its own swimming pool and sauna, and it can organize bike rental and other outdoor activities. A basic motel and wooded **campsite**, *Kemping Motel Tále* (☎048/617 00 42; ❶), can be found along the valley road.

Buses can take you (and a whole load of others) to the very northern reach-es of the valley, past the *Trangoška* (☎048/617 00 20; ❷), to the beginning of the chair lift. This rises in two stages to the top of Chopok: at the base is the *Hotel Srdiečko* (currently closed); between the two stages is *Hotel Kosodrevina* (☎048/617 00 15; ❹). To avoid disappointment you should **book in advance** for these hotels through the tourist office in Brezno or Bystrá. If you're walk-ing from Tále to the main ridge, it'll take you three to four hours along the yel-low-marked path to the top of **Dereše** (2003m).

The eastern peaks

East of the central Chopok ridge, the real wilderness begins. The peaks are even less pronounced and rarely raise their heads above the turbulent sea of forest where some of Slovakia's last remaining wild bears, wolves, lynx and chamois hide out. Meanwhile, the villages in the **Hron valley** are still a world of shepherds and horses and carts, with wooden houses surviving here and there among the stone, brick and cement; naturally, there's virtually nothing in the way of conventional tourist facilities. If this has whetted your appetite, the best thing to do is book your accommodation through the tourist offices in Bystrá or Brezno – or pack a tent and provisions and start walking.

The **railway** that climbs the Hron valley is one of the most scenic in the whole country (see box p.510), and if you pick the right train you can trav-el from Banská Bystrica through the Slovenský raj, finally coming to a halt at Košice, in three to four hours. The slower trains take significantly longer, stopping at even the most obscure villages, such as **HEĽPA** (1hr by slow train from Brezno), which has just one cheap hotel, *Hotel Heľpa* (☎048/618 62 35-6; ❶), at Hlavná 65. To get the magnificent view from the top of **Veľká Vápenica** (1691m), follow either the yellow- or the blue-marked tracks from the station (2–3hr), making sure the stream is on your right-hand side. One stop further on, **POHORELÁ** lies on the footpath to the next peak along, **Andrejcová** (1519m). The only campsite in the region, *Gindura* (open all year), is close by the next station along, Pohorelská Masa, but camping rough in the hills – while officially discouraged – is unlikely to cause any problems.

A lot of the slower trains pause for breath at Červená Skala, not a bad place to start one of the **best hikes** of the eastern range. Take the road to the village of **ŠUMIAC**, which sits on the broad sweep of the mountainside with a panoramic view west and south over the valley; then follow the blue-marked path up to **Kráľova hoľa** (1948m), the biggest bare-topped mountain east of Ďumbier. It's another three hours to **LIPTOVSKÁ TEPLIČKA**, once one of the most isolated communities in the Slovak mountains. If you want to remain in the Hron Valley, there's the pretty mountain hotel *Pusté Pole* (☎048/611 18 80; ❶) in **TELGÁRT**, 4km from Kráľova hoľa (get out at Švermovo-penzión zástavka), where the railway doubles back on itself before climbing to its high-est point (999m) shortly before Vernár station, on the edge of the Slovenský raj (see p.537).

The High Tatras (Vysoké Tatry)

Rising like a giant granite reef above the patchwork Poprad plain, the **High Tatras** (ⓦ www.tatry.net) are for many people the main reason for venturing this far into Slovakia. Even after all the tourist-board hype, they are still an incredible, inspirational sight – sublime, spectacular, saw-toothed and brooding. A wilderness, however, they are not. At the height of summer, visitors are shoulder to shoulder in the necklace of resorts at the foot of the mountains, and things don't necessarily improve when you take to the hills. The crux of the problem lies in the scale of the range, a mere 25km from east to west, some of which is shared with the equally eager Poles, and a lot of it out of reach to all but the most experienced climber. This is not helped by the saturation tactics of the tour operators, a logical extension of the region's overdevelopment. Yet when all's said and done, once you're above the tree line, surrounded by bare primeval scree slopes and icy blue tarns, nothing can take away the exhilarating feeling of being on top of the world.

Visiting the Tatras: transport and accommodation

Most fast trains to the Tatras arrive at the **main train station** in Poprad (known as Poprad-Tatry), which is adjacent to the **bus station**. If your budget is tight, it might be worth staying in Poprad (for which see p.514); otherwise, you may as well get straight onto one of the little red electric trains that connect all the main resorts and leave from a separate platform above the main line. There are only a few flights a day from Poprad's tiny **airport**, west of the town (take a taxi), which means you need to book in advance to be sure of a place in summer and winter high seasons; make your reservation in Poprad at the ČSA office next door to *Hotel Gerlach*.

In view of the region's popularity, sorting out **accommodation** should be your priority, though with so many places to stay now available, you should have few problems getting something. Whatever your budget, you should book in advance, or be prepared to take whatever's on offer (within reason); with your own transport, towns like Kežmarok are possible bases (see p.528). Be aware that prices fluctuate wildly depending on the season, with winter (excluding Christmas week) the most expensive time, followed by high summer. The PIA in Poprad (☎052/161 86), as well as the Tatranská informačná kancelária or TIK (☎052/442 34 40), T-Ski (☎052/442 32 65), SATUR and Slovakoturist in Starý Smokovec, can all book **pensions** and **private rooms** for around 300–500Sk per person.

One option worth considering is the **mountain chaty** dotted across the range, aimed primarily at walkers and therefore often only accessible on foot; prices are around 400Sk per person, and some also serve a limited selection of food in the evening. PIA in Poprad or Slovakoturist in Starý Smokovec have the latest on availability, although to take advantage of anything they offer you'll have to be flexible about your itinerary and plan your hiking around your accommodation.

The cheapest and most reliable option (providing the weather is warm enough) is **camping**, though having said that, the big swanky international sites are among the most expensive in either republic. The best of the dear ones are the *Eurocamp FICC* (open all year) and *Sportcamp* (May–Sept), both just south of Tatranská Lomnica (get off at Tatranská Lomnica-Eurocamp FICC station). The cheapest and most basic is the *Jupela* site (May–Sept), 1km south of Stará Lesná. If you can get there with your own transport, the *Šarpanec* site (mid-May to mid-Oct), on route 67 between Spišská Bela and Tatranská

HIGH TATRAS

▲ Osobitá
1687 m

P O L A N D

Zakopane

Banikov
2178 m ▲

Volovec
2063 m ▲
Ostrý Roháč
2084 m ▲
W E S T E R N

Bystrá
2248 m ▲
T A T R A S
Baranec
2044 m ▲
Ježová
2043 m ▲

Kasprov vrch
1985 m ▲

Svinica
2300 m ▲

Temniak
2090 m ▲

Veľká kopa
2052 m ▲

Kriváň
2494 m ▲
Hrubý vrch
2428 m ▲

Liptovský Mikuláš ►

N

Podbanské

Pribylina ●

Východná ●

Liptovský Hrádok

River Biely Váh

River Váh

Važec ●
Važecká jaskyňa

Štrba ●

Svit ●

Poprad

Lysá
Polana ●

Javorina

Ждiar ●

B E L I A N S K E
T A T R Y

Havran
2152 m ▲
Zadné Jatky
2019 m ▲
Jahňací štít
2229 m ▲

Belianska
jaskyňa
Tatranská
Kotlina

Lendak ●

Kežmarok ▲   ▲ Vrbov

Široká
2210 m ▲

Zelené pleso

Rysy
2499 m ▲
Veľké
Hincovo
pleso

Popradské
pleso

Predné Solisko
2093 m

Zelené pleso

Par Spišských
plies

Slavkovský štít
2452 m

Gerlachovský štít
2655 m

Lomnický štít
2632 m

Tatranská
Lomnica

Hrebienok
Funicular

Starý Smokovec
Tatranská
Polianka

Tatranská
Štrba

Strbské Pleso

Horní
Smokovec
Dolný
Smokovec
Nová Lesná

Starà Lesná ▲

Velká
Lomnica

Nová Lesná ●

Spišská
Sobota

River Poprad

Levoča ►

H I G H   T A T R A S

0   5 km
········· Chair lift
— — — Cable car

513

Kotlina, is relatively secluded, and the *Vrbov* site (July & Aug), to the east, has hidden advantages (see p.502).

Poprad and around

It would be difficult to dream up a more unprepossessing town than **POPRAD** (Deutschendorf) to accompany the Tatras' effortless natural beauty, with a great swathe of off-white high-rise housing encircling the town. A tiny old town centre, a museum and a couple of art galleries go some way to counterbalance initial bad impressions. And while it's no great joy to hang around, Poprad is refreshingly free of tour groups and a lot less pretentious than the higher resorts. It's also not a bad place to organize **accommodation** for the rest of your stay in the Tatras.

The Town

Poprad was originally one of the twenty or so Spiš towns (see p.526), though the only clue to this is the long, village-like main square, **námestie Svätého Egídia**, a five-minute walk south of the train station. Here you'll find the typical Spiš burgher houses, whose two storeys are distinguished by their stone facades and wooden gables, with eaves overhanging by six feet or so. If you're planning any hiking, you can stock up on provisions at the bakery and small vegetable market on the north side of the square, while the south side is taken up with a host of new shops, including a bookshop where you might be able to pick up relevant **maps** – look out for the invaluable *Tatranské strediská* one, which contains street plans of all the major resorts (excluding Poprad, which has its own map).

If you have some time to spare, you could pop into one of the town's museums. The long-established **Podtatranské Múzeum** (Tatra Museum; Tues–Sun 9am–4pm) on Vajanského, near the tourist office, traces the history of human settlement in the Tatras from the time of the earliest Neanderthal inhabitants. If this doesn't grab you, you could inspect either of the two branches of the **Tatranská Galéria Poprad**: the new Výstavná sieň (Mon–Fri 9am–5pm, Sat 9am–2pm) at Alžbetina 30 contains nineteenth- and twentieth-century landscape paintings of the Tatra and Spiš regions, while the Elektrarień (May–Sept daily 10am–6pm), in a former electric plant at Hviezdoslavova 12, focuses on the area's tradition of weaving and folk dress. Otherwise, you can swim at the public pool or bake in the sauna at the public facilities on the corner of Štefáníkova and Športová.

Spišská Sobota

If you do end up staying in Poprad, the village of **SPIŠSKÁ SOBOTA** (Georgenberg), just 2km northeast (bus #2 or #4), makes for an enjoyable outing on a cloudy afternoon. Only a handful of the thousands of visitors who pass through Poprad make it here, yet it couldn't be more different from its ugly, oversized neighbour. Except during Mass on Sundays, there are few signs of life in its leafy square, and only the burgher houses hint at the fact that this was once a thriving Spiš town. At the eastern end of the square, an entire row has been recently renovated and smartly whitewashed, while in the centre huddle the old radnica, the obligatory Renaissance belfry, and the church of **sv Juraj** (St George), whose origins go back even further than its present late-Gothic appearance. Its vaulting is incredibly sophisticated for this part of the world, as are the font and a couple of the smaller chapels, but the real treat is the main **altar** carved by Pavol of Levoča in 1516, which features a gilded George vanquishing the dragon, with a reworking of the famous *Last Supper* predella from the main church in Levoča, below. The **museum** (May–Sept Tues–Sun 9am–4pm) at no. 33, on the south side of the square, is worth a look if only to see the inside of a typical town house.

Practicalities

Poprad's **tourist office**, PIA (May–Sept Mon–Fri 8am–6pm, Sat & Sun 8am–1pm; Oct–April Mon–Fri 8.30am–noon & 1–5pm, Sat & Sun 8.30am–1pm; ℡052/161 86, ⓦwww.poprad.sk), at the western end of námestie sv Egídia, can organize private rooms in town and all types of **accommodation** elsewhere in the Tatras. The high-rise *Satel*, on Mnoheľova (℡052/716 11 11, ⓦwww.satel-slovakia.sk; ❺), has lots of excellent facilities, as does the slightly smaller *Poprad* on Partizánská (℡052/772 12 60, ⓦwww.hotel-poprad.sk; ❺). However, if you've got your own transport or don't mind taking the bus (#2 or #4), you'll get much better value for money and a friendlier welcome at the pub *U sv Juraj* (℡052/776 95 58, ⓦwww.penzion-sv-juraj.sk; ❷), one of several pensions on the main square in Spišská Sobota. Poprad has a number of cheap hostels, too: try the *Hotel Garni*, Karpatská 11 (℡052/776 38 77, ⓦwww.garniwm.sk; ❶), which has lots of cheap doubles and triples.

Eating and **drinking** in Poprad has improved a little of late. You can grab a baguette sandwich or a salad at the *Astoria*, on ulica 1 mája just off the main square, or wolf down one of the many excellent pizzas or desserts at *Pizzeria Palermo*, Štefáníkovo 4. For a more formal meal, the best place to head for is the *Egidius*, behind the *Satel* on Mnoheľova, a popular folksy restaurant specializing in traditional Slovak fare, with occasional live music. Less fancy is the smaller *Slovenská reštaurácia* on ulica 1 mája which serves up local specialities. The *kaviareň*, in the *Európa*, by the train station, has a little faded grandeur, but it's seen better days. If dancing's your thing, the *Surprise* **disco**, in the same building as the *Pizzeria Palermo*, has an animated bar as well as billiard tables.

The Tatra National Park (TANAP)

Cute, red, tram-like trains trundle between Poprad and the necklace of resorts and spas that nestle at the foot of the Tatras and lie within the **Tatra National Park** or **TANAP** (Ⓦwww.tanap.sk). To be honest, the resorts are all much of a muchness, a mixture of half-timbered lodges from the last century, interwar villas and tasteless new hotels, all set in eminently civilized spa gardens and pine woods – it's the mountains to which they give access that make them worth visiting.

Štrbské Pleso

Founded in 1873 by the local Hungarian lord József Szentiványi, **ŠTRBSKÉ PLESO**'s life as a mountain resort began in earnest some twenty years later, with the building of the rack railway that climbs 430m in just 5km from Štrba on the main line below. At 1351m, it's the highest Tatran resort. It's also the brashest, with reams of takeaway kiosks and tatty, eyesore hotel hoardings, though this has more to do with its having hosted the 1970 World Ski

Hiking, skiing and climbing in the High Tatras

It is as well to remember that the High Tatras are an alpine range and as such demand a little more respect and preparation than other Slovak mountains. Most of the trails described in the text are far from easy, and many involve the use of chains to traverse rock screes. The whole area is part of the **Tatra National Park (TANAP)**, whose often quite strict rules and regulations are designed to protect what is a valuable, fragile ecosystem – you may find that you have to pay a small fee to use some of the trails, so take some money with you. The most important rule is to stick to the marked paths; before setting out, get hold of a *Vysoké Tatry* **map**, which shows all the marked paths in the TANAP.

In the summer months, the most popular trails and summits are literally chock-a-block with Czech, German and Slovak walkers. One of the reasons for the summer stampede is that many of the most exhilarating treks are only open from July 1 to October 30. This is primarily due to the **weather**, probably the single most important consideration when planning your trek. Rainfall is actually heaviest in June, July and August; thunderstorms and even the occasional summer snowstorm are also features of the unpredictable alpine climate, and it may be scorching hot down in the valley yet below freezing on top of Rysy.

Hiking: the golden rules

Watch the **weather forecast** (easy enough to read even in Slovak – look for *počasie* in the paper).

Set out **early** (the weather is always better in the morning), and tell someone when and where you're going.

Don't leave the **tree line** (about 2000m) unless visibility is good, and when the clouds close in, start descending immediately.

Bring with you: a pair of **sturdy boots** to combat the relentless boulders in the higher reaches; a **whistle** (for blowing six times every minute if you need help); and a **flask of water**.

Championships than anything else. The ski resort part of town is north of the *pleso*, the second largest of the Tatran glacial lakes from which the spa gets its name; swimming in the lake is forbidden. There's a useful **TIK office** (Mon–Fri 8am–4pm, Sat 9am–noon; ☎052/449 23 91) close to the railway station.

In summer, the only working lift is the chair lift to Solisko, from where the climb to the top of **Predné Solisko** (2093m) takes well under an hour. As with all such lifts in the Tatras, book your ride well in advance to avoid the snake-like ticket queues that have usually formed by mid-morning. If you want to explore a whole ring of mystical glacial lakes – in folk legends known as "the eyes and windows of another sea" – make the trek over **Bystré sedlo** (2314m), which skirts the jagged Solisko range; it's a round trip of around eight hours, and best done anticlockwise, heading from east to west.

A gentle one-hour walk through the forest along the red-marked path to **Popradské pleso** is all many people manage on a lightning Tatra tour. It's a beautiful spot to have a picnic, although given its popularity, by no means tranquil. Those with sufficient stamina can try the punishing hour-long climb to the **sedlo pod Ostrvou** (1959m), which gives a fantastic bird's-eye view of the lake. This red-marked path, known as the Magistrála, skirts the tree line all the way to **Zelené pleso**, 20km away in the far east of the range. If you don't have boundless enthusiasm for walking, stroll along the yellow-marked track to the **symbolický cintorín** of wooden crosses set up to commemorate the

Skiing

The High Tatras are as popular for **skiing** in winter as they are for hiking in summer. The first snows arrive as early as November, but the season doesn't really get going for another month. By the end of March, you can only really ski on the higher slopes reached by chair (as opposed to ski) lifts. The main ski resort is Štrbské Pleso, which hosts the occasional international as well as national event; Hrebienok (near Starý Smokovec) and Sklanaté pleso (near Tatranská Lomnica) are the other two main ski areas. Lifts generally run from sunrise to sunset, and while lift operators keep things flowing as smoothly as they can, queues for the lifts can be pretty horrendous at the busiest times – if so, head out to the quieter pistes around Ždiar or even Jezersko in the **Spišská Magura** hills.

Ski hire facilities have improved enormously over the last few years, so if you haven't brought your own equipment, gear can be rented from the likes of T-Ski in Starý Smokovec. If you've cash to spare and want to have it all planned out before you go, contact the specialist agents who organize skiing holidays to the High and Low Tatras (see pp.12 & 14).

Climbing

To go **climbing** (as opposed to hiking) in the High Tatras you need to be a member of a recognized mountain-climbing club and be able to produce a membership card. Otherwise, you are required by law to hire a guide from the Horská služba (see below), which costs 3000–4000SK a day, though up to four people can share the cost of one guide. It's possible to climb throughout the year, but as with skiing, beware of avalanches. Note that *Cesta uzavretá – nebezpečenstvo lavín* means "Path Closed – Beware of Avalanches". The most popular climbs are in the vicinity of Lomnický štít, but **Gerlachovský štít**, the highest peak in the Tatras, is also high on the hit list.

For **advice** on where to and where not to climb, tips on the weather and emergency help, contact Horská služba, the **24-hour mountain rescue service** next door to SATUR in Starý Smokovec (☎052/442 28 20, ⑩www.horska-sluzba.sk).

considerable number of people who've lost their lives in the mountains.

One of the most popular climbs in the Tatras is **Rysy** (2499m), on the Slovak-Polish border, which Lenin himself once climbed (from the Polish side). If you're planning on conquering Rysy, you won't have time to picnic by the lake, since it's a good six hours' return trip from Popradské pleso. Just below the first peak of Váha (2343m), the *Chata pod Rysmi* (☎052/442 23 14; June–Oct), at 2250m the highest (and coldest) of the mountain chalets, is currently under reconstruction, having been destroyed in an avalanche. If you can find a place to sit down on the often crowded summit of Rysy, it has to be one of the best views in Europe. Another possible climb from Popradské pleso is the eight-hour sweep over **Vysoké Kôprovské sedlo** (2180m) via the largest lake of the lot, **Veľké Hincovo pleso**; while you're there, it's worth making the effort to take in the summit of Kôprovský štít (2367m) itself, less than an hour's climb.

Kriváň (2494m), the westernmost High Tatran peak (and, in comparison, relatively easy to climb), is an eight-hour return journey from Štrbské Pleso via Jaňské pleso. In 1841, Slovak nationalists Štúr and Hurban staged a patriotic march up the mountain, a tradition that is continued to this day at the end of August. Like Rysy, it's a popular route, swarming with walkers at the height of summer. If that sounds like your idea of hell, try some of the trails around Podbanské or even further afield in the Western Tatras (see p.502).

Starý Smokovec

The old Saxon settlement of **STARÝ SMOKOVEC** (Altschmecks) is the most established and most central of all the spas. Along with neighbouring settlements of Nový, Horni and Dolný Smokovec, it makes up the conglomeration known as **Smokovce**. The spa's old nucleus is the stretch of lawn between the half-timbered supermarket and the sandy-yellow *Grand Hotel*, a sight in its own right. It was built in 1904 in a vaguely alpine neo-Baroque style, and though the staff can be a bit snooty it's worth having a drink in the hotel café, if only to check out the wonderful 1920s decor. There are also two **wooden churches** worth seeking out in Smokovce: the red neo-Gothic parish church behind the *Grand Hotel*, and, in Dolný Smokovec, the turn-of-the-twentieth-century chapel perching on arcaded stilts.

The best place to head for help with **accommodation** is T-Ski (daily 9am–5pm; ☎052/442 32 65, ⓦwww.slovakiatravel.sk), up by the cable car (they also hire out skis and bikes), or, failing that, SATUR, on the main street (Mon–Fri 8am–6pm, Sat 8am–noon); the TIK office (Mon–Fri 8am–4pm, Sat 9am–noon; ☎052/442 34 40) is across from *Hotel Smokovec*, northwest of the train station. The *Grand Hotel* (☎052/442 21 54; ❻), with all conceivable amenities, is without doubt the finest guesthouse around; the high-rise *Bellevue* (☎052/442 29 41; ❺) has none of the atmosphere, but runs it a close second on the amenities. To the west in Nový Smokovec, the distinctive neo-Gothic *Vila Dr Szontagh* (☎052/442 20 61; ❹) is a decent, cheaper alternative, as are the *Panda* (☎052/442 26 14; ❹) and the *Vila Jana* (☎052/442 32 96; ❸), to the east in Horný Smokovec. You can book yourself into a **mountain chata** through Slovakoturist (Mon–Fri 8am–4pm), a couple of minutes' walk east of the main train station in Horný Smokovec (the closest station is Pekná Vyhliadka). The self-service **restaurant** in the Central supermarket, and the nearby *Tatra* restaurant, are both okay, and situated just a short step from the train station, though for a proper evening meal, you're better off heading for the *Grand* or the *Szontagh*.

If the weather's good, the most straightforward and rewarding climb is along the blue-marked path from behind the *Grand Hotel* to the summit of **Slavkovský štít** (2452m), a return journey of nine hours. Again from behind the *Grand Hotel*, a narrow-gauge **funicular** (daily 7am–7.40pm; closed for maintenance late April & Nov) climbs 250m to Hrebienok (45min by foot), one of the lesser ski resorts on the edge of the pine forest proper. The smart wooden *Bilíkova chata* (☎052/442 24 39; ❸) is a five-minute walk from the top of the funicular. Just past the *chata*, the path continues through the wood, joining up with two others, from Tatranská Lesná and Tatranská Lomnica respectively, before passing the gushing waterfalls of the **Studenovodské vodopády**.

At the fork just past the waterfall, a whole variety of trekking possibilities open up. The right-hand fork takes you up the **Malá Studená dolina** and then zigzags above the tree line to the *Téryho chata* (☎052/442 52 45; ❷), set in a lunar landscape by the shores of the **Päť Spišských plies**. Following the spectacular, hair-raising trail over the Priečne sedlo to *Zbojnicka chata* (☎0903/619 000; ❷), you can return via the Veľká studená dolina – an eight-hour round trip from Hrebienok. This is a one-way hiking path, so you have to do it this way round; note that it involves a 100-foot rock climb on a fixed chain, and is not recommended for the fainthearted. Alternatively, you could continue from the *Téryho chata* to Tatranská Javorina, nine hours away near the Polish border, and return by bus.

Another possibility is to take the left-hand fork to the *Zbojnicka chata* and continue to Zamruznuté pleso, in the shadow of **Východná Vysoká** (2428m); only a thirty-minute hike from the lake, this dishes out the best view there is for the non-climber of **Gerlachovský štít** (2655m), the highest mountain in Slovakia. To get back down to the valley, either descend the Poľský hrebeň and return to Starý Smokovec via the *Sliezsky dom* (9hr round trip without the Východná Vysoká ascent), or continue north and track the Polish border to Lysá Poľana, the Slovak border post (10hr one-way), returning by bus to Starý Smokovec.

Tatranská Lomnica

TATRANSKÁ LOMNICA, 5km northeast of Starý Smokovec, is a smaller version of the latter. It's a pleasant place to sit out bad weather, and of course gives access to **Lomnický štít** (2632m), the second highest mountain in the Tatras, accessible by cable car (*lanová dráha*). It's difficult to fault the view from Lomnický štít, but purists may disapprove of the concrete steps and handrails built to prevent the crowds from pushing each other off the rocky summit. The cable car (daily: summer 8.30am–5pm; winter 8.30am–4pm; closed for maintenance late May/early June & Nov) goes up in three stages: first to Štart, then to Skalnaté Pleso, the lake that sits below the mountain, from which you can either head for the summit, or opt for the chair lift to **Lomnický sedlo**, the craggy saddle 500m below Lomnický štít.

Hiking options are not so good from Tatranská Lomnica, and most treks are best started from other resorts. Otherwise, cloudy days can be filled with horseracing (Sun only), outdoor chess and the **TANAP museum** (Mon–Fri 8am–noon & 1–4.30pm, Sat & Sun 8am–noon), whose smart displays of stuffed Tatran animals and plants accompany a brief history of the region. It was only explored for the first time in the late eighteenth century when a Scotsman, Robert Townson (see p.544), who was botanizing his way round Hungary, ascended Kežmarský štít and a number of other peaks, against the advice of the local guides. There's also a garden where you can mug up on your Tatran flowers (May–Sept), a couple of hundred metres away.

THE MOUNTAIN REGIONS | The High Tatras (Vysoké Tatry)

9

If you're looking for **accommodation**, there's a free phone by the train station with an information panel detailing your options. Tatranská Lomnica's finest hotel is the *Grandhotel Praha* (☎052/446 79 41; ❻), a vast hotel right by the cable car, built in 1905 by the Wagons-Lits-Cook company; *Hotel Wili* (☎052/446 77 61; ❺), a postwar high-rise just east of the bus station, has been modernized to an equally high standard. Another top-class option is the newly built *Vila Beatrice* (☎052/446 71 20; ❻), to the south of the train station, between the tracks; each room has its own small kitchenette. Two cheaper but more characterful pensions are *Penzión Bělin* (☎052/446 77 78; ❸), on the north side of the park, opposite the info panel, and *Penzión Encián* (☎052/446 75 20; ❸). For **food**, the *Julia*, down from the train station, is folksy but a good bet for traditional Slovak fare nevertheless.

Kotlina, Ždiar and on to Poland

The overkill in the central part of the TANAP makes trekking from the relative obscurity of **TATRANSKÁ KOTLINA** an attractive alternative. Most people, however, come here not to walk, but to visit the **Belianska jaskyňa** (Tues–Sun: Jan–May, mid-Sept to mid-Nov & late Dec tours at 9.30 & 11am, 12.30 & 2pm; June to mid-Sept hourly tours 9am–4pm), fifteen minutes from the main road, whose pleasures include rock formations whimsically named the *Leaning Tower of Pisa* and *White Pagoda*, and an underground lake; another bad-weather time-filler.

The **Zelené pleso** makes a good hiking target, surrounded by a vast rocky amphitheatre of granite walled peaks including the mean-looking north face of Lomnický štít. To get there, take the blue-marked path from the southwest end of Tatranská Kotlina, and turn right onto the green trail which ends at the ruined *chata* by Biele pleso (2–3hr). From here it's half an hour to the fully functioning *Chata pri zelenom plese* (☎052/446 74 20; ❸), which sits by the green tarn itself. If you've still got time and energy on your hands, traverse the ridge to the north and mount the summit of Jahňaci štít (2–3hr round trip).

The mountains of the **Belianske Tatry**, which form the final alpine ridge in the north of the TANAP and are home to chamois, have recently reopened to the public and offer an alternative to skirting their southern slopes via the Kopské sedlo (30min on the blue trail from Biele pleso) and then on to Javorina (2–3hr).

On the other side of the Belianske Tatry, on the main road to Tatranská Javorina (and to Zakopane in Poland), is **ŽDIAR**, a traditional Góral community founded in the seventeenth century. The Górale are fiercely independent mountain farmers, speaking a Polish dialect, the majority of whom live on the Polish side of the border. The village has numerous wooden cottages in varying stages of modernization, a half-timbered cinema and an unremarkable brick church. One of the houses has been converted into a modest Góral folk museum, the **Ždiarska izba** (Mon–Fri 9am–4pm, Sat & Sun 9am–noon), while *Penzión Diana* (☎052/449 81 27; ❸), and numerous smaller houses, offer pine-clad rooms for the night.

If you're continuing your journey **into Poland**, a daily bus service will take you as far as Lysá Poľana, 12km west of Ždiar. From there you can walk across the border into Poland and catch a bus to the main Polish Tatra resort of Zakopane (see *Poland: the Rough Guide* for details).

Travel details

Bratislava to: Banská Bystrica (1 daily; 3hr 45min); Liptovský Mikuláš (every 2hr; 4hr); Martin (1–2 daily; 3hr); Ružomberok (every 2hr; 3hr 40min); Poprad (every 2hr; 4hr 40min); Žilina (every 2hr; 2hr 40min); Zvolen (4–5 daily; 3hr).

Banská Bystrica to: Brezno (11–12 daily; 50min–1hr 10min); Červená Skala (4 daily; 1hr 35min–2hr 15min); Košice (4 daily; 4hr); Martin (4 daily; 1hr 50min); Zvolen (hourly; 20–40min).

Kralovany to: Dolný Kubín (every 2hr; 30min); Istebné (every 2hr; 10min); Oravský Podzámok (every 2hr; 1hr); Podbiel (every 2hr; 1hr 20min); Trstená (every 2hr; 1hr 50min).

Poprad (Poprad-Tatry) to: Starý Smokovec (hourly; 35min); Štrbské Pleso (hourly; 1hr 10min).

Stary Smokovec to: Tatranská Lomnica (hourly; 15min).

Žilina to: Kraľovany (every 2hr; 30–40min); Liptovský Mikuláš (every 2hr; 1hr 10min); Martin (6–8 daily; 40min); Poprad (every 2hr; 1hr 55min); Rajecké Teplice (7–9 daily; 45min; 30min);

Ružomberok (every 2hr; 50min); Strečno (12–14 daily; 15min); Vrútky (every 1–2hr; 20–25min).

Zvolen to: Budapest (2–3 daily; 4hr 40min); Detva (7–8 daily; 30–40min); Fiľakovo (7–8 daily; 1hr–1hr 40min); Kremnica (6 daily; 1hr); Lučenec (every 2hr; 50min–1hr 20min); Martin (6 daily; 2hr); Turčianske Teplice (6 daily; 1hr 30min).

Banská Bystrica to: Banská Štiavnica (up to 5 daily; 1hr 30min); Martin (up to 8 daily; 1hr 15min); Ružomberok (up to 5 daily; 1hr 20min); Žilina (up to 8 daily; 2hr).

Liptovsky Mikulás to: Demänovská dolina/Jasná (hourly; 40min).

Martin to: Turčianske Teplice (hourly; 30min).

Poprad to: Lysá Poľana (6 daily; 1hr 25min); Ždiar (hourly; 1hr).

Žilina to: Banská Bystrica (4–10 daily; 1hr 45min); Čičmany (Mon–Fri 6–7 daily, Sat & Sun 3–4 daily; 1hr 20min); Strečno/Martin (up to 12 daily; 30min/45min); Terchová/Vrátna dolina (hourly; 45min/1hr).

East Slovakia

CHAPTER 10

Highlights

* **Rafting in the Pieniny** – Take a raft ride down the rapids of the River Dunajec, which forms the border between Slovakia and Poland. See p.531

* **Levoča** – Perfectly preserved medieval town originally settled by Germans, now home to some of the finest Gothic altarpieces in the country. See p.532

* **Spišský hrad** – Awesome ruined castle that sprawls across a prominent hill east of Levoča and provides one of the best photo opportunities in Slovakia. See p.536

* **Slovenský raj** – Scramble up ladders and cling to ropes beside the gushing wooded ravines of the Slovenský raj. See p.537

* **Slovenský kras** – A whole series of caves is dotted about the Slovak karst region, by the border with Hungary. See p.540

* **Andrassy mausoleum, Krásnohorské Podhradie** – This Art Nouveau memorial is the most remarkable single monument in the country. See p.542

* **Bardejov** – Saxon weavers' town with a beautifully preserved square and cathedral and a superb museum of icons. See p.550

* **Wooden churches** – The northeastern corner of Slovakia boasts a fascinating cluster of mostly Greek-Catholic wooden churches. See p.552

* **Košice** – Worth a visit for the showpiece main square alone, with its unrivalled Gothic cathedral. See p.556

10

East Slovakia

Stretching from the High Tatras east to the Ukrainian border, the countryside of East Slovakia (Vychodné Slovensko) is decidedly different from the rest of the country. The Carpathian mountains, which build up to a crescendo around the High Tatras, revert to gentle rolling hills, while the obligatory forests of pine and spruce give way gradually to acres of beech forests, at their best in September and October, when the hills turn into a fanfare of burnt reds and browns.

Ethnically, East Slovakia has always been the most diverse region in the country, with different groups coexisting even within a single valley. In medieval times, the towns were settled predominantly by Germans and Hungarians, who were later joined by Jews and Romanies. Even today, the Polish-speaking **Górale** minority continue to inhabit the northern border regions, as do the hill-dwelling **Rusyns**, whose chief homeland became part of the Soviet Union after 1945 and is now in Ukraine. Ethnic Hungarians survive in large numbers in the south of the region, but only a minority of the **Germans** or *Karpathendeutschen* survived the expulsions that followed World War II. The region's once-large Jewish population was decimated in the Nazi Holocaust, but the **Romanies**, for the most part, escaped the genocide, and now form a large minority, mostly residing on the edge of Slovak villages, in ghettos of almost medieval squalor. Even the **East Slovaks** themselves are thought of as some kind of separate race by other Slovaks; indeed, before 1918 there was a movement to create a separate state for them.

A short train ride east of the High Tatras, the intriguing medieval towns of the **Spiš region** constitute East Slovakia's architectural high point, while to the south, the **Slovenský raj** offers some highly unorthodox hiking possibilities. Further south still, along the Hungarian border, the karst region of the **Slovenský kras** boasts one of the longest underground cave systems in the world. Along the northern border with Poland, **Carpatho-Ruthenia** – home of the country's remaining Rusyn population – is a fascinating, isolated landscape. Rich medieval towns, like Bardejov and Prešov, originally built by German colonists, still stand today, while the countryside is replete with wooden churches. Many towns were badly damaged in the last war – in fact, the further east you go, the more densely concentrated are the Soviet monuments of former times: retired tanks still line the highways along which they liberated Slovakia at the end of World War II, and the plaques and statues that were ripped down after the revolution in other parts of the two republics still stand proudly. After spending time in the rural backwaters, **Košice**, the East Slovak capital, provides a welcome, though somewhat startling, return to city life, containing enough of interest for a stopover at least before heading east towards the Ukrainian border and the deserted beech forests of the **Vihorlat**.

The Spiš region

The land that stretches northeast up the Poprad valley to the Polish border and east along the River Hornád towards Prešov is known as the **Spiš region**, for centuries a semi-autonomous province within the Hungarian kingdom. After a series of particularly devastating Tatar raids in the thirteenth century practically wiped out the local population, the Hungarian kings began to encourage German craftsmen to colonize the area. With the whiff of valuable ore deposits in the air, families from Saxony (to whom the area was known as *Zips*) came in ever greater numbers, eventually establishing a federation of twenty-four *Zips* towns that were quickly granted special trading privileges and began to thrive.

The Saxon settlers used their wealth to build some wonderful Gothic churches, and later enriched almost every town and village with the distinctive touch of the Renaissance, a legacy that has imbued the towns with an appealing architectural coherence. Centuries of peaceful coexistence were shattered by World War II, when, first, the local Jewish population was sent to the camps, and then, following the Nazi defeat, the vast majority of the German-speaking community or *Karpathendeutschen* were expelled. Nowadays, tourism aside, the whole of the Spiš region, including its tiny residual German-speaking community, and the much larger Romany minority, continues to share the low living standards which have been the rule throughout East Slovakia for the last century.

Kežmarok and around

Just 14km northeast of Poprad and still within view of the High Tatras, **KEŽ-MAROK** (Käsmark) – its name is derived from the German for "cheese market" – is one of the easiest Spiš towns to visit. It's an odd place, combining the distinctive traits of a Teutonic town with the dozy feel of an oversized Slovak village. If you've visited nearby Spišská Sobota (see p.515), you'll recognize the familiar signs of a Spiš town: wooden gables, shingled overhanging eaves and big barn doors. Kežmarok, however, has the added attractions of a Renaissance castle, a fascinating town museum and a remarkable clutch of ecclesiastical buildings on its southern fringe. Like the chief Spiš town, Levoča (see p.532), with which it has a long-standing rivalry, Kežmarok was a royal free town, but whereas Levoča remained loyal to the crown, Kežmarok was a consistent supporter of the rebel cause in the seventeenth and eighteenth centuries.

The Town

From whichever direction you approach the town, the view of Kežmarok is dominated by the giant, gaudy **Nový evanjelický kostol** (May–Oct daily 9am–noon & 2–5pm; Nov–April Tues & Fri 9am–noon & 2–4pm), a Lutheran church built by the Danish architect Theophil Hansen, who was funded by the town's wealthy Protestant merchants and responsible for much of late-nineteenth-century Vienna. It's a seemingly random fusion of styles – Renaissance campanile, Moorish dome, Classical dimensions, all dressed up in grey-green and rouge rendering – but one of which Hansen, and presumably his patrons, were particularly fond. If you're accustomed to the intense atmosphere of the country's Roman Catholic churches, the simple whitewashed hall looks like it's been ransacked. On the right-hand side, swathed in the wreaths and sashes of the Hungarian tricolour, sits the tomb and mausoleum of the Protestant Hungarian rebel **Count Imre Thököly**, who had the Imperial army on the run for eight years or so during the anti-Habsburg Kuruc revolt of 1678, before being exiled to Turkey, where he died in 1705.

To gain entry to the Lutheran church you must buy your ticket next door in the even more remarkable, though significantly less imposing wooden church or **Drevený kostol** (times as above), built by a German craftsman, Georg Müttermann from Poprad. It abides by the strictures of the 1681 edict, which stipulated that Protestant churches could only be erected outside the town walls. Constructed entirely of wood, it couldn't be further from the Viennese cosmopolitanism of its neighbour. The interior, capable of seating almost 1500 people, is surprisingly ornate for a Protestant church, with florid Baroque furnishings: font, pulpit, organ and a limewood main altar flanked by barley-sugar columns, and full of curving flourishes and sunflowers. The ceiling is painted to look like the sky on a summer's day, while the balcony features wonderful wooden panel paintings of the Old and New Testaments.

One more building here deserves mention: the Lutheran Lycée library or **Lyceálnej knižnice** (Mon–Fri 8am–3pm), architecturally fairly nondescript but historically and culturally significant. Lutheranism, which was rife in the nether regions of the Hungarian Empire, especially those parts colonized by Germans, was also the religion of many of Slovakia's leading nineteenth-century nationalists. The Czechophile Pavol Šafárik, the poet Martin Rázus and the writer Martin Kukučín all studied here before the Hungarians closed it down in the 1860s.

The old town itself is little more than two long, leafy streets punctuated by a mixture of plane and fir trees radiating out in a V-shaped fork from the big, boxy, Neoclassical radnica at the centre. The town's fifteenth-century Catholic basilica of **sv Kríž** is tucked away in the dusty back alleys between the two prongs; once surrounded by its own line of fortifications, it's now protected by an appealing Renaissance belfry, whose uppermost battlements burst into sgraffito life in the best Spiš tradition. The church itself has been recently restored, and is well worth a look inside, not least to admire the exquisite net vaulting, and the sixteenth-century main altar, which comes from the workshop of Pavol of Levoča.

The **hrad** (May–Sept Tues–Sun hourly 9am–4pm; Oct–April Tues–Sat 9–11am & 1–4pm), at the end of the right-hand fork, is the main reason for the occasional Tatran tour group. For many years the property of the Thököly family, it was confiscated by the Habsburgs as punishment for their support of the aforementioned Kuruc revolt. It's impressively fortified with round towers, bulwarks, bastions and decorative Renaissance crenellations, but the museum of historical artefacts that now occupies its bare rooms doesn't really justify the hour-long guided tour. A much more interesting half hour can be spent in the nearby **Múzeum bytovej kultury** (May–Sept Tues–Sun 9am–noon & 1–5pm; Oct–April Tues–Sat 8am–noon & 1–4pm), housed in a late-seventeenth-century timber-framed house at Hradné námestie 55 (ask for the *anglický text*). The museum contains, among other things, the personal effects of Countess Hedviga Mária Szirmayova-Badányiova (1895–1973), last survivor of the aristocratic Badányi family. In among the beautiful gowns and period furniture, there's a brass samovar from Tula, and lots of luxury goods imported to the town to satisfy the tastes of the local wealthy German and Hungarian burgher families.

Finally, if you've time to spare, you could do worse than take a quick turn under the sycamore trees of the vast local **cemetery**, just off the ring road (at this point called Toporcerova, and the main road from Poprad), which gives out great views of the Tatras on a clear day. It's a fascinating testament to the diverse nationalities – Polish, Hungarian, German and Slovak – that have inhabited the region over the last century. The remaining Slovak peasantry continue to honour their dead with simple wooden crosses, while the vestigial German community, or *Karpathendeutschen* as they're known, stubbornly stick to their own language; *Ruhe Sanft!* (Rest in Peace) is to be seen on the more recent headstones, not just on the ornate, rusting, turn-of-the-twentieth-century graves belonging to the now displaced German and Hungarian elite.

Practicalities

Arriving in Kežmarok by **train** is by far the most pleasant introduction to the town, thanks to the yellowing late-nineteenth-century station (there's also a regular **bus** service from Poprad). Kežmarok is near enough to the High Tatras to figure as a possible base for exploring the mountains, providing you have your own transport. Few people bother to do this, though, so **accommodation**, while limited, is fairly easy to find. The **tourist office** or KIA (Mon–Fri 8.30am–5pm, Sat & Sun 9am–2pm; winter closed Sun; ⓦkezmarok.tripod .com/english), on the main square at Hlavné námestie 46, can book cheap private rooms; otherwise the best option is the excellent *Hotel Club*, on ulica MUDr Alexandra (☎052/452 4051, ⓔhotelclub@kk.sinet.sk; ❸), an efficiently run, tastefully modernized place right in the old town, with an excellent restaurant on the ground floor. Cheaper options include the *Štart* (☎052/452 2916; ❷), which lies in the woods to the north of the castle, a good twenty-minute walk from the train station.

Kežmarok's biggest cultural event is the **European folk craft fair** or *Európske ľudové remeslo* (EĽRO), which takes place in mid-July.

Strážky

Just 4km northeast of Kežmarok on route 67, on the outskirts of the village of **STRÁŽKY** (Nehre), is the Slovenská národná galéria's furthest-flung outpost, the pretty little Renaissance chateau of **Kaštieľ Strážky** (Tues–Sun 10am–5pm). Unfortunately you have to go on a guided tour in order to visit the chateau (ask for the *anglický text*), which was rather brutally converted following the death of the last inhabitant, the countess Margita Czóbel. The large gallery of nineteenth-century portraits by the likes of Peter Bohúň and Dominik Skutecký is less interesting than the collection of works by **Ladislav Medyánszky** (1852–1919) – aka Meďmanský – the wayward son of the local baron, who spent his youth in the bohemian Paris of the 1870s. His landscapes are reminiscent of early Impressionists like Corot, but his depictions of local peasants, gypsies and beggars are much more severe, and full of insight. The **Countess Margita Czóbel** was herself something of an amateur artist, producing some winsome pen and ink drawings and watercolours in the 1920s. She was also clearly quite a character, enjoying daily swims in the local river until her death aged 81, and entertaining Alain Robbe-Grillet during the filming of *L'Homme qui ment* in the 1960s (there are photos in the chateau to prove it).

Vrbov

Five kilometres south of Kežmarok is the village of **VRBOV**. Without your own set of wheels, you'll have to rely on the infrequent bus service from Kežmarok and Poprad. The village itself is no more than a couple of grubby streets and the obligatory Romany ghetto, but continuing on the road south, the rather dubious smell of bad eggs emanates from the nearby sulphurized **natural spring swimming pool** (termálne kúpalisko; daily 8am–10pm). It's an extremely popular spot in the height of summer, when, during the evening, the pool becomes something of a floodlit social centre as the locals immerse themselves in the fizzy, steaming, therapeutic water. Should you wish to stay, there's a **campsite** (July & Aug) beyond the pool, but it's not the best of sites, not least because of the steep bank on which you have to pitch your tent.

Spišský Štvrtok

Ten kilometres south of Vrbov, just off the main road from Poprad and Levoča, is **SPIŠSKÝ ŠTVRTOK** (Donnersmark), whose splendid thirteenth-century church sits atop the village hill, its masonry tower topped by an impressive wooden spire with four corner pinnacles. The perfect French late-Gothic side chapel, built by Master Puchsbaum and tacked onto the south wall of the church, was commissioned by the Zápoľskýs in 1473 as the family mausoleum, and is, without doubt, one of the most surprising architectural sights in East Slovakia.

The Pieniny

The **Pieniny** (Ⓦwww.pieniny.sk) is characterized by a small eruption of fissured limestone rocks that straddles the Dunajec river, which briefly forms the border between Poland and Slovakia. As early as the 1930s, the Polish and Czechoslovak governments declared this area a national park, the PIENAP, and today, despite the continuing isolation of the Zamagurie region (Zamagurie means literally "behind the Spišská Magura hills"), tourism in the Pieniny is flourishing for the Góral folk on both sides of the border, particularly the ever-popular **raft trips** down the Dunajec. Weather permitting, the rafting season runs from early May to late October, operating between 8.30am and 5pm from May to August, but finishing earlier in the last two months. In addition to the regular raft trips there's a canoe slalom competition on the river held over the first weekend in September, and a folk festival in mid-June.

Trips set off from various points along the seven-kilometre stretch of the river that starts just north of Spišská Stará Ves, and finishes at the main base of **ČER-VENÝ KLÁŠTOR** (Unterschwaben). At each of the embarkation points (*prístav plťí*) along the river, tour operators will relieve you of your money (around 200Sk per person) and give you a departure time and ticket (the earlier you get here, the less likely it is you'll have to queue). Each *plť* (raft) is made up of five log pontoons lashed together with rope and capable of carrying up to ten passengers, plus two navigators, who are dressed up in the traditional Góral rafters' costume. Though the waters are not particularly rapid, the river winds through beautiful rocky scenery, and the guides can be a barrel of laughs. River meanderings make the whole excursion about an hour in length, but if you'd prefer to do your own thing, the trip can be made on foot by following the red-marked path 10km along the tree-lined river bank.

At the end of the gorge you can catch a bus, organize a minibus or taxi or else walk the 3km along the road to Lesnica, then 5km across the hills back to Červený Kláštor. The town gets its name from the **Kartuziánsky kláštor** (April & Oct Tues–Sat 10am–4pm; May–Sept Tues–Sun 9am–5pm), or monastery, founded in the fourteenth century and occupied by first the Carthusians and then the Camaldolensians. In the nineteenth century, the monks here compiled the first Slovak grammar and the first complete Slovak translation of the Bible, and there are also valuable sixteenth-century murals to see. The nearest **hotel** is the *Pltník* (☏055/482 2525; ❷), about 1km upriver from Červený Kláštor, which offers doubles and hostel beds. Alternatively, there's the *Motorest Dunajec* (Jan, Feb & May–Sept; ☏052/439 7105; ❸), a wood-clad *chaty* complex with its own restaurant, 2km southeast of Červený Kláštor along route 543. In addition, there are plenty of very small family-run pensions, and a **campsite** (mid-June to mid-Sept) by the river, just downstream from the town.

Stará Ľubovňa

The slightly forlorn town of **STARÁ ĽUBOVŇA** (Altlublau), 25km north-east of Kežmarok and linked by road and rail, is another possible jump-off point for the Pieniny. The town itself has little to detain you, though if you've time to spare, head in the direction of the mostly ruined castle, **Ľubovniansky hrad** (May–Sept daily 9am–5.30pm; Oct–April Mon–Sat 10am–3pm), which occupies a dramatic, high spur overlooking the town, 2km north of the centre. From the fifteenth to the eighteenth century, it was the main residence of the local Polish despot, who lorded it over the thirteen *Zips* towns pawned to the Polish crown by the Hungarians in the fifteenth century. Certain sections have remained intact and now contain local folk art, crafts and costumes, as well as a memorial commemorating those who were tortured in the castle by the Nazis.

Far more interesting than the above, however, is the **Múzeum zamagurskej dediny** (daily 9am–5pm), an open-air folk museum, or *skanzen*, set up in the grassy meadow below the castle in the late 1970s to preserve the precious wooden architecture of the Zamagurie region, to the west of Stará Ľubovňa. In the late nineteenth century, malnutrition was the norm in rural parts of East Slovakia, and people emigrated in droves to other parts of Europe and the United States. Many of the cottages brought here from the surrounding villages were simply abandoned, and some of them now contain mementoes and personal details of the last owners (in Slovak only). It's a well-thought-out museum, and includes an early-nineteenth-century wooden Greek-Catholic church originally from Matysová, whose richly decorated interior, including an eighteenth-century iconostasis, can be viewed on request for the key.

The most convenient **accommodation** option is the friendly *Penzión pod hradom Peters* (☎052/432 4891, ⓦwww.peters.sk; ❶), right by the castle. For food, you could try the *pivovar* (brewery) pub on the town's pleasant main square. If you're continuing **north into Poland**, six trains a day cross the border to the Polish spa town of Muszyna (change at Plaveč on the Slovak side), two of them continuing on to Kraków; the nearest border checkpoint on the roads is 15km north of Stará Ľubovňa, on route 68 at Mníšek nad Popradom.

Levoča

Twenty-five kilometres east from Poprad across the broad sweep of the Spiš countryside, the walled town of **LEVOČA** (Leutschau), positioned on a slight incline, makes a wonderfully medieval impression. Capital of one of the richest regions of Slovakia for more than four centuries, its present-day population of around 11,000 is, if anything, less than it was during its halcyon days. The town's showpiece main square is hit by the occasional tour group from the Tatras, but otherwise its dusty backstreets are yours to explore.

The first attempts at founding a town here were completely trashed by the Tatars. Then, in the thirteenth-century wave of Saxon immigration that followed, Levoča became the capital of the Spiš towns, a position it maintained until its slow but steady decline in the eighteenth and nineteenth centuries. This led to a kind of architectural mummification, and it's the fifteenth and sixteenth centuries – the golden age of Levoča – that still dominate the town today.

The old town

The Euclidian efficiency with which the old town is laid out, chessboard-style, means that wherever you breach the walls, you'll inevitably end up at the main square, **námestie Majstra Pavla**, itself a long, regular rectangle. Most of Levoča's treasures are located here, and a foursome of free-standing buildings occupies the central space: the Protestant church, the old town hall, the Catholic church and the new town hall. The latter, by the small park and bandstand, is possibly the least distinguished, but, in its former incarnation as the *Waaghaus* or municipal **weigh-house**, by far the most important building on the square, and the focus of the town's financial might during its trading hey-

LEVOČA

N

Ⓐ Ⓑ RUŽOVÁ

Ⓒ ⓘ NÁM. KOŠICKÁ ❶❷ Barokový   Košická
MAJSTRA   Kostol   brána
Mestské ❸ PAVLA   Thurzov dom   NÁM.
divadlo   Weigh House   SLOBODY   Bus
sv Jakub Ⓓ   Station
Radnica

Dom Majstra
Pavla z Levoče
Poľská ❹
brána Spišské
Gymnasium múzeum Evanjelický
Kostol
Gynazíalny
Kostol Menhardská
brána

ACCOMMODATION

Arkáda	4
Barbakan	2
Faix	5
Penzión pri Košickej bráne	1
Satel	3

RESTAURANTS

Pizzeria	B
U Janusa	C
U troch apoštolov	D
Vegeterián	A

0   100 m

10

EAST SLOVAKIA | The Spiš region

day. In 1321 King Charles Robert granted the town the Law of Storage, an unusual medieval edict that obliged every merchant passing through the region to remain in Levoča for at least fourteen days, pay various taxes and allow the locals first refusal on all their goods. In addition, Levoča merchants were later exempted from such laws when passing through other towns. Small wonder then that the town burghers were exceptionally wealthy.

Of the freestanding buildings on the main square that were paid for with these riches, it's the Roman Catholic church of **sv Jakub** (June & Sept Mon & Sun 1–4.30pm, Tues–Sat 8.30am–4.30pm; July & Aug Mon & Sun 1–6pm, Tues–Sat 9am–6pm; Oct–May Mon & Sun 1–4pm, Tues–Sat 8.30–11.30am) that contains the most valuable booty. Every nook and cranny of the building is crammed with medieval religious art, the star attraction being the early sixteenth-century wooden altarpiece by **Master Pavol of Levoča**, topped by a forest of finials and pinnacles, which, at 18.6m in height, makes it reputedly the tallest of its kind in the world. At the time, the clarity and characterization of the figures in the predella's *Last Supper* must have seemed incredible: they were modelled on the local merchants who commissioned the work (Pavol and his apprentices can also be seen behind the figure of St James in the central panel). The disciples are depicted in various animated poses – eating, caught in conversation or, in the case of St John, fast asleep across Christ's lap. Only Judas, with thirty pieces of silver over his shoulder, has a look of anguish, while Christ presides with serene poise. The work took over ten years to complete, and is only one of the many Gothic altars in the church that deserve attention. The church can be visited only with a guide, and tours leave every half hour (every hour in winter) from the *kassa* opposite the main entrance.

533

To the south of the church is the most attractive of the central buildings, the former **radnica** (Tues–Sun: May–Oct 9am–5pm; Nov–April 8am–4pm), built in a sturdy Renaissance style. Downstairs, the local administration still holds sway, along with a few tables and chairs for ice-cream eaters; upstairs (where you get your ticket) there's a museum on the Spiš region, and some fairly dubious contemporary art exhibitions on the top floor. Close by the southeastern corner of the town hall stands the **Klietka hanby** (Cage of Disgrace), a rather beautiful wrought-iron contraption erected by Protestants in around 1600 as a pillory for women. The third building in the centre of the square is the oddly squat domed **Evanjelický kostol** (Lutheran church), which replaced its wooden predecessor in the early nineteenth century in an uncompromisingly Neoclassical style, its bare pudding-basin interior not worth the search around for the key.

The square is otherwise lined with some fine sixteenth-century burgher houses, at their most eye-catching in the **Thurzov dom** at no. 7 – at first glance a flamboyant Renaissance structure, though in fact its most striking feature, the sgraffito decoration around the windows, dates from restoration work in 1824. Further down on the east side of the square at no. 20 is a simple two-storey building, **Dom majstra Pavla z Levoče** (daily 9am–5pm), which was the house of Master Pavol. All that's known about him is what little can be gleaned from the town-hall records: he was born around 1460; sat briefly on the town council; died in 1537; and his son was accidentally murdered by a man from Kraków. Even this much is missing from the house's exhibition, which concentrates more on the Kotrba brothers who made good the woodworm of the centuries in the 1950s. Unless you're a real fan of Master Pavol's work it hardly seems worth the effort, since it contains only copies of the same work displayed in the church; however, it does allow you to get a closer look at some of the carving. If you've come this far in search of art, the **Spišské múzeum** (Tues–Sun: May–Sept 9am–5pm; Nov–April 8am–4pm) at no. 40 by the post office, is also worth a peek for its icons, paintings and furniture culled from the Spiš region, dating as far back as the fourteenth century. Among the most important works is a beautiful Renaissance portal and accompanying frescoes, carved out from a local church.

The rest of the town's grid plan is made up of modest one-storey houses, once the exclusive abodes of Saxon craftsmen, now crumbling homes to the town's Slovaks and Romanies. You could spend an enjoyable hour wandering the streets and doing the circuit of the run-down walls: the late nineteenth-century German Gymnasium in the southwest of the town has a certain curiosity value, and the sandy-coloured **Barokový kostol**, the former Franciscan monastery church next to the Košická brána, has a glorious Baroque interior complete with frescoes.

Practicalities

If you arrive by **train** along the branch line from Spišská Nová Ves (see below), you'll find yourself a short walk southeast of the old town; the **bus station** is adjacent, although there is also a bus stop close to the Košická brána in the northeast corner of town. There's a **tourist office** on the northwest corner of the main square (May–Sept Mon–Fri 10am–4.30pm, Sat & Sun 9.30am–1.30pm; Oct–April Mon–Fri 9am–4.30pm; ☏053/451 3763, Ⓦwww.levoca.sk), though outside the annual pilgrimage (see box on previous page), **accommodation** shouldn't be hard to find, the most luxurious option being the stylish *Satel* (☏053/451 2943, Ⓦwww.satel-slovakia.sk; ❺), right on the main square, which retains a beautiful arcaded Renaissance courtyard. The *Arkáda* (☏053/451 2372; ❹), also on the main square, is cheaper and also comfortable inside. The *Barbakan* (☏053/451 4310, Ⓦwww.barbakan.sk; ❸), on Košická, is less attractive but still very good value, while the *Faix* (☏053/451 2335; ❷) is positively spartan. In addition, there are a couple of inexpensive pensions, the best of which is the *Penzión pri Košickej bráne* (☏053/451 2879; ❷), right next door to the *Barbakan*. There's also a **campsite**, *Kováčova vila* (open all year), 3km north of Levoča, in the woods by Levočská dolina.

With a fairly steady trade from locals and passing tourists, **eating** options are pretty good. Authentic Slovak pub food can be had from *U Janusa*, Kláštorská 22 (closed Sat & Sun), and from *U troch apoštolov*, above a butcher's at no. 11 on the east side of the main square. There's also a lunchtime-only veggie restaurant, *Vegeterián* at Uhoľná 3, and a pizzeria at Vetrová 4, both off the northwest corner of the main square. Of the hotel restaurants the one at the *Satel*, predictably enough, rises above the others in terms of standards and price, and, like the *Arkáda*'s, is in an atmospheric Gothic vaulted cellar.

Spišská Nová Ves and around

Thirteen kilometres south of Levoča, **SPIŠSKÁ NOVÁ VES** (Neudorf) is the modern-day capital of the Spiš region, a relatively industrious town with a population of around 40,000, whose origins are as old as Levoča's, but which has borne the brunt of the changes wreaked on the region over the twentieth century. Pawned to the Poles at the height of the Hussite Wars, along with twelve other Spiš towns, it fell to the Habsburgs when Poland was partitioned in 1772, and was immediately made the Spiš capital, a fact that played a significant part in the demise of its old rival, Levoča. As a mining town, it was virtually guaranteed to get itself on the main Košice–Bohumín railway line, built in the nineteenth century. Today, therefore, it's a good place from which to visit both the Slovenský raj and Levoča by train, but otherwise has only a few residual pleasures.

The main square, **Radničné námestie**, is a very long, leafy spindle-shaped avenue in the style of Prešov and Košice, with **Zimná ulica** (Winter Street) to the south, and **Letná ulica** (Summer Street), which gets the sun, to the north. The central space between the two is dotted with important-looking buildings, not least the municipal theatre, **Spišské divadlo**, a grand turn-of-the-twentieth-century building topped by a gilded swan, and worth a peek inside if only to gape at the awesome light fittings. The massive Gothic **Rímsko-katolícky kostol** contains a couple of minor works by Master Pavol of Levoča, and there's a small **Múzeum Spiša** (Tues–Fri 8am–noon & 12.30–4.30pm, Sat 9am–noon & 12.30–5pm), housed in the best-looking building in town, Letná 50, which laboriously documents the mining history of the town.

The **train station** lies ten minutes' walk northwest of the main square, where there's a useful **tourist office** (summer Mon–Fri 8am–5pm, Sat & Sun 9.30am–1.30pm; winter Mon–Fri 8am–4.30pm), a couple of doors down from the museum, who can help you find **accommodation**. Of the town's hotels, the monstrous high-rise *Metropol* (☎053/442 2241; ❹), west of the main square on Štefánikovo námestie, has recently been refurbished, and now offers "luxury sweets" (sic); not so the *Preveza* (☎053/442 2371; ❷), a Communist-era hotel ten minutes' walk south of the main square down Kožuchova and across the river. Decent local **food** can be had from the *Nostalgie*, a café-restaurant in a lovely building next door to the tourist office.

Markušovce

A possible day-trip from Spišská Nová Ves, or from the Slovenský raj, is **MARKUŠOVCE**, 5km to the southeast on the River Hornád and on the main railway line to Košice. Here, in this raggle-taggle village, are the **Kaštieľ and Letohrádok Dardanely** (Tues–Fri & Sun 8am–noon & 12.30–4pm), originally built for the Hungarian Mariássy family in 1643. The main kaštieľ is a wonderful yellow chateau, built four-square with big corner drum towers topped with wooden shingled onion domes. Inside, two floors of rooms contain the best period furniture and costumes that survive from the Spiš region, including a great room of hunting-themed furnishings. Behind the main chateau stands the smaller, matching summer house or Letohrádok Dardenely, built by Wolfgang Mariássy in order to entertain Joseph II, though in the end the emperor never turned up. It's an unusual building: named after the Dardanelles simply because Wolfgang liked Turkey, and not completed until the 1970s when the Communists decided to add the two wings. It now houses a collection of musical keyboard instruments, from organs to clavichords and grand pianos; concerts take place in the fine acoustics of the Great Hall, which is lavishly decorated in amateurish mythological trompe l'oeil frescoes.

East to Spišský hrad

The road east from Levoča takes you to the edge of the Spiš territory, clearly defined by the Branisko ridge, which blocks the way to Prešov, and through which the new motorway is currently being tunnelled. Even if you're not planning on going any further east, you should at least go as far as Spišské Podhradie for arguably the most spectacular sight in the whole country.

En route, you might spot the palatial neo-Baroque chateau at **Spišský Hrhov** peeping through its half-tamed grounds (only the latter are open to the public as the chateau is now an orphanage). There's no point in stopping off, at least until just past the village of Klčov, at which point you get your first glimpse of the **Spišský hrad** (daily: April & Oct 9am–5pm; May–Sept 9am–6pm), its chalk-white ruins strung out on a bleak, green hill in the distance – an irresistibly photogenic shot, and one that finds its way into almost every tourist brochure in the country. As a supremely strategic spot, the place was occupied from Neolithic times onwards, but the majority of what you see now dates from the thirteenth to the fifteenth century, when it served as the seat of the lords of Spiš; burnt to the ground in 1781, it has been ruined ever since. It's difficult to resist the impulse to get nearer but the ruins are less impressive from close up; the view from the top is undeniably good, however. If you do wish to wander round the castle, stay on the bus until **SPIŠSKÉ PODHRADIE** (literally "below the castle") and then follow the signs to the hrad; Spišské Podhradie also has a **train station**, linked to Spišské Vlachy by a small branch line. For **accommodation**, the *Penzión Podzámok* at Podzámková 28 (T & F 053/454 1755; ❷) has rooms and a garden with superb views up to the castle and can organize horseriding. If you've time to spare, and energy to expend, take the path from Spišský hrad towards Dreveník, the limestone hill 2km southeast of the ruins, and continue another kilometre as far as the village of **ŽEHRA**. The lure here is the perky thirteenth-century church of **sv Duch**, which sports a delicately balanced shingled onion dome and matching white perimeter walls. Inside this compact little church are faded frescoes painted around 1400, and a wonderful set of richly decorative black-and-gold early Baroque altarpieces.

Spišská Kapitula

One kilometre west of Spišské Podhradie, and more rewarding than a wander round Spišský hrad, is the walled, one-street city of **SPIŠSKÁ KAPITULA** (Zipser Kapitel), once the ecclesiastical capital of the Spiš region, whose plain monastic towers are often featured in the foreground of the aforementioned photographs. From the front, the **Katedrála of sv Martin** is clearly a Romanesque church, built as a defiant outpost of Christianity shortly after the Tatar invasions. To get inside, you must buy a ticket from the **tourist office** (Tues–Sat 10am–noon & 1–6pm, Sun closes 3pm) in the belfry, opposite the north door of the cathedral. The interior was originally decorated with colourful fourteenth-century frescoes celebrating the coronation of the Hungarian king Charles Robert. Here and there these have been restored after their whitewashing by Protestants during the Reformation. The furnishings are, for the most part, neo-Gothic, but there is one altarpiece worth noting in the Zápoľský chapel south of the main nave, where a fifteenth-century depiction of the Virgin Mary clearly shows the influence of Pavol of Levoča's workshop. Outside, a couple of graceful cypress trees stand at the top of the town's single street, which is lined with canons' houses, all of which are currently being restored since the re-establishment of the local Catholic seminary, where the likes of Andrej Hlinka once studied.

The Slovenský raj

After the upfront post-glacial splendour of the High Tatras, the low-key pine forests of the **Slovenský raj** (pronounced "rye" – meaning "paradise", W www.slovenskyraj.sk), 20km or so to the southeast of Poprad, might seem more than a little anticlimactic at first glance. No hard-slog hiking or top-of-the-world views here, but, if your inclination is towards more frivolous out-door pursuits, such as scrambling up rocky gorges and clinging onto chains and ladders beside shooting waterfalls, then the Slovenský raj may not be far from nirvana after all.

Covered in a thick coat of pine forest, the terrain – covering just twenty square kilometres – is typically karstic, with gentle limestone hills whittled away in places to form deep, hairline ravines and providing a dank, almost tropical escape from the dry summer heat of the Poprad plain. To the north, the Hornád river has made the deepest incision into the rock, forming a fast-flowing, snaking canyon flanked by towering jagged bluffs that attract some of the country's dedicated rock-climbers. The most dramatic ravines climb up to the grassy plateau of the Vel'ká pol'ana at the centre of the region. To the south, the geography becomes more conventional in the hills around Dedinky, and in winter the whole area turns into a popular ski resort.

Practicalities

It's perfectly possible to explore the area from Poprad (see p.514) by taking the **local train** to Vydrník, Letanovce or Spišské Tomášovce. However, as Poprad is not particularly conducive to lingering, it might be more pleasant to hole up at **Čingov**, where you can **stay** at the friendly, family-run *Flóra* (℡053/911 30; ❺), which also rents out bikes and will generally do anything possible to help you, or the *Čingov* (℡053/336 63; ❸). You could also use the village of Hrabušice as a base, as it sports a number of cheap private rooms; Smižany, 3km northeast of Čingov, on the edge of Spišská Nová Ves, also contains a good handful of pensions. Dedinky (see p.539) offers up a large number of private rooms, or you could even stay in Spišská Nová Ves (see p.535). If you've got a tent or caravan, the ATC Podlesok **campsite** near Hrabušice (℡053/449 02

81) is the most convenient and open May to September. The ATC Tatran at Čingov is more basic, open all year and less crowded at the height of summer (☎053/449 11 05). Both have bungalow (*chaty*) accommodation (❶–❷).

Transport from the north to the south of the region is difficult, though there are buses from Poprad; otherwise you're best approaching from the picturesque Hron valley railway from Brezno (see p.510). Better still is to rely on your own two feet if the weather's good – it's not much more than 10km cross-country from Podlesok to Dedinky, but take adequate provisions with you. **Walking** is also the only way of seeing the canyons, and it's not a bad idea to try to get hold of a detailed walking map, marking all the one-way paths, before you arrive in the area. The most exhilarating tracks are those designated one-way – a strange concept to get your head round until you've been up one – and it's important to stick to the direction indicated. However much you're walking, it's best to bring a pair of sturdy boots, preferably with a good grip and at the very least splash-proof – it's extremely wet and slippery underfoot all year round. Bear in mind, too, that if you're at all scared of heights, you might encounter a few problems with some of the deeper canyons. Note that occasionally some of the one-way paths are closed off to walkers, either for repairs or to give the ravine a rest.

Dedinky and the Dobšiná ice cave

Since the creation of the nearby reservoir, Palcmanská Masa, **DEDINKY** has become a thriving little tourist spot all year round, and with good reason. Nestling below Gačovská skala (1106m), whose spruce trees spill down to the grassy banks of the reservoir, it's the ideal recreational centre, with plenty of opportunities for swimming, rowing, cycling, hiking and, of course, visiting the great Dobšiná ice cave. There's a wide choice of private rooms and one pension, the *Pastierňa* (☎058/798 11 75; ❷), close to the reservoir. The only hotel, the simply furnished *Priehrada* (☎058/788 16 82; ❷), is by the reservoir and the Dedinky–Geravy chair-lift, and also features wooden chalets and camping facilities (mid-June to mid-Sept, ☎058/798 12 12; ❶). There are more options in Mlynky, 3km east of the lake, including the stylish *Pension Salamander* on Palcmanská Maša 293 (☎053/449 35 45, ℱ444 32 53; ❸), close to the Placmanská Maša dam, plus the Pension Šafrán in Stratená, 4km west of Dedinky (☎058/798 11 18 or 444 05 55; ❶) in the beautiful Stratenská dolina valley.

Dobšiná ice cave

The most obvious day-trip from Dedinky is the **Dobšiná ice cave** (Dobšinská ľadová jaskyňa; Tues–Sun: mid-May to late May & Sept guided tours at 9am, 11am, 12.30pm & 2pm; June–Aug guided tours hourly 9am–4pm), by far the more impressive of Slovakia's two accessible ice caves (the other is in the Low Tatras), at its best in spring or early summer although a steady 0°C year-round. Opened to the public in 1871, and the first in Europe to be electrically illuminated, in 1887, it's basically one vast underground lake frozen to a depth of over 20m and divided into two halls, the biggest of which, the *Veľká sieň*, is over 100m across. Although the ice formations are a long way from the subtleties of your average limestone cave, it rarely fails to impress by the brute force of its size and weight.

From Podlesok, it's a three-and-a-half-hour hike, mostly through the forest. From Dedinky, simply take the train two stops in the direction of Brezno, after which it's a twenty-minute walk into the hills. It's worth bearing in mind that the caves are very popular (so get there early) and very cold (so take something

With the 1:50,000 *Slovenský raj* hiking map, you can plan your own routes. If you're staying at Podlesok and follow the green markers, you immediately enter the **Suchá Belá**, one of the most exciting river beds to explore, but also one of the most accessible and therefore extremely popular at the height of the season, causing the occasional queue at crucial ladders. With so many obstacles en route, it takes nearly everyone a full two hours to stumble up this one-way ravine to the top. Similarly breathtaking stuff can be experienced up the gladed ravine of **Piecky**, which starts from 3km along the green-marked track to the Dobšinská ľadová.

Should you need a rest after the morning's exertions, head down to **Kláštorisko**, whose sunny, sloping meadow is perfect for picnicking. If you've forgotten your packed lunch, the small *reštaurácia* at the top of the field might oblige. At the bottom of the clearing is an ongoing archeological dig where local Slavs built a monastery to give thanks for their safe deliverance from the Tartar invasions of the mid-thirteenth century.

If you continue for another half an hour along the green-marked path to the Dobšinská ľadová jaskyňa past the bottom of Piecky, you come to the deepest one-way gorge of the lot, **Veľký Sokol**, another succession of wooden ladders slung over rock pools and rapids, up the side of waterfalls and riverine gulleys. From the top, you can either walk north across the Veľká poľana plateau to Kláštorisko (1hr 30min) or head west to the top of the Malý Sokol, which swings round to join the last two-way quarter of the Veľký Sokol gorge.

The third main area to head for is the **Prielom Hornádu**, a sheer-sided breach (*prielom*) in the limestone rock forced by the Hornád river and Slovakia's longest river canyon. Until recently it was impossible to enter the gorge except on ice skates in winter or by kayak in summer. Now, in keeping with the vaguely vandalistic tendencies of the nation's trekkers, steel steps have been jammed into the rocks and rope bridges slung across the river, and the whole trip takes just three and a half hours from Podlesok to Čingov. If you're doing a round trip, take the yellow-marked path on the way back, which follows the limestone ridge high above the Hornád. The views are amazing, especially from the **Tomášovský výhlad**, a stick of exposed rock some 150m above the Prielom Hornádu.

warm to put on). Should you wish to **stay over**, there's the *Hotel Ruffiny* (☎058/798 12 77; ❸), which appears to be slipping slowly into the road, plus a clutch of pensions and private rooms.

Moving on

Dedinky lies on the wonderful Červená Skala–Margecany branch line, one of the prettiest **train journeys** in Slovakia. It's a slow run if you're going all the way to Košice (2hr 30min), considerably less on the midday *Horehronec* express. If you're heading south to the Slovenský kras, you may have to walk the 9km to the unprepossessing old German mining town of Dobšiná, since there's only a couple of buses a day – if you do make it, it's a spectacular thousand-foot drop from the Palcmanská Maša. Most buses continue from Dobšiná to Rožňava, or you could take one of the seven trains a day which also cover the route.

The Slovenský kras

Like the Moravian karst region north of Brno, the **Slovenský kras** boasts some of the finest limestone caves in central Europe, the highlight of which is the Domica caves, stretching right under the border into Hungary (where they're known as the Aggtelek caves). Even now, the surrounding hills are still plundered for their ores – copper, iron and, once upon a time, gold – and the largest town in the area, Rožňava, continues to make its living from the local mines, even if the original intrepid German miners have long since gone. The towns and villages are for the most part dusty, characterless places; people are by far the dominant feature of the landscape, with large communities of Hungarians, Slovaks and Romanies living side by side.

Rožňava and around

Once the seat of a bishopric and a flourishing German mining centre, **ROŽŇAVA** (Rozsnyó) enjoys a great setting, at the meeting point of several dramatic valleys lined with rocky bluffs. Nowadays, it's a sleepy, mostly Hungarian-speaking, garrison town, though it's also an undeniably useful base when it comes to making excursions into the karst region and the nearby aristocratic haunts of Krásna Hôrka and Betliar.

The town does have a couple of redeeming features of its own: it once boasted a mint, a cathedral and an episcopal palace. Of the three, only the former **Biskupská katedrála** (now just a parish church) is worth bothering about, largely on account of its sixteenth-century altarpiece depicting the life of local miners; you'll find it just to the northwest of the expansive main square, námestie Baníkov. Also worth a look on the main square is the late-Gothic watchtower or **Strážna veža**, and the statue of the much-mourned Františka Andrássy (see p.542), with Dionysus looking on adoringly as she comforts (someone else's) children. Lastly, there's the **Banícke múzeum** (Mining Museum; Tues–Fri 9am–4pm), set in a lovely *fin-de-siècle* block, five minutes' walk along the road to Šafárikovo – it's the second museum building you want, not the first one you come to. The museum is run by a lively retired Hungarian miner who does his best to make up for the lack of information in English. Ask to see the reconstructed (and somewhat over-clean) mine shaft tucked round the back of the building (along with an iron statue of the Hungarians' hero, Kossuth), bearing the traditional, though rather ominous, inscription *Zdar Boh* (Good Luck).

All **transport** in the region has to pass through Rožňava at some point, although three train stations still seem a mite excessive. The one closest to the centre is Rožňava mesto, ten minutes' walk west along **Stítnicka**; the main one, called simply **Rožňava**, is a two-and-a-half-kilometre walk from town (bus #1, #2 or #6 from the station); the bus station is just southeast of the main square. **Accommodation** is fairly limited, though the **tourist office** (May–Oct Mon–Fri 8am–6pm, Sat 8am–2pm; Nov–April Mon–Fri 8am–4pm; ☎058/732 8101 or 732 93 55, ⓦwww.roznava.sk), at námestie Baníkov 32, can help if you get stuck. The ugly green *Hotel Kras* (☎058/732 4243, ⓔhotel.kras@nextra.sk; ❹), on the corner of Štítnicka and Šafárikova, is comfortable enough inside, though you'll do much better at the *Čierny orol* (☎058/732 8186; ❸), a lovely place at no. 17 on the main square, with all requisite mod cons. *Penzión Fan-Fan Club* (☎058/732 1246; ❷), southeast of the centre on route 50, is a good budget option, though the location, near the Avanti petrol station, is nothing to write home about. In addition to the fine **restaurant** in the *Čierny orol*, the *Átrium*, just north of the main square, does some very good Slovak dishes, or you can try the *Sabi* pizzeria on the main square.

Krásnohorské Podhradie and around

Plenty of buses run the 5km to the village of **KRÁSNOHORSKÉ PODHRADIE** (Krasznahorkaváralja), which means literally "below Krásna Hôrka castle". Dramatically situated on top of the nearby limestone col to protect the trade route between the Spiš region and Košice, the gaunt Gothic fortress of **Krásna Hôrka** (Tues–Sun: May–Oct 8am–4.30pm; Nov–April 9am–2pm) looks utterly impregnable. The original owners, the Bebeks, fell from favour when it was discovered that they had been counterfeiting money, and the castle was subsequently confiscated and handed over to the Andrássy family. Such was the wealth of the Andrássys that they were able to turn the whole place into a family museum in 1910, having a number of other places in which they actually lived. Sadly, the compulsory guided tours are overlong (1hr 20min) and of limited general appeal.

A better bet down in the western part of the village is the original Rožňava mining museum, a fabulous Secession building from 1906, which has been recently restored and turned into the **Andrássy galéria** (Tues–Sun 9am–noon & 1–4pm). The main glass-roofed hall now contains portraits of the Andrássy family, including the two buried in the mausoleum described below, plus a large, dramatic canvas by the Hungarian painter, Ferenc Paczka, depicting the death of Attila the Hun. Look out, too, for the stork's nest on one of the building's chimneys.

Within sight of both castle and village, and without doubt the most beautiful Art Nouveau building in Slovakia, is the **Andrássy Mausoleum** (Tues–Sun: May–Oct 8am–4.30pm; Nov–April 9am–2pm), east of Krásnohorské Podhradie along route 50. It was built in 1903–04 at great expense by Count Dionysus Andrássy, in memory of his wife, the celebrated Czech opera singer Františka Hablavcová, who died in 1902. Dionysus himself was disowned by the family for marrying below his station, an action which no doubt stiffened his resolve to build an even more extravagant resting place for his lover. Set in its own carefully laid-out gardens with sombre wrought-iron gates and characteristic angelic janitors, the mausoleum itself is a simple dome structure of austere classicism. Inside, though, it bursts into an almost celebratory orgy of ornamentation: Venetian gold for the cupola, coloured marble from every corner of the globe, and as the centrepiece, two white Carrara marble sarcophagi in which both Františka and Dionysus (who died not long after the building was completed) are buried.

If you're looking for a **place to stay**, ignore the rather grim motel in favour of the more upmarket *Vila Erika* at Lípová 39 (☎058/734 61 84; ❷), with bikes for hire. There's also a **campsite**, *Pod hradom* (June–Aug), to the north of the village en route to the castle.

Betliar

Though owned by the same aristocratic family, the frivolous hunting chateau at **BETLIAR**, 5km northwest of Rožňava by train, couldn't be further from the brooding intensity of Krásna Hôrka. It was adapted as late as the 1880s in an "indefinite style", as the local tourist brochures put it, to accommodate the Andrássys' popular hunting parties. The guided tour takes you past a fairly surprising array of artefacts, including some exotic arms and armour from the Far East, an Egyptian mummy, a giant elephant tusk, as well as the usual period furniture, dull portraits, and (naturally enough) rows of hunting trophies. If the tour wears you down, though, the large, well-groomed English-style park easily makes up for it, with its playful, folksy rotundas, Japanese bridge, and various mock-historic edifices. If you're looking for somewhere to stay, the

Apartmán Barbierik at Pokroku 340 is worth a shot (☎058/798 31 09; ❷), providing private accommodation in and around Betliar.

The Gombasek, Domica and Ochtina caves

The majority of the cave systems in the Slovenský kras lie within 30km to the south and west of Rožňava, though without your own transport it's difficult to explore them in a day. As it is one of the prime tourist destinations in Slovakia, a separate pricing system has been introduced for foreigners, and it's possible that you may have to queue for the more popular caves.

Gombasecská jaskyňa

The most impressive of the cave systems, featuring on the UNESCO World Heritage list since 1995 (along with the Ochtinská, Domica and Jasovská caves), the **Gombasecská jaskyňa** (Tues–Sun: April to mid-May & mid-Sept to Oct guided tours at 9.30am, 11am, 12.30pm & 2pm; mid-May to mid-Sept tours hourly 9am–4pm) is also one of the most accessible. To reach the caves, you can catch a direct bus from Rožňava, or take the train one stop south of Rožňava to Slavec Jaskyňa station, whence it's 2km further south. There's a rudimentary **campsite** near the caves, and every June the nearby village of Gombasek (Gömbaszog) is the venue for the largest annual Hungarian folk bash in Slovakia.

The Jaskyňa Domica and Silická ľadnica

Ten kilometres due south of Gombasek, hard by the Hungarian border, are the **Jaskyňa Domica** (Tues–Sun: Feb to mid-May & mid-Sept to Dec, tours at 9am, 10.30am, 12.30pm & 2pm; mid-May to mid-Sept tours at 9am, 10.30am, 12.30pm, 2pm, 3pm & 4pm): at 22km in length, this is the longest cave system in the country. The short passage from Robert Townson (see p.544), one of the caves' earliest explorers, should give you an idea of the gushing prose they often inspire. The tours last less than an hour and include a quick boat trip on the underground river. Theoretically, it should soon be possible to continue on a longer tour over the border into Hungary, where most of the cave system lies, but so far this is possible only from the Hungarian side.

Given Domica's inaccessibility – there are around six buses a day to Plešivec (Pelsöc), 10km away, but few at weekends – perhaps the easiest and most rewarding way of getting there is to follow the yellow-marked track from Gombasek. The path climbs up onto the *planina* (see p.544) and through the oak trees via the **Silická ľadnica** cave (1hr). The cave itself is closed to the public, but its ominous entrance is impressively encrusted with ice throughout the summer, melting to a dribble by late autumn, only to be replenished when the first cold spell of November arrives. Keep following the yellow markers east for 500m or so, then hang a right when you hit the red-marked path, from where it's a two-hour trek across the pockmarked tableland to Domica.

Ochtinská aragonitová jaskyňa

Of all the cave systems, the **Ochtinská aragonitová jaskyňa** (Tues–Sun: April to mid-May & mid-Sept to Oct guided tours at 9.30am, 11am, 12.30pm & 2pm; mid-May to mid-Sept tours hourly 9am–4pm) is without doubt the thinking person's cave, set apart from the others geographically and geologically. Though by no means as spectacular in scale as the other limestone caves, it has the unique and breathtakingly beautiful feature of spiky aragonite "flowers", which form like limpets on the cave side. From Plešivec, there's an infrequent

The following is an extract from Robert Townson's Travels in Hungary, *published in 1793. Townson, a Scottish scientist, botanized his way around the old kingdom of Hungary, staying with a lot of good-humoured Calvinists on the way, and in the passage quoted below recounts a visit to the Domica caves, long before the days of safety barriers and electric lighting.*

I descended rapidly for a short distance and then I found myself in an immense cave . . . where large stalactites, as thick as my body, hung pendant from the roof, and I was shown others where the sides were ornamented in the manner of the most curious Gothic workmanship. In some the stalactites were so thick and close together that we were in danger of losing one another if we separated but a few yards. Here aged stalactites, overloaded with their own weight, had fallen down and lay prostrate; and there an embryo stalactite was just shooting into existence.

After I had wandered about for three or four hours in this awful gloom and had reached the end of the caverns in one direction, I thought it time to come out, and I desired my guide to return. After we returned, as we thought, some way, we found no passage further; yet the guide was sure he was right. I thought I recognized the same rocks we had just left, and which had prevented our proceeding further, but the guide was positive he was in a right direction. Luckily for us I had written my name on the soft clay of the bottom of the cave, which had been the extent of our journey; on seeing this the guide was thunderstruck, and ran this way and that way and knew not where he was, nor what to do. I desired him not to be frightened, but to go calmly to work to extricate us from this labyrinth . . .

After wandering about till all our wood was nearly exhausted, we found a great stalactite from which, on account of its remarkable whiteness, I had been induced to knock off a specimen as I came by: I recollected how I stood when I struck it: this at once set us right, and after walking a little further we made ourselves heard to the other guide, from whom we got fresh torches, and we continued our route homewards without further difficulty.

So complete a labyrinth as these caverns are in some places, is not I am sure to be found in similar caverns: large open passages proved cul de sacs, whilst our road was over and under, through and amongst grotto work of the most intricate nature. I finally believe that though a man should have lights and food enough to last him a month – he would not be able to find his way out.

---

train service to Ochtiná (35min), after which the cave is a three-kilometre walk uphill southwest along the blue-marked path; from Rožňava, there are even more infrequent buses (40min). If you're travelling by car, you can reach the cave most easily from the turn-off to Hrádok on route 526 from Štítnik to Jelšava.

Zádielska dolina and the caves at Jasov

One of the more bizarre karstic features of the Slovenský kras is the forested sheets of **planina** or tableland which rise above the plains like the coastal cliffs of a lost sea. In fact, the opposite is the case, the rivers having whittled down what would otherwise be a featureless limestone plateau. Mostly, these erosions form broad sweeping valleys, but in a few cases cracks appear in the more familiar form of riverine crevices.

The most dramatic of these is the **Zádielska dolina**, a brief but breathtaking three or four kilometres of sky-scraping canyon. To get there, take the train or bus to Dvorníky, 25km east of Rožňava and 1km south of the Hungarian-speaking village Zádiel (Szádelö), at the entrance to the dolina. There's none of the Slovenský raj assault course on this hike, just a gentle yet magnificent stroll between the two bluffs. For something slightly more death-defying, return along the blue-marked track, which ascends the right-hand ridge and shadows the canyon back to Zádiel, then drops down 2.5km east of Dvorníky near the cement works of Turnianske Podhradie. For a longer hike (15km) you could follow the blue-marked path over the hills to Jasov, or take the green- then red-marked track to Pipitka (1225m), 10km away, returning to Rožňava by bus from the Úhornianske sedlo down below.

Jasov

The Premonstratensian monastery at **JASOV** (Jászó) is visible across the fields long before you reach the town. It's actually much older than its eighteenth-century Baroque appearance would suggest. The monastery church contains some superb, recently restored frescoes by the Austrian painter J.L. Kracker, who also embellished the ceiling of the library, to which you may be able to gain access. The formal gardens behind the monastery are also worth exploring. The chief reason most locals visit Jasov, though, is to see the **Jasovská jaskyňa** (Tues–Sun: April to mid-May & mid-Sept to Oct guided tours at 9.30am, 11am, 12.30pm & 2pm; mid-May to mid-Sept tours hourly 9am–4pm), the least-hyped caves in the karst region, which specialize in forests of "virgin stalactites" and contain some amazing graffiti scrawled on the walls by fugitive Czech Hussites in 1452. The only accommodation is the village's lively **campsite** (open all year), which also rents out *chaty*, but if you're coming from Košice, Jasov can easily enough be done as a day-trip. If you're in need of sustenance, be sure to pay a visit to the cellars of the *Zámocká pivnica*, opposite the monastery, which serves wonderful local beer and wine and hearty food.

Carpatho-Ruthenia

Carpatho-Ruthenia★ is one of those places where people hail from rather than go to. Infamous media mogul Robert Maxwell and the parents of Andy Warhol were just a few of the million or so inhabitants who left the northeastern corner of what was then the Austro-Hungarian Empire (and later Czechoslovakia) in the late nineteenth and early twentieth centuries to seek fame and fortune elsewhere, mostly in North America.

They left to escape not so much the region's unerring provinciality, but its grinding poverty and unemployment, only quite recently abated. Even in the 1950s, an estimated 41 percent of Rusyn villages were still without electricity, and by 1968 their living standards were less than half the national average. Today, the villages are still visibly poorer and more isolated than their western counterparts – until recently, few visitors had passed through since the Russians in 1945 (and again in 1968). Some things have changed, though not always for the best: parts of the region took a hammering in the last war, and wooden buildings, once the norm, have gradually been replaced by concrete and brick; traditional costumes are now worn almost exclusively by the over-seventies; and the heavy industry, which was crudely implanted here by the Communists to try to stem the continuing emigration, is now struggling to survive.

---

*Carpatho-Ruthenia or Sub-Carpatho-Ruthenia (Podkarpatská Rus in Slovak) was the name for the easternmost province of Czechoslovakia taken as war booty by the Soviet Union in 1945. Here, the term is used loosely to refer to the East Slovak districts on the border with Poland and Ukraine, where the Rusyn minority still predominate.

From a visitor's point of view, **Prešov** and **Bardejov** are both easy to reach and immediately appealing. Further afield, transport becomes a real problem (as it is for the local inhabitants), the north–south axis of the valleys in particular hindering the generally eastbound traveller. Accommodation also peters out and declines in quality the deeper you go, so unless you have a car, you'll want to book rooms in advance. Nevertheless, it's worth persevering, if only to visit the region's most unusual sight, the Andy Warhol Museum in **Medzilaborce**.

Prešov

PREŠOV (Eperjes) has a long and chequered ethnic history. Situated on a major north–south trade route, it was a Hungarian Royal Free Town from medieval times, and one, like Levoča, where Saxons were encouraged to settle. Nowadays, with few Germans and Hungarians remaining, it serves as the capital of the Slovak Šariš region and the cultural centre of the outlying Rusyn community. With a population approaching 100,000, Prešov is a large, and – for the most part – unattractive town. However, in the centre, there are glimpses of the town's past prosperity in those buildings that survived the 1887 fire. The old town, in particular, has been treated to a wonderful facelift, and although there's not much of interest beyond its main square, Prešov is a refreshingly youthful and vibrant university town worth at least a half day's halt.

The Town

The lozenge-shaped main square, **Hlavná ulica**, is flanked by creamy, pastel-coloured, almost edible eighteenth-century facades, some topped by exceptionally appealing and varied gables and pediments, others, as at no. 22, embellished with frolicking cherubs, angels and even monkeys. Prešov's Catholic and Protestant churches vie with each other at the widest point of the square. Naturally enough, the fourteenth-century Roman Catholic church of **sv Mikuláš** has the edge, not least for its Gothic vaulting, its modern Moravian stained-glass windows and its highly theatrical Baroque altarpiece, flanked by barley-sugar columns and complete with matching pulpit and side altars.

Behind sv Mikuláš, the much plainer **Evnjelický chrám** (Lutheran Church), built in the mid-seventeenth century, bears witness to the strength of religious reformism in the outer reaches of Hungary at a time when the rest of the Habsburgs' lands were suffering the full force of the Counter-Reformation. In the 1670s, the tide turned, and a wave of religious persecution followed, culminating in the "1687 Blood Tribunal" in which 24 leading Lutherans were publicly hanged in Prešov's main square. The prime mover behind the trial was **Count Caraffa**, the papal nuncio in Vienna, whose moustached figure, flanked by a hooded executioner, stands above the grim memorial (in Hungarian) on the corner of the Protestant Lycée, next door to the church.

To the south is Prešov's **radnica**, from whose unsuitably small balcony the Czechoslovak Republic was declared in October 1918. Eight months later, Béla Kun's Hungarian Red Army declared the Slovak Socialist Republic, which lasted a mere three weeks. Searching for a socialist tradition that never really existed in this part of the country, the Slovak Communists made much of this brief episode in Prešov's history. In fact, it used to be the main subject of the town's Šarišské múzeum, situated in the splendid dogtooth-gabled **Rákócziho dom** at no. 86 (Tues–Fri 9am–5pm, Sat 9am–1pm, Sun 1–5pm). There's still plenty of material on that chaotic period, as well as the usual stuffed birds and animals, and a room on the early twentieth-century Slovak composer, Mikuláš Moyzes.

Train & Bus Stations (1 km)

In front of the town hall is a small garden, centred around a turn-of-the-twentieth-century Neptune fountain featuring a foursome of frog, fish, crocodile and tortoise, somewhat unusually commemorating the arrival of the first Jews to Prešov in 1780. Further along on the west side of the square, the **Šarišská galéria** (Tues, Wed & Fri 9am–5pm, Thurs 9am–6pm, Sat 9am–1pm, Sun 2–6pm) puts on temporary exhibitions of Slovak art on the ground floor and in the atmospheric cellar. Finally, at the square's southern tip, is the splendid **Grécko-katolícka katedrála**, its exterior decorated with delicate Rococo stuccowork. Inside, the cathedral is filled with Orthodox furnishings, including a fabulously huge iconostasis, topped by some wonderful gilded filigree work. For the first time since the imprisonment of Pavel Gojdič (see box on p.548), the cathedral and the bishop's palace next door actually have an extant Greek-Catholic bishop and are enjoying a cultural renaissance.

Prešov may appear to be little more than the sum of its main square, but there are a couple of points of interest hidden away in the quiet backstreets. On the east side, the old town has preserved some of its ancient walls, along which you can walk, while in the northwest corner, the town's disused **synagogue** has recently been restored, and a memorial to the region's prewar Jewish community of over 6000 placed outside. The flamboyant turn-of-the-twentieth-century

The **Rusyns** or Ruthenians are one of the lost peoples of central Europe. Even their name is the subject of debate, since *Rusyn* is often taken to mean Little Russian or Ukrainian, though in the Hungarian kingdom it simply referred to any non-Roman Catholic Slavs. As to their political history, the picture is equally confusing. Their language is considered by scholars to be a western Lemko dialect of Ukrainian, but their homeland actually never was part of Ukraine, and the mountains in which they had settled soon became a permanent political barrier, dividing their territory between Hungary and Poland.

Meanwhile, the Rusyns' great cultural institution, the Orthodox Church, underwent a series of crises and schisms which resulted in the Act of Union of 1596; this established the Uniate Church as part of the Roman Catholic Church, and after 1772 it became known as the Byzantine-Catholic or **Greek-Catholic Church**. This unique religion, tied to Rome but with all the trappings of Eastern Orthodoxy, became (and still is) the carrier of the Rusyn national identity. In every other way – dress codes, mores and folklore – they were hardly distinguishable from their Magyar and Slovak neighbours. Throughout this period, they remained, as they still do to a great extent, hill-dwelling peasants with no political or economic influence.

The first national leaders to emerge in the nineteenth century were, predictably enough, Greek-Catholic priests, and – like many Slovaks at the time – fiercely Russophile and pro-tsar. They played little part in the downfall of the Habsburg Empire, and when Ruthenia became a province of the new Czechoslovak Republic in 1918, it was largely due to the campaigning efforts of a handful of well-connected Ruthenian immigrants in the USA. The Slovaks laid claim to most of the land west of the River Uh (Uzh in Ukrainian), an area containing around 100,000 Rusyns; the actual province of Ruthenia, to the east, which contained not only 370,000 Rusyns but large numbers of Hungarians, Jews, Romanies and even Romanians, was annexed by the Soviet Union following "liberation" in 1945, when the area around the River Uh became a permanent border.

Orthodox synagogue, which faces onto Baštova, but which you must approach from Okružná, now houses an **Expozícia Judaík** (Tues & Wed 11am–4pm, Thurs 3–6pm, Fri 10am–1pm, Sun 1–5pm), with an exhibition in the women's gallery explaining Jewish religious practices (captions are in English and Slovak). Finally, in a passage off the main square near the radnica is the **Múzeum vín** (Mon–Fri 8am–7pm, Sat 8am–noon), more a vast underground wine shop than a museum, though the proprietors do lead informative tours of the contents for visitors. Most of the stuff is Slovak, but you can also learn about (and buy) anything from French to Ukrainian tipple as well.

Practicalities

The **bus** and **train stations** are situated opposite one another about 1km south of the main square, and connected by trolleybus (take any one which stops at Na Hlavnej). There's a **tourist office** (Mon–Fri 10am–6pm, Sat 9am–1pm; ☎051/773 1113) at Hlavná 67, very near to the radnica. Prešov's best **hotels** are the *Senátor* (☎051/773 1186; ❺), a newly done-up place above the tourist office with small self-catering apartments, or the nicely refurbished Communist-era *Dukla*, south of the main square (☎051/772 2741; ❺). There are a few smaller **pensions** in the streets west of the square, such as the *Átrium* (☎051/773 3025; ❹), at Floriánova 4, while the cheapest option in town is the *Sen* **hostel**, Vajanského 65 (☎051/773 3170; ❶).

On the surface, the Rusyns who remained in Czechoslovakia were treated better than any other minority since the war. Scratch this surface, however, and things begin to look much less rosy. Given a free choice (as they were between the wars and before 1948), the Rusyns tended to opt for either the local dialect or Russian as the language of instruction in their schools. After the 1948 coup, however, the Communist regime intervened and ruled that the term *Rusyn* was "an anti-progressive label" – all Rusyns became officially known as Ukrainians, and the language of instruction in Rusyn schools was changed to literary Ukrainian. The reaction of the Rusyns to the resulting pedagogical chaos was to opt for Slovak rather than Ukrainian schools. Secondly, collectivization, which disrupted all peasant communities in Eastern Europe, encouraged urbanization (and therefore Slovak assimilation). Lastly, and perhaps most cruelly of all, following the example of the Stalinist authorities, the Greek-Catholic Church was forcibly amalgamated into the Orthodox Church. Its priests and dissenting laity were, for the most part, rounded up and thrown in prison, including the Church's one and only Slovak bishop, **Pavel Gojdič**, who received a life sentence and died in Leopoldov prison in 1960.

Hardly surprising then that in the last three censuses, fewer than 40,000 declared themselves as Rusyn. No one knows the real numbers, but it's estimated that as many as 130,000 Rusyns still live in East Slovakia. Since the Velvet Revolution things have begun to look up. The Greek-Catholics (who include large numbers of Slovaks) have managed to get back much of the property handed over in the 1950s to the Orthodox community (reckoned to be as few as 30,000). Meanwhile, **Ján Hirka** was ordained as Prešov's Greek-Catholic bishop in 1990, and the martyr Pavel Gojdič was beatified. In 1991, the first World Congress of Rusyns was held in Medzilaborce; in 1995, literary Rusyn was officially codified and proclaimed before government, state and academic officials in Bratislava; and in 1997, a second Greek-Catholic bishopric was established in Košice.

Away from the big hotels, **eating** possibilities are improving. If it's lunch you're looking for, a freshly baked Slovak baguette from *Bagetéria*, on the main square at no. 36, is probably your best bet; for coffee and cakes, Habsburg-style, head for the *Victoria*, on the corner of Svätoplukova, with its high ceiling and chandeliers. A few restaurants spill out onto the square in summer, including the *Melódia* at no. 61, which has a satisfyingly long menu that doesn't overlook the needs of vegetarians. For more traditional fare, the *Slovenská reštaurácia* (closed Sun), at no. 11, is pleasant and unpretentious, and the basement *U richtára*, nearby at no. 71, is also appealing. Also worth checking out are *Caffeteria Solárium*, a stylish café on ulica Ku Kumštu, and its neighbouring pizzeria *La Cucaracha*.

Prešov prides itself on its cultural traditions, with two large-scale **theatres** in town, and an annual *Hudobná jar* (Musical Spring), a cultural feast that takes place in April and May. The mainstream Divadlo Jonáša Záborského (DJZ) is south of the main square, while the more famous Divadlo Alexandra Duchnoviča (DAD), is based in a theatre on Jarková, west off the square, and is home to the renowned PUĽS Dukla Folk Ensemble (Ⓦ www.lemko.org); though a Rusyn/Ukrainian theatre, plays are generally performed in Rusyn. It's also worth checking out what's on at the Čierny orol **concert hall**, down the passage beside the *Savoy*.

Bardejov and around

Over 40km north of Prešov, not far from the Polish border, **BARDEJOV** (Bartfeld) was built by Saxon weavers who colonized the area in the twelfth century. Today, it is an almost perfectly preserved walled medieval town, comfortably positioned on its own rock with the obligatory sprawl of postwar development below. However, while the buildings remain remarkably intact, the population of the town has changed immeasurably since World War II. Bardejov's Jewish community (over 50 percent of the town's total population) was devastated in the Holocaust, and the rest of its German-speaking population were kicked out after the war. Nowadays, like Prešov, Bardejov acts as a commercial and administrative centre for the outlying Rusyn villages, most obviously during the Saturday morning market.

The Town

The **staré mesto** (a 5min walk southwest of the bus and train stations) remains remarkably unchanged since its Saxon days, retaining most of its Gothic fortifications, including four of the original bastions along the eastern wall. The pristine cobbled main square, **Radničné námestie**, with its characteristic triangular gables (many of which are still faced with wooden slats), is straight out of the German Middle Ages. Along the north side is the **Bazilika** (Mon & Thurs 9.30–5pm, Tues, Wed & Fri 9am–5pm, Sat 10am–3pm, Sun 11.30am–2pm), a suitably vast Gothic church thanks to the burghers' wealth at the time. The interior is stuffed full of fifteenth-century carved wooden side altars – eleven in all – though only two sculptures and one painting survive from the original main altar by Pavol of Levoča; the current work is neo-Gothic. The fifteenth-century stone tabernacle is also noteworthy, as are the pew ends which feature grinning half-dog, half-monkey creatures.

The sandy-coloured building in the centre of the square is the town's Renaissance **radnica**, whose eastern facade boasts a beautiful stone staircase and oriel window, and whose gables sport sculptures of strange animals and figures. No longer a town hall, the radnica now forms part of the **Šarišské múzeum** (Tues–Sun: May–Sept 8.30am–noon & 12.30–5pm; Oct–April 8am–noon & 12.30–4pm), housing a number of striking fifteenth-century wooden sculptures and epitaphs, as well as the original of the rather battered statue of Roland, a copy of which adorns the apex of the gable. The finest selection of exhibits is housed in another branch of the museum on the corner of Rhódyho, at the top end of the square (same times as above). Inside, there's an impressive collection of sixteenth- to nineteenth-century icons (many in need of serious restoration) and a fascinating series of models of the region's Greek-Catholic churches (see p.552).

A couple of blocks west of the old town is the former **Jewish quarter**, from which 3700 local Jews were rounded up and dispatched to the camps; a small plaque depicting two hands tearing through Hebrew script was erected on Mlýnská, ten minutes' walk west along Dlhý rad from the Republika, to mark the spot. There are now just two Jews in Bardejov, one of whom administers the cluster of buildings remaining along Mlýnská, which are undergoing slow restoration. The plaque itself is mounted on the walls of the former ritual baths, the domed building next door to what was the kosher butcher's, and behind them is the former eighteenth-century **synagogue**, which is currently rented out to a plumbing supply firm; they are only too happy to show visitors the building's rich ceiling decoration and its Polish-style four-pillared interior.

Map labels:

Bardejovské Kúpele ▲

KUTUZOVA UL.
TOPLIANSKA UL.
Topl'a
KÚPEL'NÁ UL.
KELLEROVA UL.
NÁBREŽNÁ UL.
PŘEROVSKÁ UL.
Bus Station
UL. 29. AUGUSTA
UL. B.S. TIMRAVY
UL. J. JESENSKÉHO
SLOVENSKÁ UL.
Stará L'ubovňa
N
UL. NOVÝ SAD
Train Station
ČESKÁ UL.
KAČVINSKÉHO UL.
KELLEROVA UL.
HURBANOVA UL.
UL. DLHÝ RAD
Mlýnská
ŠTEFÁNIKOVA UL.
UL. DLHÝ RAD
UL. DLHÝ RAD
UL. POD KALVÁRIOU
JIRÁSKOVA UL.
✝ Bazilika
IIVIEZDOSLAVOVA UL.
RADNIČNÉ NÁM.
Šarišské galéria
UL. KRÁTKY RIADOK
PARTIZÁNSKA UL.
Radnica Ⓐ
STÖCKLOVA UL.
BÁŠTOVÁ UL.
KLÁŠTORSKÁ UL.
ⓘ
UL. POD KALVÁRIOU
FRANTIŠKÁNOV
VETERNÁ UL.
KOMENSKÉHO UL.
Šarišské múzeum (príroda)
Šarišské múzeum (ikony)
UL. DLHÝ RAD
POMPIKOU
JIRÁSKOVA UL.
STANCOVÁ UL.
UL. STARÝ BLICH
UL. F. KRÁL'A

BARDEJOV

ACCOMMODATION	
Penzion Semafor	2
Rolland	3
Šport	1
RESTAURANT	
Roland	A

0   200m

▼ Prešov

Practicalities

It's possible to come here on a day-trip from Prešov, though given the added attractions of the nearby spa, Bardejovské kúpele (see below), and the proximity of several wooden churches, you might prefer to stay overnight. That said, **accommodation** is pretty limited, with the town's chief hotel, the *Republika*, still out of action. The **tourist office** (Mon–Fri 9am–4.30pm; ☎054/472 6273, ⓦwww.bardejov.sk), on the main square at no. 21, can be valuable in helping to arrange private rooms, or you might consider heading over to Bardejovské Kúpele, where there's more choice. In Bardejov, there's just *Penzión Semafor* (☎0905/830 984; ❸), an excellent family pension at Kellerova 13, or the basic, hostel-style *Šport* (☎054/472 4949; ❷), on Kutuzova ulica, on the north bank of the River Topl'a, some ten minutes' walk from the old town. Adequate **food** and beer can be had at the *U zlatej koruny* café-restaurant and snack-bar complex on the main square, but for a proper sit-down meal, your best bet is the *Roland*, a congenial wine bar in the cellar under no. 12 on the main square, which serves passable pizzas. For decent **beer**, head for the cellar pub *U smädného Mnícha* on Radyho.

The wooden churches of Carpatho-Ruthenia

In the villages around Bardejov, Svidník and Humenné, a remarkable number of **wooden churches** have survived to the present day. Many (but by no means all) are Greek-Catholic churches located within Rusyn villages, and most date from around the eighteenth century, when the influence of Baroque was beginning to make itself felt even among the carpenter architects of the Carpathians. A threesome of shingled onion domes, as at Dobroslava, is the telltale sign, though the humbler churches opt for simple barn-like roofs. Below is a list of eight of the best, though there are plenty of other superb examples out there.

To visit many of the churches *in situ*, you really need your own transport, although there's a whole cluster within easy walking distance of the main road from Svidník to the Polish border. The tourist office in Bardejov organizes trips to four of the nearest wooden churches for around 260Sk per person, or can give contact details as you'll need to get hold of a key (*kľúč*). Most custodians will charge a small entrance fee to let you in. The easiest way of having a close look, of course, is to visit one of the **skanzens** at Bardejovské kúpele, Svidník or Humenné, each of which contains a wooden church.

The dark and intimate interior of a Greek-Catholic/Orthodox church is divided into three sections (from west to east): the narthex or entrance porch, the main nave, and the naos or sanctuary. Even the smallest Greek-Catholic church boasts a rich iconostasis all but cutting off the sanctuary, with the familiar icons of (from left to right) St Nicholas, the Madonna and Child, Christ Pantocrator and, lastly, the saint to whom the church is dedicated. Above the central door of the iconostasis (through which only the priest may pass) is the Last Supper, while to the left are busy scenes from the great festivals of the church calendar – the Annunciation, the Assumption and so on. The top tier of icons features the Apostles (with St Paul taking the place of Judas). Typically, the Last Judgement covers the wall of the narthex, usually the most gruesome of all the depictions, with the damned being burned, boiled and decapitated with macabre abandon.

Dobroslava, 7km north of Svidník. A delightful pagoda-style Orthodox (formerly Greek-Catholic) church, with a wide cruciform ground plan, distinctive triplet of shingled onion domes and an amazing Bosch-style *Last Judgement*.

Hervatov, 8km southwest of Bardejov. This Roman Catholic church, erected in the 1490s, is the oldest in the country, and features some remarkable seventeenth-century murals depicting "wise and crazy virgins".

Ladomírová, 4km northeast of Svidník. Greek-Catholic church on the main road to the Dukla Pass, with an eccentric mishmash of pagodas, baubles and cupolas.

Lukov, 14km west of Bardejov. Orthodox, previously Greek-Catholic, church, which boasts a fantastic red-black, sixteenth-century, diagrammatical depiction of the *Last Judgement* on the iconostasis.

Miroľa, 12km east of Svidník. Eighteenth-century Greek-Catholic/Orthodox church, one of the most perfect examples of the triple Baroque cupolas descending in height from west to east.

Nižný Komárnik, 12km northeast of Svidník. An unusual Greek-Catholic church, built with a hint of Neoclassicism in 1938, not in the usual Lemko style, with the central cupola higher than the other two.

Tročany, 15km south of Bardejov. Eighteenth-century Greek-Catholic church with simple cupolas like candle extinguisher caps; renowned for its lurid, rustic icon of the *Last Judgement*.

Uličské Krivé, 35km northeast of Snina. Eighteenth-century Greek-Catholic church rich in seventeenth-century icon paintings, including one depicting the archangel Michael casually pulverizing Sodom and Gomorrah.

Bardejovské kúpele

Hourly buses cover the 4km north from Bardejov to the spa town of **BARDEJOVSKÉ KÚPELE** (Bad Bartfeld), once a favourite playground of the Austro-Hungarian and Russian nobility. A series of devastating fires in 1910–12 destroyed most of the spa's old wooden buildings, and nowadays, only a few surviving nineteenth-century mansions hint at its former glory. Still, there's lots of greenery and traffic-free streets, and you can sample the hot waters at the 1970s concrete **Kolonáda** (daily 6–8am, 10.30am–1pm & 4.30–6.30pm), in the centre of the spa.

The major attraction for non-patients, however, is the excellent *skanzen*, **Múzeum ľudovej architektúry** (Tues–Sun: April–Sept 9am–6pm; Oct–March 8am–3.30pm), clearly signposted on the far northwestern side of the spa, which contains a whole series of timber-framed buildings, thatched cottages and two eighteenth-century wooden Greek-Catholic churches transferred from the surrounding Rusyn villages of Mikulášová and Zboj (for more on the region's wooden churches, see opposite). Tickets for the *skanzen* also give entry to the Vila Rákoczi, which puts on interesting temporary exhibitions on the ground floor, and has permanent displays on the history of the spa and on the local folk traditions.

The spa's only other claim to fame is its seated bronze statue of the **Empress Elisabeth**, wife of the Habsburg Emperor Franz-Josef I, who was a frequent visitor to the spa until her death at the hands of an Italian anarchist in 1898. A group of Hungarian admirers erected the statue in 1903, but wisely left the empress's name off the plinth, allowing her real identity to remain hidden during the ideological vicissitudes of the last century. The statue stands in front of the *Hotel Dukla*, just east of the *skanzen*.

Accommodation choices are limited if you're not actually receiving spa treatment. The most impressive place (on the outside at least) is the *Hotel Astória* (☎054/472 4122; ❸), a yellow and salmon-pink hotel built in 1898 and situated opposite the Kolonáda – however, it's seen better days; or else there's the gargantuan *Hotel Minerál* (☎052/472 4122; ❹), a Communist-era high-rise at the southern edge of the spa, that's probably improved slightly since it was first built.

Svidník and the Dukla Pass

Twenty kilometres or so due east of Bardejov and almost completely obliterated in the heavy fighting of October 1944, **SVIDNÍK** today is, not surprisingly, a characterless concrete sprawl. However, it does contain a clutch of intriguing museums and an open-air *skanzen* of Rusyn folk architecture, and hosts a Rusyn folk festival each year in the middle of June. It's also by far the most convenient base from which to explore the wooden Greek-Catholic churches in the Rusyn villages, chiefly those near the Dukla Pass.

The town's main street is **Sovietskych hrdinov** (Soviet Heroes' Street), which heads north towards the Dukla Pass and boasts a statue of Ludvík Svoboda, leader of the Czechoslovak Army during World War II. The first turning on the right is Centrálna, a pedestrianized street, on which you'll find the **Múzeum ukrajinsko-rusínskej kultúry** (Tues–Fri 8.30am–4pm, Sat & Sun 10am–4pm), containing a fine array of Rusyn folk gear and models of various Greek-Catholic churches, as well as a beautiful collection of traditional painted Easter eggs. Ten minutes' walk further east up Centrálna past the bus station, and clearly signposted round town, is the **Galéria Dezidera Millyho**, on Partizánska (Tues–Fri 8.30am–4pm, Sat & Sun 10am–4pm), mostly given over to contemporary Rusyn artists but with a couple of retrospective rooms

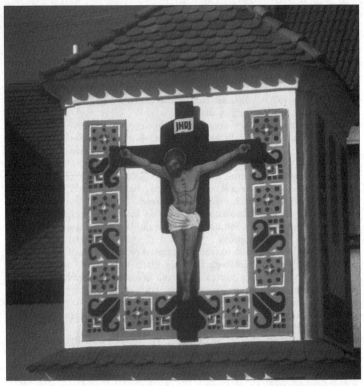

△ Roadside chapel, East Slovakia

devoted to Milly, one of the first Rusyn artists to win acclaim for his Expressionist paintings of local peasant life. The gallery also houses some weird and wonderful sixteenth- to nineteenth-century icon paintings, among the finest in East Slovakia.

Back at the town's main crossroads, and looking something like the Slovak answer to New York's Guggenheim Museum, is the **Vojenské múzeum** (Tues–Fri 8am–4pm, Sat & Sun 10am–2pm), housing a fairly standard exhibition on World War II, with plenty of military paraphernalia and a diorama of the "Valley of Death" (see "The Dukla Pass", below). If you follow the path past the military detritus behind the museum, you'll eventually reach the town's gigantic **Soviet war memorial** (Pamätník sovietskej armáde), commemorating the many thousands who fell in the fighting. It's a typically overblown affair, full of reliefs of victorious soldiers and sprinkled with quotes from Czechoslovakia's postwar Communist leader, Klement Gottwald.

Crossing the main road to Bardejov, to the south of the memorial, there are signs to Svidník's open-air folk *skanzen*, **Múzeum ukrajinskej a rusínskej dediny** (May–Sept Tues–Fri 8.30am–6pm, Sat & Sun 10am–6pm), on Festivalová. If you're not planning to visit any of the less-accessible villages, this is a great opportunity to get a close look at some thatched Rusyn cottages and a typical wooden Greek-Catholic church, transplanted from the nearby village of Nová Polianka.

Svidník really has few redeeming features, and the only decent **accommodation** is at the *Hotel Rubín* (☎054/752 4210; ❷), one of the many eyesores on Centrálna, where the rooms are at least clean, even if the service isn't up to much – if it's full, head for the **tourist office** (Mon–Fri 7.30am–3.30pm; ☎0937/16186, ⓦwww.svidnik.sk), in the local cultural building on the corner of the main crossroads, at Sovietskych hrdinov 38. Trains don't run to Svidník, but the **bus station** is ten minutes southeast of the centre along Centrálna.

The Dukla Pass

The **Dukla Pass** (Dukliansky priesmyk), a fifteen-kilometre bus trip north of Svidník, was for centuries the main mountain crossing on the trade route from the Baltic to Hungary. This location has ensured a bloody history, the worst episode occurring in the last war, when some 60,000 Soviet soldiers and 6500 Czechs and Slovaks died trying to capture the valley from the Nazis. There's a giant granite memorial to the "Dukla Heroes" at the top of the pass, 1km from the Polish border, as well as an open-air museum of underground bunkers, tussling tanks and sundry armoured vehicles, strung out along the road from Višný Komárnik, the first village to be liberated in Czechoslovakia (on Oct 6, 1944), to Krajná Poľana.

Humenné

HUMENNÉ, like Prešov and Bardejov, is another Slovak town serving as a centre for the neighbouring Rusyn villages. It is a modern and spacious place, with more charm than you'd expect from a town based on the chemical industry; the few visitors who do make it this far (mostly Slovak emigrés) head straight down the leafy main boulevard, Námestie slobody, from the train station to Humenné's one and only sight, the stately seventeenth-century **zámok** (May–Oct Tues–Fri 9am–noon & 12.30–5.30pm, Sat 9am–1pm, Sun 1–5pm), which is guarded by two female and two male lead lions. However, the local museum inside is not really worth visiting unless you need to escape from the rain. Instead, head northeast across the adjacent park to the open-air folk *skanzen* or **Múzeum ľudovej architektúry** (May–Oct Tues–Sun 10am–5pm) round the back of the chateau gardens. Set in a pretty little meadow-cum-orchard, there's a whole series of thatched cottages and farmhouses, and a characteristic eighteenth-century wooden Greek-Catholic church from Nová Sedlica; ask for the information sheet in English (*anglický text*).

To get into town from the main **bus** and **train stations**, turn right and continue along the main road, Staničná ulica, until you come to the leafy pedestrianized promenade of Námestie slobody, which leads up to the zámok. If you need to **stay**, the *Karpatia* (☎057/775 2038; ❷) is conveniently located opposite the main train station, but pretty dreadful. A better bet is the *Hotel Chemes* (☎057/776 2609, ⓦwww.chemes.sk; ❸), behind the Hummené mesto train station on Námestie slobody, which is at least newly refurbished, or the small *Penzión Albina* (☎057/775 6303; ❷), also on the main square at no. 61. For **food**, there's the inexpensive *Gastrocentrum* on the main square, or the *Zámocká vináreň*, in the chateau itself, which has a disco more or less every night.

Medzilaborce

Although actually closer to Svidník, **MEDZILABORCE** is best approached by train from Humenné, 42km to the south. The main reason for making the long journey out here is to visit the town's **Múzeum moderného umenia**

(Tues–Sun 10am–5pm; ⓦ www.warhol.sk), one of the most surreal experiences this side of the Carpathians.

The inspiration for the museum came from local Rusyn artists and relatives of **Andy Warhol**, both from the US and the area around Medzilaborce, following the death of the artist in 1987. Although Warhol was born in Pittsburgh, the steel, aluminium and glass capital of the US, his real name was Andrej Varchola and his parents hailed from the Rusyn village of Miková, 8km northwest of Medzilaborce; his father was a coal miner who, like many Rusyns, emigrated to the States shortly before World War I and was joined by the rest of the family in 1918. When fame and fortune hit in the 1960s, Warhol rarely made reference to his Slav origins, either in his work or conversation – "I come from nowhere" was his favourite enigmatic response.

Since Medzilaborce is a one-street town, it's impossible to miss the museum, a strikingly modern building, with two giant Campbell's soup cans standing guard outside the main entrance, and the modest collection of original screen prints, on loan from the Andy Warhol Foundation in New York, are displayed upstairs in the main hall – the psychedelic *Red Lenin* and *Hammer & Sickle* are particularly appropriate choices – along with biographical details and quotes from Warhol (in Slovak, Rusyn and English) and a smattering of works by Ultra Violet. In the upper gallery, there are some derivative prints by Andy's brother, Paul, and his nephew, James, followed by a room of family portraits.

In addition to the Warhol stuff, the museum hosts temporary exhibitions, ranging from work by other Pop artists to contemporary Rusyn art, and organizes various cultural events, gigs and talks throughout the year. The gallery shop sells Warhol souvenirs (including tins of Campbell's soup) as well as information on Rusyn culture and language.

Medzilaborce has two **train stations**: the main one, Medzilaborce, is 1km south of the museum; the minor one, Medzilaborce mesto, is 1km north of the museum; two trains a day continue across the border into Poland. **Accommodation** is scarce, so it might be good to book ahead from Svidník or Humenné; the only option is *Penzión Andy* (☎057/732 1640, ⓦ www.penzionandy.host.sk; ❹), a **restaurant** with newly furnished rooms above it, not far from the museum on ulica A. Warhola.

Košice

Rather like Bratislava, **KOŠICE** was, until relatively recently, a modest little town on the edge of the Hungarian plain. Then, in the 1950s, the Communists established a giant steelworks on the outskirts of the city. Fifty years on, Slovakia's second largest city has a population of over 250,000, a stunningly rejuvenated main square, a number of worthwhile museums, arguably the finest cathedral in the republic, and a lively cosmopolitanism that's reassuring after a week in the Slovak back of beyond. Just 21km north of the Hungarian border, Košice also acts as a magnet for the Hungarian community – to whom the city is known as *Kassa* – and for the terminally underemployed and neglected Romanies of the surrounding region, lending it a diversity and vibrancy absent from many provincial Slovak towns.

Arrival and accommodation

The **train** and **bus stations** are opposite each other, ten minutes' walk east of the old town, which is little more than five or six blocks across from east to

KOŠICE

- Wooden Church
- NÁM MARATÓNU MIERU
- Východoslovenské múzeum
- HVIEZDOSLAVOVA
- BAČÍKOVA
- ŠTEFÁNIKOVA
- KMEŤOVA
- KASÁRENSKÉ NÁMESTIE Ⓐ
- ZBROJNIČNÁ
- MÄSIARSKA
- MOYZESOVA
- HLAVNÁ ULICA
- Kostol františkánov
- KOVÁČSKA
- VODNÁ
- Slovenské technické múzeum
- Ⓑ BIELA
- Mestský park
- POŠTOVA
- HRADBOVÁ
- Ⓓ
- Miklušova väznica Ⓒ
- Kostol jezuitov
- UNIVERZITNÁ
- Ⓔ
- HRNČIARSKA
- Katova bašta
- Romathan
- Jakabuv palác
- Štátne divadlo
- Kostol dominikánov
- HLAVNÉ NÁMESTIE
- CYRILOMETODEJSKÁ
- Singing Fountain
- Ⓕ Urbanova veža Ⓖ
- MLYNSKÁ
- Former synagogue
- Ⓗ
- Ⓘ
- Stoličný dom
- PUŠKINOVA
- ALŽBETINA
- Dóm
- sv Micháľ
- Múzeum Vojtecha Löfflera
- Ⓙ NÁM SLOBODY
- OHLA
- MOYZESOVA
- Galéria Júliusa Jakobyho
- Entrance to Tunnels
- ZVONÁRSKA
- Ⓔ
- VRÁTNA
- HLAVNÁ ULICA
- ROOSEVELTOVA
- TIMONOVA
- Thália
- Ⓖ
- Puppet Theatre
- Dom umenia
- PRIBINOVA
- ČSA
- ⓘ
- GREŠÁKOVA
- ⓼
- RÁZUSOVA
- ŠTÚROVA
- Ⓖ 0 ——— 200 m

- ◀ ②
- ◀ ③ (1500m)
- ◀ Rožňava & ⑥ (4km)
- ▶ ①
- 10 EAST SLOVAKIA | Košice
- ▶ Train & Bus Stations (300 m)
- ▶ Prešov
- ▼ Campsite (5 km)

ACCOMMODATION

Alessandria	1
Atlantik	8
Centrum	9
Domov mládeže	3
Európa	4
Kohal	6
Krmanová	5
Penzión pri radnici	2
Slovan	7

RESTAURANTS, CAFÉS & BARS

Ajvega	I
Caravella	H
Carpano	F
Dobrá čajovna	D
Green Crow Club	A
Irish pub	E
Jazz Club	C
Kleopatra Pizza Bar	J
Sedliacky dvor	B
Slávia	G

557

west. From the stations, head across the park to the fanciful neo-Gothic **Jakabov palác** (now the British Council), on Mlynská, built with stone left over from the renovation of the city's cathedral. The city **tourist office** (Mon–Fri 9am–6pm, Sat 9am–1pm; ☎055/16186, ⓦwww.pangea.sk or www.kosice.sk) is at Hlavná ulica 2, at the southern end of the spectacular main square; another, equally useful information service is located in the Dargov department store at the base of the square (same hours). Given the compact nature of the city's old town, you shouldn't need to use the efficient **public transport** system, unless you're staying out in the suburbs. In any case, it's easy enough to use; just buy your ticket from the tourist office or machines, which is valid for trams, buses and trolleybuses, beforehand and punch it when you get on board in the little devices to hand.

Accommodation

You might want to leave it to the city tourist office to help you book your accommodation, since they can deal with anything from hotels to small pensions and **private rooms**. With one or two exceptions, the city's hotels are overpriced Communist-era places, with little to recommend them. *Domov mládeže* (☎055/643 56 88; ❶) is a year-round **hostel** on Medická, west of the centre via bus #17 or #34, or follow Poštovna to Vojenská, which becomes Ondavská, and turn left on Považská. Cheap dorm beds are also available at the *Student Hostel* (July–Aug; ☎055/633 34 37; ❶) at Podhradová 11. The nearest **campsite** (mid-April to Sept) is 5km south of the city centre and also rents out bungalows; take tram #1 or #4, or bus #22 or #52, from the *Slovan* hotel to the flyover, then get off and walk the remaining 500m west along Alejová, the road to Rožňava.

Alessandria Jiskrova 3 ☎055/622 59 03. Košice's newly modernized top hotel, with doubles going for nearly 3000Sk, but inconveniently located ten minutes' walk northeast of the old town. ❾

Atlantik Rázusova 1 ☎055/622 65 01. Small, simple, central pension that's often fully booked, so it's worth calling well in advance. ❷

Centrum Južná trieda 2a ☎055/76 31 01. A short stroll south of the old town and, from the outside, a pretty ugly high-rise. Inside, however, it's probably the best of a bad bunch. ❺

Kohal Trieda SNP 61 ☎055/642 42 40. Large, cheap place amid the concrete high-rises, with dorm-room doubles for 320Sk and a decent restaurant. Ten to fifteen minutes by tram from the centre (#6 from Šturova or #9 or #R3 from

námestie Maratónu mieru to Západ-Ferrocentrum). ❸

Krmanová Krmanová 14 ☎055/623 05 65. New pension in the old town. A good alternative if the others are full, though the decor is rather sterile. ❻

Penzión pri radnici Bacíkova 18 ☎055/622 78 24. Small pension with self-catering apartments, above a good restaurant in the backstreets of the old town, that offers, without a doubt, the most welcoming stay in the city for those with the dosh. ❾

Slovan Hlavná ul. 1 ☎055/622 73 78. There seems little point in paying the extra at this heavily tarted-up high-rise hotel, although it has access to an indoor pool, garden and tennis courts. ❾

The staré mesto

You'll find almost everything of interest on Košice's long, pedestrianized main square, which is called **Hlavná ulica** at its northern and southern extremities, **Hlavné námestie** to the north of the cathedral, and **Námestie slobody** to the south of the cathedral. The whole area has been sensitively and superbly restored in the last few years, and, lined with a handsome parade of Baroque and Neoclassical palaces, it's really looking like the city's showpiece square nowadays, a favourite place for the local version of the evening *passeggiata*. Much of the credit for the square's wonderful revival is given to Rudolf

Schuster, Košice's mayor until 1999, when he was elected president of Slovakia. Schuster put heavy emphasis on the idea that a physically attractive city is the keystone of urban renewal, and he mobilized his finances to assure that one of the republic's most beautiful old towns would remain as such.

At the centre, dominating the scene, is the city's unorthodox – and Europe's easternmost – Gothic **Dóm**, whose charcoal-coloured stone has been sand-blasted back to its original honeyed hue. Begun around 1390, the cathedral was paid for by the riches of the salt trade, which reached their peak in the following century. It's dedicated to St Elizabeth (sv Alžbeta), patron saint of the cathedral, despite the fact that the city had a long and bitter row with her father, Charles of Anjou, over its monopoly of the salt trade. From the outside, it's an unusual, slightly misshapen building, with striped roof tiles like those of Vienna's Stephansdom, and a great gilded copper cupola that sits like a helmet on the main clock tower. Inside, the stellar vaulting and Gothic furnishings create quite an impression, particularly the main gilded altar which has a total of 48 panels depicting the Passion and the life of the Virgin. Also worth a closer inspection is the tall Gothic pastophory on the north side of the presbytery. One of the best features of the church is the intricate relief work above the north and west doors, their tympana respectively depicting the frantic scenes of the Last Judgement, and Christ and his sleepy disciples squeezed onto the Mount of Olives.

South of the cathedral is the similar but much smaller Gothic church of **sv Michal**, converted into a storehouse for weapons and ammunition during the sixteenth century when the threat of a Turkish invasion caused a mass exodus from the region and turned the town into little more than a military barracks. Opposite sv Michal, at no. 27 on the east side of the square, is the pale, ice-blue Baroque **Stoličný dom**, where the postwar government was declared by President Edvard Beneš on April 4, 1945, in what became known as the Košice Agreement. For the first time, the Slovaks were given equal nation status with the Czechs, but this was overshadowed by the fact that, for many, Beneš had sealed the fate of the country by handing over four key ministries to the Communists, including the Ministry of the Interior. The Communists also saw this as a turning point, and chose the house as the venue for Košice's museum of the working class; it now contains a branch of the Galéria Júliusa Jakobyho (see p.560).

Opposite the Stoličný dom is a small park in which a newly built passage leads down to a series of **tunnels** underneath the city. These tunnels were only discovered in 1996 during the installation of new utility pipes as part of the square's revitalization effort, and after archeological work had been carried out on them, they were opened to the public for half-hour tours in 1998. Used during the Middle Ages for shelter and storage, the tunnels wiggle past sections of the old city walls, moat and alongside the foundation of the cathedral. To visit, you must wait for enough people to form a group at the tourist office at Hlavná 8 (Tues–Sun 11am–6pm; free), though claustrophobes might not enjoy them as they are rather dark and narrow.

On the busy north side of the cathedral, Košice's trickle of tourists dutifully admire the fourteenth-century **Urbanova veža**, the town tower which stands on its own set of mini-arcades, lined with gravestones discovered under the building during nineteenth-century renovation. Though the tower's top gallery is no longer open, the elaborate *Zvon urban* out front is a huge bell dating from 1557, which used to ring from on high. The public park and fountains at the centre of the main square are a favourite spot for hanging out and make an appropriately graceful foil for the city's grandiose **Štátné divadlo**, designed by the Austro-Hungarian firm of theatre-builders, Helmer & Fellner, in 1899.

Close by, on the east side of the square, are two very fine facades dating from the same period: the one at no. 63 is the Art Nouveau *Café Slavia*, which features ceramic murals of storks and a large ceramic rondel on its central gable; no. 71, beyond the **Kostol jesuitov**, sports a neo-Gothic stepped gable topped by a statue of a guy doffing his cap, and has wonderful lion brackets holding up its balcony. Further up on the same side, you might want to take a closer look at the **Kostol františkánov**, whose Baroque facade is adorned with an intricate Gothic stone relief of the Crucifixion, flanked by stucco curtains and cherubs added later on for dramatic effect; the ceiling frescoes inside the church will look great once they're restored to their former glory.

The tiny **water channel** you see running down the length of the square is another Schuster-inspired project. Centuries ago the cathedral and the small parks surrounding it stood on a small island in a stream; the stream was diverted so that Hlavná ulica could be built, but today's townsfolk wanted their stream back, so a narrow stone gulley was inlaid and the water again trickles through. This is topped by an – admittedly kitsch – "singing fountain" in the middle of the square, replete with recorded music and night-time coloured lights.

Museums and galleries

Košice's most gruesome museum is the **Miklušova väznica** (Mikluš Prison; Tues–Sat 9am–5pm, Sun 9am–1pm), down Univerzitná, whose original dimly lit dungeons and claustrophobic cells graphically transport you into the house's murky history as the city prison. Tickets for the prison must be bought from the ticket office of the geological and zoological museum in the **Katova bašta** (Hangman's bastion), through the arches diagonally opposite. If you're interested in Ferenc Rákóczi II, the museum also contains a few personal belongings and a mock-up of the rebel's house. A couple of blocks south, on Puškinova, is another grim reminder of human cruelty, the city's former **synagogue**, a pink crenellated affair built in 1927, with a memorial to the 12,000 local Jews sent to the camps during World War II. Back on the main square at Hlavná 88, opposite the Kostol františkánov, the **Slovenské technické múzeum** (Tues–Fri 8am–5pm, Sat 9am–2pm, Sun noon–5pm) holds a large and eclectic selection of "technical" exhibits, from a giant pair of seventeenth-century bellows to a Braille map of Europe. The emphasis, though, is on the wrought ironwork for which the region is famous – everything from gates to lampposts and church bells.

The city's **Galéria Júliusa Jakobyho** (June–Sept Tues–Sat 11am–7pm, Sun 11am–5pm; Oct–May Tues–Sat 10am–6pm, Sun 10am–2pm) usually puts on interesting temporary exhibitions culled from its large collection of twentieth-century Slovak, Hungarian and Austrian art: it has two branches, at Alžbetina 22, and in the **Stoličný dom** on Námestie slobody. Next door to the former is the peculiar and fascinating **Múzeum Vojtecha Löfflera** (Tues–Sat 10am–6pm, Sun 1–5pm), which features the work and private collections of Košice's most prominent Communist-sanctioned sculptor. Löffler is the man we have to thank for many of the country's most conspicuous Socialist Realist monuments of the 1960s and 1970s (a few of which litter the back courtyard), though he himself preferred working on abstract, wooden sculptures. More intriguing, though, is Löffler's collection of Slovak artists' self-portraits, which spans the entire twentieth century, and a display of local ceramics and crucifixes.

At the northern tip of the main square is námestie Maratónu mieru, named after the city's annual marathon, whose winners' names are etched into the monument at the centre of the square. On either side are the two bulky late-nineteenth-century buildings that make up the **Vychodoslovenské múzeum** (Tues–Sat 9am–5pm, Sun 9am–1pm) on Hviezdoslavova 3. The museum building to the west is the one you want for its basement collection of extremely valuable fifteenth- to seventeenth-century **gold coins** – 2920 in all – minted at Kremnica, but stashed away by city burghers loyal to the Habsburgs when Imre Thököly's rebel force took Košice briefly in the 1670s. They were discovered by accident in 1935 by builders renovating no. 74 on the main square, appropriately enough the city's Finance Directorate. And just for good measure, if you haven't yet seen one, hidden round the back of the museum is a **wooden Greek-Catholic church**, brought here from Kožuchovce in Carpatho-Ruthenia.

Eating, drinking and entertainment

Košice's choice of places to **eat and drink** is underwhelming to say the least, though it has improved by leaps and bounds since 1989. The best places are mostly located in the streets to the east of the main square: *Ajvega*, Orlia 10, is a popular vegetarian place with a summer terrace, and serves soya versions of standard Slovak dishes, washed down with fresh juices. The seafood and fish restaurant *Caravella*, just up the street at Orlia 4, does an admirable job considering its distance from the ocean. *Sedliacky dvor*, at Biela 3, is a hymn to Slovak folk culture and cuisine.

Several cafés line the west side of Hlavná ulica: *Carpano*, north of the cathedral at no. 42, aspires to be Italian and offers a limited menu of salads and light fare, while *Kleopatra Pizza Bar*, south of the cathedral at no. 24, occupies one of the finest settings of all, with outdoor tables overlooking a small park. The ubiquitous *Irish pub* buzzes at Hlavná 92, and the *Green Crow Club* in a one-time nuclear shelter at Kasárenské námestie offers jazz along with the booze. Sadly, the atmosphere at the city's most attractive **café**, the Art Nouveau *Slávia* at Hlavná 65, is too snooty to be relaxing, but the soothing *Dobrá čajovna*, Mäsiarská 42, does the job admirably and serves a wide variety of teas.

As for **nightlife**, mainstream culture still predominates, particularly during the *Hudobná jar* (Musical Spring) festival in May. Full-scale **operas**, **ballets** and **plays** go on all year round at the wonderfully ornate Státna divadlo (also known as the Divadlo Janka Borodáča) at Hlavná 58. Košice's philharmonic orchestra plays regular **concerts** at the Dom umenia on Grešákova and occasionally inside the cathedral itself. Košice has a **Hungarian theatre**, Thália, on Mojmírova, and also boasts Slovakia's one and only **Romany theatre**, Romathan (Štefánikova 4), which puts on a whole range of events from concerts to plays. You can catch **live jazz** most nights at the city's smoky *Jazz Club*, Kováčska 39 (daily 5pm–2am), and the occasional **folk gig** takes place at *Klub M*, Moldavská 37. The city's **nightclubs** are mostly worth avoiding, though if you're really keen to disco, head for the tacky *Jumbo Centrum*, on Masarykova, to the east of námestie Maratónu mieru, or you can club hop through the short string of places near *Kleopatra Pizza Bar* on Hlavná, south of the cathedral. To find out what's on at any of the above venues, and on the city's cinema screens, get hold of the free **listings booklet** *Kultúrny informátor* from the tourist office.

East to Michalovce and the Vihorlat

One of the most unusual sights in East Slovakia is the spectacular **Herľany geyser**, 22km northeast of Košice in the foothills of the Slanské vrchy, which shoots a jet of tepid water over thirty metres into the air for about twenty minutes or so every 32 to 34 hours. To get there, turn off route 50, up route 576 at Bidovce; Košice's tourist office will have the expected time of the next eruption, so you can plan your arrival to coincide with the geyser. East of Bidovce, route 50 winds its way over the **Dargov Pass** (Dargovský priesmyk), which cuts the low-lying north–south ridge of the Slanské vrchy in two – that is, until the motorway supersedes it. The pass is gentle enough to the eye, but it was captured at a cost of over 22,000 Soviet soldiers in World War II, a fact recorded by two tanks and a vast **war memorial** at the top of the pass. Coming down from the hills, you can see the hazy **Zemplín plain** below, stretching south into Hungary's Tokaj wine region and east into Ukraine.

Michalovce

Just under 60km east of Košice, and 35km west of the Ukrainian border, **MICHALOVCE** (Ⓦwww.michalovce.sk) is the main point of arrival for people heading for the Zemplínska Šírava or Slovak Sea. Frequent buses and trains run from Košice to Michalovce, though for some train services, you may have to change at Bánovce nad Ondravou. Note, too, that the train station is a good 2km west of the town centre, whereas the bus station is just east of the main square.

Other than to change buses, there's no compelling reason to hang around in Michalovce. However, if you do find yourself with an hour to spare between departures, you could head for the **Zemplínske múzeum** (April–Oct Tues–Fri 9am–noon & 1–4pm, Sat 9am–noon, Sun 2–5pm; Nov–March Tues–Sat only), housed in the chateau behind the bus station. The elongated, pedestrianized main square, **Námestie osloboditeľov**, makes for a pleasant stroll; note the great turquoise former bank from 1911, now housing the *Bohéma* café, topped by a giant beehive and decorated with attractive stuccowork.

If you're **staying the night**, there are just two mid-range modern hotels to choose from: the *Hotel Jalta* (Ⓣ056/642 6086, Ⓦwww.jalta.sk; ❹), Námestie osloboditeľov 70, is the newcomer, and probably has the edge over the *Hotel Družba* (Ⓣ056/642 0451; ❹), by the bus station, though both are pretty comfortable. For local Zemplín **cuisine**, try *Lagúna*, a block north of the main square in the Park študentov.

Zemplínska šírava (Slovak Sea)

A large artificial lake created in the 1960s for industrial purposes, the **Zemplínska šírava** (Slovak Sea), to the east of Michalovce, is a popular summer destination for Slovaks. Brash, cheek-by-jowl *chata* colonies make up the resorts that merge into one another along the lake's northern shores; not everyone's cup of tea, to be sure, but there are compensations – it's hotter here than anywhere else in the country, with the sun continuing to shine well into October. The water is far from crystal clear, but there are plenty of opportunities for **hiking** in the hills of the Vihorlat to the north of the lake (see p.563). **VINNÉ**, the first settlement you come to from Michalovce, isn't actually on the lake shore, but has its own swimming possibilities in the much cleaner mini-lake, Vinianske jazero, a short walk northeast of town, plus there's the ruined **Viniansky hrad** above the village (1hr 30min by foot). There is also a nice **campsite** along the lake shore here with cheap bungalows – preferable to the sites along the Slovak Sea itself. The resorts along the sea are much of a concrete muchness, though the further east you go, the less crowded they get. In August, **accommodation** can be a problem unless you have a tent, although many campsites have cheap bungalows to rent. The *Šírava* (☎056/649 2556, ⓦwww.hotelsirava.sk; ④) in Kamenec is no aesthetic beauty, but it's clean and modern and has views over the sea; another option, further along the shore, is the newly built *Penzión Family* (☎056/648 2025, ⓦwww.penzionfamily.sk; ❸), with very spacious en-suite rooms above a restaurant. Of the many lakeside **campsites**, your best bet is the site just past Klokočov (mid-May to mid-Sept).

The Vihorlat

The volcanic hills of the **Vihorlat** offer some of the most rewarding **hiking** outside the main Tatra ranges, in particular the trek up to the glacial lake of **Morské oko**. The best time to come is in late September, when the beech trees turn the hills a brilliant golden brown. There are plenty of buses as far as **Remetské Hámre**, the village 7km south of (and a gentle 2hr hike from) the lake. In July and August, a daily bus from Michalovce should take you right to the car park just below Morské oko. Unfortunately, it's not possible to swim in the lake since the whole area has been declared a nature reserve, but you can picnic wherever you please.

Alternatively, it's an hour or so from the shores of the lake to **Sninský kameň** (1005m), a slab of sheer rock rising up above the tree line and accessible only by ladder. The view from the top is outstanding – the blue-green splodge of Morské oko, the Slovak Sea and Zemplín plain beyond are all clearly visible, and on a good day you can see over into Ukraine, just 15km to the east. If you'd prefer not to backtrack, it's less than an hour's walk north to the village of Zemplínske Hámre, from where it's a further 5km to Belá nad Cirochou (a short train ride from Humenné).

Into Ukraine

The main **road crossing** between Slovakia and Ukraine is the 24-hour one at Vyšné Nemecké, 35km east of Michalovce; the 24-hour border crossing at Ubľa, 30km or so to the north, is for Slovaks and Ukrainians only. The **rail crossing** is at Čierna nad Tisou, whose railway siding was the scene of the last-ditch talks between the Soviets and Dubček's reformists shortly before the invasion of August 1968. You can obtain **Ukrainian visas** on the spot at border crossings for around £40/$60 in any hard currency, but be warned that stories of the **customs officials** at Uzhgorod (Užgorod) and Chop (Čop) on the Ukrainian side extorting cash or confiscating desirable items from travellers abound; delays of hours (even days) have been known, so a day-trip may prove impossible. The reason for this becomes apparent once you enter Trans-Carpathia; once an integral part of Czechoslovakia, it's now a forgotten corner of central Europe.

Travel details

Connections with Bratislava: Čierná nad Tisou (2 daily; 8hr); Humenné (2 daily; 8hr 10min); Košice (every 2hr; 6hr); Prešov (1 daily; 6hr 20min); Rožňava (2 daily; 5hr 50min).
Humenné to: Medzilaborce (10–12 daily; 40min–1hr 20min); Lupków (2 daily; 1hr 50min).
Košice to: Čierná nad Tisou (every 1–2hr; 1hr 10min–1hr 45min); Kiev (1 daily; 22hr); Kraków (2 daily; 6hr); Lučenec (3 daily; 2hr 30min); Plešivec (7–8 daily; 1hr 20min–2hr); Rožňava (8–9 daily; 1hr–1hr 40min).
Poprad to: Kežmarok (every 2hr; 25min); Košice (every 2hr; 1hr 15min); Markušovce (5 daily; 30–40min); Prešov (2 daily; 1hr 20min); Spišská Nová Ves (every 1–2hr; 20min); Stará Ľubovňa (every 2hr; 1hr 10min).
Prešov to: Bardejov (6–8 daily; 1hr 15min); Humenné (8 daily; 1hr 40min–2hr); Košice (up to 14 daily; 50min).

Košice to: Michalovce (1–2 hourly; 1hr 30min); Miskolc (1–2 daily; 2hr); Uzhgorod (8 daily; 4hr).
Levoča to: Poprad (up to 12 daily; 30–50min); Spišské Podhradie (up to 10 daily; 30min).
Poprad to: Červený Kláštor (2 daily; 1hr); Prešov (up to 10 daily; 2hr); Rožňava (2–3 daily; 2hr); Spišské Podhradie (up to 6 daily; 45min–1hr 20min).
Prešov to: Košice (every 30min; 40min–1hr); Medzilaborce (1–2 daily; 2hr 20min); Michalovce (up to 10 daily; 1hr 45min); Uzhgorod (3 daily; 4hr).
Rožňava to: Krásnohorské Podhradie (up to 1 hourly; 10min); Ochtiná (4–5 daily; 40min); Dobšiná (every 1–2hr; 45min).
Stará Ľubovňa to: Červený Kláštor (4–5 daily; 40min); Prešov (up to 14 daily; 2hr); Bardejov (up to 12 daily; 1hr 20min); Svidník (1–2 daily; 1hr 45min).
Svidník to: Prešov (up to 9 daily; 1hr 40min); Dukla Pass (up to 4 daily; 35min); Bardejov (up to 10 daily; 1hr 5min); Medzilaborce (1 daily; 1hr 30min).

10

Contexts

Contexts

The historical framework..567–592

Books 593–601

The historical framework

Czechoslovakia had been in existence for a mere 74 years when it officially split on January 1, 1993. Before that period, its constituent parts – Bohemia, Moravia and Slovakia – enjoyed quite separate histories: the first two under the sway of their German and Austrian neighbours, and Slovakia under the Hungarian crown. Only in the early days of Slav history were all three loosely linked together as the Great Moravian Empire; later, Bohemia consistently played a pivotal role in European history, prompting the famous pronouncement (attributed to Bismarck) that "he who holds Bohemia holds mid-Europe".

Beginnings

According to Roman records, the area now covered by the Czech and Slovak republics was inhabited as early as 500 BC by **Celtic tribes**: the Boii, who settled in Bohemia (which bears their name), and the Cotini, who inhabited Moravia and parts of Slovakia. Very little is known about either tribe except that around 100 BC they were driven from these territories by two **Germanic tribes**: the Marcomanni, who occupied Bohemia, and the Quadi, who took over from the Cotini. These later seminomadic tribes proved awkward opponents for the Roman Empire, which wisely chose the River Danube as its natural eastern border.

The disintegration of the Roman Empire in the fifth century AD corresponded with a series of raids into central Europe by eastern tribes: firstly the **Huns**, who displaced the Marcomanni and Quadi, and later the **Avars**, who replaced the Huns around the sixth century, settling a vast area including the Hungarian plains and parts of what are now the Czech and Slovak republics. About the same time, the **Slav tribes** entered Europe from east of the Carpathian mountains, and appear to have been subjugated by the Avars, at the beginning at least. Their first successful rebellion seems not to have taken place until the seventh century, under the Frankish leadership of **Samo** (624–658 AD), though the kingdom he created died with him.

The Great Moravian Empire

The next written record of the Slavs in this region isn't until the eighth century, when East Frankish (Germanic) chroniclers reported that a people known as the **Moravians** had established themselves around the River Morava, a tributary of the Danube, which now forms part of the border between the Czech and Slovak republics. It was an alliance of Moravians and Franks (under Charlemagne) that finally expelled the Avars from central Europe in 796 AD, clearing the way for the establishment of the **Great Moravian Empire**, which at its peak included Slovakia, Bohemia and parts of Hungary and Poland. Its significance in terms of Czech-Slovak relations is that this was the first and last time (until the establishment of Czechoslovakia, for which it served as a useful precedent) that Czechs and Slovaks were united under one ruler (though both sides argue over whether the empire was more Czech or Slovak in character).

The first attested ruler of the empire, **Mojmír** (836–846 AD), found himself at the political and religious crossroads of Europe, under pressure from two sides: from the west, where the Franks and Bavarians (both Germanic tribes) were jostling for position with the Roman papacy; and from the east, where the patriarch of Byzantium was keen to extend his influence across eastern Europe. The Germans pulled off the first coup, by helping to oust Mojmír and replace him with his nephew, **Rastislav** (846–870 AD). However, Rastislav proved to be nobody's puppet and, dissatisfied with the German missionaries, he called on the Byzantine emperor to send some missionaries who knew the Slav language. SS **Cyril and Methodius** were sent and given the job of making a written language and introducing Christianity, using the Slav liturgy and Eastern rites. Rastislav, in turn, was captured and blinded by his nephew, **Svätopluk** (871–894 AD), again in cahoots with the Germans. Eventually, however, Svätopluk also managed to shake free of the Germans, defeating them at the Battle of Devín in 873. During Svätopluk's reign of nearly a quarter of a century, the empire reached its greatest extension.

Svätopluk died shortly before the **Magyar invasion** of 896, an event that heralded the end of the Great Moravian Empire and a significant break in Czech and Slovak history. The Slavs to the west of the River Morava (ie the Czechs) swore allegiance to the Frankish emperor, Arnulf; while those to the east (ie the Slovaks) found themselves under the yoke of the Magyars. This separation, which continued for the next millennium, is one of the major factors behind the distinct social, cultural and political differences between Czechs and Slovaks, which culminated in the separation of the two nations in 1993.

The Přemyslid dynasty

There is evidence that Bohemian dukes were forced in 806 to pay a yearly tribute of 500 pieces of silver and 120 oxen to the Carolingian Empire (a precedent the Nazis were keen to exploit as proof of German hegemony over Bohemia). These early Bohemian dukes "lived like animals, brutal and without knowledge", according to one chronicler. All that was to change when the earliest recorded Přemyslid duke, **Bořivoj** (852/53–888/89 AD) appeared on the scene. The first Christian ruler of Prague, Bořivoj was baptized in the ninth century, along with his wife Ludmilla, by the Byzantine missionaries Cyril and Methodius (see above). Other than being the first to build a castle on Hradčany, nothing very certain is known about Bořivoj, nor about any of the other early Přemyslid rulers, although there are numerous legends, most famously that of **Prince Václav** (St Wenceslas), who was martyred by his pagan brother Boleslav the Cruel in 929 AD (see p.72).

Cut off from Byzantium by the Hungarian kingdom, Bohemia lived under the shadow of the **Holy Roman Empire** from the start. In 950, Emperor

Otto I led an expedition against Bohemia, making the kingdom officially subject to the empire and its king one of the seven electors of the emperor. In 973 AD, under Boleslav the Pious (967–999 AD), a bishopric was founded in Prague, subordinate to the archbishopric of Mainz. Thus, by the end of the first millennium, German influence was already beginning to make itself felt in Bohemian history.

The **thirteenth century** was the high point of Přemyslid rule over Bohemia. With the emperor Frederick II preoccupied with Mediterranean affairs and dynastic problems, and the Hungarians and Poles busy trying to repulse the Mongol invasions from 1220 onwards, the Přemyslids were able to assert their independence. In 1212, Otakar I (1198–1230) managed to extract a "**Golden Bull**" (formal edict) from the emperor, securing the royal title for himself and his descendants (who thereafter became kings of Bohemia).

The discovery of silver and gold mines throughout the Czech Lands and Slovakia heralded a big shift in the population from the countryside to the towns. Large-scale **German colonization** was generally encouraged by the Přemyslids in Bohemia and Moravia, and by the Hungarian Árpád dynasty in Slovakia. German miners and craftsmen founded whole towns in the interior of the country, where German civil rights were guaranteed them, for example Kutná Hora, Jihlava, Banská Bystrica and Levoča. At the same time, the territories of the Bohemian crown were increased to include not only Bohemia and Moravia, but also Silesia and Lusatia to the north (now divided between Germany and Poland).

The beginning of the fourteenth century saw a series of dynastic disputes – messy even by medieval standards – that started with the death of Václav II from consumption and excess in 1305. The following year, the murder of his heirless teenage son, Václav III, marked the **end of the Přemyslid dynasty** (he had four sisters, but female succession was not recognized in Bohemia). The nobles' first choice of successor, the Habsburg Albert I, was murdered by his own nephew, and when Albert's son, Rudolf I, died of dysentery not long afterwards, Bohemia was once more left without any heirs.

The Luxembourg dynasty

The crisis was finally solved when the Czech nobles offered the throne to **John of Luxembourg** (1310–46), who was married to Václav III's youngest sister. German by birth and educated in France, King John spent most of his reign participating in foreign wars, with Bohemia footing the bill, until his death on the field at Crécy in 1346. His son, **Charles IV** (1346–78), was wounded in the same battle but, thankfully for the Czechs, lived to tell the tale.

It was Charles who ushered in the Czech nation's **golden age**. Although born and bred in France, Charles was a Bohemian at heart (his mother was Czech and his real name was Václav); he was also extremely intelligent, speaking five languages fluently and even writing an autobiography. In 1346, he became not only king of Bohemia, but also, by election, Holy Roman emperor. Two years later he founded a university in Prague and began to promote the city as the cultural capital of central Europe, erecting rich Gothic monuments – many of which still survive – and numerous ecclesiastical institutions. As emperor, Charles issued many Golden Bull edicts that strengthened Bohemia's position, promoted Czech as the official language alongside Latin and German, and presided over a period of relative peace in central Europe, while western Europe was tearing itself apart in the Hundred Years' War.

Charles' son, **Václav IV** (1378–1419), who assumed the throne in 1378, was no match for such an inheritance. Stories that he roasted a cook alive on his own spit, shot a monk whilst hunting, and tried his own hand at lopping off people's heads with an axe, are almost certainly myths. Nevertheless, he was a legendary drinker, prone to violent outbursts, and so unpopular with the powers that be that he was imprisoned twice – once by his own nobles, and once by his brother, Sigismund. His reign was also characterized by religious divisions within the Czech Lands and Europe as a whole, beginning with the **Great Schism** (1378–1417), when rival popes held court in Rome and Avignon. This was a severe blow to Rome's centralizing power, which might otherwise have successfully rebuffed the assault on the Church that got under way in the Czech Lands towards the end of the fourteenth century.

The Czech Reformation

The attack was led by the peasant-born preacher **Jan Hus**, who gave sermons at Prague's Betlémská kaple. A follower of the English reformer John Wycliffe, Hus preached in the language of the masses (ie Czech) against the wealth, corruption and hierarchical tendencies within the Church at the time. Although a devout, mild-mannered man, he became embroiled in a dispute between the conservative clergy, led by the archbishop and backed by the pope in Rome, and the Wycliffian Czechs at the university. When the archbishop gave the order to burn the book of Wycliffe, Václav backed Hus and his followers, for political and personal reasons (Hus was, among other things, the confessor to his wife, Queen Sophie).

There can be little doubt that Václav used Hus and the Wycliffites to further his own political cause. He had been deposed as Holy Roman emperor in 1400 and, as a result, bore a grudge against the current emperor, Ruprecht of the Palatinate, and his chief backer, Pope Gregory XII in Rome. His chosen battleground was Prague's university, which was divided into four "nations" with equal voting rights: the Saxons, Poles and Bavarians, who supported Václav's enemies, and the Bohemians, who were mostly Wycliffites. In 1409 Václav issued the **Kutná Hora Decree**, which rigged the voting within the university giving the Bohemian "nation" three votes, and the rest a total of one. The other "nations", who made up the majority of the students and teachers, left Prague in protest.

Three years later the alliance between the king and the Wycliffites broke down. Widening his attacks on the Church, Hus began to preach against the sale of religious indulgences to fund the inter-papal wars, thus incurring the enmity of Václav, who received a percentage of the sales. In 1412, Hus and his followers were expelled from the university and excommunicated, and spent the next two years as itinerant preachers spreading their reformist gospel throughout Bohemia. Hus was then summoned to the **Council of Constance** to answer charges of heresy. Despite a guarantee of safe conduct from the emperor Sigismund, Hus was condemned to death and, having refused to renounce his beliefs, was burned at the stake on July 6, 1415.

Hus' martyrdom sparked off a **widespread rebellion** in Bohemia, initially uniting virtually all Bohemians – clergy and laity, peasant and noble (including many of Hus' former opponents) – against the decision of the council and, by inference, against the established Church and its conservative clergy. The Hussites immediately set about reforming Church practices, most famously by administering communion *sub utraque specie* ("in both kinds", ie bread and wine) to the laity, as opposed to the established practice of reserving the wine for the clergy.

The Hussite Wars: 1419–34

In 1419, Václav inadvertently provoked large-scale rioting by endorsing the readmission of anti-Hussite priests to their parishes. In the ensuing violence, several Catholic councillors were thrown to their death from the windows of Prague's Novoměstská radnice, in Prague's **first defenestration** (see p.113). Václav himself was so enraged (not to say terrified) by the mob that he suffered a heart attack and died, "roaring like a lion", according to a contemporary chronicler. The pope, meanwhile, declared an international crusade against the Czech heretics, under the leadership of Václav's brother and heir, the emperor Sigismund.

Already, though, cracks were appearing in the Hussite camp. The more radical reformers, who became known as the **Táborites**, after their south Bohemian base, Tábor, broadened their attacks on the Church hierarchy to include all figures of authority and privilege. Their message found a ready audience among the oppressed classes in Prague and the Bohemian countryside, who went round eagerly destroying Church property and massacring Catholics. Such actions were deeply disturbing to the Czech nobility and their supporters, who backed the more moderate Hussites – known as the **Utraquists** (from the Latin *sub utraque specie*) – whose criticisms were confined to religious matters.

For the moment, however, the common Catholic enemy prevented a serious split among the Hussites, and, under the inspirational military leadership of the Táborite **Jan Žižka**, the Hussites' (mostly peasant) army enjoyed some miraculous early victories over the numerically superior "crusaders", most notably at the Battle of Vítkov in Prague in 1420. The Bohemian Diet quickly drew up the **Four Articles of Prague**, which were essentially a compromise between the two Hussite camps, outlining the basic tenets on which all Hussites could agree, including communion "in both kinds". The Táborites, meanwhile, continued to burn, loot and pillage ecclesiastical institutions from Prague to the far reaches of Slovakia.

At the **Council of Basel** in 1433, Rome reached a compromise with the Utraquists over the Four Articles in return for ceasing hostilities. The peasant-based Táborites rightly saw the deal as a victory for the Bohemian nobility and the status quo, and vowed to continue the fight. However, the Utraquists, now in cahoots with the Catholic forces, easily defeated the remaining Táborites at the Battle of Lipany, outside Kolín, in 1434. The Táborites were forced to withdraw to the fortress town of Tábor. Poor old Sigismund, who had spent the best part of his life fighting the Hussites, died just three years later.

Compromise

Despite the agreement of the Council of Basel, the pope refused to acknowledge the Utraquist church in Bohemia. The Utraquists nevertheless consolidated their position by electing the gifted **George of Poděbrady** as first regent and then king of Bohemia (1458–71). The first and last Hussite king, George

(Jiří to the Czechs), is remembered primarily for his commitment to promoting religious tolerance and his far-sighted efforts to establish some sort of "Peace Confederation" in Europe.

On George's death, the Bohemian Estates handed the crown over to the **Polish Jagiellonian dynasty**, who ruled in absentia and effectively relinquished the reins of power to the Czech nobility. In 1526, the last of the Jagiellonians, King Louis, was decisively defeated by the Turks at the Battle of Mohács and died fleeing the battlefield, leaving no heir to the throne. The Roman Catholic Habsburg Ferdinand I (1526–64) was elected king of Bohemia – and what was left of Hungary (see below) – in order to fill the power vacuum, marking the **beginning of Habsburg rule** over what are now the Czech and Slovak republics. Ferdinand adroitly secured automatic hereditary succession over the Bohemian throne for his dynasty, in return for which he accepted the agreement laid down at the Council of Basel back in 1433. With the Turks at the gates of Vienna, he had little choice but to compromise at this stage, but in 1545, the international situation eased somewhat with the establishment of an armistice with the Turks.

In 1546, the Utraquist Bohemian nobility provocatively joined the powerful Protestant Schmalkaldic League in their (ultimately unsuccessful) war against the Holy Roman emperor Charles V. When armed conflict broke out in Bohemia, however, victory fell to Ferdinand, who took the opportunity to extend the influence of Catholicism in the Czech Lands, executing several leading Protestant nobles, persecuting the reformist Unity of Czech Brethren who had figured prominently in the rebellion, and inviting Jesuit missionaries to establish churches and seminaries in the Czech Lands.

Like Václav IV, **Emperor Rudolf II** (1576–1611), Ferdinand's eventual successor, was moody and wayward, and by the end of his reign Bohemia was once more rushing headlong into a major international confrontation. But Rudolf also shared characteristics with Václav's father, Charles, in his genuine love of the arts, and in his passion for Prague, which he re-established as the royal seat of power, in preference to Vienna, which was once more under threat from the Turks. Czechs tend to regard Rudolfine Prague as a second golden age, but as far as the Catholic Church was concerned, Rudolf's religious tolerance and indecision were a disaster. In the early 1600s, Rudolf's melancholy began to veer dangerously close to insanity, a condition he had inherited from his Spanish grandmother, Joanna the Mad. And in 1611, the heirless Rudolf was forced to abdicate by his brother **Matthias**, to save the Habsburg house from ruin. Ardently Catholic, but equally heirless, Matthias proposed his cousin **Ferdinand II** as his successor in 1617. This was the last straw for Bohemia's mostly Protestant nobility, and the following year conflict erupted again.

The Thirty Years' War: 1618–1648

On May 23, 1618, two Catholic nobles were thrown out of the windows of Prague Castle – the country's **second defenestration** (see p.68) – an event that's now taken as the official beginning of the complex religious and dynastic conflicts collectively known as the **Thirty Years' War**. Following the defenestration, the Bohemian Diet expelled the Jesuits and elected the youthful Protestant "winter king", Frederick of the Palatinate, to the throne. In the first decisive set-to of the war, the Protestants were utterly defeated at the **Battle of Bílá hora** (Battle of the White Mountain), which took place on November 8, 1620, on the outskirts of Prague. In the aftermath, 27 Protestant nobles were executed on Prague's Staroměstské náměstí, and the heads of ten of them displayed on the Charles Bridge.

It wasn't until the Protestant Saxons occupied Prague in 1632 that the heads were finally taken down and given a proper burial. The Catholics eventually drove the Saxons out, but for the last ten years of the war, Bohemia and Moravia became the main battleground between the new champions of the Protestant cause – the Swedes – and the imperial Catholic forces. In 1648, the final battle of the war was fought in Prague, when the Swedes seized Malá Strana, but failed to take Staré Město, thanks to the stubborn resistance of Prague's Jewish and newly Catholicized student populations on the Charles Bridge.

Counter-Reformation to Enlightenment

The Thirty Years' War ended with the **Peace of Westphalia**, which, for the Czechs, was as disastrous as the war itself. An estimated five-sixths of the Bohemian nobility went into exile, their properties handed over to loyal Catholic families from Austria, Spain, France and Italy. The country was devastated, towns and cities laid waste, and the total population reduced by almost two-thirds. On top of all that, the Czech Lands and Slovakia were now decisively under Catholic influence, and the full force of the **Counter-Reformation** was brought to bear on its people. All forms of Protestantism were outlawed, the education system handed over to the Jesuits and, in 1651 alone, over two hundred "witches" burned at the stake in Bohemia.

The next two centuries of Habsburg rule are known to the Czechs as the **Dark Ages**. The focus of the empire shifted back to Vienna, the Habsburgs' absolutist grip catapulted the remaining nobility into intensive Germanization, while fresh waves of German immigrants reduced Czech to a despised dialect spoken by peasants, artisans and servants. The situation was so bad that Prague and most other urban centres became practically all-German cities. By the end of the eighteenth century, the Czech language was on the verge of dying out, with government, scholarship and literature carried out exclusively in German. For the newly ensconced Germanized aristocracy, of course, the good times rolled, and the country was endowed with numerous Baroque palaces and monuments.

After a century of iron-fisted Habsburg rule, the accession of Charles VI's daughter, **Maria Theresa** (1740–80), to the throne, marked the beginning of the **Enlightenment** in the empire. The empress acknowledged the need for reform and, despite her own personal attachment to the Jesuits, followed the lead of Spain, Portugal and France in expelling the order in 1773. But it was her son, **Joseph II** (1780–90), who brought about the most radical changes to the social structure of the Habsburg lands. His 1781 Edict of Tolerance allowed a large degree of freedom of worship for the first time in over 150 years, and went a long way towards lifting the restrictions on Jews. The following year, he ordered the dissolution of the monasteries and embarked upon the abolition of serfdom. Despite all his reforms, though, Joseph was not universally popular. Catholics – by now some ninety percent of the population – viewed him with disdain. His centralization and bureaucratization placed power in the hands of the Austrian civil service, and thus helped to entrench the **Germanization** of the Czech Lands. He also offended the Czechs by breaking with tradition and not bothering to hold an official coronation ceremony in Prague.

The Slovaks under Hungarian Rule

Following the fall of the Great Moravian Empire (see p.567), the Slovaks became subjects of the Hungarian crown for the next one thousand years. For most of those centuries, modern-day Slovakia was simply known as the Feldivék or **Upper Hungary**, with the idea of Slovakia as a nation-state, or the Slovaks as a separate people, emerging only in the wake of nineteenth-century nationalism. In fact, over the centuries, the Slovaks proved themselves pretty loyal Hungarian subjects. In those days, Hungary was home to numerous minorities: Rusyns, Germans, Poles, Romanians, Jews and Romanies, as well as Slovaks. Magyar nationalism as such didn't yet exist and Latin was the language of correspondence, with a bit of Hungarian at a local level – if there was oppression, it was feudal in nature, which affected all the kingdom's peasants, whether Magyar or Slav.

Once or twice, in times of civil war, Upper Hungary became a semi-independent fiefdom, most notably under **Matúš Čák** (1271–1321), who held sway from Trenčín on the River Váh, and again under the Czech **Jan Jiskra** (1420–1466), who made his base in Zvolen. However, it was Hungary's defeat at the hands of the Turks in 1526 that had the biggest impact on Upper Hungary, with the Turks then controlling most of the Hungarian plain, with Transylvania as a loyal ally. What little remained of the Hungarian kingdom – essentially Upper Hungary – was claimed for the **Habsburgs** by Ferdinand I (1526–64).

As in the Czech Lands, Hungary was by this time mostly Protestant, but although the Hussites reached parts of Slovakia during their military campaigns, the **Reformation** didn't arrive in Slovakia until a century later. The Germans in the mining towns of central Slovakia were among the first to convert to Lutheranism, followed by the Slovaks; the Magyars tended to convert to Calvinism. However, the Habsburgs were determined to re-convert the masses and pursue the **Counter-Reformation** just as they had done in the Czech Lands. Eventually, the Jesuits were brought in to lead the campaign, founding a university in Trnava in 1635.

Things didn't go as smoothly in Upper Hungary as they had in Czech Lands, and periodically the country was caught up in religious rebellions. At the beginning of the seventeenth century, a Transylvanian nobleman of Slovak origin, **Štefan Bocskay** (1577–1606), revolted against the emperor Rudolf and succeeded in gaining religious concessions. At the outbreak of the Thirty Years' War, another Transylvanian prince, Gabor Bethlen (1580–1629) invaded Upper Hungary. Military campaigns such as these helped stave off the worst excesses of the Counter-Reformation, but they could do nothing in the face of the **Turkish invasion**. In 1663, the Turks burst into Upper Hungary, capturing towns across the south region from Nitra to Košice, forcing the Habsburgs to hand over parts of what is now southern Slovakia.

The Hungarian nobles were outraged and in 1678, the Protestant noble **Imre Thököly** (1657–1705) launched a *kurucz* (crusader) revolt. For a while Thököly had the Habsburgs on the run, and once again they made religious concessions, but when Thököly helped the Sultan besiege Vienna in 1683, he backed the wrong side, and ended his days in exile in Turkey. The last time the Slovaks, Hungarians and Rusyns united against the Habsburgs was during the 1703 *kurucz* revolt of **Ferenz Rákoczi II** (1635–1735). Ultimately, they were defeated by superior Habsburg power and the desertion of their ally, Louis XIV of France.

The Slovak national revival

In Hungary, the eighteenth-century Enlightenment boosted the **Magyar national revival**, and in 1792 Hungarian finally replaced Latin as the official state language throughout the Hungarian Kingdom. But Magyar nationalism was essentially chauvinistic, furthering the interests only of the Magyarized nobility, and the idea that non-Magyars might want to assert their own identity was regarded as highly subversive.

With a thoroughly Magyarized aristocracy, and a feudal society with virtually no Slovak middle class, the **Slovak national revival** or *národné obrodenie* was left to the tiny Slovak intelligentsia, comprising mostly Lutheran clergymen – passionately pro-Czech and anti-Magyar, but alienated from the majority of the (by now) devoutly Catholic Slovak peasantry on account of their religious beliefs. The leading Slovak figure throughout this period was **Ľudovít Štúr** (see p.452), son of a Lutheran pastor. Although a pan-Slavist, he was also, unlike many of his contemporaries, an ardent advocate of a separate Slovak language based on his own central Slovak dialect.

The Czech national revival

The Habsburgs' enlightened rule inadvertently provided the basis for the economic prosperity and social changes of the **Industrial Revolution**, which in turn fuelled the Czech national revival of the nineteenth century. The textile, glass, coal and iron industries began to grow, drawing ever more Czechs in from the countryside and swamping the hitherto mostly Germanized towns and cities. An embryonic Czech bourgeoisie emerged and, thanks to Maria Theresa's educational reforms, new educational and economic opportunities were given to the Czech lower classes.

For the first half of the century, the **Czech national revival** or *národní obrození* was confined to the new Czech intelligentsia, led by philologists like Josef Dobrovský and Josef Jungmann at Prague's Charles University or Karolinum. Language disputes (in schools, universities and public offices) remained at the forefront of Czech nationalism throughout the nineteenth century, only later developing into demands for political autonomy. The leading figure of the time was the Moravian Protestant and historian **František Palacký**, who wrote the first history of the Czech nation, rehabilitating Hus and the Czech reformists in the process. He was in many ways typical of the early Czech nationalists – pan-Slavist and virulently anti-German, but not yet entirely anti-Habsburg.

1848 and all that

The fall of the French monarchy in February 1848 prompted a crisis in the Habsburg Empire. The new bourgeoisie, of Czech-, German- and Hungarian-speakers, began to make political demands: freedom of the press, of assembly, of religious creeds and, in the nature of the empire, more rights for its constituent nationalities. In the **Czech Lands**, liberal opinion became polarized between the Czech- and German-speakers. Palacký and his followers were against the dissolution of the empire and argued instead for a kind of multinational federation. Since the empire contained a majority of Slavs, the ethnic Germans were utterly opposed to Palacký's scheme, campaigning instead for unification with Germany to secure their interests. So when Palacký was invited to the Pan-German National Assembly in Frankfurt in May, he refused to go. Instead, he convened a **Pan-Slav Congress** the following month, which met in Prague. Meanwhile, the radicals and students (on both sides) took to the streets in protest, erecting barricades and giving the forces of reaction an excuse to declare martial law. In June, the Habsburg military commander bombarded Prague; the following morning the city capitulated – the counter-revolution in the Czech Lands had begun.

In the **Hungarian Kingdom**, the 1848 revolution successfully toppled the Habsburgs, and a liberal, constitutional government was temporarily set up in Budapest. However, Hungarian liberals like Lajos Kossuth (himself from a Magyarized Slovak family) showed themselves to be more reactionary than the Habsburgs when it came to opposing the aspirations of non-Magyars. The "Demands of the Slovak Nation", drafted by Štúr, were refused point-blank by the Hungarian Diet in May 1848. Incensed by this, Štúr and his small Slovak army went over to the Habsburgs and into battle (mostly unsuccessfully) against Kossuth's revolutionaries. Only in August 1849 was Habsburg rule reinstated, thanks to the intervention of imperial Russian troops on the streets of Budapest.

In both cases, the upheavals of 1848 left the absolutist Habsburg Empire shaken but fundamentally unchanged. The one great positive achievement in 1848 was the **emancipation of the peasants** and the emancipation of the empire's **Jewish population**. Otherwise, events only served to highlight the sharp differences between German and Czech aspirations in the Czech Lands, and between Hungarian and Slovak aspirations in the Hungarian Kingdom. The Habsburg recovery was, however, short-lived. In 1859 and again in 1866, the new emperor, Francis Joseph II, suffered humiliating defeats at the hands of the Italians and Prussians respectively. In order to buy some more time, the compromise or *Ausgleich* of 1867 was drawn up, establishing the so-called **Dual Monarchy** of Austria-Hungary – two independent states united under one ruler.

Dualism: The Czech lands

The *Ausgleich* came as a bitter disappointment for the Czechs, who remained second-class citizens while the Magyars became the Austrians' equals. The Czechs' failure to bend the emperor's ear was no doubt partly due to the absence of a Czech aristocracy that could bring its social weight to bear at the Viennese court. Nevertheless, the *Ausgleich* did mark an end to the absolutism of the immediate post-1848 period, and, compared to the Hungarians, the Austrians were positively enlightened in the wide range of civil liberties they granted, culminating in universal male suffrage in 1907.

Under Dualism, the Czech **national revival** flourished – and splintered. The liberals and conservatives known as the **Old Czechs**, backed by the new Czech industrialists, advocated working within the existing legislature to achieve their aims. By 1890, though, the more radical **Young Czechs** had gained the upper hand and instigated a policy of non-co-operation with Vienna. The most famous political figure to emerge from the ranks of the Young Czechs was the Prague university professor **Tomáš Garrigue Masaryk** (see p.164), who founded his own Realist Party in 1900 and began advocating the (then rather quirky) concept of closer co-operation between the Czechs and Slovaks.

Dualism: Slovakia

For the Slovaks, the *Ausgleich* was nothing less than a catastrophe. In the 1850s and 1860s, direct rule from Vienna had kept Magyar chauvinism at bay, allowing the Slovaks to establish various cultural and educational institutions. After 1867, the Hungarian authorities embarked on a maniacal policy of **Magyarization**, which made Hungarian (and only Hungarian) compulsory in both primary and secondary schools. Large landowners were the only ones to be given the vote (a mere six percent of the total population), while the majority of non-Magyars remained peasants. Poverty and malnutrition were commonplace throughout Upper Hungary, and by 1914, twenty percent of the Slovak population had emigrated, mostly to the USA.

Given the suffocating policies of the Magyars, it's a miracle that the Slovak national revival (and even the language itself) was able to survive. The leading Slovak political force, the **Slovenská národná strana** (Slovak National Party), was driven underground, remaining small, conservative, and for the most part Lutheran, throughout the latter part of the nineteenth century. The one notable exception was the Catholic priest **Andrej Hlinka** (see p.505), whose unflinching opposition to Magyar rule earned him increasingly wide support among the Slovak people.

World War I

At the outbreak of **World War I**, the Czechs and Slovaks showed little enthusiasm for fighting alongside their old enemies, the Austrians and Hungarians, against their Slav brothers, the Russians and Serbs. As the war progressed, large numbers defected to form the **Czechoslovak Legion**, which fought on the Eastern Front against the Austrians. Masaryk travelled to the USA to curry favour for a new Czechoslovak state, while his two deputies, the Czech Edvard

Beneš and the Slovak Milan Štefánik, did the same in Britain and France.

Meanwhile, the Legion, now numbering around 100,000 men, became embroiled in the Russian revolutions of 1917 and, when the Bolsheviks made peace with Germany, found itself cut off from the homeland. The uneasy co-operation between the Reds and the Legion broke down when Trotsky demanded that they hand over their weapons before heading off on their legendary **anabasis**, or march back home, via Vladivostok. The soldiers refused and became further involved in the Civil War, for a while controlling large parts of Siberia and, most importantly, the Trans-Siberian Railway, before arriving back to a tumultuous reception in their new joint republic.

In the summer of 1918, the Allies finally recognized Masaryk's provisional government. On October 28, 1918, as the Habsburg Empire began to collapse, the first **Czechoslovak Republic** was declared in Prague. Two days later, a group of Slovaks gathered in Martin, not realizing what had taken place in Prague, but wishing to scupper any of the compromise plans put forward by the Hungarians. They issued the **Martin Declaration**, demanding self-determination and accepting in principle the union with the Czechs. Meanwhile, the German-speaking border regions of Bohemia and Moravia (later to become known as the Sudetenland) declared themselves autonomous provinces of the new republic of Deutsch-Österreich (German-Austria), which it was hoped would eventually unite with Germany itself. The new Czechoslovak government was having none of it, but it took the intervention of Czechoslovak troops before control of the border regions was wrested from the secessionists.

In Slovakia, any qualms the Slovaks may have had about accepting rule from Prague were superseded by fear of Hungarian military action. Košice (Kassa), Bratislava (Poszony) and various other Hungarian-speaking regions were only rested from Hungarian control in January 1919. Not long afterwards, Béla Kun's Hungarian Red Army reoccupied much of the country, and were only booted out by the Czechoslovak Legion in the summer of 1919. In June 1920, the **Treaty of Trianon** confirmed the controversial new Slovak-Hungarian border along the Danube, leaving some 750,000 Hungarians on Czechoslovak soil, and a correspondingly large number of Slovaks within Hungarian territory.

Last to opt in favour of the new republic was **Ruthenia** (officially known as Sub-Carpatho-Ruthenia), a rural backwater of the old Hungarian Kingdom that became officially part of Czechoslovakia in the Treaty of St Germain in September 1919. Its incorporation was largely due to the campaigning efforts of Ruthenians who had emigrated to the USA. For the new republic, the province was a strategic bonus but a huge drain on resources.

The First Republic

The new nation of Czechoslovakia began **postwar life** in an enviable economic position – tenth in the world industrial league table – having inherited seventy to eighty percent of Austria-Hungary's industry intact. Less enviable was the diverse make-up of its population – a melange of minorities that would in the end prove its downfall. Along with the six million Czechs and two million Slovaks who initially backed the republic, there were over three million Germans and 600,000 Hungarians, not to mention sundry other Ruthenians (Rusyns), Jews and Poles.

That Czechoslovakia's democracy survived as long as it did is down to the powerful political presence and skill of **Masaryk**, the country's president from 1918 to 1935, who shared executive power with the cabinet. It was his vision of social democracy that was stamped on the nation's new constitution, one of the most liberal of the time (if a little bureaucratic and centralized), aimed at ameliorating any ethnic and class tensions within the republic by means of universal suffrage, land reform and, more specifically, the Language Law, which ensured bilinguality to any area where the minority exceeded twenty percent.

The elections of 1920 reflected the mood of the time, ushering in the left-liberal alliance of the **Pětka** ("The Five"), a coalition of five parties led by the Agrarian Antonín Švehla, whose slogan "We have agreed that we will agree" became the keystone of the republic's consensus politics between the wars. Gradually, all the other parties (except the Fascists and Communists) – including even Hlinka's Slovak People's Party (HSMS) and most of the Sudeten German parties – began to participate in (or at least not disrupt) parliamentary proceedings. On the eve of the Wall Street Crash, the republic was enjoying an economic boom, a cultural renaissance and a temporary *modus vivendi* among its minorities.

The 1930s

The 1929 Wall Street Crash plunged the whole country into crisis. Economic hardship was quickly followed by **political instability**. In Slovakia, the HSMS fed off the anti-Czech resentment fuelled by Prague's manic centralization, and the appointment of Czechs to positions of power throughout the region. Taking an increasingly nationalist/separatist position, the HSMS was by far the largest party in Slovakia, consistently polling around thirty percent. In Ruthenia, the elections of 1935 gave only 37 percent of the vote to parties supporting the republic, the rest going to the Communists, pro-Magyars and other autonomist groups.

But the most intractable of the minority problems was that of the Sudeten Germans, who lived in the heavily industrialized border regions of Bohemia and Moravia. Nationalist sentiment had always run high in the Sudetenland, many of whose German-speakers resented being included in the new republic, but it was only after the Crash that the extremist parties began to make significant electoral gains. Encouraged by the rise of Nazism in Germany, and aided by rocketing Sudeten German unemployment, the far-right **Sudeten German Party** (SdP), led by a bespectacled gym teacher named Konrad Henlein, was able to win over sixty percent of the German-speaking votes in the 1935 elections.

Although constantly denying any wish to secede from the republic, the activities of Henlein and the SdP were increasingly funded and directed from Nazi Germany. To make matters worse, the Czechs suffered a severe blow to their morale with the death of Masaryk late in 1937, leaving the country in the less capable hands of his Socialist deputy, Edvard Beneš. With the Nazi annexation of Austria (the *Anschluss*) on March 11, 1938, Hitler was free to focus his attention on the Sudetenland, calling Henlein to Berlin on March 28 and instructing him to call for outright autonomy.

The Munich Crisis

On April 24, 1938, the SdP launched its final propaganda offensive in the **Karlsbad Decrees**, demanding (without defining) "complete autonomy". As this would clearly have meant surrendering the entire Czechoslovak border defences, not to mention causing economic havoc, Beneš refused to bow to the SdP's demands. Armed conflict was only narrowly avoided and, by the beginning of September, Beneš was forced to acquiesce to some sort of autonomy. On Hitler's orders, Henlein refused Beneš's offer and called openly for the secession of the Sudetenland to the German Reich.

On September 15, as Henlein fled to Germany, the British prime minister, Neville Chamberlain, flew to Berchtesgaden on his own ill-conceived initiative to "appease" the Führer. A week later, Chamberlain flew again to Germany, this time to Bad Godesburg, vowing to the British public that the country would not go to war (in his famous words) "because of a quarrel in a far-away country between people of whom we know nothing". Nevertheless, the French issued draft papers, the British Navy was mobilized, and the whole of Europe fully expected war.

Then, in the early hours of September 30, in one of the most treacherous and self-interested acts of modern European diplomacy, prime ministers Chamberlain (for Britain) and Daladier (for France) signed the **Munich Diktat** with Mussolini and Hitler, agreeing – without consulting the Czechoslovak government – to all of Hitler's demands. The British and French public were genuinely relieved, and Chamberlain flew back to cheering home crowds, waving his famous piece of paper that guaranteed "peace in our time".

Betrayed by his only Western allies and fearing bloodshed, Beneš capitulated, against the wishes of most Czechs. Had Beneš not given in, however, it's doubtful anything would have come of Czech armed resistance, surrounded as they were by vastly superior hostile powers. Beneš resigned on October 5 and left the country. In Slovakia many Slovaks viewed the Munich Diktat as a blessing in disguise, and on October 6 they declared their own autonomous government in Žilina. On October 15, **German troops occupied Sudetenland**, to the dismay of the forty percent of Sudeten Germans who hadn't voted for Henlein (not to mention the half a million Czechs and Jews).

However, the "rump" **Second Republic** (officially known as Czecho-Slovakia), was not long in existence before it too collapsed. On March 15, 1939, Hitler informed Hácha of the imminent Nazi occupation of what was left of the Czech Lands, and persuaded him to demobilize the army, again against the wishes of many Czechs. The invading German army encountered no resistance (nor any response from the Second Republic's supposed guarantors, Britain and France) and swiftly set up the Nazi **Protectorate of Bohemia and Moravia**. At the same time, with the approval of the Germans, **Slovak independence** was declared. The Hungarians, however, had other plans, crushing Ruthenia's one-day-old republic, and occupying parts of southern Slovakia, including Košice.

World War II

In the Czech Lands, during the first few months of the occupation, left-wing activists were arrested and Jews placed under the infamous Nuremburg Laws, but Nazi rule in the Protectorate at that time was not as harsh as it was to become – the economy even enjoyed a mini-boom. Then in late October and November 1939, Czech students began a series of demonstrations against the

Nazis, who responded by closing down all institutions of higher education. Calm was restored until 1941, when Himmler's deputy in the SS, **Reinhard Heydrich**, was put in charge of the Protectorate. Arrests and deportations followed, reaching fever pitch after Heydrich was assassinated by the Czech resistance in June 1942 (see p.114). The reprisals were swift and brutal, culminating in the destruction of the villages of Lidice (see p.163) and Ležáky (see p.319). Meanwhile, the "final solution" was meted out on the country's remaining Jews, who were transported first to the ghetto in Terezín (see p.258), and then on to the extermination camps. The rest of the Czech population was frightened into submission, and there were very few acts of active resistance in the Czech Lands until the Prague Uprising of May 1945.

In independent Slovakia, **Jozef Tiso**'s government met with widespread support, since, for the first time ever, the Slovaks were able to establish and run their own national institutions. For many, wartime Slovak independence, which lasted from 1939 to 1944, was a genuine expression of Slovak statehood, even if, at the end of the day, the country was little more than a Nazi puppet state, whose Jews shared the fate of their brethren in the Nazi-occupied Protectorate. The Nazification of Slovak society was inevitable, however, as the extremist Hlinka Guards (the paramilitary wing of the HSMS), under Vojtech Tuka, got the upper hand. Tiso maintained his position as president, but from 1942 was known as *Vodca* (the Slovak equivalent of *Führer*). And it was at this point that the Tiso government agreed to oversee the deportation of Slovakia's Jewish population.

The resistance movement was slow to start, but, with Nazi defeat looking more and more likely, it became strong enough by August 1944 to attempt an all-out rebellion in the central mountains. The **Slovak National Uprising** (see p.480), as it was later dubbed by the Communists, was seen by many as yet another plea for sovereignty, rather than a call for the re-establishment of Czechoslovakia. However, when the hoped-for Soviet offensive failed to materialize, the uprising was brutally suppressed and any pretence at Slovak independence abandoned for full-scale Nazi occupation.

By the end of 1944, Czechoslovak and Russian troops had begun to liberate the country, starting with Ruthenia, which Stalin decided to take as war booty despite having guaranteed to maintain Czechoslovakia's pre-Munich borders. On April 4, 1945, under Beneš's leadership, the provisional **Národní fronta** government – a coalition of Social Democrats, Socialists and Communists – was set up in Košice. On May 5, the people of Prague finally rose up against the Nazis, many hoping to prompt an American offensive from Plzeň, recently captured by General Patton's Third Army. In the end, the Americans made the politically disastrous (but militarily wise) decision not to cross the previously agreed upon demarcation line. The Praguers held out against the Nazis until May 9, when the Russians finally entered the city.

The Third Republic

Violent reprisals against suspected collaborators and the German-speaking population in general began as soon as the country was liberated. All Germans were given the same food rations as the Jews had been given during the war. Starvation, summary executions and worse resulted in the deaths of thousands of ethnic Germans. With considerable popular backing and the tacit approval of the Red Army, Beneš began to organize the **forced expulsion of the German-speaking population**, referred to euphemistically by Czechs and Slovaks as the *odsun* (transfer). Only those Germans who could prove their antifascist credentials were permitted to stay – the Czechs and Slovaks were not called on to prove the same – and by the summer of 1947, nearly 2.5 million Germans had been kicked out or had fled in fear. On this occasion, Sudeten German objections were brushed aside by the Allies, who had given Beneš the go-ahead for the *odsun* at the postwar Potsdam Conference. Attempts by Beneš to expel Slovakia's Hungarian-speaking minority in similar fashion, however, proved unsuccessful.

On October 28, 1945, in accordance with the leftist programme thrashed out at Košice, sixty percent of the country's industry was nationalized. Confiscated Sudeten German property was handed out by the largely Communist-controlled police force, and in a spirit of optimism and/or opportunism, people began to join the Communist Party (KSČ) in droves, membership more than doubling in less than a year. In the **May 1946 elections**, the Party reaped the rewards of their enthusiastic support for the *odsun*, of Stalin's vocal opposition to Munich, and of the recent Soviet liberation, emerging as the strongest single party in the Czech Lands, with up to forty percent of the vote (the largest ever for a European communist party in a multiparty election). In Slovakia, however, they achieved just thirty percent, while the Democratic Party got over sixty percent. President Beneš appointed the KSČ leader, **Klement Gottwald**, prime minister of another Národní fronta coalition, with several, strategically important, cabinet portfolios going to Party members, including the ministries of the Interior, Finance, Labour and Social Affairs, Agriculture, and Information.

Gottwald assured everyone of the KSČ's commitment to parliamentary democracy and, initially at least, even agreed to participate in the Americans' Marshall Plan (the only Eastern Bloc country to do so). Stalin immediately summoned Gottwald to Moscow, and on his return the KSČ denounced the plan. By the end of 1947, the Communists were beginning to lose support as the harvest failed, the economy faltered and malpractices within the Communist-controlled Ministry of the Interior were uncovered. In response, the KSČ began to up the ante, constantly warning the nation of imminent "counter-revolutionary plots", and arguing for greater nationalization and land reform as a safeguard.

Then in February 1948 – officially known as **Victorious February** – the latest in a series of scandals hit the Ministry of the Interior, prompting the twelve non-Communist cabinet ministers to resign en masse in the hope that this would force a physically weak President Beneš to dismiss Gottwald. No attempt was made, however, to rally popular support against the Communists. Beneš received over 5000 resolutions supporting the Communists and just 150 opposing them. Stalin sent word to Gottwald to take advantage of the crisis and ask for military assistance – Soviet troops began massing on the Hungarian border. It was the one time in his life when Gottwald disobeyed Stalin; instead, by exploiting divisions within the Social Democrats, Gottwald was able to maintain his majority in parliament. The KSČ took to the streets (and the airwaves), arming "workers' militia" units to defend the country against counter-revolution, calling a general strike and finally, on February 25, organizing the country's biggest-ever demonstration in Prague. The same day, Gottwald went to an indecisive (and increasingly ill) Beneš with his new cabinet, all Party members or "fellow travellers". Beneš accepted Gottwald's nominees, and the most popular Communist coup in eastern Europe was complete, without bloodshed and without the direct intervention of the Soviets. In the aftermath of the coup, thousands of Czechs and Slovaks fled abroad.

The People's Republic

Following Victorious February, the Party began to consolidate its position, a relatively easy task given its immense popular support and control of the army, police force, workers' militia and trade unions. A **new constitution** confirming the "leading role" of the Communist Party and the "dictatorship of the proletariat" was passed by parliament on May 9, 1948. President Beneš refused to sign it, resigned in favour of Gottwald, and died (of natural causes) shortly afterwards. Those political parties that were not banned or forcibly merged with the KSČ were prescribed fixed-percentage representation and subsumed within the so-called "multiparty" Národní fronta.

With the Cold War in full swing, the **Stalinization** of Czechoslovak society was quick to follow. In the Party's first Five Year Plan, ninety percent of industry was nationalized, heavy industry (and, in particular, the country's defence industry) was given a massive boost, and compulsory collectivization forced through. Party membership reached an all-time high of 2.5 million, with "class-conscious" Party cadres rewarded with positions of power. "Class enemies" (and their children), on the other hand, suffered discrimination, and it wasn't long before the Czechoslovak mining "gulags" began to fill up with the regime's political opponents – "kulaks", priests and "bourgeois oppositionists" – who numbered over 100,000 at their peak.

Having incarcerated most of its external opponents, the KSČ, with a little prompting from Stalin, embarked upon a ruthless period of internal bloodletting. As the economy nose-dived, the press was filled with calls for intensified "class struggle", rumours of impending "counter-revolution" and reports of economic sabotage by fifth columnists. An atmosphere of fear and confusion was created to justify **large-scale arrests of Party members** with an "international" background – those with a wartime connection with the West, Spanish Civil War veterans, Jews and Slovak nationalists.

In the early 1950s, the Party organized a series of Stalinist **show trials** in Prague, the most spectacular of which was the trial of Rudolf Slánský, who had been second only to Gottwald in the KSČ before his arrest. He, Vladimír Clementis, the former KSČ foreign minister, and twelve other leading Party members (eleven of them Jewish, including Slánský) were sentenced to death as "Trotskyist-Titoist-Zionists".

After Stalin

Gottwald died in mysterious circumstances in March 1953, nine days after attending Stalin's funeral in Moscow (some say he drank himself to death). The whole nation heaved a sigh of relief, but the regime seemed as unrepentant as ever, and the arrests and show-trials continued. Then, on May 30, the new Communist leadership announced a drastic currency devaluation, effectively reducing wages by ten percent while raising prices. The result was a wave of isolated **workers' demonstrations** and rioting in Prague, Plzeň and the Ostrava mining region. Czechoslovak army units called in to suppress the demonstrations proved unreliable, and it was left to the heavily armed workers' militia and police to disperse the crowds and make the predictable arrests and summary executions.

In 1954, in the last of the show trials, Gustáv Husák, the post-1968 president, was given life imprisonment, along with other leading Slovak comrades. So complete were the Party purges of the early 1950s, so sycophantic (and scared) was the surviving leadership, that Khrushchev's 1956 thaw was virtually ignored by the KSČ. An attempted rebellion in the Writers' Union Congress was rebuffed and an enquiry into the show trials made several minor security officials scapegoats for the "malpractices". The genuine mass base of the KSČ remained blindly loyal to the Party for the most part; Prague basked under the largest statue of Stalin in the world; and in 1957, the dull, unreconstructed neo-Stalinist **Antonín Novotný** – alleged to have been a spy for the Gestapo during the war – became first secretary and president.

Reformism and Invasion

The first rumblings of protest against Czechoslovakia's hardline leadership appeared in the official press in 1963. At first, the criticisms were confined to the country's worsening economic stagnation, but soon they developed into more generalized protests against the KSČ leadership. Novotný responded by ordering the belated release and rehabilitation of victims of the 1950s purges, permitting a slight cultural thaw and easing travel restrictions to the West. In effect, he was simply buying time. The half-hearted economic reforms announced in the 1965 **New Economic Model** failed to halt the recession, and the minor political reforms instigated by the KSČ only increased the pressure for greater reforms within the Party.

In 1967, Novotný attempted a pre-emptive strike against his opponents. Several leading writers were imprisoned, Slovak Party leaders were branded as "bourgeois nationalists", and the economists were called on to produce results or else forgo their reform programme. Instead of eliminating the opposition, however, Novotný unwittingly united them. Despite Novotný's plea to the Soviets, Brezhnev refused to back a leader whom he regarded as "Khrushchev's man in Prague". On January 5, 1968, Novotný was replaced as First Secretary by the young Slovak leader **Alexander Dubček**, and on March 22 was dislodged from the presidency by the Czech war hero Ludvík Svoboda.

1968: The Prague Spring

By inclination, Dubček was a moderate, cautious reformer, the perfect compromise candidate – but he was continually swept along by the sheer force of the reform movement. The virtual **abolition of censorship** was probably the single most significant step Dubček took. It transformed what had hitherto been an internal Party debate into a popular mass movement. Civil society, for years muffled by the paranoia and strictures of Stalinism, suddenly sprang into life in the dynamic optimism of the first few months of 1968, the so-called **"Prague Spring"**. In April, the KSČ published their Action Programme, proposing what became popularly known as "socialism with a human face" – federalization, freedom of assembly and expression, and democratization of parliament.

Throughout the spring and summer, the reform movement gathered momentum. The Social Democrat Party (forcibly merged with the KSČ after 1948) re-formed, anti-Soviet polemics appeared in the press and, most famously of all, the writer and lifelong Party member Ludvík Vaculík published his personal manifesto entitled "**Two Thousand Words**", calling for radical de-Stalinization within the Party. Dubček and the moderates denounced the manifesto and reaffirmed the country's support for the Warsaw Pact military alliance. Meanwhile, the Soviets and their hardline allies – Gomułka in Poland and Ulbricht in the GDR – took a very grave view of the Czechoslovak developments on their doorstep, and began to call for the suppression of "counter-revolutionary elements" and the reimposition of censorship.

As the summer wore on, it became clear that the Soviets were planning military intervention. Warsaw Pact manoeuvres were held in Czechoslovakia in late June, a Warsaw Pact conference (without Czechoslovak participation) was convened in mid-July and, at the beginning of August, the Soviets and the KSČ leadership met for **emergency bilateral talks** at Čierná nad Tisou on the Czechoslovak-Soviet border. Brezhnev's hardline deputy, Alexei Kosygin, made his less-than-subtle threat that "your border is our border", but did agree to withdraw Soviet troops (stationed in the country since the June manoeuvres) and gave the go-ahead to the KSČ's special Party Congress scheduled for September 9.

In the early hours of August 21, fearing defeat for the hardliners at the forthcoming KSČ Congress and claiming to have been invited to provide "fraternal assistance", the Soviets gave the order for the **invasion of Czechoslovakia** to be carried out by Warsaw Pact forces (only Romania refused to take part). Dubček and the KSČ reformists immediately condemned the invasion before being arrested and flown to Moscow for "negotiations". President Svoboda refused to condone the formation of a new government under the hardliner Alois Indra, and the people took to the streets in protest, employing every form of nonviolent resistance in the book. Apart from individual acts of martyrdom, like the self-immolation of **Jan Palach** on Prague's Wenceslas Square (see p.100), casualties were light compared to the Hungarian uprising of 1956 – the cost in terms of the following twenty years was much greater.

Normalization

In April 1969, there were anti-Soviet riots during the celebrations of the country's double ice hockey victory over the Soviets. On this pretext, another Slovak, **Gustáv Husák**, replaced the broken Dubček as First Secretary and instigated his infamous policy of "**normalization**". Over 150,000 fled the country before the borders closed, around 500,000 were expelled from the Party, and an estimated one million people lost their jobs or were demoted. Inexorably, the KSČ reasserted its absolute control over the state and society. The only part of the reform package to survive the invasion was **federalization**, which gave the Slovaks greater freedom from Prague (on paper at least), though even this was severely watered down in 1971. Dubček, like countless others, was forced to give up his job, working for the next twenty years as a minor official in the Slovak forestry commission.

An unwritten social contract was struck between rulers and ruled during the 1970s, whereby the country was guaranteed a tolerable standard of living (second only to that of the GDR in Eastern Europe) in return for its passive collaboration. Husák's security apparatus quashed all forms of dissent during the early 1970s, and it wasn't until the middle of the decade that an organized opposition was strong enough to show its face. In 1976, the punk rock band "The Plastic People of the Universe" was arrested and charged with the familiar "crimes against the state" clause of the penal code. The dissidents who rallied to their defence – a motley assortment of people ranging from former KSČ members to right-wing intellectuals – agreed to form **Charter 77** (*Charta 77* in Czech and Slovak), with the purpose of monitoring human rights abuses in the country (which had recently signed the Helsinki Agreement on human rights). One of the organization's prime movers and initial spokespersons was the absurdist Czech playwright **Václav Havel**. Over the next decade, Havel, along with many others, endured relentless persecution (including long prison sentences) in pursuit of its ideals. The initial gathering of 243 signatories increased to over 1000 by 1980, causing panic in the moral vacuum of the Party apparatus, but consistently failed to stir a fearful and cynical populace into action.

The 1980s

In the late 1970s and early 1980s, the inefficiencies of the economy prevented the government from fulfilling its side of the social contract. As living standards began to fall, cynicism, alcoholism, absenteeism and outright dissent became widespread, especially among the younger (post-1968) generation. The arrest and imprisonment in the mid-1980s of the **Jazz Section** of the Musicians' Union, who disseminated "subversive" pop music (like pirate copies of "Live Aid"), highlighted the ludicrously harsh nature of the regime. Pop concerts, annual religious pilgrimages and, of course, the anniversary of the Soviet invasion all caused regular confrontations between the security forces and certain sections of the population. Yet still a mass movement like Poland's Solidarity failed to emerge.

With the advent of **Mikhail Gorbachev**, the KSČ was put in an extremely awkward position, as it tried desperately to separate perestroika from comparisons with the reforms of the Prague Spring. Husák and his cronies had prided themselves on being second only to Honecker's GDR as the most stable and orthodox of the Soviet satellites – now the font of orthodoxy, the Soviet Union, was turning against them. In 1987, **Miloš Jakeš** – the hardliner who oversaw Husák's normalization purges – took over smoothly from Husák as general (first) secretary and introduced *přestavba* (restructuring), Czechoslovakia's lukewarm version of perestroika.

The Velvet Revolution

Everything appeared to be going swimmingly for the KSČ as it entered 1989. Under the surface, however, things were becoming increasingly strained, with divisions developing in the KSČ leadership as the country's economic performance worsened. The protest movement, meanwhile, was gathering momentum: even the Catholic Church had begun to voice dissatisfaction, compiling a staggering 500,000 signatures calling for greater freedom of worship. But the 21st anniversary of the Soviet invasion produced a demonstration of only 10,000, which was swiftly and violently dispersed by the regime.

During the summer, however, more serious cracks began to appear in Czechoslovakia's staunch hardline ally, the GDR. The trickle of East Germans fleeing to the West turned into a mass exodus, forcing Honecker to resign and, by the end of October, prompting nightly mass demonstrations on the streets of Leipzig and Dresden. The opening of the Berlin Wall on November 9 left Czechoslovakia, Romania and Albania alone on the Eastern European stage, still clinging to the old truths.

All eyes were now turned upon Czechoslovakia. Reformists within the KSČ began plotting an internal coup to overthrow Jakeš, in anticipation of a Soviet denunciation of the 1968 invasion. Their half-baked plan to foment unrest backfired, however. On Friday, **November 17**, a 50,000-strong peaceful demonstration organized by the official Communist youth organization was viciously attacked by the riot police. Over 100 arrests, 500 injuries and one death were reported – the fatality was in fact an StB (secret police) *agent provocateur*. Ultimately, events overtook whatever plans the KSČ reformists may have had. The demonstration became known as the *masakr* (massacre), and Prague's students immediately began an occupation strike, joined soon after by the city's actors, who together called for an end to the Communist Party's "leading role" and a general strike to be held for two hours on November 27.

Civic Forum and the VPN

On Sunday, November 19, on Václav Havel's initiative, the established opposition groups such as Charter 77 met and agreed to form Občanské fórum or **Civic Forum**. Their demands were simple: the resignation of the present hardline leadership, including Husák and Jakeš; an inquiry into the police actions of November 17; an amnesty for all political prisoners; and support for the general strike. In Bratislava, a parallel organization, Verejnosť proti nasiliu, or **People Against Violence** (VPN), was set up to co-ordinate protest in Slovakia.

On the Monday evening, the first of the really big **nationwide demonstrations** took place – the biggest since the 1968 invasion – with more than 200,000 people pouring into Prague's Wenceslas Square. This time the police held back, and rumours of troop deployments proved false. Every night for a week people poured into the main squares in towns and cities across the country, repeating the calls for democracy, freedom and the end to the Party's monopoly of power. As the week dragged on, the Communist media tentatively began to report events, and the KSČ leadership started to splinter under the strain, with the prime minister, **Ladislav Adamec**, alone in sticking his neck out and holding talks with the opposition.

The end of one-party rule

On Friday evening, Dubček, the ousted 1968 leader, appeared alongside Havel before a crowd of over 300,000 in Prague, and in a matter of hours the entire Jakeš leadership had resigned. The weekend brought the largest demonstrations the country had ever seen – over 750,000 people in Prague alone. At the invitation of Civic Forum, Adamec addressed the crowd, only to get booed off the platform. On Monday, November 27, eighty percent of the country's workforce joined the two-hour **general strike**, including many of the Party's previously stalwart allies, the miners and engineers. The following day, the Party agreed to the end of one-party rule and the formation of a new "coalition government".

A temporary halt to the nightly demonstrations was called and the country waited expectantly for the "broad coalition" cabinet promised by Prime Minister Adamec. On December 3, another Communist-dominated line-up was announced by the Party and immediately denounced by Civic Forum and VPN, who called for a fresh wave of demonstrations and another general strike for December 11. Adamec promptly resigned and was replaced by the Slovak **Marián Čalfa**. On December 10, one day before the second threatened general strike, Čalfa announced his provisional "**Government of National Understanding**", with Communists in the minority for the first time since 1948 and multiparty elections planned for June 1990. Having sworn in the new government, President Husák, architect of the post-1968 "normalization", finally threw in the towel.

By the time the new Čalfa government was announced, the students and actors had been on strike continuously for over three weeks. The pace of change had surprised everyone involved, but there was still one outstanding issue, the election of a new president. Posters shot up all round the capital urging "**HAVEL NA HRAD**" (Havel to the Castle – the seat of the presidency). The students were determined to see his election through, continuing their occupation strike until Havel was officially elected president by a unanimous vote of the Federal Assembly on December 29.

The 1990 elections

Czechoslovakia started the new decade full of optimism for what the future would bring. On the surface, the country had a lot more going for it than its immediate neighbours (with the possible exception of the GDR). The Communist Party had been swept from power without bloodshed, and, unlike the rest of Eastern Europe, Czechoslovakia had a strong, interwar democratic tradition with which to identify – Masaryk's First Republic. Despite Communist economic mismanagement, the country still had a relatively high standard of living, a skilled workforce and a manageable foreign debt.

In reality, however, the situation was somewhat different. Not only was the country economically in a worse state than most people had imagined, it was environmentally devastated, and its people were suffering from what Havel described as "post-prison psychosis" – an inability to think or act for themselves. The country had to go through the painful transition "from being a big fish in a small pond to being a sickly adolescent trout in a hatchery". As a result, it came increasingly to rely on its new-found saviour, the humble playwright-president Václav Havel.

In most people's eyes, "Saint Václav" could do no wrong, though he himself was not out to woo his electorate. His call for the rapid withdrawal of Soviet troops was popular enough, but his apology for the postwar expulsion of Sudeten Germans was deeply resented, as was his generous amnesty which eased the country's overcrowded prisons. The amnesty was blamed by many for the huge **rise in crime**; in the first year of freedom, every vice in the book – from racism to homicide – raised its ugly head.

In addition, there was still plenty of talk about the possibility of "counter-revolution", given the thousands of unemployed StB at large. Inevitably, accusations of previous StB involvement rocked each political party in turn in the run-up to the first free elections. The controversial **lustrace** (literally "lustration" or "cleansing") law, which barred all those on StB files from public office for the following five years, ended the career of many a politician and public figure, on the basis of often highly unreliable StB reports.

Despite all the inevitable hiccups and the increasingly vocal Slovak nationalists, Civic Forum/VPN remained high in the opinion polls. The **June 1990 elections** produced a record-breaking 99 percent turnout. With around sixty percent of the vote, Civic Forum/VPN were clear victors (the Communists got just thirteen percent), and Havel immediately set about forming a broad "Coalition of National Sacrifice", including everyone from Christian Democrats to former Communists.

The main concern of the new government was how to transform an outdated command-system economy into a **market economy** able to compete with its EU neighbours. The argument over the speed and model of economic reform caused Civic Forum to split into two separate parties: the centre-left Občánské hnutí or Civic Movement (OH), led by the foreign minister and former dissident Jiří Dienstbier, who favoured a more gradualist approach; and Občánská demokratická strana or the right-wing **Civic Democratic Party** (ODS), headed by the finance minister **Václav Klaus**, whose pronouncement that the country should "walk the tightrope to Thatcherism" sent shivers up the spines of those familiar with the UK in the 1980s.

One of the first acts of the new government was to pass a **restitution law**, handing back small businesses and property to those from whom it had been expropriated after the 1948 Communist coup. This proved to be a controversial issue, since it excluded Jewish families driven out in 1938 by the Nazis, and, of course, the millions of Sudeten Germans who were forced to flee the country after the war. A law has since been passed to cover the Jewish expropriations, but the Sudeten German issue remains a tricky one.

The Slovak crisis

One of the most intractable issues facing post-Communist Czechoslovakia – to the surprise of many Czechs – turned out to be the **Slovak problem**. Having been the victim of Prague-inspired centralization from just about every Czech leader from Masaryk to Gottwald, the Slovaks were in no mood to suffer second-class citizenship any longer. In the aftermath of 1989, feelings were running high, and, more than once, the spectre of a "Slovak UDI" was threatened by Slovak politicians hoping to boost their popularity by appealing to voters' nationalism. Despite the tireless campaigning and negotiating by both sides, a compromise agreement failed to emerge.

The differences between the Czechs and Slovaks came to a head in the summer of 1990, when it came to deciding on a new name for the country. In what became known as the **great hyphen debate**, the Slovaks insisted that a hyphen be inserted in "Czechoslovakia". The demand was greeted with ridicule by most Czechs; Havel was one of the few who understood that what was just a hyphen to the Czechs meant a whole lot more to the Slovaks.

The **June 1992 elections** soon became an unofficial referendum on the future of the federation. Events moved rapidly towards the break-up of the republic after the resounding victory of the Movement for a Democratic

Slovakia (HZDS), under the wily, populist politician and former boxer **Vladimír Mečiar**, who, in retrospect, was quite clearly seeking Slovak independence, though he never explicitly said so during the campaign. In the Czech Lands, the right-wing ODS emerged as the largest single party, under the leadership of Václav Klaus, who – ever the economist – was clearly not going to shed tears over losing the economically backward Slovak half of the country.

Talks between the two sides got nowhere, despite the fact that opinion polls in both republics consistently showed majority support for the federation. The HZDS then blocked the re-election of Havel, who had committed himself entirely to the pro-federation cause. Havel promptly resigned, leaving the country without a president, and Klaus and Mečiar were forced to discuss the terms of what has become known as the "Velvet Divorce". On January 1, 1993, after 74 years of troubled existence, Czechoslovakia was officially divided into two countries: the Czech Republic (Česká republika) and Slovakia (Slovensko) or the Slovak Republic (Slovenská republika).

Independent Slovakia

Compared to the Czechs, the Slovaks have had a much harder time in the ten years since independence. Economically, the situation is bleaker, but more worrying by far has been the country's **political instability**. Throughout his first term as Slovak prime minister, Vladimír Mečiar was plagued by allegations of corruption and charges of political interference in the media, and made inflammatory comments about the country's large Hungarian and Romany minorities. Finally in March 1994, the Slovak president, Michal Kováč – no angel himself and once an HZDS ally of Mečiar – orchestrated his removal from office and replaced him with Jozef Moravčík, another former HZDS ally of Mečiar who had recently fallen from grace.

Moravčík's attempt to put Slovakia back on the right track lasted just six months until the **September 1994 elections**, in which Mečiar's HZDS emerged once more as the largest party with 35 percent of the vote. Back at the helm, in coalition with, among others, the extreme nationalist Slovak National Party (SNS), Mečiar continued his uncompromising political style, repeating most of the gaffes of his first term of office. He conducted a relentless (but unsuccessful) campaign to remove Kováč from office – the president's son was kidnapped and later dumped, soaked in vodka, in the boot of a car abandoned in Vienna, an act he alleges was carried out by the Slovak secret service.

Perhaps the single most embarrassing episode in the country's recent history was the **national referendum**, which took place in May 1997. Along with questions on NATO membership, there was a question asking whether the president should be elected by popular vote (as Kováč and the opposition wanted) rather than by members of parliament (as Mečiar preferred). So as not to lose the vote, the interior minister removed the question from most (but not all) of the ballot papers, and the voters showed their disgust with only ten percent casting ballots. When Mečiar was asked by reporters why the question had been removed, he replied "that's none of your business". The Constitutional Court ruled that the interior minister should be prosecuted, but, not for the last time, the government ignored the Court's decision.

As a result, Slovakia was not included in the first batch of East European countries to join the EU or NATO. However, the referendum debacle ultimately proved disastrous for Mečiar. In the **September 1998 elections**, the HZDS emerged once more as the largest single party with 27 percent of the vote, but ultimately lost out to the opposition Slovak Democratic Coalition (SDK), who took 26.2 percent. The difference between the two parties was that the SDK were able to form a coalition government with three other smaller parties, including the Hungarian coalition bloc (SMK) and the former Communists (SDĽ). The new government, under premier Mikuláš Dzurinda, concentrated on winning back friends in the West, and got Slovakia back on track for EU and NATO membership. Mečiar suffered a further blow in the 1999 presidential elections, when he was beaten by the former mayor of Košice, **Rudolf Schuster**.

Unfortunately, however, Mečiar can't be written off. As this book went to press, Mečiar was under investigation for corruption, yet the HZDS may still emerge as the largest party in the upcoming parliamentary elections. The country is still very much split between those who think Mečiar is the only one who can stand up for Slovak interests, and those, like the SDKÚ (as the SDK are now known), who are prepared to form a coalition with anyone, in order to keep the HZDS out. Slovakia's future still hangs in the balance.

The Czech Republic

Generally speaking, the 1990s have been much kinder to the Czechs than to the Slovaks. Under Klaus, the country enjoyed a long period of **political stability**, jumped to the front of the queue for the EU and NATO, and was widely held up as a shining example to the rest of the former Eastern Bloc. Klaus and his party, the ODS, proved themselves the most durable of all the new political forces to emerge in the former Eastern Bloc. Nevertheless, in the **May 1996 parliamentary elections**, although the ODS again emerged as the largest single party, it failed to gain an outright majority. They repeated the failure again in November 1996 during the elections for the Czech Senate, the upper house of the Czech parliament. The electorate was distinctly unenthusiastic about the whole idea of another chamber full of overpaid politicians, and a derisory thirty percent turned out to vote in the second round. In the end, however, it was – predictably enough – a series of corruption scandals that eventually prompted **Klaus's resignation** as prime minister in November 1997.

One of the biggest problems to emerge in the 1990s was the issue of Czech racism towards the **Romany minority** within the country. The issue became headline news across the world in late 1997, when a misleading documentary broadcast on Czech TV showed life for the handful of Czech Romanies who had emigrated to Canada as a proverbial bed of roses. At last, the documentary seemed to be suggesting, they had found a life free from the racism and unemployment that is the reality for most of the Czech Republic's estimated quarter of a million gypsies. The programme prompted a minor exodus of up to one thousand Czech Romanies to Canada. Another Nova documentary, this time extolling life for Czech Romanies in Britain, had a similar effect, with several hundred Czech and Slovak Romanies seeking political asylum on arrival at Dover.

The **1998 elections** proved that the Czechs had grown sick and tired of Klaus's dry, rather arrogant, style of leadership. However, what really did for Klaus was that for the first time since he took power, the economy had begun to falter. The Social Democrats (ČSSD), under Miloš Zeman, emerged as the largest single party, promising to pay more attention to social issues. Unable to form a majority government, Zeman followed the Austrian example, and decided to make an **"opposition agreement"** with the ODS. This Faustian pact was dubbed the "Toleranzpatent" by the press, after the 1781 Edict of Tolerance issued by Joseph II (see p.573). The Czech public were unimpressed, seeing the whole deal as a cosy stitch-up, and in 2000, thousands turned out in Wenceslas Square for the *Díky a odejděte* (Thank you, now leave) protest, asking for the resignation of both Zeman and Klaus.

Havel, Czech President since 1993, has been dogged by ill health, and steps down in 2003 – whoever succeeds him is unlikely to command the same moral respect. That said, Havel's standing is nowhere near as high as it used to be, particularly at home. His marriage to the actress Dagmar Veškrnová, seventeen years his junior, in January 1997, less than a year after his first wife, Olga, died of cancer, was frowned upon by many. And his very public fall-out with his sister-in-law, Olga Havlová, over the family inheritance of the multi-million crown Lucerna complex in Prague, didn't do his reputation any favours either.

Czech Romanies featured large in the European media again in 1999 over the planned building of a wall to separate Romanies and non-Romanies in the north Bohemian city of **Ústí nad Labem**. The central government, under pressure from the EU, condemned the construction of the wall, and eventually the local council rehoused the white Czechs elsewhere. This is an issue that won't go away easily – only a concerted campaign of anti-racism, grass roots social work and the implementation of equal opportunities policies, will effectively counter the prejudices of the vast majority of Czechs.

Meanwhile, Czechs have become more and more disillusioned with their politicians, with just 58 percent turning out for the **2002 elections**, and 18 percent of them voting for the Communists. The ČSSD, under Vladimír Špidla, again emerged as the single largest party, with ODS in second place – this time, however, Špidla was able to form a government with the newly-formed centre party of Coalition 2, giving them the slimmest of majorities. Once more, the new government has put their social policies at the top of their agenda, but with EU entry looming near, the crucial issue is how well the ČSSD can handle the economy.

Books

Publishers are detailed below in the form of British publisher/American publisher, where both exist. Where books are published in one country only, UK or US follows the publisher's name. Out of print books are designated o/p; University Press is abbreviated UP. Books tagged with the ⊡ symbol are particularly recommended.

History, politics and society

Peter Demetz *Prague in Black and Gold; Scenes from the Life of a European City* (Penguin/Hill & Wang). Demetz certainly knows his subject, both academically and at first hand, having been brought up here before World War II (where his account ends). His style can be a little dry, but he is determinedly un-partisan and refreshingly antinationalist in his reading of history.
R.J.W. Evans *Rudolf II and His World* (Thames & Hudson, UK). First published in 1973, and still the best account there is of the alchemy-mad emperor, but not as salacious as one might hope given the subject matter.
Jan Kaplan & Krystyna Nosarzewska *Prague: The Turbulent Century* (Könemann, Prague). This is the first real attempt to cover the twentieth-century history of Prague with all its warts. The text isn't as good as it should be, but the book is worth it just for the incredible range of photographs and images from the century.
Karel Kaplan *The Short March: The Communist Takeover in Czechoslovakia, 1945–48* (o/p); *Report on the Murder of the General Secretary* (o/p). *The Short March* is an excellent account of the electoral rise and rise of the Communists in Czechoslovakia after the war, which culminated in the bloodless coup of February 1948.

Report on the Murder of the General Secretary is a detailed study of the most famous of the anti-Semitic Stalinist show trials, that of Rudolf Slánský, number two in the Party until his arrest.
⊡ **Callum MacDonald** *The Killing of SS Obergruppenführer Reinhard Heydrich* (Macmillan/Da Capo). Gripping account of the build-up to the most successful and controversial act of wartime resistance, which took place in May 1942, and prompted horrific reprisals by the Nazis on the Czechs.
Callum MacDonald & Jan Kaplan *Prague in the Shadow of the Swastika* (Quartet, UK). Excellent account of the city under Nazi occupation, with an incisive, readable text illustrated by copious black-and-white photos.
Jiří Musil (ed) *The End of Czechoslovakia* (Central European UP). Academics from both the Czech and Slovak Republics attempt to explain why Czechoslovakia split into two countries just at the point when it seemed so successful.
Derek Sayer *The Coast of Bohemia* (Princeton UP). A very readable cultural history, concentrating on Bohemia and Prague, which aims to dispel the ignorance shown by the Shakespearean quote of the title, and particularly illuminating on the subject of twentieth-century artists.
R.W. Seton-Watson *The History of*

the Czechs and Slovaks (o/p). Seton-Watson's informed and balanced account, written during World War II, is hard to beat. The Seton-Watsons were lifelong Slavophiles but maintained a scholarly distance in their writing, rare among emigré historians.

Kieran Williams *The Prague Spring and its Aftermath: Czechoslovak Politics, 1968-70* (Cambridge UP). This book draws on declassified archives to analyse the attempted reforms under Dubček and to take a new look at the 1968 Prague Spring.

★ **Elizabeth Wiskemann** *Czechs and Germans* (o/p). Researched and written in the build-up towards Munich, this is the most fascinating and fair treatment of the Sudeten problem. Meticulous in her detail, vast in her scope, Wiskemann manages to suffuse the weighty text with enough anecdotes to keep you gripped. Unique.

Essays, memoirs and biography

Margarete Buber-Neumann *Milena* (Arcade). A moving biography of Milena Jesenská, one of interwar Prague's most beguiling characters, who befriended the author while they were both interned in Ravensbrück concentration camp.

Karel Čapek *Talks with T. G. Masaryk* (Catbird Press). Čapek was a personal (and political) friend of Masaryk, and his diaries, journals, reminiscences and letters give great insights into the man who personified the First Republic.

Jana Černá *Kafka's Milena* (Souvenir Press/Northwestern UP). Another biography of Milena Jesenská, this time written by her daughter, a Surrealist poet, whose own works were banned under the Communists.

Timothy Garton Ash *We The People: The Revolutions of 89* (Penguin/Vintage). A personal, anecdotal, eyewitness account of the Velvet Revolution (and the events in Poland, Berlin and Budapest) – by far the most compelling of all the post-1989 books. Published as *The Magic Lantern* in the US.

Patrick Leigh Fermor *A Time of Gifts* (Penguin). The first volume of Leigh Fermor's trilogy based on his epic walk along the Rhine and Danube rivers in 1933–34. In the last quarter of the book he reaches Czechoslovakia, indulging in a quick jaunt to Prague before crossing the border into Hungary. Written forty years later in dense, luscious and highly crafted prose, it's an evocative and poignant insight into the culture of Mitteleuropa between the wars.

Václav Havel *Living in Truth* (Faber); *Letters to Olga* (Faber/Holt); *Open Letters: Selected Prose; Disturbing the Peace; Summer Meditations* (all Faber/Vintage); *The Art of the Impossible* (Fromm, US). The first essay in *Living in Truth* is "Power of the Powerless", Havel's lucid, damning indictment of the inactivity of the Czechoslovak masses in the face of "normalization". *Letters to Olga* is a collection of Havel's letters written under great duress (and heavy censorship) from prison in the early 1980s to his wife, Olga – by turns philosophizing, nagging, effusing, whingeing. *Disturbing the Peace* is probably Havel's most accessible work, a series of autobiographical questions and answers in which he talks interestingly about his childhood, the events of 1968 when he was in Liberec, and the path to Charter 77 and beyond (though not including his reactions to being thrust into the role of president). *Summer Meditations* are post-1989 essays by the playwright-president, while *The Art of the Impossible* is a collection of speeches given since he took office in 1990.

Václav Havel et al *Power of the Powerless* (M. E. Sharpe, US). A collection of essays by leading Chartists, kicking off with Havel's seminal title-piece. Other contributors range from the dissident Marxist Petr Uhl to devout Catholics like Václav Benda.

Miroslav Holub *The Dimension of the Present Moment* (Faber & Faber, UK); *Shedding Life: Disease, Politics and Other Human Conditions* (Milkweed, US). Two books of short philosophical musings/essays on life and the universe by this unusual, clever scientist-poet.

Leoš Janáček, *Intimate Letters* (Princeton UP, US). Selection of the countless letters written by the elderly composer Leoš Janáček to Kamila Strösslová, a young married woman with whom he fell passionately in love.

John Keane *Vaclav Havel: A Political Tragedy in Six Acts* (Bloomsbury, UK). The first book to tell both sides of the Havel story: Havel the dissident playwright and civil rights activist who played a key role in the 1989 Velvet Revolution, and Havel the ageing and increasingly ill president, who has, in many people's opinion, simply stayed on the stage too long.

Antonín Klimek & Zbyněk Zeman *The Life of Edvard Beneš: Czechoslovakia in Peace & War* (Clarendon Press). Beneš is a fascinating figure in Czech history, revered as number two to Masaryk while the latter was alive, only to find himself held responsible first for the Munich debacle, and lastly for allowing the Communists into power in 1948.

★ **Heda Margolius Kovaly** *Prague Farewell* (Orion/Holmes & Meier). An autobiography starting in the concentration camps of World War II, and ending with the author's flight from Czechoslovakia in 1968.

Married to one of the Party officials executed in the 1952 Slánský trial, she tells her story simply, and without bitterness. The best account there is on the fear and paranoia whipped up during the Stalinist terror. Published as *Under a Cruel Star* in the US.

Benjamin Kuras *Czechs and Balances, Is There Life After Marx?* and *As Golems Go* (all Baronet, Prague). The first two are witty, light, typically Czech takes on national identity and Central European politics; the latter is a more mystical look at Rabbi Löw's philosophy and the Kabbalah.

Ota Pavel *How I Came to Know Fish* (New Directions US). Pavel's childhood innocence shines through particularly when his Jewish father and two brothers are sent to a concentration camp and he and his mother have to scrape a living.

★ **Angelo Maria Ripellino** *Magic Prague* (Picador/University of California Press). A wide-ranging look at the bizarre array of historical and literary characters who have lived in Prague, from the mad antics of the court of Rudolf II to the escapades of Jaroslav Hašek. Scholarly, rambling, richly and densely written – unique and recommended.

Josef Škvorecký *Talkin' Moscow Blues* (Faber/Ecco Press). Without doubt the most user-friendly of Škvorecký's works, containing a collection of essays on his wartime childhood, Czech jazz, literature and contemporary politics, all told in his inimitable, irreverent and infuriating way. Published as *Head for the Blues* in the US.

Elizabeth Sommer-Lefkovits *Are You Here in This Hell Too?* (Menard Press/Central Books). Harrowing Holocaust experience told by a Slovak Jewish woman who worked as a pharmacist in Prešov until 1944.

Ludvík Vaculík *A Cup of Coffee With My Interrogator* (Readers International). A Party member until

1968, and signatory of Charter 77, Vaculík revived the feuilleton – a short political critique once much loved in central Europe. This collection dates from 1968 onwards.
Zbyněk Zeman *The Masaryks – The Making of Czechoslovakia* (I. B. Tauris, UK). Written in the 1970s

while Zeman was in exile, this is a very readable, none too sentimental biography of the country's founder Tomáš Garrigue Masaryk, and his son Jan Masaryk, the postwar Foreign Minister who died in mysterious circumstances shortly after the 1948 Communist coup.

Czech and Slovak fiction

Alexandra Buchler (ed) *Allskin and Other Tales by Contemporary Czech Women* (Women in Translation). This collection of short stories and excerpts from novels spans more than thirty years and contains a range of writing which the editor attempts to put into context.
Josef Čapek *Stories about Doggie and Pussycat* (Albatros, Prague). Josef Čapek (Karel's older brother) was a Cubist artist of some renown, and also a children's writer. These simple stories about a dog and a cat are wonderfully illustrated, and seriously postmodern.
Karel Čapek *Towards a Radical Centre* (Catbird Press, US); *Nine Fairy Tales* (Northwestern University Press in US); *Three Novels: Hordubal, Meteor, An Ordinary Life* (Catbird Press). Karel Čapek was the literary and journalistic spokesperson for Masaryk's First Republic, but he's better known in the West for his plays, some of which, such as R.U.R., feature in the anthology, *Towards a Radical Centre*. Probably the best of his novel writing is contained in the trilogy, *Three Novels*, set in Czechoslovakia in the 1930s.
Daniela Fischerová *Fingers Pointing Somewhere Else* (Catbird Press). Subtly nuanced, varied collection of short stories from dissident playwright Fisherová.
Ladislav Fuks *The Cremator* (Marion Boyars); *Mr Theodore Mundstock* (Four Walls Eight Windows, US). Two readable novels:

the first about a man who works in a crematorium in occupied Prague, and is about to throw in his lot with the Nazis when he discovers that his wife is half-Jewish; the second set in 1942 Prague, as the city's Jews wait to be transported to Terezín.
Jaroslav Hašek *The Good Soldier Švejk* (Penguin/Viking). This classic, by Bohemia's most bohemian writer, is a rambling, picaresque tale of Czechoslovakia's famous fictional fifth columnist, Švejk, who wreaks havoc in the Austro-Hungarian army during World War I.
Václav Havel *Selected Plays 1963–87, Selected Plays 1984–87* (Faber, UK), *The Garden Party and Other Plays* (Grove Press, US). Havel's plays are not renowned for being easy to read (or watch). *The Memorandum* is one of his earliest works, a classic absurdist drama that, in many ways, sets the tone for much of his later work, of which the *Three Vaněk Plays*, featuring Ferdinand Vaněk, Havel's alter ego, are perhaps the most successful. The 1980s collection includes *Largo Desolato*, *Temptation* and *Redevelopment*; freedom of thought, Faustian opportunism and town planning as metaphors of life under the Communists.
★ **Bohumil Hrabal** *Closely Observed Trains* (Abacus/Northwestern UP); *I Served the King of England* (Picador/Vintage); *Too Loud a Solitude* (Deutsch/Harcourt Brace). A thoroughly mischievous writer,

Hrabal's slim but superb *Closely Observed Trains* is a postwar classic, set in the last days of the war and relentlessly unheroic; it was made into an equally brilliant film by Jiří Menzl. *I Served the King of England* follows the antihero Dítě, who works at the *Hotel Paříž*, through the decade after 1938. *Too Loud a Solitude*, about a waste-paper disposer under the Communists, has also been made into a film, again by Menzl.

Alois Jirásek *Old Czech Legends* (Forest Books/Dufour). A major figure in the nineteenth-century Czech *národní obrození*, Jirásek popularized Bohemia's legendary past. This collection includes all the classic texts, including the story of the founding of the city by the prophetess Libuše.

★ **Franz Kafka** *Kafka: the Complete Novels*; *The Complete Short Stories*; *Letters to Felice*; *Diaries* (all Penguin/Vintage). A German-Jewish Praguer, Kafka has drawn the darker side of central Europe – its claustrophobia, paranoia and unfathomable bureaucracy – better than anyone else, both in a rural setting, as in *The Castle*, and in an urban one, in one of the great novels of the twentieth century, *The Trial*.

Ivan Klíma *A Summer Affair* (Penguin, UK); *My Merry Mornings* (Readers International); *My First Loves* (Penguin/Norton); *Love and Garbage* (Penguin/Vintage); *Judge on Trial* (Vintage); *My Golden Trades* (Penguin/Macmillan)*; Waiting for the Dark, Waiting for the Light* (Penguin/Picador); *The Spirit of Prague* (Granta, UK); *Ultimate Intimacy* (Granta/Grove-Atlantic). A survivor of Terezín, Klíma is another writer in the Kundera mould as far as sexual politics goes, but his stories are a lot lighter. *Judge on Trial*, written in the 1970s, is one of his best, concerning the moral dilemmas of a Communist judge. *Waiting for the Dark, Waiting for the Light* is a pessimistic novel set before, during and

after the Velvet Revolution of 1989. *The Spirit of Prague* is a very readable collection of biographical and more general articles and essays on subjects ranging from Klíma's childhood experiences in Terezín to the current situation in Prague. *Ultimate Intimacy* is his latest novel, set in the cynical post-revolutionary Czech Republic.

Pavel Kohout *I am Snowing: The Confessions of a Woman of Prague* (Harcourt Trade/Harvest Books) is set in the uneasy period just after the fall of Communism amid accusations of collaboration. *The Widow Killer* (St Martin's Press, UK) is a thriller about a naive Czech detective partnered with a Gestapo agent in the last months of World War II.

★ **Milan Kundera** *Laughable Loves*; *The Farewell Party*; *The Joke*; *The Book of Laughter and Forgetting*; *The Unbearable Lightness of Being*; *The Art of the Novel*; *Immortality*; *Slowness*; *Identity*; *Testaments Betrayed* (all Faber/HarperCollins); *Life is Elsewhere* (Faber/Penguin). Milan Kundera is the country's most popular writer – at least with non-Czechs. His books are very obviously "political", particularly *The Book of Laughter and Forgetting*, which led the Communists to revoke Kundera's citizenship. *The Joke*, written while he was still living in Czechoslovakia and in many ways his best work, is set in the very unfunny era of the Stalinist purges. Its clear, humorous style is far removed from the carefully poised posturing of his most famous work, *The Unbearable Lightness of Being*, set in and after 1968, and successfully turned into a film some twenty years later. *Slowness* is a slim volume set in France, and his first work written in French. *Identity* is his latest novel, a series of slightly detached musings on the human condition that is typical of his later works. *Testaments Betrayed*, on the other hand, is a fascinating series of essays about a range of subjects, from the formation of historical reputation to the problems of translations. His latest novel, *No Saints and Angels* (Granta), is set in bleak, contemporary Prague.

Arnošt Lustig *Diamonds of the Night; Night and Hope* (both Quartet/Northwestern UP); *Darkness Casts No Shadow* (Quartet/Avon, o/p); *A Prayer for Kateřina Horovitová* (Quartet/Overlook Press); *Lovely Green Eyes* (Harvill/Arcade). A Prague Jew exiled since 1968, Lustig spent World War II in Terezín, Buchenwald and Auschwitz, and his novels and short stories are consistently set in the Terezín camp.

Ladislav Mňačko *The Taste of Power* (o/p). Now living in Israel, Mňačko is one of the few Slovak writers to have been widely published abroad, most frequently this novel about the corruption of ideals that followed the Communist takeover.

Gustav Meyrink *The Golem* (Dedalus/Dover); *The Angel of the West Window* (Dedalus/Ariadne). Meyrink was another of Prague's weird and wonderful characters who started out as a bank manager, but soon became involved in cabalism, alchemy and drug experimentation. His *Golem*, based on Rabbi Löw's monster, is one of the classic versions of the tale, set in the Jewish quarter. *The Angel of the West Window* is a historical novel about John Dee, an English alchemist invited to Prague in the late sixteenth century by Rudolf II.

Jan Neruda *Prague Tales* (Central European UP). Not to be confused with the Chilean Pablo Neruda (who took his name from the Czech writer), these are short, bitter-sweet snapshots of life in Malá Strana at the close of the last century.

Ivan Olbracht *The Sorrowful Eyes of Hannah Karajich* (Central European UP). A moving novel set in the vanished world of a Jewish village in sub-Carpatho-Ruthenia which

shows the effects of Zionism and the terrors of Hitler.

Iva Pekarková *Truck Stop Rainbows* (Farrar Strauss & Giroux, US). A heroine who attempts to fight, often by using sexual politics, against the grim realities of the Communist system in Czechoslovakia in the 1980s.

Peter Petro *A History of Slovak Literature* (Liverpool UP/ McGill-Queen's UP). Comprehensive overview of Slovak literature from 800 to 1990.

Karel Poláček *What Ownership's All About* (Catbird Press/Independent Publishers Group). A darkly comic novel set in a Prague tenement block, dealing with the issue of fascism and appeasement, by a Jewish-Czech Praguer who died in the camps in 1944.

Robert Pynsent (ed) *Modern Slovak Prose* (Macmillan, UK). Literary criticism on Slovak fiction since 1954 by Slovaks and Western Slavists; hardback only.

Rainer Maria Rilke *Two Stories of Prague* (UP of New England, US). Both tales deal with the artificiality of Prague's now defunct German-speaking community, whose claustrophobic parochialism drove the author into self-imposed exile in 1899 (for more on Rilke see Poetry, below).

Peter Sís *The Three Golden Keys* (Frances Foster, US). Short, hauntingly illustrated children's book set in Prague, by Czech-born American Sís.

Martin Šimečka *The Year of the Frog* (Scribner, US). Largely autobiographical account of a young Slovak intellectual, whose father is a prominent dissident, living through the last years of Communism in Bratislava.

Josef Škvorecký *The Cowards*; *The Miracle Game* (both Faber/Norton); *The Swell Season*; *The Bass Saxophone* (both Vintage/Ecco Press); *Miss Silver's Past*; *Dvořák in Love* (both Vintage/Norton); *The Engineer of Human Souls* (Vintage/Dalkey

Archive); *The Republic of Whores* (Faber/Ecco Press). A relentless anti-Communist, Škvorecký is typically Bohemian in his bawdy sense of humour and irreverence for all high moralizing. *The Cowards* (which briefly saw the light of day in 1958) is the tale of a group of irresponsible young men in the last days of the war, an antidote to the lofty prose from official authors at the time, but hampered by its dated Americanized translation.

Josef Škvorecký *The Mournful Demeanor of Lieutenant Boruvka; Sins for Father Knox; The Return of Lieutenant Boruvka; The End of Lieutenant Boruvka* (all Faber & Faber/Norton). Less well known (and understandably so) are Škvorecký's detective stories featuring a podgy, depressive Czech cop, which he wrote in the 1960s at a time when his more serious work was banned. His latest book, *Two Murders in My Double Life,* (Picador) is a mystery story set in Canada, where he now lives, and the Czech Republic.

Božena Slančíková-Timrava *That Alluring Land: Slovak Stories* (Pittsburgh UP, US). Not strictly a feminist as such, Slančíková-Timrava tells her Slovak tales from a decidedly female perspective.

★ **Zdena Tomin** *Stalin's Shoe* (Hutchinson/Dodd Mead); *The Coast of Bohemia* (Everyman/Den). Although Czech-born, Tomin writes in English (the language of her exile since 1980); she has a style and fluency all her own. *Stalin's Shoe* is the compelling and complex story of a girl coming to terms with her Stalinist childhood, while *The Coast of Bohemia* is based on Tomin's experiences of the late 1970s dissident movement, when she was an active member of Charter 77.

Ludvík Vaculík *The Guinea Pigs* (Northwestern UP, US). Vaculík was expelled from the Party in the midst of the 1968 Prague Spring; this novel, set in Prague, catalogues the slow dehumanization of Czech society in the aftermath of the Soviet invasion.

Jiří Weil *Life With a Star; Mendelssohn is on the Roof* (both Northwestern UP, US). Two novels written just after the war and based on Weil's experiences as a Czech Jew in hiding in Nazi-occupied Prague.

Poetry

Jaroslav Čejka, Michal Černík and Karel Sýs *The New Czech Poetry* (Bloodaxe/Dufour). Slim but interesting volume by three Czech poets all in their late forties, all very different. Čejka is of the Holub school, and comes across simply and strongly; Černík is similarly direct; Sýs the least convincing.

Sylva Fischerová *The Tremor of Racehorses: Selected Poems* (Bloodaxe/Dufour). Poet and novelist Fischerová is one of the new generation of Czech writers, though in many ways she is continuing in the Holub tradition. Her poems are by turns powerful, obtuse and personal, as was necessary to escape censorship during the late 1980s.

Josef Hanzlík *Selected Poems* (Bloodaxe/Dufour). Refreshingly accessible collection of poems written over the last 35 years by a poet of Havel's generation.

Miroslav Holub *Supposed to Fly; The Jingle Bell Principle; Poems Before & After* (all Bloodaxe/Dufour); *Vanishing Lung Syndrome* (Faber/Oberlin College Press). Holub is a scientist and scholar, and his poetry reflects this unique fusion of master poet and chief immunologist. Regularly banned in his own country, he is the Czech poet *par excellence* – classically trained, erudite, liberal and Westward-leaning. *Vanishing*

Lung Syndrome is his most recent volume; the other two are collections.

Rainer Maria Rilke *Selected Poetry* (Picador/Vintage). Rilke's upbringing was unexceptional, except that his mother brought him up as a girl until the age of six. In his adult life, he became one of Prague's leading German-speaking authors of the interwar period.

Jaroslav Seifert *The Poetry of Jaroslav Seifert* (Catbird Press, US). Czechoslovakia's only author to win the Nobel prize for literature, Seifert was a founder-member of the Communist Party and the avant-garde arts movement *Devětsil*, later falling from grace and signing the Charter in his old age. His longevity means that his work covers some of the most turbulent times in Czechoslovak history, but his irrepressible lasciviousness has been known to irritate.

Miroslav Válek, Miroslav Cipar, Ewald Osers *The Ground Beneath Our Feet: Selected Poems* (Bloodaxe, UK). The first-ever Slovak poets to be published in Britain.

Literature by foreign writers

David Brierley *On Leaving a Prague Window* (Warner, UK). A very readable thriller set in postcommunist Prague which shows that past connection with dissidents can still lead to violence.

Bruce Chatwin *Utz* (Pan, UK). Chatwin is one of the "exotic" school of travel writers, hence this slim, intriguing and mostly true-to-life account of an avid crockery collector from Prague's Jewish quarter.

Lionel Davidson *The Night of Wenceslas* (Reed Consumer Books/St Martin's Press). A Cold War thriller set in pre-1968 Czechoslovakia that launched Davidson's career as a spywriter.

Sue Gee *Letters from Prague* (Arrow, UK). The central character fell in love with a Czech student in England in 1968, but he returned home when the Russians invaded. Twenty years later, together with her ten-year old daughter, she goes in search of him.

Martha Gellhorn *A Stricken Field* (o/p). The story of an American journalist who arrives in Prague just as the Nazis march into Sudetenland. Based on the author's own experiences, this is a fascinating, if sentimental, insight into the panic and confusion in "rump" Czecho-Slovakia after the Munich Diktat. First published in 1940.

⭐ **Jill Paton Walsh** *A Desert in Bohemia* (Black Swan/Plume). A gripping story set against the aftermath of World War II and the subsequent political upheaval in Czechoslovakia.

Philip Roth *Prague Orgy* (Vintage). A novella about a world-famous Jewish novelist (ie Roth) who goes to Communist Prague to recover some unpublished Jewish stories. Prague "is the city I imagined the Jews would buy when they had accumulated enough money for a homeland", according to Roth. A coda to Roth's Zuckerman trilogy.

Art, photography and film

Czech Modernism 1900–1945 (Bullfinch Press/Museum of Fine Arts, Houston). Wide-ranging and superbly illustrated, this American publication records the journey of the Czech modern movement through Cubism and Surrealism to Modernism and the avant-garde. The accompanying essays by leading art and film critics cover fine art, architecture, film, photography and theatre.

Devětsil – Czech Avant-Garde Art, Architecture and Design of the 1920s and 30s (Museum of Modern Art, Oxford, UK). Published to accompany the 1990 Devětsil exhibition at Oxford, this is the definitive account of interwar Czechoslovakia's most famous left-wing art movement, which attracted artists from every discipline.

Disorientations – Eastern Europe in Transition (Thames & Hudson, UK). A self-explanatory book of photos accompanied by Pavel Kohout's text.

Nature Illuminated Lee Hendrix (Thames & Hudson). Exquisite paintings of flora and fauna, commissioned by Rudolf II to illuminate a master calligrapher's manuscript.

Prague – A guide to Twentieth-century Architecture Ivan Margolius (Ellipsis London UK). Dinky little pocket guide to all the major modern landmarks of Prague (including a black-and-white photo of each building), from the Art Nouveau Obecní dům, through functionalism and Cubism, to the Fred & Ginger building.

Language

Language

Pronunciation 605

A Czech/Slovak language guide...607

Czech food and drink glossary..610

Slovak food and drink glossary 612

An A–Z of Czech and Slovak

street names 614

A glossary of Czech and Slovak words and terms 614

An architectural glossary 618

Historical and political terms 618

Abbreviations 619

Language

The official language of the Czech Republic is Czech (*český*), that of the Slovakia, Slovak (*slovenský*). Both are mutually intelligible, highly complex Slav tongues. Whether they are separate languages or simply diverse dialects of a common one is still a hotly disputed issue. However, for the non-Slav, they are sufficiently distinct to cause serious problems of understanding. Unless you're here for some time, however, it's all rather academic, since you're not likely to make any great inroads into either.

That said, any attempt to speak Czech or Slovak will be heartily appreciated, though don't be discouraged if people seem not to understand, as most will be unaccustomed to hearing foreigners stumble through their language. If you know some German already, brush up on that, since, among the older generation in particular, German is the most widely spoken second language. Russian, once the compulsory second language (and therefore theoretically spoken by most of the middle-aged population), has been practically wiped off the school curriculum. English is now the foreign language most commonly taught in schools, and the number of English-speakers has been steadily increasing.

Pronunciation

English-speakers often find Czech impossibly difficult to pronounce, Slovak less so. In fact, neither are half as daunting as they might first appear from the traffic jams of consonants that crop up on the page, as Patrick Leigh Fermor put it. Apart from a few special letters, each letter and syllable is pronounced as it's written, with virtually no letter unvoiced. The trick is always to **stress the first syllable** of a word, no matter what its length; otherwise you'll render it unintelligible.

Short and long vowels

Czech and Slovak have both **short** and **long vowels** (the latter being denoted by a variety of accents). The trick here is to lengthen the vowel without affecting the principal stress of the word, which is invariably on the first syllable.

a like the u in c**u**p
á as in f**a**ther

There are very few **teach yourself Czech** guides available – even fewer for Slovak – and each has drawbacks. *Colloquial Czech* and *Colloquial Slovak*, both by James Naughton, are good, but a bit fast and furious for most people; *Teach Yourself Czech* is a bit dry for some. The best portable **dictionaries** are the *kapesní slovník* for Czech and the *vreckový slovník* for Slovak, most easily purchased in the Czech and Slovak republics themselves. The Rough Guides also produces an excellent dictionary-style **Czech phrasebook**.

ä closer to the e in let than an a
e as in pet
é as in fair
ě like the y in yes
i or y as in pit
í or ý as in seat
o as in not
ó as in door
ô like the u in lurid
u like the oo in book
ů or ú like the oo in fool

Vowel combinations & diphthongs

There are very few diphthongs in Czech, substantially more in Slovak. Combinations of vowels not mentioned below should be pronounced as two separate syllables.

au like the ou in foul
ie like the ye in yes
ia like the ya in yak
iu like the u in flute
ou like the oe in foe

Consonants and accents

There are no silent **consonants**, but it's worth remembering that r and l can form a syllable if standing between two other consonants or at the end of a word, as in Brno (Br–no) or Vltava (Vl–ta–va). The consonants listed below are those that differ substantially from the English. Accents look daunting, but the only one that causes a lot of problems is ř (Czech only), probably the most difficult letter to say in the entire language – even Czech toddlers have to be taught how to say it.

c like the **ts** in boats
č like the **ch** in chicken
ch like the **ch** in the Scottish loch
ď like the **d** in duped
g always as in goat, never as in general
h always as in have, but more energetic
j like the **y** in yoke
kd pronounced as **gd**
ľ like the **lli** in colliery
mě pronounced as mnye
ň like the **n** in nuance
p softer than the English p
r as in rip, but often rolled
ř like the sound of **r** and **ž** combined
š like the **sh** in shop
ť like the **t** in tutor
ž like the **s** in pleasure; at the end of a word like the **sh** in shop

A Czech/Slovak language guide

In many instances the **Czech** and **Slovak words** for things are the same. Where they're different, we've separated them below, giving the Czech word first and the Slovak word second.

Basic words and phrases

Yes – ano/áno or hej
No – ne/nie
Excuse me/please/don't mention it – prosím
You're welcome – není zač/nemáte začo
Sorry – pardon/pardón
Thank you – djkuju/ďakujem
OK – dobrá/dobre
Bon appétit – dobrou chuť
Bon voyage – šťastnou cestu
Hello/goodbye (informal) – ahoj
Goodbye (formal) – na shledanou/do videnia
Good day – dobrý den
Good morning – dobré ráno
Good evening – dobrý veber
Good night (when leaving) – dobrou noc
Today – dnes
Yesterday – včera

Tomorrow – zítra/zajtra
The day after tomorrow – pozítra/pozajtra
Now – hnet/teraz
Later – pozděje/neskôr
Leave me alone – dej mi pokoj/nechaj ma osamote
Go away – jdi pryč/choď preč
Help! – pomoc!
This one – tento
A little – trochu
Large–small – velký–malý
More–less – více–méně/ – viac–menej
Good–bad – dobrý–zpatný
Hot–cold – horký–studený/horúci–studený
With–without – s–bez
How are you – jak se máte/ako sa máte?

Getting around

Over here – tady/tuná
Over there – tam
Left – nalevo/nanavo
Right – napravo
Straight on – rovně/priamo
Where is . . .? – kde je . . .?
How do I get to Zvolen? – jak se dostanu do Zvolena/ako sa dostanem do Zvolena?
How do I get to the university? – jak se dostanu k univerzitě/ako sa dostanem k univerzite?

By bus – autobusem/autobusom
By train – vlakem/vlakom
By car – autem/autom
By foot – pěšky/pešo
By taxi – taxíkem/taxíkom
Ticket – jízdenka/lístok
Return ticket – zpátečá jízdenka/spiatočný lístok
Railway station – nádraží/železničná stanica
Bus station – autobusové nádraží/autobusová stanica
Bus stop – autobusová zastávka

When's the next train to Prague? - kdy jede
další vlak do Prahy/kedy ide najbližší vlak do
Prahy?
Is it going to Brno? - jede to do Brna/ide to
do Brna?

Do I have to change? - musím přestupo-
vat/musím prestupovat?
Do I have to have a reservation? - musím
mit místenku?

Questions and answers

Do you speak English? - mluvíte
anglicky/hovoríte anglicky?
I don't speak German - nemluvím
německy/nehovorím nemecky
I don't understand - nerozumím/nerozumiem
I understand - rozumím/rozumiem
Speak slowly - mluvte pomalu/hovorte poma-
lzie
How do you say that in Czech/Slovak? -
jak se tohle vekne česky/ako sa to povie
slovenský?
Could you write it down for me? - mužete
mí to napsat/mohli by ste mi to napísať?
What - co/čo
Where - kde
When - kdy/kedy

Why - proč/prečo
How much is it? - kolík to stojí/koľko stojí?
Are there any rooms available? - máte
volné pokoje/máte voľné izby?
I want a double room - chtěl bych dvou
lůžkovy pokoj/chcem dvojpostľovú izbu
For one night - na jednu noc
With shower - se sprchou/se sprchy
Are these seats free? - je tu volno/sú tieto
miesta vonná?
May we (sit down)? - můžeme/môžme?
The bill please - zaplatím prosím
Do you have . . .? - máte . . .?
We don't have - nemáme
We do have - máme

Some signs

Entrance - vchod
Exit - východ
Toilets - záchod
Men - muži
Women - ženy
Gentlemen - pánové
Ladies - dámy
Open - otevřeno/otvorené
Closed - zavřeno/zavreté

Danger! - pozor!
Hospital - nemocnice/nemocnica
No smoking - kouření zakázáno/zákaz fajčiť
No bathing - koupání zakázáno/ zákaz kúpa-
nia
No entry - vstup zakázáno
Arrivals - příjezd/príchod
Departure - odjezd/odchod
Police - policie/polícia

Days of the week

Monday - pondělí/pondelok
Tuesday - úterý/utorok
Wednesday - středa/streda
Thursday - čtvrtek/žtvrtok
Friday - pátek/piatok
Saturday - sobota

Sunday - neděle/nedľa
Day - den/deň
Week - týden/týždeň
Month - měsíc/mesiac
Year - rok

Numbers

0 - nula
1 - jeden
2 - dva
3 - tří/tri

4 - čtyří/štyri
5 - pět/päť
6 - šest/šest
7 - sedm/sedem

L

LANGUAGE

8 - osum/osem	60 - šedesát/šesťdesiat
9 - devět/deväť	70 - sedmdesát/sedemdesiat
10 - deset/desať	80 - osumdesát/osemdesiat
11 - jedenáct/jedenásť	90 - devadesát/deväťdesiat
12 - dvanáct/dvanásť	100 - sto
13 - třínáct/trinásť	101 - sto jedna
14 - čtrnáct/žtrnásť	155 - sto padesát pět/stodpäťdesiatpäť
15 - patnáct/pätnásť	200 - dvě stě/dvesto
16 - šestnáct/šestnásť	300 - tři sta/tristo
17 - sedmnáct/sedemnásť	400 - čtyři sta/štyristo
18 - osmnáct/osemnásť	500 - pět set/päťsto
19 - devatenáct/devätnásť	600 - šest set/šesto
20 - dvacet/dvadsat	700 - sedm set/sedemsto
21 - dvacetjedna/dvadsaťjeden	800 - osum set/osemsto
30 - třícet/tridsať	900 - devět set/deväťsto
40 - čtyřícet/štyridsať	1000 - tisíc
50 - padesát/päťdesiat	

Months of the year

Czechs and Slovaks use completely different words to denote the **months of the year**. While the Slovaks copy the Roman calendar names, Czech uses the highly individual Slav system, in which the names of the month are descriptive nouns – sometimes beautifully apt for the month in question.

Czech

January - leden – ice
February - únor – renewal
March - březen – birch
April - duben – oak
May - květen – blossom
June - červen – red
July - červenec – redder
August - srpen – sickle
September - zaří – blazing
October - říjen – rutting
November - listopad – leaves falling
December - prosinec – slaughter of the pig

Slovak

January - január
February - február
March - marec
April - apríl
May - máj
June - jún
July - júl
August - august
September - september
October - október
November - november
December - december

Some foreign countries in Czech

Australia Austálie
Austria Rakousko
Canada Kanada
Ireland Irsko
Germany Německo

Great Britain Velká Britanie
Hungary Maďarsko
Netherland Nizozemí
New Zealand Nový Zéland
USA Spojené státy americké

Some foreign countries in Slovak

Australia - *Austrália*
Austria - *Rakúsko*
Canada - *Kanada*

Czech Republic - *Česká republika*
Germany - *Nemecko*
Great Britain - *Veľká Británia*

Hungary - *Maďarsko*
Ireland - *Írsko*
Netherlands - *Nizozemí*
New Zealand - *Nový Zéland*

Poland - *Polsko*
Ukraine - *Ukrajina*
USA - *Spojené štáty americké*

Czech food and drink glossary

Basics

chléb - bread
chlebíček - (open) sandwich
cukr - sugar
hořice - mustard
houska - round roll
jídla na - main dishes
objednávku - to order
knedlíky - dumplings
křen - horseradish
lžíce - spoon
maso - meat
máslo - butter
med - honey
mléko - milk
moučník - dessert
nápoje - drinks
nůž - knife
oběd - lunch
obloha - garnish
ocet - vinegar
ovoce - fruit

pečivo - pastry
pepř - pepper
polévka - soup
předkrmy - starters
přílohy - side dishes
rohlík - finger roll
ryby - fish
rýže - rice
sklenice - glass
snídaně - breakfast
sůl - salt
šálek - cup
talíř - plate
tartarská omáčka - tartare sauce
těstoviny - noodles, pasta
večeře - supper/dinner
vejce - eggs
vidlička - fork
volské oko - fried egg
zeleniny - vegetables

Soups

boršč - beetroot soup
bramborová - potato soup
čočková - lentil soup
fazolová - bean soup
hovězí vývar - beef broth

hrachová - pea soup
zelná - sauerkraut and meat soup
kuřecí - thin chicken soup
rajská - tomato soup
zeleninová - vegetable soup

Fish

kapr - carp
losos - salmon
makrela - mackerel
platýs - flounder
pstruh - trout
rybí filé - fillet of fish

sardinka - sardine
štika - pike
treska - cod
úhoř - eel
zavináč - herring/rollmop

Meat dishes

bažant - pheasant
biftek - beef steak
čevapčiči - spicy meatballs
dršťky - tripe
drůbež - poultry
guláš - goulash
hovězí - beef
husa - goose
játra - liver
jazyk - tongue
kachna - duck
karbanátky - minced meat rissoles
klobásy - sausages
kotleta - cutlet
kuře - chicken

kýta - leg
ledvinky - kidneys
řízek - steak
roštěná - sirloin
salám - salami
sekaná - meat loaf
skopové - maso mutton
slanina - bacon
svíčková - fillet of beef
šunka - ham
telecí - veal
vepřové - pork
vepřové řízek - breaded pork cutlet or
 schnitzel
žebírko - ribs

Vegetables

brambory - potatoes
brokolice - broccoli
celer - celery
cibule - onion
česnek - garlic
chřest - asparagus
čočka - lentils
fazole - beans
houby - mushrooms
hranolky - chips, French fries
hrášek - peas
karotka - carrot
květák - cauliflower

kyselá okurka - pickled gherkin
kyselé - zelí sauerkraut
lečo - ratatouille
lilek - aubergine
okurka - cucumber
pórek - leek
rajče - tomato
ředkev - radish
řepná bulva - beetroot
špenát - spinach
zelí - cabbage
žampiony - mushroom

Fruit, cheese and nuts

banán - banana
borůvky - blueberries
broskev - peach
bryndza - goat's cheese in brine
citrón - lemon
grep - grapefruit
hermelín - Czech brie
hrozny - grapes
hruška - pear
jablko - apple
jahody - strawberries
kompot - stewed fruit
maliny - raspberries
mandle - almonds
měkký sýr - soft cheese
meruňka - apricot

niva - semi-soft, crumbly, blue cheese
oříšky - peanuts
ostružiny - blackberries
oštěpek - heavily smoked curd cheese
parenica - rolled strips of lightly smoked curd
 cheese
pivní sýr - cheese flavoured with beer
pomeranč - orange
rozinky - raisins
švestky - plums
třešně - cherries
tvaroh - fresh curd cheese
urda - soft, fresh, whey cheese
uzený sýr - smoked cheese
vlašské ořechy - walnuts

Common terms

čerstvý - fresh
domácí - home-made
duzený - stew/casserole
grilovaný - roast on the spit
kyselý - sour
na kmíně - with caraway seeds
na roztu - grilled
na smetaně - in cream sauce
na zdraví - cheers!
nadívaný - stuffed
nakládaný - pickled
(za)pečený - baked/roast

plněný - stuffed
m.m. (maštěny máslem) - with melted butter
sladký - sweet
slaný - salted
smažený - fried in bread-crumbs
studený - cold
syrový - raw
sýrový - cheesy
teplý - hot
uzený - smoked
vařený - boiled
znojemský - with gherkins

Drinks

burčák - young wine
bílé víno - white wine
čaj - tea
červené víno - red wine
destiláty - spirits
káva - coffee
koňak - brandy
láhev - bottle

led - ice
minerálka - mineral water
mléko - milk
pivo - beer
suché víno - dry wine
svařák - mulled wine
vinný střik - white wine with soda
víno - wine

Slovak food and drink glossary

Basics

chlebíček - open sandwich
chlieb - bread
chren - horseradish
čierne korenie - pepper
cukor - sugar
horčica - mustard
jedálny lístok - menu
jidla na objednávku - main dishes to order
knedle - dumplings
lyžica - spoon
máslo - butter
mäso - meat
med - honey
mlieko - milk
múčnik - dessert
nôž - knife
obed - lunch
ocot - vinegar
ovocie - fruit

pečivo - pastry
pohár - glass
polievka - soup
predkrmy - starters
raňajky - breakfast
rezance - noodles/pasta
rohlík - finger roll
ryba - fish
ryža - rice
šalát - salad
šálka - cup
soľ - salt
tanier - plate
tartarská omáčka - tartare sauce
vajcia - eggs
večera - supper/dinner
vidlička - fork
zeleniny - vegetables

Soups

boršč - beetroot soup
fazuľová - bean soup
hovädzia - beef soup
hrachová - pea soup
kapustnica - sauerkraut and meat soup

kuracia - thin chicken soup
paradajková - tomato soup
šošovicová - lentil soup
zeleninová - vegetable soup
zemiaková - potato soup

Fish

losos - salmon
kapor - carp
makrela - mackerel
pstruh - trout

sardinka - sardine
šťuka - pike
treska - cod
zavináč - herring/rollmop

Meat dishes

baranina - mutton
bracvové - pork
bravčové rezeň breaded pork cutlet/schnitzel
čevabčiče - spicy meatballs
dršky - tripe
hovädzie - beef
hydina - poultry
jazyk - tongue
klobásy - sausages
kotleta - cutlet
kurča - chicken

kačica - duck
stehno - thigh
obličky - kidneys
pečeň - liver
saláma - salami
sekaná - meat loaf
slanina - bacon
sviečková - sirloin
šunka - ham
teľacie - veal
rebierko - ribs

Vegetables

cibuľa - onion
cesnak - garlic
cukrová repa - beetroot
fazuľa - beans
hranolky - chips, French fries
hrášky - peas
huby - mushrooms
kapusta - cabbage
karfiol - cauliflower
kyselá okurka - pickled gherkin
kyselá kapusta - sauerkraut

liečo - ratatouille (canned)
mrkva - carrots
paradajka - tomato
rajčina - tomato
reďkovka - radish
šošovica - lentils
špargľa - asparagus
špenát - spinach
uhorka - cucumber
zemiaky - potatoes

Fruit, cheese and nuts

banán - banana
borievky - blueberries
broskyňa - peach
bryndza - goat's cheese in brine
čerešňa - cherry
černica - blackberries
citrón - lemon
hrozienky - raisins

hrozny - grapes
hruška - pear
jablko - apple
kompot - stewed fruit
jahody - strawberries
maliny - raspberries
mandle - almonds
marhuľa - apricot

613

niva - semi-soft crumbly blue cheese
orechy - walnuts
oriezky - peanuts
pomoranč - orange

slivky - plums
tvaroh - fresh curd cheese
údený syr - smoked cheese
urda - soft, fresh whey cheese

Common terms

čerstvý - fresh
domáci - home-made
dušený - stew/casserole
grilovaný - roast on the spit
kôpar - dill
kyslý - sour
miešaný - mixed
na rasci - with caraway seeds
na ražni - grilled
nadívaný - stuffed
nakládaný - pickled

(za)pečený - baked/roast
plnený - stuffed
sladký - sweet
slaný - salted
studený - cold
surový - raw
teplý - hot
údený. - smoked
varený - boiled
vyprážený - fried in breadcrumbs
znojmský - served with gherkins

Drinks

biele víno - white wine
čaj - tea
červené víno - red wine
destiláty - spirits
káva - coffee
koňak - brandy
fľaša - bottle

led - ice
mlieko - milk
pivo - beer
suché víno - dry wine
víno - wine
nazdravie - cheers!

An A–Z of Czech and Slovak street names

After 1989, most of the streets named after erstwhile stars of the Communist Party disappeared. This was not the first (nor the last) time that the sign writers had put their brushes to use: after World War I, the old Habsburg names were replaced by Czech and Slovak ones; then under the Nazis, the streets were named after Hitler and his cronies, only for the Czech and Slovak names to be reinstated in 1945; while under the Communists, the names were changed once (or twice) more. Since independence in 1993, the Slovaks have expunged a few Czechs and supplanted them with newly rehabilitated Slovak nationalists, and so the process continues. The following names are currently the most popular in the Czech and Slovak republics; remember that street names always appear in the genitive or adjectival form, eg Palacký street as Palackého or Hus street as Husova.

5 května (May 5). The day of the Prague Uprising against the Nazis in 1945.

17 listopadu (November 17). In fact, this street name commemorates the anti-Nazi demonstration of November 17, 1939, after which the Nazis closed down all Czech institutions of higher education. The November 17, 1989 demonstration was held to commemorate the 1939 one, but, after the attack by the police, signalled the beginning of the Velvet Revolution.

28 října (October 28). Anniversary of the foundation of Czechoslovakia in 1918.

29 August. The day the unsuccessful Slovak National Uprising against the Nazis began in 1944.

Beneš, Edvard (1884–1948). Hero to some, traitor to others, Beneš was president from 1935 until 1938, when he resigned, having refused to lead the country into bloodshed over the Munich Crisis, and again from 1945 until 1948, when he acquiesced to the Communist coup.

Bernolák, Anton (1762–1813). Slovak theologian and pioneer in the Slovak written language. Author of the first Slovak dictionary.

Bezruč, Petr (1867–1958). Pen name of the Czech poet Vladimír Vayek, who wrote about the hardships of the Ostrava mining region.

Čapek, Karel (1890–1938). Czech writer, journalist and unofficial spokesperson for the First Republic. His most famous works are *The Insect Play* and *R.U.R.*, which introduced the word robot into the English language.

Čech, Svatopluk (1846–1908). Extreme Czech nationalist and poet whose best-known work is *Songs of a Slave*.

Chelčicky, Petr (born c.1390). Extreme pacifist Hussite preacher who disapproved of the violence of Žižka and his Taborite army.

Dobrovský, Josef (1753–1829). Jesuit-taught pioneer in Czech philology. Wrote the seminal text *The History of Czech Language and Literature*.

Duklianské hrdiny (The Dukla Heroes). The name given to the soldiers who died capturing the Dukla Pass in October 1944, the first decisive battle in the liberation of the country from the Nazis.

Dvořák, Antonín (1841–1904). Perhaps the most famous of all Czech composers, whose best-known work, the *New World Symphony*, was inspired by his extensive sojourn in the USA.

Havlíček-Borovský, Karel (1821–56). Satirical poet, journalist and nationalist, exiled to the Tyrol by the Austrian authorities after 1848.

Hlinka, Andrej (1864–1938). Leader of the Slovak People's Party, which went on to form the government of the Slovak Nazi puppet state (see p.505).

Hodža, Milan (1878–1944). Slovak politician who was in favour of the establishment of Czechoslovakia, led the Agrarian Party, and served as prime minister for a brief period in the 1930s.

Horáková, Milada (1901–1950). Socialist parliamentary deputy who was killed in the Stalinist purges.

Hurban, Jozef Miroslav (1817–88). Slovak writer and journalist who edited various pioneering Slovak-language journals.

Hus, Jan (1370–1415). Rector of Prague University and reformist preacher who was burnt at the stake as a heretic by the Council of Constance (see p.180).

Hviezdoslav, Pavol Orságh (1849–1921). The father of Slovak poetry, who lived in the Orava region working as a court official until his retirement.

Janáček, Leoš (1854–1928). Moravian-born composer, based in Brno for most of his life, whose operas in particular have become quite widely performed in the West.

Jánošík (1688–1713) Fabled Slovak folk hero, modelled along the lines of Robin Hood, who operated in the Malá Fatra range (see p.496).

Jesenský, Janko (1874–1945). Slovak poet who accompanied the Czechoslovak Legion in its long trek across the Russia during the Bolshevik Revolution.

Jirásek, Alois (1851–1930). Writer for both children and adults who popularized Czech legends and became a key figure in the national revival.

Jiří z Poděbrad (1458–71). The only Hussite and last Czech king of Bohemia, better known to the English as George of Poděbrady.

Jungmann, Josef (1773–1847). Prolific Czech translator and author of the seminal *History of Czech Literature* and the first Czech dictionary.

Karl IV (1346–78). Luxembourgeois king of Bohemia and Holy Roman Emperor responsible for Prague's golden age in the fourteenth century. Better known to the English as Charles IV.

Kollár, Ján (1793–1852). Professor of Slav archeology in Vienna and Slovak poet who wrote in Czech and opposed the formation of a separate Slovak written language.

Komenský, Jan Amos (1592–1670). Leader of the Protestant Unity of Czech Brethren.

Forced to flee the country and settle in England during the Counter-Reformation. Better known to the English as Comenius.

Kráľ Janko (1822–76). A Slovak poet who wrote folk ballads, while **Fraňo** (1903–55) is a Slovak Communist poet and no relation to the former.

Lidice. Bohemian village outside Prague which fell victim to the Nazis in June 1942 in retaliation for the murder of Reinhard Heydrich: the male inhabitants were shot, the women and children were sent to the camps and the entire place was burnt to the ground.

Mácha, Karel Hynek (1810–36). Romantic nationalist poet and great admirer of Byron and Keats, who, like them, died young. His most famous poem is *Máj*, published just months before his death.

Masaryk, Tomáš Garrigue (1850–1937). Professor of Philosophy at Prague University, President of the Republic (1918–35). His name is synonymous with the First Republic and was removed from all street signs after the 1948 coup. Now back with a vengeance.

Nálepka, Ján (1912–43). Slovak teacher and partisan in World War II who won fame through his daring antics in Nazi-occupied Ukraine, where he eventually died.

Němcová, Božena (1820–62). Highly popular writer who got involved with the nationalist movement and shocked with her unorthodox behaviour. Her most famous book is *Grandmother*.

Neruda, Jan. (1834–91). Poet and journalist for the *Národní listy*. Wrote some famous short stories describing Prague's Malá Strana.

Opletal, Jan (1915–39). Czech student killed by Nazis in 1939 during anti-Nazi demonstration.

Palach, Jan (1947–69). Philosophy student who committed suicide by self-immolation in protest against the 1968 Soviet invasion.

Palacký, František (1798–1876). Nationalist historian, Czech MP in Vienna and leading figure in the events of 1848.

Pavlov, I.P. (1849–1936). Russian Nobel prize-winning scientist, famous for his experiments on dogs (hence, "Pavlov's dogs"), from which he developed the theory of conditioned reflexes.

Purkyně, Jan Evangelista (1787–1869). Czech doctor, natural scientist and pioneer in experimental physiology who became professor of physiology at Prague and then WrocΔœaw universities.

Ressel, Josef (1793–1857). Fascinatingly enough, the Czech inventor of the screw-propeller.

Rieger, Ladislav (1818–1903). Nineteenth-century Czech politician and one of the leading figures in the events of 1848 and its aftermath.

Šafárik, Pavol Jozef (1795–1861). Slovak scholar and son of a Slovak Lutheran pastor whose major works were actually written in Czech and German.

Sládkovič, Andrej (1820–72). Slovak poet who lived and worked in the Detva region and whose pastoral love poem *Marína* is regarded as a classic.

Smetana, Bedřich (1824–84). Popular Czech composer and fervent nationalist whose *Má vlast* (My Homeland) traditionally opens the Prague Spring Music Festival.

SNP (Slovenské národné povstanie). The ill-fated Slovak National Uprising against the Nazis which took place in August/September 1944.

Sokol (Falcon). Physical education movement founded in 1862 and very much modelled on its German counterpart. The organization was a driving force during the Czech national revival, but was banned by the Nazis and later the Communists.

Štefánik, Milan Rastislav (died 1919). Slovak explorer and fighter pilot who fought and campaigned for Czechoslovakia during World War I.

Štúr, Ľudovít (1815–56). Slovak nationalist who led the 1848 revolt against the Hungarians and argued for a Slovak language distinct from Czech.

Svoboda, Ludvík (1895–1979). Victorious Czech general from World War II who acquiesced to the 1948 Communist coup and was Communist president during the Prague Spring in 1968 and until 1975.

Tajovský, Jozef Gregor (1874–1940). Slovak dramatist and short-story writer whose moral ethics and identification with the underdog made him a sharp social critic of the times.

Tyl, Josef Kajetán (1808–56). Czech playwright and composer of the Czech national anthem, *Where is my Home?*

Vajanský, Svetozár Hurban (1847–1916).

Romantic Slovak novelist whose Russophile views were as unpopular then as now.

Wilson, Woodrow (1856–1924). US president who oversaw the peace settlement after World War I, and was therefore seen by many as one of the founders of Czechoslovakia.

Wolker, Jiří (1900–24). Czech Communist who died of TB aged 24 and whose one volume of poetry was lauded by the Communists as the first truly proletarian writing.

Žižka, Jan (died 1424). Brilliant, blind military leader of the Táborites, the radical faction of the Hussites.

A glossary of Czech and Slovak words and terms

brána gate.
čajovna teahouse
český Bohemian.
chata chalet-type bungalow, country cottage or mountain hut.
chrám large church.
cintorín cemetery (Slovak).
cukrárna/cukáreň pastry shop.
divadlo theatre.
dolina valley (Slovak).
dóm cathedral.
dům/dom house.
dům kultury/dom kúltury communal arts and social centre; literally "house of culture".
hrad castle.
hranice/hranica border.
hřbitov cemetery (Czech).
hora mountain.
hospoda pub.
hostinec pub.
jeskyně/jaskyňa cave.
jezero/jazero lake.
kámen/kameň rock.
kaple/kaplnka chapel.
kaštieľ manor house (Slovak).
katedrála cathedral.
kavárna/kaváreň coffee house.
klášter/kláštor monastery.
kostel/kostol church.
koupaliště/kúpalisko swimming pool.
kúpele spa (Slovak).
Labe River Elbe.
lanovka funicular or cable car.
lázně spa (Czech).
les forest.
město/mesto town; staré město – old town, nové město – new town, dolní město – lower town, horní město – upper town.
moravský Moravian.
most bridge.

nábřeží/nábrežie embankment.
nádraží train station (Czech).
náměstí/námestie square, as in náměstí svo-body/námestie slobody – freedom square.
Nisa River Neisse.
Odra River Oder.
ostrov island.
paneláky prefabricated high-rise housing.
památník/pamätník memorial or monument.
pivnice/pivnica pub.
planina valley basin (Slovak).
pleso mountain lake (Slovak).
pramen natural spring.
prohlídka/prehliadka viewpoint.
radnice/radnica town hall.
řeka/rieka river.
restaurace/reštaurácia restaurant.
sad park.
sál room or hall (in a chateau or castle).
schody steps.
sedlo saddle (of a mountain).
skála/skala crag/rock.
skansen/skanzen an open-air folk museum, with reconstructed folk art and architecture.
slovenský Slovak.
stanica train station (Slovak).
staré město/staré mesto old town.
štít peak (Slovak).
svatý/svätý saint – often abbreviated to sv.
teplice spa.
třída/trieda avenue.
ulice/ulica street.
věž/veža tower.
vinárna/vináreň wine bar or cellar.
Vltava River Moldau.
vrchy hills.
vrchovina uplands.
výstava exhibition.
zahrada/záhrada gardens.
zámek/zámok chateau.

An architectural glossary

Ambulatory Passage round the back of the altar, in continuation of the aisles.

Art Nouveau Sinuous and stylized form of architecture and decorative arts. Imported from Vienna and Budapest from 1900–10 and therefore known in Czechoslovakia as the Secession rather than Jugendstil, the German term.

Baroque Expansive, exuberant architectural style of the seventeenth and mid-eighteenth centuries, characterized by ornate decoration, complex spatial arrangement and grand vistas.

Beautiful Style Also known as the Soft Style of painting. Developed in Bohemia in the fourteenth century, it became very popular in Germany.

Chancel Part of the church where the altar is placed, usually at the east end.

Empire A highly decorative Neoclassical style of architecture and decorative arts practised in the first part of the nineteenth century.

Fresco Mural painting applied to wet plaster, so that the colours immediately soak into the wall.

Functionalism Plain, boxy, modernist architectural style, prevalent in the late 1920s and 1930s in Czechoslovakia, often using plate-glass curtain walls and open-plan interiors.

Gothic Architectural style prevalent from the twelfth to the sixteenth century, characterized by pointed arches and ribbed vaulting.

Loggia Covered area on the side of a building,

often arcaded.

Nave Main body of a church, usually the western end.

Neoclassical Late eighteenth- and early nineteenth-century style of architecture and design returning to classical Greek and Roman models as a reaction against Baroque and Rococo excesses.

Oriel A bay window, usually projecting from an upper floor.

Predella Small panel below the main scenes of an altarpiece.

Romanesque Solid architectural style of the late tenth to thirteenth centuries, characterized by round-headed arches and geometrical precision.

Rococo Highly florid, fiddly though (occasionally) graceful style of architecture and interior design, forming the last phase of Baroque.

Secession Style of early-twentieth-century art and architecture based in Germany and Austria and a reaction against the academic establishment (see also "Art Nouveau").

Sgraffito Monochrome plaster decoration effected by means of scraping back the first white layer to reveal the black underneath.

Shingle Wooden roof tiles.

Stucco Plaster used for decorative effects.

Trompe l'oeil Painting designed to fool the onlooker into believing that it is actually three-dimensional.

Tympanum Area above doorway or within a pediment.

Historical and political terms

Czech Lands A phrase used to denote Bohemia and Moravia.

First Republic The new Czechoslovak Republic founded by Masaryk after World War II, made up of Bohemia, Moravia, Silesia, Slovakia and Ruthenia, dismantled by the Nazis in 1938–39.

Great Moravian Empire The first Slav state covering much of what is now Czechoslovakia, which ended shortly after the Magyar invasion of 896 AD.

Greek-Catholic Church Formed from various

breakaways from the Eastern (Orthodox) Church in the sixteenth century, the Greek-Catholic Church retains many Orthodox practices and rituals but is affiliated to the Roman Catholic Church. Also known as the Uniate Church.

Habsburgs The most powerful royal family in central Europe, whose power base was Vienna. They held the Bohemian and Hungarian thrones from 1526 to 1918, and by marriage and diplomacy acquired territories all over Europe.

Historic Provinces Land traditionally belonging to the Bohemian crown, including Bohemia, Egerland, Moravia, Silesia and Lusatia.

Holy Roman Empire Name given to the loose confederation of German states (including for a while the Czech Lands) which lasted from 800 until 1806.

Hussites Name given to Czech religious reformers who ostensibly followed the teachings of Jan Hus (1370–1415).

Jagiellonians Polish-Lithuanian dynasty who ruled the Czech Lands from 1471 to 1526.

Magyars The people who ruled over the Hungarian Kingdom and now predominate in modern-day Hungary.

Mitteleuropa Literally German for "central Europe", but it also conveys the idea of a multi-lingual central European culture, lost after the break-up of the Habsburg Empire.

Národní fronta Literally the National Front, the dummy coalition of parties dominated by the Communists which ruled the country until December 1989.

Národní obrození/národné obrodenie Czech/Slovak "national revival" movements of the nineteenth century, which sought to rediscover the lost identities of the Czech and Slovak people, particularly their history and language.

Přemyslid The dynasty of Czech princes and kings who ruled over the Historic Lands of Bohemia from the ninth century to 1306.

Ruthenia Officially Sub-Carpatho-Ruthenia, the easternmost province of the First Republic, annexed by the Soviet Union at the end of World War II.

Sudetenland Name given to mostly German-speaking border regions of the Czech Lands, awarded to Nazi Germany in the Munich Diktat of September 1938.

Velvet Revolution The popular protests of November/December 1989 which brought an end to 41 years of Communist rule. Also known as the Gentle Revolution.

Abstract — Abbreviations

Abbreviations

CKM (Cestovní kanceláu mládeže) Youth Travel Organization.

ČEDOK Former state travel and tourist agency in Czech Republic.

ČD (české dráhy) Czech Railways.

ČSAD (česká státní automobilová doprava) Czech state bus company.

HDĽS Andrej Hlinka's Slovak People's Party, the largest political party in Slovakia between the wars, and later the leading political force in the wartime clerico-fascist state.

HZDS Movement for a Democratic Slovakia.

KSČ (Komunistická strana československá) The Czechoslovak Communist Party (now defunct).

KSČM Communist Party of Bohemia and Moravia (still functioning).

ODS (Občanská demokratická strana) Civic Democratic Party – right-wing faction of Civic Forum.

SAD (Slovenská automobilová doprava) Slovak bus company.

SATUR Former state travel and tourist agency in Slovakia.

SdP Sudeten German Party (Sudetendeutsche Partei), the main proto-Nazi Party in Czechoslovakia in the late 1930s.

SNS (Slovenská národná strana) Slovak National Party – extremist Slovak nationalists.

StB (Státní bezpečnost) The Communist secret police (now disbanded).

ŽSR (Železnice Slovenskej republiky) Slovak Railways.

Index

and small print

Index

Map entries are in colour

A

absinthe 44
accommodation
  in the Czech Republic 37
  in Slovakia......................420
addresses 24
Adršpach 300
airlines
  in Australia & New Zealand 14
  in Britain & Ireland 12
  in the US & Canada 13
alphabet........................24
Antýgl..........................208
art galleries, Czech
  Republic......................46
Aussig 264–266
Austerlitz, Battle of 349

B

Babiččino údolí 306
banks 22
Banská Bystrica ..475–480
Banská Bystrica ...478–479
Banská Štiavnica.483–485
Banská Štiavnica 484
Bardejov 550–553
Bardejov 551
Bardejovské kúpele 553
Baťa, Tomáš................374
Báthori, Countess
  Elizabeth 468
Bechyně......................178
Beckov........................467
beer
  in the Czech Republic 44
  in Slovakia......................424
Belianska jaskyňa 520
Belianske Tatry.............520
Benešov 158
Benešov nad Ploučnicí ..272
Beskydy............406–413
Betlém........................313
Betliar........................542
Bezděz........................273
Bílá hora, Battle of..128, 573
Bílá Lhota....................395
Bílek, František 121
Bítov..........................359
Blansko 348
Blatnica......................489
Bohdaneč 318

Bohemia, East 285–323
Bohemia, East..............286
Bohemia, North ...247–281
Bohemia, North 248–249
Bohemia, South...169–209
Bohemia, South 170
Bohemia, West 213–243
Bohemia, West.............214
Bohunice......................466
Bojnice 500
books 593–601
Boubín 204
Bouzov........................395
Brahe, Tycho................93
Bratislava 429–451
Bratislava 432–433
Bratislava, central 436
accommodation...............434
arrival 431
Devín..........................450
Dóm sv Martina 440
drinking 448
eating 447
entertainment................448
Hrad 380
Jewish quarter 440
Kamzík 450
listings.........................449
Muzeum mimoeurópskych
  kultúr..........................440
Námestie SNP 445
Nový most.....................443
Pálffyho palác 438
Petržalka 442
Primaciálny palác...........439
Rusovce......................451
Slavín Monument.............446
Slovenská národná galéria
 444
Slovenské národné múzeum
 444
Stará radnica 438
Staré mesto.............435–439
tourist information...........434
Zlaté Piesky 450
Brezno........................510
Brezová pod Bradlom...453
Brhlovce......................465
Brno 329–345
Brno 332–333
accommodation................331
Cathedral 335
drinking 344
eating 343
entertainment................344
Fuchs, Bohuslav 341
Janáček, Leoš................338
Mendelianum 341

Místodržitelský palác 339
Moravské zemské muzeum
 334
Muzeum města Brna 340
Náměstí Svobody 336
Pražákův palác 339
Špilberk......................340
UPM 339
Vila Tugendhat 342
Výstaviště....................341
Zelný trh......................334
Broggio, Octavio..........262
Broumov......................301
Bruntál 398
Bučovice......................350
Buchlov......................372
Buchlovice....................372
Budatínsky zámok 494
Budvar brewery 189
Budweiser....................189
Burian, Zdeněk 408
Busabout 17
buses
  in the Czech Republic 34
  in Slovakia......................418
  to the Czech & Slovak
    republics.......................16
Bystřice nad Olší 407
Bystrá........................510

C

Čachtice......................467
camping in the Czech
  Republic......................38
camping in Slovakia 420
car ferries from Britain 17
car rental in the Czech
  Republic......................36
Carlsbad...............237–242
Carpathians, Small
 451–454
Carpatho-Ruthenia
 545–556
Casanova, Giacomo 254
castles in the Czech
  Republic......................45
castles in Slovakia 424
Častolovice 311
Čeňkova Pila................208
Černá v Pošumaví 200
Černová 505
Černý Kříž 201
Červená Lhota 185

Červený Kláštor 531
Česká Kamenice...........271
Česká Lípa...................272
Česká Skalice 306
České Budějovice..187–190
České Budějovice........187
České středohoří 264
České Švýcarsko ..266–272
Ceské Švýcarsko 270
Český kras 161
Český Krumlov 192–197
Český Krumlov.............193
Český ráj 285–293
Český ráj 288
Český Šternberk 157
Český Těšín 413
changing money 21
Charles IV 569
Charter...................77, 586
Cheb 231
Cheb 231–234
children 27
Chlum 413
Chlumec nad Cidlinou ..315
Chodové 223
Chomutov 253
Chopin, Frédéric 227
Chopok 509
Chrudim 319
Chýnov.........................179
Čičmany 498
Čierná nad Tisou 563
cinema in the Czech
    Republic...................48
Čingov..........................538
coaches to the Czech &
    Slovak republics......16
Comenius, John............394
Communist coup 582
consulates abroad, Czech
   18
consulates abroad, Slovak
   19
crime 25
cross-channel ferries 18
currency 21
customs allowances 19
cycling in the Czech
    Republic...................37
cycling in Slovakia........419
Czech tourist offices.......22
Czechoslovak Legion ...577

D

Ďumbier 509
Dalibor 75
Danube Basin 460–465

Dargov Pass 562
Děčín 267
Děčín 267–269
Děčínský Sněžník.........270
Dedinky........................539
Demänovská dolina 509
Destinnová, Ema..........184
Detva............................487
disabled travellers...........26
discount agents
    in Australia & New Zealand..15
    in the US & Canada............14
Ditters von Dittersdorf, Karl
   399
Dobroslava...................552
Dobšiná ice cave 539
Doksy...........................273
Dolní Věstonice............353
Dolní Vltavice 200
Dolný Kubín 500
Domažlice 222–224
Domica caves 543
Doudleby......................311
drink
    in the Czech Republic 45
    in Slovakia....................423
driving
    in the Czech Republic 35
    in Slovakia....................419
    to the Czech & Slovak
    republics.....................17
Dubček, Alexander 446
Duchcov.......................254
Dukla Pass 555
Dukla Praha 159
Dvořák, Antonín
    ....116, 118, 144, 293
Dvůr Králové nad Labem
   313

E

Edict of Tolerance.........573
Edward VII....................227
Eger......................231–234
Egerland.......................232
electricity.......................27
email
    in the Czech Republic 40
    in Slovakia....................422
embassies abroad
    Czech....................18
    Slovak....................19
emergencies (money)......22
emergencies 25
Eurail 16
Eurolines......................17
Eurostar 15
Eurotunnel....................17

F

Fatra, Lúčanska 492
Fatra, Malá 422–427
Fatra, Veľká 489
festivals
    in the Czech Republic 47
    in Slovakia....................425
Fiľakovo........................487
film in the Czech Republic
   49
flights
    from Australia & New Zealand
   14
    from Britain & Ireland 12
    from the US & Canada 13
    within the Czech Republic..37
food
    Czech...................41, 610
    Slovak 423, 612
football
    in the Czech Republic 49
    in Slovakia....................426
Františkovy Lázně
   234–237
Františkovy Lázně........235
Franz Ferdinand, Archduke
   157
Franzensbad 234–237
Frenštát pod Radhoštěm
   410
Freud, Sigmund 409
Frýdek-Místek...............412
Frýdlant 280
Frýdštejn 293
Frymburk.......................200
Fuchs, Bohuslav 341

G

Gabčíkovo-Nagymaros
    Dam..........................461
Gaderská dolina............489
gay life 27
Gerlachovský štít 519
Gočár, Josef 310, 318
Goethe, Johann Wolfgang
    von 228
Gojdič, Pavel.................549
Gombasecká jaskyňa..543
Good King Wenceslas 72
Gottwald, Klement..120, 582
Great Moravian Empire
    ....370, 567
Greek-Catholic Church ..548
Guty 407
Gypsies 591

INDEX

H

Harrachov 297
Hašek, Jaroslav 116, 181
health 20
Hejnice 280
Heľpa...........................511
Helfštýn 393
Henlein, Konrad 277
Hermany geyser...........562
Heydrich, Reinhard 114
High Tatras...........512–521
High Tatras 513
hiking
in the Czech Republic 37
in Slovakia......................420
Hirka, Ján....................549
history 567–592
Hlinka, Andrej..............505
Hlohovec......................354
Hluboká nad Vltavou 190
Hodslavice 407
Holašovice 191
Holešov........................381
holidays (public)
in the Czech Republic 47
in Slovakia......................425
Hořice v Podkrkonoší ...314
Horní Planá 200
Horšovský Týn 224
hostels
in the Czech Republic 38
in Slovakia......................420
hotels
in the Czech Republic 33
in Slovakia......................420
hours of business 22
Hrabyně 402
Hradec Králové ...306–311
Hradec Králové 307
Hradec nad Moravicí 402
Hrebienok 519
Hřensko 270
Hron valley 510
Hronsek.......................481
Hrubá skála..................287
Hrubý Jeseník 398
Hrubý Rohozec 287
Hukvaldy 410
Humenné 555
Hummel, Johann Nepomuk
..................................439
Humprecht 289
Hungarians of Slovakia
..................................463
Hus, Jan
.......91, 97, 203, 204, 570
Husinec.......................203

I

ice hockey in the Czech
Republic 49
information offices 22
internet cafés in the Czech
Republic 40
internet travel 11
InterRail........................16
Istebné 501

J

Jablonec nad Nisou......279
Jablonné v Podještědí ..273
Jáchymov 243
Jakeš, Miloš.................586
Janáček, Leoš 338, 410
Janák, Pavel 318
Jánošík, Juraj...............496
Janské Lázně 299
Jaroměř.......................311
Jaroměřice nad Rokytnou
..................................361
Jasná 509
Jasov 545
Jasovská jaskyňa..........545
Javoříčko 395
Javorník 399
Jedovnice 347
Jenišov........................201
Ještěd 278
Jeseník 399
Jeseníky 397–402
Jesenská, Milena 113
Jetřichovice.................271
Jetřichovické stěny 270
Jews in Slovakia 441
Jičín 290–292
Jihlava 364–368
Jihlava 365
Jindřichův Hradec
..........................182–185
Jindřichův Hradec........183
Jizerské hory................280
Josefov 312
Jurkovič, Dušan 373

K

Kačina 154
Kadaň..........................251
Kafka, Franz
.......75, 93, 102, 120, 147
Kaliště 181
Kámen.........................179

Kamenice gorge...........271
Karlová Studánka 398
Karlovy Vary........237–242
Karlovy Vary 238
Karlsbad 237–242
Karlštejn 160
Kašperské Hory 207
Kežmarok.............528–530
Kladno.........................163
Kladruby.......................220
Klášterec nad Ohří........252
Klatovy.........................221
Kleť Mount 192
Klimt, Gustav 240
Klokoty........................177
Kmoch, František..........151
Kokořín........................147
Kolín............................150
Komárno 462
Komenský, Jan Ámos...394
Koněpruské jeskyně 161
Konopiště.....................157
Kopřivnice....................408
Košariská 453
Košice 556–561
Košice.........................557
Kost.............................289
Kotěra, Jan 309
Kráľ, Janko 506
Kralupy nad Vltavou 143
Krásna Hôrka 542
Krásnohorské Podhradie
..................................542
Kratochvíle 191
Křivoklát 162
Kremnica 485
Krkonoše............293–300
Krkonoše 295
Krnov 400
Kroměříž 378–380
Kroměříž 378
Křtiny..........................347
Krušné hory 252
Kubová Huť..................204
Kuks............................312
Kunčice pod Ondřejníkem
..................................407
Kunerad 498
Kutná Hora..........151–155
Kutná Hora 151
Kvilda 208
Kysuce 497

L

Ladomírová 552
Lake Lipno 199
Lake Orava...................503

language 605–614
Lány 164
laundry 27
Lazisko 507
Lázně Jeseník 399
Lázně Kynžvart 230
Lázně Libverda 281
Lednice 353
Lehár, Franz 462
Lemberk 274
Lendl, Ivan 406
Lenora 204
Leštiny 501
lesbian life 27
Lety 171
Levoča 532–535
Levoča 533
Ležáky 319
Liběchov 146
Liberec 274–279
Liberec.........................274
Libkovice 254
Libochovice 249
Lidice 163
Liechtensteins 352
Lietava 498
Lipnice nad Sázavou 181
Lipno nad Vltavou........199
Liptov region........504–508
Liptovská Štiavnica.......506
Liptovská Teplička 511
Liptovský Mikuláš
..........................506–508
Litoměřice 261–264
Litoměřice 261
Litomyšl 319–321
Litomyšl 320
Litvínov........................254
Loděnice 162
Loket 242
Lomnický štít 519
Loos, Adolf...................128
Louka 357
Louny 250
Low Tatras 508–511
Löw, Rabbi...................99
Lúčanska Fatra 492
Lučenec 487
luggage, left 27
Luhačovice...................373
Lukov 552
Lysá Poľana 520
Ľysohorsky, Óndra........412

M

Mácha, Karel Hynek 118
Máchovo jezero 273
Mahler, Gustav
..................181, 366, 389
Malá Fatra...........492–500
Malá Fatra 493
Malá Morávka 398
Malá Skála 293
Malé karpaty 451–454
Malužina.......................509
maps.............................23
Marian Pilgrimage at
Levoča 534
Mariánské Lázně..225–230
Mariánské Lázně.........225
Marienbad 225–230
Markušovce 536
Martin 489–492
Martin 490
Martinů, Bohuslav.........322
Marx, Karl 241
Masaryk, Jan 79
Masaryk, Tomáš Garrigue
..................................164
Matica slovenská 489
Maxwell, Robert............465
Mečiar, Vladimír 590
Medzilaborce 555
Mělník 145
Mendel, Gregor 341
Mezná 271
Mezní Louka 271
Michalovce...................562
Mikulov 351
Milevsko.......................178
Miroľa 552
Mladá Boleslav 148
Mladečské jeskyně 395
Mnichovo Hradiště........290
Mochovce 466
Modra...........................452
Modrava.......................208
Mohyla míru 349
money...........................21
Moneygram...................22
Mór, Jókai 462
Moravia, North.....385–413
Moravia, North 386
Moravia, South 327–381
Moravia, South 328–329
Moravský kras.....345–348
Moravský Krumlov........348
Most..............................254
motorway tax discs ..17, 35
mountain huts
in the Czech Republic 38
in Slovakia.........................421
Mozart, Wolfgang
Amadeus.....................82
Mucha, Alfons.......112, 348
Munich Diktat................579
museums

in the Czech Republic 46
in Slovakia.........................424
Mužský.........................289

N

Náchod.................302–304
Náměšť nad Oslavou 361
Námestovo...................504
Napajedla.....................377
national holidays
in the Czech Republic 47
in Slovakia.........................425
Navrátilová, Martina......161
Nedvědice....................348
Nelahozeves 143
Němcová, Božena 306
Neruda, Jan 83
newspapers
in the Czech Republic 40
in Slovakia.........................422
Nitra...................457–460
Nitra 458
Nízke Tatry 508–511
Nižné Kamence............496
Nižný Komárnik............552
Nová Pec 201
Nová Ves......................289
Nové Město nad Metují 2
Nový Bor......................273
Nový Jičín 406

O

Obyčtov 369
Ochtinská jaskyňa........543
Olomouc.............385–393
Olomouc......................388
online travel agents 11
Opava 400–402
opening hours
in Czech castles 45
in Czech churches 46
in Czech museums 46
in Slovak castles................424
in Slovak churches 424
in Slovak museums 424
Opočno 305
Orava Folk Museum 502
Orava region........500–504
Oravice.........................503
Oravský hrad 502
Orlík 171
Osek.............................255
Ostrava.................403–406
Ostrava.........................403
Ostrov nad Oslavou......369
Otrokovice 377

P

Palach, Jan 103, 108
Pálava 352
Palúdza 507
Panská skála 272
Pardubice 315–318
Pardubice 315
Párkány 464
Pavlovské vrchy 351
Pec pod Sněžkou 298
Pelhřimov 180
Pernštejn 348
petrol
 in the Czech Republic 36
 in Slovakia 419
Petrov 373
pharmacies 20
Pieniny 531
Piešťany 465–467
Pilsner Urquell 217
Písek 173
plague columns 336
Plastic People of the
 Universe 586
Plasy 220
Plechý 201
Plicka, Karol 489
Ploskovice 264
Plumlov 395
Plzeň 215–219
Plzeň 216
Plzeňský Prazdroj 217
Podbiel 502
Poděbrady 149
Podkost 289
Podlesok 538
Podyjí 358
Pohorelá 511
Pohořelice 350
police 25
Polička 322
Poprad 514–516
Poprad 514
post in the Czech Republic
39
post in Slovakia 421
Prachatice 202
Prachovské skály 292
Praděd 398
Prague and around 53
Prague 53–142
 accommodation 62–67
 accommodation 64–65
 addresses 60
 arrival 56
 Astronomical clock 92
 bike rental 61
 Bílá hora 129
 boat trips 61

Café Slavia 111
cafés 132
car parking 61
cemeteries
 New Jewish 120
 Old Jewish 101
 Olšany 120
 Vyšehrad 118
Changing of the Guard 70
Charles Bridge 88
churches
 Betlémská kaple 97
 Emauzy 116
 Loreta 79
 Nejsvětější Srdce Páně .119
 Panna Maria pod řetězem
85
 Panna Maria Sněžná 110
 Panna Maria Vítězná 86
 St Vitus Cathedral 71
 Strahovský klášter 79
 sv Cyril and Metoděj 114
 sv František z Assisi 89
 sv Jakub 95
 sv Martin ve zdi 96
 sv Mikuláš (Malá Strana) .82
 sv Mikuláš (Staré Město) .92
 sv Salvátor 90
 Týn church 93
 Zrcadlová kaple 90
eating and drinking ...129–137
eating and drinking
130–131
entertainment 137
gay and lesbian nightlife ...138
history 55
Holešovice 121
Holocaust memorial 101
Hradčany 67–80
Hradčany 68–69
Hus Monument 92
Hvězda 128
Jewish Quarter 98–104
Josefov 98–104
Josefov 100
Kampa 85
Karlův most 88
Karolinum
 (Charles University) 96
Klementinum 90
listings 141
Malá Strana 80–87
Malá Strana 80
metro 59, 60
metro 59
Müllerova vila 128
museums
 Anežský klášter 95
 Bertramka (Mozart
 Museum) 129
 Bílkova vila 121
 Dům U černé Matky boží
 (Czech Cubism Museum)
94
 Dům U zlatého prstenu
 (House of the Golden
 Ring) 94

Kafka Museum 102
Mucha Museum 112
Muzeum Bedřicha Smetany
 (Smetana Museum) 97
Muzeum hraček (Toy
 Museum) 76
Muzeum loutkářských kultur
 (Puppet Museum) 90
Náprstkovo muzeum 89
Národní muzeum 108
Národní technické muzeum
123
Pedagogické muzeum 84
UPM (Applied Arts
 Museum) 103
Veletržní palác (Modern Art
 Museum) 123–127
Vila Amerika (Dvořák
 Museum) 116
Vojenské historické
 muzeum (Military History
 Museum) 77
Wax Museum Prague 110
Národní divadlo 111
Nové Město 104–117
Nové Město 106–107
Obecní dům 112
palaces
 Černínský palác 78
 Lobkovický palác
 (Hradčany) 76
 Lobkovický palác (Malá
 Strana) 83
 palác Kinských 93
 Schönbornský palác 83
 Starý královský palác 73
 Šternberský palác 77
 Valdštejnský palác 84
Petřín 86
Prague Castle 68–77
Pražský hrad 68–77
pubs and bars 134
restaurants 135
Senát 84
Staré Město 87–98
Staré Město 88
Staroměstské náměstí 92
Stavovské divadlo 96
Tančící dům (Dancing House)
116
taxis 61
tea-houses 133
tourist information 57
trams 60
transport 58
Troja 127
Týn 93
Václavské náměstí 104
Vinohrady 119
Vyšehrad 117–119
Výstaviště 127
Wenceslas Square 104
Žižkov 120
Zbraslav 129
Zlatá ulička 75
zoo 128
Prague Spring 584

Pravčická brána 271
Přemyslids 568
Přerov 393
Přerov nad Labem 148
Prešov 546–549
Prešov 547
Příbor 409
Příbram 158
Prievidza 499
Příhrazy 289
Princip, Gavrilo 260
private rooms
in the Czech Republic 38
in Slovakia......................420
pronunciation 605
Prostějov 394
Průhonice....................155
public holidays
in the Czech Republic 47
in Slovakia......................425
Punkevní jeskyně 346

R

Rabí...............................206
Radhošť 407
radio
in the Czech Republic 40
in Slovakia......................422
rail passes....................15
Rajecká Lesná 498
Rajecké Teplice.............498
Ralsko 273
Ratibořice....................306
Reichenberg, see Liberec
Řevnice 161
Roháčska dolina 503
Rohe, Mies van der.......342
Romanies.....................591
Rožmberk nad Vltavou...198
Rožňava 541
Rožnov pod Radhoštěm
.....................................411
Rudolf II 572
Rusyns 548
Ružomberok 504–506
Rybí...............................407
Rysy 518

S

Saint Agnes...................95
Saint Benedikt Junior ...460
Saint Cyril 371
Saint John of Nepomuk
.................................73, 89
Saint Methodius............371
Saint Ondrej Svorad 460

Saint Prokopius 156
Saint Wenceslas 72
Santini, Giovanni..........368
Sázava 156
Schiele, Egon...............195
Schindler, Oskar...........322
Sedlec 152
Seifert, Jaroslav 111
Semtex..........................316
Senec............................461
Senetářov....................347
Silesia..........................401
Silická ľadnica..............543
Škoda............................149
Škvorecký, Josef 303
Slanica 504
Slavkov 349
Slavonice 363
Slavoňov 305
Sliač 481
Slnečné jazerá 462
Slovácko 369–373
Slovak National Uprising
.....................................480
Slovak Sea....................562
Slovak tourist offices 23
Slovakia, Central ..475–521
Slovakia, Central..........476
Slovakia, East 525–564
Slovakia, East...........526–527
Slovakia, West 429–471
Slovakia, West 430
Slovenský kras 540–465
Slovenský raj 537–540
Slovenský raj...............538
Smetana, Bedřich
.....................97, 118, 320
smoking 27
Smokovce....................518
Sněžka 298
SNP...............................480
Sobotka 289
Soos..............................236
spas 226
speed limits
in the Czech Republic 36
in Slovakia......................419
spirits
in the Czech Republic 45
in Slovakia......................423
Špičák...........................208
Špilberk........................340
Špindlerův Mlýn............296
Spiš region 526–537
Spišská Kapitula 537
Spišská Nová Ves 535
Spišská Sobota.............515
Spišské Podhradie........537
Spišský hrad 536
Spišský Hrhov..............536

Spišský Štvrtok.............530
sport
in the Czech Republic 49
in Slovakia......................426
Srbsko...........................161
Srní...............................208
Stará Ľubovňa 531
Starý hrad 497
Starý Smokovec 518
Štefánik, Milan Rastislav
.....................................453
Štefanová.....................496
Šternberk.....................396
Stifter, Adalbert 200
Stoppard, Tom 377
Stožec..........................201
Střekov.........................266
Stříbro 220
Strakonice....................205
Štramberk 407
Strážky 530
Strážnice......................372
Štrbské Pleso...............516
Strečno 497
street names 614
student rooms
in the Czech Republic 38
in Slovakia......................420
Štúr, Ľudovít.................452
Štúrovo 464
Súľovské skály 498
Šumava 197–209
Šumava..................196–197
Šumiac 511
Šumperk 397
Sušice 206
Švankmajer, Jan...........78
Svatá hora....................159
Svatý Kopeček..............395
Svidník 553
Švihov 222
Svitavy 322
Svojanov 323
Sychrov 293

T

Tábor 174–177
Tábor 174–175
Tále 510
tampons........................27
Tatra National Park
.........................516–520
Tatranská Kotlina 520
Tatranská Lomnica........519
Tatras, High..........512–521
Tatras, High 513
Tatras, Low 508–511

INDEX

Tatras, Western 502
Telč...............................362
telephones
  in the Czech Republic 39
  in Slovakia.......................421
television
  in the Czech Republic 40
  in Slovakia.......................422
Telgárt 511
Temelín..........................172
Teplá 230
Teplice 255–258
Teplice 256
Teplice nad Metují........301
Terchová 495
Terezín 258–261
Terezín 258
theatre and opera in the
  Czech Republic............49
Theresienstadt 258–261
Thomas Cook 22
Tiesňavy........................496
time...............................27
tipping............................28
Tisá 270
Tiské stěny....................270
Tišnov 348
toilets 28
tour operators
  online 11
  in Australia & New Zealand..15
  in Britain.............................12
  in the US & Canada...........15
tourist information offices
 22
traffic laws
  in the Czech Republic 35
  in Slovakia.......................419
train passes 15
trains
  in the Czech Republic 33
  in Slovakia.......................417
  to the Czech & Slovak
    republics.........................15
transport
  in the Czech Republic........34
  in Slovakia.......................417
travel agents
  online 11
  in Australia & New Zealand..15
  in Britain.............................12
  in the US & Canada...........14
travel insurance 19
Třebechovice pod Orebem
 311
Třebíč 359–361
Třeboň...........................185

Trenčianske Teplice.......470
Trenčín 469
Trnava..................454–457
Trnava...........................455
Tročany 552
Troja 127
Troppau 340–342
Trosky............................287
Trstená 503
Trump, Ivana 377
Trutnov..........................299
Turčianske Teplice 488
Turnov 286
Tvrdošín 503

U

Uherské Hradiště 370
Ukrainian visas..............563
Uličské Krivé 552
Uniate Church...............548
Úštěk.............................264
Ústí nad Labem 264–266

V

Váchal, Josef 321
Valdice 291
Valdštejn 287
Valečov 289
Valtice 354
Važec 508
vegetarians
  in the Czech Republic 43
  in Slovakia.......................423
Veľká Fatra 489
Veľký Kriváň 497
Velehrad 371
Velké Losiny 397
Veltrusy 144
Velvet Revolution, the
  ....110, 586
vignettes 17
Vihorlat..........................563
Vimperk.........................205
Vinné 562
visa requirements............18
Vlčnov 373
Vlkolínec........................506
Volary 202
Vranov 358
Vrbov.............................530
Vrchlabí 296

Vrútky 491
Východná......................508
Vysoké Tatry.........512–521
Vyšší Brod....................198

W

Waldstein, Albrecht von
  ....233, 290, 291
Wallachian culture.........408
Warhol, Andy 556
websites, Czech & Slovak
 23
Wenceslas, Good King ...72
Western Tatras 502
Western Union 22
White Lady, the.............182
wine
  in the Czech Republic 44
  in Slovakia.......................423
wooden churches...407, 552

Y

youth hostels in the Czech
  Republic.....................38

Z

Žatec............................250
Zádielska dolina............544
Zákupy 273
Zbraslav 129
Žďár nad Sázavou 368
Ždiar.............................520
Žehra............................537
Železná Hora 208
Železná Ruda...............208
Železný Brod.................292
Žilina....................492–495
Žilina.............................494
Žižka, Jan......................571
Zemplínska šírava.........563
Zlatá Koruna 192
Žleby 154
Zlín 374–377
Zlín 375
Znojmo 355–358
Znojmo 356
Zuberec.........................502
Žulová...........................399
Zvíkov 172
Zvolen 482

INDEX

Twenty years of Rough Guides

In the summer of 1981, Mark Ellingham, Rough Guides' founder, knocked out the first guide on a typewriter, with a group of friends. Mark had been travelling in Greece after university, and couldn't find a guidebook that really answered his needs.There were heavyweight cultural guides on the one hand – good on museums and classical sites but not on beaches and tavernas – and on the other hand student manuals that were so caught up with how to save money that they lost sight of the country's significance beyond its role as a place for a cool vacation. None of the guides began to address Greece as a country, with its natural and human environment, its politics and its contemporary life.

Having no urgent reason to return home, Mark decided to write his own guide. It was a guide to Greece that tried to combine some erudition and insight with a thoroughly practical approach to travellers' needs. Scrupulously researched listings of places to stay, eat and drink were matched by careful attention to detail on everything from Homer to Greek music, from classical sites to national parks and from nude beaches to monasteries. Back in London, Mark and his friends got their Rough Guide accepted by a farsighted commissioning editor at the publisher Routledge and it came out in 1982.

The Rough Guide to Greece was a student scheme that became a publishing phenomenon. The immediate success of the book – shortlisted for the Thomas Cook award – spawned a series that rapidly covered dozens of countries. The Rough Guides found a ready market among backpackers and budget travellers, but soon acquired a much broader readership that included older and less impecunious visitors. Readers relished the guides' wit and inquisitiveness as much as the enthusiastic, critical approach that acknowledges everyone wants value for money – but not at any price.

Rough Guides soon began supplementing the "rougher" information – the hostel and low-budget listings – with the kind of detail that independent-minded travellers on any budget might expect. These days, the guides – distributed worldwide by the Penguin Group – include recommendations spanning the range from shoestring to luxury, and cover more than 200 destinations around the globe. Our growing team of authors, many of whom come to Rough Guides initially as outstandingly good letter-writers telling us about their travels, are spread all over the world, particularly in Europe, the USA and Australia. As well as the travel guides, Rough Guides publishes a series of dictionary phrasebooks covering two dozen major languages, an acclaimed series of music guides running the gamut from Classical to World Music, a series of music CDs in association with World Music Network, and a range of reference books on topics as diverse as the internet, pregnancy and unexplained phenomena. Visit **www.roughguides.com** to see what's cooking.

SMALL PRINT

Rough Guide credits

Text editor: Alison Murchie and
Geoff Howard
Series editor: Mark Ellingham
Editorial: Martin Dunford, Jonathan Buckley,
Kate Berens, Ann-Marie Shaw, Helena Smith,
Judith Bamber, Orla Duane, Olivia Swift, Ruth
Blackmore, Claire Saunders, Gavin Thomas,
Alexander Mark Rogers, Polly Thomas, Joe
Staines, Richard Lim, Duncan Clark, Peter
Buckley, Lucy Ratcliffe, Clifton Wilkinson,
Matthew Teller, Andrew Dickson, Fran
Sandham (UK); Andrew Rosenberg, Stephen
Timblin, Yuki Takagaki, Richard Koss, Hunter
Slaton, Julie Feiner (US)
Production: Susanne Hillen, Andy Hilliard,
Link Hall, Helen Prior, Julia Bovis, Michelle
Draycott, Katie Pringle, Zoë Nobes,

Rachel Holmes, Andy Turner, Michelle Bhatia
Cartography: Melissa Baker, Maxine Repath,
Ed Wright, Katie Lloyd-Jones
Cover art direction: Louise Boulton
Picture research: Sharon Martins,
Mark Thomas
Online: Kelly Cross, Anja Mutic-Blessing,
Jennifer Gold, Audra Epstein,
Suzanne Welles, Cree Lawson (US)
Finance: John Fisher, Gary Singh,
Edward Downey, Mark Hall, Tim Bill
Marketing & Publicity: Richard Trillo, Niki
Smith, David Wearn, Chloë Roberts, Demelza
Dallow, Claire Southern (UK); Simon Carloss,
David Wechsler, Kathleen Rushforth (US)
Administration: Tania Hummel, Julie
Sanderson

Publishing information

This sixth edition published November 2002
by **Rough Guides Ltd**,
80 Strand, London WC2R ORL
Penguin Putnam, Inc., 375 Hudson Street,
NY 10014, USA
Distributed by the Penguin Group
Penguin Books Ltd,
80 Strand, London WC2R ORL
Penguin Putnam, Inc.,
375 Hudson Street, NY 10014, USA
Penguin Books Australia Ltd,
487 Maroondah Highway, PO Box 257,
Ringwood, Victoria 3134, Australia
Penguin Books Canada Ltd,
10 Alcorn Avenue, Toronto, Ontario,
Canada M4V 1E4
Penguin Books (NZ) Ltd,
182–190 Wairau Road, Auckland 10,
New Zealand
Typeset in Bembo and Helvetica to an
original design by Henry Iles.

Printed in Italy by LegoPrint S.p.A.

©Rob Humphreys 2002

No part of this book may be reproduced in
any form without permission from the
publisher except for the quotation of brief
passages in reviews.

664pp, includes index
A catalogue record for this book is available
from the British Library.

ISBN 1-85828-904-1

Help us update

We've gone to a lot of effort to ensure that
this edition of **The Rough Guide to the
Czech and Slovak Republics** is accurate
and up to date. However, things change –
places get "discovered", opening hours are
notoriously fickle, restaurants and rooms
raise prices or lower standards. If you feel
we've got it wrong or left something out,
we'd like to know, and if you can remember
the address, the price, the time, the phone
number, so much the better.

We'll credit all contributions, and send a
copy of the next edition (or any other Rough

Guide if you prefer) for the best letters.
Everyone who writes to us and isn't already a
subscriber will receive a copy of our full-
colour thrice-yearly newsletter. Please mark
letters: "**Rough Guide Czech and Slovak
Republics Update**" and send to: Rough
Guides, 80 Strand, London WC2R ORL, or
Rough Guides, 4th Floor, 345 Hudson St,
New York, NY 10014. Or send an email to
mail@roughguides.com
    Have your questions answered and tell
others about your trip at
www.roughguides.atinfopop.com

Acknowledgements

Big thanks go to Alison for keeping going even when her mind was on other things, and to Geoff for picking up the baton. Thanks, too, to Gordon for coming out again, to Elizabeth for letting us share her penthouse, to Tim and Susie for trawling the provinces, to Tim Burford for tips, to Val for the biblio and other bits, and to Petr, as ever, for a warm welcome. Thanks, too, to Mandy Muggridge for the cartography, Link Hall for layout, Julia Bovis and Louise Boulton for picture research, and Jan Wiltshire for proofreading.

Readers' letters

Lastly, thanks to anyone who wrote or emailed or provided help and information, especially those listed below (apologies for any misspellings): Alex Hetwer, Mr & Mrs E.T. Hancock, Julia Miller, M. Chambers, Cheryl Berriman, David Somerville, Rev & Mrs R.J. Blakeway-Phillips, Cassandra Morris, Joseph Gow, Gerard Gorman, John Perkins, Mary Radley, Vera Lethbridge, Erica Clarke, Tim Bewer, Simon Gill, Adrian Marsden, James King, Janet Reeve, Fay Atkinson & John Owen, Jill Lambert, Michael Leahy, David Harrison, C.S.B. Pyke, G. Piper, James Foley, Andrew Metcalfe & Kirsty Jarvis, Erica Head, M.T. Sowerby, Lily Bennett, M.N., Rosemary Johnstone, A.J. Assheton, Elizabeth L'Estrange, Gerard MacSweeny, Andrew Quaye, Phil Haywood, Mark Humphries, Les & Elizabeth Smith, Dr M.H. Milnes, Alan Wilkins, and Norbert Kopco.

Photo Credits

Cover
Main front picture Telč
Front (small top image) High Tatras
© Robert Harding
Front (small bottom image) Harrachov
© Robert Harding
Back (top) Strečno castle, Slovakia
© Robert Harding
Back (lower) Frýdlant Castle, Czech Republic
© Robert Harding

Colour introduction
Beckov © Helene Hartl
High Tatras © James Strachan/
Robert Harding
Valtice, South Moravia © James
Strachan/Robert Harding
Karlštejn hrad © Mirek Frank
Wooden church, Lukov © Sean Gallup
New Bridge © TRIP/M. Barlow
Path signs © Rob Humphreys
Church of sv Mikuláš, Mala Strana © Michael
Jenner/Robert Harding
Train through the Tatras © with kind
permission of www.slovenskyraj.com
Folk festival, South Moravia © Robert Harding

Things not to miss
1. Budvar beer © TRIP/H Rogers
2. Třeboňsko, carp fish pond © John Probert
3. Český raj © Mirek Frank
4. The Kamenice Gorge, Česke Švýcarsko
© Tim Nollen
5. Terezín © John Probert
6. Jindřichův Hradec, Zámek © John Probert
7. Rafting © Liba Taylor/SELECT/
Robert Harding
8. Altar detail, Gothic church, Levoca
© James Strachan/Robert Harding
9. Castle at Litomyšl © TRIP/B. Crawshaw
10. Rožnov pod Radhoštěm
© Rob Humphreys
11. Plzeň Brewery © Gavin Hellier/
Robert Harding
12. Žďár nad Sazavou, Zelena Hora
© John Probert
13. High Tatras © James Strachan/
Robert Harding
14. Banská štiavnica © James Strachan/
Robert Harding
15. Španělska synagoga © John Probert
16. Spišský hrad © TRIP/M. Barlow

17. Moravský Kras © James Strachan/
Robert Harding
18. Veletržni palác © Rob Humphreys
19. Karlovy Vary © Phil Robinson/
Robert Harding
20. Mariánské Lazně © L. Bond/
Robert Harding
21. Slovenský raj © with kind permission of
www.slovenskyraj.com
22. Český Krumlov Castle © Rolf
Richardson/ Robert Harding
23. Sgraffito facade, Slavonice
© John Probert
24. Obecni dům café © TRIP/M. MACLAREN
25. Vlkolinec © Rob Humphreys
26. Prague Castle © John Probert
27. Bardejov © Sean Gallup
28. Pernštejn © James Strachan/
Robert Harding
29. Telč © Mirek Frank

Black and white photos
Prague © Tim Nollen (p.52)
Rooftops, Prague © Chris Coe/Axiom (p.81)
Pisek Bridge © Hans-Horst Skupy (p.168)
Tábor © Hans-Horst Skupy (p.176)
Kladruby Monastery
© Hans-Horst Skupy (p.212)
Cheb © Rob Humphreys (p.233)
České Švýcarsko © Tim Nollen (p.246)
Liberec Town Hall
© Hans-Horst Skupy (p.276)
Kuks, East Bohemia © James
Strachan/Robert Harding (p.284)
Pardubice © Tim Nollen (p.317)
Telč © John Probert (p.326)
St John Nepomuk statue, Telč © Phil
Robinson/Robert Harding (p.337)
Rožnov pod Radhoštěm
© Hans-Horst Skupy (p.384)
Olomouc © Mirek Frank (p.396)
Bratislava Palace © Hans-Horst Skupy
(p.428)
Trnava, University Church, facade detail
© James Strachan/Robert Harding
(p.457)
Tatras © Mirek Frank (p.474)
Čičmany © Hans-Horst Skupy (p.499)
Spišsky hrad © James Strachan/
Robert Harding (p.524)
Roadside chapel, East Slovakia
© Rob Humphreys (p.554)

SMALL PRINT

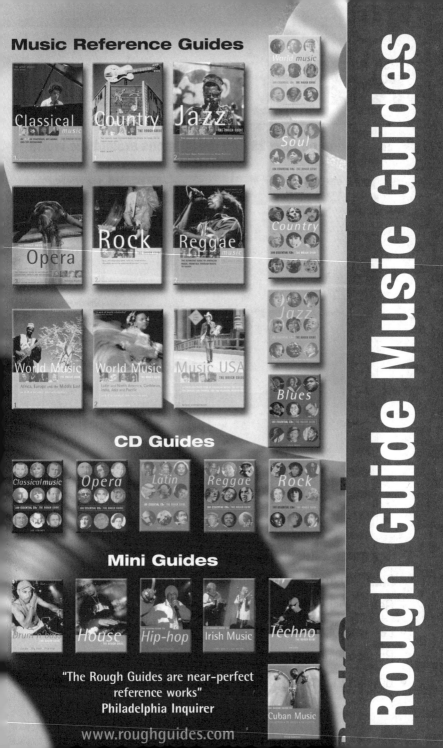

Music Reference Guides

CD Guides

Mini Guides

Rough Guide Music Guides

www.roughguides.com

around the world

Alaska ★ Algarve ★ Amsterdam ★ Andalucía ★ Antigua & Barbuda ★ Argentina ★ Auckland Restaurants ★ Australia ★ Austria ★ Bahamas ★ Bali & Lombok ★ Bangkok ★ Barbados ★ Barcelona ★ Beijing ★ Belgium & Luxembourg ★ Belize ★ Berlin ★ Big Island of Hawaii ★ Bolivia ★ Boston ★ Brazil ★ Britain ★ Brittany & Normandy ★ Bruges & Ghent ★ Brussels ★ Budapest ★ Bulgaria ★ California ★ Cambodia ★ Canada ★ Cape Town ★ The Caribbean ★ Central America ★ Chile ★ China ★ Copenhagen ★ Corsica ★ Costa Brava ★ Costa Rica ★ Crete ★ Croatia ★ Cuba ★ Cyprus ★ Czech & Slovak Republics ★ Devon & Cornwall ★ Dodecanese & East Aegean ★ Dominican Republic ★ The Dordogne & the Lot ★ Dublin ★ Ecuador ★ Edinburgh ★ Egypt ★ England ★ Europe ★ First-time Asia ★ First-time Europe ★ Florence ★ Florida ★ France ★ French Hotels & Restaurants ★ Gay & Lesbian Australia ★ Germany ★ Goa ★ Greece ★ Greek Islands ★ Guatemala ★ Hawaii ★ Holland ★ Hong Kong & Macau ★ Honolulu ★ Hungary ★ Ibiza & Formentera ★ Iceland ★ India ★ Indonesia ★ Ionian Islands ★ Ireland ★ Israel & the Palestinian Territories ★ Italy ★ Jamaica ★ Japan ★ Jerusalem ★ Jordan ★ Kenya ★ The Lake District ★ Languedoc & Roussillon ★ Laos ★ Las Vegas ★ Lisbon ★ London ★

in twenty years

London Mini Guide ★ London Restaurants ★ Los Angeles ★ Madeira ★ Madrid ★ Malaysia, Singapore & Brunei ★ Mallorca ★ Malta & Gozo ★ Maui ★ Maya World ★ Melbourne ★ Menorca ★ Mexico ★ Miami & the Florida Keys ★ Montréal ★ Morocco ★ Moscow ★ Nepal ★ New England ★ New Orleans ★ New York City ★ New York Mini Guide ★ New York Restaurants ★ New Zealand ★ Norway ★ Pacific Northwest ★ Paris ★ Paris Mini Guide ★ Peru ★ Poland ★ Portugal ★ Prague ★ Provence & the Côte d'Azur ★ Pyrenees ★ The Rocky Mountains ★ Romania ★ Rome ★ San Francisco ★ San Francisco Restaurants ★ Sardinia ★ Scandinavia ★ Scotland ★ Scottish Highlands & Islands ★ Seattle ★ Sicily ★ Singapore ★ South Africa, Lesotho & Swaziland ★ South India ★ Southeast Asia ★ Southwest USA ★ Spain ★ St Lucia ★ St Petersburg ★ Sweden ★ Switzerland ★ Sydney ★ Syria ★ Tanzania ★ Tenerife and La Gomera ★ Thailand ★ Thailand's Beaches & Islands ★ Tokyo ★ Toronto ★ Travel Health ★ Trinidad & Tobago ★ Tunisia ★ Turkey ★ Tuscany & Umbria ★ USA ★ Vancouver ★ Venice & the Veneto ★ Vienna ★ Vietnam ★ Wales ★ Washington DC ★ West Africa ★ Women Travel ★ Yosemite ★ Zanzibar ★ Zimbabwe

also look out for our maps, phrasebooks, music guides and reference books

ROUGH GUIDES | TWENTY YEARS

The ideas expressed in this code were developed by and for independent travellers.

Learn About The Country You're Visiting

Start enjoying your travels before you leave by tapping into as many sources of information as you can.

The Cost Of Your Holiday

Think about where your money goes - be fair and realistic about how cheaply you travel. Try and put money into local peoples' hands; drink local beer or fruit juice rather than imported brands and stay in locally owned accommodation. Haggle with humour and not aggressively. Pay what something is worth to you and remember how wealthy you are compared to local people.

Embrace The Local Culture

Open your mind to new cultures and traditions - it will transform your experience. Think carefully about what's appropriate in terms of your clothes and the way you behave. You'll earn respect and be more readily welcomed by local people. Respect local laws and attitudes towards drugs and alcohol that vary in different countries and communities. Think about the impact you could have on them.

Exploring The World – The Travellers' Code

Being sensitive to these ideas means getting more out of your travels - and giving more back to the people you meet and the places you visit.

Minimise Your Environmental Impact

Think about what happens to your rubbish - take biodegradable products and a water filter bottle. Be sensitive to limited resources like water, fuel and electricity. Help preserve local wildlife and habitats by respecting local rules and regulations, such as sticking to footpaths and not standing on coral.

Don't Rely On Guidebooks

Use your guidebook as a starting point, not the only source of information. Talk to local people, then discover your own adventure!

Be Discreet With Photography

Don't treat people as part of the landscape, they may not want their picture taken. Ask first and respect their wishes.

We work with people the world over to promote tourism that benefits their communities, but we can only carry on our work with the support of people like you. For membership details or to find out how to make your travels work for local people and the environment, visit our website.

www.tourismconcern.org.uk

TourismConcern

Campaigning for Ethical and Fairly Traded Tourism